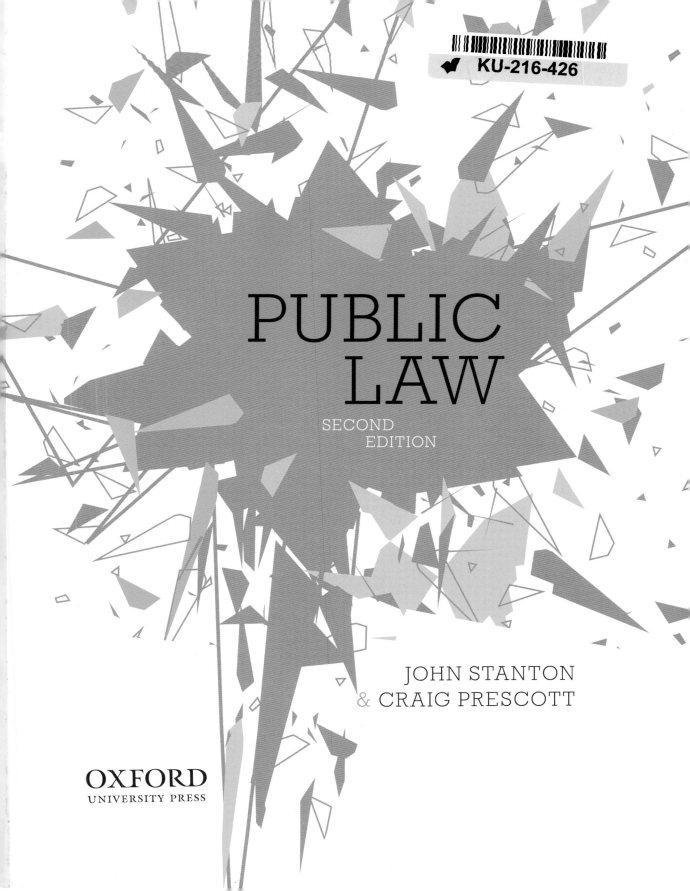

PUBLIC LAW

SECOND EDITION

JOHN STANTON
& CRAIG PRESCOTT

OXFORD

UNIVERSITY PRESS

OXFORD
UNIVERSITY PRESS

Great Clarendon Street, Oxford, OX2 6DP,
United Kingdom

Oxford University Press is a department of the University of Oxford.
It furthers the University's objective of excellence in research, scholarship,
and education by publishing worldwide. Oxford is a registered trade mark of
Oxford University Press in the UK and in certain other countries

First Edition 2018
Impression: 1

Published in the United States of America by Oxford University Press
198 Madison Avenue, New York, NY 10016, United States of America

British Library Cataloguing in Publication Data
Data available

Library of Congress Control Number: 2020932172

ISBN 978–0–19–885227–8

Printed in Great Britain by
Bell & Bain Ltd., Glasgow

Contents in brief

PREFACE   xi
ACKNOWLEDGEMENTS   xii
NEW TO THIS EDITION   xii
GUIDED TOUR OF THE BOOK   xiii
GUIDED TOUR OF THE ONLINE RESOURCES   xvi
TABLE OF CASES   xviii
TABLE OF LEGISLATION   xxvii

1 The UK Constitution   1
2 The institutions of government and the separation of powers   34
3 The rule of law   72
4 Parliamentary sovereignty: an overview   115
5 Parliamentary sovereignty, the European Union, and Brexit   154
6 The royal prerogative and constitutional conventions   203
7 Central government   259
8 Parliament   305
9 Devolution and local government   356
10 Judicial review: access to review and remedies   409
11 Judicial review: illegality   445
12 Judicial review: irrationality and proportionality   487
13 Judicial review: procedural impropriety   511
14 Administrative justice: tribunals, ombudsmen, and public inquiries   559
15 The European Convention on Human Rights and the Human Rights Act 1998   620
16 Human rights in the UK: public order and police powers   671

GLOSSARY   719
INDEX   729

Detailed contents

PREFACE   xi
ACKNOWLEDGEMENTS   xii
NEW TO THIS EDITION   xii
GUIDED TOUR OF THE BOOK   xiii
GUIDED TOUR OF THE ONLINE RESOURCES   xvi
TABLE OF CASES   xviii
TABLE OF LEGISLATION   xxvii

---

1 The UK Constitution   1

   1.1 Introduction to public law   2

   1.2 Defining a constitution   3

   1.3 The nature of the UK constitution   5

   1.4 The historical development and sources of the UK constitution   15

   1.5 Constitutional conventions   25

   1.6 Do we have a UK constitution?   27

   1.7 Summary   32

---

2 The institutions of government and the separation of powers   34

   2.1 Introduction   35

   2.2 The institutions of government   36

   2.3 The principle of the separation of powers   41

   2.4 Exploring the separation of powers in the UK constitution   45

   2.5 The UK constitution and the separation of powers: a *pure* or *partial* Separation?   65

   2.6 Summary   69

---

3 The rule of law   72

   3.1 Introduction   73

   3.2 Defining the rule of law and its historical development   73

   3.3 Dicey and the rule of law   78

3.4   Broader considerations of the rule of law   87

3.5   What does the rule of law mean in the modern UK constitution?   101

3.6   Summary   112

4   Parliamentary sovereignty: an overview   115

4.1   Introduction   116

4.2   Parliamentary sovereignty defined   117

4.3   Historical development of sovereignty   117

4.4   The legal basis of parliamentary sovereignty: a look at wade,
      jennings, and goldsworthy   121

4.5   Parliamentary sovereignty explored   125

4.6   The courts and parliamentary sovereignty today   146

4.7   Summary   152

5   Parliamentary sovereignty, the European Union, and Brexit   154

5.1   Introduction   155

5.2   The origins of the EU and its institutions   156

5.3   The instruments and principles of EU law   162

5.4   The UK's accession to the EU: reconciling EU supremacy with parliamentary
      sovereignty   172

5.5   The political controversy over the UK's membership of the EU   181

5.6   Article 50 TEU and *R (Miller) v Secretary of State for Exiting the European Union*   184

5.7   Preparing UK law for Brexit—European Union (Withdrawal) Act 2018   188

5.8   The Withdrawal Agreement and the European Union (Withdrawal)
      Agreement Act 2020   194

5.9   The future relationship   199

5.10 Summary   200

6   The royal prerogative and constitutional conventions   203

6.1   Introduction: what is the 'Crown'?   204

6.2   The nature and scope of the royal prerogative   206

6.3   Outline of prerogative powers   213

6.4	Constitutional conventions	217
6.5	Regulating the exercise of the ministerial prerogatives	221
6.6	*R (Miller) v Secretary of State for Exiting the European Union*	229
6.7	*R (Miller) v Prime Minister*	232
6.8	Royal Assent to legislation	236
6.9	The appointment of the Prime Minister	238
6.10	The Fixed-term Parliaments Act 2011	244
6.11	Reforming or abolishing the prerogative?	250
6.12	The broader constitutional role of the monarch	253
6.13	Summary	255

7 Central government — 259

7.1	Introduction	260
7.2	The Prime Minister	262
7.3	Appointment of ministers	264
7.4	Cabinet reshuffles	268
7.5	The role of cabinet	270
7.6	Government departments	278
7.7	Political accountability to parliament	281
7.8	The civil service and special advisers	296
7.9	Public bodies	300
7.10	Summary	302

8 Parliament — 305

8.1	Introduction	306
8.2	The 'life' of a parliament	308
8.3	The House of commons	310
8.4	The House of Lords	325
8.5	Primary legislation	332
8.6	Secondary legislation	343

8.7   Scrutiny of government   349

8.8   Summary   354

9   Devolution and local government   356

9.1   Introduction   356

9.2   Devolution, decentralization, and federalism   358

9.3   The formation of the United Kingdom   361

9.4   Devolution in the UK Constitution   363

9.5   Local government   389

9.6   Summary   407

10   Judicial review: access to review and remedies   409

10.1 Introduction   410

10.2 Defining judicial review   410

10.3 Legal basis and process   418

10.4 Standing   421

10.5 The public/private law divide   434

10.6 Remedies   441

10.7 Summary   442

11   Judicial review: illegality   445

11.1 Introduction   446

11.2 Illegality, *ultra vires*, and the rule of law   447

11.3 'Simple' or 'narrow' *ultra vires*   450

11.4 Errors of law and errors of fact   451

11.5 Discretionary powers   457

11.6 Controlling discretionary power   462

11.7 Delegation of power   469

11.8 Improper purpose   473

11.9 Irrelevant considerations   477

11.10 The Public Sector Equality Duty   481

11.11 Summary 484

12 Judicial review: irrationality and proportionality 487

12.1 Introduction 488

12.2 Defining irrationality and *Wednesbury* unreasonableness 488

12.3 The development of unreasonableness 491

12.4 The development of proportionality 498

12.5 Unreasonableness and proportionality 502

12.6 Summary 509

13 Judicial review: procedural impropriety 511

13.1 Introduction 512

13.2 Failing to follow statutory procedure 514

13.3 Rules of natural justice: introduction 520

13.4 Rules of natural justice: the right to be heard 522

13.5 The hearing 529

13.6 Rules of natural justice: rule against bias 537

13.7 A duty to give reasons? 545

13.8 Legitimate expectations 550

13.9 Summary 557

14 Administrative justice: tribunals, ombudsmen, and public inquiries 559

14.1 Introduction: what is administrative justice? 560

14.2 Tribunals 561

14.3 Ombudsmen 583

14.4 Public inquiries 603

14.5 Summary 617

15 The European Convention on Human Rights and the Human Rights Act 1998 620

15.1 Introduction 621

15.2 What are human rights? 622

15.3 The Council of Europe and the European Convention on Human Rights   625

15.4 Human rights protection in the UK pre-1998: the common law and the
       road to incorporation   635

15.5 Human Rights Act 1998   639

15.6 The future of human rights in the UK: a british bill of rights?   668

15.7 Summary   669

16   Human rights in the UK: public order and police powers   671

16.1 Introduction   671

16.2 Public order and the freedoms of association and assembly   672

16.3 Common law public order offences and powers   674

16.4 The Public Order Acts   681

16.5 Powers of the police and the law   695

16.6 The right to liberty and the right to a private and family life   696

16.7 The Police and Criminal Evidence Act 1984   699

16.8 Summary   716

GLOSSARY   719

INDEX   729

Preface

The UK's constitutional and governmental system is founded on a rich history that can be traced back to King John's sealing of Magna Carta in 1215. Since that time, through Acts of Parliament, judgments of the courts, and conventions of the government, this system has evolved and developed into the one that prevails today. Along the way, fundamental features and principles of the constitution have been established, confirmed, and clarified, and it is many of these that form the focus of our book. We look at the core constitutional principles of the rule of law, the separation of powers, and the sovereignty of Parliament. We consider the institutions of the constitution, such as government, Parliament, and those beneath the central level in Scotland, Wales, and Northern Ireland and at the local government level, looking at their various powers as well as broader questions concerning the way in which they function and relate to one another. We also explore the role and powers of the courts, focusing on judicial review of administrative action and the legal framework within which individual human rights and freedoms are protected.

Our constitutional and political system, though, is currently going through a period of profound flux and development. In the past ten years, we have seen the creation of the UK Supreme Court, debates concerning Scottish independence and the future nature of the UK itself, proposals for parliamentary reform and for a new Bill of Rights, and—perhaps most fundamentally of all—a referendum giving rise to the UK's departure from the European Union. Indeed, 'Brexit' in particular, and the legal questions it raises and the enactments it has inspired, will come to shape the future of the UK Constitution, as Chapters 5 and 6 discuss in detail. All this makes now an especially exciting time to be studying public law and we hope that this book will provide a useful aid to your exploration of the subject.

We consider the most distinctive feature of this book to be the way it uses problem scenarios to enhance the discussion of each topic. Every chapter opens with a problem scenario, exploring a hypothetical situation which relates to a particular topic or theme that is the focus of the chapter. That problem scenario is then referred to in 'Discussing the problem' boxes throughout the chapter, inviting consideration of specific aspects of the scenarios and how topics and issues discussed affect or impact upon them. More detailed discussion of each problem scenario is available within the book's accompanying online resources (www.oup.com/he/stanton-prescott2e). The idea behind this feature is to clearly show our readers how public law—which can sometimes seem quite abstract compared with subjects such as criminal law—applies to real-life scenarios: we aim to help students to understand not only the law and the theory, but also how it is relevant to circumstances that arise in the day-to-day operation of the UK Constitution and government. We hope that you find this feature useful.

Acknowledgements

There are a number of people who have helped in the process of updating *Public Law* and in preparing the text for second edition to whom we would like to express sincere thanks. Tom Young and Emily Cunningham at OUP have been most helpful in guiding the project forward and keeping things on track, whilst various academics kindly took the time to review the first edition and provide comments on improvements and potential updates. Thank you!

John would like to express his heartfelt thanks to his wife, Theresa, for her love and support, and for her tolerance when textbook-writing remained a central focus. Craig would like to express his thanks to his Mum and Dad for their support.

John Stanton, London
Craig Prescott, Winchester
October 2019

New to this edition

- Fully updated to cover the implications of Brexit, looking in particular at the European Union (Withdrawal) Act 2018 and the status of retained EU law in domestic legislation
- Thorough analysis of the impact of *R (on the application of Miller) v The Prime Minister* and *Cherry and others v Advocate General for Scotland* (2019) in the context of parliamentary sovereignty, the separation of powers, judicial control of the exercise of prerogative powers, and the principle of justiciability
- Expanded coverage of common law constitutionalism, devolution (*Re UK Withdrawal from the European Union (Legal Continuity) (Scotland) Bill* and *Re Northern Ireland Human Rights Commission's application for judicial review*), and local government
- Updated coverage of Cabinet collective responsibility and the updated *Ministerial Code*
- Explanation of the Fixed-term Parliaments Act 2011 and the Early Parliamentary General Election Act 2019
- Discussion of recent judicial review cases, including *R (on the application of Privacy International) v Investigatory Powers Tribunal and others* (2019) and *R (D and Others) v Parole Board* (2018)

Guided tour of the book

Public Law is a rich learning resource, enhanced with a range of features that have been designed to help you get the most from your studies in three main ways.

Setting the law into its real-world context

Problem scenarios

Each chapter begins by setting out a hypo-thetical scenario—sometimes based on a real-life event—which frames the topic and grounds it in real life, helping you to understand how the theory and concepts of public law apply in practice, and how they relate to events you read about in the news.

> **Problem scenario**
>
> Having been Prime Minister for the past two-and-half years, Patricia King has d shuffle her Cabinet. King has become increasingly frustrated with the performa Cabinet ministers, particularly her Chancellor, Neil Houlihan. However, Houlihan amongst his colleagues in the House of Commons, particularly those who are c 'wing' of the party, which supports low taxes whenever possible. There have be that Houlihan is unhappy with the direction of the government and is considerir bid for the leadership of the party. On reflection, the Prime Minister chooses to as Chancellor for the time being and appoints a new Secretary of State for Edu Marsden.

'Discussing the problem' boxes

'Discussing the problem' boxes throughout each chapter unpick the opening scenario, helping you to explore elements of it and consider how it and the people involved would be affected by the concepts and issues that have been discussed in the main chapter.

> **" Discussing the problem**
>
> Have another look at the problem scenario at the start of the chapter. To you think that the 2024 Act's reduction of the number of government mir of being drawn from Parliament will impact upon this relationship and, the UK Constitution's respect for the separation of powers?
>
> The provision to reduce the number of government ministers capable of being drawn to a maximum of thirty goes right to the heart of the apparent fusion of power tha between the legislature and the executive. This chapter has already explained that, a imum of ninety-five government ministers may be drawn from the House of Commo tributes to the overlap that currently exists between government and Parliament ins

Developing your ability to fully engage with and critically reflect on the law

'Case in depth' boxes and in-text extracts

'Case in depth' boxes and in-text extracts from commentators ease you in to being able to read and digest primary material. The authors discuss the subject's most influ-ential cases in more depth, highlighting the key points you should consider in relation to them, and share important quotations from some of public law's most prominent thinkers.

> **Case in depth:** *R v Secretary of State for the Home Departn ex p Jeyeanthan* [2000] 1 WLR 354
>
> An asylum seeker, whose claim had been rejected, appealed successfully befor The Secretary of State applied to appeal against the adjudicator's decision by using the specified form as required by rule 13(3) of the Asylum Appeals (Procec Other than the statement of trust as detailed on the form, the letter provided a required. Lord Woolf MR set out the approach that courts should take, following guidance in *London & Clydeside Estates Ltd v Aberdeen District Council*.[23] Lord
>
> I suggest that the right approach is to regard the question of whether a re directory or mandatory as only at most a first step. In the majority of cas

'Counterpoint' boxes

'Counterpoint' boxes highlight issues on which commentators and academics disagree, helping you to critically reflect on the law, appreciate its contested and continually evolving nature, and form your own opinions.

> **Counterpoint: Does the decision in *Corner House Re*: further or undermine the rule of law?**
>
> On the face of it, by ensuring that the decision-maker, the Director of the SFO decision to stop the investigation, the conclusion of the House of Lords can b principles explained so far in this section. In this way, the courts are seeking to e tion of Parliament as required by the rule of law as explained in 11.2.
>
> However, the High Court reached the opposite conclusion and also justified th the rule of law. They concluded that the Director of the SFO in yielding to such made by Saudi Arabia actually weakened the rule of law. Moses LJ stated:
>
> [75] Such threats . . . are particularly within the scope of the courts respo

'Pause for reflection' boxes

'Pause for reflection' boxes raise points and pose questions that will help you to think more carefully about the laws discussed: their wider impact, potential future reforms and implications for policy, and how they relate to other key principles and issues.

> **‖ Pause for reflection**
>
> Different Prime Ministers have exercised this power in different ways. When bo Gordon Brown were Prime Minister, they were criticized for reshuffling their i quently. During Labour's thirteen years in office from 1997 to 2010, there were s taries, eight trade and industry secretaries, eight business secretaries, and six (including three in four years).[38] This raised concerns that such frequent reshuf ernment, as continuity of policy is lost and for a period the new minister will be they need to learn about their new position and policy area. Cameron's appro ministers in office for far longer. This shows how flexible the practices are at the government with different Prime Ministers taking different approaches.

Further reading

Suggestions for further reading (both books and websites) give you a starting point from which to broaden and deepen your knowledge of the topic. Those suggestions marked with an asterix (*) indicate particularly useful resources.

> **Further reading**
>
> **Office of Prime Minister**
>
> Mark Bennister and Richard Heffernan, 'Cameron as Prime Minister: The Intra-E Britain's Coalition Government' (2012) 65(4) *Parliamentary Affairs* 778
>
> *Keith Dowding, 'The Prime Ministerialisation of the British Prime Minister' (201: *Affairs* 617
>
> Peter Hennessy, *The Prime Minister: The Office and Its Holders Since 1945* (Pe
>
> House of Commons Political and Constitutional Reform Committee, *Role and p Minister* (HC 2014–15, 351)

Acquiring, reinforcing, and revising your knowledge of key concepts

Glossary terms

Key terms are highlighted throughout each chapter and defined in clear, straightforward language in the glossary at the end of the book. These will help you to remind yourself of the meaning of important terms and to check your understanding as you learn, or when you come to revise.

> varded by the Administrative Court at the conclusion of a judicial review The objectives for this chapter are:
>
> • to define judicial review and to explain the role and jurisdiction of regards to judicial review applications;
> • to set out the legal basis for judicial review and to explain the process applications proceed, as set out in the Civil Procedure Rules;
> • to explore the requirement of standing and to discuss the manne courts have applied the test;
> • to consider the public law/private law divide, the exclusivity pri way in which the courts define a public body for the purposes of jud
> • to set out the remedies available in judicial review cases and to exp which they work.

'Quick test questions'

A list of quick-fire questions at the end of each chapter will allow you to track your progress and identify any issues or sections that you need to spend more time on, and will help you with your revision.

Learning objectives

The introduction to each chapter concludes with a list of its key objectives. These show you the aspects and themes that will be covered, giving you a sense of where the chapter's narrative will take you, and will again help you to structure your revision, acting as a checklist of the important elements of each topic.

Quick test questions

1. What are the main functions of Parliament and how effective are the H and House of Lords at fulfilling those functions?
2. Should the electoral system used for general elections be changed?
3. Does the House of Lords need reform? If so, which reforms would you
4. Is the English Votes for English Laws procedure misnamed? Would it as an English Veto?
5. How are disagreements over legislation between the House of Comm Lords resolved? What political considerations apply?

The chapter's objectives are:

* to explain the principle of devolution and its constitutional benet
* to consider the relevance of devolution to the UK Constitution a form of devolutionary attempts in Scotland, Wales, and Northern
* to discuss current and future proposals for further devolution in mind discussions in the aftermath of the 2014 Scottish Independ Brexit; and recently enacted legislative reforms;
* to discuss the importance of local government and the role that Constitution;
* to explore the nature of local government, its powers and respor various structures within which it operates.

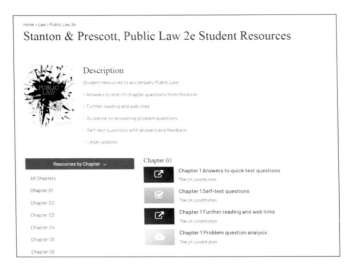

 www.oup.com/he/stanton-prescott2e

For students

Full analysis of each problem scenario in the book

A full analysis of each problem scenario included in the book helps you understand the overall and cumulative impact upon it of the issues discussed in the relevant chapter.

Guidance on approaching and analysing problem scenarios

The authors share advice on how to read a problem scenario, quickly identify the key information within it, and structure an answer to a problem question. An example of an exam problem question and a model answer are also provided.

Additional material for two chapters

Additional material for Chapter 7, on the Freedom of Information Act 2000, and Chapter 8, on parliamentary privilege, will further develop your understanding of central government and parliament, respectively.

Multiple-choice questions

A bank of over 160 multiple-choice questions allow you to check your grasp of the essentials of each topic and to identify gaps in your knowledge, or areas in which you are less confident.

Legal updates

Regular updates from the authors on developments that affect public law, including new cases and Brexit-related changes, will help you stay up to date on what's new within this fast-moving subject area.

Answers to the quick test questions

Answers to the questions included at the end of each chapter allow you to check that you have correctly understood the key points.

Further reading and useful web links

More further reading suggestions from the authors, along with links to useful webpages and sites, offer ideas of possible directions you could take as you look into topics in more depth.

For lecturers

Guidance on using this book in your teaching

Guidance and suggestions from the authors will help spark ideas for ways in which you might use this book and its problem scenarios in your teaching.

Table of Cases

United Kingdom

A v Secretary of State for the Home department [2004] UKHL 56 . . . 112

A and others v Secretary of State for the Home Department [2004] UKHL 56 . . . 81–2

AA v Chief Constable of Thames Valley [2019] EWHC 1499 (QB) . . . 712

AA (Nigeria) v Secretary of State for the Home Department [2010] EWCA Civ 773 . . . 577

Agricultural Sector (Wales) Bill—Reference by the Attorney-General for England and Wales, Re [2014] UKSC 43 . . . 379

AH (Sudan) v Secretary of State for the Home Department [2007] UKHL 49 . . . 569

Albert v Lavin [1982] AC 546 . . . 678

Alford v Chief Constable of Cambridgeshire [2009] EWCA Civ 100 . . . 709

Ali v Birmingham City Council [2010] UKSC 8 . . . 535

Anisminic Ltd v Foreign Compensation Commission [1969] 2 AC 147 . . . 53, 101, 109–10, 134–5, 411, 415–16, 452–3

Anon (1593) Poph 12, 79 ER 1135 . . . 674

Associated Provincial Picture Houses Ltd v Wednesbury Corporation [1948] 1 KB 223 . . . 367, 482, 488–92, 494, 496–8, 500–9, 551, 556, 638, 667, 708, 728

Aston Cantlow PCC v Wallbank [2003] UKHL 37 . . . 660–2

Atkin v DPP (1989) 89 Cr App R 199 . . . 687

Attorney-General v De Keyser's Royal Hotel Ltd [1920] AC 508 . . . 151, 210, 212, 230–1

Attorney-General v Fulham Corporation [1921] 1 Ch 440 . . . 395–6, 450–1

Attorney-General v Guardian Newspapers (No 2) [1990] 1 AC 109 . . . 638

Attorney-General v Jonathan Cape Ltd [1976] QB 752 . . . 26

Attorney-General of New South Wales v Trethowan [1932] AC 526 . . . 143–5

Audit Commission for England and Wales v Ealing London Borough Council [2005] EWCA Civ 556 . . . 466

Austin v Commissioner of Police for the Metropolis [2009] UKHL 5 . . . 679, 697, 716

Austin v Metropolitan Police Commissioner [2005] EWHC 480 . . . 673

AXA Insurance v Lord Advocate [2011] UKSC 46 . . . 367, 370, 386, 437

Baggs Case (1615) 11 Co Rep 93b . . . 522

Bank Mellat v HM Treasury [2013] UKSC 39 . . . 500–2, 507–9, 527–9

Barnard v National Dock Labour Board [1953] 2 QB 18 . . . 470–1

Bastionspark LLP v The Commissioners for Her Majesty's Revenue and Customs [2016] UKUT 0425 (TCC) . . . 562

Bates's Case (Case of Imposition) (1606) 2 St Tr 371 . . . 118

Bauer v DPP (Liberty intervening) [2013] 1 WLR 3617 . . . 694

BBC v Johns [1965] Ch 32 . . . 205, 209

Beatty v Gillbanks (1882) 9 QBd 308 . . . 673

Bellinger v Bellinger [2003] UKHL 21 . . . 651–4

Black v DPP (1995), unreported . . . 702

Blackburn v Attorney-General [1971] 1 WLR 1037 . . . 131, 227, 360, 413

BN v Secretary of State for the Home Department (Article 8—Post Study Work) Kenya [2010] UKUT 162 (IAC) . . . 461

Board of Education v Rice [1911] AC 179 . . . 523

Brackling v Secretary of State for Work and Pensions [2013] EWCA Civ 1345 . . . 483

Bradbury v Enfield London Borough Council [1967] 1 WLR 1311 . . . 514–15, 517

Bribery Commissioner v Ranasinghe [1965] AC 172 . . . 144–5

British Coal Corporation v The King [1935] AC 500 . . . 131

British Oxygen Company Ltd v Minister of Technology [1971] AC 610 . . . 464–5, 469

British Railways Board v Pickin [1974] AC 765 . . . 137, 147, 150

Bromley London Borough Council v Greater London Council [1983] 1 AC 768 . . . 400

Brown v Stott [2003] 1 AC 681 . . . 646

Brutus v Cozens [1973] AC 854 . . . 688–9

Burmah Oil Co Ltd v Lord Advocate [1965] AC 75 . . . 53, 54, 108, 132, 208

Campaign for Nuclear Disarmament v The Prime Minister [2002] EWHC 2777 . . . 67

Campbell v MGN Ltd [2004] UKHL 22 . . . 666

Carltona Ltd v Commissioners of Works [1943] 2 All ER 560 . . . 471–3, 485

Case of Proclamations (1611) 12 Co Rep 74 . . . 76–7, 118–19, 151

Castorina v Chief Constable of Surrey (1988) LG Rev R 241 . . . 708–9

Chalfont St Peter Parish Council v Chiltern District Council [2014] EWCA Civ 1393 . . . 456

Cherry v Advocate General [2019] CSIH 49 . . . 234

Christian Institute and others v The Lord Advocate [2016] UKSC 51 . . . 367

Christie v Leachinsky [1947] AC 573 . . . 708

Clark v University of Lincolnshire and Humberside [2000] 1 WLR 1988 . . . 436

Clarke Homes Limited v Secretary of State for the Environment and East Staffordshire District Council (1993) 66 P & CR 263 . . . 548

Commissioner of Police of the Metropolis v DSD and another [2018] UKSC 11 . . . 647

Commissioner of Police of the Metropolis v MR [2019] EWHC 888 (QB) . . . 707

Coney v Choyce [1975] 1 WLR 422 . . . 515, 517

Conway v Rimmer [1968] AC 910 . . . 101, 411

Cooper v Wandsworth Board of Works (1863) 14 CB (NS) 180 . . . 523, 526, 527

Council of Civil Service Unions v Minister for the Civil Service [1985] AC 374 . . . 67, 227–9, 411–13, 437, 443, 446–7, 454, 488–9, 492, 498, 505, 509, 512–13, 550, 552, 667

Crédit Suisse v Waltham London Borough Council [1997] QB 362 . . . 470

Day v Savadge (1614) Hobart 85 . . . 119

DB v Chief Constable of police Service of Northern Ireland [2017] UKSC 7 . . . 691

de Freitas v Permanent Secretary of Agriculture, Fisheries, Lands and Housing [1999] 1 AC 69 . . . 499, 500

De Keyser Case . . . see Attorney-General v De Keyser's Royal Hotel Ltd [1920] AC 508

Dehal v CPS (2005) 169 JP 581 . . . 694

Derbyshire County Council v Times Newspapers Ltd [1992] QB 770; [1993] AC 534 . . . 636, 637, 638

Dhesi v Chief Constable of West Midlands (9 May 2000) The Times . . . 707

Dimes v The Proprietors of the Grand Junction Canal (1852) 3 HL Cas 759 . . . 539

Director of Public Prosecutions . . . see DPP

Douglas v Hello! Ltd [2005] EWCA Civ 595 . . . 665

Dover District Council v CPRE Kent [2017] UKSC 79 . . . 549, 550

DPP v Haw [2007] EWHC 1931 (Admin) . . . 472–3

DPP v Hawkins [1988] 1 WLR 1166 . . . 707

DPP v Jones and Lloyd [1999] UKHL 5 . . . 695

DPP v Woolmington [1935] AC 462 . . . 698

DPP of the Virgin Islands v Penn [2008] UKPC 29 . . . 514

Dr Bentley's Case (R v University of Cambridge (1723) 1 Str 557) . . . 522

Dr Bonham's Case (1609) 8 Co Rep 113b, 114 . . . 16, 119

D'Souza v DPP [1992] 1 WLR 1073 . . . 713

Duncan v Jones [1936] 1 KB 218 . . . 677

Duport Steels Ltd, and Others v Sirs and Others [1980] 1 WLR 142 . . . 65

E (A Child), Re [2008] UKHL 66 . . . 686

E v Secretary of State for the Home Department [2004] EWCA Civ 49 . . . 456

Edinburgh and Dalkeith Railway Co v Wauchope (1842) 8 ER 279 . . . 135–7, 150

Ellen Street Estates Ltd v Minister of Health [1934] 1 KB 590 . . . 139–40

Emerald Supplies Ltd v British Airways [2015] EWHC 2201 (Ch) . . . 545

Entick v Carrington (1765) 95 ER 807; (1765) 2 Wils KB 275 . . . 61–3, 76–7, 79–85, 87, 101, 104, 636–7, 710

Evans v Information Commissioner [2012] UKUT 313 (AAC) . . . 219, 254

See also R (Evans) v Attorney-General [2015] UKSC . . . 21

Finucane's application for Judicial Review (Northern Ireland), Re [2019] UKSC 7 . . . 556, 607

Fitzpatrick v Sterling Housing Association Ltd [1999] UKHL 42 . . . 652

Flockhart v Robinson [1950] 2 KB 498 . . . 693

FP (Iran) v Secretary of State for the Home Department [2007] EWCA Civ 13 . . . 575

Garland v British Rail Engineering Ltd [1983] 2 AC 751 . . . 175

GCHQ case . . . *see* Council of Civil Service Unions v Minister for the Civil Service [1985] AC 374

Ghaidan v Godin-Mendoza [2004] UKHL 30 . . . 52, 648, 652–4, 656–7, 666

Gibson v Lord Advocate [1975] SLT 13 . . . 361

Gillies v Secretary of State for Work and Pensions [2006] UKHL 2 . . . 543, 574

Golden Chemical Products Ltd, Re [1976] Ch 300 . . . 472

Gough v DPP [2014] ACD 49 . . . 689

Governor's Wall's Case 28 St Tr 51 . . . 83

Gudanaviciene v The Director of Legal Aid Casework [2014] EWCA Civ 1622 . . . 577

H v Lord Advocate [2012] UKSC 24 . . . 181, 372

Hanratty v Lord Butler [1971] 115 SJ 386 . . . 226–7, 413

Harris v Minister for the Interior [1952] 1 TLR 1245 . . . 144–5

Hayes v Chief Constable of Merseyside Constabulary [2011] EWCA Civ 911 . . . 707

Helow v Secretary of State for the Home Department [2008] UKHL 62 . . . 541

Re HK (An Infant) [1967] 2 QB 617 . . . 525

Holgate-Mohammed v Duke [1984] AC 437 . . . 706

Huang v Secretary of State for the Home Department [2007] UKHL 11; [2007] 2 AC 167 . . . 500

Humphries v Connor (1864) 17 ICLR 1 . . . 674

I v DPP [2001] UKHL 10 . . . 684

Imperial Tobacco v Lord Advocate [2012] UKSC 61 . . . 368

Inland Revenue Commissioners v National Federation of Self-Employed and Small Businesses Ltd [1982] AC 617 . . . 420, 422–5, 427–30

International Transport Roth GmbH v Home Secretary [2002] EWCA Civ 158 . . . 667

IRC v Rossminster Ltd [1980] AC 952 . . . 80–2, 105

James v DPP [2015] EWHC 3296 (Admin) . . . 694

Kandamwala v Cambridgeshire Constabulary HQs (2017), unreported . . . 708

Kay v Commissioner of the Police of the Metropolis [2008] UKHL 69 . . . 691–3

Keyu v Secretary of State for Foreign and Commonwealth Affairs [2015] UKSC 69 . . . 506, 507

Kulkarni v Milton Keynes Hospital NHS Foundation Trust [2009] EWCA Civ 789 . . . 536

Lavender & Son Ltd v Minister of Housing and Local Government [1970] 1 WLR 1231 . . . 466–8

Lawal v Northern Spirit Ltd [2003] UKHL 35 . . . 537

LDRA Ltd v Secretary of State for Communities and Local Government [2016] EWHC 950 (Admin) . . . 484

Lee v Bude and Torrington Junction Railway Co (1871) LR 6 CP 576 . . . 150

Lee v Department of Education (1967) 66 LGR 211 . . . 517

Lee v Showmen's Guild of Great Britain [1952] 2 QB 329 . . . 454

Liversidge v Anderson [1942] AC 206 . . . 104, 113, 523

Lloyd v McMahon [1987] AC 625 . . . 528–30

Locabail (UK) Ltd v Bayfield Properties Ltd [2000] QB 451 . . . 538, 539–40

Local Government Byelaws (Wales) Bill 2012— Reference by the Attorney-General for England and Wales [2012] UKSC 53 . . . 379

Lodwick v Sanders [1985] 1 WLR 382 . . . 702

London & Clydeside Estates Ltd v Aberdeen District Council [1980] 1 WLR 182 . . . 515, 516

M, Re [1994] 1 AC 377 . . . 62–3, 84–5, 105–6

McCaughey's application for judicial review, Re [2012] 1 AC 725 . . . 607

M v Home Office [1993] 3 WLR 433 . . . 105, 176

Macarthy's Ltd v Smith [1979] ICR 785 . . . 174–5

MacCormick v Lord Advocate [1953] SC 396 . . . 361–2

McCann v DPP [2015] EWHC 2461 (Admin) . . . 709

McCarthy & Stone (Developments) Ltd v Richmond-upon-Thames London Borough Council [1992] 2 AC 48 . . . 397

McInnes v Onslow-Fane [1978] 1 WLR 1520 . . . 525–6

Madzimbamuto v Lardner-Burke [1969] 1 AC 645 . . . 133

Malone v Metropolitan Police Commissioner [1979] Ch 344; [1979] 2 All ER 620 . . . 24, 111–12, 637–8

Mandalia v Secretary of State for the Home Department [2015] UKSC 59 . . . 553

Manuel v Attorney-General [1983] Ch 77 . . . 136

Re Medicaments and Related Classes of Goods (No 2) [2001] 1 WLR 700 . . . 537, 538, 543

Mitchell v News Group Newspapers Ltd; Rowland v Mitchell [2014] EWHC 4014 (QB) . . . 293

Moohan v Lord Advocate (Advocate General for Scotland intervening) [2014] UKSC 67 . . . 647

Mortensen v Peters (1906) 8 F(J) 93 . . . 128–9

Moss v McLachlan [1985] IRLR 76 . . . 677, 678

Mostyn v Fabregas Cowp 161 . . . 83

Musgrave v Pulido 5 App Cas 102 . . . 83

Nakkuda Ali v Jayaratne [1951] AC 66 . . . 523

Northern Ireland Human Rights Commission's application for judicial review, Re [2018] UKSC 27 . . . 385

Nottinghamshire Country Council v Secretary of State for the Environment [1986] AC 240 . . . 493–4, 497

Oakley v South Cambridgeshire District Council [2017] EWCA Civ 71 . . . 549–50

O'Hara v Chief Constable for the Royal Ulster Constabulary [1997] AC 286 . . . 709–10

O'Kelly v Harvey (1882) 10 LR Ir 287 . . . 674

O'Loughlin v Chief Constable of Essex [1998] 1 WLR 374 . . . 713

O'Moran v DPP [1975] QB 864 . . . 681

O'Reilly v Mackman [1983] 2 AC 237 . . . 434–6, 440, 452, 502, 722

Osman v DPP [1999] EWHC 622 (Admin) . . . 701

Padfield v Minister of Agriculture, Fisheries and Food [1968] AC 997 . . . 101, 411, 462–3, 473–4

Parker v Chief Constable of Essex [2018] EWCA Civ 2788 . . . 709

Percy v DPP [1995] 1 WLR 1382 . . . 675

Percy v DPP [2001] EWHC 1125 (Admin) . . . 689

Philips v Eyre LR 4 QB 225 . . . 83

Pickin v British Railways Board [1974] AC 765 . . . 137, 147, 150

Pickstone v Freemans [1989] AC 66 . . . 179

Poplar Housing and Regeneration Community Association Ltd v Donoghue [2001] EWCA Civ 595 . . . 650, 659–60

Porter v Magill [2001] UKHL 67 . . . 475, 542–4

Powlesland v DPP [2014] 1 WLR 2984 . . . 692–3

Practice Direction (Upper Tribunal: Judicial Review Jurisdiction) [2009] 1 WLR 327 . . . 570

Practice Direction (Upper Tribunal: Judicial Review Jurisdiction) (No 2) [2012] 1 WLR 16 . . . 570

Prohibitions del Roy (1607) 12 Co Rep 63 . . . 16, 76

R (on the application of Name of party) . . . *see as* R (Name of party)

R (Abbasi) v Foreign Secretary [2002] EWCA Civ 1598 . . . 664

R (Alconbury Developments Ltd) v Secretary of State for the Environment, Transport and the Regions [2003] 2 AC 295; [2001] UKHL 23 . . . 504, 536, 642–4, 667

R (Anderson) v Secretary of State for the Home Department [2002] 3 WLR 1800 . . . 643

R (Animal Defenders International) v Secretary of State for Culture, Media and Sport [2008] UKHL 15 . . . 646

R (Anufrijeva) v Secretary of State for the Home Department [2004] 1 AC 604 . . . 93

R (Association of British Civilian Internees: Far East Region) v Secretary of State for Defence [2003] EWCA Civ 473 . . . 503, 505, 554, 590

R (Baker) v Secretary of State for Communities and Local Government (Equality and Human Rights Commission intervening) [2009] PTSR 809 . . . 483

R (Balchin) v Parliamentary Commissioner for Administration (No 3) [2002] EWHC 1876 (Admin) . . . 597

R (Bancoult) v Secretary of State for Foreign and Commonwealth Affairs (No 1) [2007] EWCA Civ 498 . . . 216

R (Bancoult) v Secretary of State for Foreign and Commonwealth Affairs (No 2) [2008] UKHL 61 . . . 228, 413, 556

R (BAPIO Action Ltd) v Secretary of State for the Home Department [2007] EWCA Civ 1139 . . . 518–20

R (Black) v Secretary of State for Justice [2017] UKSC 81 . . . 213

R (Bourgass and another) v Secretary of State for Justice [2015] UKSC 54 . . . 98–100

R (Bradley) v Secretary of State for Work and Pensions [2008] EWCA Civ 36 . . . 600–1

R (Brehony) v Chief Constable of Greater Manchester Police [2005] EWHC 640 (Admin) . . . 694

R (Brent London Borough Council) v Risk Management Partners [2009] EWCA Civ 490 . . . 397–8

R (Bulger) v Secretary of State for the Home Department [2001] EWHC Admin 119 . . . 424

R (Cabot Global Ltd and others) v Barkingside Magistrates' Court and Another [2015] EWHC 1458 (Admin) . . . 712

R (Carmichael) v Secretary of State for Work and Pensions [2016] UKSC 58 . . . 483

R (Cart) v Upper Tribunal [2009] EWHC 3052 (Admin) . . . 417, 450

R (Cart) v Upper Tribunal [2011] UKSC 28 . . . 571–3

R (Chester) v Secretary of State for Justice [2013] UKSC 63 . . . 645

R (Corner House Research and Campaign Against Arms Trade) v Director of the Serious Fraud Office [2009] 1 AC 756 . . . 467–8

R (Cornwall Council) v Secretary of State for Health and another [2015] UKSC 46 . . . 404

R (Daly) v Secretary of State for the Home Department [2001] UKHL 26 . . . 499, 500–4, 508–9, 631, 667

R (DSD and NBV and others) v The Parole Board and others [2018] EWHC 694 (Admin) . . . 426–7, 505

R (Evans) v Attorney-General [2015] UKSC 21 . . . 43, 44, 52, 109–10, 448

See also Evans v Information Commissioner [2012] UKUT 313 (AAC)

R (Faisaltex Ltd) v Preston Crown Court and Others [2008] EWHC 2832 (Admin) . . . 712

R (G) v Governors of X School [2011] UKSC 30 . . . 536

R (Gillan) v Commissioner of Police of the Metropolis [2006] UKHL 12 . . . 702–3, 705

R (Haralambous) v Crown Court at St Albans and another [2016] EWHC 916 (Admin) . . . 712

R (Heather) v Leonard Cheshire Foundation [2002] EWCA Civ 366 . . . 660

R (Hicks and others) v Commissioner of Police of the Metropolis [2014] EWCA Civ 3 . . . 643

R (Hicks and others) v Commissioner of Police of the Metropolis [2017] UKSC 9 . . . 697

R (Holborn Studios Ltd) v Hackney LBC [2017] EWHC 1662 (QB) . . . 519

R (HS2 Action Alliance Ltd) v Secretary of State for Transport [2014] UKSC 3 . . . 138, 146, 149–52, 181

R (Iran) v Secretary of State for the Home Department [2005] EWCA Civ 982 . . . 456, 568

R (Jackson) v Attorney-General [2005] UKHL 56 . . . 21, 53, 55, 122, 134, 138, 146–9, 151–2, 341

R (Jackson) v HM Attorney-General [2005] EWCA Civ 126 (CA) . . . 127

R (Jones) v First-tier Tribunal (Social Entitlement Chamber) [2013] UKSC 19 . . . 568–9, 573

R (Justice for Health Ltd) v Secretary of State for Health [2016] EWHC 2338 (Admin) . . . 67

R (Laporte) v Chief Constable of Gloucestershire Constabulary [2006] UKHL 55 . . . 674, 677–9

R (Lumba) v Secretary of State for the Home Department [2011] UKSC 1 . . . 553

R (MA) v Secretary of State for Work and Pensions [2016] UKSC 58 . . . 484

R (MA) v Work and Pensions Secretary [2013] EWHC 2213 (QB) . . . 482

R (Miller) v Prime Minister [2019] UKSC 41 . . . 29, 63, 77, 151, 206, 221, 229, 234, 236, 238, 261–2, 281, 306, 310, 413, 506

R (Miller) v Secretary of State for Exiting the European Union [2017] UKSC 5 . . . 173, 181, 184, 187, 210, 221, 229, 231–2, 372, 506

R (Miller) v Secretary of State for Exiting the European Union [2016] EWHC 2768 (Admin) . . . 6, 58

R (Moos and McClure) v Commissioner of the Metropolis [2011] HRLR 24 . . . 678

R (Moseley) v Haringey LBC [2014] UKSC 56 . . . 517–18

R (Mullins) v Appeal Board of the Jockey Club [2005] EWHC 2197 (Admin) . . . 520

R (Murray) v Parliamentary Commissioner for Administration [2002] EWCA Civ 1472 . . . 591

R (Nadarajah) v Secretary of State for the Home Department [2005] EWCA Civ 1363 . . . 551

R (Nicklinson and another) v Ministry of Justice [2014] UKSC 38 . . . 655–6

R (Osborn) v Parole Board [2013] UKSC 61 . . . 521, 530, 533, 535

R (Owusu-Yianoma) v Chief Constable of Leicestershire [2017] EWHC 576 (Admin) . . . 687, 690

R (Oxford Study Centre Ltd) v British Council [2001] EWHC 207 (Admin) . . . 440

R (P) v Secretary of State for the Home Department and others [2019] UKSC 3 . . . 655

R (Patel) v General Medical Council [2013] EWCA Civ 327 . . . 555–6

R (Pearce) v Commissioner of Police of the Metropolis [2013] EWCA Civ 866 . . . 715

R (Plantagenet Alliance Ltd) v Secretary of State for Justice [2014] EWHC 1662 (QB) . . . 519

R (Pretty) v DPP [2001] UKHL 61 . . . 666

R (Privacy International) v Investigatory Powers Tribunal and others [2019] UKSC 22 . . . 416–17, 452–3

R (Prolife Alliance) v BBC [2003] UKHL 23 . . . 666

R (Rashid) v Secretary of State for the Home Department [2005] EWCA Civ 744 . . . 553

R (Razgar) v Secretary of State for the Home Department [2004] 2 AC 368 . . . 500

R (Reilly (No 1) and another) v Secretary of State for Work and Pensions [2013] UKSC 68 . . . 93

R (Reilly (No 2) and another) v Secretary of State for Work and Pensions [2014] EWHC 2182 (Admin) . . . 93–5, 107–8

R (Roberts) v Commissioner of Police of the Metropolis and another (Liberty intervening) [2015] UKSC 79 . . . 703–5

R (Rotherham Metropolitan Borough Council and others) v Secretary of State for Business, Innovation and Skills [2015] UKSC 6 . . . 405

R (S) v Secretary of State for the Home Department [2007] EWCA Civ 546 . . . 465–6

R (SK Zimbabwe) v Secretary of State for the Home Department [2011] UKSC 23 . . . 553

R (Steinfeld and Keidan) v Secretary of State for International Development [2018] UKSC 32 . . . 655–6

R (TL) v Surrey Police [2017] EWHC 129 (Admin) . . . 714–15

R (Ullah) v Special Adjudicator [2004] UKHL 26 . . . 643–5, 647, 669

R (Unison) v Lord Chancellor [2017] UKSC 51 . . . 95, 107, 448

R (Weaver) v London and Quadrant Housing [2009] EWCA Civ 587 . . . 663

R (Wheeler) v Prime Minister and Foreign Secretary [2008] EWHC 1409; [2008] ACD 70 . . . 227

R v A (No 2) [2001] UKHL 25 . . . 649–51, 654, 656, 658

R v Badham [1987] Crim LR 202 . . . 714–15

R v Barnsley Metropolitan Council, ex p Hook [1976] 1 WLR 1052 . . . 498

R v Board of Visitors of HM Prison, the Maze, ex p Hone [1988] 1 AC 379 . . . 532

R v Board of Visitors of Hull Prison, ex p St Germain [1979] QB 425 . . . 434

R v Board of Visitors of Hull Prison, ex p St Germain and Others (No 2) [1979] 1 WLR 1401 . . . 532

R v Bow Street Metropolitan Stipendiary Magistrate, ex p Pinochet (No 2) [2000] 1 AC 119 . . . 540–1

R v Brent London Borough Council, ex p Gunning (1985) 84 LGR 168 . . . 518

R v Bristol Betting and Gaming Licensing Committee, ex p O'Callaghan [2000] QB 451 . . . 539

R v Camborne Justices, ex p Pearce [1955] 1 QB 41 . . . 539

R v Chief Constable of Kent, ex p Absalom, 5 May 1993 . . . 498

R v Chief Constable of Sussex, ex p International Trader's Ferry [1999] 2 AC 418 . . . 507

R v Chief Rabbi of the United Hebrew Congregations of Great Britain and the Commonwealth, ex p Wachmann [1992] 1 WLR 1036 . . . 438–9

R v Civil Service Appeal Board, ex p Cunningham [1992] ICR 816 . . . 547–8

R v Commissioner for Local Administration, ex p Croydon London Borough Council [1989] 1 All ER 1033 . . . 594

R v Criminal Injuries Compensation Board, ex p Lain [1967] 2 QB 864 . . . 226, 437–8

R v Derbyshire CC, ex p Times Supplements Ltd (1991) 3 Admin LR 241 . . . 473

R v Disciplinary Committee of the Jockey Club, ex p Aga Khan [1993] 1 WLR 909 . . . 438–9, 520

R v Emu [2004] EWCA 2296 . . . 714

R v Felixstowe JJ, ex p Leigh [1987] QB 582 . . . 425, 428

R v Fiak [2005] EWCA Crim 2381 . . . 706

R v Fleming and R v Robinson [1989] Crim LR 658 . . . 685

R v Foreign Secretary, ex p Everett [1989] QB 811 . . . 227

R v Fulham, Hammersmith and Kensington Rent Tribunal, ex p Zerek [1951] 2 KB 1 . . . 451, 453

R v Gaming Board for Great Britain, ex p Benaim and Khaida [1970] 2 QB 417 . . . 534

R v General Council of the Bar, ex p Percival [1990] 1 QB 212 . . . 421

R v Gough [1993] AC 646 . . . 542–4

R v Grant [1957] 1 WLR 906 . . . 532

R v Higher Education Funding Council, ex p Institute of Dental Surgery [1994] 1 WLR 242 . . . 548

R v HM Treasury, ex p Smedley [1985] QB 657 . . . 425

R v Home Secretary, ex p Pierson [1998] AC 539 . . . 43, 513

R v Home Secretary, ex p Bentley [1994] QB 349 . . . 227

R v Home Secretary, ex p Khawaja [1984] AC 74 . . . 454

R v Horseferry Road Magistrates, ex p Siadatan [1991] 1 QB 260 . . . 688

R v Howell [1982] QB 416 . . . 675–7, 716, 719

R v Hull University Visitor, ex p Page [1993] AC 682 . . . 452–3

R v Inner West London Coroner, ex p Dallaglio [1994] 4 All ER 139 . . . 542

R v Inspectorate of Pollution, ex p Greenpeace (No 2) [1994] 2 CMLR 548 . . . 430–3

R v International Stock Exchange, ex p Else [1992] BCC 11 . . . 498

R v Jordan and Tyndall [1963] Crim LR 124 . . . 683

R v Kelleher [2015] EWCA Crim 691 . . . 714

R v Lamb [1990] Crim LR 58 . . . 675

R v Lattimore (1976) 62 Cr App R 53 . . . 699

R v Liverpool Corporation, ex p Liverpool Taxi Fleet Operators' Association [1972] 2 QB 299 . . . 552

R v Local Commissioner for Administration for the North and East Area of England, ex p Bradford Council [1979] 1 QB 287 . . . 587

R v Lord Chancellor, ex p Witham [1998] QB 575 . . . 97–8, 102, 348, 417, 448, 636–7

R v Mahroof (1989) 88 Cr App R 317 . . . 684–6

R v Medical Appeal Tribunal, ex p Gilmore [1957] 1 QB 574 . . . 416

R v Metropolitan Police Commissioner, ex p Parker [1953] 1 WLR 1150 . . . 523

R v Ministry of Defence, ex p Smith [1996] QB 517 . . . 495–8, 500, 502, 504, 509

R v National Joint Council for the Craft of Dental Technicians (Disputes Committee), ex p Neate [1953] 1 QB 704 . . . 438

R v North and East Devon Health Authority, ex p Coughlan [2001] EWCA Civ 1870; [2001] QB 213 . . . 102, 551, 553, 555–6

R v Oakes [1986] 1 SCR 103 . . . 500

R v Panel on Takeovers and Mergers, ex p Datafin plc and others [1987] QB 815 . . . 437–9, 443

R v Parliamentary Commissioner for Administration, ex p Balchin (No 1) [1997] JPL 917 . . . 586, 596–7

R v Parliamentary Commissioner for Administration, ex p Balchin (No 2) (2000) 79 P & CR 157 . . . 597

R v Podger [1979] Crim LR 524 . . . 676

R v Rand (1866) LR 1 QB 230 . . . 539

R v Secretary of Health, ex p Wagstaff [2001] 1 WLR 292 . . . 613

R v Secretary of State for Education and Employment, ex p Begbie [2000] 1 WLR 1115 . . . 553–4, 556

R v Secretary of State for the Environment, ex p National and Local Government Officers' Association (1992) 5 Admin LR 785 . . . 495–6

R v Secretary of State for Foreign Affairs, ex p Rees-Mogg [1994] QB 552 . . . 227, 413, 426–8, 433

R v Secretary of State for Foreign and Commonwealth Affairs, ex p World Development Movement [1995] 1 WLR 386 . . . 432

R v Secretary of State for Home Affairs, ex p Fire Brigades Union [1995] 2 AC 513 . . . 102, 211

R v Secretary of State for the Home Department, ex p Brind [1991] 1 AC 696 . . . 494–6, 498, 500, 508, 638

R v Secretary of State for the Home Department, ex p Daly [2001] UKHL 26 . . . see R (Daly) v Secretary of State for the Home Department [2001] UKHL 26

R v Secretary of State for the Home Department, ex p Doody [1994] AC 531 . . . 512, 546–9

R v Secretary of State for the Home Department, ex p Fayed [1997] 1 All ER 763 . . . 533–4, 545

R v Secretary of State for the Home Department, ex p Fire Brigades Union [1995] 2 AC 513 . . . 69, 151

R v Secretary of State for the Home Department, ex p Hargreaves [1997] 1 All ER 397 . . . 498

R v Secretary of State for the Home Department, ex p Jeyeanthan [2000] 1 WLR 354 . . . 516–17

R v Secretary of State for the Home Department, ex p Khan [1984] 1 WLR 1337 . . . 553

R v Secretary of State for the Home Department, ex p Leech (No 2) [1994] QB 198 . . . 102, 417

R v Secretary of State for the Home Department, ex p Northumbria Police Authority [1989] QB 26 . . . 208–10

R v Secretary of State for the Home Department, ex p Pierson [1998] AC 539 . . . 102–3, 108

R v Secretary of State for the Home Department, ex p Rose Theatre Trust [1990] 1 QB 504 . . . 429–33

R v Secretary of State for the Home Department, ex p Saleem [2001] 1 WLR 443 . . . 561

R v Secretary of State for the Home Department, ex p Simms [1999] UKHL 33 . . . 102

R v Secretary of State for the Home Department, ex p Tarrant [1985] QB 251 . . . 532–3

R v Secretary of State for the Home Department, ex p Venables [1998] AC 407 . . . 479

R v Secretary of State for Social Services, ex p Child Poverty Action Group [1989] 1 All ER 1047; [1990] 2 QB 540 . . . 422, 433

R v Secretary of State for Social Services, ex p Sherwin (1996) 32 BMLR 1 . . . 473

R v Secretary of State for Transport, ex p Factortame (No 1) [1990] 2 AC 85 . . . 175

R v Secretary of State for Transport, ex p Factortame (No 2) [1991] 1 AC 603 . . . 16–18, 53, 151, 175, 177–80

R v Sherlock (Kyle) [2014] EWCA Crim 310 . . . 684

R v Somerset County Council, ex p Fewings [1995] 1 WLR 1037 . . . 480

R v Soneji [2006] 1 AC 340 . . . 516

R v Sussex Justices, ex p McCarthy [1924] 1 KB 256 . . . 521, 538

R v University of Cambridge (1723) 1 Str 557 (Dr Bentley's Case) . . . 522

Rabone v Pennine Care NHS Foundation Trust (INQUEST intervening) [2012] UKSC 2 . . . 647

Raissi v Commissioner of Police of the Metropolis [2008] EWCA Civ 1237 . . . 709

Raymond v Honey [1982] 1 All ER 756 . . . 417

Redknapp v Commissioner of Police of the Metropolis [2008] EWHC 1177 (Admin) . . . 712

Redmond-Bate v DPP [1999] Crim LR 998; [2000] HRLR 249 . . . 673, 677

Rees v John [1970] Ch 345 . . . 522

Ridge v Baldwin [1964] AC 40 . . . 101, 411, 522–5, 557

RM v Scottish Ministers [2012] UKSC 58 . . . 474

Roberts v Hopwood [1925] AC 578 . . . 478, 491–2, 509

Robinson v Secretary of State for Northern Ireland [2002] UKHL 32 . . . 383

Roy v Kensington and Chelsea and Westminster Family Practitioner Committee [1992] 1 AC 624 . . . 436

Re S (Minors) (Care Order: Implementation of Care Plan) [2002] UKHL 10 . . . 650–2, 654

Secretary of State for Education and Science v Tameside Metropolitan Borough Council [1977] AC 1014 . . . 455, 492

Semayne's Case (1604) 5 Coke Rep 91 . . . 710

Short v Poole Corporation [1926] Ch 66 . . . 492

Singh v Secretary of State for the Home Department [2015] EWCA Civ 74 . . . 461

Smith v Ministry of Defence [2014] AC 52 . . . 645

Smith v Scott [2007] SC 345 . . . 312

South Buckinghamshire District Council v Porter (No 2) [2004] UKHL 33 . . . 549

Stubbs v The Queen [2018] UKPC 30 . . . 544–5

Surrey County Council v P (Equality and Human Rights Commission intervening) [2014] UKSC 19 . . . 647

Syed v DPP [2010] EWHC 81 (Admin) . . . 713

Taylor v Lawrence [2002] EWCA Civ 90 . . . 543–5

Thoburn v Sunderland City Council [2002] EWHC 195 (Admin); [2003] QB 151 . . . 7, 150, 180, 372

Turner v East Midland Trains [2012] EWCA Civ 1470 . . . 666

UK Withdrawal from the European Union (Legal Continuity) (Scotland) Bill, Re [2018] UKSC 64 . . . 369

Vauxhall Estates v Liverpool Corporation [1932] 1 KB 733 . . . 139–40

Venables v News Groups Newspapers Ltd [2001] Fam 430 . . . 665

Vine v National Dock Labour Board [1957] AC 488 . . . 470

Virdi v Law Society of England and Wales [2010] EWCA Civ 100 . . . 544

Walker v Commissioner of Police of the Metropolis [2014] EWCA Civ 897 . . . 677–8

Wandsworth London Borough Council v Winder [1985] AC 461 . . . 436

Westminster Corporation v London & North Western Railway Co [1905] AC 426 . . . 476–7

Wheeler v Leicester City Council [1985] AC 1054 . . . 102, 474–5, 477, 490–92

White and Collins v Minister of Health [1939] 2 KB 838 . . . 450–1

Wilson v First County Trust Ltd (No 2) [2003] UKHL 40 . . . 150, 657

Yiacoub v The Queen [2014] UKPC 22 . . . 544–5

YL v Birmingham City Council and others [2007] UKHL 27 . . . 661–3

European Court of Human Rights

Austin v UK (2012) 55 EHRR 14 . . . 679–80

Brannigan and McBride v UK (1994) 17 EHRR 539 . . . 634

Colon v The Netherlands (2012) 55 EHRR SE45 . . . 704

Davies v UK (2002) 35 EHRR 29 . . . 536

Dudgeon v UK (1982) 4 EHRR 149 . . . 634

Evans v UK (2008) 46 EHRR 34 . . . 634

Gillan v UK (2010) 50 EHRR 1105 . . . 701, 703–4

Handyside v UK (1979–80) 1 EHRR 737 . . . 628, 633

Hirst v UK (No 2) (2006) 42 EHRR 41; [2005] ECHR 681 . . . 312, 645

Jecius v Lithuania (2000) 35 EHRR 400 . . . 643

Klass v Germany (1979–80) 2 EHRR 214 . . . 634

McGonnell v UK (2000) 30 EHRR 289 . . . 57

McLeod v UK [1998] 27 EHRR 493 . . . 675

Malone v UK (1984) 7 EHRR 14 . . . 637

National & Provincial Building Society v UK (1997) 25 EHRR 127 . . . 97

Ostendorf v Germany (2013) 34 BHRC 738 . . . 643

Salesi v Italy (1998) 26 EHRR 187 . . . 535

Saunders v UK (1997) 23 EHRR 313 . . . 646

Smith and Grady v UK (1999) 29 EHRR 493 . . . 496–7, 499, 500, 503–4

Steel and Others v UK (1999) 28 EHRR 603 . . . 675–6

Sunday Times v UK (1979–80) 2 EHRR 245 . . . 628, 634

Tsfayo v UK (2009) 48 EHRR 18 . . . 535

Verein gegen Tierfabriken v Switzerland (2001) 34 EHRR 159 . . . 646

Zielinkski v France (1999) 31 EHRR 532 . . . 94

European Union

Amministrazione delle Finanze dello Stato v Simmenthal SpA Case 106/77 [1978] ECR 629 . . . 168

Commission v Italy Case 39/72/EC [1973] ECR 101 . . . 163

Costa v ENEL Case 6/64 [1964] ECR 585 . . . 16, 167–8, 172

Internationale Handelsgesellschaft mbH v Einfuhr- und Vorratsstelle für Getreide und Futtermittel Case 11/70 [1970] ECR 1125 . . . 167–8

Macarthy's Ltd v Smith Case 129/79 [1980] ECR 1275 . . . 174

NV Algemene Transport- en Expeditie Onder- neming Van Gend en Loos v Nederlandse Tariefcommissie . . . *see* Van Gend en Loos

R v Minister of Agriculture, Fisheries and Food, ex p Fedesa Case C-331/88 [1990] ECR I–4023 . . . 167

R v Secretary of State for Transport, ex p Factortame Ltd Case C-213/89 [1990] ECR I-2433 . . . 176

Van Duyn v Home Office Case 41/74 [1974] ECR I 1337 . . . 171

Van Gend en Loos v Nederlandse Administratie der Belastingen Case 26/62 [1963] ECR 1 . . . 127, 163, 170–1

Variola v Amministrazione delle Finanze Case C 34/73 [1972] ECR 981 . . . 170–1

Wightman v Secretary of State for Exiting the European Union Case C-621/18 [2019] 1 CMLR 29 . . . 230

Australia

Project Blue Sky Inc v Australian Broadcasting Authority (1998) 194 CLR 355 . . . 516

Canada

Roncarelli v Duplessis (1959) 16 DLR (2d) 689 . . . 467

New Zealand

CREEDNZ Inc v Governor General [1981] 1 NZLR 172 . . . 477

United States

Marbury v Madison, 5 US (1 Cranch) 137 (1803) . . . 40, 116

Shelby County, Alabama v Holder, 570 US (2013) . . . 40, 116

Table of Legislation

UK Statutes

Acquisition of Land Act 1919 . . . 139
  s 2 . . . 139
  s 7 . . . 139–40
  s 7(1) . . . 139
Act of Settlement 1701 . . . 42, 121, 150, 207, 254, 312
  s 3 . . . 312
Acts of Union 1706 . . . 718, 139, 150, 361–3, 365, 377
Act of Union with Ireland 1800 . . . 19, 362
Agricultural Marketing Act 1958 . . . 463
  s 19 . . . 463
Anti-Social Behaviour Act 2003
  s 57 . . . 693
Anti-Terrorism, Crime and Security Act 2001 . . . 81, 112, 333
  s 21 . . . 81
  s 23 . . . 81
Appellate Jurisdiction Act 1876 . . . 327
Apprenticeships, Skills, Children and Learning Act 2009
  s 127 . . . 300
Assembly Members (Reduction of Numbers) Act (Northern Ireland) 2016 . . . 384
Australia Act 1986 . . . 130, 132
  s 1 . . . 130
  s 2(2) . . . 130

Baths and Wash-Houses Acts 1846–78 . . . 395, 450
Bill of Rights 1688 . . . 16, 24, 32, 42, 76, 116–17, 120–1, 123, 180–1, 205, 207, 308, 622, 726
  Art 1 . . . 207
  Art 2 . . . 207
  Art 4 . . . 207
  Art 6 . . . 207, 221
  Art 9 . . . 16, 120, 136, 149–50, 181, 308
Bishoprics Act 1878 . . . 326
  s 5 . . . 326
Bristol and Exeter Railway Act 1836
  s 259 . . . 137
British Nationality Act 1981

  s 6(2) . . . 533
  s 44(2) . . . 533–4
  s 71 . . . 312
British Railways Act 1968 . . . 137
  s 18 . . . 137
Broadcasting Act 1981 . . . 494
  s 4 . . . 494
Burghs and Police (Scotland) Act 1833 . . . 390

Canada Act 1982 . . . 130–2, 136
  s 1 . . . 130
  s 2 . . . 130
  Sch B . . . 130
Chancel Repairs Act 1932 . . . 660–1
  s 2(1) . . . 660
Childcare Act 2014 . . . 345
Children Act 1989 . . . 650–1
  s 20 . . . 404
Children and Young People (Scotland) Act 2014 . . . 367
Cinematograph Act 1909 . . . 489
Cities and Local Government Devolution Act 2016 . . . 37, 394
  s 2 . . . 394
Civil Justice Act 1988 . . . 211–12
Civil Partnership Act 2004 . . . 655
  s 1 . . . 655
  s 3 . . . 655
Claim of Rights Act 1689 (Scotland) . . . 150
Colonial Boundaries Act 1895 . . . 228
Colonial Laws Validity Act 1865
  s 5 . . . 143
Communications Act 2003 . . . 641
Constitutional Reform Act 2005 . . . 7, 22, 23, 32, 45, 55–60, 64, 70, 150, 180, 327, 418, 570
  Pt 1 . . . 72
  s 1 . . . 57, 74, 94
  s 2 . . . 60
  s 3 . . . 574
  s 17 . . . 57
  s 25 . . . 59

Pt 4, Chap 2 (ss 63–107) . . . 59
ss 85–93 . . . 573
Sch 8(1) . . . 59
Sch 12 . . . 58
Sch 12(1) . . . 58
Sch 12(2)–(3) . . . 59
Sch 14 . . . 573
    Pt 3 . . . 58
Constitutional Reform and Governance Act
    2010 . . . 203, 214–15, 225–7, 296–7, 345
s 3(1) . . . 296
s 5 . . . 296
s 8 . . . 299
s 10(2) . . . 296
s 11 . . . 296
s 15 . . . 298
ss 20–25 . . . 214
s 20 . . . 225–6
s 20(1) . . . 225
s 20(4) . . . 225
s 20(8) . . . 225
s 22 . . . 225
s 41 . . . 312
s 51 . . . 345
Consumer Credit Act 1974
s 127(3) . . . 657
Continental Shelf Act 1964 . . . 130, 132
s 1 . . . 130
Counter-Terrorism Act 2008 . . . 527–9
    Pt 4 (ss 40–61) . . . 528
Courts and Legal Services Act 1990 . . . 22
Courts and Tribunals (Judiciary and Functions of
    Staff) Act 2018 . . . 580
Crime and Courts Act 2013 . . . 59, 688
s 57 . . . 686
Crime and Disorder Act 1998 . . . 687
s 31(1) . . . 687
Criminal Appeal Act 1968
s 3 . . . 685
Criminal Injuries Compensation
    Act 1995 . . . 212
Criminal Justice Act 1967
s 61 . . . 547
Criminal Justice Act 1987
s 1(3) . . . 467
Criminal Justice Act 1991 . . . 479
s 35(2) . . . 103

Criminal Justice Act (Northern Ireland) 1945
s 25(1) . . . 385
Criminal Justice and Courts Act 2015
s 84(1) . . . 418
Criminal Justice and Public Order Act 1994 . . . 687
s 60 . . . 678, 700, 701–4
Crown Proceedings Act 1947
s 21 . . . 62–3, 84
s 22 . . . 176

Damages (Asbestos-related Conditions) (Scotland)
    Act 2009 . . . 367
Declaration of Abdication Act 1936 . . . 255
Dentists' Act 1878 . . . 139
Disability Discrimination Act 1985 . . . 138

Early Parliamentary General Election Act
    2019 . . . 248, 250, 309
Education Act 1944 . . . 515
s 68 . . . 455
Education (Schools) Act 1997 . . . 554
Electoral Administration Act 2006
s 18 . . . 312
Equal Pay Act 1970 . . . 138, 174, 478
Equality Act 2010 . . . 478, 481–3, 704
ss 54–67 . . . 478
s 149 . . . 481–4
s 149(1)–(7) . . . 481
s 149(2) . . . 481
s 149(3) . . . 481
s 149(7) . . . 481
s 211(2) . . . 138
Sch 27 . . . 138
Equitable Life (Payments) Act 2010 . . . 600
European Communities Act 1972 . . . 16, 17, 24,
    150, 172–5, 177–83, 186, 189, 192, 195–6, 198,
    200, 229–32, 348, 639
s 2 . . . 175, 189, 196
s 2(1) . . . 172–5, 179, 189–90, 229–31
s 2(2) . . . 173, 189
s 2(4) . . . 173–5, 179
European Communities (Amendment) Act 1993
s 1(2) . . . 426
European Parliament Elections Act 1999 . . . 21,
126
European Parliamentary Elections Act 1978 . . . 426
s 6 . . . 426
European Parliamentary Elections Act 1999 . . . 341

European Parliamentary Elections Act 2002
  s 8 . . . 645

European Union Act 2011 . . . 183, 227, 230, 232
  s 18 . . . 183

European Union (Notification of Withdrawal) Act
  2017 . . . 187–8, 231, 262, 337
  s 1(1) . . . 187

European Union Referendum Act 2015 . . . 184
  s 1 . . . 184

European Union (Withdrawal) Act 2018 . . . 10, 17,
  48, 155–6, 173, 188–98, 337, 348–9, 369, 371
  s 1 . . . 189
  s 1A . . . 195–6
  s 1B . . . 196
  ss 2–5 . . . 196
  s 2 . . . 191, 196
  s 2(1) . . . 189–90
  s 3 . . . 190–1, 193, 196
  s 3(1) . . . 190
  s 4 . . . 190–1, 193, 196
  s 4(1) . . . 190
  s 5 . . . 191–2
  s 5(1) . . . 191
  s 5(2) . . . 191
  s 6(7) . . . 189
  s 7 . . . 192
  s 7(1) . . . 189
  s 7(2) . . . 190
  s 7(3) . . . 190
  s 7(6) . . . 190
  s 7A . . . 196
  s 8 . . . 192–4
  s 8(1) . . . 192, 349
  s 8(2) . . . 192
  s 8(2)(a) . . . 192
  s 8(2)(b) . . . 192
  s 8(2)(g) . . . 192
  s 8(7) . . . 192
  s 15A . . . 195
  s 19 . . . 192
  s 20 . . . 190
  s 20(4) . . . 189
  Sch 7 . . . 193
    paras 1(2), (3) . . . 193
    para 3 . . . 193
    para 3(7) . . . 193
  Sch 8 . . . 190, 193
    paras 3, 4 . . . 190, 193
    para 4(1)–(3) . . . 193

European Union (Withdrawal) Act 2019 . . . 237,
  324–5

European Union (Withdrawal) (No 2) Act
  2019 . . . 195, 237, 262, 324–5
  s 1 . . . 195
  Sch . . . 195

European Union (Withdrawal Agreement)
  Act 2020 . . . 156, 188–8, 194–6, 198, 336,
  348–9
  s 1 . . . 195
  s 2 . . . 196
  s 5 . . . 196
  s 25 . . . 196
  s 32 . . . 225
  s 33 . . . 195

Fixed-term Parliaments Act 2011 . . . 30, 204, 210,
  215, 227, 232–3, 242–4, 246–50, 256, 263, 281,
  308–10, 323, 726
  s 1 . . . 308
  s 1(2) . . . 246
  s 1(3) . . . 246, 248
  s 1(4) . . . 246
  s 2(1) . . . 247, 250, 309
  s 2(2) . . . 247, 309
  s 2(3)(a) . . . 246
  s 2(3)(b) . . . 246
  s 2(4) . . . 246, 250, 309
  s 2(5) . . . 246, 250, 309
  s 2(7) . . . 246, 247–8, 309
  s 3(1) . . . 48, 247, 309
  s 4 . . . 365
  s 4(4)–(6) . . . 249

Foreign Compensation Act 1950 . . . 415
  s 4(4) . . . 53, 109, 134, 415–6, 452

Freedom of Information Act 2000 . . . 109–10, 345
  s 35 . . . 272
  s 53 . . . 43, 44, 52
  s 53(2) . . . 109

Gaelic Language (Scotland) Act 2005
  s 3(1) . . . 405

Government of Ireland Act 1914 . . . 21, 126, 341

Government of Ireland Act 1920 . . . 19, 362, 382
  s 4 . . . 382

s 4(1) . . . 382

s 6(1) . . . 382

s 6(2) . . . 382

Government of Wales Act 1998 . . . 19, 180, 192, 363, 377–80

Government of Wales Act 2006 . . . 378

s 45 . . . 381

s 93(2) . . . 378

s 94(2) . . . 378

s 103 . . . 379

s 103(1) . . . 379

s 108(1)–(2) . . . 379

s 108(6)(c) . . . 380

s 108A(2)(e) . . . 380

Sch 5 . . . 378

Sch 7A . . . 380

Great Reform Act 1832 . . . 307

Great Reform Act 1867 . . . 307

Great Reform Act 1884 . . . 307

Greater London Authority Act 1999 . . . 392

Health Act 2006 . . . 213

Pt 1, Chap 1 . . . 213

s 23 . . . 213

Health and Safety Work etc. Act 1974

s 14(2)(b) . . . 606

Health Service Commissioner Act 1993 . . . 584

Health and Social Care Act 2012

s 31 . . . 396

Health and Social Care (Community Health and Standards) Act 2004 . . . 342

Herring Fisheries (Scotland) Act 1889 . . . 128

High Speed Rail (London–West Midlands) Act 2017 . . . 332

House of Commons Disqualification Act 1975 . . . 46, 313

s 1 . . . 46, 313

s 2 . . . 46

s 2(1) . . . 265

s 4 . . . 313

Sch 1 . . . 46

Pt I 313

Pt II 313

Pt III 313

House of Lords Act 1999 . . . 22, 127, 329, 337, 723

s 2(2) . . . 326

House of Lords (Expulsion and Suspension Act) 2015 . . . 329, 331

House of Lords Reform Act 2014 . . . 329, 331

s 1 . . . 329

s 2 . . . 329

Housing Act 1925 . . . 139

s 46 . . . 139–40

Housing Act 1936

s 74 . . . 450–1

s 75 . . . 450

Housing Act 1985 . . . 470

s 32 . . . 475

Housing Act 1996

s 51 . . . 584

Sch 2 . . . 584

Human Rights Act 1998 . . . 7, 24, 30, 86, 108, 111–12, 128, 150–1, 180, 192, 251, 433, 479, 498–9, 504, 535, 577, 622, 625, 635–7, 639–42, 645, 651–3, 655–6, 659–69, 671–3, 681–2, 689, 698, 704, 711, 713

s 2 . . . 497, 499, 500, 641, 642–4, 646, 659, 669

s 2(1) . . . 642, 643–4

s 2(1)(a) . . . 642

s 3 . . . 641, 647–59, 669, 673, 682, 711

s 3(1) . . . 52, 647, 657

s 4 . . . 53, 94, 312, 570, 641, 647–8, 650–1, 654–9, 704, 721

s 4(2) . . . 654, 656–7

s 6 . . . 440, 642, 644, 658–66, 669–70, 673

s 6(1) . . . 642, 659, 666, 704

s 6(3) . . . 659

s 6(3)(a) . . . 642

s 6(3)(b) . . . 662

s 7 . . . 440, 658–9, 666–7, 669, 679

s 7(1) . . . 433

s 7(1)(a) . . . 694

s 7(1)(b) . . . 666, 682

s 7(3) . . . 666

s 7(5) . . . 667

s 8(1) . . . 667

s 8(2) . . . 667

s 10 . . . 39, 654–5

s 10(2) . . . 48

s 19 . . . 641

Sch 1 . . . *see* European Convention on Human Rights

Human Tissue Act 2004 . . . 617

Hunting Act 2004 . . . 21, 53, 55, 126–7, 146, 341

Immigration Act 1971
　s 33 . . . 454
Inquiries Act 2005 . . . 506, 606–7, 612, 614–7
　s 1(1) . . . 506
　s 6 . . . 606
　s 10 . . . 611
　s 11 . . . 612
　s 14 . . . 616
　s 17 . . . 612
　s 18(1) . . . 613
　s 19 . . . 614
　s 25(4)–(5) . . . 615
Insolvency Act 1986
　s 426C . . . 312
Intelligence Services Act 1994 . . . 252
Interpretation Act 1978
　Sch 1 . . . 279
Irish Free State (Agreement) Act 1922 . . . 19

Jobseekers Act 1995 . . . 94
Jobseekers (Back to Work Schemes)
　Act 2013 . . . 94

Land Transaction Tax and Anti-Avoidance of
　Devolved Taxes (Wales) Act 2017 . . . 381
Legal Aid, Sentencing and Punishment of
　Offenders Act 2012 . . . 577
　s 10 . . . 577
Life Peerages Act 1958 . . . 218, 326, 331
Limitation Act 1980 . . . 419
Liverpool Corporation Act 1921 . . . 708
Local Democracy, Economic Development and
　Construction Act 2009 . . . 394
　s 104 . . . 394
　s 105 . . . 394
Local Government Act 1888 . . . 390, 392
Local Government Act 1894 . . . 390, 402
　s 3(1) . . . 402
Local Government Act 1899 . . . 392
Local Government Act 1963 . . . 392
Local Government Act 1972 . . . 391, 402
　s 1(9) . . . 402
　s 2(1) . . . 395
　s 9 . . . 401
　s 20(6) . . . 402
　s 27 . . . 402

　s 111 . . . 397, 470
　s 120 . . . 480
Local Government Act 1974
　ss 23–34 . . . 584
Local Government Act 1985 . . . 391
Local Government Act 1992 . . . 391
Local Government Act 2000 . . . 393–4, 397, 402
　s 1 . . . 402
　s 2 . . . 397
　s 2(1) . . . 397, 402
Local Government Act 2003
　s 99 . . . 466
Local Government Act (Northern Ireland)
　2014 . . . 399
　s 21(2) . . . 393
　s 79(10 . . . 399
Local Government (Boundaries) Act (Northern
　Ireland) 1971 . . . 391
Local Government (Boundaries) Act (Northern
　Ireland) 2008 . . . 391
Local Government Finance Act 1992
　s 13A . . . 517
　Sch 1A
　　para 3 . . . 517
Local Government in Scotland Act 2003
　s 20(1) . . . 398
　s 34 . . . 396
Local Government (Ireland) Act
　1898 . . . 390
Local Government (Northern Ireland) Act
　1972 . . . 391
Local Government Planning and Land Act
　1980 . . . 493
Local Government and Public Involvement in
　Health Act 2007 . . . 393
　Sch 5 . . . 402
Local Government (Scotland) Act 1889 . . . 390
Local Government (Scotland) Act 1929 . . . 390
Local Government (Scotland) Act 1973 . . . 391
　s 51(1) . . . 402
　s 51(2) . . . 402
　s 69 . . . 398
　s 87(1) . . . 401
Local Government (Scotland) Act 1994 . . . 391
Local Government (Wales) Act 1994 . . . 391
Local Government (Wales) Measure 2011
　s 46 . . . 401
　s 126(1) . . . 402

Localism Act 2011 . . . 212, 394, 398–9, 401
  s 1 . . . 398, 722
  s 1(2) . . . 398
  s 72 . . . 401
  s 105 . . . 212
  Sch 2 . . . 401
  Sch 5 . . . 401
  Sch 10 . . . 401
Lords Spiritual (Women) Act 2015 . . . 326

Magistrates' Court Act 1980
  s 1(1) . . . 706
Magna Carta 1215 . . . 15–8, 24, 31, 75–6, 79, 82, 101, 150, 229, 622
Magna Carta 1297 . . . 180
  cl xxIx . . . 79
Marriage (Same Sex Couples) Act 2013 . . . 655
Matrimonial Causes Act 1973 . . . 651–2
  s 11(c) . . . 651
Meeting of Parliament Act 1797 . . . 234
Mental Health (Care and Treatment) (Scotland) Act 2003 . . . 474
  Pt 17, Chap 3 (ss 264–73) . . . 474
Merchant Shipping Act 1894 . . . 17
Merchant Shipping Act 1988 . . . 17, 53, 175–7, 179
  s 14 . . . 176
  s 14(1) . . . 17, 176
  s 14(2) . . . 176
  s 14(7) . . . 176
Metropolis Management Act 1855 . . . 392, 478
  s 76 . . . 523
Ministerial and Other Salaries Act 1975 . . . 265
  s 1(2)(a) . . . 265
  Sch 1
    para 2(a) 265
Misuse of Drugs Act 1971 . . . 302, 702
  s 23(2) . . . 700, 701
  s 23(4)(a) . . . 702
Municipal Corporations Act 1835 . . . 390
Municipal Corporations (Ireland) Act 1840 . . . 390

National Assistance Act 1948
  s 21 . . . 662
  s 21(1)(a) . . . 404
National Health Service Act 1948 . . . 457
National Health Service Act 2006 . . . 67

Nationality, Immigration and Asylum Act 2002
  s 7(1) . . . 533
Northern Ireland Act 1998 . . . 19, 192, 363, 383–6, 722
  s 1 . . . 383
  s 6(2)(b) . . . 385
  s 16 . . . 383
  s 24 . . . 385
  s 24(1)(a)–(b) . . . 385
  s 32(3)(b) . . . 386
  Sch 1 . . . 383
  Sch 2 . . . 385
  Sch 3 . . . 384
Northern Ireland Constitution Act 1973 . . . 382
Northern Ireland (Emergency Provisions) Act 1978 . . . 638
Northern Ireland (Executive Formation etc) Act 2019 . . . 234, 385
  s 3 . . . 234
Northern Ireland (St Andrews Agreement) Act 2006 . . . 386
  Preamble . . . 386

Obscene Publications Acts 1959 . . . 633–4
Obscene Publications Acts 1964 . . . 633–4
Offences Against the Person Act 1861
  ss 58, 59 . . . 385
Official Secrets Act 1989
  s 11(2) . . . 596
Overseas Development and Co-operation Act 1980
  s 1(1) . . . 432

Parliament Act 1911 . . . 20, 21, 26, 127, 146–8, 236, 244–5, 306, 329, 339–40, 347
  Preamble . . . 21, 329
  s 2 . . . 148
  s 2(1) . . . 146–8, 340–1
  s 7 . . . 244
Parliament Act 1949 . . . 20, 21, 26, 53, 126–7, 146–8, 306, 339–41, 347
Parliamentary Commissioner Act 1967 . . . 585–6, 590, 595, 600–2
  s 1(2) . . . 585
  s 1(2B) . . . 585
  s 1(3) . . . 585
  s 4 . . . 593
  s 4(2) . . . 593

s 5 . . . 586

s 5(1) . . . 593

s 5(1A)–(1C) . . . 593

s 5(2) . . . 594

s 6(3) . . . 594

s 7 . . . 595

s 7(2) . . . 596

s 8(1) . . . 596

s 8(2) . . . 596

s 8(3) . . . 596

s 8(4) . . . 596

s 9 . . . 596

s 10(1) . . . 596

s 10(2) . . . 586, 596

s 10(3) . . . 598

s 12 . . . 587

s 12(3) . . . 587

Sch 2 . . . 278, 593

Sch 3 . . . 593

    para 9 . . . 593

Parliamentary Voting System and Constituencies
    Act 2011 . . . 311

Petition of Right 1628 . . . 16, 75, 150

Planning Act (Northern Ireland) 2011 . . . 396

Police Act 1964 . . . 209

Police Act 1996

s 49 . . . 606

Police and Criminal Evidence Act 1984
    (PACE) . . . 672, 696, 699–700, 704, 706–8,
    710–16

s 1 . . . 701, 716

s 1(1) . . . 700

s 1(2)(a) . . . 700

s 1(2)(b) . . . 700

s 1(3) . . . 700

s 1(6) . . . 700

s 1A(b) . . . 712

s 2 . . . 700, 701

s 2(9) . . . 700

s 3 . . . 700

s 8 . . . 711–15

s 8(1) . . . 711

s 8(1)(d) . . . 711

s 8(1C) . . . 711

s 8(2) . . . 711

s 8(3) . . . 711

s 16 . . . 715

s 17 . . . 712–13, 716

s 17(1) . . . 712

s 17(1)(e) . . . 712–13

s 17(2)(a) . . . 713

s 18 . . . 711, 714–16

s 18(1) . . . 714–15

s 18(2) . . . 714

s 18(4) . . . 714

s 19 . . . 715–16

s 24 . . . 706–7, 710

s 24(1) . . . 706

s 24(2) . . . 706, 708–9

s 24(3) . . . 706–8, 710

s 24(4) . . . 706

s 24(5) . . . 706–7

s 24(5)(e) . . . 714

s 24A . . . 706

s 28 . . . 706

s 28(1) . . . 707, 710

s 28(2) . . . 707

s 28(4) . . . 707

s 32 . . . 711, 714

s 32(1) . . . 714

s 32(2)(b) . . . 714

s 32(6) . . . 714–15

s 60 . . . 700

s 60A . . . 700

s 66 . . . 700

s 78 . . . 711

s 117 . . . 700

Prevention of Terrorism (Temporary provisions)
    Act 1984 . . . 638

s 12(1) . . . 709

Protection of Freedoms Act 2012 . . . 700–1

Public Health (London) Act 1891

s 44 . . . 476

Public Order Act 1936 . . . 681–3, 688

s 1 . . . 681–3

s 2 . . . 683

s 2(1) . . . 682

ss 3–4 . . . 683

s 5 . . . 683, 688–9

Public Order Act 1986 . . . 683–5, 687–9, 690,
    693, 716

s 1 . . . 683–6, 690

s 1(4) . . . 684

s 1(6) . . . 683

s 2 . . . 683–4, 686, 690

s 2(3) . . . 684

s 2(5) . . . 683

s 3 . . . 683–4, 686, 690

s 3(2) . . . 684

s 3(4) . . . 684

s 3(5) . . . 684

s 3(7) . . . 683

s 4 . . . 683, 685–90, 716

s 4(1) . . . 685, 687

s 4A . . . 683, 686–7, 689–90, 716

s 5 . . . 683, 686–7, 689–90, 716

s 7(3) . . . 685

Pt II (ss 11–16) . . . 690

s 11 . . . 691–3

s 11(1) . . . 691

s 11(2) . . . 691–2

s 11(3) . . . 691

s 11(5) . . . 691

s 12 . . . 692–3

s 12(1) . . . 692

s 12(5) . . . 692

s 13 . . . 693

s 13(1) . . . 692

s 14 . . . 693–5

s 14(1) . . . 693

s 14A . . . 693, 695

s 14A(1) . . . 695

s 14A(9) . . . 695

s 14B . . . 695

s 14C . . . 695

s 16 . . . 693

Public Processions (Northern Ireland)
Act 1998

s 6(7) . . . 691

Race Relations Act 1976 . . . 138

s 71 . . . 475, 483

Radioactive Substances Act 1960 . . . 430

Recall of MPs Act 2015 . . . 313–14

Regency Acts 1937–1953 . . . 253–4

s 2 . . . 254

s 4 . . . 254

s 4(2) . . . 254

Regulation of Investigatory Powers Act
2000 . . . 416

s 67(8) . . . 416

Rent Act 1977 . . . 652

Representation of the People Act
1832 . . . 180, 390

Representation of the People Act 1867 . . . 180

Representation of the People Act 1884 . . . 180

Representation of the People Act 1918 . . . 307

Representation of the People Act 1928 . . . 307

Representation of the People Act 1981

s 1 . . . 313

s 3 . . . 313

s 160 . . . 313

s 173 . . . 313

Representation of the People Act 1983

s 1(1) . . . 311

s 1(1)(b) . . . 311

s 1(1)(d) . . . 311

s 1(2) . . . 311

s 2(1)(c) . . . 311

s 3 . . . 312

s 3(1) . . . 645

s 3A . . . 311

Representation of the People Act 1985

s 1 . . . 312

s 2 . . . 312

Road Traffic Act 1972

s 159 . . . 702

Road Traffic Act 1988 . . . 646

s 163 . . . 700

Royal Assent Act 1967 . . . 237, 339

s 1(1) . . . 237

Royal Marriages Act 1772 . . . 255

Scotland Act 1978 . . . 364

Scotland Act 1998 . . . 19, 151, 180, 192, 337,
363–6, 368, 373–4, 726

s 2(2) . . . 365

s 28 . . . 365, 371

s 28(7) . . . 365, 370, 372

s 29 . . . 366, 367–70, 385

s 29(1) . . . 366

s 29(2) . . . 366–8

s 29(2)(b) . . . 370

s 29(2)(c) . . . 370

s 29(2)(d) . . . 367, 370

s 29(3)–(4) . . . 367

s 37 . . . 365

Sch 4 . . . 367–8

Sch 5 . . . 366–8

Sch 5(H1) . . . 370

Scotland Act 2012 . . . 364, 366, 372

s 12 . . . 372

Scotland Act 2016 . . . 366, 374–5, 381

s 1 . . . 374

s 2 . . . 371–2, 374

s 4 . . . 374

s 11 . . . 374

Pt 2 (ss 13–21) . . . 374

Pt 3 (ss 22–35) . . . 374

Scrap Metal Dealers Act 2013 . . . 343–5

s 11 . . . 343

s 11(2) . . . 343

s 11(3) . . . 343

s 20 . . . 344

s 23(2) . . . 344–5

Sea Fisheries (Scotland) Amendment Act
1885 . . . 128

Security Services Act 1989 . . . 252

Senior Courts Act 1981 . . . 98, 418–9, 422, 434,
441–2

s 30 . . . 441

s 31 . . . 418, 441–2

s 31(1) . . . 441

s 31(2) . . . 442

s 31(3) . . . 421, 666

s 31(4)(b) . . . 442

s 31(5) . . . 441

s 31A(2) . . . 570

s 130 . . . 98

s 130(1) . . . 98

Serious Organised Crime and Police Act
2005 . . . 706, 711

s 134 . . . 473

Sex Discrimination Act 1986 . . . 138

Sexual Offences Act 2003

s 72 . . . 130

Sexual Offences (Amendment) Act 2000 . . . 21,
126, 341

Smoking, Health and Social Care (Scotland) Act
2005 . . . 366

Southern Rhodesia Act 1965 . . . 133

Statute Law (Repeals) Act 1989 . . . 134

Statute of Proclamations 1539 . . . 39

Statute of Westminster 1931 . . . 130–1

s 4 . . . 130–1

Statutory Instruments Act 1947

s 6 . . . 346

Succession to the Crown Act 2013 . . . 255

s 1 . . . 255

s 2 . . . 255

s 3 . . . 255

Suicide Act 1961

s 2 . . . 656

Sunday Entertainments Act 1932

s 1(1) . . . 489

Supreme Court Act 1981 . . . see Senior Courts
Act 1981

Taxes Management Act 1970

s 20C . . . 80

Terrorism Act 2000 . . . 700–1, 703

s 13(1) . . . 682

s 41 . . . 709

s 44 . . . 701, 702–3

s 44(1) . . . 703

s 44(2) . . . 703

s 45 . . . 701–3

s 45(1) . . . 701

s 45(1)(b) . . . 703

s 47A . . . 700, 702

s 47A(1) . . . 701–2

s 47A(5) . . . 700

Tobacco and Primary Medical Services (Scotland)
Act 2010 . . . 368

Transport (Scotland) Act 2001

s 52(1)(b) . . . 401

Tribunals, Courts and Enforcement Act
2007 . . . 565, 568, 569–74, 578–9, 582–3, 618

s 1 . . . 574

s 2 . . . 573

s 3 . . . 565

s 3(5) . . . 565

s 7(9) . . . 565

s 9 . . . 567

s 10 . . . 567

s 11(1) . . . 567

s 11(5) . . . 567

s 12 . . . 567

s 13(1) . . . 567

s 13(6) . . . 567

s 14(2) . . . 568

ss 14A–C . . . 568

s 15 . . . 570

s 15(1) . . . 570

s 18(4) . . . 570

s 18(5) . . . 570

s 18(6) . . . 570

s 22 . . . 578

s 39 . . . 574

s 43 . . . 573

Sch 17

   para 13 . . . 561

Triennial Act 1641 . . . 120

Wales Act 1978 . . . 377

Wales Act 2014 . . . 381

Wales Act 2017 . . . 380–1, 726

s 1 . . . 381

s 2 . . . 381

s3(1) . . . 380

Pt 2 (ss 23–58) . . . 380

War Crimes Act 1991 . . . 21, 126, 341

War Damages Act 1965 . . . 53, 54, 108, 132

s 1 . . . 53

Weights and Measures Act 1985 . . . 180–1

Welfare Reform Act 2012

s 94 . . . 279

Welsh Church Act 1914 . . . 21, 126, 341

Youth Justice and Criminal Evidence Act 1999

s 41 . . . 649, 658

s 41(3)(c) . . . 649–50

Statutory Instruments

Appeals from the Upper Tribunal to the Court of Appeal Order 2008 (SI 2008/2834) . . . 567

Asylum Appeals (Procedure) Rules 1993 (SI 1993/1661)

r 13(3) . . . 516

Civil Procedure Rules 1998 (SI 1998/3132) . . . 410, 418–20, 434, 437

Pt 54 . . . 419–20

r 54.1(2)(a) . . . 411

r 54.1(2)(a)(ii) . . . 437

r 54.5 . . . 419

r 54.6 . . . 419

r 54.7 . . . 419

r 54.7A . . . 572

r 54.8 . . . 420

r 54.10 . . . 420

Defence (General) Regulations 1939

reg 18B . . . 104

Defence of the Realm Regulations 1914 . . . 210–11

Dock Workers (Regulation of Employment) Order 1947 (SI 1947/1189) . . . 470

European Union (Withdrawal) Act 2018 (Exit Day) (Amendment) (No 3) Regulations 2019 (SI 1423/2019)

reg 2 . . . 189

Food and Drink, Veterinary Medicines and Residues (Amendment etc.) (EU Exit) Regulations 2019 (SI 2019/865) . . . 194

Gibraltar Constitution Order 2006 . . . 216

Immigration Rules 2007 . . . 460–1

r 57 . . . 459

Income Support (General) Regulations 1987 (SI 1987/1967)

reg 70(3A) . . . 93

Inquiry Rules 2006 (SI 2006/1838)

rr 13–15 . . . 615

Jobseeker's Allowance (Employment, Skills and Enterprise Scheme) Regulations 2011 (SI 2011/917) . . . 93

Local Government (Boundaries) Order (Northern Ireland) 2012 (SR 2012/421) . . . 391

Prison Rules 1999 (SI 1999/728) . . . 99

r 45(1) . . . 99

r 45(2) . . . 99

Public Bodies (Abolition of Administrative Justice and Tribunals Council) Order 2013 (SI 2013/2042)

Sch 1

   para 36 . . . 561

Public Contracts Regulations 2006 (SI 2006/5) . . . 398

Rules of the Supreme Court (SI 1965/1776)
   Order 53 . . . 418–9, 434–5, 441–2
   r 3(7) . . . 425

Scrap Metal Dealers Act 2013 (Commencement
   and Transitional Provisions) Order 2013 (SI
   2013/1966) . . . 345
Scrap Metal Dealers Act 2013 (Prescribed
   Documents and Information for Verification
   of Name and Address) Regulations 2013 (SI
   2013/2276) . . . 343
   reg 2 . . . 343
Single Use Carrier Bags Charge (Wales) Regulations 2010 (WSI/2010/2880) . . . 381
   r 6 . . . 381
Supreme Court Fees Order 1980 (SI
   1980/821) . . . 98

Tribunal Procedure (First-Tier Tribunal) (General
   Regulatory Chamber) Rules 2009 (SI 2009/1976)
   r 2 . . . 578
Tribunal Procedure (First-Tier Tribunal) (Social
   Entitlement Chamber) Rules 2008 (SI 2008/2685)
   r 2 . . . 578

Units of Measurement Regulations 1994
   (SI 1994/2867) . . . 180

European Legislation

Conventions and Treaties

Agreement on the withdrawal of the United
   Kingdom of Great Britain and Northern Ireland
   from the European Union and the European
   Atomic Energy Community (Official Journal of
   the European Union, 2019/C/66 I/01, 19 Febru-
   ary 2019) . . . 194–200, 225, 233, 324
   Art 4 . . . 196
   Art 4(3), (4) . . . 196
   Art 15 . . . 197
   Art 16 . . . 197
   Art 18 . . . 197
   Art 126 . . . 194–5
   Art 127 . . . 195
   Art 54(2) . . . 198
   Art 132 . . . 195

Merger Treaty 1965 . . . 158

Single European Act (SEA) 1987 . . . 158–9, 182
   Art 13 . . . 158

Treaty establishing a Constitution for Europe
   2004 . . . 160, 182
   Art I-34 . . . 160
Treaty establishing the European Atomic Energy
   Community (EUROTOM) 1957 . . . 156
Treaty establishing the European Community
   (EC Treaty) 1957 . . . 160
   Art 177 . . . 167
Treaty establishing the European Economic Com-
   munity (EEC) (Treaties of Rome) 1957 . . . 157–9
   Art 8a . . . 158
   Art 100a . . . 159
   Art 119 . . . 174–5
Treaty of Amsterdam 1999 . . . 159, 163,
Treaty of Lisbon 2009 . . . 159–60
Treaty of Nice 2003 . . . 159, 163, 182
Treaty on European Union (TEU) (Maastricht
   Treaty) 1993 . . . 159–61, 163, 182, 426
   Art 1 . . . 160
   Art 3 . . . 160
   Art 4(3) . . . 169
   Art 4(6) . . . 165
   Art 5(1) . . . 166
   Art 5(3) . . . 11, 166, 358
   Art 5(4) . . . 167
   Arts 13–19 . . . 161
   Art 14(2) . . . 162
   Art 15(1) . . . 161
   Art 16(4) . . . 161
   Art 17(1) . . . 161
   Art 17(2) . . . 161
   Art 17(3) . . . 161
   Art 17(5) . . . 161
   Art 19(1) . . . 162
   Art 27 . . . 161
   Art 47 . . . 160
   Art 49 . . . 160
   Art 50 . . . 10, 58, 155, 161, 184–9, 194, 199,
      229–34, 324
   Art 50(1) . . . 185
   Art 50(2) . . . 185, 187, 229
   Art 50(3) . . . 185
   Protocol on Social Policy . . . 426, 428
Treaty on the Functioning of the European Union
   (TFEU) 2009 . . . 159, 162–3, 166, 190–1
   Art 2(2) . . . 166
   Art 3 . . . 165

Art 4 . . . 166
Art 4(5) . . . 166
Art 5 . . . 166
Art 18 . . . 190
Art 20 . . . 190
Art 20(2)(c) . . . 190
Art 21(1) . . . 190
Art 28 . . . 170–1, 190
Art 30 . . . 190
Art 34 . . . 190
Art 35 . . . 190
Art 36 . . . 190
Art 37(1) . . . 191
Art 37(2) . . . 191
Art 45(1)–(3) . . . 191
Art 49 . . . 176, 191
Art 56 . . . 191
Art 57 . . . 191
Art 63 . . . 191
Art 101(1) . . . 191
Art 102 . . . 191
Art 106(1) . . . 191
Art 106(2) . . . 191
Art 107(1) . . . 191
Art 108(3) . . . 191
Art 110 . . . 191
Art 112 . . . 191
Art 114 . . . 159
Art 157 . . . 174, 191
Art 258 . . . 170
Art 267 . . . 162, 167, 170–1
Art 288 . . . 163, 169, 171
Protocol 5 . . . 191
Protocol 7 . . . 191
Treaty establishing the European Coal and
Steel Community (ECSC) (Treaty of Paris)
1951 . . . 157
Art 2 . . . 157

European Directives

Directive 80/836/EEC
Art 6 . . . 430
Directive 2000/43/EC . . . 189
Directive 2000/78/EC . . . 189
Directive 2004/18/EC . . . 398
Directive 2004/113/EC . . . 189
Directive 2006/54/EC . . . 189

European Regulations

Regulation 404/93/EEC . . . 163
Regulation 1083/2006/EC . . . 406
Regulation 1907/2006/EC . . . 163
Regulation 1151/2012/EU . . . 154, 166, 172, 175,
188, 193, 198–9
Regulation 666/2013/EU . . . 163
Regulation 1303/2013/EU . . . 406

Other National Legislation

Australia

Constitution Act 1902 (NSW) . . . 143–4
s 7A . . . 144
Constitution (Legislative Council) Amendment
Act 1929 (NSW) . . . 143–4

Canada

Constitution . . . 130
Constitution Act 1982 . . . 130

Germany

Constitution . . . 168

Italy

Constitutional Code . . . 167

New Zealand

Constitution . . . 8

United States

Constitution 1787 . . . 5–8, 14, 23, 40, 116, 388,
621, 669, 720
Art 1 . . . 4, 11
Art 1(1) . . . 13
Art 1(7) . . . 13
Art 2 . . . 4, 11, 13
Art 2(1) . . . 13
Art 2(2) . . . 225
Art 3 . . . 4, 11
Art 4 . . . 4
Art 5 . . . 7
Bill of Rights . . . 23, 621, 636, 669
Tenth Amendment . . . 11

Declaration of Independence 1776 . . . 4–6, 621–3

Voting Rights Act 1965
  s 4 . . . 40

War Powers Act . . . 223

International Legislation

Anglo-Irish Treaty 1921 . . . 19, 362

European Convention on Human Rights
  (ECHR) . . . 24, 52, 86, 94, 111–12, 128, 151,
  367, 371, 494, 497–8, 500–1, 503, 504, 507,
  535, 607, 622, 624–35, 637–42, 644–8, 650–1,
  653–6, 658–60, 662–9, 671–4, 679–82, 686,
  689–90, 693–6, 698–9, 701, 704–5, 708,
  716, 721
  Art 2 . . . 605, 607–8, 626, 628, 665
  Art 3 . . . 385, 501, 605, 626–7, 630, 644,
    658, 686
  Art 4 . . . 626–7
  Art 5 . . . 81–2, 112, 501, 626, 628–30, 644,
    657–8, 664, 671, 679–80, 696–8, 701, 704,
    706, 716
  Art 5(1) . . . 628, 680, 696, 701
  Art 5(1)(a) . . . 630, 680
  Art 5(1)(b) . . . 680
  Art 5(1)(c) . . . 643, 679–80, 697
  Art 5(1)(d)–(f) . . . 680
  Art 5(2) . . . 697
  Art 5(3) . . . 697
  Art 5(4) . . . 697
  Art 5(5) . . . 697
  Art 6 . . . 57, 94, 513–14, 520, 535–7, 545, 557,
    577, 626, 643, 646, 649–50, 657, 698
  Art 6(1) . . . 94, 698
  Art 6(2) . . . 698
  Art 6(3) . . . 698
  Art 7 . . . 627
  Art 8 . . . 112, 371, 385, 495, 497, 499, 501, 626,
    627, 630–1, 634, 637, 652, 655–6, 659–61,
    663, 665–6, 671, 696, 698, 703–4, 712–13,
    716, 726
  Art 8(2) . . . 627
  Art 9 . . . 626–7, 644
  Art 10 . . . 494, 626–7, 633–4, 638, 641, 665–6,
    671, 673–4, 679, 682, 686, 689, 694–5, 703,
    716, 726

Art 11 . . . 626, 627, 671, 673–4, 679, 682, 686,
  694–5, 703, 716
Art 12 . . . 626
Art 13 . . . 626, 640
Art 14 . . . 82, 112, 385, 626, 652, 655,
  666, 704
Art 15 . . . 82, 626, 627, 629
Art 16 . . . 626
Art 17 . . . 626
Art 18 . . . 626
Arts 19–52 . . . 631
Art 20 . . . 632
Art 22 . . . 632
Art 23 . . . 632
Art 25 . . . 635
Art 33 . . . 632
Art 34 . . . 632
Art 35 . . . 632
Art 35(1) . . . 632
Art 35(2) . . . 632
Art 35(3) . . . 632
Art 35(4) . . . 632
Art 40(1) . . . 632
Art 43 . . . 632
Art 44(1) . . . 632
Art 45 . . . 632
Art 46 . . . 632, 635
Protocol 1 . . . 629, 630, 660
  Art 1 . . . 367, 629, 657
  Art 2 . . . 629
  Art 3 . . . 312, 629, 630, 645
Protocol 4 . . . 629, 630
  Art 2 . . . 629
  Art 3 . . . 629
Protocol 6 . . . 629, 630
  Art 2 . . . 629
Protocol 7 . . . 629, 630
  Art 3 . . . 629
  Art 4 . . . 629
Protocol 11 . . . 631
Protocol 12 . . . 629, 630
  Art 1 . . . 629
Protocol 13 . . . 629, 630
  Art 1 . . . 629
Protocol 14 . . . 629

Protocol 15 . . . 629, 632
Protocol 16 . . . 629

Good Friday Agreement 1998 . . . 382–3, 387

International Covenant on Civil and Political
Rights
Preamble . . . 624

North Sea Fisheries Convention 1883 . . . 128–9

Statute of the Council of Europe
Art 1 . . . 625, 631
Art 3 . . . 625, 631

UN Convention on the Rights of the Child
1989 . . . 224
United Nations Resolution 1441 . . . 67
United Nations Universal Declaration on Human
Rights 1948 . . . 624–5
Art 25 . . . 624

The UK Constitution

Problem scenario

Following the death of King William V, his son, George VII, succeeds him, becoming King of the United Kingdom. George is keen to reassert the historical power of the monarchy and within the first year of his reign takes the following (fictitious) actions:

- Following that year's General Election, and since he does not like the leader of the political party that achieves a majority in the House of Commons, George VII decides to summon the leader of the second largest party in the House of Commons to Buckingham Palace, asking her to become Prime Minister and to form a government.

- When a bill amending the Devolution settlements with Scotland, Wales, and Northern Ireland is brought to George VII for Royal Assent, he amends it heavily, effectively abolishing the Devolution Settlements on the basis that he wishes the country 'to be one, United Kingdom, under one Monarch and one Parliament'. Once the amendments have been made, he signs the bill, passing it into law.

- Finally, and late in the year, when the government seeks to introduce a bill into Parliament that would severely limit the King's ability to influence the political process and the passing of laws, George VII instructs the House of Lords to veto the bill and threatens to strip members of the Lords of their peerages if they do not obey.

1.1 Introduction to public law

Public law is concerned with the exercise of power within a state,[1] explaining both how and by whom it is exercised and the manner in which it can be regulated. It refers, in this sense, to two distinct areas of law that further explain its nature: constitutional and administrative law. Explaining these two areas of law, and their relationship to the broader discipline of public law, Sir Stephen Sedley, former Court of Appeal judge and eminent public lawyer, notes that '[b]y public law I mean the body of law, embracing both administrative and constitutional law, by which the state is regulated both institutionally and in its dealings with individuals'.[2] When we refer to constitutional law, as a part of public law, we are concerned with the laws and principles that determine the allocation of power, that identify the institutions that legitimately wield it, and that set out the manner of these institutions' operation, clarifying the relationship they enjoy with one another and with citizens. Such laws and principles are invariably set out and protected through a state's constitution, as the name suggests. Administrative law, by contrast, refers to laws determining the manner in which power can be controlled and regulated, and the way in which the rights of citizens are protected amid the day-to-day administration of the state. Public law, therefore, is fundamental to the working of a legal system since its laws and principles help determine who has the power to make law, to make policy, and to adjudicate disputes, as well as the way in which those powers should be exercised and controlled. Certain aspects of human rights law are also included in this discussion as it is an area of law that deals with the regulation of state power on the basis of the protection of citizens' rights. This book, therefore, covers a broad and far-reaching area of law. It is structured, first, to explain the constitutional laws and principles underpinning the UK system, secondly, to deal with administrative law, and thirdly, to address human rights. Before we embark upon this exploration, however, we must first examine the form and nature of the UK Constitution itself.

The laws and principles determining the allocation and use of power in a state are typically set out in a constitution, that instrument being central to all that the state and its citizens can do, and underpinning and explaining the relationships between the different state actors. On this foundation, the study of constitutional law involves consideration of the way in which constitutions carry out this function and fulfil this role, including an exploration of the issues that arise as a consequence. In the UK, however, constitutional law is a particularly complex discipline, chiefly due to the way in which the 'peculiar' UK Constitution differs from many other systems across the world. This opening chapter aims to provide an introduction to the UK Constitution and to set out a foundation upon which

---

[1] See, for fuller discussion, Mark Elliott and David Feldman (eds), *The Cambridge Companion to Public Law* (Cambridge University Press 2015) Introduction. 'The state' refers to the broad institution which seeks to exercise authority over a territory or region. Loughlin defines it as 'that institution which claims the ultimate allegiance of its citizens and which maintains "the monopoly of the legitimate use of physical force within a given territory"' (Martin Loughlin, *The Idea of Public Law* (OUP 2003) 6, citing Max Weber, 'Politics as a Vocation' (1919) in HH Gerth and C Wright Mills (eds), *From Max Weber* (Routledge & Kegan Paul 1948) 77, 78).

[2] Stephen Sedley, *Lions under the Throne: Essays on the History of English Public Law* (Cambridge University Press 2015) 1. Sedley cites Loughlin who notes that public law is concerned with 'the constitution, maintenance and regulation of government authority', see Martin Loughlin, *The Idea of Public Law* (OUP 2003) 1.

discussions in later chapters can further develop. In doing this, it starts by exploring established definitions of constitutions, placing the unique UK system within commonly accepted themes and characteristics. It then moves to explain the nature and form of the UK Constitution and some of the sources of which it is constructed, as well as exploring some of the more theoretical considerations as regards its character, including the way in which it is legitimized. The final section of the chapter then entertains academic questions concerning whether or not the UK can be said to have a constitution, including discussion of the case for and against a codified system. On this basis, the aims of this chapter are:

- to consider the meaning of the term 'constitution';
- to explore the basic nature and sources of the UK's Constitution;
- to consider the legitimacy of power and authority within the UK's Constitution;
- to provide an introduction to some theoretical discussions relating to the character of the constitution including questions regarding whether or not the UK can be said to have a constitution;
- to discuss arguments pertaining to whether or not the UK needs a codified constitution.
- These objectives are set within a broader context framed by the problem scenario, above, which will be revisited throughout the chapter.

1.2 Defining a constitution

Defining a constitution is a difficult task. The term means different things for different countries, institutions, and organizations and it takes no standard form. This section considers various definitions of a 'constitution' and explores the role it fulfils in a democratic system of government.

Many constitutional theorists have offered a definition of a constitution. Professor KC Wheare, for instance, notes that '[t]he word "constitution" . . . is used to describe the whole system of government of a country, the collection of rules which establish and regulate or govern the government. These rules are partly legal . . . and partly non-legal . . .'.[3] Hilaire Barnett adds that:

> The constitution of a state . . . forms the backcloth of government and its powers . . . [it] is a set of rules, written or unwritten, which identifies the principal institutions of the state, their powers and relationships with other state institutions and the relationship between government and citizen.[4]

Finally, Colin Munro considers that a constitution means 'the body of rules and arrangements concerning the government of the country'.[5]

From these three definitions we can extract the following: a constitution is the highest source of power within a system of government; it is a collection of rules that identify, regulate, and govern the manner in which a state's institutions operate and relate to one

---

[3] KC Wheare, *Modern Constitutions* (OUP 1966) 1.
[4] Hilaire Barnett, *Britain Unwrapped: Government and Constitution Explained* (Penguin 2002) 1.
[5] Colin R Munro, *Studies in Constitutional Law* (LexisNexis Butterworths 1999) 1.

another; and it draws the parameters within which a relationship between the state and individuals can be fostered. Constitutional documents the world over exemplify these features. In the USA, for instance, provision is made for the powers of Congress, the President, and the courts' as well as for the way in which the individual states relate to the federal institutions.[6] If this is what a constitution *is*, however, then what role is it intended to fulfil?

A constitution is invariably regarded as the source of all power within a state and the highest authority of law in a system of government. This is widely accepted, not least by Thomas Paine, an eighteenth-century political and constitutional theorist, who noted that:

> A Constitution is a Thing antecedent to Government, and a Government is only the Creature of a Constitution. The Constitution of a Country is not the act of its Government, but of the People constituting a Government. It is the Body of Elements to which you can refer and quote article by article; and which contains the principles upon which the Government shall be established, the manner in which it shall be organized, the powers it shall have, the Mode of Elections, the Duration of Parliaments . . . the powers which the executive part of the Government shall have; and, in fine, every thing that relates to the compleat organization of a civil government, and the principles upon which it shall act, and by which it shall be bound.[7]

Paine here explains the sanctity with which the authority of a constitution should be regarded, particularly in relation to the power of a government. According to Paine, a constitution authorizes and limits government action insofar as its provisions and principles determine the establishment of that government, the powers with which it is blessed, and the manner in which it can use those powers. On this basis, constitutions make provision for individual rights; they legitimize and set out the scope of executive power and provide the foundation for the relationships between the institutions of a state as well as between citizens and those institutions. As Paine implies, government institutions are bound by these rights and by the limits of executive power and they must honour the boundaries that exist between the various institutions. It is also notable that Paine emphasizes the importance of 'people constituting a Government'.[8] This not only underlines the fact that a constitution should be regarded as more powerful than any government or legislative institution, but also that democracy should be at the very heart of the system. A constitution does not exist primarily to justify political agendas but to ensure that the citizenry can live and enjoy a peaceful life in a system that adheres to due legal process, protects social order, and prevents both abuses of power and the infringement of individual rights. It is this that a constitution ultimately serves to uphold. These values are reflected in words taken from the United States Declaration of Independence:

> We hold these truths to be self-evident, that all men are created equal, that they are endowed by their Creator with certain unalienable Rights, that among these are Life, Liberty and the pursuit of Happiness. That to secure these rights, Governments are instituted among Men, deriving their just powers from the consent of the governed, that whenever any Form of Government becomes destructive of these ends, it is the Right of the People to alter or to abolish it, and to institute new Government, laying its foundation on such principles and organizing its powers in such form, as to them shall seem most likely to effect their Safety and Happiness.[9]

[6] See Articles 1, 2, 3, and 4 of the US Constitution, 1787.
[7] Thomas Paine, *The Rights of Man* (1791).   [8] Ibid.
[9] US Declaration of Independence, 1776.

Pause for reflection

What do you think this Declaration of Independence means when it says that governments derive 'their just powers from the consent of the governed'? How do citizens give their consent to be governed and to the way in which a government operates?

As US President Abraham Lincoln noted in the century after Paine wrote *The Rights of Man*, 'government of the people, by the people and for the people'[10] is a central value of a constitution. The role that a constitution should fulfil and the way in which it relates to the institutions of government, therefore, is clear: it should provide the ultimate source of power for the good of the people. Building on this notion, the next section now considers the particular nature of the UK Constitution.

1.3 The nature of the UK Constitution

Consideration of the nature of the UK Constitution requires exploration of its key features, as well as a comparison with alternative systems around the world. In doing this, three themes are acknowledged: first, the features of the constitution, second, the distinction between a legal and a political constitution, and third, the structure of the constitution. We consider each matter in turn.

1.3.1 The features of the UK Constitution

The chapter started by noting the 'peculiar' nature of the UK Constitution, which stems from its most defining feature: its uncodified nature. This refers to the location in which the constitution can be found and the form that it takes. In all but three countries of the world—the United Kingdom, Israel, and New Zealand—constitutions take the form of a codified document. Though differing hugely in specific character and contents from country to country, this codified nature means that a constitution is written down in one place, created at a given point in time, and possibly with written amendments added in later years. By contrast, an uncodified constitution—such as that which prevails in the UK—is neither created at a given point nor contained within one single document. It is, in our case, set out across a range of sources, both legal and non-legal, written and unwritten, and introduced at various points across our history. Some of these sources are explored in detail later in this chapter; generally speaking, though, they fall into one of the following three categories: Acts of Parliament, case law, and constitutional conventions.[11]

The circumstances underpinning whether a country has a codified or uncodified constitution are linked to the manner in and the point at which that constitution came into being. In general, codified constitutions come about following a major event, such as a revolution, after which a country has needed to establish a fresh process and structure of government swiftly. The US Constitution, for instance, dates from 1787 and immediately

---

[10] Abraham Lincoln in the Gettysburg address, 19 November 1863.

[11] Relevant to conventions as a source of the constitution are government documents, such as the *Cabinet Manual* or the *Ministerial Code*, both of which are discussed in 1.6.

followed the American Revolution and Declaration of Independence. The written document was intended to provide the foundations for a new legal order and system of government, following a successful break from British rule. By contrast, uncodified systems evolve over a period of time, with new sources over that period adding to and constantly changing the nature and contents of the constitution. In the UK, for instance, apart from a period of Republican rule by Oliver Cromwell in the mid-seventeenth century, the system of government and democracy has developed continuously and incrementally since the Norman Conquest in 1066. The constitution has evolved through various sources since that time and has moulded into the system of rules and principles that govern our country today. Echoing this, the Supreme Court noted in *R (Miller) v Secretary of State for Exiting the European Union*[12] that '[u]nlike most countries, the United Kingdom does not have a constitution in the sense of a single coherent code of fundamental law which prevails over all other sources of law. Our constitutional arrangements have developed over time in a pragmatic as much as in a principled way, through a combination of statutes, events, conventions, academic writings and judicial decisions'.[13] Though the uncodified nature of the UK Constitution is its defining feature, this characteristic has consequences for the authority with which we regard the constitution and the manner in which it is changed and altered.

The circumstances that usually underpin the creation of a codified constitution mean that such documents invariably set out, before anything else, the basis on which a system of government will be established, as well as the functions and authority of the institutions of government. This is consistent with Paine's observation, noted above in section 1.2.[14] What this also means, however, is that the constitution is a higher source of law, fundamentally different—both in terms of its creation and its ongoing force—from ordinary laws that might thereafter be enacted by the legislature under the constitution. It is superior to all institutions and individuals in that state, including the legislature. This is a reality of the US Constitution. In an uncodified system such as the UK, however, because the system has evolved gradually over time, it consists of various sources enacted and introduced at different points throughout history. As a consequence, those laws which relate to constitutional matters and which can be said to equate to sources of the constitution are no different from those that are not. They are 'ordinary law' rather than of some special status and are subordinate to the sovereign authority of the legislature.[15]

This has a consequence for the ease with which the constitution can be amended. Because a codified constitutional document is a higher source of law, different in form from 'ordinary law' and created through an extraordinary process, it makes sense that amendment of that constitution should be through an equally extraordinary process, requiring a higher standard of approval than that required for ordinary laws. In the USA, for instance, whereas ordinary law is passed and repealed on the basis of a simple majority in both Houses of Congress and approval from the President, additions and amendments to the constitution must pass through a more rigorous process. They must be approved by

---

[12] [2017] UKSC 5.   [13] [2017] UKSC 5, [40].

[14] See Thomas Paine, *The Rights of Man* (1791).

[15] See Chapter 4 for further discussion. Orthodox theory states that Parliament is sovereign, which means that is has 'the right to make or unmake any law whatever' (AV Dicey, *Introduction to the Study of the Law of the Constitution* (JWF Allison ed, first published 1885, OUP 2013) 27).

two-thirds of both Houses of Congress and accepted by three-quarters of all the states.[16] By contrast, because the uncodified UK Constitution is predominantly contained within ordinary law, it can be adjusted and amended relatively easily through the ordinary process; that is, by laws passed through a simple majority in both Houses of Parliament and assented to by the Monarch. For example, the UK Parliament can legally repeal the Human Rights Act 1998 or the Constitutional Reform Act 2005—acts which are central to the constitutional system in the UK—as easily as any other Act of Parliament.

The differences in the way in which codified and uncodified constitutions can be amended alludes to a commonly noted distinction: 'constitutions may be classified according to the method by which they may be amended . . . Where no special process is required to amend a Constitution it is "flexible"; where a special process is required, a Constitution is labelled "rigid"'.[17] The general argument is that codified constitutions offer greater rigidity while uncodified constitutions, being made up of differing and constantly evolving sources that are easily changed, offer greater flexibility. This is readily apparent through further comparison between the US and UK systems. The process through which the US Constitution can be amended is lengthy and requires widespread acceptance. This means that constitutional laws are considerably harder to amend than ordinary laws, thereby explaining the rigidity of the US Constitution. This perhaps explains why there have been only twenty-seven amendments in the last 240 years.

By contrast, the flexible nature of the UK Constitution rests on the fact that we do not distinguish between laws pertaining to the constitution and other laws dealing with more day-to-day, 'non-constitutional' matters. Legally, they are all of the same force.[18] Legislation is easily enacted and repealed, while the rules of judicial precedent and the court hierarchy result in cases that are easily overturned by higher authority.[19] This means that:

> [The UK constitution] unlike the more common codified constitution, . . . retains sufficient flexibility to allow adaptation to suit the changing circumstances of society with minimum procedural restraints. This ability to change carries with it a danger that nothing is sacred; no principle secure from the priorities of the current government.[20]

The comparative benefits and disadvantages of rigid and flexible systems are often discussed. Flexible constitutions are seen as affording relevance and adaptability to cultural and societal changes, while rigidity brings consistency and certainty of long-lasting protection. Indeed, Wicks comments that an uncodified constitution offers the ability to adapt and shift with these changes at the expense of constitutional sanctity, while a codified constitution sacrifices the ability to change easily with the times in order to be more set in stone and sacred.[21]

---

[16] See Article 5 of the US Constitution, 1787.

[17] KC Wheare, *Modern Constitutions* (OUP 1966) 15–16.

[18] While this is indeed the case, it is interesting that the courts have on occasion acknowledged such a distinction. In *Thoburn v Sunderland City Council* [2002] EWHC 195 (Admin), Laws LJ noted a distinction between ordinary statutes and constitutional statutes, the latter being of important constitutional status and harder to repeal. This distinction has been noted more recently in *R (Miller) v Secretary of State for Exiting the European Union* [2017] UKSC 5.

[19] See, for further discussion on judicial precedent and the court hierarchy: Emily Allbon and Sanmeet Kaur Dua, *Elliott & Quinn's English Legal System* (Pearson 2019), chapter 1.

[20] Elizabeth Wicks, *The Evolution of a Constitution: Eight Key Moments in British Constitutional History* (Hart Publishing 2006) 1.

[21] Ibid.

Pause for reflection

Do you think that it is preferable for a constitution to be 'easy to change' and flexible or for it to be 'set in stone' and rigid?

The distinction between flexible and rigid constitutions, therefore, raises a number of issues—particularly with regards to the sanctity of a constitutional document compared with the ease with which that constitution can be amended. There are those, however, who argue that it is a rather academic distinction.

 Counterpoint: Is it helpful to distinguish between flexible and rigid constitutions?

Barendt considers that the distinction between flexible and rigid constitutions is 'now rather unhelpful'.[22] He bases this on two reasons. The first is that 'the group of flexible constitutions, those that can be amended by ordinary legislative procedure, is far too small: it may comprise now only the United Kingdom and New Zealand'.[23] The contention is that since so few countries in the world have what we might term a flexible constitution it is a category that is not widely recognized. This being so, the flexibility of the UK system is accepted, regardless of whether the label itself is one that cannot be widely given.

Barendt's second reason for noting the distinction as unhelpful is based on the diverse nature of the constitutions we might term rigid. He says that it is misleading 'to suggest that in practice rigid constitutions are necessarily impossible or very difficult to amend. In fact, this varies considerably from one constitution to another'.[24] Barendt exemplifies this by comparing the US Constitution, which has been amended twenty-seven times, with the younger German Constitution which has been through more than fifty amendments.[25] Simply to class constitutions as 'rigid', therefore, belies a more complex reality. Codified constitutions the world over differ greatly both in the ease with which they can be amended and the procedure through which those amendments can be enacted. Indeed, the chief common factor is simply that amendments are introduced through a special procedure, separate from the ordinary legislative process.

One final feature of comparison to note with regards to the UK and US Constitutional systems is the role of the Supreme Court. In the US, due to the prevalence of a codified constitutional document, the key institutions of the state are seen as equal under that constitution. The codified constitutional document provides supreme authority to which all institutions and legal processes are inferior; even ordinary legislative authority is subordinate to the constitution. Where power is exercised beyond the authority of the constitution, it falls to the US Supreme Court to strike such action out and to protect and uphold the provisions of the constitution. As such, the Supreme Court is the ultimate interpreter of the constitution and, in this role, has the power to scrutinize legislative and executive action in line with the constitution and set aside primary

---

[22] Eric Barendt, *An Introduction to Constitutional Law* (OUP 1998) 9.
[23] Ibid.   [24] Ibid.   [25] Ibid.

legislation and executive decisions on those grounds, if the need arises. In the UK, however, due to the lack of a codified constitutional document and the consequent prevalence of parliamentary sovereignty, the UK Supreme Court—replacing as it did the Appellate Committee of the House of Lords as the highest appeal court in the jurisdiction—acts simply as the highest court of appeal, sitting atop the domestic judicial hierarchy. It has no special powers to challenge the authority of the sovereign Parliament and its scope and ability to question the acts and decisions of the executive is limited by the concept of justiciability.[26] The uncodified constitution, found as it is across various sources, is subordinate to the authority of Parliament.

This section has explored the peculiar nature of the UK Constitution and the features that make it so different from other systems across the world, notably the US system. As the next section explains, though, the UK Constitution can be described as both legal and political.

1.3.2 A legal and political constitution

Much of what this chapter has considered and goes on to consider relates to what we call the legal constitution. This refers to the legal principles, statutory provisions, and common law rules that provide the substance of the constitution, enforced and implemented through the various institutions of the state—Parliament, executive, and the courts. In the UK, due to the uncodified nature of this legal constitution, the political machinery that takes place within the institutions and that seeks to influence and legitimize the exercise of power is also a defining factor—more so than in codified systems, where the legal framework is both clearer and stronger. This refers to what we call the political constitution. In short, our constitution is not just legal in nature, but also political. Emphasizing the prominence of this trait, Griffith, whose article explains the political nature of the UK Constitution, considered that '[t]he constitution of the United Kingdom lives on, changing from day to day; for the constitution is no more and no less than what happens. Everything that happens is constitutional. And if nothing happened that would be constitutional also'.[27]

In other words, the day-to-day political events of our governmental system are as much a part of the constitution as the various legal sources this chapter identifies and discusses. Indeed, when we consider the nature of these political aspects of the constitution, we start to see the extent to which they form a key part of its nature. In part due to the working of the parliamentary executive system, for example, the substance and content of legislation is underpinned by the political policies of those supporting the bill and the views of those opposing it. For further example, general elections, fought and contested on the basis of political manifestos, determine not only the formation of a government but also the numbers of MPs representing certain political parties in the House of Commons. Consequently, this can determine whether or not the government has a strong majority or a weak majority. The most recently prominent example of politics impacting upon the working of the Constitution, though, is Brexit. As a result of the political views of the British public, expressed through a referendum in 2016, the UK has recently gone through the process of leaving the European Union. Though that process involves and

---

[26] See 6.5.3 and 10.2.1.
[27] JAG Griffith, 'The Political Constitution' (1979) 42(1) *Modern Law Review* 1, 19.

has been punctuated by legal provision and procedure,[28] at its heart it is a process rooted in political policy and opinion.[29] The 2016 referendum itself was merely an expression of political will, with no legal requirements tied to its result, whilst the Government's negotiation of a deal with the European Council and the process through which that has been debated and discussed in the House of Commons are also evidence of the political constitution at work.[30] Politics, therefore, plays a crucial part in the broader constitution within the legal framework set out by the various legal sources.

A particularly notable feature of this distinction between the legal and political aspects of the UK Constitution, however, is the principle of constitutionalism. Constitutionalism refers to the notion of governments operating and acting in adherence to and in accordance with the constitutional principles of a state. If a government acts in contravention of the rules of a constitution it is said to have acted 'unconstitutionally'. Explaining this further, former Law Lord Lord Steyn notes that:

> [T]he principle of constitutionalism . . . is a political theory as to the type of institutional arrangements that are necessary in order to support the democratic ideal. It holds that the exercise of government power must be controlled in order that it should not be destructive of the very values which it was intended to promote.[31]

This notion of constitutionalism is reflected in practical terms by the various mechanisms which ensure that a government acts legitimately and is accountable for its actions. In keeping with both the legal and political nature of the UK system, that accountability comes in the form of both legal *and* political constitutionalism. Legal constitutionalism refers to the manner in which government can be held to legal account in the courts, while political constitutionalism is reflected in the political processes that work to keep the government in check. These include the democratic process, most prominent through elections, mechanisms of accountability in the House of Commons such as Question Time (discussed at 2.4.1 and 8.7), and the conventions of ministerial responsibility. Both the legal and political features of our system combine to ensure that it operates effectively and that the exercise of power is kept in check. In later chapters we explore in much greater detail some of these legal and political features that are so central to the operation of the constitution. It has been helpful at this point, however, to highlight the legal and political nature of the UK Constitution, further exemplifying its nature and the manner in which it operates. We look now at the structure of the UK Constitution.

1.3.3 The structure of the UK Constitution

Chapter 2, which discusses the separation of powers, will explain that there are typically three core constitutional functions: the legislative function for making laws, the executive function for executing policy and making decisions, and the judicial function for resolving and adjudicating disputes. The separation of powers doctrine states that

---

[28] See, for example, Article 50 TEU and the European Union (Withdrawal) Act 2018.

[29] See Chapter 5 for more discussion and detail.

[30] For further discussion on Brexit and the political constitution, see Michael Gordon, 'Parliamentary sovereignty and the political constitution(s): From Griffith to Brexit' (2019) 30(1) *King's Law Journal* 125, and Michael Gordon, 'Brexit: A challenge for the UK constitution of the UK constitution' (2016) 12(3) *European Constitutional Law Review* 409.

[31] Lord Steyn, 'The weakest and least dangerous department of government' (1997) *Public Law* 84, 87, cited in Dawn Oliver, *Constitutional Reform in the UK* (OUP 2003), 26.

these functions should be exercised separately from one another and by different people and institutions.[32] This is so as to prevent a concentration of power in one place and the consequent risk of abuse of that power. In systems guided by a codified constitutional document, this separation of power is invariably ensured and upheld through the text of that constitution. This can be seen in the USA, for example, where Articles 1–3 of the Constitution allocate legislative, executive, and judicial power, clarifying the limited capabilities of the institutions tasked with their execution. In the UK, however, where there is no codified constitutional document, the nature of these institutions and the relationships that they enjoy is markedly different and is what ultimately makes the UK constitutional system so unique. This section seeks to identify and highlight some of the structural features of the UK system.

The first notable feature of the UK Constitution's structure is its centralized nature. The UK is one of the most centralized systems in the world. It is often described as a 'unitary' constitution insofar as both executive and legislative power ultimately lie in one place: at Westminster. Central government and the UK Parliament together have the ability and power to make decisions and laws impacting on the whole of the UK and, while there is a complex network of local authorities, serving smaller areas across the country, as well as the shifting devolution[33] settlements seeing increasing power devolved to institutions in Scotland, Wales, and Northern Ireland, these are legally dependent upon the powers and resources allocated to them by central government and the sovereign Parliament—they act in line with centralized policy and law and the UK Parliament has the legal power to strip them of all authority.

The opposite to a unitary constitution is a federal system. Federal constitutions are those in which there are two (or more) levels of executive and legislative authority in a country, with each having their own allocation of powers and responsibilities. A common example of a federal constitution is the US,[34] where executive and legislative authority is divided between centralized, or federal, powers, exercised by the US Government and the US Congress, and the individual states, who each have their own institutions. Matters that concern the country as a whole are dealt with at the central level, with consequent laws and policies applying nationwide. By contrast, where matters are likely to differ from state to state, then the power lies with the relevant state authorities to decide and make laws appropriate to their peculiar and particular circumstances. In America, the allocation of power between federal and state authorities is dealt with by the constitution. While Article 1 of the Constitution lists all the powers vested in the national government, the Tenth Amendment provides that the 'powers not delegated to the United States by the Constitution . . . are reserved to the states respectively, or to the people'.[35] The presumption, then, is in favour of subsidiarity.[36] Save for those powers expressly stipulated in the

---

[32] See Montesquieu, *L'Esprit des Lois* (1748) and Chapter 2.

[33] Devolution refers to the process through which power is decentralized away from the centre and to regional or local institutions across the UK. See Chapter 9 for further discussion.

[34] Russia and Germany are further examples of developed federal constitutions.

[35] 10th Amendment to the US Constitution, 1791. Also see M Tushnet, *The Constitution of the United States of America: A Contextual Analysis* (Hart Publishing 2009) 159–60.

[36] Subsidiarity is a principle that has relevance under EU law. Article 5(3) of the Treaty on the European Union defines the principle in the following terms: 'Under the principle of subsidiarity, in areas which do not fall within its exclusive competence, the Union shall act only if and in so far as the objectives of the proposed action cannot be sufficiently achieved by the Member States, either at central level or at regional and local level, but can rather, by reason of the scale or effects of the proposed action, be better achieved at Union level' (Consolidated Version of the Treaty on European Union [2012] C326/13, Article 5(3)). Also see 5.3.3.

constitution as resting with centralized authorities, everything else is presumed to fall within the authority of the individual states. This makes sense since, as Founding Father James Madison notes, '[t]he powers reserved to the several States will extend to all the objects which, in the ordinary course of affairs, concern the lives, liberties, and properties of the people, and the internal order, improvement, and prosperity of the State'.[37] A natural consequence of these federal arrangements is that different states regulate the lives of its citizens in sometimes contrasting ways. Capital punishment, for instance, is an example of US states adopting differing approaches and therefore contrasting laws. The death penalty is used in thirty-one states across America, while its use is illegal in the remaining nineteen states. Other examples include the laws relating to divorce, which differ slightly across all the states as do those relating to real estate. The legal and constitutional arrangements in the USA's federal constitution, therefore, are markedly different from those that prevail in the UK's unitary system.

The second notable feature of the UK Constitution's structure is the way in which the government is drawn from Parliament. It has already been discussed in 1.3.1 that Parliament's Acts are the highest source of authority in the constitution. In addition to this, however, and in view of the lack of a codified constitutional document, it should also be understood that Parliament provides the basis and authority for the government in what is called a 'parliamentary executive'.[38] This refers to the fact that the Prime Minister and the heads of the various government departments[39] (as well as officials holding junior ministerial positions) sit in the legislature. The practical consequences of this is that, in the UK, parliamentary and governmental elections take place through the same process, the members of the government being drawn from the political party that commands the most seats in its election to the House of Commons. There is, then, a fusion of power between the executive and legislative branches of the state, with senior members of the government being drawn directly from and exerting power within the UK Parliament. As 2.4.1 discusses in further detail, this arrangement is central to the consideration of the separation of powers in the UK. While the Prime Minister and other ministers have their places in Parliament,[40] however, it should also be noted that those working lower down, within the government departments and for the Civil Service, are not a part of the legislature. Furthermore, where the fusion of power does exist, through Ministers and the Prime Minister sitting in the legislature, there are mechanisms of accountability that enable Parliament to keep the government in check. That accountability exists in a range of forms, from elections and Question Time to Select Committees.[41]

The parliamentary executive system that prevails in the UK Constitution is contrasted with America's presidential executive, so called because the President and other members of the executive do not sit in the legislature. This means that the legislative powers of the Congress and the executive powers of the President are separate from one another, that

---

[37] *The Federalist* 45—as cited in M Tushnet, *The Constitution of the United States of America: A Contextual Analysis* (Hart Publishing 2009) 159–60.

[38] See KC Wheare, *Modern Constitutions* (OUP 1966) 26.

[39] Which together form the Cabinet (see 7.5).

[40] By convention, the Prime Minister must be drawn from the House of Commons; all Ministers must sit in one of the Houses of Parliament (see 7.2).

[41] See 2.4.1.

separation being protected by the codified constitution and with the President and Congress elected through two different procedures.[42]

The existence of a President in America is also indicative of another key difference between the UK and US constitutional systems. The US, like France and Russia, is a republic, so called because the position of head of state is filled by the elected president. By contrast, in the UK, the head of state is the Queen, Elizabeth II, making the UK a constitutional monarchy. The Queen is the unelected head of state and, in that role, is the formal head of the legislature, the executive, and the judiciary. Alongside the head of state, the head of government is the Prime Minister, the leader of the political party that commands a majority in the House of Commons.[43] In the UK, the practical consequences of this distinction are defined by the fact that the monarch's role is generally ceremonial, though she does exercise certain constitutional functions. The Queen, for instance, performs the state opening of Parliament, formally appoints government ministers and members of the judiciary, and grants Royal Assent to enact a bill into law. As later chapters will illustrate, these functions are generally carried out on the advice of the government of the day, falling as they do within what are known as royal prerogative powers.[44] It is the Prime Minister's job, alongside the government, then, to carry out the important executive functions critical to the day-to-day running of the country, including the role of engaging with the legislature in the manner we have discussed. In a constitutional monarchy, while the Queen is the unelected head of state the process of passing laws and of executing policy and making decisions falls to the democratically elected Parliament and the government; she 'reigns but does not rule'.[45]

In a republic, by contrast, the head of state's role is fulfilled by an *elected* president. In some republic systems, such as France, a president serves as the elected head of state and a Prime Minister serves alongside them as elected head of government. In certain other republic systems, including America, the President is elected to serve as both head of state and head of government, there being no separate prime ministerial position. This means that, in America, the President fulfils both legislative and executive functions. They must sign bills before they can be enacted as laws and, unlike Royal Assent under the UK Constitution, the President has the power to veto laws.[46] The executive functions enjoyed by the US President are set out in detail in Article 2 of the Constitution and they include power over military forces and the ability to make treaties (with the advice and consent of the Senate). Both of these legislative and executive roles sit alongside the President's formal position as Head of State, which itself comes with various ceremonial

---

[42] See Articles 1(1) and 2(1) of the US Constitution, 1787.

[43] Typically, a Prime Minister is leader of their political party before and in the run up to an election and are therefore indirectly elected to the position when their party wins the necessary majority. Occasionally, though, the leader of the party—and therefore the Prime Minister—changes mid-term. This was the case with Gordon Brown, Theresa May, and Boris Johnson—though while Brown and Johnson were elected through their respective party processes, May was appointed following elimination and resignation of other prime ministerial candidates.

[44] See Chapter 6.

[45] Vernon Bogdanor, *The Monarchy and the Constitution* (OUP 1995) 1.

[46] Where a US President refuses to sign a bill, thereby preventing a law from being passed, that bill returns to Congress where it must now be passed with a heightened majority of two-thirds of both houses (Article 1(7) of the US Constitution, 1787).

roles. A republic constitution, therefore, differs hugely from a constitutional monarchy in terms of the way in which a head of state assumes office and the powers they might enjoy once there.

Discussing the problem

Look at the problem scenario set out at the beginning of the chapter. If King George VII sought to act in the manner set out in the question, how do you think the constitutional arrangements here described would be changed?

The most significant change would be to the characterization of the constitution as a 'constitutional monarchy'. It has already been noted that, in such a system, the monarch 'reigns but does not rule',[47] the latter responsibility (in our system) falling to the elected Parliament and government. By seeking to choose who should be Prime Minister and by changing the laws passed by Parliament, it can be argued that King George VII is seeking to exercise functions and responsibilities that typically fall to the legislative and executive branches of government.

Another of King George's actions that would impact upon the nature of the UK Constitution concerns its classification as a parliamentary executive, this being determined by the manner in which the Prime Minister, and their government, is drawn from the party that commands a majority in the House of Commons. By calling the leader of the second largest party to be Prime Minister, King George is upsetting the accepted and ordinary arrangements that determine the operation of our parliamentary executive.

This section of the chapter has explored and considered the fundamental characteristics of the UK Constitution, focusing both on its peculiar nature and its structure. Partly written and uncodified, it is distinct from other constitutions across the globe, in particular the USA's, in chief because constitutional laws have no special legal status over and above ordinary domestic laws. As a consequence, the constitution is flexible and is susceptible to easy change and alteration. The UK system operates within a parliamentary executive, under a monarchy, with power exercised and allocated across the institutions of the state, but predominantly focused at the centre. In terms of understanding more fully the way in which the UK Constitution has evolved and developed to take this form, however, it is necessary now to explore some of the key sources by which it is constituted.

Pause for reflection

Having explored the characteristics of constitutions and the nature of the UK constitutional arrangements, to what extent would you say that the UK has a constitution? How different is it from the US Constitution?

---

[47] Vernon Bogdanor, *The Monarchy and the Constitution* (OUP 1995) 1.

1.4 The historical development and sources of the UK Constitution

The sources of the UK Constitution fall within three broad categories—Acts of Parliament, case law, and constitutional conventions. In this section, we explore how certain Acts of Parliament and cases make up the UK Constitution and the role that they play. Constitutional conventions (and government codes) are dealt with in section 1.5. This section does not attempt to consider each and every source, but engages in a contextual and thematic discussion considering the broader and continued development of the constitution, exploring how particularly notable sources have helped to shape its function and operation. We will consider the following themes: the allocation of sovereign power; the establishment of the United Kingdom and the distribution of power; institutional arrangements and the separation of powers; and the protection of individual rights.

1.4.1 The allocation of sovereign power

Over the centuries, the allocation of sovereign power[48] in the UK Constitution has been a constantly evolving issue, something that is indicative of its flexible and uncodified nature. Whereas in the past, sources generally focused on the determination to set out where the balance of sovereign legislative power lay in respect of the Crown, the courts, and Parliament, more recently the issue has shifted towards the need to clarify the relationship between the UK, its sovereign Parliament, and other, international sources of law, such as the European Union.

In medieval times, the 'feudal system . . . operated on the basis that the King's barons or nobles held their lands from the King in exchange for an oath to him of loyalty and obedience'.[49] The barons and noblemen were subject to monarchical authority, and would have had to obey the laws and decisions set out by the King. It was on this basis that after becoming King in 1199, King John sought to impose arbitrary taxes on the barons to fund his various activities overseas. The 'barons were dissatisfied with what they regarded as a form of unjust taxation, and they were sufficiently united to prevail over the King'.[50] This led to the sealing of Magna Carta in 1215. The context for this is that, having seized London, the barons forced King John to negotiate and agree to a settlement whereby they would have certain rights and freedoms recognized at law and the King would be restricted in his ability to exercise arbitrary power. The King would, in short, be subject to the law rather than acting above its authority. Often cited as the first notable source of the UK Constitution, Magna Carta (or 'Great Charter') played a key role in shaping the foundation of the UK Constitution. Though its modern-day significance is generally historical rather than legally authoritative, since just three of the original sixty-three clauses remain in force,[51] Magna Carta nonetheless took what Wicks describes as the first

---

[48] Sovereign power refers to the source of fundamental authority within a constitution.

[49] Peter Leyland, *The Constitution of the United Kingdom: A Contextual Analysis* (Hart Publishing 2007) 9.

[50] Ibid.

[51] The clauses providing for the freedom of the Church of England; the protection of the liberties and free customs of the City of London; and the protection of individuals from imprisonment or punishment without due process.

steps towards the rule of law, 'establish[ing] the rights of subjects against authority and maintain[ing] the principle that authority was subject to law'.[52]

The subjection of monarchical rule to the authority of the law is a recurring theme in UK constitutional history and, after the significant events of the thirteenth century, the powers of the monarch and its relations both with the courts and Parliament continued to be a matter of wider concern and dispute. Indeed, throughout the sixteenth and seventeenth centuries, the question of the allocation of sovereign authority was frequently entertained by the courts, with the monarch and Parliament constantly vying for supreme power.[53] All this culminated in the Glorious Revolution of 1688 and was settled by way of a political contract[54] between Parliament and the monarchy. King William and his Queen, Mary, were invited to take the throne following the turbulent rule of King James II on the condition that they agreed to the settlement set out in the Bill of Rights 1688. The Bill of Rights limited the power of the monarch in favour of parliamentary authority, with its provisions setting out a wide range of instances where the Crown would be prevented from acting without parliamentary consent, also making clear that Parliament could not be questioned.[55]

Magna Carta and the Bill of Rights, therefore, represent a limitation of monarchical power, leading to the determination of Parliament as the sovereign authority, thereby providing the foundation for the modern-day concept of parliamentary sovereignty, which we will discuss in Chapter 4. Though it cannot be said that Parliament was immediately and widely accepted as sovereign in 1688, developments throughout the eighteenth and nineteenth centuries further established the idea, and by the start of the twentieth century the principle was generally accepted as constitutional orthodoxy.[56] As the twentieth century progressed, though, the increasing relevance of international sources of law posed questions once more about the appropriate allocation of sovereign power. This time, however, the question was not so much about the internal allocation of power within the constitution, but instead concerned the UK Constitution's external relationship with bodies of international law.

The most notable issue that has arisen in this regard is the UK's accession to the European Union. The UK acceded to what was then the European Communities on 1 January 1973, pursuant to the provisions of the European Communities Act 1972. The Communities themselves were already fifteen years old by this point and the supremacy of EC law had already been established and settled by the European Court of Justice.[57] Upon joining, however, questions regarding the relationship between the established sovereignty of the UK Parliament and the newly accepted supremacy of EC Law soon arose. Throughout the 1970s and 1980s, UK judges gradually accepted the primacy of EC law over UK domestic law, though often stopped short of accepting that the sovereignty of the UK Parliament had been limited. The issue reached its climax, though, in the leading case of *R v Secretary of State for Transport, ex p Factortame (No 2)*.[58]

---

[52] JC Holt, *Magna Carta* (2nd edn, Cambridge University Press 1992) 19, as cited in Elizabeth Wicks, *The Evolution of a Constitution: Eight Key Moments in British Constitutional History* (Hart Publishing 2006) 4.

[53] See, for example, *Dr Bonham's Case* (1609) 8 Co Reports 113b; *Prohibitions del Roy* (1607) 12 Co Rep 63; and Petition of Right 1628 (discussed further in Chapters 3 and 4).

[54] See HWR Wade, 'The Basis of Legal Sovereignty' (1955) 13(2) *Cambridge Law Journal* 172, and 4.4.1.

[55] See Article 9, Bill of Rights 1688.

[56] See AV Dicey, *Introduction to the Study of the Law of the Constitution* (JWF Allison ed, first published 1885, OUP 2013) 27.

[57] See Case 6/64 *Costa v ENEL* [1964] ECR 585, and 5.3.3.

[58] [1991] 1 AC 603.

Case in depth: *R v Secretary of State for Transport, ex p Factortame (No 2) [1991] 1 AC 603*

Factortame Ltd, a company incorporated under UK law but whose directors were Spanish nationals and residents, owned a number of fishing vessels that were registered as British vessels under the Merchant Shipping Act 1894. Owing to a change in the law brought in by the Merchant Shipping Act 1988, all vessels registered under the 1894 Act had to be re-registered under the new Act. Factortame's vessels, however, failed to qualify for re-registration as they failed to satisfy one of the 1988 Act's new requirements. Section 14(1) of the Act stipulated that:

> a fishing vessel shall only be eligible to be registered as a British fishing vessel if—
> (a) the vessel is British-owned;
> (b) the vessel is managed, and its operations are directed and controlled, from within the United Kingdom; and
> (c) any charterer, manager or operator of the vessel is a qualified person or company.

Factortame's directors were Spanish and it was from Spain that they sought to direct the company. As such, they fell short of the Act's requirements for registration. Factortame therefore sought review of the 1988 Act's new provisions on the basis that they were in contravention of EU Law, enforceable as a result of the European Communities Act 1972.

Following a preliminary reference to the European Court of Justice, made by the Divisional Court, which questioned the enforceability of EU Law in light of conflicting domestic law, the House of Lords held that interim relief from the application of the 1988 Act should be granted and the Act set aside to give effect to supreme provisions of EU Law.

The effect of this judgment was to acknowledge the supremacy of EU law over Acts of the UK Parliament with the House of Lords 'disapplying' the Merchant Shipping Act 1988 and arguably thereby limiting the sovereign power of the legislature. Section 5.4 discusses in much greater detail the impact that this has had on Parliament's sovereignty. For now, though, it is necessary to understand the importance of the *Factortame (No 2)* case in clarifying the allocation of sovereign power with regards to the UK's membership of the European Union. Further development in this area has been and will be, effected by the passing of the European Union (Withdrawal) Act 2018, as amended by the European Union (Withdrawal Agreement) Act 2020, and the realization of the Brexit process generally, as Chapter 5 explains.

 Discussing the problem

Have another look at the scenario set out at the beginning of the chapter. Do you think that King George VII's actions would upset the allocation of sovereign power in the UK Constitution?

In the centuries since the Bill of Rights, it has become accepted constitutional practice that the monarch appoints as Prime Minister the individual who, in the aftermath of a General Election, commands the confidence of the House of Commons and that they grant Royal Assent—thereby passing into law—a bill that has been agreed by both Houses of Parliament, having no further input into that process. The basis for these practices is explained in 1.5, which discusses constitutional conventions.

→

→

King George VII's actions in the problem scenario, however, go beyond the accepted role of the monarch in the modern constitution. He is not only seeking to choose who he would like to have as Prime Minister, in preference to the individual elected in the usual fashion, but also seeking to usurp the democratically legitimized legislative process by both amending the bill dealing with the Devolution settlements and by instructing the House of Lords on how they should deal with particular legislative proposals. These are actions that disrupt the exercise of Parliament's sovereign power and that are reminiscent of the monarch's activities pre-1688 insofar as they can be interpreted as an assertion of monarchical authority, in preference to that exercised by the legislature.

Numerous sources, both Acts and cases, then, have shaped and contributed to the allocation of sovereign power in the UK Constitution. From disputes between the King and the barons in medieval England, partly settled by Magna Carta, to the UK's accession to the European Union and the partial limitation of domestic sovereignty recognized in *Factortame (No 2)*, the manner in which power has shifted in the UK Constitution over the centuries demonstrates the flexibility and evolution which defines its nature.

1.4.2 Establishment of the United Kingdom and the distribution of power

Against the backdrop of Parliament's sovereign role, there have also been adjustments to the way in which both executive and legislative power has been dispersed amongst the regions of the United Kingdom. In this section we will explore how power has moved about in the UK Constitution and discuss the key constitutional sources that have been instrumental in allocating that power.

The establishment of the United Kingdom as England, Wales, Scotland, and Northern Ireland is relatively recent. Though Wales was conquered by England in 1282, coming under English Law shortly thereafter, Scotland and (what was then just) Ireland joined in 1707 and 1800 respectively. The Act of Union with Scotland 1707 was agreed by the Parliaments in England and Scotland, this giving effect to the creation of a new Parliament of Great Britain, in London, that served England, Wales, and Scotland together. The 1707 Act of Union still enforces Scotland's membership of the (now) United Kingdom to this day, despite a referendum considering and rejecting independence in 2014, which—had it been successful—would have seen the separation of Scotland from the rest of the United Kingdom.

 Pause for reflection

If the 2014 Scottish Independence Referendum had resulted in a vote in favour of independence, how would a constitution for the newly independent Scotland have been drafted? What sort of things do you think would have been included?

The Act of Union with Ireland 1800, by contrast, effected a union that lasted just 120 years. The Act abolished the Irish Parliament and brought the whole of Ireland under the authority of the UK Parliament and joined Ireland with England, Wales, and Scotland. In the early part of the twentieth century, however, a republican movement opposed to the union and in favour of home rule for Ireland gathered momentum. In 1920, following a turbulent revolutionary period involving conflict between the unionists (supporting the union with the UK) and the nationalists (supporting an independent Ireland, free from the union), the Government of Ireland Act 1920 was passed, recognizing that Ireland was divided. The Act set out a devolution of power separately to the six northern counties, exercised by a Parliament for Northern Ireland in Belfast, and the remaining twenty-six counties exercised by a Parliament for Southern Ireland, located in Dublin. This proved unsatisfactory, however, since Northern Ireland 'had not requested home rule', while the southern counties 'wanted far more, namely secession from the union'.[59] While the six northern Irish counties remained a part of the UK, retaining the level of devolution granted through the 1920 Act (until it was recentralized in 1972), the southern counties seceded from the union just a year later. The 1921 Anglo-Irish Treaty established the independence of the twenty-six southern counties and, through the Irish Free State (Agreement) Act 1922, saw the creation of the Irish Free State, which became the Republic of Ireland in 1949.

On the foundation of these constitutional developments the United Kingdom as we know it today was established, with the various regions being overseen by the UK Parliament and central government in Westminster. In more recent decades, however, the structure of the United Kingdom and the relationship between the various regions and the centre has been defined by devolution.[60] Though Northern Ireland enjoyed a degree of devolved power from 1921 to 1972, power and authority effecting the various regions of the UK was exercised by central government and the UK Parliament at Westminster right up until New Labour's period in government in the late 1990s. Tony Blair's government, which entered power in 1997, introduced the Scotland Act 1998, Government of Wales Act 1998, and Northern Ireland Act 1998, each of which sought to implement a devolution settlement for the respective regions, creating new institutions and empowering them with various executive and legislative powers. Later Acts have adjusted and impacted upon the form of these settlements. Though the predominance of the sovereign Parliament means that the UK cannot really be regarded as a federal state on the basis of these devolved arrangements, the decentralization of executive and legislative authority to regional institutions has meant that power is now allocated at different levels, impacting on the unitary nature of the UK Constitution as 9.4 will further explain. These key sources, therefore, have shaped both the make-up of the United Kingdom and the manner in which power continues to be distributed amongst the regions.

---

[59] Elizabeth Wicks, *The Evolution of a Constitution: Eight Key Moments in British Constitutional History* (Hart Publishing 2006) 171.
[60] See Chapter 9.

Discussing the problem

Take another look at the problem scenario at the start of the chapter. What would the consequences be for the UK Constitution if King George VII abolished these devolution settlements?

The consequence of King George VII's abolition of the devolution settlements would be to re-inforce the unitary nature of the constitution and to strengthen the notion that power ultimately lies in London. While it would, of course, depend on the specific provisions of this hypothetical bill, the apparent desire for there 'to be one, United Kingdom, under one Monarch and one Parliament' implies that power would rest with the government and Parliament at Westminster. This being the case, centralized institutions would—once more—make *all* laws and decisions for people across Scotland, Wales, and Northern Ireland.

1.4.3 Institutional arrangement and the separation of powers

Questions regarding the allocation of power in the UK Constitution do not just concern devolution and the regional institutions, but also the way in which power is organized amongst the centralized institutions of the state. There are three key institutions in the UK constitutional system—Parliament, the government, and the courts—and these have important roles to play in the constitution. As this section will explain, a number of constitutional sources have shaped these roles and have sought to ensure that each can fulfil its functions appropriately.

Historically, Parliament was merely 'an advisory body to the King'.[61] Made up of two houses—making it bicameral—the House of Lords was 'made up of the land-owning aristocracy and the established church', while the House of Commons was composed of 'elected representatives of the gentry on a roughly geographical basis'.[62] Over the centuries, though, and amid the tumultuous relationship with the unelected monarch discussed above, Parliament's legislative function developed until the Bill of Rights formally established the sovereignty of Parliament. As time went on and suffrage became more widespread, the institution gradually evolved into the democratically representative legislature that operates today. The relationship between the Commons and the Lords was historically an equal one, ensuring a balance of elected representatives and unelected peers. Growing concerns regarding hereditary entitlement to peerages in the early twentieth century, however, led to changes to the level of power the Lords possessed alongside the Commons. The Parliament Act 1911, amended by the Parliament Act 1949, was passed to alter the balance of power within the legislature, establishing the Commons as the superior chamber. Prior to the Act, both the House of Commons and the House of Lords had the power to veto a bill and prevent a law from being enacted. In 1909, however, this caused considerable difficulty for the Liberal Government. With a significant Conservative majority in the Lords, the government had a number of key policies blocked by the Upper Chamber, including the Finance Bill 1909, which attempted to bring into effect parts of the government's budget. The Parliament Act 1911 was therefore

---

[61] Peter Leyland, *The Constitution of the United Kingdom: A Contextual Analysis* (Hart Publishing 2007) 82.
[62] Ibid.

passed, setting out provisions permitting the Commons to push a bill through to royal assent after two years and three parliamentary sessions without the Lords' consent. The 1949 Act, enacted using the 1911 Act's procedure, amended this to one year and two sessions. The Parliament Acts were therefore enacted to ensure that the democratically elected Commons would not be hindered by the appointed Lords, though this has been a procedure rarely used.[63] It has, though, been tested in the courts, notably in the case of *R (Jackson) v Attorney-General*.[64]

Case in depth: *R (Jackson) v Attorney-General* [2005] UKHL 56

This case concerned a challenge by the Countryside Alliance to the validity of the Hunting Act 2004 and its prohibition of hunting with dogs. Although it had strong political undertones, the grounds on which the case was brought related to the manner in which the legislation had been passed, enacted as it was using the procedures set out in the Parliament Acts 1911 and 1949.

It was argued in the case that the Parliament Act 1911 delegated to the Commons and the monarch the power to pass secondary legislation.[65] On the basis of the maxim *delegatus non potest delegare* (delegated power cannot be used to increase one's own authority), it was then argued that this delegated authority—set out in the 1911 Act—could not be used to increase the scope of the Commons and monarch's legislative powers. The Countryside Alliance's case was that the 1949 Act sought to do just this and was, therefore, invalid. By extension, the Hunting Act 2004 must also be seen as invalid.

The House of Lords, however, found in favour of the Attorney-General and held that the 1949 and 2004 Acts were valid, emphasizing that Parliament has the power to alter its own legislative procedure. While enacted by an altered Parliament, therefore, the Hunting Act 2004 and the Parliament Act 1949 were regarded as Acts of Parliament, rather than a form of secondary legislation.

The Parliament Acts 1911 and 1949, however, were merely intended as temporary measures, dealing with constitutional issues and concerns relevant at the time and pending more fundamental reform of the Upper Chamber. The preamble to the 1911 Act explains that restriction of the House of Lords' powers, as effected by the Act, was introduced on the basis that further legislative provision was intended to be passed 'regulating the relations between the two Houses of Parliament' and substituting its hereditary basis for a model involving popular selection.[66] The two Acts remain in force, however, and now sit at the centre of a broader, ongoing debate concerning the need for fundamental reform of the unelected, and still partly hereditary, House of Lords. As Wicks notes, 'House of Lords reform has been a thorn in the side of many governments since 1911'.[67]

---

[63] It has been used on just seven occasions: Government of Ireland Act 1914, Welsh Church Act 1914, Parliament Act 1949, War Crimes Act 1991, European Parliament Elections Act 1999, Sexual Offences (Amendment) Act 2000, and Hunting Act 2004.

[64] [2005] UKHL 56.

[65] Distinct from primary legislation (which refers to Acts passed by Parliament), secondary legislation refers to laws passed by an institution subordinate to Parliament—such as government ministers or local councils—but who are empowered by Parliament to make such laws.

[66] Preamble to the Parliament Act 1911.

[67] Elizabeth Wicks, *The Evolution of a Constitution: Eight Key Moments in British Constitutional History* (Hart Publishing 2006) 106.

Attempt at a degree of reform was made by the New Labour Government in the late 1990s. The House of Lords Act 1999 reduced the size of the chamber and abolished all but ninety-two of the hereditary peers, also creating at the same time a significant number of new life peers.[68] Since 1999, further reform has also been considered. A House of Lords Reform Bill 2012, sponsored by Nick Clegg (the Deputy Prime Minister in the 2010–15 Coalition Government), for instance, explored the various options concerning an elected or partly elected house, though these proposals lacked support and were eventually dropped. The issue is far from resolved and it is not unthinkable that proposals for House of Lords reform could be up for discussion again before long.

The House of Lords Act 1999, however, was not the Labour Government's only contribution to reform of the constitutional institutions in the UK. The Constitutional Reform Act 2005 is one of the most recently significant pieces of legislation in this area, seeking to introduce as it did a clearer separation of powers in the UK, something it sought to achieve in three ways. First, through abolishing the Appellate Committee of the House of Lords. This had been the highest appeal court in the UK and was, as its name suggests, a committee of the upper chamber of Parliament. As such, there was a perceived overlap between the judicial and legislative arms of the state. Law Lords (those judges sitting in the Appellate Committee) were free to sit in and take part in debates in the legislative chamber. This lack of any clear separation meant that the general perception was that the legislator played a key role in deciding cases in the highest court of the land, even if this wasn't the case in practice.[69] The 2005 Act, therefore, abolished the Appellate Committee and replaced it with a new UK Supreme Court which began operation in October 2009. The judges were the same and its functions were identical. Crucially, however, the court was seen to cut all ties with the House of Lords. The judges were rebranded as 'Supreme Court Justices', headed by a President of the Supreme Court, and they were moved to a new location, away from a committee room in the Palace of Westminster to a publicly accessible building across Parliament Square.

The second key reform introduced by the 2005 Act was an alteration of the role of Lord Chancellor.[70] Previously, the Lord Chancellor's position involved a function in each of the three institutions of the state—the legislature, in which the Lord Chancellor was Speaker of the House of Lords; the executive, within which the Lord Chancellor was a member of the Cabinet; and the judiciary, of which the Lord Chancellor was head. As 2.4.3 will further discuss, this amounted to a substantial breach of the separation of powers in that one individual worked across all three institutions of the state which, according to the principle, should ideally be independent

---

[68] At the time, this was motivated by a desire and a need to correct the political composition of the House which was heavily Conservative (due to the large numbers of hereditary peers) and to create a more politically balanced chamber.

[69] Law Lords exercised their legislative role 'rarely' (Adam Tomkins, *Public Law* (OUP 2003)), 37. Tomkins explains, though, that '[e]ven 15 years ago [i.e. the late 1980s] the law lords were still actively engaged in the legislative process: witness for example the extensive judicial contributions during the passage of the Bill that became the Courts and Legal Services Act 1990' (37).

[70] In addition to the creation of the UK Supreme Court and the alteration to the role of Lord Chancellor, the 2005 Act also created the Judicial Appointments Commission which sees a change in the way in which judges are appointed and works to ensure greater independence in the process (see, for further discussion, 2.4.3).

of one another. To rectify this, the 2005 Act abolished the Lord Chancellor's positions as speaker of the House of Lords and head of the judiciary, leaving him as a member of the executive in the form of the Secretary of State for Justice (the head of the Ministry of Justice). As will be discussed in 2.4.3, the operation of a parliamentary executive means that, as a Cabinet member, the Lord Chancellor still sits in the legislature as an MP and, indeed, also retains an important role in relation to the judiciary through the work of the Ministry of Justice.

The third key reform introduced by the 2005 Act was in relation to judicial appointments. Prior to the Act, judges were selected for appointment by the Lord Chancellor and then formally appointed by the Queen. Where judges were appointed to senior positions within the higher courts, the Prime Minister was also involved. Due to concerns that the process lacked transparency and independence, however, coupled with issues already noted with the Lord Chancellor's other functions, the 2005 Act created the Judicial Appointments Commission. This is an independent and transparent body that selects appropriately qualified candidates for judicial office, recommending suitable candidates to the Lord Chancellor for appointment in the traditional fashion.[71] This new Commission further enhanced the manner in which one of the institutions of the state (the courts) is constituted, ensuring fairness, equality, and independence in the selection process.

Over the past century or so, key legislation has worked to react to various constitutional concerns and debates surrounding the separation of powers and the appropriate allocation of authority within the bicameral Parliament, thereby further emphasizing and demonstrating the flexibility of the UK system.

1.4.4 Protection of individual rights

The final theme that this chapter considers in its exploration of constitutional history and the sources of the constitution relates to the protection of individual rights. In systems with codified constitutional documents, individual rights are often protected by an entrenched, constitutionally superior, document. In the USA, for instance, the Bill of Rights exists as the first ten amendments to the Constitution to ensure the protection of individual rights, as do many other such Charters across the world. In the UK, by contrast, predominantly due to the lack of such a codified constitutional document, the protection of rights comes in a rather different form.

 Pause for reflection

Keeping in mind our discussions concerning the nature of the UK Constitution as compared with other systems across the world, what do you think are the benefits of protecting human rights through an entrenched constitutional document? Are there other features of a constitutional system that might similarly benefit from such protection?

---

[71] See: Judicial Appointments Commission, *What the JAC does*, https://jac.judiciary.gov.uk/what-jac-does.

Recognition of the importance of individual rights goes all the way back to Magna Carta in 1215, where the settlement between King John and his Barons sought to ensure individuals' protection from arbitrary authority. Though other authorities already discussed, such as the Bill of Rights 1688, built upon this acknowledgement that individual liberties should be protected from arbitrary power, what we might now call 'human rights' have traditionally found protection at the common law. Indeed, as will be explored in more detail in 3.3.3, Dicey, a jurist whose writing left a long-lasting legacy on the constitution, noted in the late nineteenth century that 'the general principles of the constitution (as for example the right to personal liberty, or the right of public meeting) are with us the result of judicial decisions determining the rights of private persons in particular cases brought before the Courts'.[72]

This courts-based protection of rights ensured what came to be known as a civil liberties approach—namely, that anything and everything was regarded as lawful, except those things that were expressly prohibited at law. An example of this in practice is provided by the case of *Malone v Metropolitan Police Commissioner*.[73] Here, the tapping of Malone's phone as part of a criminal investigation was held not to be unlawful. This was due not only to the fact that it could be justified by existing non-statutory powers, but also since a right to privacy and confidentiality was not recognized by the law of England.[74] The police's actions were lawful since they were not expressly prohibited at law.

This civil liberties approach changed, however, with the enactment of the Human Rights Act 1998. Like the European Communities Act before it, this was a significant constitutional statute, bringing into the UK Constitution sources of law external to domestic processes. Though the UK Government had ratified the European Convention on Human Rights and Fundamental Freedoms in 1951, it then coming into force in 1953, it wasn't until the 1998 Act that the rights and freedoms contained within the Convention were incorporated into UK domestic law, only thereafter being directly enforceable in UK courts. Before October 2000 (when the Act came into force) and pursuant to the Government's ratification of the Convention in 1951, those seeking remedies for alleged violations of human rights were limited to bringing vertical actions against state bodies in the European Court of Human Rights in Strasbourg, this being the case only following the court's establishment in 1959 and the granting of 'individual petition'[75] to UK citizens in 1966. Following the 1998 Act, however, applicants seeking redress following an alleged breach of their human rights by a public authority no longer have to go to Strasbourg but can, instead, bring actions in the UK domestic courts. The Human Rights Act 1998, therefore, is a key constitutional source, changing the approach to rights protection in the UK and ensuring a clearer avenue for citizens seeking to uphold their individual freedoms in domestic courts. It is discussed in greater detail in Chapter 15.

This section has explored a number of key themes and in so doing it has considered the way in which the UK Constitution has developed incrementally and gradually over the centuries. Over this time, various Acts and cases have contributed to fundamental aspects

---

[72] AV Dicey, *Introduction to the Study of the Law of the Constitution* (JWF Allison ed, first published 1885, OUP 2013) 115.

[73] [1979] 2 All ER 620.

[74] Though subsequent appeal to the European Court of Human Rights in Strasbourg led to a finding in favour of Malone (see 15.4.1).

[75] 'Individual petition' refers to the right of citizens to bring their case before the European Court of Human Rights.

of the UK system, often altering the way in which the constitution operates. Consideration of the allocation of sovereign power, the relationships between institutions as well as the various regions of the UK, and the protection of individual rights prove that the UK Constitution is unique. Its sources demonstrate its uncodified nature, its flexibility, and the extent to which it has evolved—and is still evolving—with the times. Acts and cases, however, are just two categories of constitutional source. We will now consider constitutional conventions.

1.5 Constitutional conventions

Constitutions the world over all have conventions to some degree, but the uncodified nature of the UK system means that they play a particularly important role in shaping the day-to-day processes of our constitution. The unique and peculiar nature of conventions rests on the fact that they are non-legal sources, meaning that they are unenforceable in the courts, but also in the fact that they are nonetheless binding on those whom they affect.

The much-quoted words of Dicey provide a clear definition of the nature of constitutional conventions. He states that 'conventions, understandings, habits or practices which, though they may regulate the conduct of the several members of the sovereign power . . . are not in reality laws at all since they are not enforced by the courts'.[76] Conventions, therefore, are constituted by traditions, practices, and habits that assist in the day-to-day operation of the constitutional system. Indeed, as Jennings adds: 'The short explanation of the constitutional conventions is that they provide the flesh which clothes the dry bones of the law; they make the legal constitution work; they keep it in touch with the growth of ideas.'[77]

As traditions, practices, and habits, conventions are not enacted or created at a given point, but rather become established over a period of time based on precedent and what has been deemed constitutionally necessary over a given period. The position of Prime Minister, for instance, is conventional; there is no statutory provision for the position. In the early eighteenth century, following the establishment of sovereign legislative power in Parliament, the seat of executive power at that time—the Crown—came to require a point of contact within Parliament to ensure that executive action could complement the legislative process. The position of First Minister—now Prime Minister—was recognized to enable the Crown to communicate with a member of the legislature. Over time, and amidst the increasingly democratic nature of the House of Commons, the Prime Minister and a group of selected senior ministers came to exercise more and more of this executive authority on behalf of the monarch. The position of Prime Minister, therefore, and that of the Cabinet, came to be established; not at a given point in history but gradually and by convention. Constitutional conventions, though, continue to play a part in the day-to-day running of the governmental and parliamentary process. It is convention, for instance, that the leader of the political party that commands a majority in the House of Commons will be called to form a government and appointed Prime Minister by the monarch; and it is convention that the monarch give Royal Assent to a bill that

[76] AV Dicey, *Introduction to the Study of the Law of the Constitution* (JWF Allison ed, first published 1885, OUP 2013) 20.
[77] Sir Ivor Jennings, *The Law and the Constitution* (5th edn, University of London Press 1963) 81.

has been passed by both Houses of Parliament, thereby making it enacted law.[78] In giving Royal Assent, as in the appointment of the Prime Minister, the monarch does not exercise independent authority, but rather is said to be acting on the advice of their Government and Parliament in carrying out its wishes, whether that be signing its bills into law or appointing the appropriate politician as Prime Minister. That the monarch acts on the advice of their Government is itself a convention, known as the Cardinal Convention.[79]

The manner in which the role of Prime Minister has changed over the centuries, though, is indicative of another feature of conventions: they can change and evolve over time, depending on prevailing constitutional needs. Another convention that reflects this is that the royal prerogative powers are exercised by the government on behalf of the monarch; no parliamentary involvement is typically necessary. One such power is the ability to declare war, capable of being exercised by the Prime Minister alone. As decisions to engage in military action in both Tony Blair and David Cameron's premierships were taken following votes in Parliament, however, some have suggested that the convention could be changing.[80] As with the creation of conventions, however, where changes take place they do so incrementally over time, as the new habit becomes gradually established.

As we have already noted, the peculiarity of constitutional conventions rests on the fact that they are non-legal, yet binding. This means that the courts do not have the power to enforce conventions since they are not provisions of law, though they have at least gone so far as to acknowledge the existence of constitutional conventions and have, on occasion, even been called upon to decide as to their scope. In the *Crossman Diaries* case, for instance, the courts did not enforce the convention of collective ministerial responsibility, but accepted that it was underpinned by existing common law rules.[81] With regards to conventions' binding nature, this is linked to the notion that they are seen as 'rules of constitutional morality'.[82]

The connection between conventions and morality is often noted and goes some way to explaining their binding nature.[83] Discussing what this means in practice, Marshall states that:

> conventions are what we might call the positive morality of the Constitution—the beliefs that the major participants in the political process as a matter of fact have about what is required of them. On this view the existence of a convention is a question of historical and sociological fact. The alternative possibility is that conventions are the rules that the political actors *ought* to feel obliged by, if they have considered the precedents and reasons correctly. This permits us to think of conventions as the critical morality of the Constitution.[84]

---

[78] With the exception of those passed pursuant to the Parliament Act 1911, as amended by the Parliament Act 1949. As discussed in 1.4.3, here the monarch would give Royal Assent to bills that have only been passed by the House of Commons.

[79] See section 6.4.3.

[80] See, for further discussion on this, Gavin Phillipson, '"Historic" Commons' Syria Vote: The Constitutional Significance (Part I), (19 September 2013) *UK Constitutional Law Association blog*, https://ukconstitutionallaw.org/2013/09/19/gavin-phillipson-historic-commons-syria-vote-the-constitutional-significance-part-i/. Also see 6.5.1.

[81] See *Attorney-General v Jonathan Cape Ltd* [1976] QB 752.

[82] Eric Barendt, *An Introduction to Constitutional Law* (OUP 1998) 40.

[83] See, for further discussion, David Feldman, 'Constitutional Conventions' in Matt Qvortrup (ed), *The British Constitution: Continuity and Change. A Festschrift for Vernon Bogdanor* (Hart Publishing 2013) 93.

[84] Geoffrey Marshall, *Constitutional Conventions: The Rules and Forms of Political Accountability* (OUP Clarendon Press 1984) 11–12, as cited in David Feldman, 'Constitutional Conventions' in Matt Qvortrup (ed), *The British Constitution: Continuity and Change: A Festschrift for Vernon Bogdanor* (Hart Publishing 2013) 93, 98.

This demonstrates that the moral force behind conventions is linked to their historic and precedential nature. In terms of understanding how this translates into a binding expectation, however, Feldman explains that conventions 'are obeyed because they encapsulate right behaviour. Disobedience is likely to precipitate criticism on the ground that the behaviour is seriously unconstitutional because it is regarded as wrong'.[85]

Constitutional conventions, therefore, though non-legal sources, have a crucial role to play in the running of the UK constitutional system, reflecting as they do many of the day-to-day practices and traditions that have come to typify the way in which the constitution operates. Further examples of constitutional conventions in action are discussed in detail in Chapter 6.

 Discussing the problem

Have a look at the problem scenario set out at the beginning of the chapter. What do you think the consequence might be of King George VII going against the convention regarding the appointment of the Prime Minister and selecting the leader of the second largest party in the Commons to be head of the government?

It has already been explained that, by convention, the monarch appoints as Prime Minister the leader of the political party that commands a majority in the House of Commons following a General Election. In making this appointment, the monarch does not exercise independent judgment or authority, but formally appoints the individual already in that position. In this scenario, King George VII has arguably breached constitutional convention in seeking to exercise his own judgment and authority in going against the election result and appointing the leader of the second largest party in the Commons as Prime Minister. Since one of the defining features of constitutional conventions is the reality that they are constitutionally binding but legally unenforceable, it would not be possible to challenge the actions of the King in any court of law, but one possible consequence might be that Parliament could seek to pass a law altering and limiting the power and involvement of the monarch in the constitutional process, though this would—under current arrangements—require the monarch's Royal Assent.

1.6 Do we have a UK Constitution?

In view of the unique and peculiar nature of the UK constitutional arrangements, and the extent to which these differ from other systems across the world, the question of whether the UK can be said formally to have a constitution at all is often considered. Though consideration of this question in the affirmative is very much the basis on which this chapter has considered the nature, characteristics, themes, and sources of the UK Constitution, it is important, in this final section, to explore this debate and to highlight some of the key arguments in this area.

For some, the crux of the issue rests on the understanding of the term 'constitution'. Though this may be reminiscent of the discussion that opened this chapter, different interpretations of the term distinguish between a wide and a narrow view, each imposing

---

[85] David Feldman, 'Constitutional Conventions' in Matt Qvortrup (ed), *The British Constitution: Continuity and Change: A Festschrift for Vernon Bogdanor* (Hart Publishing 2013) 93, 95.

particular terms on what is and what is not regarded as a constitution. Simply put, the narrow view of the term 'constitution' requires a codified document, while the wide view requires the satisfaction of certain broader characteristics not necessarily set out in such a document. Acknowledgement of the two interpretations of the term is noted by Jennings and Wheare, who consider this distinction and illustrate the UK Constitution's position in its regard. Wheare states that:

> The word constitution is commonly used in at least two senses in ordinary discussion of political affairs. First of all, it is used to describe the whole system of government, the collection of rules which establish and regulate it. These rules are partly legal and partly non-legal. When we speak of the British constitution that is the normal, if not the only possible meaning the word has. Everywhere else it is used in the sense of legal rules embodied in one document.[86]

Echoing this point, Jennings—writing before Wheare—also notes that:

> If a constitution means a written document, then obviously Great Britain has no constitution. In countries where such a document exists, the word has that meaning. But the document itself merely sets out the rules determining the creation and operation of governmental institutions, and obviously Great Britain has such institutions and such rules. The phrase 'British constitution' is used to describe those rules.[87]

If one were to argue, therefore, that the UK Constitution did not have a constitution then that might be to suggest—in line with the narrow view set out by Wheare and Jennings—that a constitution *requires* a codified document setting out the 'rules determining the creation and operation of governmental institutions'.[88] Such a view has merits and accords with some of the constitutional characteristics explored earlier in the chapter. A codified document would provide rigidity and consistency, ensuring the sanctity of the constitutional document and the values it might seek to uphold. The strength of this view, however, is not merely founded in the mere existence of a constitutional document and the clarity and rigidity which that would ensure, but rather in the consequences of having a codified, constitutional document. Ridley explains that 'Constitutions . . . have certain essential characteristics, none of them found in Britain';[89] and these are characteristics which are borne out of a codified document. These characteristics, he suggested, are that a constitution:

(1) . . . establishes, or constitutes, the system of government. Thus, it is prior to the system of government, not part of it, and its rules can not be derived from that system.

(2) It therefore involves an authority outside and above the order it establishes.

(3) It is a form of law superior to other laws—because (i) it originates in an authority higher than the legislature which makes ordinary law and (ii) the authority of the legislature derives from it and is thus bound by it.

(4) It is entrenched—(i) because its purpose is generally to limit the powers of government, but also (ii) again because of its origins in a higher authority outside the system. It can

---

[86] KC Wheare, *Modern Constitutions* (OUP 1966) 1.
[87] Sir Ivor Jennings, *The Law and the Constitution* (5th edn, University of London Press 1963) 36.
[88] Ibid.
[89] FF Ridley, 'There is No British Constitution: A Dangerous Case of the Emperor's Clothes' (1988) 41(3) *Parliamentary Affairs* 340, 342.

thus only be changed by special procedures, generally (and certainly for major change) requiring reference back to the constituent power.[90]

These characteristics are central to the very nature of a constitution, as explored earlier in the chapter by Paine.[91] The sanctity, superiority, primacy, and entrenched nature of a constitution can be guaranteed through a codified constitutional document and it is on the lack of these characteristics in the UK system that Ridley bases his argument that the UK cannot be said to have a constitution.

By contrast, arguing that the UK *does* have a constitution is to offer an approach based on the wider view set out by Wheare and Jennings above. The fact that the UK does, through various Acts, cases, and other non-legal sources, set out 'rules determining the creation and operation of governmental institutions',[92] equates to a constitution on the broader understanding of that term. The view is that, despite the lack of a superior, sacred, primary, and entrenched document which is 'antecedent to Government',[93] the collection of legal and non-legal sources that make up the UK Constitution, combined with established rules and principles, fulfil the fundamental and necessary requirements of a constitution. In other words, through various sources and principles, the UK Constitution makes provision for, *inter alia*, the protection of human rights, the appropriate allocation of power between the various institutions and regions of the UK, the sovereignty of Parliament, and the workings of a democratic system. Those sources may not offer any higher source of law or entrenched protection, but they offer the mechanisms through which the constitution can operate effectively on a day-to-day basis. Indeed, this understanding would also appear to be consistent with Bentham's interpretation of the term 'constitution', which is 'used to refer to the "aggregate of those laws in a state which are styled collectively the public law"'.[94] That the UK can be said to have a constitution on these terms is also explained by the Supreme Court. In *R (Miller) v Prime Minister*,[95] the court noted:

> Although the United Kingdom does not have a single document entitled 'The Constitution', it nevertheless possesses a Constitution, established over the course of our history by common law, statutes, conventions and practice. Since it has not been codified, it has developed pragmatically, and remains sufficiently flexible to be capable of further development.[96]

There are key arguments, therefore, surrounding the existence of the UK Constitution, which centre on the predominance or lack of a codified document. Proceeding, then, on the basis that the UK *does* have a constitution, there is no denying that that constitution and the system to which this gives rise is notably different from other systems around the world. Rather than being a primary document, put together in the aftermath of a revolution, in the UK the constitution is merely a product and ongoing construct of the parliamentary system—made up, in part, of Acts of Parliament, which while the highest

---

[90] Ibid 342–3.   [91] See 1.2.

[92] Sir Ivor Jennings, *The Law and the Constitution* (5th edn, University of London Press 1963) 36.

[93] Thomas Paine, *The Rights of Man* (1791).

[94] Jeremy Bentham, *Of Laws in General* (HLA Hart ed, first published 1782, Continuum International Publishing Group Ltd 1970) 12, cited in Colin R Munro, *Studies in Constitutional Law* (LexisNexis Butterworths 1999) 1.

[95] [2019] UKSC 41   [96] [2019] UKSC 41 [39].

form of law are not entrenched and do not have any special legal or constitutional status compared with other Acts of Parliament.

Ridley's view, then, that 'the term British constitution is near meaningless' and that we have instead 'merely a system of government',[97] fails to recognize the wider role that the constitution plays, particularly in view of its political features. Indeed, and with these in mind, it is useful to recall the words of Griffith, which more accurately explain the unique and peculiar nature of the UK Constitution:

> The constitution of the United Kingdom lives on, changing from day to day; for the constitution is no more and no less than what happens. Everything that happens is constitutional. And if nothing happened that would be constitutional also.[98]

This quotation reflects not only the flexible and ever-changing nature of the UK constitutional system, but also its inherent political nature. Rather than being led by the predominance of superior legal sources, the day-to-day operation of the political and legal institutions is what underpins the way in which the constitution works.

This chapter has set out to define and identify the nature of the UK's uncodified constitution, identifying many of the features of which it is made up. In discussing, in this section, whether or not the UK can be said to have a constitution in the formal sense, however, it is impossible to ignore recent consideration and discussion of the case for codification—the possible creation of a codified constitutional document.

It is true to say that more of our constitution is written down than ever before. In part, this is linked to the increasing volume of legislation, some of which refers to and deals with fundamental constitutional issues. In the past, while we might have thought of individual human rights or the rules concerning the calling of general elections as being aspects of our system determined either by the common law or by long-standing conventional rules, for example, both are now set out in statute in the form of the Human Rights Act 1998 and the Fixed Term Parliament Act 2011 respectively. More than this, though, documents such as the *Ministerial Code* and the *Cabinet Manual* have come to regulate and clarify further elements of our system. The first of these was created during the 1990s—though has been updated many times since—to regulate the manner in which government ministers carry out their duties and responsibilities,[99] while the *Cabinet Manual*, published in final form in 2011, sets out broader rules of operation for the government.[100] More than ever before, therefore, less of the constitution is left to unwritten and conventional or political rules; more is set out in clear and certain, written guides. This has led to some to argue that this process should reach its logical conclusion and that the UK should adopt a fully codified constitution.

---

[97] FF Ridley, 'There is No British Constitution: A Dangerous Case of the Emperor's Clothes' (1988) 41(3) *Parliamentary Affairs* 340, 341–2.

[98] JAG Griffith, 'The Political Constitution' (1979) 42(1) *Modern Law Review* 1, 19.

[99] Cabinet Office, *Ministerial Code* (August 2019), https://assets.publishing.service.gov.uk/government/uploads/system/uploads/attachment_data/file/826920/August-2019-MINISTERIAL-CODE-FINAL-FORMATTED-2.pdf.

[100] Cabinet Office, *The Cabinet Manual: A guide to laws, conventions and rules on the operation of government* (October 2011), https://www.gov.uk/government/uploads/system/uploads/attachment_data/file/60641/cabinet-manual.pdf.

Counterpoint: A codified constitution for the UK?

The development over the past twenty years of an increasing amount of legislation affecting the constitution, and the adoption of more formal rules that regulate those non-legal areas of the constitution, has led to increased debate in respect of the possible introduction of a codified constitution for the UK. There have been academic articles exploring the case for and against codification,[101] and, perhaps most significantly, the House of Commons Political and Constitutional Reform Select Committee has engaged in a thorough and far-reaching consultative process, exploring options for what it calls *A New Magna Carta*.[102]

The case in favour of a codified constitution is rooted in the fact that, in the Committee's own words:

> [T]he UK has a 'sprawling mass' of common law, Acts of Parliament . . . and . . . 'conventions' that govern administration, but the full picture is unclear and uncertain to electors in our democracy . . . [I]t has 'become too easy for governments to implement political and constitutional reforms to suit their own political convenience' . . . The present uncodified constitution is 'an anachronism riddled with references to our ancient past, unsuited to the social and political democracy of the 21st century and the future aspirations of its people'.[103]

On this basis, *A New Magna Carta?* proposes the introduction of a written, codified constitution having 'the highest legal status',[104] over and above all other laws, and susceptible to a repeal process requiring 'approval by two-thirds of the members of both the [House of Commons and House of Lords] . . . and the majority of people voting in a referendum'.[105] On this foundation, the report goes on to make a number of possible suggestions, from a directly elected Head of State,[106] to a Bill of Rights of 'special legal status',[107] and permanent devolved institutions in Scotland, Wales, and Northern Ireland, free to create their own constitutions within the UK's 'federal constitution'.[108] Most significantly, perhaps, is the acknowledgement of a guaranteed separation of powers, including a Parliament subordinate to the codified constitution and an independent judiciary.[109] The proposals, therefore, published in spring 2015 offer a radical change in the way in which the UK Constitution works, fundamentally altering many of the unique and peculiar aspects that this chapter has highlighted as being at the heart of the UK system currently constituted. Whether or not there is a genuine need for a codified constitutional document for the UK is a question that has often been considered by constitutional scholars; the case is perhaps stronger now than it has ever been. Whether or not we will see such fundamental reform of a constitutional system, however, will become clearer in the fullness of time.

[101] See, for instance, Robert Blackburn, 'Enacting a Written Constitution for the United Kingdom' (2015) 36(1) *Statute Law Review* 1, NW Barber, 'Against a Written Constitution' (2008) *Public Law* 11, and Jeff King, 'A democratic case for a written constitution' in Jeffrey Jowell and Colm O'Cinneide (eds), *The Changing Constitution* (Oxford: OUP, 9th edn, 2019), 421.

[102] House of Commons Political and Constitutional Reform Committee, *A New Magna Carta*? (HC 2014–15, 463).

[103] House of Commons Political and Constitutional Reform Committee, 'A New Magna Carta?' (Leaflet), https://www.parliament.uk/documents/commons-committees/political-and-constitutional-reform/ Magna% 20Carta%20Report%20leaflet.pdf.

[104] House of Commons Political and Constitutional Reform Committee, 'The UK Constitution: A Summary, With Options for Reform' (March 2015), https://www.parliament.uk/documents/commons-committees/political-and-constitutional-reform/The-UK-Constitution.pdf 5.

[105] Ibid 6.   [106] Ibid 7.   [107] Ibid 19.   [108] Ibid 14.   [109] Ibid 5, 10–11, 15.

1.7 **Summary**

This chapter has provided an introduction to the UK Constitution. It has explained what we mean by the term 'constitution' and, within this, the manner in which the UK system is different from other constitutions across the world. Following this, the chapter has explored a number of key themes to which the major sources of the constitution contribute in setting out the way in which the UK constitutional system operates. This has explained how the various legal and non-legal sources work to provide a framework of laws and practices which clarify such issues as the allocation of power, the relationship between the various regions and institutions of the state, and the protection of individual rights. With all this in mind, the chapter has then concluded by exploring academic arguments which discuss the characteristics of the UK Constitution in a more theoretical context and which seek to justify or disprove its nature in comparison with more typical constitutional systems.

The nature of the UK system is undoubtedly unique and peculiar. It is one steeped in a long history and in incremental development and evolution. In this way, though, it has drawn together the various sources and rules which determine the way in which the UK constitutional system operates and functions. The next few chapters of the book build on this foundation and explore the principles which determine crucial questions relevant to the working of the UK constitution.

Quick test questions

1. How does Jennings define a constitution and on what basis does he distinguish the British system from others across the world?

2. What are constitutional conventions? How did Dicey define the expression?

3. What is the difference between legal and political constitutionalism?

4. What is significant about the Bill of Rights 1688?

5. What changes of note did the Constitutional Reform Act 2005 introduce?

6. How has the allocation of sovereign power shifted over the centuries?

7. What was Ridley's argument as regards whether or not the UK has a constitution?

8. What are the arguments in favour of codifying the UK Constitution and having a written document?

Further reading

The nature of the UK Constitution

Walter Bagehot, *The English Constitution* (first published 1867, OUP 2001)

Michael Gordon, 'Parliamentary sovereignty and the political constitution(s): From Griffith to Brexit' (2019) 30(1) *King's Law Journal* 125

*JAG Griffith, 'The Political Constitution' (1979) 42(1) *Modern Law Review* 1

Sir Ivor Jennings, *The Law and the Constitution* (5th edn, University of London Press 1963)

KC Wheare, *Modern Constitutions* (OUP 1966)

Sources of the Constitution

AV Dicey, *Introduction to the Study of the Law of the Constitution* (JWF Allison ed, first published 1885, OUP 2013)

Mark Elliott, 'Constitutional Legislation, European Union Law and the Nature of the United Kingdom's Contemporary Constitution' (2014) 10(3) *European Constitutional Law Review* 379

Rt Hon The Lord Falconer of Thoroton, 'The Role of the Lord Chancellor after the 2005 Reforms' (2015 Bentham Association Presidential Address, Bentham Association, UCL, 11 March 2015), http://www.laws.ucl.ac.uk/wp-content/uploads/2015/03/The-Role-of-The-Lord-Chancellor-After-the-2005-Reforms-Lord-Falconer-of-Thoroton-PC-QC.pdf

*Joseph Jaconelli, 'Do constitutional conventions bind?' (2005) 64(1) *Cambridge Law Journal* 149

*Anthony Lester and Kate Beattie, 'Human Rights and the British Constitution' in Jeffrey Jowell and Dawn Oliver (eds), *The Changing Constitution* (6th edn, OUP 2007) 59

Tom Mullen, 'The Brexit case and constitutional conventions' (2017) 21(3) *Edinburgh Law Review* 442

Alison L Young, 'Hunting Sovereignty: *Jackson v Her Majesty's Attorney-General*' (2006) *Public Law* 187

For and against a codified constitution

*NW Barber, 'Against a Written Constitution' (2008) *Public Law* 11

Robert Blackburn, 'Enacting a Written Constitution for the United Kingdom' (2015) 36(1) *Statute Law Review* 1

House of Commons Political and Constitutional Reform Committee, *A New Magna Carta?* (Second Report, Session 2014–15), HC 463

*Jeff King, 'The democratic case for a written constitution' in Jeffrey Jowell and Colm O'Cinneide (eds), *The Changing Constitution* (9th edn, OUP 2019) 421

*FF Ridley, 'There is no British Constitution: A Dangerous Case of the Emperor's Clothes' (1988) 41(3) *Parliamentary Affairs* 340

 Visit this book's **online resources** for additional materials relating to this chapter, including a full analysis of the start-of-chapter problem scenario.
www.oup.com/he/stanton-prescott2e

2

The institutions of government and the separation of powers

Problem scenario

Following Brexit, an Act of Parliament is passed to rebalance the allocation of power in the UK Constitution. Its chief aims are to reduce the power of the government; to assert the sovereignty of the elected Parliament; and to ensure the loyalty of the judiciary to Parliament's enactments. To this end, the (fictitious) Constitutional Reform (Allocation of Power) Act 2024 makes the following provisions:

- It reduces the number of government ministers capable of being appointed from Parliament to a maximum of thirty. Any further ministerial appointments can be drawn from elsewhere.

- It requires a vote in the House of Commons upon the formation of a government to approve ministerial appointments and plans for government.

- It requires all judicial appointments to be approved by a vote in the House of Commons, with all judges capable of being removed from office in the event of a vote of no confidence supported by two-thirds of the Commons.

2.1 **Introduction**

In Chapter 1, the nature of the UK Constitution was defined and explained. This showed that the lack of any written, codified document is striking and leads to a constitutional settlement that is both unique and peculiar. At the heart of the uncodified UK Constitution, however, are three principles that guide and shape the day-to-day operation of our system and the relationships between the various institutions of government. These will be discussed and explored over the next few chapters and are: the separation of powers, the rule of law, and parliamentary sovereignty. We deal with the first of these in this chapter. The separation of powers is a doctrine that is concerned with the three principal constitutional functions: the making of laws, the making of decisions and execution of policies in the process of government, and the judging and adjudication of disputes. These are traditionally fulfilled by the legislature, the executive, and the judiciary respectively. As this chapter will discuss, at the heart of the separation of powers doctrine is a need to respect a practical and institutional demarcation in respect of these constitutional functions, concerned for the dangers that could result where boundaries or functions are obfuscated. To this end, it 'is concerned with the avoidance of concentrations of power'.[1]

On this basis, the chapter defines the doctrine and explores its historical foundations, with particular reference to the UK Constitution. It then discusses in detail the manner in which the legislative, executive, and judicial functions are exercised in the UK and how well these can be said to adhere to and respect values central to the separation of powers. This consideration is mindful of the problem scenario set at the outset of the chapter, which requires critical analysis of the relationship between the institutions of the constitution and an examination of the way in which the various fictitious legislative provisions impact upon the way in which the institutions operate and relate to one another. In considering the separation of powers, however, it is important first to understand the nature and functions of the three institutions of our constitutional system: the legislature, the executive, and the judiciary. On this basis, the first section of this chapter will explain the functions fulfilled by these institutions, including an examination of their structure and key roles, thereafter allowing fuller exploration of the separation of powers in the UK Constitution. In respect of the doctrine, the chapter identifies a common distinction drawn between what is known as the *pure* and *partial* separation of powers. One favours total separation, the latter allowing a degree of overlap to the point of ensuring a system of checks and balances. Application of this distinction enables broader analysis of the UK's application of the doctrine.

With all this in mind, the objectives for this chapter are as follows:

- to explain the three main institutions of government in the UK Constitution and to define their roles;
- to define the theory of the separation of powers, including an illustration of its historical origins;
- to explore and discuss the relevance of the separation of powers in respect of the UK Constitution;

---

[1] Eric Barendt, *An Introduction to Constitutional Law* (OUP 1998) 15.

- to consider whether or not the UK Constitution can be said to adhere to theories of the separation of powers;

- to identify the distinction between *pure* and *partial* separations of power and to place the UK Constitution in the context of this distinction.

2.2 The institutions of government

Section 2.1 highlighted the three core constitutional functions: the making of laws, the making of decisions and execution of policies in the process of government, and the judging and adjudication of disputes. This section explores each in turn, identifying the institution responsible for each function, the structure of that institution, and the manner in which its functions are carried out. We start with the legislature.

2.2.1 Legislature

The legislature is the institution of government that passes legislation; that is, it makes law. In the UK Constitution, this function is fulfilled by Parliament. Parliament has met on a site in Westminster for over 750 years, and does so nowadays in the Palace of Westminster, a nineteenth-century London landmark. The UK Parliament is, as we noted in 1.4.3, a bicameral institution as it is made up of two chambers—the House of Commons and the House of Lords. The former is elected by eligible voters across the country, the latter—for the most part—appointed by the monarch, on the advice of the Prime Minister.[2]

Detailed exploration of Parliament's legislative process is reserved for Chapter 8. In brief, though, bills pass through both Houses of Parliament before receiving Royal Assent and being formally enacted as law. Bills can start in either House and in both they go through a first and second reading. While, at the first, the bill is merely read out, the second provides a valuable opportunity for open debate and discussion, culminating in a vote. After this second reading, at the committee stage, the bill is scrutinized by a standing committee of members who 'are appointed . . . specifically for each bill'.[3] These *ad hoc* committees take into account any necessary evidence and examine the bill's provisions carefully and in great detail.[4] The third reading is then a final examination of the bill in the full house and a vote on its provisions. Once complete, the bill will proceed to the other chamber for either debate or agreement and, thereafter, to Royal Assent, at which point the monarch formally signs a bill into law. Though Royal Assent is a key part of the process and the stage through which bills must go to be formally recognized as Acts of Parliament, it is nowadays a formality, reflecting the limited authority that the monarch can legally exercise. Indeed, the last time a monarch chose to refuse to grant Royal Assent was at the beginning of the eighteenth century. It is a prerogative power— the monarch assents to the passing of a bill on the advice of the government and on the basis that it has passed through the various parliamentary stages.

---

[2] See, for further discussion, 8.4. In addition to the appointed life peers, there are ninety-two hereditary peers and the twenty-six most senior Bishops of the Church of England.

[3] Robert Rogers and Rhodri Walters, *How Parliament Works* (6th edn, Pearson Longman 2006), 211.

[4] The Committee Stage of bills is discussed in more detail in 8.5.4.

Parliament's functions, however, go beyond mere law-making. As the main centrally, democratically elected forum in the country, it serves generally to provide a representative voice for citizens nationwide. This not only informs the law-making process but also means that political debates can take place on important matters affecting the whole country. Indeed, and in view of this, one of the most important functions fulfilled by Parliament, and in particular the House of Commons, is scrutiny of the government. It is a unique characteristic of the UK Constitution that the government—at least certain members of the government—sit in the House of Commons and have an instrumental role to play in the legislative process as well. To ensure, however, that the government does not abuse this position and exert unduly arbitrary power, various mechanisms exist to ensure that other Members of Parliament—chiefly, backbenchers, the opposition parties, and the House of Lords—can hold the government to account and keep it in check. Having now explained and defined the functions of the legislature, it is important to consider the executive.

2.2.2 Executive

The executive is the body that broadly fulfils the function of government; that is, the body that makes decisions and implements policy on a wide variety of matters relevant to the day-to-day government of the country. In our system, it is fulfilled by a range of institutions—chief amongst which is central government—and its main purpose is to execute laws made by Parliament. Due to the unique structure of our governmental institutions and the manner in which the formation of government is so closely linked to the legislature, as will be discussed below, the executive also has a role to play in the pre-legislative phase. Through its decision- and policy-making role, central government must react to and lead forward the push for change and development. A vast majority of the bills debated in Parliament derive from government policy for this very reason. The Cities and Local Government Devolution Act 2016, for example, is an Act setting out the legal framework for and giving statutory recognition to the policy underpinning the Northern Powerhouse—a key initiative set out by the then Chancellor of the Exchequer, George Osborne, during the early days of the 2015 Conservative Government.[5]

In the UK Constitution, the executive operates within a hierarchical structure. At the top are the centralized institutions of government, and beneath these are other bodies appropriate to the day-to-day government of the country, answerable to and guided by central government, including the armed forces, the police, and local authorities. In terms of our discussion here, we are chiefly concerned with those acting within central government. At the very top of the central governmental hierarchy is the Prime Minister, who is responsible to Parliament and the public for all the decisions that the government makes and the policies it pursues.

---

[5] The idea behind the Northern Powerhouse policy is the decentralization of power to certain cities in the north of England, alongside the establishment of combined authorities and the adoption of directly elected mayors (see 9.5.4 for further discussion).

Pause for reflection

The Prime Minister is the head of government and, as one person, is ultimately responsible for everything that goes into the process of government. Why do you think it is important to have one single individual taking this responsibility?

Beneath the Prime Minister is the most important part of the governmental structure, the Cabinet. Made up predominantly of senior ministers and headed by the Prime Minister, the Cabinet makes decisions on key government policy. Each senior minister is head of and responsible for one of the government departments. For example, the Chancellor of the Exchequer is head of HM Treasury; the Foreign Secretary head of the Foreign and Commonwealth Office; the Home Secretary head of the Home Office; and the Secretary of State for Defence head of the Ministry of Defence, to list just four examples.[6] In Cabinet meetings, these senior ministers discuss and decide key aspects of government-wide policy and though each minister represents an individual department, they only bring department-specific matters to Cabinet where they affect another department or if it is a sufficiently important part of policy to warrant a full Cabinet discussion. Guidance on how senior ministers should fulfil their responsibilities or conduct their affairs is set out in the *Cabinet Manual*, with the *Ministerial Code*—serving ministers more broadly—overlapping with this.

Despite the importance of their roles within central government, neither the Prime Minister nor the Cabinet are provided for in or protected by legislation and statutory mention of both is scant. Their roles exist purely by convention, as they have done for almost 300 years. The origins of these positions stem from the Glorious Revolution and the subsequent Bill of Rights 1688, a document which sought to clarify the relationship between the Crown and Parliament, formally establishing the sovereignty of the latter. Post-1688, Parliament was established as the primary law-maker, with the Crown[7] formally holding executive power. By 1721, however, the practice had developed for there to be a Prime Minister in the Houses of Parliament.[8] In view of the demarcation between legislative and executive power between Parliament and the Crown, this new position was primarily intended as a means of communication between the law-making institution and the base of executive authority. Gradually, this role developed further and the Prime Minister came to act as more than a mere communicator, the holder gradually taking on more power and the role slowly evolving into the democratically elected government position that we recognize today.[9] As the executive functions became too onerous for one man,

---

[6] The number of government departments can vary, depending on the order and structure a Prime Minister might wish to adopt. As of October 2019, there are twenty-five government departments.

[7] The Crown refers to the monarch, which is the formal seat of executive power. Before the development of modern democratic government, the Crown used to exercise a large degree of executive authority itself (see 6.1 for further discussion).

[8] Though the Prime Minister is now drawn from the House of Commons, many early Prime Ministers initially came from the Lords. What is more, though the first holder of the office, Robert Walpole, took office in 1721, it was William Pitt the Younger, later in the eighteenth century, who first adopted the title of Prime Minister.

[9] See 7.2.

the Cabinet thereafter slowly developed, with individual ministers taking on functions in specific policy areas, in a manner that continues today.[10]

This all said, the Crown—as personified by the monarch—is still the *formal* head of the executive, though now exercises very little actual power. The current system is reminiscent of these origins. The Prime Minister has a weekly audience with the Queen, at which matters of government are reported and discussed. The Prime Minister, with the Cabinet, is at the centre of government, therefore. Underneath them, however, and within each of the government departments, junior ministers deal with more specific areas of that department's portfolio, being answerable to their respective senior minister. Beneath these junior ministers, a number of civil servants work across the government departments, carrying out the vast range of day-to-day functions that are necessary to ensure the appropriate functioning of government.[11]

Within this hierarchical structure, central government has an important constitutional function to fulfil; that is, to make decisions and execute policy to govern the country. In doing this, it draws power from notable sources. Generally speaking, government authority is derived from statute. Parliament legislates to bestow upon central government departments jurisdiction over certain executive matters, also setting out the various instances in which government should act and what it is empowered to do. Such legislation is invariably broad, affording central government considerable discretion in relation to the manner in which it is able to fulfil its statutory duties and exercise its power. This statutory power also manifests itself in the form of a delegated legislative function. Discussed in 2.4.1, this basically gives central government a secondary law-making power, with some forms of such power—known as Henry VIII clauses—giving ministers the authority to amend primary legislation.[12] Alongside powers derived and enabled by statute, government also holds certain prerogative powers. These are considered in greater detail in Chapter 6, but for the sake of our exploration here, these are common law powers formally derived from the Crown and exercised by the government. Having now explained and identified the core aspects of the executive, it is necessary now to proceed with an explanation of the judicial function.

2.2.3 Judiciary

The final constitutional function is judicial; that is, the adjudication and settlement of disputes in court. Within this, judges have certain key responsibilities that are necessary to ensure the effective working of the UK Constitution. In England and Wales, the courts operate within a hierarchical structure, as shown in Figure 2.1. The lower courts include the Magistrate's Courts, County Courts, and Crown Courts and these deal predominantly with questions of fact relating to the particular cases that arise. The higher courts, or appellate courts as they are also known, include the High Court, the Court of Appeal, and the UK Supreme Court. These deal with questions of law and are often faced with difficult legal issues sometimes requiring the law to be taken in a new direction.

---

[10] See 7.5.

[11] For further discussion on the establishment of the Civil Service, see Stephen Sedley, *Lions under the Throne: Essays on the History of English Public Law* (Cambridge University Press 2015) 53–6. Also see 7.7.1.

[12] So called because Henry VIII was given such powers under the Statute of Proclamations. See, for example, s 10 of the Human Rights Act 1998. See also 8.6.1.

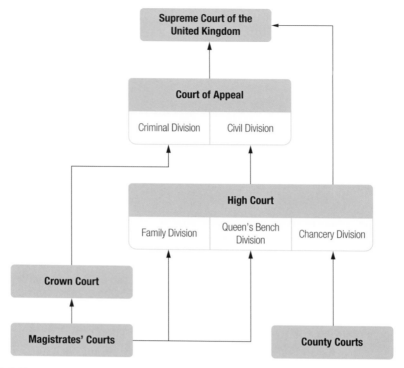

Figure 2.1 The court structure in England and Wales

 Counterpoint: Supreme Courts: comparing the UK with the US

Though it has a similar title, the UK Supreme Court fulfils a very different function from the US Supreme Court. As the constitutional court of America, the US Supreme Court has a vital role to play in upholding and protecting the provisions and rights contained within the US Constitution.[13] This includes the power to set aside pieces of primary legislation on the grounds that they are contrary to the constitution. Unlike the USA, however, the UK does not have a written or codified constitution, as Chapter 1 explained. Sovereign authority instead rests with the elected UK Parliament. As such, and with the courts not having a codified document to which they can refer and rely, UK judges cannot fulfil the same constitutional role as their counterparts in America. Instead, the UK Supreme Court acts merely as the highest court of appeal in the land, subordinate to the authority of Parliament, and it has no power to set aside legislation.

That said, the higher courts in the UK do still have a crucial constitutional role to fulfil. While Parliament is law-maker, it is the courts who are ultimately responsible for interpreting that law and for determining the manner in which it should be applied. On this basis, and in line with the principle of parliamentary sovereignty, the courts must always give effect to will of Parliament. This is discussed in more detail below.

[13] See *Marbury v Madison*, 5 US (1 Cranch) 137 (1803). An example of the US Supreme Court setting aside legislation that contravened the US Constitution can be seen in *Shelby County, Alabama v Holder*, 570 US (2013) where the court struck down s 4 of the Voting Rights Act 1965. Also see Mark Tushnet, *The Constitution of the United States of America: A Contextual Analysis* (2nd edn, Hart Publishing 2015) 134–6.

This section has identified the three main institutions of the constitution and explained the core functions that they fulfil. In later chapters,[14] some of these institutions will be explored in greater detail, but for now, this overview allows us to discuss the separation of powers principle.

2.3 The principle of the separation of powers

2.3.1 Definitions of the separation of powers

The separation of powers is a principle that can be traced back to ancient Greece. It advocates that the three core constitutional functions—legislative, executive, and judicial—should be practised by three entirely separate institutions, with no overlap or conflict. Along these lines, Aristotle stated that:

> There are three elements in each constitution and a good legislator must bear these in mind when he considers what is suitable in each case. If all these elements are in good order, then the whole constitution will also be in good order and, to the extent that these elements differ, so constitutions will also differ. The first of the three is the deliberative element concerned with common affairs: the second is the element concerned with public offices . . . the third is the judicial elements.[15]

Other theorists since Aristotle have also offered their own understandings of the principle. Locke, for instance, in his *Two Treatises of Government* states that:

> it may be too great a temptation to human frailty, apt to grasp at power, for the same persons who have the power of making laws to have also in their hands the power to execute them, whereby they may exempt themselves from obedience to the laws they make.[16]

Locke's exposition is, according to Sedley, 'doubly misleading' for the manner in which it 'came close to overlooking the role of the judicial function'.[17] The most commonly cited definition of the separation of powers doctrine, however, and the starting point for the purposes of this discussion, is the writing of Charles Louis de Secondat Montesquieu, a French political philosopher. He states, in *L'Esprit des Lois*, that:

> When the legislative and executive powers are united in the same person, or in the same body of magistrates, there can be no liberty; because apprehensions may arise, lest the same monarch or senate should enact tyrannical laws, to enact them in a tyrannical manner. Again, there is no liberty, if the judiciary power be not separated from the legislature and executive. Were it joined with the legislative, the life and liberty of the subject would be exposed to arbitrary control; for the judge would then be the legislator. Were it joined to

---

[14] See Chapters 4–8.   [15] Aristotle, *Politics*, Book IV, 14 (1297ᵇ) 35.

[16] John Locke, *Second Treatise of Government and A Letter Concerning Toleration* (Mark Goldie ed, first published 1689, OUP 2016) 73, cited in Stephen Sedley, *Lions under the Throne: Essays on the History of English Public Law* (Cambridge University Press 2015) 174.

[17] Stephen Sedley, *Lions under the Throne: Essays on the History of English Public Law* (Cambridge University Press 2015) 174–5. Sedley goes on to acknowledge that 'It is probable that, when he spoke of an independent executive power to carry out the law, Locke had in mind judicial as well as ministerial enforcement' (at 175).

the executive power, the judge might behave with violence and oppression. There would be an end to everything, were the same man, or the same body, whether of the nobles or of the people, to exercise those three powers, that of enacting laws, that of executing public resolutions, and of trying the causes of individuals.[18]

Montesquieu's formulation was based on his perception of the British Constitution as it was in the eighteenth century, which Barendt describes as an 'odd interpretation' since 'the United Kingdom constitutional arrangements did not then, and certainly do not now, observe the separation of powers as Montesquieu understood it'.[19] Indeed, as Sedley notes, '[i]n 1748, when Montesquieu commended England as a model of the separation of powers in a democracy, judges still sat in Cabinet and the final court of appeal was the upper chamber of the legislature'.[20]

This is not to say, however, that the UK Constitution has never worked to recognize demarcations of responsibility and function between the various institutions. Some of the early constitutional sources, discussed in Chapter 1, reflect an understanding of the values at the heart of the doctrine and a desire to protect citizens from the dangers of concentrated power. The Bill of Rights 1688, for example, was predicated on the recognition of a division of authority between the Crown and Parliament. Similarly, and shortly thereafter, the Act of Settlement 1700 was passed, *inter alia*, to ensure the independence of the judiciary from the other institutions. The modern constitution has evolved from these beginnings with the three institutions developing and emerging on this basis. There are some, however, who see the relevance of the separation of powers doctrine in the UK Constitution in a somewhat different way.

 Counterpoint: Tomkins—an alternative view

The approach of Aristotle and Montesquieu discussed in the first part of this chapter, with the legislature, executive, and judiciary forming a tripartite division of power, is not the only view offered. Others have considered that the core functions of the constitution can be divided on different lines. Tomkins, for instance, states that 'far from being based on a separation of powers between legislature, executive, and judiciary, to the extent that there is a separation of powers in English public law it is a separation between the Crown on the one hand, and Parliament on the other'.[21] Tomkins' alternative perspective is founded on the observation that:

> the traditional [tripartite] account of the separation of powers was formulated by eighteenth century theorists in France and in America . . . The structure of the English constitution, at least as far as the legal relationship between the institutions of State is concerned, was already largely in place by the end of the seventeenth century, secured by the Bill of Rights and the Act of Settlement. How could a seventeenth century construct (such as the English constitution) be based on an eighteenth century theory?[22]

→

---

[18] Montesquieu, *L'Esprit des Lois*, Book 11 (1748) Ch 6.
[19] Eric Barendt, *An Introduction to Constitutional Law* (OUP 1998) 14.
[20] Stephen Sedley, *Lions under the Throne: Essays on the History of English Public Law* (Cambridge University Press 2015) 172.
[21] Adam Tomkins, *Public Law* (OUP 2003) 44.   [22] Ibid 45.

→

Tomkins' understanding of the separation of powers being discussed on the basis of a bipartite division of authority between the Crown and Parliament is rooted in the fact that the Civil War and, shortly thereafter, 'the peace settlements of 1660–1662 and 1689–1700' were based on conflict between the Crown and Parliament.[23] These events provide the foundation for the modern UK Constitution, as Chapter 1 has discussed. Even today, though, and as Tomkins also observes, the Crown and Parliament are the only two powers in the constitution ever to have exercised sovereign authority, with every constitutional actor falling 'on one side or the other of this great divide' and ultimately drawing their power from one or the other.[24] Tomkins goes on to discuss the importance of accountability to this 'Crown versus Parliament' dynamic and he explains how wider constitutional principles are similarly founded on this divide.[25]

Tomkins' view of the separation of powers is markedly different from the more orthodox understandings established by Montesquieu and developed incrementally over the course of time. While it offers an alternative perspective, this chapter proceeds on the foundation established by the more widely recognized tripartite division of authority.

2.3.2 Justifications for the principle

Montesquieu has already been quoted as explaining that the separation of powers is necessary for the protection of individual liberty and the prevention of arbitrary rule. In short, it was felt that if the same institution exercised legislative, executive, and judicial authority simultaneously, then that institution would have unfettered power over individuals and would be acting without independence or any appropriate check on its authority. It is, in this way, a necessary condition for what is known as 'the rule of law'—the principle which demands that a process of government operate according to law, rather than on the basis of arbitrary powers.[26] The relevance of the separation of powers to the rule of law has been widely noted. Lord Donaldson MR stated, in *R v HM Treasury, ex p Smedley*,[27] that it 'is a constitutional convention of the highest importance that the legislature and the judicature are separate and independent of one another, subject to certain ultimate rights of Parliament over the judicature'.[28] Equally, Henderson writes that '[t]his threefold division of labour between a legislator, an administrative official, and an independent judge, is a necessary condition for the rule of law in modern society and . . . for democratic government itself'.[29]

The constitutional importance of the separation of powers, particularly with regard to the rule of law, recently came to the fore in the case of *R (Evans) v Attorney-General*.[30] Here, the Attorney-General, acting on behalf of the government, sought to overturn the decision of the Upper Tribunal in permitting the disclosure of letters sent by Prince Charles to various government departments. The Supreme Court upheld the Tribunal's decision and permitted publication of the letters. Though the Attorney-General was acting pursuant to a statutory power,[31] Lord Neuberger noted that:

> it is a basic principle that a decision of a court is binding as between the parties, and cannot be ignored or set aside by anyone, including (indeed it may fairly be said, least of all) the

[23] Ibid 46.   [24] Ibid.   [25] Ibid 46–54.
[26] See, further, Chapter 3.   [27] [1985] QB 657.   [28] Ibid 666.
[29] Edith Henderson, *Foundations of English Administrative Law: Certiorari and Mandamus in the Seventeenth Century* (Harvard University Press 1963) 5.
[30] [2015] UKSC 21.   [31] Section 53 of the Freedom of Information Act 2000.

executive. Secondly, it is also fundamental to the rule of law that decisions and actions of the executive are, subject to necessary well established exceptions . . . and jealously scrutinised statutory exceptions, reviewable by the court at the suit of an interested citizen. Section 53, as interpreted by the Attorney General's argument in this case, flouts the first principle and stands the second principle on its head. It involves saying that a final decision of a court can be set aside by a member of the executive (normally the minister in charge of the very department against whom the decision has been given) because he does not agree with it.[32]

This decision further underlines the importance of the separation of powers as a value consistent with the rule of law and as a principle that serves to limit potentially arbitrary uses of executive authority. The Supreme Court in *Evans* ensured that the executive did not abuse its position in overturning the decision of the Upper Tribunal. We return to this case in Chapter 3.

The separation of powers, though, can also be justified on the basis of principles necessary for efficient governance and an effective working democratic and just system. On this, Barber notes that:

an alternative approach to the separation of powers claims that the point of the doctrine is to promote efficient state action by ensuring that powers are allocated to the institution best able to make use of those powers. [To this end t]here is a long tradition of scholars who place efficiency, rather than just liberty, as at the heart of the separation of powers.[33]

Barber goes on to identify examples that support this view. The process of democracy, for instance, is important in ensuring that 'the bodies that set the direction of the state are under the control of its citizens'.[34] Elected MPs sit in the House of Commons—part of the legislature—to play a part in the law-making process and it would be contrary to the value of democracy if laws and policies could be passed by those unelected to the legislature, such as members of the executive or judiciary. Equally, though, 'there must [also] be some mechanism that allows the integration of expertise into the process'.[35] There is a place for unelected experts, provided 'that their influence on legislation be mediated through elected representatives'.[36] The unelected House of Lords, subordinate to the House of Commons, is consistent with this justification.

The independence of the judiciary is another vital feature of a system consistent with the separation of powers. Not only because judges must 'make decisions according to the relevant law and not because of bribes or political pressure',[37] but more broadly

---

[32] [2015] UKSC 21 [52]. Also see Mark Elliott, 'Of Black Spiders and Constitutional Bedrock: The Supreme Court's Judgment in Evans' (*Public Law for Everyone*, 26 March 2015), https://publiclawforeveryone.com/2015/03/26/of-black-spiders-and-constitutional-bedrock-the-supreme-courts-judgment-in-evans/.

[33] Nicholas W Barber, 'The Separation of Powers and the British Constitution' (2012) Oxford Legal Studies Research Paper No 3/2012, https://papers.ssrn.com/sol3/papers.cfm?abstract_id=1995780. In referring to this 'long tradition of scholars', Barber cites Ann Stuart Anderson, 'A 1787 Perspective on the Separation of Powers', in Robert A Goldwin and Art Kaufman (eds), *The Separation of Powers—Does it Still Work?* (AEI Press 1987) 145; David Gwynn Morgan, *The Separation of Powers in the Irish Constitution* (Round Hall Ltd 1997) 4; Peter Laslett in John Locke, *Two Treatises of Government* (Peter Laslett ed, Cambridge University Press 1988) 118–20; Bruce G Peabody, and John D Nugent, 'Toward a Unifying Theory of the Separation of Powers' (2003–2004) 53 *American University Law Review* 1, 26.

[34] Nicholas W Barber, 'The Separation of Powers and the British Constitution' (2012) Oxford Legal Studies Research Paper No 3/2012, 14.

[35] Ibid 15.   [36] Ibid.   [37] Ibid.

because it would be contrary to the process of justice if the court system—hearing as that does disputes between private and public parties—were to overlap and be influenced by those institutions that execute policy and make law.

 Pause for reflection

Barber is critical of justifying the separation of powers on grounds of liberty. He states that '[t]here are a number of difficulties with accounts that treat liberty as the sole objective of the separation of powers'.[38] They assume, he suggests, 'that liberty and a strong state are inevitably opposed to each other, [and] that the citizen can only be truly free within a state whose power for concerted action is limited by institutional conflict'.[39] Furthermore, he notes that 'the simple liberty model of the separation of powers cannot explain why a particular power should be allocated to a particular institution, nor why a particular type of person should exercise these powers'.[40]

Do you agree with him? To what extent is the separation of powers justified by the protection of individual liberties, or efficiency of process, or both?

The separation of powers has far-reaching constitutional justifications, some of which lie at the heart of the principle elucidated by Montesquieu, and others that—more broadly—ensure the effective and efficient operation of the constitutional institutions. In terms of understanding the manner in which the principle applies in respect of the UK Constitution, however, the next section now examines the relationships between each of the three institutions, exploring the characteristics that both complement the principle and raise questions of its relevance in the UK.

2.4 Exploring the separation of powers in the UK Constitution

Due to the unique, uncodified nature of the UK Constitution and the institutions operating within that system, discussion of the separation of powers is both interesting and highly contentious. In exploring the manner in which the doctrine applies in the UK, this section is divided into three sections, each looking at a particular relationship between the institutions of the constitution. The first explores the relationship between legislature and executive, the second, legislature and judiciary, and the third, executive and judiciary. Within these sections, we will explore important themes, such as judicial independence and parliamentary accountability, and also consider recent developments that have been introduced with prime concern for the separation of powers, such as the Constitutional Reform Act 2005.

2.4.1 Legislature and executive

In the UK constitutional and governmental system, the relationship between the legislature (Parliament) and executive (central government) is particularly interesting. In chief, this is because there is ostensibly very little separation between the two institutions since

[38] Ibid 13.   [39] Ibid.   [40] Ibid.

each government is established from the ranks of Parliament following a General Election. This happens because the leader of the political party that commands a majority in the House of Commons is, by convention, invited to become Prime Minister and to form a government, also having the power to appoint ministers to that government. Those whom the Prime Minister appoints as ministers within the government must be a member of one of the Houses of Parliament,[41] with the Prime Minister always drawn from the Commons. The reality of government ministers in this way representing a lack of separation of powers between the legislature and executive is noted by Walter Bagehot. He stated that the:

> efficient secret of the English Constitution may be described as the close union, the nearly complete fusion of the executive and legislative powers. According to the traditional theory, as it exists in all the books, the goodness of our constitution consists in the entire separation of the legislative and executive authorities, but in truth its merit consists in their singular approximation. The connecting link is *the cabinet*.[42]

Members of government being within the make-up of Parliament is an obvious concern from the perspective of the separation of powers. It is tempered, though, by legislation that seeks to place limitations on who can sit in the House of Commons. The House of Commons Disqualification Act 1975, for example, states in section 1 that 'a person is disqualified for membership of the House of Commons' if they are one of the Lords Spiritual,[43] a holder of judicial office, a civil servant, a member of the Armed Forces or a Police Force, 'a member of the legislature of any country or territory outside the Commonwealth (other than Ireland)', or a member of one of a range of bodies listed in Schedule 1 to the Act.[44] What is more, while government ministers are elected to sit in the House of Commons, and are selected for government office on this basis, this is the extent of the personnel overlap between the legislature and the executive. Indeed, section 2 of the 1975 Act limits ministers that can be drawn from the House of Commons to 95. The restrictions imposed by the 1975 Act, *inter alia*, serve to ensure that other members of the executive and those holding judicial office are prevented from sitting in the House of Commons. As Barber has acknowledged:

> whilst there is a strong connection between the legislature and executive branches—with the political part of the government tying the two together—there are also profound differences. The executive branch in the United Kingdom is very large: . . . there are hundreds

---

[41] The majority of Government ministers come from the House of Commons. In June 2017, when Theresa May announced her administration after that year's election, only 21 per cent of ministers came from the House of Lords. Lords filling Cabinet positions is particularly rare: while Lord Carrington (Foreign Secretary under Margaret Thatcher, 1979–82); Lord Falconer (Lord Chancellor and Secretary of State for Constitutional Affairs, then Justice Secretary under Tony Blair, 2003–07); and Lord Mandelson (First Secretary of State and Secretary of State for Business, Innovation and Skills under Gordon Brown, 2008–10) are notable examples in recent decades, there have only been ten Cabinet ministers drawn from the Lords since 1979 (not including Lord Chancellors or leaders of the House of Lords). See Lucinda Maer, 'Ministers in the House of Lords' (House of Commons Library Briefing Paper 05226, 4 September 2017).

[42] Walter Bagehot, *The English Constitution* (first published 1867, OUP 2001) 11.

[43] Lords Spiritual are the twenty-six Bishops of the Church of England who are members of the House of Lords.

[44] Such bodies include the judiciary, the Charity Commission, the Care Quality Commission, the Office of Fair Trading, the Scottish Law Commission, as well as many more (see Sch 1 to the House of Commons Disqualification Act 1975).

of thousands, perhaps even a million, people working in the executive. There are civil servants, soldiers, policemen, nurses, all of whom could be considered part of this branch of the state. They, for the most part, do not sit in Parliament. Indeed, in a clear instance of the separation of persons, civil servants are barred from sitting in the House of Commons. In their working life, these state employees are expected to be apolitical.[45]

While the overlap in personnel between the government and Parliament has been widely acknowledged as representing a fusion of authority between the two institutions, therefore, it is to a point controlled by rules that limit the people qualified to sit in the House of Commons.

 Discussing the problem

Have another look at the problem scenario at the start of the chapter. To what extent do you think that the 2024 Act's reduction of the number of government ministers capable of being drawn from Parliament will impact upon this relationship and, more broadly, the UK Constitution's respect for the separation of powers?

The provision to reduce the number of government ministers capable of being drawn from Parliament to a maximum of thirty goes right to the heart of the apparent fusion of power that currently exists between the legislature and the executive. This chapter has already explained that, at present, a maximum of ninety-five government ministers may be drawn from the House of Commons, and this contributes to the overlap that currently exists between government and Parliament insofar as the Prime Minister and the senior and junior ministers of the government are all drawn from one of the Houses of Parliament; typically, though not exclusively, the House of Commons. With regards to the separation of powers, though, the question behind this particular provision of the 2024 Act is whether a reduction in the number of government ministers drawn from Parliament would impact upon the relationship between the legislature and the executive and improve the separation of powers in the UK Constitution. While such a reduction would inevitably reduce the number of people serving both Parliament and the government, the basis for the fusion of authority would still exist, just to a lesser degree.

Above and beyond this fusion of membership between the legislature and executive, government ministers also possess certain powers that could be said to amount to more of a legislative function than an executive one. Ministers, for example, have the power to enact delegated, or secondary legislation. Often in the form of statutory instruments, members of government have the authority under various enabling Acts 'to change the law to meet changing circumstances without the sledgehammer (and the delay) of new primary legislation'.[46] Statutory instruments can take a number of forms, including 'orders, regulations, Orders in Council, schemes, rules, [and] codes of practice'.[47] A particularly notable, and previously mentioned, example of such delegated legislative powers can come in the form of what are known as Henry VIII clauses. These empower ministers

---

[45] Nicholas W Barber, 'The Separation of Powers and the British Constitution' (2012) Oxford Legal Studies Research Paper No 3/2012, 10.

[46] Robert Rogers and Rhodri Walters, *How Parliament Works* (6th edn, Pearson Longman 2006) 253.

[47] Ibid.

to alter or amend primary legislation. Section 10(2) of the Human Rights Act 1998, for instance, is an example of such a provision. This states that 'a Minister of the Crown . . . may by order make such amendments to . . . legislation as he considers necessary to remove' an incompatibility with Convention rights. These Henry VIII clauses are also prominent in the context of Brexit. The European Union (Withdrawal) Act 2018, which set out the legal framework for the UK's departure from the EU, provides that applicable EU law, in force at the time of the UK's departure, would be retained as 'part of [UK] domestic on and after exit day'.[48] The Act then gave 'Ministers time-limited powers to amend domestic law (including but not only, retained EU law) to address "deficiencies" arising from Brexit; this extend[ed], subject to certain exceptions, to allowing Ministers to do anything that could be done by Act of Parliament'.[49] These powers are examples of Henry VIII clauses, and permit ministers to exercise far-reaching powers to adjust the law post-Brexit. Powers to pass secondary legislation are therefore notable and give members of the executive the authority to act as legislators.

This close fusion between legislative and executive authority in the UK constitution could be seen as a threat to the values espoused by Montesquieu concerning individuals' protection from arbitrary uses of power, and, more broadly, principles at the heart of the rule of law. It is a point fairly made that a particularly strong government, backed up by a large majority in the House of Commons, might be at risk of exerting commanding authority in the legislature. In 1997, for example, Tony Blair's Labour Party won 418 seats in the House of Commons, leaving just 232 MPs on the opposition benches. While this book does not deign to pass judgement on any laws or policies that were presented to the Commons at that time, the Labour Government found it easier to win votes than Theresa May's 2017 Conservative Government, which was a minority government, falling short of the requisite 326 seats and propped up by ten MPs from the Democratic Unionist Party. The dangers this can present are discussed by the former Lord Chancellor, Lord Hailsham, who in a lecture in October 1976 identified the risks of what he called the 'elective dictatorship'.[50] This is the notion that a government, while elected by the people through a General Election, can be capable of exerting considerable influence over the House of Commons, and the rest of Parliament, party whips, the party machine and the civil service.[51] To counter these risks and the close fusion of power between Parliament and government, a number of mechanisms exist within the UK system to ensure that government can be controlled and the dangers of arbitrary authority prevented.

Many of these mechanisms function within Parliament itself, through the ordinary course of debates, discussion, and parliamentary procedure. The opposition parties, while ordinarily collectively fewer in number than those MPs who are members of the party in power,[52] through these mechanisms provide a measure of scrutiny and accountability

---

[48] European Union (Withdrawal) Act 2018, section 3(1).

[49] Mark Elliott, '1,000 words / The European Union (Withdrawal) Act 2018' (*Public Law for Everyone*, 28 June 2018), https://publiclawforeveryone.com/2018/06/28/1000-words-the-european-union-withdrawal-act-2018/, citing European Union (Withdrawal) Act 2018, section 8.

[50] Lord Hailsham, 'Elective Dictatorship—The Richard Dimbleby Lecture' *The Listener* (21 October 1976) 496, 500.

[51] Ibid, 496.

[52] Unless there is a minority government where there are a greater number of MPs on the opposition benches than on the government benches.

over the actions of the government; the government being accountable to Parliament by virtue of the convention of Ministerial Responsibility.[53] The most prominent way in which this accountability exists is through parliamentary question time. In the House of Commons, question time involves a member of the government—that is, the Prime Minister or the head of a particular government department—facing questions from opposition parties and backbenchers. Questions seek to challenge and scrutinize government actions and decisions and demand answers and explanations in respect of recent activity. The most prominent form of question time is Prime Minister's Questions, which takes place every Wednesday at 12 noon for half an hour. Here, the leader of the government receives questions from the House, particularly from the leader of the opposition.

Over and above the valuable function that opposition parties play in the process of Commons' question time, MPs from opposition parties also have opportunity during the course of policy debates and bill readings to question and challenge the government's course of action. Indeed, on occasion there are also votes in the House of Commons determining whether or not the government should pursue a particular policy. While various votes during the 2017–19 Parliament to seek endorsement of the government's plans to proceed with Brexit is an example of the Commons voting on government policy, it is notable that a Commons vote in 2013 declined to support military action against Syria, David Cameron's Coalition Government honouring that decision. While, in one sense, the general process of debate enhances the process and ensures a rigorous and robust policy or law, in another sense, it serves to provide yet another form of accountability for the government, responding as they must to questions and challenges from the opposition benches and having government action determined by votes in the House.

 Pause for reflection

While these various mechanisms—Question Time, opposition parties, debates, and votes—act as a check on government power, in practice government victory is particularly common; it is more notable when it loses. This is perhaps unsurprising when we also consider the substantial number of MPs who are on the government payroll (118, as of June 2017).[54]

With this in mind, how effective do you think these various mechanisms in the House of Commons are at keeping the government in check?

Another prominent way in which the House of Commons provides a measure of accountability over the government is through Select Committees. These are permanent Committees, which exist in respect of each government department, and whose job it is 'to examine the expenditure, administration and policy of [the relevant government department] and associated public bodies'.[55] The Committees vary in size, though they

[53] For further discussion on Ministerial Responsibility, see 7.7.

[54] Lucinda Maer and Richard Kelly, 'Limitations on the Number of Ministers' (House of Commons Library Briefing Paper 03378, 10 August 2017).

[55] Robert Rogers and Rhodri Walters, *How Parliament Works* (6th edn, Pearson Longman 2006) 347–8. This is a form of words that is generally provided as Terms of Reference in respect of the Select Committees by the House of Commons Standing Orders. See, for instance, House of Commons, *Standing Orders of the House of Commons—Public Business 2017* (20 April 2017, HC 4) [121]–[152D].

must reflect the relative strength of the political parties in the House itself. The Committees carry out ongoing investigations into the workings of their respective departments as well as specific enquiries into a particular policy area. They can call upon oral and written evidence as well as the work of special advisers, appointed for a particular enquiry. At the end of a given investigation, a Committee publishes a report that outlines its thoughts on the government's action as well as any considerations it might have for how the particular area might develop in the future. An example of this Select Committee process at work is provided by the Education Committee, which has recently been engaged in an inquiry on '[s]pecial educational needs and disabilities'.[56] The Committee drew from a wealth of evidence and published its report in October 2019.[57]

The House of Commons provides valuable mechanisms for accountability that serve to keep the government in check and ensure that it does not abuse its position as the most powerful part of the legislature. Outside the House of Commons, though, the unelected House of Lords also exists to provide a measure of scrutiny and accountability for the government. Like the Commons, there is question time in the Lords. Here, at the beginning of each day's sitting (except Fridays), a maximum of thirty minutes is set aside during which 'four questions for oral answer . . . may be put to the government'.[58] There are also Select Committees in the House of Lords, though unlike the Commons, these are not tied to particular departments but instead focus on specific, specialist subjects, such as science and technology, economic affairs, and the constitution.[59] As unelected peers, members of the House of Lords are not influenced by public opinion or the desire to remain in political office and can therefore be more independent and rigorous in their scrutiny of government policies and bills. Indeed, some members of the House of Lords, known as cross-benchers, are not connected to any political party, which further increases the independence of their scrutiny.

> ## ❞ Discussing the problem
>
> **Have another look at the problem scenario. The 2024 Act provides that a vote in the House of Commons be held upon the formation of a government, to approve ministerial appointments and plans for government. How far do you think this would bolster existing mechanisms in ensuring that the House of Commons can hold the government to account and what impact does this have on the separation of powers?**
>
> This particular provision of the 2024 Act is designed to supplement and improve the existing mechanisms through which Parliament is able to hold the government to account and keep it in check. Currently, and as this chapter has already discussed, Question Time, general debate and discussion, as well as Select Committee work, all serve to ensure that the government's exercise of power is checked and scrutinized by the House of Commons. The idea behind this provision of the 2024 Act, however, would be to improve this check and provide a further level of scrutiny. It would, however, raise questions about the separation of powers insofar as ministerial appointments are very much an executive function, within the remit of the Prime Minister. Requiring
>
> →

---

[56] Education Committee, *Special educational needs and disabilities* (HC 2019–20, 20).   [57] Ibid.
[58] Robert Rogers and Rhodri Walters, *How Parliament Works* (6th edn, Pearson Longman 2006) 338–9.
[59] Ibid 378.

> →
>
> Commons approval for appointments could be seen as Parliament interfering to an unnecessary degree in the operation and process of government, actions that would compromise the separation of powers.

Within Parliament, therefore, there are various ways through which members of the government are held to account and scrutinized during the ordinary process of debate, policy, and law making. While it is difficult to ignore that the government—bolstered by the payroll vote[60]—is the largest and, therefore, the most powerful part of the House of Commons, these mechanisms serve to ensure, *inter alia*, that any potential abuses or arbitrary uses of power that might occur as a result of the close fusion between the government and the legislature are balanced by mechanisms of accountability. Indeed, and ultimately, the opportunity that citizens have to participate in frequent elections also serves as a mechanism to keep the government of the day in check. A government will not necessarily wish to behave in such a way that discourages the public from re-electing them. Other mechanisms, external to the parliamentary and governmental process, derive from the jurisdiction of the Administrative Court and judicial review and these are discussed in 2.5.

2.4.2 Legislature and judiciary

The relationship between the legislative and judicial functions under the UK Constitution is, in one sense, relatively clear. Parliament makes the law, whilst the primary judicial function is to interpret legislation and give effect to the will of Parliament, adjudicating disputes on this basis. This satisfies, at least, an ostensible separation of function. But it is rather more complicated than this. The relationship between the two functions is, in part, defined by the principle of parliamentary sovereignty. While literal consideration of Montesquieu's doctrine might lead one to suppose that the legislative and judicial functions should be both separate from and equal to one another, the superiority of Parliament in the UK Constitution gives rise to characteristics that ensure this cannot be the case. It has already been noted that in the USA, the Supreme Court has the authority to adjudicate alleged breaches of the constitution and strike down primary legislation if it is found to be unconstitutional.[61] In the absence of any codified constitutional document in the UK, however, the UK Supreme Court has no such authority and must instead look to Parliament as the highest source of law. The courts are subordinate to the legislature and must interpret Acts so as to give effect to the latest, express will of Parliament.

A consequence of this relationship between the legislature and the judiciary is that Parliament has the power to make laws affecting the courts. Above and beyond the conventional tools of statutory interpretation,[62] for example, Parliament has on occasion

---

[60] The payroll vote simply refers to MPs who are on the government payroll and who can be relied upon to vote in support of government policies and decisions.

[61] See 2.2.3.

[62] The rules of statutory interpretation are: the literal rule, the golden rule, the mischief rule, and the purposive approach (see Emily Allbon and Sanmeet Kaur Dua, *Elliott & Quinn's English Legal System* (19th edn, Pearson 2018) ch 3).

set out how far the courts can and should go in interpreting legislative provisions. Section 3 of the Human Rights Act 1998, for instance, states that 'primary legislation and subordinate legislation must be read and given effect in a way which is compatible with the Convention rights'.[63] Though this has generated a great deal of judicial discussion—explored in Chapter 15—Lord Nicholls observes in *Ghaidan v Godin-Mendoza*[64] that Parliament has, through section 3, effectively established a new form of statutory interpretation, inviting judges to stretch the wording of legislative provisions—even where no ambiguity exists—to achieve compatibility with the European Convention on Human Rights.

The role that the courts play in interpreting statutes, alongside the sovereignty of Parliament, though, is also an important constitutional function, above and beyond merely giving effect to the will of Parliament. Lord Neuberger, for instance, who went on to become President of the UK Supreme Court, noted in 2011:

> In our present complex fast-moving society, the judges have a vital role to play. First, we must not just interpret the law enacted by Parliament in a blinkered unimaginative way. With the welter of legislation, much of it ill-drafted, we should interpret statutes in a practical way . . . Secondly, we must develop the common law so it reflects the changing needs and standards of society. That sometimes means moving the law on when Parliament has not got the legislative time, or even sometimes when it has not got the political will to do so. Thirdly, we must be vigilant to protect individuals against any abuses or excesses of an increasingly powerful executive.[65]

The UK courts have a vital function to fulfil, therefore, considering the words of legislation alongside broader constitutional and societal factors, as well as upholding the rule of law through protecting individuals from potentially abusive exercise of executive power. While, as Lord Neuberger goes on to stress, the courts 'should never forget that, however we develop or apply the law, we cannot go against Parliament's will when it is expressed through a statute',[66] it often falls to the courts to uphold and protect values at the heart of the constitution, something that can occasionally require them to compromise on the intentions of Parliament. Indeed, in fulfilling their statutory interpretative role, judges have on occasion strayed from obedience to the clear and express words of Parliament in order that other, competing constitutional values be upheld. In the already considered case of *Evans*, for instance, though section 53 of the Freedom of Information Act 2000 set out a clear power through which the Attorney-General could overturn the decision of the Upper Tribunal and prevent disclosure of Prince Charles' letters, the Supreme Court felt that to afford the executive the power to overturn courts' decisions would be contrary both to the separation of powers and the

---

[63] Section 3(1) of the Human Rights Act 1998.

[64] [2004] UKHL 30.

[65] Lord Neuberger MR, 'Who are the Masters Now?' (Second Lord Alexander of Weedon Lecture, 6 April 2011), para 72, http://webarchive.nationalarchives.gov.uk/20131203081513/http://www.judiciary.gov. uk/Resources/JCO/Documents/Speeches/mr-speech-weedon-lecture-110406.pdf.

[66] Ibid para 73, citing Sir John Laws, 'Illegality and the Problem of Jurisdiction' in Michael Supperstone and James Goudie (eds), *Judicial Review* (Butterworths 1997) para 4.17, cited in Jeffrey Goldsworthy, 'The Myth of the Common Law Constitution' in Douglas E Edlin (ed), *Common Law Theory* (Cambridge University Press 2007) 204.

rule of law. Similarly, in the case of *Anisminic v Foreign Compensation Commission*,[67] the courts refused to read section 4(4) of the Foreign Compensation Act 1950—which stated that '[t]he determination by the Commission of any application made to them under this Act shall not be called in question in any court of law'—as ousting the scope of judicial review, in order that the accessibility of judicial review as a means of upholding the rule of law should be protected.[68]

Over and above compromising the interpretation of statutes in view of competing constitutional values, however, the courts have also, on occasion, been called upon to examine the validity of primary legislation. In *R v Secretary of State for Transport, ex p Factortame (No 2)*, the House of Lords disapplied the Merchant Shipping Act 1988 due to its confliction with EU law,[69] while in *R (on the application of Jackson) v Attorney-General*, the same court examined the validity of the Parliament Act 1949 and, by extension, the Hunting Act 2004. Perhaps most significantly, though, section 4 of the Human Rights Act 1998 permits the courts to issue declarations of incompatibility where provisions of primary legislation are found to be incompatible with ECHR rights. Though falling short of a power to set aside legislation, section 4 does, at least, provide an example of the courts examining Parliament's enactments.[70] The relationship between the courts and Parliament is complex and important. While parliamentary sovereignty ultimately means that the courts are inferior to the legislature and bound by its laws, the courts still have a vital role to fulfil in protecting values at the heart of the constitution, a role that can sometimes justify them departing from the apparent will of Parliament.

Parliament's sovereignty, though, also means that it has the power to overturn judgments and alter judicial decisions, something that also sits uneasily with the separation of powers. One case that exemplifies this is *Burmah Oil Co Ltd v Lord Advocate*.[71]

Case in depth: *Burmah Oil Co Ltd v Lord Advocate* [1965] AC 75

In 1942, at the height of the Second World War and with the Japanese having recently invaded Burma, Burmese oil fields were destroyed by British forces so as to render them unusable should they fall into the hands of the enemy and help their war effort. Though it was accepted that the authority to destroy the oil fields derived from the royal prerogative powers to conduct the war, a case was brought seeking compensation for the damage that had been caused by the fields' destruction. The case went to the House of Lords which held that, while the order to destroy the fields had indeed been taken lawfully, the Burmah Oil Company Ltd was entitled to compensation for the damage caused. Such compensation, held the court, should come from public funds.

Notably, however, and despite the judgment in the case, the War Damages Act 1965 was enacted with retrospective effect. Section 1 of the Act states:

> No person shall be entitled at common law to receive from the Crown compensation in respect of damage to, or destruction of, property caused (whether before or after the

→

---

[67] [1969] 2 AC 147.

[68] See: Lord Woolf, 'Droit Public—English Style' (1995) *Public Law* 57, 69, citing *Anisminic v Foreign Compensation Commission*.

[69] [1991] 1 AC 603. See, for further discussion on this, 5.4.2.

[70] See, for further discussion on this, 15.5.4 and 15.5.5.   [71] [1965] AC 75.

> →
>
> passing of this Act, within or outside the United Kingdom) by acts lawfully done by, or on the authority of, the Crown during, or in contemplation of the outbreak of, a war in which the Sovereign was, or is, engaged.
>
> The Act was passed to overturn the judgment of the House of Lords.

The constitutional significance of the *Burmah Oil* case and the War Damages Act 1965 is matched by the uniqueness of the situation and the circumstances in which it arose. While Parliament has the power to make or unmake any law whatsoever,[72] where it does so with retrospective effect, concerns are raised for the rule of law, as Chapter 3 will further discuss. Nonetheless, and in the context of the current discussion, the fact that Parliament acted to overturn retrospectively a judgment of the House of Lords demonstrates the manner in which the sovereignty of the legislature impacts upon the separation between the legislative and judicial functions. Viscount Dilhorne noted during the War Damage Act's progression through the House of Lords:

> this Bill confuses the separate functions of the Judiciary and the Legislature, and threatens the independence of the Judges . . . Parliament is supreme, and can legally do anything that is physically possible. But my submission is that it is a most dangerous thing for Parliament to abrogate the right of action possessed by a subject who is seeking to enforce it in a court of law. The particular feature of this Bill which causes me so much anxiety is not merely the retrospective factor but the proposal that Parliament should, by means of this subsection, empower the Crown to compel a court in which it is being sued to '. . . forthwith set aside or dismiss the proceedings' . . . the words of the Bill—. . . thus deprive the plaintiff of an acquired right, namely, the decision which he has obtained from our Appellate Committee.[73]

The judgment in the *Burmah Oil* case had interesting implications for the separation of powers and the relationship between the judiciary and the sovereign legislature. That Parliament could both retrospectively overturn a judgment and impose limitations on future cases interferes with the judicial function and arguably represents a breach of Montesquieu's conception of the doctrine.

Another issue that is often considered in respect of the relationship between Parliament and the courts, *vis-à-vis* the separation of powers, is the extent to which judges can be said to make law. While it has already been explained that judges' primary function is to interpret legislation to give effect to the latest will of Parliament, due to the concept of judicial precedent and the broader operation of the common law system, judges' statements and principles are applied and followed as case law, beyond the limits of any one specific case. This gives rise to assertions that judges are making law, something that potentially affects the separation of powers, insofar as the legislative function is being exercised by a body other than the accepted law-maker. The contention of the judicial law-making function

---

[72] See AV Dicey, *Introduction to the Study of the Law of the Constitution* (JWF Allison ed, first published 1885, OUP 2013) 27 and Chapter 4.

[73] HL Deb 25 March 1965, vol 264, col 763.

continues to inspire debate, with some suggesting that judges are merely 'declaring' the common law, and 'interpreting' statutes.[74] Whether declaratory or legislative, however, the role that judges play in the process of deciding cases, in the broader context of the common law, is undoubtedly significant. This is because it falls within the natural function of the courts—the higher courts in particular—to establish common law principles and interpret legislation in certain ways, thereby contributing to the broad fabric of UK law and arguably usurping—to a small degree—the role of the legislative Parliament. This said, parliamentary sovereignty ensures that the courts remain inferior to the legislature.

The relationship between the legislature and the judiciary is an important one, particularly with regards to the sovereignty of Parliament, and consequences of this sovereignty, coupled with the historical role that judges play as interpreters of legislation and protectors of the common law, have raised certain questions over the application of the separation of powers principle. Before 2005, though, questions concerning a demarcation of function between Parliament and the courts were even more prominent. Prior to the Constitutional Reform Act 2005, the highest court of appeal in the UK was the Appellate Committee of the House of Lords. As its name suggests, this was one of the Committees of the upper chamber of Parliament. While its function was purely judicial, composed of twelve Law Lords, its existence as part of—and indeed, its placement within the same building as—the legislature gave rise to the appearance that the two functions were adjoined in some way. Indeed, while the judicial function has, since the mid-nineteenth century,[75] been the exclusive domain of the Law Lords, the legislative function has been one in which the Law Lords were able fully to participate. Until the coming into force of the 2005 Act, Law Lords could take part in debates and vote on bills that came before the house, though this was generally quite a rare occurrence. Where Law Lords did participate in legislative debates and votes, though, this would disqualify them from hearing cases relevant to that legislation. Indeed, two Law Lords voted on the Hunting Act 2004, meaning that they were not permitted to hear the *Jackson* case—one that tested the Act's validity—when it came before the court in 2005.

The 2005 Act established the UK Supreme Court, as a replacement to the Appellate Committee of the House of Lords, which ensured a greater separation between the judiciary and the legislature. Its function is essentially the same as the House of Lords—the highest court of appeal—but its appearance is of greater independence, separate from the legislature with which it had previously been more closely associated. In part, this appearance stems from the Court's relocation away from the Palace of Westminster, to the old Middlesex Crown Court building on the opposite side of Parliament Square. More than this, though, the apparent separation also stems from a clearer demarcation of personnel. The twelve Justices of the Supreme Court, who are not permitted to participate in House of Lords proceedings, are also now appointed through a more independent process than that which previously existed, following the Act's creation of a Judicial Appointments Commission, discussed in 2.4.3.

We can see that the 2005 Act, then, has altered a key aspect of the relationship between the legislature and judiciary. While the sovereignty of Parliament means that a certain imbalance will continue to affect the way in which Parliament interacts with the

---

[74] See, for fuller discussion, JAG Griffith, *The Politics of the Judiciary* (5th edn, Fontana Press 1997) ch. 8.
[75] It used to be that all members of the House of Lords could hear appeals and vote on cases; however, the last time lay members of the house heard cases was in 1834.

judiciary, the prevailing view is that—particularly since the Act—the greatest degree of separation now exists between the legislature and the judiciary.

2.4.3 Executive and judiciary

One thing that the creation of the UK Supreme Court did was further cement the importance of judicial independence as a part of the UK constitutional system. Recalling the discussion earlier in the chapter identifying the rule of law as a justification for the separation of powers, securing the independence of the judiciary is vital because it ensures that the courts 'will be free from extraneous pressures and independent of all authority save that of the law'.[76] Beyond the changes introduced by the 2005 Act, however, the relationship between the executive and the judiciary is one that also relies heavily on the ability of independent judges to fulfil their judicial functions impartially, unaffected by external influences, as this section explains.

Unlike the relationship between the legislature and judiciary, which is defined by the predominance of the sovereign Parliament, the relationship between the executive and judiciary is in one sense more balanced. Government, and the wider executive, exercise powers largely (though not exclusively) derived from statute. These powers, as we have discussed, relate to the execution and implementation of policy and the general day-to-day governance of the country. The courts, by contrast, deal with the resolution of disputes and the interpretation and application of the law, as has already been explained. In terms of functions and personnel, there is minimal overlap between the executive and the judiciary, with each being constituted by very different people and fulfilling very different functions. Indeed, the only real connection between the two institutions is the position of Lord Chancellor, a role that historically raised genuine challenge to the separation of powers in the UK.

Position of the Lord Chancellor

Before 2005, the Lord Chancellor fulfilled a number of functions across each of the three institutions. He was the speaker of the House of Lords (legislative), he was a member of the Cabinet (executive), and he was head of the judiciary (judicial). The position is one steeped in history, dating back to the period immediately after the Norman Conquest in the eleventh century.[77] Though initially an ecclesiastical position, with various administrative functions, 'as custodians of the King's seal', the position of Lord Chancellor grew and developed—particularly under the reign of the Tudor monarchs, when they 'would often be left to run the country' when wars were being fought overseas.[78] Gradually, the role picked up other facets, including a judicial dimension, to the point that—as Lord Falconer acknowledged in the 2015 Bentham Lecture—'it was a dazzling amalgamation of titles and duties across the executive, legislature and judiciary'.[79] That a position exercising such a wealth of authority in each of the three institutions represents a breach of Montesquieu's principle of the separation of powers, however, is clear to see. Indeed, Barnett,

---

[76] Joseph Raz, 'The Rule of Law and its Virtue' (1977) 93 *Law Quarterly Review* 195, 201.

[77] Rt Hon The Lord Falconer of Thoroton, 'The Role of the Lord Chancellor after the 2005 Reforms' (2015 Bentham Association Presidential Address, Bentham Association, UCL, 11 March 2015), 2, http://www.laws.ucl.ac.uk/wp-content/uploads/2015/03/The-Role-of-The-Lord-Chancellor-After-the-2005-Reforms-Lord-Falconer-of-Thoroton-PC-QC.pdf.

[78] Ibid.　　[79] Ibid 3.

writing a couple of years prior to the 2005 Act, states that '[t]he role of the Lord Chancellor is particularly difficult to reconcile with the idea of separation of powers . . . [it] appears to be fundamentally unconstitutional, violating every aspect of' the principle.[80]

The difficulties that the Lord Chancellor's former position in the legislative, executive, and judiciary might have presented to the separation of powers, and the UK Constitutional system more broadly, can be seen from a parallel drawn with the case of *McGonnell v United Kingdom*.[81] This case concerned McGonnell's application for planning consent on the island of Guernsey, which was rejected on the basis that the States of Deliberation, the island's law-maker, had passed a Detailed Development Plan, reserving the land in question for agricultural purposes alone. The point of contention was that the Guernsey Royal Court Bailiff, who dismissed the appeal of the planning rejection acting in his judicial capacity, had also played a role in his legislative capacity in passing the Development Plan.

It was argued that his involvement in both the legislative and judicial elements of the matter undermined his impartiality, an application being made to the European Court of Human Rights on the basis of the Article 6 right to a fair trial. The Strasbourg Court allowed the application, finding that the Bailiff's involvement in both aspects of the case cast 'doubt on his impartiality when he subsequently determined . . . the applicant's planning appeal'.[82] While a case concerning Guernsey, brought in the Strasbourg Court, cannot be seen as binding on the UK Constitution, a parallel can be drawn between the Royal Court Bailiff's legislative and judicial capacity and the Lord Chancellor's involvement in legislative, judicial, and executive affairs. In view of this, it is hardly surprising that Lord Irvine, the then Lord Chancellor, stressed in a subsequent debate in the House of Lords that 'the Lord Chancellor would never sit in any case concerning legislation in the passage of which he had been directly involved nor in any case where the interests of the executive were directly engaged'.[83] In view of the Lord Chancellor's former position, it is clear that the concerns regarding the separation of powers were evident, with the Lord Chancellor himself keen to stress that there were limitations on his position. For this, and other concerns already identified, it is hardly surprising that substantial changes were introduced to the position of Lord Chancellor. The Constitutional Reform Act 2005 provided that the Lord Chancellor would no longer be the speaker of the House of Lords or head of the judiciary, predominantly exercising executive functions, which are now combined with the position of Secretary of State for Justice. The holder of this combined office can have a seat in either the House of Commons or the House of Lords and in this way are in fact still a member of the legislature.

It is in the Lord Chancellor's membership of the Cabinet, however, combined with their responsibilities to the judiciary, that we still see a degree of overlap between the executive and the judiciary. The 2005 Act explains that the Lord Chancellor's 'constitutional role in relation to' the rule of law is 'not adversely' affected by the Act, while the Lord Chancellor's oath, set out in section 17 of the Act, expects that he or she will 'respect the rule of law' and 'defend the independence of the judiciary'.[84] Though seemingly uncontentious, that the Lord Chancellor must protect judges creates a link between executive and judiciary and establishes a delicately balanced constitutional position insofar as the Lord Chancellor is a member of the government, but must transcend party politics to represent

---

[80] Hilaire Barnett, *Britain Unwrapped: Government and Constitution Explained* (Penguin 2002) 37.
[81] (2000) 30 EHRR 289.
[82] Ibid [57].   [83] HL Deb 23 February 2000, vol 610, col 33WA.
[84] See ss 1 and 17 of the Constitutional Reform Act 2005.

and protect the judiciary, even from his or her own government, potentially creating an interesting dynamic.[85] Indeed, the relevance of this role in defending the independence of the judiciary was evident following the High Court's decision in *R (Miller) v Secretary of State for Exiting the European Union*,[86] certain tabloid newspapers published headlines and articles that criticized the judges for deciding that Parliament must have a part to play in the UK's invocation of Article 50 TEU, giving effect to Brexit.[87] In view of these headlines, Liz Truss, the then Lord Chancellor, was called upon to stand up for and defend the independent role of the judiciary, even though the judges had found against the government.

Appointment of judges

Even after the Constitutional Reform Act 2005, however, the position of Lord Chancellor still involves a degree of overlap with other institutions. Not only does the position within the Cabinet mean that they remain a part of the legislature, but also, as head of the Ministry of Justice—the department overseeing the judiciary—they still play a role in the appointment of judges. Before the 2005 Act, judges were formally appointed by the monarch, on the advice of the Prime Minister and the Lord Chancellor. On this, Barendt, writing in 1998, noted that with two essentially executive positions deciding on the appointment of judges, party political considerations could be a concern.[88] More significantly, he also stated that:

> [I]t is difficult to mount a principled defence of the government's monopoly power of appointment, which moreover is exercised in private, without public scrutiny. It would be preferable to set up a body such as a Judicial Services Commission, with judicial and lay members, with powers to appoint the judges and to discharge other functions, for instance, considering complaints and perhaps dismissing judges in extreme cases.[89]

The lack of transparency, coupled with concerns that the process could potentially be politically driven, led to reforms akin to those suggested by Barendt. The 2005 Act established the Judicial Appointments Commission, which, in its own words, exists to provide 'a fair and transparent process for selecting candidates for judicial office in courts and tribunals in England and Wales and for some posts in Scotland and Northern Ireland'.[90] The Commission is independent and separate from the operation of government, the body itself being constituted by a range of possible persons. Indeed, Schedule 12 to the 2005 Act sets out that the Commission must consist of a Chairman and fourteen other Commissioners.[91] The Commissioners are appointed by the monarch on the 'recommendation of the Lord Chancellor', and of the fourteen, five must be judicial members, two must be professional members, five must be lay members, one must be 'the holder of an office listed in Part 3 of Schedule 14 or of an office listed in sub-paragraph (2A)',[92] and

---

[85] See, for further discussion, Rt Hon The Lord Falconer of Thoroton, 'The Role of the Lord Chancellor after the 2005 Reforms' (2015 Bentham Association Presidential Address, Bentham Association, UCL, 11 March 2015), 2.   [86] [2016] EWHC 2768.

[87] The *Daily Mail*, for example, published a headline under pictures of the three High Court judges that read 'Enemies of the People', suggesting their decision had frustrated the democratic vote in the EU referendum (James Slack, 'Enemies of the People' *Daily Mail* (London, 4 November 2016) 1).

[88] Eric Barendt, *An Introduction to Constitutional Law* (OUP 1998) 134. Though Barendt did also acknowledge that 'There is admittedly no evidence that party political considerations play any part in this process' (at 134).   [89] Ibid 134.

[90] Judicial Appointments Commission, https://jac.judiciary.gov.uk.

[91] Schedule 12(1) to the Constitutional Reform Act 2005.

[92] These sections cover a range of possible positions, relevant to various specific tribunals and arbitration.

one must be a lay member.[93] In addition, and with regards to appointments to the UK Supreme Court specifically, a different ad hoc Commission is established. This consists of the President and Deputy President of the Supreme Court, plus a member each of the Judicial Appointments Commission, the Judicial Appointments Board for Scotland, and the Northern Ireland Judicial Appointments Commission.[94]

One rationale behind the creation of the Judicial Appointments Commission is not only to ensure that the appointments process is independent from government, but that it is also *seen* to be as independent as possible. This has meant that the Lord Chancellor's role has changed significantly. Whereas, before, they played a central role in judicial appointments, their role is now far more limited. Their power to recommend Commissioners, for instance, is limited to those who are nominated by the Judges' Council or by a panel that includes the Lord Chief Justice; and, later on in the process, while they can reject the appointment of a potential candidate or ask the Commission to reconsider its choice, these actions can only be taken once.[95] Further limitations to the Lord Chancellor's role in the judicial appointment process were also introduced by the Crime and Courts Act 2013. This took away the Lord Chancellor's power to appoint judges to courts beneath the High Court, such appointments now being made by the Lord Chief Justice, and it took away the power to appoint judges to First-Tier and Upper Tribunals, this role now being fulfilled by the Senior Presidents of Tribunals.[96] The Lord Chancellor, therefore, plays much less of a role with regards to judicial appointments following the 2005 Act and its creation of the Judicial Appointments Commission.

The new appointments process is also more transparent. While, in the past, judges were simply selected by the Lord Chancellor, the new Commission must now apply certain criteria in selecting candidates and making appointments. The 2005 Act sets out, in section 25, the criteria for selecting Justices of the Supreme Court, while Chapter 2 of Part 4 of the Act covers the criteria for the various other judicial positions, these being different depending on the level of the court. The creation of the Commission, complete with its strict criteria for membership and appointment, ensures that judicial appointments now take place in a forum that is fair, equal, and transparent, thereby combatting previous concerns under the old system and promoting values at the heart of the separation of powers doctrine.

 Counterpoint: Is it a good idea to appoint non-lawyers to the position of Lord Chancellor?

Another notable, though more subtle, change to the position of Lord Chancellor relates to the recent appointments of non-lawyers to the position. Rozenberg notes that, with the changes introduced by the 2005 Act and the reduction of the Lord Chancellor's position to that of Secretary of State, 'it was going to happen sooner or later' that we saw politicians appointed to the post

→

---

[93] Schedule 12(2) and (3) to the Constitutional Reform Act 2005.
[94] Schedule 8(1) to the Constitutional Reform Act 2005.
[95] See further Mark Elliott and Robert Thomas, *Public Law* (3rd edn, OUP 2017) 274–6.
[96] Ibid 274.

→

who did not have a background in the law.[97] While some of those that have been appointed since the Act—Jack Straw, Ken Clarke, David Gauke, and Robert Buckland—have been lawyers, Chris Grayling, a Lord Chancellor under David Cameron's recent governments, was the first non-lawyer to hold the post in 440 years,[98] with Michael Gove, Liz Truss, and David Lidington following, also with no legal qualifications.

In one sense, the shift is a natural consequence of the 2005 reforms, which now set out broader criteria for the position. Indeed, section 2 of the Act notes that a person may be appointed to the position of Lord Chancellor only if they have experience as a Minister of the Crown, as a member of either House of Parliament, as a qualifying practitioner, as a teacher of law in a university, and any other experience that the Prime Minister deems relevant.[99] With this section in mind, and also in view of the fact that the Lord Chancellor is no longer a judge and no longer plays a directing role in the appointment of judges, it can be argued that the position need not be filled by a lawyer.[100] Indeed, David Allen Green, writing in 2014, defended the appointment of non-lawyers to the historic position, stressing that 'it is now rare for any first-rate lawyer to also be in the first rank of politics', adding that 'there is no reason to believe that [those with legal qualifications] would be any better than [a non-lawyer] at policy or upholding the court system'.[101]

Equally, though, there can also be scepticism about the move away from having lawyers as Lord Chancellor. In one sense, it is a question of expertise. Green's points notwithstanding, the minister tasked with working closely with the court system, with judges and with lawyers must be able to understand the legal profession and the particular challenges it poses, separate from any political questions. In addition, the political agenda and challenges the Lord Chancellor faces as a government minister might at times run contrary to their role in defending the judiciary and respecting the rule of law. Rozenberg, for instance, writing at a time when Grayling was Lord Chancellor, suggests that the fact that Grayling might have reasonably regarded himself 'as on the way up in politics' meant that he would 'find there are easy headlines to be won by attacking the judges for being soft on sentencing or for upholding the human rights of unpopular members of society', making it hard to 'achieve the effective working relationship that [the position of Lord Chancellor] needs to have with the Lord Chief Justice'.[102] The difficulties Liz Truss may have faced in defending High Court judges following the *Miller* judgment have already been noted in this regard. The appointment of non-lawyers to the position of Lord Chancellor is therefore another notable change effected by the 2005 Act, and one that inspires a great deal of discussion and debate.

---

[97] Joshua Rozenberg, 'Chris Grayling, Justice Secretary: Non-Lawyer and "On the Up" Politician' *The Guardian* (4 September 2012), https://www.theguardian.com/law/2012/sep/04/chris-grayling-justice-secretary-non-lawyer.

[98] Joshua Rozenberg, 'Legacy of a Lay Lord Chancellor' *The Law Society Gazette* (16 March 2015), https://www.lawgazette.co.uk/comment-and-opinion/legacy-of-a-lay-lord-chancellor/5047494.article.

[99] Section 2 of the Constitutional Reform Act 2005.

[100] See David Allen Green, 'Does a Lord Chancellor Really Need to be a Lawyer?' *Financial Times* (5 June 2014), http://blogs.ft.com/david-allen-green/2014/06/05/does-a-lord-chancellor-really-need-to-be-a-lawyer/.

[101] Ibid.

[102] Joshua Rozenberg, 'Chris Grayling, Justice Secretary: Non-Lawyer and "On the Up" Politician' *The Guardian* (4 September 2012).

Judicial independence

One of the most significant aspects of the relationship between executive and judiciary, however, relates to the ability of the courts to hold the government to account, a function that requires a degree of overlap insofar as judges must be able to examine and scrutinize government action to fulfil this role. With such broad powers and the ability to make decisions and policies potentially affecting the lives of citizens all across the country, it is important that the government is kept in check and that it does not abuse or exceed its powers, or exercise arbitrary authority. While the principle of parliamentary sovereignty means that it is the duty of judges always to interpret legislation and uphold the will of Parliament, government, by contrast, is open and susceptible to scrutiny by the courts and, indeed, this is a fundamental part of our constitutional and democratic system. It is here that the principle of judicial independence comes in once again, since it is vital that the government is checked and scrutinized by an institution that is impartial and separate from external influences. Speaking at an event at University College London in February 2011, the then President of the Supreme Court, Lord Phillips, echoed this, stating that:

> The rule of law is the bedrock of a democratic society. It is the only basis upon which individuals, private corporations, public bodies and the executive can order their lives and activities. If the rule of law is to be upheld it is essential that there should be an independent judiciary. The rule of law requires that the courts have jurisdiction to scrutinise the actions of government to ensure that they are lawful. In modern society the individual citizen is subject to controls imposed by the executive in respect of almost every aspect of life. The authority to impose most of those controls comes, directly or indirectly, from the legislature. The citizen must be able to challenge the legitimacy of executive action before an independent judiciary. Because it is the executive that exercises the power of the State and because it is the executive, in one form or another, that is the most frequent litigator in the courts, it is from executive pressure or influence that judges require particularly to be protected.[103]

The principle of judicial independence serves to provide a fundamental basis both for the manner in which judges should act and carry out their functions and, more broadly, the way in which the courts relate to the other institutions, particularly the executive. In one sense it promotes a separation of powers, insofar as it is founded on the judiciary being separate from the other institutions. In another sense, though, it requires a degree of overlap with other institutions, and consequently a compromise with regards to the separation of powers. This overlap is necessary since, in order that the independent judiciary can check and scrutinize the acts and decisions of the executive, they must be able to investigate the way in which the government works and even strike out their decisions if the law so requires. The consequences of this reality, with regards to the separation of powers, are discussed below. For now, though, it is important to expand on this principle of judicial independence and the practice of the courts checking and scrutinizing the executive through exploration of relevant case law. We start with *Entick v Carrington*.[104]

---

[103] Lord Phillips of Worth Matravers, 'Judicial Independence and Accountability: A View from the Supreme Court' (Judicial Independence Research Project Launch, UCL, 8 February 2011), https://www.ucl.ac.uk/constitution-unit/events/judicial-independence-events/launch.

[104] (1765) 95 ER 807.

Case in depth: *Entick v Carrington* (1765) 95 ER 807

King's messengers entered Entick's house to search for and seize some of his papers. Entick sued the messengers, challenging the entry on the basis that it was unlawful. The defendants pleaded not guilty, however, on the basis that their entry and search had been with a warrant. That warrant was issued by the Earl of Halifax, who was one of the King's Secretaries of State. The warrant authorized the defendants:

> to make strict and diligent search for the plaintiff, mentioned in the said warrant to be the author, or one concerned in the writing of several weekly very seditious papers, [entitled] *The Monitor, or British Freeholder* . . . containing gross and scandalous reflections and invectives upon His Majesty's Government, and upon both Houses of Parliament, and him the plaintiff having found, to seize and apprehend and bring together with his books and papers in safe custody.[105]

The court found, however, that the warrant was unlawful on the basis that there was no statutory or judicial authority which supported the Secretary of State issuing such a warrant.

Entick v Carrington exemplifies the importance of judicial independence and, with this, the importance of scrutinizing executive action and holding the government to account. Mr Entick's rights were infringed as a result of unlawful and unauthorized executive action, and, as a consequence, the court was able to act—separate from the executive and free from undue influence—to provide a remedy. A similar situation arose in the more recent case of *Re M*.[106]

Case in depth: *Re M* [1994] 1 AC 377

This case involved an application for asylum by a citizen of Zaire (now known as the Democratic Republic of the Congo). This was rejected by the Secretary of State, with an attempted judicial review of that decision also later refused. Shortly before the individual's removal back to Zaire, a fresh application for judicial review was brought on new grounds. The Divisional Court, knowing of the citizen's imminent removal, ordered that his departure be postponed pending proper and appropriate consideration of this new application for judicial review. The Home Office officials in charge of the Zairean citizen, however, failed to take him off the plane before its departure, failing again to do so when the plane stopped in Paris. Hearing this, the judge made an order requiring the Secretary of State to effect the citizen's immediate return to the UK. Though such arrangements were initially followed, the Secretary of State felt that the decision to reject the application for asylum was correct and, being advised that the judge's order (a mandatory interim injunction) had been imposed without appropriate jurisdiction, the Secretary of State gave up on attempts to return the Zairean citizen to the UK. The applicant sought proceedings against the Home Office on the basis that they had breached court orders against them to prevent his departure from and effect his return to the UK. These proceedings were rejected, however, on the basis that, pursuant to section 21 of the Crown Proceedings

→

---

[105] See (1765) 95 ER 807, 808.   [106] [1994] 1 AC 377.

> →
>
> Act 1947, the Crown, including those departments or ministers working for the Crown in the course of their duties, were immune from injunctions and could not be found in contempt of court in the event of their breach. The Court of Appeal overturned this decision, however, finding that the Secretary of State was personally guilty of contempt of court. The House of Lords, though finding that the Secretary of State was acting in his official, not personal, capacity, also agreed that he was in contempt of court.

As with *Entick*, *Re M* demonstrates another instance of the judiciary serving to protect individuals from potential abuses of executive authority, thereby serving as a check on the governmental system. The most recently prominent example of the courts acting as a check on the government, though, is reflected in the case of *R (Miller) v Prime Minister*.[107]

> ### Case in depth: *R (Miller) v Prime Minister* [2019] UKSC 41
>
> This case concerned a challenge to the Prime Minister's five-week prorogation of Parliament in September 2019. Boris Johnson, who became Leader of the governing Conservative Party— and therefore Prime Minister—in July 2019, acted under the prerogative in advising the Queen to prorogue (or suspend) Parliament for a five-week period from mid-September to mid-October 2019. He explained that such prorogation would permit a fresh Queen's Speech to be held in October, thereby ushering in a new parliamentary session and a fresh legislative agenda for the Government. The timing, however, was contentious since the UK's departure from the European Union was at that point due to take effect on 31 October 2019, no deal yet having been agreed between the UK and the EU as to the future of their relationship. The default position, therefore, was that the UK would leave without a deal. In view of this, it was felt that the prorogation of Parliament would prevent opportunity for parliamentary debate on the issue. As a consequence, two actions were brought challenging the Prime Minister's prorogation of Parliament. One, in Scotland, was brought by Joanna Cherry MP *et al* and argued that the prorogation itself was unlawful; the other, in England, was brought by Gina Miller and argued that the Prime Minister's advice to the Monarch in seeking prorogation was unlawful. At first instance, Cherry won her case, whilst Miller lost. Both challenges were joined in the Supreme Court on appeal. The Supreme Court in the UK held that the prorogation was unlawful because it frustrated the operation of Parliament in its law-making activities and in its role in holding the Government to account. The Court went to great lengths to emphasize the constitutional importance of these two functions. As a consequence, the Court declared the prorogation as void and of no-effect, effectively quashing it and declaring that it had never taken place. The parliamentary session was immediately resumed.

As with the cases explored, above, therefore, the *Miller* case exemplifies the important role that the courts can play in holding the government to account.

That there is a separation in functions and personnel between the executive and judiciary, therefore, is clear to see. Apart from the delicately balanced position of the Lord Chancellor, there is little by way of overlap between the two functions. Due to the nature

---

[107] [2019] UKSC 41.

of the government's position within our constitutional system, however, and the need to ensure that its exercise of power is kept in check, the courts exercise a degree of authority over the government, including the power to quash decisions and force new decisions to be taken, and the power to enforce remedies against government ministers for abuses of power. Judicial independence ensures that this can take place effectively and impartially.

Pause for reflection

Having now explored the relationships between the various institutions in the UK, and before we move on to the last section, to what extent do you think the UK's constitutional arrangements are consistent with the principle of the separation of powers as espoused by Montesquieu?

This section's exploration of the relationships between the various institutions of the constitution has enabled a close examination of the separation of powers in the UK. It is clear to see, on this basis, that the institutional arrangements that prevail under our constitution are rather more complex than the clear demarcation of functions and re-sponsibilities as required by Montesquieu's conception of the principle. The next section, though, now explores arguments considering the extent to which the separation of pow-ers is nonetheless relevant to the UK's constitutional arrangements.

Discussing the problem

Look at the problem scenario again. The 2024 Act requires all judicial appointments to be approved by a vote in the House of Commons, also setting out a process through which judges can be removed from office by a vote in the chamber. To what extent does this impact upon the relationship between the legislature and the judiciary and, more broadly, what effect does it have on the separation of powers?

This final provision, listed in the problem scenario, concerns the relationship between the legislature and the judiciary and the notion of judicial independence. This section of the chapter has explained that, since the enactment of the Constitutional Reform Act 2005, judges have been appointed through a process involving the Judicial Appointments Commission. This was created by the Act to improve the transparency and independence of a process that previously involved the Lord Chan-cellor to a much larger degree. Judicial independence, as this chapter has explained, is important not only for the process of justice and in ensuring the impartiality of case judgments, but more broadly the rule of law, a value itself linked to the important principle of the separation of powers. The notion, however, of requiring all judicial appointments to be approved by a vote in the House of Com-mons as per the 2024 Act, and providing for a process through which judges can be removed by a two-thirds majority vote raises further questions for the separation of powers in the UK Constitution. The rationale underlying the creation of the Judicial Appointments Commission was to improve the independence of the judiciary and to increase the separation of powers between the courts and Parliament and the government. Permitting the House of Commons to play such an important role in the appointment of judges, however, dilutes this independence and means that the judiciary is essentially tied to the legislature, lessening the separation of functions introduced by the 2005 Act.

THE UK CONSTITUTION AND THE SEPARATION OF POWERS: A *PURE* OR *PARTIAL* SEPARATION?

65

2.5 The UK Constitution and the separation of powers: a *pure* or *partial* separation?

The previous section of this chapter explored in detail the nature of the relationships that exist between the key institutions in the UK—Parliament, as legislature, central government, as a part of the broader executive, and the courts, exercising the judicial function. That the UK Constitution operates in a unique fashion is evident from this exploration and from an understanding of these institutions' functions. Whether or not the UK Constitution can be said to adhere to a separation of powers, however, remains a contested and debated issue, with some dismissing the relevance of the doctrine altogether and others going so far as to laud it as being at the centre of the UK Constitution.

Griffith and Street, for instance, comment that '[t]he doctrine is so remote from the facts that it is better disregarded altogether'.[108] A similar view is voiced by de Smith who goes so far as to say:

> Mention the theory of the separation of powers to an English constitutional lawyer, and he will forthwith put on parade the Lord Chancellor, the Law Lords, the parliamentary executive, delegated legislation and administrative adjudication and shift the conversation to more significant topics. He tends to regard the theory as . . . an irrelevant distraction for the English law student and his teachers . . . No writer of repute would claim that it is a central feature of the modern British constitution.[109]

But such views are tempered by those shedding a rather more positive light on UK application of the doctrine. Lord Diplock, for instance, notes that '[i]t cannot be too strongly emphasized that the British Constitution, although largely unwritten, is firmly based on the separation of powers; Parliament makes the laws, the judiciary interpret them'.[110] Bogdanor, too, in explaining the manner in which the UK Constitution has shifted from being 'based upon the sovereignty of Parliament', suggests that it is now 'based on the idea of a constitutional state based upon a separation of powers'.[111] That there is a difference of opinion on the point is clear to see. This section explores the arguments underpinning both sides and sets out the principle of 'checks and balances' which itself typifies the application of the separation of powers doctrine in the UK.

On the foundation of theories identified, a common distinction that is drawn with regards to the separation of powers distinguishes between what is called a *pure* separation of powers and a *partial* separation of powers.[112] A *pure* separation can be associated with the formulation explained by Montesquieu and rests on the belief that there must be a complete demarcation between the three constitutional functions—legislature, executive, and judiciary—with the institutions exercising those functions completely separate from one another. By contrast, a *partial* separation 'does not require that only one institution exercises a particular function of government',[113] but instead recognizes the broader benefit of allowing a degree of overlap between the various functions and institutions. The purpose

---

[108] JAG Griffith and H Street, *Principles of Administrative Law* (Pittman 1952) 16.

[109] SA de Smith, 'The Separation of Powers in New Dress' (1966–1967) 12 McGill LJ 491, 491.

[110] *Duport Steels Ltd and Others v Sirs and Others* [1980] 1 WLR 142, 157.

[111] Vernon Bogdanor, *The New British Constitution* (Hart Publishing 2009) 285.

[112] See Eric Barendt, *An Introduction to Constitutional Law* (OUP 1998) 15.

[113] Ibid.

of such an overlap is, according to Barendt, so that 'each branch of government . . . is able to check the exercise of power by the others, either by participating in the functions conferred on them, or by subsequently reviewing the exercise of that power'.[114] The benefits of such overlaps are widely noted, particularly by those who laud the importance of the separation of powers as a foundation for the rule of law. Allan, for instance, notes that '[t]he principle of separation of powers enables the law to serve as a bulwark between governors and governed, excluding the exercise of arbitrary power'.[115]

This *partial* model of the separation of powers is also commonly known as the system of 'checks and balances' due to the manner in which these permitted overlaps in functions and institutions is necessary to provide a degree of check and balance on the functions of the constitution. In reality, this *partial* model of the separation of powers exists more prominently than the *pure* separation, in chief because it is more workable. Indeed, it is a point fairly made that ensuring a clear and total separation of functions and authority between legislature, executive, and judiciary gives rise to a system that is disjointed, with less communication between the main institutions. As such, this section argues that the *partial* model of the separation of powers, or the system of checks and balances, is prevalent in respect of the UK Constitution, this being evident from the various relationships we have discussed. In particular, there are two examples relevant to these relationships that demonstrate the nature of the *partial* separation of powers in the UK.

The first example is the principle of judicial review of administrative action. As Chapter 10 further explains, judicial review is a valuable process whereby acts and decisions of the executive (and other public bodies) can be challenged in the courts on grounds of legality, rationality, proportionality, and procedural propriety.[116] The purpose of this is to protect those affected by government's acts and decisions from abuses of power and exercises of arbitrary authority. The process of judicial review, however, requires the courts to scrutinize government activity, potentially going so far as to set aside acts or decisions taken illegally, irrationally, or improperly. This amounts to a degree of overlap between the judiciary and the executive, insofar as the courts are examining, in detail, the activities and decisions that are at the heart of the day-to-day operation of government and determining whether or not they can lawfully be upheld. Such overlap, however, is entirely justified in the manner already explained by Barendt: the courts are able to 'check the exercise of power by the [government] . . . by subsequently reviewing the exercise of that power'.[117] Judicial review, while exemplifying a degree of overlap in the UK Constitution, amounts to a check and a balance on the governmental system, ensuring that those wielding executive authority are kept within the confines of the law.

Further issues are inevitably raised by this process. Government makes decisions and implements policy for the overall governance of the country, as the first section of this chapter explained. There might be concern, however, that unelected judges, concerned with the enforcement of the law, and having the ability not only to examine and scrutinize executive action, but set it aside if it does not accord with legal principle and

---

[114] Ibid.

[115] TRS Allan, *Constitutional Justice: A Liberal Theory for the Rule of Law* (OUP 2001) 3 (cited in and also see Keith Syrett, *The Foundations of Public Law: Principles and Problems of Power in the British Constitution* (2nd edn, Palgrave Macmillan 2014) 26).

[116] See Chapter 10 and, also, *Council for Civil Service Unions v Minister for the Civil Service* [1985] AC 374.

[117] Eric Barendt, *An Introduction to Constitutional Law* (OUP 1998) 15.

process, itself amounts to a breach of the separation of powers. Judges are perhaps ill-equipped to understand and appreciate the full range of challenges inherent within the government process, yet possess the power to quash and mandate nonetheless. While the judiciary's involvement in the process is justified in the manner we have explored, this concern is mitigated by limitations preventing judges from involving themselves in the executive process where issues are of a particularly political or important policy nature. First, in entertaining applications for judicial review, the courts are exercising a supervisory jurisdiction, as opposed to an appellate jurisdiction. This is explained more fully in 10.2.1, but, in brief, it means that they are supervising and reviewing application of the law, rather than hearing appeals and deciding cases on their legal merits. A government act or decision is only susceptible to remedies imposed under judicial review if it is deemed to have been taken illegally, irrationally, or improperly. The process provides no recourse for review where the political aspect of the action is at issue; that would be a matter solely for the government. In *R (on the application of Justice for Health Ltd) v Secretary of State for Health*,[118] for example, a case involving judicial review of the imposition of junior doctors' contracts, the High Court was satisfied that the Secretary of State was acting within his powers under the National Health Service Act 2006. The Court said that the Act gave him 'a broad margin of discretion . . . to introduce the new contract',[119] demonstrating judicial restraint to get involved in what might be seen as a matter of political policy. Only if the issue is one that is arguably taken against legal authority do the courts step in.

The second example illustrating the nature of the *partial* separation of powers is the fact that the concept of justiciability also serves to limit the potential for courts to involve themselves in political or policy-related matters. Justiciability refers to the courts' ability to hear cases on a given issue, with a matter that is deemed non-justiciable outside the court's jurisdiction. In this context, a matter is deemed non-justiciable if it is of a particularly political nature. Though this is also explained more fully in 6.5.3. and 10.2.1, for now, it is rooted in Lord Roskill's judgment from *Council of Civil Service Unions v Minister for the Civil Service*.[120] Here, Lord Roskill provided a list of exemplifying areas that might be deemed non-justiciable and therefore outside the power of the courts to review. This list included the signing of treaties, matters of national security, defence of the realm, the appointment of ministers, the dissolution of Parliament, and the granting of honours.[121] The justiciability of the UK Government's decision to engage in military action in Iraq in 2003 is a notable example of the principle at work. In *Campaign for Nuclear Disarmament v The Prime Minister*,[122] an application for judicial review was brought on the contention that United Nations Resolution 1441 did not authorize military action. The crux of the judgment focused on the court's inability to declare the meaning of international legal provisions, and in dismissing the application, the judges stressed that '[f]oreign policy and the deployment of the armed forces remain non-justiciable'.[123] Through application of the concept of justiciability, judges are restricted in the extent to which they can

---

[118] [2016] EWHC 2338 Admin.

[119] Ibid [12].   [120] [1985] AC 374.   [121] Ibid 418.

[122] [2002] EWHC 2777. Also see, for further discussion, Lord Sumption, 'Foreign Affairs in the English Courts since 9/11' (Lecture at the Department of Government, LSE, 14 May 2012), https://www.supremecourt.uk/docs/speech_120514.pdf.

[123] [2002] EWHC 2777 [H12].

review the acts and decisions of the executive, serving as a safeguard for the protection of executive authority and ensuring the 'check' provided by judicial review is 'balanced' with the separation of powers.

The second example of checks and balances in the UK system relates to the relationship between the legislature and the executive. It has already been noted that there is a fusion of power between government and Parliament insofar as government ministers must be members of one of the Houses of Parliament, the legitimacy of that membership deriving from an MP's election. The manner in which this fusion of power is tempered by the various mechanisms of accountability, however, equates to another form of checks and balances. While government is a notable part of Parliament's membership, the ability of opposition parties, backbenchers, and members of the House of Lords to question, examine, and scrutinize government activity, through their respective opportunities for Question Time, general debate, and Select Committee work, acts as a valuable and constant check on the government's operation, working to ensure that it exercises its power properly, responsibly, and transparently.

It is clear that Montesquieu's elucidation of the separation of powers principle is far removed from the realities of the modern UK Constitution. It has been widely recognized that the UK has no formal separation of powers[124] since there is no clear demarcation between the institutions, and varying degrees of overlap and interference existing across all the relationships between legislature, executive, and judiciary. There is, however, a strong argument in favour of the UK's subscription to a *partial* separation of powers. In many instances, the overlaps that exist between the institutions facilitate a check and a balance on the exercise of authority, as this section has explained: the courts, in the example of judicial review, providing a check on the lawful use of governmental power; and the House of Commons, through various mechanisms ensuring that the government does not abuse its power, to cite just two examples.

> **₎₎ Discussing the problem**
>
> Have a final look at the problem scenario, set out at the beginning of the chapter. How far do the various provisions of the Constitutional Reform (Allocation of Power) Act 2024 impact upon the separation of powers in the UK? Under that Act, do you think the UK would be said to have more of a *pure* or *partial* separation of institutions and functions?
>
> This chapter has already explained that, under current arrangements, the UK Constitution can be characterized as adopting a partial separation of powers, insofar as there are various overlaps between the institutions, which in turn permit a level of scrutiny. The provisions of the 2024 Act, however, arguably do little to change this. While a reduction in the number of government ministers capable of being drawn from Parliament might be seen as a weakening of the fusion between the legislative and executive branches, the fusion remains nonetheless. What is more, requiring a vote in the Commons upon the formation of a government to approve ministerial
>
> ➞

[124] See, for instance, Tony Wright, 'The Politics of Accountability', in Mark Elliott and David Feldman (eds), *The Cambridge Companion to Public Law* (Cambridge University Press 2015) 96, 106.

→ appointments, and requiring all judicial appointments to be approved by the Commons could be seen as a way of strengthening the level of scrutiny that particular institutions can exercise, rather than a reduction in the institutional overlaps that have already been identified. Under the 2024 Act, the UK constitutional system would still, it is argued, be classified as recognizing a partial separation of powers.

The question concerning the separation of powers in the UK Constitution is a complex one. It is, however, neatly summed up by an extract from Lord Mustill's judgment in *R v Secretary of State for the Home Department, ex p Fire Brigades Union*,[125] which Syrett notes as reflecting this *partial* separation of powers. This quote neatly concludes this section:

It is a feature of the peculiarly British conception of the separation of powers that Parliament, the executive and the courts have each their distinct and largely exclusive domain. Parliament has a legally unchallengeable right to make whatever laws it thinks right. The executive carries on the administration of the country in accordance with the powers conferred on it by law. The courts interpret the laws, and see that they are obeyed. This requires the courts on occasion to step into the territory which belongs to the executive, to verify not only that the powers asserted accord with the substantive law created by Parliament but also that the manner in which they are exercised conforms with the standards of fairness which Parliament must have intended. Concurrently with this judicial function Parliament has its own special means of ensuring that the executive, in the exercise of delegated functions, performs in a way which Parliament finds appropriate.[126]

2.6 Summary

This chapter has offered a detailed exploration of the key institutions—the legislature, the executive, and the judiciary—and considered the relevance of the principle of the separation of powers in respect of the UK Constitution. In doing this, it has examined a range of views and perspectives both of the abstract principle and of its application in the UK, and it has explored each of the relationships in turn, identifying their unique characteristics relevant to the separation of powers.

Questions concerning the separation of powers continue to inspire a great deal of debate, though the distinction drawn between a *pure* and *partial* separation of powers enables us not only to understand the various ways in which the principle can work but, also, to examine more easily how it can be said to be relevant to the UK's peculiar constitutional arrangements. The overlaps between our institutions rebut any consideration that we subscribe to a *pure* separation, though the checks and balances that are embedded within our system are indicative of a *partial* separation of powers, mindful as that is of the importance of ensuring each institution broadly remains within its powers and functions. The principle derived from Aristotle and famously expounded by Montesquieu remains of considerable importance in the UK Constitution.

---

[125] [1995] 2 AC 513.

[126] Ibid 567. Also see Keith Syrett, *The Foundations of Public Law: Principles and Problems of Power in the British Constitution* (2nd edn, Palgrave Macmillan 2014) 227–8.

Quick test questions

1. What are the three institutions of the constitution and what are their main functions and responsibilities?

2. What is the essence of Montesquieu's conception of the separation of powers?

3. What key changes did the Constitutional Reform Act 2005 introduce with regard to the separation of powers in the UK?

4. Which feature of the UK system did Walter Bagehot describe as the 'efficient secret of the constitution'?

5. What is the distinction between a *pure* separation of powers and a *partial* separation of powers? Which model do you think is most relevant to the UK's constitutional arrangements?

6. What is judicial review and how important is it in terms of the separation of powers in the UK?

7. What does Tomkins identify as the bipartite separation of powers?

Further reading

Defining the separation of powers

*Montesquieu, *L'Esprit des Lois*, Book 11 (1748) Ch 6

Stephen Sedley, *Lions under the Throne: Essays on the History of English Public Law* (Cambridge University Press 2015) Chapter 9

The separation of powers in the UK Constitution

David Allen Green, 'Does a Lord Chancellor Really Need to be a Lawyer?' *Financial Times* (5 June 2014), http://blogs.ft.com/david-allen-green/2014/06/05/does-a-lord-chancellor-really-need-to-be-a-lawyer/

*NW Barber, 'The Separation of Powers and the British Constitution' (2012) Oxford Legal Studies Research Paper No 3/2012, https://papers.ssrn.com/sol3/papers.cfm?abstract_id=1995780

Eric Barendt, 'Case Comment: Constitutional Law and the Criminal Injuries Compensation Scheme' (1995) *Public Law* 357

Richard Cornes, '*McGonnell v UK*, the Lord Chancellor and the Law Lords' (2000) *Public Law* 166

*SA de Smith, 'The Separation of Powers in New Dress' (1966–1967) 12 McGill LJ 491

Rt Hon The Lord Falconer of Thoroton, 'The Role of the Lord Chancellor after the 2005 Reforms' (2015 Bentham Association Presidential Address, Bentham Association, UCL, 11 March 2015), http://www.laws.ucl.ac.uk/wp-content/uploads/2015/03/The-Role-of-The-Lord-Chancellor-After-the-2005-Reforms-Lord-Falconer-of-Thoroton-PC-QC.pdf

*Roger Masterman and Se-shauna Wheatle, 'Unpacking Separation of Powers: Judicial Independence, Sovereignty and Conceptual Flexibility in the UK Constitution' (2017) *Public Law* 469

Lord Neuberger MR, 'Who are the Masters Now?' (Second Lord Alexander of Weedon Lecture, 6 April 2011), http://webarchive.nationalarchives.gov.uk/20131203081513/http://www.judiciary.gov.uk/Resources/JCO/Documents/Speeches/mr-speech-weedon-lecture-110406.pdf

Joshua Rozenberg, 'Legacy of a Lay Lord Chancellor' *The Law Society Gazette* (16 March 2015), https://www.lawgazette.co.uk/comment-and-opinion/legacy-of-a-lay-lord-chancellor/5047494.article

Joshua Rozenberg, 'Chris Grayling, Justice Secretary: Non-Lawyer and "On the Up" Politician' *The Guardian* (4 September 2012), https://www.theguardian.com/law/2012/sep/04/chris-grayling-justice-secretary-non-lawyer

 Visit this book's **online resources** for additional materials relating to this chapter, including a full analysis of the start-of-chapter problem scenario.
www.oup.com/he/stanton-prescott2e

3

The rule of law

Problem scenario

Fred is a journalist for one of the major London newspapers. He is currently dating Toby, who is a junior government minister in the Department of Health. One evening, when Fred is visiting Toby at his flat, Fred discovers highly confidential documents that outline legislative plans to abolish the National Health Service. Shocked that such plans have not been made public and knowing the outcry that they would cause, Fred intends to write an article for his newspaper revealing the government's plans.

The next morning, Fred calls the Department of Health, which denies that the National Health Service will be abolished. He is warned against spreading 'false rumours'. Three hours later, however, the police arrive at Fred's house and place him under immediate arrest for 'meddling in government business', later detaining him at the police station. When Fred angrily points out to the police officers that he has not committed any offence, he is told: 'You're being detained under the authority of the Secretary of State. She can do what she likes; she works for the government!'

In order that Fred's detention and silence can be lawfully guaranteed, the Secretary of State for Health introduces a short bill into Parliament—the Freedom from the Press (Government Privacy) Bill 2023, which provides that '[t]he publication or revelation of Government policies and decisions before formal announcement is unlawful'. The Act is passed within the week and as soon as it receives Royal Assent, Fred is formally charged and a date set for his trial.

3.1 Introduction

The rule of law is a complex and heavily theoretical principle which underpins the way in which constitutional systems operate. This chapter starts by defining the rule of law, explaining its importance, and placing its origins in Ancient Greece and the writings of Aristotle. Offering a brief consideration of how the principle has developed since that time, the chapter then moves to discuss the consideration provided by Dicey who, writing his seminal text—*An Introduction to the Study of the Law of the Constitution*—in 1885, explored the meaning of the rule of law and its place in the UK Constitution. Following this, the chapter then considers broader theories of the rule of law, dividing these into those that support what are known as 'formal conceptions' of the rule of law, and 'substantive conceptions' of the rule of law.[1] Finally, the chapter explores the way in which the rule of law—as both a formal and substantive principle—can be said to apply in the UK Constitution, both historically and in terms of modern day authorities. In doing this, it discusses the relevance and importance of the principle with regards to broader aspects of constitutional law, considering, for instance, how the rule of law sits alongside parliamentary sovereignty; how it works in relation to the use and restraint of executive power; and how the rule of law relates to the protection of human rights.

With these issues in mind, the problem scenario is designed to engage with various aspects of the rule of law discussion, including the manner in which it applies in the UK Constitution. The objectives for this chapter are:

- to explore the historical development of the rule of law and to consider what the basic principle means;
- to consider the orthodox principle espoused by Dicey and to consider its relevance to the modern constitutional order;
- to discuss formal and substantive conceptions of the rule of law, considering how each relates to the UK Constitution;
- to consider how the rule of law relates to wider aspects of the UK Constitution, including parliamentary sovereignty, judicial review, and human rights.

3.2 Defining the rule of law and its historical development

The rule of law, in simple terms, refers to the principle that the law should rule. What we mean by this is that, rather than a country's constitutional and governmental system being run on the basis of arbitrary decisions, often-changing and subjective values, and the personal preferences of those in power, we should be governed and ruled by a system that operates according to accepted law and established legal principle. What this means in practice, and in more detail, is open for debate, as this chapter will demonstrate.

---

[1] This distinction relates to whether or not the rule of law can be said to have any 'moral content', as will be explored in 3.4. As is explained further in 3.4.2, in particular, 'moral content' in this context can take a number of meanings, though generally reflects notions that core values, such as rights protection, justice, equality, and democracy—to name just a few—are contained within our understandings of the rule of law principle.

For now, though, the principle is important for the manner in which it represents the values that should underpin and guide the operation of a law-making and governmental system. Before we seek to explore these values, though, and the varying ways in which the rule of law is explained, it is necessary in this first section to define the principle and to outline its origins and development.

Section 1 of the Constitutional Reform Act 2005 is the first statutory acknowledgement of the principle of the rule of law. It states that: 'The Act does not adversely affect—(a) the existing constitutional principle of the rule of law, or (b) the Lord Chancellor's existing constitutional role in relation to that principle.'[2] Although the meaning of that provision is relevant to the manner in which that Act altered the role of the Lord Chancellor and the wider reforms the legislation sought to introduce,[3] it is notable that Parliament expressly acknowledges the rule of law as a principle and also hints at its importance with respect to the UK Constitution. This Act falls short, though, of offering any definition of the rule of law or further guidance on how the principle relates more broadly to the working of the constitution. It is in this reality that we catch a glimpse, for the first time, of the complexities faced when exploring the principle and the difficulty we have in reaching a commonly agreed definition.

Many academics and theorists have sought to interpret the meaning of the rule of law and have done so from many different perspectives. Jowell, for instance, considers that '[t]he Rule of Law is not a principle of moral law, yet it is a principle of institutional morality. As such, it guides all forms both of law enforcement and of law making.'[4] By contrast, Tomkins states that:

> In English public law the rule of law has at its core a single, simple, and clear meaning. It is a rule that concerns the power of the executive, of government . . . and it governs the relationship of the executive to the law. The rule of law provides that *the executive may do nothing without clear legal authority first permitting its actions*.[5]

At the very least, we can say that the principle has, at its heart, a concern for the proper and lawful actions of the institutions of government. It determines, in one sense, that power should be exercised in line with the law, but in another sense it sets out a moral code on the basis of which a constitutional system must operate. Though we talk here about the rule of law in the context of the UK Constitution, it is a principle that goes back to the birth of democratic government. Indeed, Bingham notes that the idea at the heart of the rule of law can be traced back as far as Aristotle.[6] It is here that our discussion starts.

Aristotle states that '[i]t is better for the law to rule than one of the citizens . . . so even the guardians of the laws are obeying the laws'.[7] Understanding this proposition is vital to grasping the various theories, which we will explore, that consider the ways in which the rule of law operates. Whatever view we take with regards to the content of the principle, though, or the role that it should play, at the rule of law's very foundation is an acceptance of the preference for the supremacy of law over the supremacy of man. In other

---

[2] Section 1 of the Constitutional Reform Act 2005.   [3] See 2.4.3.

[4] Jeffrey Jowell, 'The Rule of Law and its Underlying Values' in Jeffrey Jowell and Dawn Oliver (eds), *The Changing Constitution* (7th edn, OUP 2011) 11, 24.

[5] Adam Tomkins, *Public Law* (OUP 2003) 78.

[6] Tom Bingham, *The Rule of Law* (Allen Lane 2010) 3.

[7] Aristotle, *Politics and Athenian Constitution*, Book III, s. 1287 (John Warrington ed and trs, Dent 1959) 97, cited in Tom Bingham, *The Rule of Law* (Allen Lane 2010) 3.

words, the law—set by due legal process—should govern and guide rather than the arbitrary wishes of one individual person. On these foundations, as this chapter illustrates, the rule of law has developed as a defining characteristic of the modern UK Constitution. It is not, however, merely a British phenomenon. As Loughlin explains, '[t]he English idea of "the rule of law" finds its correlative formulations in continental European concepts of *Rechsstaat, l'Etat de droit, Stato di diritto, Estado de derecho*, and so on'.[8] Despite the principle's wide appeal, however, our focus in this chapter is purely on the rule of law in the UK system.

In terms of the UK Constitution, Magna Carta 1215 is often regarded as the starting point from which we can trace the importance of a process of government under law. Indeed, the historical setting of Magna Carta exemplifies the idea at the heart of Aristotle's consideration of the rule of law that those in power (or 'guardians of the law') should be restrained under the law and due legal process. Though it is of little legal relevance nowadays, Magna Carta's historical legacy is where its modern values lie. As 1.4.1 explained in greater detail, the 'Great Charter' concerned a limitation of the monarch's power insofar as it sought to limit the authority of 'Bad King John', who was imposing arbitrary taxes on his barons. It therefore represents the restraint of a tyrannical monarch's power and the limitation of that power under the law. Citing Holt and underlining the importance of Magna Carta to the rule of law in the UK, Wicks explains that:

> It is difficult to imagine the modern UK constitution without [the rule of law] . . . at its heart, and the first steps towards it can be traced back to 1215 and the Magna Carta which 'sought to establish the rights of subjects against authority and maintained the principle that authority was subject to law'.[9]

Writing at a similar time to Magna Carta, Bracton also noted that '[t]he King must not be under man but under God and under the law, because the law makes the King'.[10] This statement is, in the first instance, indicative of a very different time. Unlike in the modern UK Constitution, outlined in Chapter 1, the monarch in thirteenth-century England was said to derive their authority directly from God, a view that persisted at least until the seventeenth century and the Glorious Revolution. It is in the context of this 'divine right of Kings' that Bracton writes and that sets the scene for challenges in establishing values at the heart of the rule of law against monarchical authority. Ultimately, though, Bracton's assertion echoes both the Aristotelian idea of the rule of law, relevant to the UK system, and the principle at the heart of Magna Carta itself.

In the centuries that followed Bracton and Magna Carta, issues concerning the allocation of power and the nature of relationships between the monarch, the citizens of the UK, and the institutions of government, shaped the way in which we think about the rule of law and the authorities that support the values at the heart of the principle. In the seventeenth century, for example, the importance of Magna Carta was reiterated and reinforced by the Petition of Right 1628. Drafted by Sir Edward Coke as a reaction

---

[8] Martin Loughlin, *Foundations of Public Law* (OUP 2010) 313.

[9] Elizabeth Wicks, *The Evolution of a Constitution: Eight Key Moments in British Constitutional History* (Hart Publishing 2006) 3–4, citing JC Holt, *Magna Carta* (2nd edn, Cambridge University Press 1991) 19.

[10] Henry de Bracton, *On the Laws and Customs of England* (Samuel E Thorne trs, Harvard University Press 1968) vol II, 33, cited in Keith Syrett, *The Foundations of Public Law: Principles and Problems of Power in the British Constitution* (2nd edn, Palgrave Macmillan 2014) 40.

to excessive monarchical power, it sought to restrain Charles I's arbitrary practices that included the imposition of taxes without parliamentary approval and the imprisonment of those refusing to pay such taxes. It was later in the seventeenth century, however, that we see an ultimately more permanent limitation of unelected monarchical power through the Glorious Revolution and the settlement reached through the Bill of Rights 1688.

Before the 1688 settlement, and throughout the seventeenth century, there had been much debate and dispute as regards whether Parliament or the monarch should be regarded as holding sovereign power, with the courts often being called upon to consider exercises of both monarchical and statutory authority. As 4.3.2 will discuss in greater detail, the Bill of Rights 1688 settled the issue, formally establishing the sovereignty of Parliament. In doing so, however, the settlement reached through the bill represented a permanent restriction on monarchical authority and meant that power would be exercised predominantly under the authority of a democratically elected Parliament[11] and subject to legal principle, rather than at the whim of an unelected monarch. The Bill of Rights, in this way, further underlined the values at the heart of the rule of law, and of Magna Carta, and sought to uphold the supremacy of law over the supremacy of man.

Alongside these various proclamations regarding the rule of law and its relevance in the UK constitutional system, there have also been a number of cases and judicial statements underling the importance with which values at the heart of the principle should be regarded. The first such case, pre-dating the Bill of Rights, is *Prohibitions del Roy*.[12] This case concerned a question regarding the powers of King James I to settle disputes, in particular between the ecclesiastical courts and the courts of the common law.[13] Though it was argued that the King had a divine right to resolve disputes himself and that judges were mere delegates of the King, the court disagreed and held that the King had no such power and should, instead, leave it to the judges. To decide this case in favour of King James would have been to find that the monarch, in many respects, was above the law. Four years later, the principle emerged in another key case, the *Case of Proclamations*.[14] This case involved a challenge to the King's alleged power to make law by royal proclamation. In finding that 'the King by his proclamation . . . cannot change any part of the common law, or statute law, or customs of the realm',[15] the court emphasized that 'the King hath no prerogative, but that which the law of the land allows him'.[16] This reflects the rule of law principle insofar as it makes clear that the King is beneath the established law and can only act pursuant to lawful authority. Another notable case, which shows the relevance of values at the heart of the rule of law, is *Entick v Carrington*.[17]

---

[11] In the late seventeenth century, though, Parliament was not the democratic institution that we recognize today, as Chapter 8 will further explain.

[12] (1607) 12 Co Rep 63.

[13] See, for further discussion, Ann Lyon, *Constitutional History in the UK* (Cavendish Publishing Ltd 2003) 201.

[14] (1611) 12 Co Rep 74.   [15] (1611) 12 Co Rep 74, 75.   [16] (1611) 12 Co Rep 74, 77.

[17] (1765) 95 ER 807.

> ### Case in depth: *Entick v Carrington* (1765) 95 ER 807
>
> King's messengers entered Entick's house to search for and seize some of his papers. Entick sued the messengers, challenging the entry on the basis that it was unlawful. The defendants pleaded not guilty, however, on the basis that their entry and search had been with a warrant issued by the Earl of Halifax, 'one of the Lords of the King's Privy Council, and one of his principal Secretaries of State'. The warrant authorized the defendants:
>
> > to make strict and diligent search for the plaintiff, mentioned in the said warrant to be the author, or one concerned in the writing of several weekly very seditious papers, intitled The Monitor, or British Freeholder . . . containing gross and scandalous reflections and invectives upon His Majesty's Government, and upon both Houses of Parliament, and him the plaintiff having found, to seize and apprehend and bring together with his books and papers in safe custody.[18]
>
> The court held, however, that the warrant was unlawful, since the Earl of Halifax had had no statutory or judicial authority to issue such a warrant.

The judgment in *Entick v Carrington* is notable for the manner in which it represents the courts seeking to bring the executive within the law, a notion fundamental to the rule of law principle. Indeed, and in commenting on the lack of legal authority for the warrant at issue, Lord Camden CJ famously stated that:

> if this is law it would be found in our books, but no such law ever existed in this country; our law holds the property of every man so sacred, that no man can set his foot upon his neighbour's close without his leave; if he does he is a trespasser, though he does no damage at all; if he will tread upon his neighbour's ground, he must justify it by law.[19]

This statement underlines the importance of acting with appropriate legal authority, particularly where that action is taken by 'a principal Secretary of State' who is, by virtue of their role, in a position of power. Ultimately, the rule of law is there to ensure that a government cannot act in a certain way just because it is the government, even if it truly and honestly believes that the action is both necessary and good. Indeed, an example of this principle still at work in the modern UK Constitution is provided by the case of *R (Miller) v Prime Minister*,[20] the details of which are set out at 2.4.3.

In reaching its decision, the Supreme Court cited the *Case of Proclamations* and *Entick v Carrington* and explained that there were legal limits to the powers of the Government, in respect of which 'the courts . . . [could exercise] a supervisory jurisdiction'.[21] There are, of course, other cases which reflect the importance and relevance of the rule of law in the UK Constitution. These are discussed within this chapter, but for now, it is important to consider, on the foundation of the early historical development, what the rule of law principle means today.

---

[18] Ibid 808.   [19] Ibid 817.   [20] [2019] UKSC 41   [21] [2019] UKSC 41 [31]-[32].

3.3 Dicey and the rule of law

The previous section has explained the historical development of the rule of law both in terms of its origins generally and also with regards to its emergence in the early UK Constitution. Despite this long history, however, modern day considerations of the principle in the UK context generally start with an exploration of the writings of Dicey, who discussed the rule of law in his text *An Introduction to the Study of the Law of the Constitution*. The value of Dicey's contributions in this field should not be underestimated. Bingham notes that '[c]redit for coining the expression "the rule of law" is usually given to Professor A. V. Dicey . . . But the point is fairly made that even if he coined the expression he did not invent the idea lying behind it'.[22] Bingham also adds elsewhere that:

> whether as the late Professor Lawson wrote, Dicey 'coined' the phrase 'the Rule of Law', or whether he merely popularized it, he was effectively responsible for ensuring that no discussion of modern democratic government can properly omit reference to it.[23]

Dicey's contribution, therefore, provides an appropriate and authoritative starting point for our discussion, though it must be noted that his views have met with much criticism over the years. Indeed, rather than providing a general explanation of constitutional law, some of his observations are an evolution of his own *political* views. Nonetheless, it is important to single out Dicey's explanation of the rule of law and to consider the definition to which he attributed it. He explained that:

> When we say that the supremacy or the rule of law is a characteristic of the English constitution, we generally include under one expression at least three distinct kindred conceptions. We mean, in the first place, that no man is punishable or can be lawfully made to suffer in body or goods except for a distinct breach of law established in the ordinary legal manner before the ordinary Courts of the land. In this sense the rule of law is contrasted with every system of government based on the exercise by persons in authority of wide, arbitrary or discretionary powers of constraint . . . We mean in the second place . . . not only that with us no man is above the law, but . . . that here every man, whatever be his rank or condition, is subject to the ordinary law of the realm and amendable to the jurisdiction of the ordinary tribunals . . . [Finally, w]e may say that the constitution is pervaded by the rule of law on the ground that the general principles of the constitution (as for example the right to personal liberty, or the right of public meetings), are with us the result of judicial decisions determining the rights of private persons in particular cases brought before the Courts; whereas under many foreign constitutions the security . . . given to the rights of individuals results, or appears to result, from the general principles of the constitution.[24]

As this extract highlights, Dicey identifies three parts to his consideration of the rule of law. The first is that there should be no punishment without a breach of law; the second, that the law should apply equally to all; and the third, that the general principles of the constitution are protected through the courts, rather than through an entrenched legal document. Our discussion looks at each of these in turn.

---

[22] Tom Bingham, *The Rule of Law* (Allen Lane 2010) 3.

[23] Tom Bingham, *Lives of the Law: Selected Essays and Speeches 2000–2010* (OUP 2011) 53, citing FH Lawson, *The Oxford Law School 1850–1965* (OUP Clarendon Press 1968) 72.

[24] AV Dicey, *Introduction to the Study of the Law of the Constitution* (by JWF Allison ed, first published 1885, OUP 2013) 97–114.

Pause for reflection

This chapter has already explained that the rule of law has its origins in the writings of Aristotle. To what extent, though, do you think this statement set out by Dicey reflects Aristotle's notion of the supremacy of law, in preference to the supremacy of man?

3.3.1 No punishment without breach of law

Central to Dicey's conception of the rule of law is the notion that punishment and sanction should only be imposed in line with the written word of the law, and not on the basis of any arbitrary or discretionary authority. This is consistent with one of the few provisions of Magna Carta that remain in force today, which provides that:

> No freeman shall be taken or imprisoned, or be disseised[25] of his Freehold, or Liberties, or free Customs, or be outlawed or exiled, or any other wise destroyed; nor will we not pass upon him, nor condemn him, but by lawful judgment of his Peers, or by the Law of the Land. We will sell to no man, we will not deny or defer to any man either Justice or Right.[26]

In modern language, this clause ensures that nobody can be punished or have sanctions imposed against him unless they have been found, through due legal process, to have broken and breached the established law. This, and Dicey's echoing of the principle, is consistent with Lord Camden CJ's judgment in *Entick v Carrington*, which we have already considered. Lord Camden CJ was quoted in 3.2 as saying that 'if this is law it would be found in our books, but no such law ever existed in this country'.[27] Dicey's justification for this view was that 'wherever there is discretion there is room for arbitrariness, and that in a republic no less than under a monarchy discretionary authority on the part of the government means insecurity for legal freedom on the part of subjects'.[28]

In one sense, Dicey's reasoning is acceptable and reflects the evolution of a value that is at the very heart of the rule of law. Namely, that a society should be governed and guided by laws and due legal process, rather than by arbitrary rule. The rationale is simple: we should know and be able to predict the rules and laws by which we are governed in order that we can act and go about our lives in a lawful fashion. Arbitrariness does not always make allowance for this and means that the course of decision-, policy-, and law-making and implementation can be unpredictable and potentially unfair. As Syrett explains, Dicey's 'central concern is that governmental power should be exercised in a manner which is relatively certain, clear, open and predictable, free from the whim or personal prejudice of the decision-maker'.[29] This is a view consistent with other conceptions of the rule of law, including that of Joseph Raz, who considers that 'the making of particular laws should be guided by open and relatively stable general rules'.[30] Raz also adds, much later, that '[t]he rule of law consists of principles that constrain the way government actions

---

[25] Meaning disseized or disposed of.   [26] Clause XXIX, Magna Carta 1297.

[27] (1765) 95 ER 807, 817.

[28] AV Dicey, *Introduction to the Study of the Law of the Constitution* (JWF Allison ed, first published 1885, OUP 2013) 98.

[29] Keith Syrett, *The Foundations of Public Law: Principles and Problems of Power in the British Constitution* (2nd edn, Palgrave Macmillan 2014) 43.

[30] Joseph Raz, 'The Rule of Law and its Virtue' (1977) 93 *Law Quarterly Review* 195, 198.

change and apply the law – to make sure, among other things, that they maintain stability and predictability, and thus enable individuals to find their way and to live well'.[31]

In another sense, however, Dicey's contention that 'discretionary authority on the part of the government means insecurity for legal freedom on the part of subjects'[32] is problematic. The predominant concern is that, while exercise of arbitrary power is not desirable for reasons already stated, discretionary authority is a vital and necessary part of any effective system of government. This was true at the time that Dicey was writing and is even more so today. As Jennings states: '[i]f we look around us we cannot fail to be aware that public authorities do in fact possess wide discretionary powers. Many of them formed part of the law even when Dicey wrote in 1885'.[33] Jennings then goes on to identify examples of discretionary power, saying:

> Any court can punish me for contempt of court by imprisoning me for an indefinite period. If I am convicted of manslaughter, I may be released at once or imprisoned for life. If I am an alien, my naturalisation is entirely within the discretion of the Home Secretary. If the Queen declares war against the rest of the world, I am prohibited from having dealings abroad. If the country is in danger, my property can be taken, perhaps without compensation. If a public health authority wants to flood my land in order to build a reservoir, it can take it from me compulsorily. I can be compelled to leave my work for a month or more, in order to serve on a jury.[34]

The point is plainly made: discretionary authority exists and is a necessary part of the governmental system. Dicey perhaps goes a little too far in suggesting that such uses of discretionary power should not be an acceptable part of a working legal system, but his view that *arbitrary* uses and abuses of power should be prevented remains a fundamental part of the rule of law in the UK. As Raz echoes: 'powerful people and people in government, just like anybody else, should obey the law'.[35] This is a point substantiated by the already considered case of *Entick v Carrington*, where the Earl of Halifax's general warrant was issued unlawfully, without the authority of any statute or common law principle, and as such, entry to and the searching of Entick's house could not be justified. Another, more recent case representing this principle is *IRC v Rossminster Ltd*.[36]

Case in depth: *IRC v Rossminster Ltd* [1980] AC 952

The Inland Revenue obtained warrants to search the premises of Rossminster Ltd, a financial services company that was suspected of tax fraud, in order to seize 'anything which they had reasonable cause to believe might be required as evidence in proceedings in respect of tax fraud', pursuant to section 20C of the Taxes Management Act 1970.[37] Accompanied by police officers, revenue officers arrived at and searched the premises of Rossminster Ltd pursuant to the warrant. This warrant, however, contained no particulars and the officers carrying out the search failed to inform those present on the premises of the offences alleged against them or the

→

---

[31] Joseph Raz, 'The Law's Own Virtue' (2019) 39(1) *Oxford Journal of Legal Studies* 1, 2.

[32] AV Dicey, *Introduction to the Study of the Law of the Constitution* (JWF Allison ed, first published 1885, OUP 2013) 98.

[33] Sir Ivor Jennings, *The Law and the Constitution* (5th edn, University of London Press 1963) 55.

[34] Ibid.

[35] Joseph Raz, 'The Rule of Law and its Virtue' (1977) 93 *Law Quarterly Review* 195, 197, cited in Keith Syrett, *The Foundations of Public Law: Principles and Problems of Power in the British Constitution* (2nd edn, Palgrave Macmillan 2014) 42.   [36] [1980] AC 952.   [37] Ibid 953.

→

identity of the alleged suspects. Rossminster Ltd applied for judicial review to quash the warrants to search their premises and seize any evidence, claiming that the officers did not have proper authority to seize the documents taken. The Divisional Court rejected the application, however, this decision was reversed by the Court of Appeal but later reinstated in the House of Lords.

Although the final decision in *IRC v Rossminster Ltd* did not find there to be anything amiss with the government's actions, the Court of Appeal made interesting comments concerning the requirement for action to be taken with lawful authority and, more broadly, the continued relevance of this requirement with regards to the rule of law. Lord Denning MR stated:

> [W]e have to see in this case whether this warrant was valid or not. It all depends of course upon the statute . . . When the officers of the Inland Revenue come armed with a warrant to search a man's home or his office, it seems to me that he is entitled to say: 'Of what offence do you suspect me? You are claiming to enter my house and to seize my papers.' And when they look at the papers and seize them, he should be able to say: 'Why are you seizing these papers? Of what offence do you suspect me? What have these to do with your case?' Unless he knows the particular offence charged, he cannot take steps to secure himself or his property. So it seems to me, as a matter of construction of the statute and therefore of the warrant—in pursuance of our traditional role to protect the liberty of the individual—it is our duty to say that the warrant must particularise the specific offence which is charged as being fraud on the revenue. If this be right, it follows necessarily that this warrant is bad. It should have specified the particular offence of which the man is suspected. On this ground I would hold that certiorari should go to quash the warrant.[38]

We return again to *IRC v Rossminster Ltd* later on; its significance here, though, is notable in affirming and updating principles established over 250 years ago in *Entick v Carrington* underlying the importance of acting with appropriate lawful authority. The most recent case concerning this first head of Dicey's conception of the rule of law, however, is *A and others v Secretary of State for the Home Department*,[39] which involves the detention without trial of suspected terrorists.

Case in depth: *A and others v Secretary of State for the Home Department* [2004] UKHL 56

This case concerned nine foreign nationals who were suspected terrorists, allegedly causing a potential threat to national security in the UK. On this basis, and pursuant to sections 21 and 23 of the Anti-Terrorism, Crime and Security Act 2001, the foreign nationals were detained without trial. Though they were free to return to their native countries, the individuals were fearful of the possibility that they would be tortured if they did. Their decisions to remain in the UK meant that they were subject to detention without trial for an indefinite period of time, pursuant to the 2001 Act. Though such detention could be deemed contrary to the right to liberty, protected under Article 5 of the European Convention on Human Rights,[40] the UK Government had sought to

→

---

[38] Ibid 974.   [39] [2004] UKHL 56.   [40] Subsequently ECHR.

→

derogate from this right—under Article 15—in order that detention in such circumstances could be allowed.[41] The applicants, however, sought to challenge the legality of their detention on the basis that the provisions of the 2001 Act were more than 'strictly required by the exigencies of the situation', as required under Article 15, and that the UK Government's derogation was unlawful.

Though the House of Lords addressed a number of issues in giving judgment, they ultimately held that the indefinite detention was unlawful, not only on the basis that it exceeded the permitted grounds for derogation contained within Article 15, but also on the basis that it contravened the right to liberty in Article 5 and discriminated against non-British nationals, contrary to Article 14 of the Convention.

This case is relevant to this discussion for the manner in which the House of Lords upheld the principle espoused by Dicey stating that no man can be punished or made to suffer unless there has been a breach of the law. As Lord Nicholls said in giving judgment: 'indefinite imprisonment without charge or trial is an anathema in any country which observes the rule of law . . . Wholly exceptional circumstances must exist before this extreme step can be justified'.[42] Such exceptional circumstances were not found to exist in this case. As such, and since the foreign nationals were never charged with an offence, their indefinite detention could not be justified consistently with the rule of law.

A more recent and extreme example of the importance of not subjecting individuals to punishment without an established breach of the law is highlighted not by a case, but by the extrajudicial killings of suspected terrorists. In August 2015, the UK Government confirmed that it had recently executed two British citizens who were fighting for Isis in Syria.[43] Their execution, it is reported, came not following any trial or conviction but as a result of 'meticulous planning' and preparation on the basis of received intelligence.[44] The government's actions with regards to these killings received a great deal of criticism in the press, with many emphasizing concern for the fact that the suspects were essentially executed without any recourse to due legal process, something that sits uneasily with orthodox understandings of the rule of law.

The principle that there should be appropriate lawful authority for state action remains a vital part of the rule of law, as *Entick v Carrington*, *IRC v Rossminster*, and *A and others v Secretary of State for the Home Department* all serve to demonstrate. It is reflective of a value that dates back to Magna Carta and one that is placed firmly at the centre of orthodox understandings of the rule of law principle.

3.3.2 No man is above the law

The second aspect of Dicey's orthodox principle of the rule of law is one that supports the idea of equality before the law. Dicey himself acknowledged that this meant two things: '[N]ot only that with us no man is above the law, but (what is a different thing) that here

---

[41] Article 15 of the ECHR provides that a country may take measures to derogate from its obligations under the Convention in time of war or public emergency, provided such measures are no more than those strictly required by the exigencies of the situation.

[42] [2004] UKHL 56 [74].

[43] Gary Younge, 'State-Sanctioned Killings Without Trial: Are These Cameron's British Values?' *The Guardian* (8 September 2015), https://www.theguardian.com/commentisfree/2015/sep/08/state-sanctioned-executions-cameron-british-values.   [44] Ibid.

every man, whatever be his rank or condition, is subject to the ordinary law of the realm and amenable to the jurisdiction of the ordinary tribunals'.[45]

The underlying idea here is that all people, whatever their position in society, their profession, or their status, should be subjected to the same laws. As Dicey explains: 'With us every official, from the Prime Minister down to a constable or a collector of taxes, is under the same responsibility for every act done without legal justification as any other citizen.'[46]

This aspect of the Diceyan conception of the rule of law is widely accepted. Raz and Allan, for instance, both stress the importance of the general and equal application of law, though whether it suffices as a procedural value or should be supplemented by more substantive characteristics lies at the heart of where Raz and Allan differ in their rule of law conceptions, as will be discussed in 3.4.[47] The underlying value of this aspect, though, is fairness. It would be fundamentally unfair and improper if those in a position of power, such as a government minister or a Member of Parliament, were to enjoy exemptions and immunity to the effect that they did not have to obey the law in the same way as ordinary citizens.

 Counterpoint: Is everyone really treated the same under the law?

Dicey's conception that everyone is subject to the law in the same way is sometimes criticized. There are some who argue that Dicey fails to account for those members of society who are subject to different or additional laws and responsibilities. For example, Jowell, citing Dobson, considers that in Dicey's time there were '"colossal distinctions" between the rights and duties of private individuals and those of the administrative organs of government . . . Public authorities possessed special rights and special exemptions and immunities'.[48] Even today, the monarch is immune from criminal prosecution in her own courts; MPs enjoy a range of privileges and immunities for actions done or statements made in the House of Commons; and police officers have special powers to stop and search individuals, to list just a few examples.

Do you agree that Dicey's idea that everybody is at law treated the same seems, in the case of a few examples, somewhat artificial in today's constitution?

Returning to Dicey's words and considering a different reading of his proposition that 'every man, whatever be his rank or condition, is subject to the ordinary law of the realm and amenable to the jurisdiction of the ordinary tribunals',[49] we can see that this can also be read as suggesting that, regardless of an individual's rank or position in society, sanctions for breach of the law should always be consistent and equal. As a notion, this is broadly correct, as can be seen in a number of cases. We have already examined

---

[45] AV Dicey, *Introduction to the Study of the Law of the Constitution* (JWF Allison ed, first published 1885, OUP 2013) 100.

[46] Ibid. Dicey cites *Entick v Carrington*; *Philips v Eyre* LR, 4 QB 225; *Mostyn v Fabregas* Cowp 161; *Musgrave v Pulido* 5 App Cas 102; *Governor's Wall's Case* 28 St Tr 51 as examples of cases where officials have been brought before the courts to account for alleged breaches of the law.

[47] See Joseph Raz, 'The Rule of Law and its Virtue' (1977) 93 *Law Quarterly Review* 195; and TRS Allan, *Constitutional Justice: A Liberal Theory for the Rule of Law* (OUP 2001) 31.

[48] Jeffrey Jowell, 'The Rule of Law and its Underlying Values' in Jeffrey Jowell and Dawn Oliver (eds), *The Changing Constitution* (7th edn, OUP 2011) 11, 14, citing William A Robson, *Justice and Administrative Law* (2nd edn, Stevens 1947) 345.

[49] AV Dicey, *Introduction to the Study of the Law of the Constitution* (JWF Allison ed, first published 1885, OUP 2013) 100.

Entick v Carrington and this is perhaps one of the notable examples of the extent and manner to which the law should apply equally to all, regardless of their position. Just because the Earl of Halifax was a 'principal Secretary of State', this did not automatically justify what was essentially an unlawful warrant. Its declaration as unlawful meant that the consequences of his actions were the same as if he were an ordinary citizen: those who purported to enter Entick's property, not having lawful authority to support their entry, were committing a trespass. Another, more recent case that exemplifies this issue further, and that also involves a government minister abusing his position, is *Re M*.[50]

Case in depth: *Re M* [1994] 1 AC 377

This case involved an application for asylum by a citizen of Zaire (now the Democratic Republic of the Congo), which was rejected by the Home Secretary, with an attempted judicial review of that decision also later refused. Shortly before the claimant's removal back to Zaire, however, he brought a fresh application for judicial review on new grounds. The Divisional Court, knowing of the citizen's imminent removal, ordered that his departure be postponed pending proper and appropriate consideration of this new application for judicial review. The Home Office officials in charge of the Zairean citizen, however, failed to take him off the plane before its departure, failing again to do so when the plane stopped in Paris. Hearing this, the judge made an order requiring the Home Secretary to effect the citizen's immediate return to the UK. Although such arrangements were initially followed, the Home Secretary felt that the decision to reject the application for asylum was correct and, being advised that the judge's order (a mandatory interim injunction) had been imposed without appropriate jurisdiction, the Home Secretary gave up on attempts to return the Zairean citizen to the UK. The applicant sought proceedings against the Home Office on the basis that they had breached a court order against them to prevent his departure from and effect his return to the UK. These proceedings were rejected, however, on the basis that, pursuant to section 21 of the Crown Proceedings Act 1947, the Crown—including those departments or ministers working for the Crown, in the course of their duties—was immune from injunctions and could not be found in contempt of court in the event of their breach. The Court of Appeal overturned this decision, however, finding that the Secretary of State was personally guilty of contempt of court. The House of Lords, although finding that the Home Secretary was acting in his official, not personal, capacity, also agreed that he was in contempt of court.

The finding that the Home Secretary was in contempt of court is notable here for two reasons. First, it supports the equal subjection of persons before the law point, as discussed. Following Dicey and the authority that goes back to *Entick v Carrington*, the Home Secretary's position alone did not and should not justify the ability to violate a court order. Secondly, and more significantly, the judgment is notable insofar as it represents the authority whereby a Minister of the Crown can be held in contempt of court. Before *Re M*, the Crown, including a minister of the Crown acting in their official role, could not be found in contempt due to the lack of legal personality. This position was pursuant to section 21 of the Crown Proceedings Act 1947 and, indeed, was a view that had been upheld by the Court of Appeal in *Re M*. The House of Lords, however, sought to distinguish

---

[50] [1994] 1 AC 377.

between the Crown as the monarch and Ministers of the Crown, as those merely working on the monarch's behalf and in their name, and on this basis found that the minister could be held in contempt of court. Lord Woolf said:

> Nolan LJ [in the Court of Appeal] . . . considered that the fact that proceedings for contempt are 'essentially personal and punitive' meant that it was not open to a court, as a matter of law, to make a finding of contempt against the Home Office or the Home Secretary. While contempt proceedings usually have these characteristics and contempt proceedings against a government department or a minister in an official capacity would not be either personal or punitive . . . this does not mean that a finding of contempt against a government department or minister would be pointless. The very fact of making such a finding would vindicate the requirements of justice.[51]

 Discussing the problem

Have another look at the problem scenario. In what way does the arrest of Fred for 'meddling in government business' fail to comply with the first and second aspects of Dicey's conception of the rule of law?

Dicey's two observations that 'no man is punishable or can be lawfully made to suffer in body or goods except for a distinct breach of law' and that 'no man is above the law' are both relevant to the government's actions in seeking to silence Fred by arresting him. At the time that Fred is arrested, for allegedly 'meddling in government business', it is not—as he points out—an offence. The police's persistence in arresting him anyway means that he is being made 'to suffer', despite no breach of the law, contrary to Dicey's conception that someone should only be arrested for breaching the law. What is more, when Fred is told that he is being arrested 'under the authority of the Secretary of State' who 'can do what she likes [since] she works for the government', the government is essentially seeking to maintain that it is 'above the law' contrary to Dicey's second point. *Entick v Carrington* is a relevant case here since, like the Secretary of State in that case unlawfully authorizing entry and search of Entick's property, the government is here ordering the arrest of Fred with no lawful authority.

The judgment in *Re M*, following the principle espoused in *Entick v Carrington*, underlines the importance of Dicey's second point: that individuals, whatever their rank or position in society, should be subjected to the equal application of laws.

3.3.3 General principles of the constitution protected by the courts through the ordinary law of the land

The third and final aspect of Dicey's consideration of the rule of law concerns the protection of the constitution and, in particular, constitutional rights. In view of the fact that the UK has no codified constitutional document, Dicey felt it was for the independent courts to uphold and protect constitutional principles and, in particular, fundamental rights. As a result, and as Jowell observes, '[l]ike Bentham before him, [Dicey] was against

---

[51] Ibid 425.

a basic document setting out a catalogue of human rights and saw our law and liberties as arising from decisions in the courts—the common law'.[52] Dicey stated:

> We may say that the constitution is pervaded by the rule of law on the ground that the general principles of the constitution (as for example the right to personal liberty, or the right of public meeting), are with us the result of judicial decisions determining the rights of private persons in particular cases brought before the Courts.[53]

This position is, said Dicey, in contrast to 'many foreign constitutions [where] the security (such as it is) given to the rights of individuals results, or appears to result, from the general principles of the constitution'.[54] Instead:

> the English constitution, [has] not been created at one stroke, and far from being the result of legislation in the ordinary sense of that term, [is] the fruits of contests carried on in the Courts on behalf of the rights of individuals. Our constitution, in short, is a judge-made constitution, and it bears on its face all the features, good and bad, of judge-made law.[55]

In short, the third aspect of Dicey's conception of the rule of law is one that observes that the general principles of the constitution, including and especially the rights of individuals, are protected through the common law system on which the UK Constitution is founded, and not on the basis of any entrenched constitutional document.

 Pause for reflection

The third part of Dicey's definition of the rule of law considers the importance of the courts in upholding constitutional principles and fundamental rights, in preference to an entrenched constitutional document. On this basis, how differently do you think the rule of law can be said to apply in countries that have such a document protecting fundamental rights?

In one sense, the UK courts have fulfilled a role consistent with this principle. Historically, the UK Constitution's attitude to rights protection has been based on the notion of civil liberties whereby everything was deemed lawful unless expressly prohibited. In another sense, however, the broader constitutional landscape within which this particular aspect of Dicey's conception was initially framed has altered somewhat since the late nineteenth century. As such, the modern relevance of Dicey's view as regards the protection of constitutional rights and principles is something to be questioned. The ratification of the European Convention on Human Rights in 1951 and its incorporation through the Human Rights Act 1998, for instance, has altered the manner in which rights are protected in the UK. We no longer have just a 'civil liberties' approach to rights protection, but also a culture of rights that are protected through the Act and supplemented by jurisprudence from the European Court of Human Rights in Strasbourg.

---

[52] Jeffrey Jowell, 'The Rule of Law and its Underlying Values' in Jeffrey Jowell and Dawn Oliver (eds), *The Changing Constitution* (7th edn, OUP 2011) 11, 13.

[53] AV Dicey, *Introduction to the Study of the Law of the Constitution* (JWF Allison ed, first published 1885, OUP 2013) 115.

[54] Ibid 116.   [55] Ibid.

3.3.4 **Concluding remarks on Dicey**

Dicey's contribution to modern thinking with regards to the rule of law is notable. Returning to Bingham's earlier observation, Dicey is responsible for the prominence with which we now regard the principle of the rule of law in the UK Constitution and while the UK Constitution has evolved and developed since the late nineteenth century, his conceptions do still have a relevance to the modern UK system. Dicey's views, however, are not the final word on the rule of law and, indeed, can rightly be regarded as just one consideration of the principle. This chapter now moves on to explore broader considerations of the rule of law, drawing from a range of scholars who have sought to consider its meaning.

3.4 **Broader considerations of the rule of law**

There are many ways of thinking about the rule of law and of categorizing the various conceptions that have been offered over the centuries. One of the most commonly accepted distinctions, however, on the basis of which we can break down these differing views for further consideration, lies between what are termed the 'formal' and 'substantive' conceptions. The 'formal conception' of the rule of law is concerned with procedural rules and formal values, while the 'substantive conception' builds on the formal conception and contends that the rule of law requires the law itself to honour certain, substantive characteristics. This section considers and discusses the difference between these two conceptions and explores the writings of a number of theorists in their regard.

3.4.1 **Formal conceptions of the rule of law**

To the distinction between formal and substantive considerations of the rule of law, some add a third—namely, a conception that the principle represents nothing more than the simple notion of abiding by the written word of the law. In one sense, this is the very essence of the rule of law. As Jowell explains: '[a]t its most fundamental, the Rule of Law requires everyone to comply with the law',[56] an idea that forms a part of Dicey's consideration that nobody should be punished or made to suffer in the absence of appropriate legal authority. If we return to *Entick v Carrington*, for instance, the issue was that the Earl of Halifax did not have a legal basis for the general warrant, thereby rendering it unlawful.

 Counterpoint: Is there a limit to the formal conception of the rule of law?

If we are to take the rule of law as amounting to nothing more than a question of legality, then a situation arises whereby actions and decisions which might seem unethical or improper can arguably be viewed as consistent with the rule of law. For example (as 4.5.1 will discuss in greater detail), Stephen said of Parliament's sovereignty that it had the power to legislate to have all blue-eyed babies put to death.[57] If Parliament enacted such a law, would the killing of 'all blue-eyed babies' be consistent with the rule of law?

---

[56] Jeffrey Jowell, 'The Rule of Law and its Underlying Values' in Jeffrey Jowell and Dawn Oliver (eds), *The Changing Constitution* (7th edn, OUP 2011) 11, 17.

[57] Sir Leslie Stephen, *The Science of Ethics* (GP Putnam's Sons 1907) 137.

There is, though, something inherently problematic in viewing the rule of law as consisting of nothing more than a requirement to obey the written word of the law. As Allan explains:

> On an interpretation of the rule of law which reflected only the ordinary requirement of legality, every dictatorship whose authority is acknowledged by the courts would be a *Rechsstaat*; and the grant of unlimited discretion to officials to pursue their own ideas of the public good, unfettered by legislative guidance or judicial review, would be consistent with the rule of law.[58]

The notion of unlimited or unfettered discretionary authority is—as we have already seen—far removed from common understandings of the rule of law; most notably Dicey's. It is for this reason that, as Allan goes on to note, '[i]t is . . . widely accepted that we should seek an explanation of the rule of law which is more fruitful and ambitious than the jejune idea of legality'.[59] On this basis, and accepting Allan's point, we move now to consider the formal conception of the rule of law.

 Discussing the problem

In the problem scenario, Parliament passes the Freedom from the Press (Government Privacy) Act 2023, which provides that '[t]he publication or revelation of Government policies and decisions before formal announcement is unlawful'. Viewing the rule of law as nothing more than a principle requiring adherence to the written word of the law, to what extent has the government acted contrary to the rule of law?

Arguably, not at all, since the government has acted within the provisions of the newly enacted 2023 Act in preventing the proposed abolition of the National Health Service from being released by Fred before the government has itself had opportunity formally to announce the policy decision. The only issue concerns the fact that the Act is passed *after* Fred is arrested; at the time of arrest, Fred had not committed a crime. This argument, though, touches more on formal conceptions of the rule of law, as the section now explains.

For those espousing a formal conception, the rule of law means that there should be a set of guiding principles that provide a framework for the way in which a system of government should operate. Under such conceptions, though, the content of the law is not regarded as relevant. Craig explains that:

> Formal conceptions of the rule of law address the manner in which the law was promulgated (was it by a properly authorised person, in a properly authorised manner, etc.); the clarity of the ensuing norm (was it sufficiently clear to guide an individual's conduct so as to enable a person to plan his or her life, etc.); and the temporal dimension of the enacted norm (was it prospective or retrospective, etc.). Formal conceptions of the rule of law do note however seek to pass judgment upon the actual content of the law itself. They are not concerned with whether the law was in that sense a good law or a bad law, provided that the formal precepts of the rule of law were themselves met.[60]

---

[58] TRS Allan, 'The Rule of Law as the Rule of Reason: Consent and Constitutionalism' (1999) 115 *Law Quarterly Review* 221, 221–2.   [59] Ibid 221.

[60] Paul P Craig, 'Formal and Substantive Conceptions of the Rule of Law: An Analytical Framework' (1997) *Public Law* 467, 467.

Dicey's elucidation of the principle is regarded as falling within the formal conception of the rule of law,[61] since his consideration is founded on the view that requires laws to be 'passed in the correct legal manner', for the law to apply equally to all, and for rights to be protected through the common law rather than through an entrenched constitutional document.[62] Although, as Craig rightly admits, 'the words used by Dicey could bear substantive meaning',[63] Dicey's conception is concerned with how laws are made, applied, and enforced, *not* with the substantive content of those laws.

There are many other theorists, though, who also offer a formal conception of the rule of law. Hayek, for instance, echoes Dicey's dislike for discretionary authority in noting that:

> stripped of all technicalities [the rule of law] means that government in all its actions is bound by rules fixed and announced beforehand—rules which make it possible to foresee with fair certainty how the authority will use its coercive powers in given circumstances, and to plan one's individual affairs on the basis of this knowledge.[64]

Hayek's conception of the rule of law is undoubtedly formal and reflects a minimalist view of the state. Indeed, just as Dicey's conception can be said to be in part reflective of his own conservative politics, so Hayek's desire for a minimalist state can be said to be consistent with his own classically liberal ideological beliefs. He was opposed to the 'welfare state' on the basis that it promoted distributive justice, which in turn allowed for the exercise of discretionary governmental authority.[65] Hayek's conception is a relatively straightforward example of a formal view of the rule of law, insisting as it does on the strict adherence to openly publicized rules which allow citizens to predict the course of government action and 'plan his or her life'.[66]

Another, particularly notable, proponent of the formal conception of the rule of law is Raz. In his view, the rule of law 'has two aspects: (1) that people should be ruled by the law and obey it, and (2) that the law should be such that people will be able to be guided by it'.[67] He elaborates on this second point by adding that 'if the law is to be obeyed *it must be capable of guiding the behaviour of its subjects*'.[68] To this end, Raz considered that the law should possess certain formal or procedural characteristics that could guide the behaviour of individuals in society. Although he felt that it was not possible to provide a detailed or conclusive list of all these formal characteristics, Raz did consider that they should include the following:

- 'All laws should be prospective, open and clear';
- 'Laws should be relatively stable';

---

[61] Ibid 470.   [62] Ibid 470–4.   [63] Ibid 470.

[64] Friedrich Hayek, *The Road to Serfdom* (Routledge 1944) 54, cited in Keith Syrett, *The Foundations of Public Law: Principles and Problems of Power in the British Constitution* (2nd edn, Palgrave Macmillan 2014) 49, and Joseph Raz, 'The Rule of Law and its Virtue' (1977) 93 *Law Quarterly Review* 195, 195.

[65] See Friedrich Hayek, *The Road to Serfdom* (Routledge 1944), generally, and in particular 102.

[66] Paul P Craig, 'Formal and Substantive Conceptions of the Rule of Law: An Analytical Framework' (1997) *Public Law* 467, 467.

[67] Joseph Raz, 'The Rule of Law and its Virtue' (1977) 93 *Law Quarterly Review* 195, 198.

[68] Ibid 198.

- 'The making of particular laws (particular legal orders) should be guided by open, stable, clear and general rules';

- 'The independence of the judiciary must be guaranteed';

- 'The principles of natural justice must be observed';

- 'The courts should have review powers over the implementation of the other principles';

- 'The courts should be easily accessible';

- 'The discretion of the crime preventing agencies should not be allowed to pervert the law'.[69]

Pause for reflection

Raz's list is far from exhaustive. What other 'general characteristics' do you think might be relevant to a formal conception of the rule of law?

One of the consequences of viewing the rule of law from a purely formal or procedural perspective is that it does not take account of other values which might be deemed fundamental to the operation of a constitutional system, such as, for example, justice, fairness, equality, and the protection of individual rights. Though such values are included within certain substantive conceptions of the principle, as we will discuss, the formal conception's emphasis on procedural characteristics means that these are necessarily excluded due to the manner in which they refer to the substance of the law, rather than merely to the way in which it applies. Understanding this point is central to Raz's consideration of the rule of law, who explains that the principle 'is just one of the virtues which a legal system may possess and by which it is to be judged. It is not to be confused with democracy, justice, equality (before the law or otherwise), human rights of any kind or respect for the persons or for the dignity of man.'[70] It is not to say, however, that such values are by any means unimportant; rather, they are separate from the rule of law. For Raz, a conception of the rule of law that seeks to include these various other virtues (democracy, justice, equality, human rights) purports to set out 'a complete social philosophy'.[71]

A consequence of viewing such values as separate from the rule of law, though, is that a system that fails to promote equality or protect human rights can arguably still be consistent with the rule of law. Indeed, it follows from this that the rule of law, in its formal conception and devoid of any moral content, can be used either for good or for evil. As Raz himself goes on to state:

> A non-democratic legal system, based on the denial of human rights, on extensive poverty, on racial segregation, sexual inequalities and religious persecution may, in principle, conform to the requirements of the rule of law better than any of the legal systems of the more enlightened western democracies.[72]

---

[69] Ibid 198–202.   [70] Ibid 196.   [71] Ibid.   [72] Ibid.

Counterpoint: The moral content of the rule of law

Relevant to Raz's argument that the formal conception could be used either for good or evil purposes, it is interesting to observe that the notion of the rule of law is often employed as a political label to mark out differences in 'good' and 'bad' states, with castigation of those against whom we might seek action often justified on the perceived lack of compliance with the rule of law. For example, Tony Blair stated in a speech to the US Congress in 2003 that '[o]urs are not Western values, they are the universal values of the human spirit . . . freedom not tyranny; democracy not dictatorship; the rule of law not the rule of secret police'.[73]

This being so, do you think that this aspect of the formal conception of the rule of law presupposes a degree of moral content?

With this reality that the rule of law can be used for good or for evil in mind, it is interesting that Raz revisited his conception of the rule of law in an article published in 2019.[74] In it he remains loyal to the formal conception, explaining that

> rule of law principles are not about the content of the law, but about its mode of generation and application: they require that legal decisions and rules be anchored in stable general legal doctrines, made for publicly available reasons, applied faithfully observing due process, etc.[75]

Raz goes on to discuss, however, that commonly stated principles espousing the need for, *inter alia*, clarity, stability, and generality of rules, inadequately explain *how* governments should comply with the rule of law. On this basis, he goes on to elucidate an explanation of the principle that emphasizes the 'commonly agreed, aim of the rule of law . . . to avoid *arbitrary government*' and the notion that 'governments may act only in the interests of the governed'.[76]

Raz also revisits his previous contention that the rule of law is separate from other 'virtues which a legal system may possess and by which it is to be judged'.[77] Though he repeats this claim, noting that '[t]he law should conform to a variety of moral principles and display a number of distinct moral virtues. The rule of law is one of them, but not the only one', he nonetheless goes on to concede that 'while the rule of law does not secure conformity to the other principles the law should conform to, it is close to being a condition for the law's ability to conform to them'.[78] In his most recent consideration of the rule of law principle, therefore, Raz both defends the formal basis for the rule of law, separate from other moral virtues, and goes further in emphasizing how governments should comply with the principle in avoiding the use of arbitrary power.

---

[73] Tony Blair, speech to US Congress, 2003—noted on the back cover of Tom Bingham, *The Rule of Law* (Allen Lane 2010).

[74] See: Joseph Raz, 'The Law's Own Virtue' (2019) 39(1) *Oxford Journal of Legal Studies* 1.

[75] Joseph Raz, 'The Law's Own Virtue' (2019) 39(1) *Oxford Journal of Legal Studies* 1, 2.

[76] Joseph Raz, 'The Law's Own Virtue' (2019) 39(1) *Oxford Journal of Legal Studies* 1, 5, and 14.

[77] Joseph Raz, 'The Rule of Law and its Virtue' (1977) 93 *Law Quarterly Review* 195, 196.

[78] Joseph Raz, 'The Law's Own Virtue' (2019) 39(1) *Oxford Journal of Legal Studies* 1, 9, and 15.

Another proponent of the rule of law is Tom Bingham, who offers 'an account of the value of the rule of law, focusing upon the extent to which the maintenance of the rule of law can provide the foundation for a fair and just society which respects fundamental rights and civil liberties'.[79] Bingham's conception, while demonstrating certain characteristics of a substantive view,[80] is ultimately and generally formal insofar as it requires that the law fulfil certain characteristics to ensure it is accessible to all, passed correctly, and used appropriately. Indeed, Bingham himself notes that at the heart of the rule of law is the idea 'that all persons and authorities within the state . . . should be bound by and entitled to the benefit of laws publicly made, taking effect (generally) in the future and publicly administered in the courts'.[81] He underlines the ultimate importance of formal values in ensuring that the rule of law is universally upheld. Although, as Young notes, Bingham's conception emphasizes the importance of providing a 'foundation for a fair and just society which respects fundamental rights and civil liberties',[82] the acknowledgement that the rule of law *contributes* to this foundation, rather than contains the substantive rights and liberties to be protected, further underlines the formal nature of his conception. On this foundation, Bingham identifies eight principles on which his view of the rule of law is based:

1. 'The law must be accessible and so far as possible intelligible, clear and predictable';[83]

2. 'Questions of legal right and liability should ordinarily be resolved by application of the law and not the exercise of discretion';[84]

3. 'The laws of the land should apply equally to all, save to the extent that objective differences justify differentiation';[85]

4. 'Ministers and public officers at all levels must exercise the powers conferred on them in good faith, fairly, for the purpose for which the powers were conferred, without exceeding the limits of such powers and not unreasonably';[86]

5. 'The law must afford adequate protection of fundamental human rights';[87]

6. 'Means must be provided for resolving, without prohibitive cost or inordinate delay, bona fide civil disputes which the parties themselves are unable to resolve';[88]

7. 'Adjudicative procedures provided by the state should be fair';[89]

8. 'The rule of law requires compliance by the state with its obligations in international law as well as in national law'.[90]

Echoing aspects of Raz's conception, Bingham's rule of law goes right to the very heart of what the formal view is about—ensuring the protection of due legal process; the clear, open, and general publication and application of laws and the ultimate provision of a platform upon which a legal system sympathetic to values of equality and human rights can be built.

---

[79] Alison L Young, 'The Rule of Law in the United Kingdom: Formal or Substantive?' (2012) 6 *International Journal of Constitutional Law* 259, 260.

[80] Indeed, Young argues that Bingham's consideration of the rule of law displays 'elements of the substantive rule of law', insofar as it requires the laws to ensure protection of fundamental human rights and adhere to principles of procedural fairness and natural justice (ibid 261).

[81] Tom Bingham, *The Rule of Law* (Allen Lane 2010) 37.

[82] Alison L Young, 'The Rule of Law in the United Kingdom: Formal or Substantive?' (2012) 6 *International Journal of Constitutional Law* 259, 260.

[83] Tom Bingham, *The Rule of Law* (Allen Lane 2010) 37.   [84] Ibid 48.   [85] Ibid 55.

[86] Ibid 60.   [87] Ibid 66.   [88] Ibid 85.   [89] Ibid 90.   [90] Ibid 110.

Exploration of Dicey, Raz, Hayek, and Bingham's considerations of the rule of law helps to explain the formal conception of the principle, as this section has sought to demonstrate. In terms of understanding the way in which the formal view rule of law might apply in the UK Constitution, however, it is necessary to look closely at a number of cases, the first being *R (Anufrijeva) v Secretary of State for the Home Department*.[91]

Case in depth: *R (Anufrijeva) v Secretary of State for the Home Department* **[2004] 1 AC 604**

In this case, the claimant was an asylum seeker who was receiving benefits for income support. When her application to remain in the UK was rejected, her benefits were stopped immediately, pursuant to regulation 70(3A) of the Income Support (General) Regulations 1987, which she no longer satisfied. These benefits had been stopped, however, before the applicant had been notified about the outcome of her asylum application. She sought to challenge the rejection of the asylum application by way of judicial review. Finding in favour of the claimant, the House of Lords determined that Anufrijeva should have received benefits right up until the moment that she was told of the application's outcome.

Demonstrating the relevance of this decision to formal considerations of the rule of law, Lord Steyn set out a 'view . . . reinforced by the constitutional principle requiring the rule of law to be observed', finding that 'a constitutional state must accord to individuals the right to know of a decision before their rights can be adversely affected'.[92] Such a requirement was not stipulated by positive law, but was nonetheless deemed to be a procedural value that should be followed, enabling adherence to the characteristics of openness and clarity that a legal system must possess if it is to adhere to the rule of law.

Another case that touches upon aspects of the formal conception of the rule of law is the more recent case of *R (on the application of Reilly (No 2) and another) v Secretary of State for Work and Pensions*.[93]

Case in depth: *R (on the application of Reilly (No 2) and another) v Secretary of State for Work and Pensions* **[2014] EWHC 2182 (Admin)**

Reilly was unemployed and receiving Jobseeker's Allowance. Pursuant to the Jobseeker's Allowance (Employment, Skills and Enterprise Scheme) Regulations 2011, she was required to undertake unpaid work while claiming the allowance. If she did not participate in the scheme, the regulations provided that her allowance could be withdrawn. Participation in this scheme, however, meant that Reilly was unable to continue volunteering in a local museum, a position she held with a view to pursuing a career in that field. By contrast, the position given to her under the Jobseeker's scheme (a job at Poundland) did not, she thought, offer any long-term career prospects. Reilly sought to challenge the policy requiring her to work for Poundland in order that she could obtain her allowance.[94]

→

---

[91] [2004] 1 AC 604.   [92] Ibid [28].   [93] [2014] EWHC 2182 (Admin).

[94] See *R (on the application of Reilly (No 1) and another) v Secretary of State for Work and Pensions* [2013] UKSC 68.

→

The Court of Appeal held that the 2011 Regulations were *ultra vires* the Jobseekers Act 1995. Before the Supreme Court had heard the subsequent appeal, the Jobseekers (Back to Work Schemes) Act 2013 had been enacted, which retrospectively validated the 2011 Regulations, even though the Court of Appeal had found them *ultra vires*. The Supreme Court, in view of the new Act, found in favour of the government.

This case (*Reilly (No 2)*) was therefore brought to challenge the compatibility of the 2013 Act with the European Convention on Human Rights. It was there argued that its retrospective (rather than prospective) force and the manner in which it had impacted on simultaneous legal proceedings contravened the Article 6 right to a fair trial, insofar as the Act effectively gave the Court no option but to find against Reilly. The Administrative Court found in favour of Reilly and issued a declaration of incompatibility, pursuant to section 4 of the Human Rights Act 1998.

Though the implications of this judgment for the relationship between the rule of law and parliamentary sovereignty are discussed later in the chapter, it is relevant to the discussion here for the manner in which the court sought to uphold the importance of formal values, even in the face of opposing statutory authority. On this, Mrs Justice Lang stated, in giving judgment, that:

> [A]lthough Parliament is not precluded in civil matters from adopting new retrospective provisions to regulate rights arising under existing laws, the principle of the rule of law and the notion of a fair trial and equality of arms contained in Article 6(1) 'precludes any interference by the legislature . . . with the administration of justice designed to influence the judicial determination of a dispute' or 'influencing the judicial determination of a dispute to which the State is a party'.[95]

These principles, she continued:

> accurately reflect fundamental principles of the UK's unwritten constitution. The constitutional principle of the rule of law was expressly recognised in section 1, Constitutional Reform Act 2005. It requires, *inter alia*, that Parliament and the Executive recognise and respect the separation of powers and abide by the principle of legality. Although the Crown in Parliament is the sovereign legislative power, the Courts have the constitutional role of determining and enforcing legality. Thus, Parliament's undoubted power to legislate to overrule the effect of court judgments generally ought not to take the form of retrospective legislation designed to favour the Executive in ongoing litigation in the courts brought against it by one of its citizens, unless there are compelling reasons to do so. Otherwise it is likely to offend a citizen's sense of fair play.[96]

Reilly (No 2) exemplifies the court's protection of what can be seen as formal values relevant to the rule of law. The rejection of retrospective legislation, of note, was a characteristic identified by Raz as being contrary to the guidance of effective action, while Parliament's interference in ongoing legal action jeopardizes both the clarity and predictability of the law and hinders the resolution of disputes through the ordinary legal process.

---

[95] [2014] EWHC 2182 (Admin) [81], citing *Zielinkski v France* (1999) 31 EHRR 532 [57], and *National & Provincial Building Society v United Kingdom* (1997) 25 EHRR 127 [112].

[96] [2014] EWHC 2182 (Admin) [82].

The most recently significant case demonstrating protection of values aligned to a formal conception of the rule of law, however, is *R (Unison) v Lord Chancellor.*[97] Here, a challenge was brought in respect of the Employment Tribunals and the Employment Appeal Tribunal Fees Order 2013, which introduced a more stringent regime for the payment of fees in cases brought before the relevant tribunals. The challenge was made on the basis that the new regime served as a restriction on the right of access to the courts. In upholding the challenge, the Supreme Court emphasized that:

> The constitutional right of access to the courts is inherent in the rule of law . . . Courts exist in order to ensure that the laws made by Parliament, and the common law created by the courts themselves, are applied and enforced. That role includes ensuring that the executive branch of government carries out its functions in accordance with the law. In order for the courts to perform that role, people must in principle have unimpeded access to them. Without such access, laws are liable to become a dead letter, the work done by Parliament may be rendered nugatory, and the democratic elections of Members of Parliament may become a meaningless charade.[98]

In both *Reilly (No 2)* and the *Unison* case, the courts' identification of the Article 6 right to fair trial and the right of access to the courts, respectively, might inspire consideration of the substantive conception of the rule of law, that being rooted more firmly in the requirement of certain rights and moral principles. However, it is clear from both judgments and from this discussion that we are concerned not with the content of the law, but with the formalities required in administering the law and ensuring an effective working system. Indeed, we can see that Raz identified the procedural protection of rights as being crucial to the formal conception, including—and specifically—the right of access to the courts. Having now explained and explored formal conceptions of the rule of law, it is necessary to consider those offering a substantive approach to the rule of law.

3.4.2 Substantive conceptions of the rule of law

Substantive conceptions of the rule of law build on and accept the values and procedural characteristics offered by the formal conception of the rule of law. They are also concerned, though, with the content of the law, arguing that it should include certain moral content in some form. Returning to Craig, he explains that:

> Those who espouse substantive conceptions of the rule of law seek to go beyond [the formal conception]. They accept that the rule of law has the formal attributes mentioned above, but they wish to take the doctrine further. Certain substantive rights are said to be based on, or derived from, the rule of law. The concept is used as the foundation for these rights, which are then used to distinguish between 'good' laws, which comply with such rights, and 'bad' laws which do not.[99]

Substantive conceptions of the rule of law are generally more complex and varied than those which underpin the formal approach. Some, such as Dworkin, espouse a theory focusing on the individual, ensuring the protection of their rights, for instance.

---

[97] [2017] UKSC 51.   [98] [2017] UKSC 51 [66] and [68].
[99] Paul P Craig, 'Formal and Substantive Conceptions of the Rule of Law: An Analytical Framework' (1997) *Public Law* 467, 467.

Others, like Allan, offer a view that focuses more on government institutions and the need to ensure adherence to proper procedure. Indeed, Allan's substantive conception makes for an appropriate starting point.

Allan was sympathetic to Raz's view and his acknowledgement of 'the dangers of subscribing to a substantive conception'.[100] Equally, though he was also concerned that Raz's conception was 'unduly modest' and capable of expansion and elaboration 'without [the] danger of collapse into a full-scale theory of social justice'.[101] Though Allan also rejects 'any rigid distinction between procedure and substance, as artificial and unworkable',[102] he is undoubtedly substantive in his own conception. Central to his consideration of the rule of law is the view that formal conceptions are in fact founded upon substantive values, a point he makes in arguing that the procedural value of 'generality of laws' is insufficient of itself to ensure the preservation of equality and that substantive values must also be included. Making the point, Allan argues that:

> The formal or procedural canons that constitute an essential strand of any coherent account of the rule of law must be interpreted in the light of further principles that explain the connection between law and justice. Formal equality must be supplemented by a more substantive conception: rules of fair procedure, narrowly conceived, must be expanded to include principles of due process, requiring the rational justification of the laws according to consistent principles of public policy; and judicial independence must be annexed to a more fully elaborated separation of powers, denying the executive government power to alter the law at the same time as it asserts its authority in any particular case.[103]

Elsewhere, Allan goes on to explore what this substantive equality entails and considers the manner in which the common law works to uphold, enforce, and apply its values and principles when deciding cases.[104] On this, he suggests that:

> [t]he common law articulates the content of the common good, according to the society's shared values and traditions . . . [its] strength . . . lies in its inherent commitment to rationality and equality. Adherence to precedent ensures that like cases are treated alike, ensuring equality of treatment.[105]

Although it is not a view without its critics,[106] Allan offers a conception of the rule of law founded on the view that substantive values of equality underpin the very meaning of the rule of law and are, as a consequence of our common law system, protected through decisions and principles applied in the courts. Allan's conception, and particularly his views with regards to the common law, can be linked to another proponent of the substantive conception—Ronald Dworkin. Dworkin's discussion of the rule of

---

[100] Ibid 481.

[101] TRS Allan, 'The Rule of Law as the Rule of Reason: Consent and Constitutionalism' (1999) 115 *Law Quarterly Review* 221, 222.

[102] TRS Allan, *Constitutional Justice: A Liberal Theory for the Rule of Law* (OUP 2001) 1.

[103] Ibid 59.

[104] See TRS Allan, 'The Rule of Law as the Rule of Reason: Consent and Constitutionalism' (1999) 115 *Law Quarterly Review* 221, generally and, in particular, 239–44.

[105] Ibid 239.

[106] It is worth reading Craig's reservations regarding Allan's view: Paul P Craig, 'Formal and Substantive Conceptions of the Rule of Law: An Analytical Framework' (1997) *Public Law* 467, 481–4.

law centres on a distinction he identifies between a 'rule book' conception of the rule of law and a rights conception.[107] The first of these can be associated with the formal view and is, in a broad sense, compatible with Raz. Dworkin states that the rule book conception:

> insists that, so far as is possible, the power of the state should never be exercised against individual citizens except in accordance with rules explicitly set out in a public rule book available to all. The government as well as ordinary citizens must play by these public rules until they are changed, in accordance with further rules about how they are to be changed.[108]

Drawing similarities with proponents of the formal view, we can here pick out from Dworkin's rule book conception values of, *inter alia*, openness, prospectivity, generality of laws; features of Raz's own conception of the rule of law. Though he identifies this aspect of the rule of law, however, Dworkin sees the rule book conception as being insufficient of itself for the achievement of justice. Instead, he views it simply as a part of a broader 'theory of law and adjudication'[109] that takes account of his conception of rights. Dworkin's rights conception:

> assumes that citizens have moral rights and duties with respect to one-another, and political rights against the state as a whole. It insists that these moral and political rights be recognized in positive law, so that they may be enforced *upon the demand of individual citizens* through the courts and other judicial institutions of the familiar types, so far as this is practicable. The rule of law on this conception is the ideal of rule by an accurate public conception of individual rights.[110]

Like Allan, Dworkin therefore acknowledges the important role played by the courts in upholding and protecting substantive values, which in Dworkin's case consist of individual rights.

There are, of course, many other views that might fairly be said to encapsulate the substantive conception of the rule of law. This section's discussion of Allan and Dworkin, however, has demonstrated the manner in which the rule of law, in the form of a substantive conception, might be said to include content, over and above formal characteristics already identified. Though the precise nature of this moral content can differ in details from conception to conception, as this section's discussion of Allan and Dworkin has shown, it can be exemplified by the protection of fundamental values and qualities that seek to preserve and protect individual rights, freedoms, and liberties.

Like the formal conception, support for a substantive conception of the rule of law is evident in case law. The first case we consider is *R v Lord Chancellor, ex p Witham*.[111]

---

[107] See Ronald Dworkin, *A Matter of Principle* (OUP 1985) 11–13.

[108] Ibid 11–12.

[109] Paul P Craig, 'Formal and Substantive Conceptions of the Rule of Law: An Analytical Framework' (1997) *Public Law* 467, 478.

[110] Ronald Dworkin, *A Matter of Principle* (OUP 1985) 11–12.   [111] [1998] QB 575.

> ## Case in depth: *R v Lord Chancellor, ex p Witham* [1998] QB 575
>
> The Lord Chancellor, using powers of secondary legislation granted under section 130(1) of the Supreme Court Act 1981 (now Senior Courts Act 1981), sought to repeal a statutory instrument—the Supreme Court Fees Order 1980—that provided relief to those on income support from the obligation to pay court fees. The issue had arisen when Witham, on income support, had sought to bring an action for malicious falsehood and libel, but had found the rules regarding his obligation to pay fees changed by the Lord Chancellor. Unable to pay these fees, he brought an application for judicial review, arguing that the section 130 power could not be used to deny individuals their constitutional right of access to the courts and that the 1996 Order was therefore *ultra vires*. The court found in favour of Witham and held that the exercise of discretionary power must take account of fundamental rights.

In the context of the rule of law, *Witham* is an interesting decision. Laws J, in giving the leading judgment, explained the common law basis for the constitutional right of access to the courts and stressed that the right could only be limited by primary legislation. In the absence of such legislation here, Laws J stated that the constitutional right acted as an implied limitation on the exercise of the secondary legislative power.[112] The consistency of this judgment with substantive conceptions of the rule of law is evident in the fact that, above and beyond the wording of section 130—which provided simply that the Lord Chancellor had the power to 'prescribe the fees to be taken in the . . . [Senior] Court'[113]—the court found the constitutional right of access to the courts as being significantly implied as to justify this particular use *ultra vires*. Indeed, echoing this view, Forsyth and Elliott note that *Witham* exemplifies a 'mode of statutory construction' on which enabling legislation can be 'subjected to a form of constitutional interpretation which leads to the implication of principles of good administration founded upon the rule of law'.[114]

 Pause for reflection

Do you agree with the decision in *R v Lord Chancellor, ex p Witham*? How fair is it that the courts should be able to imply constitutional rights into the law, altering the reading of an otherwise straightforward statutory provision?

Another, more recent, case exemplifying the relevance of substantive values to rule of law judgments is *R (on the application of Bourgass and another) v Secretary of State for Justice*.[115]

---

[112] Ibid 579–80.   [113] Section 130(1) of the Senior Courts Act 1981.

[114] Christopher Forsyth and Mark Elliott, 'The Legitimacy of Judicial Review' (2003) *Public Law* 286, 304. For a more in-depth discussion of *Witham*, see Mark Elliott, *The Constitutional Foundations of Judicial Review* (Hart Publishing 2001) 213–14.   [115] [2015] UKSC 54.

> ### Case in depth: *R (on the application of Bourgass and another) v Secretary of State for Justice* [2015] UKSC 54
>
> This case concerned the solitary confinement of three prisoners already serving time for a number of serious offences. Pursuant to rule 45(1) of the Prison Rules 1999, and following fights with other prisoners, the claimants were placed in solitary confinement for several months.
>
> Rule 45(1) of the Prison Rules provides that prisoners can be placed in solitary confinement, where desirable for the maintenance of good order, for a period not exceeding seventy-two hours in the first instance, with the permission of the Secretary of State needed to extend that confinement for a further fourteen days, that permission being susceptible to renewal after the fourteen days is passed. These procedural requirements were met, with the claimants' confinement being reviewed and extended at regular intervals, albeit by a prison manager rather than the Secretary of State directly.
>
> The claimants sought judicial review of their continued solitary confinement, first on the grounds of breach of their ECHR rights (Article 6) and, secondly, on the contention that the prison manager did not have sufficient authority to extent their confinement under the Prison Rules. The Supreme Court upheld their appeal on both grounds, finding that while a prisoner did not enjoy a right to be with the general population under Article 6, the common law standard of procedural fairness had not been met since insufficient information pertaining to the claimants' continued confinement had not been imparted. On the second ground, the Supreme Court held that while the initial seventy-two hours of the prisoners' solitary confinement had been appropriately authorized, it was thereafter unlawful as the Secretary of State's permission had not been sought and granted; a prison manager could not grant an extension since he was not impartial.[116]

Though the facts of *Bourgass* raise a number of issues, relevant to this discussion is the court's finding that the common law standard of procedural fairness had not been appropriately observed. Putting aside the fact that the court held that the decision to extend the period of confinement was *ultra vires* the Prison Rules, the implication of their judgment is such that it expects a basic standard of fairness to be observed in abiding by the rules, such that information must be provided to those prisoners subject to solitary confinement, explaining the rationale for their continued separation from the general population. In terms of our discussion here, the requirement that certain standards of justice and fairness be read into legal provisions in this way, and observed in their basic application, is consistent with the substantive conception of the rule of law.[117] Indeed, this is supported by the following statement by Lord Reed:

> a prisoner should normally have a reasonable opportunity to make representations before a decision is taken by the Secretary of State under rule 45(2). That follows from the

---

[116] For further discussion of the complex facts surrounding this case: Matrix Legal Information Team Case Comments, 'Case Comment: R (Bourgass & Anor) v Secretary of State for Justice [2015] UKSC 54' (UK Supreme Court Blog, 17 August 2015), http://ukscblog.com/case-comment-r-bourgass-anor-v-secretary-of-state-for-justice-2015-uksc-54/; and Mark Elliott, 'Bourgass in the Supreme Court: Solitary Confinement, the Carltona Doctrine and Procedural Fairness' (Public Law for Everyone, 29 July 2015), https://publiclawforeveryone.com/2015/07/29/bourgass-in-the-supreme-court-solitary-confinement-the-carltona-doctrine-and-procedural-fairness/.

[117] It is helpful, at this point, to refer back to 3.4.1 where the notion of fairness, as a part of Bingham's conception of the rule of law, was identified as reflecting more of a substantive aspect.

seriousness of the consequences for the prisoner of a decision authorising his segregation for a further 14 days; the fact that authority is sought on the basis of information concerning him, and in particular concerning his conduct or the conduct of others towards him; the fact that he may be able to answer allegations made, or to provide relevant information; and, in those circumstances, from the common law's insistence that administrative power should be exercised in a manner which is fair.[118]

Bourgass then provides further authority supporting a substantive conception in respect of the UK Constitution's approach to the rule of law.

This section has explored broader theories of the rule of law, namely formal and substantive conceptions, examining theorists who offer views in line with those conceptions and case law that support their relevance in respect of the UK Constitution. Although it is easy to think of the rule of law as starting with Dicey's principle, in truth the rule of law has its origins much, much earlier, and as this section has demonstrated, his view is merely one amongst many. Others, arguing both for a formal and a substantive conception of the rule of law, demonstrate the complex nature of the principle and the broader debate concerning what the rule of law actually entails. Having explored in detail the various conceptions of the rule of law, however, it is necessary now to consider how the rule of law applies more broadly in the UK Constitution.

 Discussing the problem

Have another look at the problem scenario. Keeping in mind the Freedom from the Press (Government Privacy) Act 2023, to what extent do the actions of the government conflict with a formal or a substantive conception of the rule of law?

One aspect of the problem scenario that raises a number of points is the Freedom from the Press (Government Privacy) Act 2023's provision which states that '[t]he publication or revelation of Government policies and decisions before formal announcement is unlawful' and Fred's subsequent charge under this provision. This raises a number of issues from the perspective of both a formal and a substantive conception of the rule of law. With regards to the formal conception of the rule of law, this provision is problematic from the point of view of retroactivity. The Act is passed by Parliament and *then* Fred is charged under its provision. The effect this has is that Fred is essentially charged with something that was not actually an offence when he carried out the actions in question. This goes against the formal conception of the rule of law and, in particular, features of the principle identified by Raz. With regards to the substantive conception, the provision and Fred's subsequent charge for its offence raise a number of issues concerning potential breaches of fundamental rights. The whole episode arises, it seems, to prevent Fred from exercising 'free speech', though he later experiences violations of his right to liberty and his right to a fair trial (through the unlawful arrest and detention), both of which are protected under the ECHR.

[118] [2015] UKSC 54 [98].

WHAT DOES THE RULE OF LAW MEAN IN THE MODERN UK CONSTITUTION?

101

3.5 What does the rule of law mean in the modern UK Constitution?

The beginning of this chapter discussed how Magna Carta, in 1215, represented the establishment of core values that are today reflected at the heart of the rule of law. Since that time, however, the relevance and significance of the principle has developed and the nature of its application in the UK Constitution, particularly bearing in mind the variance of thinking, is something that has become increasingly complex. This section aims to bring together the various considerations of the rule of law and to explore the manner in which the principle can be said to apply in the modern UK Constitution. In doing this, it explores three themes: first, the rule of law, executive power, and judicial review; secondly, the relationship between the rule of law and parliamentary sovereignty; and finally, the role that human rights plays alongside the rule of law.

3.5.1 Rule of law, executive power, and judicial review

In the UK Constitution today, one of the most significant roles that the rule of law plays is in the monitoring of executive power and discretion. Indeed, this is a role that goes back to and that has developed since the case of *Entick v Carrington*.[119] Over the past century, however, the nature and the role of the executive has changed and, as a consequence, the manner in which the rule of law can be said to apply has become increasingly prominent.

The most significant way in which the rule of law serves as a check on executive power is through the development of judicial review of administrative action. As a set form of action, judicial review has only really been a part of the UK constitutional system since the 1960s and a line of cases that established the principles on which it is now founded.[120] Judicial review is explored in detail throughout Chapters 10–13. For now, though, note that it is a process whereby applications can be brought before the courts by interested and affected persons on the basis of executive or administrative decisions, policies, or actions that are allegedly illegal, irrational, disproportionate, or procedurally improper. It is seen as a way in which the exercise of discretionary power or authority, usually conferred on the executive by Parliament, can be checked and scrutinized by the courts. On this basis, the courts have a supervisory jurisdiction to scrutinize the acts and decisions of the executive, but not to substitute their decisions with that of the court. It is, in essence, a way in which the courts can hold the executive to account and, in this way, it is a mechanism for the rule of law insofar as it seeks to ensure the lawfulness of executive action. Jowell emphasizes the importance of judicial review in providing the rule of law with 'its most significant recent development', also noting that '[t]he practical application of the rule of law' through judicial review demonstrates both its formal and substantive values.[121] He explains further:

> The first two 'grounds' of judicial review, illegality and procedural impropriety, are based in large part on the rule of law. Under the ground of illegality the courts act as guardians of Parliament's intent and purpose, seeking to ensure that officials act within the scope of

---

[119] See 3.2.

[120] Adam Tomkins, *Public Law* (OUP 2003) 171, citing *Ridge v Baldwin* [1964] AC 40; *Padfield v Minister of Agriculture, Fisheries and Food* [1968] AC 997; *Conway v Rimmer* [1968] AC 910; and *Anisminic v Foreign Compensation Commission* [1969] 2 AC 147.

[121] Jeffrey Jowell, 'The Rule of Law's Long Arm: Uncommunicated Decisions' (2004) *Public Law* 246, 246.

their lawful powers. Even failure to implement a scheme authorised by Parliament can fall foul of the rule of law [as in *R v Secretary of State for Home Affairs, ex p Fire Brigades Union*[122]]. The content of the rule of law broadens under the ground of procedural impropriety, where the courts require a fair trial and lack of bias on the part of the decision-maker. The protection of the 'legitimate expectation' is itself grounded in the rule of law's core requirement of legal certainty.

Under the third ground of judicial review, that of irrationality (or unreasonableness), the courts tread more warily before interfering with the decision of the primary decision-maker, but have nevertheless justified their intervention . . . upon the rule of law's substantive content.[123]

There are a number of cases that Jowell uses to illustrate the relationship between judicial review, the principle of legality, and the rule of law,[124] a couple of which are worth further consideration here. The first case is *Wheeler v Leicester City Council*.[125]

Case in depth: *Wheeler v Leicester City Council* [1985] AC 1054

Here, Leicester City Council sought to prevent members of the local rugby club from travelling to South Africa for a rugby tour during the apartheid regime. The council believed that going ahead with the tour would signal support for the racist regime that prevailed at that time. By contrast, certain members of the club believed that the tour would serve to show support for those who suffered at the hands of the apartheid regime and act as a force for good. On this basis, they proceeded with the tour and travelled to South Africa, against the council's instructions. As punishment, the local council imposed a one-year ban on the rugby club, preventing them from using the local recreation ground. The club challenged this decision through an application for judicial review, arguing that the council had exercised its powers for an improper purpose. The rugby club was successful, with the House of Lords finding that the punishment had been imposed improperly on the basis that the rugby club had done nothing wrong, other than merely going against the wishes of the council.

This case demonstrates the role that judicial review can play in upholding the rule of law by providing an example of the notion that punishment should not be imposed where there is no breach of the law, an aspect of the principle highlighted, most notably, by Dicey. The relevance of this particular aspect is highlighted by the view of Browne-Wilkinson LJ, who noted that '[i]n my judgment it is undoubtedly part of the constitution of this country that, in the absence of express legislative provision to the contrary,

---

[122] [1995] 2 AC 513.

[123] Jeffrey Jowell, 'The Rule of Law's Long Arm: Uncommunicated Decisions' (2004) *Public Law* 246, 246–7.

[124] Ibid 247. Also see: *Wheeler v Leicester City Council* [1985] AC 1054 (HL); *R v Secretary of State for the Home Department, ex p Leech (No 2)* [1994] QB 198; *R v Lord Chancellor, ex p Witham* [1997] 1 WLR 104; *R v Secretary of State for the Home Department, ex p Pierson* [1998] AC 539; *R v North and East Devon Health Authority, ex p Coughlan* [2001] EWCA Civ 1870; *R v Secretary of State for the Home Department, ex p Simms* [1999] UKHL 33.   [125] [1985] AC 1054.

each individual has the right to hold and express his own view'.[126] Another, more recent, case, though, which exemplifies the relationship between judicial review and the rule of law, is *R v Secretary of State for the Home Department, ex p Pierson*.[127]

Case in depth: *R v Secretary of State for the Home Department, ex p Pierson* [1998] AC 539

Pierson was convicted of murdering his parents and was sentenced to two concurrent life sentences. The trial judge and the Lord Chief Justice stipulated that Pierson should serve at least fifteen years of his sentence. In 1993, however, following changes to the regime relating to the policy concerning mandatory life sentences, the Secretary of State felt that, due to the conviction for a double murder, twenty years should be the appropriate length of time to be served, increasing Pierson's sentence accordingly.

Pierson brought an application for judicial review of the Secretary of State's decision, noting that there had been no new aggravating features since the original sentence had been imposed. The House of Lords found for Pierson and agreed that the decision to impose the increased sentence had been made in the absence of any exceptional circumstances and that, furthermore, the Secretary of State had not had the power to increase the length of time where it had previously been fixed. The decision was quashed.

The need to honour values consistent with the rule of law was noted by Lord Steyn in this case, who stated in the House of Lords that:

> Unless there is the clearest provision to the contrary, Parliament must be presumed not to legislate contrary to the rule of law. And the rule of law enforces minimum standards of fairness, both substantive and procedural . . . It is true that the principle of legality only has prima facie force. But in enacting section 35(2) of the [Criminal Justice] Act of 1991, with its very wide power to release prisoners, Parliament left untouched the fundamental principle that a sentence lawfully passed should not retrospectively be increased. Parliament must therefore be presumed to have enacted legislation wide enough to enable the Home Secretary to make decisions on punishment on the basis that he would observe the normal constraint governing that function. Instead the Home Secretary has asserted a general power to increase tariffs duly fixed. Parliament did not confer such a power on the Home Secretary. It follows that the Home Secretary did not have the power to increase a tariff lawfully fixed.[128]

The issue in *Pierson*, and the House of Lords' judgment, went right to the very heart of the rule of law principle in upholding the need to ensure prospectivity of laws and policies. The importance of this notion has been emphasized by various theorists, as we have seen. As these cases serve to demonstrate, judicial review of administrative action provides a crucial medium through which the rule of law can be upheld. Through enabling the courts to scrutinize and review acts and decisions of the executive, judicial review affords the opportunity to consider whether the executive is honouring fundamental aspects of law-making and governance that go to the heart of the rule of law principle. The courts, however, have not always been so ready and willing to scrutinize the actions of

---

[126] Ibid 1063.   [127] [1998] AC 539.   [128] Ibid 591.

the executive to assess their consistency with the rule of law. In *Liversidge v Anderson*,[129] a case that pre-dates the development of modern judicial review, the court was rather more restrained in its approach.

Case in depth: *Liversidge v Anderson* **[1942] AC 206**

During the Second World War, an emergency power was given to the Home Secretary by regulation 18B of the Defence (General) Regulations 1939, under which he had the authority to detain individuals he had reasonable cause to believe were of hostile association. This was a power exercised against Liversidge who, when detained, brought an action for false imprisonment against the Home Secretary. The court held that the Home Secretary was not obliged to give particulars of the reasonable cause for believing the individual to be of hostile association and, as such, Liversidge's case failed.

The court's discussions in *Liversidge v Anderson* focused primarily on whether or not the Home Secretary's reasonable cause for believing Liversidge to be of hostile association could be assessed objectively by the court, or whether a subjective test would suffice (ie the Home Secretary informing the court that his causes for detaining the individual were reasonable and the court accepting this). In the House of Lords, by a majority of 4–1, the subjective test was favoured. Lord Atkin dissented. The basis for the majority view was the question of justiciability.[130] Their Lordships felt that whether or not the Home Secretary's belief was reasonable was an executive or political decision and not one that was within the remit of the courts to determine. It therefore sufficed for the Home Secretary to inform the court that he had reasonable cause for believing Liversidge to be of hostile association. He was not required to go further and explain either the basis for that belief or have that subjected to judicial scrutiny. In terms of the rule of law, this decision is striking since, though the courts were called upon to decide a question relating to the exercise of executive power, they were reluctant to explore the matter in too much detail, instead finding that the issue was out of their remit.

Compared with many of the judicial review cases that came after *Liversidge*, and indeed keeping in mind earlier cases such as *Entick v Carrington*, it is interesting that the courts were reluctant to intervene here, particularly since the matter at issue—detention without due process—is one that goes right to the very heart of the rule of law principle. There are many potential reasons underlying this, however, including the fact that the country was at war when the case was heard, so the courts may have been reluctant to overrule executive action taken with the war effort in mind. It is hardly surprising, however, that the courts have since been inclined and more willing to investigate executive action, in the name of the rule of law, as the cases we have discussed demonstrate.

 Pause for reflection

In view of the judgment in *Liversidge v Anderson*, to what extent to you think the power assigned under the regulation permits unquestioned executive authority, or do you think that the question of reasonableness should be for a court to determine?

---

[129] [1942] AC 206.   [130] See 10.2.1.

Almost forty years after *Liversidge v Anderson*, the courts were once again called upon to consider the lawfulness of executive action in the case of *IRC v Rossminster*.[131] Similar to *Liversidge*, this case involved consideration of a provision empowering the executive to act in the event of a 'reasonable cause'. Unlike *Liversidge*, however, the courts felt able to assess the lawfulness of the warrant. Though it was ultimately deemed lawful, it is interesting that the House of Lords rejected the previous authority. Indeed, Lord Diplock stated that '[f]or my part I think the time has come to acknowledge openly that the majority of this House in Liversidge v. Anderson were expediently and, at that time, perhaps, excusably, wrong and the dissenting speech of Lord Atkin was right'.[132]

Counterpoint: Criticisms of *Liversidge v Anderson*

The majority decision in *Liversidge v Anderson* has often been the source of much discussion and debate, with some suggesting that it deferred to the government's decision at the expense of allowing a situation that might, in other circumstances, be deemed unlawful. Indeed, Lord Atkin criticized his colleagues in stating that the majority view was 'more executive-minded than the executive'.[133] Stable J also wrote to Lord Atkin in the aftermath of the case and similarly criticized the majority judges for being no longer 'lions under the throne, but mice squeaking under a chair in the Home Office'.[134]

In view of these criticisms and in the context of the wider judgment, do you think that the decision in *Liversidge v Anderson* would have been different if the country had not been at war at the time?

The courts' willingness to investigate executive action in the name of the rule of law is also evident in the previously considered case of *Re M*.[135] It has already been explained that this case was notable for the manner in which the court affirmed the equal subjection of all people before the law, on the basis that a government minister was as susceptible to criminal conviction as any ordinary citizen. In addition, it is also significant that the court found a Minister of the Crown to be in contempt of court, distinguishing his position from the individual monarch, who is immune from criminal prosecution. Despite these significant aspects of the judgment, however, there are some who consider that *Re M* amounts merely to a partial fulfilment of the rule of law.[136] The basis for this view is that, while, consistently with the rule of law, the Secretary of State was found personally to be in contempt of court, 'Lord Woolf [only] talked of contempt orders as lying either against the Minister "in his official capacity" or against "the office"'.[137] In other words, despite the finding of contempt of court, these were seen as 'ultimately unenforceable'[138] and therefore could not lie personally against the Minister. Nonetheless, the

---

[131] [1980] AC 952.   [132] Ibid 1011.

[133] [1942] AC 206, 244. Also see Stephen Sedley, *Lions under the Throne: Essays on the History of English Public Law* (Cambridge University Press 2015) 38.

[134] RFV Heuston, 'Liversidge v. Anderson in Retrospect' (1970) 86 *Law Quarterly Review* 33. Also see, for fuller discussion, Ian Loveland, *Constitutional Law, Administrative Law and Human Rights* (8th edn, OUP 2018) 61–3.   [135] [1994] 1 AC 377.

[136] Carol Harlow, 'Accidental Death of an Asylum Seeker' (1994) 57 *Modern Law Review* 620.

[137] Ibid 623, citing *M v Home Office* [1993] 3 WLR 433, 466.   [138] Ibid.

courts finding of contempt, and the willingness of the judiciary to investigate executive action in this case indicates the extent to which the rule of law can be used to ensure and monitor the lawfulness of executive action where that comes to impact negatively on the lives of others. Indeed, the significance of *Re M* is noted by Harlow, who comments that the case 'moved to cut down to size prerogative powers asserted by government and subject them to controls appropriate to a modern democracy'.[139] That is, in essence, what the rule of law is about.

It is clear that the judiciary have a fundamental role to play in upholding and protecting values at the heart of the rule of law. This is evident through judicial review proceedings, but more widely, through actions where the courts have been called upon to consider acts, policies, and decisions of the executive. The line of cases discussed has shown an increasing willingness on the part of the judiciary to strike down decisions of the executive where it appears that values consistent with the rule of law are not upheld. As the next section will explain, however, the rule of law has a somewhat different relationship with Parliament.

3.5.2 The rule of law and the legislative function

Although the rule of law can be used as a basis on which to examine executive action, as the previous section has explained, the way in which it works in relation to Parliament is different, chiefly due to the sovereign nature of the legislature and the consequent understanding that Parliament cannot be questioned or challenged by other institutions of the constitution. In exploring the relationship between the rule of law and the sovereign legislative function, we must start by turning back to Dicey, who himself considered the relationship between the two principles. He stated that:

> The sovereignty of Parliament and the supremacy of the law of the land—the two principles which pervade the whole of the English constitution—may appear to stand in opposition to each other, or to be at best only counterbalancing forces. But this is not so; the sovereignty of Parliament . . . favours the supremacy of law, whilst the predominance of rigid legality throughout our institutions evokes the exercise and thus increases the authority of Parliamentary sovereignty.[140]

Dicey goes on to explain this on a number of grounds. First, the compatibility of the sovereignty of Parliament with the rule of law is justified by the fact that 'Parliament . . . has never, except at periods of revolution, exercised direct executive power or appointed the officials of the executive government', but is instead confined to acting 'through the combined action of its three constituent parts', the will of Parliament capable only of being expressed through Acts of Parliament.[141] Secondly, Dicey observed that 'Parliament, though sovereign . . . has never been able to use the powers of the government as a means of interfering with the regular course of law',[142] and that, once enacted, Acts immediately became 'subject to judicial interpretation'.[143] Thirdly, Dicey believed that the rule of law was itself compatible with the sovereignty of Parliament, a belief he based on the view

---

[139] Ibid 626.
[140] AV Dicey *Introduction to the Study of the Law of the Constitution* (JWF Allison ed, first published 1885, OUP 2013) 180.   [141] Ibid 180.
[142] Ibid 181.   [143] Ibid 180.

that any discretionary uses of executive power which are, at times, an essential part of governance, must always be exercised under the authority of an Act of Parliament.[144] This, says Dicey, 'places the government even when armed with the widest authority, under the supervision . . . of the Courts'.[145] In a sense, these propositions appear supported by *R (Unison) v Lord Chancellor*, a Supreme Court case concerning access to the courts. In the course of their judgment, Lord Reed explained the important role that the courts play, alongside Parliament, in upholding the rule of law. He stated that:

> At the heart of the concept of the rule of law is the idea that society is governed by law. Parliament exists primarily in order to make laws for society in this country. Democratic procedures exist primarily in order to ensure that the Parliament which makes those laws includes Members of Parliament who are chosen by the people of this country and are accountable to them. Courts exist in order to ensure that the laws made by Parliament, and the common law created by the courts themselves, are applied and enforced. That role includes ensuring that the executive branch of government carries out its functions in accordance with the law.[146]

 Counterpoint: The rule of law and the relationship between the executive and legislature

Whilst it is, in theory, true that executive power is limited to the extent that it must always be exercised under the authority of statute, tensions arise when we consider the fusion of power between the executive and legislature,[147] the result of which means that a government—particularly one with a significant number of seats in the House of Commons—is capable of dominating the legislative process and ensuring enactment of legislation to legitimize executive authority. The consequences of this is that, while the rule of law requires government to point to legislation authority for any action it might undertake, the close fusion of power between the executive and legislature potentially means that a government could ensure that such authority always exists. Indeed, and in a manner of speaking, the facts of *Reilly (No 2)* highlight at least the manner in which the government is able to clarify the authority underpinning its use of executive power, in this instance retrospectively.

In Dicey's view, the rule of law and parliamentary sovereignty are concepts capable of complementing one another. An issue arises, however, when it is considered that Parliament could legislate contrary to the rule of law. On the understanding that Parliament can make and unmake any law,[148] there is technically no force of law or authority stopping Parliament from passing Acts that stand in the way of the characteristics that make the operation of the rule of law possible. In such circumstances, it would be down to the courts to protect values at the heart of the rule of law, to the extent that their

---

[144] Ibid 182–4.   [145] Ibid 183.

[146] [2017] UKSC 51 [68]. Also see Mark Elliott, 'Unison in the Supreme Court: Tribunal Fees, Constitutional Rights and the Rule of Law' (*Public Law for Everyone*, 26 July 2017), https://publiclawforeveryone.com/2017/07/26/unison-in-the-supreme-court-employment-fees-constitutional-rights-and-the-rule-of-law/.

[147] See 2.4.1.

[148] See AV Dicey, *Introduction to the Study of the Law of the Constitution* (JWF Allison ed, first published 1885, OUP 2013) 27.

subordination to the sovereign Parliament might permit. In terms of the courts' approach in this regard, Lord Steyn's words from *Pierson* have already been noted, where he said that '[u]nless there is the clearest provision to the contrary, Parliament must be presumed not to legislate contrary to the rule of law'.[149] This statement suggests that, in the absence of any contrary provision, the courts will always work to uphold the rule of law in their interpretations of primary legislation. This position notwithstanding, conflicts between legislation and the rule of law have arisen in the past. The War Damages Act 1965, for example, was enacted to overturn the authority of the House of Lords' decision in *Burmah Oil Company Ltd v Lord Advocate*,[150] relating to the paying of compensation for the wartime destruction of the Burmah Oil Company's installations. Though the predominance of parliamentary law over judicial decisions is accepted, the effect of the 1965 Act was retrospectively to overrule the House of Lords judgment, arguably going against a value that is central to the rule of law.

A similar scenario arose more recently in the case of *Reilly (No 2)*,[151] where the courts considering retrospective legislation expressly acknowledged the clash with the rule of law and the Human Rights Act 1998. The extent to which the enactment of legislation retrospectively to legitimize use of executive power offends principles at the heart of the rule of law has already been discussed. What we are concerned with here, though, is the manner in which the dilemma facing the court effectively required a departure from orthodox understandings of sovereignty to ensure that the values consistent with the rule of law could be upheld. On this, Mrs Justice Lang has already been quoted as saying:

> Although the Crown in Parliament is the sovereign legislative power, the Courts have the constitutional role of determining and enforcing legality. Thus, Parliament's undoubted power to legislate to overrule the effect of court judgments generally ought not to take the form of retrospective legislation designed to favour the Executive in ongoing litigation in the courts brought against it by one of its citizens, unless there are compelling reasons to do so. Otherwise it is likely to offend a citizen's sense of fair play.[152]

The judgment in *Reilly (No 2)* can be contrasted with that in the *Burmah Oil* case. Whilst accepting that Parliament's sovereign power includes the ability to enact retrospective legislation, where that legislation interferes with the rights of citizens party to ongoing legal action, the High Court held that courts must find a way to preserve the rule of law and protect those rights. Going further than legislation enacted retrospectively, however, it has been suggested that if Parliament were *expressly* to legislate contrary to the rule of law, then the courts could be justified in actually disobeying that particular Act of Parliament. As 4.5.2 addresses in greater detail, Lord Woolf, writing extrajudicially, has in the past noted a partnership between the courts and Parliament, with 'both engaged in a common enterprise involving the upholding of the rule of law'.[153] With this in mind, he observes that:

> There are . . . situations where . . . in upholding the rule of law, the courts have had to take a stand . . . if Parliament did the unthinkable, then I would say that the courts would also be required to act in a manner which would be without precedent . . . there are even limits on the supremacy of Parliament which it is the courts' inalienable responsibility to

---

[149] [1998] AC 539, 591.   [150] [1965] AC 75.   [151] [2014] EWHC 2182 (Admin).
[152] Ibid [82].
[153] Lord Woolf, 'Droit Public—English Style' (1995) *Public Law* 57, 69.

identify and uphold. They are limits of the most modest dimensions which I believe any democrat would accept. They are no more than are necessary to enable the rule of law to be preserved.[154]

One example, notes Woolf, is *Anisminic v Foreign Compensation Commission*.[155] Here, the courts refused to read a legislative provision 'that the Commission's decision "shall not be called in question in any court of law"'[156] as ousting the scope of judicial review, thereby protecting something that—as this chapter has already shown—is vital to due process and the ability to uphold the rule of law.

The most recently significant example of case law exploring the tensions arising where Parliament passes law that flies in the face of values at the heart of the rule of law is the case of *R (Evans) v Attorney-General*.[157]

Case in depth: *R (Evans) v Attorney-General* [2015] UKSC 21

This case concerned a number of private letters that had been written by Prince Charles—the Prince of Wales and heir to the throne—and sent to various government departments. Evans, who was a journalist, felt that these should be made public and so made a freedom of information request, seeking their disclosure. The interest and contention in respect of the letters was principally based on the understanding that members of the Royal Family—particularly the heir to the throne—should be seen to be politically impartial, so as not to exert any influence on the democratic political process. In addition, while the Queen meets the Prime Minister once a week to discuss affairs of state, the notion that the Prince of Wales should be permitted to write to and advise government departments was thought to exceed his role. Though the initial request was rejected, a later appeal to the Upper Tribunal overturned this and permitted the letters to be disclosed. Following this, the Attorney-General issued a certificate, pursuant to section 53 of the Freedom of Information Act 2000, endorsing the government's refusal to disclose. Evans challenged this in the Supreme Court, where he won. Disclosure of the letters was permitted and they were later published in the national press.

The appeal in *Evans* turned on the wording of section 53(2) of the 2000 Act, which provides that the Attorney-General has the power to issue a certificate refusing disclosure of information provided he or she has 'on reasonable grounds formed the opinion that' disclosure ought to be refused. On a plain and literal reading of this provision, the Act gives the Attorney-General a broad power to overturn decisions of the Upper Tribunal. Though giving effect to such an interpretation would be consistent with parliamentary sovereignty and the role of the courts in giving effect to the express will of Parliament, the majority of the Supreme Court felt that such an interpretation was contrary to values at the heart of the rule of law. Amongst these were the independence of the judiciary from the executive, the separation of powers between executive and judiciary, and—fundamentally—the role of the court to review and scrutinize acts and decisions of the executive. It is for these reasons that a majority of the Supreme Court found in favour of Evans.

---

[154] Ibid.   [155] [1969] 2 AC 147.
[156] Lord Woolf, 'Droit Public—English Style' (1995) *Public Law* 57, 69, citing *Anisminic v Foreign Compensation Commission* [1969] 2 AC 147. Also see s 4(4) of the Foreign Compensation Act 1950.
[157] [2015] UKSC 21.

The court's decision in *Evans*, though, has motivated a great deal of further discussion and debate. Elliott, for instance, highlights the significance of the case and notes that '[s]uch judicial activism does not sit comfortably with the notion of parliamentary sovereignty'.[158] He goes on to note, however, that 'it does not follow that the two [principles] are wholly irreconcilable', explaining how the case demonstrates the manner in which the principles of the rule of law, parliamentary sovereignty, and the separation of powers relate to one another, with the sovereign legislature always being afforded the 'last word'.[159] The significance of this decision has also been the focus of analysis by Ekins and Forsyth, who go further in noting that even if, on a strict interpretation, the 2000 Act can be taken as compromising the rule of law, the judges themselves arguably compromised the rule of law by failing to give effect to the clear, express words of Parliament.[160] This case of *Evans* highlights yet further the tensions that exist between parliamentary sovereignty and the rule of law. Whilst the provision of the 2000 Act was clear and Parliament's intention unambiguous, the Supreme Court felt that to give effect to a literal interpretation would have flown in the face of values central to the rule of law principle.

 Discussing the problem

In view of the court's decision in *Evans* and the potential conflict it reflects between parliamentary sovereignty and the rule of law, how do you think a court would deal with the Freedom from the Press (Government Privacy) Act 2023 explained in the problem scenario, keeping in mind the manner in which the actions of the government impacts upon the rule of law?

This section has already explained that, in the *Evans* case, the Supreme Court had to consider the government's action in preventing disclosure of letters between Prince Charles and the government, ostensibly in line with the written word of Parliament's legislation. In finding that the government had acted unlawfully, the courts upheld the rule of law and, in so doing, seemingly departed from the clear words of Parliament. The courts could, it seems, be faced with a similar dilemma here: that is, a question as to whether to uphold the written word of the Freedom from the Press (Government Privacy) Act 2023 in prohibiting 'publication or revelation of Government policies and decisions before formal announcement' and thereby justify government action that arguably contravenes a number of features of the rule of law.

The relationship between the rule of law and parliamentary sovereignty is a complex one. One principle seeks to uphold and insist upon adherence to due process in governance and law-making, taking into consideration numerous values that are vital to a just working system, while the other sets out the supremacy of parliamentary law over any other, suggesting that nothing can limit the actions of Parliament. Whilst on the face of it irreconcilable, notable judgments in *Anisminic* and *Evans* have seemingly ensured the continued importance of the rule of law and have determined, at least, that Parliament's legislative

---

[158] Mark Elliott, 'A Tangled Constitutional Web: The Black-Spider Memos and the British Constitution's Relational Architecture' (2015) *Public Law* 539, 549.

[159] Ibid 549–50.

[160] Richard Ekins and Christopher Forsyth, 'The Rule of Law vs. the Rule of Courts—A Rejoinder' (*Judicial Power Project*, 13 January 2016), https://judicialpowerproject.org.uk/the-rule-of-law-vs-the-rule-of-courts-a-rejoinder/.

authority is exercised according to values consistent with that principle. More than the few notable judgments of the courts, however, and outside any power the courts might possess—hypothetical or otherwise—Parliament's acceptance of values at the heart of the rule of law is tied to its democratic legitimacy. Parliament is dependent upon the electoral process for its authority and, in carrying out its functions, it represents the electorate. Were Parliament to legislate contrary to the rule of law in an express fashion, though Diceyan principle might suggest that it is legally possible, politically there could be ramifications.

3.5.3 The role of human rights

The role that human rights plays with regards to the rule of law in the UK Constitution is notable, though the nature of that role differs depending upon whether one follows a formal or substantive conception of the principle. Under a formal conception, a system of government should comply with various procedural characteristics to provide a foundation on which human rights can be suitably protected, those rights being important, but not a part of the rule of law. A relationship between the formal conception and human rights on these terms is evident from Bingham's consideration, in respect of which it has already been explained that it is important to provide a 'foundation for a fair and just society which respects fundamental rights and civil liberties',[161] which is different from stipulating precisely what those substantive rights should be.[162] By contrast, under a substantive conception, protection of such rights is integral to the rule of law itself and part of its content. Undoubtedly, protection of human rights is something that goes right to the heart of what the rule of law is about. This section explores the manner of rights protection in the UK Constitution, demonstrating the extent to which this touches upon values that are consistent with the rule of law principle.

In the UK, human rights protection has developed significantly in recent years. Recalling Dicey's third limb of his rule of law conception, there has been a shift from what might be called the 'civil liberties' approach to rights protection, whereby anything was permissible except for that which was expressly prohibited by law, to a system that also includes protection through the European Convention on Human Rights and the Human Rights Act 1998. The effect this has had on rights protection in the UK Constitution and the rule of law can be seen by a comparison between the following two cases. The first is *Malone v Metropolitan Police Commissioner*.[163]

Case in depth: *Malone v Metropolitan Police Commissioner* **[1979] 2 All ER 620**

Malone was on trial for handling stolen property. During the course of the proceedings, it transpired that Malone's phone had been tapped by the police. Though it was supported by a warrant, signed by the Secretary of State, Malone argued that it was unlawful and brought an action for breach of privacy and confidentiality. The court held, however, that the right to privacy and confidentiality was not recognized by the law of England and that accordingly the tapping in this case could not be deemed unlawful.

---

[161] Alison L Young, 'The Rule of Law in the United Kingdom: Formal or Substantive?' (2012) 6 *International Journal of Constitutional Law* 259, 260.
[162] See 3.4.1.
[163] [1979] 2 All ER 620.

The finding of the court, here, was based on a reluctance to develop the law in an entirely new way and to pass judgment on an issue that Parliament had not yet considered. Despite the House of Lords finding the action to be lawful, however, the case was appealed to Strasbourg and the European Court of Human Rights where it was found that the phone tapping contravened the Article 8 right to respect for a private and family life.

Focusing on the discussion at hand and the relevance of human rights to the rule of law, this judgment is obviously consistent with the civil liberties approach to individual rights protection that prevailed before the Human Rights Act 1998. The domestic courts found that the police's actions were lawful since they were not expressly prohibited at law. As this case shows, however, this approach also gave public authorities much wider scope for action that might, under newer laws, have been found inconsistent with human rights and the rule of law.[164] Indeed, demonstrating this point further is the case of *A v Secretary of State for the Home Department*,[165] which was discussed earlier in the chapter. It is recalled that this case concerned a declaration by the court that provisions of the Anti-Terrorism, Crime and Security Act 2001 were incompatible with the European Convention on Human Rights, on the basis that it authorized the indefinite detention of foreign nationals suspected of terrorist activities, contrary to both Articles 5 and 14 of the Convention. Unlike *Malone*, however, the court refused to endorse the executive action—even where it was supported by legislation—on the basis that it contravened the suspects' human rights. Comparing these two cases shows a stark difference of approach. Whereas, in the past, the courts have been happy to find that acts and decisions of the executive were legal provided they were not expressly prohibited by law, as in *Malone*, since the enactment of the Human Rights Act 1998 they have more readily examined the lawfulness of executive, and indeed legislative action, on the basis of rights set out in the Convention. This greater willingness to investigate and scrutinize the executive's acts and decisions, in line with human rights, demonstrates stronger protection for the rule of law.

Human rights has a key role to play with regards to the rule of law principle and, as these two cases have demonstrated, a shift in the law to the protection of positive rights has meant that the courts are more ready and willing to investigate executive action and can fulfil their role more fully in upholding the rule of law.

3.6 Summary

This chapter has explained the rule of law and explored the way in which it applies in respect of the UK Constitution. As these discussions have shown, the principle can be interpreted in a number of different ways, demonstrated by numerous theorists' explanations and definitions and the distinction drawn between formal and substantive conceptions. The last section of the chapter, though, including its focus on a number of cases, has emphasized the importance of the rule of law in the UK Constitution, demonstrating the way in which the courts serve to uphold its values, often against the acts

---

[164] See, for example, the judgment of the European Court of Human Rights in *Malone v UK* (1984) 7 EHRR 14, where the simple absence of any clear laws justifying and governing phone tapping, meant that the gathering of evidence via phone tapping contravened the Article 8 right to a private and family life (see, for further discussion of this case, 15.4.1).

[165] [2004] UKHL 56.

and decisions of the executive and even, on occasion, Acts of Parliament. Building on Aristotle's assertion that '[i]t is better for the law to rule than one of the citizens',[166] this chapter has shown that the rule of law is a central feature of the UK Constitution, serving to ensure appropriate and legitimate exercise of authority.

Quick test questions

1. What are the origins of the rule of law principle?

2. What are Dicey's three points for the rule of law?

3. What are formal conceptions of the rule of law and how do they differ from substantive conceptions of the rule of law?

4. What is the central feature of Raz's understanding of the rule of law? How and why does Allan disagree with Raz?

5. Do you find the formal or substantive conception of the rule of law more convincing in view of the UK constitutional order?

6. In *Liversidge*, did Lord Atkin favour an objective or subjective test? Do you agree with his judgment in that case?

7. To what extent does judicial review of administrative action uphold the rule of law?

8. How does parliamentary sovereignty relate to the rule of law?

Further reading

Understanding the rule of law

TRS Allan, *Constitutional Justice: A Liberal Theory of the Rule of Law* (OUP 2001)

*Tom Bingham, *The Rule of Law* (Allen Lane 2010)

*AV Dicey, *Introduction to the Study of the Law of the Constitution* (JWF Allison ed, first published 1885, OUP 2013)

Friedrich A Hayek, *The Road to Serfdom* (Routledge 1944)

Jeffrey Jowell, 'The Rule of Law's Long Arm: Uncommunicated Decisions' (2004) *Public Law* 246

Martti Koskenniemi, 'Imagining the Rule of Law: Rereading the Grotian "Tradition"' (2019) 30(1) *European Journal of International Law* 17

Formal and substantive conceptions

TRS Allan, 'The Rule of Law as the Rule of Reason: Consent and Constitutionalism' (1999) 115 *Law Quarterly Review* 221

*Paul P Craig, 'Formal and Substantive Conceptions of the Rule of Law: An Analytical Framework' (1997) *Public Law* 467

---

[166] Aristotle, *Politics and Athenian Constitution*, Book III, s 1287 (John Warrington ed and trs, Dent 1959) 97, cited in Tom Bingham, *The Rule of Law* (Allen Lane 2010) 3.

*Joseph Raz, 'The Rule of Law and its Virtue' (1977) 93 *Law Quarterly Review* 195

*Joseph Raz, 'The Law's Own Virtue' (2019) 39(1) *Oxford Journal of Legal Studies* 1

Alison L Young, 'The Rule of Law in the United Kingdom: Formal or Substantive?' (2012) 6 *International Journal of Constitutional Law* 259

The rule of law in the UK Constitution

Richard Ekins and Christopher Forsyth, 'The Rule of Law vs. the Rule of Courts—A Rejoinder' (*Judicial Power Project*, 13 January 2016), https://judicialpowerproject.org.uk/the-rule-of-law-vs-the-rule-of-courts-a-rejoinder/

*Mark Elliott, '*Unison* in the Supreme Court: Tribunal Fees, Constitutional Rights and the Rule of Law' (*Public Law for Everyone*, 26 July 2017), https://publiclawforeveryone.com/2017/07/26/unison-in-the-supreme-court-employment-fees-constitutional-rights-and-the-rule-of-law/

*Mark Elliott, 'A Tangled Constitutional Web: The Black-Spider Memos and the British Constitution's Relational Architecture' (2015) *Public Law* 539, 549

C Harlow, 'Accidental Death of an Asylum Seeker' (1994) 57 *Modern Law Review* 620

Jo Eric Khushal Murkens, 'Judicious Review: The Constitutional Practice of the UK Supreme Court' (2018) 77(2) *Cambridge Law Journal* 349

 Visit this book's **online resources** for additional materials relating to this chapter, including a full analysis of the start-of-chapter problem scenario.
www.oup.com/he/stanton-prescott2e

4

Parliamentary sovereignty: an overview

Problem scenario

Parliament passes the (fictitious) Foreign and Domestic Taxes Act 2024 with the aim of protecting the UK economy following years of recession. This provides that all British citizens residing in the UK and all those who have expatriated abroad within the past five years must pay a standard £250 yearly tax to the British Government, on top of other existing tax provisions. In addition, to ensure long-term financial security and to protect the Act from being repealed too easily, it provides that 'this Act is only subject to repeal in the event that a two-thirds majority is achieved in the House of Commons'.

Consider the constitutional validity of this Act of Parliament, thinking in particular about the following factors and circumstances, which we will discuss as the chapter progresses:

* If the UK Government were to sign an international treaty setting out rules concerning the payment of taxes, would the enactment be deemed thereafter invalid if it were contrary to that treaty?

* Can Parliament require that a two-thirds majority be achieved before repeal?

* What if a later Parliament were to enact legislation that conflicted with the Foreign and Domestic Taxes Act 2024 but which did not expressly address its repeal?

* If the Foreign and Domestic Taxes Act 2024 is repealed by a simple majority and not with a two-thirds majority, would the courts be able to challenge the parliamentary process?

* While Parliament has the power to legislate with regards to British nationals residing in the UK, what about expatriates?

4.1 Introduction

In countries that have a codified constitution, the written constitutional document provides supreme authority, with all legislative and executive authority exercised subordinate to that constitution. For example, in the USA, legislative and executive authority is exercised pursuant to the provisions of the written constitutional document and the US Supreme Court is empowered to protect the constitution, even having the authority to strike out primary legislation to that end.[1] In the UK, by contrast, the lack of a codified constitutional document means that supreme or sovereign authority must lie elsewhere. Legal philosophers have explained that there must be a single point from which all laws and constitutional legitimacy must derive[2] and while over the centuries questions regarding the allocation of this sovereign power in the UK Constitution have been oft disputed and discussed, orthodox theory states that it lies with Parliament.

The principle of parliamentary sovereignty has been described as a cornerstone[3] of our constitution insofar as the consequent relationship that Parliament has with the executive, the courts, and with citizens underpins the constitution and the way in which other institutions of the state behave. On this basis, this chapter discusses and explores the way in which parliamentary sovereignty has developed within the UK Constitution and what it means—in legal terms—for the day-to-day operation of our system. It defines the principle in orthodox terms set out by Dicey and explains the manner in which it has developed, historically, out of the Bill of Rights and on the back of the unsettled constitutional times that prevailed during the seventeenth century. The chapter then sets out the legal basis for sovereignty, calling on the authority of Wade, Jennings, and Goldsworthy to explain the importance of the courts' role in determining and providing the foundation for Parliament's authority. It then explores the fundamental aspects of the orthodox theory, explaining how that operates in practice and discussing the various challenges and limitations that have arisen since the late nineteenth century. The chapter then concludes by considering the position of parliamentary sovereignty today, analysing the extent to which orthodox Diceyan theory can be said still to be relevant. The objectives of this chapter are:

- to explain orthodox Diceyan theory of parliamentary sovereignty, drawing from constitutional history to discuss its origins;
- to discuss the underlying legal theories supporting parliamentary sovereignty;
- to explore varying and often competing authorities that both support and challenge orthodox sovereignty;
- to consider the extent to which Parliament can still be regarded as sovereign in today's twenty-first-century constitution.

---

[1] See *Marbury v Madison*, 5 US (1 Cranch) 137 (1803). Section 2.2.3 noted an example of the US Supreme Court setting aside legislation that contravened the US Constitution in the case of *Shelby County, Alabama v Holder*, 570 US (2013). Also see Mark Tushnet, *The Constitution of the United States of America: A Contextual Analysis* (2nd edn, Hart Publishing 2015) 134–6.

[2] See, for example, Hans Kelsen's theory of norms and the basic norm (Hans Kelsen, *General Theory of Law and State* (2nd edn, Harvard University Press 1946)).

[3] See, for a recent instance, Lord Neuberger MR, 'Who are the Masters Now?' (Second Lord Alexander of Weedon Lecture, 6 April 2011), http://webarchive.nationalarchives.gov.uk/20131203081513/http://www.judiciary.gov.uk/Resources/JCO/Documents/Speeches/mr-speech-weedon-lecture-110406.pdf.

4.2 **Parliamentary sovereignty defined**

Our consideration of parliamentary sovereignty starts with a statement of the orthodox theory, famously set out by Dicey in the late nineteenth century in his seminal text *An Introduction to the Study of the Law of the Constitution*. He stated that:

> The principle of parliamentary sovereignty means neither more nor less than this, namely, that parliament thus defined has, under the English constitution, the right to make or unmake any law whatever; and, further, that no person or body is recognised by the law of England as having the right to override or set aside the legislation of Parliament.[4]

Having defined the principle in these terms, Dicey then goes on to identify, within this definition, two limbs of the orthodox theory. He continues by saying that:

> The principle . . . of Parliamentary sovereignty may, looked at from its positive side, be thus described; Any Act of Parliament, or any part of an Act of Parliament, which makes new law, or repeals or modifies an existing law, will be obeyed by the courts. The same principle, looked at from its negative side, may be thus stated; there is no person or body of persons who can, under the English constitution, make rules which override or derogate from an Act of Parliament, or which (to express the same thing in other words) will be enforced by courts in contravention of an Act of Parliament.[5]

Dicey's definition of parliamentary sovereignty is widely cited and while there are those who criticize his approach,[6] his statement is acknowledged as an accepted starting point for consideration of the principle. Though in Chapter 5 we will examine the way in which membership of the European Union and the Brexit process have raised questions of the sovereign authority of Parliament, this chapter explores the continued relevance of Dicey's definition as well as subtle challenges to the principle that have often derived from the internal workings of the UK Constitution itself. Before these various challenges are discussed, however, it is necessary to explore in detail the origins of the orthodox theory.

4.3 **Historical development of sovereignty**

Despite the authority with which Dicey states the principle of parliamentary sovereignty, he is by no means its founder. As this section demonstrates, parliamentary sovereignty, at least in historical terms, is derived from the Glorious Revolution of 1688 and the Bill of Rights 1688, which was enacted to settle the turbulent relationship between the competing authority of the Crown[7] and Parliament. Our consideration starts with an examination of the situation before 1688, a discussion of the constitutional developments leading up to the Glorious Revolution, and the effects of the Bill of Rights itself.

---

[4] AV Dicey, *Introduction to the Study of the Law of the Constitution* (JWF Allison ed, first published 1885, OUP 2013) 27. Dicey defines Parliament, in this sense, as consisting of the monarch, the House of Lords, and the House of Commons acting together (27).

[5] Ibid 27.

[6] See, for instance, Chijioke Dike, 'The Case Against Parliamentary Sovereignty' (1976) *Public Law* 283.

[7] The Crown is discussed in more detail in 6.1. For the purposes of this discussion, we mean the Crown as monarch and note that the monarch, exercising their inherent authority, would seek to exercise power recognized by common law as belonging to them as part of the royal prerogative.

4.3.1 **Pre-1688**

Historically, supreme authority rested with the Crown, the 'system . . . operat[ing] on the basis that the King's barons or nobles held their lands from the King in exchange for an oath to him of loyalty and obedience'.[8] This meant that the monarch could exercise full executive power primarily through the Privy Council but also exercise some legislative power through making royal proclamations under the royal prerogative. Gradually, though, Parliament emerged as an alternative legislative body, particularly during the Tudor period and the reigns of Henry VIII and Elizabeth I when Parliament provided the key mechanism though which the monarch could 'legalise their actions'.[9] In apparent conflict with this growing power of Parliament, when the Stuart Kings took to the throne during the seventeenth century, there was a clear monarchical desire to 'claw back the initiative from Parliament by re-asserting the divine right of Kings to govern'.[10] In 1610, for example, King James I stated in a speech to Parliament that:

> The state of Monarchy is the supremest thing upon earth; for kings are not only God's lieutenants upon earth and sit upon God's throne, but even by God himself they are called gods . . . Kings are justly called gods for that they exercise a manner or resemblance of Divine power upon earth; . . . they make and unmake their subject; they have power of raising and casting down; of life and death; judges over all their subjects and in all causes, and yet accomptable to none but God only. They have power to exalt low things and abase high things, and make of their subjects like men at the chess, a pawn to take a bishop or a knight, and to cry up or down any of their subjects as they do their money. And to the King is due both the affection of the soul and the service of the body of his subjects.[11]

The belief of the Stuart Kings in the Divine Right of the monarch meant that when Parliament refused to comply with the monarch's demands, the resultant conflict became a battle to assert supremacy over the other. This led to the courts being required to decide on the authority of each institution and to determine the legality of their actions.

In *Bates's Case (Case of Imposition)*,[12] for example, Bates had refused to pay an import duty that had been imposed by James I without any parliamentary approval. The court upheld the validity of the duty and therefore the power of the King to introduce and impose his own taxes. Equally, though, the courts, on other occasions, sought to restrict the authority of the monarch. In the *Case of Proclamations*,[13] for example, the King claimed the power to legislate by proclamation to 'prohibit new buildings in and about London . . . [and to] prohibit the making of starch of wheat'.[14] In giving judgment to the effect that the King could not legislate without the authority of Parliament, Coke CJ famously stated that:

> [T]he King by his proclamation or other ways cannot change any part of the common law, or statute law, or the customs of the realm . . . also the King cannot create any offence by his prohibition or proclamation, which was not an offence before, for that was to change the law, and to make an offence which was not; . . . also . . . the King hath no prerogative, but that which the law of the land allows him.[15]

---

[8] Peter Leyland, *The Constitution of the United Kingdom: A Contextual Analysis* (Hart Publishing 2007) 9.
[9] Ibid 10.
[10] Ibid 10. Also see Elizabeth Wicks, *The Evolution of a Constitution* (Hart Publishing 2006) 16–17.
[11] James VI and I on the Divine Right of Kings (given as a speech to Parliament, 21 March 1610), https://faculty.history.wisc.edu/sommerville/351/Jamesdrk.htm. Also cited in Ian Loveland, *Constitutional Law, Administrative Law, and Human Rights: A Critical Introduction* (8th edn, OUP 2018) 22.
[12] (1606) 2 St Tr 371.   [13] (1611) 12 Co Rep 74.   [14] Ibid.   [15] Ibid.

It was not only the power of the King, however, that the courts saw fit to limit and control; they were equally restrictive of the authority of Parliament, as can be seen from *Dr Bonham's Case*.[16]

Case in depth: *Dr Bonham's Case* (1609) 8 Co Rep 114

Dr Bonham was summoned to appear before the London College of Physicians when he was found to be practising medicine in London without the appropriate licence. He was fined, arrested, and ordered to undertake further examination. When Bonham refused, however, and claimed that the London College of Physicians had no authority to make such an order to arrest him, he brought an action for false imprisonment against the President and Censors of the College of Physicians. In defence, the College relied on its Statute of Incorporation, which they argued gave it the authority to regulate all physicians in London and to punish those practitioners not licensed by the college. The court found in favour of Dr Bonham on the basis that, since the fine ordered to be paid went to the College itself, it was not acting fairly.

The most significant aspect of *Dr Bonham's Case* is the judgment of Coke CJ, which explains the relationship between the courts and Parliament at that time, particularly with the authority of statutes in mind. He stated that:

> [I]t appears in our books, that in many cases, the common law will controul Acts of Parliament, and sometimes adjudge them to be utterly void: for when an Act of Parliament is against common right and reason, or repugnant, or impossible to be performed, the common law will controul it, and adjudge such Act to be void.[17]

This is a view that was endorsed and followed just a few years later in *Day v Savadge*,[18] a case concerning an action for trespass, where Hobart CJ stated in giving judgment that 'an Act of Parliament, made against natural equity, as to make a man Judge in his own case, is void in itself'.[19] In the midst of these turbulent relations between the Crown and Parliament in the early seventeenth century, the judgments in the *Case of Proclamations* and *Dr Bonham's Case* are particularly significant. They demonstrate not only the extent of the conflicting powers that existed between Parliament and the Crown but, more importantly, they show that it was often down to the courts to police the limits of those powers.

Yet, it remained that the weakness in the power of Parliament was that the monarch had the power under the royal prerogative to summon Parliament and to prorogue it (prorogue in this context means to adjourn Parliament so that it did not sit). This meant that Parliament sat only when the monarch desired. One of the flash points between the monarch and Parliament during this period was taxation, where it was long recognized that for the Crown to impose taxation it needed the consent of Parliament. Shortly after taking the throne in the 1625, Charles I attempted to impose taxes without Parliament's consent and to summon and dismiss Parliament at will.

Charles I summoned Parliament in 1629; however, Parliament refused to allow him to raise the necessary taxes, as they were opposed to the King's policies on religion

---

[16] (1609) 8 Co Rep 114.   [17] Ibid.   [18] (1614) Hobart 85.   [19] Ibid.

following his marriage to the Catholic Henrietta Maria of France. The response of Charles I was to adjourn Parliament for the following eleven years, meaning that he ruled without Parliament by exercising his executive powers. In 1641, under the leadership of John Pym, a longstanding critic of the King, a group of Parliamentarians presented to Charles I the 'Grand Remonstrance', a list of grievances as to how the country was being run under the prerogative. One consequence of this was the Triennial Act 1641, which required that the monarch call Parliament to meet at least once every three years.

The power-struggle and turbulent relations between the Crown and Parliament continued, however, and in time led to civil war. Resisting and opposing the King's demands and powers, parliamentary forces overcame the Crown, and executed Charles I in 1649.[20] Oliver Cromwell took up the position of Lord Protector of the Commonwealth, succeeded briefly by his son, before the accession of Charles II in 1660 saw the monarchy reinstated. When James II ascended the throne, upon the death of Charles II in 1685, the turbulent relationship between Crown and Parliament once again came to the fore. A Catholic King for whom religion came before the welfare of his own country, James II showed complete disregard for the authority of Parliament[21] and 'exercised his prerogative powers without caution or restraint and set himself against the popular will of his people'.[22] As a result, opposition to the monarchy grew once more and some of those opposed to James II negotiated with William of Orange (who had married James II's daughter Mary) to come to England and seize the throne from James II. William landed at Torbay in Devon with a large army, which proceeded to gain control of a large portion of the country. James, sensing 'the prospect of revolt on the horizon, dissolved Parliament in 1688' and later fled the country.[23] These events formed part of and gave rise to one of the most significant moments in UK constitutional history—the Glorious Revolution.[24]

4.3.2 The Glorious Revolution and the Bill of Rights 1688

With the throne vacant, William of Orange and Mary were invited to take it jointly on the condition that they accepted the terms of the Bill of Rights. The Bill of Rights 1688 represented a settlement between the Crown and Parliament and clarified their previously turbulent relationship, seeking to establish Parliament as the superior and sovereign authority. To this end, the bill set out various statements to the effect that the Crown could not generally exercise authority without the consent of Parliament. Notable amongst these provisions is Article 9. This required 'that the Freedom of Speech and Debates or Proceedings in Parliament ought not to be impeached or questioned in any Court or Place out of Parliament', thereby setting out the authority whereby Parliament's

---

[20] See Peter Leyland, *The Constitution of the United Kingdom: A Contextual Analysis* (Hart Publishing 2007) 10.   [21] Ibid 11.

[22] Elizabeth Wicks, *The Evolution of a Constitution* (Hart Publishing 2006) 12.

[23] Peter Leyland, *The Constitution of the United Kingdom: A Contextual Analysis* (Hart Publishing 2007) 11.

[24] Wicks suggests that the revolution was termed 'glorious' for the manner in which the settlement 'set the foundations for a peaceful kingdom with limited government, individual rights and liberties and an evolutionary constitution' (16).

workings and processes cannot be questioned.[25] In addition to this, the Bill of Rights also provided that 'Parliament should meet on a regular basis' and set out 'a right to free speech and debate for MPs, and . . . the right to regulate their own proceedings without limitation or interference either from the Crown or from the courts'.[26] These provisions served to ensure that Parliament, as law-maker, would meet frequently and that it could do so without interference from the monarch or any other institution, establishing it as the sovereign legislature.

The effect of these provisions and of the Bills of Rights more generally was profound. By settling the long-standing tension between the Crown and Parliament, it ensured constitutional stability and provided the historical foundations on which the doctrine of parliamentary sovereignty has since grown and developed. As Judge states, 'what was asserted in 1688 was the principle of *parliamentary sovereignty*, whereby parliament secured legal supremacy', most notably over the Crown.[27] Parliament's supremacy was later confirmed by the Act of Settlement 1700, which made clear that the line of succession to the Crown is regulated by Parliament through statute. This establishment of Parliament's sovereignty is justified on the basis that Parliament is elected and therefore holds the democratic mandate to legislate in line with its accountability to the electorate.

 Pause for reflection

This justification has even greater relevance today as the nature of Parliament's democratic base has broadened significantly since the seventeenth century. To what extent is Parliament 'more democratic' today compared with the Parliament at the time of the Bill of Rights?

This section has explored the historical development of the principle of parliamentary sovereignty and demonstrated the manner of its foundations and origins in constitutional history. These various sources and developments, however, merely show how the orthodox principle came to be established in an historical sense; they do not account for the legal power of Parliament or provide justification for the law-making powers that Parliament possesses. In the next section, we consider explanations for the *legal* basis for sovereignty, determining why it is that Parliament is regarded as sovereign and how that sovereignty is manifested.

4.4 The legal basis of parliamentary sovereignty: a look at Wade, Jennings, and Goldsworthy

In order that this section can explain why Parliament is regarded as legally sovereign we must go beyond the historical origins and developments that are founded on the Bill of Rights. As Tomkins notes, 'the Bill of Rights is concerned with the relationship of the Houses of Parliament to the Crown. Legislative supremacy, by contrast, is concerned with

---

[25] Article 9 is explained in greater detail in the Online Resources.
[26] Peter Leyland, *The Constitution of the United Kingdom: A Contextual Analysis* (Hart Publishing 2007) 11.
[27] David Judge, *The Parliamentary State* (Sage 1993) 20, cited in Brian Thompson and Michael Gordon, *Cases and Materials on Constitutional and Administrative Law* (11th edn, OUP 2014) 45.

the relationship of Acts of Parliament to the law'.[28] This alludes to the legal basis of parliamentary sovereignty, an area rife with academic theory, discussion, and debate, some of which we now consider through this section.

The legal basis for parliamentary sovereignty rests with the courts. Simply put, Parliament is sovereign because the courts recognize its Acts as sovereign. Though this reality is generally accepted, the underlying reasons are numerous and contrasting, having consequences for the perceived authority of Parliament, as this chapter will later go on to explore.

4.4.1 Wade and the rule of judicial obedience

For Wade, parliamentary sovereignty was linked to the rule of judicial obedience; that is, the notion that judges obey and abide by the wishes and enactments of the democratically elected Parliament. Explaining the significance of this rule, Wade notes that:

> The rule of judicial obedience is in one sense a rule of common law; but in another sense— which applies to no other rule of common law—it is the ultimate *political* fact upon which the whole system of legislation hangs. Legislation owes its authority to the rule: the rule does not owe its authority to legislation. To say that Parliament can change the rule, merely because it can change any other rules, is to put the cart before the horse.[29]

This statement effectively sums up what Wade regards as the basis of legal sovereignty and from it we can take three key points. The first has already been noted and is widely accepted—that Parliament is sovereign because the courts recognize its Acts as sovereign. Lord Steyn, for instance, agreed in the case of *R (Jackson) v Attorney-General*[30] that parliamentary sovereignty 'is a construct of the common law. The judges created this principle'.[31]

The second point to take from Wade's conception is that he sees it not as a legal principle, but as a political one. This view is founded on the argument that 'Parliament could not, in the first place, have conferred sovereign (or any other) legislative power upon itself . . . the constitutional principle which accords supreme law-making power to Parliament must lie beyond Parliament's legislative reach'.[32] Indeed, if Parliament's sovereignty were to depend on the authority of an enabling statute, then Parliament's authority would thereafter be constantly dependent on and subject to that particular Act, thereby undermining the continuing sovereignty of Parliament. The reasoning behind this view is explained by Wade through reference to the following extract by Salmond:

> All rules of law have historical sources. As a matter of fact and history they have their origin somewhere, though we may not know what it is. But not all of them have legal sources. Were this so, it would be necessary for the law to proceed *ad infinitum* in tracing the descent of its principles. It is requisite that the law should postulate one or more first causes, whose operation is ultimate and whose authority is underived . . . The rule that a man may not ride a bicycle on the footpath may have its source in the by-laws of a municipal council; the rule that these by-laws have the force of law has its source in an Act of Parliament. But whence comes the rule that Acts of Parliament have the force of law? This is legally ultimate;

---

[28] Adam Tomkins, *Public Law* (OUP 2003) 103.
[29] HWR Wade, 'The Basis of Legal Sovereignty' (1955) 13(2) *Cambridge Law Journal* 172, 188.
[30] [2005] UKHL 56.   [31] Ibid [102].
[32] Mark Elliott, *The Constitutional Foundations of Judicial Review* (Hart Publishing 2001) 45.

its source is historical only, not legal . . . It is the law because it is the law, and for no other reason that it is possible for the law itself to take notice of. *No statute can confer this power upon Parliament, for this would be to assume an act on the very power that is to be conferred.*[33]

If sovereignty, based on the rule of judicial obedience, cannot be derived from a legal source, from where must it originate? The answer lies in Wade's previously mentioned description of sovereignty as the 'ultimate *political* fact' of our system.[34] As a political fact, sovereignty is rooted outside the realms of the law and derived from the political settlement which underpins the relationship between the institutions of state.[35] This takes us back to the agreement reached in 1688 whereby Parliament, the Crown, and the courts effectively accepted the sovereign authority of Parliament. In short, for Wade, the Bill of Rights 1688 and the agreement reached upon William and Mary's accession to the throne had no legal basis but can, instead, be seen as a political reality. A consequence of that settlement is the court's acceptance and recognition of parliamentary sovereignty.[36]

This brings us to the third and final aspect of Wade's conception of sovereignty. Since parliamentary sovereignty cannot be said to derive from any Act of Parliament but lies instead in the political reality of Parliament's relationship with the courts, it stands to reason that Parliament cannot itself alter or change its own sovereignty. Such a change can only come about through a shift in that political reality, an event which Wade describes as a 'revolution', by which he means the courts change their allegiance from one sovereign body to another.[37] Wade provides historical example of such a political shift altering the allocation of sovereign power: in 1649 following the execution of Charles I, the courts changed their allegiance from the King in Parliament to the kingless Parliaments overseen by Oliver Cromwell, thereby bringing about, according to Wade, a judicial revolution.[38] The same thing then happened in 1688: the courts changed their allegiance from the Parliament that had existed under James II's rule and—pursuant to the political settlement reached through the Bill of Rights—shifted it to the Parliament under William and Mary, which operated on the basis of a new agreement.[39]

For Wade, Parliament's sovereignty is rooted outside legal authority and is, instead, derived from political fact. This fact, according to Wade, explains not only the relationship between the courts and Parliament but also the sovereignty of Parliament itself. Wade's view, however, is not the only conception seeking to explain the legal basis for parliamentary sovereignty. Jennings, for instance, takes a different approach, as the next section now explains.

4.4.2 Jennings and the common law

In contrast to Wade's understanding of parliamentary sovereignty, Jennings argues that it is a common law principle established as a result of the evolution and growth of the UK Constitution.[40] He states that:

[T]he power of a legislature derives from the law by which it is established. In nearly every country . . . this law is to be found in the written Constitution. In the United Kingdom, which has no written Constitution, it derives from the accepted law, which is the common law.[41]

---

[33] HWR Wade, 'The Basis of Legal Sovereignty' (1955) 13(2) *Cambridge Law Journal* 172, 187 (emphasis in original).

[34] Ibid 188.   [35] Ibid 188–9.   [36] Ibid.   [37] Ibid 188.   [38] Ibid.   [39] Ibid 188–9.

[40] See Sir Ivor Jennings, *The Law and the Constitution* (5th edn, University of London Press 1959) 156–7.

[41] Ibid 156.

On this basis and according to Jennings, Parliament is sovereign because it has, over the centuries, become established as sovereign through recognition at the common law, since the courts have not historically sought to question the validity of Parliament's Acts.[42] As a result, 'there are no principles of the common law which Parliament cannot repeal . . . [and] there is no recent precedent for declaring an Act of Parliament to be *ultra vires* because it offends against the powers of Parliament conferred by the common law'.[43] Consequently, 'the modern trend is towards admitting the supremacy of Parliament over the common law'.[44] According to Jennings, Parliament is sovereign because the courts have always recognized it as sovereign and the authority with which the courts regard Acts of Parliament has become embedded within the common law. Parliamentary sovereignty, on this conception, then, is merely 'a legal concept, a form of expression which lawyers use to express the relations between Parliament and the courts. It means that the courts will always recognize as law the rules which Parliament makes by legislation'.[45] This means that, according to Jennings, Parliament could itself alter the nature of its own sovereign powers by simply changing the common law rules that give rise to its sovereignty. We return to this possibility in exploring the 'manner and form' theory, below.[46]

 Counterpoint: Goldsworthy and parliamentary sovereignty

Jennings' conception of parliamentary sovereignty, however, is not without its critics. Goldsworthy discusses the principle at length and suggests that the root of the issue stems from Jennings' mistaken 'claim that the doctrine of parliamentary sovereignty was a creature of common law'.[47] He explains:

> The problem is that the doctrine is quite unlike ordinary common law rules and principles, because it was not made by the judges and cannot be unilaterally revised by them. By the same token, it was not made by Parliament: it was not, and could not have been, prescribed by statute, since any such statute would beg the question of Parliament's authority to enact it. It is deeper and more enduring than both statute law and ordinary common law. Since it is the source of Parliament's authority, it is prima facie superior to Parliament, and the notion that Parliament can alter it at will is therefore implausible. It is a creature of consensus among the senior legal officials of all branches of government. It can be altered by Parliament unilaterally only if there is a consensus to that effect among senior officials, and there is little evidence that there is.[48]

Not only, then, does this go against Jennings' consideration of sovereignty, but it also departs somewhat from the conception offered by Wade. Goldsworthy is, to a point, reminiscent of Wade insofar as he sees sovereignty as deriving not from parliamentary legal authority but instead from

→

---

[42] Ibid 158.   [43] Ibid 160.   [44] Ibid.   [45] Ibid 149.   [46] See, for further discussion, 4.5.3.

[47] Jeffrey Goldsworthy, *Parliamentary Sovereignty: Contemporary Debates* (Cambridge University Press 2010) 115, citing Peter C Oliver, *The Constitution of Independence: The Development of Constitutional Theory in Australia, Canada and New Zealand* (OUP 2005) 82. Also see Michael Gordon, *Parliamentary Sovereignty in the UK Constitution: Process, Politics and Democracy* (Hart Publishing 2015) 101–7.

[48] Jeffrey Goldsworthy, *Parliamentary Sovereignty: Contemporary Debates* (Cambridge University Press 2010) 115.

→

'consensus among the senior legal officials'.[49] Unlike Wade, though, Goldsworthy places much less emphasis on the courts and suggests that it would be undemocratic for the courts to have the power to determine the sovereignty of Parliament. Offering clear rationale for neither the courts *nor* Parliament having sole responsibility for the allocation of sovereign power, Goldsworthy goes on to explain that:

> If the courts had authority unilaterally to change the doctrine, they could impose all kinds of limits on Parliament's authority without any democratic input. This would amount to a profoundly undemocratic process of constitutional change. And if Parliament had such authority, a political party with temporary control of both Houses could protect its partisan policies, enacted into law, from amendment or repeal by majorities in future Parliaments, which would also be undemocratic.[50]

Wade, Jennings, and Goldsworthy offer very different legal justifications for parliamentary sovereignty. For one, it is founded on a political relationship and changed only by a judicial revolution; for another, it is a common law principle that has been accepted over the centuries; and for the third, it is dependent on wider consensus amongst the legal officials of the state. These views, however, have very different consequences when we explore questions regarding the power of Parliament to entrench legislation and bind itself in 4.5.3.

4.5 Parliamentary sovereignty explored

So far, this chapter has explored the historical foundations on which the principle of parliamentary sovereignty has developed and it has discussed, at length, various arguments pertaining to the legal basis for the principle. It is necessary now, however, to explain in more detail what Dicey's orthodox theory means in practice and to consider the challenges and limitations that have affected Dicey's conception since it was elucidated in the late nineteenth century. In doing this, this section breaks Dicey's definition down into three key points, which are commonly identified as reflecting the essence of the orthodox principle:[51]

1. Parliament can make and unmake any law on any subject matter (the positive aspect);

2. no person or body has the power to override or derogate from an Act of Parliament (the negative aspect);

3. Parliament cannot be bound by its predecessors or bind its successors.

---

[49] Ibid 115. Also see Michael Gordon, *Parliamentary Sovereignty in the UK Constitution: Process, Politics and Democracy* (Hart Publishing 2015) 101.

[50] Ibid 116.

[51] For further discussion of these three aspects, see AV Dicey, *Introduction to the Study of the Law of the Constitution* (JWF Allison ed, first published 1885, OUP 2013) 27–8 and 39–40. Young also discusses them, for instance, at Alison L Young, *Parliamentary Sovereignty and the Human Rights Act* (Hart Publishing 2009) 2–3.

4.5.1 Parliament can make any law on any subject matter

Laws by Parliament are enacted in the form of Acts of Parliament. These are passed by the House of Commons, the House of Lords, and formally signed by the monarch at Royal Assent. Only after Royal Assent is granted are Acts passed as law. With this in mind, the first aspect of orthodox theory, described by Dicey as the positive limb,[52] is the notion that Parliament can make and unmake any law on any subject matter. Legally speaking, there are no limits to what Parliament can do, something that is reflected in hypothetical examples given by Jennings and Stephen. They say, for instance, that if Parliament 'enacts that smoking in the streets of Paris is an offence, then it *is* an offence',[53] also noting that Parliament could legislate to have all blue-eyed babies put to death.[54] Though the enforceability of these examples would in reality encounter difficulties, political and jurisdictional to name just two, it would nonetheless be legally possible for Parliament to pass such laws.

 Pause for reflection

What would happen, do you think, if the UK Parliament actually passed a law that sought to outlaw smoking in Paris? Would the French courts enforce such a law and, if not, why?

While these statements by Jennings and Stephen are hypothetical and serve to exemplify the theoretical breadth of Parliament's sovereign law-making capability, there are a number of statutes which exemplify the reality of Parliament's broad law-making powers, as this section now explains through consideration of Acts that demonstrate Parliament's ability to change itself; to legislate contrary to international law; and to pass laws with extra-territorial effect. We look at each of these in turn.

Parliament changing itself

Parliament is capable of altering itself, in terms both of its composition and the procedures through which it enacts law, and this is something that it has sought to do on a number of occasions. The Parliament Act 1911, for example, introduced a new procedure through which legislation could be passed.[55] The Act, as amended by the Parliament Act 1949, made it possible for statutes to be enacted by the House of Commons and Royal Assent alone if it should be that the unelected House of Lords has delayed the passage of a bill for more than a year. Though it is a procedure that has rarely been used,[56] it provides an

---

[52] See AV Dicey, *Introduction to the Study of the Law of the Constitution* (JWF Allison ed, first published 1885, OUP 2013) 27.

[53] Sir Ivor Jennings, *The Law and the Constitution* (5th edn, University of London Press 1959) 170. Jennings does note that it would be 'an offence by English law and not by French law' and, as such, the 'Paris police would not at once begin arresting all smokers, [and] nor would French criminal courts begin inflicting punishments upon them' (170–1).

[54] Sir Leslie Stephen, *The Science of Ethics* (GP Putnam's Sons 1907) 137, cited in AV Dicey, *Introduction to the Study of the Law of the Constitution* (JWF Allison ed, first published 1885, OUP 2013), 47.

[55] See 8.5.9 for further discussion.

[56] Only seven Acts have been passed using this procedure: Government of Ireland Act 1914; Welsh Church Act 1914; Parliament Act 1949; War Crimes Act 1991; European Parliament Elections Act 1999; Sexual Offences (Amendment) Act 2000; and the Hunting Act 2004.

important mechanism through which the elected House of Commons can push through legislation that is being hindered by the unelected House of Lords.

The constitutional nature of this procedure was explored in the case of *R (Jackson) v Attorney General*, in which a challenge was brought to the validity of the Parliament Act 1949 and Hunting Act 2004. Though the case is discussed in much greater detail in 4.6, for the purposes of this discussion it is important here to note the arguments raised in court. The grounds for the challenge were that the Parliament Act 1911 established a new process through which delegated legislation could be enacted, meaning that laws passed pursuant to that process could not be regarded as primary legislation. In chief, this was seen as being due to the view that they rely on the provisions of the 1911 Act for their validity. Consequently, said the appellants, the Parliament Act 1949 (itself passed using the 1911 Act procedure) and, by extension, the Hunting Act 2004 (passed using the 1949 Act's amended procedure) could not be regarded as valid legislation. In joining with other members of the House of Lords in dismissing this argument, however, and upholding the validity of Acts passed pursuant to the Parliament Acts, Lord Carswell endorsed a statement expressed in the Court of Appeal to the effect that:

> [T]here is, in our judgment, no constitutional principle or principle of statutory construction which prevents a legislature from altering its own constitution by enacting alterations to the very instrument from which its powers derive by virtue of powers in that same instrument, if the powers, properly understood, extend that far. This is not performing an act of bootstrap levitation, provided the power exercised is duly derived, directly or indirectly, from a sufficient original sovereign power and authority.[57]

The House of Lords' judgment in *Jackson* had the effect of accepting the legislative sovereignty of Parliament as including the power to alter its own procedures. The Parliament Acts, however, are not the only example of this in action. The House of Lords Act 1999 made various changes to the membership of the legislative chamber of the House of Lords. These substantially reduced the number of hereditary peers in the House from over 700 to just ninety-two and increased significantly the number of Life Peers. Further House of Lords reform has been frequently discussed over the years and, indeed, a House of Lords Reform Bill was laid before Parliament in 2012, setting out proposals to introduce elections to the chamber. This was later abandoned, though, due to a lack of support. As these examples demonstrate, Parliament's sovereign authority includes the ability to change both its procedure and its composition, a power that has been endorsed and accepted by the courts.

Parliament and international law

Another factor that demonstrates the breadth of Parliament's law-making powers is the relationship between domestic parliamentary law and international law. Though 5.4 discusses in great detail the specific way in which membership of the European Union has impacted on the sovereignty of Parliament,[58] this section here considers treaties and other provisions of international law more widely and the manner in which this affects the sovereignty of the UK Parliament.

---

[57] [2005] EWCA Civ 126 [68], cited at [2005] UKHL 56 [174].

[58] EU law is seen as different from other forms of international law. As the European Court of Justice stated in Case 26/62 *Van Gend en Loos v Nederlandse Administratie der Belastingen* [1963] ECR 1, the European Union can be seen as a 'new legal order of international law' (12).

There are two theories that illustrate differing relationships between international laws and national laws. These are monism and dualism. In a monist state, once a treaty has been signed its international legal provisions become a part of that state's domestic law immediately; the two bodies of law exist as one. In a dualist state, by contrast, international and national laws exist on two levels, with only the national laws having domestic legal force. Even once an international treaty is signed, it does not create any legal obligations in that state or have any legal force in the domestic courts until it is also and subsequently 'incorporated' and made a part of national law. The UK is a dualist state and the signing of treaties is a prerogative power exercised by the government.[59] Once a treaty has been signed it will not give rise to any domestic legal obligations or be regarded as a part of UK law until that treaty has also been incorporated into UK law, something that only Parliament has the power to do. For example, in 1951 the UK Government was one of the first countries to sign and ratify the European Convention on Human Rights. As such, at the international level, the UK had various obligations on the basis of the Convention and actions could be brought challenging alleged breaches of its rights in the European Court of Human Rights in Strasbourg, after the granting of individual petition in 1966.[60] The Convention, however, did not become a part of UK law and therefore did not create enforceable obligations in the domestic courts until it was incorporated into UK law by Parliament under the Human Rights Act 1998.

The UK's relationship with international law and the constitution's dualist characteristics stem from the principle of parliamentary sovereignty and the relationship between the legislature and the executive. Orthodox conceptions of sovereignty accept that Parliament is the highest authority in the UK Constitution and that other institutions—including the government—are subordinate. This means that when the UK Government signs an international treaty it does so as a purely executive act, having no legally binding effect on the sovereign Parliament. Indeed, parliamentary sovereignty means that Acts of Parliament, superior to the government, could be passed contrary to the provisions of that treaty. This only changes once the treaty has been incorporated and the international law has been made a part of UK domestic law as an Act of Parliament. In a sense, it is as if the Treaty were a contract between international organizations and governments. This contract binds a government to its terms, but these do not apply to ordinary citizens and domestic law unless and until Parliament decides that it should take effect through statute. This relationship between Parliament's sovereignty and international law is illustrated by the case of *Mortensen v Peters*.[61]

Case in depth: *Mortensen v Peters* (1906) 8 F(J) 93

Mortensen, a native of Denmark, was charged in contravention of the Sea Fisheries (Scotland) Amendment Act 1885 and the Herring Fisheries (Scotland) Act 1889. These Acts conferred upon the Fishery Board for Scotland the power to make byelaws. One such byelaw outlawed a method of fishing known as otter-trawling in an area that was marked by a line drawn from Duncansby Head in Caithness to Rattray Point in Aberdeenshire; an area that included a part of the Moray Firth. Mortensen was found to have been otter-trawling in the Moray Firth and within the area stipulated in the byelaw. Following conviction for the offence, Mortensen appealed. He argued that Denmark and the UK were signatories to the North Sea Fisheries Convention 1883, which provided

→

---

[59] See, for further explanation, 6.5.2.   [60] See 1.4.4.

[61] (1906) 8 F(J) 93.

that fishermen had the exclusive right to fish in waters within 3 miles off their native shore. Since the area of the Moray Firth in which Mortensen was found to be fishing was more than 3 miles from the Scottish coast, he argued it was an area in which he was entitled to fish. Furthermore, Mortensen claimed that the convention limited the UK's jurisdiction over the Moray Firth. The conviction was upheld, however, as the courts acknowledged the supremacy of the domestic legislation and said that it applied, regardless of the international agreement.

Explaining the basis for this decision, Lord Dunedin stated:

> In this Court we have nothing to do with the question of whether the Legislature has or has not done what foreign powers may consider a usurpation in a question with them. Neither are we a tribunal sitting to decide whether an Act of the Legislature is ultra vires as in contravention of generally acknowledged principles of international law. For us an Act of Parliament duly passed by Lords and Commons and assented to by the King, is supreme, and we are bound to give effect to its terms.[62]

The case of *Mortensen v Peters* emphasizes the extent to which Acts of the sovereign Parliament are upheld by the courts, even where there might be conflicting provisions of international law.

〉〉 Discussing the problem

Have a look at the problem scenario at the beginning of this chapter. In view of the judgment in *Mortensen v Peters*, what would the situation be with regards to the UK Government signing an international treaty making it party to a Tax Code? Would the Foreign and Domestic Taxes Act 2024 be invalid?

We have noted that the UK is a dualist state, which means that when the UK Government signs international treaties—as per its prerogative power—then the provisions of those treaties only have domestic legal force once the UK Parliament passes legislation 'incorporating' them into UK law. Until that point, Acts of the UK Parliament remain superior to any treaty by virtue of the fact that the sovereign legislature is superior to the government that signed the treaty. It follows that, as in the case of *Mortensen v Peters*, the UK could pass legislation contrary to any international treaty that the UK Government had signed. In this instance, such a treaty would not affect the validity of the Foreign and Domestic Taxes Act 2024.

Legislating with extra-territorial effect and grants of independence

Jennings has already been quoted as saying that Parliament could legislate to ban smoking in Paris.[63] While, as he also concedes, questions of enforceability in the French courts would limit the scope and application of any such law,[64] the fact remains that Parliament

---

[62] (1906) 8 F(J) 93, 100–1.
[63] See Sir Ivor Jennings, *The Law and the Constitution* (5th edn, University of London Press 1959) 170.
[64] Ibid 170–1.

can legally pass any law that it so chooses, including laws purporting to have effect outside the geographical boundaries of the United Kingdom. Examples of Parliament's power over territories outside the UK are not confined to the hypothetical, however, with a few Acts passed over the years applying to and affecting persons outside the country. Section 72 of the Sexual Offences Act 2003, for example, provides that where a UK national or resident commits an act outside the UK that would, if done in England and Wales, constitute a sexual offence, then the individual can be guilty of the offence under the Act. Also, the Continental Shelf Act 1964 provides in section 1 that '[a]ny rights exercisable by the United Kingdom outside territorial waters with respect to the sea bed and subsoil and their natural resources, except so far as they are exercisable in relation to coal, are hereby vested in Her Majesty'.

More significantly, though, there is a body of legislation that deals with the allocation of power following the independence of countries formerly under the British Empire. The Canada Act 1982, for instance, sets out a constitution for Canada, enacted to ensure that remaining legislative powers up until that time still vested in the UK Parliament could be transferred entirely to the Canadian Constitution. To this end, it states in section 1 that: 'The Constitution Act, 1982 set out in Schedule B to this Act is hereby enacted for and shall have the force of law in Canada and shall come into force as provided in that Act.'[65] In a similar vein, the Australia Act 1986 grants powers, again formerly held by the UK Parliament, to the Parliament in Australia. It states in section 2(2) that:

> [T]he legislative powers of the Parliament of each State include all legislative powers that the Parliament of the United Kingdom might have exercised before the commencement of this Act for the peace, order and good government of that State but nothing in this sub-section confers on a State any capacity that the State did not have immediately before the commencement of this Act to engage in relations with countries outside Australia.[66]

Chief amongst these various Acts granting power to former imperial states, though, is the Statute of Westminster 1931. This grants the dominions freedom to make their own laws, save for where they wish to remain under the authority of the UK Parliament. Section 4 of the Act states that:

> No Act of Parliament of the United Kingdom passed after the commencement of this Act shall extend, or be deemed to extend, to a Dominion as part of the law of that Dominion, unless it is expressly declared in that Act that that Dominion has requested, and consented to, the enactment thereof.

This section of the Statute of Westminster, along with those already identified in respect of the Canada Act and Australia Act, provide further example of Acts of Parliament impacting upon countries outside the United Kingdom.

---

[65] Section 2 of the Canada Act 1982 also provides that 'No Act of the Parliament of the United Kingdom passed after the Constitution Act 1982 comes into force shall extend to Canada as part of its law'.

[66] Section 1 of the Australia Act 1986 also notes that 'No Act of the Parliament of the United Kingdom passed after the commencement of this Act shall extend, or be deemed to extend, to the Commonwealth, to a State or to a Territory as part of the law of the Commonwealth, of the State or of the Territory'.

Counterpoint: Grants of independence and the positive limb

These statutes granting independence to the dominions, however, also raise another notable issue, namely one concerning the UK Parliament's ability to repeal such Acts. Central to orthodox theory is the notion that Parliament has the legal power to repeal any law that it has passed. In considering these Acts granting independence to the dominions, however, this particular strand of orthodox theory presents a potentially difficult issue: if Parliament *were* to repeal the Canada Act or the Statute of Westminster, for example, this would have the effect of returning the various powers transferred to the Canadian or dominion legislatures through those Acts back to the UK Parliament, thereby disempowering the Canadian or other dominion legislatures from making their own laws.

The issue here is one that hinges on two competing factors—the legal sovereignty of Parliament on the one hand and the political reality of its Acts on the other. Despite the strength of orthodox theory, the view on this matter is generally settled. While Parliament might be legally competent to repeal Acts dispersing power to independent dominions, it would not reflect political reality for it to take such a course, as the courts have often explained. In *British Coal Corporation v The King*,[67] for instance, the Privy Council was called upon to consider the Statute of Westminster 1931 and in relation to questions regarding its repeal, Viscount Sankey stated that 'the Imperial Parliament could, as a matter of abstract law, repeal or disregard s. 4 of the Statute. But that is theory and has no relation to realities'.[68] Equally, in *Blackburn v Attorney General*,[69] a case questioning the lawfulness of Britain's accession to the European Communities, Lord Denning, in discussing the Statute of Westminster, cited the words of Viscount Sankey and famously stated that:

> We have all been brought up to believe that, in legal theory, one Parliament cannot bind another and that no Act is irreversible. But legal theory does not always march alongside political reality. Take the Statute of Westminster 1931, which takes away the power of Parliament to legislate for the Dominions. Can any one imagine that Parliament could or would reverse that Statute? Take the Acts which have granted independence to the Dominions and territories overseas. Can anyone imagine that Parliament could or would reverse those laws and take away their independence? Most clearly not. Freedom once given cannot be taken away. Legal theory must give way to practical politics.[70]

While Parliament's sovereign authority includes the power to legislate with extra-territorial effect, where Acts seek to grant power to legislatures in other countries, political questions are raised in connection to whether Parliament would be able to exercise its legal authority in retaking that power. As these various judicial statements show, though, the courts have adopted the view that while the situation does not necessarily alter the legal sovereignty of Parliament, political reality is such that Parliament would not exert its authority in repealing such Acts. While 5.4 further discusses the extent to which European Union membership has impacted on the sovereignty of the UK Parliament, the words of Lauterpacht are notable at this point in observing that 'sovereignty ends where Britain's international obligations begin'.[71]

---

[67] [1935] AC 500.

[68] Ibid 520. Also see, for further discussion, Michael Gordon, *Parliamentary Sovereignty in the UK Constitution: Process, Politics and Democracy* (Hart Publishing 2015) 87.

[69] [1971] 1 WLR 1037.   [70] Ibid 1040.

[71] Eli Lauterpacht, 'Sovereignty—Myth or Reality?' (1997) 73 *International Affairs* 137, 149.

Dicey's consideration that Parliament can make or unmake any law whatsoever is re-flective of a broad legislative ability. Beyond ordinary domestic law-making, Parliament has the power to alter its own procedures and composition; it can legislate superior to unincorporated international law; and it can legislate with extra-territorial effect, albeit within the limits of political and practical reality. But this list is far from exhaustive. Section 3.5.2 considers, for instance, from the perspective of the rule of law, the power of Parliament to legislate with retrospective effect. The War Damages Act 1965, which was enacted by Parliament to overrule a judgment handed down by the House of Lords in *Burmah Oil v Lord Advocate*,[72] arguably offends values at the heart of the rule of law but demonstrates the scope of Parliament's sovereign authority. This section, however, has at least provided an insight into the law-making capabilities of Parliament and the manner in which this reflects orthodox claims of parliamentary sovereignty. It is necessary now to discuss the second aspect of orthodox Diceyan theory.

Discussing the problem

Have another look at the problem scenario set out at the beginning of this chapter: the Foreign and Domestic Taxes Act 2024 purports to require expatriates to pay taxes. To what extent is this possible?

Though there are examples cited throughout this section of the chapter, such as the Australia Act 1986, the Canada Act 1982 and the Continental Shelf Act 1964, that demonstrate Parliament's ability to legislate on matters that are relevant beyond the shores of Britain, the question of whether Parliament could impose taxes on expatriates is more uncertain. Jennings has already been quoted as hypothesizing that Parliament could ban smoking on the streets of Paris.[73] While this is indeed the case in form—Parliament could easily pass such a law—the enforceability of such legislation is less likely. French police and the French courts would not give effect to that particular law because they do not recognize the authority of the UK Parliament.[74] They exist to enforce and uphold French law. Similarly here, then, expatriates would be susceptible to the laws of the country in which they resided, not to the laws passed by the UK Parliament.

4.5.2 No person or body has the power to question the validity of an Act of Parliament

The negative limb of Dicey's conception of parliamentary sovereignty states that no person or body—in particular any court of law—can question the validity of an Act of Parliament.[75] If such people or bodies were to question the validity of legislation, this would undermine the authority of the sovereign Parliament and its law-making ability. Consideration of this negative limb, however, raises two issues: the first relating to the substance of legislation, the second to the procedure by which it is passed. We start with the former.

---

[72] [1965] AC 75.

[73] See Sir Ivor Jennings, *The Law and the Constitution* (5th edn, University of London Press 1959) 170.

[74] Ibid 170–1.

[75] See AV Dicey, *Introduction to the Study of the Law of the Constitution* (JWF Allison ed, first published 1885, OUP 2013) 27.

Substance of legislation

If Parliament, under the positive limb of Dicey's conception of sovereignty, can make or unmake any law on any subject matter and if, under the negative limb, the courts do not have the power to question that legislation,[76] then Parliament essentially has the legal power to pass laws that could be outrageous, immoral, unethical, or unconstitutional. Jennings and Stephen have already provided hypothetical support for this,[77] but there is judicial authority as well. In the Privy Council case of *Madzimbamuto v Lardner-Burke*,[78] in which the validity of the Southern Rhodesia Act 1965 was considered,[79] Lord Reid stated that:

> It is often said that it would be unconstitutional for the United Kingdom Parliament to do certain things, meaning that the moral, political and other reasons against doing them are so strong that most people would regard it as highly improper if Parliament did these things. But that does not mean that it is beyond the power of Parliament to do such things, If Parliament chose to do any of them the courts could not hold the Act of Parliament invalid.[80]

This not only underlines the potential breadth of Parliament's sovereign authority but also demonstrates that the courts do not have the power to strike down legislation, even where it might be regarded as immoral or unconstitutional. The issue of Parliament enacting immoral legislation was something which Dicey himself discussed. He said that 'Acts of Parliament . . . are invalid if they are opposed to the principles of morality . . . Parliament . . . cannot make a law opposed to the dictates of private or public morality'.[81] Though this might seem to offend the very foundation of orthodox theory and set out a limitation to Dicey's conception, it is notable that he goes on to add that:

> There is no legal basis for the theory that judges, as exponents of morality, may overrule Acts of Parliament . . . The plain truth is that our tribunals uniformly act on the principle that a law alleged to be a bad law is *ex hypothesi* a law, and therefore entitled to obedience by the Courts.[82]

The negative limb of parliamentary sovereignty, while serving to protect the legislative authority of Parliament, appears also to leave open the possibility for immoral, unethical, or unconstitutional statutes to be enacted. It is therefore not surprising that on other occasions, the courts have suggested that there is a point at which they might be obliged to step in and declare invalid statutes enacted contrary to certain core values and principles. In 1995, for instance, the then Lord Chief Justice, Lord Woolf, writing extra-judicially, felt that there were extreme instances in which the courts could perhaps question the validity of legislation. In stating that 'I see the courts and Parliament as

---

[76] Ibid 27.

[77] See Sir Ivor Jennings, *The Law and the Constitution* (5th edn, University of London Press 1959) 170; and Sir Leslie Stephen, *The Science of Ethics* (GP Putnam's Sons 1907) 137, cited in AV Dicey, *Introduction to the Study of the Law of the Constitution* (JWF Allison ed, first published 1885, OUP 2013) 47.

[78] [1969] 1 AC 645.

[79] An Act that purported to declare that Southern Rhodesia was a part of the UK colonies and not an independent state.

[80] [1969] 1 AC 645, 723.

[81] AV Dicey, *Introduction to the Study of the Law of the Constitution* (JWF Allison ed, first published 1885, OUP 2013) 38.

[82] Ibid 38–9.

being partners both engaged in a common enterprise involving the upholding of the rule of law'[83] he noted that:

> There are . . . situations where already, in upholding the rule of law, the courts have had to take a stand. The example that springs to mind is the Anisminic case. In that case even the statement in an Act of Parliament that the Commission's decision 'shall not be called in question in any court of law' did not succeed in excluding the jurisdiction of the court. Since that case Parliament has not again mounted such a challenge to the reviewing power of the High Court. There has been, and I am confident there will continue to be, mutual respect for each other's roles.[84]

With this in mind, the point that Lord Woolf goes on to make is that:

> [I]f Parliament did the unthinkable, then I would say that the courts would also be required to act in a manner which would be without precedent . . . there are even limits on the supremacy of Parliament which it is the courts' inalienable responsibility to identify and uphold. They are limits of the most modest dimensions which I believe any democrat would accept. They are no more than are necessary to enable the rule of law to be preserved.[85]

This extra-judicial view was also endorsed by a number of the Law Lords in *R (Jackson) v Attorney-General*.[86] Lord Steyn, for instance, there noted that parliamentary sovereignty:

> is a construct of the common law. The judges created this principle. If that is so, it is not unthinkable that circumstances could arise where the courts may have to qualify a principle established on a different hypothesis of constitutionalism. In exceptional circumstances involving an attempt to abolish judicial review or the ordinary role of the courts, the Appellate Committee of the House of Lords or a new Supreme Court may have to consider whether this is a constitutional fundamental which even a sovereign Parliament acting at the behest of a complaisant House of Commons cannot abolish.[87]

There are substantive limits to the negative limb of orthodox sovereignty. If Parliament were to err into the immoral, unethical, or unconstitutional, for example, it is perhaps not unthinkable—to use Lord Woolf's terminology—that the courts might step in to uphold certain values aligned with the rule of law. While such an eventuality has not yet occurred, an example of sorts can be seen by the judgment in *Anisminic Ltd v Foreign Compensation Commission and others*,[88] a case mentioned by Lord Woolf in the passage we have just examined. *Anisminic* involved a consideration by the House of Lords of a statutory provision that attempted to exclude judicial review through an ouster clause.[89] That provision stated that '[t]he determination by the [Foreign Compensation] Commission of any application made to them under this Act shall not be called in question in any court of law'.[90] Wary

---

[83] Lord Woolf, 'Droit Public—English Style' (1995) *Public Law* 57, 69. Also see 3.5.2.
[84] Ibid 69, citing *Anisminic Ltd v Foreign Compensation Commission* (1969) 2 AC 147. Also see 3.5.2.
[85] Ibid 69.
[86] See the judgments of Baroness Hale [142], Lord Hope [104], and Lord Steyn [71].
[87] [2005] UKHL 56 [102].   [88] [1969] 2 AC 147.
[89] Judicial review is the process through which the courts scrutinize and review the acts and decisions of the executive (see Chapters 10–13).
[90] Section 4(4) of the Foreign Compensation Act 1950. This section was repealed by the Statute Law (Repeals) Act 1989.

of the fundamental role that judicial review plays in affording accountability against the executive, however, the House of Lords held that the statute could not be interpreted as completely restricting enquiry and scrutiny on the part of the courts.

The negative limb of orthodox parliamentary sovereignty works to protect the legislative authority of Parliament by preventing the courts from questioning the validity of statutes. There are, however, potential limits to this approach, as Lord Woolf and Lord Steyn observe, and as is perhaps also implied by the judgment in *Anisminic*. There are certain principles and values that the courts might seek to uphold, even in the face of sovereign legislation to the contrary. Having now examined the extent to which there are, or could be, substantive issues with regards to the negative limb of parliamentary sovereignty, it is necessary now to examine the procedural issues, which brings us to the Enrolled Bill Rule.

Enrolled Bill Rule and continued judicial obedience

The Enrolled Bill Rule serves to ensure that the courts do not question the validity of legislation. It defines the nature of a valid Act of Parliament and stipulates that, once passed through the House of Commons, House of Lords, and Royal Assent, an Act cannot be questioned by the courts. The rule derives from the judgment in *Edinburgh and Dalkeith Railway Company v Wauchope*,[91] though has been upheld and affirmed by the courts more recently, too.

Case in depth: *Edinburgh and Dalkeith Railway Company v Wauchope* (1842) 8 ER 279

The Edinburgh and Dalkeith Railway Company were constructing a railway that was to run through land owned by Wauchope. By virtue of a private Act of Parliament, passed in 1826, the Railway Company was required to pay a tonnage duty for both goods and passengers transported along this particular stretch of line. For many years, however, Wauchope received monies from the Railway Company only for goods and articles, and not for passengers. In 1835, Wauchope sought to claim unpaid money due for the transportation of passengers across his land. The Railway Company contested his right to do this, however, claiming that even if the Act of Parliament had originally conferred upon Wauchope the right to claim such sums in respect of passengers it was now at an end because Wauchope had, for so long, sought only to claim monies in respect of goods and articles only. On this point, the House of Lords found for Wauchope and held that just because he had not, to date, charged for the passengers being carried across his land, this did not preclude him from later seeking money in that regard.

One issue that was discussed in the case concerned the passing of an Act of Parliament that purported to repeal *some* of the provisions of the former Act, extend other provisions, and continue the rest.[92] On this point, the appellants argued that a new Act of Parliament had taken away some of the duties of the former Act. By contrast, the respondent argued that 'the right conferred by [the original Act of Parliament] . . . was not affected by the [more recent Act of Parliament] . . . or . . . if it was, then that latter Act could not

---

[91] (1842) 8 ER 279.   [92] Ibid 280.

be made applicable to him, for that it was private Act affecting a vested right, and had been introduced without due notice of its introduction being served on him'.[93] Though this point was actually dropped in the House of Lords appeal, their lordships nonetheless felt that the contention relating to the lack of notice of the private bill was worthy of comment. On this, Lord Brougham noted:

> I will only add one word on a point which has been abandoned at this bar . . . namely, that the want of notice in one of the preliminary stages of an Act of Parliament, operates to prevent that Act from affecting the rights of the parties to whom such notice ought to have been given. Such a doctrine is wholly without justification.[94]

The House of Lords felt that the validity of an Act of Parliament could not be challenged on the grounds that a preliminary requirement in the legislative process had been ignored or overlooked. It is this aspect of the decision that establishes the Enrolled Bill Rule, a notion that serves to substantiate and support Dicey's negative limb that no institution should have the power to question an Act of Parliament.[95] In considering this point further and explaining the broader principle underlying the Enrolled Bill Rule, Lord Campbell also stated in *Wauchope* that:

> I think it right to say a word or two upon the point that has been raised with regard to an Act of Parliament being held inoperative by a Court of Justice because the forms prescribed by the two Houses to be observed in the passing of a bill have not been exactly followed . . . All that a Court of Justice can do is to look to the Parliamentary roll: if from that it should appear that a bill has passed both Houses and received the Royal assent, no Court of Justice can inquire into the mode in which it was introduced into Parliament, nor into what was done previous to its introduction, or what passed in Parliament during its progress in its various stages through both Houses.[96]

Since the mid-nineteenth century and the case of *Wauchope*, the Enrolled Bill Rule has become central to orthodox understandings of parliamentary sovereignty and, indeed, courts continue to acknowledge its relevance and importance today. In *Manuel v Attorney General*,[97] for example, Sir Robert Megarry VC stated that:

> I have heard nothing in this case to make me doubt the simple rule that the duty of the court is to obey and apply every Act of Parliament, and that the court cannot hold any such Act to be ultra vires. Of course there may be questions about what the Act means, and of course there is power to hold statutory instruments and other subordinate legislation ultra vires. But once an instrument is recognised as being an Act of Parliament, no English court can refuse to obey it or question its validity . . . There has been no suggestion that the copy before me is not a true copy of the [Canada] Act [1982] itself, or that it was not passed by the House of Commons and the House of Lords, or did not receive the Royal Assent. The Act is therefore an Act of Parliament and the court cannot hold it to be invalid.[98]

---

[93] Ibid 280.   [94] Ibid 283.

[95] See AV Dicey, *Introduction to the Study of the Law of the Constitution* (JWF Allison ed, first published 1885, OUP 2013) 27.

[96] (1842) 8 ER 279, 284–5, a statement that is consistent with Article 9 of the Bill of Rights 1688.

[97] [1983] Ch 77.

[98] [1983] Ch 77, 86. Sir Robert Megarry VC then went on to cite Lord Campbell's obiter statement from *Edinburgh and Dalkeith Railway Company v Wauchope* (1842) 8 ER 279, 284–5.

Similarly, in *Pickin v British Railways Board*,[99] Lord Reid cited Lord Campbell's words from *Wauchope* and added that '[t]he function of the court is to construe and apply the enactments of Parliament . . . [It] has no concern with the manner in which Parliament or its officers carrying out its Standing Orders perform [their] . . . functions'.[100]

The principle underpinning the Enrolled Bill Rule is widely supported. Lord Reid's statement, however, was not the only observation of the principle in *Pickin*. The case serves today more generally as a notable authority for the reluctance of the courts to question both the validity of Acts of Parliament and the parliamentary process itself.

Case in depth: *British Railways Board v Pickin* [1974] AC 765

Pursuant to section 259 of the Bristol and Exeter Railway Act 1836 (a private Act), where a railway line has become abandoned the land which the line occupies is acquired by the owner(s) of the adjoining land. In time, this section came to be repealed by another private Act, the British Railways Act 1968, which had the effect of ensuring that *inter alia* land occupied by abandoned lines vested in the British Railways Board. In this case, Pickin, having come into possession of land adjoining the abandoned track in question, brought an action under section 259 of the 1836 Act to the effect that he was the owner of the land. The Railways Board argued against this, however, claiming that section 18 of the 1968 Act served to vest the land in the Board itself. Against this, Pickin argued that the Railways Board had fraudulently misled Parliament in getting the bill passed by falsely declaring that the requisite documents had been deposited with the necessary authority and that, as such, section 18 was ineffective and could not be relied upon. The Board sought to have the action struck down. Though early hearings found in favour of the Board, the Court of Appeal, reversed this decision. The House of Lords then allowed the Board's appeal and found that they did not have the power to question the validity of the 1968 Act.

The House of Lords' judgment in *Pickin* is notable due to the way in which the Law Lords sought to underline the continued importance of parliamentary sovereignty, there demonstrating an ongoing commitment to orthodox Diceyan theory.[101] Lord Reid stated in *Pickin* that:

> The idea that a court is entitled to disregard a provision in an Act of Parliament on any ground must seem strange and startling to anyone with any knowledge of the history and law of our constitution . . . In earlier times, many learned lawyers seem to have believed that an Act of Parliament could be disregarded in so far as it was contrary to the law of God or the law of nature or natural justice, but since the supremacy of Parliament was finally demonstrated by the Revolution of 1688 any such idea has become obsolete . . . The function of the court is to construe and apply the enactments of Parliament. The court has no concern with the manner in which Parliament or its officers carrying out its Standing Orders perform these functions.[102]

The Enrolled Bill Rule, supported by *Wauchope* and *Pickin*, is a well-established principle at common law. It underlines the importance of Dicey's negative limb of parliamentary

---

[99] [1974] AC 765.   [100] Ibid 787.
[101] See Michael Gordon, 'The Conceptual Foundations of Parliamentary Sovereignty: Reconsidering Jennings and Wade' (2009) *Public Law* 519, 520.
[102] [1974] AC 765 at 782 and 787.

sovereignty and ensures that no institution has the power to question the validity of primary legislation.

Within the confines of domestic law[103] the courts have, historically, been generally willing to uphold the validity of parliamentary legislation, as a number of cases support. As this section has highlighted, however, there are perhaps moral or ethical boundaries to Parliament's sovereignty, which would fall to the courts to police. While such an eventuality has not yet occurred, statements by both Lord Woolf and Lord Steyn suggest that if Parliament did 'cross the line', the courts might well be called upon to question the validity of Acts of Parliament. Indeed, more recent concerns with the unquestionable power of Parliament are discussed in the following sections in respect of the judgments in *Jackson* and *HS2*. For now, though, we move to the final aspect of orthodox Diceyan theory of parliamentary sovereignty.

4.5.3 No Parliament is bound by its predecessors or can bind its successors

As this section has so far explained, the positive and negative limbs of orthodox theory explain the essence of the principle and clarify why and how it is that Parliament is regarded as sovereign in the UK Constitution. If we are to accept that Parliament is sovereign, however, then we must also accept that there is one fundamental restriction upon its power. Simply put, Parliament cannot bind succeeding Parliaments or be bound by those that have gone before it. The underlying rationale for this is that if Parliament were to bind its successors, then future incarnations of the legislature would be limited in their law-making abilities, thereby rendering them no longer sovereign. As Dicey himself explains, quoting Todd, 'it is certain that a Parliament cannot so bind its successors by the terms of any statute, as to limit the discretion of a future Parliament, and thereby disable the Legislature from entire freedom of action at any future time'.[104] By requiring, then, that Parliament cannot bind succeeding Parliaments, the future and continued sovereignty of the legislature is ensured.

It is a peculiar facet of the principle, therefore, that a seemingly supreme authority should have limits upon its power, but it is also a necessary feature to ensure the continued sovereignty of Parliament. The most significant way in which this aspect of orthodox theory is given effect is through the doctrine of implied repeal.

Implied repeal

Repeal is the process of revoking legislation, and it is capable of being done either by express words or by implication. Express repeal is so called by virtue of the fact that the repealing legislation acknowledges all or part of the previous Act and makes explicit provision for its repeal and possibly its replacement. For example, section 211(2) and Schedule 27 to the Equality Act 2010 expressly list a number of statutes that are repealed as a result of its new legislative provisions.[105] Implied repeal, by contrast, takes place

---

[103] Section 5.4 explores the extent to which the courts have been faced with questions concerning the validity of Acts of Parliament in line with EU law.

[104] Alpheus Todd, *Parliamentary Government in the British Colonies* (Longmans, Green and co, 1880) 192, as cited in AV Dicey, *Introduction to the Study of the Law of the Constitution* (JWF Allison ed, first published 1885, OUP 2013) 41.

[105] That schedule provides that, inter alia, the Race Relations Act 1976, Equal Pay Act 1970, Sex Discrimination Act 1986, and the Disability Discrimination Act 1985 are repealed in their entirety.

not on the basis of express wording of legislation but by virtue of contradictions and conflicts between two Acts of Parliament. Premised on the understanding that no two pieces of conflicting legislation can co-exist, where an Act is passed that conflicts with and goes against the provisions of an existing statute, then the more recent Act is said to have impliedly repealed the former Act, or sections of it. Implied repeal does not involve Parliament but is instead a rule employed by the courts for the purposes of ensuring that the latest will of Parliament is upheld, thereby making it impossible for Parliament to bind its successors as new legislation will always overrule previous legislation.

The reality of the doctrine of implied repeal, in the context of parliamentary sovereignty, is noted by Dicey who explains that '[s]hould the Dentists' Act, 1878, unfortunately contravene the terms of the Act of Union, the Act of Union would be *pro tanto* repealed'.[106] In addition to this, there is also strong judicial support for implied repeal, demonstrated by two key cases: *Vauxhall Estates v Liverpool Corporation*[107] and *Ellen Street Estates Ltd v Minister of Health*.[108]

Case in depth: *Vauxhall Estates v Liverpool Corporation* [1932] 1 KB 733

Pursuant to the Housing Act 1925, the Corporation of Liverpool set out a scheme under which a particular area of the city would be improved. The chosen area included land owned by Vauxhall Estates Ltd. An issue arose, however, as to the manner in which compensation to be paid to Vauxhall Estates was assessed. The Corporation appointed an official arbitrator, under the Acquisition of Land Act 1919, to consider the question of compensation. Section 2 of the 1919 Act set out provisions relating to the assessment of compensation and, under section 7(1) of the Act, any subsequent statutory provisions on the same matter should only 'have effect subject to this Act, and so far as inconsistent with this Act those provisions shall cease to have or shall not have effect'. Vauxhall Estates sought to argue, however, that section 46 of the 1925 Act (a further provision for the assessment of compensation and under which the Corporation sought to base their claim) was inconsistent with the 1919 Act and had repealed the scheme introduced under the 1919 Act. The question that the Divisional Court sought to consider was whether section 7 of the 1919 Act was capable of requiring future provisions to be in line with the 1919 Act or whether section 46 of the 1925 Act succeeded in repealing the earlier statute. The court found that section 7 of the 1919 Act could not bind future Parliaments; consequently the 1925 Act was found to have impliedly repealed the 1919 Act.

In reaching this decision and in giving the leading judgment, Avory J stated that:

> [W]e are asked to say that by a provision of this Act of 1919 the hands of Parliament were tied in such a way that it could not by any subsequent Act enact anything which was inconsistent with the provisions of the Act of 1919. It must be admitted that such a suggestion as that is inconsistent with the principle of the constitution of this country. Speaking for myself, I should certainly hold, until the contrary were decided, that no Act of Parliament can effectively provide that no future Act shall interfere with its provisions.[109]

---

[106] AV Dicey, *Introduction to the Study of the Law of the Constitution* (JWF Allison ed, first published 1885, OUP 2013) 78.
[107] [1932] 1 KB 733.   [108] [1934] 1 KB 590.   [109] [1932] 1 KB 733, 743.

In the later case of *Ellen Street Estates Ltd v Minister of Health*, the same facts arose. There was again a conflict between section 7 of the Acquisition of Land Act 1919 and section 46 of the Housing Act 1925 as to how much compensation should be paid in respect of an improvement scheme on land owned by the Ellen Street Estates company. This time, though, the case went to the Court of Appeal, which followed and approved the decision that the Divisional Court had reached in *Vauxhall Estates*. Maugham LJ there stated that:

> The legislature cannot, according to our constitution, bind itself as to the form of subsequent legislation, and it is impossible for Parliament to enact that in a subsequent statute dealing with the same subject-matter there can be no implied repeal. If in a subsequent Act Parliament chooses to make it plain that the earlier statute is being to some extent repealed, effect must be given to that intention just because it is the will of the legislature.[110]

The two cases of *Vauxhall Estates* and *Ellen Street Estates* provide authority for the doctrine of implied repeal. As both the decisions make clear, the notion that Parliament might pass legislation seeking to bind future Parliaments, as section 7 of the Acquisition of Land Act 1919 arguably purported to do, does not sit easily with orthodox theory. If Parliament is to maintain its sovereign power, then whenever it enacts legislation contradicting or conflicting with existing legislative provisions, the more recent enactment must be taken to have impliedly repealed the earlier provision or Act.

 Discussing the problem

In the problem scenario set out at the beginning of this chapter, if Parliament were to pass a statute that conflicted with the provisions of the Foreign and Domestic Taxes Act 2024, but did not mention it explicitly, what effect would this have on the 2024 Act?

According to the orthodox principle, if Parliament enacted legislation that conflicted with the Foreign and Domestic Taxes Act 2024 but which did not expressly address its repeal, then under the authority of the *Vauxhall Estates* and *Ellen Street Estates* cases, the new Act would have impliedly repealed the 2024 Act.

The doctrine of implied repeal supports orthodox theory insofar as it ensures that Parliament cannot bind succeeding Parliaments or be bound by those that have already been. This is not, however, the only thing to consider when discussing this particular aspect of parliamentary sovereignty.[111] We must also consider the contrasting views of continuing and self-embracing sovereignty, which raise questions that go to the very heart of the principle of parliamentary sovereignty.

 Pause for reflection

To what extent do you think the courts' use of the implied repeal doctrine interferes with parliamentary intention? If Parliament did not expressly revoke an Act, should the courts have the ability to infer repeal through subsequent parliamentary enactment?

---

[110] [1934] 1 KB 590, 597 (also see HWR Wade, 'The Basis of Legal Sovereignty' (1955) 13(2) *Cambridge Law Journal* 172, 175).
[111] We return to this in 5.4.

Continuing and self-embracing sovereignty

The orthodox view that Parliament cannot be bound by its predecessors or bind its successors, while supported by the doctrine of implied repeal, has been a point of contention for some theorists. This contention is based on an apparent conflict between the illimitable ability of Parliament to pass laws on any subject matter and the notion that Parliament cannot bind its successors. On the one hand, the argument is that, if Parliament can pass any law it wants, then surely this includes the power to bind itself. On the other hand, however, as soon as Parliament has bound itself, it no longer has the power to make or unmake any law, as has already been explained. This contention, then, gives rise to two competing schools of thought—those espousing a theory of continuing sovereignty and those supporting the notion of self-embracing sovereignty. This section explores these competing ideas, starting with continuing sovereignty.

Continuing sovereignty

Continuing sovereignty is an explanation of orthodox theory. It suggests that Parliament's sovereignty is ongoing and continuous and that every time Parliament meets it is not bound by any previous enactments, having free and limitless power to pass any law whatsoever. The only thing it cannot do is bind future Parliaments, as per the exposition from Dicey that we have just considered.

Wade discusses continuing sovereignty in terms of the importance of implied repeal, arguing that no legislation is immune from being repealed by implication. He states that the idea of Parliament entrenching legislation 'is a legal impossibility . . . all . . . legislation . . . [is] repealable by any ordinary Act . . . Parliament cannot bind its successors . . . there is one, and only one, limit to Parliament's legal power: it cannot detract from its own continuing sovereignty'.[112] This argument fits neatly with Wade's explanation of the basis of sovereignty. It is recalled briefly that he considers the sovereignty of Parliament to be ultimate, established as a result of the political settlement reached in 1688 and continued through the ongoing political relationship between Parliament and the courts. Recalling, too, that sovereignty is dependent upon the courts' acceptance of Parliament's sovereign power, it follows from Wade's conception that Parliament does not have the power to alter this political relationship or its own sovereignty unilaterally. It is capable only of being altered by way of a revolution, which would only come about where the courts acknowledge an alternative sovereign body. Enacting laws that purport to bind future Parliaments and that demand some form of entrenchment over future legislation requires the courts to accept an alteration of the political relationship and while Parliament can pass such laws, the courts would not necessarily acknowledge their validity.[113] Continuing sovereignty is therefore consistent with orthodox theory. Accepting that, as Dicey noted, the one thing Parliament cannot do is bind future Parliaments, the otherwise illimitable power of Parliament to pass any law whatsoever remains.

---

[112] HWR Wade, 'The Basis of Legal Sovereignty' (1955) 13(2) *Cambridge Law Journal* 172, 174.

[113] Ibid 189 and for further discussion, Mark Elliott and Robert Thomas, *Public Law* (3rd edn, OUP 2017) 232–41.

Self-embracing sovereignty

In contrast to continuing sovereignty, proponents of self-embracing sovereignty accept that Parliament is capable of binding itself and entrenching legislation. This goes against a key plank of orthodox theory but is rooted in the notion that *if* Parliament is sovereign and has supreme law-making power, then this must surely mean that it has the power to do anything that it wants, *including* bind itself. Jennings, discussed earlier in the chapter, was a proponent of self-embracing sovereignty and he explained that:

> [T]he legislature has for the time being power to make laws of any kind in the manner required by the law. That is, a rule expressed to be made by the Queen, 'with the advice and consent of the Lords . . . and Commons . . .' will be recognised by the courts, *including a rule which alters this law itself* . . . the 'legal sovereign' may impose legal limitations upon itself, because its power to change the law includes the power to change the law affecting itself.[114]

Recalling Jennings' observation of sovereignty as a common law principle, expressing the relationship between Parliament and the courts,[115] self-embracing sovereignty can be justified on the following basis:

   (a) Parliament is dependent on the common law for acknowledgement of its sovereign power;

   (b) Parliament, as sovereign legislature, is superior to the common law;

   (c) Parliament can thus change the common law rules determining its own sovereignty.[116]

Simply put, if Parliament enacts a law that purports to bind future Parliaments, then in view of the common law's subordination to Parliament, the courts will be bound to follow and apply that law, regardless of its content. Crucially, this view also means that Parliament could pass a law effectively seeking to 'unbind' itself and the courts would also be bound to give effect to that law. The sovereignty of Parliament would be maintained through its continuing ability to pass any law whatsoever. If Parliament can be said to have the power to bind itself and entrench legislation, however, it is important to consider the way in which this might be achieved in practice.

When we talk of entrenchment, we mean that a law is in some way protected from repeal or revocation through the ordinary legislative process,[117] or to put it another way, it means employing 'a mechanism . . . to enhance the level of protection of a particular statute from amendment or repeal'.[118] Mechanisms employed to offer that protection might include requirements for a particular result in a referendum to be achieved before repeal can be effective; or the need for a heightened majority in a legislative chamber before repealing provisions can be passed.

---

[114] Sir Ivor Jennings, *The Law and the Constitution* (5th edn, University of London Press 1959) 153.

[115] Ibid 149.   [116] Ibid 159–63.

[117] We can distinguish between procedural and substantive entrenchment. Procedural entrenchment exists where an Act of Parliament sets out a different procedure for repeal, beyond the ordinary legislative process, making that Act harder to repeal; substantive entrenchment exists where a particular substantive area of law or policy is protected from ordinary parliamentary activity.

[118] Han-Ru Zhou, 'Revisiting the "Manner and Form" Theory of Parliamentary Sovereignty' (2013) 129 *Law Quarterly Review* 610, 614.

Discussing the problem

Have another look at the problem scenario at the beginning of the chapter. You can see that the Foreign and Domestic Taxes Act 2024 requires a two-thirds majority before it can be repealed. Under continuing and self-embracing sovereignty, to what extent is this provision valid?

This issue goes right to the very heart of Dicey's conception of parliamentary sovereignty. Specifically, it highlights the problem that derives from Parliament's ability, on the one hand, to pass any law on any subject matter and, on the other, the limitation that Parliament cannot bind future Parliaments. Under the positive limb of Dicey's principle, Parliament could easily include in the Foreign and Domestic Taxes Act a provision that stipulated the need for a two-thirds majority before it could be repealed. However, if it sought to do so, future Parliaments would be bound by this requirement and therefore limited in their ability to pass 'any law'. Parliament would only be able to repeal the 2024 Act *if* they met the requirement stipulated in the Act. It is this conundrum that has inspired a great deal of discussion and debate, as this chapter has explained, most notably through the opposing arguments of Wade and Jennings. If we accept that the provision of the 2024 Act, requiring a two-thirds majority for repeal, can be seen as an attempt by Parliament to alter the terms of the settlement and change the basis on which its Acts are regarded as sovereign, then Wade and Jennings reach different conclusions about the validity of this particular provision of the 2024 Act. Wade argues that parliamentary sovereignty is a political fact that can only be changed by an alteration in the political settlement established by the Bill of Rights 1688; it cannot be changed by Parliament alone. As such, the provision in the Foreign and Domestic Taxes Act 2024 requiring a two-thirds majority would not be required to be followed by subsequent Parliaments, since it is merely Parliament seeking to alter its own sovereignty. It would not, on this view, be valid. Jennings, by contrast, stresses that, since the courts ultimately give Parliament its sovereignty through their recognition of Acts as sovereign, then Parliament can simply use its superiority over the courts to change the terms of its sovereignty. It could be argued that this is what Parliament is seeking to do here and that the provision of the Foreign and Domestic Taxes Act 2024 is valid on this view. This feature of the 2024 Act raises a particularly thorny issue, rife with academic debate and discussion.

Despite the theoretical support for self-embracing sovereignty and the arguments suggesting that Parliament has the ability to bind itself, there are no instances under the UK Constitution of legislation that has been in any way entrenched. The most commonly cited examples are cases in former imperial constitutions, which discuss the authority of UK Acts of Parliament. It is these that we explore now, starting with *Attorney-General of New South Wales v Trethowan*.[119]

Case in depth: *Attorney-General of New South Wales v Trethowan* [1932] AC 526

This appeal to the Privy Council from the High Court of Australia involved a challenge to the validity of provisions seeking to alter the Constitution Act 1902, which sets out the Constitution for New South Wales, by abolishing the legislative council. The 1902 Act, amended in 1929, provided in section

→

[119] [1932] AC 526.

→

7A that 'no Bill for abolishing the Legislative Council should be presented to the Governor for His Majesty's assent until it had been approved by a majority of the electors voting upon a submission to them made in accordance with the section', with the same provision applying to any bill attempting to repeal section 7A. In 1930, however, two Acts were passed that sought to repeal section 7A and abolish the legislative council without a referendum. This case was consequently brought by two members of the legislative council on the grounds that the requirements of section 7A had not been met in seeking its repeal or the abolition of the legislative council. The Supreme Court of New South Wales held that, pursuant to section 5 of the Colonial Laws Validity Act 1865 (an Act of the UK Parliament), the legislature of New South Wales had the power 'to make laws respecting the constitution, powers and procedure of the legislature, provided that the laws should have been passed in such "manner and form" as might from time to time be required by any Act of Parliament, letters patent, Order in Council, or colonial law in force in the colony'. On this basis, it determined that the requirements of section 7A should be upheld and injunctions granted preventing the enforcement of the consequent attempts to repeal section 7A and abolish the legislative council. Appeals to the High Court of Australia and the Privy Council were unsuccessful, with those courts agreeing that section 7A of the Constitution Act 1902, amended in 1929, was a valid provision and should be followed.

Putting these facts in the context of our discussion, section 7A of the Constitution Act 1902, amended in 1929, sought to entrench the position of the legislative council by requiring an extraordinary procedure to be followed in the event of its abolition; a provision that the court upheld. In setting out the Privy Council's judgment, Viscount Sankey stated that:

> The question . . . arises, could . . . a repealing Bill, after its passage through both chambers, be lawfully presented for the Royal assent without having first received the approval of the electors in the prescribed manner? In their Lordships' opinion, the Bill could not lawfully be so presented. The proviso in the second sentence of s. 5 of the Act of 1865 states a condition which must be fulfilled before the legislature can validly exercise its power to make the kind of laws which are referred to in that sentence. In order that s. 7A may be repealed . . . the law for that purpose must have been passed in the manner required by s. 7A.[120]

The court held that section 7A was an entrenched provision. Requiring assent through a referendum before it could be repealed, the two bills purporting to repeal section 7A and abolish the legislative chamber were not valid because they had not been passed with a referendum, pursuant to the requirements set out in section 7A itself. Commenting on this case, Jennings notes that '[t]he Judicial Committee [of the Privy Council] decided that the Act of 1929 provided the "manner and form" which were to be followed in respect of any Bill of the kind mentioned in that Act'.[121]

The judgment in *Trethowan* shows an example of a legislative procedure binding future Parliaments as to the way in which laws should be passed. It is not, however, an isolated example, with two subsequent cases—*Harris v Minister for the Interior*[122] and *Bribery Commissioner v Ranasinghe*[123]—finding that Acts of the UK Parliament are capable of binding legislatures in South Africa and Ceylon (now Sri Lanka) as to the procedure through

---

[120] [1932] AC 526, 540–1.
[121] Sir Ivor Jennings, *The Law and the Constitution* (5th edn, University of London Press 1959) 154.
[122] [1952] 1 TLR 1245.   [123] [1965] AC 172.

which certain legislative reforms can be enacted. The three cases together demonstrate an acceptance of manner and form provisions and provide authority for courts' willingness to accept that a legislature's provisions can legally bind later enactments with regards to the way in which they should be passed.

While invoked to exemplify the workings and authority of self-embracing sovereignty and the notion that a parliament can bind itself, however, all three of these cases have a crucial characteristic in common: they all involved former imperial constitutions testing the authority of UK Acts of Parliament over legislatures that are inferior to the UK Constitution.[124] As such, their relevance as authority for self-embracing sovereignty is at best persuasive.[125] The UK Parliament has not sought to bind itself through entrenched legal provisions in the same form and, as such, there is no judicial authority explaining how this should or might be regarded if it did.

 Discussing the problem

In the problem scenario outlined at the beginning of this chapter, the Foreign and Domestic Taxes Act 2024 requires a two-thirds majority before it can be repealed. If Parliament passes a repealing Act through a simple majority, however, could the courts question the validity of such an Act and strike this down on the basis that the requisite majority has not been met?

This question refers to an issue that is presented, on the one hand, by the debate already highlighted concerning whether or not Parliament could impose a condition requiring a heightened majority be achieved before legislation is repealed and, on the other hand, the negative limb of Dicey's orthodox conception. The negative limb states that no body, including a court of law, can question the validity of Acts of Parliament. This is buttressed by the 'Enrolled Bill Rule', which operates on the basis that, provided an Act has been passed by the House of Commons, the House of Lords, and received Royal Assent, it is regarded as an Act of Parliament and cannot be questioned by the courts. On this view, legislation repealing the 2024 Act through a simple majority would be seen as valid and could not be challenged by the courts. The alternative argument, however, rests on the view put forward by Jennings and is supported by the manner and form cases, such as *Trethowan*. This suggests that Parliament could enact a provision requiring a two-thirds majority be achieved before repeal, thereby altering the nature of its sovereign power. On this basis, the courts could find that the provision of the 2024 Act, requiring a heightened majority to be achieved, is lawful.

We can see that the notion of self-embracing sovereignty in respect of the UK Parliament has little practical authority. The theory is supported by cases dealing more with the relationship between supreme and subordinate legislatures than with parliamentary attempts at entrenchment and it is not possible, as a result, to say how the UK courts would treat such attempts. Nonetheless, Jennings' consideration of sovereignty is interesting and serves to highlight the problematic nature of aspects of orthodox Diceyan theory. While it is a key tenet of sovereignty that no Parliament be able to bind succeeding Parliaments,

---

[124] *Trethowan* was a case relating to New South Wales, *Harris* related to South Africa, and *Ranasinghe* related to Ceylon (now known as Sri Lanka).

[125] See Han-Ru Zhou, 'Revisiting the "Manner and Form" Theory of Parliamentary Sovereignty' (2013) 129 *Law Quarterly Review* 610, 615.

questions of entrenchment have equally become a central part of recent theoretical debates. Having now explored in detail orthodox parliamentary sovereignty, founded as that is on Dicey's nineteenth-century statements, the next section now examines the principle's continued relevance in the modern UK Constitution.

4.6 The courts and parliamentary sovereignty today

4.6.1 The approach of the courts and the preservation of parliamentary sovereignty

Section 5.4 discusses the principle of parliamentary sovereignty in light of the European Communities Act and the UK's membership of the European Union. This will enable further consideration of whether or not Parliament can still be regarded as sovereign specifically in light of the supremacy of EU Law. For now, however, it is necessary to close this chapter by exploring recent considerations of sovereignty by the House of Lords and the Supreme Court. To this end, this section discusses two notable cases: *R (Jackson) v Attorney General*[126] and *R (on the application of HS2 Action Alliance Limited) v Secretary of State for Transport*.[127] We take one at a time.

Case in depth: *R (Jackson) v Attorney General* [2005] UKHL 56

This case involved a challenge to the validity of the Parliament Act 1949 and the Hunting Act 2004, the latter being passed to make hunting with dogs unlawful. The legal background to the case is the procedure set out in the Parliament Act 1911. As previously noted, the 1911 Act introduced a legislative procedure whereby a bill could be passed without the House of Lords' consent, after the Lords had delayed the process by two years. The Parliament Act 1949 Act amended this, providing that the Lords could only delay the passage of a bill by one year instead of two.

At the heart of the challenge was the contention that since the Parliament Act 1949 had itself been passed using the 1911 Act procedure it could not be regarded as a valid Act of Parliament and, as a result, the Hunting Act 2004 was also invalid. This challenge was based on the argument that the 1911 Act created a procedure for passing merely delegated legislation and that both the 1911 and 1949 Acts created a subordinate non-sovereign legislature, with power delegated to it by the full Westminster Parliament. On this basis, and at the heart of suggestions that the 1949 and 2004 Acts were invalid, it was argued that changes to the procedure set out in the 1911 Act could only be made with the consent of the full Parliament—including the House of Lords. As a consequence, the Parliament Act 1949 was argued as invalid, as was legislation passed in its name—in this case, the Hunting Act 2004.

The challenge was rejected, however, with the Divisional Court, Court of Appeal, and House of Lords setting out various reasons why the Parliament Act 1911 could be used to pass primary legislation, including Acts that altered that Act's legislative procedure. The Parliament Act 1949 and, as a result, the Hunting Act 2004 were upheld as valid.

Above and beyond the finding that the Parliament Act 1949 and the Hunting Act 2004 were valid and that section 2(1) of the Parliament Act 1911 was capable of giving rise to primary legislation, the judgment in *Jackson* is also notable due to the House of Lords'

---

[126] [2005] UKHL 56.   [127] [2014] UKSC 3.

various obiter statements considering the relevance of parliamentary sovereignty in the modern UK Constitution, with Lords Hope and Steyn, along with Baroness Hale, discussing the principle at length.

In view of the prevailing authority at the time (most notably the judgment in *Pickin*), it is significant that the House of Lords was even called upon to consider the issues raised in *Jackson*, involving as it did questions of legislative validity. As Lord Nicholls noted in the case:

> These proceedings are highly unusual. At first sight a challenge in court to the validity of a statute seems to offend the fundamental constitutional principle that the courts will not look behind an Act of Parliament and investigate the process by which it was enacted. Those matters are for Parliament, not the courts.[128]

In giving judgment in *Jackson*, however, their lordships distinguished the issue on the basis that, unlike *Pickin*, they were being called upon not to *question* parliamentary procedure, but to *interpret* section 2(1) of the Parliament Act 1911 and consider whether Acts passed pursuant to its provisions could be considered 'enacted law'.[129] This, said Lord Bingham, raises 'a question of law which cannot . . . be resolved by Parliament' and is instead one that should be resolved by the courts.[130]

In resolving this issue, the House of Lords unanimously held in favour of the sovereignty of Parliament, stating that 'Parliament can do anything', including 'redesign itself' as it purportedly did through section 2(1) of the Parliament Act 1911.[131] Much discussion in the House, however, also considered the *nature* of this sovereignty, the development of orthodox theory and whether the principle could be said to have been altered by the Parliament Acts. In exploring these, it is necessary first to consider the wording of section 2(1) of the 1911 Act, as amended by the Parliament Act 1949, which states that:

> If any Public Bill (other than a Money Bill or a Bill containing any provision to extend the maximum duration of Parliament beyond five years) is passed by the House of Commons in two successive sessions . . . and, having been sent up to the House of Lords at least one month before the end of the session, is rejected by the House of Lords in each of those sessions, that Bill shall, on its rejection for the second time by the House of Lords, unless the House of Commons direct to the contrary, be presented to His Majesty and become an Act of Parliament on the Royal Assent being signified thereto, notwithstanding that the House of Lords have not consented to the Bill: Provided that this provision shall not take effect unless one year has elapsed between the date of the second reading in the first of those sessions of the Bill in the House of Commons and the date on which it passes the House of Commons in the second of these sessions.[132]

One of the contentions with regard to this section, and particularly the words 'a Bill containing any provision to extend the maximum duration of Parliament beyond five years', is that it effectively binds future Parliaments as regards the power—or rather lack thereof—to extend the life of Parliament beyond five years.[133] As Lord Nicholls points out, not only does this section prevent the use of the 1911 Act to extend the life

---

[128] [2005] UKHL 56 [49].   [129] Ibid [27] and [51].   [130] Ibid [27].
[131] Ibid [159] and [160].   [132] See, for further discussion, 8.5.9.
[133] See: Alison L Young, 'Hunting Sovereignty: Jackson v Her Majesty's Attorney-General' (2006) *Public Law* 187, 193–4.

of Parliament but, in addition, it can also not be used 'to force through a Bill deleting' these words from section 2 (thereby removing the restriction and giving Parliament the power to extend itself using the 1911 Act).[134] As Young notes, this effectively makes section 2(1) an entrenched provision insofar as 'Parliaments wishing to overturn its provisions can only do so by adopting a specific manner and form—legislation that has the consent of the House of Lords'; an argument that points towards a form of self-embracing sovereignty.[135]

By contrast, however, the judgments of Lords Hope, Nicholls, and Carswell consider that section 2(1) of the 1911 Act preserves continuing sovereignty.[136] This is founded on a Wadean perspective of the principle and suggests that section 2(1) 'modified the way in which valid legislation can be enacted', thereby altering the political fact of parliamentary sovereignty itself.[137] This means that, in practice and through section 2(1), the courts, already recognizing the sovereignty of Parliament, now recognize sovereignty on an altered understanding—namely, that Parliament can pass Acts through a different process (ie without the House of Lords' consent). This view is substantiated by the fact that, as Lord Hope also acknowledged, 'the 1949 Acts proclaims itself to be, and appears on the Parliamentary Roll as, an Act of Parliament'.[138]

Regardless of whether the judgment in *Jackson* can be said to support a continuing or self-embracing conception of sovereignty, though, the House of Lords was clear and unanimous in the view that parliamentary enactments under section 2(1) of the Parliament Act 1911 were valid and that what Parliament had sought to do through that section it was able to do by virtue of its sovereignty. As Baroness Hale stated:

> The concept of parliamentary sovereignty which has been fundamental to the constitution of England and Wales since the 17th century . . . means that Parliament can do anything . . . If Parliament can do anything, there is no reason why Parliament should not decide to redesign itself, either in general or for a particular purpose . . . [and] it follows that Parliament can allow its redesigned self further to modify the design.[139]

Mindful of the consequences of such allegedly unfettered authority, however, and wary of the changed constitutional landscape in which the courts' relationship with Parliament was now placed, the House of Lords was acutely aware of the potential dangers that could lie within the power of section 2(1) of the Parliament Act 1911. Lord Steyn stated that:

> [T]he 1949 Act could . . . be used to introduce oppressive and wholly undemocratic legislation. For example, it could theoretically be used to abolish judicial review of flagrant abuse of power by a government or even the role of the ordinary courts in standing between the executive and citizens. This is where we may have to come back to the point about the supremacy of Parliament . . . The classic account given by Dicey of the doctrine of the supremacy of Parliament, pure and absolute as it was, can now be seen to be out of place in the modern United Kingdom. Nevertheless, . . . [it] is still the general principle of our constitution. It is a construct of the common law. The judges created this principle. If that is so, it is not unthinkable that circumstances could arise where the courts may have to qualify a principle established on a different hypothesis of

---

[134] See [2005] UKHL 56 [58] and [59].

[135] Alison L Young, 'Hunting Sovereignty: Jackson v Her Majesty's Attorney-General' (2006) *Public Law* 187, 194.

[136] Ibid 193–4.   [137] Ibid 194.   [138] [2005] UKHL 56 [125].   [139] Ibid [159]–[160].

constitutionalism. In exceptional circumstances involving an attempt to abolish judicial review or the ordinary role of the courts, the Appellate Committee of the House of Lords or a new Supreme Court may have to consider whether this is a constitutional fundamental which even a sovereign Parliament acting at the behest of a complaisant House of Commons cannot abolish.[140]

This is a notable statement and one that underlines the importance of the *Jackson* judgment. While the court's decision in the case had the effect of upholding the sovereignty of Parliament, Lord Steyn's considerations of how far the courts *might* have gone in more severe circumstances is telling and reflective of a potentially changing constitutional landscape. The acknowledgement that Dicey is 'out of place' is hardly surprising; while the statement that 'it is not unthinkable that circumstances could arise where the courts may have to qualify a principle [of sovereignty] established on a different hypothesis of constitutionalism'[141] endorses the earlier, extra-judicial view of Lord Woolf, already discussed.[142] This emphasizes the degree of change which the constitution has witnessed since Diceyan orthodox theory was espoused in 1885 and the form that the principle of parliamentary sovereignty now takes in the modern constitution. The recent *HS2* case, though, demonstrates this further, as this section now explains.

 Pause for reflection

In *Jackson*, Lord Steyn states that 'it is not unthinkable that circumstances could arise where the courts may have to qualify a principle established on a different hypothesis of constitutionalism'. Aside from the hypothetical abolition of judicial review mentioned in his judgment, what other circumstances can you think of where the courts might be forced to 'qualify the principle' of parliamentary sovereignty?

The significance of the Supreme Court decision in *R (on the application of HS2 Action Alliance Limited) v Secretary of State for Transport* stems from judgments of Lords Neuberger and Mance, which offered insight into the continuing application and constitutional importance of certain established principles, including that set out in Article 9 of the Bill of Rights 1688.

The appeal itself was concerned with questions relating, first, to whether strategic environmental assessments should have been carried out before the government set out its plans for the High-Speed 2 rail link, pursuant to EU law, and secondly, whether the hybrid bill procedure proposed for the relevant legislation was compliant with EU law. In the case, the Supreme Court was asked 'not only to consider the adequacy of . . . information placed before members of both Houses of Parliament, but also to take the step of scrutinising the likely adequacy . . . of their procedures and debates' in line with the Environmental Impact Assessment Directive.[143] Recalling that Article 9 of the Bill of Rights provides that 'the Freedom of Speech and Debates or Proceedings in Parliament

---

[140] [2005] UKHL 56 [102]. This is a concern with which Lord Hope also agrees ([127]).
[141] [2005] UKHL 56 [102].
[142] See Lord Woolf, 'Droit Public—English Style' (1995) *Public Law* 57, 69.
[143] [2014] UKSC 3 [200].

ought not to be impeached or questioned in any Court or Place out of Parliament',[144] the Supreme Court considered whether they could, in honouring obligations placed within EU law, scrutinize the workings of the UK Parliament. This was, in essence, a consideration of a possible clash between two constitutional statutes: namely, the European Communities Act 1972 and Article 9 of the Bill of Rights 1688.[145] To put this issue another way, the question was whether an investigation into the workings of Parliament, as required at EU Law and mandated by the European Communities Act 1972, would have the effect of impliedly repealing Article 9 of the Bill of Rights, which itself forbade such investigation.

In considering the issue, Lords Neuberger and Mance emphasized that '[t]he principle enshrined in article 9 is recognised and buttressed by a series of constitutional cases'.[146] Acknowledging the accepted supremacy of EU law and the limitations that that has historically imposed upon the UK Constitution,[147] they then continued by noting that:

> Scrutiny of the workings of Parliament and whether they satisfy externally imposed criteria clearly involves questioning and potentially impeaching (i.e. condemning) Parliament's internal proceedings, and would go a considerable step further than any United Kingdom court has ever gone.

> The United Kingdom has no written constitution, but we have a number of constitutional instruments. They include Magna Carta, the Petition of Right 1628, the Bill of Rights and (in Scotland) the Claim of Rights Act 1689, the Act of Settlement 1701 and the Act of Union 1707. The European Communities Act 1972, the Human Rights Act 1998 and the Constitutional Reform Act 2005 may now be added to this list. The common law itself also recognises certain principles as fundamental to the rule of law. It is, putting the point at its lowest, certainly arguable (and it is for United Kingdom law and courts to determine) that there may be fundamental principles, whether contained in other constitutional instruments or recognised at common law, of which Parliament when it enacted the European Communities Act 1972 did not either contemplate or authorise the abrogation.[148]

The effect of the *HS2* judgment is notable. Though it is relevant to a broader discussion exploring the relationship between UK law and EU law, it is here significant as discussing the relationship between two constitutionally important statutes and the legal status of certain constitutional values, recognized at common law. The Supreme Court found that the fundamental constitutional principle set out in Article 9 of the Bill of Rights was recognized at common law and was capable of binding future Parliaments. This not only meant that the investigation into parliamentary procedure, as required at EU law, could not be deemed constitutional, but moreover had the effect of demonstrating that constitutional principles, protected at common law, could act as a restraint

---

[144] Article 9 of the Bill of Rights 1688.

[145] In *Thoburn v Sunderland City Council* [2002] EWHC 195 (Admin), discussed further in 5.4.3, Laws LJ identified a hierarchy of statutes: ordinary statutes and constitutional statutes. He suggested that constitutional statutes were immune from implied repeal [62].

[146] [2014] UKSC 3 [204]. They refer to cases cited by Lord Reed [78]: *Edinburgh and Dalkeith Railway Co v Wauchope* (1842) 8 ER 279; *Lee v Bude and Torrington Junction Railway Co* (1871) LR 6 CP 576; *Pickin v British Railways Board* [1974] AC 765; and *Wilson v First County Trust Ltd (No 2)* [2003] UKHL 40.

[147] See 5.3 and 5.4.   [148] [2014] UKSC 3 [206]–[207].

upon Parliament's sovereign authority. As Elliott notes: 'on the view adopted in *HS2*, constitutional norms operate as *legal* constraints upon Parliament's legislative capacity, denying it the authority to effect their disturbance other than through express or specific provision'.[149]

Both *HS2* and *Jackson* demonstrate that whether through Lord Steyn's obiter comments suggesting that there might be a point at which the courts would step in to protect fundamental values against an Act of Parliament or through the Supreme Court's decision to bind Parliament to core constitutional values protected at the common law, the nature of parliamentary sovereignty has changed. Amidst broader constitutional controls[150] and the impact that these have on our domestic institutions, the emboldened courts are seemingly willing to play a more prominent role in determining the nature of parliamentary sovereignty, not afraid to impose limits if competing constitutional interests should require. This being so, where no circumstances arise for this more prominent and emboldened action, then the courts have always been plain in their protection of parliamentary sovereignty. The House of Lords' decision in *Jackson* reflects this; comments hypothesizing a possible state of affairs where the courts might step in to protect fundamental values against an Act of Parliament are obiter.

Most recently, though, the Supreme Court decision in *R (Miller) v Prime Minister* represents a resounding restatement of the importance of parliamentary sovereignty in the UK Constitution. *Miller* was discussed in detail in 2.4.3 and this section does not seek to replicate those discussions here. In brief, the case concerned a challenge to the Prime Minister's prorogation of Parliament in September 2019. With just weeks to go until the date at which the UK was then due to leave the European Union and with no deal in place, the Prime Minister asked the Queen to prorogue Parliament for five weeks. On appeal from challenges in the English and Scottish Courts, the Supreme Court held that the prorogation was unlawful because it frustrated the operation of Parliament in its law-making activities and in its ability to hold the Government to account. In so doing, though, the Court emphasized the importance of the principle of parliamentary sovereignty. They said:

> Time and again, in a series of cases since the 17th century, the courts have protected Parliamentary sovereignty from threats posed to it by the use of prerogative powers, and in doing so have demonstrated that prerogative powers are limited by the principle of Parliamentary sovereignty . . . [Similarly here, t]he sovereignty of Parliament would . . . be undermined as the foundational principle of our constitution if the executive could, through the use of the prerogative, prevent Parliament from exercising its legislative authority for as long as it pleased . . . the power to prorogue cannot be unlimited.[151]

---

[149] Mark Elliott, 'Constitutional Legislation, European Union Law and the Nature of the United Kingdom's Contemporary Constitution' (2014) 10(3) *European Constitutional Law Review* 379, 392. Also see Paul Craig, 'Constitutionalising Constitutional Law: HS2' (2014) *Public Law* 373.

[150] Lord Steyn himself identifies these, stating that: 'We do not in the United Kingdom have an uncontrolled constitution . . . In the European context the second *Factortame* decision [1991] 1 AC 603 made that clear. The settlement contained in the Scotland Act 1998 also point to a divided sovereignty. Moreover, the European Convention on Human Rights as incorporated into our law by the Human Rights Act 1998, created a new legal order' ([2005] UKHL 56 [102]).

[151] [2019] UKSC 41, [41], [42], and [44]. The court cites as examples of these 'cases since the 17th century' the *Case of Proclamations* (1611) 12 Co Rep 74; *Attorney General v De Keyser's Royal Hotel Ltd* [1920] AC 508; and *R v Secretary of State for the Home Department, ex p Fire Brigades Union* [1995] 2 AC 513.

The above discussion notwithstanding, therefore, and despite the courts' clear thinking that they might be required to step in to protect certain constitutional values from Parliament or bind Parliament to certain principles, the courts have nonetheless consistently upheld the importance of parliamentary sovereignty.

4.6.2 Common law constitutionalism

Consideration of these various cases and their explanation of the way in which parliamentary sovereignty applies and is relevant in the UK Constitution brings us to one final consideration; namely, common law constitutionalism. In 1.3.2, constitutionalism was identified as 'the notion of governments operating and acting in adherence to and in accordance with the constitutional principles of a state'.[152] Constitutionalism can be presented in different forms. Political constitutionalism, for instance, refers to the manner in which the political machinery of a state provides the rules and principles upon which the constitution is founded, whilst legal constitutionalism sees this as being routed in legal provision, perhaps even a codified constitutional document. A strand of legal constitutionalism, however, concerns 'the creative development of the common law as a way of ensuring that legal values permeate the current constitutional system. We can label this strand of thought "common law constitutionalism"'.[153] What this means is that, particularly in the UK where no codified constitutional document exists, we can—in certain areas and in respect of certain principles—rely on and draw from the common law as providing the basis for constitutional principle. This reality is evident from a number of matters, including aspects of judicial review of administrative action and, pre-1998, the protection of human rights and civil liberties in the UK. For the purposes of this explanation, though, we can say that through the various judicial rules and principles espoused through a number of cases—many of which have been discussed throughout this chapter—constitutional rules and principles have been developed. They reflect, in other words, common law constitutionalism. The notion, for example, that Parliament might hypothetically be bound as to the manner and form of legislation, discussed in 4.5.3, or the idea that the courts might step in to protect constitutional values eroded by Acts of Parliament, provide just two examples of common law constitutionalism and its impact in this area.

4.7 Summary

This chapter, then, has considered and explored the orthodox theory of parliamentary sovereignty. It has demonstrated the foundations of the principle, rooted as it is in constitutional history, and it has explained the Diceyan conception of sovereignty. There have, over the years, been various challenges to this principle, most notably those based on arguments supporting self-embracing sovereignty, and these have even led some to suggest that the principle is out of place in our modern UK Constitution.[154] Whether or not this is seen as the case, discussions in both *Jackson* and *HS2* highlight the extent to which it has changed over the centuries. These both show that while parliamentary sovereignty remains a fundamental principle of UK constitutional law, it now sits amidst a range of other constitutional doctrines and relationships that often fall to the courts to examine. Chief amongst these is the relationship between UK law and EU law, on which Chapter 5 now focuses.

---

[152] See: 1.3.2.

[153] Andrew Le Sueur, Maurice Sunkin, and Jo Eric Khushal Murkens, *Public Law* (4th edn, OUP 2019) 28.

[154] See Lord Steyn at [2005] UKHL 56 [102].

Quick test questions

1. Identify the main points of the orthodox theory of parliamentary sovereignty.

2. Explain the historic importance of the Bill of Rights in terms of parliamentary sovereignty.

3. How does the doctrine of implied repeal ensure that Parliament is not bound by its predecessors or bind its successors?

4. Explain the rules relating to 'manner and form' provisions.

5. What is the Enrolled Bill Rule?

6. Explain the significance of the judgment in *Dr Bonham's* case.

7. How did Wade view the sovereignty of Parliament? What, according to Wade, is needed for there to be a change in this allocation of sovereign power?

Further reading

Understanding parliamentary sovereignty

*AV Dicey, *Introduction to the Study of the Law of the Constitution* (JWF Allison ed, first published 1885, OUP 2013)

Martin Loughlin and Stephen Tierney, 'The Shibboleth of Sovereignty' (2018) 81(6) *Modern Law Review* 989

*HWR Wade, 'The Basis of Legal Sovereignty' (1955) 13(2) *Cambridge Law Journal* 172

Continuing and self-embracing sovereignty

Michael Gordon, 'The Conceptual Foundations of Parliamentary Sovereignty: Reconsidering Jennings and Wade' (2009) *Public Law* 519

*Michael Gordon, *Parliamentary Sovereignty in the UK Constitution: Process, Politics and Democracy* (Hart Publishing 2015)

Han-Ru Zhou, 'Revisiting the "Manner and Form" Theory of Parliamentary Sovereignty' (2013) 129 *Law Quarterly Review* 610

Parliamentary sovereignty today

Anthony Bradley, 'The Sovereignty of Parliament—Form or Substance?' in Jeffrey Jowell and Dawn Oliver (eds), *The Changing Constitution* (7th edn, OUP 2011) 35

*Paul Craig, 'Constitutionalising Constitutional Law: HS2' (2014) *Public Law* 373

Mark Elliott, 'Constitutional Legislation, European Union Law and the Nature of the United Kingdom's Contemporary Constitution' (2014) 10(3) *European Constitutional Law Review* 379

Jeffrey Goldsworthy, *Parliamentary Sovereignty: Contemporary Debates* (Cambridge University Press 2010)

*Alison L Young, 'Hunting Sovereignty: *Jackson v Her Majesty's Attorney-General*' (2006) *Public Law* 187

 Visit this book's **online resources** for additional materials relating to this chapter, including a full analysis of the start-of-chapter problem scenario.
www.oup.com/he/stanton-prescott2e

5

Parliamentary sovereignty, the European Union, and Brexit

Problem scenario

Given the result of the 2016 referendum to leave the European Union, the Stilton Cheese Producers Association is concerned about the impact of Brexit on the businesses of its members. In particular they are concerned about the effect of EU law no longer applying to the UK following the withdrawal of the UK from the EU on 31st January 2020.

This is because under EU Regulation 1151/2012[1] Stilton cheese is protected by 'Protected Designation of Origin' status, which means that Stilton cheese can only be produced in the English counties of Leicestershire, Derbyshire, and Nottinghamshire and must be produced according to the traditional method. Even if a producer of cheese, elsewhere in the UK or in another EU Member State, uses exactly the same ingredients and production methods as the producers who are based within those three counties, it is unlawful for them to call their cheese 'Stilton'. Essentially, EU law protects the name 'Stilton' and ensures that consumers of Stilton cheese can be sure that what they buy in the supermarkets is genuinely Stilton cheese produced according to traditional methods.

[1] Parliament and Council Regulation (EU) 1151/2012 on quality schemes for agricultural products and foodstuffs [2012] OJ L343/1.

5.1 **Introduction**

At a referendum held on 23 June 2016, 52 per cent of voters opted to leave the EU, with 48 per cent voting to remain.[2] The day after, the government announced that it would start to prepare to begin the process of the UK's withdrawal from the EU, commonly referred to as 'Brexit'.

The UK became a member of the European Economic Community ('EEC') on 1 January 1973. As explained in 5.4, a significant motivation for joining was economic, as the UK's economy lagged behind the Member States of the EEC. The EEC later became known as the European Community (EC) and then the European Union (EU).

Given our discussion of parliamentary sovereignty in Chapter 4, the key constitutional question that arose of the UK's entry into the EU was how to take account of the supremacy of EU law. EU law is binding on the legal systems of all its Member States and takes priority over all domestic laws and decisions. In the UK, this inevitably impacts significantly on parliamentary sovereignty as it is a constitutional impossibility to have two supreme entities making laws and decisions for a country; one must be superior over the other. Consequently, on numerous occasions, the courts have addressed the question of how EU law applies in the UK and the manner in which it has impacted on parliamentary sovereignty. This case law is the focus of the first half of this chapter as it seeks to map out how EU law is applied in the UK.

Concerns about the impact of EU membership on parliamentary sovereignty fed into broader questions held by some about the UK's continuing membership. These concerns grew as successive reforms increased the EU's powers as it acquired competencies to act in new policy areas. These issues contributed to a demand for a referendum on the UK's membership. The vote to leave set the government and Parliament the challenge of establishing the terms of departure, and the new relationship with the EU. Whatever is agreed with the EU, the UK's broader standing in the world will be changed, particularly in the field of international trade, a policy area which since 1973 has been addressed through the EU.

The political and legal backdrop to the referendum, its aftermath, and the emerging future relationship form the focus of the second half of this chapter. In legal terms this requires considering the process of withdrawal as laid down by Article 50 TEU ('Article 50') and the outcome of that process, and addressing how the UK legal system will deal with all the EU law that has become part of the UK's legal system during its membership of the EU. This will require considering the European Union (Withdrawal) Act 2018.

In November 2018, the UK and the EU agreed a Withdrawal Agreement and Framework for Future Relationship as required by Article 50, but this was rejected three times by the House of Commons. This ultimately led to Theresa May's resignation as Prime Minister. Her replacement, Boris Johnson, renegotiated aspects of the Withdrawal Agreement, but the House of Commons refused to approve it unconditionally. The government's response was to seek a general election, which was held in December 2019. The Conservative Party's clear victory with an eighty-seat majority gave Johnson the mandate he needed to go on to ratify and implement the Withdrawal Agreement as he had agreed with the EU. From a UK perspective, the last significant stage of this process was the

---

[2] This is a fast-developing area of law and policy and this chapter is up to date as of 21 November 2019. See the online resources for up-to-date information and ongoing discussion on Brexit.

enactment of the European Union (Withdrawal Agreement) Act 2020, which amended the European Union (Withdrawal) Act 2018. The 2020 Act was enacted in time for the UK's departure from the EU on 31 January 2020.

At the time of writing, attention has now shifted to negotiating the ongoing future relationship between the UK and the EU, which may take effect on 1 January 2021.[3]

Overall, this chapter aims:

- to introduce the European Union, explain its origins and its key institutions;

- to explain the supremacy of EU law;

- to explore the nature of the UK's membership of the EU, discussing in particular the way in which the supremacy of EU law impacts upon the sovereignty of the UK Parliament;

- to examine the political and legal background to the Brexit process and how EU law that has become part of UK law through the UK's EU membership will remain part of UK law under the European Union (Withdrawal) Act 2018;

- to consider the Withdrawal Agreement and Framework for Future Relationship as negotiated between the UK and the EU, and how this will be implemented into UK law by discussing the main features of the European Union (Withdrawal Agreement) Act 2020; and

- to briefly consider the future relationship between the UK and the EU, once the UK has left the EU.

5.2 The origins of the EU and its institutions

To comprehensively consider the workings of the EU, a specialist text should be consulted.[4] As this chapter aims to consider the effect of EU membership on parliamentary sovereignty and the UK legal system more generally, the following sketch of the origins of the EU and its institutions provides the backdrop for the next three sections which explain the supremacy of EU law, how and why the UK joined the EU, and the relationship between UK and EU law, given the doctrine of parliamentary sovereignty.

After the atrocities of the Second World War, and the devastation that gripped Europe, in the years that followed there was a collective determination to ensure that the same thing could not and would not happen again. On this basis, the European Coal and Steel Community (ECSC) and European Economic Community (EEC) were established in the 1950s with the aim of fostering greater unity and security across Europe, laying the foundations for what is now the European Union.[5]

---

[3] As this is a developing issue, please consult the online resources for up-to-date information regarding the negotiation of the future relationship between the UK and the EU.

[4] See: Paul Craig and Gráinne de Búrca, *EU Law: Text, Cases and Materials* (7th edn, OUP 2020) or Margot Horspool, Matthew Humphreys, and Michael Wells-Greco, *European Union Law* (10th edn, OUP 2018).

[5] Alongside the creation of the EEC, the European Atomic Energy Community (Euratom) was created under a separate treaty. This is primarily concerned with the development of the nuclear energy industry. Although all members of the EU are also members of Euratom, it is governed by a separate treaty to the present-day EU. As the UK also left Euratom as well as the EU on 31 January 2020, it is not discussed further in this chapter.

5.2.1 The European Coal and Steel Community

The first such community, the European Coal and Steel Community, was established in 1951 by the Treaty of Paris with the intention of contributing 'to economic expansion, the development of employment and the improvement of the standard of living'.[6] In particular, the treaty sought to 'establish conditions which . . . [would] assure the most rational distribution of production at the highest possible level of productivity, while safeguarding the continuity of employment and avoiding . . . fundamental and persistent disturbances in the economies of the member States'.[7] The objective here was to ensure that individual countries in Europe could not have exclusive access to the coal and steel industry that had been instrumental in providing resources during the Second World War. As the then French foreign minister, Robert Schuman, stated, sharing these resources in this way would 'make it plain that any war between France and Germany becomes not merely unthinkable, but materially impossible'.[8]

The Treaty of Paris created four main institutions. The High Authority would exercise executive power, with each Member State government appointing one member. The High Authority would be required to consult the Council, which was formed by a representative of the government of each Member State. The Assembly would supervise the actions of the ECSC and be formed from representatives from the parliaments of each Member State. The Court of Justice would determine the definitive meaning of the Treaty.

5.2.2 European Economic Community

A continuing desire to develop the level of integration and unity in Europe led to the Treaty of Rome ('EEC Treaty'), which established the European Economic Community ('EEC') in 1957.[9] The founding Member States were Belgium, France, West Germany, Italy, Luxembourg, and the Netherlands. Although the eventual objective may well have been to achieve a deepening level of political integration, through 'an ever closer Union', initially the focus of the EEC was on economic integration. Primarily, this would be achieved by removing barriers to trade such as tariffs and quotas through establishing a customs union and a common or single market. A customs union is an agreement between several countries that aims to eliminate tariffs on goods traded between them, with the same tariffs imposed on goods that originate from countries outside the customs union. Central to the single market are the four freedoms of goods, services, capital, and workers. In principle, if a good could be sold lawfully in one Member State, it could be sold lawfully in the other EEC Member States. To ensure fair access to the market, anti-competitive practices were outlawed and national governments were unable to support their own industries and producers at the expense of those in other Member States.

The EEC shared the Assembly and Court of Justice with the ECSC. However, the Treaty of Rome also established a separate Council of Ministers, formed of a representative from the government of each Member State, and with executive power being exercised by the Commission. The Commission would represent the interests of the Community and

---

[6] Treaty constituting the European Coal and Steel Community, Art 2 (this Treaty expired in July 2002).

[7] Ibid.

[8] Robert Schuman, 'The Schuman Declaration' (9 May 1950), https://europa.eu/european-union/about-eu/symbols/europe-day/schuman-declaration_en.

[9] Formally called the Treaty Establishing the European Economic Community.

propose legislation to further the objectives of the EEC Treaty. The Council of Ministers would vote on these legislative proposals, often using qualified majority voting, which would give the larger Member States a greater say than smaller ones. The Assembly had a right to be consulted, but little more.

Following the Merger Treaty in 1965, these institutions were later shared with the ECSC, with the Commission taking over the functions of the High Authority.

5.2.3 Enlargement and evolution

The two key features of the development of the Communities until the mid-1980s were enlargement and evolution. In 1973, the new Member States acceded to (meaning joined) the Communities for the first time. These were the UK (after two aborted attempts), Ireland, and Denmark. The UK's Accession is discussed in 5.4. Greece joined in 1981, with Spain and Portugal following in 1986, meaning that the number of Member States had doubled from six to twelve.

Within the EEC, the Member States wrestled with the *supranational* aims of the EEC Treaty while protecting and advancing their own national interests through a more *intergovernmental* approach. Supranationalism would require that the aims of the Treaty should be pursued for the benefit of the broader Community, even if that damaged the interests of individual Member States, particularly in the short-term. While an intergovernmental approach would ensure that Member States could protect national interests more effectively, agreement of all Member States would be needed for any proposal at Community level. This would inevitably slow down the progress of the Community.

Attempts at resolving this tension run through the continuing evolution of the EEC and, later, the EU. The Luxembourg Accords meant that even if the EEC Treaty provided for decisions to be made by a majority of Member States in the Council of Ministers, an issue would not proceed any further if a Member State argued that its 'very important interests' were at stake. Similarly, from 1974 the European Council, at which the Heads of Government from each Member State met twice a year, would set the broad direction of the EEC, further increased the role that the national interest would play in decision-making. However, other institutions, particularly the Court of Justice, furthered supranationalism with a series of landmark decisions that furthered the aims of the EEC Treaty over the interests of Member States. Several of these decisions formed the basis of the supremacy of EEC, and then, later, EU law, over the law of Member States and are discussed in 5.3. From 1979, the Assembly became the European Parliament and elected through direct elections held in each Member State.

The first significant amendment to the EEC came with the Single European Act in 1986 ('SEA'). The main aim of the SEA was sought to enable 'The Community shall adopt measures with the aim of progressively establishing the internal market over a period expiring on 31 December 1992', with the internal market defined as 'an area without internal frontiers in which the free movement of goods, persons, services and capital is ensured in accordance with the provisions of this Treaty'.[10]

To complete the single market, the Community was given the power to approximate the laws of the Member States (meaning to bring them into closer alignment with each other), including through the harmonization of laws across Member States. In order to complete the internal market, measures were needed to eliminate as far as possible non-tariff barriers to

---

[10] Single European Act, Art 13, inserting Art 8a EEC.

trade, such as the need to comply with different regulations across Member States. For example, if a car manufacturer in Germany needed to comply with different environmental standards in each Member State, they may need to produce different models for different countries, which would be difficult, expensive and so form a substantial barrier to trade. It would be much easier if a single standard applied across all Member States, meaning that the German car manufacturer only needs to comply with one set of standards. In addition, consumers in Member States other than Germany could purchase German produced cars safe in the knowledge that it complies with the same standards as cars produced within their own Member State.

To pass such harmonizing measures, the SEA created a new legislative-making procedure, known as the cooperation procedure.[11] The power of the European Parliament was increased and it could, if supported by the Council, block measures proposed by the Commission. More significantly, under this procedure, the Council of Ministers would use qualified majority voting, rather than unanimity, making it much easier for measures to pass and become law. At least as regards the internal market, this was a distinctive shift towards supranationalism.

5.2.4 Maastricht Treaty

Although the SEA revitalized the Community, and significant progress was made, the single market was still some way from 'completion'. This momentum was carried forward with the Maastricht Treaty, which entered into force in 1993. The Maastricht Treaty, formally known as the Treaty on European Union (TEU), established the creation of the European Union, and adopted a three-pillar structure. This pillar structure enabled both the supranational and governmental approaches to European integration to continue. Within the first pillar sat what was the European Economic Community, now renamed the European Community (with the formal title of the EEC Treaty now changed to the Treaty Establishing the European Community, or EC Treaty for short). As discussed, the increasing use of qualified majority voting in the Council highlighted how the Community had increasingly adopted a more supranational approach as it strived to complete the single market.

The next two pillars were contained in the TEU, and were the Common, Foreign and Security Policy, and Policy in Justice and Home Affairs respectively. As these issues were felt to impinge upon the sovereignty of Member States to a greater extent than most issues related to the single market, these two pillars adopted a strongly intergovernmental approach, with little or no role for the Commission, the Parliament, or the CJEU, as decisions were made either in the Council of Ministers or the European Council.

The longer-term significance is that the TEU laid down the foundations and established the timetable for the creation of Economic and Monetary Union, and the adoption of the Single European Currency—the euro. For those Member States taking part, this was a significant increase in economic integration, as significant aspects of economic policy would increasingly be determined by a new institution, the European Central Bank.

5.2.5 The Constitutional Treaty and Treaty of Lisbon

The Treaty of Amsterdam and Treaty of Nice were both intended to prepare the EU for enlargement. By now the EU had fifteen Member States, following the accession of Austria, Finland, and Sweden in 1995, and preparations were required for the accession of ten

---

[11] Originally, this was Article 100a EEC, now it is Art 114 TFEU.

more in 2004, with eight being former Communist countries within the USSR.[12] At least symbolically, this was the biggest stride towards the European unity sought since the aftermath of the Second World War. However, as we have seen, the institutional structure of the EU was created with six Member States in mind and had been amended to work for fifteen Member States. Some felt that the leap to twenty-five, and eventually even more, would ultimately require fundamental reform to the EU's institutional structure.

Treaty Establishing a Constitution for Europe

These concerns led to the negotiation of the Treaty Establishing a Constitution for Europe, which as its name suggests included aspects more readily seen in texts of state constitutions rather than treaties creating international organizations. The pillar structure adopted by the Maastricht Treaty was to be abandoned, with the EU obtaining full and single legal personality, with the ability to create 'European laws' and 'framework laws'.[13] The EU would legally adopt a flag, a motto ('United in diversity'), and an anthem. Some were concerned that the EU was moving towards acquiring the character of a state with aspects of the Treaty such as the creation of the position of Union Minister for Foreign Affairs. These and many other aspects of the Constitution proved controversial as the Treaty was rejected in referendums in France and the Netherlands. This ultimately caused the Constitution to be abandoned.[14]

The Lisbon Treaty

However, many aspects of the Constitution were salvaged by the Lisbon Treaty. Entering into force in 2009, its primary aim was to amend rather than replace the existing treaties, the TEU and EC Treaty. As with the Constitution, the Lisbon Treaty abolished the pillar structure, with the EC pillar now falling as part of the broader EU. All references to 'Community' were replaced with 'Union'. The EC Treaty was renamed as the Treaty on the Functioning of the European Union, or TFEU for short.

Treaty on European Union

The TEU reaffirms the fundamental goal 'of an ever closer union among the peoples of the Europe',[15] which is achieved through pursuing the objectives of the EU. These include the internal market; the euro; providing EU citizens an area of freedom, security, and justice 'without internal frontiers, in which the free movement of persons is ensured'; and conducting relations with the 'wider world'.[16] The TEU provides for the legal personality of the EU.[17] Other fundamental institutional matters addressed by the TEU include provision for the TEU and TFEU to be amended according to a simplified revision procedure, the process by which a 'European State' can apply to become an EU member.[18]

---

[12] The eight former Soviet countries that joined in 2004 were Czech Republic, Estonia, Latvia, Lithuania, Hungary, Poland, Slovenia, and Slovakia. Also, Cyprus and Malta joined in 2004. In 2007, Bulgaria and Romania joined, and Croatia followed in 2013.

[13] Treaty Establishing a Constitution for Europe, Art I-34.

[14] This meant that the UK Government did not need to hold its promised referendum on the Constitutional Treaty.

[15] TEU Art 1.   [16] TEU Art 3.   [17] TEU Art 47.

[18] TEU Art 49. The use of 'European State' is interesting, as this indicates a distinctive limit to the geographical reach of the EU. For instance, in 1987, Morocco applied to join the (then) EC, but this was rejected on the basis that Morocco was not a 'European State'.

Conversely, and importantly for the second half of this chapter, the TEU outlines the process by which a Member State can withdraw from the EU.[19]

The TEU consciously avoids any of the state apparatus that proved so controversial with the Constitution, meaning that there is no reference to a flag, motto, or anthem and the Union Minister for Foreign Affairs was amended to become a High Representative of the Union for Foreign Affairs.[20] Although the pillar structure from the Maastricht Treaty has been abolished, at least the spirit of the pillars remains in the TEU as particular rules apply to the Common Foreign and Security Policy, which place the emphasis on decision-making within the Council and European Council, which, as explained in the next section, are separate institutions of the EU.

Institutions of the EU

The TEU also establishes the institutions of the EU—the key features of each are now discussed in turn.[21]

European Council—Composed of the Heads of Government of the Member States and headed by its President, the main role of the European Council is to outline the 'general political direction and priorities' of the Union.[22] For example, for the period 2019–24, the European Council has set four broad priorities: (1) protecting citizens and freedoms; (2) developing a strong and vibrant economic base; (3) building a climate-neutral, green, fair, and social Europe; and (4) promoting European interests and values on the global stage.[23]

European Commission—Within the framework laid down by the European Council, the Commission must 'promote the general interest of the Union'.[24] It achieves this by exercising two key functions. Firstly, by monitoring how Member States apply and comply with EU law, and if necessary taking enforcement actions against a Member State in the Court of Justice of the European Union.[25] Secondly, it initiates proposals for new legislation as discussed below.[26] The Commission is headed by a President and is composed of one commissioner from each Member State, each serving a term of five years.[27]

Council (separate from the European Council)—Once the Commission has issued a legislative proposal, it will be considered by the Council. This is formed of representatives of the government of each Member State, with the relevant Minister attending the relevant Council meetings. For example, the Minister with responsibility for the environment from each Member State will attend to discuss environmental matters. Unless stated otherwise in the Treaties, the Council acts by a qualified majority, meaning that for the Council to make a decision it must be agreed by '55% of members, comprising of at least fifteen of them', who together represent at least 65 per cent of the population of the EU.[28]

European Parliament—The other institution that must agree to a legislative proposal from the Commission is the European Parliament. The procedure by which the Council and

---

[19] TEU Art 50.   [20] TEU Art 27.

[21] TEU Arts 13–19. In addition, there is the Court of Auditors and the European Central Bank, but these are not discussed in this chapter.

[22] TEU Art 15(1) TEU. The President of the European Commission is also a member of the European Council.

[23] European Council, *A new strategic agenda 2019–2024* (European Council, June 2019) https://www.consilium.europa.eu/en/eu-strategic-agenda-2019-2024/.

[24] TEU Art 17(1).   [25] TEU Art 17(1).   [26] TEU Art 17(2).

[27] TEU Art 17(3), (5).   [28] TEU Art 16(4).

Parliament agree or amend proposals is discussed at the end of this section. The European Parliament is composed of 750 Members of the European Parliament (MEPs) elected in constituencies from each Member State. Some Member States have more MEPs than others depending on their population size, though each country must have at least six MEPs and no more than ninety-six.[29] At the last European Parliamentary Elections in 2019, Germany had ninety-six and France seventy-four, with the smallest EU Member States, Malta, Luxembourg, Estonia, and Cyprus, each having six MEPs.

The Court of Justice of the European Union (CJEU, formerly ECJ)—This is formed of the Court of Justice, the General Court (formerly the Court of First Instance), and the specialized courts. One judge from each Member State sits in the Court of Justice, with *at least* one judge from each Member State sitting in the General Court. Usually, cases are heard first by the General Court, with the possibility of appeal to the Court of Justice. The CJEU's primary function is to 'ensure that in the interpretation and application of the Treaties the law is observed'.[30] Primarily, this is through the preliminary reference procedure, where an issue of EU law has arisen in a case in the court of a Member State, and that refers a question to the CJEU which then gives its ruling.[31] The domestic court then applies that ruling in the case before it.

Treaty on the Functioning of the European Union

The TFEU provides for more detailed rules, elaborating on how the objectives of the EU are to be realized within the areas of competence allocated to it. There are provisions regarding the different areas in which the EU acts, the customs union, the internal market, and provisions on the four freedoms: goods, services, workers and capital, the common agricultural policy, and more detailed provisions regarding how the institutions operate. The TFEU also explains how regulations and directives are adopted according to the ordinary legislative procedure, which is discussed in the next section.

5.3 The instruments and principles of EU law

As can be seen from the previous sections, the EU has a broad range of responsibilities aimed at achieving far-reaching objectives, such as 'an ever closer Union', which if taken to its logical conclusion could raise profound questions about the role of the Member States. These questions are managed by the EU acting through the adoption of new EU laws, which can take one of several forms, the most important of which are regulations and directives. This then leads to the question as to when and how far the EU can act. This requires the consideration of the principles of competency, subsidiarity, and proportionality, which in different ways all demarcate the limits of when and how far the EU can act in any given area. This leads on to the final question, which is to consider the effect that EU law has on the laws of each Member State. As will be explained in this section, in order for EU law to operate effectively it must apply with equal force across the Union, and cannot be disapplied by Member States at their whim. Consequently, this means that EU law is supreme over the laws of each Member State, to the extent that some provisions of EU have direct effect, which means that they can be invoked before the courts of the Member States, even if not provided for by the domestic law of that Member State.

---

[29] TEU Art 14(2).   [30] TEU Art 19(1).   [31] TFEU Art 267.

This reflects how the Treaties, now expressed through the TEU and TFEU, have created a 'new legal order in international law'.[32]

5.3.1 Regulations and directives

EU law distinguishes between primary and secondary legislation. Only the two treaties, the TEU and TFEU, fall into the category of primary legislation. The most important categories of secondary legislation are regulations and directives. Both of these are usually adopted according to the ordinary legislative procedure as discussed in 5.3.3. There are approximately 20,000 pieces of EU legislation in force, of which 5,000 are regulations.[33] The following outlines the key differences between regulations and directives.

Regulations

Regulations are binding in their entirety and are directly applicable.[34] This means that regulations have immediate and automatic force across all of the Member States, without any requirement that each Member State enact domestic legal provisions to activate or enforce the regulation.[35] As is discussed in 5.4, regulations also have direct effect, which means that they can be enforced by EU citizens against their national governments in their own domestic courts.[36] Examples of regulations range from those concerning energy efficiency[37] and protection from harmful chemicals and substances,[38] to those determining that all bananas imported into the EU must be of a certain shape, size, and ripeness.[39]

Directives

Directives, by contrast, are not directly applicable. They are 'binding [only] as to the result to be achieved',[40] which means that Member States must enact legislative provisions to enforce them and give them domestic legal effect, it being up to the individual Member States to decide on the most appropriate form of domestic implementation. Directives, unlike regulations, can also be addressed to certain specific Member States to the exclusion of others.[41]

5.3.2 Ordinary legislative procedure

Regulations and directives are adopted by the EU according to the ordinary legislative procedure. This was first introduced into the Treaties by the Maastricht Treaty, and has since become the default decision-making process following further reforms in the Treaty of Amsterdam and the Treaty of Nice.[42] The existing version of the procedure as provided for in the TFEU is as explained in Figure 5.1.

---

[32] Case 26/62 *NV Algemene Transport- en Expeditie Onderneming Van Gend en Loos v Nederlandse Tarief-commissie*, [1963] ECR 1, 12 (subsequently *Van Gend en Loos*).

[33] Vaughne Miller, 'Legislation for Brexit: directly applicable EU law' (House of Commons Library, Briefing Paper 7863, 12 January 2017).

[34] TFEU Art 288.   [35] TFEU Art 288.   [36] See Case 39/72 *EC Commission v Italy* [1973] ECR 101.

[37] Commission Regulation (EU) 666/2013 of 8 July 2013 implementing Directive 2009/125/EC of the European Parliament and of the Council with regard to ecodesign requirements for vacuum cleaners.

[38] Regulation (EC) 1907/2006 of the European Parliament and of the Council of 18 December 2006 concerning the Registration, Evaluation, Authorisation and Restriction of Chemicals (REACH) and establishing a European Chemicals Agency.

[39] Council Regulation (EEC) 404/93 of 13 February 1993 on the common organisation of the market in bananas.

[40] TFEU Art 288.   [41] TFEU Art 288.

[42] The Treaty of Amsterdam entered into force in 1999, the Treaty of Nice in 2003.

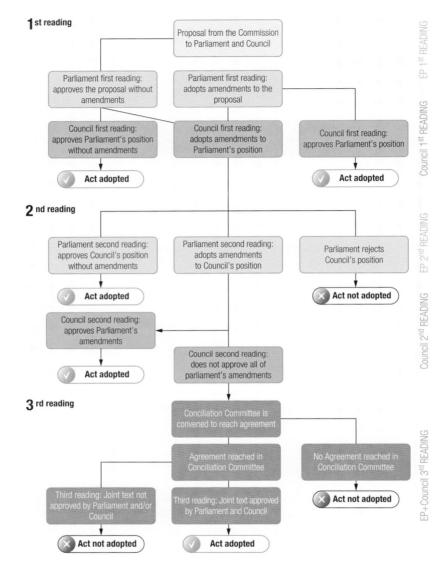

Figure 5.1 Ordinary legislative procedure—step by step
Source: © European Union, 2019. European Parliament, *Handbook on the Ordinary Legislative Procedure: A guide to how the European Parliament co-legislates* (November 2019), http://www.epgencms.europarl. europa.eu/cmsdata/upload/e3fba5b5-853b-440b-b9d3-c896e340615f/handbook-olp-en.pdf

First reading

The Commission makes a legislative proposal, which is considered separately by the European Parliament and the Council. If both the Parliament and the Council adopt the proposal without proposing any amendments, then it becomes law without any further process. Alternatively, if the Parliament amends the proposal and the Council accepts that amended proposals, then that becomes the adopted Act. Between 2014 and 2019, 89 per cent of legislative proposals were approved at first reading.

If the Council either amends the proposal itself or amends the position taken by the Parliament, then the proposal will progress to the second reading.

Second reading

At second reading, the Parliament could reject the amendments made by the Council, and the proposal will progress no further. Alternatively, it could accept the Council's amendments, and the legislation is adopted. If the Parliament makes further amendments, then the proposal will have to go to the Council for a second time.

If the Council accepts the amendments of the Parliament, the proposal is adopted, if the Council rejects the amendments, then the third-reading stage is required.

Third reading

This takes the form of a Conciliation Committee, where representatives of the Council and Parliament meet to reach a negotiated position as facilitated by the Commission. If the Conciliation Committee reaches an agreement, then this needs to be approved by the Council and the Parliament. If it is approved, then the proposal is adopted; if rejected, the process is exhausted, and the proposal does not become law. Similarly, if the Conciliation Committee fails to reach agreement, the process comes to an end without the proposal being adopted. Between 2014 and 2019, no legislative proposals reached the third-reading stage.

As can be seen from this discussion, the European Parliament is a full player in the legislative process, and its powers have shifted from being merely consulted, to possessing an outright veto. Although in practice this veto is rarely exercised, its very existence means that the views of the Parliament are taken seriously at the formative stage of any proposal and once it has made any amendments. Increasing the powers of the European Parliament has also been the primary method in which the EU has sought to address its perceived 'democratic deficit'. This is the concern that as the Commission is unelected and the primary proposer of legislation, increasing the powers of the Parliament which is directly elected by citizens of the Member States seeks to addresses this concern. The ordinary decision-making procedure resembles the two-chamber structure of many European legislatures, with the Council and the Parliament each playing an equal role.

5.3.3 Competency, subsidiarity, and proportionality

Competency

A key consideration when developing a legislative proposal is whether it is appropriate or indeed legal for the EU law to adopt it. The key starting point is whether it is within the competency of the EU to act. The Union is required to 'pursue its objective by appropriate means commensurate with the competencies which are conferred upon it in the Treaties',[43] and with any competencies 'not conferred upon the Union in the Treaties remain with the Member States'.[44]

Under the principle of conferral, the Union 'shall act only within the limits of the competencies conferred upon by the Member States in the Treaties'.[45] As explained in the TFEU, there are three types of competency that are conferred to the EU. These are as follows:

- *Exclusive competency*—This applies in areas such as the single currency or the customs union, and only the EU can act in these fields.[46]

---

[43] TEU Art 4(6).   [44] TEU Art 5(1).   [45] TEU Art 5(1).   [46] TFEU Art 3.

- *Shared competency*—This applies in areas including the single market, the common agricultural policy, and consumer protection.[47] Member States can exercise their competence in this field to the extent that the EU has not yet exercised its competence. For example, a Member State is free to make whatever provision they wish in the area of consumer protection, say, electrical safety. However, if the EU then exercises its competency in consumer protection to introduce EU rules on electrical safety then that Member State must adopt the new EU rules at the expense of its existing domestic rules.[48]

- *Competency to support, co-ordinate, or supplement* ('supporting competence')—This is the weakest form of competency, which enables the EU to support the activities of Member States in a range of areas, including culture, tourism, and education.[49]

Subsidiarity

Even if the EU has the competency to act in a particular area, the TEU makes clear that the 'use of Union competencies is governed by the principles of subsidiarity and proportionality'.[50] These two principles serve to limit when the EU can act.

Subsidiarity applies the shared or the supporting competencies, and requires the Union to 'act only if and in so far as the objectives of the proposed action cannot be sufficiently achieved by the Member States, either at central level or at regional and local level, but can rather, by reason of the scale or effects of the proposed action, be better achieved at Union level'.[51] This significantly restrains the scope of these competencies, as they can only be exercised when the objective of the act is better achieved at the Union level. This ensures that power should always be exercised at the most appropriate level, which could be at the Union, national, or even the local level. For example, transport is a matter of shared competence, but it would be contrary to the principle of subsidiarity for the EU to exercise its competence in this area to pass a regulation setting the speed limit on certain streets in London. Clearly, it is appropriate for such a decision to be made by national and local institutions.

 Discussing the problem

An example of subsidiarity

Regulation 1151/2012, which protects Stilton, is an example of the subsidiarity principle in practice. It is clear that a common system of protection across all Member States of the EU protects products, such as Stilton, most effectively. Had this been left to national governments, each implementing their own scheme, then in order for a producer to protect their product they would have to apply to each Member State. This would be costly and time consuming, and creates the possibility that different Member States might apply different criteria, meaning that some products may only be protected in some Member States. It is much easier for there to be single scheme with producers required to make a single application to the European Commission, and if the application for protection is approved, for it to apply across all Member States uniformly.

---

[47] TFEU Art 4.   [48] TFEU Art 2(2).   [49] TFEU Art 5.
[50] TEU Art 5(1).   [51] TEU Art 5(3).

Proportionality

The second limitation on all competencies is proportionality. This requires that 'the content and form of Union action shall not exceed what is necessary to achieve the objectives of the Treaties'.[52] Proportionality is a key principle of EU law and means that when the EU acts, it should do so only in such a way that is proportionate to achieve the particular objective at issue. This is a principle that the CJEU has considered over the years, explaining in *R v Minister of Agriculture, Fisheries and Food, ex p Fedesa* that proportionality required consideration of whether a particular measure at issue 'was appropriate and necessary to achieve the objectives legitimately pursued by the law in question'.[53]

5.3.4 **Supremacy**

The need for such restraints on the EU's competence is partly due to the principle of supremacy. This means that EU law is supreme over all domestic law in each Member State, so that the courts of the Member States are required to apply EU law ahead of any conflicting provision of domestic law. This makes EU law extraordinarily powerful and in principle allows it to penetrate deep into the core of the constitutional arrangements of Member States. Just how deeply the principle of supremacy goes into the domestic legal order of each Member State has been a permanent part of the debate of the UK's entry into, membership of, and now exit from the EU.

The CJEU first expressed the concept of sovereignty in the case of *Costa v ENEL*.

Case in depth: Case 6/64 *Costa v ENEL* [1964] ECR 585

Costa was an Italian individual who was opposed to the nationalization of the electricity sector in Italy. He was also a shareholder of an electricity company affected by the nationalization. In protest, he refused to pay his electricity bill. When proceedings were launched against Costa, in pursuit of his unpaid bill, he challenged the lawfulness of the nationalization, claiming that it was contrary to provisions of the Italian Constitutional Code and to articles of the EC Treaty. On the question of whether the relevant provisions of the EC Treaty were applicable, the court in Italy—the *Giudice Conciliatore*—referred the question to the CJEU, under Article 177 of the EC Treaty (now Article 267 TFEU).[54] The Italian Government argued that this reference was itself inadmissible, since the national courts were bound to apply national law, but the CJEU held that the EC Treaty contained directly enforceable rights which individuals could invoke in their national courts and that that national law could not take precedence over Union law.

The CJEU explained the rationale for the principle of the supremacy of EU law as follows:

> By creating a Community of unlimited duration, having its own institutions, its own personality, its own legal capacity . . . and, more particularly, real powers stemming from a limitation of sovereignty or a transfer of powers from the States to the Community, the Member States have limited their sovereign rights, albeit within limited fields, and have thus created a body of law which binds both their nationals and themselves. The

[52] TEU Art 5(4).

[53] [1990] ECR 1–4023 [2]. Also see Case 11/70 *Internationale Handelsgesellschaft mbH v Einfuhr- und Vorratsstelle für Getreide und Futtermittel* [1970] ECR 1125.

[54] Preliminary reference refers to the procedure, set out in Art 267 TFEU, whereby national courts of Member States can refer questions of EU law to the CJEU for clarification.

integration into the laws of each Member State of provisions which derive from the Community, and more generally the terms and the spirit of the Treaty, make it impossible for the States, as a corollary, to accord precedence to a unilateral and subsequent measure over a legal system accepted by them on a basis of reciprocity. Such a measure cannot therefore be inconsistent with that legal system. The executive force of Community law cannot vary from one State to another in deference to subsequent domestic laws, without jeopardizing the attainment of the objectives of the Treaty.[55]

The CJEU finds that the supremacy of EU law is a necessary implication of the Treaties, and is an integral and conditional part of EU membership. When Member States agreed to join the EU, they accepted a limitation of their sovereign right to make law as they saw fit. Any previous ability, held by institutions in any given Member State, to pass laws within their legal system is curtailed by the supremacy of EU law.

 Pause for reflection

Do you agree with the CJEU judgment in *Costa v ENEL*? Why do you think that it is important for the laws of the EU to be supreme across all the Member States?

In *Internationale Handelsgesellschaft mbH v Einfuhr und Vorratsstelle für Getreide und Futtermittel*,[56] EU laws relating to the payment and repayment of performance deposits under export licences were argued as being in conflict with 'the elementary, fundamental rights guaranteed by the German Constitution'.[57] In upholding the supremacy of EU law again, the CJEU emphasized that:

> Recourse to the legal rules or concepts of national law in order to judge the validity of measures adopted by the institutions of the Community would have an adverse effect on the uniformity and efficacy of Community Law. The validity of such measures can only be judged in the light of Community law. In fact, the law stemming from the Treaty, an independent source of law, cannot because of its very nature be overridden by rules of national law, however framed, without being deprived of its character as Community law and without the legal basis of the Community itself being called in question. Therefore the validity of a Community measure or its effect within a Member State cannot be affected by allegations that it runs counter to either fundamental rights as formulated by the constitution of that State or the principles of a national constitutional structure.[58]

The importance of the *Futtermittel* judgment is that it was not an ordinary provision of domestic law that was invoked, but a provision of the German Constitution. Yet this had no impact on the reasoning of the CJEU, for any rule of national law, no matter how fundamental it is to that legal system of the Member State, cannot be applied if contrary to EU law. The need for the uniform application of EU law is a greater consideration than the needs of individual Member States.

Finally, the case of *Amministrazione delle Finanze dello Stato v Simmenthal SpA*[59] concerned a challenge to a veterinary and public health inspection fee that was imposed under Italian law to beef imported from France. Though Simmenthal SpA argued that

---

[55] [1964] ECR 585, 593–4.   [56] [1970] ECR 1125.   [57] Ibid 1128.   [58] Ibid [2].
[59] Case 106/77 *Amministrazione delle Finanze dello Stato v Simmenthal SpA* [1978] ECR 629.

this fee was a barrier to the free movement of goods within the EU, it was argued by the Italian Government that, since the Italian law setting out and requiring this fee to be imposed was passed more recently, this should take precedence over the EU law. The question was referred to the CJEU, which held once again that EU law should prevail over national law. In explaining the rationale underpinning the judgment, the CJEU stated:

> [14] . . . rules of Community law must be fully and uniformly applied in all the Member States from the date of their entry into force and for so long as they continue in force.
>
> . . .
>
> [17] . . . in accordance with the principle of the precedence of Community law, the relationship between provisions of the Treaty and . . . measures of the institutions on the one hand and the national law of the Member States on the other is such that those provisions and measures not only by their entry into force render automatically inapplicable any conflicting provision of current national law but - in so far as they are an integral part of, and take precedence in, the legal order applicable in the territory of each of the Member States - also preclude the valid adoption of new national legislative measures to the extent to which they would be incompatible with Community provisions.
>
> [18] Indeed any recognition that national legislative measures which encroach upon the field within which the Community exercises its legislative power or which are otherwise incompatible with the provisions of Community law had any legal effect would amount to a corresponding denial of the effectiveness of obligations undertaken unconditionally and irrevocably by Member States pursuant to the Treaty and would thus imperil the very foundations of the Community.[60]

Again, the CJEU stresses the strength of the obligation that Member States accept when joining the EU to accept and apply EU law in its entirety. Once the EU has acted, by adopting a regulation or a directive, the Member States are bound by the Treaties to act according to that regulation or directive, without exception. This duty to uphold EU law is also placed on the courts in each Member State, which must 'apply Community law in its entirety and . . . must accordingly set aside any provision of national law which may conflict with it, whether prior or subsequent to the Community rule'.[61]

The supremacy of EU law has since been referred into the Treaties, with Member States now required to 'take any appropriate measure . . . to ensure fulfilment of the obligations arising out of the Treaties or resulting from the acts of the institutions of the Union. The Member States shall facilitate the achievement of the Union's tasks and refrain from any measure which could jeopardise the attainment of the Union's objectives.'[62]

5.3.5 Direct applicability

As stated in 5.3.1, regulations are directly applicable. This is provided for in Art 288 TFEU, which states that a regulation 'shall be binding in its entirety and directly applicable in all Member States'. This is an expression of the supremacy of EU law and highlights the particular relationship between EU law and the legal systems of each Member State.

---

[60] Ibid [14]–[18].   [61] Ibid [21].   [62] TEU Art 4(3).

For countries, such as the UK, that adopt the dualist system, changes in international law do not take effect in domestic law until domestic legislation is enacted which either places the relevant provisions of international law into domestic law, or at least makes reference to them. The EU makes many regulations each year, and the law-making process would become even slower, if not halt entirely, if each Member State needed to pass their own domestic legislation incorporating each new regulation.

The direct applicability of regulations avoids this problem. Directly applicable means that once it has been adopted by the EU institutions, the regulation is part of the law of each Member State without them taking any action. Indeed, the CJEU has held that it in some circumstances it is unlawful for Member States to pass legislation incorporating a regulation into their domestic law.[63] Each Member State is bound by the regulation, and should they fail to act according to its requirements, then an individual from a Member State could take their government to the national courts for breaching EU law. Alternatively, the Commission may commence enforcement action under Art 258 TFEU, which may ultimately reach the CJEU.

5.3.6 Direct effect

In *Van Gen den Loos*, the CJEU established the doctrine of direct effect.

Key case: C 26/62 *NV Algemene Transport- en Expeditie Onderneming Van Gend en Loos v Nederlandse Tariefcommissie* [1963] ECR 1

Van Gend en Loos imported chemicals into the Netherlands from Germany. They were charged a tariff at a rate that was contrary to (what is now) Article 28 TFEU. When challenging the tariffs before the domestic courts in the Netherlands, Van Gen den Loos raised Article 28 TFEU in argument. Under the preliminary reference procedure, the domestic court asked the CJEU whether Article 28 TFEU directly applies within a Member State, and whether nationals of a Member State can claim individual rights arising from the Treaty that the courts must give effect to?

The CJEU made reference to the preamble which emphasized the involvement of just the governments of each Member State, but the peoples of each Member State to take part in the functioning of the Community. Importantly, this is consistent with the preliminary reference procedure of (what is now) Art 267 TFEU, which confirmed 'that the [Member States] have acknowledged that Community law has an authority which can be invoked by their nationals before [domestic] courts and tribunals'.[64]

This led the court to conclude that the Community:

> constitutes a new legal order of international law for the benefit of which the states have limited their sovereign rights, albeit within limited fields, and the subjects of which comprise not only Member States but also their nationals. Independently of the legislation of Member States, Community law therefore not only imposes obligations on individuals but is also intended to confer upon them rights which become part of their legal heritage. These rights arise not only where they are expressly granted by the

→

---

[63] C 34/73 *Variola v Amministrazione delle Finanze* [1972] ECR 981.
[64] C 26/62 *NV Algemene Transport- en Expeditie Onderneming Van Gend en Loos v Nederlandse Tariefcommissie* [1963] ECR 1, 12.

> Treaty, but also by reason of obligations which the Treaty imposes in a clearly defined way upon individuals as well as upon the Member States and upon the institutions of the Community.
>
> Because Article 28 TFEU contained a clear and unconditional prohibition and placed the Member State under a negative obligation, it was designed to have direct effects on the legal relationship between a Member State and its citizens. The effect of having direct effect was that Article 28 TFEU created individual rights that the domestic courts must protect in order to comply with the law.

The effect of *Van Gend en Loos* is that if a provision of EU law was clear, unconditional, negative in nature (in that it required the Member State not to do something), and required no legislative intervention, then it had direct effect and could be invoked by individuals before the domestic courts in their Member State. This meant that only those Treaty provisions that meet these criteria have direct effect.

As regards regulations, in *Fratelli Variola SpA v Amministrazione italiana delle Finanze*, the CJEU held that due to their 'very nature and . . . place in the system of sources of Community law, a regulation has immediate effect and, consequently, operates to confer rights on private parties which the national courts have a duty to protect'.[65] Essentially, by definition the direct applicability of regulations means that they have direct effect, because being directly applicable means that regulations automatically become part of the law of each Member State which the courts must uphold.

Directives

The question of whether and which directives have direct effect has proven challenging. This is perhaps understandable, because directives are not directly applicable, and are only binding as to the 'result to be achieved'.[66] This means that that the requirements for direct effect laid down in *Van Gend en Loos* of being clear, unconditional, and not requiring any implementation measures are absent. The choice of adopting a directive over a regulation may well be intentional, as the policy area in question may require that Member States should exercise some discretion as to how to achieve a particular goal and it may not be necessary to require a uniform approach across each Member State.

Despite these concerns, in *Van Duyn v Home Office*, the CJEU advanced two reasons why some directives have direct effect. The first reason is that a failure to recognize direct effect 'would be incompatible with the binding effect attributed to a directive . . . to exclude, in principle, the possibility that the obligation which it imposes may be invoked by those concerned'.[67] Essentially, that the unity of EU law would be better secured if incorrectly or unimplemented directives could be invoked before domestic courts. The second reason is similar to that advanced in *Van Gend en Loos* itself, that the preliminary reference procedure as now provided for by Art 267 TFEU allows national courts to refer questions regarding any provision of EU law to the CJEU. By implication, this must mean that individuals can raise questions of EU law before the national courts, including questions relating to directives.

---

[65] C 34/73, [1973] ECR 981 [8].
[66] TFEU Art 288.
[67] Case 41/74 *Van Duyn v Home Office* [1974] ECR I 1337 [12].

Discussing the problem

Have another look at the problem scenario at the beginning of this chapter and consider it in the light of direct applicability, direct effect, and the regulation.

A key feature of regulations is that they are directly applicable. This means that regulations, such as Regulation 1151/2012, once adopted automatically become the law of each Member State, without them passing any further legislation. This means that regulations can be invoked before the courts of each Member State. This ensures that the regulation applies to, and can be enforced in, each Member State, including the UK. Consequently, the aim of the regulation, to introduce a common scheme to protect the production of certain foods such as Stilton, is achieved.

5.4 The UK's accession to the EU: reconciling EU supremacy with parliamentary sovereignty

After much debate, the UK joined what became the EU on 1 January 1973. The UK had first applied to become a member in 1961, though its application was twice blocked by the French President, Charles de Gaulle, in 1963 and 1967. Permission to start negotiations for the UK's membership was granted in 1969, after which the UK and the EU negotiated and concluded the Accession Treaty which provided for the UK's membership. In constitutional terms, the process for joining the EU was clear; the government conducted the negotiations under the royal prerogative, which, as explained in Chapter 6, is a source of government power recognized by the common law as belonging to the Crown.[68]

5.4.1 The European Communities Act 1972

The greater challenge was to make the necessary changes in UK law to give effect to the UK's membership of the EU. As explained in 5.3, the Treaties created a 'new legal order', generating both laws that are directly applicable, so becoming part of the laws of each Member State, and rights that citizens can invoke directly before their national courts. More generally, as explained in *Costa v ENEL*, EU law is supreme. As explained in 4.5.1, due to the dualist nature of the UK, in order to give effect to a treaty that the UK has agreed, Parliament must pass an Act of Parliament giving effect to that treaty in UK law. The challenge was that the amount and content of EU law that needed to be incorporated into UK law was dynamic, as it would change as the EU institutions continued to enact regulations or directives. To incorporate EU law into UK law, Parliament enacted the European Communities Act 1972. Section 2(1) states:

> All such rights, powers, liabilities, obligations and restrictions from time to time created or arising by or under the Treaties, and all such remedies and procedures from time to time provided for by or under the Treaties, as in accordance with the Treaties are without further enactment to be given legal effect or used in the United Kingdom shall be recognised and available in law, and be enforced, allowed and followed accordingly.

[68] See 6.4.2.

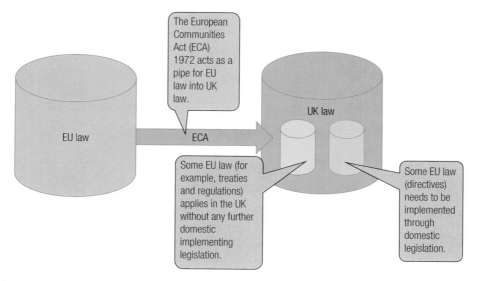

Figure 5.2 The European Communities Act 1972 as a 'conduit pipe' by which EU law becomes part of UK law
Source: Explanatory Notes to the European Union (Withdrawal) Act 2018, para 18. Content available under the Open Government Licence v3.0

Although the provision is complex, the effect of this section is to make provisions of EU law automatically part of UK domestic law. The structure of the provision is that *'all rights, powers, liabilities, obligations and restrictions from time to time created or arising by or under the Treaties'* aim to capture all provisions of EU law that are directly applicable and reflects the principle of direct effect. The use of the phrase *'from time to time'* ensures that this provision is dynamic rather than static, so that it covers changes in the content of those 'rights, powers, liabilities' etc., as the institutions adopt new regulations and directives and repeal old ones. The key element is that these 'rights, powers, liabilities' etc. are *'without further enactment to be given legal effect or used in the United Kingdom'* and *'shall be recognised and available in law'*, which means that no further legislation is required for each provision of EU law caught by this section to take effect in UK law.

Section 2(4) takes this a step further, and gives explicit effect to the general principle of the supremacy of EU law, stating that *'any enactment passed or to be passed . . . shall be construed and have effect subject to the foregoing provisions of this section'*. This means that *all* legislation only has effect to the extent that it complies with EU law. This includes legislation that is enacted *after* the 1972 Act. The third key provision is section 2(2), which gives ministers a broad power to enact secondary legislation to give effect to directives.

These provisions of the ECA 1972 have led to it being referred to as the 'conduit pipe' by which EU law enters UK law.[69] This can be seen in Figure 5.2.

The difficulty is whether and how section 2(1) and (4) of the ECA 1972 can be reconciled with parliamentary sovereignty, as explored in Chapter 4. It is impossible for both EU law and Parliament to be supreme. Section 2(1) appears to contradict the negative

---

[69] *R (Miller) v Secretary of State for Exiting the European Union* [2017] UKSC 5 [65], quoting John Finnis who first adopted the term.

limb of sovereignty as explained by Dicey, that 'no person or body is recognized as having a right to override or set aside the legislation of Parliament'.[70] Arguably, section 2(4) presents a greater challenge, as it seeks to bind future parliaments, so that Parliament cannot legislate in a manner that contradicts EU law. In particular, it attempts to ensure that later legislation does not impliedly repeal the ECA 1972, but only takes effect subject to the ECA 1972 and the requirements of EU law.

The first notable case in which the provisions of the ECA 1972 were applied was *Macarthy's Ltd v Smith*.[71]

Case in depth: *Macarthy's Ltd v Smith* [1979] ICR 785

The Equal Pay Act 1970 made provision for equal pay in situations of simultaneous employment, meaning that men and women should receive the same salary when employed in the same role at the same time. Wendy Smith, who was employed as a stockroom manager, discovered that she received a lower wage than the man who had previously held her job. This was not a case of simultaneous employment, but of subsequent employment which was not covered by the 1970 Act. Smith argued that her employers contravened the principle of equal pay, then set out in Article 119 of the EEC Treaty (now Article 157 TFEU), which required that Member States were required to uphold and apply the principle that 'that men and women should receive equal pay for equal work', and that the principle applies to situations of subsequent, and not just simultaneous employment. The Court of Appeal referred a question on the application of Article 119 EEC to the CJEU.

The CJEU held that that Article 119 EEC:

> applies directly, and without the need for more detailed implementing measures on the part of the Community or the Member States, to all forms of direct and overt discrimination . . .[72]

This means that the provision had direct effect, and could be invoked directly by Smith in the UK courts. When the Court of Appeal continued to hear the case following the CJEU's judgment, they applied Article 119 EEC and found that Smith had been discriminated against, and should have been paid the same as the man who previously held her job.[73]

In the Court of Appeal, Lord Denning explained the impact of the ECA 1972 as follows:

[The] principle [set out in Article 119 EEC] is part of our English law. It is directly applicable in England. So much so that, even if we had not passed any legislation on the point, our courts would have been bound to give effect to [it] . . . Under section 2(1) and (4) of the European Communities Act 1972 the principles laid down in the Treaty are 'without further enactment' to be given legal effect in the United Kingdom: and have priority over 'any enactment passed or to be passed' by our Parliament. So we are entitled—and think bound—to look at article 119 of the Treaty because it is directly applicable here . . . If on

---

[70] AV Dicey, *Introduction to the Study of the Law of the Constitution* (JWF Allison ed, first published 1885, OUP 2013) 27–8. See further 4.5.

[71] [1979] ICR 785.

[72] Case 129/79 *Macarthy's Ltd v Smith* [1980] ECR 1275 [10].

[73] *Macarthy's Ltd v Smith* [1981] QB 180.

close investigation it should appear that our legislation is deficient—or is inconsistent with Community law—by some oversight of our draftsmen—then it is our bounden duty to give priority to Community law. Such is the result of section 2(1) and (4) of the European Communities Act 1972.[74]

The requirements of the ECA 1972 as outlined by Lord Denning were followed in subsequent cases. However, they involved instances when Parliament had expressed no intention of acting contrary to EU law, meaning that the courts could use the tools provided by the ECA 1972 to resolve the inconsistency in favour of EU law.[75]

 Discussing the problem

Have a look at the problem set out at the beginning of the chapter. How does the ECA 1972 interact with the regulation?

As a regulation, Regulation 1151/2012 is covered by the ECA 1972, section 2 when it states: '*all rights, powers, liabilities, obligations and restrictions from time to time created or arising by or under the Treaties.*' Regulation 1151/2012 has been created by the EU institutions under powers granted to them by the Treaties, and its provisions, generate rights, powers, liabilities, obligations, and restrictions, as Stilton cheese meets the requirements of the regulation to qualify for the protection that it provides, then the producers of Stilton have a right for that product to be protected. The effect of being covered by ECA 1972, section 2 is that the regulation becomes part of UK law; in short, the ECA 1972 recognizes that the regulation is directly applicable.

5.4.2 The *Factortame* litigation

The more difficult situation for the courts was how to respond to the situation when Parliament had legislated directly in contravention of EU law. In *Macarthy's Ltd v Smith*, as obiter, Lord Denning considered that the later Act of Parliament would prevail over the requirements of EU law and the ECA 1972. He stated that:

> If the time should come when our Parliament deliberately passes an Act—with the intention of repudiating the Treaty or any provision in it—or intentionally of acting inconsistently with it—and says so in express terms—then I should have thought that it would be the duty of our courts to follow the statute of our Parliament.[76]

The scenario envisaged by Lord Denning arose in the *Factortame* litigation.[77] Under the Common Fisheries Policy, the relevant Member States are each granted a quota for fishing. Spanish fishermen were circumventing these quotas by registering their vessels under UK law as British vessels, meaning that in addition to having access to the Spanish quota, they also had access to the UK's quota. The response of the UK government and Parliament was to enact the Merchant Shipping Act 1988, to ensure that those who accessed the UK's

---

[74] *Macarthy's Ltd v Smith* [1979] ICR 785, 788–9.

[75] See for example, *Garland v British Rail Engineering Ltd* [1983] 2 AC 751, which also discussed (what was then) Art 119 EEC.

[76] Ibid 789.   [77] [1991] 1 AC 603.

fishing quota had a genuine link with the UK. Fishing vessels could only be registered in the UK if they met the following criteria as laid down in section 14(1):

(a) the vessel is British-owned;

(b) the vessel is managed, and its operations are directed and controlled, from within the United Kingdom; and

(c) any charterer, manager or operator of the vessel is a qualified person or company.

A 'qualified person' was defined as British citizen resident and domiciled in the UK, and a 'qualified company' was defined as a company incorporated in the UK, with at least 75 per cent of its directors being qualified persons and 75 per cent of its shares also required to be owned by qualified persons.[78]

Prima facie, these provisions of the Merchant Shipping Act 1988 breached the freedom of establishment, now provided for by Art 49 TFEU, which, in broad terms, allows a citizen of a Member State who operates a business in one Member State 'to carry on an economic activity in a stable and continuous way in another Member State'.

Merchant Shipping Act 1988, section 14 was challenged by Factortame Ltd, a company that had registered vessels in the UK before the 1988 Act came into effect but now, because its directors were Spanish nationals and residents, fell foul of the new rules. In the following case, they argued that the new rules breached EU law.

Case in depth: *R v Secretary of State for Transport, ex p Factortame* [1990] 2 AC 85 and *R v Secretary of State for Transport, ex p Factortame (No 2)* [1991] 1 AC 603

Factortame Ltd argued that the registration requirements laid down in the 1988 Act breached EU law, and that the courts should enforce EU law ahead of the 1988 Act as required by the European Communities Act 1972. The High Court sent a reference to the CJEU on the question of whether EU law should prevail over UK law.

The second argument was that interim relief should be granted against the application of the 1988 Act, pending the judgment of the CJEU. This would mean that the operation of the 1988 Act would be suspended until the CJEU had made its decision. Interim relief was granted by the High Court, but was overturned by the Court of Appeal because as a matter of UK law, the courts have no power to award interim relief against the Crown.[79] The House of Lords agreed with the Court of Appeal, due to Crown Proceedings Act 1947, section 22 which explicitly stated that the courts do not have this power. Consequently, the House of Lords sent a second question on whether EU law required that interim relief should be granted.

In hearing the references, in Case C-213/89 *R v Secretary of State for Transport, ex p Factortame Ltd*,[80] the CJEU held that, in line with the principle of supremacy, that EU law should take precedence over conflicting provisions of national law. Furthermore, the Court said that relief

→

---

[78] Merchant Shipping Act 1988, s 14(2), (7).

[79] Although this has now changed, and the courts can now do this—see *M v Home Office* [1994] 1 AC 377.   [80] [1990] ECR I-2433.

should be granted from the application of the 1988 Act, and if the only obstacle to such relief was a provision of national law, then it should be set aside in preference for EU law.

Following these clarifications, the case returned to the House of Lords (as *Factortame (No 2)*), which held that interim relief from the application of the 1988 Act should be granted and the Act disapplied[81] to give effect to EU law.

In *Factortame (No 2)*, Lord Bridge gave the leading judgment, and considered the effect and consequences of disapplying the Merchant Shipping Act 1988. In particular, he explained, how the supremacy of EU law had been established before the UK acceded to the treaties that the UK joined the EU aware of the fact that it entailed limiting its sovereignty. He stated that:

> Some public comments on the decision of the European Court of Justice, affirming the jurisdiction of the courts of member states to override national legislation if necessary to enable interim relief to be granted in protection of rights under Community law, have suggested that this was a novel and dangerous invasion by a Community institution of the sovereignty of the United Kingdom Parliament. But such comments are based on a misconception. If the supremacy within the European Community of Community law over the national law of member states was not always inherent in the EEC Treaty it was certainly well established in the jurisprudence of the European Court of Justice long before the United Kingdom joined the Community. Thus, whatever limitation of its sovereignty Parliament accepted when it enacted the European Communities Act 1972 was entirely voluntary. Under the terms of the Act of 1972 it has always been clear that it was the duty of a United Kingdom court, when delivering final judgment, to override any rule of national law found to be in conflict with any directly enforceable rule of Community law. Similarly, when decisions of the European Court of Justice have exposed areas of United Kingdom statute law which failed to implement Council directives, Parliament has always loyally accepted the obligation to make appropriate and prompt amendments. Thus there is nothing in any way novel in according supremacy to rules of Community law in those areas to which they apply and to insist that, in the protection of rights under Community law, national courts must not be inhibited by rules of national law from granting interim relief in appropriate cases is no more than a logical recognition of that supremacy.[82]

While—as Chapter 4 explained—various constitutional factors over the years have led to developments and, arguably, erosion to the principle of parliamentary sovereignty, never before had such a blatant exception to the principle been acknowledged by the courts.

In particular, the approach of Lord Bridge poses a particular problem for Dicey's negative limb of sovereignty, which as discussed in 4.2 states that 'there is no person or body of persons who can, under the English constitution, make rules which override or derogate from an Act of Parliament, or which (to express the same thing in other words) will be enforced by courts in contravention of an Act of Parliament'.[83] The disapplication of the Merchant Shipping Act 1988 in *Factortame*, in favour of EU law, seems to breach

---

[81] It is important to note that this does not mean that the 1988 Act was *invalid*, merely that there was an injunction against its application in favour of EU law.

[82] [1991] 1 AC 603, 658–9.

[83] AV Dicey, *Introduction to the Study of the Law of the Constitution* (JWF Allison ed, first published 1885, OUP 2013) 40.

this principle. However, it must be noted that Lord Bridge described the limitation of sovereignty as 'voluntary',[84] which suggests that if Parliament willingly and actively accepted the limitation of its own sovereignty, then it can pass another Act that voluntarily repudiates the UK's obligations under the EU Treaties, thereby bringing this sovereign power back to Westminster. Until such an Act is passed, Parliament has chosen to constrain its sovereignty to defer to the supremacy of EU law. The consequence of this approach is that the positive limb of parliamentary sovereignty that Parliament can 'make or unmake any law whatsoever' remains, as Parliament can repeal the ECA 1972 removing the voluntary limitation on its own sovereignty.

Wade, was critical of the approach adopted by Lord Bridge, noting that 'he did not appear to recognise that there was any problem of a constitutional kind' with the facts of *Factortame* or the decision that the House of Lords ultimately reached.[85] For Wade, the passing of the 1972 Act and the effect that the supremacy of EU law consequently has had on the UK system has meant that 'Parliament's powers had suffered a seismic change . . . the results were revolutionary'.[86] As explained, Wade's approach to sovereignty can be summed up neatly in three points:

- Parliament is sovereign because the courts recognize its Acts as sovereign;
- the principle of sovereignty is an ultimate political fact, founded on the political settlement realized in the Bill of Rights; and
- the ultimate political fact of sovereignty can only be changed by revolution.[87]

It is in this context that Wade goes on to discuss the events in *Factortame* in the following terms:

> As previously supposed, the rule was that an Act of Parliament in proper form had absolutely overriding effect, except that it could not fetter the corresponding power of future Parliaments. It is a rule of unique character, since only the judges can change it. It is for the judges, and not for Parliament, to say what is an effective Act of Parliament. If the judges recognise that there must be a chance, as by allowing future Parliaments to be fettered, this is a technical revolution. That is what happens when the judges, faced with a novel situation, elect to depart from the familiar rules for the sake of political necessity . . . in *Factortame* the House of Lords elected to allow the Parliament of 1972 to fetter the Parliament of 1988 in order that Community law might be given the primacy which practical politics obviously required. This in no way implies that the judges . . . decided otherwise than for what appeared to them to be good legal reasons. The point is simply that the rule of recognition is itself a political fact which the judges themselves are able to change when they are confronted with a new situation which so demands . . . In *Factortame* it arose from the creation of new ties with Europe.[88]

The constitutional revolution that Wade hypothetically described back in his 1955 article had, he thought, been realized by the events in *Factortame*. Taking this argument to its logical conclusion, it also means that the UK—through Parliament—cannot unilaterally

---

[84] [1991] 1 AC 603, 658–9.
[85] HWR Wade, 'Sovereignty—Revolution or Evolution?' (1996) 112 *Law Quarterly Review* 568, 575.
[86] Ibid 574.
[87] HWR Wade, 'The Basis of Legal Sovereignty' (1955) 13(2) *Cambridge Law Journal* 172.
[88] HWR Wade, 'Sovereignty—Revolution or Evolution?' (1996) 112 *Law Quarterly Review* 568, 574.

withdraw from the EU since it is the EU and the EU alone that holds sovereign power and a non-sovereign power (ie the UK Parliament) cannot re-exert their previous power without the new sovereign's consent, unless of course the courts were to effect another revolution.

By contrast, other commentators, such as Allen, see *Factortame (No 2)* as 'only [an] example of evolution', not revolution, and sits alongside other similar cases.[89] In support of this approach Allen cites *Pickstone v Freemans*,[90] in which:

> the House of Lords adopted a purposive construction of [legislative] provisions intended to enable the United Kingdom to comply with a . . . Directive, even though on a more natural or literal construction they had failed to achieve their object. Ordinary principles of interpretation were abandoned in order to avoid a result thought unacceptable on general constitutional grounds.[91]

Similarly, he suggests that the House of Lords in *Factortame* interpreted the 1972 Act and the 1988 Act in such a way that would avoid an unacceptable constitutional result; namely, that Parliament would be seen as sovereign against the supremacy of EU law, in contravention of well-established and accepted EU legal principles.[92]

 Pause for reflection

Having now explored the various academic views commenting on the *Factortame* judgment and its impact on the principle of parliamentary sovereignty, with which do you most agree?

5.4.3 **Constitutional statutes**

The challenge posed to orthodox understandings of sovereignty is highlighted when implied repeal is considered. Implied repeal is an expression of the principle that no Parliament can bind a future Parliament, in that if two pieces of legislation conflict, the latter one is said to impliedly repeal the earlier Act.[93] If this was applied to *Factortame*, then the Merchant Shipping Act 1988, which conflicted with rules of EU law, would have impliedly repealed the ECA 1972, section 2(1) and (4), which would have had far-reaching constitutional consequences over and above the mere implied repeal of a piece of legislation. It would have served as a repudiation of the UK's obligations under the Treaty and potentially call into question the UK's membership of the EU, if Parliament was said to have even impliedly repealed the provisions of UK law that give effect to EU law. Consequently, given the result in *Factortame (No 2)*, it appears the ECA 1972 is not subject to implied repeal. The following case provides an explanation for this, by considering that the ECA 1972 is a 'constitutional statute', which at common law is not subject to implied repeal 'ordinary statutes'.

---

[89] TRS Allan, 'Parliamentary Sovereignty: Law, Politics, and Revolution' (1997) 113 *Law Quarterly Review* 443, 447.   [90] [1989] AC 66.

[91] TRS Allan, 'Parliamentary Sovereignty: Law, Politics, and Revolution' (1997) 113 *Law Quarterly Review* 443, 447.

[92] A similar view is put forward by PP Craig, 'Sovereignty of the United Kingdom Parliament after *Factortame*' (1991) 11 *Yearbook of European Law* 221.

[93] See 4.5.3.

> ### Case in depth: *Thoburn v Sunderland City Council* [2002] EWHC 195 (Admin)
>
> An Act of the UK Parliament, the Weights and Measures Act 1985, when originally enacted provided that both imperial (such as ounces, pounds, and stones) and metric (grams and kilograms) measurements could be used. Then the EU adopted the Units of Measurement Regulations 1994, which required that only metric units could be used for business purposes. The UK amended the 1985 Act to comply with the EU regulation.
>
> Thoburn, a fruit seller, was convicted under the 1985 Act (as amended) for using weighing machines that did not measure in metric units and so contravening the EU regulation. Two others were also convicted for failing to use metric units, and a fourth wished to challenge the imposition from his local authority of a condition that required him to sell products using metric units.
>
> The four individuals' defences were based on the legal argument that, since the Weights and Measures Act 1985 had been passed after the European Communities Act 1972, it impliedly repealed its provisions, thereby rendering the imposition of any subsequent regulations—including that in 1994—unlawful. Their cases were dismissed in both the High Court and Court of Appeal.

In the High Court, LJ Laws essentially confirmed the decision of *Factortame (No 2)*, but then provided his own analysis that rejected the implied repeal argument of the claimants.

> We should recognise a hierarchy of Acts of Parliament: as it were 'ordinary' statutes and 'constitutional' statutes. The two categories must be distinguished on a principled basis. In my opinion a constitutional statute is one which (a) conditions the legal relationship between citizen and state in some general, overarching manner, or (b) enlarges or diminishes the scope of what we would now regard as fundamental constitutional rights . . . The special status of constitutional statutes follows the special status of constitutional rights. Examples are Magna Carta 1297, the Bill of Rights 1689, the Union with Scotland Act 1706, the Reform Acts which distributed and enlarged the franchise (Representation of the People Acts 1832, 1867 and 1884), the Human Rights Act 1998, the Scotland Act 1998 and the Government of Wales Act 1998. The 1972 Act clearly belongs in this family. It incorporated the whole corpus of substantive Community rights and obligations, and gave overriding domestic effect to the judicial and administrative machinery of Community law. It may be there has never been a statute having such profound effects on so many dimensions of our daily lives. The 1972 Act is, by force of the common law, a constitutional statute. Ordinary statutes may be impliedly repealed. Constitutional statutes may not.[94]

 Pause for reflection

To what extent do you think that Laws LJ's consideration that '[w]e should recognise a hierarchy of Acts of Parliament' would sit with Dicey's orthodox conception of parliamentary sovereignty?

---

[94] [2002] EWHC 195 (Admin) [62]–[63].

According to Laws LJ, constitutional statutes (including the ECA 1972) are immune from implied repeal and can only be expressly repealed. In the absence of such express provisions in the amended Weights and Measures Act 1985 for any repeal or amendment of the ECA 1972, it still applied. Furthermore, as the earlier decision in *Factortame* shows, where an Act of Parliament conflicts with an earlier, *constitutional* statute, then the court will uphold the constitutional statute in preference to the more recent enactment.

Laws LJ's concept of constitutional statutes has since been approved by the Supreme Court on several occasions. In *H v Lord Advocate*, the Court noted the 'fundamental constitutional nature of the [devolution] settlement that was achieved by the Scotland Act' 1998.[95] In *R (on the application of HS2 Action Alliance Limited) v Secretary of State for Transport*, the Supreme Court described both the Bill of Rights, the European Communities Act 1972, and other statutes as 'constitutional instruments'.[96] Lord Neuberger in *R (Miller) v Secretary of State for Exiting the European Union*, observed that '[t]he primacy of EU law means that, unlike other rules of domestic law, EU law cannot be implicitly displaced by the mere enactment of legislation which is inconsistent with it'.[97] The support given to the concept of constitutional statutes gives it weight as an explanation, albeit perhaps only up to a point, of how the supremacy of EU law has been squared with parliamentary sovereignty.

5.5 The political controversy over the UK's membership of the EU

Since the end of the Second World War, a dominant and recurrent theme in British politics has been the question of the UK's relationship with its European neighbours and, as it developed, the EU. From the mid-1950s onwards, answering this question became more pressing. The British Empire was winding down at a pace, and its successor organization the Commonwealth proved to be ineffective in the context of the Cold War between the United States and the Soviet Union. The UK's position in the world was diminishing rapidly. Prior to becoming Prime Minister, Harold MacMillan expressed the concerns of some senior politicians when stating, 'I do not like the prospect of a world divided into the Russian sphere, the American sphere and a united Europe of which we are not a member'.[98] Addressing these concerns raised a series of difficult questions, as Harrison explains:

> there was much indecision in Britain about how to respond, together which much wishful thinking and nostalgia. Should kinship, sentiment and wartime loyalties make the Commonwealth the national anchor? Or were shifting economic relationships gradually enhancing the appeal of a European alignment? Or should Britain try to get the best of both worlds by pursuing the so-called 'special relationship' with the USA? . . . Dean Acheson [foreign policy advisor to four US presidents] claimed that 'Great Britain has lost an empire and had not yet found a role'.[99]

---

[95] [2012] UKSC 24 [30].

[96] [2014] UKSC 3 [208]. This case is discussed at length in 4.6 and is notable for its consideration that EU law might have to yield to fundamental provisions of domestic constitutional law, such as the Bill of Rights 1688, Article 9.

[97] [2017] UKSC 5 [66].

[98] Quoted in Anthony King, *The British Constitution* (OUP 2017) 92.

[99] Brian Harrison, *Seeking a Role: The United Kingdom 1951–1970* (OUP 2009) xvii.

Such indecision could be seen in how, when negotiations to establish the EEC took place, the UK declined to take part. Instead, in 1960, the UK preferred to join the European Free Trade Association,[100] which had a similar aim of advancing free trade amongst its members, but avoided the supranational elements of the EEC, operating more like a traditional international organization, on an intergovernmental basis. France also made the UK's position more difficult, twice rejecting her application to join the EEC in 1963 and 1967. It was ultimately the UK's sluggish economic growth compared with the EEC Member States that underpinned these attempts to join. The third attempt was successful, and the UK became a member of the EU on 1 January 1973.

Joining the EEC was controversial—the second reading of the European Communities Act 1972, giving effect to the UK's membership was passed only by 309 votes to 301.[101] In particular, the Labour Party was split on the issue. After winning the October 1974 General Election, the Labour Government renegotiated the UK's terms of membership, and then held a referendum on whether the UK should remain a member of the EEC. 68.7 per cent voted to remain a member, with 31.3 per cent against.[102] The focus of political debate was on the economic benefits, and despite the principles of supremacy and direct effect already being established, concerns regarding national sovereignty and parliamentary sovereignty were secondary to the economic benefits.

If joining was controversial, so was remaining a member, and both the Labour and Conservative parties constantly shifted their positions on the EEC as it developed into the EU. Despite the result of the referendum in 1975, Labour campaigned at the 1983 General Election on a manifesto commitment to leave the EEC. At this time, the Conservatives were in their most pro-Europe phase and were eager for the EEC to adopt the Single European Act to complete the internal market. By the 1990s, the Labour Party viewed the EU more sympathetically, as the regulations and directives adopted by the EU enhanced employment protection to a greater extent than laws passed by the UK Parliament during periods of Conservative government.

For many within the Conservative Party, the Maastricht Treaty and the creation of the EU, together with its timetable for the creation of the euro—the single European currency—were too great an erosion of national sovereignty in favour of EU control. The UK secured an opt-out from the euro, but a referendum promised by both the Conservative and Labour parties on adopting the euro at a later stage never materialized, as public opinion stood firmly against losing the pound. Concerns about national sovereignty grew as the EU acquired more competencies through the Treaty of Nice and the Treaty of Amsterdam. The negotiation of the Constitutional Treaty further increased concerns regarding future direction of the EU. A referendum promised on that Treaty was never held, because as discussed in 5.2.5, this was abandoned following its rejection in referendums held in the Netherlands and France. In opposition, David Cameron made it Conservative Party policy to hold a referendum on the Lisbon Treaty, which sought to resurrect aspects of the Constitutional Treaty. However, he was unable to deliver on this promise as the Lisbon Treaty entered into force before he became Prime Minister after the 2010 General Election.

---

[100] This was formed by Austria, Denmark, Norway, Portugal, Sweden, Switzerland, and the UK. Only Norway and Switzerland have since not joined the EU, and remain members of th European Free Trade Association along with Iceland and Liechtenstein.

[101] HC Deb, 17 February 1972, vol 831, col 754–7.

[102] Colin Rallings and Michael Thrasher (eds), *British Electoral Facts 1832–2012* (Biteback 2012) 241.

The Coalition Government, implementing a manifesto commitment of the Conservative Party, enacted the European Union Act 2011. The 2011 Act sought to address concerns of sovereignty and deepening integration with the EU, by introducing a 'referendum lock', that before any further powers could be transferred to the EU there would have to be a referendum. In addition, the 2011 Act sought to declare that all 'directly applicable or directly effective EU law . . . falls to be recognised and available in law in the United Kingdom only by virtue of the [ECA 1972]'.[103] As Gordon states, although this provision did not change the legal position, the primary concern of the government was to address 'the possibility that it might become accepted that EU law had acquired some kind of autonomous legal authority in the UK, transcending that which had been afforded by Parliament in the ECA [1972]'.[104]

5.5.1 The 2016 referendum

The 2011 Act had only a limited impact on the continuing argument over the UK's relationship with the EU. While the referendum lock attempted to provide a guarantee that the UK would not integrate further into the EU without a referendum, this did little to reassure those who felt that EU integration had already gone too far. Concerns over the rate of immigration, including from nationals of Member States whose economies were struggling as a result of the eurozone financial crisis, also contributed to the unease felt by some over EU membership.

In January 2013, David Cameron announced that if the Conservative Party won a majority at the next general election, due in 2015, then that future Conservative Government would renegotiate the UK's terms of membership with the EU, and hold a referendum on whether to remain on those renegotiated terms or to leave the EU.[105] Cameron acknowledged the concerns held by some within his own party, and the broader public, stating that 'public disillusionment with the EU is at an all time high . . . [p]eople feel that the EU is heading in a direction that they never signed up to', and that 'democratic consent for the EU in Britain is now wafer thin'.[106]

 Pause for reflection

Although there have been several referendums in Scotland and Wales on issues of devolution or, in the case of Scotland, independence, to date there have only ever been three UK-wide referendums—the 1975 referendum on remaining a member of the EEC, the referendum in 2011 on changing the electoral system, and the 2016 referendum on EU membership.

To what extent are referendums an appropriate way of resolving important and fundamental constitutional issues? Or are such matters best left to elected politicians to decide through the ordinary processes of representative democracy?

---

[103] European Union Act 2011, s 18.

[104] Michael Gordon, *Parliamentary Sovereignty in the UK Constitution: Process, Politics and Democracy* (Hart 2015) 248.

[105] Cabinet Office, PM's Office, 10 Downing Street, and David Cameron, 'EU speech at Bloomberg' (*HM Government*, 23 January 2013), https://www.gov.uk/government/speeches/eu-speech-at-bloomberg.

[106] Ibid.

After the Conservatives won a narrow majority of twelve seats at the 2015 General Election, David Cameron, continuing as Prime Minister, set about the renegotiations. The renegotiated terms of membership included an acknowledgement that 'the United Kingdom . . . is not committed to further political integration into the European Union . . . [and] that references to ever closer union do not apply to the United Kingdom',[107] greater recognition for those Member States (including the UK) whose currency is not the euro, and a concession on the payment of benefits to EU migrants.[108] Although for some, the renegotiations were successful as they carved out a special position for the UK within the framework of the Treaties, for others they were merely cosmetic changes which did not meet their demands for more fundamental reform to the UK's terms of membership.

Legally, provision was made for the referendum by enacting the European Union Referendum Act 2015. The referendum was held on 23 June 2016, with the 2015 Act setting voters the question 'Should the United Kingdom remain a member of the European Union or leave the European Union', to which 52 per cent answered 'leave the European Union' and 48 per cent answered 'remain a member of the European Union'.[109] The result was a surprise to many, including to Cameron, who had committed the government to implement the outcome of the referendum. Having campaigned so strongly to remain, only for that argument to be rejected, Cameron felt he could not be the Prime Minister and Conservative Party leader who negotiated the terms of the UK's exit from the EU.[110] Theresa May won the ensuing Conservative Party leadership contest, and succeeded Cameron as Prime Minister.

 Pause for reflection

The European Union Referendum Act 2015 only provided for the *holding* of the referendum on EU membership. The 2015 Act was entirely silent as to its consequences. This meant that the referendum was not binding, but could be viewed merely as a statement of the political will of the electorate. Despite that, is the government or Parliament always required to implement the result of a referendum?

5.6 Article 50 TEU and *R (Miller) v Secretary of State for Exiting the European Union*

5.6.1 Article 50 TEU in outline

The process by which a Member State can leave the EU is outlined in Article 50 TEU. Article 50 provides as follows:

1. Any Member State may decide to withdraw from the Union in accordance with its own constitutional requirements.

---

[107] European Council, 'European Council meeting (18 and 19 February 2016)—Conclusions' (*European Council*, 19 February 2016) 16, https://www.consilium.europa.eu/media/21787/0216-euco-conclusions.pdf.

[108] Ibid.

[109] European Union Referendum Act 2015, s 1.

[110] David Cameron, 'EU referendum outcome: PM statement, 24 June 2016' (gov.uk, 24 June 2016) https://www.gov.uk/government/speeches/eu-referendum-outcome-pm-statement-24-june-2016.

2. A Member State which decides to withdraw shall notify the European Council of its intention. In the light of the guidelines provided by the European Council, the Union shall negotiate and conclude an agreement with that State, setting out the arrangements for its withdrawal, taking account of the framework for its future relationship with the Union. . . . It shall be concluded on behalf of the Union by the Council, acting by a qualified majority, after obtaining the consent of the European Parliament.

3. The Treaties shall cease to apply to the State in question from the date of entry into force of the withdrawal agreement or, failing that, two years after the notification referred to in paragraph 2, unless the European Council, in agreement with the Member State concerned, unanimously decides to extend this period.[111]

Essentially, the withdrawing Member State must decide to withdraw and then notify the European Council of its intention to withdraw. This became known as 'triggering Article 50'. Once triggered, there is a two-year time period within which to negotiate and conclude two documents. The first is a withdrawal agreement, which takes into account the second document, the framework for the future relationship. The withdrawal agreement will be an international treaty between the EU and the withdrawing Member State, and the framework for the future relationship will be a non-legally binding political declaration. As hinted at by Article 50(2) TEU, the longer-lasting relationship between the EU and the withdrawing Member State will be negotiated once they have left the EU under the terms of the withdrawal agreement. If these two documents are not agreed within two years of Article 50 being triggered, then the negotiating period can be extended, otherwise the Member State will leave without any terms establishing the terms of withdrawal, which in the context under discussion has become known as a 'No Deal Brexit'.

5.6.2 Triggering Article 50—*R (Miller) v Secretary of State for Exiting the European Union*

For the UK, the first stage of Brexit—'triggering Article 50'—raised difficult constitutional questions. Under the UK Constitution, which institution has the authority to issue the notification as required by Article 50(2)? Could the government act alone, under the royal prerogative, as normal for negotiating an international treaty, or is the consent of Parliament required?[112] When the government announced its intentions to act under the royal prerogative, others argued that, legally, Parliament was required to authorize the government to act.[113] These arguments formed the heart of *R (Miller) v Secretary of State for Exiting the European Union.*[114]

---

[111] Art 50(1)–(3) TEU.

[112] See 6.5.2. Only if a treaty requires a change to domestic law will Parliament be involved, as in 1972.

[113] N Barber, T Hickman, and J King, 'Pulling the article 50 trigger: Parliament's indispensable role' (*UK Constitutional Law Association*, 27 June 2016), https://ukconstitutionallaw.org/2016/06/27/nick-barber-tom-hickman-and-jeff-king-pulling-the-article-50-trigger-parliaments-indispensable-role/ and D Pannick, 'Why giving notice of withdrawal from the EU requires act of Parliament' *The Times* (London, 30 June 2016), https://www.thetimes.co.uk/article/c8985886–3df9–11e6-a28b-4ed-6c4bdada3.

[114] [2017] UKSC 5.

> **Case in depth:** *R (Miller) v Secretary of State for Exiting the European Union* [2017] UKSC 5
>
> Gina Miller, a British businesswoman, supported by various other groups and parties, brought a case against the UK Government, arguing that Article 50 could not be triggered without parliamentary involvement and approval. The main argument was that, since triggering Article 50 will set in motion Brexit and will involve fundamental changes to UK law, including to the rights of British citizens, Parliament's consent is needed before Article 50 can be invoked. Against this, the government argued that Parliament, in enacting the European Communities Act 1972, intended that the Crown retained the prerogative power to sign and withdraw from Treaties. The Divisional Court unanimously found against the government, holding that there was nothing in the 1972 Act to this effect and that, since Brexit would come to involve change to domestic law, fundamental constitutional principle required Parliament to be involved; the government cannot change the law on its own. On subsequent appeal to the Supreme Court, Miller's case was upheld by a majority of eight to three.

The legal question, concerning the relationship between Parliament and the royal prerogative, as raised by this case, is discussed more fully in 6.6 and only a brief summary is given here. Essentially, the Supreme Court held that EU law is an 'independent and overriding source of domestic law', which cannot be changed without Parliament's involvement. Indeed, the court said that since:

> the 1972 Act effectively constitutes EU law as an entirely new, independent and overriding source of domestic law . . . [withdrawal] will constitute as significant a constitutional change as that which occurred when EU law was first incorporated in domestic law by the 1972 Act . . . [w]e cannot accept that [such] a major change to UK constitutional arrangements can be achieved by ministers alone; it must be effected in the only way that the UK constitution recognises, namely by Parliamentary legislation.[115]

This is particularly the case, because leaving the EU would have the effect of changing the 'rights of UK citizens'.[116] Dissenting judgments, by contrast, held that the legal effect of the EU Treaties in the UK is conditional on the UK's membership of the EU, effected by the government's exercise of the prerogative back in 1972. As a result, and since the 1972 Act 'imposes no requirement, and manifests no intention, in respect of the UK's membership of the EU, [it] does not, therefore, affect the Crown's exercise of prerogative powers in respect of UK membership'.[117] In addition, Lord Carnwath noted that triggering Article 50 'will not, and does not purport to, change any laws or affect any rights. It is merely the start of an essentially political process of negotiation and decision-making'.[118] Parliament would be involved later in the process. Alongside this main issue, the Supreme Court was also asked to consider whether or not there was a legal requirement that the devolved institutions be involved in the Brexit process, a question which was answered unanimously in the negative, as 9.4.1 further explains.[119]

---

[115] Ibid [81] and [82].   [116] Ibid [83].   [117] Ibid [177].
[118] Ibid [259].   [119] Ibid [126]–[152].

5.6.3 European Union (Notification of Withdrawal) Act 2017

Following the judgment of the Supreme Court, the European Union (Notification of Withdrawal) Act 2017 was enacted, providing in section 1(1) that:

> The Prime Minister may notify, under Article 50(2) of the Treaty on European Union, the United Kingdom's intention to withdraw from the EU.

Under the terms of the Act, Theresa May triggered Article 50 on 29 March 2017, formally starting the negotiations of the UK's withdrawal from the EU.[120]

 Counterpoint: What did *R (Miller) v Secretary of State for Exiting the European Union* achieve?

Ewing questions whether *Miller* was ultimately worth it, stating:

> When all is said and done . . . it is not clear precisely what the Remainers' demand for a legislative response to the referendum has achieved, the 57 words of the Act being scant reward for bitter litigation. In the end it all seems rather pointless, seeking to compel the House of Commons in particular to do something for which it had no stomach, and which it had the power to do anyway had the will been present. Passed without amendment, the 2017 Act as a precondition to trigger Article 50 failed spectacularly to fulfil the ambitions of those who saw Parliament as a means of containing the Government or even derailing Brexit.[121]

Ewing's point is that all that *Miller* led to was for Parliament to enact the European Union (Notification of Withdrawal) Act 2017, which simply gave the Prime Minister an entirely unrestricted power to trigger Article 50 at a time of her choosing. This power appears very similar to the royal prerogative power that the claimants successfully argued was unlawful. Arguably, the value of the *Miller* case was to empower Parliament and make clear that, as a matter of constitutional principle, it could not be shut out of the Brexit process by the government exercising the royal prerogative.

5.6.4 British politics during the Article 50 negotiation period

In triggering Article 50, Theresa May also started one of the most turbulent times in British politics in living memory, as the Brexit process has stress-tested the UK's constitutional arrangements to the brink of destruction, with almost no area of the constitution immune from becoming embroiled in Brexit. The Brexit process has raised fundamental questions ranging from the exercise of royal prerogative powers, the conduct of cabinet government, to the devolution settlement. These questions and others are addressed throughout the remainder of this book, and the longer-term impact of the Brexit process on the constitution more generally may take several years to emerge. During the Article 50 period, May resigned as Prime Minister to be replaced by Boris

---

[120] Theresa May, 'Prime Minister's letter to Donald Tusk triggering Article 50' (29 March 2017, gov.uk) https://www.gov.uk/government/publications/prime-ministers-letter-to-donald-tusk-triggering-article-50.
[121] Keith Ewing, 'Brexit and Parliamentary Sovereignty' (2017) 80(4) *Modern Law Review* 685, 724.

Johnson and general elections have been held in June 2017 and December 2019 as UK politics grappled with how best to deliver on the outcome of the 2016 referendum. The failure to achieve a clear outcome meant that the two-year period provided by Article 50 TEU was extended three times—first from 29 March 2019 to 12 April, then to 31 October, and then finally to 31 January 2020, the date of the UK's eventual departure from the EU.

The following sections provide an overview of the following aspects of the Brexit process:

- how the European Union (Withdrawal) Act 2018 prepared the UK legal system for Brexit;

- the key features of the Withdrawal Agreement, and how that Agreement has been implemented into UK law through the European Union (Withdrawal Agreement) Act 2020; and

- finally, the chapter will consider what shape the future relationship between the UK and EU may take now that the UK has left the EU,

Discussing the problem

Effect of triggering Article 50

It is important to note that the mere act of triggering Article 50 changed nothing about the status of EU law within the UK legal system. EU law, including Regulation 1151/2012, remained part of UK law and had the same effect as before Article 50 was triggered on 29 March 2017. This means that the protected status of Stilton cheese continued throughout the negotiating period as provided for by Article 50. This also means that the regulation continued to apply throughout the successive extensions of Article 50 from 29 March 2019, when it was originally expected to end, until 31 January 2020, the date of the UK's departure from the EU.

5.7 Preparing UK law for Brexit—European Union (Withdrawal) Act 2018

The most important piece of legislation that prepared the UK legal system for Brexit is the European Union (Withdrawal) Act 2018. The aim of the 2018 Act is to ensure that the UK statute book remains operational and cogent after Brexit. The difficulty was that by necessity, this legislation was enacted while negotiations as to the precise form of Brexit were ongoing with the EU. Consequently, the 2018 Act provided for the most legally challenging scenario—that the UK left the EU at the end of the Article 50 negotiating period without any withdrawal agreement, in a 'No Deal Brexit'. This meant that to take account of the Withdrawal Agreement reached with the EU, and in particular the transition period it provides for, the 2018 Act had to be amended. Consequently, the 2018 Act was amended by the European Union (Withdrawal Agreement) Act 2020. These amendments are discussed in 5.8.

5.7.1 The repeal of the European Communities Act 1972 and 'exit day'

The 2018 Act, at section 1, states that '[t]he European Communities Act 1972 is repealed on exit day'. 'Exit day' was initially defined as 29 March 2019, at 11.00 p.m., the precise time when the UK was expected to leave the EU under Article 50 TEU. However, 'exit day' was amended to 31 January 2020 to reflect the three extensions to the Article 50 negotiation period as described in 5.6.4.[122] The definition of 'exit day' is important, because by default many provisions of the 2018 Act became operational on 'exit day'. However, as we will see shortly, when discussing the European Union (Withdrawal Agreement) Act 2020 in 5.8, the effect of this repeal is less dramatic than it initially appears.

5.7.2 'Retained EU law'

As explained in 5.4, the ECA 1972 is the lynchpin of the complex relationship between UK and EU law, providing the basis by which EU law becomes part of UK law. Provisions of EU law that are directly applicable, such as regulations and those provisions of the treaties that have direct effect, are part of UK law via ECA 1972, section 2(1), without any further legislation being enacted. Most directives passed by EU institutions are implemented into UK law by ministers enacting secondary legislation under section 2(2). The concern is that if the ECA 1972 was simply repealed, as provided for by section 1, then on 'exit day' these laws would also be repealed, leaving significant gaps in the legal system. Consequently, the 2018 Act seeks to achieve legal continuity on 'exit day' by effectively creating a 'snapshot' of all EU law which has become part of UK law via the ECA 1972 and then retaining it as UK law.[123] To achieve this, the snapshot the Act seeks to take covers the following three categories of EU law, which together form a body of UK law called 'retained EU law':[124]

- *Section 2: 'EU-derived domestic legislation'*—This category includes the secondary legislation enacted under ECA 1972, section 2(2) to implement directives.[125] The category also includes other provisions of UK law that implemented directives, for example the Equality Act 2010, which implemented four directives into UK law.[126] Section 2(1)

---

[122] Section 20(4), and the European Union (Withdrawal) Act 2018 (Exit Day) (Amendment) (No 3) Regulations 2019, SI 1423/2019, reg 2.

[123] The word 'snapshot' was first used by Mark Elliott to describe this process. See Mark Elliott, '1,000 words / The European Union (Withdrawal) Act 2018' [https://publiclawforeveryone. com/2018/06/28/1000-words-the-european-union-withdrawal-act-2018/].

[124] The 2018 Act itself uses the term 'retained EU law' at s 6(7).

[125] This then continues to be part of UK law after exit day under EU(W)A 2018, s 7(1). Some directives have been implemented into UK law by primary legislation, which means that those provisions of EU law do not rely on the ECA 1972 and would remain part of UK law after the repeal of the ECA 1972. However, they are included within the EU(W)A 2018, s 2(1) as EU-derived domestic legislation, meaning that the provisions of amending other types of EU-derived domestic legislation can apply where appropriate to this type of legislation.

[126] These were: Council Directive 2000/43/EC implementing the principle of equal treatment between persons irrespective of racial or ethnic origin; Council Directive 2000/78/EC establishing a general framework for equal treatment in employment and occupation; Council Directive 2004/113/EC implementing the principle of equal treatment between men and women in the access to and supply of goods and services; European Parliament and Council Directive 2006/54/EC on the implementation of the principle of equal opportunities and equal treatment of men and women in matters of employment and occupation (recast).

provides that 'EU-derived domestic legislation, as it has in effect in domestic law imme-diately before exit day, continues to have effect in domestic law on and after exit day'.

- *Section 3: 'Direct EU legislation'*—This category primarily includes regulations, which became part of UK law via ECA 1972, section 2(1).[127] Section 3(1) ensures that EU law covered by this category 'so far as operative immediately before exit day, forms part of domestic law on and after exit day'.

- *Section 4: 'rights, powers, liabilities'*—which otherwise became part of UK law via under ECA 1972, section 2(1). In particular, this category includes provisions of EU law that have direct effect. This primarily includes specific articles of the Treaties. Section 4(1) ensures that they remain part of UK law and 'continue on and after exit day to be recognised' so that they continue to have effect and are available to be invoked in UK law.

In the Explanatory Notes to the 2018 Act, the UK government provides the following indicative list of TFEU articles that have direct effect (Table 5.1), and so will be converted into UK law on exit day under section 4.

TABLE 5.1 An indicative list of TFEU articles that have direct effect, and so converted into UK law on exit day.

(i) **Article 18**	Non-discrimination on ground of nationality
(ii) **Article 20 (except Article 20(2)(c))**	Citizenship rights
(iii) **Article 21(1)**	Rights of movement and residence deriving from EU citizenship
(iv) **Article 28**	Establishes customs union, prohibition of customs duties, common external tariff
(v) **Article 30**	Prohibition on customs duties
(vi) **Article 34**	Prohibition on quantitative restrictions on imports
(vii) **Article 35**	Prohibition on quantitative restrictions on exports
(viii) **Article 36**	Exception to quantitative restrictions

---

[127] This is further complicated because EU(W)A 2018, s 7(2), (3), and (6) splits the category of direct EU legislation into two, as provided for by s 3: 'retained direct minor EU legislation' and 'retained direct principal legislation'. 'Retained direct minor EU legislation' broadly means EU tertiary legislation, which is defined in s 20 as including secondary legislation within EU law, such as provisions made *under* a EU regulation or EU directive. 'Retained direct principal EU legislation' is all other EU legislation which falls within s 3 as direct EU legislation. The consequence of this distinction is technical and, essentially, secondary legislation enacted under Sch 8(3) and (4) amending retained direct principal EU legislation which is subject to the same procedure that applies to secondary legislation that amends primary legisla-tion. Secondary legislation enacted under these powers that amends retained direct minor EU legislation is subject to the procedures that apply to secondary legislation that amends other secondary legislation.

(ix) **Article 37(1) and (2)**	Prohibition on discrimination regarding the conditions under which goods are procured
(x) **Article 45(1), (2), and (3)**	Free movement of workers
(xi) **Article 49**	Freedom of establishment
(xii) **Article 56**	Freedom to provide services
(xiii) **Article 57**	Services
(xiv) **Article 63**	Free movement of capital
(xv) **Article 101(1)**	Competition
(xvi) **Article 102**	Abuse of a dominant position
(xvii) **Article 106(1) and (2)**	Public undertakings
(xviii) **Article 107(1)**	State aid
(xix) **Article 108(3)**	Commission consideration of plans regarding state aid
(xx) **Article 110**	Internal taxation
(xxi) **Article 112**	Non-discrimination in indirect taxes
(xxii) **Article 157**	Equal pay
(xxiii) **Protocol 5—Articles 13, 20(2), 23(1) and (4), 26, 27 (second and third sub-paragraphs), 28(4)**	EIB
(xxiv) **Protocol 7—Article 21**	Privileges and immunities of the EIB

Source: European Union (Withdrawal) Act 2018, Explanatory Notes, para 94

5.7.3 **Supremacy after Brexit**

Sections 2, 3, and 4 are all subject to section 5. This provides that on or after exit day, the principle of the supremacy of EU law over UK law only applies 'so far as relevant to the interpretation, disapplication or quashing of any enactment or rule of law passed or made before exit day'.[128] For laws passed after exit day, the principle of supremacy 'does not apply'.[129] This means that retained EU law will only continue to be supreme over domestic legislation enacted before exit day. Any domestic legislation enacted after exit day will not be subject to the supremacy of EU law.

---

[128] European Union (Withdrawal) Act 2018, section 5(2).
[129] Ibid s 5(1).

5.7.4 **Amending 'retained EU law'**

Legally, it is section 5 which removes the limitation on sovereignty that Parliament imposed on itself when enacting the ECA 1972. This means that Parliament will be able to amend or repeal any provision of retained EU law at any point after exit day. Section 7 makes this explicit, providing that all retained EU law can be amended or repealed by an Act of Parliament or, if within their respective competencies, by primary legislation passed by the Scottish Parliament, Northern Irish Parliament, and/or Welsh Parliament.[130] In a sense, the ability of the UK to pass its own laws in areas once governed by the EU is the very essence of Brexit, but given the extent to which EU law is currently part of the UK legal system, the exercise of this regained sovereignty is likely to be a gradual process. The 2018 Act is clear that nothing within its provisions precludes the UK from mirroring any provision of EU law, or taking part or having a formal relationship with any agencies of the EU after exit day.[131] The extent to which UK law will mirror or diverge from EU law will depend on the nature of the UK's future relationship with the EU.

However, because the Act is intended to ensure legal continuity, this is not its focus. A more immediate concern is that the EU law captured as 'retained EU law' has been originally drafted to apply to the Member States of the EU. This means that much retained EU law contains terms or expressions that make little sense to a non-Member State. Having ensured legal continuity in retaining EU law as domestic law, the Act then provides ways in which the statute book can be amended so that it operates effectively when the UK leaves the EU.

Primarily, this has been achieved by granting the government extensive powers to amend retained EU law through secondary legislation. The Act provides two methods to do this: first by creating new powers, and second by extending existing powers.

Section 8—new power to amend retained EU law

The new power to amend retained EU law is contained in section 8. This allows ministers to enact secondary legislation to correct any 'failure' of or a 'deficiency' in retained EU law.[132] The Explanatory Notes to the Act state that a 'failure' is when the 'law doesn't operate effectively', whereas a 'deficiency' 'covers a wider range of cases where it does not function appropriately or sensibly'.[133]

'Deficiency' is defined in the Act as including situations when retained EU law:

- 'contains anything which has no practical application in relation to the United Kingdom or any part of it or is otherwise redundant or substantially redundant';[134]

- 'confers functions on, or in relation to, EU entities which no longer have functions in that respect under EU law in relation to the United Kingdom or any part of it';[135]

- 'contains EU references which are no longer appropriate'.[136]

Secondary legislation made under this power can 'make any provision that could be made by an Act of Parliament',[137] but cannot be used to impose new taxes, create criminal offences, establish a new public authority, and amend or repeal the Human Rights Act 1998, the Scotland Act 1998, the Government of Wales Act 2006, or the Northern Ireland Act 1998.[138]

---

[130] Ibid s 7.   [131] Ibid s 19.
[132] Ibid s 8(1).
[133] Explanatory Notes to the European Union (Withdrawal) Act 2018, para 123.
[134] Ibid s 8(2)(a).   [135] Ibid s 8(2)(b).   [136] Ibid s 8(2)(g).
[137] Ibid s 8(2).   [138] Ibid s 8(7).

Generally, any secondary legislation made under this section 8 power is subject to the negative resolution procedure.[139] However, if any regulation seeks to allocate a function of an EU entity or public authority in a Member State to a public authority in the UK, 'creates or widens the scope of a criminal office', or creates or amends a power to legislate, then the regulations are subject to the affirmative procedure.[140] The procedures for making secondary legislation are explained in 8.6.

The 2018 Act requires the House of Commons and the House of Lords to each create a committee to 'sift' through regulations that the government intend to be subject to the negative procedure.[141] The committees have the power to recommend that despite the government's intention, the regulation should be subject to the positive procedure. If the government disagrees, it must make a statement explaining why it disagrees with the recommendation of the committee.[142]

Extending existing powers to amend retained EU law

Existing powers to amend primary legislation via secondary legislation (so-called 'Henry VIII powers') in any Act of Parliament can be used to amend any retained direct EU legislation as provided for by section 3, or any retained EU law as provided for by section 4.[143] This would be subject to the same procedure as would apply to that legislation if it were amending or repealing primary legislation.[144] Originally, these Henry VIII powers were enacted on the basis that they would only be used in compliance with EU law. Now these powers can be used free from that restriction, and can also be used to amend, revoke, or modify retained EU law.[145] The procedure for the exercise of this power is the same as provided for in the Act of Parliament that establishes the Henry VIII power in question. A similar structure applies to devolved institutions. This is potentially a significant increase in government power, as in theory this allows the government via secondary legislation to diverge from EU law, using powers that were not initially designed for this purpose. There are other technical powers to amend legislation contained in Sch 8 of the Act.

 Discussing the problem

How does the European Union (Withdrawal) Act 2018 apply to the regulation?

The European Union (Withdrawal) Act 2018 seeks to ensure that all EU that has become part of the UK law will be converted to 'retained EU law' and remain part of UK law even after the repeal of the ECA 1972. Regulation 1151/2012 will fall under the category of 'retained direct EU legislation'. As the regulation was written to apply to Member States, it contains references to

→

---

[139] Ibid Sch 7, para 1(3).

[140] Ibid Sch 7, para 1(2).

[141] Ibid Sch 7, para 3. In the House of Commons, the European Statutory Instruments Committee has been created to fulfil this function. In the House of Lords, this function has been allocated to the Secondary Legislation Scrutiny Committee.

[142] Ibid Sch 7, para 3(7).

[143] Ibid Sch 8, para 3.

[144] Ibid Sch 8, para 4.

[145] Ibid Sch 8, para 4(1)–(3).

→

EU concepts and terms, such as 'Member States', 'Commission', and the 'Union' (meaning EU), which will not apply to the regulation as it is converted into retained EU law that applies to the UK only.

As described by section 8, these references are known as 'deficiencies' and can be amended by secondary legislation. Consequently, under powers granted by the 2018 Act, the government has prepared the Food and Drink, Veterinary Medicines and Residues (Amendment etc.) (EU Exit) Regulations 2019,[146] which removes these deficiencies, for example, by replacing references to the 'Commission' with 'Secretary of State', and 'Union' with 'United Kingdom'.

Both the conversion of the regulation into retained EU law and its amendment by the regulations were due to come into force on 'exit day' as defined by the 2018 Act.

5.8 The Withdrawal Agreement and the European Union (Withdrawal) Agreement Act 2020

In November 2018, the EU and UK announced that, as required by Art 50 TEU, they had concluded negotiations on the Withdrawal Agreement and the Framework for the Future Relationship.[147] However, several of its provisions, particularly those relating to what became known as the 'Northern Ireland Backstop', proved extremely controversial, and the House of Commons voted against the Withdrawal Agreement three times. The first two of these defeats were the largest government defeats in the House of Commons in modern times.[148] These defeats were ultimately the cause of the repeated extensions of the Article 50 negotiating period until 31 October 2019. In June 2019, when it was clear that the House of Commons would ultimately reject the Withdrawal Agreement a fourth time, Theresa May announced her intention to resign as Prime Minister and Conservative Party leader.

Her replacement, Boris Johnson, fought the Conservative Party leadership contest on a clear platform to address MPs' (particularly Conservative MPs who voted against the deal) concerns on the Northern Ireland Backstop. In October 2019, Johnson managed to secure several amendments to the Withdrawal Agreement and the Framework for the Future Relationship.[149] In the first Saturday sitting of Parliament since 1982,[150] the House

---

[146] SI 2019/865.

[147] Agreement on the withdrawal of the United Kingdom of Great Britain and Northern Ireland from the European Union and the European Atomic Energy Community (Official Journal of the European Union, 2019/C/66 I/01, 19 February 2019) Article 126.

[148] Firstly, on 15 January 2019 by 432 votes against to 202 in favour, and then on 12 March by 391 votes against to 242; HC Debs 15 January 2019, vol 652, cols 1222–5; 12 March 2019 vol 656, cols 291–5. The third defeat was narrower with 344 votes against to 286 in favour, HC Deb 29 March 2019, vol 657, cols 771–5.

[149] European Commission, 'Working document – Consolidated version of the Withdrawal Agreement following revision of Protocol on Ireland/Northern Ireland and technical adaptations to Article 184 "Negotiations on the future relationship" and Article 185 "Entry into force and application" (document TF50(2019)64), as agreed at negotiators' level and endorsed by the European Council', (TF50(2019)66, 17 October 2019).

[150] When Parliament met to discuss the Argentinian invasion of the Falkland Islands, HC Debs 3 April 1982, vol 21, cols 633–88.

of Commons declined to give its explicit backing to the amended deal, at least until the legislation, the European Union (Withdrawal Agreement) Bill ('WAB'), which implements the Withdrawal Agreement into UK law, has been passed by Parliament.[151] This meant that as required by European Union (Withdrawal) (No 2) Act 2019, Johnson requested a further extension until 31 January 2020, which was agreed to by the EU.[152]

When the WAB was introduced into Parliament, the House of Commons granted it a second reading, but did not support the government's timetable for the rest of its passage through the House of Commons. Concerned that this was a precursor to MPs blocking the WAB entirely, Johnson sought a general election, held on 12 December 2019, on which he pledged to 'get Brexit done' by promising that the first act of a Conservative government would be to enact the WAB, which would allow the UK leave to the EU on 31 January 2020. Following the Conservatives' victory with an eighty-seat majority, the government reintroduced the WAB into Parliament, and it was enacted as the European Union (Withdrawal Agreement) Act 2020.

The following seeks to address the key elements of the Withdrawal Agreement and how the 2020 Act seeks to implement these provisions into UK law; in particular, how it amends the European Union (Withdrawal) Act 2018 as discussed in 5.7.

5.8.1 Transition period

The Withdrawal Agreement provides for a transition period[153] lasting from 31 January 2020, the date of the UK's departure from the EU, until 31 December 2020.[154] This period can be extended once for either one or two years.[155] During this time, the UK will continue to be bound by EU law in its entirety.[156]

Clearly, this raises questions about how this will sit with the European Union (Withdrawal) Act 2018, which requires on the date the UK leaves the EU, known as 'exit day', for the European Communities Act 1972 to be repealed and for retained EU law to take effect. The 2020 Act addresses this issue by continuing to allow the ECA 1972 to be repealed on exit day, but stating that, despite being repealed, under a new section 1A inserted into the 2018 Act, stating that the ECA 1972, 'as it has effect . . . before exit day, continues to have effect . . . on and after exit day'.[157] Such linguistic gymnastics reduces the repeal of the ECA 1972 to only the barest political symbols as the new section 1A means that EU law will continue to be part of UK law as before exit day, despite the repeal of the ECA 1972.

---

[151] HC Debs 19 October 2019, vol 666, cols 570–653.

[152] The letter was sent according to the requirements of the European Union (Withdrawal) (No 2) Act 2019, at s 1 and the Schedule to the Act.

[153] Both the European Union (Withdrawal) Act 2018 and European Union (Withdrawal Agreement) Act 2020 use the phrase 'implementation period'; however, this is commonly referred to as the transition period, and this is the phrase used in this chapter.

[154] European Commission (n 149), Art 126.

[155] European Commission (n 149), Art 132. Although the European Union (Withdrawal Agreement) Act 2020, s 33 inserts s 15A into the European Union (Withdrawal) Act 2018, which makes it unlawful, as a matter of UK law, for the UK Government to seek an extension to the transition period. Although, should the government wish to seek an extension, this provision could be repealed or amended by further legislation.

[156] European Commission (n 149), Art 127.

[157] European Union (Withdrawal Agreement) Act 2020, s 1, inserting s 1A into the European Union (Withdrawal) Act 2018.

This new section 1A will only have effect until the end of the transition period, after which the ECA 1972, or more precisely its effect, will be repealed entirely.

Given that the ECA 1972 will still be repealed, the 2020 Act ensures that specific provision is made to ensure that 'EU-derived domestic legislation', a category of retained EU law as described in 5.7.2, continues to have the same legal status after exit day and during the transition period.[158] More generally, the 2020 Act amends the provisions regarding retained EU law, as outlined above in 5.7.2, so that sections 2, 3, and 4 of the European Union (Withdrawal) Act 2018 only take effect at the end of the transition period rather than exit day.[159]

5.8.2 Direct effect and supremacy of the Withdrawal Agreement

At Article 4, the Withdrawal Agreement provides that:

> the provisions of this Agreement and the provisions of Union law made applicable by this Agreement shall produce in respect of and in the United Kingdom the same legal effects as those which they produce within the Union and its Member States.

Consequently, this means that the Agreement is governed by EU law and its provisions 'shall be interpreted and applied in accordance with the methods and general principles of Union law' and according to the case law of the CJEU as handed down before the end of the transition period.[160] More importantly, the concept of direct effect applies to the Withdrawal Agreement for any provision that meets the conditions for direct effect under pre-existing EU law. Finally, the UK is under an obligation to ensure that any UK law that is inconsistent or incompatible with the Withdrawal Agreement is disapplied, meaning that the principle of supremacy is retained.[161]

The 2020 Act, at section 5, makes provision for this by introducing a new section 7A into the European Union (Withdrawal) Act 2018. In language eerily reminiscent of ECA 1972, s 2, it provides for the following:

(1)   . . .

    (a)   all such rights, powers, liabilities, obligations and restrictions from time to time created or arising by or under the withdrawal agreement, and

    (b)   all such remedies and procedures from time to time provided for by or under the withdrawal agreement,

as in accordance with the withdrawal agreement are without further enactment to be given legal effect or used in the United Kingdom.

5.8.3 Citizens' rights

A key element of EU membership is the freedom of movement of citizens between Member States. Millions of EU citizens have exercised this right to move to another Member State. This has led to approximately 3 million citizens from other Member States

---

[158] European Union (Withdrawal Agreement) Act 2020, s 2, inserting s 1B into the European Union (Withdrawal) Act 2018.

[159] European Union (Withdrawal Agreement) Act 2020, s 25, amending European Union (Withdrawal) Act 2018, ss 2–5.

[160] European Commission (n 149), Art 4(3)–(4).

[161] European Commission (n 149), Art 4.

living in the UK, and 1.2 million UK citizens living elsewhere in the EU.[162] Unless citizens are lawfully resident in their adopted, 'host' country in some other way under the law of that Member State (for example, family connections or length of residency), then Brexit threatens the lawful basis on which these EU citizens have exercised their right of freedom of movement.

The Withdrawal Agreement avoids this by providing EU citizens who have exercised their right of freedom of movement to reside in the UK before the end of the transition period can continue to reside in the UK afterwards. Once these EU citizens have been continuously resident in the UK for five years, they acquire the right of permanent residency.[163] This five-year period can be accumulated either before or after the end of the transition period.[164] The same provisions apply to UK nationals who have exercised their right to reside in another EU Member State. The UK, in relation to EU citizens and the other Members States in relation to UK nationals, may require that they apply for this new residence status.[165] The UK has required that EU citizens must apply for settled status to prove their status.[166]

The Withdrawal Agreement also makes more detailed provisions regarding the rights of EU citizens, including the coordination of social security systems, and the creation of the Independent Monitoring Authority to oversee the implementation in the UK of the citizens' rights aspects of the Withdrawal Agreement. These provisions have also been implemented into UK law by the 2020 Act.

5.8.4 **Northern Ireland Backstop**

The Northern Ireland Backstop has proven to be the most controversial aspect of the Withdrawal Agreement, and was the primary focus of Boris Johnson's renegotiations. The concern is essentially what happens after the UK leaves the EU, especially after the end of the transition period when EU law will no longer apply in the UK. The issue is that the UK, including Northern Ireland, shares many rules and customs arrangements with the Republic of Ireland, due to both countries being Member States of the EU. This means that goods can travel freely across the border between Northern Ireland and the Republic, and this has, at least to some extent, underpinned the peace process in Northern Ireland.

As discussed in 5.9, if the UK and the EU fail to agree the future relationship by the end of the transition period, then by default, different customs rules apply between the UK, (including Northern Ireland) and the Republic of Ireland. Usually, when two neighbouring countries have two different customs regimes, border checks are required to ensure that all customs requirements for both countries are met. This is thought to be entirely out of the question for the Northern Ireland–Republic of Ireland border, not only in terms

---

[162] Carlos Vargas-Silva and Mariña Fernández-Reino, 'EU Migration to and from the UK' (The Migration Observatory, 30 September 2019), https://migrationobservatory.ox.ac.uk/resources/briefings/eu-migration-to-and-from-the-uk/; BBC News, 'Reality Check: How many EU nationals live in the UK?' (BBC News, 8 July 2016), https://www.bbc.co.uk/news/uk-politics-uk-leaves-the-eu-36745584.

[163] European Commission (n 149), Art 15.

[164] European Commission (n 149), Art 16.

[165] European Commission (n 149), Art 18.

[166] Gov.uk. 'Apply to the EU Settlement Scheme (settled and pre-settled status)', https://www.gov.uk/settled-status-eu-citizens-families.

of the peace process, but also logistically as there are more than 200 roads that cross the border, carrying an extensive amount of traffic each day.

To try to resolve this dilemma, the UK and EU have agreed the 'Northern Ireland Backstop', so that, should the UK and EU not agree the future trading relationship, the backstop will take effect. Although highly complex, it can be boiled down to the following basic principles. In terms of customs, Northern Ireland has a form of hybrid status. If goods are entering Northern Ireland from the rest of the UK, then no tariff is charged because Northern Ireland remains part of the customs territory of the UK. Similarly, if goods enter Northern Ireland from the Republic of Ireland, then there will also be no tariffs to pay. However, if a good entering Northern Ireland from the rest of the UK is 'at risk' of being moved into the EU, then the EU tariff will be payable. For this to work, goods moving from the rest of the UK to Northern Ireland will be subject to checks.

For some, this is controversial because they believe that this threatens the unity of the UK, as there is essentially a customs border in the North Sea between Northern Ireland and the rest of the UK. These concerns are furthered when it is considered that Northern Ireland will also be required to stick to many of the EU rules that regulate the single market. By contrast, the rest of the UK will be able to diverge from EU rules. If the backstop ever takes effect, then four years after the end of the transition period the Northern Ireland Assembly will be able to vote on whether to continue with the backstop. Further votes would then be held every four years after that. If the Assembly votes against the backstop, then it will cease to apply two years after that vote.[167]

 Discussing the problem

How do the European Union (Withdrawal Agreement) Bill and the Withdrawal Agreement apply to the regulation?

The transition period, as provided for under the Withdrawal Agreement, means that Regulation 1151/2012 will continue to apply in UK law until the end of the transition period. The European Union (Withdrawal Agreement) Act 2020 serves to change the legal base on which the regulation remains part of UK law, because although the ECA 1972 is repealed, its effect is preserved by amendments that the 2020 Act makes. These last for the duration of the transition period, after which the main provisions of the European Union (Withdrawal) Act 2018 will take effect, meaning that the regulation will remain part of UK law, as retained EU law. This means that Stilton cheese, and all the other products in the UK protected by the regulation, will continue to be protected.

Furthermore, under the Withdrawal Agreement as agreed with the EU, the UK has committed that those products protected by the regulation (including products from the EU, protected in the UK) 'shall be granted at least the same level of protection under the law of the United Kingdom' as under EU law.[168] This requirement will last until the EU and the UK have agreed the terms of their future relationship, which, in theory, could be after the end of the transition period.

---

[167] Alex Stojanovic, 'Brexit deal: the Northern Ireland protocol' (Institute for Government, 17 October 2019), https://www.instituteforgovernment.org.uk/explainers/brexit-deal-northern-ireland-protocol.

[168] European Commission (n 149), Art 54(2).

5.9 **The future relationship**

As can be seen from 5.8, the Withdrawal Agreement is limited to focusing on the terms of the UK's withdrawal from the EU. Decisions regarding how the UK and the EU will trade with each other depend on a new trade deal being agreed. The transition period until 31 December 2020, provided for in the Withdrawal Agreement, is meant to serve as a bridge between when the UK leaves the EU to when the future relationship takes effect. As required by Article 50, the UK and the EU have agreed the Framework for the Future Relationship, which although not legally binding, indicates the form that the future relationship may take.[169]

As renegotiated by Boris Johnson, the Framework commits the UK and the EU to agreeing an 'ambitious' relationship, based on a free trade agreement with 'deep' regulatory co-operation, which suggests that the UK may co-operate with several EU agencies. This means that, even after EU law no longer applies to the UK, EU regulations will, at the very least, influence the development of UK laws and regulations. However, it appears unlikely that the UK will remain a member of the customs union, meaning that some tariffs and checks will be required for goods moving between the UK and the EU. How this will apply in relation to Northern Ireland, given the difficulties explained in 5.8.4, remains unclear. The UK has indicated that, at the end of the transition period, the freedom of movement between the UK and the EU, as provided for by EU law will end, with EU nationals subject to similar rules as non-EU nationals, which are more restrictive. Both the UK and the EU intend to allow visa-free travel for short trips.

Even allowing for the fact that negotiations are starting from the situation where the UK and the EU share common rules, this new agreement is likely to run to hundreds, if not thousands, of pages, with technical provisions dealing with many different sectors of the economy. This includes transport, intellectual property, energy, public procurement, fishing, and financial services. At the time of writing, the intention is for this agreement to take effect from 1 January 2021, the end of the transition period, although this can be extended by either one or two years.

> **⁙ Discussing the problem**
>
> **What does the Framework for the Future Relationship say as regards Regulation 1151/2012?**
>
> Under the Withdrawal Agreement, the protection provided by Regulation 1151/2012 continues until the future relationship between the UK and EU takes effect. The Framework for the Future Relationship states as follows:
>
> →

---

[169] European Commission, 'Revised text of the Political Declaration setting out the framework for the future relationship between the European Union and the United Kingdom as agreed at negotiators' level on 17 October 2019, to replace the one published in OJ C 66I of 19.2.2019' (TF50(2019)65, 17 October 2019).

> Noting the protection afforded to existing geographical indications in the Withdrawal Agreement, the Parties should seek to put in place arrangements to provide appropriate protection for their geographical indications.[170]

Clearly, details are scarce, but this appears to suggest that the future relationship will seek to replicate the protection of foods such as Stilton as provided in the Withdrawal Agreement. This is perhaps an example of how although the UK has now left the EU, and soon EU law will no longer apply, the UK will not entirely leave the EU's orbit, and in certain areas, UK law will closely mirror EU law.[171]

5.10 Summary

This chapter has explained the origins, fundamental rationale, and evolution of the EU and its institutions. In order to achieve its objectives of a greater interdependence, and an 'ever closer union' between its Member States, the EU has an extraordinary effect on their domestic legal systems. Initially, the UK, unsure of its position in the world following the Second World War, and with its rapidly diminishing Empire, chose not to join. When the UK did become a Member State in 1973, it did so after the principles of direct applicability, direct effect, and supremacy had been well established in EU law.

As a matter of domestic law, giving effect to these principles through the ECA 1972 raised fundamental questions of parliamentary sovereignty, which perhaps have never been answered conclusively. Concerns about sovereignty, and the UK's ability to make its own laws, as the EU acquires more competencies to make law in an increasingly large number of areas, fed into broader questions about the UK's membership of the EU. These questions have been a key feature of British politics ever since 1973. When David Cameron sought to answer those questions with a referendum, the electorate answered by voting to leave.

Brexit has proven to be a challenging technical, political, and legal process and despite the UK's actual exit taking place on 31 January 2020, it is still ongoing. Focus has shifted to the next stage of negotiations, which seek to establish the UK's future relationship with the EU. At the time of writing, the UK Government is committed to the deadline of 31 December 2020, the end of the transition period and the point at which the UK will no longer be bound by EU law. Yet, as the Framework for the Future Relationship shows, UK law will continue to be influenced by EU law. The question facing the UK Government and Parliament is to decide by just how much. In essence, this is the same question that has concerned many since the end of the Second World War: just what form should the relationship between the UK and Europe take? The future relationship will have to provide an answer, whatever it may be.

---

[170] Ibid para 43.

[171] For a full discussion of the issues raised in the problem question see Craig Prescott, Manuela Pilato, and Claudio Bellia, 'Geographical indications in the UK after Brexit: An uncertain future?' (2020) *Food Policy* (Vol 90, Article 101808), available at https://doi.org/10.1016/j.foodpol.2019.101808.

Quick test questions

1. What are the aims of the EU?

2. Which cases established the supremacy of EU law?

3. What are the key provisions of the European Communities Act 1972 and what was their effect?

4. What are the facts underpinning the *Factortame* litigation? Why was the House of Lords' judgment so significant?

5. What is the distinction, with regard to implied repeal, between ordinary and constitutional statutes?

6. What was the basis of the Supreme Court's decision in *Miller*?

7. What are the main aims of the European Union (Withdrawal) Act 2018?

8. What amendments did the European Union (Withdrawal Agreement) Act 2020 make to the European Union (Withdrawal) Act 2018 so that the 2018 Act takes account of the transition period, as provided for by the Withdrawal Agreement?

Further reading

The EU in general

Paul Craig & Gráinne de Búrca, *EU Law: Text, Cases and Materials* (7th edn, OUP 2020)

Catherine Barnard & Steve Peers (eds) *European Union Law* (3rd edn, OUP 2020)

Parliamentary sovereignty

TRS Allan, 'Parliamentary Sovereignty: Law, Politics, and Revolution' (1997) 113(Jul) *Law Quarterly Review* 443

NW Barber, 'The Afterlife of Parliamentary Sovereignty' (2011) 9(1) *International Journal of Constitutional Law* 144

PP Craig, 'Sovereignty of the United Kingdom Parliament after *Factortame*' (1991) 11 *Yearbook of European Law* 221

PP Craig, 'Constitutionalising Constitutional Law: HS2' [2014] *Public Law* 373

Michael Gordon, *Parliamentary Sovereignty in the UK Constitution: Process, Politics and Democracy* (Hart 2015)

*HWR Wade, 'The Basis of Legal Sovereignty' (1955) 13(2) *Cambridge Law Journal* 172

HWR Wade, 'Sovereignty—Revolution or Evolution?' (1996) 112(Oct) *Law Quarterly Review* 568

The Brexit process and *R (Miller) v Secretary of State for Exiting the European Union*

N Barber, T Hickman, and J King, 'Pulling the Article 50 Trigger: Parliament's Indispensable Role' (UK Constitutional Law Association Blog, 27 June 2016), available at https://ukconstitutionallaw. org/2016/06/27/nick-barber-tom-hickman-and-jeff-king-pulling-the-article-50-trigger-parliaments-indispensable-role/

Keith Ewing, 'Brexit and Parliamentary Sovereignty' (2017) 80(4) *Modern Law Review* 685

*Gavin Phillipson, 'A Dive into Deep Constitutional Waters: Article 50, the Prerogative and Parliament' (2016) 79(6) *Modern Law Review* 1064

Gavin Phillipson, 'EU Law as an Agent of National Constitutional Change: *Miller v Secretary of State for Exiting the European Union'* (2017) 36(1) *Yearbook of European Law* 46

Alison L Young, 'Case Comment: *R. (Miller) v Secretary of State for Exiting the European Union*: Thriller or Vanilla?' (2017) 42(2) *European Law Review* 280

The European Union (Withdrawal) Act 2018

*Paul Craig, 'Constitutional Principle, the Rule of Law and Political Reality: The European Union (Withdrawal) Act 2018' (2019) 82(2) *Modern Law Review* 319

*Mark Elliott and Stephen Tierney, 'Political Pragmatism and Constitutional Principle: The European Union (Withdrawal) Act 2018' [2019] *Public Law* 37

European Union (Withdrawal Agreement) Act 2020

Graeme Cowie, 'Withdrawal Agreement Bill: Implementing the transition period'? (House of Commons Library, 22 October 2019) available at https://commonslibrary.parliament.uk/brexit/the-eu/withdrawal-agreement-bill-implementing-the-transition-period/?preview=true&_thumbnail_id=23637

Michael Gordon, 'The European Union (Withdrawal Agreement) Bill: Parliamentary Sovereignty, Continuity and Novelty', (UK Constitutional Law Association Blog, 22 October 2019) available at https://ukconstitutionallaw.org/2019/10/22/mike-gordon-the-european-union-withdrawal-agreement-bill-parliamentary-sovereignty-continuity-and-novelty/

House of Lords Constitution Committee, *European Union (Withdrawal Agreement) Bill: Interim Report* (HL 2019, 21)

 Visit this book's **online resources** for additional materials relating to this chapter, including a full analysis of the start-of-chapter problem scenario.
www.oup.com/he/stanton-prescott2e

6

The royal prerogative and constitutional conventions

Problem scenario

In early 2022, the Conservative Government has negotiated a new international treaty with the USA. The government, concerned at the growing costs of replacing Trident, the UK's existing nuclear deterrent, has agreed with the USA to use its nuclear technology. As part of this agreement, the UK has agreed that the USA can store nuclear missiles at US military bases located on UK territory. Prior to this agreement, the USA last stored missiles in the UK in 2006, when the last missiles were withdrawn.

Since its announcement, the treaty has provoked enormous controversy, as some believe that it reduces the UK's standing in the world to that of a mere colony of the USA, and others are outraged by the principle of replacing the UK's own nuclear deterrent and believe that existing nuclear missiles should be destroyed rather than replaced. Others believe that the agreement ensures the UK's security for the foreseeable future. This debate over the treaty has come to dominate politics throughout most of 2022. Protests against the treaty have been led by several campaign groups who are now urging the Queen to intervene. They are asking Her Majesty to speak out against the treaty and prevent the government from ratifying it.

As required by the Constitutional Reform and Governance Act 2010, the government laid the treaty before Parliament. Immediately, the Opposition tabled a motion in the House of Commons, stating that the treaty should not be ratified. The next day, MPs voted against the treaty, triggering an immediate political crisis. The government is concerned that the controversy is only going to continue as MPs may block the government's other measures as a protest over the treaty.

Consequently, the Prime Minister feels that the crisis can only be resolved through an early general election, and requested that the House of Commons voted to hold an election in

→

accordance with the Fixed-term Parliaments Act 2011. The main opposition party agreed, and more than 580 MPs out of 650 voted for an early general election.

The general election held in November 2022 delivered the result shown in Figure 6.1.

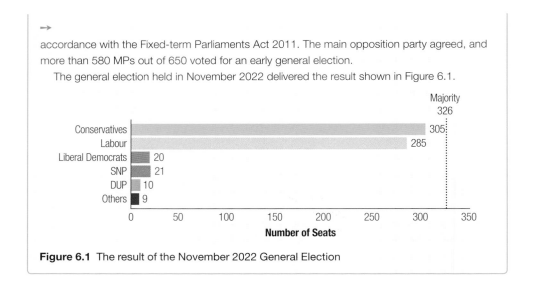

Figure 6.1 The result of the November 2022 General Election

6.1 Introduction: what is the 'Crown'?

The rule of law requires that government acts according to the law. This means that the powers of the government must be derived from the law. Usually the government's powers stem from statute. However, within the UK Constitution, some powers of the government are part of the royal prerogative, as recognized by the common law. Indeed, it is the 'royal' part of that label, which reveals that not all the powers of government are derived from statutes passed by Parliament.

Historically, the monarch was seen as the source of executive, legislative, and judicial power.[1] The inherent status and importance of the monarch was such that they personally exercised the powers of government, giving rise to the notion that governmental power belonged to 'the Crown'. These powers became collectively referred to as the royal prerogative.

From the early middle ages onwards, monarchs governed personally but took advice from advisers who formed the Council. By the Tudor period, the Council had become the Privy Council, with the monarch's advisers dealing with routine matters of government on behalf of the monarch. Intervention by the monarch started to reduce significantly by the eighteenth century, as the monarch's advisers met in the Cabinet Council. Initially the monarch would regularly attend Cabinet meetings, but George III attended only very rarely and later monarchs not at all, leaving day-to-day government to ministers.[2] This formed the origin of modern cabinet government and as the importance of the monarch diminished, the focus was placed on ministers who led government departments staffed with civil servants. The nature and functions of central government is discussed in more detail in Chapter 7.

---

[1] *Halsbury's Laws* (5th edn, 2014) vol 20, para 14.

[2] Although the Queen, as part of her Diamond Jubilee celebrations, did observe part of a Cabinet meeting in 2012. BBC News, 'The Queen Visits Downing Street for Cabinet meeting' (BBC News, 18 December 2012), http://www.bbc.co.uk/news/av/uk-20769759/the-queen-visits-downing-street-for-cabinet-meeting.

The important point for present purposes is that although these powers are exercised by government ministers and civil servants, legally they do so in the name of the Crown. Retaining this concept of the Crown has meant that the exercise of the powers under royal prerogative gradually shifted from the monarch to ministers without the need for any further conceptual or legal development. This means that unlike many other countries, the UK has never really developed the legal concept of the 'state', instead persisting with the concept of the Crown. So even today, central government is carried on in the name of the Crown.

This concept of the Crown is important, because as Maitland states, when lawyers mention the 'Crown', they are not referring to the crown worn by monarchs, for that 'does nothing but lie in the Tower of London to be gazed at by sight-seers'.[3] Instead, within a legal context, when someone is referring to the Crown, they are referring to the government. As Diplock LJ stated in *BBC v Johns*, the Crown 'personifies the executive government of the country'.[4] The Crown, in this sense, means the monarch, ministers, and civil servants who all collectively form the government.[5]

As indicated, the monarch also possessed legislative and judicial power. However, gradually, the majority of these powers of the monarch have been abolished, or transferred to Parliament or the courts. Yet, some legislative and judicial powers remain. These include the granting of Royal Assent to legislation, and the granting pardons to those found guilty of a criminal offence.

The exercise of the Crown's powers caused a series of constitutional disputes, particularly during the seventeenth century, when several monarchs clashed with Parliament over who exercised sovereign power within the constitution.[6] Ultimately, Parliament prevailed. The enactment of the Bill of Rights 1688 made clear that the Crown was subject to Parliament, meaning that Parliament through passing an Act can abolish specific powers of the royal prerogative, or place legally binding conditions on how specific powers can be exercised. Yet, given that royal prerogative powers do not derive from Parliament, concerns remain over how Parliament can scrutinize the exercise of the royal prerogative. This is because of the fundamental need to ensure that the exercise of the royal prerogative reflects the democratic nature of today's constitution. A further question is the extent to which courts can scrutinize government actions or decisions made under the royal prerogative.

The concepts of the Crown and the royal prerogative mean that although the Queen is Head of State, it is generally the ministers who form the government that exercise the prerogative powers of the Crown. For this reason, many prerogative powers are often referred to as the 'ministerial prerogatives', and the few prerogative powers still exercised personally by the monarch are referred to as the 'personal prerogatives'. As this chapter explains, the exercise of the prerogative can be heavily regulated by non-legal rules called constitutional conventions (these were briefly introduced in 1.5). As regard the personal prerogatives, these conventions significantly reduce the ability for any direct intervention by the monarch.

---

[3] FWR Maitland, *The Constitutional History of England* (CUP 1908) 395–6, 418.
[4] [1965] Ch 32, 79.
[5] Adam Tomkins, *Public Law* (OUP 2003) 61. Central government is discussed in detail in Chapter 7.
[6] These are described in 4.3.

Although the focus of this chapter is very much on the legal aspects of the monarchy, it cannot be ignored that the monarch and the broader royal family continue to exercise an important symbolic role for the nation both at home and abroad, and this chapter concludes with a brief consideration of the legal and constitutional issues that the Queen's record-breaking reign as the longest-ever serving monarch may raise in the future.

In summary, this chapter is a mixture of history, law, and politics. This includes very recent politics, as the Brexit process generated a series of fundamental constitutional questions that placed the royal prerogative and the functions of the monarchy into the heart of political debate in a manner not seen for centuries. This culminated in the seminal case of *R (Miller) v Prime Minister*,[7] decided by the Supreme Court in September 2019 and the General Election held in December 2019.

The objectives for this chapter are:

- to explain the nature of the royal prerogative;
- to consider the scope of the royal prerogative and how to establish the *existence* of a specific prerogative power;
- to briefly consider the legislative and judicial powers of the prerogative;
- to determine how the royal prerogative is *exercised* and to distinguish between the 'ministerial' and 'personal' prerogative powers;
- to consider how the exercise of royal prerogative power can be restrained or controlled by statute, the courts, and constitutional conventions; and
- to consider the broader constitutional functions of the monarch and legislation that relates to the monarch.

6.2 The nature and scope of the royal prerogative

From the discussion in 6.1, to understand the royal prerogative there are two key issues to consider. First, there is the question of establishing the scope of the royal prerogative and whether a specific prerogative power exists. This can only be explained by considering the nature of the royal prerogative and how it interacts with statute. The second issue is how prerogative powers are exercised, and what controls are placed on the exercise of the prerogative. These controls can be legal or non-legal in the form of constitutional conventions. This is important, because as explained in 6.1, prerogative powers derive from the concept of the Crown and the common law rather than Parliament. This means that generally, there is no legal requirement that Parliament is informed about the exercise of the prerogative powers. By contrast, if the government acts under a statutory power, this is because Parliament has granted the government the power in question. At least in theory, these powers are transparent as they are granted to the government after undergoing the debate and scrutiny required by the legislative process.[8] This lack of transparency raises questions about how the government is accountable for the exercise of the royal prerogative.

The rest of this section will discuss the nature of the prerogative and the rules that have been established to determine its scope and whether any specific prerogative power

[7] [2019] UKSC 41.
[8] The legislative process is discussed in detail in Chapter 8, particularly in 8.5.

exists. The chapter will then consider some examples of specific prerogative powers and explain the different ways in which the exercise of the prerogative can be restrained, through constitutional conventions, statute, or judicial scrutiny.

6.2.1 The nature of the royal prerogative

The royal prerogative was described by Blackstone in the eighteenth century as:

> That special pre-eminence which the King hath, over and above all other persons, and out of the ordinary course of the common law, in right of his Royal dignity . . . it can only be applied to those rights and capacities which the King enjoys alone, in contradistinction to others.[9]

This remains a valuable definition today. It reflects the ancient relationship between the monarch and their subjects. In return for the subject's allegiance to the monarch, the monarch in return provided security to the subject. Although, the concept of citizenship has overridden most aspects of this relationship, Blackstone's approach reflects how prerogative powers are not ordinary powers that can be shared with individuals. They are recognized as belonging to the monarch because of their pre-eminent status within the law.

Historically, these powers were personally exercised by the monarch exercising their inherent authority over all others. Tudor monarchs chose to govern through the Privy Council, a group of officials and advisers close to the monarch. However, the emergence of Parliament as a legislative body raised the question as to the extent to which the monarch could continue to govern without recourse to Parliament. By the start of the seventeenth century, the prerogative was undefined, with the monarch exercising full executive power through the Privy Council while also exercising some legislative and judicial powers. As explained in 4.3, the question of the relationship between the Crown and the prerogative on the one hand, and Parliament on the other, led to a series of constitutional skirmishes throughout the seventeenth century. This question was ultimately resolved in favour of Parliament, as shown by the enactment of the Bill of Rights in 1688 and Act of Settlement in 1700.

While not entirely abolishing the royal prerogative, several provisions of the Bill of Rights restricted or abolished key prerogative powers that conclusively proved the supremacy of Parliament over the Crown. These included the abolition of the monarch's ability to suspend or dispense with the operation of statutes;[10] the levying of taxes without the consent of Parliament was made illegal;[11] and that a standing army could thereafter only be held with the consent of Parliament.[12]

This new constitutional settlement led to the development of government accountability to Parliament and the emergence of the cabinet system of government as monarchs could no longer govern themselves through the Privy Council. Instead, ministers, including the Prime Minister, while appointed by the monarch, came to be chosen by virtue of their seat in either the House of Commons or the House of Lords. This is an important point because even today this is how the royal prerogative relates to 'the general power of

---

[9] William Blackstone, *Commentaries on the Laws of England I* (first published 1765–69, OUP 2016) 155.
[10] Bill of Rights 1688, Arts I and II.   [11] Bill of Rights 1688, Art IV.
[12] Bill of Rights 1688, Art VI.

the government to govern, a power both *political* in that ministers are drawn from those forming the *elected* majority in Parliament and *legal* in that *ministers* are the Crown's principal servants and are entrusted with the Crown's powers'.[13] The uniqueness of the royal prerogative, in contrast to statute, is that the power granted to ministers is 'original, not electorally derived'.[14] Overall, the exercise of most prerogative powers has passed from the monarch to ministers who are accountable to Parliament. This ensures that the historic nature of monarchical power is squared with the modern concept of democracy.

6.2.2 The scope of the royal prerogative

The relationship between Parliament and the Crown as explained in the previous section is fundamental to understanding the scope of the royal prerogative today. This section outlines three key considerations that apply when determining whether a prerogative power exists. These are, first, whether a prerogative power has been said to previously exist, second, if so, whether it has been abolished or restricted by statute, and finally that the Crown is not bound by a statute unless expressly so, or by necessary implication.

Does a prerogative power exist?

Having established that Parliament is supreme over the Crown, the next question is to consider is the scope of the royal prerogative today. Parliament has exercised its supremacy over the Crown to gradually replace powers previously exercised under the royal prerogative, with statutory powers. In this sense, Dicey captures the essence of the royal prerogative as representing those powers that are still derived from the Crown because they have been left untouched by Parliament when he describes it as the:

> residue of discretionary or arbitrary authority, which at any given time is legally left in the hands of the Crown.[15]

On the foundation of this definition, there are three principles that assist in determining the nature and existence of prerogative powers in the UK Constitution. The first such principle is as stated by Nourse LJ in *R v Secretary of State for the Home Department ex p Northumbria Police Authority*: 'it has not at any stage in our history been practicable to identify all the prerogative powers of the Crown. It is only by piecemeal decisions over a period of centuries that particular powers are seen to exist or not to exist.'[16] This means that we have to consider the case law in order to gain an understanding of the prerogative today, as it remains for the courts to consider whether or not a particular prerogative power exists.

The second principle is stated by Lord Reid in *Burmah Oil Company Ltd v Lord Advocate* as:

> It is not easy to discover and decide the law regarding the royal prerogative and the consequences of its exercise . . . we must try to see what the position was after it had become clear that sovereignty resided in the King in Parliament. Any rights thereafter exercised by the King (or the executive) alone must be regarded as a part of sovereignty which Parliament chose to leave in his hands.[17]

---

[13] David Pollard, Neil Parpworth, and David Hughes, *Constitutional and Administrative Law Text with Materials* (4th edn, OUP 2007) 78.   [14] Ibid.

[15] AV Dicey, *Introduction to the Study of Government* (10th edn, Macmillan 1959) 424.

[16] [1989] QB 26, 56.   [17] [1965] AC 75, 99–100.

This means that, to determine whether a prerogative power exists, it must be considered whether the prerogative power existed before 1688, the date at which Parliament exerted its supremacy over the Crown. It follows from this that the final principle is that no new prerogative powers can be created, as stated by Diplock LJ in *BBC v Johns*:

> it is 350 years and a civil war too late for the Queen's courts to broaden the prerogative. The limits within which the executive government may impose obligations or restraints on citizens of the United Kingdom without any statutory authority are now well settled and incapable of extension.[18]

These principles assist in establishing the nature of the prerogative power. The difficulty with defining the royal prerogative, however, is determining the scope of a prerogative power before 1688 and then applying the historic prerogative power to modern situations. One example is the following case.

Case in depth: *R v Secretary of State for the Home Department, ex p Northumbria Police Authority* [1989] QB 26

The Home Secretary informed all police forces that baton rounds and CS gas would be available for use in the event of serious public disorder. The Home Secretary would supply this equipment from a central store they maintained. This would be available to the police even if the local police authority objected. The Northumbria Police Authority argued that this policy was unlawful on the grounds that it was not authorized under the Police Act 1964 or under the royal prerogative. The Court of Appeal disagreed, holding that the Home Secretary's policy was authorized by the Police Act 1964, but also under the royal prerogative.

In reaching this conclusion, the Court of Appeal had to consider whether a prerogative power to keep the peace existed and if so, whether it survived the enactment of the Police Act 1964. Although the Court of Appeal struggled to find positive authority for the existence of such a prerogative power, Purchas LJ reasoned that there was a duty on the Crown to protect its subjects in return for their allegiance. Consequently, the prerogative includes the power to preserve the Queen's peace and the 'continued existence of this prerogative has never been questioned' as there was no evidence that the monarch in 'assenting to any of the enactments referred to . . . any way derogated from the royal prerogative to maintain the peace of the realm'.[19]

In short, there was no express and unequivocal inhibition sufficient to abridge the prerogative powers, otherwise available to the Secretary of State, 'to do all that is reasonably necessary to preserve the peace of the Realm'.[20] Purchas LJ further stated, that when 'considering the powers of the ministers exercising as a Secretary of State the royal prerogative, one must distinguish between the existence of the prerogative and the machinery set up to enable the expeditious and efficient use of that prerogative'.[21]

---

[18] [1965] Ch 32, 79.   [19] [1989] QB 26, 56.
[20] Ibid 53.   [21] Ibid 56.

Counterpoint: *Northumbria Police Authority* **and the rule of law**

While clearly there is a prerogative power to ensure the defence of the realm against external threats, *Northumbria Police Authority* involves making preparations to protect against internal threats. The finding of a royal prerogative power on the basis that its existence was never questioned before has been criticized by some. As Adam Tomkins states:

> that the courts are prepared to grant to the Crown such elastic and ill-defined powers [shows that] the executive will find the rule of law a much less onerous check on its powers than might first have seemed.[22]

Given that the rule of law requires lawful authority for the exercise of government powers, to what extent do cases such as *Northumbria Police Authority* comply with the rule of the law if the government's powers under the prerogative are so vague?

All three principles—that there is no complete list of prerogative powers, that no new prerogative powers can be created and that historic prerogative powers need to be interpreted in light of modern circumstances—can be seen in action in *R (Miller) v Secretary of State for Exiting the European Union*, which is discussed in detail in 6.6.[23]

Abolishing or restricting prerogative powers by statute

The principle of parliamentary sovereignty[24] means that Parliament can pass legislation to abolish a prerogative power,[25] or restrict how that prerogative power can be exercised.[26] This is clearly the case if the statute in question either expressly abolishes a prerogative power or does so by necessary implication. Yet, as the case of *Attorney-General v De Keyser's Royal Hotel Ltd* shows, Parliament often creates a statutory scheme which overlaps with a prerogative power that covers the same subject area, without making clear its intention regarding the future of the prerogative power. The question here, then, is whether the Crown can continue to rely on the prerogative or whether it is required to follow the statutory scheme.

Case in depth: *Attorney-General v De Keyser's Royal Hotel Ltd* [1920] AC 508

In 1916, the Crown took possession of a hotel to house the headquarters of the Royal Flying Corps. At the time, the Crown argued that they were acting under the Defence of the Realm Regulations, and refused to compensate the owners of the hotel. The owners brought an action and argued that they were entitled to compensation under the regulations. In response, the Crown argued that there existed a prerogative power to take land from a subject during wartime without paying compensation to the owner. This was despite the Defence of the Realm

→

---

[22] Adam Tomkins, *Public Law* (OUP 2003) 82.   [23] [2017] UKSC 5.

[24] Parliamentary sovereignty is considered in detail in Chapter 4.

[25] For example, the Fixed-term Parliaments Act 2011 abolished the prerogative power to dissolve Parliament, triggering a general election. This is discussed in detail in 6.10.

[26] This is discussed in detail in 6.5.2.

→

Regulations providing for compensation in these circumstances. The issue was whether the Crown in taking possession of the hotel was acting under the royal prerogative where compensation was not payable, or under the statute where compensation was payable. The House of Lords held that compensation was payable as the Crown was acting under statute.

Lord Dunedin stated:

> if the whole ground of something which could be done by the prerogative is covered by the statute, it is the statute that rules. On this point I think the observation of the learned Master of the Rolls [who heard the petition in the Court of Appeal] is unanswerable. He says: 'What use would there be in imposing limitations, if the Crown could at its pleasure disregard them and fall back on the prerogative?'[27]

Furthermore, Lord Dunedin stated:

> Inasmuch as the Crown is a party to every Act of Parliament [through granting Royal Assent] it is logical enough to consider that when the Act deals with something which before the Act could be effected by the prerogative, and specially empowers the Crown to do the same thing, but subject to conditions, the Crown assents to that, and by that Act to the prerogative being curtailed.[28]

It follows from the supremacy of Parliament that if a scheme is enacted which overlaps with a prerogative power, then the statutory scheme should take precedence over the prerogative power. As explained by Lord Dunedin, the rationale for this principle is that as the Crown, through the monarch, has given Royal Assent to the legislation in question, they are consenting to the changes that the Act of Parliament makes to the royal prerogative. It would be strange if the Crown could effectively change its mind about the matter without the involvement of Parliament. A variation of this principle can be seen in the case of *R v Secretary of State for the Home Department, ex p Fire Bridges Union*. In this case, the issue was whether the Home Secretary could choose not to implement a statute which would replace a prerogative power, and instead rely on the existing prerogative power that the statute would have replaced had it been brought into force.

Case in depth: *R v Secretary of State for the Home Department, ex p Fire Brigades Union* [1995] 2 AC 513

In 1964, a criminal injuries compensation scheme was created under the royal prerogative. Parliament decided that this scheme would be placed on a statutory footing under the Civil Justice Act 1988. For the statutory scheme to come into force, the statute required the Home Secretary to bring the relevant sections of the Act into legal effect on a date he chose. The Home Secretary decided against bringing this statutory scheme into force, instead choosing to use the royal

→

---

[27] [1920] AC 508, 526.   [28] Ibid.

→

prerogative to replace the existing scheme with a wholly new scheme, which would be cheaper. The decision to not implement the statutory scheme was challenged.

The case raised profound constitutional questions regarding the relationship between the Crown and Parliament, and the House of Lords was split 3:2. Those in the minority were of the view that this was a political issue and for the courts to interfere or require the Home Secretary to bring into force the statutory scheme would be 'an unwarrantable intrusion by the court into the political field and a usurpation of the function of Parliament'.[29] Essentially, the minority considered that if there was a breach of duty on these facts it was a duty owed to Parliament and it is for Parliament to consider its response. The majority viewed the case as raising legal rather than purely political issues; they took the view that the Home Secretary was abdicating the statutory power given to him by deciding never to bring into force the 1988 Act. This was contrary to the will of Parliament as expressed in the legislation. As Lord Browne-Wilkinson stated:

> it would be most surprising if, in the present day, prerogative powers could be validity exercised by the executive, so as to frustrate the will of Parliament as expressed in a statute.[30]

In a similar manner to *De Keyser*, the principle is that the prerogative cannot be used to thwart the will of Parliament as expressed in legislation. In effect, the decision of the Home Secretary never to bring the provisions of the 1988 Act into force and introduce a new scheme under the royal prerogative was essentially an attempt to informally repeal the Act. The real solution to this issue was not to use the royal prerogative in this manner, but to go back to Parliament and introduce legislation repealing the provisions of the 1988 Act, replacing them with a new statutory scheme. This is precisely what the government did when enacting the Criminal Injuries Compensation Act 1995.

The Crown is not bound by statute unless expressly stated or by necessary implication

A related issue is the principle of statutory interpretation that statutes do not bind the Crown unless expressly stated or by necessary implication. This means that for a statute to restrict a prerogative power such an intention must be clear on the face of the statute. A straightforward example of this can be found in the Localism Act 2011, which at section 105 states that 'this Chapter binds the Crown'. This means that those sections of the Act which fall under that Chapter apply to the Crown.

In this context, the concept of the Crown, as discussed at the beginning of this chapter, is important as the Crown extends from the monarch personally to government ministers and their departments, civil servants, and public bodies established by central government. One example of this principle in action is that the Crown is not subject to taxation. This clearly makes sense regarding government departments, because as de Smith and Brazier state there is no reason 'why an intention should be imputed to Parliament to raise money *from* the government'.[31] This also means that the monarch as a matter of law

---

[29] [1995] 2 AC 513, 546.   [30] Ibid 552.
[31] Stanley de Smith and Rodney Brazier, *Constitutional and Administrative Law* (8th edn, Penguin 1998) 142.

is exempt from taxation—although since 1992, in response to some public criticism, the Queen has voluntarily paid income tax, capital gains tax, and inheritance tax. The effects of this rule of statutory interception can be seen in the following case.

Case in depth: *R (Black) v Secretary of State for Justice* **[2017] UKSC 81**

The issue was whether Chapter 1 of Part 1 of the Health Act 2006, which introduced a ban against smoking in most workplaces and enclosed public spaces, applied to the Crown. The claimant was a prisoner detained at a prison operated directly by the government and was complaining that the ban was not being wholly enforced in their prison.

Had the prisoner been detained at a prison operated by a private company on behalf of the government, then it was clear that the Health Act 2006 would have applied to the prison. When the bill was going through Parliament, there was no intention that prisons operated by the government would be exempt from the ban.[32] Indeed, when the Act came into force, the Prison Service took the view that the smoking ban applied to all prisons.[33]

The Supreme Court concluded that the Crown was not bound by Chapter 1, Part 1 of the Health Act 2006. This was because there was no language in the Act stating that these provisions applied to the Crown. This conclusion was all the more inevitable when section 23 of the 2006 Act made clear that other provisions of the Act, unconnected with the smoking ban, did apply to the Crown. This meant that Parliament had considered the specific issue of which sections of the Act applied to the Crown, and had decided against making the Crown bound by the relevant provisions. As Lady Hale stated, if 'Parliament intended Part 1 of Chapter 1 of the 2006 Act to bind the Crown, nothing would have been easier than to insert such a provision into that Part'.[34] This meant that the smoking ban did not apply to prisons operated directly by the government.

In *Black*, the Supreme Court also considered whether to they should revisit or modify the rule. The Court declined to take either option. It is difficult to revisit the rule because it is so well established, and many statutes are drafted on the basis of the rule as it presently exists.[35] Modifying the rule was also rejected on a similar reasoning. Given that the rule is so well established, revisiting the test or adding further elements to the test was unnecessary and undesirable.[36] The Supreme Court did suggest that Parliament and the Law Commission should consider whether the rule should be abolished or to reverse the presumption so that statutes apply to the Crown unless they expressly state otherwise. Ultimately, this was not an option the Supreme Court could pursue in an individual case.

6.3 Outline of prerogative powers

The previous section considered the nature of the prerogative and the general rules that apply to determine whether a prerogative power exists in a given situation. This section outlines the most important prerogative powers. From that point, we can then consider the role that constitutional conventions and statutes play in regulating how these powers are exercised.

---

[32] [2017] UKSC 81 [20].   [33] Ibid.   [34] Ibid [48].   [35] Ibid [35].   [36] Ibid [37].

Although no complete collection of prerogative powers has ever been compiled, it is possible to list some key prerogative powers.[37] The ministerial prerogatives include:

- the power to acquire and cede territory;
- the making of and, subject to the Constitutional Reform and Governance Act 2010, ratification of treaties;[38]
- the conduct of diplomacy, including the recognition of states, the relations (if any) between the United Kingdom and other governments, and the appointment of ambassadors and High Commissioners;
- the governance of British Overseas Territories;
- the deployment and use of the armed forces overseas, including involvement in armed conflict, or the declaration of war (the Royal Navy is still maintained by virtue of the prerogative; the Army and the RAF are maintained under statute);
- the use of the armed forces within the United Kingdom to maintain the peace in support of the police;
- the Prime Minister's ability to appoint and remove ministers, peerages, and honours (save for the four Orders within the Queen's own gift mentioned within the list of personal prerogatives), patronage appointments (eg in the Church of England), and the appointment of senior judges;
- recommendations for honours by the Foreign Secretary and the Defence Secretary;
- the creation of and allocation of responsibilities to government departments;
- the grant and revocation of passports;
- the grant of pardons (subject to recommendations by the Criminal Cases Review Commission) and the Attorney-General's power to stop prosecutions.

The personal prerogatives include:

- appointment of Prime Minister;
- power to dismiss government;
- granting the Royal Assent to legislation;
- power to prorogue Parliament;
- granting of honours, decorations, arms, and regulating matters of precedence, with some honours, the Order of the Garter, the Order of the Thistle, the Royal Victorian Order, and the Order of Merit being in the personal gift of the monarch.

To this list could be added a range of other miscellaneous prerogative powers, covering relatively minor matters such as the right to construct and supervise harbours, the right to mint coinage, the right to mine precious metals, and the right of the Crown to claim the ownership of any sturgeon, dolphins and whales, and swans on certain stretches of the River Thames. These miscellaneous powers are generally viewed as historical anachronisms, with some, such as the right to impress men into the Royal Navy (in this context 'impress' means be required to join), thought to be of little practical effect today.

---

[37] This list has been adapted from House of Commons Public Administration Select Committee, *Taming the Prerogative: Strengthening Ministerial Accountability* (HC 2003–04, 422) para 9.

[38] Constitutional Reform and Governance Act 2010, ss 20–5. See 6.5.2.

6.3.1 'Ministerial' and 'personal' prerogative powers

The list at the start of this section is split between the ministerial and personal prerogative powers. This is an informal separation but reflects the difference in who exercises these powers. The term 'ministerial prerogatives' shows how historically the monarch came to act by constitutional convention on the advice of their ministers and how these powers are in substance now exercised by ministers on the monarch's behalf. Ministers are responsible to Parliament for how they have chosen to exercise these powers.

The involvement of the monarch varies according to the power in question. Some prerogative powers, such as the issue of passports, are wholly exercised by government departments, while others retain a formal role for the monarch. For example, under the prerogative of mercy, a decision to grant a pardon to an individual is made by the Home Secretary, but this will be sent to the monarch for formal approval, who will approve the decision following the advice of the Home Secretary. The ministerial prerogative powers are discussed in more detail in the following section, with particular reference to the royal prerogative to enter into and ratify treaties and to deploy the armed forces overseas.

The personal prerogatives, by contrast, are those powers which are personally exercised by the monarch. These powers include granting Royal Assent to bills in order for them to become Acts of Parliament, the power to prorogue Parliament, the appointment of the Prime Minister, and the concurrent capacity (at least in theory) to dismiss the government. While in law these powers are hugely significant, the exercise of these powers is constrained by constitutional convention. It used to be the case that until the enactment of the Fixed-term Parliaments Act 2011, another personal prerogative power was the monarch's ability to dissolve Parliament, triggering a general election. This power was only exercised on the advice of the Prime Minister. The operation of the 2011 Act is discussed in 6.10.

 Discussing the problem

Consider the problem scenario outlined at the start of the chapter. Which powers of the prerogative are relevant to the question and who will exercise them?

The main issue raised by the problem is the controls over the prerogative power to enter into and ratify international treaties—in this case, the free trade agreement with the United States. This can be classified as a ministerial prerogative power, and so is exercised by ministers on behalf of the monarch. The problem also highlights (as considered in 6.5.2) how Parliament, and especially the House of Commons, has become involved and voted against the treaty. This is due to the Constitutional Reform and Governance Act 2010. This serves as an example of how a royal prerogative power can only be exercised according to a procedure that Parliament has laid down in statute.

The campaign groups seeking the intervention of the Queen are asking Her Majesty to become involved in the conduct of government. This raises questions that involve the relationship of the monarch to politics and the government. As we will see, constitutional conventions play an extremely important role here.

Finally, the results of the 2022 General Election raise the question as to whether the government can continue in office or whether a new Prime Minister should be appointed who could then form a new government. As seen in the list at 6.3, the appointment of the Prime Minister is a personal prerogative power, exercised by the Queen herself. As considered in 6.9, the choice that the Queen makes is determined by a series of constitutional conventions.

6.3.2 The legislative and judicial functions of the prerogative

As stated at the beginning of this chapter, the monarch was originally seen as source of legislative and judicial power. However, as seen from the list of prerogative powers in the previous section, very few prerogative powers of a judicial or legislative function still exist today. One example of a legislative prerogative power that remains is the granting of Royal Assent to legislation. Once a bill has been approved by both the House of Commons and the House of Lords, the final stage of the legislative process is for the Royal Assent to be granted by the monarch.[39] Other legislative powers include passing Orders in Council through the Privy Council which are discussed in more detail in the following section.

The remaining judicial powers include the prerogative of mercy, which involves granting a pardon to someone convicted of a criminal offence. The effect of this is to remove the punishments imposed as a result of the criminal conviction. Should someone be granted a pardon while serving a prison sentence, they would be released. The prerogative can also be used to stop legal proceedings, with the Attorney-General entering a *nolle prosequi*, which will stop the proceedings from continuing. This is different to a pardon because the defendant will not be convicted of a criminal offence as the trial is stopped before any verdict can be given by the jury.

That the monarch is the source of judicial power still exists in the sense that appeals from the courts from some Commonwealth countries heard by the Privy Council are in the form of a petition to the monarch, with the Judicial Committee of the Privy Council (which is formed by the Justices of the Supreme Court) technically advising the monarch as to how to dispose of the appeal. The judgment of the Judicial Committee is formally approved at a Privy Council meeting.

 Pause for reflection

From the list in 6.3, consider the examples of prerogative powers. Is it misleading to describe the prerogative as a mere 'residue' of power?

6.3.3 The Privy Council

So what of the Privy Council today? Once of great importance, it now only plays a minor role in the modern constitution.

The main business of the Privy Council is to pass Orders in Council which is a form of legislation. Some Orders in Council are made under the royal prerogative, these include amending or adopting new constitutions for British Overseas Territory, such as Gibraltar.[40] As the *Bancoult (No 2)* case (discussed in 6.4.4) shows, these Orders in Council are considered as equivalent to an Act of Parliament and a form of primary legislation. However, the great majority of Orders in Council are made under powers granted to the

---

[39] Although, as discussed in 8.5.9, if the Parliament Act procedure applies, then Royal Assent can be given to legislation which has passed only the House of Commons.

[40] Gibraltar Constitution Order 2006.

Privy Council by Acts of Parliament and are a form of secondary or delegated legislation.[41] Other business of the Privy Council includes approving the text of a Royal Charter establishing a new institution such as a new university. The BBC is granted a Royal Charter that must be renewed every ten years.

Appointments to the Privy Council are made by the monarch on the Prime Minister's advice and are for life (although they can be removed on advice from the Prime Minister or by their own request). Privy Councillors are entitled to be addressed as 'the Right Honourable', and in the House of Commons should be referred to by other MPs as 'my Right Honourable friend'. By convention, all Cabinet ministers are Privy Counsellors and it is customary to appoint those who hold other significant positions of office.[42]

Meetings of the Privy Council usually, but not always, take place at Buckingham Palace and are held in secret with the monarch in attendance along with three or four Privy Councillors, who are usually government ministers. Meetings are usually extremely short, with those present standing. The title of each Order to be made at the meeting is read out, and the Queen simply responds with 'approved'.

6.4 Constitutional conventions

6.4.1 The importance of constitutional conventions

The following sections make frequent reference to constitutional conventions as rules that regulate how the royal prerogative is exercised. While constitutional conventions are important in other areas of the constitution, and frequent reference is made conventions throughout this book,[43] conventions are particularly important with the exercise of the royal prerogative. This is because by its nature, and the fact that ministers exercise prerogative powers on behalf of the monarch, constitutional conventions are necessarily involved. These conventions have reduced the need for Parliament to regulate or abolish specific prerogative powers. Conventions are also important in relation to those prerogative powers the monarch exercises personally. This means that it is worth considering constitutional conventions in more detail.

6.4.2 Identifying constitutional conventions

As explained in 1.5, a key feature of constitutional conventions is that they are rules of practice or behaviour rather than law. This means that there is no single authoritative source outlining the existence or the scope of any given convention. This is different to legislation where the rules are definitively laid out in the relevant Act of Parliament or delegated legislation. Should the interpretation of legislation be contested, this dispute can be conclusively resolved by the courts. If the existence or scope of a convention is disputed there is no equivalent mechanism to conclusively resolve the question.

---

[41] Orders *in* Council should be distinguished from Orders *of* Council, which are made without the monarch's formal approval. These are a form of secondary legislation, and are usually concerned with changing the bylaws or rules of governing bodies of the professions, such as those involving surgeons, vets, or learned societies.

[42] These include the Archbishops of Canterbury and York, the Leader of the Opposition, the Speaker of the House of Lords, the Lord Speaker, and the Mayor of London.

[43] For example, the Salisbury Convention plays a key role in regulating the relationship between the House of Commons and the House of Lords.

One of the most useful ways to determine whether a convention exists is to adopt the three-part test proposed by Jennings:

> We have to ask ourselves three questions; first, what are the precedents; secondly, did the actors in the precedents believe that they were bound by the rule; and thirdly, is there a good reason for the rule.[44]

This is a useful test because it makes clear that not every non-legal practice is a convention. For a practice to become a convention, there must be a 'good reason' for its existence. In this context, Jennings considered that a 'good reason' was whether the practice 'accords with the prevailing political philosophy', such as facilitating the principles of democracy to operate in practice, or 'enabling the machinery of the state to run more smoothly'.[45]

This distinction between a convention and a practice can be seen in the following two examples. The rule that a minister must either have a seat in the House of Lords or the House of Commons is clearly a constitutional convention because the reason for following this rule is that it enables Parliament to hold government to account.[46] If a minister did not sit in either House then Parliament could not adequately question or scrutinize the actions of that minister. By contrast, the tradition that the Chancellor of the Exchequer would drink alcohol while delivering the budget speech in the House of Commons (Geoffrey Howe would drink a gin and tonic, and Kenneth Clarke would drink whisky) could only ever be a mere practice, as there are no constitutional reasons for it. Subsequent Chancellors discontinued this tradition, drinking water while delivering their budget speeches, and no constitutional consequences have flowed from this change.

Yet, the issue of a lack of an authoritative source remains. One element of the Jennings test is to consider the precedents. As Bradley, Ewing, and Knight state,[47] to find these precedents one starting point is to consult one of the leading works on particular areas of the constitution such as *Cabinet Government* by Jennings,[48] *Constitutional Conventions* by Marshall,[49] *Whitehall* by Hennessy,[50] or *Constitutional Practice* by Brazier.[51] These works focus on historical precedents to determine the constitutional position on controversial issues. However, caution must be exercised as there may be more than one interpretation of any given set of precedents. More recent works such as *Politics of the Coalition* by Hazell and Yong can also be extremely helpful.[52]

---

[44] Sir Ivor Jennings, *The Law and the Constitution* (5th edn, London University Press 1959) 136.

[45] Ibid.

[46] Should the government wish to appoint someone who does not sit in either House, they will be given a life peerage under the Life Peerages 1958 to allow them to sit in the House of Lords. For example, Rosalind Altman was appointed as Pensions Minister in May 2015 and was given a peerage to facilitate this appointment.

[47] AW Bradley, KD Ewing, and CJS Knight, *Constitutional and Administrative Law* (16th edn, Pearson 2015) 28.

[48] Sir Ivor Jennings, *Cabinet Government* (3rd edn, CUP 1969).

[49] Geoffrey Marshall, *Constitutional Conventions* (OUP 1984).

[50] Peter Hennessy, *Whitehall* (Fontana Press 1989).

[51] Rodney Brazier, *Constitutional Practice* (4th edn, OUP 1999).

[52] Robert Hazell and Ben Yong, *Politics of the Coalition* (Hart 2012).

The *Cabinet Manual*

One document worthy of special attention is the *Cabinet Manual*, and repeated reference is made to this throughout the following sections in this chapter. The *Cabinet Manual* was written by the Civil Service under the direction of the Cabinet Secretary (the most senior civil servant).[53] He stated in the preface that the intention behind the Manual was to provide 'a guide for those working in government, recording the current position rather than driving change. It is not intended to be legally binding or set issues in stone' and is 'not intended to be the source of any rule'.[54] In short, as the Cabinet Secretary stated in a lecture, it is 'by the executive for the executive'.[55] The first full edition was published in 2011 after extensive consultation with responses from the public and academics. The focus of the Manual is largely on different aspects of the executive ranging from the monarch, the principles of government formation following a general election, the structure of government, and decision-making within the Cabinet.

The Manual has been scrutinized by various committees in Parliament, and while the House of Lords Constitution Committee was sceptical about the idea of the Manual, the House of Commons Political and Constitutional Reform Select Committee were more positive, believing that it might provide the basis for a greater public understanding of the constitution.[56] Yet, importantly, all were agreed that the publication of the rules and principles underpinning government formation after a general election was to be welcomed. These rules are referred to in 6.9.2, however it must be remembered that the *Cabinet Manual* is intended to record the rules, rather than create them.

6.4.3 The 'cardinal' convention

There is one particularly important constitutional convention which underpins the exercise and the very basis of the royal prerogative. Known as the 'cardinal' convention, the rule is that the monarch always acts on the advice of ministers.[57] Particularly in relation to the exercise of the ministerial prerogatives, the monarch's role is one of formally approving decisions that have been made elsewhere. In return, the monarch has the right to 'be consulted, the right to encourage and the right to warn' the government.[58] Moreover, as Brazier states:

> a sovereign cannot offer advice nor support action, counsel against proposed action without knowing what ministers are doing. Perhaps, therefore, it is more accurate to say. . . that the sovereign has five constitutional rights rather than three—to be informed, to be consulted, to advise, to encourage and to warn.[59]

[53] Cabinet Office, *The Cabinet Manual* (1st edn, Cabinet Office 2011), https://www.gov.uk/government/uploads/system/uploads/attachment_data/file/60641/cabinet-manual.pdf.

[54] Ibid iv.

[55] Sir Gus O'Donnell, Speech on the *Cabinet Manual* at the Institute for Government, London, 24 February 2011.

[56] House of Lords Constitution Committee, *The Draft Cabinet Manual* (HL 2010–11 107), House of Commons Political and Constitutional Reform Committee, *Cabinet Manual* (HC 2010–11, 734) para 9.

[57] This term was recognized by the Upper Tribunal in *Evans v Information Commissioner* [2012] UKUT 313 (AAC) [76].

[58] Walter Bagehot, *The English Constitution* (originally published in 1867, OUP 2001) 64.

[59] Rodney Brazier, 'The Monarchy' in Vernon Bogdanor (ed), *The British Constitution in the 20th Century* (British Academy/OUP 2003) 78.

The monarch most vividly exercises these rights in her weekly audiences with the Prime Minister, and is informed about government business by receiving government papers, Cabinet documents, and updates from ambassadors overseas. A famous example of the monarch exercising the right to warn the Prime Minister took place during the Second World War, when George VI strongly advised the Prime Minister, Winston Churchill, not to be present at the D-Day landings in 1944.[60] Eventually, Churchill followed the King's advice.

For the monarch to function as a figurehead for the nation (a role discussed in more detail in 6.12), it is important that the monarch retains her impartiality and political neutrality.[61] Otherwise, these rights cannot be exercised effectively. For this reason, these rights are exercised in confidence. This means it is difficult to be clear as to what extent these rights are used by the monarch, although Ben Pimlott in his autobiography of the Queen suggests that she rarely criticizes government policy; instead she may refer to others that hold alternative views.[62] Indeed, any leaks regarding the use of these rights, such as concerns apparently expressed by the Queen during Margaret Thatcher's government in 1986, were ultimately embarrassing to both the monarch and Prime Minister.[63] The extent to which the monarch's advice has any impact on government policy will depend on the Prime Minister's view of the advice, who has to take into account many other considerations from other sources, including the opinion of Cabinet, MPs, the media, and the electorate. However, Prime Ministers have often stated in their memoirs that they valued their meetings with the Queen as she shared the knowledge she has accumulated over her long reign.[64]

 Discussing the problem

Take a moment to remind yourself of the problem scenario set out at the beginning of the chapter. Which part of the scenario raises issues that involve the 'cardinal' convention?

The relevant part of the problem are those campaign groups that are urging the Queen to intervene and speak out against the ratification of the treaty with the United States. This runs directly contrary to the cardinal convention, which is that the Queen acts on the advice of her ministers, and does not get personally involved in matters of political controversy.

This means that the Queen will not follow any demand to speak out publicly against the treaty as it would call into question her political impartiality. However, in her confidential audiences with the Prime Minister, the Queen could exercise her right to 'be advised, to warn and to encourage'; in this case, the right to warn is the most relevant. The Queen may raise the issue of the treaty, and as Pimlott suggests, refer to arguments made by others against ratifying the treaty. Yet ultimately, the decision to ratify the treaty is one for the government and not the Queen to make.

---

[60] The correspondence from the King to Churchill is available at https://www.royalcollection.org.uk/sites/royalcollection.org.uk/files/ra_ps_pso_gvi_c_069_43-5.pdf.

[61] Before the Scottish Independence Referendum in 2014, the Queen was quoted as saying that she hoped that voters thought 'carefully about the future' when casting their vote. This was seen by some as a coded statement of support for Scotland to remain part of the UK. BBC News, 'Scottish independence: Queen urges people to "think carefully about future"' (BBC News, 14 September 2004), http://www.bbc.co.uk/news/uk-scotland-scotland-politics-29200359.

[62] Ben Pimlott, *The Queen: Elizabeth II and the Monarchy* (HarperCollins 2012).

[63] Ibid 501; Geoffrey Marshall, 'The Queen's Press Relations' [1986] *Public Law* 505.

[64] For example, John Major, *The Autobiography* (HarperCollins 1999) 508, stated that particularly in relation to Commonwealth affairs, 'I hope Tony Blair [Major's successor as Prime Minister] seeks her advice and heeds her response. I found them invaluable on many occasions'.

6.5 Regulating the exercise of the ministerial prerogatives

Having considered in previous sections the existence of the prerogative and examples of specific prerogative powers, we can now start to focus in more detail on how the prerogative power is exercised. In particular, this section focuses on the different ways the exercise of the prerogative power is regulated or scrutinized. This could be by convention or legislation. As an example of a prerogative power being constrained by convention, this section considers the emergence of a convention that the consent of the House of Commons is required before the government uses the prerogative power to deploy the military overseas. This is followed by a discussion of the role of Parliament in the ratification of treaties, which is a prerogative power, now subject to requirements imposed by legislation. The next two sections then consider how these issues applied in the two seminal cases of *R (Miller) v Secretary of State for Exiting the European Union*[65] and *R (Miller) v Prime Minister*.[66]

6.5.1 Regulation by convention—deployment of armed forces

The list of prerogative powers in 6.3 includes the power of the government to send the armed forces abroad. Once this power was personally exercised by monarchs, but now by convention, this is now exercised by ministers, in particular the Prime Minister. As this is a prerogative power there is no legal obligation on the government to consult Parliament. Considering that the decision to send the armed forces abroad is one of the most important decisions a government can make, the lack of formal parliamentary involvement raises profound constitutional questions, as Brazier said:

> How odd, perhaps bizarre—it is that the approval of both Houses of Parliament is required for pieces of technical and often trivial, subordinate legislation, whereas it is not needed at all before men and women can be committed to the possibility of disfigurement or death![67]

The traditional approach would be that the Prime Minister and the broader government would account to Parliament, particularly the House of Commons, for the exercise of this prerogative power. This would be achieved by making statements informing the House of Commons that forces have been deployed and Parliament would be updated through further statements. This may have followed substantial discussion and debate in the months or weeks leading up to this decision, but Parliament would have no formal role in making the actual decision. Instead, the formal role of the House of Commons in relation to the armed forces is to pass an Armed Forces Act every five years and grant the necessary funds for their operations.[68]

The government approached the Iraq War in 2003 in a different manner to previous deployments. Instead of the House of Commons merely being informed of the decision to deploy, MPs were actively involved in the decision, with three debates being held before troops were deployed.[69] At the time, the view of the government was that this was

---

[65] [2017] UKSC 5.   [66] [2019] UKSC 41.

[67] Rodney Brazier, *Constitutional Reform* (1st edn, OUP 1991) 103–4.

[68] This is to comply with the requirement in the Bill of Rights 1688, Art VI, referred to in 6.2.1, that there can be no standing army without the consent of Parliament.

[69] HC Debs, 25 November 2002, vol 395, col 133; 26 February 2003, vol 400, col 295; 18 March 2003, vol 401, col 760.

a special case and no precedent for the future was being set. The Attorney-General, Lord Goldsmith stated that:

> the decision to use military force is, and remains a decision within the royal prerogative and as such does not, as a matter of law or constitutionality, require the prior approval of Parliament.[70]

This view was not shared several years later by the Leader of the House of Commons, Sir George Young, who stated that:

> a convention has developed in the House [of Commons] that before troops are committed, the House should have an opportunity to debate the matter. We propose to observe that convention except when there is an emergency and such action would not be appropriate.[71]

It was in 2013 that the convention was seen in action when the government held a vote before deploying armed forces in Syria, dramatically losing it by 285 votes to 272. The Prime Minister, David Cameron, in response stated that he recognized 'that the House of Commons does not want to see British military action . . . and the government will act accordingly'.[72] Military action did not start in Syria. Further votes have been held before deploying the military to Iraq in 2014,[73] and a second vote on action in Syria was held in 2015.[74] Using the Jennings test referred to in 6.4, the existence of these further precedents appear to confirm the existence of a convention that the House of Commons is usually consulted before the military is deployed overseas.

 Counterpoint: Does the convention need to be refined?

In 2011, MPs voted in favour of taking military action in Libya, but this vote was held *after* rather than *before* military action.[75] Similarly, in April 2018, evidence suggested that the government of Syria had used chemical weapons as part of the ongoing civil war. Concerned about the potential normalization of chemical weapons, the USA, France, and the UK agreed to a series of air strikes aimed at destroying the Syrian government's stock of chemical weapons. Theresa May authorized the involvement of the UK without the prior approval of the House of Commons.[76]

Given the previous votes on military action, and especially since the Syria vote in 2013, this was a controversial approach to take. This suggests that our understanding of the convention needs to be refined, as the precedents do not all point towards a Commons vote *before* action

---

[70] HL Deb, 19 February 2003, vol 644, col 1138–9.

[71] HC Deb, 10 March 2011, vol 524, col 1066. See also Sir Michael Fallon who as Defence Secretary stated in 2016 that the government would 'keep Parliament informed and . . . of course seek its approval before deploying British forces in combat roles into a conflict situation', HC Deb 18 April 2016, vol 608, col 630.

[72] HC Deb, 10 March 2011, vol 524, col 1556–7.

[73] HC Deb, 26 September 2014, vol 585, cols 1255–366.

[74] HC Deb, 2 December 2015, vol 603, cols 323–500.

[75] HC Deb, 21 March 2011, vol 525, col 700.

[76] A Labour backbencher, Alison McGovern, made an application for an emergency debate on the motion 'That this House has considered the current situation in Syria and the UK Government's approach', which was approved by 314 votes to 36 against, HC Deb 16 April 2018, vol 639 cols 105–54. Similarly, Jeremy Corbyn, Leader of the Opposition, was granted an urgent debate on the rights of Parliament in relation to the approval of military action by British forces overseas, HC Deb 17 April 2018, vol 639, col 192–246.

is taken. May justified not seeking Commons approval before taking action on the basis that the level of force was the minimum necessary to avoid the 'humanitarian catastrophe' that would occur if chemical weapons were used again.[77]

The Public Administration and Constitutional Affairs Select Committee held an inquiry into the role of the House of Commons on decision to take military action.[78] There was broad acceptance with Sir George Young's description of the convention as outlined above, but considered the part of his statement that vote would not be held 'when there is an emergency and such action would not be appropriate' needed further clarification.[79] In evidence to the Committee's inquiry, the government suggested that a vote would not be held in the following four circumstances:[80]

> First, where it could compromise the effectiveness of our operations and the safety of British service men and women. Second, to protect our sources of secret intelligence. Third, so as not to undermine the effectiveness or security of operational partners. Fourth, where the legal basis for action has previously been agreed by Parliament.

While the Committee noted the explanation of these exceptions, it considered that the inherent vagueness in these exceptions still means that effectively the government will still decide if and when the Commons should be consulted. Consequently, the Committee suggested a clarification of the *Cabinet Manual*, which currently refers to Sir George Young's statement,[81] to outline the circumstances when a Commons vote is not necessary.[82]

Despite the ambiguity of the exceptions to the convention, many see the increased role of Parliament as a positive development, while others argue that this falls short of what is acceptable in a modern democratic society. Though the power to send troops abroad derives from the Crown, the government is in effect making the decision and is merely seeking approval from the House of Commons. This is still unlike other countries such as the United States who have a specific War Powers Act, specifying the procedure by which Congress is involved in the process and acts as a check on the constitutional power of the President to commit forces without the approval of Congress. Some prefer the principle that the power to deploy troops stems from Parliament and not the Crown, and this can only happen by similar legislation to that in United States.

Not only is there the question of the constitutional principle of the role of Parliament, but there is also a range of practical arguments in favour or against a greater role for Parliament. These are summarized in Table 6.1.[83] The arguments also extend to whether the greater involvement should take place through a constitutional convention or through a process set out in statute.

---

[77] HM Government, 'Syria action – UK government legal position' (gov.uk, 14 April 2018), https://www.gov.uk/government/publications/syria-action-uk-government-legal-position/syria-action-uk-government-legal-position.

[78] Public Administration and Constitutional Affairs Committee, *The Role of Parliament in the UK Constitution: Authorising the Use of Military Force* (HC 2017–19, 1891).

[79] Ibid [67]–[68].　　[80] Ibid quoted at [57].

[81] Cabinet Office, *Cabinet Manual* (n 58) [5.38].

[82] Public Administration and Constitutional Affairs Committee, *The Role of Parliament in the UK Constitution: Authorising the Use of Military Force* (n 81) [68].

[83] The arguments in Table 6.1 are taken from House of Lords Constitution Committee, *Waging War: Parliament's Role and Responsibility* (HL 2005–06, 236).

TABLE 6.1 Arguments for and against greater parliamentary involvement in decision to deploy troops abroad

For	Against
Legitimacy—The decision to deploy armed forces carries with it the risk of life. This means that the decision is so important that it can only be legitimate if Parliament authorizes action.	*Legal Impact of Legislation*—There is a need to ensure that the ability to surprise enemies is retained; a public debate in Parliament beforehand is likely to compromise this. The need to consult Parliament is likely to slow down decision-making and may compromise the effectiveness of operations.
Increased Accountability—Ministers should be required to explain their reasons for deploying armed forces to Parliament. This reflects that Ministers are accountable to Parliament.	*Executive Responsibility*—Essentially, the power to deploy troops is an executive power, and it needs to be clear that the executive is responsible for the decision. Involving Parliament risks diffusing responsibility amongst many more people. The executive should be responsible for the conduct of military operations.
Better Decision-Making—If the government is accountable to Parliament, who will scrutinize the decision, then the government will develop detailed arguments justifying their decision.	*Lack of Informed Decision-Making*—The government, not Parliament will be most informed about whether to take military action as they have access to the necessary intelligence information.
Impact on Military Morale—If the decision to deploy forces is approved by the people's democratically elected representatives this would show the military that the public support the action.	*Impact on Military Morale*—The need to consult Parliament may introduce uncertainty as the force prepare for action. Also, if the vote on action is only narrowly passed, it might weaken the commitment of government to the proposed military action. Both of these factors are likely to compromise morale.

 Pause for reflection

Having considered some of the arguments for and against greater involvement, which view do you prefer? If you believe that Parliament should have a greater role, should this be through a convention or a statutory procedure?

6.5.2 Regulation by statute—ratification of treaties

As could be seen in the list in 6.3, another power the government enjoys under the royal prerogative is the power to ratify international treaties. This has become an increasingly significant power as treaties deal with an ever-greater variety of matters, including the European Union, defence (such as membership of NATO), or specific issues such as the UN Convention on the Rights of the Child. Treaties are first negotiated by the governments of two or more countries, and then each state needs to ratify it.[84] Some countries require that the legislature must approve the treaty before the government can ratify it. For example, in the United States, two-thirds of senators need to approve a treaty before it can be ratified by the government.[85]

In the UK, the stark legal position is that the government both negotiates and ratifies international treaties acting under the royal prerogative. On the face of it, this is a very significant power for the government, with seemingly little role for Parliament. However, the Constitutional Reform and Governance Act 2010 outlines a procedure by which Parliament is involved.[86]

Section 20 of the 2010 Act provides that a treaty can only be ratified once it has been laid before both Houses for twenty-one sitting days and neither House has passed as a resolution stating that the treaty should not be ratified.[87] However, if such a motion is passed and the government still wishes to ratify the treaty, a minister can lay a statement before Parliament explaining why the government still wishes to ratify the treaty. The House of Commons then has a further twenty-one sitting days to pass a second resolution stating that the treaty should not be ratified.[88] If no second resolution has been passed, the government can go ahead and ratify the treaty.[89] Note that the House of Lords has no role to play at this stage. Under section 22, the government can bypass the need to lay a treaty before Parliament if it is an exceptional case. Although what qualifies as an exceptional case is not defined by the Act, the government would have to explain to Parliament why the procedure outlined in section 20 should not apply to that treaty.[90]

In terms of the royal prerogative, this aspect of the Constitutional Reform and Governance Act 2010 shows how the exercise of the royal prerogative can be controlled by statute. This also provides an example of how the royal prerogative can be reformed, making it subject to legal controls imposed by Parliament.

 Pause for reflection

Given that the government can ratify a treaty even though the House of Commons has voted against it, to what extent can the procedure outlined in the Constitutional Reform and Governance Act 2010 be accurately described as a control on the government?

---

[84] Ratify in this context means approve.   [85] US Constitution, Art II, s 2.

[86] Parliament can exclude the requirements of the Constitutional Reform and Governance Act 2010 for specific treaties, or for certain types of treaties. For example, the European Union (Withdrawal Agreement) Act 2020, section 32 disapplied the requirements of the Constitutional Reform and Governance Act 2010 for the Withdrawal Agreement between the UK and the EU, meaning that once the 2020 Act was enacted, the Agreement could be ratified without needing the twenty-one sitting-day requirement to be met. This allowed the UK to leave the EU on 31 January 2020. Looking to the future, the Trade Bill, as introduced into Parliament during the 2017–19 session, cl 7 made clear that free trade agreements would be excluded from the requirements of the Constitutional Reform and Governance Act 2010, with their ratification being subject to their own procedure as outlined in the bill. However, this bill was lost at the end of the session, and at the time of writing, it has yet to be reintroduced into Parliament following the December 2019 General Election.

[87] Constitutional Reform and Governance Act 2010, s 20(1).

[88] Ibid s 20(4).   [89] Ibid s 20(8).

[90] However, the 2010 Act is clear that s 22 cannot be invoked after either the Commons or the Lords has voted against a treaty under s 20. In other words, it cannot be used to override a vote against a treaty, as the procedure in s 20 must be complied with.

Discussing the problem

Take a moment to remind yourself of the problem scenario set out at the beginning of the chapter. Why can the government not ratify the treaty with the United States?

As we have seen, the power to ratify the treaty with the United States is a royal prerogative power. However, section 20 of the Constitutional Reform and Governance Act 2010 places a procedure by which the government is required to follow. The 2010 Act requires that the government lays the treaty before both Houses of Parliament, and if either House wishes to, they can hold a vote on whether the government should ratify the treaty. As required, the government laid the treaty before both Houses of Parliament; however, the House of Commons has voted against its ratification. The 2010 Act does allow the government to lay a statement before Parliament setting out its reasons in favour of ratifying the treaty, and require that the House of Commons votes on the treaty a second time.

However, in situations such as this, political considerations can be just as important as legal ones. Rather than setting out their reasons why the treaty should be ratified, the Prime Minister has decided to abide by the view of the House of Commons and instead has decided to go for a general election. The rationale behind this is that should they win the general election with a majority in the House of Commons, they would be able to ratify this treaty and proceed with implementing their manifesto.

6.5.3 Regulation by the courts—judicial control of the *exercise* of prerogative powers

As seen in 6.2.2, the courts have long held that they have the power to examine and decide whether a particular royal prerogative power exists; the traditional view was that the courts had no power to examine how that prerogative power had been *exercised*. By contrast, statutory powers given to the government by Parliament have always been subject to the principles of judicial review. In outline, judicial review requires that a decision or action must be made according to the law, comply with the principles of natural justice, and not be unreasonable or irrational. These principles are discussed in detail in Chapters 10–13.

It used to be the case that the courts felt that they could not review decisions made under the royal prerogative. To give one example, *Hanratty v Lord Butler* held that the courts could not determine whether the monarch had been advised correctly by the Home Secretary in relation to the exercise of the prerogative of mercy.[91] However, in *R v Criminal Injuries Compensation Board, ex p Lain*,[92] the court could review decisions made by the Criminal Injuries Compensation Board, a body set up under the royal prerogative. Parker CJ stated:

> I can see no reason either in principle or in authority why a board set up as the board was is not a body of persons amenable to the jurisdiction of this court. True, it is not set up by statute but the fact that it is set up by executive government, i.e. under the prerogative, does not render its acts any the less lawful.[93]

Essentially Lord Parker CJ reflected on the fact that although the source of the power may differ, whether it is statutory or the prerogative, the effect of the exercise of the power in law is very similar.

This point was further explained in *Council of the Civil Service Unions v Minister of State for the Civil Service ('GCHQ')*.[94] The Minister for the Civil Service, who was the Prime Minister, decided to ban trade union membership at the General Communications Headquarters (GCHQ). GCHQ is one of the intelligence services and the government felt that previous strikes had threatened national security. To prevent further strikes, the government decided that the decision to ban trade union membership should be implemented without consulting the staff at GCHQ beforehand. The decision was made under an Order in Council passed under the royal prerogative and justified on the grounds of national security.[95] The decision was challenged by the trade unions.

The House of Lords confirmed that the decision could in principle be reviewed by the courts. Lord Diplock, giving the leading judgment, stated that:

> I see no reason why simply because a decision making power is derived from common law and not from a statutory source it should *for that reason only* be immune from judicial review.[96]

Implicit in Lord Diplock's statement is that a prerogative power could be excluded from review for other reasons. Lord Roskill highlighted that there are some prerogative powers which 'because of their subject matter are such as not to be amenable to the judicial process'.[97] Examples his Lordship gave include the making of treaties, the granting of honours, the appointment of ministers, or the deployment of the armed forces.[98] In *GCHQ* the prerogative power involved was essentially the employment conditions of civil servants.[99] As this did not fall under any of the exceptional categories outlined by Lord Roskill, the decision of the government was in principle subject to judicial review. However, the House of Lords declined to intervene on this occasion on grounds of national security.

Since the *GCHQ* case, the courts have frequently held that the exercise of certain prerogative powers are subject to judicial review. These include the prerogative power to issue passports[100] and, in contrast to *Hanratty v Lord Butler* discussed earlier, the prerogative of mercy has since been found to be subject to judicial review.[101] However, other powers, particularly those relating to foreign policy such as the ratification of treaties, are generally thought not to be subject to judicial review.[102]

---

[94] [1985] AC 374.

[95] As discussed in 13.8.2, previous changes to employment conditions had given rise to a legitimate expectation that future changes could only be made after consulting the staff and the trade unions.

[96] Ibid 410.   [97] Ibid 418.

[98] Lord Roskill also included the dissolution of Parliament, but this prerogative power has since been abolished by the Fixed-term Parliaments Act 2011.

[99] Although elements of the Civil Service have now been placed on a statutory footing in the Constitutional Reform and Governance Act 2010.

[100] *R v Foreign Secretary, ex p Everett* [1989] QB 811.

[101] *R v Home Secretary, ex p Bentley* [1994] QB 349.

[102] *Blackburn v Attorney-General* [1971] 1 WLR 1037. See also *R v Secretary of State for Foreign and Commonwealth Affairs, ex p Rees-Mogg* [1994] QB 552. Although treaties relating to the European Union could, in theory be subject to judicial review. In *R (Wheeler) v Office of the Prime Minister* [2008] EWHC 1409, [2008] ACD 70, [55] it was conceded by counsel for the government in argument that if the procedure to ratify a treaty was set out in statute (as was the case with the European Union Act 2011, since repealed), then in principle judicial review would be available so that the courts can ensure compliance with the statutory procedure. Arguably, the same would apply to treaties required to be laid before Parliament under the Constitutional Reform and Governance Act 2010, or any other legislation. However, this is a very different point to the question of whether judicial review could challenge the substantive *content* of a treaty.

The issue as to the extent to which some royal prerogative powers are not justiciable was considered in the following case.

Case in depth: *R (Bancoult) v Secretary of State for Foreign and Commonwealth Affairs (No 2)* [2008] UKHL 61

The Chagos Islands were part of Mauritius, which was a British colony. However, the Islands became known as the British Indian Ocean Territory (BIOT) as a colony, now a British Overseas Territory separate from Mauritius. The British Government negotiated with the United States Government to allow the USA to establish a military base on the main island of BIOT. This required the removal of the population of the BIOT, which was legally authorized by an Order in Council made under the Colonial Boundaries Act 1895. In *R (Bancoult) v Secretary of State for Foreign and Commonwealth Affairs* it was held that this was executed unlawfully because the 1895 Act did not allow for such orders to be made.[103] It was thought that the Chagos islanders could return to the islands.

However, the government issued two further Orders in Council under the royal prerogative preventing the islanders' return. In *R (Bancoult) (No 2)*, these two later Orders in Council were challenged. The issue was whether these Orders in Council, made purely under the royal prerogative (note, not under any legislation), could be reviewed by the courts. This was a different question to that in the *GCHQ* case because, in that case, the question was whether executive action taken under an Order in Council could be reviewed rather than the Order in Council itself which was the case here.

The government argued that the courts have no power to review an Order in Council such as this, as it is the equivalent to an Act of Parliament. The House of Lords disagreed with the government on this point, holding that an Order in Council could be reviewed.

However, as Elliott and Varuhas state, this finding is of 'little more than rhetorical significance', as the majority in the House of Lords held that while in principle an Order in Council could be reviewed by the courts, they also held the prerogative in this area was a 'plenary' power 'that could be used for any purpose'.[104] Lord Rodger went as far as to hold that, in theory, the prerogative power could be used to enact legislation allowing torture.[105] This meant that it was extremely difficult to find the Order in Council unlawful given the enormous scope the prerogative power gives to the government.

 Pause for reflection

To what extent does *R (Bancoult) (No 2)* mean that challenges to the exercise of the royal prerogative are likely to be more successful?

---

[103] [2001] QB 1067.
[104] Mark Elliott and Jason Varuhas, *Administrative Law: Text and Materials* (5th edn, OUP 2017) 122.
[105] [2008] UKHL 61 [109].

This section highlights how judicial scrutiny of prerogative powers, particularly since the *GCHQ* case, has increased and many areas of the prerogative, such as the grant of passports, are now subject to similar judicial scrutiny as statutory powers. Although the courts were reluctant to hold that all prerogative powers are subject to review of the courts, and even if they were, they may be subject to limited scrutiny from the courts. These issues are considered further in the next two sections which discuss *R (Miller) v Secretary of State for Exiting the European Union*[106] and *R (Miller) v Prime Minister*.[107]

6.6 *R (Miller) v Secretary of State for Exiting the European Union*

Following the referendum on Britain's membership of the EU, the government indicated its intention to issue the notification under Article 50 TEU by the end of March 2017.[108] Initially, it was assumed that the government could issue the notification using the royal prerogative power to enter into and withdraw from international treaties. The government intended to proceed on that basis.

Undeniably, this was controversial. This meant that Parliament would have no formal role to play in one of the most significant constitutional decisions of recent decades. Many felt that as a matter of constitutional principle, Parliament needed to be involved in the process to invoke Article 50 and start the process of leaving the EU. The government was unmoved by these arguments. Gina Miller, a successful businesswoman, spearheaded a campaign that led to a legal challenge to the government's approach, arguing that the government would need the consent of Parliament before invoking Article 50. This relatively narrow legal question raised many of the points regarding the legal nature of the prerogative raised in this chapter. After the High Court found in favour of Miller, the government appealed, and the case was sent straight to the Supreme Court who delivered their judgment in January 2017.

6.6.1 The arguments

The central issue of the case was the legal effect of the European Communities Act 1972. The key provision was section 2(1) which states:

> All such rights, powers, liabilities, obligations and restrictions from time to time created or arising by or under the Treaties, and all such remedies and procedures from time to time provided for by or under the Treaties, as in accordance with the Treaties are without further enactment to be given legal effect or used in the United Kingdom shall be recognised and available in law, and be enforced, allowed and followed accordingly . . .

This section provides the link between rights arising under EU law and UK law because it gives effect to EU law rights in UK law. The aim was for this process to be automatic, because the content of rights arising under EU law would vary as the EU institutions, under the EU Treaties, increase, amend, or remove rights arising under the EU law. The

---

[106] [2017] UKSC 4.   [107] [2019] UKSC 41.

[108] BBC News, 'Conservative Conference: Theresa May's speech in full' (BBC News, 5 October 2016), http://www.bbc.co.uk/news/av/uk-politics-37563510/conservative-conference-theresa-may-s-speech-in-full.

effect of this section is that those changes become part of UK law without any further legislation. This is because the section uses the phrase 'from time to time'. Consequently, the government's argument was that because section 2(1) only gives effect to
rights arising under EU law at any one particular moment, when Article 50 is invoked,
and ultimately the UK leaves the EU, section 2(1) would still be complied with, even if
no EU rights were part of UK law.[109] In other words, the effect of section 2(1) is to give
effect to EU rights for as long as the UK is a member of the EU, but it is silent on the
issue of whether the UK should be a member of the EU. Consequently, the government
argued that this 'statutory silence'[110] on the UK's membership of the EU meant the issue
remained part of the general royal prerogative to negotiate, enter into, and withdraw
from international treaties.

Essentially, this is an argument which reflects a traditional approach to the royal prerogative as being the 'residue' of powers left in the hands of the Crown. It is always open
to Parliament to abolish or regulate any prerogative power, either expressly or through
necessary implication. The government argued that the 1972 Act did not do this, and
neither did any subsequent legislation. The European Union Act 2011 curtailed the prerogative regarding international treaties by making many decisions in relation to the EU
subject either to a referendum or parliamentary approval but did not make any specific
provision regarding Article 50. Similarly, the Constitutional Reform and Governance Act
2010 (as discussed in 6.5.2) did not address Article 50. Consequently, the argument is that
because Parliament has not addressed the issue, the prerogative power to withdraw from
a treaty is left untouched.

As is to be expected, the arguments from Miller were the opposite to the government.
They argued that because invoking Article 50 will necessarily cause the treaties to no
longer to apply to the UK,[111] some legal rights that citizens currently enjoy through the
UK's membership of the EU will be lost when the UK leaves the EU after the negotiations on the terms of exit are concluded. Given that the UK would leave following the
Article 50 notification, the principle from the *De Keyser* case was argued as showing that
the prerogative cannot be used to change the common law or the law as provided by
Parliament. Invoking Article 50 would necessarily cause the loss of rights provided for
by section 2(1) of the 1972 Act; consequently the royal prerogative could not be used to
remove those rights, because that is changing the law as provided by Parliament through
the 1972 Act.

As can be seen, the arguments from the government and Miller were both reasonably
strong, grounded on existing principles drawn from the case law on the prerogative.

---

[109] This could be subject to the terms of any exit agreement that the UK reaches with the EU. It is
possible that some rights remain even after Britain leaves the EU. Whether any retained rights would
require a similar provision to that of s 2(1) will depend on what is agreed between the UK and EU.

[110] A term used by David Howarth to explain the issues in *Miller*: see David Howarth, 'On Parliamentary Silence', UK Const L Blog (13 December 2016), https://ukconstitutionallaw.org/2016/12/13/
david-howarth-on-parliamentary-silence/.

[111] The case was argued by both sides on the basis that issuing a notification under Art 50(2) would be
irreversible, although Art 50 itself is silent on this question. However, the CJEU in C-621/18 *Wightman
v Secretary of State for Exiting the European Union* [2019] 1 CMLR 29 decided that a notification under Art
50 could be revoked unilaterally by the Member State that had previously notified their intention to
withdraw.

6.6.2 **Judgment of the Supreme Court**

As discussed in Chapter 5, a majority of eight out of the eleven Supreme Court judges that heard the case, took the view that the 1972 Act, as an exercise of Parliament's sovereignty created a new source of law for the legal system of the UK. The Supreme Court described the 1972 Act as the 'conduit pipe' by which EU law is introduced into UK domestic law,[112] with the majority concluding that as 'long as the 1972 Act remains in force, its effect is to constitute EU law [as] an independent and overriding source of domestic law'.[113]

Once that decision about the effect of the 1972 Act had been made, it was then a relatively small step to find that Article 50 could not be triggered by the royal preroga-tive. This is because to trigger Article 50 would ultimately remove EU law as a source of domestic law in the UK. This would clearly be changing the law, which, as held in cases such as *De Keyser*, cannot be undertaken under the royal prerogative. While the majority judgment accepted that section 2(1) of the 1972 Act, meant that the quantity and scope of rights could change over time, this did not extend to Parliament allowing ministers to remove those rights entirely.[114] The majority interpreted the 1972 Act as forming the approval by Parliament of Britain's entry into the EU:

> and gave effect to the United Kingdom's membership of what is the now the European Union under the EU Treaties in a way which is inconsistent with the future exercise by ministers of any prerogative power to withdraw from such treaties.[115]

Overall, the key difference between the majority and the minority judgments was their conclusion over the status of EU law within the UK legal system. From this flowed their disagreement over whether the prerogative could be used to trigger Article 50.

The immediate consequence of the case was the enactment of the European Union (Notification of Withdrawal) Act 2017, which granted the Prime Minister the legal au-thority to trigger Article 50. Theresa May exercised this authority by sending the EU the UK's notification of withdrawal on 29 March 2017. Based on the discussion of the major-ity judgment, the consequences of *Miller* for the royal prerogative appear to be limited. This is because the discussion of the royal prerogative relied on existing principles and the Supreme Court emphasized the exceptional nature of the 1972 Act.[116] There is little indication that the prerogative power to withdraw from other non-EU treaties is limited in the same way.

 Counterpoint: Must fundamental constitutional change be made by legislation?

There is an ambiguity in the Supreme Court's judgment, which may give rise to a broader inter-pretation. It is obvious, and was recognized as such by the majority judgment, that withdrawal from the EU will be a very significant change to the UK's Constitution.[117] They also indicated that withdrawing from the EU 'will constitute as significant a constitutional change as that which

➡

---

[112] *R (Miller) v Secretary of State for Exiting the European Union* [2017] UKSC 5 [65].
[113] Ibid [65].   [114] Ibid [81].   [115] Ibid [77].   [116] Ibid [90].   [117] Ibid [82].

→

occurred when the EU was first incorporated in domestic law by the 1972 Act'.[118] Given that the UK will leave the EU under the terms of Article 50, the UK will leave whether the 1972 Act is repealed or not.

The Supreme Court then concluded that:

> It would be inconsistent with long-standing and fundamental principle for such a far-reaching change to the UK constitutional arrangements to be brought about by ministerial decision or ministerial action alone. All the more so when the source in question was brought into existence by Parliament through primary legislation, which gave that source an overriding supremacy in the hierarchy of domestic law sources.[119]

This led to the majority judgment making what appears to be an extremely broad point:

> We cannot accept that a major change to UK constitutional arrangements can be achieved by ministers alone; it must be effected in the only way that the UK constitution recognises, namely by Parliamentary legislation. This conclusion appears to us to follow from the ordinary application of basic concepts of constitutional law to the present issue.[120]

This is problematic for several reasons. First, the majority did not cite any authority to support this conclusion and they did not develop this point, which appears to limit the prerogative in a novel way.[121] Secondly, this approach of creating a broad restriction on the power of the prerogative in this manner runs counter to the traditional understanding of the prerogative as explained by Dicey as the 'residue' of powers left in the hands of the Crown, with prerogative powers being removed only by express provision or necessary implication. As Lord Reed highlighted in his dissenting judgment:

> it is a basic principle of our constitution that the conduct of foreign relations, including the ratification of treaties, falls within the prerogative powers of the Crown. That principle is so fundamental that it can only be overridden by express provision or necessary implication . . . No such express provision exists in the 1972 Act.[122]

Consequently, after reviewing legislation passed since 1972, including the European Union Act 2011, Lord Reed concluded that Article 50 could be invoked by the royal prerogative.

6.7 *R (Miller) v Prime Minister*

If *R (Miller) v Secretary of State for Exiting the European Union* could be explained as an application of pre-existing principles, the same cannot be said about *R (Miller) v Prime Minister*.[123] A key feature is that it involved a personal prerogative power—the power to prorogue Parliament. The next two sections will consider two remaining personal prerogative powers: the granting of Royal Assent to legislation, and the appointment of a new Prime Minister. There used to be another personal prerogative power—the power to dissolve Parliament, which would trigger an early general election. This was abolished by the Fixed-term Parliaments Act 2011, replacing the prerogative power of dissolution with a

---

[118] Ibid [81].   [119] Ibid.   [120] Ibid [82].

[121] James Grant, 'Prerogative, Parliament and Creative Constitutional Adjudication: Reflections on *Miller*' (2017) 28(1) *King's Law Journal* 35, 50.

[122] *R (Miller) v Secretary of State for Exiting the European Union* [2017] UKSC 5 [194].

[123] [2019] UKSC 41.

series of statutory rules to determine when Parliament is dissolved, and general elections are held. Although now a statutory power, the 2011 Act is considered in this chapter because the issue of general elections and the appointment of Prime Minister are so deeply intertwined that the Act needs to be considered within this context.

6.7.1 The power to prorogue Parliament

The case revolves around the prerogative power to prorogue Parliament. This is exercised by the monarch on the advice of the Prime Minister, with the decision formally made through an Order in Council made at a meeting of the Privy Council, and put into effect by Royal Commissioners acting on behalf of the Queen at a ceremony held in the House of Lords.[124] As explained in more detail in 8.2.4, sittings of Parliament are organized into sessions. Prorogation is the legal power to end a session and set the date of the start of the new session, which starts with a new Queen's Speech. This is when the government announces its legislative programme for the new session of Parliament. Although practice has varied, the gap between the end of one session and the start of the next is typically around a week. During this period, Parliament is prorogued. This means that it cannot sit, hold debates, or pass any legislation. If a bill has not completed its passage through Parliament, then usually it is lost and will have to start again in the following session.[125]

Since the Fixed-term Parliaments Act 2011 established the legal default of elections taking place every five years in May, the expectation has been that each five-year-long Parliament would see five sessions, starting and ending in or around May. Following the surprise 2017 general election, the government announced that the next session of Parliament would last two years, instead of one. This would match with the two-year period to negotiate Brexit as outlined in Article 50 TEU, which started on 29 March 2017. During this period, the government would be able to get through Parliament the complex legislation necessary to implement Brexit. Presumably, the intention was that once the UK left the EU on the expected date of 29 March 2019, the government would then start a new session of Parliament and the Queen's Speech would outline its post-Brexit legislative agenda.

6.7.2 The decision of 28 August 2019

As explained in Chapter 5, events did not follow this expected course. Theresa May failed to obtain the approval of the House of Commons for the Withdrawal Agreement that she concluded with the EU, and ultimately, she was required to resign as Conservative Party leader and Prime Minister. The UK extended the Article 50 period to 31 October 2019.[126]

During the Conservative Party leadership contest, some candidates raised the prospect of proroguing Parliament for an extended time period, including until after 31 October 2019. This would mean that as Parliament could not sit while prorogued, this would allow the government to decide whether the UK should leave without an agreement with the EU on 31 October. Parliament would be powerless to stop this. To address this concern, some backbench MPs strongly opposed to leaving the EU without a deal, amended a bill

---

[124] The monarch could prorogue Parliament in person, but no monarch has done so since Queen Victoria in 1854.

[125] Exceptionally, some bills can be 'carried over' from one session to the next to complete the remaining stages of the legislative process.

[126] The Art 50 period has since been extended to 31 January 2020. See Chapter 5.

relating to Northern Ireland so that Parliament would be required to sit from 14 October, even if it has been previously prorogued.[127]

In July 2019, Boris Johnson became Prime Minister and committed himself to delivering Brexit by 31 October, if necessary on a no deal basis. On 28 August 2019, a Privy Council meeting was held at Balmoral Castle and an Order in Council was made proroguing Parliament 'on a day no earlier than Monday the 9th September and no later than Thursday 12th September' to 14 October 2019.[128] As required by the cardinal convention, the Queen approved the order. Parliament was prorogued on 9 September. Johnson justified this on the basis that the government needed this period to prepare for a new Queen's Speech, and its programme of future legislation. Others were concerned that Parliament would be unable to prevent leaving the EU without an agreement, as there would be little time to act once Parliament returned on 14 October.[129]

6.7.3 The Supreme Court's judgment

The decision to prorogue was enormously controversial, and faced legal challenges in both Scotland and England and Wales. The Court of Session held that the prorogation was unlawful, whereas the High Court found the matter was non-justiciable.[130] On this point, as explained in 10.2.1, the Supreme Court agreed with the Court of Session.

The Supreme Court stated that there are two issues to address when the justiciability of the prerogative is questioned. As explained in 6.2.2, the first question is whether the prerogative power exists, and if so, what its extent is. It is uncontroversial that the courts determine this question. The second question is as explored in 6.5.3, which is when a prerogative power has been exercised within its legal limits, but, just like a statutory power, would be subject to review under the ordinary principles of judicial review.[131]

The Supreme Court focused its analysis onto the first question: what are the legal limits on power to prorogue Parliament? After reciting the importance of parliamentary sovereignty as a 'fundamental principle of constitutional law',[132] the Court then considered that an unlimited power to prorogue Parliament would be 'incompatible with the legal principle of Parliamentary sovereignty'.[133] The Court then explained how an unlimited power to prorogue would also conflict with a second constitutional principle, that of parliamentary accountability. The Supreme Court explained this principle in the following way:

> Ministers are accountable to Parliament through such mechanisms as their duty to answer Parliamentary questions and to appear before Parliamentary committees, and through Parliamentary scrutiny of the delegated legislation which ministers make. By these means,

---

[127] As required under the Northern Ireland (Executive Formation etc) Act 2019 s 3, a royal proclamation requesting that Parliament meets would be issued under the Meeting of Parliament Act 1797.

[128] Privy Council, 'Orders Approved at the Privy Council held by the Queen at Balmoral on 28th August 2019' (Privy Council Office, 2019), available at https://privycouncil.independent.gov.uk/wp-content/uploads/2019/09/2019-08-28-List-of-Business.pdf.

[129] In particular, there was scheduled to be an EU Council summit meeting of the Heads of Government, who could decide how to respond to any request for a further extension to the Art 50 period beyond 31 October.

[130] *Cherry v Advocate General* [2019] CSIH 49; *R (Miller) v Prime Minister* [2019] EWHC 2381 (QB).

[131] Namely, illegality, procedural impropriety, and unreasonableness/irrationality, as explained in Chapters 11, 12, and 13.

[132] [2019] UKSC 41 [41].   [133] Ibid [42].

the policies of the executive are subjected to consideration by the representatives of the electorate, the executive is required to report, explain and defend its actions, and citizens are protected from the arbitrary exercise of executive power.[134]

Although a short prorogation would not challenge this principle, 'the longer that Parliament stands prorogued, the greater the risk that responsible government may be replaced by unaccountable government: the antithesis of the democratic model'.[135]

Essentially, both constitutional principles raised the same question: how should the power to prorogue Parliament be limited so that Parliament can 'carry out its constitutional functions'?[136] The Supreme Court answered this question as follows:

> that a decision to prorogue Parliament (or to advise the monarch to prorogue Parliament) will be unlawful if the prorogation has the effect of frustrating or preventing, without reasonable justification, the ability of Parliament to carry out its constitutional functions as a legislature and as the body responsible for the supervision of the executive. In such a situation, the court will intervene if the effect is sufficiently serious to justify such an exceptional course.[137]

The Court then applied this test to the decision of 28 August, finding that:

> This was not a normal prorogation in the run-up to a Queen's Speech. It prevented Parliament from carrying out its constitutional role for five out of a possible eight weeks between the end of the summer recess and exit day on 31 October.[138]

The issue is that during this five-week period, in the run up to 31 October (then scheduled to be the date of the UK's exit from the EU), Parliament would be unable to ask questions of the government about its Brexit policy. This is particularly important as the House of Commons appeared to disagree with government policy over leaving without reaching an agreement with the EU. The democratically elected House of Commons 'has a right to have a voice' in how Brexit takes place, and this prorogation would have the effect of excluding the Commons from the debate at this critical stage. The government needed to put forward a reasonable justification for a prorogation that has this effect. However, the justification that it advanced—that the government needed the time to prepare for a Queen's Speech—was contested by evidence from the former Prime Minister, Sir John Major, who made clear that a more typical period would be four to six days.[139] Given that this evidence was unchallenged by the government, the Supreme Court arrived at the natural conclusion that the five-week period could not be justified.

This meant that this prorogation was outside the scope of the power to prorogue Parliament, meaning that the advice the Prime Minister gave to the Queen was unlawful. The upshot being that everything that happened in consequence of that advice was 'unlawful, null and of no effect'.[140] Consequently, the Order in Council made on 28 August 2019 was quashed, and in legal terms, the prorogation ceremony carried out by the Commissioners was based 'on a blank sheet of paper'.[141] All of this meant that Parliament had never been prorogued and that both Houses should resume business as soon as possible.[142] The Speaker of the House of Commons and the Lord Speaker made arrangements for their respective chambers to sit the day after the Supreme Court gave its judgment on

---

[134] Ibid [46].   [135] Ibid [48].   [136] Ibid [48].
[137] Ibid [50].   [138] Ibid [55].   [139] Ibid [59].
[140] Ibid [69].   [141] Ibid.   [142] Ibid [70].

24 September. Shortly after resuming the session, Parliament was later prorogued, this time lawfully, from 8 to 14 October 2019.

> **Counterpoint: What are the implications of *R (Miller) v Prime Minister* on other conventions?**
>
> The main effect of *R (Miller) v Prime Minister* is to limit the power to prorogue Parliament, so that it cannot be used to unjustifiably undermine the key constitutional functions of Parliament. As the Supreme Court explained, this includes the ability of Parliament to hold the government to account—parliamentary accountability—and described as a fundamental principle of the constitution, sitting alongside parliamentary sovereignty.
>
> The accountability of the government underpins the convention described in 6.5.1, that before the armed forces are deployed overseas, the government seeks the approval of the House of Commons. As Chowdhury has questioned, could the approach of *R (Miller) v Prime Minister* be applied to situations such as in April 2018, when the armed forces were deployed without the prior approval of the Commons?[143] Would the lack of a vote have a similar effect to a long prorogation in frustrating the ability of Parliament to fulfil its constitutional function of holding the government to account?
>
> Potentially, this could mean that *any* occasion a vote is not held would frustrate Parliament. The government could be in the position of having to invoke before the courts one of the justifications it advanced before the Public Administration and Constitutional Affairs Select Committee for not seeking prior Commons approval (outlined in 6.5.1). These were, when a vote would:
>
> • compromise the effectiveness and the safety of the armed forces;
> • compromise intelligence sources;
> • undermine the effectiveness or security of the UK's operational partners; or
> • when Parliament has already agreed the legal basis for action.
>
> Traditionally it has been felt that the courts are unable to address these questions, as the courts are not best placed to deal with such issues as they may not have ready access to the same information, particularly intelligence information, as the government. However, similar considerations regarding the political sensitivities surrounding prorogation did not apply in *R (Miller) v Prime Minister*, as the Court sought to frame the issues as questions of law, not politics.[144]
>
> *R (Miller) v Prime Minister* opens up the question that a failure to gain Commons approval before a more pre-meditated, pre-emptive, or anticipatory strike could be reviewed by the courts because the justifications of urgency, security, or humanitarian considerations of Syria made for 2018 might not apply.[145]
>
> What this discussion shows is that the implications of *R (Miller) v Prime Minister* on the prerogative and the relationship between the government and Parliament are potentially far-reaching. It remains to be seen how courts will address these issues in light of the Supreme Court's judgment.

6.8 Royal Assent to legislation

The other remaining personal prerogative power relates to the Crown operating in a legislative capacity and is more minor. Once a bill in Parliament has been agreed by both Houses of Parliament (or only the House of Commons should the Parliament Act 1911

---

[143] Tanzil Chowdhury, '*Miller (No 2)*, the Principle-isation of Ministerial Accountability and Military Deployments', UK Const L Blog (24 October 2019), available at https://ukconstitutionallaw.org/2019/10/24/tanzil-chowdhury-miller-no-2-the-principle-isation-of-ministerial-accountability-and-military-deployments/.
[144] [2019] UKSC 41 [31].   [145] Ibid.

apply to the bill), the final process is the granting of Royal Assent by the monarch.[146] Despite no monarch refusing Royal Assent since Queen Anne refused the Scottish Militia Bill in 1707, Royal Assent remains at common law a prerogative power and is exercised personally by the monarch.

It was once the practice that the monarch would personally grant Royal Assent in Parliament, with Queen Victoria the last to do this in 1854. Today, Royal Assent is granted by the monarch signing letters patent (a legal document issued by the monarch) to which the Great Seal is affixed.[147] At a convenient break amongst other parliamentary business, the fact that Royal Assent has been granted is announced in both the House of Lords and the House of Commons. It is at this point that a bill becomes an Act of Parliament.[148]

Counterpoint: Can the monarch refuse to grant the Royal Assent?

Usually, parliamentary business is controlled by the government, which means that most legislation passed by Parliament is introduced by the government that is seeking to change the law so that it can implement its new policies. As required by the 'cardinal' convention, the Royal Assent is always granted, regardless of the personal views of the monarch.

Highly unusually, in March and September 2019, MPs voted to take control of what the House of Commons debated, and despite the government's wishes voted to pass two pieces of legislation—the European Union (Withdrawal) Act 2019 and the European Union (Withdrawal) (No 2) Act 2019. Both pieces of legislation were aimed at ensuring that the UK did not leave the EU without an agreement.

However, on both occasions, there was speculation that ministers might advise the Queen to refuse to grant Royal Assent.[149] On the face of it, this would indicate that the Queen should follow the cardinal convention, and follow the advice of ministers. However, in these circumstances, this clearly breaches the principle of parliamentary sovereignty, which requires that Parliament plays the primary role in legislation, not the monarch. The true constitutional situation is perhaps best understood as follows: by convention the monarch always grants Royal Assent, and this convention is underpinned by the need to reflect parliamentary sovereignty. As Elliott states, the cardinal convention only arises when 'there is uncertainty as to what the Queen ought to do. There is absolutely no uncertainty when it comes to granting Royal Assent, and so the ["cardinal" convention] is beside the point.'[150] However, other commentators hold alternative views.[151]

In the event, on both occasions, Royal Assent was granted in the ordinary way.

---

[146] The place of Royal Assent in the legislative process is discussed in 8.5.8.

[147] Royal Assent Act 1967, s 1(1).

[148] Rodney Brazier, 'Royal Assent to Legislation' (2013) 129 LQR 184, 191.

[149] Some academics had floated this possibility: see Geoffrey Marshall, *Constitutional Conventions: The Rules and Forms of Political Accountability* (OUP 1984) 22.

[150] Mark Elliott, 'Can the Government Veto Legislation by Advising the Queen to Withhold Royal Assent' (Public Law for Everyone, 21 January 2019), https://publiclawforeveryone.com/2019/01/21/can-the-government-veto-legislation-by-advising-the-queen-to-withhold-royal-assent/.

[151] Robert Craig, 'Could the Government Advise the Queen to Refuse Royal Assent to a Backbench Bill?', UK Const L Blog (22 January 2019), available at https://ukconstitutionallaw.org/2019/01/22/robert-craig-could-the-government-advise-the-queen-to-refuse-royal-assent-to-a-backbench-bill/); Rodney Brazier, 'Ministerial Advice and the Queen' (*The Times*, 4 April 2019) (https://www.thetimes.co.uk/past-six-days/2019-04-04/comment/times-letters-brexit-deadlock-and-the-art-of-negotiation-86k78vrnz); Sir Stephen Laws and Richard Ekins, 'Endangering Constitutional Unsettlement' (Policy Exchange, 2019), https://policyexchange.org.uk/wp-content/uploads/2019/03/Endangering-Constitutional-Government.pdf.

6.8.1 The effect of *R (Miller) v Prime Minister*

Royal Assent can also be given during the prorogation ceremony in the House of Lords. This is particularly useful when legislation has been rushed through both Houses prior to prorogation in order to avoid it being lost by the end of that parliamentary session. As previously discussed, the Supreme Court in *R (Miller) v Prime Minister* declared that the prorogation of Parliament from 9 September 2019, based on the Order of Council approved on 28 August 2019, was unlawful. However, in its judgment, the Supreme Court did not address the implications of this decision on Parliamentary Buildings (Restoration and Renewal) Bill, which was granted Royal Assent during the prorogation ceremony that now had no legal effect. Consequently, to remove any doubt over the validity of Royal Assent to the bill, it was granted for a second time when Parliament was again prorogued, this time lawfully in October 2019.[152]

6.9 The appointment of the Prime Minister

As discussed in more detail in Chapter 7, the Prime Minister is the effective Head of the Government, responsible for its overall conduct. Although the monarch appoints the Prime Minister, the choice the monarch makes is heavily regulated by constitutional convention. Primarily, the Prime Minister must by constitutional convention be an MP[153] and be able to command the confidence of the House of Commons. The following discussion focuses first on what happens when one party has an overall majority of the seats in the House of Commons, before discussing the more complex situation of when no party has an overall majority.

6.9.1 Single party majority governments

Usually, the position is straightforward. Following a general election, the Prime Minister is the leader of the political party which has a majority of seats in the House of Commons. If that person is already the Prime Minister, no new appointment is required because they have retained the confidence of the House of Commons. For example, in 1992, John Major was the Prime Minister and leader of the Conservative Party and after the election continued as Prime Minister as the Conservatives retained a majority of twenty-one MPs. Similarly, in 2019, Boris Johnson went into the election as Prime Minister and leader of a Conservative minority government; when the Conservatives won an eighty-seat majority, Johnson remained Prime Minister. In these circumstances, the monarch does not 'reappoint' the Prime Minister.

A new appointment will be required if, after an election, a different political party has won a majority of the seats in the House of Commons. The Prime Minister has 'lost' their majority and will resign, to be replaced by the leader of the party that now enjoys a majority in the Commons. This was most clearly seen after the 1997 General Election. The existing Prime Minister, John Major, lost his majority as his Conservative Party won only 165 seats.

---

[152] This issue is explored in more detail in the online materials that consider parliamentary privilege.

[153] The last member of the House of Lords to be Prime Minister was the Marquess of Salisbury in 1901. In 1963, Sir Alec Douglas-Home had to renounce his seat in the House of Lords and take a seat in the House of Commons in order to become Prime Minister.

Labour, led by Tony Blair, won 418 seats and a massive majority of 179. This meant that Major, having lost his majority and so the confidence of the House of Commons, resigned as Prime Minister, and the Queen appointed Blair as the new Prime Minister.

The other straightforward scenario is when the Prime Minister decides to resign as Prime Minister and party leader between general elections. This happened in June 2016 when David Cameron announced that he was going to resign as Prime Minister and leader of the Conservative Party. Cameron had rightly concluded that his position was untenable following his failed campaign to keep Britain in the EU at the referendum. Cameron's resignation triggered a leadership election within the Conservative Party. The early stages whittled down five candidates to the final two, who were Andrea Leadsom and Theresa May. However, following some negative press reports, Leadsom withdrew, leaving May as the sole remaining candidate and became by default, the new leader of the Conservatives. When this was confirmed, two days later, David Cameron tendered his resignation to the Queen at Buckingham Palace, who then appointed Theresa May as the new Prime Minister.

Similarly, in June 2019, Theresa May announced that she intended to resign as Prime Minister. When Boris Johnson won the Conservative Party leadership contest, the following day, May tendered her resignation and Johnson was appointed as her successor. As all the main political parties have rules outlining how the leader is to be appointed,[154] there is now no scope for the monarch to make a choice in these situations.[155]

6.9.2 Hung Parliaments

A more complex situation is when no one party has a majority of the seats in the House of Commons, described as a 'hung Parliament'. The complexity arises from the different options as to who could form the government and which political parties may be involved. There has been substantial debate amongst constitutional scholars as to how the constitutional conventions operate in these situations and what scope there is for intervention by the monarch.[156] The fundamental problem is that an unelected, hereditary monarch should not be seen to be determining the result of the general election by choosing one possibility over another. This would be seen as an affront to the democratic process and would challenge the political neutrality of the monarch.

Consequently, there is a need to unpack the constitutional conventions at play when it comes to forming the government. These conventions are explained in the *Cabinet Manual*. The overriding principle is that the Prime Minister is whoever can command

[154] Similar circumstances occurred when Tony Blair resigned as Prime Minister in 2007. Blair announced that he would resign as Prime Minister, so triggering a leadership contest within the Labour Party. In the event, Gordon Brown was the only candidate for the leadership. Once Brown became the Labour leader according to the rules of the Labour Party, Tony Blair resigned as Prime Minister and Gordon Brown was appointed by the Queen soon afterwards.

[155] This has not always been the case. In 1957 and 1963 the incumbent Conservative Prime Minister, Sir Anthony Eden and Harold Macmillan respectively, both resigned while in office. At the time, there was no process by which the Conservatives chose a new leader. In 1957, the Queen consulted a range of senior Conservative figures, including Sir Winston Churchill and acted on their advice in appointing Harold Macmillan. In 1963, when Macmillan resigned, there were several candidates for the leadership and the Queen relied on the controversial advice of Macmillan to appoint Sir Alec Douglas-Home instead of other candidates such as Rab Butler.

[156] See, for example, Robert Blackburn, 'Monarchy and the Personal Prerogatives' [2004] *Public Law* 546; Rodney Brazier, '"Monarchy and the Personal Prerogatives": A Personal Response to Professor Blackburn' [2005] *Public Law* 45.

the confidence of the House of Commons. The basic challenge is in determining who that person is when there is more than one possibility without the monarch making any active decision or exercising any discretion. The *Cabinet Manual* spells out two core principles which govern the situation. First, 'Prime Ministers hold office unless and until they resign'[157] and, secondly, it is the 'responsibility of those in the political process . . . to seek to determine and communicate clearly to the [Monarch] who is best placed to command the confidence of the House of Commons'.[158]

With a hung Parliament, these principles operate so that the government remains in office unless and until the Prime Minister resigns. The Prime Minister is perfectly entitled to wait until Parliament meets to see whether it has the confidence of the House of Commons, as shown through the vote on the Queen's Speech (which sets out the government's legislative programme).[159] However, as the *Cabinet Manual* states they are expected to resign 'if it becomes clear that it is unlikely to be able to command that confidence and there is a clear alternative'.[160] If there are a range of potential different governments, then the political parties can hold negotiations 'to establish who is best able to command the confidence of the House of Commons and form the next government'.[161]

6.9.3 **2010—coalition**

These rules could be seen in operation after the 2010 General Election when, as Figure 6.2 shows, no party won an overall majority.

The Labour Party, led by the then Prime Minister Gordon Brown, had lost their majority and the Conservative Party became the largest party, although twenty seats short of an overall majority. The Liberal Democrats were the third party and could possibly have formed a government with either Labour or the Conservatives, although only a coalition between the Conservatives and the Liberal Democrats would have created a government

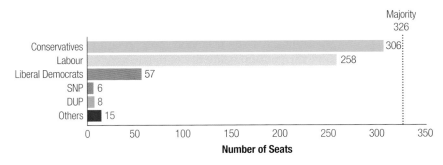

Figure 6.2 The result of the 2010 General Election

[157] Cabinet Office, *The Cabinet Manual* (1st edn, Cabinet Office 2011) para 2.8.

[158] Ibid para 2.9.

[159] The last time a Prime Minister waited to face the new Parliament and test the confidence of the House of Commons in this was Stanley Baldwin, the Conservative Prime Minister in 1924 following the General Election in December 1923. After Baldwin lost the vote of confidence, he resigned and Ramsay MacDonald, leader of the Labour Party, was invited to form a government.

[160] Cabinet Office, *The Cabinet Manual* (1st edn, Cabinet Office 2011) para 2.12.

[161] Ibid para 2.13.

with an overall majority. During the five days that followed the election, the political parties negotiated with each other. Both Labour and the Conservatives negotiated with the Liberal Democrats with the aim of forming a government with their support. When it became clear that the Conservatives and the Liberal Democrats were going to work together, and that Gordon Brown as leader of the Labour Party would no longer have the confidence of the House of Commons, he resigned as Prime Minister. The Queen then appointed David Cameron, the leader of the Conservatives, to form a government. This government was a coalition between the Conservatives and the Liberal Democrats, with MPs and members of the House of Lords from both parties being appointed as ministers to form the government.[162]

 Pause for reflection

Two days after the 2010 General Election, the headline in *The Sun* newspaper was 'Squatter Holed Up in No 10'.[163] This was a reference to how Gordon Brown remained in Downing Street after the election as Prime Minister, despite the Labour Party winning forty-eight seats fewer than the Conservatives. These reflected the arguments made by some that Brown should have resigned immediately after the General Election and make way for the 'clear winner' David Cameron, leader of the Conservatives, even though it was not certain by that point that the Conservatives and Liberal Democrats were going to enter into a coalition together.

Had Gordon Brown resigned immediately after the General Election, without it being clear that there was an alternative government, would this have been consistent with the rules as outlined in the *Cabinet Manual*?

At the 2015 General Election, the Conservatives gained an overall majority, no resignation or appointment of the Prime Minister was necessary as David Cameron was already in situ and would continue to enjoy the confidence of the House of Commons.[164] However, it is worth noting that the nature of the government changed from a coalition with the Liberal Democrats to a single party majority government.

6.9.4 **2017—confidence and supply**

At the surprise 2017 General Election (the circumstances of which are discussed in 6.10), the Conservatives came just short of retaining their majority by seven seats but were still comfortably the largest party, winning fifty-five more seats than Labour, the second largest party. The results can be seen in Figure 6.3.

---

[162] Accounts of the formation of the coalition government include Vernon Bogdanor, *The Coalition and the Constitution* (Hart 2011) Ch 1; Robert Blackburn, 'The 2010 General Election Outcome and Formation of the Conservative-Liberal Democrat Coalition Government' [2011] *Public Law* 30; David Laws, *22 Days in May* (Biteback 2010).

[163] Tom Newton Dunn, 'Squatter Holed Up in No 10' *The Sun* (London, 8 May 2010) 1.

[164] The Conservatives won an overall majority of eleven seats with 330 seats.

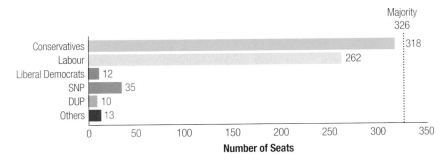

Figure 6.3 The result of the 2017 General Election

The day after the election, Theresa May indicated that she intended to continue as Prime Minister and announced that she intended to form an agreement with the Democratic Unionist Party (DUP), a party with ten MPs who represented constituencies in Northern Ireland.[165]

As can be seen from Figure 6.3, the support of these ten MPs would ensure that the Conservatives had the support of a majority of the House of Commons. This meant that May could continue to command the confidence of the House of Commons and govern with a degree of stability. A failure to reach this agreement would have meant that the Conservatives would not be certain of winning certain key votes, such as the Queen's Speech or the Budget (which ensures that the government can raise the necessary taxes for their policies). Any defeat on these votes would raise serious questions as to whether the government continued to have the confidence of the House of Commons to govern and could trigger the provisions of the Fixed-term Parliaments Act which are discussed in the next section.

This agreement the Conservatives and the DUP reached is known as a Confidence and Supply Agreement.[166] This agreement commited the DUP to agree to support the Conservative Government on all motions of no confidence. Importantly for the 2017 Parliament, the DUP also committed to support the government on Brexit. The DUP would decided whether to support the government on all other votes not covered by the agreement on a case-by-case basis. In return for reaching this agreement, the DUP secured up to £1 billion of extra funding for public services in Northern Ireland.[167] As can be seen, this falls significantly short of a coalition, as agreed after the 2010 election, as the DUP would not play any active role in government, but merely support the Conservatives in office. As required by the terms of the agreement, the ten DUP MPs supported the government when it faced a motion of no confidence in January 2019. The motion was defeated by 325 votes to 306.[168]

---

[165] Prime Minister's Office, 'PM statement: General Election 2017' (Prime Minister's Office, 9 June 2017), https://www.gov.uk/government/speeches/pm-statement-general-election-2017.

[166] Prime Minister's Office, 'Confidence and Supply Agreement between the Conservative and Unionist Party and the Democratic Unionist Party' (Prime Minister's Office, 26 June 2017), https://www.gov.uk/government/publications/conservative-and-dup-agreement-and-uk-government-financial-support-for-northern-ireland/agreement-between-the-conservative-and-unionist-party-and-the-democratic-unionist-party-on-support-for-the-government-in-parliament.

[167] Prime Minister's Office, 'UK Government Financial Support for Northern Ireland' (Prime Minister's Office, 26 June 2017), https://www.gov.uk/government/publications/conservative-and-dup-agreement-and-uk-government-financial-support-for-northern-ireland/uk-government-financial-support-for-northern-ireland.

[168] HC Deb, 16 January 2019, vol 652, cols 1171–1273.

6.9.5 A minority?

In all of the above examples, the issue has been how a political party, occasionally with the aid of another party, can acquire the confidence of the House of Commons to either become or remain in office. A different question emerged in September 2019, when despite only having a small majority, Boris Johnson sacked twenty-one of his MPs by withdrawing the Conservative Party whip from them, meaning that they could no longer sit as Conservative MPs. This meant that the government became forty-three seats short of a majority, even with the support of the DUP. However, despite losing a succession of votes in the House of Commons, a no confidence motion was not tabled. This shows how Prime Ministers hold office until they resign, and that it is up to the House of Commons to move a motion of no confidence to show that the government has lost the confidence of the House.

Partly in response to this succession of defeats, the government sought to hold an early general election, but as the next section discusses, the Fixed-term Parliaments Act 2011 posed an obstacle that needed to be overcome.

 Discussing the problem

Consider the result of the 2022 General Election as outlined in the problem scenario presented at the start of the chapter. The result is displayed in Figure 6.4. Who would be most likely to form a government?

As the Conservatives formed the government before the general election, they would remain in office immediately after the general election, this is because the result of the general election is unclear as no one party has obtained an overall majority. Out of the precedents of 2010 and 2017, this result appears closer to 2010 rather than 2017. This is because in 2017, the Conservatives were the largest party and very close to an overall majority and just needed the support of a smaller party (in that case the DUP) to ensure that they remained in office. At this election, the Conservatives remain the largest party, but Labour are close enough to suggest that they could potentially form a viable government with the support of one or two other parties.

Perhaps to a greater extent than was the case in 2010, there is a range of possibilities as to what government could be formed. The Conservatives could reach an agreement with the Liberal Democrats to form a viable minority government. This could be further secured with the support of the

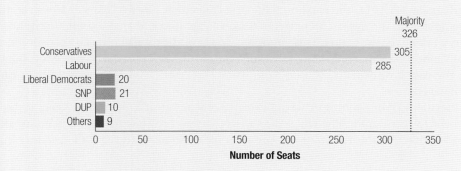

Figure 6.4 The result of the 2022 General Election

→

Democratic Unionist Party and those three parties together would have an overall majority. The likelihood of this may depend on the view of the Liberal Democrats on the treaty with the USA.

Given fundamental disagreement between the SNP and the Conservatives over Scottish independence and many other areas of policy, it would be unlikely that they would work together. It would be more likely that the SNP would work with the Labour Party, who could also attempt to work with the Liberal Democrats. If those three parties worked together, they would just get an overall majority. The likelihood of either of these possibilities (or any other) would depend on politics, in particular, the policies contained in party manifestos and given the context of this election, and their views on the treaty with the United States.

This means that the events that followed the 2010 General Election, as provided for by the *Cabinet Manual*, would be likely to be repeated. The political parties would hold negotiations to determine which political parties would be willing to work with each other and to what extent. The options include a full coalition between two or possibly three parties or either the Labour Party or Conservatives could attempt to govern on their own, but with confidence and supply agreements from other parties to ensure that they had the confidence of the House of Commons.

If the Conservatives reached an agreement, and were able to form a government, then no new appointment of a Prime Minister would be needed. The existing Prime Minister would continue in office. However, if Labour formed a government, then once this was clearly going to be the case, the Conservative Prime Minister would tender their resignation to the Queen, who would then appoint the Leader of the Labour Party to be next Prime Minister and form a new government. As can be seen, there is little scope for the Queen to exercise her own personal judgment.

6.10 The Fixed-term Parliaments Act 2011

To understand the effect of the Fixed-term Parliaments Act 2011, it is necessary to understand the situation before the 2011 Act was passed.

6.10.1 Before the Fixed-term Parliaments Act 2011

It used to be the case that the other significant personal prerogative power of the monarch was the power to dissolve Parliament and trigger a general election. Under the Parliament Act 1911, the maximum life of a Parliament was five years.[169] However, this was subject to the monarch's power to dissolve Parliament at any point up until the expiry of the five-year period. This enormous power of the monarch was by constitutional convention exercised on the advice of the Prime Minister. Consequently, it was common in the media to hear speculation as to when the Prime Minister would 'call' an early general election.

Inevitably, Prime Ministers would exercise this power at a time most likely to be of benefit to them politically, when they were likely to continue to have a majority after the election. For this reason, it was common for Parliaments to last for four rather than

---

[169] Parliament Act 1911, s 7, now repealed by the Fixed-term Parliaments Act 2011.

the full five years.[170] The other situation when an early general election would have been held is when the Prime Minister lost a vote of no confidence in the House of Commons. This could have been on a specific confidence motion or on a vote considered to be matter of confidence such as the Queen's Speech or Budget.[171] Occasionally Prime Ministers would announce that a vote was of such seriousness that if the government lost it they would either call a general election or tender their resignation to the Queen.[172] The government last lost a specific vote of no confidence in 1979, after which the Prime Minister James Callaghan requested that the Queen dissolve Parliament and trigger a general election.[173]

One issue with this prerogative power was whether the monarch was always required to grant the request of a Prime Minister. In general, the monarch was 'obliged to act upon the advice and direction of the Prime Minister in all questions of dissolution, except where that advice is manifestly unconstitutional and in breach of convention'.[174] Although much would depend on the circumstances at the time, an example of manifestly unconstitutional advice would be if a Prime Minister had lost their majority at an election, clung on to office, and, after losing a vote of no confidence, requested a second general election.[175] In such extreme circumstances, the Queen would have been bound to reject such advice and dismiss the Prime Minister from office. The Queen would then appoint the Leader of the Opposition to form a government.

The situation could have been more complicated in a hung Parliament. Although the presumption would be that the Prime Minister would be able to call an election when they desired, relevant factors would include how recently the previous general election has been and how the minority government arose. For example, if a Prime Minister had lost their majority but remained in office they may not have been able to request a dissolution straight after the previous election.[176] Beyond this, it was difficult to envisage all the circumstances when the monarch could have refused the request of a Prime Minister to dissolve Parliament.

6.10.2 The operation of the 2011 Act

The old rules under the prerogative form the background for the Fixed-term Parliaments Act 2011, which radically reformed this area of the constitution by abolishing the prerogative power to dissolve Parliament. While many proposals for fixed-term Parliaments had been made, persuading a Prime Minister to surrender this power was always going to be unlikely. The situation changed after the 2010 General Election. The agreement

---

[170] Indeed, it was Prime Ministers leading troubled governments that usually lasted for the full five years, knowing that their electoral prospects looked bleak. This occurred with John Major in 1997 and Gordon Brown in 2010. Both lost in the elections that followed.

[171] More accurately, the vote on the Queen's Speech would be a vote on an amendment to the Queen's Speech, with the amendment expressing that this House has no confidence in Her Majesty's Government.

[172] Philip Norton, 'The Fixed-term Parliaments Act and Votes of Confidence' (2016) *Parliamentary Affairs* 3.

[173] HC Deb, 28 March 1979, vol 965, cols 461–590.

[174] Robert Blackburn, 'The Monarchy and the Personal Prerogatives' [2004] *Public Law* 546, 556.

[175] Ibid 557.

[176] AW Bradley, KD Ewing, and CJS Knight, *Constitutional and Administrative Law* (16th edn, Pearson 2015) 246.

between the Conservatives and Liberal Democrats to form a coalition was founded upon a commitment that this Parliament should last the full five-year term. This was a purely political agreement, ensuring that neither party could withdraw from the coalition before the end of the Parliament, potentially bringing the government down when it suited their own political interests.[177]

Five-year fixed terms

The result of this commitment is the Fixed-term Parliaments Act 2011. This provides for fixed terms, by first providing that the next general election would (and did) take place on Thursday 7 May 2015.[178] The default position is that future general elections will take 'place on the first Thursday in May in the fifth calendar year following' the date of the previous election.[179] This meant that the date of the next general election was due to be 7 May 2020, yet as will be seen below, two general elections have been held before that date.

Votes of no confidence

An early election will be held under the 2011 Act if the government loses the confidence of the Commons and a specific series of events take place.

- First, the government loses a confidence motion in the House of Commons in the form required by the 2011 Act, stating 'that this House has no confidence in Her Majesty's Government'.[180]
- The second stage is that fourteen days have elapsed without the House of Commons passing a motion 'that this House has confidence in Her Majesty's Government'.[181] If this motion is not passed within the fourteen days, then an early general election will take place on a date set by the Prime Minister.[182] Parliament will be dissolved twenty-five working days before that date.[183]

Although not expressly stated in the Act, the implication is that within those fourteen days, the political parties should negotiate and attempt to form a government that has the necessary support to pass the second motion.[184] For example, a government that narrowly lost the first motion may attempt to come to an agreement with a smaller party to allow the second motion to be passed, so remaining in government and avoiding an early general election.

One unanswered question is when: does the Prime Minister who has lost the confidence of the House come under a duty to resign? Before the 2011 Act, if they lost a motion of no confidence, the Prime Minister could either seek a dissolution and hold a general election or resign. Now, under the 2011 Act, is a Prime Minister entitled to wait throughout the fourteen-day period and force a general election? The Public Administration and Constitutional Affairs Select Committee has taken the view that the Prime Minister should

---

[177] Rodney Brazier, 'A Small Piece of Constitutional History' (2012) *Law Quarterly Review* 315.
[178] Fixed-term Parliaments Act 2011, s 1(2).
[179] Ibid, s 1(3). But under s 1(4) if an early election is held before the first Thursday in May, then the next election will take place in the first Thursday in May in the *fourth* calendar year following the previous election.
[180] Fixed-term Parliaments Act 2011, s 2(3)(a), (4).
[181] Ibid s 2(3)(b), (5).   [182] Ibid, s 2(7)   [183] Ibid, s 3(1).
[184] Cabinet Office, *The Cabinet Manual* (1st edn, Cabinet Office 2011), para 2.20.

resign when an alternative government that is likely to have the confidence of the House has emerged, otherwise they remain in office.[185] This does have the advantage of carrying over the broad approach of what happens following an election that has returned a hung Parliament, as in 2010 when Gordon Brown remained Prime Minister until it was clear that the Conservatives and the Liberal Democrats were going to work together.

To date, only the motion of no confidence tabled in January 2019 has complied with the wording required by the Act and been voted on. This motion was defeated, and so the second stage of the process and the question of what happens during the fourteen-day period did not arise.

An early election if 66 per cent of MPs vote in favour

The other method to hold an early general election is when 66 per cent of MPs vote in favour of the motion 'That there shall be an early parliamentary general election'.[186] The 66 per cent threshold is calculated on the basis of the number of seats, which means that with 650 seats in the House of Commons, at least 434 MPs need to vote in favour.

It was this method that Theresa May used to hold the (surprise) 2017 General Election. On 18 April 2017, Theresa May announced her intention to seek an early general election, with the House of Commons voting on the motion the following day, which was approved by 522 votes to 13.[187] Exercising the power granted to the Prime Minister in the Act, May set the date of the general election as 8 June 2017, with Parliament dissolved on 3 May, twenty-five working days before the election.[188]

Ostensibly, May's reasons for seeking an early election were based on seeking a mandate from the electorate for her approach towards Brexit.[189] However, politically, the fact that the Conservatives had a very large lead in the opinion polls and the opportunity for May to secure a large majority (having become Prime Minister following David Cameron's resignation) and obtain her own personal mandate were presumably important factors in her decision to hold an election. However, the 2017 General Election did not go as planned for May, and instead of increasing her majority, she ended up losing it.

On taking over from Theresa May, Boris Johnson sought to hold an election by tabling a motion for an early general election under the 2011 Act three times, on 4 September, 9 September, and 28 October. On each occasion, the 66 per cent threshold (434 seats) was not met, with many MPs simply abstaining.[190] The concern of some MPs was that Johnson would exercise the power granted to him under the 2011 Act to set the date of the early election to after 31 October 2019—the date when the UK was due to leave the EU—meaning that Parliament would have been powerless to have prevented the UK leaving the EU without an agreement.

---

[185] Public Administration and Constitutional Affairs Committee, *The Role of Parliament in the UK Constitution Interim Report – The Status and Effect of Confidence Motions and the Fixed-term Parliaments Act 2011* (HC 2017–19, 1813) para 35.

[186] Ibid s 2(1)–(2).

[187] HC Deb, 19 April 2017, vol 624, cols 681–712.

[188] Fixed-term Parliaments Act 2011, ss 2(7), 3(1).

[189] BBC News, 'Theresa May's general election statement in full' (BBC News, 18 April 2017), http://www.bbc.co.uk/news/uk-politics-39630009.

[190] The results of the three votes were as follows: 4 September, 298 votes to 56 in favour of an early election; 9 September, 293 votes to 46 in favour; 28 October, 299 votes to 70 in favour. HC Debs, 4 September 2019, vol 664, cols 291–315; 9 September, vol 664, cols 616–39; 28 October 2019, vol 667, cols 54–79.

6.10.3 Early Parliamentary General Election Act 2019

The third vote took place after the UK had secured an extension to the Article 50 period to 31 January 2020. However, the Commons had rejected the government's expedited timetable to enact the European Union (Withdrawal Agreement) Bill, which needed to be enacted in order for the government to ratify the agreement the UK has reached with the EU and leave the EU on 31 January 2020. Although there was time for a longer timetable for the bill, the government was concerned that opposition to the timetable was an indication of opposition to the bill itself. Consequently, the government sought an election for a third time; when this was rejected, Johnson stated that 'we will not allow the paralysis to continue, and one way or another we must proceed straight to an election'.[191]

The way ahead was to introduce another bill into Parliament, the Early Parliamentary General Election Bill, which set the date of the general election to 12 December 2019. This reflects parliamentary sovereignty, as the Parliament of 2019 cannot be bound by the Parliament of 2011, as only a simple majority of the votes, and not 66 per cent of seats, is needed for the bill to become law and change the operation of the 2011 Act. The Liberal Democrats and the SNP had indicated that they would support a general election, making it likely that a simple majority of MPs would support the bill. Labour then switched position to support the bill and a general election, after previously insisting that Brexit needed to be resolved before any election was held. The bill was approved at third reading, its final stage in the Commons, by 438 votes to twenty, and was approved by the House of Lords the following day.[192]

The Early Parliamentary General Election Act 2019 set the date for the election by effectively creating a legal fiction. For the purposes of the Act, 12 December is deemed to be the date set by the Prime Minister under s 2(7) of the 2011 Act as if an early election has been triggered by the 2011 Act. The 2011 Act has not been amended and continues to operate as before. This means that Parliament was dissolved, as required by the 2011 Act, twenty-five working days before 12 December on 6 November. Similarly, under the Act, the next election is due to be held under the terms of the 2011 Act on the first Thursday in May, in the fifth calendar year following the previous election, setting the date to Thursday 2 May 2024.[193]

 Counterpoint: What is the point of the Fixed-term Parliaments Act 2011?

The Early Parliamentary General Election Act 2019 points to a fundamental weakness of the 2011 Act. As shown by the 2019 Act, its provisions, including the requirement that an early general election can only be held if the 66 per cent threshold is met, can be overridden by another Act of Parliament passed by a simple majority of both Houses. This means that a majority government

→

---

[191] HC Deb, 28 October 2019, vol 667, col 79.

[192] Ironically, the 438 votes exceeded the 66 per cent threshold (434 votes) required to hold an election under the 2011 Act.

[193] Fixed-term Parliaments Act 2011, s 1(3).

could effectively decide to call an election whenever it wished, knowing that its MPs would vote in favour of any legislation setting the date of the next election. Indeed, as eventually took place in 2019, the opposition parties may find that politically they would have to support the legislation. To do otherwise suggests that they are not willing to put their policies and ideas to the electorate.

Despite this flaw, there may still be a principled argument for the 2011 Act. The previous rules, as described in this chapter, were part of the royal prerogative and the decision to dissolve Parliament and hold an election was made by the monarch on the advice of the Prime Minister. Effectively, the executive is deciding when elections to the legislature take place. The principle the 2011 Act advances is that the House of Commons, the elected part of the legislature, is responsible for when elections are held. This better reflects the separation of powers.

Potentially, these two points could be combined and amend the Fixed-term Parliaments Act 2011, so that an early election is called when a majority of MPs vote in favour of one. This would reflect the reality that if there is a majority in the House of Commons for an election, that majority can override the 66 per cent requirement, while ensuring that at least in principle, the decision is made by Parliament and not the executive.

In any event, reform appears highly likely in the near future. At the 2019 General Election, both the Conservative and Labour parties pledged to repeal the 2011 Act.[194] However, neither party gave any indication as to what would replace it, or whether an attempt will be made to restore the pre-2011 Act position.[195]

Discussing the problem

Consider the result from the 2022 General Election shown in the problem scenario. What effect would the Fixed-term Parliaments Act 2011 have on the House of Commons?

On the face of it, the Fixed-term Parliaments Act 2011 would indicate that the next general election would take place in May 2027. However, any government that emerges from the 2022 General Election is unlikely to be stable as Labour or the Conservatives will, one way or another, be reliant on the support of other political parties in order to have the confidence of the House of Commons.

It is also likely that the demands of government would place any agreement reached by the political parties under pressure. They could become divided over particular policies and the Conservatives may struggle to keep several parties in agreement with government policy. If any of

→

---

[194] Conservative Party, *Get Brexit Done – Unleash Britain's Potential* (Conservative and Unionist Party, 2019) 48. The Labour Party, *It's Time for Real Change – The Labour Party Manifesto 2019* (Labour Party, 2019) 82.

[195] Robert Craig, 'Restoring Confidence: Replacing the Fixed-term Parliaments Act 2011' (2018) 81(3) *Modern Law Review* 480. Even if it is not repealed, a review of the 2011 Act is required to be held between June and November 2020, with the review able to make recommendations as to the repeal or amendment of the Act, Fixed-term Parliaments Act 2011, s 4(4)–(6).

→

the smaller parties withdrew their support for the government, it would then be in a minority and at any time could lose a vote of no confidence as provided for in section 2(4) of the 2011 Act.

If the government did lose a vote of no confidence then, according to the *Cabinet Manual*, the political parties would then have fourteen days during which they could see whether a new government could be formed. The assumption made by the 2011 Act is that if a new government is formed within the fourteen days with different political parties then, when this became clear, the existing Prime Minister would resign and a new Prime Minister would be appointed. The House of Commons would then pass a motion that it now had confidence in the government under section 2(5). For example, if a Conservative government lost the no confidence motion and the Labour Party formed an agreement with the Liberal Democrats and the SNP, it would now have a majority and the confidence of the House of Commons. Once this was clear, the leader of the Labour Party would be appointed as the new Prime Minister.

The effect of this is that there would be a change of government without a general election being held. This would be hugely controversial and would raise serious questions about the legitimacy of the new government.

This conclusion could be avoided if the process that triggered the 2017 General Election was used when 66 per cent of MPs voted for an early general election under section 2(1) of the Act. Alternatively, if a simple majority of MPs agree that an election is necessary, they could pass legislation similar to the Early Parliamentary General Election Act 2019, which set the date of the 2019 General Election. This would enable the electorate, rather than the politicians, to decide who should form the next government. Whether this would happen instead of the no confidence procedure outlined earlier in this section would very much depend on the politics at the time.

6.11 Reforming or abolishing the prerogative?

A key theme of this chapter is that the relationship between the prerogative and the legislature is a complex. The exercise of prerogative powers is subject to a range of statutory or conventional restrictions. However, some are concerned that the history of the prerogative, and the transfer of the exercise of most prerogative powers from the monarch to ministers, has effectively granted considerable power to the government without any systematic oversight by Parliament.[196]

Although this chapter has discussed examples of how statute and constitutional conventions require that Parliament is involved in the exercise of certain prerogative powers in the opinion of some, these restrictions or checks are too limited. The House of Commons Public Administration Select Committee expressed concern that the exercise of some prerogative powers, including the ability to grant and remove passports, may have profound consequences for the individuals concerned, but there is no formal role for Parliament to scrutinize these decisions.[197] Similarly, significant political powers such as the government appointments for major public offices are not subject to any systematic

---

[196] House of Commons Public Administration Select Committee, *Taming the Prerogative: Strengthening Ministerial Accountability* (HC 422, 2003–04).
[197] Ibid para 32.

control. The Committee concluded that to reform the prerogatives would enhance the effectiveness of Parliament and would reflect the importance of both the rule of law and parliamentary supremacy.[198]

In its response to the report, the government suggested that these concerns were misplaced, emphasizing that the powers are subject to judicial review and the Human Rights Act.[199] The government also felt that the actions of ministers under both the prerogative or statute are adequately scrutinized by Parliament, as ministers are accountable to Parliament through questions and appearing before select committees. As Pollard, Parpworth, and Hughes state: '*political* accountability was considered to be sufficient without any further legal control'.[200] The government did accept that there may occasionally be the case for individual prerogative powers to be subject to greater control.[201]

 Pause for reflection

Clearly, the Public Administration Committee and the government held contrasting views about the desirability of greater control over the royal prerogative. Which view do you prefer?

As we have seen in this chapter, since the Public Administration Committee published its report, some powers under the royal prerogative have been:

- abolished (such as the power to dissolve Parliament);
- made subject to greater statutory control (the ratification of treaties); or
- made subject to new constitutional conventions (the deployment of the armed forces abroad).

Alongside these developments, the constitution has undergone many significant reforms, and it is perhaps surprising that apart from these specific prerogative powers, the fundamental issue of oversight of the royal prerogative in general remains relatively untouched.

When in opposition, Jack Straw, who later became a Cabinet minister throughout Labour's period in power from 1997–2010, stated that 'where power is based not upon statute but upon the royal prerogative it is accountability that suffers' and that the royal prerogative is used 'as a smoke-screen by ministers to obfuscate the use of power for which they are insufficiently accountable'.[202]

The basic issue that prerogative powers do not derive from Parliament but from the Crown, and that Parliament does not necessarily have the opportunity to scrutinize the

[198] Ibid paras 44–5.

[199] Department for Constitutional Affairs, 'Government Response to the Public Administration Select Committee's Fourth Report of the 2003–4 Session', July 2004, http://webarchive.nationalarchives.gov.uk/+/http://www.dca.gov.uk/pubs/reports/prerogative.htm.

[200] David Pollard, Neil Parpworth, and David Hughes, *Constitutional and Administrative Law Text with Materials* (4th edn, OUP 2007) 114.

[201] Department for Constitutional Affairs, 'Government Response to the Public Administration Select Committee's Fourth Report of the 2003–4 Session', July 2004, http://webarchive.nationalarchives.gov.uk/+/http://www.dca.gov.uk/pubs/reports/prerogative.htm.

[202] Jack Straw, 'Abolish the Royal Prerogative' in Anthony Barnett (ed), *Power and the Throne: The Monarchy Debate* (Vintage 1994) 125, 126.

exercise of those powers, remains. This is the core of the principled argument based on the separation of powers and the rule that all powers of the government should derive from Parliament, where the House of Commons is elected, rather than having power derived from the Crown largely for historical reasons.

As the House of Commons Public Administration Select Committee outlines, there are two ways to reform the prerogative. The entire prerogative could be abolished and placed on a statutory basis, or the current approach of individual prerogative powers being replaced by statute on a case-by-case basis could be continued. As Mark Fisher MP stated:

> the Government ought to make clear and there ought to be a list of what the prerogative powers that presently exist are, and only then can one go on to look at both principles and the distinction between necessary and desirable powers and those that are totally unnecessary for the conduct of government, and then possibly proceed to thinking about a Prerogative Powers Act.[203]

The government did express some sympathy with this view in *The Governance of Britain*, a policy paper suggesting a series of possible constitutional reforms.[204] The difficulty with this approach is that no complete list of prerogative powers has ever been created and, as discussed in 6.2.2, such a task is almost impossible, given how vague the prerogative is as a concept. A further difficulty with wholesale reform of the prerogative is that any legislation is likely to be complex given the range of powers involved. Also, such a task is unlikely to be a priority for any government, which will usually have other more immediate political objectives to pursue. This point is furthered when several prerogative powers are minor or of little practical use to modern government. In addition, for the foreseeable future both government and Parliament are preoccupied with Brexit, making other, perhaps less urgent, constitutional reforms increasingly unlikely.

All of these reasons suggest that the current approach is likely to continue for the foreseeable future. Lord Hurd gave the example of placing the intelligence services (MI5, MI6, and GCHQ, which were created under the royal prerogative) on a statutory basis stating:

> every now and then a reform, a change, becomes clearly necessary . . . two Acts of Parliament which put under statutory power or identity the three intelligence services: The Security Services Act 1989 and the Intelligence Services Act 1994. There were, if anyone is interested, very practical, cogent reasons which persuaded even the Prime Ministers of the day, and certainly the heads of the services, that this was a good and necessary move.[205]

Given the developments described in this chapter, it appears that this *ad hoc* approach to reforming the royal prerogative will continue.

---

[203] House of Commons Public Administration Select Committee, *Taming the Prerogative: Strengthening Ministerial Accountability* (HC 2003–04, 422) para 47.

[204] HM Government, *The Governance of Britain* (Cm 7170, 2007).

[205] House of Commons Public Administration Select Committee, *Taming the Prerogative: Strengthening Ministerial Accountability* (HC 2003–04, 422) para 39.

6.12 **The broader constitutional role of the monarch**

The Queen, as the monarch, in addition to her constitutional role in relation to the royal prerogative, holds many other important constitutional positions. These include holding the positions of the Supreme Governor of the Church of England and Head of the Commonwealth, and as well as being the Head of State of the UK, the Queen is also the Head of State of fifteen other nations, including Canada, Australia, and New Zealand.

6.12.1 **Head of State and Head of Nation**

There are also other aspects to her role. The official British Monarchy website states that in addition to her formal role as Head of State, the

> Monarch has a less formal role as 'Head of Nation'. The Sovereign acts as a focus for national identity, unity and pride; gives a sense of stability and continuity; officially recognises success and excellence; and supports the ideal of voluntary service.[206]

The combination of these elements of her role means that on a day-to-day basis the formal constitutional role of the monarch requires that she spends several hours each day signing state papers granting legal effect to decisions made elsewhere, receiving ambassadors from abroad, holding investitures to formally grant honours to recipients, holding audiences with the Prime Minister, and attending meetings of the Privy Council. The role of Head of State requires visiting other countries on state visits and hosting state visits from other Heads of State.[207] The informal role, described in the quotation as 'Head of Nation' requires the monarch to 'be seen to be believed' and to attend functions or engagements across the country, such as visiting charitable causes or public institutions including universities, hospitals, and schools. In this role, the Queen is supported by other members of the Royal Family.

6.12.2 **The line of succession and regency**

As the Queen is now in her nineties and continues her record-breaking reign as the longest-ever serving monarch, questions regarding the future are inevitably raised. The Queen has indicated that she is extremely unlikely to abdicate and vacate the throne in favour of Prince Charles.[208] Yet legally, Acts requiring the approval of the monarch cannot simply be fulfilled by other members of the Royal Family. Should the situation occur where the monarch cannot fulfil their constitutional functions due to illness, then to prevent legal and constitutional difficulties, an alternative to abdication could be a regency declared under the Regency Acts 1937 to 1953. A regent would exercise all the powers of a monarch other than being able to give assent to legislation which changes the line

---

[206] The British Monarchy, 'The Role of the Monarchy', https://www.royal.uk/role-monarchy.

[207] Although given the Queen's age, she now travels abroad far less frequently than she used to; instead other members of the Royal Family, including Prince Charles and Prince William, represent the Queen abroad on visits to other countries.

[208] On her twenty-first birthday, in 1947, the Queen (then Princess Elizabeth) declared in an address to the Commonwealth that 'I declare before you all that my whole life whether it be long or short shall be devoted to your service'.

of succession to the throne or a bill that made changes to the position of the Church of Scotland.[209] Under section 2, one ground for declaring a regency is if the monarch 'is by reason of infirmity of mind or body incapable for the time being of performing the royal functions'. The Regent would be the next in line to the throne as long as they are over the age of eighteen. Should the situation be less serious, then under section 4, some functions of the monarch could be transferred to Counsellors of State, which may include the next four in line to the throne, and the spouse of the monarch.[210]

Informally, the Queen is passing an ever-greater share of her more ceremonial duties to other members of the Royal Family, particularly to Prince Charles. This in turn increases the scrutiny he faces. While the Queen has strived never to say in public anything controversial for fear that this may compromise her political neutrality and ability to act as source of national unity and pride, some argue that the same cannot be said about Prince Charles. As shown by *Evans v Information Commissioner* and the following disclosure of exchanges of letters between the Prince and government ministers, he has actively raised issues with ministers.[211] When this is combined with his public statements about genetically modified crops, architecture, and the environment,[212] and decisions including not to attend a state banquet held for the President in China (which was viewed as a statement about China's treatment of Tibet), the impression is one of a more politically active prince.[213] In 2018, Prince Charles stated that when King, he will operate within 'the constitutional parameters' that limit that role, indicating that he accepts the need for the monarch to be politically impartial.[214] Despite this, some continue to question whether the Crown should 'skip' a generation and pass to Prince William.

Yet, the legal and constitutional position on this is clear. When Parliament invited William and Mary to take the throne in 1689 (at the conclusion of the constitutional disputes of the seventeenth century discussed in 4.3) this confirmed that Parliament controlled the line of succession to the Crown. The law regulating line of succession of the Crown is contained in the Act of Settlement 1700, which states that the Crown shall 'remain and continue to the said most excellent Princess Sophia [the granddaughter of James I] and the heirs of her body being protestant'. The essential point is that the line of succession is regulated by statute and on the death of the monarch the immediate heir instantly accedes to the throne.

---

[209] Regency Acts 1937 to 1953, s 4(2).

[210] For a discussion of potential problems that may be caused by the decisions (for very different reasons) of Prince Andrew and Prince Harry to step back from carrying out royal duties, at least for the foreseeable future, see Craig Prescott, 'Harry and Meghan, Regency, Counsellors of State and a "Slimmed Down" Royal Family' (UK Constitutional Law Association Blog, 21 January 2020) available at https://ukconstitutionallaw.org/2020/01/21/craig-prescott-harry-and-meghan-regency-counsellors-of-state-and-a-slimmed-down-royal-family/

[211] [2012] UKUT 313 (AAC); the letters and their responses from ministers are available at Cabinet Office, 'Prince of Wales Correspondence with Government Departments' (Cabinet Office, 13 May 2015), https://www.gov.uk/government/collections/prince-of-wales-correspondence-with-government-departments.

[212] For example, in 2015, Prince Charles addressed the opening session of the UN Conference on Climate Change, urging delegates 'to think of your grandchildren' and saying we 'risk the tipping point of failure of catastrophe' unless action is taken. The Prince of Wales, 'A speech by HRH The Prince of Wales at the COP21 Opening Session, Paris' (30 November 2015), https://www.princeofwales.gov.uk/media/speeches/speech-hrh-the-prince-of-wales-the-cop21-opening-session-paris.

[213] This is also discussed in detail in Catherine Mayer, *Charles: The Heart of a King* (WH Allen 2015).

[214] BBC One, *Prince, Son and Heir: Charles at 70* (BBC, 8 November 2018), https://www.bbc.co.uk/programmes/p06r4v3k.

6.12.3 **The Succession to the Crown Act 2013**

The Succession to the Crown Act 2013 has modernized the line of succession to the throne.[215] Most notably, it removed the rule of primogeniture, the rule giving males preference over females in the line of succession for those born after 28 October 2011.[216] Such a change has been discussed for many years, the initiative to act came from fears that if the first-born child of Prince William and the Duchess of Cambridge was female, and a second child was male, it would be the second child that would eventually take the Crown. In the event, Prince George was born before Princess Charlotte, meaning the issue did not arise. However, due to the Act, Princess Charlotte is ahead of her younger brother Prince Louis in the line of succession.

The 2013 Act also repealed the Royal Marriages Act 1772, which, subject to certain exceptions, required those in the line of succession, no matter how distant, to seek the consent of the monarch in order to marry, otherwise their marriage was void. Now under the 2013 Act, only the first six in the line of succession require the consent of the monarch. If they marry without the monarch's consent, then instead of the marriage being void, they (and their descendants) lose their place in the line of succession.[217] This provision was first used when Prince Harry, then fifth in line of succession, sought consent to marry Meghan Markle.[218]

Finally, the 2013 Act removed the disqualification of those who married Catholics from the line of succession.[219] As this was clearly discriminatory against Catholics (those who married those of other faiths were not affected), this rule was increasingly hard to justify. However, given the monarch's position as Supreme Governor of the Church of England, the requirement that the monarch is a protestant in communion with the Church of England remains.

6.13 **Summary**

This chapter has explored the historical, legal, and political nature of the Crown and the royal prerogative. The historic nature of the Crown explains why the law has not developed a clear idea of 'the state'; instead central government is organized around the concept of the Crown. The battle for the balance of power between the Crown and Parliament during the seventeenth century showed how Parliament became supreme over the Crown and curtailed the powers of the prerogative. As *R (Miller) v Prime Minister* shows, the balance between Crown and Parliament continues to change.

Yet the scope of the royal prerogative remains significant and in recent decades the ability to scrutinize the exercise of these prerogative powers has been questioned both in Parliament and in the courts. However, it remains the case that despite significant reforms

---

[215] The only other change since 1700 was when Edward VIII abdicated by signing His Majesty's Declaration of Abdication Act 1936, in favour of his younger brother George VI. The effect of this was that George VI's children were then next in line to the throne, meaning that Princess Elizabeth, the present Queen, became monarch on her father's death in 1952.

[216] Succession to the Crown Act 2013, s 1.   [217] Ibid s 3.

[218] By contrast, due to the 2013 Act, Princess Eugenie did not require the consent of the Queen for her marriage Jack Brooksbank, as on her wedding day, she was ninth in the line of succession.

[219] Succession to the Crown Act 2013, s 2.

elsewhere in the constitution, the fundamentals of the royal prerogative remain largely unchanged. Some individual prerogative powers such as the ratification of treaties and deployment of the armed forces abroad have been made subject to greater parliamentary scrutiny. There is some demand for comprehensive reform of the royal prerogative, but it seems that in the near future, further piecemeal reform focused on individual powers is more likely.

As regards the prerogative powers personally exercised by the monarch, the Royal Assent to legislation has long lost any substance, the Fixed-term Parliaments Act 2011 has abolished the role of the monarch in dissolving Parliament and any doubt about the role of the monarch when appointing a Prime Minister has been significantly reduced by the exposition of the relevant constitutional conventions in the *Cabinet Manual*. In terms of the ceremonial role of the monarch, the Queen is gradually handing over greater responsibilities to other members of the royal family, particularly the next in line to the throne, in an attempt to ensure that the monarchy continues to deliver its key symbolic and constitutional function: stability.

Quick test questions

1. While power lies with the Crown, who is responsible for exercising that power? Is it the Queen or ministers?

2. Writing in 1908, Maitland once observed that identifying the royal prerogative is 'set about with difficulties, with prerogatives disused, with prerogatives of doubtful existence, with prerogatives which exist by sufferance, merely because no one has thought it worthwhile to abolish them' (FW Maitland, *Constitutional History of Britain* (CUP 1908) 421).

    To what extent does this still apply today?

3. How is the exercise of the royal prerogative subject to control by:

    (a) the courts;

    (b) Parliament?

4. To what extent does the *Cabinet Manual* provide clear rules that regulate the appointment of the Prime Minister?

5. To what extent did the majority judgment in *R (Miller) v Secretary of State for Exiting the European Union* depart from established principles when deciding that the government did not have the power under the royal prerogative to invoke Article 50 TEU?

6. 'This is unfinished constitutional business. The prerogative has allowed powers to move from Monarch to Ministers without Parliament having a say on how they exercised. This should no longer be the acceptable to Parliament or the people. It is now time for this unfinished business to be completed.'[220]

    Do you agree with this statement?

[220] House of Commons Public Administration Select Committee, *Taming the Prerogative: Strengthening Ministerial Accountability to Parliament* (HC 422, 2003–04) para 61.

Further reading

The royal prerogative in general

Mark Elliott and Amanda Perreau-Saussin, 'Pyrrhic Public Law: Bancoult and the Sources, Status and Content of Common Law Limitations on Prerogative Power' [2009] *Public Law* 697

BV Harris, 'Judicial Review, Justiciability and the Prerogative of Mercy' (2003) 62(3) *Cambridge Law Journal* 631

*House of Commons Public Administration Select Committee, *Taming the Prerogative: Strengthening Ministerial Accountability* (HC 422, 2003–04)

Deploying the armed forces overseas

Veronika Fikfak and Hayley Hooper, 'Whither the War Powers Convention? What Next for Parliamentary Control of Armed Conflict after Syria?' (UK Constitutional Law Association Blog, 20 April 2018), available at https://ukconstitutionallaw.org/2018/04/20/veronika-fikfak-and-hayley-j-hooper-whither-the-war-powers-convention-what-next-for-parliamentary-control-of-armed-conflict-after-syria/

Gavin Phillipson, '"Historic" Commons' Syria Vote: The Constitutional Significance (Part I)' (UK Constitutional Law Association Blog, 19 September 2013), available at http://ukconstitutionallaw.org/2013/09/19/gavin-phillipson-historic-commons-syria-vote-the-constitutional-significance-part-i/

Public Administration and Constitutional Affairs Committee, *The Role of Parliament in the UK Constitution: Authorising the Use of Military Force* (HC 2017–19, 1891)

R (Miller) v Secretary of State for Exiting the European Union

Paul Craig, 'Miller, Structural Constitutional Review and the Limits of Prerogative Power' [2017] (Brexit Special Extra Issue) *Public Law* 48

Keith Ewing, 'Brexit and Parliamentary Sovereignty' (2017) 80(4) *Modern Law Review* 685

*James Grant, 'Prerogative, Parliament and Creative Constitutional Adjudication: Reflections on Miller' (2017) 28(1) *King's Law Journal* 35

Gavin Phillipson, 'A Dive Deep into Constitutional Waters: Article 50, the Prerogative and Parliament' (2016) 79 *Modern Law Review* 1064

R (Miller) v Prime Minister and prorogation

Nick Barber, 'Prorogation, Prerogative and the Supreme Court' (Harvard Law Review Blog, 3 October 2019), available at https://blog.harvardlawreview.org/prorogation-prerogative-and-the-supreme-court/

Tanzil Chowdhury, '*Miller (No 2)*, the Principle-isation of Ministerial Accountability and Military Deployments' (UK Constitutional Law Association Blog, 24 October 2019), available at https://ukconstitutionallaw.org/2019/10/24/tanzil-chowdhury-miller-no-2-the-principle-isation-of-ministerial-accountability-and-military-deployments/

Anne Twomey, 'How to decide whether prorogation was exercised for an improper purpose' (LSE British Politics and Policy Blog, 22 September 2019), available at https://blogs.lse.ac.uk/politicsandpolicy/prorogation-improper-purpose/

Fixed-term Parliaments Act 2011 and appointment of the Prime Minister

Robert Blackburn, 'The 2010 General Election Outcome and Formation of the Conservative–Liberal Democrat Coalition Government' [2011] *Public Law* 30

Andrew Blick, 'Constitutional Implications of the Fixed-Term Parliaments Act 2011 (2016) 69(1) *Parliamentary Affairs* 19

Cabinet Office, *Cabinet Manual* (1st edn, 2011) Ch 2, available at https://assets.publishing.service.gov.uk/government/uploads/system/uploads/attachment_data/file/60641/cabinet-manual.pdf

*Robert Craig, 'Restoring Confidence: Replacing the Fixed-term Parliaments Act 2011' (2018) 81(3) *Modern Law Review* 480

*Philip Norton, 'The Fixed-term Parliaments Act and Votes of Confidence' (2016) 69(1) *Parliamentary Affairs* 3

*Public Administration and Constitutional Affairs Committee, *The Role of Parliament in the UK Constitution Interim Report – The Status and Effect of Confidence Motions and the Fixed-term Parliaments Act 2011* (HC 2017–19, 1813)

Royal Assent

*Rodney Brazier, 'Royal Assent to Legislation' (2013) 129(Apr) *Law Quarterly Review* 184

Mark Elliott, 'Can the Government veto legislation by advising the Queen to withhold royal assent' (Public Law for Everyone, 21 January 2019), available at https://publiclawforeveryone.com/2019/01/21/can-the-government-veto-legislation-by-advising-the-queen-to-withhold-royal-assent/

More generally on the monarchy

Walter Bagehot, *The English Constitution* (first published in 1867, OUP 2001)

Robert Blackburn, *King and Country: Monarchy and The Future King Charles III* (Politico's 2006)

Ben Pimlott, *The Queen: Elizabeth II and the Monarchy* (HarperCollins 2012, Diamond Jubilee edn)

Craig Prescott, 'Harry and Meghan, Regency, Counsellors of State and a "Slimmed Down" Royal Family' (UK Constitutional Law Association Blog, 21 January 2020), available at https://ukconstitutionallaw.org/2020/01/21/craig-prescott-harry-and-meghan-regency-counsellors-of-state-and-a-slimmed-down-royal-family/

 Visit this book's **online resources** for additional materials relating to this chapter, including a full analysis of the start-of-chapter problem scenario.
www.oup.com/he/stanton-prescott2e

7

Central government

Having been Prime Minister for the past two-and-half years, Patricia King has decided to re-shuffle her Cabinet. King has become increasingly frustrated with the performance of some Cabinet ministers, particularly her Chancellor, Neil Houlihan. However, Houlihan is very popular amongst his colleagues in the House of Commons, particularly those who are on the right 'wing' of the party, which supports low taxes whenever possible. There have been rumours that Houlihan is unhappy with the direction of the government and is considering mounting a bid for the leadership of the party. On reflection, the Prime Minister chooses to keep Houlihan as Chancellor for the time being and appoints a new Secretary of State for Education, Joshua Marsden.

The following events then occur:

- One of the policies Marsden introduces is a new IT system, which all schools would be required to use. While this would initially be very expensive, costing £5 billion, the intention is that in the long term this will save money, as a common system would be cheaper for each school. However, the costs of the project have increased to £7.5 billion, an increase of 50 per cent. The civil servant in charge of the project is aware of this, but he has not told the Secretary of State. When Marsden discovers this, he is furious with his officials. The Prime Minister has unilaterally decided to cancel the entire project to prevent it becoming a further embarrassment to the government.

- The Prime Minister has become very concerned with housing, believing that high house prices are destabilizing the economy. She is considering increasing the top rate of income tax to 55 per cent. This would fund a new 'House Building and Infrastructure Fund', the aim of which would be to prevent house prices from spiralling out of control. The Chancellor, Neil Houlihan, profoundly disagrees. The Prime Minister and Chancellor argue over this policy in one of their regular meetings. Newspaper reports state that 'Prime Minister and Chancellor at loggerheads over tax and housing policy' and contain detailed information about the proposed policy. Several Conservative MPs are concerned about this policy and seek assurances from the Prime Minister that the story does not reflect government policy.

→

- Finally, a Sunday newspaper has just published photos of Olivia Hill, the Secretary of State for International Development, entering a hotel in London late on Wednesday night with a man who is not her husband. They were also photographed at a restaurant earlier that evening. The newspapers have identified this man as Charles Holloway, a convicted fraudster. Further stories are published in the newspapers the following week, indicating that Hill has been seeing Holloway for at least six months and alleges that they are having an affair. It also emerges that Holloway has recently been appointed a director of Compassionate Food, a charity that provides food to war-torn countries, especially in the Middle East. It has since emerged that the Department for International Development has just agreed to award Compassionate Food a grant of £1.5 million to support their activities.

7.1 Introduction

It may surprise many but written on the famous black door of Number 10 Downing Street is not 'Prime Minister' but 'First Lord of the Treasury'. This is because, historically, the most important minister advising the monarch in matters of government was the Lord High Treasurer, who was responsible for the Treasury and charged with collecting taxes on behalf of the monarch. Since the early seventeenth century, the position of Lord High Treasurer was placed in commission, meaning that the office was carried out by several appointed 'commissioners' who worked together. The most important of these was the First Lord of the Treasury, who became the leader of a small group of ministers who met to make the key decisions of government.

Robert Walpole, on becoming First Lord of the Treasury in 1721, increasingly became referred to as the 'Prime Minister'. This reflected the perception that he had become the principal adviser to the monarch, particularly after George II took to the throne in 1727.[1] During the nineteenth century, this group of ministers, led by the Prime Minister became known as the Cabinet, and the structure of central government gradually emerged into what is seen today. To this day, the Prime Minister also takes the position of First Lord of the Treasury.

Chapter 6 described how power shifted from the monarch to ministers whilst retaining the concept of the Crown, which was explained as referring to the monarch, ministers, and civil servants. This chapter explores how that power is now distributed within central government. At its most basic, the Prime Minister leads the Cabinet, which is composed of a group of ministers who each lead government departments staffed by civil servants.

In many ways, the structure of central government remains the archetypal area of the uncodified constitution. The present structure is the product of centuries of incremental development, with a heavy emphasis on practice and convention rather than law. This has developed in recent years to a proliferation of 'codes', statements of conventions, or practices which guide different aspects of government. These have become particularly

---

[1] FWR Maitland, *The Constitutional History of England* (CUP 1908) 395–6, 418.

important within central government and frequent reference will be made in this chapter to the *Ministerial Code*[2] and the *Cabinet Manual*.[3] These documents explain key features of central government, including the powers of the Prime Minister and the code of conduct that ministers are expected to maintain.[4]

This emphasis on non-legal rules has allowed the structure of central government to mould and meet the constantly changing political dynamics at the heart of government without the need for significant legal reform. Recent developments include the increasing importance of special advisers working with government ministers and the civil service, and the emergence of public bodies such as executive agencies and non-ministerial departments who fulfil functions of government in addition to traditional government departments.

It is also the case that this flexibility means that each Prime Minister can approach their role differently. Sometimes this is through choice, but sometimes this is due to the underlying political circumstances under which they hold office. This particularly affects how the Prime Minister interacts with their Cabinet.

This chapter aims to examine the structure and role of central government, with the later part of the chapter focusing on the key constitutional principle as expressed in *R (Miller) v Prime Minister* that Parliament is able to hold the government to account, which in turn reflects the democratic nature of the constitution.[5] Chapter 8, which considers the role of Parliament in detail, examines the different processes used to hold the government to account.

As indicated, the phrase 'central government' refers to the Prime Minister, Cabinet, ministers, government departments, and civil servants. Informally, these parts of central government are often referred to as 'Whitehall', reflecting how most government departments and the Prime Minister are based around that area of central London close to Westminster. A more constitutionally appropriate phrase is the 'executive'. However, this term can also be taken to mean other elements which include the governments of Scotland, Northern Ireland, and Wales, as well as local government and organizations such as the police. These are all discussed elsewhere,[6] leaving this chapter to focus on those aspects of the executive located at the centre of the national government of the UK.

The aims of the chapter are:

- to give an overview of the structure of central government;
- to outline the role and functions of the Prime Minister;
- to explain the nature of the Cabinet;
- to describe the role of ministers and the functions of government departments;
- to explain the role of the Civil Service and special advisers;
- to outline and give examples of how the government is held to account.

---

[2] Cabinet Office, *Ministerial Code* (August 2019).

[3] Cabinet Office, *The Cabinet Manual* (1st edn, Cabinet Office 2011) Introduction, para 13.

[4] For a discussion of the importance of codes in this area of the constitution, see Andrew Blick, *Codes of the Constitution* (Bloomsbury 2016).

[5] [2019] UKSC 41 [46]–[47].

[6] The governments of Scotland, Wales, and Northern Ireland are discussed in Chapter 9 and the police are discussed in Chapter 16.

7.2 **The Prime Minister**

As discussed in Chapter 6, government is carried on in the name of the Crown, with the role of the monarch being predominantly ceremonial. One of the most important powers the monarch exercises is the appointment of the Prime Minister, which she possesses in her capacity as Head of State. The Prime Minister, on appointment, is the head of the government and is responsible for the conduct of the government as a whole. The Prime Minister, like other ministers, is accountable to both Parliament and the public. Accountability to Parliament is facilitated by the convention that the Prime Minister must have a seat in the House of Commons.

As the introduction to this chapter described, the office of the Prime Minister has emerged through a process of evolution and continues to evolve as the nature of government continues to adapt to modern demands. It is still the case that relatively few statutes explicitly mention the Prime Minister,[7] meaning that there is no definitive list of functions or duties that the Prime Minister must fulfil. However, practice over time indicates that the Prime Minister's powers include the following:[8]

1. *Appointment and dismissal of ministers* Primarily, the Prime Minister is responsible for the overall organization and conduct of government.[9] The Prime Minister achieves this through appointing ministers, allocating them to lead a government department, and, if necessary, dismissing them. This is discussed in more detail in 7.3.

2. *Cabinet* The Prime Minister also determines who attends Cabinet and Cabinet committees and sets the agenda for Cabinet meetings. Cabinet is discussed in more detail in 7.5.

3. *Organization of government and the Civil Service* The Prime Minister has the power to alter the organization of government through abolishing or creating government departments. In addition, the Prime Minister is also the Minister for the Civil Service, meaning that they are responsible for the appointments of senior civil servants and other significant appointments in the public sector. The Prime Minister may also choose to pursue their own policies that are of special interest to them, in conjunction with the relevant ministers. When combined with the powers to appoint ministers and set the Cabinet agenda, this gives the Prime Minister significant control over the direction of the government.

4. *Constitutional role* The Prime Minister also has a key constitutional role. The Prime Minister is the primary constitutional adviser to the monarch and enjoys a weekly audience with the monarch. When giving advice to the monarch, in the Prime Minister has as constitutional responsibility to have regard to all the relevant interests and act responsibly.[10] The Prime Minister also meets the Heir to the Throne occasionally and is responsible for the overall relationship between the government and the monarch.

[7] The European Union (Notification of Withdrawal) Act 2017 and the European Union (Withdrawal) (No 2) Act 2019 are two examples of statutes referring to the Prime Minister.

[8] This is a list adapted and updated from one prepared by (Lord) Peter Hennessy, originally published in 2011 as written evidence to the House of Commons Political and Constitution Reform Select Committee, *Role and Powers of the Prime Minister* (HC 2012–13, 351) published as written evidence 842vw. See also Peter Hennessy, *Distilling the Frenzy* (Biteback 2011) Ch 7.

[9] Cabinet Office, *The Cabinet Manual* (1st edn, Cabinet Office 2011), Introduction, para 13.

[10] *R (Miller) v Prime Minister* [2019] UKSC 41 [30].

An increasingly important role is managing the relationships between UK Central Government and devolved administrations in Scotland, Wales, and Northern Ireland. The Prime Minister is assisted here by the Secretaries of State for Scotland, Wales, and Northern Ireland respectively.

In addition, as shown by the events of 2017 and 2019, the Prime Minister can decide when the government requests that the House of Commons dissolves Parliament under the Fixed-term Parliaments Act 2011 by voting for a general election.[11]

5. ***Security and intelligence matters*** The Prime Minister has overall responsibility for matters relating to national security and intelligence matters. This includes appointing the heads of the intelligence agencies, MI5, MI6, and GCHQ. The Prime Minister also chairs a weekly meeting of the National Security Council, which sets the government's priorities according to the National Security Strategy.[12]

6. ***The armed forces*** In terms of the military, the Prime Minister is responsible for decisions to deploy the armed forces either abroad or to support the police within the UK.[13] Outside an ongoing conflict, the Prime Minister authorizes the deployment of drone strikes.[14] Should it ever be necessary, the Prime Minister would take any decision to shoot down a hijacked aircraft before it reached a major population centre and, in the most extreme of circumstances, authorize the use of the UK's nuclear weapons.

7. ***International relations and Brexit*** The Prime Minister is responsible for representing the UK at various international meetings, including the international defence alliance, NATO,[15] the G7,[16] and the biannual Commonwealth Heads of Government Meeting. When the UK was a member of the EU, the Prime Minister, along with the heads of government of the other Member States, attended meetings of the European Council. Since the 2016 referendum, the Prime Minister had overall responsibility to negotiate the UK's exit from the EU. Now, following the UK's departure, the Prime Minister has primary responsibility to negotiate the UK's future and ongoing relationship with the EU.

From this account, it can be seen that the powers of the Prime Minister are extensive, giving them a unique perspective at the apex of central government. It is also the case that the role of the Prime Minister has increased over the past forty years;[17] some functions such as representing the UK at international summits have increased in frequency as issues such as climate change require greater co-operation between countries. Similarly,

[11] Although, in 2019 the Commons refused Prime Minister Boris Johnson's request three times. The Fixed-term Parliaments Act 2011 is discussed in 6.10.

[12] HM Government, *National Security Strategy and Strategic Defence and Security Review 2015* (CM 9161, 2015).

[13] Although the deployment of the armed forces overseas now appears to be subject to the approval of Parliament. The convention of consulting the House of Commons is discussed in 6.5.1.

[14] An example of this was the drone strike which killed two British citizens who were fighting for Islamic State in Syria. The then Prime Minister, David Cameron, authorized the drone strike. HC Deb, 7 September 2015, vol 599, col 23.

[15] North Atlantic Treaty Organization.

[16] The Group of 7, which in addition to the UK includes the United States, Japan, Germany, France, Italy, and Canada.

[17] Keith Dowding, 'The Prime Ministerialisation of the British Prime Minister' (2013) 66(3) *Parliamentary Affairs* 617, 635.

functions involving security and defence have become more critical as the UK faces different terrorist threats including cyberterrorism and the ability to conduct drone strikes. The process of constitutional change means that the Prime Minister has acquired further responsibilities, particularly with devolution. These issues, when combined, have considerably increased the importance of the Prime Minister ahead of other Cabinet ministers.

However, as we have seen, the lack of a clearly defined role means that the way each Prime Minister goes about their role can differ markedly. This can depend on a variety of factors, including the relationship that a Prime Minister has with their Cabinet ministers, which in turn depends on the underlying political situation. This issue is explored after the Cabinet and the nature of government departments have been outlined.

7.3 Appointment of ministers

Having discussed the role of the Prime Minister, this section considers those on the level below the Prime Minister: government ministers. The most senior ministers are Cabinet ministers, who lead government departments and are supported by junior ministers and civil servants. This section considers how Cabinet ministers and junior ministers are appointed, with the following section considering government departments.

7.3.1 Cabinet ministers

Once appointed by the monarch, the Prime Minister has the task of forming a government. As discussed in Chapter 6, government ministers are formally appointed under the royal prerogative by the monarch, on the advice of the Prime Minister. However, in substance, the power to hire and fire ministers rests with the Prime Minister. Most ministers are chosen to serve in a specific government department, as indicated by their title.

There is a range of ministerial positions available. The most senior ministers will be part of the Cabinet. The Cabinet is chaired by the Prime Minister, containing all secretaries of state, who oversee government departments.[18] As of February 2020, there were twenty-four government departments, covering areas of policy such as health, education, and transport, each having representation in Cabinet.[19]

Two government departments require special mention. First, the Treasury, which is the most significant department, responsible for setting economic policy, including taxation and setting budgets for the other government departments. The head of this department is the Chancellor of the Exchequer, which, after the Prime Minister, is the second most significant ministerial position in government and can have a significant impact on government policy. Secondly, the Cabinet Office, which historically supported all Cabinet ministers, now mainly supports the Prime Minister. It is headed by the Cabinet Secretary, who as Head of the Civil Service is the most senior civil servant in the country and is responsible for the maintenance of the civil service.

---

[18] The current Cabinet is available at this link from the following website: https://www.gov.uk/government/ministers.

[19] A list of government departments is available at this link from the following website: https://www.gov.uk/government/organisations. The Department for Exiting the European Union was closed following the UK's exit from the EU on 31 January 2020.

It is worth noting that certain ministerial positions are more prestigious than others. In addition to the Chancellor of the Exchequer, two other particularly important offices are the Foreign Secretary and Home Secretary. These three positions form the 'Great Offices of State' responsible for three of the most important areas of policy.

Two unusual offices include the Leader of the House of Commons and Leader of the House of Lords. These two roles have the primary responsibility for ensuring that the government gets its 'business' through each House of Parliament. This really means ensuring that the government's programme of legislation is enacted by Parliament as easily as possible.

Some ministers hold sinecure titles, which are positions which come with little or no responsibility. The advantage of these positions is the flexibility they give to the Prime Minister as to who they appoint. These include the Chancellor of the Duchy of Lancaster, the Lord Privy Seal, and Lord President of the Council. They can be combined with other positions,[20] with the main benefit of these titles being that they allow the holder to receive a ministerial salary under the Ministerial and Other Salaries Act 1975, as we will go on to discuss.

It may appear that the Prime Minister has a free choice as to who is appointed. However, the Prime Minister's choice is restrained by a variety of factors. These can be categorized as legal, conventional, and political.

Legal restrictions

By law, the number of ministers that can receive a ministerial salary is limited to 109,[21] of which a maximum of ninety-five can sit in the House of Commons.[22] Out of these 109, twenty-one ministers are allowed to receive the salary of a Secretary of State.[23] The Lord Chancellor receives their own specific salary.[24] While more than 109 ministers could be appointed, any further ministers must be unpaid.[25]

Conventional restrictions

By convention, ministers must either come from the House of Commons or the House of Lords. This forms the crucial link between the executive and the legislature and enables the government to be accountable to Parliament through its ministers. Most ministers are MPs, reflecting the dominance that the Commons enjoys over the Lords within Parliament. Ministers can be appointed without a seat in either the House of Commons or the House of Lords, but will usually be given a seat in the Lords shortly after their ministerial appointment.[26]

---

[20] For example, as of February 2020, the Lord Privy Seal is also the Leader of the House of Lords and the Lord President of the Council is the Leader of the House of Commons.

[21] Ministerial and Other Salaries Act 1975, Sch 1, para 2(a).

[22] House of Commons Disqualification Act 1975, s 2(1).

[23] Ministerial and Other Salaries Act 1975, Sch 1, para 2(a).

[24] Ibid s 1(2)(a).

[25] For example, before the 2019 General Election, within the Conservative Government, James Cleverly was an unpaid Minister without Portfolio (meaning that he is appointed as minister but has no responsibility for a government department). Cleverly was the Conservative Party Chairman, meaning that he had responsibility for campaigning within the Conservative Party. His appointment as a minister allowed him to be part of the Cabinet.

[26] For example, Rosalind Altman was appointed as Minister of State for Pensions shortly after the 2015 General Election. Eight days later she was made a member of the House of Lords as Baroness Altman. An unusual circumstance happened at the 2019 General Election. The Secretary of State for Digital, Culture, Media and Sport, Nicky Morgan, chose to stand down as an MP. However, she was then made a member of the House of Lords, as Baroness Morgan, in order to continue to serving as Secretary of State.

Political restrictions

This leads to the political restrictions. Given the status of that some positions carry, certain senior figures within the party may 'expect' a Cabinet position based on their standing within the party and previous experience in government. Political parties contain many different views and philosophies about key issues. Consequently, the Prime Minister, when appointing ministers, will usually ensure that relevant shades of political opinion within the party are reflected. This shows that although the Prime Minister leads the government and will seek to place their own stamp on the government, they are subject to some indirect control Brexit by their party. For example, given his standing in the Labour Party, Gordon Brown was practically guaranteed the position of Chancellor of the Exchequer when Tony Blair became Prime Minister in 1997.

Similarly, Theresa May's appointments on becoming Prime Minister in 2016 after the EU referendum highlight the political limitations on this power. May was able to place her own stamp on her Cabinet by replacing George Osborne, who was very close to David Cameron, the outgoing Prime Minister, but her freedom to choose was tempered by the need to reflect both sides of the argument (particularly because she campaigned to remain in the EU herself) to foster party unity. This meant that her appointments needed to reflect both sides of the post-referendum debate between those who wished the government to pursue a 'soft Brexit', meaning that despite leaving the EU, the UK should continue to have a close relationship with the EU, and those who advocated a 'hard' Brexit, with the UK placing greater reliance on trade with other countries around the world, not just the EU.[27] Had May failed to do this, it would have left one-half of the party feeling frozen out and deeply sceptical of her government, particularly with regard to Brexit.

By contrast, when in July 2019 Boris Johnson took office following May's resignation, he felt he had no such restriction. During the Conservative Party leadership contest, Johnson made clear that he was prepared to leave the EU on a 'no deal' basis if Theresa May's 'deal' could not be renegotiated. Emboldened by his victory in the leadership contest with 66 per cent of Conservative Party members voting for him, Johnson made support for his Brexit strategy the key criteria for a ministerial appointment. This led to the resignation of six ministers who served under May, as under no circumstances were they willing to support a 'no deal' Brexit.[28] On taking office, Johnson made sweeping changes to the Cabinet, with only three ministers retaining their positions from May's prime ministership.

[27] This included Boris Johnson (Foreign Secretary), Liam Fox (International Trade Secretary), and Chris Grayling (Transport Secretary), who were all leading campaigners to leave the EU and were given Cabinet positions. Philip Hammond (Chancellor of the Exchequer), Amber Rudd (Home Secretary), and Sir Michael Fallon (Defence Secretary) all campaigned to remain.

[28] Philip Hammond (Chancellor of the Exchequer), David Gauke (Lord Chancellor and Justice Secretary), Rory Stewart (International Development), David Liddington (Chancellor of the Duchy of Lancaster), Alan Duncan (Minister of State in the Foreign Office), and Anne Milton (Minister of State in Department for Education).

Counterpoint: The ousting of Margaret Thatcher—how Prime Ministers must retain the confidence of their Cabinet

The political restraints on the Prime Minister show how the Prime Minister must retain the confidence of their Cabinet. Should a Prime Minister lose this then, as Margaret Thatcher discovered in 1990, they are unlikely to remain Prime Minister for much longer and will be placed under pressure to resign. Thatcher led a Conservative Government which was increasingly divided over Britain's membership of the EU. At the same time, she decided to press ahead with the introduction of the Poll Tax. This proved to be one of her greatest errors as this became a profoundly unpopular policy. The combination of these two factors meant that she lost popularity within the party and with the general public, ultimately being challenged for the leadership of the party.

Some Cabinet ministers withdrew their support for their Prime Minister; others, notably Ken Clarke, informed her that she could not win the leadership contest. Thatcher then withdrew, ultimately paving the way for John Major to win the leadership contest. On becoming the Conservative leader, Major replaced Thatcher as Prime Minister.

As Rodney Brazier concludes: 'Prime Ministers—even the mightiest—are completely dependent in the end on their parties and colleagues for their personal power, and that what the parties give they can also take away.'[29] Ultimately, while Prime Ministers possess enormous powers, these must be exercised in such a manner that ensures Cabinet and parliamentary support.

7.3.2 Junior ministers and parliamentary private secretaries

Within a government department, there are different levels of minister. Each government department is headed by a Secretary of State. Below this are junior ministers, who are appointed as either a Minister of State or as Parliamentary Under Secretary of State, which is the most junior level of government minister. While the Secretary of State has overall responsibility for the department, the junior ministers will have responsibilities for aspects of that department's work. For example, the Foreign Secretary is supported by five other ministers who each have responsibility for policy for specific parts of the world, with a Minister of State for Europe and the Americas and other ministers responsible for relations with Asia and the Pacific, the Middle East, Africa, and finally the Commonwealth and UN.

Many ministers also have a parliamentary private secretary (PPS), an unpaid assistant to a minister 'whose main role is to be the "eyes and ears" of the Minister in the House of Commons' and to provide a line of communication between ministers and their backbench MPs.[30] Although not part of the government, PPSs are expected to vote with the government on all votes in Parliament. Service as a PPS may lead onto a junior ministerial job when the opportunity arises.

---

[29] Rodney Brazier, 'The Downfall of Margaret Thatcher' (1991) 54 *Modern Law Review* 471, 491.

[30] Michael Everett and Lucinda Maer, 'Parliamentary Private Secretaries' (House of Commons Library Briefing Paper, No 04942) 15, http://researchbriefings.parliament.uk/ResearchBriefing/Summary/SN04942#fullreport.

7.4 **Cabinet reshuffles**

Prime Ministers sometimes 'reshuffle' their Cabinet, moving ministers from a junior position in one department to a more senior position in another department. For example, David Cameron reshuffled his Cabinet after the 2015 General Election, with seven Secretaries of State either being appointed to the Cabinet for the first time or moving departments.[31] Sometimes a reshuffle is sparked when a minister resigns from the government. Over the life of a government, periodic reshuffles, however they arise, usually allow a Prime Minister to gradually cast the government in their image, easing out those less sympathetic to the direction that the Prime Minister wishes to take the government and appointing and promoting ministers who align themselves more closely to the Prime Minister. They may also look to bring into government those who they believe have potential or are popular MPs within the party.

There are limitations to this, as the most senior ministers can be difficult to move without causing major difficulties within their parliamentary party. One notable example is how Tony Blair ultimately felt he was unable to sack his Chancellor Gordon Brown despite the breakdown in their relationship and the difficulties that this was causing his government.[32] There is no doubt that given the divisions then existing within the Labour Party between the 'Blairites' (ministers and MPs who supported Blair) and 'Brownites' (those who supported Brown), had Blair sacked Gordon Brown this would have furthered those existing divisions and could have plunged the government into crisis, as other ministers could have resigned in sympathy with Brown.

Indeed, the requirements of collective responsibility mean that all ministers must in public support government policy[33] and this may lead to a Prime Minister deciding, on balance, to retain a troublesome minister within the government. This means that the minister must support government policy rather than giving them free reign to criticize the government once released from the strictures of collective responsibility. John Major, leading a Conservative Government bitterly divided over Britain's signing of the Maastricht Treaty, chose not to sack three Cabinet ministers who were at odds with him over his policy, fearing the problems they could cause outside of government.[34]

By contrast, under the Coalition Government, led by David Cameron, reshuffles occurred much less frequently, with several ministers remaining in office for the full five-year term. There are arguably two reasons for this. First, this was a coalition government and, reflecting the political situation, Cameron was subject to restrictions that did not apply to Blair or Brown, who both led the Labour Party with their own majority. Under the terms of the coalition agreed between the Conservatives and the Liberal Democrats, there needed to be a balance of ministers from each party reflecting the number of seats each party had in the Commons. This led to a ratio of six Conservative minsters to every one Liberal Democrat. Secondly, the Deputy Prime Minister, a Liberal Democrat, had the right to choose the Liberal Democrat ministers. Finally, any re-allocation of portfolios

---

[31] Michael Gove, Justice Secretary; Sajid Javid, Business Secretary; Amber Rudd, Energy and Climate Change Secretary; John Whittingdale, Culture, Media and Sport Secretary; Greg Clark, Communities and Local Government Secretary; Alun Cairns, Wales Secretary; David Mundell, Scottish Secretary.

[32] Tony Blair, *A Journey* (Hutchinson 2010). 494, 498-500.

[33] This is discussed in 7.7.1.

[34] John Major, *The Autobiography* (HarperCollins 1999) 343.

between the parties needed the agreement of both party leaders.[35] As Bogdanor states, this was a surrender of the Prime Minister's power to appoint and dismiss ministers, for 'if the Prime Minister believed that a Liberal Democrat minister had been at fault in the administration of his department . . . he would not be able, as in a single-party government to secure his resignation' without the agreement of the Deputy Prime Minister.[36]

The second reason reflects how different Prime Ministers undertake the office differently, as despite the constitutional concerns this arrangement raised, in practice Cameron may not have been unduly concerned by these restrictions. He disapproved of the Blair and Brown years stating that:

> I'm not a great believer in endlessly moving people between different jobs . . . We had 12 energy ministers in nine years. And the tourism minister changed more often than people got off planes at Heathrow. It was hopeless. I think you've got to try to appoint good people and keep them.[37]

 Pause for reflection

Different Prime Ministers have exercised this power in different ways. When both Tony Blair and Gordon Brown were Prime Minister, they were criticized for reshuffling their ministers too frequently. During Labour's thirteen years in office from 1997 to 2010, there were six defence secretaries, eight trade and industry secretaries, eight business secretaries, and six home secretaries (including three in four years).[38] This raised concerns that such frequent reshuffles harmed government, as continuity of policy is lost and for a period the new minister will be less effective as they need to learn about their new position and policy area. Cameron's approach was to keep ministers in office for far longer. This shows how flexible the practices are at the heart of central government with different Prime Ministers taking different approaches.

Prime Ministers themselves must adapt their approach according to the prevailing political climate. For example, when she took office as Prime Minister in July 2016, Theresa May was at the peak of her powers, and had the political space to sack the Chancellor George Osborne, who had been a key figure under David Cameron. By contrast, after triggering the 2017 General Election, reports emerged that she wanted to replace Philip Hammond as Chancellor with someone more aligned with her position on Brexit.[39] Yet, the surprise election result, with the Conservatives losing their majority, caused May's authority to ebb away. Much diminished, May was unable to conduct a broader Cabinet reshuffle, and practically all the leading members of her Cabinet, including those who constantly urged that she adopted a different course with Brexit, remained in office.[40]

---

[35] Cabinet Office, *Coalition Agreement for Stability and Reform* (Cabinet Office 2010) paras 1.1–1.5.

[36] Vernon Bogdanor, *The Coalition and the Constitution* (Hart 2011) 49.

[37] 'PM's 1 year vow: I'll get Britain back on Track', *The Sun* (10 May 2011), quoted in House of Commons Political and Constitutional Reform Committee, *The impact and effectiveness of ministerial reshuffles* (HC 2013–14 255) para 10.   [38] Ibid para 2.

[39] Christopher Hope, 'Amber Rudd lined up to Replace Philip Hammond as Chancellor after Conservative landslide victory', *The Telegraph* (1 June 2017), http://www.telegraph.co.uk/news/2017/06/01/amber-rudd-lined-replace-philip-hammond-chancellor-conservative/.

[40] Gavin Freeguard, 'The government reshuffle, in eight charts' (Institute for Government, 20 June 2017) available at https://www.instituteforgovernment.org.uk/blog/government-reshuffle-eight-charts.

This also meant that she was unable to sack Hammond as her Chancellor as he supported the softest possible form of Brexit. May's fundamental inability to dictate the direction of her Cabinet over Brexit was ultimately the cause of the unprecedented number of resignations from the Cabinet and broader government during her time as Prime Minister, as she constantly attempted to compromise between the different factions in her party.

> **” Discussing the problem**
>
> **Take a moment to look at the problem scenario outlined at the beginning of the chapter. Was the Prime Minister right to keep Neil Houlihan as Chancellor?**
>
> This is largely a matter of political judgment. The Prime Minister clearly has the power to sack his Chancellor. However, given Houlihan's standing in the party, it seems unlikely that Houlihan would be happy with another Cabinet position, as any other position is likely to be considered as a demotion. The dilemma for the Prime Minister is that if she sacks the Chancellor, he may ultimately launch a leadership bid. Consequently, keeping the Chancellor in position shows how the powers of the Prime Minister are, in practice, more restricted than it may initially appear. Keeping Houlihan also means that he remains bound by collective responsibility, which may be to the Prime Minister's advantage as this ensures that Houlihan is bound to support government policy.

7.5 The role of Cabinet

The previous sections outlined the position of the Prime Minister and their role in appointing ministers to lead government departments. The next issue to consider is the Cabinet and its role today. In 1918, the Haldane Committee identified the following functions of Cabinet.

(a) the final determination of the policy to be submitted to Parliament;

(b) the supreme control of the national executive in accordance with the policy presented to Parliament;

(c) the continuous co-ordination and determination of the activities of the several departments of state.[41]

These functions would indicate that Cabinet is a collective body, with ministers debating policy amongst themselves, working together to ensure that government is operating coherently. A more modern formulation is provided by the *Cabinet Manual*.

> Cabinet is the ultimate decision-making body of government. The purpose of Cabinet and its committees is to provide a framework for ministers to consider and make collective decisions on policy issues. Cabinet and its committees are established by convention but it is a matter for the incumbent government to determine the specific arrangements for collective decision-making.[42]

---

[41] Ministry of Reconstruction, *Report of the Machinery of Government Committee* (Cmnd 9230, 1918) para 6.

[42] Cabinet Office, *Cabinet Manual*, para 4.1.

While there is reference to collective decision-making, there is a distinct weakening of the language used by the *Cabinet Manual* compared to the Haldane Committee. The Cabinet is no longer described as exercising anything even remotely close to the 'supreme control of the national executive' as indicated by the Haldane Committee. As has already been discussed in 7.2, this function is now fulfilled by the Prime Minister, who has overall responsibility for the conduct of government.

The relationship between the Prime Minister and the Cabinet is the main point of tension in this area of the Constitution. The traditional theory is that Cabinet was the forum to coordinate government activity and exercise supreme control over the government, making decisions that bind other parts of the government. However, the demands of modern government, a more personality-led form of politics focused on the leadership of political parties and the functions of modern Prime Ministers, all point towards increased prime ministerial power at the expense of Cabinet. This development can be exaggerated by the character and approach of individual Prime Ministers. To analyse this, we need to consider the traditional approach before discussing how recent Prime Ministers have interacted with their Cabinet.

7.5.1 The traditional approach

The *Cabinet Manual* emphasizes that the Cabinet is responsible for making decisions within the government and that decisions should be reached collectively rather than individually by the Prime Minister. For this reason, traditionally the UK is said to have a system of Cabinet government rather than a presidential system, which sees decisions made by a presidential figure who then instructs ministers to implement the policy.

The Cabinet itself is a weekly meeting of the most senior ministers, at which the most significant decisions are made. Matters which are said to go to Cabinet include:

- decisions to take military action;
- the government's legislative priorities to be set out in the Queen's Speech;
- issues of a constitutional nature, including matters relating to the monarchy, reform of Parliament, and changes to the devolution settlements;
- the most significant domestic policy issues;
- the most significant international business;
- issues that impact on every member of Cabinet; and
- national emergencies, including terrorism.[43]

Below the Cabinet sit Cabinet committees, which are effectively subcommittees of the full Cabinet. These Cabinet committees are formed by the Prime Minister, who also determines who sits on them. Their membership is usually a combination of Cabinet ministers and more junior ministers. The *Cabinet Manual* describes Cabinet committees in the following terms:

> Cabinet committees help to ensure that government business is processed more effectively by relieving pressure on Cabinet. The committee structure also supports the principle of collective responsibility, ensuring that policy proposals receive thorough consideration without an issue having to be referred to the whole Cabinet. Cabinet committee decisions have the same authority as Cabinet decisions.[44]

[43] Ibid para 4.18.   [44] Ibid para 4.9.

As this description highlights, the main advantage of Cabinet committees is efficiency, as they allow for issues to be discussed without needing to go to the full Cabinet.

The emphasis on collective decision-making reflects the fundamental principle of Cabinet government—collective responsibility. This means that all government ministers are bound by the decisions of the Cabinet or one of its committees,[45] 'regardless of whether they were present when the decision was taken or their personal views'.[46] The expectation is that the relevant ministers are able to discuss matters frankly within Cabinet or one of its committees with the Prime Minister or the chair of the Cabinet committee summarizing what decision has been reached. This is then recorded in the minutes by the civil servants. The minutes are then circulated to the relevant parties across government.[47] Once a decision has been reached, ministers should not publicly criticize it and, when necessary, defend it. This allows the government to maintain a common position, both towards the public and to Parliament. It also follows that in order for this common position to be maintained, discussions within Cabinet and its committees should be confidential.[48]

7.5.2 Modern practice

Over the course of the past century, the practice has not necessarily met the high ideals laid out by the theory. As Brazier states:

> Meeting for once a week for a couple of hours with a full agenda, and being composed overwhelmingly of Ministers with heavy departmental responsibilities, the Cabinet could not possibly now be the forum for either the close control of the activities of government or for the co-ordination of actives of state.[49]

Simply put, modern government is too extensive, too demanding, and too complex to be controlled by a select few ministers at the apex of government, personally coordinating government by meeting for a few hours once a week. This means that out of the three functions outlined by the Haldane Committee in 1918, only one, the final approval of policy, has any validity today. Even here, the emphasis should be on the word *final*, for in recent decades, decisions have increasingly been taken outside the Cabinet structure.

This development is envisaged by the *Cabinet Manual*, which makes it clear that 'it is a matter for the incumbent government to determine the specific arrangements for collective decision-making'.[50] The concern is that over the past few decades, particularly under the prime ministerships of Margaret Thatcher and Tony Blair, the Cabinet machinery was undermined through their preference to govern outside the Cabinet structure. A common feature of both Prime Ministers was to use informal groups which met outside the Cabinet structure to develop policy. The advantage was greater flexibility as the membership of these groups could be manipulated so that the Prime Minister could reach the conclusions they desired.

---

[45] Ibid para 4.2.   [46] Ibid para 4.3.   [47] Ibid.

[48] For this reason, at s 35, the Cabinet and Cabinet Committees have an exemption from the provisions of the Freedom of Information Act 2000, s 35.

[49] Rodney Brazier, *Constitutional Practice* (3rd edn, OUP 1999) 107–8.

[50] Cabinet Office, *Cabinet Manual*, para 4.1.

A powerful Prime Minister can use this method to overcome disagreement, as ministers are less likely to disagree with the Prime Minister within a group of three or four compared to the full Cabinet. This led to a sidelining of Cabinet as a decision-making body. For example, Nigel Lawson, Chancellor of the Exchequer in Margaret Thatcher's Government, stated that, 'as Chancellor, I used to look forward to Cabinet Meetings as the most restful and relaxing event of the week' as the 'Cabinet's customary role was to rubber stamp decisions that had already been taken'.[51]

7.5.3 Cabinet Government under Blair

When Prime Minister, Tony Blair took things one stage further. As soon as he formed a government in 1997, one of his earliest decisions, announced by the Chancellor, was to allow the Bank of England to have full independence from the government to set interest rates. This decision was made by the Prime Minister and Chancellor after consulting only the Deputy Prime Minister and the Foreign Secretary. Tony Blair's new Cabinet had not even met for the first time before this decision was made, yet this was arguably the most significant decision of economic policy that Blair made as Prime Minister.[52]

Blair was criticized for holding short Cabinet meetings which made few decisions as matters had already been decided elsewhere. While Cabinet continued to meet, Blair preferred to hold bilateral meetings with individual ministers, where matters of policy would be decided. In addition, Blair would seek the advice of a few chosen ministers or advisers, rather than the whole Cabinet. Those who were in Blair's closest circle would change depending on who was in favour at the time. However, this was not a phenomenon unique to Blair as both Thatcher's Government and the Coalition Government operated along similar lines at times.

Pause for reflection

It used to be said that the Prime Minister was *primus inter pares* (first amongst equals) in relation to their Cabinet. To what extent was this ever the case and did this retain any validity during Blair's time as Prime Minister?

Blair's approach placed tremendous pressure on collective decision-making as in effect decisions were 'taken in Blair's preferred way some distance from the Cabinet and its apparatus'.[53] However, the flip side of collective responsibility, of ministers being required to support government policy in Parliament and in public, remained. This meant that ministers had to support decisions over which they had little input with limited opportunities to express their disagreement within the Cabinet. Even if the Cabinet did discuss an issue, Blair's view would prevail. One example of this was the Cabinet discussion about whether the government continue with the construction of the Millennium

---

[51] Quoted in Peter Hennessy, *The Prime Minister: The Office and its Holders Since 1945* (Penguin 2000) 401.
[52] Ibid 481.   [53] Ibid 518.

Dome (now The O2 Arena), in Greenwich, which started under the previous Conservative Government. At a Cabinet meeting Blair took the view that the Dome should proceed; however, a clear majority of the Cabinet was against. Blair had to leave the meeting and the Deputy Prime Minister, John Prescott, took over. When Prescott summed up the discussion, to the surprise of other ministers, he declared that the collective view was that 'the decision should be left to Tony' and that the Dome would go ahead. Later, some Cabinet ministers discovered that a press release stating that the Dome was going ahead had already been released.[54] As King states, 'so much for cabinet government, at least under Blair'.[55]

The concerns about the decline of Cabinet government under Blair were laid bare by the Butler Review which considered the use of intelligence before the invasion of Iraq in 2003. The Butler Review highlighted that discussion regarding Iraq in Cabinet was informal, with the Cabinet restricted to oral briefings by the Prime Minister, Foreign Secretary, and Defence Secretary. The key process used to make decision was a series of informal meetings attended by a 'small number of key ministers, officials and military officers'.[56] The concern was that the shift away from using the Cabinet or its committees to make decisions led to an informal decision-making, derided as 'sofa government', with decisions being reached by small groups of ministers and advisers.[57]

As the Butler Review stated, the 'inescapable consequence of this was to limit wider collective discussion and consideration by the Cabinet', which meant that it was 'obviously much more difficult for members of the Cabinet outside the small circle directly involved to bring their political judgement and experience to bear on the major decisions for which the Cabinet as a whole must carry responsibility'.[58] This is particularly the case when relying on intelligence data which requires judgment and advice from experts. The Butler Review concluded by suggesting problems with Blair's approach to government, stating that:

> We do not suggest that there is or should be an ideal or unchangeable system of collective Government, still less that procedures are in aggregate any less effective now than in earlier times. However, we are concerned that the informality and circumscribed character of the Government's procedures which we saw in the context of policy-making towards Iraq risks reducing the scope for informed collective political judgement. Such risks are particularly significant in a field [such as the use of intelligence] where hard facts are inherently difficult to come by and the quality of judgement is accordingly all the more important.[59]

One cost of this approach was that Britain's role in the Iraq War triggered the resignations of Robin Cook and Claire Short from the government, as discussed in 7.6.

---

[54] This is based on an account given by Claire Short, *An Honourable Deception? New Labour, Iraq and the Misuse of Power* (Free Press 2004) 69.

[55] Anthony King, *The British Constitution* (Oxford 2007) 328.

[56] Review of Intelligence on Weapons of Mass Destruction, *Report of a Committee of Privy Councillors* (HC 2003–04, 898) para 609.

[57] Ibid para 606.   [58] Ibid para 610.   [59] Ibid para 611.

Counterpoint: The Westland affair—how a Prime Minister can dominate their Cabinet

The Westland affair, which started in 1985, during Thatcher's time as Prime Minister, shows the level of dominance that a Prime Minister can exercise over their Cabinet through avoiding collective decision-making.

Westland plc, which provided the Ministry of Defence with helicopters, had descended into financial difficulty and required a bail out. There were two options on the table. One was from an American consortium and one from Europe. Government policy was to be neutral, as the matter was for the board of Westland to decide. However, Michael Heseltine, Secretary of State for Defence, preferred the European option and began to advocate this policy. The matter became more controversial and it was decided at Cabinet that ministers' statements about Westland needed to be checked by the Cabinet Office to ensure that they complied with government policy. This served as a rebuke to Heseltine, who was the minister responsible for the issue. When Heseltine sought to discuss the matter with the Prime Minister, she cancelled a meeting that had been arranged and later refused for this to be discussed in Cabinet. In January 1986, Heseltine resigned at the Cabinet meeting, collecting his papers and leaving Downing Street. Later, Heseltine stated that his resignation was due to a 'breakdown in constitutional government', meaning that the Prime Minister had frustrated collective decision-making and he was unable to continue to serve in her government, as he felt that he did not have the trust and support of the Prime Minister.

This was the first resignation which expressed concern for Thatcher's approach to her Cabinet, and was followed by the resignations of Nigel Lawson in 1989 and, most notably, Geoffrey Howe in November 1990. In his resignation speech to the House of Commons, Howe stated that collective government is about 'Government by persuasion—persuading colleagues and the nation . . . but I realise now that the task has become futile: trying to stretch the meaning of words beyond what was credible, and trying to pretend that there was a common policy when every step forward risked being subverted by some casual comment or impulsive answer'.[60]

Howe's resignation ultimately sowed the seeds of Thatcher's eventual downfall, as it was clear that she had lost the support of her Cabinet as discussed in 7.3.1.

Discussing the problem

Consider the problem scenario outlined at the start of the chapter. What considerations apply to the disagreement between the Prime Minister and the Chancellor?

There are several issues to discuss here. First, it is notable how the debate regarding housing has taken place outside a Cabinet meeting; this shows how the most significant policy debates can be resolved through more informal meetings. This may be appropriate if the matter is at an early stage but means that the views from other ministers have not been sought. The situation also indicates that the Chancellor has become an influential figure within the government, possibly due to the level of support he enjoys amongst MPs.

→

---

[60] HC Deb, 13 November 1990, vol 180, col 465.

→

It is also an example of how the Prime Minister has the potential to drive the policy agenda of the government, even without the initial approval of the relevant ministers. It's notable that the Secretary of State for Housing, Communities and Local Government has not been part of these discussions. If they find that collective responsibility means that they must defend this policy and they disagree with it, this could cause problems for the Prime Minister. Ultimately, they could choose to resign from the government.

7.5.4 How Cabinet can support a coalition government—the Conservative/Liberal Democrat Coalition 2010 to 2015

The creation of the coalition government between the Conservatives and Liberal Democrats following the 2010 General Election showed how, despite the predilections of Prime Ministers not to use the structures of Cabinet to their fullest extent, the Cabinet machinery still existed and was ready to be revitalized. As a coalition is an arrangement between two parties, there was a need to ensure that each side felt they were appropriately involved in making decisions. Had David Cameron operated as Prime Minister in the same manner as Blair or Thatcher, this would have frozen out his coalition partners, who could have ultimately withdrawn from the coalition and their support from the government in the House of Commons, causing the government to collapse.

The belief at the start of the coalition was that this necessitated a move towards a more traditional form of government that respected the procedures of Cabinet and its committees. As Christopher Foster states:

> Solidarity is an important characteristic of a well-functioning Cabinet. While Cabinet ministers must recognise that practicality does not permit all to be involved in every Cabinet decision, all need enough involvement and trust in the system not to think they are being misled.[61]

The procedures of Cabinet would give the best opportunity to foster the necessary solidarity between ministers from different political parties. In addition to the guarantees regarding the balance between Conservative and Liberal Democrat ministers,[62] there was an effort to ensure that the Liberal Democrats were involved in as many aspects of government as possible.

Given the need for agreement between the parties on policy, efforts were made to ensure that most departments had at least one Liberal Democrat minister. However, given the limited number of places for the Liberal Democrats as the junior partner to the coalition, this was not always possible. It was anticipated that Cabinet committees, with representation from both parties, would become the natural place for any disagreement to be resolved.

To this end, Cabinet committees were 'revived' and met more frequently than had been the case under either Blair or Brown. The Coalition Committee was created, which had five members from the Conservatives and five from the Liberal Democrats. This was

---

[61] Christopher Foster, *The British Government in Crisis* (Hart 2005) 282.
[62] These are discussed in 7.4.

intended to be the most senior committee below Cabinet and would meet weekly to resolve disagreements on policy when the relevant other Cabinet committees had failed to reach agreement. Yet, in the first three months of the coalition, it had met only twice, and it met even more infrequently after that. An adviser to Downing Street was quoted as saying, that 'it [was] important that it exist[ed], but better that it never meets',[63] because anything that was referred to this committee would mean that there had been a serious disagreement within the coalition.

However, despite occasional disagreements, the coalition proved more stable than many imagined. This meant that Cabinet Committees were still useful, but were used for their more traditional purpose, which was to resolve disputes between departments rather disputes between the two political parties.[64] It remained the case that ministers were still involved to a far greater extent than under Blair or Thatcher.

Instead, policy disputes between parties were often resolved informally. This would have been through discussions between the Prime Minister and Deputy Prime Minister, or a meeting between the Prime Minister and the relevant minister (sometimes the Deputy Prime Minister would also attend). More important was the emergence of the 'Quad'.[65] This was an informal meeting of the Prime Minister and the Chancellor of the Exchequer (both Conservatives) and the Deputy Prime Minister and the Chief Secretary to the Treasury (both Liberal Democrats). All of these informal mechanisms share similarities with Blair's government, in that they took place outside the structures of Cabinet. However, unlike with Blair, coalition meant that any agreement reached had to be sent to the relevant Cabinet committee for approval.[66] Often, with Blair, there would have been no further discussion as the matter had already been decided by Number 10.

 ## Counterpoint: Theresa May's tenure as Prime Minister

Theresa May's period as Prime Minister was dominated to such an extent by attempting to deliver Brexit that it was difficult to discern a distinctive style of government. The political agenda was set largely by the progress of the negotiations, while she sought to maintain the support of her divided Cabinet and parliamentary party for her Brexit strategy. In addition, after the 2017 General Election, she faced a hung Parliament, meaning that only a few rebels from her parliamentary party would mean that she would be defeated in the Commons. This made seeking a consensus amongst the Cabinet even more critical. However, May's approach was often to shut out Cabinet as much as possible when developing the approach to Brexit, including her own Secretary of State for Exiting the European Union.[67] Brexit policy was effectively presented to Cabinet on a 'take or leave it' basis, and if the compromise was too difficult for a minister to swallow so that they could no longer support May's approach, they had little choice other than to resign from the government.

→

---

[63] Robert Hazell and Ben Yong, *The Politics of the Coalition: How the Conservative-Liberal Democrat Government Works* (Hart 2012) 53.

[64] Ibid 54.   [65] Ibid 58.   [66] Ibid 55–61.

[67] Both David Davies and Dominic Raab resigned as Brexit Secretary due to feeling undermined by Theresa May and her advisors.

→

The loss of the government's majority at the election significantly weakened May to the extent that ministers could resign safe in the knowledge that she was unlikely to remain Conservative Party leader for long, even if she had delivered Brexit on the default date of 29 March 2019. Although throughout much of the time she retained the support of a majority of Conservative MPs,[68] once it was clear that she was unable to deliver Brexit, it was clear that she would have to resign as Conservative Party leader and Prime Minister.

It is clear from May's tenure as Prime Minister that a strong Prime Minister requires a sizeable majority in the House of Commons and a relatively united parliamentary party and Cabinet. When those things are absent, and the Prime Minister is faced with delivering something as complex and multifaceted as Brexit, any Prime Minister would struggle.

7.5.5 Summary on Cabinet

This discussion over the past four sections has outlined the role of the Prime Minister, ministers, government departments, and the Cabinet. As we have seen, the functions of the Prime Minister have increased over the past forty years.[69] This has combined with two Prime Ministers who have sought to dominate their Cabinet, creating a far stronger government at the centre. This increase in power has to some extent come at the expense of the Cabinet and, particularly with Blair, the very notion of Cabinet government itself. Yet, as Cameron's period as Prime Minister has shown, it is possible for ministers to play a greater role, as part of a more collegiate form of government. However, it remains difficult to determine whether this was due in part to Cameron's own temperament or whether it was a necessary response to the dynamics of coalition. As Cameron led a single party government for only one year after the general election, it is difficult to establish any distinct change in patterns in such a short time period. However, to be an effective Prime Minister, as Theresa May's tenure showed, Prime Ministers are also dependent on external factors, including the size of their majority and the level of support from their MPs and Cabinet.

7.6 Government departments

As discussed in the previous section government ministers will be responsible for a government department. There is no precise legal definition of a government department,[70] but the core elements can be found as follows. It is headed by a Secretary of State and other ministers, responsible to Parliament for its actions, staffed by civil servants, and derives its legal powers from statute or the royal prerogative. However, for legal purposes, lists of government departments can be found in legislation.[71]

---

[68] Including winning a confidence vote in the leadership of the Conservative Party in December 2018.

[69] Keith Dowding, 'The Prime Ministerialisation of the British Prime Minister' (2013) 66(3) *Parliamentary Affairs* 617.

[70] Colin Turpin and Adam Tomkins, *British Government and the Constitution* (7th edn, Cambridge 2011) 429.

[71] For example, Parliamentary Commissioner Act 1967, Sch 2.

More commonly, should a statute confer a power on a government minister, this will usually be achieved by conferring the power to the Secretary of State. This means that the power can be exercised by any one of the Secretaries of State.[72] However, in practice, the most relevant Secretary of State will exercise the power.[73]

Ministers within government departments will develop policies and, if required, will develop legislation for approval in Parliament. Very often the party of government will have presented their proposed policies to the electorate at an election manifesto and the election of that political party into government gives them the mandate to pursue those policies.

Otherwise, government departments will continue to govern according to the existing laws and policies. The day-to-day work of the government is conducted by permanent civil servants, who are politically impartial and remain in post no matter who is in government and whichever policies are pursued.

Most members of the Cabinet lead government departments, which fulfil the functions of central government in specific policy areas. The ministers leading these departments are responsible for the development and implementation of policy within their departments. For example, the Education Secretary leads the Department for Education and, as the title suggests, is responsible for policy regarding education from pre-school to universities. However, as the discussion in 7.5 shows, this is subject to the extent to which the Prime Minister may seek to intervene in the affairs of a department from Downing Street.

7.6.1 Reorganizing government departments

The Prime Minister 'is responsible for the overall organisation of the government and the allocation of functions between ministers'.[74] This is a function of the royal prerogative, which means that changes can be made without reference to Parliament. In practice, the number of departments is limited by the fact that only twenty-one ministers can receive the salary of a Cabinet minister.[75] This power allows the Prime Minister to recast the structure of government according to their policy priorities.

With some exceptions, it is notable how extensively these powers have been used, with few government departments being immune from change. For example, the Department of Health and Social Security was split into two in 1998, creating a Department of Health and a Department of Social Security. The latter proved to be short lived, as in 2001 this merged with part of the Department of Education and Employment to create the Department of Work and Pensions, reflecting the intention of the government to link the social security system with tackling unemployment and encouraging claimants to seek employment.

On appointment as Prime Minister, Theresa May created two new departments: the Department for Exiting the European Union and the Department for International Trade. This reflected the importance to the government of Brexit and the need to take preparatory steps to agree trade deals with other countries once the UK has left the EU. To create

---

[72] The Interpretation Act 1978, Sch 1, states that '"Secretary of State" means one of Her Majesty's Principal Secretaries of State'.

[73] For example, the Welfare Reform Act 2012, s 94 gave the Secretary of State the power to make regulations regarding Personal Independence Payment, a benefit paid to the disabled. Regulations made under this power are made by the Secretary of State for Work and Pensions.

[74] Cabinet Office, *Cabinet Manual*, para 3.48.   [75] See 7.3.1.

a space in the Cabinet, the Department for Energy and Climate Change and the Department for Business, Innovation and Skills were both abolished, with the functions of these departments being merged to create the Department for Business, Energy and Industrial Strategy. During May's tenure as Prime Minister two departments were renamed, with the Department for Culture, Media and Sport becoming the Department for *Digital*, Culture, Media and Sport, while the Department for Communities and Local Government became Ministry of *Housing*, Communities and Local Government. Both changes of name were designed to reflect the shifting priorities of those departments.

Decisions to create or abolish government departments are inevitably political decisions. They can cause considerable disruption and the effectiveness of such changes can be a matter of debate. Merging departments or creating new ones can risk losing the expertise accumulated within the defunct department as the new department seeks to establish itself within Whitehall.

7.6.2 Functions of government departments

Government departments have two main functions. First, they will maintain the operation of government according to existing law and policy. This can simply be referred to as 'running the country': the collection of taxes, ensuring that social security benefits are paid on time, considering applications for passports, and funding the NHS, schools, the police, and other public services. The government can be legally accountable for decisions made before the courts through an application for judicial review. This is a highly developed area of law and is discussed in detail in Chapters 10–13.

Politically, the government is accountable to Parliament. From time to time, the government will have to respond to emergencies or new developments according to existing law and government policy. Clearly, the demands of government have long meant that ministers are unable to make all the decisions that their departments are required to.

Consequently, departments are staffed by civil servants who will make most decisions on behalf of the minister according to the existing law and policy. This means that a key issue here considers the extent to which ministers are responsible and accountable to Parliament and the public for decisions that have been made by civil servants on their behalf. The more complex, important or controversial the decision to be made is, the more likely it is that the decision will be made by the relevant minister after taking advice from their civil servants.[76]

The second function of government is to develop new policy. When this requires new legislation to provide the legal basis for the new policy, the government will introduce new legislation for approval in Parliament. As discussed in Chapter 8, Parliament usually responds to and scrutinizes legislative proposals from the government rather than initiating proposed legislation itself. Civil servants will assist ministers in developing new policy and will be able to advise on the practicality of policy using their administrative expertise. However, civil servants must remain politically impartial and should not stray into providing advice about the political consequences of a proposed policy. Consequently, the practice has emerged where ministers, particularly senior ministers, appoint their own special

[76] As discussed in 11.7.1, critical to the functioning of government departments is the *Carltona* doctrine. This means that although legislation may grant the power to the Secretary of State, civil servants can act in the name of the minister.

advisers, not drawn from the civil service, who provide advice of a more political nature. Civil servants and special advisers are considered in 7.8. Once a decision has been made or a new policy has been developed, ministers are required to support that decision. This allows Parliament to scrutinize the government and hold it to account. The requirement that ministers must support the government is explained in more detail in the following section.

7.7 Political accountability to Parliament

No matter how the government is run by the Prime Minister, the core constitutional fundamental remains that the government, through its ministers, is accountable to Parliament. In practice this means that because ministers are a member of either House of Parliament, their actions can be scrutinized through questions, debate, and investigations by select committees. In addition, because the House of Commons is elected, this link between Parliament and the government allows the electorate to hold the government to account at general elections. The principle of government accountability has been described as 'a democratic bulwark of the British constitution'.[77] Furthermore, in *R (Miller) v Prime Minister*, the Supreme Court described accountability of the government to Parliament as a constitutional principle established at common law.[78]

7.7.1 Collective responsibility

As the government is drawn from Parliament, chiefly the House of Commons, it requires the confidence of that House. This is gained by ministers being collectively responsible to the House of Commons as a government. The Prime Minister is asked to form a government that will enjoy the confidence of the House of Commons. Should the government lose the confidence of the House, as expressed by passing a motion of no confidence, then if an alternative government can be formed, the Prime Minister will resign on behalf their government.[79] If the provisions of the Fixed-term Parliaments Act 2011 have been complied with, then there could be an early general election. Such occasions are rare; as shown by the discussion of the principles of government formation in 6.5, if the government has an overall majority in the House of Commons then party solidarity will ensure that it retains the confidence of the House.

Governments lose the confidence of the House very rarely (ie twice in 1924 and once in 1979). All three occasions involved a minority government. Yet it remains the case that government is predicated on having the confidence of the House. For this reason, following the 2017 General Election, and finding that she was now leading a minority government, Theresa May felt that she needed the security of a Confidence and Supply Agreement with the Democratic Unionist Party to ensure that she retained the confidence of the House of Commons.[80]

The paradox here is that the House of Commons holds the government to account, but many MPs of the same political party as the government view their role as an MP is to

---

[77] Stanley de Smith and Rodney Brazier, *Constitutional and Administrative Law* (8th edn, Penguin 1998) 195.
[78] [2019] UKSC 41, see 6.7 for a detailed discussion of the case.
[79] Cabinet Office, *Cabinet Manual*, para 2.19.   [80] See 6.9.

maintain and support the government. However, as Turpin and Tomkins state, this does not mean that accounting to Parliament has little content:

> the ultimate, collective responsibility of the government to Parliament is not without meaning. The need to retain the confidence of the House imposes restraints. It compels governments to explain, justify, bargain and concede.[81]

Particularly if the government has a small or no majority, out of necessity it will have to consider the views of MPs from other parties to ensure that it can still get its legislation through the House of Commons.

The *Ministerial Code* makes clear that collective responsibility applies to all government ministers, which means that government ministers must support and defend government policy.[82] This is the other side of the coin to Cabinet government as discussed in 7.6. In theory, because ministers have opportunity to debate policy within government, they must defend it in Parliament, and they are bound by decisions made within the Cabinet. This has the basic and fundamental effect of establishing government policy, as ministers must support a single policy, allowing Parliament to scrutinize that policy. If disagreements about policy between government ministers were made public, then not only would this be embarrassing for the government, but if ministers blamed each other for policy failures, it would be more difficult for Parliament to hold the government accountable.

To this end, the *Ministerial Code* states that 'Ministers should be able to express their views frankly in the expectation that they can argue freely in private while maintaining a united front when decisions have been reached'.[83] This is furthered when the Code states that 'decisions reached by the Cabinet or Ministerial Committees are binding on all members of the government'.[84]

However, it is important to recognize the limitations of collective responsibility. These limitations are both formal and informal.

7.7.2 Limits on collective responsibility

Setting collective responsibility aside

Formally, collective responsibility can be suspended, or 'set aside' by the Prime Minister when government ministers fail to agree on government policy, meaning that they can express their different views in public. Since 1945, there have been three notable examples.

First, in 1975, the Cabinet was split over whether the UK should remain in the EEC (European Economic Community—now EU). The overall government position was to remain and government recommended that the electorate should vote to remain in a referendum. However, Cabinet ministers were given the express permission by the Prime Minister to campaign against this position.

The second example took place during the 2010 coalition—one of the natural consequences of a coalition government is that the two political parties disagree in some

---

[81] Colin Turpin and Adam Tomkins, *British Government and the Constitution* (7th edn, Cambridge University Press 2011) 569.

[82] Cabinet Office, *Ministerial Code* (Cabinet Office 2019) para 2.1.

[83] Ibid para 2.1.   [84] Ibid para 2.3.

areas. In 2010, one such area was electoral reform and whether to change the electoral system used for general elections: the Liberal Democrats have long been in favour of this policy, with the Conservatives remaining committed to the existing system. Consequently, in order for the two parties to enter into coalition, it was agreed that a referendum should be held on the issue, with the proposal that the electoral system should change from the existing first-past-the-post system to the alternative vote. It was agreed that collective responsibility would be lifted to allow Conservative ministers to campaign against the new electoral system. In the event, the electorate chose to retain the existing voting system.[85]

The third example was when, in 2016, David Cameron as Prime Minister was again forced to suspend collective responsibility on the issue of Britain's membership of the EU and allowed ministers to campaign against the government's recommendation to remain in the EU. Had Cameron not yielded, it was certain that he would have faced several resignations from his government. As it was, the campaign saw some of the most vicious campaigning of recent times, with government ministers robustly debating each other in public.

Informal limits—leaking

An expression of collective responsibility in its barest form could give the impression of a minister being required to make a commitment of unyielding loyalty to the government. This would be very misleading, for as Brazier states, 'in order to preserve the essentials of the doctrine at all a number of safety valves have been developed'. Of these, the 'life-saver of collective responsibility' is the unattributable leak.[86]

Should a minister present their view in Cabinet or in a Cabinet committee, but is in the minority and the decision goes the other way, the minister has two options. They could accept defeat or resign from the government. Yet, neither of these options is attractive, as becoming a government minister could be the highlight of their political career or they may have designs on achieving even higher office. One solution is for the minister to 'brief' the press, explaining his opposition to the decision of the government. The result is 'that all the world knows that he opposes the policy, just as if he had resigned, but by using an unattributable leak, the façade of collective responsibility is maintained and the Minister, press and Prime Minister are happy'.[87] Leaking is so frequent that most newspapers will contain stories containing information that could only be obtained by a leak, with many newspaper stories referring to 'Cabinet sources' or some other such term. Occasionally, leaking descends into the dark arts of politics, with ministers, including the Prime Minister, leaking in order to embarrass a particular minister to achieve a political objective. In 2016, Theresa May warned that leaks would not be tolerated, especially regarding Brexit, and that it would result in instant dismissal. However, somewhat ironically, this was then leaked to the newspapers.[88]

Following the 2017 election, the leaks continued, increasing further as May's position as Prime Minister became more tenuous as the House of Commons rejected her Brexit

---

[85] The referendum is discussed in 8.3.2.
[86] Rodney Brazier, *Constitutional Practice* (3rd edn, OUP 2009) 145.   [87] Ibid 145.
[88] BBC News, 'Leak inquiry into leaking of letter warning about leaks' (BBC News, 5 December 2016) available at http://www.bbc.co.uk/news/uk-politics-38212447.

deal three times in early to Spring 2019. Ministers felt that they could leak with impunity as May was unlikely to remain as Prime Minister for much longer. Blow-by-blow accounts of Cabinet meetings were shared via WhatsApp messages to journalists, as ministers jock-eyed for position in advance of the inevitable Conservative Party leadership contest as May's position at No 10 became ever more untenable as she failed to obtain the approval of the House of Commons for her Brexit deal.

This reached its nadir in April 2019, when details of a meeting of the National Security Council were leaked. This meets in private, with ten Cabinet ministers attending and receiving briefings from the armed forces and the security services, MI5, MI6, and GCHQ. At the meeting, Cabinet ministers were split over whether the Chinese telecoms company Huawei should be allowed to take part in building the UK's new 5G phone network. The concern was that if Huawei was involved, cyberattacks on the network originating from China could be made easier than if another, Western company was used instead. The Prime Minister decided that Huawei could help build 'non-core' parts of the network to safeguard against any risk to national security.

The suspicion is that one of the five Cabinet members who voted against any involvement from Huawei leaked this information to show that they would take a strong line on national security as part of positioning themselves for a bid for the Conservative Party leadership. The former Cabinet Secretary Lord O'Donnell described the leak as a 'complete outrage', and an inquiry was immediately launched.[89] Evidence from the inquiry suggested that Gavin Williamson, the Secretary of State for Defence, was responsible for the leak. Williamson denied this, and after he refused to resign, Theresa May sacked him from the government, stating that 'no other credible version of events to explain the leak has been identified'.[90]

 Discussing the problem

Consider the scenario outlined at the beginning of the chapter. What appears to have happened regarding the disagreement between the Prime Minister and Chancellor?

It appears that their disagreement over taxation and house building has been leaked to the newspapers. It's unclear who is the source of the leak. It may be the Chancellor, with the aim of preventing the policy from developing any further. By contrast, the Prime Minister may have leaked it in an attempt to undermine the Chancellor. On this occasion, it appears to have worked to the Chancellor's benefit, given the support he has from MPs. Should the Prime Minister pursue this policy despite the views of her MPs, she may find that she loses their support on other issues. This shows an informal, political constraint on the power of the Prime Minister.

---

[89] Dan Sabbagh and Rowena Mason, 'Ultimatum to cabinet ministers in Huawei leak investigation' (The Guardian, 26 April 2019) available at https://www.theguardian.com/technology/2019/apr/25/may-faces-calls-for-inquiry-over-huawei-leak.

[90] BBC News, 'Exchange of letters between Theresa May and Gavin Williamson' (BBC News, 1 May 2019), available at https://www.bbc.co.uk/news/uk-48126671

7.7.3 When collective responsibility becomes too much—resignation

Should a government minister profoundly disagree with government policy, then their only option could be to resign as a minister (they would however remain an MP or member of the House of Lords). Should the resigning minister so wish, they can make a statement to the House of Commons setting out their reasons why. For example, Robin Cook resigned as Leader of the House of Commons in 2003 over the government's intention to invade Iraq. Cook resigned so that he could vote against the government over the issue the following day.

By contrast, the Prime Minister may be willing to tolerate some dissent and not insist that a minister resigns. For example, Claire Short, Secretary of State for International Development, chose to publicly criticize the government's approach to the Iraq War, describing it as 'reckless'. Yet Short did not resign nor was she sacked by the Prime Minister. Although Short did resign a few months later over Iraq, a comparison between Short and Cook remains instructive as to how flexible collective responsibility can be. The Prime Minister may calculate that it is better to overlook and accept a certain level of open dissent if that is the politically expedient course of action. Indeed, this is arguably what happened with Short, as sacking her could have led to her becoming more vocal with her opposition to the Iraq War and caused greater problems for the Prime Minister.

Clearly, if a minister is going to go as far as voting against the government, then their position is intolerable, and they must resign from the government. The second feature is that unless the minister chooses to resign—the consequences for breaching collective responsibility—a conventional rule is political. The *Ministerial Code* makes this clear, stating that 'Ministers only remain in office for so long as they retain the confidence of the Prime Minister. She is the ultimate judge of the standards of behaviour expected of a Minister and the appropriate consequences of a breach of those standards'.[91] Any consequences of a breach of collective responsibility, without any prior agreement to differ, are for the Prime Minister to determine.

Indeed, as we have noted, one consequence of the Coalition Government was that the Prime Minister's power to sack Liberal Democrat ministers was limited, which in turn allowed the Liberal Democrats to criticize government policy with some level of immunity. This meant that Vince Cable, a particularly popular Liberal Democrat minister, appeared to have been granted some leeway as he repeatedly criticized government policy and the Conservatives in general[92] yet He remained a minister. Had Cameron unilaterally sacked a Liberal Democrat minister, against the wishes of the Liberal Democrat Deputy Prime Minister, this would have breached the terms of the coalition and would have plunged the government into crisis, potentially even causing its collapse.

Before Brexit, the most notable recent resignation over policy in recent times was that of Iain Duncan Smith. Duncan Smith was responsible for a major reform to the benefits system with the introduction of Universal Credit which aimed to replace several other benefits, including Jobseeker's Allowance (paid to those out of work), Employment

---

[91] Cabinet Office, *Ministerial Code* (Cabinet Office 2019) para 1.6.

[92] For example, Patrick Wintour, 'Vince Cable should resign over immigration remarks, says Tory MP', *The Guardian* (23 December 2013), https://www.theguardian.com/uk-news/2013/dec/23/vince-cable-immigration-tory-mp-enoch-powell.

Support Allowance (paid to those out of work with certain medical conditions), and Housing Benefit. However, Duncan Smith became disillusioned with the constraints he was operating under to implement this major policy, as his department's budget was cut time and time again.

The final straw for Duncan Smith came at the 2016 Budget when he was asked by the Prime Minister and Chancellor to cut benefits paid to disabled people when other provisions of the budget benefited high earners with tax cuts. Duncan Smith, in his resignation letter, felt that he was 'unable to watch passively while certain policies are enacted in order to meet the fiscal self-imposed restraints that I believe are more and more perceived as distinctly political rather than in the national economic interest' and that there had not been 'enough awareness from the Treasury, in particular, that the government's vision of a new welfare-to-work system could not be repeatedly salami-sliced'.[93]

Again, Duncan Smith felt that he was unable to remain in the government as the priorities of the government had shifted away from his flagship policy. Somewhat ironically, the first action of his successor, Stephen Crabb, was to announce that the government would not proceed with the benefit cuts that Duncan Smith resigned over.

 Discussing the problem

Consider the dispute between the Home Secretary and the Prime Minister outlined in the problem scenario. Are there any other remaining considerations?

Should the Prime Minister insist on the policy there is the prospect that other ministers may feel undermined, particularly the Secretary of State for Housing, Communities and Local Government, as housing is their responsibility. They are likely to be distinctly unhappy that they were not involved in discussions over the policy. It will also be the case that the Chancellor will have to announce the tax rise. If the Prime Minister persists despite their opposition to the policy, they may feel so undermined by the Prime Minister that they have no other option than to resign.

Since the 2016 referendum, Brexit has placed collective responsibility under extreme and unique pressure. The combination of the gravity of the issue and the lack of an agreed policy, outlined when Theresa May became Prime Minister, meant that she was faced with the difficult task of steering a course between a variety of options, each of which had support within Cabinet. As we have seen in 7.3.1, May appointed ministers who took a variety of positions on Brexit. This meant that the ministers which May appointed who voted to remain in the EU at the 2016 referendum tended to want to maintain a closer relationship with the EU (a 'soft Brexit'), and those who voted to leave wanted a looser relationship and were willing to countenance leaving the EU without an agreement (a 'hard Brexit'). As the Brexit process unfolded, it proved impossible to satisfy everyone. Some ministers resigned because May was pursuing a hard Brexit,[94] and many more resigned because the form of Brexit on offer was not hard enough.[95] Others later resigned over the

---

[93] Available at https://blogs.spectator.co.uk/2016/03/iain-duncan-smiths-resignation-letter-full-text/.

[94] Such as Philip Lee, who resigned in June 2018, and Jo Johnson who resigned in November 2018.

[95] For example, Boris Johnson and David Davis both resigned from the Cabinet, and five junior ministers resigned following the Chequers Agreement, which stated that the government would seek a closer continuing relationship with the EU than they wished.

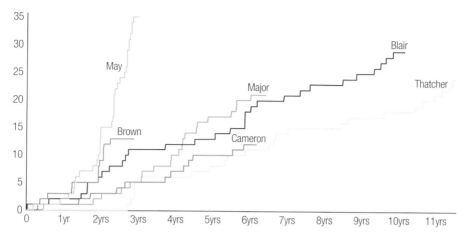

Figure 7.1 The number of ministerial resignations outside reshuffles, 4 May 1979 to 13 July 2019
Source: Institute for Government. Reproduced under the terms of the Creative Commons Attribution 4.0 licence https://creativecommons.org/licenses/by-nc/4.0/.

eventual Withdrawal Agreement that Theresa May concluded, including Dominic Raab, her then Brexit Secretary, who, at least ostensibly, took part in negotiating elements of the agreement.[96] Some ministers took the unusual step of voting against the government, with the effect that they were taken to have resigned at that moment.[97] During May's time in office, two other ministers resigned over policy differences unrelated to Brexit.[98] As Figure 7.1 from the Institute for Government highlights, May's government saw more resignations, more quickly, than any of her immediate predecessors, particularly following the 2017 General Election. This placed May under considerable pressure and ultimately contributed to her resignation.

As stated in 7.3.1, Boris Johnson made support for his Brexit strategy a condition of being appointed a minister. Consequently, when two ministers changed their mind and felt that they could no longer support this, they had to resign from the government. This included Amber Rudd, who had supported Johnson during the Conservative Party leadership contest, and Jo Johnson, who also happens to be the brother of the Prime Minister.

7.7.4 Individual ministerial responsibility

Ministers are individually accountable and responsible to Parliament for the conduct of their department, the actions of their civil servants, and for their own personal conduct. This means that individual ministerial responsibility essentially has three main elements. Individually, as ministers, they are under a duty not to mislead Parliament, they should take responsibility for the actions of their department, and they should ensure that their private conduct is that expected of a minister. This section discusses these three elements in turn.

[96] Other ministers to resign included Esther McVey, who resigned from the Cabinet, and seven other junior ministers.

[97] For example, three ministers resigned by voting against the government whip and in favour of the House of Commons holding 'indicative votes' in an attempt to establish an agreed position.

[98] Tracey Couch (over fixed-odds betting terminals) and Greg Hands (over the expansion of Heathrow Airport).

Misleading Parliament

The most fundamental rule is that a minister is under a duty not to mislead Parliament. The *Ministerial Code* states the following:

> It is of paramount importance that Ministers give accurate and truthful information to Parliament, correcting any inadvertent error at the earliest opportunity. Ministers who knowingly mislead Parliament will be expected to offer their resignation to the Prime Minister.[99]

The most famous example remains the Profumo Affair. In 1963, John Profumo was the Secretary of State for War. He was having an affair with Christine Keeler, who was also having a relationship with a Soviet naval attaché, a spy for the Soviet Union. Given that these events took place during the Cold War, Profumo's conduct raised security concerns, of which the Opposition took advantage. In a statement to the House of Commons, Profumo stated that there was no impropriety between him and Christine Keeler. When it emerged that this was untrue, he had no option other than to resign because he had misled Parliament.[100]

In 2018, Amber Rudd resigned when she 'inadvertently misled' the Home Affairs Select Committee. This took place in the context of the Windrush scandal, when the Home Office sought to deport illegal immigrants; however, some migrants from Commonwealth countries who settled in the UK from the late 1940s to 1973 were mistakenly identified as illegal immigrants, with some being incorrectly deported by the Home Office. When giving evidence to the Select Committee, Rudd stated that the Home Office did not have any targets for deportations. However, the *Guardian* reported that a memo written by a civil servant in 2017, copied to Rudd's office, made a clear reference to introducing targets. In addition, Rudd had written to Theresa May with details of her intention to increase deportations by 10 per cent.[101] In her resignation letter, Rudd admitted that she should have been aware of the targets and took responsibility for not being aware of this when giving evidence to the committee.

The strictness of this rule is critical because this ensures that Parliament is provided with the information it needs in order to scrutinize the activities of government through its ministers. This in turn allows ministers to fulfil their 'duty to Parliament to account and be held to account for the policies, decisions and actions other departments and agencies'.[102]

It is important to establish what is meant by 'accountability'. At one level it requires answering questions and making statements to Parliament explaining the policies pursued and the decisions taken. Each minister is responsible for this form of explanatory accountability to Parliament. A stronger element of accountability is the aim that Parliament holds ministers responsible for failures of policy. If it is a serious failure then, in theory, the minister should resign.

---

[99] Cabinet Office, *Ministerial Code* (August 2019) para 1.2(c).

[100] Profumo also resigned as an MP.

[101] Nick Hopkins and Heather Stewart, 'Amber Rudd was sent targets for migrant removal, leak reveals' (*The Guardian*, 28 April 2018) available at https://www.theguardian.com/politics/2018/apr/27/amber-rudd-was-told-about-migrant-removal-targets-leak-reveals.

[102] Cabinet Office, *Ministerial Code* (Cabinet Office 2019) para 1.3(b).

Responsibility for a department

A high water mark of **individual ministerial responsibility** remains Lord Carrington's resignation as Foreign Secretary over the failure of the Foreign Office to monitor and anticipate Argentina's intentions before they invaded the Falkland Islands (a British Overseas Territory) in 1982. Lord Carrington resigned because of the failure within his department, yet he was not personally responsible for the failure. Viewed in this context, it appears that the scope of ministerial responsibility is extremely broad and begs the question as to how a minister can be responsible for everything that takes place within their department. Arguably, Lord Carrington's resignation can be justified on the basis that the invasion of the Falklands caused a loss of confidence in the organization and leadership of the Foreign Office. This could only be restored with a new Secretary of State.

However, it is not the case that on every occasion something goes wrong within a department, ministers are deemed to be responsible and must resign. The reality is more complex, with the precedents of ministerial resignations building an unclear and shapeless picture. As Finer states:

> Whether a minister is forced to resign depends on three factors, on himself, his Prime Minister and his party . . . For a resignation to occur all three factors have to be just so: the minister compliant, the Prime Minister firm, the party clamorous . . . Above all it is indiscriminate—which Ministers escape and which do not is decided neither by the circumstances of the offence nor its gravity.[103]

The foundation of the modern approach to ministerial responsibility remains the fallout from the Crichel Down affair. This saw the resignation of the Minister for Agriculture, Sir Thomas Dugdale. In 1938, the Air Ministry acquired some land to be used as a bombing range. After the Second World War, this land was no longer required and it was transferred to the Ministry of Agriculture, who were allowed to let it to a tenant of their choice. One of the former owners made a request to buy back the land, but was refused, and some neighbouring landowners had an understanding that they would be allowed to bid for a tenancy. However, they were also denied this right. An official inquiry was severely critical of the department. Dugdale resigned accepting full responsibility for the conduct of his department.

Sir David Maxwell Fyfe, the Home Secretary, sought to clarify when and how ministerial responsibility applies. These can be clarified into four principles:[104]

1. if the Minister orders a civil servant to act in a particular manner they must accept responsibility;

2. when the civil servant acts properly in accordance with a policy laid down by the minister, the minister must protect the civil servant and accept responsibility;

3. if the official makes a mistake or causes a delay, the minister will acknowledge the mistake and accept responsibility, although they were not personally involved. The minister should take corrective action within the Department;

---

[103] SE Finer, 'The Individual Responsibility of Ministers' (1956) 34 *Public Administration* 377, 393.

[104] These principles are a summary of Maxwell Fyfe's statement to the House of Commons (HC Deb, 20 July 1954, vol 530, cols 1285–7).

4. if a civil servant takes an action of which the minister disapproves, which was taken without the minister's prior knowledge, and the conduct of the civil servant is reprehensible, the minister is not obliged to endorse the action. While the minister remains constitutionally responsible to Parliament for the fact that something has gone wrong, he should give an account to Parliament.

 Pause for reflection

Considering the Maxwell Fyfe principles we have discussed, was Brazier correct when he pithily summarized them as 'the further the minister was, geographically or hierarchically from the events complained of, the less he will generally be expected to take the blame for them and resign'?[105]

The precedents of Dugdale and Lord Carrington remain notable examples of when ministers feel that they should resign. However, under the Conservative Government of the 1980s and 1990s, the doctrine was said to have developed a 'policy' and 'operational' distinction. 'Policy' could be described as a combination of the first two of Maxwell Fyfe's principles and 'operational' is a combination of the last two. Ministers would be more likely to resign if the matter is one of policy as opposed to an operational issue. Yet, establishing when this distinction can be made can prove elusive. This is shown by considering the resignations such as those of Stephen Byers and Estelle Morris during Blair's Government.

Stephen Byers resigned in 2002 as Secretary of State for Transport, Environment and the Regions after a series of misjudgements. He was already under pressure for refusing to sack his special adviser who attempted to use the 9/11 terrorist attacks in New York to 'bury bad news', and amongst other matters he faced allegations that he had misled Parliament.[106] While it was unclear whether this was unintentional, it was clear that he failed to admit that he had inadvertently misled the House or apologized for doing so. Ultimately, his position became untenable and he had to resign.

Shortly afterwards, Estelle Morris unexpectedly resigned, again for a series of incidents rather than for any specific event. Morris was criticized for her handling of a crisis over the marking of A Levels. After initially refusing, she ordered an inquiry, but then was accused of improperly interfering with the inquiry's conclusions. She was also under pressure from the media because exam results were not meeting targets set by her predecessor. It appears that the accumulation of these issues caused her to resign. Woodhouse considers that '[w]hatever the reasons for the resignations of Morris and Byers, they provide additional precedents for a resigning convention within the departmental context'.[107] Considering Finer's approach indicated at the top of this section, that a ministerial resignation is dependent on the wishes of the minister, the Prime Minister, and the party, Woodhouse considers that scrutiny from the media also plays an important role, suggesting that they were the key factor, especially with Morris, who retained the support of the Prime Minister throughout.

---

[105] Rodney Brazier, *Constitutional Practice* (3rd edn, OUP 2009) 194.

[106] HC Deb, 9 May 2002, vol 385, cols 293-4.

[107] Diana Woodhouse, 'UK Ministerial Responsibility in 2002: The Tale of Two Resignations' (2004) 82 *Public Administration* 1, 6.

Similarly, the arbitrary nature with which ministers resign is shown when Charles Clarke as Home Secretary admitted that due to a serious failure within the department the Home Office had failed to deport 1,000 foreign criminals on the completion of their sentences. Clarke offered his resignation to the Prime Minister, who declined. Clarke then stated that he would accept responsibility, but remain in the department to act and put things right. Shortly afterwards, Clarke was offered another position in Cabinet following one of Blair's regular Cabinet reshuffles, but he declined and left the government.

A more recent example of the policy/operational distinction could be seen in the Laidlaw Review into the conduct of the Department of Transport.[108] The Department is responsible for granting franchises to train companies who then run the railway lines. Companies, including Virgin Trains, the operator until December 2019, were invited to bid for the new franchise to run trains on the West Coast Mainline, which covers trains to and from London, Birmingham, Manchester, Liverpool, and Glasgow. This process became a fiasco as the Department chose a winning bid based on an incorrect interpretation of information submitted by the bidders. This meant that the bidding process was severely flawed. When Virgin Trains realized these facts they threatened a judicial review of the decision to award the franchise to the other operator. The response of the government was to cancel the franchise process costing the taxpayer £50 million. The Laidlaw Review found that the Department lacked the skills to run the process properly and it appeared that some civil servants were aware of problems, but this was not passed on to ministers.

In this sense, it appears to mainly be an operational failure. This was the view of the Secretary of State, who blamed their civil servants, and this was accepted by the lead civil servant of the Department, the Permanent Secretary, who suspended three officials. However, arguably, there is a policy element here, in that the terms of the franchise competition were set by ministers who remained responsible for the resourcing the department. This led the House of Commons Transport Committee to lay some blame with ministers on the basis that ministers must ensure departments have the capacity to deliver the policies they introduce.[109] This shows how the policy/operational distinction can be difficult to apply in practice.

Discussing the problem

Consider the problem scenario outlined at the start of the chapter. Would the Education Secretary be required to resign for the failure of the new IT system for schools?

This is a major failure within the department, but it remains difficult to conclude that the Education Secretary must resign in this instance. The difficulties of establishing clear rules as to when ministers should resign is also shown, as this situation does not match any of the four Maxwell Fyfe principles that have been outlined. This appears to be a similar situation as to that within the Department of Transport and the franchise for the West Coast Mainline. In that instance, the blame fell on the civil servants, largely because they failed to inform the Secretary of State about the problem. This appears to have happened here with the Education Secretary.

---

[108] HM Government, *Report of the Laidlaw Inquiry: Inquiry into the lessons learned for the Department of Transport from the InterCity West Coast Competition* (HC 2012–13, 809).

[109] House of Commons Transport Committee, *Cancellation of the InterCity West Coast Franchise Competition* (HC 2012–13, 537) [32].

Counterpoint: Is ministerial accountability 'pure fantasy'?

Anthony King and Ivor Crewe conclude that ministerial accountability is

> almost pure fantasy. Most ministers who make mistakes, however egregious, do not resign and are most unlikely to be sacked. If they do leave the government, it is seldom voluntarily, never at the behest of Parliament. It is either because they have lost the backing of the Prime Minister, or the backing of their own backbenchers, or both. More often than not, they go simply because they have, for whatever reason, become a source of embarrassment to the government—or seem to be about to become.[110]

Considering the examples of ministerial resignations (or non-resignations) discussed above, do you think this is an accurate description of the state of ministerial responsibility today?

Private conduct

Most ministerial resignations involve the private conduct of the minister. This can happen when their personal conduct raises questions about their fitness for office. The *Ministerial Code* is at best unhelpful in this respect, as it baldly states that ministers 'are expected to behave in a way that upholds the highest standards of propriety' and are 'responsible for deciding how to act and conduct themselves' given the requirements of the Code.[111] If necessary, they will be required to justify their actions to Parliament and the public. Yet it remains that the minister stays in office only for as long as they retain the confidence of the Prime Minister.[112] Within this framework, and given the precedents discussed below, it is difficult to establish any coherent approach for ministerial resignations.

The past few years have seen some interesting ministerial resignations. A recurring concern is the blurring of a minister's official capacity with their own private interests.[113] This was shown most clearly with the resignation of Liam Fox as Defence Secretary in 2011. The situation revolved around his connections with Adam Werritty, who, despite lacking any official status, appeared to act as an adviser to Liam Fox and represented himself as such at meetings with senior figures in the US military (amongst others). The other concern was that Werritty, lacking any official status, was being funded by private individuals who had previously donated to Liam Fox's campaigns. The conclusion of these allegations was that Fox had allowed Werritty to act as an adviser funded by private money and may even have gone as far as conducting 'a maverick foreign policy' contrary to the government's official policy run by the Foreign Office.[114] When these facts emerged over several days, politically Fox had no option other than to resign. Later, an investigation by the Cabinet Secretary found several breaches of the *Ministerial Code*, showing that Fox's decision to resign was entirely correct.

---

[110] Anthony King and Ivor Crewe, *The Blunders of Our Governments* (OneWorld 2014) 347.

[111] Cabinet Office, *Ministerial Code* (Cabinet Office 2019) para 1.1 and 1.6.

[112] Ibid para 1.6.

[113] The *Ministerial Code* requires that 'Ministers must ensure that no conflict arises or appears to arise between their public duties and private interests'; ibid para 1.3(f).

[114] Polly Curtis, Jason Burke, and Rupert Neate, 'Liam Fox faces fresh questions on Sri Lanka links' *The Guardian* (13 October 2011), https://www.theguardian.com/politics/2011/oct/13/liam-fox-fresh-questions-over-sri-lanka.

The resignation of Priti Patel as Secretary of State for International Development shared some of the characteristics of Fox's resignation. While on a holiday in Israel, Patel met senior figures in the Israeli government, including Prime Minister Benjamin Netanyahu. These meetings were not authorized by Downing Street or the Foreign Office,[115] and British diplomats based in Israel were unaware that these meetings had taken place. At the meetings, Patel was accompanied by Lord Polak, a longstanding pro-Israel campaigner within the Conservative Party with access to wealthy donors. There were reports of further unauthorized meetings with key political figures from Israel. As this emerged, May ordered Patel to return from an official trip in Uganda, and Patel resigned from the government.[116] In her resignation letter, Patel accepted that her actions 'fell below the high standards that are expected of a Secretary of State'.[117]

The primary concern that led to the resignations of both Fox and Patel was the risk that their ministerial duties had become entangled with their own private interests. The *Ministerial Code* is strict on this, requiring that ministers 'ensure that no conflict arises, or appears to arise, between their public duties and their private interests'.[118] The perception is that both Fox and Patel placed themselves in a situation where they may have allowed themselves to be improperly influenced by donors. As one former minister was quoted as saying in regards to Patel, 'What does it say to the rest of the Middle East if a senior Cabinet minister in charge of Britain's huge aid budget disappears for 48 hours from a family holiday in Israel and is under the wing of a pro-Israeli lobbyist?'[119]

A controversial resignation remains Andrew Mitchell's resignation as Chief Whip. During an incident that became known as 'plebgate', Mitchell was alleged to have sworn at a policeman and then described him as a 'pleb' as he was leaving Downing Street. Mitchell accepted that he swore at the officer, but maintained that he did not use the word 'pleb'. Despite serious problems with the accounts of some of the policemen involved, with one even receiving a one-year prison sentence for misconduct in a public office for lying about witnessing the incident, Mitchell was ultimately forced to resign.[120]

In some circumstances, though, the minister has no option other than to resign. This is most clearly seen when the minister is charged with a criminal offence. In 2011, for example, Chris Huhne resigned as Secretary of State for Energy and Climate Change after he was charged with perverting the course of justice in relation to a speeding offence.

A large proportion of resignations involve sex scandals. In 1983, Cecil Parkinson was forced to resign after fathering a child with his former secretary. Similarly, in 1992, David Mellor was forced to resign, despite having the support of the Prime Minister, when he continued to appear in the press following reports of an extra-marital affair.

---

[115] Although Patel maintained that the then Foreign Secretary, Boris Johnson, was aware of these meetings.

[116] James Landale, 'Priti Patel held undisclosed meetings in Israel' *BBC News* (8 November 2017), https://www.bbc.co.uk/news/uk-politics-41853561.

[117] BBC News, 'Priti Patel quits cabinet over Israel meetings row' *BBC News* (8 November 2017), https://www.bbc.co.uk/news/uk-politics-41923007.

[118] Cabinet Office, *Ministerial Code* (Cabinet Office, 2019) para 1.3f.

[119] James Landale, 'Priti Patel held undisclosed meetings in Israel' *BBC News* (8 November 2017), https://www.bbc.co.uk/news/uk-politics-41853561.

[120] However, in a libel trial in the High Court, it was held 'on balance of probabilities that Mr Mitchell did speak the words alleged or something so close to them as to amount to the same, including the politically toxic word "pleb"', *Mitchell v News Group Newspapers Ltd; Rowland v Mitchell* [2014] EWHC 4014 (QB) [183].

In 2016, Stephen Crabb chose to resign when newspapers revealed that he had 'sexted' a young researcher via WhatsApp.[121] Yet, in 2006, when details of John Prescott's two-year affair with his secretary emerged, Prescott did not resign as Deputy Prime Minister and the question of his resignation was raised as a possibility. A spokesman for the Prime Minister described the issue as a 'private matter'. Similarly, Robin Cook was not required to resign when news of his affair reached the newspapers. It seems that the key factor for both Prescott and Cook was the support of the Prime Minister to remain in government.

Recently, there has been an increasing concern that some MPs have abused their position by making unwanted advances with sexual overtones towards junior parliamentary staff and journalists. Given the status of MPs within Westminster, those subject to these advances felt that they had no right of recourse. These concerns became connected with the broader #MeToo movement when victims of sexual harassment tweeted about their experiences with the aim of increasing awareness of the scale of the problem.

In this context, Jane Merrick, a journalist, informed Downing Street that, in 2003, after lunch, Sir Michael Fallon, who later became the Secretary of State for Defence, had 'lunged' at her.[122] Further allegations involving lewd remarks had been made by his Cabinet colleague, Andrea Leadsom. These allegations made Fallon's position untenable, and he resigned, accepting 'that in the past I have fallen below the high standards that we require of the armed forces that I have the honour to represent'.[123]

Damian Green's past also caught up with him. In 2008, when an Opposition MP, Green's computer was seized from his office by the police as part of an investigation into how government information was being released to the media.[124] In the aftermath of the 2017 Election in June, Damian Green was appointed as First Secretary of State (essentially the Prime Minister's deputy). Kate Maltby, an activist for the Conservative Party, wrote an article about a meeting she had with Green, when Green offered Maltby 'career advice and in the same breath made it clear he was sexually interested'.[125] Green denied these allegations.[126] At this point, the seizure of Green's computer became significant. A police officer involved in analysing the evidence on Green's computer, since retired, made a statement that he found pornography of an extreme nature on Green's computer.

Green denied the allegations and said that the allegation was 'little more than an unscrupulous character assassination', and that the police had 'never suggested to me that

[121] Siobhan Fenton, 'Stephen Crabb accused of "hypocrisy" after "sexting" woman', *The Independent* (9 July 2016), http://www.independent.co.uk/news/uk/politics/dwp-secretary-stephen-crabb-accused-of-hypocrisy-after-sexting-woman-a7128451.html.

[122] Jane Merrick, 'I won't keep my silence: Michael Fallon lunged at me after our lunch' *The Guardian*, 4th November 2017 [https://www.theguardian.com/politics/commentisfree/2017/nov/04/michael-fallon-lunged-at-me-jane-merrick].

[123] Sam Coates, Francis Elliott, and Deborah Haynes, 'Fallon denies lewd comment about Leadsom's cold hands' *The Times* (3 November 2017), https://www.thetimes.co.uk/article/fallon-denies-lewd-comment-about-leadsom-s-cold-hands-gkp3wnzn0.

[124] The circumstances of the initial raid raised questions about parliamentary privilege. This is discussed in the discussion of parliamentary privilege available in the online resources.

[125] Kate Maltby, 'Damian Green probably has no idea how awkward I felt' *The Times* (1 November 2017), https://www.thetimes.co.uk/article/kate-maltby-damian-green-you-probably-have-no-idea-how-awkward-i-felt-j2kk88frj.

[126] Henry Zeffman, 'Deputy PM denies sleaze claim as investigation begins' *The Times* (2 November 2017), https://www.thetimes.co.uk/article/deputy-pm-denies-sleaze-claim-as-investigation-begins-sq50xmdc6.

improper material' had been found.[127] A few weeks later, another police officer repeated the claims, stating that thousands of pornographic images were found.[128] A Cabinet Office inquiry found that Green's response to the pornography allegation was 'inaccurate and misleading', because the Metropolitan Police had previously informed him of their findings on two occasions.[129] This meant that he did not meet the requirements of the Seven Principles of Public Life, which are incorporated into the *Ministerial Code*. In particular by making false statements, Green failed to meet the need for honesty, which requires that 'holders of public office should be truthful'.[130] As regards the allegation from Kate Maltby, the inquiry found that although no definitive conclusion can be reached, Maltby's account was 'plausible'.[131] When the report was published, Green was 'asked to resign'.

In light of the resignations of Fallon and Green, a new paragraph has been inserted into the *Ministerial Code* stating that 'Harassing, bullying or other inappropriate or discriminating behaviour wherever it takes place is not consistent with the Ministerial Code and will not be tolerated'.[132] It is perhaps disappointing, to say the least, that this simply cannot be taken as read.

The insertion of the new section does highlight the importance of the *Ministerial Code* in all the resignations discussed in this section. If a breach of the *Ministerial Code* can be identified, then it is difficult to see that minister remaining in office. This naturally results in the *Code* being updated with more specific provisions taking account of the latest resignations.

〝 Discussing the problem

Will Olivia Hill, the Secretary of State for International Development in the problem scenario, have to resign, given the allegations that have been published about her in the newspapers?

It is possible that Hill will have to resign. The precedents regarding extra-marital affairs are unclear and only sometimes do they trigger the resignation of a minister. The additional embarrassing factor on this occasion is that the affair is with a convicted fraudster. This may raise questions about her judgment. Yet identifying a breach of the *Ministerial Code* for these facts alone is difficult.

Of greater significance is the grant made by the Secretary of State's department to Compassionate Food. Here there is a risk that the Secretary of State's public duties and private interests are in conflict. It is notable that in addition to avoiding any actual conflict of interest, the

→

---

[127] Damian Green, Statement Released on Twitter (4 November 2017: 10:59 p.m.), https://twitter.com/DamianGreen/status/926932035079491584.

[128] Danny Shaw, 'Damian Green computer porn claims: "Thousands" of images viewed' *BBC News* (1 December 2017), http://www.bbc.co.uk/news/uk-politics-42151148.

[129] 'Summary of the Cabinet Secretary's Report on Allegations about Damian Green's Conduct', https://www.gov.uk/government/uploads/system/uploads/attachment_data/file/670198/SUMMARY_OF_THE_CABINET_SECRETARY_S_REPORT_ON_ALLEGATIONS_ABOUT_DAMIAN_GREEN_S_CONDUCT.pdf

[130] Cabinet Office, *Ministerial Code* (Cabinet Office, 2019) Annex A – The Seven Principles of Public Life.

[131] Ibid.   [132] Cabinet Office, *Ministerial Code* (Cabinet Office, 2019), para 1.2.

→

Ministerial Code also refers to the need for ministers to avoid any perception of a conflict between their ministerial capacity and their private interests.[133] This is likely to cause the Secretary of State some difficulty, particularly if it was proven that she was involved in making the decision to award the grant to Compassionate Food.

However, the ultimate arbiter of the *Ministerial Code* is the Prime Minister who is the 'ultimate judge of the standards of behaviour expected of a minister'.[134] It is also notable that it is the media that are driving the situation, as they are finding out more information to embarrass the Secretary of State as they continue to investigate.

It may be that, ultimately, given the media pressure she faces, Hill will have to resign from the government.

7.8 The civil service and special advisers

As mentioned in this chapter, government departments are staffed by civil servants, taking instructions from the Secretary of State who has overall responsibility for the department. In addition, the Secretary of State is likely to appoint their own special advisers, who can assist both the Secretary of State and civil servants by acting as a go-between for the two. They ensure that the minister is informed about the activities of the department and that civil servants are aware of the priorities of the minister.

7.8.1 The civil service

The civil service are the permanent officials that form most of the staff of government departments. The civil service has a strong tradition which can be traced back to the Northcote Trevelyan report of 1854. This report developed the core principles of the civil service that it should be politically impartial, permanent, and have promotion based on merit. Entrants to the service would be able to 'expect the highest prizes in the service if they can qualify themselves for them'.[135]

Until the Constitutional Reform and Governance Act 2010, the Civil Service was maintained through the royal prerogative. This meant that legally civil servants were not employees, but servants of the Crown. Consequently, civil servants owe their duty to the government rather than to individual ministers. Now, under the 2010 Act, aspects of the civil service are on a statutory footing. In particular, the Act creates the Civil Service Commission. The main function of this Commission is to publish a set of principles that governs appointment to the service known as the Civil Service Code.[136] This Code must reflect the need for recruitment being on 'merit on the basis of fair and open competition'.[137] The management of the civil service is the responsibility of the Minister for the Civil Service,[138] who is required to publish and lay before Parliament the Civil Service Code, which regulates the conduct of civil servants.[139]

[133] Cabinet Office, *Ministerial Code* (Cabinet Office 2019) paras 1(f) and 7.1.
[134] Ibid para 1.6.
[135] Report on the Organisation of the Permanent Civil Service (C (1st Series) 3638, 1854) 22.
[136] Constitutional Reform and Governance Act 2010, s 11.
[137] Ibid s 10(2).   [138] Ibid s 3(1).   [139] Ibid s 5.

The provisions of the 2010 Act simply set out the barest of frameworks. The detail is contained in the Civil Service Code, which is based around the principles of integrity, honesty, objectivity, and impartiality. For example, objectivity requires that civil servants are expected to provide information and advice on the basis of the evidence and accurately present the options available. Constitutionally, impartiality is the most important principle, as this requires that civil servants service the government 'whatever its political persuasion, to the best of your ability in a way which maintains political impartiality'.[140] The aim, expressly stated in the Code, is that the relationship between ministers needs to be such that ministers have confidence in their officials, while being aware of the need that they will be required to establish a similar relationship with a future government which may represent a different political party.

While it is difficult to generalize across such a large organization, overall the civil service has three main functions, which can be explained as administrative, policy, and project management. Each of these is considered below.

- *Administrative*—Most roles in the civil service fulfil this function. This is the carrying out of the government's policies, for example running government schemes, issuing passports, and paying unemployment benefits and other social security payments. Depending on the department in question, many of these civil servants are likely to be based outside London in regional offices located around the country.

- *Policy*—A smaller proportion of civil servants will be involved in advising and developing policy with ministers. This will usually be based in Whitehall and is the aspect of central government of most interest to the media.

- *Project management*—Finally, some civil servants have a more managerial role, and run large projects such as preparing for the 2012 Olympic Games or building infrastructure such as new railway lines. These large projects may also be internal, particularly if a government policy requires that the way the department delivers a service requires fundamental change. One example is the introduction of Universal Credit, a wholesale reform of the benefits system, which has required the introduction of new IT systems to implement the new policy.

More recently, there have been increasing concerns that the civil service has lacked the expertise and capacity to meet the demands of modern government. This appears to have been especially the case with introducing modern technology into government. As Anthony King and Ivor Crewe highlight:

> To put it politely, the performance of successive British governments in negotiating contracts and managing projects has not been entirely satisfactory. Ministers and officials have occasionally been ripped off, they have sometimes been gulled into thinking that suppliers possessed knowledge and expertise that they did not possess; and, most commonly they have been misled into believing that their suppliers could deliver by a specified date products and services that they could not possibly deliver, then or ever.[141]

This can be seen in several major projects, including the introduction of a new IT system for the NHS. After several delays, the main elements of the project were cancelled, having cost

---

[140] HM Government, *Civil Service Code*, https://www.gov.uk/government/publications/civil-service-code/the-civil-service-code.

[141] Anthony King and Ivor Crewe, *The Blunders of Our Governments* (Oneworld 2014) 376.

the taxpayer £9.8 billion.[142] Another fiasco was the creation of regional control centres for the Fire and Rescue Services, which was cancelled after almost £500 million had been spent.[143]

The difficulty is that traditionally civil servants are not directly accountable to Parliament.[144] They act in the name of their ministers, yet remain independent from them. While civil servants are theoretically accountable to ministers, in practice this can be difficult as civil service independence means that a minister cannot sack an individual civil servant. This has led to some concerns being expressed about whether the skills of the civil service match the demands of modern government.[145] To address these concerns, and the management of large projects in particular, a rolling programme of reforms to the civil service has been introduced aimed at ensuring that it has the necessary skills, particularly in the IT and procurement sectors.[146]

7.8.2 Special advisers

In recent decades, special advisers (commonly referred to as 'Spads') have become increasingly important within central government. Their presence within Whitehall has become a source of intrigue for the national media and academics. The outcome of their greater importance and consequent scrutiny has been a greater formalization of certain aspects of their role.

Ministers select their own special advisers with their proposed appointment being approved by the Prime Minister.[147] Other than the Prime Minister, each Cabinet minister is entitled to select two special advisers to serve them.[148] If necessary, the Prime Minister can authorize additional appointments. This means that, as of December 2019, the Chancellor of the Exchequer had six, with the Foreign Secretary and the Home Secretary having four each.[149] This reflects the importance of their offices, as the great Offices of State. There appears to be no limit as to the number of special advisers the Prime Minister can appoint; as of December 2019, the then Prime Minister employed forty-four special advisers. Special advisers are classed as 'temporary civil servants' and so are subject to the requirements of the Civil Service Code like all other civil servants.[150]

---

[142] House of Commons Public Accounts Committee, *The dismantled National Programme for IT in the NHS* (HC 2013–14, 294).

[143] House of Commons Public Accounts Committee, *The failure of the FiReControl project* (HC 2010–12, 1397).

[144] Although civil servants do give evidence to Select Committees, they do so 'on behalf of their minister and under their directions'. The rules under which civil servants give evidence to Select Committees are referred to as the 'Osmotherly rules': Cabinet Office, 'Giving Evidence to Select Committees: Guidance for Civil Servants' (Cabinet Office 2014), https://www.gov.uk/government/uploads/system/uploads/attachment_data/file/364600/Osmotherly_Rules_October_2014.pdf.

[145] House of Commons Public Administration Committee, *Good Government* (HC 2008–08, 97).

[146] Civil Service, *Civil Service Workforce Plan 2016–2020*, https://assets.publishing.service.gov.uk/government/uploads/system/uploads/attachment_data/file/536961/civil_service_workforce_strategy_final.pdf.

[147] Constitutional Reform and Governance Act 2010, s 15.

[148] Cabinet Office, *Ministerial Code* (Cabinet Office, 2019) para 3.2.

[149] Cabinet Office, Annual Report on Special Advisors 2019 (Cabinet Office, 2019), https://assets.publishing.service.gov.uk/government/uploads/system/uploads/attachment_data/file/854554/Annual_Report_on_Special_Advisers.pdf.

[150] Cabinet Office, *Code of Conduct for Special Advisors* (Cabinet Office 2016), para 7, https://www.gov.uk/government/uploads/system/uploads/attachment_data/file/579768/code-of-conduct-special-advisers-dec-2016.pdf.

Special advisers are considered as 'a critical part of the team supporting ministers', adding a 'political dimension to the advice and assistance available to ministers'.[151] The intention is to supplement the politically impartial advice they receive from civil servants. Special advisers work alongside civil servants, for example by adding party political content to speeches drafted by civil servants.[152] In many ways, special advisers serve as the 'alter egos' of ministers, as they can represent the minister, both within the department and externally. For example, when working with civil servants, the special adviser may present the views of the minister and discuss the advice they have received from the civil servants.[153] Externally, a special adviser can brief the minister's political party on government policy, discuss policy with external groups or organizations, and, if authorized, represent the minister in the media. In departments with two special advisers, the general practice appears to be that one special adviser works on policy while the other works with the media.[154]

Usually, special advisers carry out their roles effectively to the benefit of both the civil service and ministers. The civil service, when developing policy, is able to gain a better understanding of the minister's aims and objectives through their special adviser as they can explain the political objectives of proposed policies. Similarly, the minister will have the ability to take advantage of the special adviser's knowledge gained through their contact with the civil service and other organizations.

Inevitably, when things do go wrong, they can become the centre of a media storm. A notable example remains Jo Moore, a special adviser for the Transport and Local Government Secretary, who in September 2001 felt that the day of the 9/11 attacks, when terrorists hijacked airplanes and flew them into, among others, the World Trade Center in New York, would be a 'very good day to get out anything we want to bury'.[155] The intention was that this would be an opportunity to release details of a slightly embarrassing change to local councillors' pensions.[156] It also appeared that she intended to repeat this trick on the day of Princess Margaret's funeral.[157] The ensuing controversy meant she had to resign.

This fed into developing controversy over the use of special advisers, which primarily arose during Blair's period as Prime Minister. The concern was that special advisers were becoming increasingly powerful, particularly with the relationship between the government and the media. Concerns were that special advisers were permeating a culture of 'spin', seeking to manipulate the presentation of policy to make a political gain.

To assist with this, Tony Blair, on becoming Prime Minister, authorized some of his special advisers to issue instructions to civil servants. Given the political role of a special adviser, this risked undermining the impartial advice that civil servants give to ministers, as they could be required to follow instructions from a political appointee. However, statute has since intervened to prevent this from reoccurring.[158]

---

[151] Ibid para 1.   [152] Ibid para 3.   [153] Ibid para 4.

[154] The Constitution Unit, 'Being a Special Advisor' (Constitution Unit 2014), https://www.ucl.ac.uk/constitution-unit/publications/tabs/unit-publications/158.

[155] Andrew Sparrow, 'Sept 11: "a good day to bury bad news"', *The Telegraph* (10 October 2011), http://www.telegraph.co.uk/news/uknews/1358985/Sept-11-a-good-day-to-bury-bad-news.html.

[156] Ibid.

[157] BBC News, *Spin memo row quit* (BBC News, 15 February 2002), http://news.bbc.co.uk/1/hi/uk_politics/1823120.stm.

[158] Constitutional Reform and Governance Act 2010, s 8.

Now that special advisers have been given statutory recognition, it is clear that special advisers have become 'indispensable to the way Whitehall works',[159] as they provide a bridge between the political nature of a minister's role and civil servants who have to remain politically impartial.[160] It can be seen that special advisers fill a gap between civil servants and ministers, ensuring that civil servants are aware of the minister's objectives and can be a useful point of contact for interest groups to seek the opinion of the Secretary of State and find out about policy.

7.9 Public bodies

The remaining part of central government to consider is what could be described as 'public bodies'. There are different types, each to some extent separate from ordinary government departments but still carrying out important functions. The range of public agencies is vast, from the well known such as the Bank of England to the very new and relatively obscure such as the Groceries Code Adjudicator. They are a vital part of government, with the latest figures indicating that there are 301 public bodies, employing over 275,000 people, with an expenditure of just over £200 billion.[161] A lack of space prevents a detailed consideration of these bodies, with the following intended to provide an outline of the different types and their connection to ordinary government departments.

Much of the work of these bodies could be carried out by a government department. However, the alleged benefit of the public agencies is their independence by being separate to the department. This comes, though, at the cost of reducing the direct political control over the functions the public body exercises. One example is Ofqual (the Office of Qualification and Examinations Regulations). Created in 2010,[162] it has responsibility to regulate and reform qualifications including GCSEs, AS Levels, A Levels, and various vocational qualifications. This involves ensuring that examinations and assessments reflect what students have achieved and that the general public has confidence in the examinations system. These functions used to be carried about by the Department for Education. The concern was that the Department for Education might allow easier exams to be set so that politicians can use improving exam results as justification for their education policies. Ensuring that politicians and the broader Department are at least one step removed from overseeing the exams system is intended to reassure parents, employers, and the broader public that exams are not being made easier.

Given the variety of functions that the government exercises, there is similarly a broad range of public bodies. As we will see, some merely advise the government, some create policies, and others enforce policy. There are broadly three different types of public agency: non-ministerial departments, non-departmental public bodies, and executive agencies.

---

[159] Ben Yong and Robert Hazell, *Special Advisers: Who They Are, What They Do and Why They Matter* (Hart 2014) 206.

[160] Ibid Ch 10.

[161] Cabinet Office, 'Public Bodies 2018–19' (Cabinet Office 2019).

[162] Under the Apprenticeships, Skills, Children and Learning Act 2009, s 127.

7.9.1 **Non-ministerial departments (NMDs)**

There are currently twenty-two NMDs. These range from the Food Standard Agency, which ensures food safety and hygiene in the UK, to the Crown Prosecution Service, the Serious Fraud Office, and the National Crime Agency. Other MNDs are responsible for regulating specific sectors of the economy such as the Water Services Regulation Authority and the Office for Gas and Electricity Markets, which is responsible for regulating the energy markets. As the category non-ministerial department suggests, they are not headed by a government minister but by a Chief Executive.

This means that NMDs are accountable directly to Parliament, through their Chief Executive, although ministers may provide some limited oversight of the body. This has led to NMDs being described as a 'misunderstood and obscure part of our governance landscape'.[163] The most important NMD is HM Revenue and Customs, which is responsible for collecting taxes. This is an NMD because it reduces the scope for direct political involvement in day-to-day decision-making, avoiding any potential political controversy over any single individual or company's tax affairs.

7.9.2 **Non-departmental public bodies (NDPBs)**

NDPBs are described by the Cabinet Office 'as enjoying a role in the process of national government, but are not part of national government'.[164] They operate at arms' length from ministers, meaning that they operate independently from ministers, yet in contrast to NMDs, a minister is accountable for them before Parliament. In this way, NDPBs are one step closer to a government department than an NMD. As of 31 March 2018, there were 242 NDPBs, and they can be split into two categories: executive and advisory.

Executive NDPBs

As the category suggests, these are NDPBs which provide an executive function separate from the relevant government department. One example is the Arts Council, which distributes funding to cultural institutions such as museums, theatres, and art galleries with the aim of benefiting the public. Although these functions could be carried out by the Department of Culture, Media and Sport, it is considered important for there to be no political interference in deciding who should receive funding. In this way, despite the significant funding from the government, the Arts Council ensures that the arts are independent from party politics.[165] This ensures that government does not succumb to the temptation to dictate which exhibits art galleries or museums display, or the plays theatres produce.

Advisory NDPBs

Usually smaller than an executive NDPB, these are created to provide advice from external experts, external in this context meaning separate from government. These are specialized around particular issues, for example the Advisory Council on the Misuse of Drugs,

[163] Institute for Government, 'The Strange Case of Non-Ministerial Departments' (Institute for Government 2013).

[164] Cabinet Office, 'Classification of Public Bodies: Guidance for Departments' (Cabinet Office 2016) 13.

[165] Department of Culture, Media and Sport, 'Tailored Review of Arts Council England' (April 2017), https://www.gov.uk/government/uploads/system/uploads/attachment_data/file/610358/FINAL_Arts_Council_England_Tailored_Review_Report.pdf.

which makes recommendations based on scientific research regarding which substances should be banned under the Misuse of Drugs Act 1971. This is sponsored by the Home Office, who has overall responsibility for this area of policy. The advantage of creating a NDPB to provide this function, is that the expertise is independent from the government.

7.9.3 Executive agencies

These are described as being part of the government department 'responsible for undertaking executive functions of that department as distinct from giving policy advice' and are accountable to ministers within their department.[166] As of 31 March 2018, there are thirty-seven executive agencies. A classic example is the DVLA, the Driver and Vehicle Licensing Agency, which is responsible for issuing drivers' licences and collecting vehicle excise duty (which is often referred to as the 'car tax'). Executive agencies are staffed by civil servants in the ordinary manner, but headed by a chief executive. In theory, the chief executive is accountable to the minister, who in turn is accountable to Parliament. In this way, the link with Parliament is one step removed. In practice, chief executives give evidence directly to parliamentary committees.

Yet the tension between operational and policy matters, described in 7.7.5, is more acute. Generally, the chief executive of the agency is responsible for operational matters as they are implementing and working to the policy established by ministers. Arguably, in 1995, Michael Howard, as Home Secretary, took advantage of the ambiguity between operational and policy matters. Following the escape of several prisoners, Howard requested the resignation of Derek Lewis, the chief executive of the Prison Service, an executive agency. In response Lewis argued that Howard had interfered in operational matters, while Howard was arguing in Parliament that this was an operational matter for which Lewis should be responsible. Howard survived, but Lewis was dismissed. This raises the prospect that ministers can take advantage of the existence of an executive agency and the distinction between policy and operational matters so that they can take the credit for successes, but blame the agency for any failures.

7.10 Summary

This chapter has explained the nature and structure of central government in the UK. The central figure is the Prime Minister, who in recent decades has become increasingly powerful at the expense of the Cabinet, formed of ministers, who usually lead government departments. The increase in power of the Prime Minister is mainly due to the increase in the functions that are reserved to them. This has also been one cause behind the decline in Cabinet government, with Prime Ministers preferring to make decisions in smaller groups outside of the Cabinet. When it comes to the appointment of ministers, the Prime Minister operates under legal, conventional, and political constraints.

However, the fundamental structure of government remains. The government as a whole is collectively accountable to Parliament and, should a Prime Minister conduct government in such a way as to lose the support of the Cabinet and their MPs then, as Margaret Thatcher discovered in 1990, in effect, they will be removed from office by their

[166] Cabinet Office, 'Classification of Public Bodies: Guidance for Departments' (Cabinet Office 2016) 12.

own Cabinet. Indeed, as the Coalition Government showed, a more traditional approach to Cabinet Government is still possible—although even this fell back on informal ways to resolve disputes on policy. Brexit has placed collective responsibility under considerable pressure, and Theresa May's tenure as Prime Minister saw an unprecedented rate of ministerial resignations and divisions over Brexit, making it hard for her to control her Cabinet.

Ministers are also individually responsible for the activities of their departments. The difficulty is establishing just how far this responsibility now reaches and under what set of circumstances a minister should be expected to resign. This is becoming increasingly difficult as modern government becomes increasingly complex, making it ever more unrealistic to expect that ministers are aware of all the activities and decisions of their department. This led to a distinction between policy and operational issues, with operational matters being the fault of civil servants or officials. The concern of some is that this has allowed ministers to evade responsibility, especially when the distinction between an operational or policy issue is at best unclear. When the issue involves public bodies, which are at least one step removed from the relevant government department, ministerial accountability to Parliament can be made even weaker.

Quick test questions

1. To what extent can it be said that the Prime Minister is *primus inter pares* today? On which factors does this depend?
2. Can it be said that we have 'Cabinet Government' today?
3. What effect did a coalition have on the conduct of government within the Cabinet?
4. Have special advisers made a positive contribution to the conduct of government? In what way is their role different from a civil servant?
5. Is collective responsibility an onerous obligation placed on ministers?
6. In what circumstances should a minister resign?

Further reading

Office of Prime Minister

Mark Bennister and Richard Heffernan, 'Cameron as Prime Minister: The Intra-Executive Politics of Britain's Coalition Government' (2012) 65(4) *Parliamentary Affairs* 778

*Keith Dowding, 'The Prime Ministerialisation of the British Prime Minister' (2013) 66(3) *Parliamentary Affairs* 617

Peter Hennessy, *The Prime Minister: The Office and Its Holders Since 1945* (Penguin 2000)

House of Commons Political and Constitutional Reform Committee, *Role and powers of the Prime Minister* (HC 2014–15, 351)

Ministers and Cabinet

Andrew Blick, *Codes of the Constitution* (Bloomsbury 2016)

House of Commons Political and Constitutional Reform Committee, *The Impact and Effectiveness of Ministerial Reshuffles* (HC 2013–14, 255)

*House of Commons Public Administration Committee, *Smaller Government: What do Ministers do?* (HC 2010–12, 530)

Christopher Foster, 'Cabinet Government in the Twentieth Century' (2004) 67(5) *Modern Law Review* 753

Accountability

Nicholas Bamforth, 'Political Accountability at Play' [2005] *Public Law* 229

Michael Gordon, 'Ministerial Responsibility After Huhne' (United Kingdom Constitutional Law Association Blog, 25 March 2013), available at https://ukconstitutionallaw.org/2013/03/25/mike-gordon-ministerial-responsibility-after-huhne/

House of Commons Public Administration Committee, *Who's accountable? Relationships between Government and arm's length bodies* (HC 2014–15, 110)

Anthony King and Ivor Crewe, *The Blunders of our Governments* (Oneworld 2014)

*Diana Woodhouse, 'UK Ministerial Responsibility in 2002: A Tale of Two Resignations' (2004) 82(1) *Public Administration* 1

Civil Service and special advisors

*Robert Hazell and Ben Yong, *Special Advisors: Who They Are, What They Do and Why They Matter* (Bloomsbury 2004)

Richard Wilson, 'Policy Analysis as Policy Advice' in Michael Moran, Martin Rein and Richard Goodwin , *The Oxford Handbook of Public Policy* (OUP 2006) Ch 7

 Visit this book's **online resources** for additional materials relating to this chapter, including coverage of the Freedom of Information Act 2000 and a full analysis of the start-of-chapter problem scenario.
www.oup.com/he/stanton-prescott2e

8

Parliament

Problem scenario

At the 2024 General Election, Amy Sanderson was re-elected as the Conservative MP for Nanchester. She was first elected to represent the constituency in 2010 and is pleased to be continuing as their MP.

Consider the implications of how Amy Sanderson MP should react to the following events.

- In December 2024, one of the major employers in Nanchester, Silver Chips plc, has announced that it is closing its factory located in Sanderson's constituency. Silver Chips produces components for leading manufacturers of mobile phones and blames the closure on the lack of labour with the relevant skills and education. On hearing the news, some residents of Nanchester constituency met Sanderson, their local MP, for advice.

- In the last Queen's Speech, Her Majesty announced that the government intends to introduce a bill into Parliament that will require businesses to register all foreign workers onto a central database held by the Home Office. The government's intention is that any new foreign employee must be registered within three working days of starting employment. Several backbench MPs, including Sanderson, profoundly disagree with this proposal, believing that it serves no useful purpose, is very illiberal, and is contrary to their political beliefs as Conservatives.

8.1 Introduction

8.1.1 An outline

This chapter considers the functions, structure, and procedures of Parliament. Parliament's main functions include serving as the forum for debate on the main issues of the day; to represent citizens; to enact legislation; and to hold the government to account.[1] As we saw in Chapter 2, Parliament has three elements: the House of Commons, the House of Lords, and the monarch. This chapter considers Parliament in more detail. As will be explained, the monarch's role, although remaining important, is almost exclusively ceremonial. This means that the focus of this chapter is very much on the two Houses, often referred to as 'chambers'.

Historically, the power of the two Houses was relatively equal, although for many centuries, the Commons has taken the primary role in matters of taxation. The balance of power has changed as the requirement for the government to have the confidence of the House of Commons emerged, increasing the authority of the Commons over the Lords. Formal restrictions on the power of the Lords were introduced in the Parliament Acts 1911 and 1949 mean that the Commons is the dominant chamber. This difference in power reflects the different composition of the two chambers. The House of Commons is elected and accountable to the people, whereas the House of Lords is unelected. As we will see when discussing the legislative process, the House of Lords and the House of Commons are both independent from each other, each having different procedures and practices.

The main output of Parliament is legislation. There are two forms of legislation. Primary legislation, referred to as Acts of Parliament, which are the exercise of Parliament's legal supremacy to change the law, either by making new law or amending or abolishing existing law. Parliament also has the power to delegate its law-making power to others, usually to the government, allowing them to make delegated legislation according to the terms set out by Parliament.

As discussed in Chapter 7 and affirmed by the Supreme Court in *R (Miller) v Prime Minister*,[2] a key constitutional principle is that the government is accountable to Parliament. This chapter considers how this accountability takes place, through Parliament's ability to question ministers and scrutinize the government. This is reflected in Parliament's constitutional independence from the other branches of government, as required by the separation of powers as discussed in Chapter 2. Although as described in that chapter, the UK Constitution does not fully realize the separation of powers as the government are members of either House of Parliament. A recurring theme in this chapter is that Parliament may not always fully assert its independence, particularly in the House of Commons due to the role of political parties.

Finally, for Parliament to fulfil its functions and to reflect its independence from both the government and the courts, it enjoys certain 'privileges' under the law which are not available to other institutions. Privilege is discussed in detail in the online resources that accompany this book.

---

[1] The further function of controlling public expenditure is not considered in this chapter. For an accessible introduction to this area, see Robert Rogers and Rhodri Walters with Nicolas Besly and Tom Goldsmith, *How Parliament Works* (8th edn, Routledge 2019) Chapter 7.

[2] [2019] UKSC 41, see 6.6.

Throughout this chapter, but especially in that section, frequent reference is made to *Erskine May: Parliamentary Practice*, which is an authoritative text on the procedure and practices of Parliament written by senior parliamentary clerks.[3]

8.1.2 History and politics

From the outset, it is important to emphasize that Parliament is a historic institution that has gradually developed over the past 750 years from when Simon De Montfort called the first recognizable Parliament in 1265. From 1377, the two-chamber structure we see today emerged. What became the House of Lords reflected how the monarch would seek advice from the owners of the most significant estates, including the Church. This was reflected in the membership of the Lords, which, until reforms made during the twentieth century, was dominated by the aristocracy and the Church.

The House of Commons was formed by elected representatives, elected from a very small electorate based on property ownership. This gradually changed following the enactment of the Great Reform Acts of 1832, 1867, and 1884 which each increased the availability of the vote, forming the basis of the mass democracy we see today. Women first acquired the vote in 1918 and then could vote on the same terms as men—on attaining 21—in 1928. In 1969, the voting age was further reduced to 18.[4] The increase of the size of the electorate served to increase the legitimacy of the House of Commons over the unelected House of Lords.

The history of Parliament explains many of Parliament's most recognizable features. For example, from the middle of the sixteenth century, the House of Commons met in St Stephen's Chapel in Westminster. The seating had three or four rows of benches facing each other, running along the building rather than across the building. This may have had a political effect, as the two banks of benches naturally led to those supporting the government sitting on one side, facing those who opposed the government sat on the other side.[5] Arguably, this gave rise to two party politics, with one party forming the government and another forming the opposition.

This led to an adversarial form of politics, with members being part of political parties and the Commons becoming the setting for political parties, through their members, to battle each other through debate. Primarily, Members owe their allegiance to their party as opposed to the Commons itself. This makes political parties extremely powerful within Parliament. As Dawn Oliver states, members of the Commons are 'captured by their parties . . . which are essentially tribal groupings' able to 'manipulate the organization of members in their own party interests'.[6] As stated in 7.7, although, constitutionally, Parliament scrutinizes the government, MPs who belong to the political party of government will use their membership of the Commons to sustain that government, with many hoping that their allegiance to the party line may lead to them being appointed by the Prime Minister as a minister in the government. By contrast, members of the main opposition party oppose the government from across the chamber and in committees, to serve

---

[3] Sir David Natzler and Mark Hutton (eds), *Erskine May: Parliamentary Practice* (25th edn, 2019 LexisNexis), also available online at https://erskinemay.parliament.uk/. Subsequently called '*Erskine May*'.

[4] The Representation of the People Act passed in 1918 and 1928 respectively.

[5] UK Parliament, 'The Commons Chamber in the 16th Century' (UK Parliament, 2017), http://www.parliament.uk/about/living-heritage/building/palace/estatehistory/reformation-1834/shaping-the-commons-/.

[6] Dawn Oliver, *Constitutional Reform in the UK* (OUP 2003) 172–3.

their party and to embarrass the government, with some hoping to bolster their status within their party so that they could be offered a ministerial position, if and when their party forms a government in the future.

This means that although, in theory, Parliament can reform itself, in practice only those reforms that are acceptable to the party of government stand a chance of being put into effect. Yet, given the adversarial nature of politics, the government is usually unwilling to surrender their power to either Parliament as a whole or to an individual chamber, as that could increase the powers of the opposing parties. This is tempered by the fact that even the most secure government realizes that one day it will be in opposition. However, it can be very difficult to introduce reforms if they do not benefit the main political parties, even though they would benefit Parliament as an institution.[7]

Overall, we will in this chapter:

- consider the composition of both the House of Commons and the House of Lords and possible reforms to both Houses;

- explore the primary legislative procedure and what happens when the House of Commons and the House of Lords disagree;

- ascertain the importance of delegated legislation, but also the problems this causes for Parliament;

- describe the various ways in which Parliament can hold the government to account;

- and, in the online resources, consider the purpose and extent of parliamentary privilege with a focus on Bill of Rights 1688, Article 9.

8.2 The 'life' of a Parliament

This section provides an overview of the 'life of a Parliament' and how elections, sessions of Parliament, and the Queen's Speech all relate to each other. This then allows us to consider in later sections the main features of Parliament including elections and the legislative process.

It may seem strange but, in strict legal terms, Parliament is not a permanent institution. Instead, it is *summoned* by the monarch and exists until it has been *dissolved* according to the provisions of the Fixed-term Parliaments Act 2011. Once dissolved there is no Parliament until a new Parliament, again *summoned* by the monarch, meets for the first time. The terminology of summoning and dissolving Parliament means that each parliamentary term, the period between elections, can be described as 'the life of a parliament'. To explain the life of a parliament, counterintuitively, it makes sense to start at the end rather than the beginning.

8.2.1 Dissolution of Parliament

Parliament can be *dissolved* (meaning that it is brought to an end) in one of three ways under the Fixed-term Parliaments Act 2011. First, it can be dissolved through the expiry of the full five-year fixed term.[8] Secondly, an early general election can be held if the

---

[7] Philip Norton, 'Speaking for Parliament' (2017) 70(2) *Parliamentary Affairs* 191.
[8] Fixed-term Parliaments Act 2011, s 1.

House of Commons passes the motion '[t]hat this House has no confidence in Her Majesty's Government'[9] and fourteen days have elapsed without the House of Commons passing a second motion that '[t]hat this House has confidence in Her Majesty's Government'.[10] As discussed in 6.10, the intention is that a new Prime Minister may have been appointed in that fourteen-day window. The final method is when 66 per cent of MPs (calculated by the number of seats as opposed to 66 per cent of votes) decide to dissolve Parliament and hold an early general election.[11]

It was this final method that was used in April 2017, when, to the surprise of many, the Prime Minister, Theresa May, announced that she wished to hold an early general election. The following day the House of Commons voted overwhelmingly by 522 votes to 13 in favour of dissolving Parliament and holding an early election.[12] Alternatively, as discussed in 6.10.3, an Act of Parliament can be passed an effectively override the Fixed-term Parliaments Act 2011, specifically setting the date of the next election. This happened with the Early Parliamentary General Election Act 2019, which set the date of the election as 12 December 2019. Whichever way the date of the election is set, under the Fixed-term Parliaments Act 2011, Parliament is dissolved twenty-five working days before the date of the election.[13]

Once Parliament is dissolved, all seats are vacated pending the election, which means that Parliament cannot meet because in law there are no longer any MPs. Someone who was an MP before the election only becomes an MP again once they are re-elected. This meant that when the country experienced terrorist attacks in Manchester and London during the 2017 General Election campaign, Parliament could not meet to discuss and debate the issues.

8.2.2 The meeting of the new Parliament

When Parliament has been dissolved, the monarch will issue a royal proclamation which sets the date by which the new Parliament is to meet. The date will be after the General Election. For the 2017 Election, the new Parliament was summoned to meet on 13 June following the General Election on 8 June. This date is before the State Opening of Parliament and the Queen's Speech (discussed in 8.2.3) and allows for the members of both Houses to be sworn in and officially take their seats. Also, in the House of Commons the Speaker of the House is elected by its members.[14]

8.2.3 The state opening of Parliament and vote on the Queen's Speech

A few days after the Parliament first meets, the State Opening of Parliament is held. This is the only occasion when all three elements of Parliament, the Commons, Lords, and monarch all meet in person. This is a moment of grand ceremony, the centrepiece of which is the Queen's Speech, when the Queen reads out the government's legislative

---

[9] Ibid s 2(4).   [10] Ibid s 2(5).   [11] Ibid s 2(1), (2).

[12] HC Deb, 19 April 2017, vol 624, cols 681–712. Under s 2(7) of the 2011 Act the Prime Minister recommended that the date of the next General Election would be 8 June 2017.

[13] Fixed-term Parliaments Act 2011, s 3(1).

[14] If the Speaker from the previous Parliament wishes to continue, then by convention they are elected unopposed.

priorities for the forthcoming session. After several days of debate, the vote on the Queen's Speech is held.[15]

8.2.4 Sessions and prorogation

Unless Parliament is dissolved earlier, it is expected that the life of the Parliament will last for five years. Using the prerogative power of prorogation, the five-year period is usually split into five sessions, each lasting around a year, running from each May.[16] *Prorogation* means the legal power to end a session of Parliament. This is significant because a bill, going through the legislative process must complete all its stages before the end of the session, otherwise it will be lost and the bill would need to be reintroduced in the following session.[17] As a prerogative power, prorogation is exercised by the monarch acting on the advice of the government. Exercise of the power also sets the date for start of the next session of Parliament. Each session is opened by another State Opening of Parliament and Queen's Speech.

The power to prorogue Parliament was thought to have become a formality with only a few days, usually a week between the end of one session and the start of the next one. After the 2017 General Election, the government announced that the first session of Parliament would last two years instead of one. The government justified this on the basis that Brexit requires a substantial amount of complex legislation and more time is needed for this legislation to pass through both Houses. As Theresa May failed to obtain agreement from the House of Commons for the Withdrawal Agreement she had negotiated with the EU, this session continued, becoming the longest session in history since the Civil War (1642–51).[18] The decision of her successor, Boris Johnson, to prorogue Parliament for five weeks in the lead up to the (then) expected Brexit date of 31 October 2019 was challenged before the courts. In *R (Miller) v Prime Minister*, the Supreme Court held that the power of prorogation cannot be used to frustrate the ability of Parliament to pass legislation or hold the government to account.[19]

The following two sections consider the composition of the House of Commons and the House of Lords.

8.3 The House of Commons

The key feature is that the House of Commons is elected, making the Commons the dominant House within Parliament. At all times, the key test of the government's capability to govern is that it maintains the confidence of the House. This means that it is important

---

[15] The vote on the Queen's Speech used to be considered by some as a test of whether the government has the confidence of the House of Commons. This has been placed into doubt by the Fixed-term Parliaments Act 2011.

[16] This is based on the practice since the passing of the Fixed-term Parliaments Act 2011. Before the passing of this Act, the practice was more variable.

[17] However, with the agreement of either the Lords or the Commons, if a bill has not completed all of its stages before the end of the session, the government can carry-over a bill from one session to the next, meaning that it can effectively start from where it left off in the new session.

[18] Edward Hick, 'Is this the longest parliamentary session ever?' (House of Commons Library, 10 May 2019) available at https://commonslibrary.parliament.uk/parliament-and-elections/parliament/is-this-the-longest-parliamentary-session-ever/.   [19] See 6.6.

to consider the electoral process and the effect that this has on the composition of the House of Commons.

8.3.1 Elections

Currently, the House of Commons is made up of 650 MPs, each representing a constituency in the UK.[20] The electoral system used to choose the MP for a constituency is described as the first-past-the-post system and is simple to explain. Those who are registered to vote in each constituency choose which one of the candidates standing in their constituency they would like to represent them. The candidate with the most votes wins and takes up their seat at Westminster.

There are other important factors to consider. Most, but not all, candidates belong to a political party and voters are likely to vote for a candidate on the basis of the party the candidate represents rather than attributes or characteristics of the candidate. This is because a voter's choice of an MP leads indirectly to their choice of a government, as the government is usually formed by the party that wins the most seats in the House of Commons.[21] For this reason, a voter may often informally say they 'voted for a Labour Government' or 'voted Liberal Democrat' rather than for an individual candidate.

The electorate

The electorate includes all those entered onto the register of electors for a constituency. The qualifications to register include:

- the voter has reached eighteen years of age by the date of the general election;[22]
- the voter is either a Commonwealth citizen or a citizen of the Republic of Ireland.[23] By implication this includes all British citizens.

This means that unless a voter is a Commonwealth or Irish citizen, EU citizens cannot vote at general elections, but can vote in local elections and elections to the European Parliament.[24] At a general election, each voter may only vote once and in one constituency.[25]

Those who are not entitled to vote include:

- persons subject to mental incapacity;[26]
- persons detained in mental health hospitals;[27]
- Members of the House of Lords;

---

[20] Under the Parliamentary Voting System and Constituencies Act 2011, the number of MPs is due to be reduced to 600. However, despite the necessary proposals being published in 2018, the government has not submitted them to Parliament for approval. See Ron Johnston, Charles Pattie, and David Rossiter, 'Boundaries in limbo: why the government cannot decide how many MPs there should be' (LSE British Politics and Policy Blog, 1 May 2019) available at https://blogs.lse.ac.uk/politicsandpolicy/boundaries-in-limbo/.

[21] As discussed in Chapter 6, this could be a majority government, a minority government, or a coalition.

[22] Representation of the People Act 1983, s 1(1)(d).

[23] Ibid s 1(1).   [24] Ibid s 2(1)(c).

[25] Ibid s 1(2).   [26] Ibid s 1(1)(b).   [27] Ibid s 3A.

- persons convicted of a criminal offence and detained in a 'penal institution' (i.e. a prison);[28]
- British and Irish citizens, who have been resident overseas for more than fifteen years.[29]

Counterpoint: Should 16- and 17-year-olds be given the vote?

In Scotland, 16- and 17-year-olds could vote at the Scottish Independence Referendum in 2014 and in the Scottish Parliamentary Elections held in 2016. Yet the same age group were unable to vote in the 2017 General Election. This led Labour and Liberal Democrats to propose that 16- and 17-year-olds across the UK should be able to vote in all elections. The argument is that 16-year-olds are legally able to marry, to have sex, and to join the armed forces, yet they cannot vote. However, others argue that 16 is too young, as these individuals have insufficient life experience and therefore the voting age should remain at 18.

What do you think? Do you think that someone as young as 16 should be able to vote at elections?

Candidates and qualification for membership

In general, there are no qualifications required to stand as a candidate in a constituency. However, some categories of people are excluded from being a member of the House of Commons:

- persons aged under 18;[30]
- nationals of countries other than Commonwealth nations (excluding Ireland).[31] If a person is domiciled for tax purposes in a country other than the UK, on becoming a member of the House of Commons, they will be treated as being domiciled in the UK. This means that they will be required to comply with UK tax law;[32]
- members of the House of Lords;[33]
- those subject to a bankruptcy order.[34] If a member becomes bankrupt, then their seat is vacated;

---

[28] Ibid s 3. This has proven to be controversial since the ECtHR in *Hirst v UK (No 2)* [2005] ECHR 681 has found this provision to be contrary to Protocol 1, Art 3 ECHR. In *Smith v Scott* [2007] SC 345, the Scottish court followed *Hirst* and issued a declaration of incompatibility under the Human Rights Act 1998, s 4. However, Parliament has chosen not to amend the legislation. See also 15.5.3.

[29] Representation of the People Act 1985, ss 1–2. In the December 2019 Queen's Speech, the government committed to abolishing the fifteen-year limit, implementing a commitment from the Conservative Party 2019 General Election manifesto, Conservative Party, *Get Brexit Done – Unleash Britain's Potential* (Conservative and Unionist Party, 2019) 48.

[30] Electoral Administration Act 2006, s 18. Previously it was twenty-one years of age.

[31] Act of Settlement 1701, s 3 states, 'no Person born out of the Kingdoms of England, Scotland or Ireland or the Dominions thereunto belonging . . . (except such as are born of English Parents) shall be capable to be . . . a Member of either House of Parliament'. However, the effect of the British Nationality Act 1981, s 71, is that this ban does not apply to citizens of Ireland or a Commonwealth country.

[32] Constitutional Reform and Governance Act 2010, s 41.

[33] At common law, see Robert Blackburn, *The Electoral System in Britain* (Macmillan, 1995) 161.

[34] Insolvency Act 1986, s 426C.

- those imprisoned for a sentence of longer than a year. If a member becomes convicted of a crime and sentenced for longer than a year, their seat is vacated;[35]

- those guilty of certain election practices.[36]

In addition, under the House of Commons Disqualification Act 1975, those holding certain offices are unable to take a seat in the House of Commons. Under section 1 of the 1975 Act, these include:

- members of the judiciary, as listed in Part I of Schedule 1 to the 1975 Act. This includes District Judges, Circuit Judges, and judges of the High Court, Court of Appeal, and Supreme Court;

- civil servants;

- members of the 'regular' armed forces, including the British Army, Royal Navy, Royal Marine, and Royal Air Force;

- members of a police force;

- Members of Parliaments or legislatures outside the Commonwealth or Ireland. This includes the European Parliament;

- members or office holders of a range of public bodies listed in Parts II and III of Schedule 1 to the 1975 Act. Usually these are bodies which are required to be independent from Parliament and/or the government.

By-elections and retiring from the House

Should a seat become vacant for any reason, for example through the death or retirement of a member, then a **by-election** is held to allow the constituency to select a new member.

It is has long been the practice that a Member cannot simply retire from their seat during the life of a Parliament.[37] To overcome this restriction, a Member wishing to retire is appointed to an office under the Crown, usually either the Steward of the Manor of Northstead or the Bailiff of Her Majesty's Three Chiltern Hundreds of Stoke, Daresborough, and Burnham. These offices are entirely nominal with no functions, and have only been retained to provide a mechanism for MPs to retire.[38] They hold this office until another member wishes to retire and is appointed in their place.

Recall of MPs Act 2015

If an MP has:

(1) been convicted of an offence and is sentenced to imprisonment for less than a year;

(2) been suspended from the House for ten days or more; or

(3) been convicted of providing false or misleading information for their expenses,

then, under the Recall of MPs Act 2015, a recall petition will be triggered. The Speaker will notify the constituency, and the 'recall petition' is opened in the constituency. If this

---

[35] Representation of the People Act 1981, s 1.

[36] Ibid ss 3, 173, and 160.

[37] This is due to a resolution passed by the House on 2 March 1624. See House of Commons Information Office, 'The Chiltern Hundreds' (April 2011); if a member wishes to retire at the next general election, they simply choose not to stand for re-election.

[38] House of Commons Disqualification Act 1975, s 4.

petition is signed by at least 10 per cent of constituents, then a by-election will be held. The member is said to have been 'recalled' back to his constituency by his constituents, and if they so wish, they can contest the by-election.

To date, three recall petitions have been triggered under the Act. Ian Paisley Jr was suspended from the Commons for thirty days for failing to declare that visits to Sri Lanka were paid for by the Sri Lankan government. However, the petition failed to meet the 10 per cent target. By contrast, the 10 per cent target was hit when Fiona Onasanya was convicted of perverting the course of justice and sentenced to three months in prison, and when Christopher Davies was convicted for making false expenses claims. Perhaps unsurprisingly, both Onasanya and Davies lost their seats at the following by-election.

8.3.2 The electoral system

The following four tables (Tables 8.1 to 8.4) show the results from the last five general elections.[39]

From these figures, the following comments can be made about the first-past-the-post electoral system, which was outlined in 8.3.1.

Disproportionality of first-past-the-post

It is difficult to conclude that the electoral system delivers results where parties get a proportion of seats broadly equivalent to their share of the vote. Indeed, the effect of this disproportionality appears to be quite random. In 2005, Labour obtained only 2.9 per cent more of the vote than the Conservatives, but still won 25 per cent more seats.

TABLE 8.1 2005 General Election (Outcome: Labour Majority Government)

Party	% of vote	Seats won	% of total seats
Conservative	32.4	198	30.7
Labour	35.2	355	55.0
Liberal Democrat	22.0	62	9.6
Scottish National Party	1.5	6	0.9
United Kingdom Independence Party	2.2	0	0.0
Others (including Northern Ireland parties and Plaid Cymru)	6.7	25	3.9
	Total Seats	**646**	

Source: Colin Rallings and Michael Thrasher, *British Electoral Facts 1832–2012* (Biteback 2012)

[39] In the following tables, the Speaker has been counted as an 'other' rather than counting for the political party to which they used to belong.

TABLE 8.2 2010 General Election (Outcome: Conservative–Liberal Democrat Coalition Government)

Party	% of vote	Seats won	% of total seats
Conservative	36.1	306	47.1
Labour	29.0	258	39.7
Liberal Democrat	23.0	57	8.8
Scottish National Party	1.7	6	0.9
United Kingdom Independence Party	2.2	0	0.0
Others (including Northern Ireland parties and Plaid Cymru)	8.0	23	3.5
	Total Seats	**650**	

Source: Colin Rallings and Michael Thrasher, *British Electoral Facts 1832–2012* (Biteback 2012)

TABLE 8.3 2015 General Election (Outcome: Conservative Majority Government)

Party	% of vote	Seats won	% of total seats
Conservative	36.8	330	50.8
Labour	30.4	232	35.7
Liberal Democrat	7.9	8	1.2
Scottish National Party	4.7	56	8.6
United Kingdom Independence Party	12.6	1	0.2
Others (including Northern Ireland Parties and Plaid Cymru)	7.6	23	3.5
	Total Seats	**650**	

Source: House of Commons Library, *General Election 2015* (Briefing Paper CBP 7186, 28 July 2015) available at http://researchbriefings.files.parliament.uk/documents/CBP-7186/CBP-7186.pdf

By contrast, in 2019, the Conservatives needed to win more than 11 per cent more of the vote than Labour to obtain a similar number of seats.

More significantly, the electoral system benefits the two largest parties, who usually end up winning a greater share of the seats than their share of the vote would seemingly justify. This is at the expense of smaller parties, particularly the Liberal Democrats, who in 2005 got 22 per cent of the vote, but only 10 per cent of the seats. A particularly egregious

TABLE 8.4 2017 General Election (Outcome: Conservative Minority Government)

Party	% of vote	Seats won	% of total seats
Conservative	42.4	317	48.8
Labour	40.0	262	40.3
Liberal Democrat	7.4	12	1.8
Scottish National Party	3.0	35	5.4
United Kingdom Independence Party	1.8	0	0.0
Others (including Northern Ireland parties and Plaid Cymru)	5.4	24	3.7
	Total Seats	**650**	

Source: House of Commons Library, *General Election 2017: Results and Analysis* (Briefing Paper CBP 7989, 2nd edn, 29 January 2019) available at http://researchbriefings.files.parliament.uk/documents/CBP-7979/CBP-7979.pdf

TABLE 8.5 2019 General Election (Outcome: Conservative majority government)

Party	% of vote	Seats won	% of total seats
Conservative	43.6	365	56.2
Labour	32.0	202	31.0
Liberal Democrat	11.5	11	1.7
Scottish National Party	3.9	48	7.4
Brexit Party	2.0	0	0
Others (including Northern Ireland parties and Plaid Cymru)	7.0	24	3.7
	Total Seats	**650**	

Source: House of Commons Library, *General Election 2019: Results and Analysis* (Briefing Paper CBP 7989, 2nd edn, 28 January 2020), available at http://researchbriefings.files.parliament.uk/documents/CBP-8749/CBP-8749.pdf

example is the United Kingdom Independence Party (UKIP) who in 2015, despite winning over 12 per cent of the vote, only had one MP, equivalent to 0.2 per cent of the seats. The explanation for this is that support for minor parties is usually spread across the country, making it more difficult for them to succeed in individual constituencies. In theory, a political party can obtain 15 per cent of the vote across every constituency yet win no seats if another party always wins a greater share of the vote for each seat.

By contrast, a political party can reap the dividends if its support is concentrated in specific constituencies. For example, the Scottish National Party (SNP) only fields candidates in the fifty-nine Scottish constituencies, and in 2015 won fifty-six of those constituencies with 50 per cent of the vote in Scotland. This meant that Labour, which won nearly a quarter of the vote in Scotland, only won one Scottish constituency.[40] The SNP's concentration of support in Scottish constituencies means that it is more successful than its national vote share would indicate.

The way the electoral system treated third parties was becoming more of an issue as voters increasingly moved away from Labour and the Conservatives to other smaller parties. For example, in 1951, 98.5 per cent of the vote went to one of the two main parties. By 2010, this had gradually reduced to 65.1 per cent. This was felt to be a continuous trend, but it has been brought to an abrupt halt with the 2017 General Election, which saw 82.4 per cent of votes being cast for either a Conservative or Labour candidate, the highest since 1979. The 2019 Election saw the Conservatives increase their share of the vote from 42.4 per cent to 43.6 per cent, but Labour's share reduced by 8 per cent from 40 per cent to 32 per cent. This hints at a possible trend where the Conservatives retain their share of the vote, while Labour's declines in favour of other, smaller parties, such as the Liberal Democrats. The issue then becomes that none of these smaller parties, including Labour, has the critical mass of support required to take advantage of disproportionate effects of the first-past-the-post system and challenge the Conservatives. Unless these smaller parties decide to work together, or even merge, this dynamic could result in extended periods of Conservative government. Consequently, those smaller parties often argue for electoral reform, and for a different electoral system to be used for general elections, but the Conservatives favour retaining first-past-the-post. We now consider the debate on electoral reform.

 Counterpoint: The effects of disproportionate results under first-past-the-post

This historic disproportionality has led to repeated calls by many to change the electoral system to one that is fairer to smaller parties and delivers more proportionate results. The need is arguably greater when turnout is considered. In 2005, Labour won the election with 35.2 per cent of the vote, on a turnout of 61.4 per cent. This meant that Labour governed with only 21.6 per cent of the electorate actually voting for them. The possibility of such results led to Lord Hailsham, in his book *The Dilemma of Democracy*, to conclude that 'I would certainly prefer almost any system of electoral reform to the prospect of elective dictatorship in any form, but particularly one based on first-past-the-post'.[41]

Electoral reformers have long argued that from the electoral system much else follows. The electoral system allows a party, being elected into government on a minority of the vote, to introduce their policies without much resistance from the House of Commons, who will slavishly pass them into law because the government has a majority. The House of Lords, historically, would provide

→

---

[40] House of Commons Library, *General Election 2015* (Briefing Paper CBP7186, 28 July 2015) 14.
[41] Lord Hailsham, *The Dilemma of Democracy: Diagnosis and Prescription* (Collins 1978) 187–8.

→

little resistance to the government.[42] Then, after an election, should the other political party form the government, they get the opportunity to undo the policies of the previous government and introduce their own, different policies. This is viewed as leading to unstable policy as political parties are encouraged to seek short-term goals rather than attempt to deal with the underlying causes for many of the country's problems. Most reformers argue that the existing system is particularly disproportionate and flagrantly breaches the principle as explained by John Stuart Mill that:

> In a really equal democracy, every or any section would be represented, not disproportionately but proportionately. A majority of the electors would always have a majority of the representatives; but a minority of the electors would always have a minority of the representatives. Man for man, they would be as fully represented as the majority. Unless they are, there is not equal government, but a government of inequality and privilege; one part of the people rule over the rest; there is a party whose fair and equal share of influence in the representation is withheld from them contrary to all just government, but above all, contrary to the principle of democracy, which professes equality as its very root and foundation.[43]

Arguments in favour of first-past-the-post

We will now examine the arguments for the existing system in turn.

Simplicity

One key argument is that the first-past-the-post system is familiar to the voters and they understand it. The candidate in the constituency with the most votes wins and represents that constituency in Parliament. Although the system has the consequence of disproportionality, the argument of simplicity is hard to refute when compared to the complexity of some electoral systems that are discussed next.

Avoiding extremism

The concern with other electoral systems is that they can allow small extremist parties into Parliament. In this vein, various fascists including Hitler are often invoked, based on the claim that they gained representation due to proportionate systems which they have traditionally struggled to get under first-past-the-post. However, Robert Blackburn states that this 'inflammatory line of oratory seems to suggest that the phenomenon of political fanaticism is somehow linked to the electoral laws of a country' and not to the underlying economic and social issues or issues of identity which make fascism or other extreme forms of politics attractive in the first place.[44]

Constituency representation

One benefit is that by having one MP per constituency, each MP becomes unambiguously responsible for representing the interests of their constituency in Parliament. This includes considering the effect of legislation and government policy on their constituency

---

[42] Although this could be more of an argument for reforming the House of Lords rather than the House of Commons, see 8.4.2 and 8.4.3 for discussion of this point.
[43] John Stuart Mill, *Considerations on Representative Government* (1861) Ch 7.
[44] Robert Blackburn, *The Electoral System in Britain* (Macmillan 1995) 393.

and raising issues relevant to their constituency in Parliament. Also, individual constituents can raise issues with their MP by writing to or emailing them who can consider the matter and raise it with government ministers, raising it in Parliament or, if relevant, refer the query to the Parliamentary Ombudsman.[45] An MP's link with their constituency has become an increasingly important aspect of their role. The concern is that this link could be lost with the multi-member constituencies that other electoral systems involve.

 Discussing the problem

Take a moment to look at the problem scenario at the beginning of the chapter. Why might you expect constituents to go to Amy Sanderson following the news that Silver Chips will be closing its factory?

As their constituency MP, Amy Sanderson is responsible for representing the interests of that constituency, she should listen to their concerns and make the government aware of them. This reflects the link between an MP and their constituency that the first-past-the-post system can achieve and how MPs can raise the concerns of their constituency in Parliament.[46] Because it is for the government to act in response to the news, as an MP there is very little that Sanderson can directly achieve for those at risk of losing their jobs. However, Sanderson can be expected to use her position as an MP to pressurize the government to act for her constituents.

Other benefits may be more subjective. As we have seen, Lord Hailsham describes first-past-the-post as leading to 'elective dictatorship'.[47] However, others might view this as representing strong government. The advantage of the current system is that it allows a single party to implement its manifesto commitments and then be judged on its record at the next election. Historically, first-past-the-post has a consistent record of returning majority governments. There had been concerns that the electoral system was increasingly failing to deliver on this basis. The 2010 and 2017 elections failed to deliver a single party majority government, and even then, the intervening election in 2015 only gave the Conservatives a slender majority of twelve. The result in 2019, and the Conservative majority of eighty, is return to the large majorities of 1983, 1987, 1997, 2001, and 2005.

Other electoral systems make it far harder for any one party to form a government, meaning that a large party must either govern with another party in a coalition or as a minority. This could lead to smaller parties holding the balance of power, acting as king-makers, as they reach a deal with a larger party. Their price for their support is likely to be the implementation of some of their policies, even though they obtained relatively little support from the electorate. For example, following the 2017 General Election, the Democratic Unionist Party in return for supporting the Conservative Government secured up to £1 billion of extra public spending specifically for Northern Ireland, which was not available to the rest of the UK.[48]

---

[45] The role of the Parliamentary Ombudsman is discussed in 14.3.

[46] It must be stated that other electoral systems that deliver one MP per constituency, such as the alternative vote, or the supplementary vote are just as able to deliver this MP–constituency link.

[47] Lord Hailsham, *The Dilemma of Democracy: Diagnosis and Prescription* (Collins 1978) 187–8.

[48] See 6.9.4.

The concern is also that smaller parties could withdraw from any coalition or refuse to support a minority government, meaning that the government will be 'weak' and unable to act decisively as they lack a majority in the House of Commons.

Alternative electoral systems

For some, the arguments in favour of first-past-the-post, the MPs' constituency presence, the probability of strong governments, and the simplicity of the system do not outweigh the problems caused by the disproportionate results it delivers. This led the Liberal Democrats, who have long been in favour of electoral reform, to demand a referendum on adopting the alternative vote system for general elections as a condition to entering into coalition with the Conservatives. This proved to be unpopular with voters and it was rejected by 67.9 per cent of those voting.[49] This reflects the difficulty for reformers who need to propose a viable alternative to first-past-the-post, as each alternative comes with its own advantages and disadvantages.

Alternative vote

This was the electoral system that was rejected in a referendum held in 2011. Each voter in a constituency ranks each of the candidates in their order of preference. If a candidate gets more than 50 per cent of the first preferences they are elected. If no candidate reaches the 50 per cent hurdle the candidate with the fewest first preferences drops out and the second preferences of those votes are allocated to the remaining candidates. This process is repeated until one candidate gets an overall majority of the votes.

The system does not guarantee proportionality, but it does allow voters to express their preferences in a more complex way than simply casting one vote. For example, if someone is a Liberal Democrat supporter, but lives in a constituency where the two main parties are Conservatives and Labour, a voter can choose the Liberal Democrat candidate as their first preference and then choose either Labour or Conservative for their second preference. This way the vote for the Liberal Democrat is not 'wasted', as that first preference is registered, but they can still have an impact on who gets elected.

Supplementary vote

This system is used for mayoral elections around the country.[50] Each voter chooses a first and second preference. Initially, all the first preferences are counted. Should a candidate receive more than 50 per cent of the first preferences, they are elected. If not, the top two candidates effectively 'run off' and the second preferences of voters whose first preference has been eliminated are counted.

Additional members system

This system is used for elections to the Scottish Parliament and Welsh Assembly. There are effectively two elections, electing two types of member. First, there is the ordinary, constituency based election conducted using the first-past-the-post system. Then, to ensure greater proportionality, 'additional' members are elected on a regional basis, using a party list. This means that voters cast a second vote for a political party. These additional seats are then allocated according to a formula that aims to achieve a more proportionate result.

[49] Colin Rallings and Michael Thrasher, *British Electoral Facts 1832–2012* (Biteback 2012) 243.
[50] Although the Conservative manifesto for the 2017 General Election proposed replacing the use of the supplementary vote with the first-past-the-post vote.

Party list

This is relatively straightforward. Electors vote for a party rather than a candidate. The seats are then allocated according to the proportion of votes cast for each party. For example, if there are ten seats and Party A wins 50 per cent of the vote, Party B 40 per cent, and Party C 10 per cent, then Party A would get five seats, Party B four seats, and Party C one seat respectively. The party list can be on a national basis or on a regional basis, with each region being allocated a number of seats based on their population. In the UK, the regional party list system was used for elections to the European Parliament.

Single transferable vote

This is the most complex of the systems used. The country is split into large multi-member constituencies. The voter ranks each candidate according to their preference. Then a quota is calculated based on the number of seats available and the number of votes cast. In a four-seat constituency, this would be equivalent to around a fifth of the votes. Any candidate who received more than the quota would be elected in the first round. If there are still some seats left to be filled, then the second preferences of those who voted for a candidate are then reallocated to the remaining candidates. If this does not fill all the seats, then the candidate with the fewest number of first preferences is eliminated and their vote is transferred according to their second preferences. While complex to explain, the system is relatively straightforward for voters, who merely rank the candidates in order of preference, and the outcome is proportionate. The problem for some is the intricate mathematics that takes place in the middle of the process.

This electoral system is used to elect members to the Northern Irish Assembly and for local government elections in Scotland.

8.3.3 Speaker of the House of Commons

Arguably the most important Member of the House of Commons is the Speaker. The Speaker has several functions both inside and outside the chamber.

Inside, the most obvious function of the Speaker is to maintain order during debates. If a member acts contrary to the rules of the House, then they are called to 'order' by the Speaker. There are a range of rules and practices that members must comply with, including addressing their remarks to the Speaker rather than to an individual member, referring to other members by the name of their constituency rather than their name, and avoiding the use of unparliamentary language, which includes terms that insult other members.[51] This helps ensure that debates in the House are conducted with a level of civility and politeness. The Speaker is supported by three Deputy Speakers.

Other important functions of the Speaker include choosing who to speak in a debate and which amendments to a bill or motion are selected for debate and a vote. John Bercow, the Speaker from 2009 to 2019, allowed significantly more urgent questions. These are questions on a matter of topical importance, which a member believes should be raised as a matter of urgency. Finally, if the House is not sitting due to a recess, the Speaker can recall the House due to the need to debate or reflect on events which cannot wait

---

[51] One relatively recent example is Tom Watson, a Labour MP, describing the Conservative minister Michael Gove as 'a miserable pipsqueak of a Man'. The use of 'pipsqueak' was considered unparliamentary by the Speaker, who asked Watson to withdraw the remark; HC Deb, 7 July 2010, vol 513, col 486.

until the House was expected to return. Examples of when the House of Commons has been recalled include the Argentinian invasion of the Falklands, the death of the Queen Mother, and the outbreak of public disorder during August 2011.

Following the introduction of English Votes for English Laws, which is discussed in 8.5.10, the Speaker is required to determine which bills are required to go through the procedure.

The Speaker also fulfils an external role and is the figurehead of the House of Commons and represents the House externally. This involves acting as the spokesperson of the House; for example, expressing the condolences of the House to the US Congress following the 9/11 attacks in New York or presenting an address to the Queen for her Diamond Jubilee.[52] Similarly, the Speaker receives ambassadors, ministers, and Speakers from other parliaments around the world when they visit Westminster.

To fulfil these functions fairly, the Speaker must be impartial between government and Opposition. Consequently, on becoming Speaker, they will resign the membership of their political party. When seeking re-election as a member, at a general election, the Speaker does so as 'the Speaker seeking re-election' rather than as a political party. By convention, the major parties do not field candidates in the Speaker's constituency. The Speaker fulfils their constituency business like any other constituency MP.

8.3.4 The political dynamic of the House—government, Opposition

As the first-past-the-post system favours the two largest parties, this naturally leads to an adversarial way of conducting business. The government proposes laws, gives statements in the House, and answers questions, and it is the role of the Opposition to criticize, challenge, and attempt to embarrass the government. The second largest party is usually designated as Her Majesty's Loyal Opposition and they form their own Shadow Cabinet, who will question and challenge their opposite number in government. The intention is that when the Prime Minister makes a statement to the House, the Leader of the Opposition will respond; similarly, when the Defence Secretary answers questions, the Shadow Defence Secretary will ask questions on behalf of the Opposition.

As stated in 8.1, the adversarial approach is furthered by the layout of the Chamber. The government sits on the front bench to the right of the Speaker and the Opposition sits on the front bench opposite. Behind the front benches on both sides are where other MPs sit (not members of either the government or Opposition), meaning that these are referred to as 'backbenchers'. The doctrine of collective responsibility, discussed in 7.7.1, means that government ministers must support the government. The Opposition is expected to maintain a consistent policy in the same manner, as its overall aim is to present itself as a viable alternative government.

Backbenchers have a freer hand and are free to choose whether to vote with their party's line or 'rebel' and vote against. Members of all parties are expected to follow the party line on any given issue and those with aspirations of ministerial office will have to show loyalty to the party. Maintaining party loyalty is the responsibility of the 'party whips'. The Chief Whip for the government side has a particularly important role and must inform the Prime Minister if any future votes hang in the balance because their backbench

---

[52] Robert Rogers and Rhodri Walters with Nicolas Besly and Tom Goldsmith, *How Parliament Works* (8th edn, Routledge 2019) 56.

MPs have indicated that they may vote against the government. Should a member be thinking of voting against the government, the whips will use their powers of persuasion and attempt to change their mind. If a large rebellion is likely, the Prime Minister may arrange to see MPs to discuss their concerns. Controversial issues are likely to be discussed in advance so that the whips and the government can ascertain the opinion of their backbenchers and decide how to approach the matter.

The whips send a document to all their MPs each week called 'The Whip'. This lists the business for the next two weeks and when key votes are expected. Votes where the Members' attendance is mandatory will be indicated with three lines: 'a three-line whip'. If the business is less important a two-line or a one-line whip will apply. Failure to attend a three-line whip will result in a political sanction from the whip, usually a written reprimand, a copy of which will also be sent to the constituency party.

Pairing

Whips are also responsible for organizing 'pairing'; this is when a member of the government party is paired with one of the opposition parties. Pairing means that if one MP cannot vote, the MP on the other side of the House will not vote. The effect is that the non-attendance of one MP who would have supported the government is cancelled out by the non-attendance from the opposition side who would have voted against the government. Although described by one MP as 'organised truancy',[53] when the government has a small majority, pairing becomes increasingly important. Pairing allows government ministers to travel overseas without being called back at short notice to vote and allows MPs to spend more time in their constituencies rather than at Westminster.

Minority government

Under a minority government, the importance of the whips increases exponentially as the government needs to ensure that party discipline is strong before even attempting to attract votes from other parties. This can increase the power of the government's backbenchers, as the government will need to be more accommodating to the concerns of backbench MPs. Although as Rogers and Walters state:

> when the boat is low in the water, people are less inclined to rock it, and, however strongly they feel, government MPs will be reluctant to risk the 'nuclear option' of defeating their party.

Yet it remains the case that a minority government is fundamentally weak because it lacks a majority and operates under the threat of collapsing if it loses support from its MPs or if it is routinely defeated in the House of Commons. Ultimately, the government could lose a no confidence motion, which may trigger an early general election under the Fixed-term Parliaments Act 2011. As discussed in 6.5.1 following the 2017 General Election, the Conservatives fell just short of an overall majority. To ensure that the government retained the confidence of the House of Commons, they entered into an arrangement, called a 'confidence and supply' agreement, with the Democratic Unionist Party. Under this arrangement, MPs from the Democratic Unionist Party supported the government on any vote of no confidence.[54]

---

[53] Paul Flynn, *How to be an MP* (rev edn, Biteback 2012) 117, quoting Dennis Skinner.

[54] On the vote of no confidence held 16 January 2019, the ten Democratic Unionist Party MPs supported the Conservative Government, which won the vote by 325 votes to 306, HC Deb, 16 January 2019, vol 652, cols 1269–73.

8.3.5 **Brexit in the House of Commons**

The agreement between the Conservatives and the DUP did not prevent the government from suffering the two largest defeats in history on the Withdrawal Agreement as negotiated by Theresa May. First, it was rejected by 230 votes in January 2019, followed by a second defeat by 149 votes in February 2019. The third vote was closer, but still the Withdrawal Agreement defeated by 58 votes. On all three occasions, significant numbers of Conservative MPs voted against the government. However, Theresa May went on to win two no confidence votes in her government following the first two defeats.

This is symptomatic of the difficulty the House of Commons has found itself in since the 2017 General Election. On Brexit, MPs were split across party lines with different groups advocating Brexit outcomes ranging from leaving the EU without a deal, to 'hard' or 'soft' variations of Brexit, to holding a second referendum to confirm the result of the first referendum in 2016 or to revoking Article 50 and abandoning Brexit entirely. This meant that obtaining a majority for any single proposed course of action within a hung Parliament proved extremely difficult. On rejecting the Withdrawal Agreement as agreed by Theresa May, the House of Commons failed to conclusively approve any alternative. These divisions led to significant numbers of MPs resigning the whip from their party, and even new political groupings being formed amongst MPs.[55] Party allegiances weakened, as some MPs, to some extent reflecting the public at large, increasingly related to 'leave' or 'remain' as much as they did to their party. This had a profound impact on the way that the House of Commons operates.

Most notably, this was seen with the enactment of the European Union (Withdrawal) Act 2019 and the European Union (Withdrawal) (No 2) Act 2019. Both pieces of legislation reflected the majority in the House of Commons against leaving the EU without any withdrawal agreement. Consequently, on both occasions, first in April 2019 and later in September 2019, backbench MPs took advantage of a ruling by the Speaker John Bercow to take control of the timetable of the House of Commons (which normally grants precedence to government business) and attempt to enact legislation that required the government to seek an extension of the Article 50 negotiating period. For this reason, both of these Acts are referred to as 'backbench legislation'.

Particularly on the second occasion in September, the government strongly opposed the legislation. Yet both pieces of legislation were enacted, and the government was required to seek an extension to the Article 50 period, to prevent a no deal Brexit.[56] The government was required to act according to the instruction of Parliament as expressed through legislation. In a sign of how the traditional party system was under pressure, twenty-one Conservative MPs voted against the government and in favour of the European Union (Withdrawal) (No 2) Act 2019. The response of Boris Johnson was to take the whip from these Conservative MPs even though that would make it harder for his government to win future votes in the House of Commons. Ultimately, despite his own

---

[55] For example, the Independent Group which was formed with the breakaway of seven Labour MPs, with another Labour MP and three Conservative MPs later joining them. However, after rebranding themselves as Change UK, five of the group later decided to join the Liberal Democrats. Some Labour and Conservative MPs have chosen to sit as independent MPs.

[56] Although, in the end, Theresa May had sought an extension in April 2019 before the European Union (Withdrawal) Act 2019 had completed its passage through Parliament.

reservations, Johnson complied with the law and sought the extension as required by the No 2 Act 2019, with the result that the EU granted a further extension until 31 January 2020, which became the date on which the UK left the EU.

Counterpoint: Backbench legislation and collective responsibility?

It is likely that the European Union (Withdrawal) Act 2019 and the European Union (Withdrawal) (No 2) Act 2019 were exceptional responses to an exceptional situation—MPs desire to avert a no deal Brexit. The eighty-seat majority that the government obtained at the 2019 election means that any repeat is now extremely unlikely. However, when and if there is another hung parliament, the precedent has now been set.

Yet, if such backbench legislation becomes a regular occurrence during hung parliaments, then our existing understanding of collective responsibility and how the government is accountable before Parliament will be challenged.[57] This works on the presumption that the government seeks to obtain authorization for *its* policy from Parliament, rather than for policy to be imposed on it by Parliament. This means that it is difficult to imagine the government taking responsibility in the ordinary way for the consequences that flow from a policy dictated to it by Parliament when it objected to that policy and voted against the legislation.

8.4 The House of Lords

The membership of the House of Lords is perhaps the strangest of any legislative assembly in a democratic state. It is a wholly unelected chamber and has never intended to be representative of the nation in the way that the Commons is said to be. To gain a sense of the House of Lords, it is necessary to consider its membership in detail before going any further.

8.4.1 Membership

There are four categories of members: hereditary peers; the Lords Spiritual; life peers; and Law Lords. Each are now considered in turn.

Hereditary peers

Hereditary peers were originally powerful landowners relied on by the monarch for their support, for example by providing knights for the battlefield. The monarch would recognize these landowners for their support by granting them a title, making them a Duke, Marquess, Earl, Viscount, or Baron. These titles form the peerage and are hereditary, which means that they pass down the family, usually to the eldest son. Holders of peerages are often referred to as 'peers'. Reflecting changes in the economy, from the eighteenth and nineteenth century onwards, hereditary peerages were also given to senior figures in industry or commerce.[58] The holders of a peerage other than a dukedom are usually referred to as 'Lord' rather than their rank of peerage. This means, for example, that Baron Strathclyde is referred to as Lord Strathclyde.

---

[57] See 7.7.

[58] Robert Rogers and Rhodri Walters with Nicolas Besly and Tom Goldsmith, *How Parliament Works* (8th edn, Routledge 2019) 36.

There are currently around 800 hereditary titles. However, since the House of Lords Act 1999, only ninety-two hereditary peers have the right to sit, debate, and vote in the House of Lords. These include the Earl Marshall and Lord Great Chamberlain due to their ceremonial roles within Parliament.[59]

Initially, the remaining ninety were allocated to the political parties according to their proportions amongst the hereditary peerage. This meant that forty-two places were allocated to the Conservatives, three to the Liberal Democrats, two to Labour, and twenty-eight to the 'crossbenchers' (who are explained later in this section). The remaining fifteen are elected by the whole House and can be from any or no political party. Should a vacancy arise, a by-election is held amongst that group's remaining hereditary peers. For example, if a vacancy arises amongst the hereditary 'crossbenchers', the other hereditary crossbenchers with seats in the Lords will elect another crossbench hereditary peer to replace them.

The Lords Spiritual

The Lords Spiritual comprise the most senior twenty-six bishops of the Church of England. The Archbishops of Canterbury and York and the Bishops of London, Durham, and Winchester always have a seat for as long as they hold those positions.[60] The remaining twenty-one seats are given to the most senior bishops according to the length of time they have served in office. Usually, when one of these bishops retires from their office (referred to as a 'see'), they lose their seat and are replaced by the next most senior bishop, by length of time served not already in the House.[61] However, since the admission of women bishops into the Church of England, it has been decided that, under the Lords Spiritual (Women) Act 2015, any vacancy arising amongst the twenty-one bishops must be filled by a woman bishop regardless of their seniority, should one be available. This ensures that women bishops will have a seat in the House of Lords far sooner than would ordinarily be the case. The first women bishop to take a seat under the act was the Bishop of Gloucester in 2015, followed by the Bishop of Newcastle in 2016. The 2015 Act applies until 2025.[62]

There is no right for representation for other religions to be represented in the same way. However, senior figures from other religions can be granted a life peerage.[63]

Life peers

Life peers are appointed to sit in the House under the Life Peerages Act 1958 by the monarch on the advice of the Prime Minister. As the name suggests, the peerage and the right to sit in the House is for life but does not pass down to the peer's eldest son. Given the reduction in the number of hereditary peers, this has made the Lords a predominantly appointed chamber.

The ability to appoint life peers has practically ended the creation of new hereditary peers.[64] This has allowed new members to be introduced from many different sectors of

---

[59] House of Lords Act 1999, s 2(2).

[60] Bishoprics Act 1878, s 5. However, it has been the practice to give a retiring Archbishop a life peerage on their retirement.

[61] Bishoprics Act 1878, s 5.

[62] When the Bishop of London, Sarah Mullally, was appointed in 2018, the 2015 Act did not apply to her, because she was entitled to her seat in the Lords as Bishop of London.

[63] For example, Lord Sacks, when Chief Rabbi, was made a life peer, but on his retirement he remained a peer, as the peerage is personal to him.

[64] Since 1965 only three non-royal hereditary titles have been created. These were the Earl of Stockton (in 1984 to Harold Macmillan, the former Prime Minister), Viscount Tonypandy (in 1983 to the former Speaker of the House of Commons), and Viscount Whitelaw (in 1983 to the former Home Secretary).

society, including finance, the arts, universities, trade unionists, local government, and former MPs and ministers.

All life peerages are at the rank of Baron in the peerage, with all male peers simply referred to as 'Lord' and female life peers referred to as 'Baroness' or 'Lady'.

Law Lords

Law Lords are peers appointed for life under the Appellate Jurisdiction Act 1876. Until 2009, the House of Lords also served as the final court of appeal. To enable judges to be appointed to hear cases, the Appellate Jurisdiction Act 1876 allowed for peers to be appointed as a Lord of Appeal in Ordinary (more commonly referred to as 'Law Lords'). While they could vote and take part in debates just like any other member, increasingly they focused solely on their judicial role. On retiring as judges, the Law Lords remained as members, and some continue to play an active part in the House.

In 2009, the Supreme Court took over the jurisdiction of the House of Lords and is a separate institution. The first judges of the Supreme Court were the existing Law Lords. However, they are now excluded by the Constitutional Reform Act 2005 from sitting in the House of Lords. However, on their retirement, they can once again take up their seat in the House like any other member. It remains a possibility for retired Supreme Court Judges (not already a peer) to be made a life peer on their retirement.[65]

Party politics and crossbenchers

Although not as important as in the House of Commons, party politics still plays a role in the House of Lords. Many peers owe their seat in the Lords to a political party and party loyalty, although not as tribal as in the Commons, remains strong. Evidence suggests that there are very few peers who rebel against the party whip.[66] However, unlike in the Commons, the whips can struggle to enforce attendance, which suggests that instead of rebelling, peers just stay away from the House when they disagree with their party. It is very difficult to sanction peers as they have their seat for life. Crossbenchers and non-affiliated peers have no such party considerations. They do not take the party whip of any party and are free to vote however they wish. They are essentially independent members and play as active a role in the House as they desire. This weakening of party politics means that debates tend to be less partisan and more reflective than those in the Commons.

Unlike the House of Commons, membership of the House of Lords is generally considered a part-time commitment, with many members engaged in other activities outside of the House. These can include university professors, lawyers, leaders of charities, businesspeople, or those engaged in public administration. Many are former MPs who have been government ministers. The intention is that they can bring their expertise from the outside world to their duties in the House. Two notable life peers are Lord (Alan) Sugar and Baroness (Karren) Brady, who both appear on BBC television in *The Apprentice*.

---

[65] The original members of the Supreme Court were the twelve Law Lords who heard appeals in the House of Lords. Those later appointed to the Supreme Court, who are not otherwise a peer, are by permission of the Queen known as 'Lord' or 'Lady' despite not having a peerage. This is known as a 'courtesy title'. To date, no retiring Supreme Court judge not already a peer has been awarded a life peerage on retirement, although those already a peer before being appointed to the Supreme Court can take up their seat on retirement.

[66] In the 2015–16 session, only 4 per cent of votes cast by Labour peers were against the party line; for the Conservatives this figure was 1 per cent, and for the Liberal Democrats 0.4 per cent: Robert Rogers and Rhodri Walters with Nicolas Besly and Tom Goldsmith, *How Parliament Works* (8th edn, Routledge 2019) 41.

TABLE 8.6 Membership of the House of Lords and party balance as of February 2020

Party	Life	Hereditary	Bishop	Total
Bishops	0	0	26	26
Conservative	199	46		245
Crossbenchers	157	29		186
Labour	176	4		180
Liberal Democrat	89	3		92
Lord Speaker	1	0		1
Non-Affiliated	42	7		49
Other	15	0		15
Total	**679**	**89[67]**	**26**	**794**

Source: https://members.parliament.uk/parties/Lords

The composition of the House of Lords as of February 2020 is shown in Table 8.6.

The composition is notable because neither Conservative nor Labour have a majority in the Lords. This means for the government to get its legislation through, it needs the support of either some crossbenchers or Liberal Democrat peers. Although the Commons may ultimately get its way, as discussed in 8.5.9, this gives the House of Lords a significant role in the legislative process.

8.4.2 Recent concerns and changes

The power to appoint new life peers is legally unrestricted. Since 1999, both Blair and Cameron have made extensive use of these powers.[68] During Blair's ten years as Prime Minister he appointed over 374 new life peers, while Cameron appointed 245 over five-and-a-half years.[69] This has raised concerns that this method of appointment is constitutionally inappropriate as it contravenes the separation of powers and gives significant power of patronage to the Prime Minister. In addition, given that there is no limit on the number of peers, this rate of appointments has led to arguments that the House of Lords now has too many members, rising from 601 in 2009 to just under 800 in 2019.

[67] In February 2020, three hereditary peers, the Marquess of Cholmondeley, the Earl of Listowel, and the Countess of Mar, took a leave of absence. This means that although entitled, they have chosen not to take part in the work of the House of Lords and are not counted as members. They can terminate their leave of absence and become active members by giving three months' notice.

[68] Neither Gordon Brown nor Theresa May were Prime Minister long enough to have any significant impact.

[69] House of Lords Library, 'In Focus—Life Peerages Created Since 1958' (House of Lords Library 2016), http://researchbriefings.files.parliament.uk/documents/LIF-2016–0040/LIF-2016–0040.pdf.

Pause for reflection

One way that membership of the House of Lords could be reduced would be to remove the remaining ninety-two hereditary peers. Can the membership of these ninety-two hereditaries be justified at all in a democracy?

Recently, there have been some minor reforms, with the House of Lords Reform Act 2014 and House of Lords (Expulsion and Suspension Act) 2015. The 2014 Act achieved three things. First, it is now possible for a member to resign their membership;[70] second, should a peer fail to attend once during a session of Parliament they cease to be a member; and third, if a Member is convicted of a serious offence leading to imprisonment of one year or more they are expelled from the House.[71] The 2015 Act makes it possible for the House of Lords to hold a vote and expel or suspend a member. A vote will be held if a member has committed a serious breach of the Code of Conduct for Members of the House of Lords. Although it is likely that should a peer be found guilty of wrongdoing, or faced with incontrovertible evidence of this, they would resign to save the embarrassment of being expelled by a vote of the House.[72]

At best, the effect of these provisions on reducing the size of the House will be minimal. The membership of the Lords has continued to hover around 800 as the number of resignations broadly match the number of new appointments to the chamber.

8.4.3 Significant reform

The concerns raised about the membership of the Lords raise the question of whether the House of Lords should undergo more significant reforms or even be entirely replaced.

This is not a new issue: the preamble to the Parliament Act 1911 states that its provisions were only to be a temporary measure as:

> it is intended to substitute for the House of Lords as it at present exists a Second Chamber constituted on a popular instead of hereditary basis, but such substitution cannot be immediately brought into operation.

Yet, over 100 years later, a popular, elected chamber remains elusive. Despite numerous attempts, no reform proposal has attracted the necessary level of support to proceed. The House of Lords Act 1999 was intended to be the first stage before introducing a democratically elected chamber. Yet, despite attempts by the Labour Government, it failed. The Coalition introduced proposals into Parliament when all three main parties stood on a manifesto commitment at the 2010 General Election (admittedly to varying degrees) to large scale reform, but backbenchers from both the Conservatives and Labour blocked the proposals. This serves as a further example of the political difficulties of reforming Parliament as described in 8.1.1.

---

[70] House of Lords Reform Act 2014, s 1.

[71] House of Lords Reform Act 2014, s 2.

[72] For example, after newspapers obtained a video of Lord Sewel allegedly taking drugs in the presence of prostitutes, Lord Sewel chose to resign, rather than wait to be expelled from the House.

The core difficulty with reforming the House of Lords is tackling a series of paradoxes which are almost impossible to resolve satisfactorily.[73]

For some, the greatest strength of the House of Lords is its membership. The House of Lords has a range of expertise from politics, business, the civil service, universities, local government, and the charitable sector that the House of Commons cannot match. The reason for this is that peers are unelected and while successful scientists and businesspeople are open to becoming members of the House of Lords,[74] they would be unlikely to put themselves forward for election. The demands of constituents and the electoral process would make membership very unattractive to someone who already has substantial commitments elsewhere. The part-time nature of the House of Lords allows them to combine their parliamentary commitments with their other interests.

If elections were introduced to the House of Lords, it would be likely to substantially change the nature of the House, with a greater level of commitment being expected, not only by their constituents but also by their political party. It would be likely that just like the House of Commons, being elected to the House of Lords would be dependent on being selected by one of the main political parties in the first place. Once elected, members would be required to act in a more party-political manner, to ensure that they were selected for re-election.[75] This would further politicize the House, as members would be less able to independently exercise their judgment when scrutinizing legislation.

As discussed in the next section, the House of Lords in its present form is more effective at scrutinizing legislation than the House of Commons. This means that if the government has a majority in both the House of Lords and the House of Commons, then they would be more confident in getting their legislation through. As Brazier states, currently one:

> benefit is the unpredictability of the House of Lords in the matter of legislation. In its tendency to treat the legislation of both parties with something approaching an impartial rigour, the House of Lords has become [a] counterweight in the British constitution to elective dictatorship.[76]

The concern is that the House of Lords is able to scrutinize legislation more effectively because of its current membership. Introducing elections may create a chamber in the shadow image of the House of Commons and reduce the level of scrutiny that government bills receive if the government enjoys a majority in both the Lords and the Commons.

This problem could be avoided by using a different electoral system to the House of Commons. This in turn may create a different problem. As seen in 8.3.2 with the discussion of the House of Commons, the electoral system usually delivers manifestly disproportionate results. Any different electoral system would be likely to deliver more proportionate results. This raises the prospect of an elected House of Lords having different composition to the Commons and, given an elected House's more overtly political nature, it may be willing to use its powers to the full and block legislation. A reformed chamber may also argue that the House of Commons should back down, as its lack of proportionality means that it is a less legitimate chamber than an elected House of Lords using proportional representation.

---

[73] Many of these arguments are rehearsed by Rodney Brazier in *Constitutional Reform* (3rd edn, OUP 2008) 70.

[74] For example, Lord Winston, a scientist with expertise in stem cell research, and Lord Bilmoria, the businessman who founded Cobra Beer.

[75] If indeed re-elections were allowed, in the Draft Bill published in 2012, members would be able to serve for a single fifteen-year term.

[76] Rodney Brazier, *Constitutional Reform* (3rd edn, OUP 2008) 70.

Counterpoint: The Burns Report: A limit on the size of the House?

One of the main concerns about the present system of appointments to the House of Lords is that there is no limit on the number of members. Currently, there is concern that the Lords is too large, and amongst parliaments around the world is unusual in being larger than the primary chamber. Consequently, the Report of the Lord Speaker's Committee on the Size of the House ('Burns Report'), made a series of recommendations aimed at reducing the size of the House of Lords gradually until it was reduced to 600.[77]

The committee believed that with Brexit dominating politics, there was little chance of new legislation dealing with the issue, so it made a series of proposals that would not need to be introduced by legislation. This also means that the twenty-six Lords Spiritual and the ninety-two hereditary peers would also remain.

The first proposal is that the Prime Minister would be required to exercise restraint in the number of new appointments made under the Life Peerages Act 1958. Appointments would be made on a 'two out, one in' basis. Over the next eleven years, this would gradually reduce the size of the House, while still allowing new members to be introduced. To encourage the process, the cross-benchers, Labour, Conservatives, and Liberal Democrats would each be given targets to encourage their existing life peers to retire. In return, each party would be given a share of new appointments in proportion to that party's vote at the last general election. Crossbenchers would continue to account for 20 per cent of seats in the Lords, ensuring that no one party would have a majority.

The final proposal is that all new peers appointed under this system sign an undertaking that they would serve a single fixed term of fifteen years. After this they would retire from the House under the House of Lords Act 2014. This would ensure that the membership of the House would be refreshed as general election results could continue to be taken into account. If a new peer did not retire according to their undertaking, they would be expelled under the House of Lords (Expulsion and Suspension) Act 2015.

The proposals are to some extent ingenious, but their fundamental weakness is that they rely on the Prime Minister of the day exercising restraint with the number of new peers they appoint. This was something neither Blair nor Cameron were able to do. Theresa May was at best lukewarm about the proposal,[78] and so far, Boris Johnson has not indicated how he intends to proceed with appointments to the Lords.

 Pause for reflection

Perhaps the fundamental problem remains that reform of the House of Lords is solely focused on the chamber as if it has no connection with the House of Commons. Given the concerns about the composition of both the House of Commons and the House of Lords, would it not be better to consider Parliament as a whole, aiming to develop proposals that benefit Parliament overall rather than each House individually?

---

[77] Report of the Lord Speaker's committee on the size of the House, 31 October 2017, available at https://www.parliament.uk/documents/lords-committees/size-of-house/size-of-house-report.pdf.

[78] Public Administration and Constitutional Affairs Committee, *Government Response to the Committee's Thirteenth report: A smaller House of Lords: The report of the Lord Speaker's committee on the size of the House* (HC 2017–19, 2005).

8.4.4 Conclusions on the composition of Parliament

This section, and the previous section, considered the composition of Parliament; this is important because it fundamentally explains their different roles in the legislative process, which we will consider in the next section. While both Houses of Parliament have questions over their composition, they are complementary to each other, meaning that they both have different roles. The House of Commons sustains the government and focuses on scrutinizing the executive, whereas the House of Lords can be more reflective and focuses on using its expertise to revise legislation. A careful balance has been struck by a series of incremental reforms and any significant reform of one House is likely to considerably impact on the other.

8.5 Primary legislation

The composition of the House of Commons and the House of Lords as discussed in the previous two sections directly impacts the legislative process, which is the focus of this section. Usually, the government will want to implement the policies contained in their manifesto. Sometimes this can be achieved through the existing law. If so, then new legislation may not be necessary. Yet, often, the government's policies will require a change to the law or new law is needed to give the government the legal authority to implement their policy. The government achieves this by introducing a bill into Parliament, which once it has completed the legislative process becomes an Act of Parliament.

There are three categories of bill: public, private, and hybrid.[79] This section discusses the legislative process for the most common form of bill: a public bill. In addition, the focus here is on government bills, which are bills introduced by the government. Bills can be introduced by any backbench MP (known as a Private Member's bill), but these are unlikely to become law without government support, because the government's business takes priority in the chamber, leaving little time for non-government business.

8.5.1 Pre-legislative stage

Policy-making process

The government will have determined what their policy is on a given subject and will have decided that it requires a change in the law. Policy can be developed in many different ways. Most policies will have been proposed in the party's manifesto at the last general election and their election into government is said to give them a mandate to implement those policies. The different political parties develop their policies in different ways. The Conservatives grant considerable latitude to their leader, while Labour and Liberal Democrats involve their party members to a greater degree, with policy being subject to internal procedures within their party and approved at their annual conferences held in the autumn.

---

[79] Private bills change the law for specific individuals or organizations, giving them particular powers or benefits which are additional to or in conflict with the general law. Hybrid bills are bills which have some elements of both a public bill and private bill. An example is the High Speed Rail (London–West Midlands) Act 2017, which creates the power to construct a new railway line between London and Birmingham.

Think tanks (such as the Institute for Economic Affairs, the Resolution Foundation, or the Institute for Government), the media, and experts (including academics) all contribute to the policy-making process. If an issue becomes one of public concern and receives media coverage, then the political parties will develop a policy on that issue to include in their manifesto. Occasionally, a decision of the courts may require the law to be changed or clarified and unanticipated events may simply require a new policy, which requires legislation.[80]

If the government has decided that legislation is required to implement its policy, it may conduct a consultation exercise to get the opinion of interested parties about their ideas. This can involve the publication of a Green Paper, which sets out the ideas behind the government's thinking and invites interested parties to respond to the government's consultation. This can be followed with a White Paper which contains more detail about the government's proposal after it has considered the responses to the consultation. During this process, policies can be debated in the media or discussed by MPs and peers. If they have concerns, they can ask questions and those concerns are considered by the government. Questions may also be asked about possible policies in Parliament.[81]

 Discussing the problem

Consider the problem scenario at the start of the chapter. Is there anything Sanderson can do about the government's proposals at this stage?

Possibly. If Sanderson believes that she has the support of other MPs, she could raise her concerns informally with government ministers. Particularly as Sanderson has no intentions of becoming a government minister, as a backbench MP, if she wished, she could strongly criticize this policy in the media. Whether it would have any effect would depend on how many other MPs agree with her, the size of the government's majority, and how strongly it felt about the issue.

Developing a bill

The government needs to draft a bill to present to Parliament. To do this, the government will determine exactly what is required and issue instructions to Parliamentary Counsel who draft the bill. While the bill is being developed, it will be discussed within government. Backbench MPs and peers may influence the bill at this early stage by raising their concerns with the relevant minister or the Prime Minister. The government will also be able to take the temperature of their backbenchers at parliamentary party meetings. The media may also play a role, particularly if a policy proves unpopular, causing the government to drop or change the policy.

Draft bills

Some bills may not be introduced into Parliament immediately; instead they are published in 'draft' first. The government publishes a paper containing details about the policy and the law, followed by a complete draft of the bill. This draft bill can then be scrutinized by the relevant select committee or a draft bill committee could be established to consider

---

[80] For example, the 9/11 attacks in New York directly led to the Anti-Terrorism, Crime and Security Act 2001.

[81] The process of asking questions is discussed in 8.8.

the draft bill. This allows individual provisions to be scrutinized and the Committee can consider expert evidence. The government can then consider any recommendations made by the committee before introducing the bill into Parliament.

Timetabling legislation

Although Parliament is legally sovereign, a restraint on the legislative power of Parliament is a practicality of enacting legislation. Generally, the government will outline its legislative proposals for the following session in the Queen's Speech. Most departments may expect one 'slot' in the Queen's Speech and will need to consider which policies to pursue. The government will also need to find a balance between eye-catching proposals, which may be controversial and may take time to go through Parliament, and less controversial and more technical measures.[82] In this way, even though the bill has yet to enter Parliament, the government is already being held to account, as the government only has the political capital to pursue so many controversial policies at once. Indeed, if the government has a small or no majority, then in order to avoid defeats in Parliament, it could avoid pursuing more controversial policies altogether.

The procedures in the House of Commons and the Lords are largely similar; the following sections focus on the House of Commons, but key elements of the process in the Lords are described. Figure 8.1 provides a visual overview of the legislative process and the following sections discuss each stage in turn.

8.5.2 First reading—introducing the bill to Parliament

This is a formality, which effectively introduces the bill to the chamber. The government usually publishes explanatory notes alongside the bill, explaining the effect of individual provisions. These do not form any part of the legislative process and are provided by the government to help explain the intentions behind the bill.

One decision the government must make is whether the bill should be considered first by the House of Commons or House of Lords. Generally, if a bill is likely to be controversial, the government will introduce it into the Commons first. This means that potentially the Parliament Act procedure, as discussed in 8.5.9, can be used. Less important or controversial bills may be first introduced into the House of Lords.

8.5.3 Second reading

This is the first time the bill is debated. This takes place in the main chamber and focuses on the general principles and objectives of the bill. It is extremely rare for a government bill to be rejected at this stage, the last occasion being in 1986 when the Commons rejected the Shops Bill, a bill designed to relax the laws on Sunday trading. In times when the government has a large majority, government backbench MPs can rebel against the government to express their dissatisfaction with a controversial bill, safe in the knowledge that the bill will still pass this stage in any event. This is more difficult when the government has only a small majority or is a minority government, because a defeat on the second reading of a bill could place the government in crisis and may trigger a no confidence motion being moved by the Opposition.

---

[82] Andrew Kennon, 'Pre-legislative Scrutiny of Draft Bills' [2005] *Public Law* 477, 479.

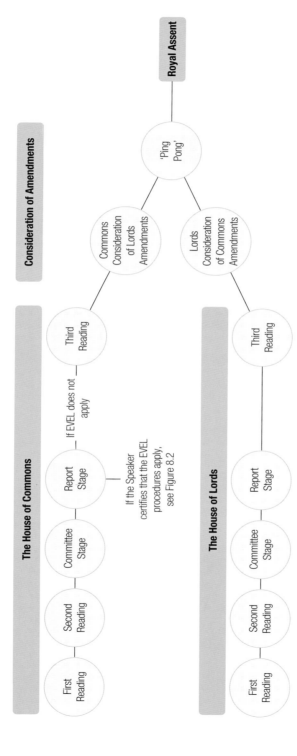

Figure 8.1 The legislative process

If a government believes that it is likely to lose a vote at second reading, then it will avoid a vote on the second reading of the bill. For example, in May 2019, once it was clear that the European Union (Withdrawal Agreement) Bill was going to be rejected at second reading, Theresa May delayed the publication of the bill, and ultimately resigned as Prime Minister. It was introduced into Parliament by her successor Boris Johnson, and was enacted following the 2019 General Election as the European Union (Withdrawal Agreement) Act 2020. Unlike May, Johnson was sure that it would pass at second reading due to the eighty-seat majority that the Conservatives won at the election.

> ### " Discussing the problem
>
> **Consider the problem scenario at the start of the chapter. If the government introduces a bill, called the Foreign Workers Bill, containing its proposals, could Sanderson rebel and vote against it at second reading?**
>
> There is a range of factors here. It is possible that the bill could be amended, making the legislation more palatable. However, if an MP feels so strongly about an issue, then it could be that no amount of amendments can satisfy them. This may lead to Sanderson rebelling against the government. Whether she would choose to do so may depend on the size of the government's majority, if it's large, then an MP can rebel safe in the knowledge that the bill will pass anyway, but can be satisfied that they have raised their concerns. This is more difficult if the government has a very small majority as it could raise questions about whether the government still has the confidence of the House of Commons.

In the House of Commons, after second reading the government will then propose (and the Commons will usually pass) a programme motion.[83] This sets out how much time will be available for debate at each of the rest of the stages in the Commons. There is no equivalent procedure in the House of Lords, meaning that government cannot restrict the time available for debate. The use of programme motions in the Commons have led to some concerns that some bills have not been debated adequately before reaching the House of Lords.

8.5.4 Committee stage

This is the process when the detailed provisions of the bill are considered individually.

Public bill committee

In the House of Commons, most bills are considered in a public bill committee. Normally between sixteen and thirty MPs will consider the bill. The parties are represented in proportion to their seats in the House of Commons. The Committee can receive evidence from campaign groups or experts about the bill.

---

[83] Occasionally, the government may decide to no longer progress with a bill if the programme motion is lost. For example, in 2012, the House of Lords Reform Bill passed its second reading, but the programme motion was rejected by the Commons. The government feared that if it progressed with the bill, it would be subject to many amendments delaying its passage, and potentially other legislation. Similarly, in October 2019, the European Union (Withdrawal Agreement) Bill was granted its second reading, but due to concerns about the lack of time offered by the government to debate the bill, the programme motion was rejected. The bill was passed following the 2019 General Election.

Backbench or Opposition amendments to the bill can be moved at this point, but given that usually the government will have a majority on the committee, it is very rare for the government to accept such amendments.

 Counterpoint: Amendments may still have an impact, even when they have been 'rejected'

Although the government may reject amendments proposed by the Opposition in Committee, this may not be the end of the matter, As Russell, Gover, and Wollter state:

> A typical scenario is for an opposition member or government backbencher to propose an amendment that the minister initially resists. But the minister, if unable to convince its proposer of the government's position, may indicate a willingness to reconsider. Consequently, the proposer will often let the amendment drop, in the hope of a government amendment at a later stage. This process can occur repeatedly, for example with an initial amendment at Commons committee stage, subsequent non-government amendments thereafter, and an ultimate government climbdown in the House of Lords.[84]

Their analysis shows that around a quarter of amendments made to bills are in response to suggestions made by either backbench MPs or the Opposition. This shows that although it may seem a thankless task to develop and propose amendments only for them to be rejected, these amendments can still have a significant effect as the bill passes through Parliament.

While this appears to be a strange process, it does mean that the government can remain in control and does not suffer any defeats in the Commons.

Committee of the whole House

Bills which are entirely uncontroversial, urgent, or of 'first-class constitutional importance' are considered in a committee of the whole House rather than in a public bill committee.[85] It is not clear what the requirements are for a bill to be of first-class constitutional importance, however legislation such as the House of Lords Act 1999, the Scotland Act 1998, the European Union (Notification of Withdrawal) Act 2017 and European Union (Withdrawal) Act 2018 all clearly qualified and were considered in a committee of the whole House.

Although still a committee, it meets in the chamber of the House of Commons. One benefit can be speed but, particularly with bills of constitutional importance, this process allows all members to contribute to the debate on the bill. The Deputy Speakers chair the debate in place of the Speaker.

In the House of Lords, the committee stage can either take place in a committee of the whole House or can be committed to a Grand Committee. Grand Committees usually meet in the Moses Room rather than the chamber of the Lords and any peer is entitled to attend. The only significant difference with a Grand Committee is that no voting is allowed and all decisions need to be taken unanimously.

---

[84] Meg Russell, Daniel Gover, and Kristina Wollter, 'Does the Executive Dominate the Westminster Legislative Process? Six Reasons for Doubt' (2016) 69 *Parliamentary Affairs* 286, 295.

[85] *Erskine May*, 555.

Discussing the problem

If the Foreign Workers Bill outlined at the start of the chapter is given a second reading, what options does Sanderson have?

MPs such as Sanderson could look to move amendments to the legislation. The requirement that all new foreign workers are registered within three working days appears particularly onerous. Sanderson could attempt to pass an amendment that extends this period, to make the requirements less demanding on business.

It is unlikely that Sanderson's amendment will succeed in the Commons without government support. However, it is possible that the issue could be raised by peers in the House of Lords. It may have a far greater chance of success because the government lacks a majority in the Lords. If the proposal has been extensively criticized, the government may move an amendment in the House of Lords itself.

8.5.5 Report stage

In both the House of Lords and the House of Commons, the bill is received from the committee stage and is reconsidered in the chamber. Further amendments can be made at this point. The role of the Speaker is crucial here in selecting the amendments to be debated and voted on. The Speaker may not select an amendment covering an issue which has already been debated fully at committee stage (unless the government has shown that it is willing to reconsider the issue), but significant matters of policy will be discussed on the basis that all MPs should have the opportunity to raise their concerns.[86]

8.5.6 Third reading

This stage is often quite brief and gives either MPs or peers a final review of the bill's contents. Once approved it goes to the other House to start at first reading.

8.5.7 Consideration of amendments: 'ping pong'

After going through the Lords or the Commons most bills will have been amended, sometimes quite heavily. These amendments need to be considered in the House that first considered the bill. If the amendments are agreed, the bill can then proceed to Royal Assent. If the amendments are not agreed, counter-amendments can be suggested and sent back to the second House. This House can choose whether to insist on their amendment or propose a compromise. This process can take place many times, with the amendments going back and forth in a form of parliamentary ping pong until the final version of the bill is agreed.

Usually, the House of Lords will give way to the House of Commons on the basis that they are the elected House and the unelected House should not thwart the wishes of elected representatives. Very often, the aim of the Lords in initially insisting on an amendment is to ensure that the Commons has thought again about the issue. Occasionally a compromise can be reached to the satisfaction of both Houses.

---

[86] Robert Rogers and Rhodri Walters with Nicolas Besly and Tom Goldsmith, *How Parliament Works* (8th edn, Routledge 2019) 207.

8.5.8 **Royal Assent**

For the bill to become law, once the final wording of the bill has been agreed by both Houses, the assent of the monarch is required.[87] By convention this is always granted; the last time assent was withheld was by Queen Anne when she refused to consent to the Scottish Militia Bill in 1708.[88]

Under the Royal Assent Act 1967, the monarch is not required to grant assent in person. Instead, the usual process is that the Lord Chancellor submits to the monarch a list of bills that require assent. The monarch then personally signs Letters Patent granting assent to those bills and the Great Seal is attached to the Letters Patent showing that assent has been granted.[89] The fact that assent has been given is communicated to both Houses by their Speakers. At this point, the bill becomes an Act of Parliament.

8.5.9 **The powers of the Lords**

Generally, the House of Lords has the same power as the House of Commons to pass amendments to legislation. Although much of the focus can be on the House of Commons, the progression of a bill through the House of Lords is often more of a challenge for the government as it lacks a majority in that House. This means that the Lords can defeat the government by passing amendments which the government does not wish to make. The Lords can go as far as blocking legislation entirely by refusing to grant it a second reading.

These substantial powers are limited in practice by the fact that the House of Commons is elected and the House of Lords is unelected, meaning that the Lords is generally said to be a 'revising chamber'. This means that it aims to amend legislation with the intention of improving it and pass amendments which may ask the government to 'think again' about an issue. As discussed in 8.6.4, the government may introduce amendments about matters raised in the Commons, but in addition the lack of a government majority in the Lords means that further amendments, against the government's wishes could be passed.

The extent to which the Lords can use this power is limited in two important ways: the Salisbury Convention and the Parliament Acts 1911 and 1949.

Salisbury Convention

On a day-to-day basis, the Salisbury Convention governs the relationship between the Houses. As the franchise for the House of Commons gradually increased, it was accepted that the government had a mandate to enact policies promised at the general election. This meant that when the Labour Government was elected in 1945, promising extensive economic and social reform, including the creation of the NHS, and an extension of the welfare state, they claimed a mandate to introduce such policies. Although Labour had a large majority of 156 in the House of Commons, the problem was that Labour only had 16 peers out of 831 in the (then, still predominantly hereditary) Lords.[90] The question was: how should the unelected Lords treat legislation that was implementing a promise made by Labour at the election?

---

[87] See also 6.8.

[88] The History of Parliament Trust states that even then, Queen Anne was acting according to the advice of the government: see History of Parliament Trust, 'Parliaments: 1705' (Institute of Historical Research), http://www.historyofparliamentonline.org/volume/1690–1715/parliament/1705.

[89] For more detail see Rodney Brazier, 'Royal Assent to Legislation' (2013) 129 *Law Quarterly Review* 184.

[90] HM Government, *House of Lords: Reform* (Cm 7027, 2007) 3.7.

Viscount Cranbourne speaking for the Conservatives stated that:

> We should frankly recognise that these proposals were put before the country at the recent General Election and that the people of this country, with full knowledge of these proposals, returned the Labour Party to power. The Government may, I think, fairly claim that they have a mandate to introduce these proposals. I believe that it would be constitutionally wrong, when the country has so recently expressed its view, for this House to oppose proposals which have been definitely put before the electorate.[91]

This developed into the Salisbury Convention whereby any 'manifesto bill' is granted a second reading as a matter of course by the House of Lords.[92] 'Manifesto bill' means a bill that seeks to implement a policy proposed in the government's manifesto at the last election. The House of Lords can still amend the legislation in later stages of the legislative process.

Parliament Acts 1911 and 1949

The powers of the House of Lords were severely curtailed by the Parliament Act 1911, as amended by the Parliament Act 1949. This was enacted following the crisis in 1909 when the Conservative-dominated Lords blocked the Liberal Party's 'People's Budget'. This caused a general election to be held in January 1910, which saw the Liberals returned as the largest party and able to govern with the support of the Irish Nationalists. The budget was then passed by the Lords. The Liberals then wanted to settle the issue of the relationship between the two Houses for good and so proposed curtailing the powers of the Lords in law. The Lords indicated that they would only agree to this if it had the explicit mandate of the electorate in another general election. This was sought at the election held in December 1910, which delivered an almost identical result to the January election. The Liberals then introduced the bill that became the Parliament Act 1911. The Lords acquiesced to its enactment as George V agreed to a request from the Liberal Government to create a sufficient number of Liberal peers to ensure that the Lords passed the bill.[93]

The main provision is section 2(1), as amended by the Parliament Act 1949, which provides the following:

> If any Public Bill (other than a Money Bill or a Bill containing any provision to extend the maximum duration of Parliament beyond five years) is passed by the House of Commons in two successive sessions (whether of the same Parliament or not), and, having been sent up to the House of Lords at least one month before the end of the session, is rejected by the House of Lords in each of those sessions, that Bill shall, on its rejection for the second time by the House of Lords, unless the House of Commons direct to the contrary, be presented to His Majesty and become an Act of Parliament on the Royal Assent being signified thereto, notwithstanding that the House of Lords have not consented to the Bill:
>
> Provided that this provision shall not take effect unless one year has elapsed between the date of the second reading in the first of those sessions of the Bill in the House of Commons and the date on which it passes the House of Commons in the second of these sessions.

Although the drafting of the section is complex, its effect is that if a bill has been passed by the House of Commons in two successive sessions and is rejected by the House of

---

[91] HL Deb, 16 August 1945, vol 137, col 47.

[92] Joint Committee on Conventions, *Report* (2005–06, HL 265-I, HC 1212-I) [99].

[93] Chris Ballinger, *The House of Lords 1911–2011: A Century of Non-Reform* (Hart 2012) 28.

Lords in both of those sessions, then after being rejected the second time by the Lords, the bill can still receive Royal Assent and become an Act of Parliament.

There are some conditions on this procedure, the most important of which is that at least one year needs to have elapsed between the bill being given its second reading in the Commons in the first session of Parliament and its third reading in the second session.

Also, the bill must be sent to the House of Lords a month before the end of both sessions. The Parliament Act procedure has been used seven times,[94] including to amend the Parliament Act itself.[95]

As can be seen from the language of section 2(1) itself, this procedure does not apply to a 'Money Bill', or a 'bill which extends the life of a parliament beyond five years'.

Money bills are bills that relate exclusively to financial matters, which include taxation, 'supply', meaning how public money is spent, and the national debt. Under section 1 of the Act, all such money bills cannot be amended by the House of Lords and are passed automatically if the House of Lords does not pass the bill within one month.

A *'Bill to extend the life of a parliament beyond five years'* has the effect that the House of Commons cannot use the Parliament Act to indefinitely delay the next general election. The only occasion the general election has been delayed was during the Second World War, when the election in 1945 took place ten years after the previous election, held in 1935.[96]

Pause for reflection

Does the Parliament Act procedure facilitate democracy or, given that the government usually enjoys a majority in the Commons, does the Act make the government too powerful?

8.5.10 English Votes for English Laws (EVEL)

In the House of Commons, in between the Report Stage and Third Reading, a new process has been introduced, called English Votes for English Laws. As explained in 9.4, this was introduced as an attempt to ensure that English MPs have a greater say over issues that only affect England, in response to increasing devolution to Scotland, Wales, and Northern Ireland. The concern is that although many issues are devolved to Scotland (for example), Scottish MPs can still vote on all legislation that the House of Commons considers, even though some legislation does not apply to Scotland because that matter has been devolved to the Scottish Parliament. This can lead to the situation when the government enacts English-only legislation with the support of Scottish, Welsh, and/or Northern Irish

---

[94] To pass the Welsh Church Act 1914, Government of Ireland Act 1914, Parliament Act 1949, War Crimes Act 1991, European Parliamentary Elections Act 1999, Sexual Offences (Amendment) 2000, and Hunting Act 2004.

[95] This was the key issue in *R (Jackson) v Attorney-General* [2005] UKHL 56; however the House of Lords unanimously held that the 1949 Act was valid, rejecting the argument that Acts passed under the Parliament Act were a form of delegated legislation.

[96] This was achieved by enacting, with the approval of the House of Lords in the ordinary manner, an annual Prolongation of Parliament Act until elections could be held in 1945 after the end of the War.

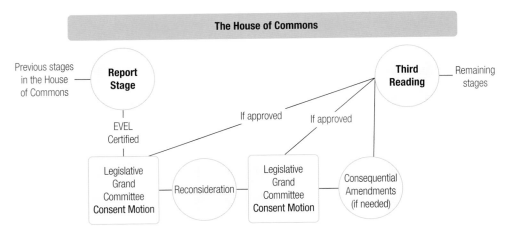

Figure 8.2 English Votes for English Laws procedure

MPs, even though a majority of English MPs voted against it.[97] EVEL is designed to ensure that legislation applying to only England has the approval of MPs representing English constituencies by following the procedure set out in this section and shown in diagrammatic form in Figure 8.2.

1. After Report Stage, the Speaker reviews the bill and will certificate any provisions that apply only to England.[98]

2. The Legislative Grand Committee then meets and only those MPs representing English constituencies can vote to approve the provisions that have been certificated. MPs from all constituencies can take part in the debate.

3. The Whole House meets again and any matters in dispute can be debated and amendments to the legislation can be made.

4. The Speaker will then review the bill and if necessary, certify the bill once again, as containing clauses that affect only England.

5. Then the Legislative Grand Committee meets again and can either:

   • give consent, meaning that the bill passes to third reading;

   • order for the clauses applying to England only to be removed; or

   • refuse consent to the whole bill meaning that the bill progresses no further.

In many ways EVEL is misnamed: it is not 'English Votes for English Laws' but rather an English Veto (Against) English Laws. English MPs cannot initiate legislation themselves but only veto legislation which has been approved by the House as a whole. Since its introduction, EVEL has yet to have any significant effect, because the Conservative government had a majority in both England and the UK as a whole. This remains the case after the 2019 General Election, when the Conservatives won 345 out of the 533 English constituencies, a majority of 158. Even following the 2017 general election, when the

---

[97] This happened with the Health and Social Care (Community Health and Standards) Act 2004.

[98] With the necessary changes, the EVEL procedure also applies to provisions that apply only to England and Wales.

Conservatives lost their majority across the UK as a whole, they retained a comfortable majority of English seats.[99] The difficulty that minority governments will experience is in getting legislation passed by all MPs in the first place. Only when a future government has a majority across the UK, but lacks a majority in England, will the EVEL procedure become a significant hurdle for the government.

8.6 Secondary legislation

Primary legislation is only part of the story. Acts of Parliament can allow for the creation of further law to be made under the authority of that Act itself. This can be called secondary or delegated legislation or referred to as statutory instruments. The following discussion of the Scrap Metal Dealers Act 2013 provides a good routine example of how secondary legislation can operate.

After concerns were raised about the industry and with frequent reports of valuable metal being stolen and then sold to dealers, Parliament enacted the Scrap Metal Dealers Act 2013. This Act introduced the requirement that scrap metal dealers must have a licence in order to deal in scrap metal. Section 11 states that scrap metal dealers can only accept scrap metal once they have verified the seller's name and address. Section 11(2) stated that this should be achieved by checking identity documents. Section 11(3) provides that:

> (3) The Secretary of State may prescribe in regulations—
>
> > (a) documents, data or other information which are sufficient for the purpose of subsection (2);

This means that the Scrap Metal Dealers Act 2013 has delegated the power to decide which documents would be suitable for this purpose to the Secretary of State. The Secretary of State's decision was given legal effect by passing the Scrap Metal Dealers Act 2013 (Prescribed Documents and Information for Verification of Name and Address) Regulations.[100] This provided that a passport would be suitable for checking a seller's identity and, for proof of address, a bank or building society statement, a credit card statement, or a council tax bill would be suitable documents.[101] The basic point is that Parliament though the Act itself laid out the general principles of the scheme in law, and the government can develop the details through legislation.

It is important to note that there is much interchangeable terminology in this area. Acts of Parliament that delegate power can be referred to as the 'parent act', the 'enabling act', or 'primary legislation'. These terms simply mean that the power to make regulations is derived from the Act of Parliament in question. In the example just given, this is the Scrap Metal Dealers Act 2013. Section 11 of the Act is said to 'confer', 'grant', or 'delegate' the power to make the further laws to the Secretary of State. This is sometimes referred to as the enabling provision.

Under this power, the Secretary of State passed the Regulations. This can be referred to as the delegated or secondary legislation or sometimes as a statutory instrument. In this example, the Secretary of State was given the power to make 'regulations'; other similar

---

[99] The Conservatives won 297 seats out of 533, giving them a majority of fifty-nine.
[100] SI 2013/2276.   [101] Ibid reg 2.

provisions in other acts may give the Secretary of State power to make an 'order' or 'rules'. Some delegated legislation must be made by 'Order in Council', which means that it must be approved at a meeting of the Privy Council.[102]

8.6.1 Why use delegated legislation?

Having explained the procedure to pass Acts of Parliament in the previous section, the question is why are not all laws made by an Act of Parliament? There are two reasons. First, the amount of delegated legislation is so large that it is beyond the capacity of Parliament to legislate for everything through Acts of Parliament. As Table 8.7 shows, there is far more delegated legislation than Acts of Parliament.

The other reason is that a significant amount of delegated legislation is uncontroversial and relates only to the minutiae of a policy or scheme. As seen in the example discussed in this section from the Scrap Metal Dealers Act 2013, the form of identity required is unlikely ever to be a controversial or significant issue. Instead Parliament had debated the principle of the need for such a scheme in the first place and that identity checks on scrap metal sellers was needed. The general view is that it is appropriate and sensible for Parliament to focus on the key matters of principle and leave the less important matters of detail to be resolved by delegated legislation.

Commencement orders

Finally, a frequent type of delegated legislation is the commencement order. Returning to the Scrap Metal Dealers Act 2013, section 23(2) states:

(2)   The provisions of this Act, except section 20 and this section, come into force on such day as the Secretary of State may appoint by order.

TABLE 8.7 Comparison between the number of Acts of Parliament and statutory instruments

Year	Number of Acts	Number of Statutory Instruments
2012	23	3,329
2013	33	3,314
2014	30	3,563
2015	37	2,059
2016	25	1,242
2017	35	1,289
2018	34	1,387

[102] See also 6.3.3. In addition, members of the Privy Council, but not in the presence of the Monarch at a meeting, may also make Orders *of* Council. These are rules or regulations that usually relate to the governing bodies of the professions or chartered institutions. Both Orders in Council and Orders of Council must be distinguished from prerogative 'Orders in Council', which is the prerogative power to pass primary legislation in a few matters, such as coinage and for changing the constitutions of British Overseas Territories such as Gibraltar and Crown Dependencies including the Channel Islands.

An Act of Parliament will come into force and take legal effect immediately on Royal Assent. However, most Acts of Parliament will contain a provision similar to section 23(2). This is known as a commencement provision in that the Act will only 'come into force', meaning that it will not have legal effect until the Secretary of State makes an order bringing the legislation into force. There are several good reasons for doing this. The government department responsible for administering the scheme may need to prepare to bring the scheme into effect. This may involve training civil servants or setting up computer systems. Some schemes need to be implemented after a public awareness campaign has been held informing the public or those involved about the introduction of the new scheme.[103]

'Henry VIII clauses'

'Henry VIII clauses' are far more controversial; they are used to amend or repeal Acts of Parliament. This means that an Act of Parliament is giving the Secretary of State the power on behalf of the government to amend an Act of Parliament. These are called 'Henry VIII clauses' because, if such powers are abused, the government could effectively act like Henry VIII, who frequently sought to suspend Acts of Parliament. In practice, Henry VIII clauses are used to give the government the power to make minor changes to legislation. Occasionally, minor problems with a new law are only discovered once the law has been put into operation.

Henry VIII powers become far more controversial when they are used more extensively and allow for more significant changes to be made by the government. It is at this point that they raise significant challenges to the separation of powers and to parliamentary sovereignty. One example is the Constitutional Reform and Governance Act 2010. This Act made provision for the civil service, the ratification of treaties, and amendments to the Freedom of Information Act 2000. The 2010 Act also allows a minister to 'make such provision' as they 'consider appropriate in consequence of any provision of this Act' and this can include the power to 'amend, repeal or revoke any existing statutory provision'.[104] This power has been described by Lord Judge as the power to 'infringe, break or subvert statute' and goes far beyond what was necessary to achieve the aims of introducing the Act.[105]

8.6.2 Concerns about delegated legislation

Lord Judge's fundamental concern is that the government could be tempted to push the use of delegated legislation further and further. The government could introduce bills into Parliament that provide for the barest of frameworks, that simply grant powers enabling the government to act through delegated legislation instead of being required to justify its policy in the Commons and Lords through the full legislative process. A particularly notorious example from recent times is the Childcare Act 2016, which was

---

[103] The Scrap Metal Dealers Act 2013 came into effect when the Scrap Metal Dealers Act 2013 (Commencement and Transitional Provisions) Order 2013, SI 2013/1966 was made.

[104] Constitutional Reform and Governance Act 2010, s 51.

[105] Lord Judge, 'Ceding Power to the Executive: the Resurrection of Henry VIII' Lecture at King's College London, 12 April 2016, https://www.kcl.ac.uk/law/newsevents/newsrecords/2015–16/Ceding-Power-to-the-Executive—Lord-Judge—130416.pdf.

described by the House of Lords as containing 'virtually nothing of substance beyond the vague "mission statement" of clause 1'.[106] The Act gives extensive powers to the government to implement its policy of creating free childcare through delegated legislation rather than setting out the scheme in the Act of Parliament itself. In substance, the legislation governing the scheme is being made by the government via delegated legislation, not Parliament.

8.6.3 Scrutiny of delegated legislation

To some extent, these concerns could be addressed if delegated legislation was sufficiently scrutinized. There is a paradox here in that if the very reason for delegated legislation is that Parliament lacks the time to deal with those matters, then it follows that any scrutiny can only be limited, otherwise the very point of delegated legislation is subverted.

The most important form of scrutiny is the Joint Committee on Statutory Instruments. This is a Joint Committee with seven members from the Commons and Lords appointed.[107] This committee provides technical scrutiny of each piece of delegated legislation, for example by considering whether its drafting is defective and that the legislation is within the scope of the power granted by the parent act. Should the committee consider that a piece of delegated legislation requires scrutiny, its report will alert both Houses.

The policy implications of delegated legislation are considered by the Secondary Legislation Scrutiny Committee. This is a committee of the House of Lords which scrutinizes each piece of delegated legislation and through a weekly report to the House seeks to draw attention to delegated legislation that may:

- be politically or legally important;
- be inappropriate due to changed circumstances since the parent Act was enacted;
- inappropriately implement European Union legislation;[108]
- imperfectly achieve its policy objectives.

Such policy issues do not always get scrutinized. Delegated legislation is approved under either the negative or affirmative procedures. Which procedure applies depends on the Act of Parliament granting the power to make the delegated legislation in the first place. If the regulations are made 'subject to annulment in pursuance of a resolution of either House of Parliament' then the negative resolution procedure will apply.[109] If the Act of Parliament states that the delegated legislation cannot be made 'unless a draft . . . has been laid before, and approved by a resolution of, each House of Parliament'[110] then

---

[106] Delegated Powers and Regulatory Reform Committee, *Childcare Bill [HL]. Regulation of Political Opinion Polling Bill [HL]. Airports Act 1986 (Amendment) Bill [HL]. Cities and Local Government Devolution Bill [HL]: Government Response. Draft Legislative Reform (Duchy of Lancaster) Order 2015* (HL 2015–16, 12) [8].

[107] Should only the House of Commons be required to consider delegated legislation, the members from the Commons meet as the House of Commons Select Committee on Statutory Instruments.

[108] Even though the UK has now left the EU, during the transitional period, which will last until 31 December 2020, EU directives taking effect during this period apply to the UK, and will need to be implemented as if the UK was still a member.

[109] Statutory Instruments Act 1947, s 6.

[110] Statutory Instruments Act 1947, s 6.

the affirmative resolution procedure will apply.[111] Some delegated legislation, usually the most uncontroversial, such as commencement orders, receive no scrutiny from Parliament at all.

Negative resolution procedure

The negative resolution procedure applies to around 75 per cent of delegated legislation. This requires that the delegated legislation is laid before the House of Commons and House of Lords and takes effect on the date stated on the legislation, unless within forty days either House votes in favour of annulling the piece of delegated legislation. If no motion is passed it remains law. The last time the House of Commons voted down delegated legislation under this procedure was in 1979, and the House of Lords in 2000.

Affirmative resolution procedure

There is a better chance of policy scrutiny with the affirmative procedure. Around 10 per cent of delegated legislation goes through this process. This requires that each House expressly approves the legislation, although it may have legal effect while approval is pending. In the House of Commons, delegated legislation subject to the affirmative procedure can either be debated in the chamber for ninety minutes, after which a vote can be taken, or it can be referred to Delegated Legislation Committee (DLC). The Committee considers the legislation in a debate with a minister for up to ninety minutes. Once considered, a motion to approve the delegated legislation is made on the Floor of the House without any debate. Whether the legislation is considered in the chamber or in the DLC, no amendments can be made.

 Counterpoint: Did the House of Lords cause a 'constitutional crisis'?

The Parliament Acts 1911 and 1949 do not apply to delegated legislation. This means that the House of Lords has an absolute veto over proposed delegated legislation that is subject to the affirmative resolution procedure. However, the Salisbury Convention does apply if the proposed regulations implement a manifesto commitment. This has meant that the Lords has rarely rejected delegated legislation and has done so on only five occasions since 1968. In 2015, the House of Lords blocked the Draft Tax Credits (Income Thresholds and Determination of Rates) Amendment Regulations 2015. The intention of the government was to reduce certain benefits paid to those on low incomes. The immediate response of the Chancellor of the Exchequer was to say that the Lords had caused a constitutional crisis by their actions, because he felt that the Lords had gone too far in blocking legislation that related to how public money was spent, which is usually a matter for the House of Commons to determine.

An inquiry held by Lord Strathclyde recommended that a new procedure should be laid out in statute, which if the Lords wished, could require the Commons to 'think again' about a piece of

→

---

[111] This is scrutinized by the Delegated and Regulatory Reform Committee, which considers each bill introduced into Parliament, and reports to the House on any bills that in its view inappropriately delegate power to the government to make delegated legislation or if it feels that the delegated legislation should be subject to a different scrutiny procedure; that is, it should be made via the affirmative rather than the negative resolution procedure.

→

delegated legislation before they could insist that it should be passed.[112] So far, this proposal has not been pursued.

The real criticism should be that the governments of all political parties have developed the habit of creating a structure where significant matters of policy have been delegated to the government to make by secondary legislation rather than being created through an Act of Parliament. This raises questions as to the balance to strike between primary and secondary legislation, in particular the use of 'skeleton bills', which allow the government to create the detailed policy through delegated legislation which Parliament cannot amend.

Scrutiny by the courts

Scrutiny in a different form can come through the courts applying the principles of judicial review. When making delegated legislation, the Secretary of State is operating under a power granted to them by Parliament. Consequently, if the legislation is outside the scope of the power granted, so making the legislation *ultra vires* (meaning outside the power), then the courts can strike the delegation legislation as being invalid. This ensures that if the parent act defines the scope of the power to make delegated legislation relatively tightly, then the courts can intervene. The courts can also imply words into the language used by Parliament to restrict the scope of the power further than it may initially appear. One notable example is *R v Lord Chancellor, ex p Witham*.[113] In this case, the Lord Chancellor's decision to set court fees at a new higher level would have excluded people on low incomes from having the right of access to courts. This was held to be a fundamental right so that Parliament, when granting the power to the Lord Chancellor, did not intend, without expressly stating so in the legislation, for the power to be used to restrict this right. The principles of judicial review are considered in more detail in Chapters 10–13.

 Pause for reflection

Lord Judge believes that '[u]nless strictly incidental to primary legislation, every Henry VIII clause, every vague skeleton bill, is a blow to the sovereignty of Parliament. And each one is a self-inflicted blow, each one boosting the power of the executive.'[114]

Is he correct?

8.6.4 **Brexit**

Following the UK's departure from the EU, and the end of the transitional period, most EU law that has become part of UK law via the European Communities Act 1972 will continue to be part of UK law, as retained EU law under the European Union (Withdrawal) Act 2018 as amended by the European Union (Withdrawal Agreement) Act 2020.

---

[112] HM Government, Strathclyde Review: Secondary legislation and the primacy of the House of Commons (Cm 9177, 2015).   [113] [1998] QB 575.

[114] Lord Judge, 'Ceding Power to the Executive: the Resurrection of Henry VIII' Lecture at King's College London, 12 April 2016, available at https://www.regulation.org.uk/library/2016_Henry_VIII_powers-Lord_Judge.pdf.

The main concern is that this retained EU law was drafted on the basis that it would apply to EU Member States. Consequently, this body of retained EU law will need to be amended so that it continues to operate effectively for the UK, once outside the EU. To achieve this, the 2018 Act gives the government broad powers to correct any 'failure' of or 'deficiency' in retained EU law.[115] This has greatly increased the amount and importance of secondary legislation.

These powers are discussed in more detail in Chapter 5, along with the rest of the discussion of the European Union (Withdrawal) Act 2018 and the European Union (Withdrawal Agreement) Act 2020.

8.6.5 Summary on delegated legislation

Lord Judge's comments highlight the two concerns with the use of delegated legislation that Henry VIII powers can allow the government to amend primary legislation and skeleton bills give the government the power to create the detailed provisions of a new scheme or policy. Amending primary legislation and legislating for new policies should be functions of Parliament, not government. The concerns over the use of delegated legislation have increased, as governments frequently rely on it to implement their policies. These concerns have increased as implementing Brexit requires a heavy reliance on delegated legislation.

8.7 Scrutiny of government

In Chapter 7 we discussed how responsible government requires that the government is accountable to Parliament. In 8.5 and 8.6 we considered how the government's legislation is scrutinized by the government. However, the scope of debates regarding legislation is restricted to the bill itself, meaning that the legislative process does not allow MPs to challenge the government on broad issues or the general implementation of their policy. Parliamentary scrutiny of other aspects of government is achieved through various opportunities to challenge and hold the government to account. This is a rolling process, taking place day in, day out. This is the hard grind of asking questions, taking part in debates, and embarking on the detailed work of select committees. Primarily, the focus of this section is on the House of Commons.

8.7.1 Prime Minister's Question Time

Prime Minister's Questions (or PMQs) is the highlight of the parliamentary week and is the most famous session of Parliament. For half an hour,[116] at 12 noon on Wednesdays, MPs can ask the Prime Minister about any aspect of government policy. The session is broadcast live on television and radio, with highlights included in news bulletins. The centrepiece of the session is the ten minutes or so where the Leader of the Opposition asks their allotted six questions to the Prime Minister. Through these questions, a form of mini debate develops between the Prime Minister and their opposite number.

---

[115] European Union (Withdrawal) Act 2018, s 8(1).

[116] Although when Speaker John Bercow increasingly let it run to as long as fifty minutes to allow backbenchers to ask more questions.

First introduced as a permanent fixture in 1961, PMQs has become a theatrical event, with backbenchers often showing their support for their leader by cheering and then jeering at the other leader. This is the Commons at its most partisan and political and PMQs often descends into cheap political point scoring. Although the exchanges are rarely enlightening, it remains a manifestation of how the government as a whole, led by the Prime Minister, is accountable to Parliament. Occasionally the Prime Minister may use the session to make an announcement in response to question, which is then reported by the media.

Counterpoint: Does PMQs show Parliament in a good or a bad light?

The Hansard Society have long been critical of Prime Minister's questions, arguing that the 'yah-boo nature of the sessions . . . risks bringing Parliament into disrepute'.[117]

An alternative view is given by Marc Geddes, who argues that PMQs provides a

> snapshot of opinion that allows both lead actors of the play—[the Prime Minister] and [Leader of the Opposition]—to give their verdict on what is important to them. This makes the weekly jousting between the leaders a battle to outline their political priorities and therefore their competing visions for the country.[118]

Geddes concludes that PMQs remains popular because it distils the week's political priorities into one theatrical contest. The purpose of PMQs is not to scrutinize the government, but rather to set the political agenda.

Watch a session of PMQs on Parliament's website, http://www.parliament.uk, focusing on the exchanges between the Prime Minister and Leader of the Opposition. Which view do you prefer?

8.7.2 Ministerial questions

There is usually a less frenetic atmosphere for the first hour each day (apart from Fridays), which is reserved for ministerial questions. This is an opportunity for MPs to question government ministers. Each day the ministers from a government department will attend according to a rota which sees each department questioned once every five weeks.

Just like PMQs, ministerial questions reflect individual ministerial responsibility and MPs can ask any question relating to the department. As Erskine May states:

> Questions addressed to Ministers should relate to the public affairs with which they officially connected, to proceedings pending in Parliament, or to matters of administration for which they responsible.[119]

---

[117] Hansard Society, 'Still Turned Off? Public Attitudes to "People's PMQs"' (Hansard Society, 12 October 2015), http://blog.hansardsociety.org.uk/pmqs2015/.

[118] Marc Geddes, 'In Defence of Prime Minister's Questions' (The Crick Centre Blog, 21 January 2015), http://www.crickcentre.org/blog/defence-pmqs/.

[119] *Erskine May*, para 22.9.

This means that ministers can be asked about government policy or what they propose to do about a particular situation that has arisen. There are some strict rules as to what questions cannot relate to, including the following:

- local authorities;

- the personal powers of the monarch;

- the affairs of other countries;

- questions concerning matters that have been devolved to Northern Ireland, Scotland, or Wales;

- questions which seek an expression of opinion on a point of law or relate to a case being heard by the courts at the time.

Questions can be oral or written. Questions for an oral answer in the chamber are tabled (meaning to give notice) at least three working days in advance. As there are usually more questions tabled than can be answered within question time, any questions not selected for an oral answer by the Speaker (who chooses at random) will be given a written answer. If the question is selected for an oral answer, once the minister has answered the question, the MP can ask a supplementary question. A skilful MP can use their supplementary question to expose poor government thinking on an issue or extract a concession from the government in relation to a policy. The last fifteen minutes of question time are dedicated to topical questions. These are not submitted in advance and give MPs the opportunity to question ministers on recent developments or events. While the political nature of the Commons cannot be excluded, oral questions can be more enlightening than PMQs and give MPs an indication as to a minister's grasp of their portfolio.

Questions put down for a written answer (or an oral question not answered during question) tend to be more factual and can be a very useful way to get information out of the government. Ordinarily, these are answered within seven days. Should the member require the question answered by a specific date, it is called a 'Named Day' question and receives an answer on that specific date.

Overall, in the 2016–17 session, nearly 40,000 questions were asked by MPs,[120] highlighting how important they can be as a method of scrutiny.

8.7.3 Opposition business

Generally, the government's business has precedence over all other business.[121] One exception is the Opposition Days allocated to the opposition parties, who are able to debate a policy area of their choice and receive a response from the government. There are twenty days per session allocated for the Opposition, seventeen go to the largest opposition party and the last three going to the second largest. This is an opportunity for the opposition parties to raise an issue or challenge government action of their own choosing.

---

[120] House of Commons, *Sessional Returns—Session 2016–17* (HC 2017–19, 1) 5.
[121] House of Commons, *Standing Orders of the House of Commons—Public Business 2018* (HC 2017–19, 1020) Standing Order 14(1).

8.7.4 Urgent questions

Another mechanism to get an issue heard is the urgent question. An MP may make an application to the Speaker for an urgent question. If the Speaker is convinced that the matter is urgent, in the public interest, and there is no other viable way for the issue to be debated, then he will grant the application. This means that a question will be asked and a government minister will have to respond explaining what the government is doing about the matter being asked. Other MPs may ask questions.

Urgent questions have increased in importance in recent years, particularly under the Speaker John Bercow, who was keen to allow more urgent questions to increase the topicality of the House, meaning that it is more responsive to current events and increases the power of backbench MPs. In the 2016–17 session, seventy-four urgent questions were asked.[122]

8.7.5 Select Committees

The most detailed scrutiny can be delivered by Select Committees, which have increased in importance, particularly since the introduction of the 'Wright Reforms': a package of reforms designed to increase the visibility and effectiveness of Select Committees.[123] During the 2010–15 Parliament, many of the most notable events took place in Select Committee hearings rather than in the chamber itself.

There are two main types of Select Committee. Departmental Committees shadow the work of a specific government department: for example, the Home Affairs Committee considers the work of the Home Secretary, while other types of committees cut across government departments, such as the Public Administration Committee, which considers the standards of administration within the government and receives the reports of the Parliamentary Ombudsman.[124]

Traditionally, committees have had a less partisan atmosphere than debates in the chamber, as backbench MPs from different parties work together to scrutinize the government. The Wright Reforms introduced secret ballots for Select Committee chairs. This removed the power of the party whips to prevent awkward MPs from becoming chairs.[125] The inherent authority in being elected by other Members of the House has allowed elected chairs to be more outspoken and independent in running their committees.

The membership of the committee is in proportion to the parties' share of the seats in the House of Commons. These are elected by a secret ballot within each party. Again, this emphasizes their independence from the government.

Departmental Select Committees have a responsibility to scrutinize the policy, administration, and expenditure of their department.[126] They achieve this by conducting inquiries. This involves announcing an inquiry, inviting those with expertise to send written

---

[122] House of Commons, *Sessional Returns—Session 2016–17* (HC 2017–19, 1) 5.

[123] House of Commons Reform Committee, *Rebuilding the House* (HC 2008–09, 1117).

[124] The Parliamentary Ombudsman is discussed in 14.3.

[125] House of Commons Reform Committee, *Rebuilding the House* (HC 2008–09, 1117) para 80.

[126] House of Commons, *Standing Orders of the House of Commons—Public Business 2018* (HC 2017–19, 1020) Standing Order 152(1). Although some departmental select committees have increasingly conducted inquiries into private companies and other organizations that are not part of government: see Craig Prescott, 'Select Committees: Understanding and Regulating the Emergence of the "Topical Inquiry"' (2019) 72 *Parliamentary Affairs* 879.

evidence, and then question witnesses in hearings. This includes government ministers, but can include civil servants and those with an interest in the topic of the inquiry including academics, businesspeople, and the charitable sector. The Committee will then consider the evidence and publish a report which usually makes recommendations for the government to consider. The government will then have to make a written response to the report and occasionally the report can be debated in the Commons chamber itself.

Serving on a committee allows MPs to acquire expertise over time and, with the assistance of specialist advisers, a committee can provide a forum for systematic scrutiny. Some select committees may also consider relevant legislation, using their expertise for the benefit of the House. In the main chamber, the Chair of a committee is likely to be selected by the Speaker to ask questions when relevant. A notable example is at the Budget, when the Chair of the Treasury Select Committee is called by the Speaker to ask a question immediately after the Leader of the Opposition has concluded their response to the Chancellor's budget statement.

The evidence is that the government have increasingly accepted either in whole or in part the recommendations of a Select Committee. Benton and Russell have found that 'committee recommendations are . . . considerably influential, both in terms in initial government acceptance and eventual implementation',[127] with 40 per cent of recommendations being accepted by the government.[128] They concluded that:

> Overall, [select committees] strengthen the policy-making process inside and outside government by exposing decision-making to rigorous tests, and by encouraging more careful consideration of options . . . it is clear that they are taken seriously.[129]

A notable committee is the Liaison Committee, of which all Select Committee chairs are members. This hears evidence twice a year from the Prime Minister in an extended session. The members of the Committee can question the Prime Minister on any issue and ask follow-up questions. This is clearly a more robust form of scrutiny than that provided at PMQs.

🗨 Discussing the problem

Consider the problem scenario set out at the start of this chapter. The news that Silver Chips is leaving raises questions about the government's policies. How can you scrutinize the government's policy?

When the announcement was made, this would be a major news story. As it is not a matter of legislation, an MP's primary method of getting the government's response would be through asking questions of ministers. This could include Prime Minister's Questions or requesting an urgent question in the House of Commons. However, whether to grant the urgent question is a decision for the Speaker, who has discretion over whether to grant the request.

It may also be that a Select Committee may investigate the matter considering that Silver Chips is leaving due to a lack of available skills. This suggests that there could be a policy problem which lies behind Silver Chip's decision. A Select Committee could gather the facts and make recommendations in a report to which the government must respond.

---

[127] Meghan Benton and Meg Russell, 'Assessing the Impact of Parliamentary Oversight Committees: The Select Committees in the British House of Commons' (2013) 66 *Parliamentary Affairs* 772, 779.
[128] Ibid 793.   [129] Ibid.

8.7.6 Conclusions on scrutinizing the government

Scrutinizing the government in the House of Commons is a thankless and unglamorous task. It involves constant effort, usually for little immediate reward. Yet the opportunities to scrutinize the government are there. Although the government's own backbenchers can be a thorn in the government's side, the use of these scrutiny mechanisms by a well-organized Opposition can, over time, chip away at the government. While a government with a large majority will not fall due to parliamentary scrutiny, many government policies are improved due to the scrutiny they receive.

8.8 Summary

This chapter has discussed the composition and functions of both the House of Commons and the House of Lords. The composition of both Houses could be questioned, although they do complement each other. This is shown through the process of enacting primary legislation. The House of Commons grants legislation the necessary democratic legitimacy and the House of Lords plays an important role in improving or revising the legislation. The rules for determining what happens when the Lords and Commons disagree are a mixture of law and convention, but make clear that, ultimately, the unelected House should give way to the elected House.

There are more concerning questions regarding the use of delegated legislation. While some delegated legislation is necessary given the demands on Parliament, the concern is that governments have increasingly relied on framework legislation and Henry VIII clauses when their use is unjustified. This raises profound questions about the separation of powers and parliamentary sovereignty.

The other key role of Parliament is to hold the government to account. As most government ministers are drawn from the House of Commons, it is naturally this chamber which takes the lead. While it is open to all MPs to scrutinize the government, and some government backbenchers do, the onus is really on the opposition to scrutinize the government through asking questions and taking part in debates. Given the support the government has from their own MPs, scrutiny will not cause a government with a large majority to fall, but can require the government to reconsider an issue, improving government policy.

Quick test questions

1. What are the main functions of Parliament and how effective are the House of Commons and House of Lords at fulfilling those functions?

2. Should the electoral system used for general elections be changed?

3. Does the House of Lords need reform? If so, which reforms would you pursue and why?

4. Is the English Votes for English Laws procedure misnamed? Would it be better described as an English Veto?

5. How are disagreements over legislation between the House of Commons and the House of Lords resolved? What political considerations apply?

6. Are the existing controls over the use of delegated legislation sufficient?

7. Is Parliament able to sufficiently scrutinize the government?

Further reading

General

*Robert Rogers and Rhodri Walters with Nicolas Besly and Tom Goldsmith, *How Parliament Works* (8th edn, Routledge 2019)

The composition of Parliament and the House of Lords

Robert Blackburn, *The Electoral System in Britain* (MacMillan 1995)

Rodney Brazier, *Constitutional Reform: Reshaping the British Political System* (3rd edn, OUP 2008)

*Philip Norton, 'Adding Value? The Role of Second Chambers' (2007) 15(1) *Asia Pacific Law Review* 3

Jonathan Tonge, 'The Recall of MPs Act 2015: Petitions, Polls and Problems' (2019) 90(4) *Political Quarterly* 713.

The legislative process

Daniel Gover and Michael Kenny, 'Answering the West Lothian Question? A Critical Assessment of "English Votes for English Laws" in the UK Parliament' (2018) 71(4) *Parliamentary Affairs* 760

Meg Russell and Philip Cowley, 'The Policy Power of the Westminster Parliament—The "Parliamentary State" and the Empirical Evidence' (2016) 29(1) *Governance* 121

*Meg Russell, Daniel Gover, and Kristina Wollter, 'Does the Executive Dominate the Westminster Legislative Process? Six Reasons for Doubt' (2016) 69(2) *Parliamentary Affairs* 286, 295

Delegated legislation

Lord Judge, 'Ceding Power to the Executive; the Resurrection of Henry VIII' (Lecture at King's College London, 12 April 2016) available at https://www.regulation.org.uk/library/2016_Henry_VIII_powers-Lord_Judge.pdf.

*Stephanie Pywell, 'Something Old, Something? New: Busting Some Myths about Statutory Instruments and Brexit' [2019] *Public Law* 102.

Select Committees

*Meghan Benton and Meg Russell, 'Assessing the Impact of Parliamentary Oversight Committees: The Select Committees in the British House of Commons' (2013) 66(4) *Parliamentary Affairs* 772

Philip Norton, 'Departmental Select Committees: The Reform of the Century' (2019) 72(4) *Parliamentary Affairs* 727

Craig Prescott, 'Select Committees: Understanding and Regulating the Emergence of the "Topical Inquiry"' (2019) 72(4) *Parliamentary Affairs* 879

Finally, Parliament's own website, www.parliament.uk, contains a wealth of information about the role of Parliament, its functions, and procedures.

 Visit this book's **online resources** for additional materials relating to this chapter, including a discussion parliamentary privilege and a full analysis of the start-of-chapter problem scenario.
www.oup.com/he/stanton-prescott2e

9

Devolution and local government

9.1 Introduction

Devolution, in the context of UK constitutional law, refers to the decentralization of power from central institutions in London to regional institutions exercising executive and legislative authority in Scotland, Wales, and Northern Ireland. As a concept, the benefits of devolution are well documented and will be explored in detail throughout this chapter. Debates calling for devolution in the UK were prominent throughout the 1970s, though these did not bear fruit. It was not until the late 1990s, and the then newly elected Labour Government's programme for pushing power away from Whitehall to newly created institutions in other parts of the UK, that devolution became established as a practical feature of UK constitutional arrangements. Since this time, the devolved institutions in Edinburgh, Cardiff, and Belfast have thrived and developed, with their founding settlements and the programme of powers devolved from Westminster constantly evolving. In the aftermath of the 2014 Scottish Independence Referendum and in the context of Brexit, calls for further devolution to the regions have gathered momentum, with recent legislation concerning Scotland and Wales delivering on these calls. This chapter explores the principle of devolution, both in terms of its historical development and its constitutional importance, and it discusses recent issues and debates relevant to the role that it continues to play in the UK Constitution through the established institutions in Scotland, Wales, and Northern Ireland. All this is tied together in consideration of the problem scenario set out in this section, which encourages discussion of the powers of the devolved institutions and their relationship with centralized authority at Westminster.

Devolved institutions overseeing government and law-making in Scotland, Wales, and Northern Ireland, though, do not represent the only form of government below the centre. At an even lower level, local councils across the UK fulfil an important administrative and constitutional function, governing and overseeing cities and small local areas. Indeed, local government long pre-dates even the establishment of central government.

With this in mind, the second focus of this chapter is local government, outlining its nature, its role and powers, and the varied structures within which it operates. It explores local government's historical development and the relationship it shares with the centre. Even more so than devolution to the regions, localism and local democratic reform has featured consistently on government agendas, with the decentralization of power and the invigoration of communities being a key part of councils' operation. With this in mind, the chapter also discusses recent issues that have arisen with regards to the reform of councils and how government policy is shaping and will continue to shape the role that local government plays in the UK Constitution. A second problem scenario, set out at the beginning of the local government section of the chapter (9.5), provides a focal point for the discussion of local government and the democratic legitimacy councils derive from local people, also inviting consideration of the relationship between councils and central government.

The chapter's objectives are:

- to explain the principle of devolution and its constitutional benefits;
- to consider the relevance of devolution to the UK Constitution and the nature and form of devolutionary attempts in Scotland, Wales, and Northern Ireland;
- to discuss current and future proposals for further devolution in the UK, bearing in mind discussions in the aftermath of the 2014 Scottish Independence Referendum; Brexit; and recently enacted legislative reforms;
- to discuss the importance of local government and the role that it plays in the UK Constitution;
- to explore the nature of local government, its powers and responsibilities, and the various structures within which it operates.

Devolution problem scenario

Across the UK, and in the aftermath of Brexit, there is a (fictitious) employment crisis. Due to new, stricter immigration laws, the departure of a great many European citizens has left a huge number of vacancies across both the public and private sectors. Furthermore, an increase in university tuition fees across the country (as a consequence of fewer students from the European Union) is discouraging students from attending university, meaning that the quality of applicants for many such jobs is declining. Devolved and centralized legislatures across the country introduce measures to combat this crisis. These include the following:

- In Scotland, a new law is passed that permits employers to require their employees to be at work six days a week; Saturday and Sunday are to be regarded as normal working days. A large majority of public and private sector employers enforce this.

- In Wales, to improve the quality of applicants to job vacancies, a law is passed that makes it compulsory for children to attend school until they are eighteen years old. It is hoped that this will motivate more students thereafter to attend university.

→

→

- Aware of its border with an EU Member (the Republic of Ireland), Northern Ireland decides to introduce its own immigration laws, different from and more lenient than those adopted by the UK Government in respect of the country as a whole. The aim is to permit EU nationals to enter Northern Ireland to work, without a visa, provided they already have a job lined up.

- Finally, the UK Parliament seeks to pass a law that requires all universities across the UK to condense all their degree programmes to two years in the hope that this will work out both cheaper and quicker for those thinking about going to university.

9.2 Devolution, decentralization, and federalism

9.2.1 Subsidiarity and devolution

Devolution 'is a process, not an event'.[1] It 'involves the dispersal of power from a superior to an inferior political authority',[2] and is founded on an awareness and appreciation of the value of localized leadership and governance. Indeed, its underlying rationale is the belief that power is best exercised at a level that is as close as possible to those whom it affects. In this way, it is linked to the principle of subsidiarity, which, though more familiar to those considering EU law, is here taken with the same meaning. Article 5(3) of the Treaty on European Union states that:

> Under the principle of subsidiarity, in areas which do not fall within its exclusive competence, the Union shall act only if and in so far as the objectives of the proposed action cannot be sufficiently achieved by the Member States, either at central level or at regional and local level, but can rather, by reason of the scale or effects of the proposed action, be better achieved at Union level.[3]

Subsidiarity effectively means that power should be exercised at the most appropriate level of governance. Applying this within the context of devolution, if there are issues concerning housing in Scotland, for example, then the effective and appropriate allocation of power would see a government institution in Scotland making the relevant decisions and policies. Similarly, if changes are required to the system of social services in Northern Ireland, then a government body in Belfast would be best placed to design and implement this. This is the reality of subsidiarity and a rationale at the heart of the devolution concept. More fundamentally, though, devolution is also about using power in a manner that is relevant and appropriate to those whom it affects. Devolution to Scotland, for example, and the establishment of the Scottish institutions was borne out of a desire to ensure that decisions and laws affecting the Scots could be made in Scotland, by Scottish institutions who would be sympathetic to and appreciative of issues affecting Scottish people. The intention was that this would, in turn, give rise to responsive and relevant decision-making and laws that are appropriate to the constitutional and legal

---

[1] Anthony King, *The British Constitution* (OUP 2007) 212. Also see Ron Davies, *Devolution—A Process Not an Event* (Gregynog Papers, Institute of Welsh Affairs 1999) 11.

[2] David M Smith and Enid Wistrich, *Devolution and Localism in England* (Ashgate 2014) 4–5 citing Vernon Bogdanor, *Devolution* (OUP 1979) 2.

[3] Article 5(3) of the Consolidated Version of the Treaty on European Union [2012] OJ C326/13.

landscape of Scotland—objectives that would be much harder to achieve by institutions acting on behalf of the whole of the UK and situated 400 miles away.

Devolution, in this sense, then, is linked to democracy insofar as Scottish institutions, for example, elected by the Scottish people can provide a legitimate base for this responsive and relevant use of power. It is borne out of a desire to achieve an efficient and effective allocation of power in the constitution that can operate to provide responsive and democratic leadership to people in specific geographical regions. More widely, though, it is also justified by a desire to break from the centralized government system that the UK has traditionally adopted—a desire that is increasing, as recent constitutional and political events serve to demonstrate and as this chapter will go on later to explore.

9.2.2 Devolution, federalism, and the unitary constitution

Before we embark on a detailed discussion of devolution, we must first consider the broader constitutional structure within which the policy operates, specifically the distinction mentioned in 1.3.3 that is drawn between unitary states and federal states. Indeed, due to the structural nature of a federal state and the practical consequences of devolution, a link is often drawn between the two principles. It is important to examine more closely the concept of federalism and to explain, in greater detail, why the UK is traditionally regarded as a unitary state on this basis.

It was noted, in 1.3.3, that a federal constitution is one in which there exist two or more levels of executive and legislative authority, each having their own allocation of exclusive powers and responsibilities. In the USA, for instance, Congress and the US Government have the ability to make laws and decisions for the country as a whole, while legislative and executive institutions within each of the fifty states have authority to make laws and decisions for their respective states. The centre cannot exercise powers held at state level and the states cannot pass laws or decisions applicable across the whole country, these respective realms of authority being preserved through the Constitution. In contrast to a federal system, the UK is a unitary state insofar as legislative and executive authority ultimately rests at the centre.

Though, as this chapter explains, there are legislative and executive institutions beneath the central level—both across the UK regions and (administratively) at the local government level—these do not have the effect of establishing the UK as a federal constitution for two key reasons. First, the sovereignty of Parliament. In the absence of a supreme, codified constitutional document, allocating power to institutions and determining the manner in which it should be exercised, Parliament is sovereign and sets out Acts of Parliament as the highest form of law in our system.[4] All legislative and executive authority, exercised either by devolved institutions in Scotland, Wales, and Northern Ireland, or by local authorities across the UK, is subordinate to Parliament and must always be exercised in line with parliamentary enactments. Unlike in the USA, lower levels of government do not have their own areas of competence, which are beyond the reach of the centre—the sovereign Parliament has the authority to legislate on any matter, including stipulating the realms of authority to be exercised by subordinate bodies. Secondly, due to the varying sizes—both geographically and in terms of population—of the UK regions, the asymmetrical nature of the way in which power is shared amongst the regions

---

[4] See 4.2.

also means that the UK cannot be a federal state. In the USA, each of the fifty states has the same level of power and autonomy under the Constitution and no one state is more powerful than another.

In the UK, by contrast, not only do the various countries vary greatly in both size and population, but so does the degree of authority devolved to each of the respective institutions. Though, as we shall see, reforms and amendments over the years have adjusted the devolution settlements, when they were initially established in the late 1990s Scotland and Northern Ireland both enjoyed legislative power, while the Welsh Assembly did not. What is more, with regards to England—which contains 84 per cent of the UK's population[5]—there is no dedicated law-making or governmental institution. The UK Parliament (since 2015 with the assistance of a Legislative Grand Committee containing MPs from English constituencies) makes laws for England, with the UK Government making decisions and implementing policy for people across the English region. The UK's constitutional arrangements, in the context of federalism and in comparison with the US system, are shown to be unitary in nature.

It is in the context of the UK's unitary status, though, that devolution has been introduced and established. In the years following the 1998 settlement, it was accepted that although power had been devolved to newly created institutions in Scotland, Wales, and Northern Ireland, the Westminster Parliament retained its sovereignty, with the relevant legislation noting this explicitly.[6] Parliament has the legal authority to repudiate the devolution settlements and to bring back to Westminster any power that has been devolved. Whether this is something that Parliament would in reality do is, of course, another question. As Lord Denning stated in respect of Acts granting independence to the Dominions, '[c]an anyone imagine that Parliament could or would reverse those laws and take away their independence? Most clearly not. Freedom once given cannot be taken away. Legal theory must give way to practical politics.'[7] Similarly, it is difficult to imagine a scenario in which Parliament might re-centralize devolved authority without any political basis. While, in the past, powers have been re-centralized in respect of Northern Ireland's devolution settlement, this has been a reaction and solution to politically difficult circumstances, rather than Parliament merely seeking to assert its sovereign authority, as this chapter goes on later to discuss.

More recently, and notwithstanding the sovereignty of Parliament, as the desire for further devolution increases and the devolved institutions become further protected in their roles, there are arguments suggesting that the current and future state of devolution in the UK is giving rise to a shift towards a more federal (or, at least, quasi-federal) state, an issue to which this chapter will later return. For now, though, we can see that the principle of devolution goes right to the heart of the UK's constitutional arrangements and plays a significant role in determining the appropriate and effective allocation of power vertically across the UK regions. This chapter now moves to consider how that role has been shaped and how the principle of devolution has evolved within the Constitution. First, though, it explains how the constituent countries of the UK came together.

---

[5] See Office for National Statistics, 'Population Estimates for UK, England and Wales, Scotland and Northern Ireland: mid-2016' (22 June 2017), https://www.ons.gov.uk/peoplepopulationandcommunity/populationandmigration/populationestimates/bulletins/annualmidyearpopulationestimates/latest.

[6] Section 28(7) of the Scotland Act 1998, for instance, states that '[t]his section does not affect the power of the Parliament of the United Kingdom to make laws for Scotland'. See 9.4.1.

[7] *Blackburn v Attorney-General* [1971] 1 WLR 1037, 1040. See, for further discussion on this point, 4.5.1.

9.3 The formation of the United Kingdom

At the heart of discussions concerning devolution in the UK are the regions to which power has been decentralized—namely, Scotland, Wales, and Northern Ireland. To understand the process better and the way in which the concept has worked in respect of the UK Constitution, our exploration must start with a consideration of the nature of the UK itself and an explanation of how the union came to be formed.

The UK has only existed in its current form for less than a century, with the geographical parts joining (and leaving) the union at various points over the past 750 years. Wales was conquered by England in the late-thirteenth century, with two Acts of the English Parliament in 1536 and 1543 formally and legally recognizing the union.[8] Unlike legislation that later brought Scotland and Ireland together under one Parliament, there was no agreed union with Wales, but rather the English Parliament's unilateral recognition of the principality's union with England.

By contrast, the Act of Union with Scotland, in 1707, was the culmination of negotiations between England and Scotland and the legal authority for the union that they created between the two countries. Though the union preserved certain aspects of Scottish national identity,[9] it joined the two countries under one Parliament in Westminster and formally recognized the creation of Great Britain, consisting of England, Wales, and Scotland, unified under the authority of that one Parliament. Representing the 'union' between the two countries, the English and Scottish Parliaments were both abolished and replaced by a new Parliament for Great Britain, created by the 1707 Treaty.

 Counterpoint: The Act of Union and parliamentary sovereignty

In Chapters 4 and 5, the principle of parliamentary sovereignty was discussed. Diceyan orthodox theory suggests not only that the UK Parliament can pass any laws it so wishes, but also that no Act is above the authority of Parliament and immune from repeal or capable of binding the authority of future Parliaments.[10] This is well supported by case law.[11]

If the Act of Union 1707, however, is credited with having formally created the (now) UK Parliament then there is a valid argument in favour of saying that the Act of Union is a superior force of law and that the UK Parliament operates only by virtue of the Act's authority, thereby binding it. This is an issue that has been discussed in the courts, with obiter statements in both *MacCormick v Lord Advocate*[12] and *Gibson v Lord Advocate*[13] considering the legality of legislation that purported to conflict with provisions of the Act of Union 1707.[14] Though the court in both

➡

---

[8] See Elizabeth Wicks, *The Evolution of a Constitution: Eight Key Moments in British Constitutional History* (Hart Publishing 2006) 168.

[9] Notably in terms of the church and legal system: see Elizabeth Wicks, *The Evolution of a Constitution: Eight Key Moments in British Constitutional History* (Hart Publishing 2006) 168.

[10] See AV Dicey, *Introduction to the Study of the Law of the Constitution* (JWF Allison ed, first published 1885, OUP 2013) 27.

[11] See 4.5 for discussion of this case law.

[12] [1953] SC 396.   [13] [1975] SLT 13.

[14] See, for more detailed discussion on all this, Colin Turpin and Adam Tomkins, *British Government and the Constitution: Text and Materials* (7th edn, Cambridge University Press 2011) 222–8.

→

cases felt that the question of an Act's validity could not be justiciable, the judgments did raise the question as to whether the 1707 Act could be seen as a fundamental law, with much academic discussion also exploring the issue over the past sixty years or so.

Smith, on the one hand, in an article written just a few years after *MacCormick*, suggests that 'the entrenched provisions [of the Act of Union] could only be superseded by revolution—in the sense of a fundamental reconstruction of the British constitution'.[15] On the other hand, Sharp observes that there are strong rejections of the supposition that the Act of Union serves as a higher law, superior to the authority of Parliament, adding that 'given the sheer number of alterations and repeals, it is simply untenable to contend that the Union legislation can in any meaningful way constitute fundamental law'.[16]

The constitutional significance of the Act of Union is self-evident, not only with regards to the creation of the union between England and Scotland, but also with regards to its authority with respect to the accepted sovereignty of Parliament.

Less than a century after the Act of Union with Scotland 1707, the Union with Ireland Act 1800 effected Great Britain's union with Ireland and formally established the United Kingdom of Great Britain with Ireland under the authority of one sovereign Parliament at Westminster. The political narrative accompanying this union, however, has meant that it was never particularly settled. Republican movements in the early part of the twentieth century were opposed to Ireland's union with Great Britain and campaigned for Home Rule. Following a period of conflict with British forces, Irish independence was achieved in the twenty-six southern counties of Ireland in 1921, with the Anglo-Irish Treaty recognizing the creation of the Irish Free State (which later declared independence as the Republic of Ireland in 1949). The remaining six counties—Northern Ireland—remained a part of the United Kingdom and pursuant to the Government of Ireland Act 1920 they were the beneficiaries of devolved power until 1972, when this was re-centralized at Westminster and Northern Ireland was again brought under direct rule. Northern Ireland—like Scotland and Wales—then remained under direct rule until the late 1990s and New Labour's programme for devolution to the UK regions.

We can see that the United Kingdom of Great Britain with Northern Ireland was created over a long and complex period of constitutional evolution and development, ultimately leading to the formation of what has traditionally been regarded as a unitary state.[17] As the next section will now explore, it is upon the foundation of these unions that devolution has been discussed and implemented over the past twenty years.

[15] Thomas B Smith, 'The Union of 1707 as Fundamental Law' [1957] *Public Law* 99, 113, quoted in Dan Sharp, 'Parliamentary Sovereignty: A Scottish Perspective' (2010) 6(1) *Cambridge Student Law Review* 135, 140.

[16] Dan Sharp, 'Parliamentary Sovereignty: A Scottish Perspective' (2010) 6(1) *Cambridge Student Law Review* 135, 140–1. Also see Elizabeth Wicks, 'A New Constitution for a New State? The 1707 Union of England and Scotland' (2001) 117 *Law Quarterly Review* 109, 118; AV Dicey, *Introduction to the Study of the Law of the Constitution* (JWF Allison ed, first published 1885, OUP 2013) 39–40 and JD Ford, 'Legal Provisions in the Acts of Union' (2007) 66(1) *Cambridge Law Journal* 106, 139.

[17] See 1.3.3.

9.4 Devolution in the UK Constitution

This section builds on the explanation of how the UK came to be unified and explores the schemes for devolution in each of the respective parts of the country. It considers both the historical development of plans for devolution as well as the specific nature of the settlements currently in force. In respect of this last point, the settlements are markedly different in each case and are typically described as asymmetrical. This asymmetry chiefly refers to the differing powers that have, in each case, been devolved to the regional authorities, though in some cases also to the institutions that have there been created.

The devolution settlements are all founded in primary legislation—the Scotland Act 1998, the Government of Wales Act 1998, and the Northern Ireland Act 1998—with further statutes since that time adding to these and adjusting the nature of the arrangements and the powers devolved. In addition to the legislative provisions, Memoranda of Understanding between the UK Government and each of the devolved governments also sets out political consensus on a number of issues relevant to the day-to-day working and cooperation of the centralized and devolved institutions. While the principle of parliamentary sovereignty and the legislative foundation to the devolution settlements might theoretically permit the UK Parliament to legislate on the matters ostensibly devolved to the regions, it is agreed between the various institutions and central government that Parliament would not exercise such authority, as we will discuss in greater detail. Each respective part of the United Kingdom is now explored in turn, starting with Scotland.

9.4.1 Devolution to Scotland

The union with Scotland, established in 1707, is still intact today, albeit in a rather different form from that initially created. Though Scotland is still under the authority of the UK Parliament, it now enjoys devolved powers and responsibilities exercised by a Scottish Parliament and Scottish Government, created through a scheme of devolution legislation that started in 1998. The 1707 Act of Union's securing of 'the independence of its legal system and Church—aspects of Scottish identity seen as critical at the time'[18]—have been crucial to the health of the union over the past 300 years; however, 'by the twentieth century it was obvious that the institutions of government were becoming more important'[19] and this, in time, led to a strong nationalist movement supporting a desire for Scottish institutions.[20]

The desire for and discussion around Scottish devolution, however, started long before its eventual realization in the late 1990s. In the mid-1970s, Harold Wilson's Labour Government embarked upon an investigation 'to examine the present functions of the central legislature and government in relation to "the several countries, nations and regions of the United Kingdom," [and] to consider possible changes in existing constitutional and

---

[18] Elizabeth Wicks, *The Evolution of a Constitution: Eight Key Moments in British Constitutional History* (Hart Publishing 2006) 172.   [19] Ibid 172.

[20] The strength of this nationalist movement is evident from the results of the two General Elections held in 1974. In the February, the Scottish National Party won 21.9 per cent of the vote in Scotland winning seven seats in the UK Parliament, whilst in October they won 30.4 per cent of the vote in Scotland, winning eleven seats in the UK Parliament (see Colin Rallings and Michael Thrasher, *British Electoral Facts 1832–2012* (Biteback 2012) 44 and 46).

economic relationships'.[21] The Royal Commission on the Constitution was appointed to this end, publishing its report (the Kilbrandon Report) in 1973.[22] Explaining the catalyst underpinning Labour's investigation, Williams notes that:

> The . . . stimulus for the appointment of the Commission came from those who reacted . . . to the apparent pressures of Scottish and Welsh nationalism. More generally, there was considerable dissatisfaction expressed in the late 1960s about the over-centralisation of government and about the remoteness of government.[23]

The report discussed the possibilities for devolution at length and proposed the introduction of legislative and executive devolution to Scotland.[24] The government took this on board and set out to create an assembly in Scotland that would enjoy a degree of legislative authority. A White Paper in 1974 was followed in 1976 by a Scotland and Wales Bill. Though this was later withdrawn, the Scotland Act 1978 was successfully passed on the condition that it be approved by a post-legislative referendum in which at least 40 per cent of the Scottish electorate voted in favour of the programme for devolution set out in the Act. In Scotland, while a majority of voters supported the Act's provisions, the turnout was such that, overall, only 33 per cent of Scotland's registered voters backed the proposals—the Act failed to attract the necessary public support and was never implemented. A year later, in 1979, Thatcher's Conservative Government was elected into power. The Conservatives had little support in Scotland and the Prime Minister was not in favour of pursuing devolution any further. Plans for the decentralization of power north of the border were shelved.

Following eighteen years of Conservative rule, however, Tony Blair's New Labour Government entered power in 1997 with a manifesto that included proposals to create devolved institutions in Scotland and Wales. Shortly after the election, White Papers were published outlining the proposals for reform[25] including the proposed creation of a Scottish Parliament. Following the White Papers, a pre-legislative referendum was held on the proposals in Scotland in September 1997, the outcome of which was markedly different from the vote that had taken place nineteen years previously. In Scotland, with a much higher turnout (60.2 per cent), devolution was supported by 74.3 per cent of voters.[26] With the support of the Scottish public, the Scotland Act 1998—broadly based on the preceding White Paper—was enacted by Parliament.

Scotland Act 1998

The Scotland Act 1998 created a Scottish Parliament and what is now termed a Scottish Government in Edinburgh[27] and it devolved to these institutions primary legislative and executive authority. Though it altered, like never before, the nature of the union between Scotland and the rest of the UK, the intention was that this devolution could take place

---

[21] DGT Williams, 'The Commission on the Constitution' (1974) 33(1) *Cambridge Law Journal* 15, 15.

[22] Home Office, *Royal Commission on the Constitution* (Cmnd 5460, 1973).

[23] DGT Williams, 'The Commission on the Constitution' (1974) 33(1) *Cambridge Law Journal* 15, 16.

[24] See Home Office, *Royal Commission on the Constitution* (Cmnd 5460, 1973).

[25] Scottish Office, *Scotland's Parliament* (Cm 3658 1997) and Welsh Office, *A Voice for Wales: The Government's Proposals for a Welsh Assembly* (Cm 3718, 1997).

[26] See Elizabeth Wicks, *The Evolution of a Constitution: Eight Key Moments in British Constitutional History* (Hart Publishing 2006) 172–3, citing HM Government, *Democracy and Devolution Proposals for Scotland and Wales* (Cmnd 5732, 1974).

[27] The Scottish Government had formerly been known as the 'Scottish Executive', this being altered by the Scotland Act 2012.

within the existing framework and consistent with the provisions of the Acts of Union 1707. To this end, the Scotland Act 1998 provided, in section 37, that '[t]he Union with Scotland Act 1706 and the Union with England Act 1707 have effect subject to this Act'. More broadly, though, the intention was also that the 1998 Act would not affect the sovereignty of the UK Parliament, the Scottish legislature being subordinate to that at Westminster. To this end, section 28 of the Act, which sets out the legislative power and process of the Scottish Parliament, states in subsection 7 that '[t]his section does not affect the power of the Parliament of the United Kingdom to make laws for Scotland'. The Act, then, though passed with the intention that broader constitutional issues of power allocation and union would not be disrupted, nonetheless created a framework within which the devolution of power to Scotland could be facilitated and implemented. The next sections explore in detail the nature of the institutions in Scotland and the powers that they have been granted.

Scottish Parliament

The Scottish Parliament, at Holyrood in Edinburgh, consists of a 129-seat unicameral Parliament. The 129 seats are made up of a mixture of members of the Scottish Parliament (MSPs) elected across the seventy-three constituencies, and fifty-six MSPs from eight parliamentary regions (each region being represented by seven MSPs).[28] As Hadfield explains, the 129 MSPs 'are elected by a mixture of the first-past-the-post electoral system for the 73 constituency MSPs, and, to ensure greater proportionality in the outcome, by the additional member system for the 56 regional list MSPs'.[29] Pursuant to section 2(2) of the Scotland Act 1998, elections to the Scottish Parliament are held every four years.[30]

The reserved powers model

Though the Scottish Parliament has primary legislative authority, this is limited to the extent that the 1998 Act only gives the Holyrood legislature the power to make laws for Scotland and, pursuant to section 28(7) of the Scotland Act 1998, this does not preclude the sovereign UK Parliament from making laws which would be superior to the Scottish institutions. This primary legislative authority, however, is also limited in scope insofar as the Scottish Parliament does not have the ability to legislate on all matters affecting Scotland and the Scottish people. This is because the devolution of power to Scotland exists within what is called a 'reserved powers model'. The Scotland Act 1998, as amended by subsequent Acts, lists certain matters or policy areas that are reserved for the exclusive competence of the UK-wide governmental and legislative institutions. Anything not listed in the Acts is presumed to be devolved. The 1998 legislation tells the Scottish institutions not what they *can* do, but rather, what they *cannot* do, something that is undoubtedly less restrictive. Legislative provision for these reserved matters means, on the one hand, that the sovereignty of the UK Parliament is preserved, while on the other, it means that the Scottish Parliament's legislative ability is also honoured and recognized.

---

[28] The 129 MSPs are separate from the fifty-nine MPs who represent differently structured constituencies in the UK Parliament.

[29] Brigid Hadfield, 'Devolution: A National Conversation?' in Jeffrey Jowell and Dawn Oliver (eds), *The Changing Constitution* (7th edn, OUP 2011) 213, 216. For an explanation of the different voting systems, see 8.3.2.

[30] Section 4 of the Fixed-term Parliaments Act 2011 sets out the alternative arrangements, which ensure that elections of the Scottish Parliament do not take place on the same day as UK-wide parliamentary elections.

The reserved matters are listed in Schedule 5 to the 1998 Act, as amended by the Scotland Acts 2012 and 2016, and they include the following areas:

- The Constitution
- Foreign affairs
- Defence
- Immigration
- National security
- Intellectual property
- Consumer protection
- Electricity, oil and gas, coal and nuclear energy
- Social security
- Health and safety
- Employment and industrial relations
- Broadcasting
- Equal opportunities

In addition to these matters reserved for the exclusive competence of the UK Parliament, section 29(2) of the 1998 Act also states that the Scottish Parliament cannot legislate in such a way that is contrary to the rights set out in the European Convention on Human Rights[31] or contrary to the UK's legal obligations under EU law. These restrictions notwithstanding, the Scottish Parliament is able to exercise legislative authority for Scotland in a broad range of areas, as seen from a number of examples. The Smoking, Health and Social Care (Scotland) Act 2005, for instance, banned smoking in enclosed public areas in Scotland before a similar law was introduced in England, Wales, and Northern Ireland and, unlike other parts of the UK, Scottish university students under the age of twenty-five do not have to pay tuition fees when attending Scottish universities. The laws that the Holyrood legislature can pass have a direct impact on Scotland and the lives of Scottish people.

Judicial review of the Scottish Parliament

As an institution created by an Act of the UK Parliament, the Scottish Parliament is susceptible to scrutiny by the courts. Judges have the ability to entertain challenges from interested parties to Scottish legislation that allegedly attempts to trespass into the realm of reserved matters, set out in the 1998 Act, or to go against obligations under the ECHR or EU law. In such cases, where the courts assess the validity of Acts of the Scottish Parliament, pursuant to section 29 of the 1998 Act, they have the power to strike down legislation as invalid. Section 29 states:

(1) An Act of the Scottish Parliament is not law so far as any provision of the Act is outside the legislative competence of the Parliament.

(2) A provision is outside that competence so far as any of the following paragraphs apply—

    (a) it would form part of the law of a country or territory other than Scotland, or confer or remove functions exercisable otherwise than in or as regards Scotland,

    (b) it relates to reserved matters,

---

[31] Hereinafter ECHR.

(c) it is in breach of the restrictions in Schedule 4,

(d) it is incompatible with any of the Convention rights or with EU law,

(e) it would remove the Lord Advocate from his position as head of the systems of criminal prosecution and investigation of deaths in Scotland.

(3) For the purposes of this section, the question whether a provision of an Act of the Scottish Parliament relates to a reserved matter is to be determined, subject to subsection (4), by reference to the purpose of the provision, having regard (among other things) to its effect in all the circumstances.

(4) A provision which—

(a) would otherwise not relate to reserved matters, but

(b) makes modifications of Scots private law, or Scots criminal law, as it applies to reserved matters,

is to be treated as relating to reserved matters unless the purpose of the provision is to make the law in question apply consistently to reserved matters and otherwise.

In view of the courts' power to review Acts of the Scottish Parliament and with section 29 in mind, there has, over the years, been case law testing and examining the boundaries of the devolved powers and the scope of the Scottish Parliament's legislative authority. In the case of *The Christian Institute and others v The Lord Advocate*,[32] for instance, a number of charities challenged the validity of the Children and Young People (Scotland) Act 2014 on three bases: first, that it dealt with matters reserved for the UK Parliament; secondly, that it was incompatible with the ECHR; and thirdly, that it was contrary to EU law. Though only the challenge alleging incompatibility with the ECHR was successful, the circumstances of this case demonstrate the court's ability to determine the validity of Scottish legislation. Another case relevant here is *AXA Insurance v Lord Advocate*.[33]

Case in depth: *AXA Insurance v Lord Advocate* [2011] UKSC 46

A case was brought challenging the validity of the Damages (Asbestos-related Conditions) (Scotland) Act 2009, which states in its Long Title that it sought to 'provide that certain asbestos-related conditions are actionable personal injuries'. The contention was that this Act of the Scottish Parliament was contrary to the right to peaceful enjoyment of one's possessions, protected under Article 1 of the First Protocol to the ECHR and was therefore in contravention of section 29(2)(d) of the 1998 Act. It was also argued that the Act was 'an irrational exercise of legislative authority', under the principles established at common law.[34]

The challenge failed, however, with the Scottish Parliament's Act being upheld as valid. The Supreme Court decided that, while the insurance companies were permitted to bring the claim, the Act could not be said to be unreasonable in its protection of the public interest.[35] Explaining this, the Court found that, as a legislative body deriving its powers from Parliament, the Scottish Parliament was subject to the supervisory jurisdiction of the courts since the scope of its powers were set out under section 29(2) of the 1998 Act and were plenary in nature (ie were general

→

---

[32] [2016] UKSC 51.   [33] [2011] UKSC 46.

[34] See Chapter 12 and, in particular, the case of *Associated Provincial Picture Houses Ltd v Wednesbury Corporation* [1948] 1 KB 223.   [35] See [2011] UKSC 46 [42].

> →
>
> insofar as they were not required to be exercised for specific purposes).[36] At the same time, however, since the Scottish Parliament was also answerable to its electorate, it was not deemed constitutionally appropriate to subject it to the common law grounds for review.[37]

The Courts can only review legislation of the Scottish Parliament in line with the UK statutory authority that devolves the power to make such legislation and they can only intervene on grounds other than those specified in section 29(2) in exceptional circumstances, understood by the court to include where decisions might interfere with fundamental rights or the rule of law.[38] Despite this limitation of common law judicial review, the importance of this case rests in its clarification of the manner in and extent to which the devolved legislatures can be subjected to the supervisory jurisdiction of the court. The novelty of this question was highlighted by Lord Hope, who noted that, historically, 'a challenge to primary legislation at common law was simply impossible while the only legislature was the sovereign Parliament of the United Kingdom at Westminster, [so] we are in this case in uncharted territory'.[39] He went on to observe, providing the constitutional foundation for this view, that the devolved institutions are not sovereign and could therefore be susceptible to review, albeit in the limited form just described.

It was Lord Hope again, just a year later, who elaborated on this and explained, in the case of *Imperial Tobacco v Lord Advocate*,[40] the way in which the courts should seek to review devolved legislation on the basis of their 1998 enabling Acts.

Case in depth: *Imperial Tobacco v Lord Advocate* [2012] UKSC 61

The Scottish Parliament enacted the Tobacco and Primary Medical Services (Scotland) Act 2010, bringing into law a prohibition on the displaying of tobacco products in shops. The Imperial Tobacco company, however, brought a case challenging the validity of the legislation, arguing that its subject matter fell within the areas of 'Sale and supply of goods' and 'Product Safety', both within the ambit of 'consumer protection', a reserved matter under the Scotland Act 1998. The case went all the way to the UK Supreme Court, which dismissed Imperial Tobacco's action, finding that the 2010 Act fell within the legislative competence of the Scottish Parliament. In giving the leading judgment, Lord Hope explained that the relevant sections of the 2010 Act had nothing to do with consumer protection and were passed, instead, 'to discourage or eliminate sales of tobacco products not to regulate how any sales are to be conducted so as to protect the consumer from unfair trade practices'.[41] The Act was therefore upheld as valid.

In judgment, the Supreme Court took time to elucidate the 'three principles that should be followed when undertaking the exercise of determining whether, according to the rules that the 1998 Act lays down, a provision of an Act of the Scottish Parliament is outside competence'.[42] Lord Hope, with others in agreement, stated that:

> First, the question of competence must be determined in each case according to the particular rules that have been set out in sec 29 of, and schs 4 and 5 to, the 1998 Act . . . Second,

---

[36] Ibid [147].   [37] Ibid [148].   [38] Ibid [149].   [39] Ibid [48].   [40] [2012] UKSC 61.
[41] Ibid [40].   [42] Ibid [12].

those rules must be interpreted in the same way as any other rules that are found in a UK statute . . . [and] Third, the description of the Act as a constitutional statute cannot be taken, in itself, to be a guide to its interpretation. The statute must be interpreted like any other statute.[43]

The intention behind this explanation was to clarify the 'exercise . . . of statutory construction' underpinning the courts' examination of devolved legislation so as to leave 'no room for doubt' regarding the process that should be used in determining alleged instances of the devolved legislatures going beyond the scope of their allocated powers.[44]

A recently prominent example of the courts reviewing devolved legislation is in the case of *Re UK Withdrawal from the European Union (Legal Continuity) (Scotland) Bill*.[45]

Case in depth: *Re UK Withdrawal from the European Union (Legal Continuity) (Scotland) Bill* [2018] UKSC 64

This case involved a reference from the Attorney General and the Advocate General for Scotland to the Supreme Court on whether the UK Withdrawal from the European Union (Legal Continuity) (Scotland) Bill was within the scope of the Scottish Parliament's legislative powers. The bill was introduced following the Scottish Parliament's refusal to consent to the passing of the European Union (Withdrawal) Act 2018, an Act passed by the UK Parliament setting out the legal framework for Brexit. Consent was sought on the basis that Brexit—and therefore the 2018 Act—would impact upon the devolution settlements and the powers of the institutions in Edinburgh. Assuming that the refusal to consent to the 2018 Act would mean that it did not apply to matters devolved to Scotland, the Scottish Parliament sought to pass its own 'Brexit legislation', providing 'for EU law to remain in effect in relation to devolved matters after exit day . . . [giving] the Scottish Ministers powers to adjust the devolved statute book in the light of Brexit'.[46]

The 2018 Act was passed by the UK Parliament, and despite the Scottish Parliament having withheld its consent, the Act also applied to matters devolved to Scotland.[47] This case arose, then, in the context of the 2018 Act having been passed, the reference asking the Supreme Court whether the Scottish bill would be—either as a whole or in part—outside the scope of the Edinburgh legislature. They held that the bill as a whole was not outside the legislative competence of the Scottish Parliament, but that *certain* specific sections were outside this competence and, therefore, they could not be regarded as law under section 29 of the Scotland Act 1998.

Chief amongst the provisions that were outside the competence of the Scottish Parliament was section 17 of the bill. This provided that the consent of Scottish Ministers would be required in respect of UK subordinate legislation where that subordinate legislation affected matters devolved to Scotland.[48] The intention here was to protect 'retained (devolved)

---

[43] Ibid [13]–[15].   [44] Ibid [9].   [45] [2018] UKSC 64.

[46] Aileen McHarg and Chris McCorkindale, 'The Supreme Court and Devolution: the Scottish Continuity Bill Reference' (2019) 2 *Juridical Review* 190, 190.

[47] See: Aileen McHarg and Chris McCorkindale, 'The Supreme Court and Devolution: the Scottish Continuity Bill Reference' (2019) 2 *Juridical Review* 190, 190.

[48] See: section 17(1) and (2), UK Withdrawal from the European Union (Legal Continuity) (Scotland) Bill 2018.

EU law', preserved by the bill post-Brexit.[49] The Supreme Court, however, held that section 17 limited 'the UK Parliament's power to make laws for Scotland', because it 'prevent[ed] legislation enacted by the UK Parliament from coming into force without the Scottish Ministers' consent'.[50] As a consequence, the Court said 'section 17 of the Bill would modify section 28(7) of the Scotland Act', which preserves the power of the UK Parliament to pass laws for Scotland, and it is therefore contrary to section 29(2)(c) of the 1998 Act and is not law.[51]

This case provides another example of the courts permitting review of legislation passed by the Scottish Parliament. Moreover, it shows the reserved powers model of devolution at work by emphasizing 'the breadth of the legislative powers that [the Scottish Parliament] . . . enjoy[s] within the limits of their competence'.[52]

Discussing the problem

Take a look at the problem scenario set out at the beginning of the chapter. Does the Scottish Parliament have the power to pass laws affecting people's term of employment? To what extent do you think the requirement to work six days a week is consistent with the ECHR right to a private and family life?

As this question makes clear, there are two issues to consider with regards to the law passed by the Scottish Parliament. The first relates to whether or not employment is an area within which the Scottish legislature has the competence to act; the second concerns the compatibility of this new law with the ECHR. We consider each in turn.

The list of reserved matters provided above sets out some of the matters that are expressly labelled as reserved matters under the Scotland Act 1998. This list includes employment and industrial relations and, indeed, Schedule 5(H1) to the 1998 Act provides that '[e]mployment rights and duties and industrial relations' are reserved matters. This means that the Scottish Parliament has no power to pass this law permitting employers to require employees to work six days a week, such power lying only with the Westminster legislature. Pursuant to section 29(2)(b) of the Scotland Act 1998, which provides that an Act of the Scottish Parliament is not law if it is a reserved matter, the Act is therefore invalid. As the Supreme Court judgment in *AXA Insurance v Lord Advocate* exemplifies, it is possible for the courts to declare the Act as invalid under the section 29 provision.

The second issue presented by this Act of the Scottish Parliament in the problem scenario concerns the compatibility of the law permitting employers to require employees to work six days a week with the ECHR. While the finding that this law relates to a reserved matter and is therefore invalid renders this point moot, it is nonetheless worth considering. Section 29(2)(d) of the Scotland Act 1998 provides that an Act of the Scottish Parliament is not law if it is outside the competence of the Scottish Parliament, an eventuality that can arise where the law is incompatible with the ECHR. While we consider the ECHR and its application in the UK in Chapters 15 and 16,

→

[49] Section 17(1)(b)(ii), UK Withdrawal from the European Union (Legal Continuity) (Scotland) Bill 2018.
[50] [2018] UKSC 64 [53].   [51] [2018] UKSC 64 [54].
[52] Aileen McHarg and Chris McCorkindale, 'The Supreme Court and Devolution: the Scottish Continuity Bill Reference' (2019) 2 *Juridical Review* 190, 196.

→

it is worth identifying at this point the right set out in Article 8 of the ECHR. This provides that '[e]veryone has the right to respect for his private and family life, his home and his correspondence'. With this in mind, it could be argued that by requiring employees to treat Saturday and Sunday as normal working days, they are deprived of valuable time with their families, contrary to Article 8 of the ECHR. As such, even if the law were found to be within the realm of matters devolved to Scotland, incompatibility with the Convention rights could also potentially render it invalid.

Scottish devolution, parliamentary sovereignty, and the Sewel Convention

Above and beyond the court's ability to review devolved exercises of legislative authority, the powers of the UK Parliament must also be considered. Indeed, though the 1998 Act is said to have devolved power to the Scottish Parliament, the continued sovereignty of the UK Parliament means that Westminster still has the legal ability to legislate on devolved matters, a reality that is consistent with orthodox understandings of parliamentary sovereignty. Parliament having the legal power to pass laws for those in Scotland, though, might be seen as a potential threat to the devolution settlements. To get around this and to ensure that the authority of the sovereign UK Parliament does not erode the devolved authority of the Holyrood Parliament, a Convention has been established. The Sewel Convention provides that the UK Parliament will not legislate on matters devolved to Holyrood without the consent of the Scottish Parliament. Named after Lord Sewel, the minister within the Scotland Office who was responsible for the Scotland bill during its passage through Parliament, this convention initially formed a key part of the Memorandum of Understanding[53] between the UK Government and the Scottish Government. It has since been placed on a statutory footing in the Scotland Act 2016, section 2 of which states:

> In section 28 of the Scotland Act 1998 (Acts of the Scottish Parliament) at the end add—
> 'But it is recognised that the Parliament of the United Kingdom will not normally legislate with regard to devolved matters without the consent of the Scottish Parliament'.

In practical terms, the effect of the Sewel Convention is that 'by conditioning the exercise of the Westminster Parliament's theoretical sovereignty, [it] ensures that the Scottish Parliament in effect enjoys exclusive competence within the realm of devolved matters'.[54] It is important to explain, however, that the Sewel Convention is not law, but rather a constitutional convention.[55] As such, the courts have no power to enforce it and no basis on which to strike out UK legislation that affects devolved matters, a reality that is consistent with orthodox parliamentary sovereignty. Indeed, demonstrating the conventional nature of the rule, it is notable that the European Union (Withdrawal) Act 2018—which provides the legal foundation for Britain's departure from the EU—was still passed even without the consent of the Scottish Parliament. The Sewel Convention's inclusion in the

---

[53] The Memoranda of Understanding is a political document that represents the agreement between Central Government and the devolved governments, providing a working foundation for their relationships and a basis for the day in which they operate.

[54] Stephen Bailey and Mark Elliott, 'Taking Local Government Seriously: Democracy, Autonomy and the Constitution' (2009) 68(2) *Cambridge Law Journal* 436, 471.

[55] See 1.5.

2016 Act also does nothing to change its nature. As Lord Neuberger commented in *R (Miller) v Secretary of State for Exiting the European Union*,[56] in considering section 2 of the 2016 Act as part of a discussion on whether or not the devolved legislatures should have a say in the government's Brexit negotiations:

> the UK Parliament is not seeking to convert the Sewel Convention into a rule which can be interpreted, let alone enforced, by the courts; rather, it is recognising the convention for what it is, namely a political convention, and is effectively declaring that it is a permanent feature of the relevant devolution settlement . . . We would have expected [the] UK Parliament to have used other words if it were seeking to convert a convention into a legal rule justiciable by the courts.[57]

Section 2 of the 2016 Act, in other words, does nothing to entrench the devolved matters and legally prevent Parliament's authority from encroaching into the realm of authority allocated to the Scottish Parliament. All it does is show 'that Parliament is not politically omnipotent, a fact which has never been in dispute'.[58] While devolution is undoubtedly a political constraint on Parliament's authority, realized through the practical realities of the Sewel Convention, legally speaking, and keeping in mind section 28(7) of the Scotland Act 1998, '[t]he legislative authority of the UK Parliament remains legally unlimited notwithstanding the creation by statute of the devolution settlement'.[59]

On a separate, though connected, point, as the Supreme Court noted in *H v Lord Advocate*,[60] the Scottish devolution settlement is of a constitutional nature.[61] Keeping in mind our discussion from 5.4.3, however, and Laws LJ's notable judgment in *Thoburn v Sunderland City Council*,[62] this classification of the Scotland Act as 'constitutional' merely renders it incapable of implied repeal: it can—as the Supreme Court noted in *H*—still be altered or removed by 'express enactment'.[63] The legal power of Parliament to adjust or remove the devolution settlement with Scotland, then, is unchanged. The Scottish Parliament created to exercise devolved legislative authority in Edinburgh is therefore placed in a unique constitutional position.

The Scottish Government

Alongside the Scottish Parliament, the Scottish Government is the executive institution in Scotland. Created as the Scottish Executive in 1998, it was renamed the Scottish Government under the Scotland Act 2012.[64] The government's role is to execute policy within the laws passed by the Scottish Parliament and to fulfil administrative responsibilities within the various matters devolved to the Scottish institutions. The government is led by a First Minister who is formally appointed by the monarch and they have the power to appoint other ministers to positions lower down within the government, including to a Cabinet. The work of both the First Minister and the Cabinet is then supported by the six Scottish Government Directorates—the equivalents of government departments

---

[56] [2017] UKSC 5.   [57] Ibid [148].

[58] Michael Gordon, *Parliamentary Sovereignty in the UK Constitution: Process, Politics and Democracy* (Hart Publishing 2015) 116.   [59] Ibid.

[60] [2012] UKSC 24.   [61] Ibid [30].   [62] [2002] EWHC 195 (Admin).   [63] Ibid.

[64] See s 12 of the Scotland Act 2012.

at Westminster—which are staffed by civil servants.[65] As with their counterparts at Westminster, the Scottish Government has a close relationship with the Scottish Parliament. The government is drawn from the political party that wins the most seats in the parliamentary elections and they are accountable to the Scottish legislature in all that they do. Indeed, each minister also fulfils the role of an MSP,[66] meaning that the Scottish Government plays a key role in the broader legislative process, ensuring the influence of government policy on what can become law.

The Scottish Parliament and the Scottish Government, created through the Scotland Act 1998, both play a fundamental role in exercising and executing devolved functions and powers in Scotland. Despite the role that these institutions have played, however, the constitutional landscape underpinning devolution to Scotland is likely to change in the coming years, particularly in the aftermath of the Scottish Independence Referendum, the Brexit process and outcome, and subsequent calls for greater devolution.

The Scottish Independence Referendum 2014

In September 2014, following a long prelude of political discussion between Edinburgh and London, a Scotland-wide referendum was held on the question of Scottish independence. The question put to the people of Scotland asked simply whether or not Scotland should be an independent country. The result was 55 per cent voting against independence and 45 per cent voting for independence.

Though referendums are notable for their non-binding nature, the Edinburgh Agreement between the UK Government and the Scottish Government, set out in October 2012, reflected political consensus on the manner in which the referendum would be carried out and the way in which the result would be respected by both governments in London and in Edinburgh. The Agreement stated:

> The governments have agreed that the referendum should:
>
> have a clear legal base;
>
> be legislated for by the Scottish Parliament;
>
> be conducted so as to command the confidence of Parliaments, government, and people; and
>
> deliver a fair test and decisive expression of the views of people in Scotland and a result that everyone will respect.[67]

True to the Agreement, following the referendum and despite the close result, further steps towards independence were not then taken. Indeed, the then Scottish First Minister, Alex Salmond, described the 2014 Referendum as a 'once in a generation opportunity',[68]

---

[65] Scottish Government, 'Government Structure', http://www.gov.scot/About/People/Directorates. These are: Learning and Justice; Health and Social Care; Communities; Finance; Enterprise, Environment and Innovation; and Strategy and External Affairs. Also the Scottish Parliament, 'The Scottish Parliament and the Scottish Government—What is the Difference?', http://www.parliament.scot/ WebSPEIR-Resources/SP_SP_SG_English_Nov_2014_web.pdf.   [66] Ibid 5.

[67] HM Government and the Scottish Government, 'Agreement between the United Kingdom Government and the Scottish Government on a reference on independence for Scotland' (Edinburgh, 15 October 2012), http://www.gov.scot/Resource/0040/00404789.pdf.

[68] Simon Johnson, 'Alex Salmond Pledges No Second Scottish Referendum' *The Telegraph* (14 September 2014), http://www.telegraph.co.uk/news/uknews/scottish-independence/11095188/Alex-Salmond-pledges-no-second-Scottish-referendum.html.

the feeling being that the decision against independence had been made and settled. Very quickly, however, it became clear that the result should not be seen so much as a Scottish rejection of independence, but more as a desire to remain a part of the United Kingdom on the condition that Scotland enjoy a greater devolution of power from London and a stronger constitutional position within the United Kingdom.[69] This desire for further devolution is linked to last minute attempts made by the UK Government and other political parties at Westminster, ahead of the referendum, to encourage people to vote against independence with promises that the Scottish institutions would be given further power and autonomy going forward. It is not surprising that issues concerning Scotland's place in the union, the desire for further devolution, and the potential for independence have—since September 2014—far from subsided. Since Scotland voted to stay in the UK, there has been continued discussion about the nature of the union and, in particular, about the powers which should be devolved to Scotland. In the immediate aftermath of the referendum, the Smith Commission was established by then Prime Minister David Cameron to explore the possibilities for further devolution of power to Scotland.[70] The report explored the need for further devolution, setting a number of proposals to this end. These included the proposed recognition of the Scottish Parliament and Scottish Government as permanent institutions and the inclusion of the Sewel Convention in legislation.[71] Proposals also included the recommended devolution of powers over the setting of tax rates, public spending, and the welfare system, as well as the ability to oversee elections to the Scottish Parliament and local governmental institutions in Scotland.[72] The proposed programme for further devolution to Scotland was notable and said to reflect wider public desire with regards to Scotland's continued place within the United Kingdom.

The Scotland Act 2016

With the Commission's proposals in mind, the Scotland bill was introduced into Parliament in May 2015, receiving Royal Assent in March 2016. According to the Explanatory Notes to the Act, the new legislation amends the Scotland Act 1998 and 'rebalances the devolved and reserved responsibilities between' the Scottish and UK administrations.[73] The Act's provisions themselves see the evolution of many of the Smith Commission's proposals, including the permanent recognition of the Scottish institutions,[74] statutory provision for the Sewel Convention,[75] and the introduction of the proposed electoral powers.[76] It also sees the introduction of a 'super-majority' procedure[77] and the ability of the Supreme Court to scrutinize bills, as well as the devolution of various powers related to income tax and the welfare system.[78]

---

[69] Indeed, amidst fears that the Scots would vote to leave the United Kingdom, the UK Government made promises for further devolution in the lead up to the referendum.

[70] The Smith Commission, 'Report of the Smith Commission for further devolution of powers to the Scottish Parliament' (27 November 2014), http://webarchive.nationalarchives.gov.uk/20151202171017/http://www.smith-commission.scot/.

[71] Ibid 13.   [72] Ibid 13–27.   [73] Explanatory Notes to the Scotland Act 2016 [2].

[74] Section 1 of the Scotland Act 2016.   [75] Section 2 of the Scotland Act 2016.

[76] Section 4 of the Scotland Act 2016.

[77] Section 11 of the Scotland Act 2016. This concerns a procedure, reserved for certain pieces of legislation, whereby a two-thirds majority of the Scottish Parliament is required for enactment.

[78] Parts 2 and 3 of the Scotland Act 2016.

The 2016 Act, then, sees an unprecedented level of devolution to Scotland and a new constitutional settlement for Scotland within the United Kingdom. Indeed, through the permanent recognition of Scottish governmental and parliamentary institutions and statutory provision for the Sewel Convention, the new devolutionary settlement arguably moves the UK closer to a quasi-federal state than ever before, an issue that is picked up again later in the chapter. Whether or not we see another Scottish Independence Referendum in the future, however, is arguably tied to the success of these reforms. The 2014 Referendum was identified as a 'once in a generation opportunity'.[79] In the aftermath of the Brexit vote, however, at which a majority of Scotland voted to remain in the European Union, discussions concerning a second referendum resurfaced, with the Scottish Parliament backing Nicola Sturgeon's plans to start discussions with Westminster concerning a second referendum.[80] The loss of more than twenty Scottish National Party seats in the UK Parliament at the 2017 General Election, however, reflected a lack of popular support for another independence referendum and it is not surprising that the plans were later shelved. As the realities of Brexit become ever more apparent, though, the question of Scottish independence is not yet settled. Regardless, the Scottish people and the parties representing Scottish constituencies need to be satisfied with the package of powers being devolved and the nature of their decentralization if they are to remain a part of the United Kingdom.

 Counterpoint: English votes for English laws: the West Lothian Question

An issue that has become increasingly prominent in the aftermath of the 2014 Scottish Independence Referendum is the question of Scottish MPs sitting in the UK Parliament and voting on matters and laws pertaining solely to England. This issue is far from new and it has drawn concern ever since the devolution settlements were agreed back in the late 1990s. It is known as the West Lothian Question, though has more recently also been framed as the English Question or 'English votes for English laws' (EVEL).

The concern here centres on the reality that issues relating to devolved matters and affecting only Scotland, Wales, or Northern Ireland are dealt with and fall within the jurisdiction of the relevant institutions in Edinburgh, Cardiff, and Belfast. Only elected officials in each of the devolved regions are empowered to debate and decide on such matters. By contrast, matters concerning only England are dealt with, debated by, and ultimately fall to the UK Parliament and UK Government. There is no specific English institution able to deal with matters only concerning England.

→

[79] Simon Johnson, 'Alex Salmond Pledges No Second Scottish Referendum' *The Telegraph* (14 September 2014).

[80] See Libby Brooks, 'Second Scottish Referendum Inevitable, Says Alex Salmond' *The Guardian* (26 July 2015), http://www.theguardian.com/politics/2015/jul/26/second-scottish-referendum-inevitable-alex-salmond and Severin Carrell, 'Scottish Parliament Votes for Second Independence Referendum' *The Guardian* (28 March 2017), https://www.theguardian.com/politics/2017/mar/28/scottish-parliament-votes-for-second-independence-referendum-nicola-sturgeon.

→

That the issue has long gone hand-in-hand with devolution discussions in the UK is evident from the reality that:

> When in 1978 Parliament legislated to introduce devolution for Scotland and for Wales (against the backdrop of a somewhat longer search for a new system of devolution for Northern Ireland) the then MP, Tam Dalyell, for the then constituency of West Lothian raised the above concerns which would henceforth bear the soubriquet of the 'West Lothian Question' . . . would it be acceptable, after the introduction of devolution, for Scottish MPs to continue to vote on English matters at Westminster when English MPs could not vote on Scottish devolved matters?[81]

In October 2015, however, a solution to the question was finally sought, albeit amidst a great deal of political discussion and debate—particularly between the government and MPs representing the Scottish National Party. The solution involves a new procedure, set out in an amended House of Commons Standing Order,[82] that requires the Speaker of the House of Commons to '"certify" bills, or clauses within them, that meet two criteria: first, they relate only to England (or England and Wales); and second, comparable policy decisions are devolved elsewhere in the UK'.[83] Where bills meet this criteria, MPs for English constituencies will have the opportunity, prior to the Third Reading in the House, to debate and agree to the bill's provisions in a Legislative Grand Committee. The consent of these MPs is required before a bill can proceed to third reading, meaning that they have a power of veto. Where the Committee withholds its consent, a bill will return to the full House for reconsideration and amendment.[84] If the Committee still withholds its consent to the entire bill, it will go no further; though if consent is only withheld in respect of certain parts of the bill, those sections can be removed from the bill, leaving it free to proceed to third reading.[85] While it does not seek to diminish the role that the full House of Commons plays in the broader, legislative process, the main purpose of this new procedure is to ensure a level of devolutionary equality between the various regions of the United Kingdom whereby MPs for English constituencies can have a directing say on laws passed for England. The procedure was used for the first time in January 2016 in respect of the Housing and Planning Bill.

---

[81] Brigid Hadfield, 'Devolution, Westminster and the English Question' (2005) *Public Law* 286, 288, citing Barry K Winetrobe, 'The West Lothian Question' (*HC Research Paper 95/58*, 6 September 1995); Barry K Winetrobe, 'The Scotland Bill: Some Constitutional and Representational Aspects' (*HC Research Paper 98/3*, 7 January 1998).

[82] These are written rules which regulate the proceedings of each House (see UK Parliament, 'Standing Orders', http://www.parliament.uk/site-information/glossary/standing-orders/).

[83] Michael Kenny and Daniel Gover, 'The Triumph of EVEL: What Next for the English Question?' (*The Constitution Unit, UCL*, 23 October 2015), https://constitution-unit.com/2015/10/23/the-triumph-of-evel-what-next-for-the-english-question/.

[84] UK Parliament, 'English Votes for English Laws: House of Commons Bill Procedure' (Biteback Publishing 2015) 15, https://www.parliament.uk/about/how/laws/bills/public/english-votes-for-english-laws/. Also see 8.5.10.

[85] Ibid.

Concluding thoughts on Scotland

The constitutional narrative underpinning Scotland's position in the United Kingdom is interesting. Founded upon the union agreed in 1707 and—for now—sustained by the 'No' vote achieved in the 2014 Scottish Independence Referendum, Scotland's place within the UK is preserved. Since 1998, though, the relationship between Edinburgh and London has been defined by the devolution of power. The initial settlement ensured that certain legislative and executive authority was devolved to Holyrood in a legal framework that sought to protect the fundamental aspects of the UK Constitution. Increasingly, though, and with proposals, calls, and plans for further devolution, the broader constitutional landscape could be changing, with some going so far as to suggest that we are moving towards a quasi-federal state.

9.4.2 **Devolution to Wales**

Though Wales' place in what is now the United Kingdom long pre-dates Scotland's formal, legal accession in the early-eighteenth century, the journey to Welsh devolution follows a path parallel, though not identical, to that which led to Scottish devolution in the late 1990s. It is the purpose of this section to explore and discuss the nature of devolution in Wales and to consider how this has developed since that time.

The 1973 Royal Commission on the Constitution was tasked with investigating the possibility of devolution not only to Scotland, but also to Wales, following increasing nationalist pressures there.[86] Similar to Scotland and following publication of the Kilbrandon Report, the realization of proposals for executive devolution to Wales were hindered first by the failed Scotland and Wales Bill 1976 and two years later by a referendum which failed to endorse the scheme for devolution set out in the Wales Act 1978. Indeed, only 12 per cent of registered voters supported the 1978 Act's plan for devolution. Come 1997, though support for Welsh devolution was not quite as strong as it was in Scotland, a pre-legislative referendum narrowly endorsed the programme for devolution set out in the *A Voice for Wales* White Paper that New Labour had published.[87] As a result, the Government of Wales Act 1998 was enacted.

Government of Wales Act 1998

The main difference between the initial devolutionary settlement for Wales, compared with that in Scotland, was the decentralization of merely executive power to Cardiff. In 1998, the newly created National Assembly for Wales (now called the Welsh Parliament) was to have the ability to make secondary legislation, but primary legislative authority would, for the time being, remain with the UK Parliament at Westminster. The chief justification for this is the different historical and legal relationship that Wales has with England, compared with Scotland. Whereas Scotland had, until 1707, its own law-making Parliament, Wales had never had such an institution and had been ruled by the UK Parliament for over 450 years. In addition, Wales had for many years been included within the English court system, whereas Scotland still had its own courts.[88]

---

[86] See 9.4.1. Also see DGT Williams, 'The Commission on the Constitution' (1974) 33(1) *Cambridge Law Journal* 15, 16.

[87] On a 50.1 per cent turnout, 50.3 per cent of voters endorsed the programme for devolution (Colin Rallings and Michael Thrasher, *British Electoral Facts 1832–2012* (Biteback 2012) 246).

[88] See Sir David Williams, 'Devolution: The Welsh Perspective' in University of Cambridge Centre of Public Law, *Constitutional Reform in the United Kingdom* (Hart Publishing 1998), 41, 44, as cited in Colin Turpin and Adam Tomkins, *British Government and the Constitution: Text and Materials* (7th edn, Cambridge University Press 2011) 246.

The Welsh devolved institution created by the 1998 Act was a unicameral Assembly, made up of sixty members who are elected every four years through a two-part process. Forty members, representing constituencies across Wales, are elected through the first-past-the-post system, while the remaining twenty members were selected from a party list across five regions of Wales. The Assembly in Wales, unlike the Scottish Parliament and separate government, was created as a statutory corporation, meaning that it was empowered with authority to make just secondary legislation and executive decisions for Wales, under the primary legislative authority of the UK Parliament. Structurally, this also meant that there was no separation of the legislative and executive functions, giving rise not only to a lack of governmental accountability—insofar as the legislative body did not exist as a separate entity to hold the government to account—but, more fundamentally, to a devolutionary settlement that was more akin to a delegation of power, rather than a devolution of authority and autonomy.

Nonetheless, the model set up by the 1998 Act was met with some success, with the Assembly seen as creating for the Welsh 'a stronger, more democratically accountable voice in Britain and in Europe'.[89] On the recommendations of the House of Commons Select Committee on Welsh Affairs and the House of Lords Select Committee on the Constitution, however, further changes were later introduced which sought to ensure that 'the Assembly Government [could] . . . secure its legislative priorities more quickly and more easily, within its current areas of responsibility'.[90] These were introduced by the Government of Wales Act 2006.

The Government of Wales Act 2006

The 2006 Act made two key alterations to the devolution settlement in Wales. First, it created a Welsh Government, working separately from the legislative authority of the Assembly. Secondly, it changed the form of the Welsh Assembly itself. As the Explanatory Notes to the Act state:

> [t]he corporate body which was set up under the Government of Wales Act 1998 with legislative and executive powers, and which was also called the 'National Assembly for Wales', will cease to exist.[91]

In its place, the Government of Wales Act 2006 saw the 'establishment of the legislative body called the National Assembly for Wales'.[92] Under the Act, this was granted the ability to pass a form of legislation known as 'Assembly Measures' in twenty specified and limited 'fields' devolved to the Assembly and set out in Schedule 5 to the Act.[93] Any measure that goes beyond the scope of these fields is 'not law'.[94] These Assembly Measures are a form of secondary legislation, rather than primary legislation, insofar as they are passed by the Assembly and approved by Order in Council, rather than by Royal Assent.[95] The 2006 Act, however, also gave the National Assembly for Wales the power to pass primary legislation, 'just like the Scottish Parliament'.[96] Known as 'Assembly Acts', this

---

[89] Wales Office, *Better Governance for Wales* (Cm 6582, 2005) 2.   [90] Ibid 3.

[91] Explanatory Notes to the Government of Wales Act 2006 [36].   [92] Ibid.

[93] These included: education, the environment, health, local government, social welfare, and planning.

[94] Section 94(2) of the Government of Wales Act 2006.

[95] Ibid s 93(2). Also see Brice Dickson, 'Devolution' in Jeffrey Jowell, Dawn Oliver, and Colm O'Cinneide (eds), *The Changing Constitution* (8th edn, OUP 2015) 249, 260.

[96] See Dickson, 'Devolution' at 249, 260.

primary legislation 'may make any provision that could be made by an Act of Parliament' provided it is within the Assembly's legislative competence,[97] that is, within the already identified twenty specified fields. Unlike the Scottish Parliament, however, the ability of the National Assembly of Wales to pass these Acts was not automatic, but had to be 'activated' by referendum.[98] Section 103 of the 2006 Act stated that 'Her Majesty may by Order in Council cause a referendum to be held throughout Wales about whether the Assembly Act provisions should come into force'.[99] A referendum to this end was held in 2011, with 63.5 per cent of those who voted deciding that the Assembly's powers to pass primary legislation, in the form of Assembly Acts, should be activated.[100] Since 2011, the Assembly has had primary legislative powers within specified fields set out in the Act.

The effect of devolving legislative authority to the Welsh Assembly in certain, specified fields was to establish a conferred-powers model of devolution. Different from the reserved-powers model that prevails in Scotland, which permits the Scottish Parliament to pass laws in any area that is not reserved, the conferred-powers model established in Wales after the 2006 Act meant that the Assembly could only legislate and govern within the twenty specified fields set out in the Act.[101] In other words, power is conferred on Wales rather than reserved to Westminster.

Similar to legislation passed in Scotland, laws passed by the Welsh Assembly under this conferred-powers model have been susceptible to review and scrutiny by the courts. In the case of *Local Government Byelaws (Wales) Bill 2012—Reference by the Attorney-General for England and Wales*,[102] for instance, the Attorney-General sought clarification from the Supreme Court of the Local Government Byelaws (Wales) Bill 2012 about whether or not it fell within the remit of conferred powers. The 2012 bill sought to simplify procedures for making and enforcing local authority byelaws in Wales by removing a requirement that the Secretary of State confirm or reject byelaws introduced by the Assembly. The contention was, though, that the bill sought to alter the powers of the Secretary of State, something it was not empowered to do. The Court held, however, that the bill was within the scope of conferred powers and was therefore valid. The basis for this decision was that the altering of the Secretary of State's powers was incidental to the main aim of the bill, which was to remove the need for Welsh ministers to seek confirmation upon the introduction of certain byelaws. Similarly, in *Agricultural Sector (Wales) Bill—Reference by the Attorney-General for England and Wales*,[103] the Attorney-General sought clarification from the Supreme Court of the Agricultural Sector (Wales) Bill 2013. Under the Government of Wales Act 2006, the Welsh Assembly has the competence to pass legislation on, *inter alia*, agriculture. It sought to do that in this case, the 2013 bill concerning agricultural wages. The Attorney-General contended, however, that the bill related to employment and industrial relationship, matters beyond the scope of the powers conferred to Wales by the 2006 Act. The Court unanimously held, though, that the bill was valid on the basis that 'agriculture' referred also to the industry and economic activity underpinning the

---

[97] Section 108(1) and (2) of the Government of Wales Act 2006.

[98] Ibid s 103.   [99] Ibid s 103(1).

[100] Turnout was low, at just 35.2 per cent. For more on the referendum, see Brice Dickson, 'Devolution' in Jeffrey Jowell, Dawn Oliver, and Colm O'Cinneide (eds), *The Changing Constitution* (8th edn, OUP 2015) 249, 260.

[101] See Robert Thomas, 'The Draft Wales Bill 2015—Part 1' (UK Constitutional Law Association, 2 December 2015), https://ukconstitutionallaw.org/2015/12/02/robert-thomas-the-draft-wales-bill-2015-part-1/.

[102] [2012] UKSC 53.   [103] [2014] UKSC 43.

agricultural sector.[104] The scope of the conferred powers has been readily explored and tested in the courts, with the Supreme Court in particular clarifying the powers devolved to the Welsh Assembly.

Wales Act 2017

This conferred-powers model, however, which had been a defining feature of the Welsh devolution settlement since 2006, was reformed again by the Wales Act 2017. This brought into force a reserved-powers model, akin to that which operates in Scotland. This means that the 2006 Act—amended by the 2017 statute—no longer limits Assembly Acts to the twenty previously defined fields, but instead lists the matters that are reserved for Westminster and in respect of which the Welsh institutions are not permitted to act. These reserved matters are set out in a newly added Schedule 7A to the 2006 Act and they include the constitution, tribunals, defence, home and foreign affairs, immigration, and consumer protection. In addition, and building on provisions already introduced in the 2006 Act,[105] the Wales Act 2017 also made clear that the Welsh Assembly could not pass laws that were contrary to the UK's obligations under EU law or that are incompatible with the ECHR.[106] Alongside this establishment of reserved matters, the 2017 Act also gave increased power to the Assembly over a range of matters, including energy and the environment, taxes, road and transport, elections, and electoral processes.[107] The final development in respect of devolution to Wales has been the passing of the Senedd and Elections (Wales) Act 2020. Section 2 of this Act, renamed the Assembly, Senedd Cymru or Welsh Parliament, reflecting its shift towards a reserved powers model.

Discussing the problem

Education in Wales was listed under the 2006 Act as being an area in which the Parliament could make primary legislation. It is not listed as a reserved matter under the 2017 Act. Returning to the problem scenario at the beginning of the chapter and keeping in mind changes recently introduced, is the Welsh Parliament acting within its powers to pass a law increasing the age at which children leave school to eighteen years of age?

On the basis that the reserved matters in the newly added Schedule 7A to the Government of Wales Act 2006 do not list education as a matter that is reserved for the exclusive competence of the Westminster Parliament, it can be concluded that it is a matter that falls within the competence of the Welsh Parliament. On this basis, this law can be regarded as valid.

This shift from a conferred-powers model to a reserved-powers model, however, also affects the way in which the Welsh Parliament relates to the UK generally, and particularly to the UK Parliament. Formerly, under the conferred-powers model, the Welsh Assembly could only act in those specifically defined fields expressly stipulated in the Government of Wales Acts of 1998 and 2006, being susceptible to the scrutiny of the courts if and when it sought to go beyond these, as cases already explored demonstrate. Though the Sewel

---

[104] Ibid [47]–[49].
[105] See s 108(6)(c) of the Government of Wales Act 2006, repealed by s 3(1) of the Wales Act 2017.
[106] See s 108A(2)(e) of the Government of Wales Act 2006, added by s 3(1) of the Wales Act 2017.
[107] See Part 2 of the Wales Act 2017.

Convention was also recognized as applying to the Welsh devolution settlement, this merely meant that Parliament would not pass laws in any of the specifically defined fields, being otherwise free and unlimited in its ability to legislate for Wales. The provisions of the 2017 Act, however, now mean that the Sewel Convention operates in a slightly different way. First, and due to the establishment of a reserved-powers model, the UK Parliament will now not legislate for Wales beyond the scope of matters expressly reserved in the 2017 Act. In addition, and similar to provisions set out in the Scotland Act 2016, the Wales Act 2017 also recognizes the convention that 'the Parliament of the United Kingdom will not normally legislate with regard to devolved matters without the consent of the Parliament'.[108] Again similar to the Scotland Act 2016, the 2017 statute also recognizes the permanence of the Welsh Parliament and Welsh Government as features of the UK's constitutional arrangements.[109] The effect of these provisions, though, similar to those already discussed in respect of Scotland, is merely to recognize the political convention that the UK legislature will not trespass into matters devolved to Wales and to recognize the existence and operation of devolved institutions exercising power in Wales. They do nothing to limit the legal power of the UK sovereign Parliament. Indeed, as in Scotland, '[t]he legislative authority of the UK Parliament remains legally unlimited notwithstanding the creation by statute of the devolution settlement' in Wales.[110] The devolution Acts are also susceptible to ordinary repeal and amendment, which means that Parliament still has the legal power to adjust or remove the devolution settlement with Wales.

The devolution settlement with Wales has undoubtedly become stronger since its creation in the late 1990s. The Parliament in Cardiff is now blessed with more power than it has ever had before, something that can be seen from recent examples of laws passed by the Parliament. The enactment of the Wales Act 2014, which conferred tax-raising powers on the Parliament, paved the way for the recent Land Transaction Tax and Anti-avoidance of Devolved Taxes (Wales) Act 2017. This was enacted to replace stamp duty land tax with a new land transaction tax, thereby giving rise to the first Welsh-only tax in almost 800 years. Going further back, the Single Use Carrier Bags Charge (Wales) Regulations 2010 introduced a charge of '5 pence for every single use carrier bag supplied' by sellers.[111] Though similar charges now exist in other parts of the UK, these came much later. The legislative ability of the Welsh Parliament means that it enjoys the power to pass laws unique to Wales, as these examples demonstrate.

Welsh Government

Before 2006, at a time when the National Assembly held both legislative and governmental responsibilities, a First Secretary, with various appointed Secretaries, formed a Cabinet that exercised executive power on behalf of the whole Assembly. Section 45 of the 2006 Act, however, changed this and created the new Welsh Government, which now operates separate from the main Parliament.

The Welsh Government is formed from the political party that commands a majority in the Parliament[112] and is headed by a First Minister, who is formally appointed by the

---

[108] Section 2 of the Wales Act 2017.   [109] Section 1 of the Wales Act 2017.

[110] Michael Gordon, *Parliamentary Sovereignty in the UK Constitution: Process, Politics and Democracy* (Hart Publishing 2015) 116.

[111] Section 6 of the Single Use Carrier Bags Charge (Wales) Regulations 2010.

[112] Welsh Government, 'Welsh Government: A Quick Guide', 4, http://gov.wales/docs/caecd/publications/150917-quick-guide-en.pdf.

Queen following nomination by the Members of the Senedd.[113] The First Minister has the power to appoint various other ministers to a Cabinet, thereby forming the main decision-making body of the government. The government, though, also includes the Counsel General, who—like the Attorney-General in the UK Government—provides legal advice and representations on matters affecting Wales.[114] In this form, the government has a number of key functions, including responsibility for proposing and implementing policy and laws which would apply in Wales and making 'decisions on matters regarding' the devolved areas.[115]

The Welsh Parliament, initially created as a mere statutory corporation, has developed and changed more than any other of the devolved institutions since 1998. Now recognizing a separate executive and legislature and exercising primary legislative authority within a reserved-powers model, the Parliament offers a greater degree of power and accountability to the Welsh people on matters affecting and relevant to Wales.

9.4.3 Devolution to Northern Ireland

As this chapter has already explained, the narrative underpinning Northern Ireland's position within the United Kingdom is markedly different from both Wales' and Scotland's own stories. This is chiefly due to the long history of Irish nationalist opposition to the union, which over the last century has seen revolution and the break-up of Ireland into the independent Republic of Ireland and Northern Ireland, the latter remaining a part of the United Kingdom.

In the midst of all this, however, Northern Ireland enjoyed a degree of devolution for half a century after the break-up of Ireland. The Government of Ireland Act 1920, enacted following the north–south separation, saw the creation of a Northern Ireland Parliament, complete with Prime Minister and executive that wielded significant devolved authority on Northern Irish matters. Section 4 of that Act provided that 'the Parliament of Northern Ireland shall respectively have power to make laws for the peace, order, and good government of . . . Northern Ireland'. Though undoubtedly broad, the provision went on to outline certain specific limitations to the power, noting that the Northern Ireland Parliament could not legislate on matters affecting the United Kingdom as a whole.[116] The Act also clarified that the UK Parliament's sovereignty was unaffected and that Westminster retained the power to legislate on matters devolved to Belfast.[117]

Though the Northern Ireland Parliament enjoyed this devolved authority until the early 1970s, this was amid increasing unrest between the nationalists and the unionists. As a result, the Northern Ireland Constitution Act 1973 was enacted to abolish the Northern Ireland Parliament, with its devolved legislative powers returning to the UK Parliament at Westminster. Far from being the end of the story, however, amid continued unrest, discussions between unionists and nationalists were ongoing throughout the 1970s, 1980s, and 1990s, eventually culminating in the 1998 Good Friday Agreement.[118] This represented

---

[113] See Welsh Government, 'First Minister of Wales', http://gov.wales/about/firstminister/?skip= 1&lang=en.

[114] Welsh Government, 'Welsh Government: A Quick Guide', 17.   [115] Ibid 2.

[116] Such matters include: the Crown, the making of peace and war, armed forces, and treaties and relations with foreign states (see s 4(1) of the Government of Ireland Act 1920).

[117] See s 6(1) and (2) of the Government of Ireland Act 1920.

[118] So called because the agreement took place on Good Friday 1998.

consensus on Northern Ireland's position within the UK and stated that this would remain the case until a majority of Northern Ireland's population voted in favour of leaving the union and becoming a part of the Republic of Ireland. On the back of the Agreement and simultaneously with the establishment of devolutionary settlements in Scotland and Wales, a referendum was held on the question of fresh devolution to Northern Ireland. An overwhelming 71 per cent of voters supported the Agreement and the proposals for devolution and, as a consequence, the Northern Ireland Act 1998 was passed.

Northern Ireland Act 1998

The Act established new institutions in Belfast and set out devolved powers with which these would be blessed. Of note, the 1998 Act also gave statutory effect to the Good Friday Agreement. Section 1 of the Act states:

(1) It is hereby declared that Northern Ireland in its entirety remains part of the United Kingdom and shall not cease to be so without the consent of a majority of the people of Northern Ireland voting in a poll held for the purposes of this section in accordance with Schedule 1.

(2) But if the wish expressed by a majority in such a poll is that Northern Ireland should cease to be part of the United Kingdom and form part of a united Ireland, the Secretary of State shall lay before Parliament such proposals to give effect to that wish as may be agreed between Her Majesty's Government in the United Kingdom and the Government of Ireland.

Reflecting the agreement reached between the British and Irish Governments and political representatives from Northern Ireland, this section of the Northern Ireland Act 1998 ensures that the achievement of devolution to Belfast and the constitutional landscape this created would not stand as a barrier to any future negotiations aimed at unifying Ireland as one country again. For now, though, Northern Ireland remains a part of the UK and enjoys devolved authority, exercised by the Northern Ireland Assembly on the Stormont Estate in Belfast. The constitutional importance of the Northern Ireland Act 1998 is evident from *Robinson v Secretary of State for Northern Ireland*.[119] This case involved a challenge to the legality of the Northern Ireland Assembly elections in 2002 on the basis that the First Minister and the Deputy First Minister were not elected into office by members of the Assembly within the required period of six weeks following the Assembly elections, pursuant to section 16 of the 1998 Act. Though an election had been held in time, the candidates did not initially attract sufficient support to take up office, meaning another election had to be held a few days later. The House of Lords, however, held that the election of the First Minister and Deputy First Minister was still valid. The basis for this decision was the view that Parliament, in including this provision in the 1998 Act, was unlikely to 'have wished to constrain local politicians . . . within such a tight straitjacket',[120] and that consequently, as a constitutional statute, the Northern Ireland Act 1998 should be interpreted broadly and generously. Though this is a view that has subsequently been criticized and has not been followed elsewhere, it underlines the constitutional importance that the courts have been willing to place on legislation giving effect to peaceful agreement with Northern Ireland.[121]

---

[119] [2002] UKHL 32.   [120] Ibid [14].

[121] See further Colin Turpin and Adam Tomkins, *British Government and the Constitution: Text and Materials* (7th edn, Cambridge University Press 2011) 88–91.

Northern Ireland Assembly

The Northern Ireland Assembly originally consisted of 108 members, these being elected through a single transferable voting system.[122] Unlike elections to the Scottish Parliament and Welsh Assembly, the Northern Irish constituencies that determine the representatives for the UK Parliament at Westminster are also used for the elections to the Northern Ireland Assembly, with each constituency electing six members to the assembly. Amid concerns, however, that a 108-strong Assembly was simply too large, the Assembly Members (Reduction of Numbers) Act (Northern Ireland) 2016 reduced its size by providing that constituencies should return five members, instead of six, thereby reducing the overall membership of the Assembly to ninety, effective from the election held in March 2017.

From the Northern Ireland Assembly is drawn an executive that has administrative and executive powers and functions within devolved areas. The executive is headed by the First Minister and Deputy First Minister, who have the authority to appoint up to ten ministers to various roles within the executive, with any remaining ministerial positions being appointed from the wider membership, proportionate to party population in the Assembly. The executive system in Northern Ireland is multi-party on the basis that the ministers and First/Deputy First Ministers are drawn from two different parties. The largest party provides the First Minister, while the second largest provides the Deputy First Minister.[123] The justification for the multi-party system is—in view of past troubles—to ensure opportunity for both unionist and nationalist parties to be represented in the executive and to ensure that administrative functions are not dominated by one political party but are carried out with a balance of competing interests.

Reserved and excepted powers

The Northern Ireland Assembly, like the Scottish Parliament, is empowered with primary legislative authority and can pass Acts of the Northern Ireland Assembly. Unlike devolution to Scotland, however, there are two different categories of legislation which apply to the devolved legislative powers of the Northern Ireland Assembly and which are relevant to its relationship with Westminster. Whereas, in Scotland, a reserved-powers model prevails on the basis of which the Parliament is able to act in a range of areas provided it does not trespass into the realm of matters reserved for Westminster, in Northern Ireland we distinguish between excepted and reserved powers. Reserved matters, rather than representing those areas which are reserved for the exclusive competence of the UK Parliament, are matters which are reserved to Westminster but which can be transferred to the Assembly by the Secretary of State following a request by the Assembly and by way of an Order in Council. Excepted matters, by contrast, like reserved matters in Scotland, are reserved for the exclusive competence of the Westminster Parliament. On the basis of this distinction, Schedule 3 to the 1998 Act identifies reserved matters as including:

- Navigation and civil aviation
- The foreshore and seabed
- Firearms and explosives
- Financial services and pensions regulation

[122] See 8.3.2.

[123] Prior to the St Andrews Agreement 2006, the First and Deputy First Ministers were elected by all members of the assembly, each appointment requiring the support of the various parties.

- Intellectual property
- Broadcasting
- Consumer safety

Excepted matters are listed in Schedule 2 and include:

- The Crown
- International relations
- Defence and armed forces
- Treason
- Nationality, immigration, and asylum
- National security
- Nuclear energy

In addition to the 1998 Act's identification of reserved and excepted matters, section 24 of the Act provides that Northern Ireland 'has no power to make, confirm or approve any subordinate legislation' that is incompatible with the ECHR rights or contrary to the UK's obligations under EU law.[124] Indeed, it is on a question of compatibility with the ECHR that legislation passed by the Northern Ireland Assembly was, in 2018, subject to challenges in the Supreme Court. *In Re Northern Ireland Human Rights Commission's application for judicial review*[125] involved a challenge to the compatibility of Northern Ireland's abortion laws, as enacted by the old Northern Ireland legislature,[126] with articles 3, 8, and 14 of the ECHR. Though there were exceptions to Northern Ireland's laws against abortion, it was not lawful to have a pregnancy terminated where the foetus had fatal abnormalities, or where the pregnancy was as a result of rape or incest. Though the Supreme Court denied the application on other grounds, it did emphasize that 'the current law is disproportionate'.[127] (It is notable that the law concerning abortion in Northern Ireland has changed since this case, pursuant to the Northern Ireland (Executive Formation etc) Act 2019, which came into force on 21 October 2019.) Though this case concerns a challenge to laws enacted by the old Northern Ireland legislation (ie that which operated between 1920 and 1972), it nonetheless shows the susceptibility of devolved legislation to review by the courts where it is alleged that the law is incompatible with the ECHR.

 Discussing the problem

Have another look at the problem scenario set at the beginning of the chapter. Do you think that the Northern Ireland Assembly is acting within its devolved authority by introducing its own immigration laws? If not, what would be the most appropriate course of action?

Schedule 2 to the Northern Ireland Act 1998 lists immigration as an excepted matter, meaning that it remains within the exclusive competence of the UK Parliament and Government. Similar to section 29 of the Scotland Act 1998, section 6(2)(b) of the Northern Ireland Act makes clear

→

---

[124] Section 24(1)(a) and (b) of the Northern Ireland Act 1998.   [125] [2018] UKSC 27.
[126] See: ss 58–9 of the Offences Against the Person Act 1861 and s 25(1) of the Criminal Justice Act (Northern Ireland) 1945.   [127] [2018] UKSC 27 [127].

→

that laws passed by the Northern Ireland Assembly dealing with an excepted matter are outside the legislative competence of the Assembly. This being the case, the law seeking to permit EU nationals entry to Northern Ireland, provided they have a job lined up, is outside the competence of the Belfast legislature and is, therefore, invalid. Furthermore, on the basis of the authority provided by the case of *AXA Insurance v Lord Advocate*, this law could be reviewed by the courts in line with the excepted powers set out in the 1998 Act and, on that basis, held to be beyond the legislative powers of the Assembly.

The Northern Ireland Act 1998 sets out full and detailed provision for the devolution of power to Belfast and the exercise of both legislative and executive authority in Northern Ireland. Since 1998, however, continued difficulties in the relationship between unionist and nationalist parties has meant that devolution has not always been an easy experience, with the Secretary of State suspending the devolution settlement on no fewer than four occasions since 1998. Following the most recent suspension, in 2002, the Northern Ireland (St Andrews Agreement) Act 2006 was passed to 'make provision for preparations for the restoration of devolved government in Northern Ireland'.[128] The St Andrews Agreement, on which the Act was founded, represented consensus on the matter that the devolved institutions should be reinstated and was reflective of a commitment from both the unionists and nationalists for a joint administration in Stormont. Since 2006, devolution has generally been more settled, with the elections in 2016 marking the completion of two uninterrupted terms of devolved power, free from suspension. Further issues early in 2017, however, meant that another election had to be held, just a year after the previous one. The circumstances are that in protest at political scandals in which the Democratic Unionist Party (DUP) leader and then First Minister, Arlene Foster, had been involved, the then Deputy First Minister, Sinn Fein's Martin McGuinness, resigned his post. Pursuant to section 16B of the 1998 Act, Sinn Fein, as the second largest party, had a week to nominate a replacement to the position. When this was not done, and in the event of the Deputy First Minister's position being vacant for more than seven days, pursuant to section 32(3)(b) an 'extraordinary' election had to be held. This took place on 2 March 2017, following which the DUP and Sinn Fein were returned again as the two largest parties. Following this election, however, the two parties were unable to reach an agreed basis for a subsequent power-sharing government, preventing any administration from taking office. In fact, Northern Ireland remained without its Government until 11 January 2020, when agreement was finally reached and the Executive and Assembly fully restored.[129] During this three-year period, though, not all power was recentralized to Westminster. Though the UK Parliament did play a more active role than normal in the law- and decision-making process of Northern Ireland at this time, '[t]he Assembly elected on 2 March 2017 was not formally suspended, as in the past, and Members of the Legislative Assembly . . . continued to carry out a range of activities, most significantly constituency work'.[130]

[128] Preamble to the Northern Ireland (St Andrews Agreement) Act 2006.

[129] In October 2019, there was an attempt to recall the Assembly as part of plans to debate and vote on the anti-abortion laws due to come into effect that month. Due to a continued lack of consensus, however, the whole Assembly did not sit and was not able to participate in the planned activities.

[130] David Torrance, 'Devolution in Northern Ireland, 1998–2020' (House of Commons Library Briefing Paper 8439, 4 February 2020) 4.

Both the manner in which Northern Ireland came to form a part of the UK and the continued nature and form of its devolution settlement is indicative of the troubles that have persisted in that region between those supporting a unified Ireland and those supporting membership of the United Kingdom. While the multi-party system that operates in Belfast has been created to ensure that political differences do not hinder the workings of a fully representative devolutionary settlement, the realization of the Good Friday Agreement in the years since 1998 has at times proved difficult. Nonetheless, the foundation established in 1998 continues to provide a basis for a unique model of devolved authority that provides legislative and executive authority to the people of Northern Ireland.

 Discussing the problem

In the problem scenario at the beginning of the chapter, the UK Parliament seeks to pass a law changing the length of degree programmes across the UK. Having now explored devolution, including a focus on the sovereignty of Parliament, what issues does this raise?

The various legislative provisions, determining the powers of the devolved legislatures in Scotland, Wales, and Northern Ireland, make clear that education is a matter that is devolved, since it is not listed as an area reserved or excepted for the exclusive competence of Westminster. On this understanding, the law passed by the UK Parliament, changing the length of degree programmes across the whole of the UK, impacts upon a devolved matter.

Unlike with regards to devolved legislation that affects a reserved matter, Acts of the UK Parliament cannot be subjected to scrutiny by the courts since Parliament is sovereign and, as Dicey made clear, no court can question the validity of any parliamentary enactment.[131] The actions of the UK Parliament, however, do engage the Sewel Convention. As this chapter has explained, this makes clear—as a matter of convention—that the UK Parliament will not normally legislate on devolved matters, without the consent of the relevant devolved institution(s). This makes sure that the authority of the legislatures in Edinburgh, Cardiff, and Belfast is protected, but as a merely political convention, it also determines that the sovereignty of Parliament is legally unaffected by the arrangements.

The consequence of all this, however, is that there are no legal ramifications in the event of Parliament passing a law such as that described in the problem scenario, despite its focus on devolved matters. Any consequences would be purely political, for example, potentially adding momentum to calls for independence from the UK or reducing support for the government in power.

Conclusion on devolution

Though the devolution settlements are only just two decades old, the workings of the institutions in Edinburgh, Cardiff, and Belfast and the settlements within which they operate have come to form a vital part of the modern UK Constitution. Each of the settlements, however, appears in a constant state of flux, with the devolved institutions having received increased powers and responsibilities since their creation in 1998. The manner in which this will continue to impact upon the nature of the UK Constitution is something to watch.

---

[131] See AV Dicey, *Introduction to the Study of the Law of the Constitution* (JWF Allison ed, first published 1885, OUP 2013) 27.

Counterpoint: Is the UK becoming a federal or quasi-federal state?

In the opening sections of this chapter, the notion of federalism was discussed alongside the principle of devolution. Though the difference between the two principles was there pointed out, the manner and extent to which the devolution settlements have evolved since 1998 has given rise to increased discussion and consideration of federalism and the question of whether the UK Constitution can be said to be moving closer to such a system. Writing in the late 1970s, shortly after the UK's accession to the European Union and at a time when discussions concerning the possible establishment of devolved institutions were taking place, Vile commented that 'we are witnessing something that would have seemed almost impossible a few years ago, [namely] a serious discussion taking place in the United Kingdom about the possibility, and the desirability, of the introduction of a federal, or "quasi-federal" system'.[132] Now, forty years down the line, with the devolution settlements firmly established and providing the foundation for increased power in the UK regions, arguments suggesting that the UK now exists within a quasi-federal constitution are stronger.

The notion that the UK is moving towards a federal system rests on the increased power of the devolved institutions. The Scottish Parliament and Welsh and Northern Irish Assemblies all have the ability to pass primary legislation for their respective regions, with reserved-powers models set out in legislation and the political operation of the Sewel Convention seeking to ensure that there is a demarcation between the devolved bodies and the Westminster institutions. Two levels of government having their own distinct powers and responsibilities is a mark of a federal state, such as that which exists in America, as this chapter has already explained. In addition, the role of the UK Supreme Court in reviewing Acts of the devolved legislatures, thereby protecting the realm of matters reserved for Westminster, is a constitutional function that seeks to uphold this demarcation of authority.

The suggestion, though, that the UK could be moving towards a 'quasi-federal' system, rather than simply a 'federal' one rests on the constitutional features that mean that power ultimately rests at the centre and that, consequently, the various UK regions and devolved regions cannot exercise their own legally exclusive realm of powers and responsibilities separate from Westminster. The main barrier to a federal system in the UK is parliamentary sovereignty. While the devolution settlements have seen increased powers and responsibilities in the various regions of the UK, they were ultimately created by Acts of the UK Parliament and can legally be revoked by ordinary repeal of that legislation. Though the Sewel Convention functions to ensure that Westminster does not legislate on matters devolved to the regions, this is a political convention and imposes no legal restriction on the sovereignty of Parliament. More than this, though, the comparable sizes of the various regions of the UK, particularly in terms of population, mean that the equality of power demanded by a federal system cannot be achieved. In America, each of the fifty states have the same powers and responsibilities under the Constitution. By contrast, in the UK, due to the different cultural, political, and social histories underpinning the relationships between the regions and the broader UK and the size of their respective populations, devolution is asymmetrical. Although there is an argument to say that we are moving towards a federal system, more fundamental constitutional arrangements and features ultimately mean that this is no more than quasi-federal.

---

[132] MJC Vile, 'Federal Theory and the "New Federalism"' (1977) 12 *Politics* 1, 1. Also see Mark Elliott, 'The Supreme Court's Judgment in Miller: In Search of Constitutional Principle' (2017) 76(2) *Cambridge Law Journal* 257, 286; Nicholas Aroney, 'Federal Models for a UK Constitution?' (UK Constitutional Law Association, 22 March 2012), https://ukconstitutionallaw.org/2012/03/22/nicholas-aroney-federal-models-for-a-u-k-constitution/.

9.5 Local government

> ### Local government problem scenario
>
> Parliament enacts the Local Housing Act 2022. This gives effect to key parts of the government's plans for solving a housing shortage by requiring local councils to subsidize private tenancies, thereby making it more affordable for poorer families and individuals to rent somewhere to live. Central government awards grants to councils, as it sees fit, for the specific purpose of subsidizing the tenancies. In the (fictional) town of Strochester, however, the council has recently been newly elected and one of the main parts of the winning party's manifesto was a pledge to ensure the building of 500 new homes in the town. Strochester Borough Council, in view of its election promises, decides to use the money granted by central government to embark on a five-year programme of home-building. The Secretary of State, learning of Strochester's refusal to use the money for the specific purpose for which it was intended, decides to cancel their grant with immediate effect.

Having now explored the principle of devolution and the manner in which it has and continues to have a relevance to the workings of the UK Constitution, it is important now to focus on an even lower level of government: local government. This second half of the chapter explores the complex network of local authorities operating in the UK and outlines the role that they play in the broader constitutional system. As part of this, the historical development of local government is discussed, with a particular focus on the way in which frequent legislative reforms impact on the way in which councils are organized and are able to operate. This part of the chapter also explores the various local governmental structures that exist across the country, as well as the functions, powers, and responsibilities that local councils exercise and fulfil. The chapter then ends by exploring the relationship between central and local government and the way in which this impacts on the power and democracy of local councils. This section is linked to the local government problem scenario, referring back to it throughout the discussions.

9.5.1 Defining the nature of local government, its structure, and its historical development

'Local government is a unique and valuable institution . . . [It] refers to the authorities . . . that . . . provide a range of specified services and represent the general interests of a specific area under the direction of a locally elected council.'[133] Fulfilling locally administrative functions for the good of a local area and overseeing the provision of local public services, councils have a crucial role to play within the broader executive structure. Similar to devolved power in Scotland, Wales, and Northern Ireland, the existence and operation of local government in the UK Constitution is justified on the grounds of subsidiarity, insofar as it is most appropriate for local towns, cities, communities, and counties to be governed and organized by an institution that is proximate to and capable of appreciating the particular concerns of a given local area. Though realization of this

---

[133] JA Chandler, *Local Government Today* (4th edn, Manchester University Press 2009) 1.

justification has often proved difficult, as this chapter goes on later to discuss, that councils are best placed to govern local areas is a notion at the heart of local government law. To explore in detail the workings of local government, however, it is necessary first to consider its historical development in the constitution.

Historically, across what is now the UK, local administration was provided by—or on behalf of—the monarch, with arrangements put in place in the eleventh, twelfth, and thirteenth centuries providing the foundations for modern local government; these remaining in place (to varying degrees) until the nineteenth century. Local government as we know it today, however, can be said to be based on legislation set out in the nineteenth century. Loughlin explains, with regards to local government in England and Wales:

> By the end of the [19th] century . . . and as a result of such reforms as the Municipal Corporations Act 1835, the extension of the principle of representative democracy to county councils in 1888 and the establishment of district councils in 1894 and the London boroughs in 1899, the framework of local government as we know it was more or less intact.[134]

The 1835 Act, while relatively minor in the grand scheme of things, was enacted in the aftermath of the Great Reform Act 1832[135] and was passed to establish a number of municipal boroughs in towns and cities across the country, with the aim of creating and putting in place a uniform model of local governance. The main push for uniformity across the country, though, came with the Local Government Acts 1888 and 1894. The 1888 Act saw the establishment of county councils across England and Wales, while the 1894 Act created district councils and made further provision for parish councils. These reforms were mirrored by similar provisions in Scotland and Ireland. The Burghs and Police (Scotland) Act 1833 and Municipal Corporations (Ireland) Act 1840 empowered municipal boroughs in their respective regions, whilst the Local Government (Scotland) Act 1889 and Local Government (Ireland) Act 1898 introduced a system of county councils in each region, similar to that created in England and Wales.

The local governmental arrangements set out by these various Acts remained largely unchanged until the 1960s.[136] Though the structure was confusing insofar as local government across the UK was a patchwork of different models, local institutions nonetheless enjoyed a generally stable and working relationship with the centre throughout this period.[137]

In the aftermath of the Second World War, various Commissions were set up to explore the possibility for local governmental reform.[138] Loughlin identifies the catalyst for this desire for reform, noting that '[w]ith continuing urban growth in the twentieth century, conflicts emerged between urban and rural authorities as the towns and cities grew beyond their administrative boundaries'.[139] This led to councils being stripped of a great many powers and responsibilities, 'the establishment of public corporations to run'

---

[134] Martin Loughlin, *Local Government in the Modern State* (Sweet and Maxwell 1986) 4.

[135] See 8.1.2 for further explanation.

[136] This said, the Local Government (Scotland) Act 1929 was somewhat more notable than the 1889 statute, the 1929 law bringing into effect fundamental changes to the structure of local government in Scotland.

[137] See Anthony King, *The British Constitution* (OUP 2007) 155–6.

[138] In England, for example, the Redcliffe-Maud Commission proposed reform of local government outside London, whilst the Herbert Commission focused on London specifically. In Scotland, the Wheatley Commission made its own recommendations for local government.

[139] Martin Loughlin, *Local Government in the Modern State* (Sweet and Maxwell 1986) 7.

various nationalized industries and, with this, 'pressures for centralisation'.[140] These Commissions, in time led to fundamental reform of local government. The Local Government Act 1972 completely overhauled the system of local government in England and Wales, introducing a two-tier system of County and District Councils across those regions. County Councils occupied the upper tier and oversaw geographical areas generally drawn on the county boundaries, while District Councils formed the lower tier and operated within and underneath County Councils, covering a smaller geographical area within a given county. The 1972 Act also recognized a distinction between metropolitan government and non-metropolitan government. Though both existed within this two-tier structure, the former was created in urban areas in the north of England, with much greater and more densely packed populations than the non-metropolitan areas elsewhere in the country. While the metropolitan county councils were abolished by the Local Government Act 1985, the metropolitan district councils still exist, effectively operating as a unitary level of government, exercising powers formerly held at the county level. The non-metropolitan County and District Councils also still exist across much of England. Structural reform in the early 1970s was mirrored in other parts of the country, too. The Local Government (Scotland) Act 1973 established regional and district councils for Scotland, and the Local Government (Boundaries) Act (Northern Ireland) 1971 provided for the creation of twenty-six local government districts across that region.[141]

Alongside the two-tier network of local authorities in some parts of the UK, there is also a growing pattern of unitary authorities. Unitary authorities are a single tier of local government, exercising powers and functions that are elsewhere or were previously divided between County/Regional and District Councils. Notably, in Scotland, Wales, and Northern Ireland more recent reforms have seen the abolition of the previous two-tier system and the creation of unitary councils right across those three regions.[142] In England, though unitary councils were first proposed under the Redcliffe-Maud Commission back in the late 1960s, it was not until the Local Government Act 1992 and its creation of the Local Government Commission that active steps were taken towards their introduction. Following the Commission's proposals, a few unitary authorities were created, though fresh motivation coming from reforms introduced under the 1997–2010 Labour Government, mean that there are now fifty-six unitary authorities across England. These exist alongside the two-tier structure elsewhere.[143] As a result, and different from Scotland, Wales, and Northern Ireland, which still operate within a uniform pattern of single-tier councils, local government in England continues to take a number of different forms, with the two tiers of County and District Councils in much of the country, juxtaposed with unitary authorities and metropolitan district councils in other parts of the country. What is more, amidst the mixed pattern of authorities across the country, Greater London itself takes a different form.

[140] Ibid 6–7.

[141] Councils for these districts were established by the Local Government (Northern Ireland) Act 1972.

[142] See: the Local Government etc. (Scotland) Act 1994; the Local Government (Wales) Act 1994; the Local Government (Boundaries) Act (Northern Ireland) 2008; and the Local Government (Boundaries) Order (Northern Ireland) 2012.

[143] Despite the stated focus of this chapter, it is worth noting that the whole of Scotland, Wales, and Northern Ireland is made up of unitary authorities of varying kinds.

Pause for reflection

The multiplicity of local governmental arrangements across England—that is, the coexistence of two-tier arrangements in some parts and unitary authorities in others—is linked to the piecemeal nature of local governmental reform. Though the two-tier arrangements were introduced uniformly in 1972, adoption of unitary tier local government has been more difficult to embed since the early 1990s. What are the comparative benefits and disadvantages of unitary authorities against a two-tier structure of local government? Though one offers a single, clearly identifiable body of governance, the other exists at a level closer to local people.

London Government has always been separate and different from the rest of the country. Even with the development of the national government in Westminster from the twelfth century, this remained separate from the established government of the City of London, itself dating back to Anglo-Saxon times.[144] Like much of the rest of the country, however, until the nineteenth century London's government was made up of a mixed patchwork of parishes and districts. Since this time, it has developed through the establishment (and abolition) of various governmental institutions across two tiers. Though the Metropolitan Board of Works had been created by the Metropolis Management Act 1855 as an unelected body, overseeing the delivery of services and infrastructure across the capital,[145] it is the establishment of the London County Council, by the Local Government Act 1888, that saw the first city-wide tier of elected government. Complemented by the London Government Act 1899, which created the initial twenty-eight boroughs at the lower tier of government, the form of government in the capital established in the late nineteenth century remained in place until the 1960s. At a similar time to the proposal for fundamental reform to countrywide local government, however, consideration for the government in the ever-growing metropolis of London was also discussed. The Herbert Commission, set up in the late 1950s to investigate possible models for reform of London Government, was followed shortly thereafter by the London Government Act 1963. This created the Greater London Council and beneath this the thirty-three London Borough Councils (including the City of London Corporation) that still operate to this day. The new Council and the Boroughs reflected the geographical expansion that the capital had witnessed in the preceding decades, now including as part of Greater London, towns and areas that had formerly been a part of neighbouring counties. Come the 1980s, however, and Thatcher's Conservative Government, political differences between the centre and the Labour-controlled Greater London Council led to the abolition of the upper tier of London Government in 1986. The powers that had previously been held at that level were decentralized to the Borough Councils. For fourteen years, until the establishment of the Greater London Authority (GLA) in 2000,[146] London Boroughs served as a unitary level of government in the capital. The GLA, however, under the leadership of a directly elected mayor[147] and the scrutiny of a twenty-five strong Assembly, now provides citywide government once more, including the provision of key services and alongside the continued operation of the thirty-three London Boroughs.

[144] See Tony Travers, *London's Boroughs at 50* (Biteback 2015) 8.   [145] Ibid 15.
[146] See Greater London Authority Act 1999.
[147] Directly elected mayors refer to the leaders of local councils or authorities that are elected directly by the people rather than indirectly through political party structures.

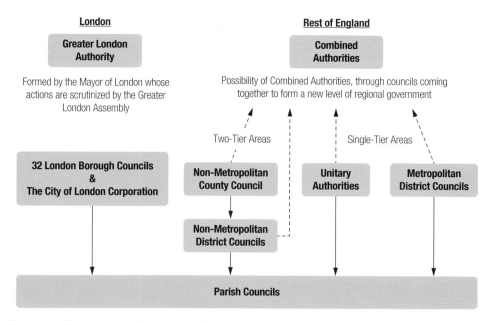

Figure 9.1 Diagram of local government institutions in England

The English local government institutions within and outside London are shown in diagrammatic form in Figure 9.1. (Combined authorities, though included on the diagram, are considered later in this section.)

Local government in the UK has in recent years been in a constant state of flux. Since the establishment of a uniform approach to local governance in the late nineteenth century, structural arrangements have been much altered, invariably due to changing political climates and challenges posed by broader social and economic factors. All this means, though, that local government in England exists within a complex network of local authorities, some unitary, others within a two-tier structure. Reforms in Scotland, Wales, and Northern Ireland have at least come to ensure a degree of uniformity.

Within these various structures and focusing on internal executive arrangements, the Local Government Act 2000, amended by the Local Government and Public Involvement in Health Act 2007, provides that councils in England and Wales should adopt a model consisting of a cabinet, overseen either by an executive leader or a directly elected mayor.[148] Councils in Scotland are led by a Council Leader, who is typically the leader of the largest political party. They have the ability to form 'the "Administration" which controls the running of the council'.[149] In Northern Ireland, councils must adopt an executive model that consists either of a 'committee of the council ("cabinet-style executive"); . . . or more than one committee of the council ("streamlined committee executive")'.[150] In terms of understanding what all this means for people within local areas across the country, however, it is important now to explore the powers and functions of local government.

---

[148] See Explanatory Notes to the Local Government and Public Involvement in Health Act 2007 [155]. Also see John Stanton, *Democratic Sustainability in a New Era of Localism* (Routledge 2014) 76.

[149] Scottish Government, 'Local authorities: factsheet', 8 May 2017, https://www.gov.scot/publications/local-authorities-factsheet/.

[150] Local Government Act (Northern Ireland) 2014, s 21(2).

Counterpoint: The introduction of combined authorities with elected mayors in England

Legislative reform in 2009 and 2016 further altered the possible ways in which local government in England could be arranged and organized. Following the abolition of metropolitan county councils in the mid-1980s, the Local Democracy, Economic Development and Construction Act 2009 Act introduced the concept of 'combined authorities'. These are created where a group of adjoining local councils agree to come together to form one combined authority across the broader geographical area. In such circumstances, the individual local councils remain unchanged and in full operation, but voluntary establishment of a combined authority gives them opportunity to combine their resources with other local councils, for the benefit of the broader area, and to receive increased powers, functions, and responsibilities for that area. For example, section 104 of the 2009 Act makes provision for combined authorities to function as Integrated Transport Authorities, thereby taking on responsibility for transport services across the given area; while section 105 imposes on combined authorities a 'duty to perform functions with a view to promoting economic development and regeneration'. Combined authorities ensure that, following the abolition of metropolitan county councils, individual local authorities could still come together to coordinate and strengthen the governance, leadership, and provision of services across broader geographical areas. Indeed, identification of existing combined authorities sees a predominance of the arrangements in particular urban areas.

The Cities and Local Government Devolution Act 2016 made further alteration to these arrangements, however, by making provision for the election of directly elected mayors to oversee combined authority areas.[151] Historically, directly elected mayors, as a part of English local government, have not been particularly well received. Though the Mayor of London was the first directly elected mayoral position, its creation being supported by citizens and councils across Greater London, the attempted introduction of mayors across the country more broadly has not been met with widespread support or enthusiasm. The Local Government Act 2000 made provision for mayors to be introduced across England, on the condition that they were supported by a majority of local voters in a referendum, with the Localism Act 2011 modifying that process by empowering the Secretary of State to invite local areas to hold referendums on the issue. Between June 2001 and October 2016, however, and under the authorities of the 2000 and 2011 Acts, fifty-three referendums have given rise to just sixteen mayors, three of which have since been or are in the process of being abolished.[152] The 2016 Act, however, in making changes to the possible leadership of combined authorities, also encouraged the wider introduction of directly elected mayors across England. Doing away with any requirement for a referendum, the Act provided that those authorities that agreed to adopt the mayoral model would enjoy a greater devolution of authority compared to those authorities led by a chair.[153] Such increased devolution depends on the nature of the particular arrangement agreed by that combined authority and

→

[151] Section 2 of the Cities and Local Government Devolution Act 2016.

[152] It is also notable that mayors were introduced in Leicester and Liverpool without a referendum, under a power in the 2007 Act which enables councillors alone to vote in favour of the model. In addition, second referendums held in Stoke-on-Trent (2008), Hartlepool (2012), and Torbay (2016) saw councils abandon the mayoral model and reverting to an executive leader arrangement.

[153] Where a combined authority is overseen by a chair, rather than a directly elected mayor, that chair is elected by the members of the combined authority from among the executive members.

central government, though can include increased powers over 'functions such as local transport, housing, skills and healthcare'.[154]

Recent reform, then, has altered the way in which local government in England is arranged, introducing not only a combined authority model but also further motivating the adoption of directly elected mayors.

9.5.2 Powers and functions of local government

Within the various structures just explored, the constitutional role and position that local authorities adopt across the UK is particularly notable. Though councils exist on a practical level to fulfil administrative functions and provide public services—typical of a governmental institution—they remain subordinate both to the sovereign legislature and central government and, in Scotland, Wales, and Northern Ireland, the respective devolved legislatures and executives. Reflecting this reality, councils only have the power to do those things expressly permitted by the relevant Parliament or Assembly. Indeed, with regards to England and Wales, section 2(1) of the Local Government Act 1972 provides that 'councils shall have all such functions as are vested in them by this Act or otherwise'. This shows that local authorities are not freely autonomous and do not exercise any residual discretionary authority in the same way that central government is empowered to do. They are, in short, statutory corporations, as Loughlin explains:

> In law, local authorities are statutory corporations which are dependent on powers given to them by statute for their ability to act; the doctrine of *ultra vires* exists to ensure that they keep within their statutory powers and are accountable to the courts; and central departments of state possess a range of powers enabling them to influence the manner in which local authorities conduct their affairs.[155]

This doctrine of *ultra vires* is explained in more detail in 11.3.[156] For the sake of discussion here, though, it is a Latin phrase meaning 'outside the power' and it refers to instances where public authorities—in this case, local councils—act beyond the scope of their allocated powers, leaving them susceptible to judicial review. We see this doctrine at work in the case of *Attorney-General v Fulham Corporation*.[157] Here, a local authority in Fulham had a power under the Baths and Wash-Houses Acts 1846–1878 to establish 'baths, wash-houses and open bathing spaces'. Using this authority, the council created a launderette that permitted customers to leave their clothes to be washed by council employees. The court held that this was *ultra vires*, or outside the power of the local authority, since it was beyond the scope of the legislative power provided.

Adding to Loughlin's explanation of the legal nature of local government and demonstrating councils' lack of residual authority to which this gives rise, Bailey also notes that: '[u]nlike a normal person who can in general do what he pleases so long as what he does is

---

[154] Colin Copus, Mark Roberts, and Rachel Wall, *Local Government in England: Centralisation, Autonomy and Control* (Palgrave Macmillan 2017) 130.

[155] Martin Loughlin, *Local Government in the Modern State* (Sweet and Maxwell 1986) 1–2.

[156] Also see 8.6.3 for brief introduction to the concept.

[157] [1921] 1 Ch 440. Also see fuller discussion of this case at 11.3.

not forbidden by law or contrary to law, a statutory corporation can do only those things which are authorised to do by statute, directly or by implication.'[158] There is, therefore, a great deal of legislation setting out the various powers and responsibilities of councils, some of which has already been explored. A couple of specific examples, though, include section 31 of the Health and Social Care Act 2012, which introduces a policy that sees certain local councils in England having the power to exercise public health functions; in Scotland, section 34 of the Local Government in Scotland Act 2003 places a duty on local authorities to 'prepare . . . integrated waste management plan[s]', and in Northern Ireland, the Planning Act (Northern Ireland) 2011 gives councils increased powers over local plan-ning applications. More broadly, the powers bestowed upon local councils differ depending on the council and the level at which it operates. In England, county councils are respon-sible for a range of county-wide services, including education, transport, planning, fire and public safety, social care, libraries, and waste management.[159] By contrast, and operating within their smaller geographical areas, district, borough, and city councils are responsible for services such as rubbish collection, council tax collection, recycling, housing, and plan-ning applications.[160] Where there are unitary authorities, then all of the services listed—for both district and county councils—fall within the remit of the single-tier authority.

Councils' position as statutory corporations, however, and restriction to the express provisions of Parliament does present fundamental issues in respect of their governmen-tal functions. As Sandford explains:

> Historically, local authorities in the UK were permitted only to do things that they had specific statutory powers to do. If an authority did something that it had no specific statutory power to do, this would be deemed *ultra vires*—illegal, and hence void. This has long been regarded as a limitation on the powers of local authorities to act in the interests of their electorate.[161]

Discussing the problem

Have a look at the problem scenario at 9.5. On the basis that Strochester Borough Council is using the money from central government to fund the building of new homes, rather than the subsidization of private tenancies, as stipulated in the 2022 Act, do you think they are acting *ultra vires*?

Yes. This scenario is reminiscent of the case of *Attorney-General v Fulham Corporation*.[162] It is re-called that, here, the local council used a power intended for the establishment of wash-houses, to create a launderette wherein council employees would wash customers' clothes. The court found that this was *ultra vires* the statutory power. Similarly, since Strochester council are seeking to use a grant of money, intended for the subsidization of private tenancies, to build new homes they can similarly be deemed to be acting *ultra vires*.

---

[158] SH Bailey, *Cross on Principles of Local Government Law* (3rd edn, Sweet and Maxwell 2004) [1]–[20] as cited in Michael Varney, 'United Kingdom—Local Government in England: Localism Delivered?' in Carlo Panara and Michael Varney (eds), *Local Government in Europe: The 'Fourth Level' in the EU Multilay-ered System of Governance* (Routledge 2015) 330, 335.

[159] HM Government, 'Understand How Your Council Works: Types of Council', https://www.gov.uk/understand-how-your-council-works/types-of-council.   [160] Ibid.

[161] Mark Sandford, 'The General Power of Competence' (House of Commons Library Briefing Paper 05687, 9 March 2016) 4.

[162] [1921] 1 Ch 440. Also see fuller discussion of this case at 11.3.

As a consequence of councils' legal position and the fact that they must rely on express legal provision for their actions, attempts have been made over the years to bestow on local authorities' across the UK broad discretionary authority, empowering them to do 'whatever activities are not expressly forbidden by statute'.[163] In England and Wales, for instance, section 111 of the Local Government Act 1972 stated that 'a local authority shall have power to do any thing . . . which is calculated to facilitate, or is conducive or incidental to, the discharge of any of their functions';[164] while section 2(1) of the Local Government Act 2000 set out a well-being power, which provided that:

> Every local authority are to have power to do anything which they consider is likely to achieve any one or more of the following objects:
>
> a) the promotion or improvement of the economic well-being of their area,
>
> b) the promotion or improvement of the social well-being of their area, and
>
> c) the promotion or improvement of the environmental well-being of their area.

Similar to section 111 of the 1972 Act, the well-being power was intended to clarify the powers of English and Welsh local authorities and make provision for them 'to take any action, unless it is subject to statutory prohibitions, restrictions or limitations specifically set out in legislation'.[165] Such broad discretion was well received:

> The provision was welcomed as providing 'councils with an important opportunity to develop a meaningful and substantive community leadership role'. It is, at first glance, a broad power allowing scope for local authorities to act as they choose, so long as it is for the benefit of their local area.[166]

While both section 111 of the 1972 Act and section 2 of the 2000 Act were intended to fashion councils with broad discretionary powers, the fact that these were set out in legislation meant that they were still subject to certain statutory restrictions and therefore fell short of the broader discretionary authority enjoyed by central government. More than this, their express provision in statute also did nothing to remove the supervisory jurisdiction of the courts, which served to establish judicial limitations to these powers. In *McCarthy & Stone (Developments) Ltd v Richmond-upon-Thames London Borough Council*,[167] for instance, an attempt to justify a charge imposed for pre-planning application advice on the basis of section 111 of the 1972 Act was rejected by the court. Lord Lowry held that such advice was 'at best, incidental to the incidental and not incidental to the discharge of the functions'.[168] Later, in *R (Brent London Borough Council) v Risk Management Partners*,[169] the 2000 Act well-being power also came to be limited.

---

[163] The Labour Party, 'The New Hope for Britain' (Labour Party Manifesto 1983) cited in Mark Sandford, 'The General Power of Competence' (House of Commons Library Briefing Paper 05687, 9 March 2016) 4.

[164] Also see Mark Sandford, 'The General Power of Competence' (House of Commons Library Briefing Paper 05687, 9 March 2016) 4.

[165] See Explanatory Notes to the Local Government Act 2000 [15].

[166] Ashley Bowes and John Stanton, 'The Localism Act and the General Power of Competence' (2014) *Public Law* 392, 392, citing Philip Swann, 'Local Government: The Modernizing Agenda' (2000) *Journal of Planning and Environment Law Supplement* 9, 13.

[167] [1992] 2 AC 48.

[168] Ibid 75. Also see Mark Sandford, 'The General Power of Competence' (House of Commons Library Briefing Paper 05687, 9 March 2016) 4.

[169] [2009] EWCA Civ 490.

> **Case in depth:** *R (Brent London Borough Council) v Risk Management Partners* [2009] EWCA Civ 490
>
> In this case, a number of London Borough Councils—including Brent—had come together to set up London Authorities Mutual Limited, an insurance company protecting councils from various risks. Brent London Borough Council, which was seeking insurance, despite having had a more financially favourable quote from Risk Management, offered the insurance contract to London Authorities Mutual Limited. This decision was challenged by Risk Management on the grounds that it breached rules of procurement, protected through Directive 2004/18/EC and the Public Contracts Regulations 2006, on the basis of which local authorities had to 'award certain contracts above a minimum value only after fair competition and to the person offering the lowest price or making the most economically advantageous offer'.[170] The Court of Appeal found in favour of Risk Management: it held that Brent London Borough Council had breached procurement rules and was therefore not permitted to seek insurance from London Authorities Mutual Limited.

Attempts to endow councils with broad discretionary powers have, as we can see, proved difficult. The well-being power was repealed by the Localism Act 2011, it now only remaining in force in Wales.[171] Its replacement, contained in section 1 of the Localism Act 2011, sets out a general power of competence for English councils. This provides that a 'local authority has power to do anything that individuals generally may do'.[172] Though a catch-all provision, there for those instances where existing powers cannot justify council's activity, the wording of the power is broader than its predecessor. That said, it is still a legislative provision, complete with various stated limitations, and it does not fall outside the scope of the supervisory jurisdiction of the Administrative Court.

Interest in empowering councils with broad discretionary powers is also evident in Scotland and Northern Ireland (Wales so far being covered by legislation applicable to—or formerly applicable to—English councils).[173] In Scotland, powers have generally mirrored those in force south of the border. Section 69 of the Local Government (Scotland) Act 1973, for instance, echoed the 1972 Act in providing that 'a local authority shall have power to do any thing . . . which is calculated to facilitate, or is conducive or incidental to, the discharge of any of their functions'; whilst section 20(1) of the Local Government in Scotland Act 2003 provides Scottish councils with a well-being power. This states that '[a] local authority has power to do anything which it considers is likely to promote or improve the well-being of—(a) its area and persons with that area; or (b) either of those'. This remains in force today and its breadth is explained by Glasgow City Council, which notes that the power covers the ability 'to incur expenditure; give financial assistance; enter into agreements; co-operate with, facilitate or co-ordinate the activities of any person; exercise on behalf of any person any function of that person;

---

[170] [2008] LGR 429 [3] cited at [2009] EWCA Civ 490 [62].

[171] Schedule 1(2) to the Localism Act 2011.

[172] Section 1 of the Localism Act 2011.

[173] It is worth noting that Wales has proposed replacing the well-being provision with a general power of competence of its own. The bill in which this was contained, however—the Local Government (Wales) Bill 2015—was never enacted.

and provide staff, goods, services or property to any person'.[174] Councils in Northern Ireland, by contrast, were not granted broad discretion in the 1970s or early 2000s similar to local authorities in other parts of the country. Indeed, it was not until the passage of the Local Government Act (Northern Ireland) 2014 that local government there was empowered with a general power of competence similar to that set out in the Localism Act 2011.[175]

Local government power is therefore founded in a range of statutes. Despite various attempts to afford UK councils with broad discretion, local authorities can only do that which is expressly permitted by Parliament.

9.5.3 Democratic role of local government

Through exercising the various powers and functions with which Parliament and central government and the devolved institutions endow local authorities, and in view of the unique constitutional position they occupy as locally elected, governmental institutions, local government has the potential to play an important democratic role in the UK Constitution. As Bailey and Elliott explain:

> Given their democratic credentials and geographical and cultural proximity to those on behalf of whom they act, one might expect local authorities to occupy a pivotal position in the democratic life of the country, pursuing distinctive agendas appropriate to the needs and mores of their respective areas. This, in turn, might be expected to form part of a virtuous circle in which the obvious importance and responsiveness of local government incentivises the participation of individuals in local politics and elections.[176]

Though issues in establishing the appropriate balance in the central–local relationship have long meant that realization of this—what Bailey and Elliott themselves describe as—utopian ideal local democracy is difficult,[177] councils have long provided a platform for local democracy and a setting for attempts at empowering the local electorate to involve themselves in local politics.

As at the central and regional governmental level, elections play a fundamental role in providing local representatives and legitimizing their use of power. Local areas are divided into wards—small geographical areas within a council's broader area. Councillors stand in a ward and, if elected, represent that ward's citizens on the local council. In England and outside London, all local elections take place on the basis of the first-past-the-post voting system. This means that councillors just need to achieve a higher portion of the vote than opposing candidates to take the seat in their respective ward. Candidates are often affiliated with a particular political party, though some stand independently. Following an election, the political party that achieves a majority of the seats on the council takes control. Due to the diverse nature of local politics, the number of parties active at the local level, and the number of independent candidates, however, it is not uncommon for no party to take overall control of a council. In this eventuality, a council may be run by a coalition of parties.

---

[174] Glasgow City Council, 'A Guide to Glasgow City Council's Statutory Duties and Powers', January 2019, https://www.glasgow.gov.uk/CHttpHandler.ashx?id=41179&p=0.

[175] See: Local Government Act (Northern Ireland) 2014, s 79(1).

[176] Stephen Bailey and Mark Elliott, 'Taking Local Government Seriously: Democracy, Autonomy and the Constitution' (2009) 68(2) *Cambridge Law Journal* 436, 436.

[177] Ibid.

As at the central governmental level, party manifestos and promises made in the run up to elections play a key part in the local governmental electoral process. Important as these are to the democratic process, however, it is necessary to understand that these create no legally binding duties to act or behave in line with said promises. In the case of *Bromley London Borough Council v Greater London Council*,[178] the Greater London Council instructed the individual London Boroughs to levy a supplementary tax in order that the London-wide authority could honour one of its electoral commitments in subsidizing the cost of bus and tube fares across London. When Bromley London Borough Council challenged this policy, arguing that it was *ultra vires*, the Greater London Council argued in return that they were bound by the promise made in the electoral manifesto. The House of Lords, however, upholding the decision of the Court of Appeal, quashed the Greater London Council's policy. They not only held that the Council owed a fiduciary duty to local tax-payers to have regard to their financial interests,[179] but also found that the Greater London Council was in error in believing itself to be bound by its electoral promise.[180]

 Discussing the problem

In view of the decision in *Bromley LBC v Greater London Council*, to what extent do you think Strochester Borough Council, in the problem scenario, should feel required to honour the election pledge to build 500 new homes? How far should councils be able to go in upholding a promise that has formed the foundation of their democratic mandate if it goes against central governmental policy?

As the decision in *Bromley* makes clear, local councils are not legally bound by promises made in an election manifesto. Indeed, it would be unreasonable to impose such expectations. What is more, 9.5.2 has already made clear that councils can only do—and must only do—that which legislation decrees and central/regional executive authority instructs. This means that Strochester council is not *required* to honour its election pledge to build 500 homes and in light of the discussion already had about the actions of the council being potentially *ultra vires*, their legal responsibilities under the 2022 Act must take priority over their political promises. This might, of course, have political ramifications, such as a petition or a different result in a subsequent election, however, election promises do not affect the legal responsibilities of councils.

In the capital, the London Mayoral elections operate on the basis of the supplementary vote system, with voting Londoners identifying two desired candidates by order of preference. The London Assembly members are elected through the first-past-the-post system for the fourteen constituency representatives and the closed party-list system for the remaining eleven London-wide members. There is also a diversity of local electoral processes in other parts of the country too. In Scotland and Northern Ireland, for instance, councillors are elected through the single transferable vote system, which permits citizens to rank the candidates in order of preference, with the least popular candidates eliminated and votes transferred until a winner has a majority. In Wales—as in England—councillors are elected through the first-past-the-post system. [181]

---

[178] [1983] 1 AC 768.   [179] Ibid 818.   [180] Ibid 830–1.
[181] For an explanation of the different voting systems, see 8.3.2.

While elections play a pivotal role in shaping the democratic nature of local politics, a recurrent issue that often affects the legitimacy of local institutions is the worrying turnout that local elections often inspire. In England, the average national turnout at local elections in 2016 and 2017 was 33.8 per cent and 35 per cent respectively.[182] It is little better elsewhere in the UK, with turnout in Scotland and Wales at the 2017 local elections 46.9 per cent and 42.4 per cent respectively.[183] Though turnout tends to increase when local elections coincide with other election and referendum events, these numbers are indicative of problems concerning low citizen engagement with local politics.

Referendums also play a key part at the local governmental level, providing a platform whereby councils can gauge local opinion on given issues and invite endorsement of certain specific projects. While the Localism Act 2011 was initially intended to introduce a general referendums power in England and Wales, enabling councils to hold referendums on any issue, this was removed from the bill before Royal Assent. As such, apart from section 9 of the Local Government Act 1972, which enables parish councils to hold referendums on any issue, all referendums powers at local government are intended for specific issues. The 2011 Act contains a number of such referendums provisions applicable in both England and Wales, including relating to council tax increases,[184] approval of neighbourhood plans,[185] and endorsing changes to local governance arrangements.[186] A referendum in Wales is also required where a local area wishes to move to executive arrangements that include a directly elected mayor.[187] Though councils in Northern Ireland do not have powers to hold local referendums, there is provision in Scotland. There, the ability to hold referendums often takes the form of a broader power to consult on a particular question or investigate an issue, without expressly directing that a referendum be held or, indeed, be the only method of enquiry. Section 87(1) of the Local Government (Scotland) Act 1973, for example, states that '[a] local authority may conduct, or assist in the conducting of, investigations into, and the collection of information relating to, any matters concerning their area or any part thereof and may make, or assist in the making of arrangements whereby any such information and the results of any such investigation are made available to any government department or the public'. Sandford notes that this power 'can provide the basis for conducting a local referendum'.[188] Also, and providing an example of a referendum being based on the power to consult, under section 52(1)(b) of the Transport (Scotland) Act 2001, Scottish local councils 'may consult . . . as they think fit' on the introduction of road user charging schemes.[189] Regardless of the power on which they are based, though, referendums provide a valuable way in which citizens can engage with local government.

Another way in which local government promotes democracy and makes use of its proximity to local people to enhance the governmental process is through parish or

---

[182] Elise Uberoi, 'Turnout at elections' (House of Commons Briefing Paper CBP 8060, 5 July 2019), 16.

[183] Elise Uberoi, 'Turnout at elections' (House of Commons Briefing Paper CBP 8060, 5 July 2019), 16.

[184] See s 72 and Sch 5 of the Localism Act 2011.

[185] See Sch 10 of the Localism Act 2011.

[186] See Sch 2 of the Localism Act 2011.

[187] See: s 46 of the Local Government (Wales) Measure 2011 and Mark Sandford, 'Local Government: Polls and Referendums' (House of Commons Briefing Paper 03409), 12.

[188] Mark Sandford, 'Local Government: Polls and Referendums' (House of Commons Briefing Paper 03409), 5.

[189] See: Mark Sandford, 'Local Government: Polls and Referendums' (House of Commons Briefing Paper 03409), 5.

community councils. These operate at the lowest level of local government in England, Wales, and Scotland, underneath the level of unitary or district councils. Northern Ireland has never had a system of parishes, at least in the manner here explained. Parish councils play a key role in the local governmental hierarchy, though with district, county, and unitary councils existing at higher levels and covering wider geographical areas, they have fewer powers and responsibilities, usually just over small, locally specific issues. In modern terms, English and Welsh parish councils derive from the Local Government Act 1894, which provided that a 'parish council for a rural parish shall be elected from among the parochial electors of that parish'.[190] The Local Government Act 1972 introduced further changes aimed at increasing the number of parish councils, including changing some existing district councils into parish councils.[191] The Act also abolished all parish councils in Wales and introduced community councils in their place.[192] Parliament then introduced—just a year later—a system of community councils in Scotland.[193] The continued relevance of this local level of government is evident from Schedule 5 to the Local Government and Public Involvement in Health Act 2007, which broadened the scope of parish councils by providing that they could be set up in London boroughs.

The powers of parish and community councils are, as noted, locally specific. Since the councils themselves tend just to cover a small geographical area, with a population of just a couple of thousand, their powers are intentionally limited. In England, they have responsibility over burial grounds and cemeteries, allotments, community centres, highways, litter, planning, and water supply,[194] and, they are also included within the Localism Act's 'general power of competence'. In Wales, the powers of community councils are largely still rooted in the 1972 Act. The Welsh Government notes that '[a]mong the services and amenities they most commonly provide are village halls, playing fields and open spaces, seats, shelters, street lighting and footpaths'.[195] What is more, and with the Local Government Act 2000's well-being power still in force in Wales, the Local Government (Wales) Measure 2011 extended the scope of the power to include community councils.[196]

In Scotland, and by contrast, community council's powers are not specifically listed or defined. Instead, section 51(2) of the Local Government (Scotland) Act 1973 states that:

> In addition to any other purpose which a community council may pursue, the general purpose of a community council shall be to ascertain, co-ordinate and express to the local authorities for its area, and to public authorities, the views of the community which it represents, in relation to matters for which those authorities are responsible, and to take such action in the interests of that community as appears to it to be expedient and practicable.

---

[190] Section 3(1) of the Local Government Act 1894.

[191] Section 1(9) of the Local Government Act 1972.

[192] See: ss 20(6) and 27 of the Local Government Act 1972.

[193] See: s 51(1) of the Local Government (Scotland) Act 1973.

[194] Laura Sharman, 'Parish Council Responsibilities' (*LocalGov*, 5 November 2013), http://www.localgov .co.uk/Parish-council-responsibilities/29135.

[195] Law Wales, 'Community Councils', https://law.gov.wales/constitution-government/government-in-wales/local-gov/communities/?lang=en#/constitution-government/government-in-wales/local-gov/communities/?tab=overview&lang=en.

[196] See: s 126(1) of the Local Government (Wales) Measure 2011, amending ss 1 and 2(1) of the Local Government Act 2000.

The key feature of parish and community councils, though, is linked to their local position. Bailey and Elliott note that: '[l]ocal government can enable citizens to participate in governance more readily and to a greater extent than would be possible if all governance occurred at a national level.'[197] More so than any other level, though, parish councils can encourage citizens to participate in local politics since the councils are made up entirely of laymembers, who are elected by other citizens across the community. This means that local issues, concerns, and knowledge directly feed into the parish council process, improving the democratic value of their work and operation.

It is clear that local government in the UK has an important democratic role to fulfil. Through various mechanisms—such as elections, referendums, and parish councils, to name just three—councils facilitate the involvement of local people and engage with those affected by its decisions and policies. There are other factors, however, that can impact negatively on councils' ability to function for the good of local people, such as its relationship with central government and an ongoing concern for a lack of local funding.

9.5.4 Central–local relations and local government finance

The final matter to consider relates to central–local relationships, that is, the manner in which Central or Devolved Government relates to and communicates with local government in the various parts of the UK. Recalling the reality, just discussed, that local authorities are 'statutory corporations . . . dependent on powers given to them by statute for their ability to act . . . and [that] central departments of state possess a range of powers enabling them to influence the manner in which local authorities conduct their affairs',[198] it stands to reason that local government and central/devolved government have an important working relationship to fulfil. It is a relationship, however, that is and has been difficult to balance and that—due to the important democratic role of local councils—is increasingly important to get right.

Part of this difficulty arises due to the fact that councils are mere creatures of statute and are constantly at the mercy of centralized policy and law-making. Consequently, local government often becomes something of a battleground between, on the one hand, the need and desire to govern, lead, and represent local people appropriately and, on the other hand, the ability and competence to be able to fulfil that within the boundaries set by the centralized institutions. Indeed, it is important to make clear that:

> Local authorities are more than mere agents of central government. They are political institutions constituted by election with a wide range of functions and the right to tax. These three fundamental features justify and legitimate their exercise of local choice on behalf of the citizens to whom they are accountable. Traditionally much legislation was drafted to give local authorities space for the development of that choice, including their level of expenditure and taxation.[199]

---

[197] Stephen Bailey and Mark Elliott, 'Taking Local Government Seriously: Democracy, Autonomy and the Constitution' (2009) 68(2) *Cambridge Law Journal* 436, 438–9.

[198] Martin Loughlin, *Local Government in the Modern State* (Sweet and Maxwell 1986), 1–2.

[199] George Jones and John Stewart, 'Local Government: The Past, the Present and the Future' (2012) 27(4) *Public Policy and Administration* 346, 347, citing Martin Loughlin, *Legality and Locality: The Role of Law in Central-Local Government Relations* (OUP, 1996).

Councils exist primarily as tools of government at the local level. They make decisions and implement policies; they provide and facilitate local services and are—before anything else—institutions of democratic government for the people. At the same time, though, local government's recent existence has been marked by considerable legislation, seeking to alter the powers it possesses in relation to central government and seeking also constantly to shift power to and from the centre. Central government possesses and retains huge power to supervise and direct the operation of local councils, something it has arguably done to a considerable extent in recent decades. In part, this power and ability to supervise is a natural consequence of the constitutional order that prevails in the modern United Kingdom. Parliament is sovereign so has the authority to pass any law, including laws that impact upon, supervise, manipulate, or—if it so chooses—abolish local governmental institutions. In addition, in Scotland, Wales, and Northern Ireland, and pursuant to legislation clarifying the scope of devolved powers, the legislatures are each empowered by Act of Parliament to pass laws impacting upon local government on the basis that local government is not a matter reserved or excepted for Westminster. Furthermore, at both the central and devolved levels, government is superior to local councils and has the power to introduce and implement policies that impact upon and influence the operation of local government. The realities of this mean that, while in a sense there to serve local people and communities, local government often finds itself merely implementing policies or decisions on behalf of higher levels of government, sometimes even having its local powers limited. This is particularly evident in England where there is no level of regional government between Whitehall and local councils. The extent to which this impacts on the day-to-day operation of local government is evident from a number of examples. In October 2016, for instance, central government overruled Lancashire County Council's rejection of an application to proceed with fracking on a site near Blackpool, against the wishes of local people. Furthermore, and in the case of *R (Cornwall Council) v Secretary of State for Health and another*,[200] a young boy (P) with multiple disabilities and lacking mental capacity was placed in care by Wiltshire council, in line with the local authority's duties under section 20 of the Children Act 1989. His carers lived in South Gloucestershire, while his parents moved to Cornwall. Upon reaching the age of eighteen, however, the question arose as to which council would be responsible for providing support and accommodation to P for the rest of his life. Pursuant to section 21(1)(a) of the National Assistance Act 1948, the decision lies with the Secretary of State. Would it be Wiltshire, who had been initially responsible for him as a baby, or South Gloucestershire, where he had resided with his carers, or Cornwall, where his parents—who still played an active role in his life—lived? While the Secretary of State decided that Cornwall Council should be responsible for P, this was later challenged through judicial review proceedings. Though the Court of Appeal held that South Gloucestershire should be responsible for P, the Supreme Court reversed this decision and found that Wiltshire Council should be responsible since it was they who had dealt with him as a baby and no change had been made to those arrangements. The circumstances of this case, though, highlight the extent to which local councils are required to act under the instruction and supervision of central government. In the other regions of the UK, the operation of a regional level of government between localities and the centre makes for a rather different dynamic between councils and those higher up the government hierarchy. There is,

---

[200] [2015] UKSC 46.

in one sense, greater balance between the different levels because devolution itself has already paved the way for a more local expression of power and autonomy. In another sense, though, the legal reality that the regional institutions in Edinburgh, Cardiff, and Belfast have authority over their local government bodies is unavoidable and can lead to centralizing tendencies similar to that experienced in England. In Wales, for example, the Assembly has been criticized for its increasingly centralized approach in its dealing with Welsh councils, particularly with regards to public services and local government structures.[201] In Scotland, cuts imposed by Holyrood have been harshly felt by local government, whilst certain Scottish Government policies are imposed in a top-down manner without regard for the particular circumstances of a specific locality. The National Gaelic Language Plan, for instance, sees the Bòrd na Gàidhlig having the power to 'require . . . [a local] authority to prepare a Gaelic language plan' potentially regardless of that authority's area and of whether the Gaelic language is a prominent part of its heritage.[202] Across the UK, therefore, the superiority of legislatures and governments over local councils means a particularly top-down approach to the process of local government.

One particularly prominent way in which central or regional government impacts upon the operation of local councils, though, is through the provision of funding. In England, Wales, and Scotland, the vast majority of councils' money comes from central or devolved government, a small amount coming from local services, council tax, and, in some instances, the EU.[203] This means that, beyond directing and supervising local government activity through decisions and policies, the centre can also restrict councils' activities by determining how much money they should have at their disposal. Indeed, and amid recent policies and initiatives aimed at tackling austerity, central and regional governments have imposed substantial cuts on local government finances across the country. Central control of local finances in Northern Ireland is noticeably less than in other parts of the UK. This is principally because '62 per cent of local government expenditure is funded by the district rates and a further 26 per cent by income from charges for services, facilities and fees, with only approximately 12 per cent from central government grants'.[204]

The discretion that central governments have over local government finance has been the subject of challenge in the courts. In *R (Rotherham Metropolitan Borough Council and others) v Secretary of State for Business, Innovation and Skills*,[205] a number of local councils

---

[201] Welsh Local Government Association, 'In Defence of Localism', June 2014, https://www.wlga.wales/SharedFiles/Download.aspx?pageid=62&mid=665&fileid=1218.

[202] Section 3(1) of the Gaelic Language (Scotland) Act 2005. The Bòrd na Gàidhlig is a non-departmental public body overseen by the Scottish Government in the delivery of its National Gaelic Language Plan (see Bòrd na Gàidhlig, 'National Gaelic Language Plan 2018–2023', https://www.gaidhlig.scot/wp-content/uploads/2018/03/BnG-NGLP-18-23-1.pdf).

[203] In Wales, 80 per cent of local government funding comes from the Welsh Government (National Assembly for Wales, 'Local Government', April 2007, http://www.assembly.wales/NAfW%20Documents/tb-07-024.pdf%20-%2028072009/tb-07-024-English.pdf). In England, roughly 75 per cent of funding comes from central government (Mark Ryan, 'Central-Local Government Relations and the UK Constitution' (2009) 14(1) *Coventry Law Journal* 20, 21, citing Communities and Local Government Select Committee, *The Balance of Power: Central and Local Government* (HC 2009, 33-I) 35). In Scotland, 85 per cent of funding comes from the centre (Scottish Government, 'Local Government', https://www.gov.scot/policies/local-government/local-government-revenue/); See generally: Philip Brien, Local Government Finances (House of Commons Briefing Paper 08431, 31 October 2018).

[204] Derek Birrell and Cathy Gormley-Heenan, *Multi-Level Governance and Northern Ireland* (Palgrave Macmillan 2015) 138.

[205] [2015] UKSC 6.

in England sought judicial review of a central government decision to allocate money from the European Union to local councils in such a way that left the claimants with only 60 per cent of the funding they had previously received.[206] Other councils received as much as 95 per cent of their previous funding. The Supreme Court, however, held that the councils had not been subjected to unequal or disproportionate treatment and that central government had exercised its powers under the EU regulation lawfully.

 Discussing the problem

In the problem scenario, central government awards Strochester Borough Council a grant for the specific purpose of subsidizing private tenancies. The council, however, goes against these instructions and uses the money to fund the building of new homes. Is the Secretary of State justified, then, in cancelling the grant?

In short, yes. As the problem scenario makes clear, central government awards grants to councils 'as it sees fit'. It is entirely within the discretion of the Secretary of State to decide whether or not to make such an award. In light of Strochester Council's misuse of the funds, it could be argued that the Secretary of State is more than justified in cancelling the money.

We can see that local government has been significantly affected by a central–local relationship that leans towards central or regional institutions and away from the important role that local authorities play in the wider constitutional and governmental system. Councils are heavily influenced by the direction and supervision of government as well as by the funding that is made available for local activities and responsibilities. Solutions to these issues have been often discussed and explored, with the Big Society and Northern Powerhouse policies[207] recently being promoted by central government and supported by legislation to strengthen and invigorate local democratic and governmental processes. The success of these schemes and initiatives, however, has been widely discussed and debated, with general opinion still reflecting concern for the balance between central or regional governments and local government. How well government policy and parliamentary enactment can effect change to the central–local dynamic is something to continue watching.

[206] Allocation of this funding was governed by Regulation (EU) No 1303/2013 of the European Parliament and of the Council of 17 December 2013 laying down common provisions on the European Regional Development Fund, the European Social Fund, the Cohesion Fund, the European Agricultural Fund for Rural Development and the European Maritime and Fisheries Fund and laying down general provisions on the European Regional Development Fund, the European Social Fund, the Cohesion Fund and the European Maritime and Fisheries Fund and repealing Council Regulation (EC) No 1083/2006.

[207] The Big Society was a Conservative-led initiative under the Coalition Government of 2010–15, which centred around values that saw a reduction in the size of the state and a correlative increase in local autonomy, authority, and status. The Northern Powerhouse, more recently, is a policy that was promoted under David Cameron's 2015 Conservative Government, which sees the establishment of combined authorities—particularly in northern urban areas—overseen by directly elected mayors.

9.6 Summary

The allocation of power within the UK Constitution is a matter that touches on a number of important constitutional themes, insofar as it seeks to ensure that power and authority are exercised at the most appropriate level, enhancing the democratic value of the process and ensuring that consequent decisions and policies are relevant to those affected. The devolution settlements pursued through the 1998 Acts were founded on this justification and, since this time, have developed and evolved, giving rise to institutions that possess notable power in Scotland, Wales, and Northern Ireland. Similarly, though founded on a historical basis that goes much further back, local government in the UK also exists to govern and lead local areas, making decisions and policies relevant to that area. Devolution and localism, however, in the context of the UK Constitution both raise important questions concerning federalism and centralism. This chapter has sought to discuss and consider these, facilitating further exploration through the problem scenarios referred to throughout the chapter.

Quick test questions

1. Which Act created the Scottish Parliament and the Scottish Executive? How, according to that Act, do the institutions in Edinburgh relate to the sovereign UK Parliament?

2. Explain the English Question. What measures have been introduced to seek an answer to this question?

3. What was the main difference between the initial devolutionary settlements in Wales and Scotland? How have they changed since 1998?

4. What does section 1 of the Northern Ireland Act 1998 provide?

5. What is the 'general power of competence' and what does it enable local authorities to do?

6. Explain the differences between unitary authorities, district councils, county councils, and parish councils.

7. How would you characterize the relationship between central and local government?

Further reading

Devolution

Mick Antoniw, 'Not a Bad Start: 20 Years of Devolution' (2019) 116(18) *Law Society's Gazette* 15

*Vernon Bogdanor, *Devolution in the United Kingdom* (OUP 2001)

*Brice Dickson, 'Devolution in Northern Ireland' in Jeffrey Jowell and Colm O'Cinneide (eds), *The Changing Constitution* (9th edn, OUP 2019) 239

Brigid Hadfield, 'Devolution: A National Conversation?' in Jeffrey Jowell and Dawn Oliver (eds), *The Changing Constitution* (7th edn, OUP 2011) 213

*Aileen McHarg and Chris McCorkindale, 'The Supreme Court and Devolution: the Scottish Continuity Bill Reference' (2019) 2 *Juridical Review* 190

*Aileen McHarg, 'Devolution in Scotland' in Jeffrey Jowell and Colm O'Cinneide (eds), *The Changing Constitution* (9th edn, OUP 2019) 270

*Richard Rawlings, 'The Welsh Way/Y Ffordd Gymreig' in Jeffrey Jowell and Colm O'Cinneide (eds), *The Changing Constitution* (9th edn, OUP 2019) 296

Elizabeth Wicks, *The Evolution of a Constitution: Eight Key Moments in British Constitutional History* (Hart Publishing 2006) Ch 8

Local government

*Stephen Bailey and Mark Elliott, 'Taking Local Government Seriously: Democracy, Autonomy and the Constitution' (2009) 68(2) *Cambridge Law Journal* 436

Derek Birrell and Amanda Hayes, *The Local Government System in Northern Ireland* (Institute of Public Administration 1999)

Ashley Bowes and John Stanton, 'The Localism Act and the General Power of Competence' (2014) *Public Law* 392

Colin Copus, Mark Roberts, and Rachel Wall, *Local Government in England: Centralisation, Autonomy and Control* (Palgrave Macmillan 2017)

*George Jones and John Stewart, 'Local Government: The Past, the Present and the Future' (2012) 27(4) *Public Policy and Administration* 346

Martin Laffin, 'Comparative British Central–Local Relations: Regional Centralism, Governance and Intergovernmental Relations' (2002) 22(1) *Public Policy and Administration* 74

Ian Leigh, 'The Changing Nature of Local and Regional Democracy' in Jeffrey Jowell and Dawn Oliver (eds), *The Changing Constitution* (7th edn, OUP 2011)

Jean McFadden, *Local Government Law in Scotland: An Introduction* (Tottel Publishing 2008)

*John Stanton, 'Rebalancing the Central–Local Relationship: Achieving a Bottom-up approach to Localism in England' (2018) 38(3) *Legal Studies* 429

Michael Varney, 'United Kingdom—Local Government in England: Localism Delivered?' in Carlo Panara and Michael Varney (eds), *Local Government in Europe: The 'Fourth Level' in the EU Multilayered System of Governance* (Routledge 2015) 330

 Visit this book's **online resources** for additional materials relating to this chapter, including a full analysis of the two problem scenarios.

www.oup.com/he/stanton-prescott2e

10

Judicial review: access to review and remedies

Problem scenario

The (fictitious) Local Education Act 2025 empowers local authorities to decide which pupils are admitted to their local state schools and what the rules are relating to progression through and graduation from those schools. The basis for the reform rests on a policy that was introduced to encourage greater local influence on education. Its aim was to enable local authorities to know local children better and to be in a better position to decide on the appropriate educational system.

One particular local authority, however, sees the power as a means through which they can guarantee the quality of pupils admitted to and progressing through local state schools in order to improve the educational reputation of their area. It decides to introduce policies across all of its five state primary schools to require pupils to pass exams before entry at the age of five and again at the end of each year in order to progress. Those pupils who fail to achieve entry to or progression at the schools are encouraged to seek education in the next town. The introduction of this policy attracts widespread criticism and outrage, with many individuals and groups considering legal action against the local authority.

The following individuals and groups are amongst those wondering whether or not they satisfy the legal requirements for a judicial review application:

- *Primary School Teachers Together* — the well-established union of primary school teachers of which the majority (80 per cent) of the local state school staff are members.

- The editor of the local newspaper who has been inundated with letters of complaint.

- *Parents for Education* — a group of local parents, whose children attend state schools in the area and who have joined forces with the aim of campaigning against this policy.

- The priest at one of the local churches (associated with one of the schools) who, whilst on sabbatical at the time the policy is published, learns of it upon his return six months later.

- The head teachers of the two private primary schools in the area who are concerned that the new policy will take the best pupils away from them.

10.1 Introduction

Judicial review of administrative action falls within the broader area of administrative law, which is chiefly concerned with the administration of the state, setting out laws policing and regulating the appropriate use of executive and administrative power. Administrative law plays a vital role in the UK Constitution by ensuring that government authority is exercised lawfully and legitimately, protecting the public from any potential abuses of power. In pursuit of this objective, judicial review seeks to provide a mechanism of legal accountability, affording those adversely affected by illegal, unreasonable, or procedurally unfair exercises of administrative authority the opportunity to seek a remedy in a court of law. It is the purpose of this chapter to introduce judicial review and its various features and requirements. This lays the foundation for subsequent chapters to explore the substantive and procedural grounds upon which applications for judicial review can be brought before the courts.

The chapter starts by exploring the meaning and purpose of judicial review, explaining the particular function that the courts fulfil and the jurisdiction that justifies their scrutiny of administrative matters. It then sets out the legal basis for judicial review and the process through which applications proceed, which, while rooted in statute, has developed incrementally through both case law and the 1998 Woolf Reforms. The chapter then goes on to consider issues relating to access to review, exploring the legal requirements that must be fulfilled before an application for judicial review can be entertained by the Administrative Court.[1] This includes discussion of standing, which determines who can bring a claim, and consideration of the issues relating to the public law/private law divide, which concerns against whom a claim can be brought and the matter upon which that claim can be founded. The chapter then concludes by setting out the potential remedies that can be awarded by the Administrative Court at the conclusion of a judicial review application.

The objectives for this chapter are:

- to define judicial review and to explain the role and jurisdiction of the courts with regards to judicial review applications;
- to set out the legal basis for judicial review and to explain the process through which applications proceed, as set out in the Civil Procedure Rules;
- to explore the requirement of standing and to discuss the manner in which the courts have applied the test;
- to consider the public law/private law divide, the exclusivity principle, and the way in which the courts define a public body for the purposes of judicial review;
- to set out the remedies available in judicial review cases and to explain the way in which they work.

10.2 Defining judicial review

Judicial review of administrative action refers to the means and process through which the Administrative Court can review and scrutinize decisions and actions of public bodies, having the power to provide remedies where challenges reveal that such actions or

---

[1] The Administrative Court is the division of the High Court that deals with judicial review cases.

decisions have been taken illegally, unreasonably, or without due regard to the necessary procedures. As Cane notes:

> A CJR [claim for judicial review] is 'a claim to review the lawfulness of (i) an enactment; or (ii) a decision, action or failure to act in relation to the exercise of a public function'. JRP [the judicial review procedure] *must* be used for making a CJR in which a quashing, prohibiting or mandatory order is sought.[2]

There are elements of judicial review that rest on a deep historical foundation. The remedies, for instance, 'date from medieval times', while the rules of natural justice on which the procedural grounds for review are partly based 'had already become established by the sixteenth century'.[3] Modern judicial review, though, as a form of action, has developed primarily over the course of the past fifty years, with anything that might previously have resembled the procedure before this time being described as '"superficial" and little more than "perfunctory"'.[4] Since the 1960s, a long line of cases and reforms have come to shape both the processes that should be followed in seeking judicial review and the grounds on which such an application can be pursued. Indeed, Tomkins emphasizes the extent to which Lord Reid was instrumental in leading this legal transformation and explains that:

> First, the law of procedural fairness was reformed; then substantive review and aspects of the relationship between the law and the Crown were reformulated and strengthened. Finally, the arcane but important area of jurisdictional review was revisited . . . Lord Reid['s] . . . mission was to sweep away what he saw as the unnecessary, and out-moded restrictions and technicalities of the past, and to replace them not with a detailed series of rules, but rather with wide-ranging judicial discretion so that the law could be further developed and clarified on a case-by-case basis in the future. Thus, a significant characteristic of modern judicial review law is that it possesses a remarkable degree of judicial discretion . . . The advantage of discretion is that it can facilitate valuable flexibility in the law . . .
>
> By 1984 the courts had developed the law of judicial review to such a point that Lord Diplock was able to synthesize it, giving it a new and authoritative framework for analysis. In his seminal judgment in the GCHQ case . . . Lord Diplock stated that there were three 'heads' or 'grounds' of judicial review, which he labelled 'illegality', 'irrationality', and 'procedural impropriety'.[5]

This statement demonstrates both the rapidity of the development of judicial review during the 1960s and how it subsequently became a valuable judicial tool for scrutiny of the executive. The grounds on which such scrutiny takes place—illegality, irrationality, and procedural impropriety—are our focus in the subsequent three chapters. With the evolution of this new form of action, however, concerning the potential examination of governmental matters, the courts were required to fulfil a unique role, as the next section now explores.

---

[2] Peter Cane, *Administrative Law* (5th edn, OUP 2011) 249, citing the Civil Procedure Rules, r 54.1(2)(a).

[3] Adam Tomkins, *Public Law* (OUP 2003) 171.

[4] Ibid 171, citing Stanley A de Smith, *Judicial Review of Administrative Action* (3rd edn, Stevens & Sons 1973) 28.

[5] Adam Tomkins, *Public Law* (OUP 2003) 171–2, citing *Ridge v Baldwin* [1964] AC 40; *Padfield v Minister of Agriculture, Fisheries and Food* [1968] AC 997; *Conway v Rimmer* [1968] AC 910; *Anisminic v Foreign Compensation Commission* [1969] 2 AC 147; and *Council for Civil Service Unions v Minister for the Civil Service* [1985] AC 374 at 410.

10.2.1 The role of the court in judicial review

In providing this mechanism for executive scrutiny, wider constitutional issues mean that judicial review affords the higher courts a significant role, different from their conventional appellate functions. Ordinarily, higher courts exercise what is termed their 'appellate jurisdiction' in hearing appeals. This involves consideration of a specific provision and judgment in respect of the merits (or demerits) of a particular legal issue.[6] By contrast, in judicial review cases, courts exercise their 'supervisory jurisdiction'; that is, they supervise the procedure, but are not able to judge the substantive merits of that issue or make a judgment on the basis of those merits.

Limiting the court in judicial review cases to this supervisory jurisdiction shows respect for the separation of powers. It was discussed, in 2.5, that consideration of this principle in the UK Constitution leads to the identification of a system of checks and balances. Different from constitutions where there is a clear demarcation between institutional roles and functions, a system of checks and balances involves a degree of overlap between the various bodies of the state, this being accepted as necessary to provide a means through which the institutions can be subjected to scrutiny, or 'checked', by one another. Judicial review is an example of such an overlap—the Administrative Court having the power to scrutinize and check the actions and decisions of the executive and other public bodies. To ensure that they do not go too far, however, and adjudicate on the merits of potentially political matters in respect of which they might lack expertise, knowledge, and jurisdiction, courts are restricted to a supervisory role—considering merely the legality, reasonableness, and fairness of administrative procedures. The practical effect of this role is, as Syrett explains, that:

> [C]ourts in judicial review cases are not empowered to substitute their view of what is the 'correct' outcome for that of the original decision-maker, as is normally possible on appeal. Rather, the court generally remits . . . the decision to the decision-maker, with its judgment forming an explanation of the manner in which the first decision was unlawful. It is therefore quite possible for the decision-maker to reach the same conclusion again . . . provided that it does so in accordance with the standards of lawfulness set out by the court.[7]

We can see that the supervisory jurisdiction enables the Administrative Court to scrutinize and review the acts and decisions of the executive without compromising the separation of powers and making decisions as to the merits of potentially political and policy-related matters.

Another way in which the Administrative Court is prevented from erring too far into political or policy-related matters is through the principle of justiciability, which applies in respect of the Court's power to review the government's use of the prerogative powers. Historically, the courts were somewhat reluctant to permit review of the prerogative powers, a reticence that stems from the formal placement of these powers in the hands of the Crown; the monarch being immune from challenge in the courts.[8] In fact, until 'the 1984 House of Lords case of *Council of Civil Service Unions v Minister for the Civil Service* . . . it was thought that the courts would not review how the prerogative powers

---

[6] Keith Syrett, *The Foundations of Public Law: Principles and Problems of Power in the British Constitution* (2nd edn, Palgrave Macmillan 2014) 186.
[7] Ibid 186–7.   [8] See 3.3.2.

were exercised, only whether they existed'.[9] Signifying a change to this approach, Lord Diplock explained in that case that 'I see no reason why simply because a decision making power is derived from the common law and not from a statutory source it should *for that reason only* be immune from judicial review'.[10] With this increased reviewability of the prerogative, though, the courts also acknowledged that certain prerogative powers existed in respect of political or policy-related matters; matters that it felt fell outside the constitutional remit of the courts. It is for this reason that the notion of justiciability came more clearly to be elucidated. As 6.5.3 has already explained, 'there are prerogative powers, which "because of their subject matter are such as not to be amenable to the judicial [review] process"'.[11] Where a matter is not amenable on these terms, we say that it is non-justiciable. There are numerous examples of what the courts regard as non-justiciable, including a decision to prevent GCHQ employees from joining trade unions to protect national security,[12] the ratification of treaties,[13] and the Home Secretary's advice to the monarch in relation to exercise of the prerogative of mercy.[14] In more recent years, though, the courts have taken an increasingly liberal approach to what is amenable to judicial review in the context of the prerogative powers and justiciability. In *R (Bancoult) v Secretary of State for Foreign and Commonwealth Affairs (No 2)*,[15] for instance, the House of Lords held that Orders in Council (that is, subordinate legislation enacted by the government under the prerogative) were reviewable,[16] whilst in the case of *R (Miller) v Prime Minister*,[17] the Supreme Court held that the Prime Minister's prorogation of Parliament under the prerogative could be reviewed by the courts. These two (and other) cases demonstrate how the courts' willingness to review exercise of the prerogative has broadened in recent years. Providing further explanation, the Supreme Court stated in *Miller* that:

> [A]lthough the courts cannot decide political questions, the fact a legal dispute concerns the conduct of politicians, or arises from a matter of political controversy, has never been a sufficient reason for the courts to refuse to consider it . . . almost all important decisions made by the executive have a political hue to them. Nevertheless, the courts have exercised a supervisory jurisdiction over the decisions of the executive for centuries. Many if not most of the constitutional cases in our legal history have been concerned with politics in that sense.[18]

The notion of the supervisory jurisdiction, therefore, alongside questions of justiciability, serve to clarify the courts' role in respect of judicial review. Having now explained both the origins of judicial review and the judicial role to which this has given rise, though, it is necessary now to examine the broader purpose of judicial review.

---

[9] Gail Bartlett and Michael Everett, 'The Royal Prerogative' (House of Commons Library Briefing Paper 03861, 17 August 2017) 7. For further explanation of the GCHQ case in this area, see 6.5.3.

[10] [1985] AC 374, 410. Also see 6.5.3.

[11] 6.5.3, citing *Council for the Civil Service Unions v Minister of State for the Civil Service* [1985] AC 374, 418 (hereinafter 'GCHQ').

[12] See, for example: *GCHQ*.

[13] See, for example: *Blackburn v Attorney-General* [1971] 1 WLR 1037 and *R v Secretary of State for Foreign and Commonwealth Affairs, ex p Rees-Mogg* [1994] QB 552.

[14] *Hanratty v Lord Butler* [1971] 115 SJ 386.   [15] [2008] UKHL 61.

[16] See, for further discussion, 6.5.3.   [17] [2019] UKSC 41.   [18] [2019] UKSC 41 [31].

10.2.2 **The purpose of judicial review**

Judicial review provides an avenue of legal accountability. It is a means through which the Administrative Court can scrutinize and supervise the acts and decisions of the executive, calling them to account in respect of challenges to the legality, reasonableness, and procedural propriety of those acts and decisions. Oliver notes that accountability entails 'being liable to be required to give an account or explanation of actions and, where appropriate, to suffer the consequences, take the blame or undertake to put matters right if it should appear that errors have been made', with *legal* accountability equating with accountability to the courts on the foundation of a duty to obey the law.[19]

One way in which judicial review represents this duty to obey the law relates to the *ultra vires* principle. A Latin term meaning 'outside one's powers', *ultra vires*—in the context of judicial review—provides a basis on which the courts can assess the extent to which public bodies have gone beyond the scope of their legislative powers. In this way, the courts can uphold the word of the sovereign Parliament and ensure accountability to the written word of the law through the judicial review process. There are, however, issues surrounding the continued suitability of *ultra vires* as a basis for judicial review. These are based on arguments claiming that *ultra vires* provides an artificial foundation insofar as it does not take account of wider factors that go beyond mere obedience to the law or the fact that public authorities' powers are increasingly drawn from non-statutory foundations. Consequently, it is necessary to consider a broader and somewhat more significant basis for judicial review—the rule of law.

The rule of law can be defined in a number of different ways, as Chapter 3 explained. The theories broadly relate to the Aristotelian principle concerning the supremacy of law, discussed and developed in 3.2, which posits that executive power should be exercised on the basis of appropriate legal authority, rather than the arbitrary whims of individuals, and in line with certain procedural characteristics or substantive objectives. On this basis, judicial review can be justified by the rule of law insofar as it seeks to ensure that public bodies operate lawfully, reasonably, and properly, thereby protecting citizens from arbitrary abuses of authority. It also encourages those in power to accord with broader ideas at the heart of the law itself, such as the procedural characteristics that are relevant to formal conceptions of the rule of law, or any moral content that is ensured by substantive conceptions. As Oliver states:

> The legal accountability of public bodies is an important aspect of the rule of law. The duty to obey the law, enforceable by action in the courts at the instigation of those affected by the actions of public bodies, imposes an obligation on a public body to explain and justify its action in legal terms if . . . subjected to judicial review, and to make amends if found to have transgressed.[20]

The relevance of the rule of law to judicial review is widely supported. Raz, for instance, in explaining the formal conception of the rule of law,[21] notes that '[t]he courts should have

---

[19] Dawn Oliver, *Constitutional Reform in the UK* (OUP 2003) 48 and 51, citing Geoffrey Marshall, *Ministerial Responsibility* (OUP 1989); Dawn Oliver and Gavin Drewry, *Public Service Reforms: Issues of Accountability and Public Law* (Pinter 1996); Diana Woodhouse, *In Pursuit of Good Administration* (OUP Clarendon Press 1997).

[20] Dawn Oliver, *Constitutional Reform in the UK* (OUP 2003) 51.   [21] See 3.4.1.

review powers over the implementation of the other principles [of the rule of law]. This includes review of both subordinate and parliamentary legislation and of administrative action . . . to ensure conformity to the rule of law'.[22] The review of primary legislation is restrained by parliamentary sovereignty, but the courts' ability to scrutinize subordinate legislation and administrative action is represented by the judicial review process and goes right to the heart of the rule of law principle. The importance of judicial review, as a means of protecting and upholding the rule of law, is also reflected in the case of *Anisminic Ltd v Foreign Compensation Commission and others*,[23] in which the House of Lords was called upon to examine statutory provisions attempting to oust the courts' powers of review.

Case in depth: *Anisminic Ltd v Foreign Compensation Commission and others* [1969] 2 AC 147

Anisminic was an English company, which owned property in Egypt that was seized by Egyptian authorities amidst the Suez Crisis in October 1956. A year later, this property was sold to the Economic Development Organization.

In February 1959, pursuant to an agreement between the UK Government and the Government of the United Arab Republic, substantial money was paid to the UK as settlement for the seizure of the British property. Pursuant to the Foreign Compensation Act 1950 and other secondary legislation, the Foreign Compensation Commission was set up to oversee and distribute this money in respect of various claims for properties that had also been taken over. In September 1959, Anisminic made a claim to the Commission for compensation; however, this was provisionally refused on the grounds that the Commission felt that Anisminic had failed to establish an appropriate claim.

As a result, Anisminic brought an action against the Foreign Compensation Commission, seeking a declaration that the provisional refusal of their claim was wrong in law and that they were, in fact, entitled to receive compensation. In defence of this, the Commission argued that, pursuant to section 4(4) of the Foreign Compensation Act 1950, the court had no jurisdiction to entertain the proceedings brought by Anisminic since, under that section, the courts' ability to review the determinations of the Commission was ousted. The House of Lords rejected this argument, however, and held that it was capable of considering the legality of the Commission's refusal.

The key point of law in this case relates to the manner in which the courts dealt with the attempted exclusion of judicial review. Section 4(4) of the Foreign Compensation Act 1950 provided that '[t]he determination by the [Foreign Compensation] Commission of any application made to them under this Act shall not be called in question in any court of law'.[24] The Commission contended that this could only have one clear meaning and that this was that proceedings considering the validity of Commission determinations are prohibited by statute. The Law Lords considered, at length, the meaning of the term 'determination' in the statute and found that:

> The provisions of section 4 (4) of the Act do not . . . operate to debar any inquiry that may be necessary to decide whether the commission has acted within its authority or

---

[22] Joseph Raz, 'The Rule of Law and its Virtue' (1977) 93 *Law Quarterly Review* 195, 201.
[23] [1969] 2 AC 147. This case is also discussed in 11.4.2.
[24] This section was later repealed by the Statute Law (Repeals) Act 1989.

jurisdiction. The provisions do operate to debar contentions that the commission while acting within its jurisdiction has come to wrong or erroneous conclusions.[25]

It is the effect of this judgment, however, that is most pertinent to considerations of the courts' role in judicial review. In *Anisminic*, if the exclusion clause in section 4(4) were to have been upheld on the basis of its strict legal meaning then it would have served to make administrative decisions made on this basis immune from judicial review. Curtailing the full scope of judicial review in this way could then have set a dangerous precedent whereby further legislative provisions might have empowered other administrative bodies to make decisions and take action free from the accountability afforded by the Administrative Court. By rejecting arguments suggesting that section 4(4) completely excluded the scope of judicial review, the House of Lords in *Anisminic* resisted an attempt by Parliament to disarm the judiciary of the important role that they play through judicial review.[26] Wade and Forsyth stress that this judgment represents a 'judicial insistence . . . that administrative agencies and tribunals must at all costs be prevented from being sole judges of the validity of their own acts. If this were allowed, to quote Denning LJ . . ."the rule of law would be at an end"'.[27]

Clauses purporting to oust the scope of judicial review came before the courts again in the 2019 case of *R (Privacy International) v Investigatory Powers Tribunal and others*.[28]

Case in depth: *R (Privacy International) v Investigatory Powers Tribunal and others* [2019] UKSC 22

In this case, Privacy International sought judicial review of a decision taken by the Investigatory Powers Tribunal concerning the issuing of thematic warrants under the Regulation of Investigatory Powers Act 2000. The High Court, however, held that judicial review of the tribunal was not possible since it was prohibited under section 67(8) of the 2000 Act. This states:

> Except to such extent as the Secretary of State may by order otherwise provide, determinations, awards and other decisions of the Tribunal (including decisions as to whether they have jurisdiction) shall not be subject to appeal or be liable to be questioned in any court.

The High Court's decision was upheld in the Court of Appeal but later overturned in the Supreme Court where, by a majority of 4–3, Privacy International won.

In allowing the appeal, the Supreme Court drew from *Anisminic* in finding that

> the exclusion [in section 67(8)] applies, not to all determinations, awards or other decisions . . . but only to those which are 'legally valid'. Thus, if the [Investigatory Powers Tribunal]'s decision . . . were found to have been reached on an erroneous interpretation . . . those words [in section 67(8)] would not save it from intervention by the courts.[29]

---

[25] [1969] 2 AC 147, 181.
[26] See HWR Wade and CF Forsyth, *Administrative Law* (10th edn, OUP 2009) 614–15.
[27] Ibid 616, citing Denning LJ in *R v Medical Appeal Tribunal ex p Gilmore* [1957] 1 QB 574, 586.
[28] [2019] UKSC 22.   [29] [2019] UKSC 22 [107].

In other words, determinations, awards, and decisions of the Tribunal are potentially only exempt from judicial examination where they are *not* otherwise legally questionable and where there is no other reason to call upon the supervisory jurisdiction of the Administrative Court.

The Court went on to consider more generally, though, whether Parliament could 'by statute "oust" the supervisory jurisdiction of the High Court'.[30] Lord Carnwath explained that 'it is ultimately for the courts, not the legislature, to determine the limits set by the rule of law to the power to exclude review. This proposition . . . [is] a natural application of the constitutional principle of the rule of law . . . and an essential counterpart to the power of Parliament to make law'.[31] He went on to make clear that it was not necessarily the case that Parliament could not oust the scope of judicial review but rather that '[t]he question in any case is . . . "what scope of judicial review . . . is required to maintain the rule of law"; it being "a matter for the courts to determine what that scrutiny should be"'.[32] The Supreme Court made clear in *Privacy International*, therefore, the importance of judicial review in respect of the rule of law and the courts' role in protecting this, even in the face of an ostensible attempt by the sovereign legislature to oust the scope of judicial review.

The judicial review process, then, involves so much more than merely 'ascertaining and enforcing the literal meaning of the words which Parliament uses'.[33] More broadly, it provides the courts with a platform on which values consistent with the rule of law can be protected and ensured. As Elliott notes, 'the exercise of the judicial review jurisdiction occurs within a constitutional setting that leads the courts to impute to Parliament an intention to legislate consistently with the rule of law. As a long line of authorities attests, the rule of law strongly favours citizens' access to the courts'.[34]

 Pause for reflection

Section 3.4 explored different conceptions and explanations of the rule of law, offered by a number of theorists and commentators. Above and beyond those already mentioned, can you think of further ways in which judicial review of administrative action upholds the rule of law? Is there an argument to suggest that the role of the courts in entertaining judicial review applications is an affront to certain aspects of the rule of law?

The important role that the courts fulfil in respect of judicial review has a firm constitutional justification and is rooted in the need both to ensure accountability to the written word of the law and, more importantly, to protect values at the heart of the rule of law, even if this means going against the literal interpretations of primary legislation.

---

[30] [2019] UKSC 22 [113].   [31] [2019] UKSC 22 [131]–[132].

[32] [2019] UKSC 22 [132], citing *R (Cart) v Upper Tribunal (Public Law Project intervening)* [2012] 1 AC 663 [133] and [102].

[33] Mark Elliott, 'The Ultra Vires Doctrine in a Constitutional Setting: Still the Central Principle of Administrative Law' (1999) 58(1) *Cambridge Law Journal* 129, 151, citing Paul P Craig, 'Ultra Vires and the Foundations of Judicial Review' [1998] 57(1) *Cambridge Law Journal* 63.

[34] Mark Elliott, 'The Ultra Vires Doctrine in a Constitutional Setting: Still the Central Principle of Administrative Law' (1999) 58(1) *Cambridge Law Journal* 129, 151, citing *Raymond v Honey* [1982] 1 All ER 756; *R v Secretary of State for the Home Department, ex p Leech* [1994] QB 198; *R v Lord Chancellor, ex p Witham* [1998] QB 575.

The next section now sets out the legal basis for judicial review and explains the procedure that must be followed in pursuing an application to the Administrative Court.

10.3 Legal basis and process

10.3.1 Senior Courts Act 1981

Though judicial review has largely developed through case law, the legal basis is now rooted in legislation and contained within section 31 of the Senior Courts Act 1981.[35] This sets out the possible remedies that can be awarded in the event of a successful application, as well as the requirements that must be satisfied in the course of bringing a judicial review claim. Both of these areas are discussed later in the chapter.[36] In terms of the procedure that must be followed in bringing an application for judicial review, however, this is now contained in the Civil Procedure Rules, which were introduced in the late 1990s to replace the Order 53 Procedure.

 Counterpoint: Restricting judicial review: the 'makes no difference' principle

Since the 1960s, judicial review has been in a state of flux with cases and frequent reforms constantly changing the way in which the procedures and remedies operate. Of particular significance, however, are proposals set out by the 2010–2015 Coalition Government. While some of these proposals were later abandoned—most notably those relating to standing—one aspect that ultimately made it through to enactment was the 'makes no difference principle'. Introduced as an amendment to the 1981 Act by virtue of section 84(1) of the Criminal Justice and Courts Act 2015, this provides that relief for a judicial review case should be refused and no remedy awarded if it is highly likely that the outcome for the applicant would not have been substantially different if the conduct complained of had not happened in the first place. This requirement emphasizes that judicial review is not a substantive appeal but merely an exercise of the court's supervisory jurisdiction.

Mark Elliott offers interesting discussion of this particular aspect of the recent reforms, explaining that:

> Nothing in the Bill suggests that *unlawful* administrative actions that cannot be successfully challenged due to the 'makes no difference' principle (either because leave will be denied or relief withheld) will be rendered *lawful*. The effect of the proposal is not to alter the legal status of the unlawful measure, but merely to shield it from judicial review.[37]

Since the general trend throughout the recent reform of judicial review has been to simplify the process and make it more accessible to those seeking redress for allegedly unlawful executive acts and decisions, it seems somewhat at odds with the very purpose of the principle that such acts and decisions should be protected from the judicial review procedure.

---

[35] This was enacted as the Supreme Court Act 1981, though it was renamed by the Constitutional Reform Act 2005 to avoid confusion with the UK Supreme Court, created by the 2005 Act.

[36] See 10.4 and 10.6.

[37] Mark Elliott, 'Judicial Review Reform (Again)' (*Public Law for Everyone*, 6 February 2014), http://publiclawforeveryone.com/2014/02/06/judicial-review-reform-again-2/.

10.3.2 **Order 53 and the Civil Procedure Rules**

Prior to 1977, there was no standard procedure for judicial review, with different processes available depending on the particular remedy being sought by the aggrieved party.[38] This meant that there was no one clearly accessible route for the review of administrative acts and decisions or the consequent remedies. The possible avenues were confusing and not conducive to the easy pursuit of administrative justice. All this changed in 1977, however, following the publication of the Law Commission's report on *Remedies in Administrative Law* in 1976.[39] As a result of the recommendations made in that report, Order 53 of the Rules of the Supreme Court was introduced,[40] with other changes later coming in the form of the Senior Courts Act 1981, as we have discussed. Order 53 provided a 'procedure for making applications for judicial review . . . regardless of the remedy sought',[41] simplifying the process and offering a clearer route for those wishing to challenge administrative acts and decisions. In time, and as a result of Lord Woolf's reforms during the late 1990s, however, the Civil Procedure Rules came to amend further the procedure for judicial review, with rule 54 contained therein replacing the Order 53 Procedure.

Pursuant to rule 54, and the Civil Procedure Rules generally, there are a number of requirements that must be fulfilled in adhering to the judicial review procedure. This includes the pre-action protocol, on the basis of which alternative forms of resolving the dispute must be considered, pursued, and raised for discussion.[42] Failing this and in the event that resort to the judicial review procedure is unavoidable, the party seeking to bring the application for judicial review must fill in a claim form and serve it upon the defendant authority.[43] It is here that the first key requirement for judicial review is encountered. Unlike in private law, where parties have a number of years in which to consider and instigate proceedings,[44] in judicial review the claim form must be submitted within three months and without undue delay, though this can be subject to alteration at the discretion of the court.[45] The rationale underlying the three-month limit in judicial review cases is so that public functions and the operation of public bodies are not unduly delayed and held up, pending a judicial review application,[46] and also to ensure

---

[38] See Peter Cane, *Administrative Law* (5th edn, OUP 2011) 250–1.

[39] Law Commission, *Remedies in Administrative Law* (Law Com No 73, 1976).

[40] The Rules of the Supreme Court set out the various civil procedures that should be followed. They were later superseded by the Civil Procedure Rules.

[41] Peter Cane, *Administrative Law* (5th edn, OUP 2011) 250.

[42] Ministry of Justice, *Pre-Action Protocol for Judicial Review*, http://www.justice.gov.uk/courts/procedure-rules/civil/protocol/prot_jrv#IDATB1HC.

[43] Civil Procedure Rules, rr 54.6 and 54.7.

[44] The corresponding time limits at private law are significantly longer (procedures in tort and contract, for example, are subject to a six-year time limit, pursuant to the Limitation Act 1980).

[45] See Civil Procedure Rules, r 54.5. The time limit for judicial review has recently been the subject of reform. In July 2013, the government introduced an amendment to the Civil Procedure Rules to the effect that the time limit for judicial review should be reduced to six weeks in respect of certain planning cases and to thirty days in respect of certain procurement cases. The intention with this change was to bring the requirements for judicial review in line with time limits for statutory appeals (see Ministry of Justice, *Judicial Review: Proposals for further reform* (Cm 8703, 2013) 5).

[46] See Peter Cane, *Administrative Law* (5th edn, OUP 2011) 253.

that public bodies are not constantly in court defending their acts and decisions. Adding further explanation, Cane notes that:

> The chief functions of the relatively short time-limit under CPR part 54 are to prevent public programmes from being unduly held up by litigation challenging their legality; and to prevent steps already taken in implementation of challenged decisions having to be reversed long after the decision was acted upon.[47]

 Pause for reflection

Despite the rationale underpinning the three-month time limit, to what extent do you think it could serve unfairly to restrict those seeking to bring an application for judicial review?

Provided the three-month time limit is honoured and following service of the claim form, though, the defendant authority has twenty-one days in which to file an Acknowledgement of Service, given to the claimant as indication that they are willing to engage with the judicial review application.[48] Once these requirements have been satisfied, the parties then proceed to the permission stage. This is the point at which the Administrative Court will consider whether or not the application for judicial review should be allowed to proceed.[49] This invariably involves consideration of whether or not the claimant has, at first glance, an arguable case, a relative chance of success,[50] and the necessary standing to proceed with the case. The need for this permission stage is explained by Lord Diplock:

> Its purpose is to prevent the time of the court being wasted by busybodies with misguided or trivial complaints of administrative error, and to remove the uncertainty in which public officers and authorities might be left as to whether they could safely proceed with administrative action while proceedings for judicial review of it were actually pending even though misconceived.[51]

Once that permission is granted by the court, the parties can then proceed to the full hearing or substantive stage in the Administrative Court. It is here that the case is finally decided and, if done so in favour of the claimant, remedies can be awarded at the discretion of the court, as will be discussed in the following sections. The full judicial review procedure is summarized in diagrammatic form in Figure 10.1.

The Civil Procedure Rules set out a clear procedure that must be followed in making an application for judicial review. This process, however, also includes a number of further requirements that must be satisfied and that are worthy of further identification and discussion. These are: standing, or *locus standi*; issues relating to the public law/private law divide; and the need for a judicial review application to be brought only against a public authority. The chapter now addresses each of these in turn, starting with standing.

[47] See further Peter Cane, *Administrative Law* (5th edn, OUP 2011) 252.

[48] Ibid 253–4.

[49] Civil Procedure Rules, r 54.8.

[50] Civil Procedure Rules, r 54.10.

[51] *Inland Revenue Commissioners v National Federation of Self Employed and Small Businesses Ltd* [1982] AC 617, 642–3.

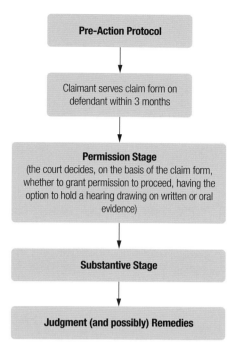

Figure 10.1 Judicial review procedure

10.4 **Standing**

Standing, or *locus standi*, is one of the most significant requirements for judicial review. This serves to restrict access to judicial review to those who can be said to have a genuine claim and who have been directly affected by the administrative act or decision at issue. The legal requirement for standing is contained within section 31(3) of the 1981 Act, which states that:

> (3) No application for judicial review shall be made unless the leave of the High Court has been obtained in accordance with rules of court; and the court shall not grant leave to make such an application unless it considers that the applicant has a sufficient interest in the matter to which the application relates.

This is known as the sufficient interest test and it provides the basis on which those eligible to bring an application for judicial review can be assessed and determined. This section of the chapter will explore many examples of how the courts have interpreted this test over the years. A fairly conventional application, however, is demonstrated by the case of *R v General Council of the Bar, ex p Percival*.[52] Here, a Queen's Counsel was reported to the General Council of the Bar by the head of their barristers' chambers on the grounds that they had behaved dishonestly and had brought the profession into

---

[52] [1990] 1 QB 212.

disrepute through ignoring the appropriate etiquette in respect of chambers' finances. The Professional Conduct Committee of the General Council of the Bar, whose duty it was to bring the case before a disciplinary hearing, decided not to charge the barrister with professional misconduct, opting instead for the lesser charge of breach of proper professional standards. As a consequence, the head of the chambers applied for judicial review of the decision on the basis that—in their view—the more serious charge should have been pressed. The court found that the applicant had sufficient standing to bring the application, stating:

> Unless the disappointed complainant is regarded as having sufficient locus standi to challenge the decision it is difficult to see who else could be expected to do it. We are fortified in our view by the fact that the applicant here was head of the chambers, his interest being the greater in order to ensure that any lapse from proper professional conduct or the observance of proper professional standards by a member of his chambers for whom he was responsible should be properly investigated and referred to a disciplinary tribunal if necessary. If that does not amount to a sufficient interest for present purposes we should find it difficult to envisage what circumstances possibly could.[53]

Despite this seemingly conventional application, however, the sufficient interest test is undoubtedly a particularly broad test, in part due to its vague nature and the fact that the legislation provides no further guidance as regards what it means to have a 'sufficient interest'. As a result of this, the question of standing is one always to be considered by the courts in each case. As Schiemann notes, writing extra-judicially, '[i]t is clear from the wording of that subsection that . . . the court must apply *its* mind to the question of standing'[54] and he goes on to cite Woolf LJ who states that 'the question of locus standi goes to the jurisdiction of the court'.[55] Because of this, it is the case law, and the various judgments made over the years, that have given rise to the rules of standing that are now applied in parallel with the statutory test and that provide further indication of what standing means and what can be regarded as a 'sufficient interest'. As Lord Diplock notes, emphasizing the important role that the courts have played in this area:

> The rules as to 'standing' for the purpose of applying for prerogative orders, like most of English public law, are not to be found in any statute. They were made by judges, by judges they can be changed; and so they have been over the years to meet the need to preserve the integrity of the rule of law despite changes in the social structure.[56]

These words of Lord Diplock formed part of his judgment in the case of *Inland Revenue Commissioners v National Federation of Self-Employed and Small Businesses Ltd*,[57] which came just a year after the Senior Courts Act 1981 and in which the House of Lords discussed in detail the sufficient interest test and the way in which it should be employed by the courts.

---

[53] Ibid 231.

[54] Konrad Schiemann, 'Locus Standi' (1990) *Public Law* 342, 345.

[55] *R v Secretary of State for Social Services, ex p Child Poverty Action Group* [1989] 1 All ER 1047, 1055, cited in ibid 346.

[56] *IRC v National Federation of Self Employed and Small Businesses Ltd* [1982] AC 617, 639. Hereinafter 'the *IRC* case'. [57] Ibid.

Case in depth: *Inland Revenue Commissioners v National Federation of Self-Employed and Small Businesses Ltd* **[1982] AC 617**

A number of casual workers, who were on occasion employed by some of the newspapers on Fleet Street, had given false names and addresses in submitting their details so that, when collecting their pay, they could not be traced by the Inland Revenue to pay their taxes. On learning about the fraudulent activities, Inland Revenue discussed the issue with employers and the workers' unions and agreed a special arrangement on the basis of which, provided correct names and details were given and future taxes paid correctly, the workers would not be ordered to pay the taxes due (estimated to be £1m a year). The National Federation of Self-Employed and Small Businesses Ltd, however, challenged this on the grounds that it differed from the attitude usually adopted by the Inland Revenue in respect of tax evasions and on the contention that the Inland Revenue had no power to grant such an amnesty. The National Federation applied for judicial review, seeking a declaration to the effect that the Inland Revenue had acted unlawfully and the imposition of a mandatory order, requiring the taxes to be assessed and collected. The Divisional Court, though granting initial leave to proceed, later held that the National Federation had no standing for judicial review, a finding that was overturned on appeal. The Court of Appeal felt that the federation was representing a body of taxpayers who could claim a genuine grievance in this case, thereby giving them standing. On further appeal, however, the House of Lords overturned the Court of Appeal's judgment. They held that, as just a body of taxpayers, the National Federation had no sufficient interest and, in addition, they had failed to demonstrate that the actions of the Inland Revenue were in any way *ultra vires* or unlawful.

The judgment in the *IRC* case is notable for two reasons: first, due to the manner in which it demonstrates and provides further guidance on the operation of the 'sufficient interest' test; and secondly, due to its consideration of the issue relating to group standing. While the second of these is dealt with in 10.4.2, it is necessary here to explore notable comments made in the House of Lords with regards to application of the 'sufficient interest' test. One particular factor that the court discussed was the point in judicial review proceedings at which the test should be considered. On this, it was held that the question of standing should be considered twice—at the permission or threshold stage and, later, at the substantive hearing. As Lord Wilberforce explained:

> There may be simple cases in which it can be seen at the earliest stage that the person applying for judicial review has no interest at all, or no sufficient interest to support the application: then it would be quite correct at the threshold to refuse him leave to apply. The right to do so is an important safeguard against the courts being flooded and public bodies harassed by irresponsible applications. But in other cases this will not be so. In these it will be necessary to consider the powers or the duties in law of those against whom the relief is asked, the position of the applicant in relation to those powers or duties, and to the breach of those said to have been committed.[58]

This approach was also endorsed by Lord Scarman, who described the necessity for sufficiency of interest to be assessed in this way as 'one legal principle, which is implicit in the

---

[58] Ibid 630.

case law and accurately reflected in the rule of court'.[59] It is Lord Diplock, however, who gives the greatest weight to this view. He states that:

> The whole purpose of requiring that leave should first be obtained to make the application for judicial review would be defeated if the court were to go into the matter in any depth at that stage. If, on a quick perusal of the material then available, the court thinks that it discloses what might on further consideration turn out to be an arguable case in favour of granting to the applicant the relief claimed, it ought, in the exercise of a judicial discretion, to give him leave to apply for that relief. The discretion that the court is exercising at this stage is not the same as that which it is called upon to exercise when all the evidence is in and the matter has been fully argued at the hearing of the application.[60]

The reasons underlying this two-pronged approach are stated throughout their lordships' judgments. The courts address the question of standing at the preliminary stage 'to prevent abuse by busybodies, cranks, and other mischief-makers',[61] and to provide a 'safeguard against the courts being flooded and public bodies harassed by irresponsible applications'.[62] Standing is then considered at the substantive stage to place a more significant emphasis on the individual facts and merits of each particular case. This emphasis on merits, considered alongside the question of standing, is notable. Since judicial review invariably concerns acts and decisions of public bodies, potentially involving important policy issues, it is only right that a particularly meritorious claim should be more likely to be heard. Fusing the question of standing at the substantive stage with this issue of merits ensures that all relevant factors are considered in deciding whether or not an application for judicial review should proceed. It also often means, though, that the courts sometimes adopt an apparently liberal approach to standing, seeming to find a sufficient interest in cases where the personal interest is not particularly convincing but the merits of the issue strong, as demonstrated in a number of cases that we will go on to discuss.

The judgment in the *IRC* case was significant in further explaining the manner in which the sufficient interest should be applied. In the years that followed, however, a number of further cases came before the courts, testing the requirements of standing and further exploring its application, as this next section will now consider.

10.4.1 **Approach to standing**

Since the seminal judgment in the *IRC* case, the courts have adopted a liberal approach to the question of standing. This observation is not novel. In *R (on the application of Bulger) v Secretary of State for the Home Department*,[63] Rose LJ emphasized that:

> It is true . . . that the threshold for standing in judicial review has generally been set by the courts at a low level. This . . . is because of the importance in public law that someone should be able to call decision makers to account, lest the rule of law break down and private rights be denied by public bodies.[64]

---

[59] Ibid 653.   [60] Ibid 643–4.   [61] Ibid 653.   [62] Ibid 630.
[63] [2001] EWHC Admin 119 [21].
[64] Ibid [20], citing HWR Wade and CF Forsyth, *Administrative Law* (10th edn, OUP 2009) 667–88. This case involved a challenge, by the victim's father, of the fixing of the tariff term to be served by James Bulger's murderers. In the case there was no standing because it related to criminal proceedings in which only the Crown and the defendant were 'proper parties' [21].

This liberal approach is widely noted and has been attributed to the reforms and the manner in which they broadened out the restrictive approach that had previously prevailed.[65] Indeed, in the case of *R v HM Treasury, ex p Smedley*,[66] Slade LJ observed that:

> The speeches of their Lordships in [the *IRC* case] well illustrate that there was been what Lord Roskill described . . . as a 'change in policy', which has in recent years greatly relaxed the rules as to locus standi. Lord Diplock referred . . . to a 'virtual abandonment' of the former restrictive rules as to the locus standi of persons seeking prerogative orders against authorities exercising governmental powers.[67]

With these words in mind, the liberal approach is evident from consideration of a number of cases. The first of these is the case of *Smedley* itself. Here, an individual challenged a draft Order in Council which set out an undertaking on the basis of which a payment would be made to the European Community to finance a budget. The individual was deemed to have standing simply by virtue of the fact that he was a British taxpayer. Slade LJ noted that 'I do not feel much doubt that Mr. Smedley, if only in his capacity as a taxpayer, has sufficient *locus standi* to raise this question by way of an application for judicial review'.[68] Bearing in mind that it is the purpose of standing to limit judicial review to those who have been directly affected by a particular decision or action and who have a genuine claim, the decision in *Smedley* seems particularly broad. It is a case, though, that demonstrates the manner in which applicants in especially meritorious cases are more likely to be granted standing. Though a taxpayer arguably no different from any other, the matter at issue in Smedley's case was sufficiently important that the courts felt it appropriate to allow the application to proceed.

Another case that demonstrates the courts' liberal approach to standing is *R v Felixstowe JJ, ex p Leigh*.[69] Here, a journalist sought an application for judicial review in respect of the refusal by judges in a trial of alleged gross indecency to reveal their identity, action they took for security reasons. Though he was deemed not to have sufficient interest to order the names to be revealed, the journalist was held to have standing to seek a declaration that the judges were not entitled to withhold their names. Watkins LJ stated in the case that:

> The application for the declaration seems to me to be brought either by the applicant himself, or possibly by the press through him, as guardian of the public interest in the maintenance and preservation of open justice in magistrates' courts, a matter of vital concern in the administration of justice. In the context of the unlawful use of power without jurisdiction, which I take the policy of the Felixstowe justices and their clerk to be, I feel that a 'public-spirited citizen' . . . would have a sufficient interest in the matter of the declaration sought by this applicant. I would so regard him at the very least as such a person.[70]

---

[65] See, further, Paul Craig, *Administrative Law* (5th edn, Sweet and Maxwell 2012) Ch 25.

[66] [1985] QB 657.

[67] Ibid 669, citing Lord Roskill in *IRC* [1982] AC 617, 656 [G]–[H]; and Lord Diplock, 640 [C].

[68] Ibid 669. Though this was a view with which Sir John Donaldson MR, who gave the leading judgment in this case, did not agree. He noted that it is worth mentioning the 'submission by Mr Laws [on behalf of the Treasury] that Mr Smedley has no sufficient interest within the meaning of RSC, Ord 53, r 3(7). Woolf J [at first instance] did not find it necessary to decide this point and neither do I, although I agree with the judge that I should be extremely surprised to find myself obliged to uphold that submission' (667).

[69] [1987] QB 582.

[70] Ibid 598, citing Lord Denning MR's citation from HWR Wade, *Administrative Law* (4th edn, OUP 1978) 608, in the *IRC* case [1980] QB 407, 422.

One of the most significant examples of the courts' liberal approach to standing, how-ever, is *R v Secretary of State for Foreign Affairs ex p Rees-Mogg*.[71]

Case in depth: *R v Secretary of State for Foreign Affairs ex p Rees-Mogg* **[1994] QB 552**

The editor of the *Times* newspaper, Lord Rees-Mogg, who was also a member of the House of Lords with an interest in constitutional affairs, applied for judicial review in respect of the govern-ment's decision to ratify the Protocol on Social Policy, as part of the Treaty on European Union ('the Maastricht Treaty'). The grounds were that it allegedly breached section 6 of the European Parliamentary Elections Act 1978 (prohibiting the ratification of any treaty agreement or protocol increasing the powers of the European Parliament without parliamentary approval) and also be-cause it purportedly and unlawfully transferred royal prerogative powers (relating to the making of foreign policy) to the EU, without parliamentary approval.

The application was dismissed, however, on the basis that the Protocol was automatically a part of the Treaty and that, pursuant to section 1(2) of the European Communities (Amendment) Act 1993, all Titles, Protocols, and Declarations of the Treaty had also been ratified without breach of the 1978 Act. In addition, the court found that this was an issue relating to exercise of the prerogative power and that, involving as it did matters unrelated to domestic law, the court did not have the jurisdiction to consider judicial review on this point.

Though the case was dismissed, it is notable that Lord Rees-Mogg was deemed to have a sufficient interest to bring the application for judicial review simply by virtue of his inter-est in constitutional affairs. As Lloyd LJ noted, '[t]here is no dispute as to the applicant's locus standi . . . we accept without question that Lord Rees-Mogg brings the proceedings because of his sincere concern for constitutional issues'.[72] This provides another example of the courts adopting a particularly liberal approach to standing. Indeed, it seems some-what tenuous to base the satisfaction of the standing criteria on merely a concern for constitutional matters. When we consider, however, the importance of the issue and the extent to which ratification of European treaties impacts on the public as a whole, we see that the merits of the case are notable, therefore making a stronger case for standing to be granted. On a connected point, also on the Court's mind in deeming Lord Rees-Mogg to have standing was the reality that 'if Lord Rees-Mogg did not have standing then no one did',[73] circumstances that would have prevented the Court from potentially reviewing this particularly meritorious issue. That this is a valid consideration is evident from the more recent case of *R (DSD and NBV and others) v The Parole Board and others*.[74] Here, amid a judicial review of the Parole Board's decision to permit release of an individual convicted in 2009 of various sexual offences, the Mayor of London—as one of the applicants— was deemed not to have standing. The reasons given were that his interest in the case was 'very general in scope, and . . . [did] not relate in any respect, even indirectly, to the

---

[71] [1994] QB 552.   [72] Ibid 561–2.   [73] [2018] EWHC 694 (Admin) [110].
[74] [2018] EWHC 694 (Admin).

workings of the Parole Board'.[75] Of particular interest, though, the court also acknowledged that the Mayor was 'in no different position from any other politician or . . . member of the public'.[76] Drawing from the decision in *Rees-Mogg*, the Court distinguished the liberal approach adopted in that case by noting that there 'are . . . obviously better-placed challengers',[77] the standing of the other applicants not being questioned.

 Counterpoint: The reasons for a liberal approach to standing

The rationale for this consistently liberal approach is provided, albeit before any of these examples were heard, by Lord Diplock. In the *IRC* case he stated that:

> It would, in my view, be a grave *lacuna* in our system of public law if a pressure group, like the [National Federation of Self-Employed and Small Business], or even a single public-spirited taxpayer, were prevented by outdated technical rules of locus standi from bringing the matter to the attention of the court to vindicate the rule of law and get the unlawful conduct stopped.[78]

A liberal, more open system offers greater accountability and protection for the rule of law, ensuring that those bringing an application for judicial review are not prevented by overly technical rules of standing from bringing their case to the Administrative Court.[79] Indeed, writing extra-judicially, Schiemann emphasizes the importance of having 'administrators who act according to law and who can be brought to account if they do not', noting that judicial review is perhaps the only way to get the courts to act.[80] The ability for an administrator to be sued subject to an 'open-system' of standing would encourage that administrator to act more carefully in line with the law.[81]

Though the courts have tended to adopt this liberal approach to standing, however, the comparative benefits of a liberal approach against a stricter, more closed system is an oft-considered debate.[82] A closed system, for instance, saves unnecessary cost and delay, and ensures the ability of administrators to be able to work free from the distractions and worries of potential claims.[83] Coming back to Schiemann's example, the 'possibility of being sued can [also] cause an administrator to concentrate less on the quality of his decision and more on making it "judge proof"'.[84] It is through balancing these two competing issues that the courts have developed a case-by-case approach to the standing test.

Do you think it more important to have an open test that encourages greater accountability and protection for the rule of law or a stricter test that saves resources and affords greater protection for public authorities?

With these justifications and examples in mind, it is clear to see how and why the courts, since 1981, have been minded to adopt a liberal approach to standing. Though in *DSD and NBV* the question of the Mayor of London's standing is distinguished from the liberal

---

[75] [2018] EWHC 694 (Admin) [109].   [76] [2018] EWHC 694 (Admin) [109].

[77] [2018] EWHC 694 (Admin) [110].

[78] [1982] AC 617, 644, cited in Konrad Schiemann, 'Locus Standi' (1990) *Public Law* 342, 346.

[79] Schiemann, 'Locus Standi' (1990) *Public Law* 346, citing Lord Diplock in *IRC* case [1982] AC 617, 644.

[80] Ibid 346.   [81] Ibid.

[82] See, for example, ibid 346, citing Lord Diplock in the *IRC* case [1982] AC 617 at 644.

[83] Ibid 348.   [84] Ibid.

approach in *Rees-Mogg*, the reality that there were other applicants better placed to bring the claim influenced this finding. One thing that all of these cases have in common, however, is that they all involve an individual party seeking to apply for judicial review. A different line of cases that involve groups of individuals, or cases brought by pressure groups on behalf of individuals, have raised their own issues, as this next section now explores.

 Discussing the problem

Have another look at the problem scenario. In view of the rules of standing discussed in this section, do you think (a) the newspaper editor, (b) the priest, or (c) the two private school head teachers would have standing to challenge the local council's policy?

(a) Newspaper editor

With regards to the newspaper editor, we are guided by the case of *ex p Rees-Mogg* in which the editor of *The Times* was held to have sufficient standing to challenge the government's ratification of the Protocol on Social Policy by virtue of his interest in constitutional matters. Such a liberal approach to standing would suggest that, in the problem scenario, the editor of the local newspaper might similarly be granted standing on the basis of an arguable interest in the local area, fuelled by the numerous letters of complaint that have been received. In addition, and borrowing Watkins LJ's words from *ex p Leigh*, it could also be argued that the newspaper editor is acting as the 'guardian of the public interest',[85] thereby strengthening the meritorious nature of the case.

(b) Priest

On the question of standing, the priest cannot be said to be directly affected by the council's policy, at least to the same degree as the pupils, parents, and teachers. This said, given the courts' liberal approach to standing, it is perhaps not inconceivable that they might theoretically find a sufficient interest on the basis of the priest's association with one of the schools, through his church. Regardless of this, however, the court would be unlikely to grant leave for the priest's application on the basis that he has exceeded the strict three-month time limit in which judicial review proceedings must be brought. Due to his absence, on sabbatical, for six months, he has been unable to make a start at an earlier point. Despite the court's ability to exercise a degree of discretion on this point, they would be unlikely to permit the priest's application to proceed for these reasons.

(c) Private school head teachers

Despite the reasons underpinning their proposed application for judicial review, the private school teachers would be unlikely to be granted standing. In the *IRC* case, the National Federation of Self-Employed and Small Businesses Ltd was not granted standing on the basis that they were just a body of taxpayers and had no legitimate interest in the way in which the Inland Revenue dealt with the casual Fleet Street workers. In a similar vein, here, it could be argued that the private school head teachers have no legitimate interest in the way in which the local council deals with state schools under its charge. Private schools are private entities, falling outside the authority of the council, so they would struggle to show themselves to be directly affected by the policy in question.

[85] [1987] QB 582, 598.

10.4.2 **Group standing**

The issue raised by these 'group cases' concerns the question of whether collective action, involving a number of people or representation by pressure groups acting on behalf of a number of individuals, can increase the likelihood of a sufficient interest being accepted.

This matter was first considered in the *IRC* case. In examining whether the National Federation of Self-Employed and Small Businesses had standing to challenge the Inland Revenue's treatment of the casual workers, the House of Lords found that:

> One taxpayer has no sufficient interest in asking the court to investigate the tax affairs of another taxpayer or to complain that the latter has been under assessed or over-assessed. And this principle applies equally to groups of taxpayers: an aggregate of individuals each of whom has no interest cannot of itself have an interest.[86]

This judgment is consistent with the view that issues of standing are linked to merits and it shows that this remains the case even where a greater number of individuals is involved. The courts will always consider the sufficient test and, based on the *IRC* judgment, an increase in numbers will not necessarily increase the chances of that test being satisfied. This is a view that was upheld eight years later in the case of *R v Secretary of State for the Home Department, ex p Rose Theatre Trust*.[87]

Case in depth: *R v Secretary of State for the Home Department, ex p Rose Theatre Trust* [1990] 1 QB 504

During the course of redevelopment on the banks of the Thames in London, the remains of the historical Rose Theatre were discovered. The Rose Theatre Trust Company was set up with the aim of preserving and protecting these remains and making them accessible to members of the public. To this end, it applied to the Secretary of State for the Environment to have the site listed in the Schedule of Monuments. Though the Secretary of State accepted that the theatre's remains were of national importance, he refused to list the site as a monument on the basis that, inter alia, there was a need to balance the desirability of preservation with the need for a city such as London to thrive. The Trust Company applied for judicial review of the decision, though, claiming that the Secretary of State had taken into account irrelevant considerations, failed to take account of relevant considerations, misdirected himself in law, and acted unreasonably. On this basis, it sought an order to quash the decision and to require a new one to be made, considering the Rose Theatre site as a monument. The application was refused on two grounds. First, because the Secretary of State had a broad discretion to list sites as monuments and had exercised this appropriately. Secondly, because the matter was a governmental one, in respect of which members of the public had insufficient interest and, therefore, no standing; something that was unchanged by the mere fact that certain members of the public had set up a Trust Company as a vehicle for their challenge.

---

[86] [1982] AC 617, 618, as per Lord Wilberforce, Lord Fraser, and Lord Roskill.
[87] [1990] 1 QB 504.

In entertaining the question of group standing in *Rose Theatre*, Schiemann J followed the judgment of the House of Lords in the *IRC* case. He stated that '[s]ince, in my judgment, no individual has the standing to move for judicial review it follows . . . that the company created by those individuals has no standing'.[88] Amidst the courts' liberal approach to standing in cases involving individuals, the general view is that there is no such thing as *cumulative* standing; that is, if a number of people come together—themselves with no or little claim of standing—then the court cannot find that sufficient standing has been established merely through their collective action. Groups of people will be assessed individually, not collectively.

The judgment in *Rose Theatre* is often contrasted with one that came just a few years later, testing the rules of group standing in a somewhat different manner. *R v Secretary of State for the Home Department, ex p Greenpeace (No 2)*[89] did not so much concern a group of individuals, but rather representation of a group by Greenpeace, a well-established and respected charity, of which a number of the affected individuals in the case were a member.

Case in depth: *R v Inspectorate of Pollution, ex p Greenpeace (No 2)* [1994] 2 CMLR 548

The Inspectorate of Pollution and the Minister of Agriculture, Fisheries and Food granted an application, made by British Nuclear Fuels pursuant to the Radioactive Substances Act 1960, to allow variations to existing authorizations to permit the company to discharge radioactive waste from its power station at Sellafield, in Cumbria, as part of a testing procedure. Greenpeace sought to challenge this variation through an application for judicial review on the grounds that a completely new authorization was required and that insufficient justification was provided, as necessary under Article 6 of Directive 80/836. Otton J, however, refused the application, finding that the variations to existing authorizations were sufficient to cover the test and that appropriate advanced justifications for the test were provided.

Though the application was refused in *Greenpeace*, the key point to consider again relates to the issue of group standing. Arguments were made in the case to the effect that Greenpeace did not have a sufficient interest or statutory right to bring the complaint and that, in light of the authority provided by *Rose Theatre* and the *IRC* case, a group of individuals or body representing such individuals did not change this. The court, however, disagreed. Otton J looked more to the nature of Greenpeace itself and found that its status as a 'responsible and respected body with a genuine concern for the environment' meant that it had an interest in the disposal of radioactive waste at Sellafield.[90] In addition, and on the basis that the charity represented some 2,500 members in the Cumbria area and that these were 'inevitably concerned about . . . a danger to their health and safety from any additional discharge of radioactive waste', the issues presented by the application were deemed 'serious and worthy of determination' by the court.[91] Indeed, in the circumstances, it was felt that if Greenpeace were to be denied standing, there might not

---

[88] Ibid 522.   [89] [1994] 2 CMLR 548.   [90] Ibid [81].   [91] Ibid.

be any other possible or effective way in which these local, concerned individuals could challenge the Inspectorate's decision.[92] Otton J rejected arguments that Greenpeace were a '"mere" or "meddlesome busybody"', stating that 'I regard the applicants as eminently respectable and responsible and their genuine interest in the issues raised is sufficient for them to be granted locus standi'.[93]

 Discussing the problem

Have another look at the problem scenario set at the outset of this chapter. In light of the judgments in both the *Rose Theatre* case and the *Greenpeace* case, consider whether or not *Parents for Education* and *Primary School Teachers Together* would be granted standing in respect of the council's policy.

(a) Parents for Education

Relevant to the circumstances surrounding any possible application for review brought by *Parents for Education* is the decision in the *Rose Theatre* case. This parallel is drawn on the basis that, like the campaigners challenging the decision of the Secretary of State not to list the Rose Theatre site on the Schedule of Monuments, the group of local parents came together for the specific purpose of challenging the council's policy. Unlike the campaigners in *Rose Theatre*, however, there is perhaps a stronger case to be made in favour of standing. It has already been noted that the campaigners in that case were assessed individually, none of them having sufficient interest to bring an application, a reality that was unchanged by the combined forces of the Trust bringing the case. *Parents for Education*, however, is made up of local parents whose children attend local state schools and who could therefore be held to have an interest in challenging the policy due to their children being directly affected by its implementation. Despite the decision in *Rose Theatre*, standing could potentially be granted to this group.

(b) Primary School Teachers Together

With regards to *Primary School Teachers Together*, we can look to the case of *Greenpeace*. The parallel with this authority is founded on the fact that, just as Greenpeace was held to have standing due to its long-standing and well-established reputation, and the fact that so many local residents were members, the proposed application in the scenario is also brought by a well-established body which represents a significant majority of teachers affected by the council's policy. What is more, the teachers will be affected by the implementation of this policy, meaning that the test for standing applied by the courts can be more easily satisfied.

Greenpeace was a notable judgment and one that can be distinguished from the earlier *Rose Theatre* decision on the basis that the circumstances in that case were different.[94] For instance, 'the interest group [in *Rose Theatre*] had been formed for the exclusive purpose of saving the Rose Theatre site and no individual member could show any personal interest in the outcome'.[95] It therefore makes sense that since no individual could show any personal interest in respect of the historic site, forming a group of those individuals

---

[92] Ibid [82].   [93] Ibid [83].   [94] Ibid [86].   [95] Ibid.

would do nothing to increase the possibility of any such interest. By contrast, however, given that a number of people would have been affected by the disposal of radioactive waste in the *Greenpeace* case, and were concerned about the possible effects of that disposal on their own lives, a group of such individuals served to increase the weight of that concern and give rise to a collective sufficient interest. Greenpeace was then able to represent those individuals because, as a respected and experienced charity, championing environmental issues and concerns, it was best placed to do so. Indeed, and bearing in mind the discussion concerning the impact that merits has on the question of standing, the matter at issue in *Greenpeace*, regarding as that did concerns for widespread health, may also have had an impact on the decision to grant standing. In other words, in addition to Greenpeace's representative standing, there was an element of public interest in permitting the application to proceed.

The *Rose Theatre* and *Greenpeace* cases provide an interesting insight into the issues that are considered when assessing group standing, exemplifying both the case-by-case nature of the question and the importance that is placed on the merits of each particular case. In *Greenpeace*, Otton J emphasized this case-by-case nature of standing questions by stressing that the *Greenpeace* judgment did not set a precedent that interest groups could always follow. He said: 'it must not be assumed that Greenpeace (or any other interest group) will automatically be afforded standing in any subsequent application for judicial review . . . this will have to be a matter to be considered on a case by case basis.'[96]

Nonetheless, just a year later, the courts were once again invited to consider the issue in *R v Secretary of State for Foreign and Commonwealth Affairs, ex p World Development Movement*.[97]

Case in depth: *R v Secretary of State for Foreign and Commonwealth Affairs, ex p World Development Movement* [1995] 1 WLR 386

Pursuant to section 1(1) of the Overseas Development and Co-operation Act 1980, a British consortium sought aid and trade provision in respect of a project to construct a hydro-electric power station on the Pergau river in Malaysia. The UK Government engaged in negotiations with the Malaysian Government with regards to the possibility of funding for the project. As part of this, the Overseas Development Administration engaged in an appraisal mission, though it reported that the project was uneconomic and that for the UK Government to involve itself in the project would be an abuse of the aid programme and not a sound development project. Regardless, on the view that it was important for the UK's credibility, the Secretary of State for Foreign and Commonwealth Affairs approved the necessary support and signed a financial agreement with the Malaysian Government, thereby providing funding for the project. The World Development Movement, an interest group 'dedicated to improving the quantity and quality of British aid to other countries,[98] sought an assurance from the Secretary of State that there would be no further funding, however, this was not provided. As a result, the World Development Movement Ltd sought an application for judicial review on grounds that the Secretary of State had acted unlawfully, and it was granted.

---

[96] Ibid [85].   [97] [1995] 1 WLR 386.   [98] Ibid at 386.

One of the main issues considered by the court related to whether the World Development Movement, as an interest group, had sufficient interest to bring the application. Rose LJ considered a number of factors and a range of previous authorities and found no reason to deny standing.[99] Indeed, in view of the range of previous cases, some of which have been discussed, Rose LJ felt that:

> The authorities referred to seem to me to indicate an increasingly liberal approach to standing on the part of the courts during the last 12 years . . . if the Divisional Court in *Ex p Rees-Mogg* [1994] Q.B. 552 . . . was able to accept that the applicant . . . had standing in the light of his 'sincere concern for constitutional issues,' . . . it seems to me that the present applicants, with the national and international expertise and interest in promoting and protecting aid to underdeveloped nations, should have standing in the present application.[100]

Drawing from previously discussed case law, the Court of Appeal acknowledged and endorsed the liberal approach that the courts have—over the years—adopted with regards to issues of standing, and they contributed to it further by accepting that the *World Development Movement*, despite not having any financial or personal interest in the matter, could have standing to challenge the government's decision. This not only represents a departure from the initially cautious approach that the courts took in *Rose Theatre* with regards to group standing, but also serves as a further example of the importance with which the courts continue to see the merits of a case being linked to the question of *locus standi*.

10.4.3 Concluding thoughts on standing

Questions of standing have been discussed at length over the years, with courts considering a range of factors and issues in determining whether applicants should be deemed to have a sufficient interest to make an application. Cases involving individuals, groups of individuals, and interest groups have all presented differing issues. The overriding approach employed by the courts, however, appears to be a liberal one. Judges have tended to go beyond simply asking whether or not the applicant has a 'sufficient interest' in the matter at issue and, instead, have placed great emphasis on the merits of the case and the importance of protecting the rule of law, of affording redress where alternative courses of action are not possible, and of resolving key, important issues in addressing questions of standing.[101] Alongside the requirement of standing, however, questions regarding the public/private law divide are often presented to the courts in entertaining judicial review applications, as the next section now discusses.

---

[99] Ibid 395. Such factors, with appropriate authority, included: 'the importance of vindicating the rule of law' (See: Lord Diplock in the *IRC* case); 'the importance of the issue raised, as in *R v Secretary of State for Social Services, ex p Child Poverty Action Group* [1990] 2 QB 540'; 'the likely absence of any other responsible challenger, as in *Ex p Child Poverty Action Group* and *Ex p Greenpeace Ltd. (No. 2)* [1994] 4 All ER 329'; and the prominent role of the applicants in giving advice and guidance (See *Ex p Child Poverty Action Group*).

[100] [1995] 1 WLR 386, 395–6.

[101] In judicial review claims brought under the Human Rights Act 1998, the test for standing is different. Pursuant to s 7(1), you must be the victim of an unlawful act to bring proceedings.

10.5 The public/private law divide

Judicial review of administrative action is a public law action, founded on the prerogative remedies of certiorari, mandamus, and prohibition,[102] which, as Lord Denning explained in *O'Reilly v Mackman*,[103] were the special remedies available in public law to regulate the affairs of public authorities.[104] These have been built on by further legislation and provision over the years, with the Senior Courts Act 1981, the Order 53 procedure, and its successor, the Civil Procedure Rules, explaining and setting out further the public nature of judicial review. The purpose of this public law procedure serves not only to protect those subject to administrative decisions from arbitrary abuses of power, but also protects those in decision-making positions from facing unnecessary, time-consuming, costly, and uncertain actions in the court. The requirements, already discussed, relating to time-limits and standing, exist to ensure that applications for judicial review have merit and are brought within reasonable time. Much of this has already been explained. This public law action, however, can be clearly distinguished from procedures and remedies available at private law with actions there often being based, for example, on contractual or tortious disputes and being subjected to different rules and procedures. This divide between public and private law, though, has been the focus of much discussion over the years, with cases considering both the notion of procedural exclusivity and the requirement that judicial review only stand against public authorities, as this section will now explain.

10.5.1 The exclusivity principle

Procedural exclusivity, or the exclusivity principle, is the idea that only matters relating to public law can be dealt with by judicial review; issues of private law must be dealt with through the relevant, private law procedures.[105] The principle derives from Lord Diplock's notable judgment in *O'Reilly v Mackman*.[106]

Case in depth: *O'Reilly v Mackman* [1983] 2 AC 237

Following a riot at a prison in Hull, a number of prisoners were brought before the Board of Visitors where they were found guilty of disciplinary offences and ordered to lose remission of sentence of 510 days. Amid complaints that the Board had breached rules of natural justice in carrying out its inquiry and in handing out the sentence, a number of the prisoners made applications for judicial review. While they were told by the Divisional Court that this was not available to them, the Court of Appeal reversed this view, resulting in the quashing of some of the decisions.[107] Four prisoners, however, long after the time limit for judicial review had expired,

→

---

[102] These are quashing orders, mandatory orders, and prohibition orders, discussed in 10.6.
[103] [1983] 2 AC 237.   [104] Ibid 255.
[105] Private law typically refers to proceedings between private parties, such as contract law or tort law.
[106] [1983] 2 AC 237.
[107] See *R v Board of Visitors of Hull Prison, ex p St Germain* [1979] QB 425.

→

brought an ordinary action by writ, on the grounds that the Board had breached Prison Rules and the rules of natural justice. The Court of Appeal and, subsequently, the House of Lords both dismissed the proceedings on the basis that action through ordinary writ was not appropriate and that, since the necessary remedies were available at judicial review, action should have been sought through an application there instead.

In the Court of Appeal, Lord Denning labelled it a 'high constitutional principle' that 'judicial review . . . should be the normal recourse in all cases of public law where a private person is challenging the conduct of a public authority or a public body, or of anyone acting in the exercise of a public duty'.[108] This is a view that was endorsed by the House of Lords on appeal, with Lord Diplock giving the leading judgment and commenting on the then recent reforms. He stated that:

> Now that . . . all remedies for infringements of rights protected by public law can be obtained upon an application for judicial review . . . it would in my view as a general rule be contrary to public policy, and as such an abuse of process of the court, to permit a person seeking to establish that a decision of a public authority infringed rights to which he was entitled to protection under public law to proceed by way of an ordinary action and by this means to evade the provisions of Order 53 for the protection of such authorities.[109]

Though the idea of placing a clear divide between public and private law matters, with regards to judicial review, was contrary to the 1977 reform's desire to simplify and clarify the procedures and remedies for judicial review, the House of Lords judgment in *O'Reilly* had the effect of limiting access to judicial review to those parties affected by public law issues.

 Pause for reflection

Do you agree with the judgment in *O'Reilly v Mackman* that the prisoners' case should be dismissed purely on the grounds that it was sought using the wrong process? What are the broader implications of dismissing applications on this basis?

In the years that followed, however, the House of Lord's decision in *O'Reilly*, and Lord iplock's judgment in particular, came to be widely criticized. Wade and Forsyth, for instance, question 'whether the logic of *O'Reilly v Mackman* is as compelling as Lord Diplock maintained', noting how it 'has produced uncertainty as to the boundary between public and private law'.[110] They describe the case as a 'setback for administrative law' and stress that the judgment 'has caused many cases, which on their merits might have succeeded, to fail merely because of choice of the wrong form of action'.[111] In view of these comments, it is

---

[108] [1983] 2 AC 237, 256.   [109] Ibid 285.
[110] HWR Wade and CF Forsyth, *Administrative Law* (10th edn, OUP 2009) 567 and 569.
[111] Ibid 567.

hardly surprising that the courts came later to impose exceptions to the application of the exclusivity principle. The two most prominent post-*O'Reilly* cases are *Wandsworth London Borough Council v Winder*[112] and *Roy v Kensington and Chelsea and Westminster Family Practitioner Committee*.[113]

In *Winder*, Wandsworth Borough Council increased the rent of council property, giving due notice to the tenant. When the tenant refused to pay the increased rate, however, the council brought private, civil law proceedings for the outstanding amount, also seeking repossession of the property. In defence, the tenant claimed that the decision to increase the rent was made *ultra vires* and was therefore void. Though the council made attempts to strike out this defence, the Court of Appeal and, subsequently, the House of Lords both upheld the view that the tenant should be allowed to pursue a public law action in defence in this way. Lord Fraser, in giving the leading judgment, accepted that the principle set out in *O'Reilly* and the basis for judicial review more widely, was to ensure good administration and speedy certainty, thereby protecting authorities from unmeritorious or dilatory challenges and ensuring certainty for third parties who may be indirectly affected by a particular decision.[114] At the same time, however, he emphasized the importance of 'preserving the ordinary rights of private citizens to defend themselves against unfounded claims'.[115] Accepting that public law judicial review proceedings could be invoked as a defence to a claim in private law meant that the scope of Lord Diplock's judgment in *O'Reilly* had become limited.

The exclusivity principle was considered again in the case of *Roy*. Here, a GP had some of his basic practice allowance withheld by the Committee on the basis that they felt he had carried out an insufficient amount of necessary work. As a result, the GP instigated private law proceedings in the High Court, issuing the Committee with a writ. In their defence and as a counterclaim, the Committee sought to have the claim struck out on the basis that, as a public law decision, it should be challenged by an application for judicial review. The Court of Appeal, and later the House of Lords, held that since the issue involved a private law right, on the basis of a contract that existed between the Committee and the GP, the proceedings could be brought through ordinary action at private law, even if those proceedings also involved a challenge to a public law decision. In both *Winder* and *Roy* the principle established in *O'Reilly v Mackman* came to be limited insofar as the court accepted that where a case involved both private and public law issues, either action could be used. Indeed, as we see in *Winder*, public law actions can be used as a defence in relation to an otherwise private law matter.

Since *O'Reilly*, the divide between public and private law has become much less of an issue. Indeed, this has been observed by the courts themselves, with the Court of Appeal holding in *Clark v University of Lincolnshire and Humberside*[116] that 'a claim against a public body for breach of contract should not be struck out merely because an application for judicial review might have been more appropriate'.[117] Since the early 1980s and the case of *O'Reilly*, the exclusivity principle, in the strict form elucidated by Lord Diplock, has come to be limited by the courts, essentially to the point that it is no longer seen as a relevant requirement for judicial review.

---

[112] [1985] AC 461.   [113] [1992] 1 AC 624.   [114] See [1985] AC 461, 508–9.
[115] Ibid 509.   [116] [2000] 1 WLR 1988.   [117] Ibid 1988.

10.5.2 Public authorities and public functions

Nowadays, the only instance in which the courts will consider the relevance of the public/
private law divide is in respect of the body against which an application for judicial review can be brought. Even in this regard, there has been a gradual liberalization of the
courts' approach, as this section explains. The Civil Procedure rules set out the procedural
basis for this rule and state that 'a "claim for judicial review" means a claim to review the
lawfulness of . . . a decision, action or failure to act in relation to the exercise of a public
function'.[118] That said, historically, questions relating to whether or not a particular authority was 'public', and therefore susceptible to judicial review, looked to the source of
that authority's power, rather than to the functions which they exercised.[119] Typically, a
public authority was one that had been created either by legislation or as a result of prerogative powers.[120] In *R v Criminal Injuries Compensation Board, ex p Lain*,[121] for instance,
the Compensation Board, created by royal prerogative, was deemed to be susceptible to
review; in *Council for Civil Service Unions v Minister for the Civil Service*,[122] it was an Order in
Council, passed by the Prime Minister herself, that was the question of review. Nonetheless, this approach was significantly expanded upon in the case of *R v Panel on Takeovers
and Mergers, ex p Datafin Plc and others*.[123]

**Case in depth: *R v Panel on Takeovers and Mergers, ex p Datafin
Plc and others* [1987] QB 815**

Datafin Plc and Prudential Bache Securities Inc were engaged in competition with Norton Opax
Plc, all bidding to take over McCorquodale Plc. It was argued, however, that Norton Opax was
acting in breach of the City Code on Take-overs and Mergers. As a result, Datafin and Prudential
Bache Securities (the applicants) complained to the Panel of Takeovers and Mergers, though the
Panel dismissed this complaint. Consequently, the applicants sought judicial review of the dismissal, seeking an order to have it quashed and another order to require reconsideration of the
complaint. The Divisional Court refused leave for the application, however, on the grounds that
the decision of the Panel was not susceptible to judicial review, a decision that was later reversed
by the Court of Appeal.

The Court of Appeal's judgment was notable for its departure from previously accepted
considerations of the source of power in determining whether or not an authority could
be regarded as 'public' for the purposes of judicial review. As Falkner explains, it was argued in the case that 'although the Panel did not exercise statutory or prerogative powers,
it should nevertheless be subject to judicial review because it was essentially a public body

---

[118] Civil Procedure Rules, r 54.1(2)(a)(ii).

[119] Section 6.5.3, for instance, discusses the line of cases that established that power derived from the
royal prerogative was equally reviewable as power derived from statute, subject to further questions of
justiciability.

[120] As the case of *AXA Insurance v Lord Advocate* [2011] UKSC 46, demonstrates, discussed in 9.4.1, the
devolved institutions are susceptible to judicial review, albeit only with regards to the scope of their
statutory powers.

[121] [1967] 2 QB 864.   [122] [1985] AC 374.   [123] [1987] QB 815.

carrying out public functions'.[124] This was a view with which Sir John Donaldson MR agreed, stating that:

> [The Panel on Takeovers and Mergers] is without doubt performing a public duty and an important one. This is clear from the expressed willingness of the Secretary of State for Trade and Industry to limit legislation in the field of take-overs and mergers and to use the panel as the centrepiece of his regulation of that market. The rights of citizens are indirectly affected by its decisions . . . it has a duty to act judicially and it asserts that its *raison d'être* is to do equity between one shareholder and another . . . Given that it is really unthinkable that . . . the panel should go on its way cocooned from the attention of the courts in defence of the citizenry.[125]

More broadly, though, Lloyd LJ placed this decision in the wider context of accepted tests in this area by stating that:

> I do not agree that the source of the power is the sole test whether a body is subject to judicial review . . . Of course the source of the power will often, perhaps usually, be decisive. If the source of power is a statute, or subordinate legislation under a statute, then clearly the body in question will be subject to judicial review. If, at the other end of the scale, the source of power is contractual, as in the case of private arbitration, then clearly the arbitrator is not subject to judicial review . . . But in between these extremes there is an area in which it is helpful to look not just at the source of the power but at the nature of the power. If the body in question is exercising public law functions, or if the exercise of its functions have public law consequences, then that may . . . be sufficient to bring the body within the reach of judicial review . . . The essential distinction . . . is between a domestic or private tribunal on the one hand and a body of persons who are under some public duty on the other.[126]

On this foundation, Lloyd LJ went on to emphasize the manner in which the Panel had been created 'under authority of the government'[127] and that, as a result, it was fulfilling not merely a public role but also a governmental one. Consequently, he was satisfied that the Panel could be regarded as a public authority for the purposes of judicial review.

The *Datafin* case substantially broadened the accepted understandings of what could be regarded as a public authority for the purpose of judicial review, inviting courts to look beyond the mere source of a body's power and to consider the nature of the powers that it exercises. The breadth of this judgment is echoed by Sir Thomas Bingham who noted that '[t]he effect of this decision was to extend judicial review to a body whose birth and constitution owed nothing to any exercise of governmental power but which had been woven into the fabric of public regulation in the field of take-overs and mergers'.[128]

The test set out in *Datafin* was subsequently applied in *R v Chief Rabbi of the United Hebrew Congregations of Great Britain and the Commonwealth, ex p Wachmann*.[129] This case concerned an application for judicial review by an Orthodox rabbi in respect of a decision

---

[124] Robert Falkner, 'Judicial Review of the Take-over Panel and Self-regulatory Organisations' (1987) 2(2) *Journal of International Banking Law* 103, 106.

[125] [1987] QB 815, 838–9.

[126] Ibid 847, citing *R v National Joint Council for the Craft of Dental Technicians (Disputes Committee), ex p Neate* [1953] 1 QB 704.

[127] Ibid 849, citing Diplock LJ in *R v Criminal Injuries Compensation Board, ex p Lain*.

[128] *R v Disciplinary Committee of the Jockey Club, ex p Aga Khan* [1993] 1 WLR 909, 921.

[129] [1992] 1 WLR 1036.

made by the applicant's Chief Rabbi to declare him 'no longer religiously and morally fit to occupy his position as rabbi', terminating his employment on those grounds.[130] In applying the test from *Datafin*, Brown J rejected arguments to the effect that the rabbi was fulfilling a public function, stating that:

> To attract the court's supervisory jurisdiction there must be not merely a public but potentially a governmental interest in the decision-making power in question . . . [the rabbi's] functions are essentially intimate, spiritual, and religious—functions which the government could not and would not seek to discharge in his place were he to abdicate his regulatory responsibility.[131]

The court in *Wachmann* distinguished the facts from *Datafin*, acknowledging that the role of the rabbi was not established by any governmental authority and his functions were also sufficiently far removed from any governmental interest for him to fall outside the scope of judicial review. Just six years after the *Datafin* judgment, however, the courts were called upon again to consider the tests for determining whether a body could be termed a public authority for the purposes of judicial review, in the case of *R v Disciplinary Committee of the Jockey Club, ex p Aga Khan*.[132]

Case in depth: *R v Disciplinary Committee of the Jockey Club, ex p Aga Khan* [1993] 1 WLR 909

Following victory in a horse race at Epsom, the winning horse—owned by the Aga Khan—underwent a routine test. This found that the horse's urine contained traces of camphor, a substance banned under the Jockey Club's Rules of Racing. The Disciplinary Committee held that the winning horse should be disqualified and its owners fined £200. Consequently, the Aga Khan sought an application for judicial review of the decision to disqualify, with the aim of having the Committee's decision quashed and the win reinstated. Addressing the preliminary question with regards to the Jockey Club's susceptibility for review, the Divisional Court dismissed the application, although it was later upheld in the Court of Appeal.

Like the Panel on Takeovers and Mergers in *Datafin*, Bingham MR accepted the 'contention that the Jockey Club . . . regulates a significant national activity, exercising powers which affect the public and are exercised in the interest of the public'.[133] Indeed, he added that 'I am willing to accept that if the Jockey Club did not regulate this activity the government would probably be driven to create a public body to do so'.[134] In going on to distinguish the facts from *Datafin*, however, Bingham MR also noted that:

> the Jockey Club is not in its origin, its history, its constitution or (least of all) its membership a public body . . . It has not been woven into any system of governmental control of horseracing, perhaps because it has itself controlled horseracing so successfully that there has been no need for any such governmental system and such does not therefore exist.

---

[130] Ibid 1036.   [131] Ibid 1041.   [132] [1993] 1 WLR 909.
[133] Ibid 923.   [134] Ibid.

This has the result that while the Jockey Club's powers may be described as, in many ways, public they are in no sense governmental.[135]

As a consequence, it was held by the Court of Appeal that the Jockey Club, though exercising public, though not governmental, functions, could not be regarded as a public authority for the purposes of judicial review. One of the most significant reasons underlying this was not so much the Jockey Club's functions, but rather the nature of its relationship with its members, which in this instance was based on a contract. As Bingham explained:

> [T]he powers which the Jockey Club exercises over those who (like the applicant) agree to be bound by the Rules of Racing derive from the agreement of the parties and give rise to private rights on which effective action for a declaration, an injunction and damages can be based without resort to judicial review. It would in my opinion be contrary to sound and long-standing principle to extend the remedy of judicial review to such a case.[136]

In short, where there is a contract the courts will regard this as indicative of a private law relationship, affecting only those party to that contract. Consequently, acts and decisions of parties to that contract will be actionable only at private law and will not be susceptible to judicial review. This is a view that has been endorsed more recently in *R (Oxford Study Centre Ltd) v British Council*,[137] where the court rejected the application for judicial review on the grounds that the body in question was not exercising a public function and also because the source of the body's power was contractual.[138]

We can see that the division between public and private law has provided much judicial discussion in respect of the scope of judicial review. Though Lord Diplock's judgment in *O'Reilly v Mackman* set out the exclusivity principle and provided an initial explanation of how judicial review could be restricted in terms of the public/private law divide, this came to be criticized and was limited in subsequent cases. Since then, the courts have broadened out the instances where judicial review is available and have expanded the rules relating to the definition of public authorities, looking predominantly to their functions and the relationships they share with their respective members in determining their suitability for review.[139] Having explored the various requirements and procedures for judicial review throughout this chapter, it is necessary finally to consider the remedies that can be awarded upon a successful application for judicial review.

 Discussing the problem

Have a look at the problem scenario at the beginning of this chapter. Assuming the relevant parties have standing to bring an application for judicial review, are they bringing proceedings against a public authority?

Yes. As Chapter 9 has already explored and explained, local councils are a branch of the government so can be classed as a public authority for the purposes of judicial review.

---

[135] Ibid.   [136] Ibid.   [137] [2001] EWHC (Admin) 207.

[138] Ibid and see further HWR Wade and CF Forsyth, *Administrative Law* (10th edn, OUP 2009) 547.

[139] Since the enactment of the Human Rights Act 1998, judicial review now has a further dimension. Under ss 6 and 7 of that Act, public authorities can be challenged in light of a duty to act compatibly with the ECHR. This is discussed further in 15.5.6.

10.6 **Remedies**

When an application for judicial review is brought, it will be the main aim of the applicant to seek the award of an appropriate remedy. These are designed to impose upon a public authority an order to the effect that illegal or improper decisions are struck down, and/or to ensure that future decisions are made legally and properly. The central role that remedies play in the judicial review procedure is reflected in section 31(1) of the Senior Courts Act 1981. This provides that judicial review consists of:

(1) An application to the High Court for one or more of the following forms of relief, namely—

(a) a mandatory, prohibiting or quashing order;

(b) a declaration or injunction under subsection (2); or

(c) an injunction under section 30 restraining a person not entitled to do so from acting in an office to which that section applies.

As this section shows, there are a number of potential remedies available, though they are awarded entirely at the discretion of the court in each case. The available remedies can be divided into two categories—prerogative remedies and ordinary remedies, which were, prior to Order 53 of the Rules of the Supreme Court, originally available under entirely different procedures. Reforms brought in in the late 1970s, however, and discussed earlier in this chapter, now mean that all these remedies are available under the same judicial review procedure, as section 31 explains.

The prerogative remedies are only available at public law and have, for centuries, formed the basis of actions against public authorities. There are three of them—quashing orders, mandatory orders, and prohibition orders. Quashing orders, if awarded, serve retrospectively to strike out the particular decision or action in respect of which an application for judicial review has been brought. In addition, as Craig observes, 'where there are grounds for quashing the decision the court can remit the case to the original decision-maker with a direction to reconsider the matter and reach a decision in accord with the judgment of the court'.[140] Prohibition orders serve prospectively to prohibit potentially unlawful action, meaning that they serve to prevent a public authority from acting in a particular way in the future. Finally, mandatory orders are imposed to demand that a public authority act in a particular way.

 Pause for reflection

Can you think of situations in which more than one of these prerogative remedies might be awarded simultaneously to quash a public authority's decision and require it to re-make a decision lawfully and legitimately?

Ordinary remedies, which can be sought at private law as well, include injunctions, declarations, and damages. Injunctions serve simply to prevent a public authority from taking a particular course of action or require them to abide by stipulations of the court, while a

---

[140] Paul Craig, *Administrative Law* (5th edn, Sweet and Maxwell 2012) 811, citing s 31(5) of the Senior Courts Act 1981.

declaration serves to 'state the rights or legal position of the parties as they stand, without changing them in any way'.[141] Both injunctions and declarations can be awarded by the court where it is 'just and convenient' to do so, in view of the nature of the matter, the nature of the parties, and the circumstances of the case.[142] Finally, and as at private law, damages for judicial review can compensate the aggrieved applicant for any loss that they might have endured as a result of the erroneous decision. Pursuant to section 31(4)(b) of the 1981 Act, however, they can only be awarded where 'the court is satisfied that such an award would have been made if the claim had been made in an action begun by the applicant at the time of making the application'.

 Discussing the problem

What, if any, remedies do you think should be awarded in respect of the local council's decision in the problem scenario?

Leaving aside the question of whether any application for judicial review would succeed on these facts—a consideration that can only be entertained once the various grounds for review (discussed in Chapters 11 to 13) have been explored—there are two remedies potentially of interest to the scenario set out at the start of the chapter. First, quashing orders. Each of the parties seeking to bring an application for judicial review does so to challenge and change the policy as it stands. They would want for a case to be made in favour of striking out—or quashing—the council's policy. Secondly, though of perhaps less importance, a court might grant a mandatory order, requiring the council to review the statutory power granted under the 2025 Act and to set out another policy.

It is clear that the remedies play a valuable role in judicial review, providing a number of potential outcomes for applicants who successfully challenge the decisions and actions of public authorities, subject of course to the discretion of the Administrative Court.

10.7 Summary

This chapter has provided an in-depth introduction to judicial review of administrative action and explained, in detail, its fundamental aspects and requirements. It has defined judicial review and provided an insight into the way in which it has developed since the 1960s, with various reforms and judgments being pivotal to the form of action as we know it today. Section 31 of the Senior Courts Act 1981 provides the legal basis for review, while the Civil Procedure Rules, replacing Order 53 of the Rules of the Supreme Court, set out the procedure that is to be followed in bringing an application for judicial review. Alongside these various provisions, there are a number of other requirements that must be fulfilled. The principle of standing ensures that only those with a 'sufficient interest' in the matter at issue are able to proceed with an application, a test which the courts

---

[141] HWR Wade and CF Forsyth, *Administrative Law* (10th edn, OUP 2009) 480.
[142] Section 31(2) of the Senior Courts Act 1981.

have explored and applied in an increasingly liberal and varying manner. In addition, the requirement that judicial review be brought only against a public authority helps to guide applicants towards the most appropriate form of action, a requirement that—since *Datafin*—the courts have again interpreted broadly. Provided these various requirements are met and procedures followed, however, then it is at the discretion of the court to award either ordinary or prerogative remedies. The next three chapters now proceed on the foundation provided by this exploration of judicial review and cover the substantive and procedural grounds on which an application can be made. These have developed through case law over many years, though were identified by Lord Diplock in *Council for Civil Service Unions v Minister for the Civil Service* as illegality, irrationality, and procedural impropriety.

Quick test questions

1. What was the significance of the judgment in *Anisminic Ltd v Foreign Compensation Commission and others*?

2. Explain the judicial review procedure.

3. What is the time limit within which an application for judicial review must be made and how strictly is this applied?

4. What is the 'sufficient interest' test and where is it contained?

5. What did the House of Lords say in *IRC v National Federation of Self-Employed and Small Businesses Ltd* with regard to the way in which the 'sufficient interest' test should be applied?

6. Why was Greenpeace granted standing in *R v Inspectorate of Pollution, ex p Greenpeace (No 2)*?

7. What tests do the courts employ to determine whether a body is a public authority for the purpose of judicial review?

8. What are the three prerogative remedies and what do they do?

Further reading

Nature and purpose of judicial review

Peter Cane, 'Private Rights and Public Procedure' (1992) *Public Law* 193

*Paul Craig, 'Ultra Vires and the Foundations of Judicial Review' (1998) 57 *Cambridge Law Journal* 63

Mark Elliott, 'The Ultra Vires Doctrine in a Constitutional Setting: Still the Central Principle of Administrative Law' (1999) 58(1) *Cambridge Law Journal* 129

Mark Elliott, *The Constitutional Foundations of Judicial Review* (Hart Publishing, 2001)

*Christopher Forsyth, 'Of Fig Leaves and Fairy Tales: The Ultra Vires Doctrine, the Sovereignty of Parliament and Judicial Review' (1996) 55(1) *Cambridge Law Journal* 122

Standing

*Peter Cane, 'Standing, Legality and the Limits of Public Law' (1981) *Public Law* 322

*Peter Cane, 'Standing up for the Public' (1995) *Public Law* 276

*Konrad Schiemann, 'Locus Standi' (1990) *Public Law* 342

The public/private law divide

Robert Falkner, 'Judicial Review of the Take-Over Panel and Self-Regulatory Organisations' (1987) 2(2) *Journal of International Banking Law* 103

Jonathan Morgan, 'A Mare's Nest? The Jockey Club and Judicial Review of Sports Governing Bodies' (2012) 12(2) *Legal Information Management* 102

*Dawn Oliver, 'Public Law Procedures and Remedies – Do We Need Them?' (2002) *Public Law* 91

 Visit this book's **online resources** for additional materials relating to this chapter, including a full analysis of the start-of-chapter problem scenario.
www.oup.com/he/stanton-prescott2e

11

Judicial review: illegality

Problem scenario

The Food Distribution Act 2024 (fictitious), at section 2, states the following:

(1) A Local Authority may operate a market which sells food. A market established under this section shall be referred to as a 'Food Market'.

(2) To operate a Food Market, a Local Authority may grant a licence to operate a stall at a Food Market to those who apply.

(3) A Local Authority can consider applications to operate a stall as they see fit and in their absolute discretion.

(4) Any decision made by a Local Authority under this section cannot be challenged in any court of law.

Ever since the Act was passed, Nanchester District Council have operated a market in the centre of Nanchester. It has been very popular, and Kendrick, Francesca, Callum, and Unusual Fruits Ltd have all recently applied for a licence.

- Kendrick applied for a licence for a stall that would sell a range of foods including pies, sausage rolls, and pastries. Kendrick's application was rejected. This was because the Council is concerned that the market is quiet after lunchtimes, and so they want to encourage stalls that sell products other than food, believing that this will attract shoppers later in the day.

- Francesca made an application for a stall to sell sandwiches. The Council instructed Francesca to send her application to the Market Manager, who was employed by Country Markets Ltd, the company that manages the market on behalf of the Council. Francesca has just heard from the Market Manager that her application has been rejected.

- The Council has accepted Callum's application for a licence on the condition that Callum, at his own expense, will spend his Friday afternoons driving pensioners to the local supermarket so they can do their grocery shopping. This is following the Council's decision to cut the

→

budget for bus services in the area, with the effect that buses no longer stop at the supermarket. Callum is surprised by this condition.

- Unusual Fruits Ltd has applied for a licence: however, their application was refused. Unusual Fruits Ltd specialize in rare fruits from around the world and wished to have a stall in the market. Their application was refused by the Council because there are already three fruit stalls, and it was the policy of the Council not to have more than three stalls of the 'same type' in the market. Unusual Fruits Ltd explained that they would sell types of fruit that are not currently sold at the market, but the Council representative told them, 'I'm sorry but that's our policy'.

11.1 Introduction

This chapter considers 'illegality' as a ground of judicial review. As will be explained, illegality is one of the three main grounds of judicial review as outlined by Lord Diplock in *Council of Civil Service Unions & Others v Minister for the Civil Service*.[1] Broadly, the aim of this ground of judicial review is to ensure that public authorities act within the scope of their powers. This means that illegality is a wide ground of judicial review and is best considered as an umbrella term for a range of different ways in which a decision by a public authority can be challenged.

A decision can be challenged under this ground of judicial review on the basis that the public authority lacks the power to make the decision in the first place, or if it does have the power, then the power has been exercised incorrectly. This could be because the power may give the public authority a discretion to act, but this discretion has not been exercised correctly. This may be because the decision made was not a genuine exercise of discretion because that discretion was 'fettered'. This could be because the decision was in substance made by someone else who was not authorized to act. Similarly, decisions made by public authorities could be made after taking into account considerations not relevant to the power granted, or be an attempt to use the power for a purpose different to that intended by Parliament. All of these issues are discussed in this chapter. Finally, Parliament may impose duties on public authorities when making decisions and if these duties are not complied with then the decision has not been made according to law. An example of this is the Public Sector Equality Duty and this is explained at the end of the chapter.

An important consideration to realize at the outset is that although the areas considered in this chapter are each distinct areas of illegality, there can be considerable overlap between these areas. This means that the same action or decision of a public authority may fall under more than one of these areas.

The objectives of this chapter are:

- to explain the relationship between illegality and *ultra vires* and how illegality as a ground of judicial review is an important way in which the intention of Parliament can be enforced against public authorities and the rule of law fulfilled;

---

[1] [1985] AC 374. Hereinafter referred to as *GCHQ* as the case involved employees of the Government Communications Headquarters.

- to show how errors or law and errors of fact are treated differently by the courts;

- to highlight the importance of discretion within government and how the law imposes controls on how that discretion can be exercised;

- to consider how the courts control powers that have been exercised in order to achieve an improper purpose or scrutinize decisions reached when irrelevant considerations have been taken into account when making a decision;

- to introduce and explain the Public Sector Equality Duty and its impact on public authorities when making decisions.

11.2 Illegality, *ultra vires*, and the rule of law

It is a basic requirement of the rule of law that public authorities act within the scope of their legal powers. When a public authority acts outside the scope of their powers then they are said to be acting *ultra vires*, a Latin phrase meaning 'outside the power'. At its most fundamental level, judicial review is about ensuring that public authorities act *intra vires*, meaning that they act within their powers. In this wider sense, whenever the court grants a judicial review over an action of a public authority, they are holding that the public authority has acted *ultra vires* in some way making the action unlawful or illegal.

As can be seen, *ultra vires* is a very broad term, but it is from this concept that the courts developed more precise grounds of judicial review. By the time of the *GCHQ* case, the law reached the state where Lord Diplock could explain the grounds of judicial review as 'illegality', 'procedural impropriety', and 'irrationality'. While older cases may simply refer to a public body acting *ultra vires*, the modern approach is that the action of the public authority will be *ultra vires* if court finds one of these three grounds of judicial review. Consequently, the remainder of this chapter will focus on the first of these grounds, illegality.

Lord Diplock explained illegality as follows:

> By 'illegality' as a ground for judicial review, I mean that the decision maker must understand correctly the law that regulates his decision-making power and must give effect to it. Whether he has or not is par excellence a justiciable question to be decided, in the event of a dispute, by those persons, the judges, by whom the judicial power of the state is exercisable.[2]

At first glance it may not be obvious how this differs from the concept of *ultra vires* as it has already been explained. For, if a decision-maker has not understood the law correctly, they are likely to have made a decision for which they lack the necessary legal authority, making the decision *ultra vires*. This is often described as 'simple' or 'narrow' *ultra vires*. However, the key phrase in Lord Diplock's statement is 'the law that regulates his decision-making power'. This means that in addition to whether there is authority for the power or decision in question, the legal context of the power is also relevant in determining *how* the decision should be made.

This in turn begs the question as to what the legal context is for any particular decision. To answer this question, the basis of judicial review needs to be considered. It used to be argued that the courts when developing the principles of judicial review are fulfilling the intention of Parliament, by ensuring that the limits of the powers Parliament grants to

[2] [1984] AC 374, 410.

public authorities are enforced. While this may explain some of the ways in which decisions can be challenged, for example when the question is one of 'simple' or 'narrow' *ultra vires*[3] or errors of law.[4] This does not adequately explain some of the other bases for a successful application for judicial review, which are based on principles developed by the courts. For example, it is established that decisions must take into account only relevant considerations and ignore irrelevant considerations or that powers must only be used for the purposes that Parliament intended. Yet these arguments are less clearly based on the interpretation of legislation as they raise arguments about which the legislation is very often silent. This question is even more pressing when considering the ground of procedural impropriety, which is based more clearly on principles developed by the courts rather than legislation.[5] The *ultra vires* principle would address this concern by arguing that the courts when developing these principles of judicial review are acting on the intention of Parliament. However, it is very difficult for the *ultra vires* principle to explain that Parliament has intended that the powers it grants to public authorities should be exercised according to requirements that it has never explicitly or even implicitly required.

This gave rise to the argument that judicial review was based on principles established by the common law rather than the intention of Parliament.[6] The benefit of this argument is that there is no need to implausibly argue that the principles of judicial review, as developed by the courts, are a manifestation of an intention that Parliament has never clearly articulated through legislation. Yet the argument that judicial review is based on the common law creates a new problem: that this approach does not sit easily with the principle of parliamentary sovereignty. Forsyth explains that:

> what an all powerful Parliament does not prohibit, it must authorise either expressly or impliedly. Likewise if Parliament grants a power to a minister, that minister either acts within those powers or outside those powers. There is no grey area between authorisation and prohibition or between empowerment and the denial of power.[7]

The problem Forsyth highlights is a weakness in the argument for the common law basis of judicial review. If Parliament grants a power to a public authority, with no implicit intention on the part of Parliament that the exercise of that power should be subject to requirements to consider only relevant considerations or be used for its proper purpose, then the courts in placing their own restrictions are taking away power that Parliament is deemed to have intended to give to that public authority. In short, basing judicial review on the common law is difficult to reconcile with parliamentary sovereignty.

The problem with both the *ultra vires* approach and the common law theory can (at least to some extent) be resolved if we take a step back, and think more broadly about the constitution. It is accepted that, in general, Parliament is sovereign. However, as explained in Chapter 4, Parliament is deemed to legislate in a way that fulfils the requirements of the rule of law. This means that the courts often interpret legislation to give effect to the rule of law.[8] It follows that judicial review is also based on this broad principle, with Parliament leaving it to the courts to develop the detailed principles necessary to ensure that powers are exercised by public authorities in a manner that complies with the requirements of the

---

[3] See 11.3.   [4] See 11.4.   [5] This is considered in detail in Chapter 13.

[6] Paul Craig, 'Ultra Vires and the Foundations of Judicial Review' [1998] *Cambridge Law Journal* 63.

[7] Christopher Forsyth, 'Of Fig Leaves and Fairy Tales: The Ultra Vires Doctrine, The Sovereignty of Parliament and Judicial Review' (1996) 55 *Cambridge Law Journal* 122, 133.

[8] See, eg, *R v Lord Chancellor, ex p Witham* [1998] QB 575; *R (Evans) v Attorney-General* [2015] UKSC 21; *R (Unison) v Lord Chancellor* [2017] UKSC 51.

rule of law, preventing discretionary power from descending into arbitrary government. This approach avoids the need to argue that the detailed principles of judicial review are based on an implicit intent of Parliament. The concerns about parliamentary sovereignty raised in the common law approach are avoided because, at least in theory, it remains open to Parliament to legislate contrary to the rule of law or explicitly state that a particular power does not need to be exercised in a way that complies with the rule of law.[9]

This approach explains the structure of the rest of the chapter, which covers the different ways in which a decision can be challenged on the grounds of illegality. As explained in 11.1, these include 'simple' or 'narrow' *ultra vires*, errors of law and or fact, the requirements that the law imposes on the exercise of discretionary power, and the need to only take into account relevant considerations and to use powers for a proper purpose. This may appear to be a rag-bag of different methods to challenge a decision and it is possible that a decision could be challenged through one or more of these ways. However, as explained in this section, the common thread throughout all of these different methods is that they all ensure that public authorities exercise their powers according to the law as intended by Parliament. The final consideration is the Public Sector Equality Duty, which is an example of Parliament placing in statute a general requirement on public authorities to consider issues relating to equality when making decisions. If this requirement has not been fulfilled the decision can be unlawful on this basis alone. The different elements that form the ground of illegality can be seen within Figure 11.1.

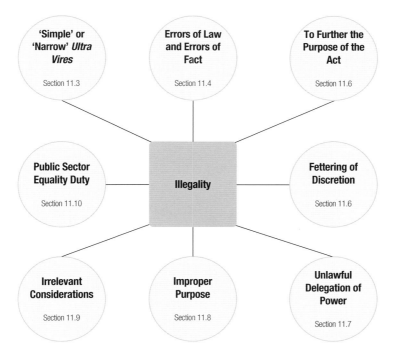

Figure 11.1 The different elements of illegality

---

[9] Christopher Forsyth, 'Of Fig Leaves and Fairy Tales: The Ultra Vires Doctrine, The Sovereignty of Parliament and Judicial Review' (1996) 55 *Cambridge Law Journal* 122, 138.

11.3 'Simple' or 'narrow' *ultra vires*

The most straightforward form of illegality is often described as simple or narrow *ultra vires*. This is when the decision of a public authority is challenged on the basis that the decision is outside the scope of the power under which the public authority made the decision. It necessarily follows that the key consideration in such a case is the statute that granted the power to the public authority to make the decision. This is the most obvious way in which the courts can ensure that the will of Parliament as expressed in statute prevails. As Laws LJ stated in *R (Cart) v Upper Tribunal*:[10]

> If the meaning of statutory text is not controlled by [the courts], it would at length be degraded to nothing more than a matter of opinion. Its scope and content would become muddied and unclear. Public bodies would not, by means of the judicial review jurisdiction, be kept within the confines of their powers prescribed by statute. The very effectiveness of statute law, Parliament's law, requires that none of these things happen.[11]

Often this involves the interpretation of words or phrases which appear straightforward, but this can be more challenging than it first appears. A classic example, *Attorney-General v Fulham Corporation*, revolves around the meaning of the word 'wash-house'.

Case in depth: *Attorney-General v Fulham Corporation* [1921] 1 Ch 440

Under the Baths and Wash-Houses Acts 1846–1878, Fulham Corporation had the power to establish 'baths, wash-houses and open bathing spaces'. The defendants had created a scheme that allowed people to leave their clothes at the facility which were then washed by the employees of the defendant. The issue was whether this was within the scope of the Act which only allowed the defendant to establish a 'wash-house'. Sargant J held that under the legislation, 'wash-house' meant that the defendant could only provide facilities for people to wash their own clothes and not to provide a service whereby clothes were washed for them. Essentially the defendant had established a laundry service, which was beyond the scope of the term 'wash-house'. This meant that Fulham Corporation lacked the legal authority to provide the laundry service they had been offering.

A similar case is *White and Collins v Minister of Health*[12] which considered the meaning of the word 'park'. Under section 74 of the Housing Act 1936, a local authority could purchase land through compulsory purchase orders to provide social housing. This was subject to a restriction in section 75 that any land that formed 'part of any park' could not be purchased under section 74. The local authority had made a compulsory purchase order under section 74 covering land that was used for grazing. The owner of the land challenged the compulsory purchase order on the basis that the land formed part of a park and so could not be compulsory purchased under section 74.

Luxmore LJ considered that the issue raised was whether the word 'park' was used in a technical sense meaning 'a tract of land enclosed and privileged for wild beasts of chase

---

[10] *R (Cart) v Upper Tribunal* [2009] EWHC 3052 (Admin) [38].
[11] Ibid.   [12] [1939] 2 KB 838.

by the "Monarch's grant or by prescription"', or whether the word 'park' was used in a more everyday sense as 'a large ornamental piece of ground usually comprising woodland and pasture, attached to or surrounding a country house or mansion and used for recreation, and often for keeping deer, cattle or sheep'.[13] Luxmore LJ held that 'park' had been used in other statutes in its ordinary sense and that was clearly the case here.[14] Because 'park' was used in its more everyday sense, this meant that the purchase order under section 74 was invalid.

Both *Attorney-General v Fulham Corporation* and *White and Collins v Minister of Health* are clear examples of the courts ensuring that the actions of public authorities are within the scope of the powers they have been granted. Should the courts be too restrictive, it is always open to Parliament to amend the legislation and make their intentions clearer.

11.4 Errors of law and errors of fact

The next way in which the intention of Parliament is maintained is when the courts address errors of law and errors of fact. As regards errors of law, this is also an exercise of statutory interpretation, but is more specific than simple *ultra vires* discussed in 11.3 as it is focused on the scope of the decision-making power that the public authority has. Central to this is the concept of 'jurisdiction'. This is a word which has caused particular difficulty in the case law.

As Wade and Forsyth state, '"jurisdiction" is a hard-worked word'.[15] Particularly in older cases, 'jurisdiction' is used instead of the language of *ultra vires*. In this context, jurisdiction is referring to a power and so acting outside jurisdiction is similar to acting *ultra vires*. However, in a more modern context, 'jurisdiction' can mean the 'power to decide', or 'power to determine'. This is more intuitive when the decision has been made by a tribunal or other decision-making body as the question is whether the body has the power to make the decision in the first place.

This section will consider errors of law first, after which errors of fact will be discussed.

11.4.1 Can the tribunal make the decision?

As we have discussed, the most natural use of 'jurisdiction' is deciding whether the decision-making body has the power to decide the issue. This is usually a preliminary issue before moving on to decide the issue in question. Necessarily, the decision-maker must come to an initial decision about the scope of its powers, but the rule of law requires that such a decision cannot be conclusive. In *R v Fulham, Hammersmith and Kensington Rent Tribunal, ex p Zerek*,[16] Lord Goddard CJ stated 'that if a certain state of facts has to exist before an inferior tribunal have jurisdiction, they can inquire into the facts in order to decide whether or not they have jurisdiction, but cannot give themselves jurisdiction by a wrong decision upon them'.[17] This means that tribunals and other decision-makers acting under statute have to come to a decision as to the scope of their powers, but this is subject to the overriding review of the courts. If a decision-maker takes a broader view

---

[13] Ibid 852.   [14] Ibid.
[15] HWR Wade and CF Forsyth, *Administrative Law* (11th edn, OUP 2014) 212.
[16] [1951] 2 KB 1.   [17] Ibid 6.

than the courts then they are acting in excess of their jurisdiction and any decisions made outside the scope of their decision-making power will be unlawful.

If the courts lacked this power to review then tribunals could decide that they have jurisdiction in excess of what was intended by Parliament, but there would be little chance of correcting this. The courts need to have overall supervision of questions of jurisdiction such as this to ensure that tribunals and other decision-makers remain within the scope of their powers.

11.4.2 Error of law within and outside jurisdiction

'Jurisdiction' in the other sense referred to in 11.4.1 is when the term is used instead of 'ultra vires' to mean when a decision-maker has made an error of law. The law adopted a distinction (which was difficult to apply in practice) between errors of law which remained *within* jurisdiction and those errors of law that were *outside* jurisdiction. The courts could only intervene with errors of law that took the tribunal or decision-maker *outside* their jurisdiction. However, this distinction has now largely been abolished since *Anisminic Ltd v Foreign Compensation Commission*,[18] with all errors of law now taking the decision-maker or tribunal *outside* their jurisdiction.

Case in depth: *Anisminic Ltd v Foreign Compensation Commission* [1969] 2 AC 147

The Foreign Compensation Commission rejected a claim for compensation from Anisminic Ltd for their loss of property during the Suez Crisis in 1956. The Commission rejected the claim on the basis that the successor in title did not have British nationality. The Act establishing the Commission stated at section 4(4) that any 'determination by the commission of any application made . . . shall not be called in question in any court of law'. However, the House of Lords held that the Commission had misinterpreted the statute regarding the nationality of successors of title and that this requirement did not apply in this case. Consequently, the Commission had acted outside its jurisdiction as it had made an error of law. This meant that the courts could judicially review the decision.

As explained by Lord Carnwath in *R (Privacy International) v Investigatory Powers Tribunal*, it was only in later cases that the full implications of *Anisminic* became clear.[19] In *O'Reilly v Mackman*, Lord Diplock explained that *Anisminic* was a 'breakthrough' which had decided that all errors of law made by a tribunal were subject to judicial review.[20] As further explained by Lord Browne-Wilkinson in *R v Hull University Visitor, Ex Page*, after '*Anisminic* . . . it was to be taken that Parliament had only conferred the decision-making power on the basis that it was to be exercised on the correct legal basis: a misdirection in law in making the decision therefore rendered the decision ultra vires'.[21] There was no scope for any distinction between an error within or outside jurisdiction, so that any decision made on the basis of an error of law was *ultra vires*.

---

[18] [1969] 2 AC 147.   [19] [2019] UKSC 22; [2019] 2 WLR 1219 [52].
[20] [1983] 2 AC 237, 278.   [21] [1993] AC 682, 701.

This conclusion also has a sound theoretical basis. In *Hull University Visitor, ex p Page*, Lord Browne-Wilkinson stated that 'the fundamental principle is that the courts will intervene to ensure that the powers of public decision-making bodies are exercised lawfully . . . [and] on the decision maker on the underlying assumption that the powers are to be exercised only within the jurisdiction conferred'.[22] More broadly, as explained by Lord Carnwath in *Privacy International*, this is consistent with the inherent supervisory jurisdiction of the High Court, which can ensure that errors of law are corrected, so enhancing the rule of law, and ensuring that the law as laid down by Parliament is complied with.[23]

 Discussing the problem

Consider the scenario outlined at the start of the chapter. Given section 2(4) of the 2020 Act, can any of the three decisions made by Nanchester District Council be challenged on the grounds before the courts?

Despite the wording of section 2(4), *Anisminic* and the discussion in 11.4 show that the courts are extremely reluctant to simply give effect to provisions such as these which are said to 'oust' the ability of the courts to review decisions made under the Act. Applying the reasoning of *Anisminic*, the argument here would be that despite section 2(4), the courts retain the ability to ensure that public bodies act within their jurisdiction. If the Council has made an error of law they would then be outside their jurisdiction. Consequently, the courts could review the decisions that the Council has made on the basis that they have made an error of law, which has taken them outside their jurisdiction.

11.4.3 Errors of fact

In addition to an error of law, it is possible for a public authority to make a decision based on an error of fact. Generally, in judicial review, the courts are reluctant to investigate claimed errors of fact, as Devlin J stated in *R v Fulham, Hammersmith and Kensington Rent Tribunal ex p Zerek*:

> Where the question of jurisdiction turns solely on a disputed point of law, it is obviously convenient that the court should determine it then and there. But where the dispute turns on a question of fact, about which there is a conflict of evidence, the court will generally decline to interfere.[24]

As long as the public authority making the decision has made a decision within their powers, then the courts will rarely intervene. This will particularly be the case if the decision-maker has arrived at the decision after considering conflicting evidence that addresses the relevant facts. This is because, at this point, the argument of the claimant seeking to challenge the decision starts to resemble an appeal rather than a judicial review claim.

---

[22] [1993] AC 682, 701.
[23] [2019] UKSC 22 [132]. *Privacy International* is also discussed in 10.2.2.
[24] [1951] 2 KB 1, 11.

11.4.4 **No supporting evidence**

However, this approach only extends so far. If the decision-maker reaches a decision which is unsupportable on the evidence before them, then the courts are minded to intervene as this is an abuse of power. The following case provides a rare example.

> **Case in depth: *Lee v Showmen's Guild of Great Britain* [1952] 2 QB 329**
>
> The committee of a guild of travelling showmen who performed at fairgrounds found that one of its workers, Lee, had breached a rule that meant one member of the guild cannot compete unfairly with another member. Lee was given a fine, which he refused to pay, and he was eventually expelled. Lee challenged this decision on the basis that his actions could not have been unfair competition, meaning that his fine and expulsion were void. The Court of Appeal agreed, stating that a question of fact should usually be decided by the decision-maker rather the courts.
>
> However, as Denning LJ stated, if:
>
>> the facts were not reasonably capable of being held to be a breach, and yet the committee held them to be a breach, then the only inference is that the committee have misconstrued the rules and exceeded their jurisdiction. The proposition is sometimes stated in the form that the court can interfere if there was no evidence to support the finding of the committee; but that only means that the facts were not reasonably capable of supporting the finding.[25]

This also serves as an example of how the three grounds of judicial review as explained by Lord Diplock in *GCHQ* can merge into each other, as there is a distinct similarity here to the ground of irrationality which is discussed in more detail in Chapter 12.

11.4.5 **Precedent fact**

The courts can treat errors of fact differently depending on the circumstances. First, there is the concept of a precedent fact, which is a fact which must be correct in order for the power to be validly exercised. An oft-cited example is the case of *R v Home Secretary, ex p Khawaja*[26] which considered the power, granted by section 33 of the Immigration Act 1971, of the Home Secretary to deport an 'illegal entrant'. The court held that this meant that it was a matter for judicial review as to whether a person deported under this power has entered the country illegally or not, as the valid use of the power depended on that fact. In this case, the reasonable belief of the immigration officer that the claimant was an 'illegal entrant' was not a sufficient basis on which to use the power. The status of the claimant as an 'illegal entrant' needed to be ascertained with some evidential proof before the power of deportation could be used. As Lord Scarman stated: '[where] the exercise of executive power depends upon the precedent establishment of an objective fact, the courts will decide whether the requirement has been satisfied.'[27] Decisions such as this ensure that powers granted by legislation are only used for the purposes and in the circumstances Parliament intended.

---

[25] [1952] 2 QB 329, 345.   [26] [1984] AC 74.   [27] Ibid 110.

11.4.6 Material error of fact

In addition to the courts intervening when there is no factual basis for the decision made, the courts have also developed the ability to intervene when the decision-maker has acted on a misunderstanding or error of a fact. The classic authority is the *Tameside* case.

> ### Case in depth: *Secretary of State for Education and Science v Tameside Metropolitan Borough Council* [1977] AC 1014
>
> Under section 68 of the Education Act 1944, the Secretary of State had the power to intervene 'if satisfied' that an education authority was 'acting unreasonably'. When it was under the control of the Labour Party, Tameside MBC in November 1975 decided to convert all secondary schools in the area to comprehensive schools (open to all abilities), meaning that the three grammar schools (which would only take pupils who had passed the 11 plus exam) would be converted. Yet this proved controversial amongst voters and in the council elections held in May 1976 the Conservatives were elected on a pledge to reconsider this decision and retain two grammar schools. When the Council, now under the control of the Conservatives, informed the Secretary of State of a Labour Government of their intention, he sought to intervene using section 68 on the basis that he was satisfied that the council were acting unreasonably. The Council challenged the Secretary of State's intervention.
>
> The court took the view that it could decide whether the Council were acting unreasonably. Lord Wilberforce held that if 'a judgment requires, before it can be made, the existence of some facts, then, although the evaluation of those facts is for the Secretary of State alone, the court must inquire whether those facts exist'.[28] The court made clear that the Secretary of State could only intervene if the Council were acting 'unreasonably'. The court took the view that unreasonably meant the decision-maker had to be not only wrong, but wrong to the extent that no reasonable person could take that view.[29]
>
> The Secretary of State was of the view that reorganizing the schools would lead to chaos, in particular when selecting the pupils who were to attend the two retained grammar schools. However, this was rejected by the House of Lords on the basis that this conclusion was based on a misconception of the facts. Although there may be some disruption, it was still possible to select pupils for the two grammar schools using a variety of methods and the Council had a duty to implement their policy for which they had been elected. Consequently, the Secretary had not directed himself properly as to the facts available as, on a proper consideration of the facts, it could not be said that the Council were acting unreasonably.

 Pause for reflection

In *Politics of the Judiciary*, Griffith took the view that in cases such as *Tameside*, 'one is often left with a feeling . . . that judges rely almost entirely on their own sense of justice or on their own personal conception of what is best'.[30] Essentially, did the courts manipulate the meaning of 'unreasonably' to allow them to conclude that the Secretary of State was acting outside his powers and so acting unlawfully?

---

[28] [1977] AC 1014, 1024.
[29] Ibid 1024. The concept of unreasonableness is discussed in Chapter 12.
[30] JAG Griffith, *The Politics of the Judiciary* (5th edn, Fontana Press 1996) 112.

11.4.7 Mistake of fact as a distinct ground of judicial review

In *E v Secretary of State for the Home Department*[31] an application for asylum in the UK was refused by the Secretary of State on the basis that the applicant did not have a well-founded fear of persecution. The decision was confirmed by the Immigration and Asylum Tribunal. The applicant sought leave to appeal on a point of law, and then during the appeal to rely on new evidence to show that the decision was made on the basis of a mistake of fact. The Court of Appeal, summarizing the law, held that 'the time has now come to accept that a mistake of fact is a separate head of challenge in an appeal on a point of law',[32] finding that a decision on a mistake of fact can be overturned if the four ingredients are present:

(1) There must have been a mistake as to an existing fact, including a mistake as to the availability of evidence on a particular matter.

(2) The fact or evidence must have been 'established', in the sense that it was uncontentious and objectively verifiable.

(3) The appellant (or his advisers) must not been have been responsible for the mistake.

(4) The mistake must have played a material (not necessarily decisive) part in the tribunal's reasoning.[33]

As Forsyth explains, these ingredients do not include the requirement that the mistake of fact generated unfairness as such, although that is a likely consequence of when all four ingredients are met.[34] In addition, ingredient (2) considerably limits the scope of this ground of review as the error that *E* seeks to capture relates to questions that deliver right or wrong answers. The fact in question can usually be proven objectively rather than requiring some form of evaluative judgment being made. Effectively, if the fact in question requires an exercise of judgment, then the decision-maker or court will remain within their jurisdiction.[35]

11.4.8 Summary on errors of law and fact

In summary, this section has shown how the courts are generally reluctant to intervene when an application for judicial review is based on an error of fact. However, the courts will consider errors of fact when there is no factual basis to support the decision made. There is some similarity between the concepts of precedent fact and material fact in that if the exercise of a power is dependent on particular key facts being correct, then the courts reserve the right to consider whether those facts exist. The overall effect of decisions discussed in this section is to ensure that the rule of law and the intentions of Parliament are upheld as the executive is prevented from reserving for itself powers which go beyond the scope of the statute that creates their decision-making power. Both with errors of law and fact, the courts are ensuring that the power in question can only be exercised when Parliament has intended for it to arise.

---

[31] [2004] EWCA Civ 49 [66].   [32] Ibid.   [33] Ibid.

[34] Christopher Forsyth, 'Error of Fact Revisited: Waiting for the "Anisminic Moment"' (2018) 23 *Judicial Review* 1, 4, citing *Chalfont St Peter Parish Council v Chiltern District Council* [2014] EWCA Civ 1393 [100].

[35] Ibid 5. A discussion of the types of matters that give rise to an error of fact can be found in Brooke LJ's discussion in *R (Iran) and others v Secretary of State for the Home Department* [2005] EWCA Civ 982.

11.5 **Discretionary powers**

The discussion in the previous two sections can be explained as examples of the courts interpreting statute to ensure that public authorities act within the scope of powers granted to them by Parliament. With discretionary powers the issue is different. This is because the decision-maker will be allowed not only to decide whether to exercise the power or not, but if the power is exercised, the decision-maker may have freedom to exercise it in different ways. Consequently, the cases in this area are examples of when the courts have developed principles to constrain the exercise of discretionary power and, as discussed in 11.2, these principles are not immediately apparent on reading the statute. Instead, the courts have developed this area of law to ensure that the existence of discretionary power is consistent with the rule of law.

11.5.1 **The importance of discretionary powers**

To understand the importance of discretionary powers within administrative law, it is necessary to consider how the role of government has changed over time. Famously, the historian AJP Taylor said that '[until] August 1914, a sensible law-abiding Englishman could pass through life and hardly notice the existence of the state, beyond the post office and policemen'.[36] Yet, as Wade and Forsyth state, such a sensible law-abiding Englishman could not 'have been a very observant citizen',[37] because already by 1914 the state employed many people to carry out the various functions it had acquired by law. These included 'the state schoolteacher, the national insurance officer, the job centre, the sanitary and factory inspectors'.[38] This accelerated after the Second World War, as the Labour Government led by Prime Minister Clement Attlee set about creating the modern welfare state, including creating the National Health Service.[39] An eventual response to this was Thatcherism, with the aim of 'rolling back the frontiers of the State',[40] seeking to reverse this trend. This was most clearly shown by privatizing many functions of government. Yet arguably this had the perverse effect of increasing state intervention as the newly privatized industries required powerful regulators to ensure fair competition.[41] Although the policies of austerity that have prevailed since the 2008 financial crash have seen the government shrink in size, the government continues to play a significant role in almost every aspect of life.

The government will make such interventions by implementing policies developed in government departments, for which Parliament has enacted the necessary legislation. It follows that it is impossible for Parliament to envisage every circumstance in which these policies are to be applied. Consequently, 'legislation may set out the general policy and establish the central principles and criteria by reference to which the policy is to be operated'.[42] By necessity, this means that discretion will have to be given to those

[36] AJP Taylor, *English History* (Oxford 1965) 1.
[37] HWR Wade and CF Forsyth, *Administrative Law* (11th edn, OUP 2014) 3.   [38] Ibid 3.
[39] National Health Service Act 1948.
[40] Nigel Lawson, 'The New Conservatism: Lecture to the Bow Group' 4 August 1980, http://www.margaretthatcher.org/commentary/displaydocument.asp?docid=109505.
[41] Jeffrey Jowell, 'Administrative Law' in Vernon Bogdanor (ed), *The British Constitution in the Twentieth Century* (OUP 2003).
[42] Mark Elliott, *Beatson Matthews and Elliott's Administrative Law* (4th edn, OUP 2010) 113.

who actually make the individual decisions, whether they are ministers, civil servants, or members of a government agency set up to implement a policy. This means that as the role of the state has increased the use of discretionary power has 'exploded'.[43] Given its importance in decision-making, it is necessary to consider what discretionary powers are and their advantages and disadvantages before considering how the courts review how they are exercised.

11.5.2 What is a discretionary power?

A discretionary power is a power granted to officials, who have flexibility when deciding how to exercise that power. In particular, they can take into account a range of factors when making decisions. Usually, this will be applying standards or guidelines that set out how decisions under the power are meant to be made, but the official may have some discretion as to how those guidelines will apply in any individual case. As Galligan states, central to the idea of discretion is:

> the idea that within a defined area of power the official must reflect upon its purposes, and then settle upon the policies and strategies for achieving them. There may be discretion in identifying and interpreting purposes; there may also be discretion as to the policies, standards, and procedures to be followed in achieving these purposes.[44]

The key benefit of discretionary powers is that they allow for the decision-maker to be flexible in how they make decisions. This means that decision-makers may consider factors that Parliament had not even contemplated when enacting the legislation.

 Counterpoint: The problem with discretionary power

While discretion is necessary in the modern state given its role in almost every area of law, discretionary power can be problematic. This is explained by Lord Bingham in his book *The Rule of Law*:

> Suppose, hypothetically, that Parliament has enacted a scheme for the making of grants to persons suffering from a disability, stipulating that decisions on eligibility shall be made by local officers responsible for social security, and shall not be challengeable in the courts. Mrs Smith, who lives in Durham, believes herself to be suffering from disability and applies to her local officer for a grant, giving the reasons for her belief that she is entitled. He refuses her application, giving no reasons. She presses to know why she has been refused. The officer replies that he considers her to be ineligible because (a) her disability is mental, not physical; (b) she has not suffered from her disability for long enough to qualify for a grant; and (c) her disability is not sufficiently severe. Mrs Smith, . . . asks the officer for the grounds on which he excludes mental disability, what

→

---

[43] Ibid.
[44] DJ Galligan, *Discretionary Powers: A Legal Study of Official Discretion* (OUP 1990) 21–2.

→

period is laid down as the qualifying period, and what is the standard severity required for a grant. She points out that her sister, Mrs Brown, who lives in Newcastle, is in a very similar position to herself, and has received a grant. The officer replies, declining to answer Mrs Smith's questions but saying that the decision is one for him alone and he has decided she shall not receive a grant. As for her sister, Mrs Brown is in Newcastle, the officer points out that he is not responsible for that area, and if the officer there takes a different view, so be it.[45]

It is clear that a major problem with discretionary power is that it can lead to inconsistent decision-making and this can generate a sense of grievance for those in the position of Mrs Smith.

As Lord Bingham states, the real issue here is that 'in the absence of an effective means to challenge the Durham officer's decision such a regime would plainly violate the rule of law. Mrs Smith's entitlement should be governed by law, not the arbitrary whim of an official'.[46] Consequently, it is critical that the exercise of discretionary power can be challenged before the courts to ensure that discretionary power has been exercised in accordance with the law.

The following section contrasts a policy which initially gave considerable discretion to decision-makers, but was later changed to remove all discretion from decision-makers. This allows us to consider in more detail the advantages and disadvantages of discretionary powers.

11.5.3 Should powers be discretionary? The advantages and disadvantages

There are many examples of discretionary powers across many different policy areas, ranging from welfare to education and planning. The following example comes from immigration law and is a useful example as one version of the rules, allowing for a significant degree of discretion on the part of the decision-maker, was replaced by rules which gave almost no discretion to decision-makers. Under the pre-2008 Immigration Rules, if a non-EU national wanted to enter the UK as a student they had to show that they had been accepted onto a course at a UK university and comply with several additional conditions. These included the following requirements, as set down by the Immigration Rules.

The requirements to be met by a person seeking leave to enter the United Kingdom as a student are that he: . . .

(vi) intends to leave the United Kingdom at the end of his studies; and

(vii) does not intend to engage in business or to take employment, except part-time or vacation work undertaken with the consent of the Secretary of State; and

(viii) is able to meet the costs of his course and accommodation and the maintenance of himself and any dependants without taking employment or engaging in business or having recourse to public funds. . .[47]

---

[45] Tom Bingham, *The Rule of Law* (Penguin 2011) 49–50.   [46] Ibid.
[47] Immigration Rules 2007, r 57.

As the House of Commons Home Affairs Select Committee found, these conditions leave 'considerable discretion to the decision-maker'.[48] For example, what is meant by 'intending to leave at the end of his studies'? Does this mean the student must leave after the last lecture, or the last exam, or graduation? Similarly, what is meant by meeting 'the costs of his course and accommodation and maintenance of himself'? What sort of sum is sufficient here?

Clearly, rules framed in this way are capable of being interpreted in a flexible manner and allow the decision-maker to consider the circumstances of the individual case. For example, as the cost of living is generally higher in London than in other parts of the country, a decision-maker is more likely to require a high amount for a student studying in London than elsewhere.[49] Rules such as this also allow for the sensitivities of a case to be considered. Arguably, under these rules a student receiving medical treatment towards the end of their course could remain after the conclusion of their studies, as long as they retained an intention to leave the country. A further advantage of rules of this nature is that they are relatively easy to draft and are short as the real decisions are made by the decision-makers who consider each case.

Yet, with an example such as this, the disadvantages of giving discretion should also be apparent. The imprecision inherent in these rules means that inconsistent decisions can be made, particularly when the government agency or department is making thousands of decisions. As described in the following sections, the law requires that discretion is genuinely exercised with each case being considered. This can be time-consuming and costly, making the administration of government inefficient. Furthermore, without a clear objective basis behind a decision, the decision-maker could be subject to criticisms of making decisions arbitrarily. This lack of objectivity can lead to decisions challenged solely on the basis of a differing interpretation of the rules. These difficulties were expressed by the Home Office, who stated that the Immigration Rules were not straightforward to administer and often involved assessing applicants' intentions, which is a subjective task.[50] Overall, the rules were thought to be inefficient for both the Home Office, who administered the rules, and for those who applied for entry into the UK.[51]

These concerns led to the introduction of a new points-based system, with the Immigration Rules being updated to reflect this. The fundamental aim of the points system was to introduce objective criteria, such as academic qualifications, age, and earnings, that left no room for decision-makers to exercise their own judgement or discretion.

For example, under the new rules, an immigration officer no longer has any discretion over what is a sufficient amount for a student entering the UK. Instead, a student seeking entry into the UK is required to show evidence that they have funds covering the fees for the first year of the course, plus either £1,265 (if in London) or £1,015 (elsewhere) to cover their living costs for the each of the first nine months of the course.[52] These requirements are extremely precise and rigid. While clearly such rigid rules address the concerns

[48] House of Commons Home Affairs Select Committee, *Immigration Control* (HC 2005–06, 775) para 100.

[49] Office for National Statistics, 'Family spending in the UK: financial year ending March 2016' (16 February 2017, Office for National Statistics), https://www.ons.gov.uk/peoplepopulation andcommunity/personalandhouseholdfinances/expenditure/bulletins/familyspendingintheuk/ financialyearendingmarch2016.

[50] Home Office, *A Points-based System: Making Migration Work for Britain* (Cm 6741, 2006) 7.

[51] Ibid.

[52] The rules also provide for how this evidence is provided and the rules also differ if the course is for a year or less.

that flow from more open ended rules such as those just highlighted, this approach creates further difficulties. First, as stated in *BN v Secretary of State for the Home Department (Article 8—Post Study Work) Kenya*,[53] injustice can arise:

> from Rules in which any opportunity for discretion has been removed. This kind of situation cries out for somebody to take a sensible and common sense approach, looking at the overall aim of the Rule in question. As was clear at the hearing, however, any opportunity to exercise discretion has been removed at all stages of the system.[54]

Secondly, to remove any discretion from a set of rules, the rules have to become extraordinarily detailed, which increases their complexity. Court of Appeal judges have complained that even for lawyers the rules are not easy to understand. In *Singh v Secretary of State for the Home Department*,[55] Underhill LJ stated:

> I fully recognise that the Immigration Rules, which have to deal with a wide variety of circumstances and may have as regards some issues to make very detailed provision, will never be 'easy, plain and short' . . . [T]he aim should be that the Rules should be readily understandable by ordinary lawyers and other advisers. That is not the case at present.[56]

Pause for reflection

Having seen the different approaches taken between the old and the new Immigration Rules, which approach do you prefer and why?

Discussing the problem

Look again at the problem scenario set out at the start of the chapter. Can you think why Nanchester District Council has been given a *discretionary* power to grant licences?

Parliament has decided that it is unable to decide which licences should be approved and that local councils will be much better placed to decide which stalls will be suitable for their markets that serve their local communities. A market in the middle of a large city will be likely to have different demands to a market in the centre of a small town. Parliament, in giving this discretion to local councils, has allowed each council to make their own assessment of their needs. In theory, local councils should be more sensitive to the needs of their local community than MPs attempting to make the same decisions for markets across the country.

Clearly, if a judicial review claim involves a precise rule which allows little room for discretion, then the case will be one of narrow *ultra vires* or illegality as explained in 11.3. However, the following section will focus on discretionary rules and the basis on which the exercise of discretionary rules can be challenged. It must be remembered that this remains within the heading of illegality, as the fundamental role of the courts is to ensure that the decision-maker must understand correctly the law that regulates his

---

[53] [2010] UKUT 162 (IAC). [54] Ibid [18]. [55] [2015] EWCA Civ 74. [56] Ibid [59].

decision-making power and give effect to it. This reflects the fundamental constitutional principles explained in 11.2 that the courts are upholding the intention of Parliament and ensuring that government acts according to the law. As we will see in the next section, a key consideration is the statute that creates the discretionary power in the first place. Other factors include ensuring that the decision-maker has in substance exercised their discretion and not allowed themselves to be improperly influenced by someone else. Similarly, in 11.7, who can exercise the discretionary power is considered.

11.6 Controlling discretionary power

Having established what a discretionary power is, the important question for judicial review is to consider how the exercise of discretionary powers can be controlled by the courts. As stated by Dicey, the rule of law requires 'the absolute supremacy of regular law as opposed to the influence of arbitrary power, and excludes the existence of arbitrariness, of prerogative or even of wide discretionary authority on the part of the government'.[57] Clearly, Dicey preferred the certainty of the regular law, as opposed to 'arbitrariness' or 'wide discretionary authority'. There is a danger that Dicey's argument can be taken to the extreme and hold that there should not be any scope for discretion, but as shown, this raises the possibility of injustice. But as Lord Bingham states, it must be clear that the purpose of rule of law in this context is to avoid arbitrary government. It aims to achieve this by requiring that 'no discretion should be unconstrained so as to be potentially arbitrary. No discretion may be legally unfettered'.[58] Consequently, the rest of this section highlights how the law prevents arbitrary government by considering controlling the exercise of discretionary powers granted to it by Parliament. The two key factors to consider are the purpose of the relevant legislation and that the decision-maker should not 'fetter' their discretion but make a genuine decision as required by the law. Both of these are considered in turn.

11.6.1 Purpose of the Act

One of the basic requirements developed by the courts is that the decision-maker must exercise their discretion to further, rather than undermine, the purpose of the Act of Parliament that gives rise to the discretionary power in the first place. This is the case even if the Act of Parliament in question appears to give the decision-maker complete discretion. The following case provides an example.

Case in depth: *Padfield v Minister of Agriculture, Fisheries and Food* **[1968] AC 997**

This case was literally an argument over the price of milk. At the time, producers of milk could only sell their milk to the Milk Marketing Board. The Board paid a fixed price for the milk and this fixed price was set according to which region the milk was supplied from. Milk producers

→

---

[57] AV Dicey, *Introduction to the Study of the Law of the Constitution* (8th edn, 1915, reprinted Liberty Fund 1982) 120.

[58] Tom Bingham, *The Rule of Law* (Penguin 2011) 54.

→

in the South East argued that the price they received was too low, believing that being near London they could get a higher price on the open market. However, the Milk Marketing Board disagreed and refused to increase their prices. Consequently, the producers complained to the Minister under the Agricultural Marketing Act 1958. Section 19 of that Act required a committee to investigate any complaint the Minister 'in any case so directs'. The Minister refused to direct the committee to investigate the complaint. The Minister argued that under the Act they had total discretion over whether to refer a complaint. The House of Lords rejected that argument.

Lord Reid stated that Parliament 'must have conferred the discretion with the intention that it should be used to promote the policy and objects of the Act'.[59] Furthermore, determining what the policy and objects of the Act are is a matter for the courts by considering the Act as a whole. Lord Reid held that in this case the purpose of the Agricultural Marketing Act 1958 was to provide 'machinery for investigating and establishing whether the scheme is operating or the board is acting in a manner contrary to the public interest'.[60] The minister had refused to forward the complaint because of the potential political embarrassment he may face should the committee uphold the complaint and the Minister chose not to give effect to this decision. The court interpreted section 19 so that the Minister did not have a total discretion over whether or not to forward complaints to the committee, but had to forward the overall purpose of the Act. In this case, by choosing not to forward the complaint, the Minister was frustrating the very purpose of the Act which was to ensure that complaints from milk producers could be considered by the board.

A key principle from *Padfield* is that the courts are seeking to interpret and then enforce the intention of Parliament. If that intention is not being fulfilled then the courts are likely to intervene. Consequently, discretionary powers have to be exercised to further the object and purpose of the Act. As the following section discusses, this also extends not only to the decision itself, but to how the decision has been made.

 Discussing the question

Consider the scenario outlined at the start of the chapter. Could the principle of *Padfield* be applied to any of the rejected applications?

On the face of it, the rejection of Kendrick's licence could appear to be the use of discretion in a manner that does not advance the purpose of the Act. The purpose of the Act is to allow local councils to run food markets. However, Kendrick's application has been rejected on the basis that his stall will not offer non-food products. The principle of *Padfield* could be used to argue that the Council are not furthering the purpose of the Act by rejecting Kendrick's application on this basis.

[59] [1968] AC 997, 1030.   [60] Ibid.

11.6.2 Fettering discretion

In addition to being exercised in accordance with the purpose of the Act granting the power, a discretionary power must not be 'fettered'. In this context 'fettered' means restricting the discretionary power in some way so that the decision-maker is no longer genuinely exercising their discretion. This means that all the relevant circumstances must be considered by the person or government agency charged by Parliament to make the decision in question.

There are several ways in which a decision may not be a genuine exercise of discretion; these include following a policy as binding rule, allowing someone else not authorized by statute to make the decision, or when the decision-maker has allowed someone else to dictate to them what decision they should make. These can be described in turn as fettering discretion through policy, abdication, and dictation. Each of these are three distinct ways in which discretion can be fettered, but the discussion will highlight how these categories can overlap and one set of facts could easily fall within more than one category. The unifying principle between the three ways to fetter discretion is that the public authority granted the discretion by Parliament has not made a *genuine* exercise of *their* discretion. In this way, this ensures that decision-makers fulfil the task they have been set by Parliament and do not allow someone else to complete that task for them. In the same manner as the other aspects of illegality described in this chapter, the courts are seeking to ensure that the intention of Parliament is enforced.

Policy

If a decision-maker has been given a discretionary power, it may choose to adopt a policy as guidance as to how that power can be exercised. This can overcome some of the disadvantages of discretionary power. It ensures that there is some consistency in decision-making, particularly when a large government department is making thousands of similar decisions. A policy should also ensure that a decision-maker does not have to make individual enquiries each time a new decision is needed. However, there is a risk that a policy can become a fixed rule, which if applied rigidly could mean that the decision-maker is no longer exercising their discretion when making individual decisions. The following case discusses the right balance to strike.

Case in depth: *British Oxygen Company Ltd v Minister of Technology* **[1971] AC 610**

The Board of Trade operated a scheme of discretionary grants to allow companies to invest in their businesses. The Board adopted a policy that grants would not be paid for items costing less than £25 each. British Oxygen had spent over £4 million on gas cylinders that cost £20 each and applied for a grant to cover the cost. Their application was rejected by the Board, as it did not comply with their policy. The House of Lords held that while the Board could adopt a policy it could not be applied rigidly to every application. Lord Reid explained that generally:

> anyone who has to exercise a statutory discretion must not 'shut his ears to an application' . . . I do not think there is any great difference between a policy and a rule.

→

> There may be cases where an officer or authority ought to listen to a substantial argument reasonably presented urging a change of policy. What the authority must not do is to refuse to listen at all. But a Ministry or large authority may have had to deal already with a multitude of similar applications and then they will almost certainly have evolved a policy so precise that it could well be called a rule. There can be no objection to that, provided the authority is always willing to listen to anyone with something new to say . . .[61]

Because the Board of Trade had considered the application of British Oxygen and their representations, but still refused the grant, the decision of the Board was upheld. This was because it was still an exercise of their discretion, as the Board did not just blindly follow their policy, but had listened to what British Oxygen had said. However, in *R (on the application of S) v Secretary of State for the Home Department* the very policy itself was so severe as to be a fettering of discretion.[62]

Case in depth: *R (on the application of S) v Secretary of State for the Home Department* [2007] EWCA Civ 546

An Afghan national claimed asylum in 1999. In January 2001, the Home Office, the government department responsible for processing asylum applications, had decided to delay considering claims made before January 2001. This was in order to meet a target agreed with the Treasury (the government department responsible for public spending and funding the Home Office) to process 60 per cent of new claims within sixty-one days. Carnwath LJ considered this to be a 'textbook case' of an unlawful fettering of discretion.[63] The Home Office had adopted a blanket policy which prevented it from considering individual cases on their merits. The effect of the policy was to 'defer a whole class of applications without good reasons and without consideration of the effects on the applicants'.[64]

Considering both *R (on the application of S)* and *British Oxygen*, the key consideration is that a policy adopted by a decision-maker must retain some flexibility so that when making decisions it remains an exercise of discretion.

Abdication

It is also possible for discretion to be fettered by being 'abdicated'. This means that instead of the decision-maker making the decision itself, it has chosen to follow the decision of another decision-maker. It may be that in form the decision has been made by the appropriate decision-maker, but in substance the decision-maker has allowed the decision to be made by someone else who has not been authorized to make the decision. Effectively, the appropriate decision-maker has abdicated their decision-making power to someone else. There is a clear overlap here between abdication and unlawfully delegating a discretionary power, discussed in 11.7.

---

[61] [1971] AC 610, 625.   [62] [2007] EWCA Civ 546.   [63] Ibid [50].   [64] Ibid.

R (on the application of S) v Secretary of State for the Home Department is discussed above and is also an example of abdication. As stated by Carnwath LJ, 'public authority may not . . . allow its treatment of applications to be dictated by agreement with another government body'.[65] The Home Office had abdicated their discretion over how to deal with applications to the Treasury, who imposed targets on the Home Office detailing how applications were to be treated. This is a fettering of discretion because it was for the Home Office, not the Treasury, to decide how to consider applications. A further example is the following case, identified by Carnwath LJ as a 'classic example'.[66]

Case in depth: *Lavender & Son Ltd v Minister of Housing and Local Government* [1970] 1 WLR 1231

The claimants had been refused planning permission to extract gravel from a plot of protected agricultural land. They then exercised a statutory right of appeal to the Minister of Housing and Local Government. When determining the application, the Minister of Housing stated that protected agricultural land such as this should not be released to extract gravel unless the Minister of Agriculture consented. As the Minister of Agriculture had not given their consent, the Minister of Housing rejected the claimants' appeal. The claimants sought a judicial review, with Willis J finding in their favour. He held that the policy of the Minister of Housing, in requiring the consent of the Minister of Agriculture before any land could be released with no exceptions, meant that in substance decisions were being made by the Minister of Agriculture. This ran against the requirement of the statute that it should have been the Minister of Housing that made the decision. Effectively, the Minister of Housing had abdicated their decision-making power to the Minister of Agriculture and had unlawfully fettered their discretion.

This should not be taken to mean that one decision-maker cannot take account of other decisions made elsewhere as shown in *Audit Commission for England and Wales v Ealing London Borough Council*.[67] Under section 99 of the Local Government Act 2003, the Audit Commission is required to rate the performance of local authorities. The Audit Commission had given Ealing London Borough Council a rating of 'weak'. This rating was partly based on the finding of another authority, the Commission for Social Care Inspection (CSCI), who had given Ealing Council's social care services a 'zero-star' rating. The Council argued that the Audit Commission had allowed its own processes to be dictated by the ratings from the CSCI when it should have made its own independent judgment. As Keene LJ stated, the Audit Commission was entitled to 'adopt the professional judgements of the CSCI',[68] as they had the necessary expertise and it would have been 'absurd' and contrary to the intention of Parliament if the Audit Commission was required to duplicate the ratings process undertaken by the CSCI.[69] Overall, the Council's rating of 'weak' was determined by the Audit Commission, who had decided themselves what weight they should attach to the rating of the CSCI. Essentially, the Audit Commission had allowed their rating to be informed by CSCI's assessment rather than abdicating their discretion to it.

---

[65] Ibid.   [66] Ibid.   [67] [2005] EWCA Civ 556.   [68] Ibid [24].   [69] Ibid.

Dictation

Discretionary power can also be fettered through dictation. This is when the decision-maker does not apply their own mind to the question to be decided because they are ordered or somehow forced by a third party to exercise their discretion in a particular way. As the decision is not as a result of applying their own mind to the question, the decision-maker has fettered their power. The Canadian case of *Roncarelli v Duplessis*[70] provides a clear example. The Quebec Liquor Commission's decision to revoke a licence to sell alcohol was invalid because the Commission was acting on the instruction of the Prime Minister of Quebec who issued the instruction for political reasons. The Liquor Commission should have exercised its powers independently and not at the instigation of the Prime Minister, who should have had no role in making the decision in question. In English law, dictation was the key issue in the following case.

Case in depth: *R (on the application of Corner House Research and Campaign Against Arms Trade) v Director of the Serious Fraud Office* [2009] 1 AC 756

Under section 1(3) of the Criminal Justice Act 1987, the Director of the Serious Fraud Office (SFO) started an investigation into allegations of corruption against BAE Systems (formerly British Aerospace). The investigation involved a contract to sell military aircraft between the British Government and Saudi Arabia, with BAE Systems being the main contractor providing the aircraft. The SFO's investigation led them to bank accounts held in Switzerland with a suspicion that they were used by BAE Systems to make payments to Saudi Arabian officials. At this point, the Saudi Arabian Government threatened that if the investigation continued Saudi Arabia would end ongoing negotiations over the contract, and, more importantly, end cooperation with the United Kingdom on counter-terrorism matters. The Director of the SFO felt that there was sufficient evidence to continue with the investigation, but chose to end it following discussions with the government (which included the Attorney-General and Prime Minister) and after being informed by UK's Ambassador to Saudi Arabia that continuing with the investigation would mean that 'British lives on British streets were at risk'.[71]

The claimants argued that the Director's decision to end the investigation in light of this threat was unlawful, because he had not exercised his powers independently but had effectively surrendered his powers to a third party, the Saudi Arabian Government. These arguments were rejected by the House of Lords, who held that the Director had carefully considered the threat made and reached his own conclusion after consulting relevant people within government. As Lord Bingham held:

> The Director was confronted by an ugly and obviously unwelcome threat. He had to decide what, if anything, he should do. He did not surrender his discretionary power of decision to any third party, although he did consult the most expert source available to him in the person of the ambassador and he did, as he was entitled if not bound to do, consult the Attorney General who, however, properly left the decision to him.[72]

---

[70] (1959) 16 DLR (2d) 689.   [71] [2009] 1 AC 756 [14].   [72] Ibid [41].

The distinction that can be made between the *Corner House Research* case and the cases such as *Lavender & Son Ltd v Minister of Housing and Local Government* is that while the threat issued by the Saudi Arabian authorities caused the Director of the SFO to suspend the investigation, he had made the decision with sufficient care for the House of Lords to find that it was still an exercise of his discretion to halt the investigation; whereas in *Lavender & Son*, the decision-maker acted directly on the influence of the third party.

 Counterpoint: Does the decision in *Corner House Research* further or undermine the rule of law?

On the face of it, by ensuring that the decision-maker, the Director of the SFO, had made the decision to stop the investigation, the conclusion of the House of Lords can be justified on the principles explained so far in this section. In this way, the courts are seeking to enforce the intention of Parliament as required by the rule of law as explained in 11.2.

However, the High Court reached the opposite conclusion and also justified their conclusion on the rule of law. They concluded that the Director of the SFO in yielding to such threats as those made by Saudi Arabia actually weakened the rule of law. Moses LJ stated:

> [75] Such threats . . . are particularly within the scope of the courts responsibility. It is difficult to identify any integrity in the role of the courts to uphold the rule of law, if the courts are to abdicate in response to a threat from a foreign power.

> [76] Mr Sales's submission [counsel for the Director of the SFO] appears to us not to be one of principle but rather one of practicality: resistance is useless, the judgment of the Government is that the Saudi Arabian Government will not listen and the authorities in the United Kingdom must surrender. That argument reveals the extent to which the Government has failed to appreciate the role of the courts in upholding and protecting the rule of law.

> [77] The courts protect the rule of law by upholding the principle that when making decisions in the exercise of his statutory power an independent prosecutor is not entitled to surrender to the threat of a third party, even when that third party is a foreign state. The courts are entitled to exercise their own judgment as to how best they may protect the rule of law, even in cases where it is threatened from abroad. In the exercise of that judgment we are of the view that a resolute refusal to buckle to such a threat is the only way the law can resist.[73]

It can be seen from this disagreement between the High Court and the House of Lords that the requirements of the rule of law in any given situation can be contentious, which reflects the lack of a clear definition of the rule of law itself.[74] Whose view do you prefer? That of the House of Lords or the High Court?

---

[73] [2008] EWHC 714 (Admin).
[74] This is discussed in detail in Chapter 3.

Discussing the problem

Consider the problem scenario outlined at the start of the chapter. Based on the discussion regarding the fettering of discretion in 11.6.2, is there any example of the Council fettering its discretion?

The reasons that the Council gave for rejecting the application of Unusual Fruits Ltd are particularly relevant here. This bears a close resemblance to the *British Oxygen* case discussed in 11.6.2 as an example of fettering discretion through having a policy which is rigidly applied to any application that is received. This means that it is not a genuine exercise of Council's discretion as Parliament intended when granting this power under section 2(2) of the Food Distribution Act 2024.

Although the *British Oxygen* case was clear that it is perfectly acceptable to have a policy, as Lord Reid states, the decision-maker must remain open to 'listen to anyone with something new to say' and deal with their application accordingly. In this case, the Council representative did not do that, showing that they had effectively fettered their discretion.

11.6.3 Summary on discretionary power

In summary, a discretionary power is one where the decision-maker must be mindful of the purposes for which he has been given the power, and set about using the power to achieve that purpose. This may involve setting standards or policies about how that power can be used and the decision-maker may have discretion about what those standards and policies are. However, the decision-maker must exercise their discretion and not simply rigidly apply any standard or policy to all cases that come before them. The room for manoeuvre that a decision-maker will have will depend on how the power is framed and the context within which it operates. When faced with a judicial review questioning whether a discretionary power has been exercised lawfully, the role of the courts is to establish the scope of the discretion accorded to the decision-maker and to consider whether the decision-maker has made a genuine exercise of their discretion.

11.7 Delegation of power

Section 11.6 considers *how* the discretionary power has been exercised. This section considers *who* should exercise the power in question. Again, the aim of the courts is to achieve the same purpose, to ensure that the intention of Parliament as expressed in statute is upheld. When Parliament grants a statutory power to a public authority, it is presumed that the intention of Parliament is for that public authority to exercise the statutory power in question. Consequently, a public authority must exercise those powers and cannot delegate their authority to another person. This is the rule against delegation based on the Latin maxim *delegatus non potest delegare*. This means 'one to whom power is delegated cannot himself further delegate' that power. Once again, like the other elements of illegality, the starting point is the statute that grants the power in question. Should Parliament intend to allow a public authority to delegate a power, Parliament can allow for this to happen either expressly or by necessary implication.

Alternatively, Parliament can allow a power to be delegated under another statute. This means that the language the statute or statutory instrument uses when granting the power to the public authority is crucial. The following case is a classic example of the non-delegation principle in action.

Case in depth: *Barnard v National Dock Labour Board* [1953] 2 QB 18

Under the Dock Workers (Regulation of Employment) Order 1947,[75] the National Dock Labour Board was in charge of a national scheme to ensure that dock workers received more regular employment and ensure that sufficient labour was available to meet the demands of the docks. As part of this, the National Dock Labour Board ('National Board') was required to delegate to Local Dock Labour Boards ('Local Board') various functions, including the power to discipline dock workers and suspend dock workers without pay. Significantly, the Local Boards were required to have equal numbers of representatives of employers and workers. However, the Local Board for London, had further delegated the power to discipline dock workers to the Port Manager. Barnard was one dock worker of several who had been suspended by the Port Manager and they challenged their suspensions.

 The Court of Appeal held that the dock workers had been suspended unlawfully. The Port Manager had made the decision during a dispute over working patterns and conditions and had suspended the dock workers without reference to the Local Board. As the Local Board did not have any lawful authority by which they could further delegate the power delegated to them by the National Board, the Local Board should have made the decision itself. As the decision was made by the Port Manager, this was unlawful, and the suspensions were overturned.

This is a useful case because it shows how power can be delegated if authorized by Parliament. A further case, *Vine v National Dock Labour Board*,[76] discussed the same scheme as in *Barnard* and made clear the reason for this principle. The Local Boards were required to have an equal number of representatives of employers and dock workers. This was to ensure that dock workers and those using the docks both had confidence in the decisions reached by the Local Boards as they each effectively had their own representatives on the boards. When these Local Boards delegated their powers to someone else, this undermined the intention of Parliament which was that the boards themselves needed to exercise the power.

 Statutes may often grant duties or functions to local authorities and a local authority may wish to delegate that function to someone under another statute. An example of this is *Crédit Suisse v Waltham London Borough Council*.[77] Under the Housing Act 1985, the local authority was under the statutory duty to provide housing for homeless persons. The local authority sought to delegate this function under the Local Government Act 1972[78] to a company it had set up with the assistance of a loan from a bank. This was found to be unlawful, because this involved transferring functions granted to the Council to this company and such a delegation of power was not allowed under the Local Government Act 1972.

---

[75] SI 1947/1189.   [76] [1957] AC 488.   [77] [1997] QB 362.   [78] Particularly under s 111.

The cases considered so far are examples of when delegation has been attempted in a direct and deliberate way. Yet the reality of decision-making is often more complex than this, and it is possible for delegation to take place more subtly, whereby it appears as though the decision has been made by the appropriate public authority, but informally the decision has in substance been taken by someone else. For example, it was suggested in *Barnard* that the Labour Board could simply ratify decisions taken by the Port Manager. However, this argument was given short shrift by Denning LJ, who stated that:

> if the board have no power to delegate their functions to the port manager, they can have no power to ratify what he has done. The effect of ratification is to make it equal to a prior command; but just as a prior command, in the shape of a delegation, would be useless, so also is a ratification.[79]

There is a clear overlap here between delegating power informally and fettering the exercise of discretionary power when the decision-maker allows the decision to be made in effect by someone else.

Discussing the problem

Consider the scenario outlined at the start of the chapter. Has there been any example of an unlawful delegation of power?

This is most relevant to Francesca's application because her application was dealt with by the Market Manager, who is employed by Country Markets Ltd, which manages the market on behalf of the Council. The Council, in allowing the Market Manager to deal with Francesca's application, have unlawfully delegated their power to the Market Manager. This is unlawful because section 2(2) of the Food Distribution Act 2024 is clear that it is councils who have the legal power to grant licences and deal with applications. There is nothing to indicate in the statute that the Council can delegate this power to someone else.

It is also clear from Lord Denning's reasoning in *Barnard v National Dock Labour Board* that if the Council had ratified the decision of the Market Manager that would have been unlawful too, as the Council would still not be actively making the decision themselves. The key consideration is that the statute has given the power to the Council to decide applications for licences who must be able to show that both in form and in substance it is they who have decided the applications in question.

11.7.1 An important exception—the *Carltona* principle

The principle of non-delegation of power is subject to one important exception, this is called the *Carltona* principle, after *Carltona Ltd v Commissioners of Works*.[80] In summary, the *Carltona* principle is a rule which allows officials within government departments to act in the name of ministers without any formal delegation of power. The rationale behind this principle is that powers are conferred by Parliament to ministers who are in charge of large government departments. Given that some government departments,

---

[79] [1953] 2 QB 18, 40.   [80] [1943] 2 All ER 560.

such as the Department of Work and Pensions or the Home Office, make many thousands of decisions a day, it is 'physically impossible for the Minister to exercise personally all the powers vested in the Minister in his or her official capacity'.[81] Parliament is assumed to accept this, so when it grants powers to ministers, it is accepted that they can be exercised by civil servants within their department on the minister's behalf.[82] In *Carltona* itself, Lord Greene MR explained the constitutional explanation for the rule:

> Constitutionally, the decision of such an official, is, of course, the decision of the minister. The minister is responsible. It is he who must answer before Parliament for anything that his officials have done under his authority, and, if, for an important matter he selected an official of such junior standing that he could not be expected competently to perform the work, the minister would have to answer for that in Parliament. The whole system of departmental organisation and administration is based on the view that ministers, being responsible to Parliament, will see that important duties are committed to experienced officials. If they do not do that, Parliament is the place where complaint must be made against them.[83]

As Lord Greene explains, the constitutional justification for the principle is that civil servants are accountable to ministers within their government department and ministers are accountable to Parliament for the activities of their department as a whole. The ways in which ministers are accountable to Parliament are explained in 8.7and include answering parliamentary questions, appearing before select committees, and taking part in debates.

 Pause for reflection

To what extent can the constitutional reason for the *Carltona* principle be questioned? As Peter Cane states, 'the main difficulty with the *Carltona* decision is that it relies on an unrealistic view of the effectiveness of ministerial responsibility as a vehicle of political accountability'.[84]

With this in mind, and considering how effective Parliament is at scrutinizing the executive, can the *Carltona* doctrine be justified?

At a more detailed level, as Elliott describes, there are questions about the scope of the *Carltona* principle. First, does this allow 'any power to be devolved to any departmental official'?[85] Arguments have attempted to limit the principle. In *Re Golden Chemical Products Ltd*[86] it was argued that if the power was expressed to be exercised by the minister personally (eg by a statute using language such as 'if it appears expedient to him, the Minister may'), then such powers would fall outside the scope of the principle and should be exercised by the minister personally. This argument was rejected by the court on the basis that it would be impossible to make a distinction between which powers could and could not be delegated in a logical manner.

More recently, in *DPP v Haw*[87] Lord Phillips MR suggested that the principle required 'refinement', and that the doctrine should be 'subject to a requirement that the seniority

---

[81] Peter Cane, *Administrative Law* (5th edn, OUP 2011) 168.   [82] Ibid.
[83] [1943] 2 All ER 560, 563.   [84] Peter Cane, *Administrative Law* (5th edn, OUP 2011) 169.
[85] Mark Elliott, *Beatson, Matthews and Elliott's Administrative Law* (4th edn, OUP 2010) 162.
[86] [1976] Ch 300.   [87] [2007] EWHC 1931 (Admin).

of the official exercising a power should be of an appropriate level having regard to the nature of the power in question'.[88]

The underlying concern of Lord Phillips in *Haw* is the scope of the *Carltona* principle. *Haw* extended the principle to the Commissioner of the Metropolitan Police, who although clearly not a government minister, could nevertheless, delegate to a superintendent a duty imposed on them by section 134 of the Serious Organised Crime and Police Act 2005 to regulate demonstrations outside Parliament. This was decided on the basis that such a delegation was necessarily implied by Parliament. Lord Phillips stated that 'when the practicalities are considered it is plain that Parliament cannot have intended that the Commissioner should determine the conditions himself'.[89] There is a real danger that approach can be become a convenient solution for the courts, extending the *Carltona* principle far and wide. This danger was highlighted by Freedland who discussed how the *Carltona* principle applied to executive agencies, that as discussed in 7.9 that are set to achieve specific tasks allocated to a government department, yet because they are one step removed from their department, the traditional methods of ministerial accountability do not apply in the same manner.[90] Yet, despite this concern, it has been accepted that civil servants working within an executive agency fall within the *Carltona* principle.[91]

11.7.2 Summary on the principle of delegation of powers

In summary, the broad principle of delegation of powers is relatively straightforward. Delegation can only be lawful if it is authorized by statute. It is also clear that the courts will not accept a mere ratification of a decision made by someone else, as in substance the decision has been made by someone not authorized by the statute. As regards government departments, the situation is more complex with the *Carltona* principle, meaning that actions of civil servants are constitutionally accepted as being actions of the minister responsible for that department. However, some questions remain over the precise scope of the principle.

11.8 Improper purpose

As discussed in 11.6 in the context of discretionary power, the main objective of the courts is to ensure that statutory powers are used to further, rather than undermine, the purpose of the Act. This means that it is an unlawful use of power for a public authority to use it for an improper purpose. What is considered to be an improper purpose will shortly be discussed in more detail, but an improper purpose is one which Parliament will not have intended the power to be used for.[92] It is clear from *Padfield* (discussed in 11.6.1)

---

[88] Ibid [29].   [89] Ibid [36].

[90] Mark Freeland, 'The Rule Against Delegation and the *Carltona* Doctrine in an Agency Context' [1996] *Public Law* 19.

[91] *R v Secretary of State for Social Services, ex p Sherwin* (1996) 32 BMLR 1.

[92] The use of 'improper' does not imply that the power must have been used with malice, spite, or personal dishonesty. Indeed, cases of this type are rare, AW Bradley, KD Ewing, and CJS Knight, *Constitutional and Administrative Law* (16th edn, Pearson 2015) 640. Although one example is *R v Derbyshire CC, ex p Times Supplements Ltd* (1991) 3 Admin LR 241, when Derbyshire County Council withdrew its advertising from the *Times Educational Supplement* after *The Sunday Times* had published a potentially libellous article about the leader of the Council. It was held that this was a misuse of power as the decision was made solely to punish the claimants for publishing the article in question.

and *RM v Scottish Ministers*,[93] that discretionary power, even if framed so that it appears that the public authority has an absolute discretion, must be exercised to give effect to the intention of Parliament.

Case in depth: *RM v Scottish Ministers* [2012] UKSC 58

In Scotland, the Mental Health (Care and Treatment) (Scotland) Act 2003 provided that patients detained in psychiatric hospitals should have the right of appeal against their detention. The Act also required that the Scottish Government should pass regulations providing for a process by which appeals can be made and that these regulations should be introduced by 1 May 2006. This deadline had passed without any regulations being made, meaning that the claimant could not make an appeal against their detention. The Supreme Court held that by imposing this dead-line, the Scottish Parliament had intended that those in the claimant's position should have had the ability to make an appeal by 1 May 2006, but that up until that date the ministers had dis-cretion as to how to make the necessary regulations. This meant that the ministers, by failing to make the regulations by the deadline, had 'thwarted the intention of the Scottish Parliament. It therefore was, and is, unlawful'.[94] As Lord Reed stated, this was a clear application of the princi-ple established in *Padfield*:

> The importance of *Padfield's* case [1968] AC 997 was its reassertion that, even where a statute confers a discretionary power, a failure to exercise the power will be unlawful if it is contrary to Parliament's intention . . . In the present case, the exercise of the power to make regulations by 1 May 2006 was necessary in order to bring Chapter 3 of Part 17 of the 2003 Act into effective operation by that date, as the Scottish Parliament intended. The Ministers were therefore under an obligation to exercise the power by that date.[95]

From *Padfield* and *RM v Scottish Ministers*, it is clear that public authorities have to use their powers to further the intention of parliament. If a public authority uses their powers for other purposes, then this will be using a power for an improper purpose. The follow-ing case provides a clear example.

Case in depth: *Wheeler v Leicester City Council* [1985] AC 1054

Three players for Leicester Football Club, a well-known rugby union club (now known as the Leicester Tigers), had chosen to take part in a tour of South Africa organized by the English Rugby Football Union (commonly called the RFU). This was a controversial decision because this was during the period of apartheid in South Africa when many sports had chosen to boycott South Africa, meaning that they would refuse to tour South Africa or allow South Africa to tour in other countries. The intention was that this was part of a series of measures aimed at increasing the pressure on the South African government to end apartheid. The Council had taken a strong

→

---

[93] [2012] UKSC 58.

[94] Ibid [12], Lord Reed (with whom Lord Hope DPSC, Lady Hale, Lord Wilson, and Lord Carnwath agreed).

[95] Ibid [47].

stance against apartheid, and although the rugby club had condemned it, they took no action against the players for taking part in the tour. In response, the Council decided to ban the rugby club from using fields owned by the Council for training and matches. The Council argued that they were acting on the basis of section 71 of the Race Relations Act 1976 and the duty on the Council to 'promote . . . relations, between persons of different racial groups'.[96]

However, the court disagreed. Essentially, the Council had requested the rugby club, a private organization, to pursue an objective that the Council wanted. When the rugby club refused to do this, in response, the Council banned the rugby club from using its field. The effect of this was that the Council was effectively punishing the club for a taking a different view on this matter. The Court considered that this was a misuse of the Council's powers. As Lord Templeman stated:

> The council could not properly seek to use its statutory powers of management or any other statutory power for the purposes of punishing the club when the club had done no wrong.[97]

Wheeler makes clear that policies intended to achieve one purpose cannot be used to achieve another unrelated purpose, even if that purpose is generally viewed as desirable. This is a classic example of a public authority acting with an excess of zeal, attempting to go beyond what is authorized by the law, in order to achieve what the public authority perceives to be a laudable aim. *Porter v Magill*[98] is an example of the opposite, showing how powers can be manipulated and used in an attempt to gain a political advantage.

Case in depth: *Porter v Magill* [2001] UKHL 67

The Conservative Party controlled Westminster City Council and the leader of the Council, Dame Shirley Porter, developed a policy to sell some of its council-owned housing. This was perfectly legal under section 32 of the Housing Act 1985. However, this policy was adopted in the belief that homeowners were more likely to vote Conservative at future elections and that this policy would create more homeowners. The Auditor of the Council (responsible for scrutinizing the Council's accounts) objected to this policy and found that Dame Shirley Porter and others were personally liable for the cost to the Council that this policy caused. Many points of administrative law were raised in this case, but one issue was whether the defendants had acted under an improper purpose.

The House of Lords found that the defendants had acted under an improper purpose. The difficulty is that, obviously, politicians will act for political motives, in the sense that they believe that their policies are in the public interest and that they will be popular so that they could be re-elected at the next election. This form of accountability is a vital feature of democracy. However, they cannot act so that powers granted to the Council are used to achieve a purely political objective. Lord Bingham explained how to strike the right balance. He recognized that elected politicians obviously wish to act in a way that is popular with the electorate and are clearly not

→

---

[96] This duty can now be found as part of the Public Sector Equality Duty and is discussed in 11.10.
[97] [1985] AC 1054, 1080–1.   [98] [2001] UKHL 67.

→

acting improperly or unlawfully if exercising the powers in ways that they hope voters will appreciate. However, the powers exercised must be used for the purposes for which they were conferred. Powers are not lawfully exercised if they are 'exercised not for a public purpose for which the power was conferred but in order to promote the electoral advantage of a political party'.[99]

Lord Bingham makes clear that while the controlling political party of a council will seek re-election, and will make decisions with that in mind, the powers of a local authority cannot be used for the purpose of securing a distinct political advantage of that political party. The powers granted to the local authority must be exercised for the purposes for which the power has been granted to them by Parliament.

11.8.1 More than one purpose?

In addition to acting with one purpose in mind, it is possible that a decision can be made with the aim of achieving more than one purpose, essentially attempting to 'kill two birds with one stone'. If both purposes pursued are lawful then there is unlikely to be any issue. However, the position is more complex when one of the purposes achieved is lawful and the other purpose is unlawful and 'improper'. The difficulty here is determining how this is to be balanced. Does the existence of the improper purpose invalidate the decision even though there was also a proper purpose behind it? This was the key question in the following case.

Case in depth: *Westminster Corporation v London & North Western Railway Co* [1905] AC 426

Under section 44 of the Public Health (London) Act 1891, Westminster Corporation had the power to build public toilets, but this did not include the power to build a public subway. Near the Palace of Westminster on Parliament Street (where Parliament meets), the Corporation had constructed public toilets underground which were accessible via a public subway. This could be accessed from either side of the road. This meant that it was possible to cross the road via the subway rather than across the busy street above. It was argued by North Western Railway, however, that the real purpose of constructing the subway was to provide an underground crossing rather than public toilets.

The House of Lords rejected this argument with Lord Macnaghten stating that although the Corporation may well have contemplated that the public may use the subway to cross the street, even though its primary purpose is to access the public toilets, this was not enough to make the decision unlawful. Lord Macnaghten stated that 'to make out a case of bad faith it must be shown that the corporation constructed this subway as a means of crossing the street under colour and pretence of providing public conveniences which were not really wanted at that particular place'.[100]

---

[99] Ibid [21].   [100] [1905] AC 426, 432.

Westminster Corporation makes clear that the presence of other purposes does not vitiate the intention to pursue the intended proper and lawful purpose if that was the main reason behind the decision. In this case, it was clear that the main reason behind constructing the public toilets in that location was to make provision as allowed by the law. While the construction of the subway was an obvious consequence of this decision, it was not the main reason for deciding to build the public toilets in that particular location.

 Discussing the problem

Consider the scenario outlined at the start of the chapter. Has Nanchester District Council exercised its powers in order to pursue an improper purpose?

It is clear from the statute that Parliament has given the power to the Council to issue licences under section 2(2) of the 2024 Act for the purposes of running a market that sells food. With Callum's application, the Council appear to have used their power of issuing licences to effectively replace bus routes that the Council have cut. While ensuring that vulnerable people can still retain access to the supermarket is an appropriate aim for the Council to pursue, cases such as *Wheeler v Leicester City Council* show that this would still be an example of using a legal power for an improper purpose as it is totally unconnected to Callum's application for a stall at the market. The conclusion would be that the condition attached to Callum's licence would be unlawful.

It would also be difficult for the Council to argue the *Westminster Corporation v London & North Western Railway* discussed in 11.8.1. In that case, the construction of a public subway below the street was an improper purpose which did not make the decision to construct the public toilets unlawful. This was because the public subway was incidental to the decision to build the public toilets. By contrast, it is hard to argue that the condition on Callum's licence is incidental to the decision to grant him a licence, because driving pensioners to the supermarket is wholly unrelated to the power to run a market.

11.9 Irrelevant considerations

Very closely related to the issue of improper purpose is the issue of irrelevant considerations. This is the requirement that when making a decision under statute a public authority must take into account all relevant factors while excluding all irrelevant factors. What constitutes a relevant consideration is a matter of statutory interpretation, as derived from the statute granting in the first place. As Cooke J in *CREEDNZ Inc v Governor General*[101] stated:

> What has to be emphasised is that it is only when the statute expressly or impliedly identifies considerations required to be taken into account by the authority as a matter of legal obligation that the court holds a decision invalid . . . It is not enough that a consideration is one that may properly be taken into account, nor even that it is one which many people, including the court itself, would have taken into account if they had to make the decision.[102]

---

[101] [1981] 1 NZLR 172.   [102] Ibid 183.

Cooke J is clear that for the courts to intervene there needs to be a legal obligation, stemming from the statute either expressly or by implication, that the factor should be taken into account. If there is no such obligation, then the courts will not intervene. Neither will courts intervene if, although the decision-maker was under no legal obligation to take a consideration into account, they could reasonably have been taken into account. Alternatively, there can be considerations which a decision-maker ought not to take into account. The issue of decision-makers taking into account irrelevant considerations was central to the following case.

Case in depth: *Roberts v Hopwood* [1925] AC 578

In 1922, Poplar Metropolitan Borough Council in East London decided to introduce a minimum wage that paid men and women equally. Under powers granted by the Metropolis Management Act 1855, the Council set the wage at the same level as the previous year despite a significant drop in the cost of living, believing that this was the minimum that a model employer should pay. The minimum wage was above the market rate for the local area. The District Auditor argued that the Council had misused their discretion and 'surcharged' the council the amount of money that, in his view, the Council had misspent under this policy. This meant that the members of the Council were personally liable to pay the sum misspent.

The House of Lords agreed with the District Auditor in holding that although the Council did enjoy discretion over the levels of pay, the Council should consider their duties to [taxpayers] as well as to their employees and needed to have regard to the market rate of labour when deciding what a fair and reasonable wage should be. However, according to Lord Atkinson, the Council did not do this, and instead allowed 'themselves to be guided in preference by some eccentric principles of socialistic philanthropy, or by a feminist ambition to secure the equality of the sexes in the matter of wages in the world of labour'.[103] Clearly, Lord Atkinson was of the view that such considerations were irrelevant to the issue as to what the correct level of pay should be.

In this case, the courts found that the Council failed to consider its fundamental duty to those paying the rates to obtain value for money when spending public money.[104] Instead, the Council based their decision on factors which the court considered to be irrelevant. Undoubtedly, a similar case reaching the courts today would reach a very different result because equal pay could not be an irrelevant consideration.[105] Although society in the 1920s was very different to today, the case remains a good example of how considering irrelevant considerations can make decision unlawful.

A further example of taking into account irrelevant considerations can be seen in the following case.

---

[103] [1925] AC 578, 594.

[104] The modern equivalent to the rates is the Council Tax. Commercial premises still pay a version of the rates known as Business Rates.

[105] Indeed, equal pay between the sexes is legally required under the Equality Act 2010, ss 54–67, replacing the provisions of the Equal Pay Act 1970. If the case occurred today, the Public Sector Equality Duty considered in 11.10 would also be relevant.

Case in depth: *R v Secretary of State for the Home Department, ex p Venables* [1998] AC 407

Under the Criminal Justice Act 1991, it used to be the case that the Home Secretary could decide the minimum sentence of a minor sentenced to prison (known as the 'tariff').[106] The Home Secretary would make the decision after consulting with the Lord Chief Justice and the trial judge. The applicants were Jon Venables and Robert Thompson, who, when aged ten, were convicted of the murder of two-year-old James Bulger. The case was extensively covered by the media. The trial judge had recommended a tariff of eight years; however, the Home Secretary chose a fifteen-year tariff. When making this decision the Home Secretary had decided to take into account public opinion as expressed through petitions from a tabloid newspaper. The applicants challenged the Home Secretary's decision.

The House of Lords found in favour of the applicants on several grounds, the most important one for present purposes being the issue over the public petitions. It was held by Lord Steyn that while the Home Secretary was entitled to consider public confidence in the penal system, the petitions organized by the newspapers were of no value, as they did not reflect 'informed public opinion'.

Lord Steyn took the view that 'informed public opinion' meant 'public opinion formed in the knowledge of all the material facts of the case. Plainly, the "evidence" to which the Home Secretary referred did not measure up to his standard. It was therefore irrelevant. But the Home Secretary was influenced by it. He gave weight to it. On this ground his decision is unlawful'.[107]

The problem with the information that the Home Secretary used was that the power exercised was of a judicial character which means that the Home Secretary should exercise the power dispassionately. As a sentencing judge would clearly ignore a newspaper campaign for a longer sentence of a prisoner, so must the Home Secretary.

 Pause for reflection

How significant was it that the newspaper petition was likely to be of little value to a judge because the newspaper coverage was likely to be exaggerated? Does this case ensure that the decision is reached fairly?

 Discussing the problem

Thinking again about the scenario outlined at the start of the chapter, have the Council considered any irrelevant considerations in how they have dealt with the applications for new stalls?

This could be another way of thinking about Kendrick's application. His application was rejected on the basis that the Council want to encourage stalls that sell non-food items. It could be argued

→

---

[106] This is now no longer the case, as, following the introduction of the Human Rights Act 1998, the power to make this decision has been taken away from the Home Secretary and is now solely made by the trial judge.

[107] [1998] AC 407, 525–6.

that this is an irrelevant consideration to the Council's power to determine applications for food stalls. The Council may well have concerns about the popularity of the market in the afternoons, but arguably, these are irrelevant as to whether Kendrick's application for a licence should or should not be granted.

One common theme of this chapter is how the different specific headings all under the label of 'illegality' can overlap with each other. This is shown most clearly with irrelevant considerations and improper purpose where the dividing line between the two is, at best, unclear. This is because many of the decisions for an improper purpose could also be viewed as a case involving irrelevant considerations. Conceptually, what is viewed as an improper purpose could also be viewed as irrelevant considerations as they both are symptoms of the same problem, which is not giving effect to the intention of Parliament. *R v Somerset County Council, ex p Fewings*[108] provides a clear example of the overlap between an irrelevant consideration and an improper purpose. Under section 120 of the Local Government Act 1972, councils have the power to manage land they owned for 'the benefit, improvement or development of their area'. Somerset County Council decided to use this power to ban deer hunting over land the Council owned. Councillors made the decision based on their own personal views regarding deer hunting, with some believing it to be 'systematically torture', 'barbaric', 'uniquely abhorrent', and that hunting involved taking 'pleasure [in] torturing animals'.[109] This decision was challenged by those who had hunted on the land. The Court of Appeal quashed the decision of the Council because the councillors had based the decision on their own personal views of hunting rather than on a consideration of section 120 of the 1972 Act, with little mention as to how a ban would be for 'the benefit, improvement or development' of the area in question.

On the face of it, the case may raise the issue of taking into account irrelevant considerations, or using a power for an improper purpose, with the ethical issues not being relevant to the use of section 120. However, as Bingham LJ made clear, the Council was not entirely prevented from banning deer hunting on council-owned land under section 120 on ethical concerns. The problem in *Fewings* was the way the decision was made, because the Council was not acting for the purposes provided for by the statute, but instead allowed its decision to be clouded by irrelevant considerations, in particular its own personal opinions. It would have been open to the Council to have considered the ethical concerns regarding deer hunting as part of considering how any ban would 'benefit' an area as required by section 120.[110]

 Discussing the problem

Does Callum's application raise questions of improper purposes and irrelevant considerations?

This overlap between improper purposes and irrelevant considerations can be seen with Callum's application. As discussed in 11.8, it can be argued that the condition on Callum's licence, to

➞

---

[108] [1995] 1 WLR 1037.   [109] Ibid 1045.   [110] Ibid 1046.

→

drive pensioners to the supermarket, is an example of an improper purpose. This could also be viewed as an irrelevant consideration, as it is difficult to consider how the issue of accessing the supermarket is relevant to the Council's power to determine Kendrick's application for a licence.

Although there can be a fine line to draw between an improper purpose and irrelevant consideration, ultimately, the difference is one of emphasis. With Callum's application, it could be argued that the Council were seeking to actually achieve an improper purpose, using legislation that allowed the Council to run the food market to provide access to the supermarket.

11.10 The Public Sector Equality Duty

Parliament can also impose general duties on public authorities when exercising any power. These duties are in addition to any requirement to exercise an individual power lawfully. One example of this is the Public Sector Equality Duty (PSED) as detailed by section 149 of the Equality Act 2010. Section 149 is reproduced here:

(1) A public authority must, in the exercise of its functions, have due regard to the need to—

   (a) eliminate discrimination, harassment, victimisation and any other conduct that is prohibited by or under this Act;

   (b) advance equality of opportunity between persons who share a relevant protected characteristic and persons who do not share it;

   (c) foster good relations between persons who share a relevant protected characteristic and persons who do not share it.

(2) A person who is not a public authority but who exercises public functions must, in the exercise of those functions, have due regard to the matters mentioned in subsection (1).

(3) Having due regard to the need to advance equality of opportunity between persons who share a relevant protected characteristic and persons who do not share it involves having due regard, in particular, to the need to—

   (a) remove or minimise disadvantages suffered by persons who share a relevant protected characteristic that are connected to that characteristic;

   (b) take steps to meet the needs of persons who share a relevant protected characteristic that are different from the needs of persons who do not share it;

   (c) encourage persons who share a relevant protected characteristic to participate in public life or in any other activity in which participation by such persons is disproportionately low.

(4)–(6)   . . .

(7) The relevant protected characteristics are—

   age;

   disability;

   gender reassignment;

   pregnancy and maternity;

   race;

   religion or belief;

   sex;

   sexual orientation.

The effect of this section is to impose two complementary requirements on public authorities when making decisions. First, public authorities must have 'due regard' of the need to 'eliminate discrimination' and other conduct that is banned by the Equality Act 2010 itself. For example, the Equality Act 2010 bans discrimination on the grounds of sex or race. The second requirement is that public authorities must foster 'good relations' and the 'equality of opportunity' between those that possess a protected characteristic (such as disability or pregnancy) and those that do not. When making a decision, if the PSED has not been complied with then the decision is unlawful. As the cases that have attempted to invoke the PSED show, the PSED can be useful for claimants challenging a decision which may otherwise have been made lawfully (and so not invoking any of the grounds discussed in this chapter) or is not unreasonable in the *Wednesbury* sense (usually because the decision in question involves the allocation of public resources and the courts are reluctant to intervene in such issues).[111]

The critical part of section 149 is the phrase 'due regard'. This makes it clear that the requirement on public authorities is not to achieve equality in practice but to ensure that the decision has been reached after considering the factors required by the section. This means that the PSED is procedural rather than substantive in nature. Essentially, if the public authority can show that as part of the decision-making process the PSED has been considered, then the duty has been complied with. In *R (MA) v Secretary of State for Work and Pensions*,[112] Laws LJ summed up the requirements of the PSED when he stated:

> [T]he duty of due regard is not a duty to achieve a particular result. The courts will not administer section 149 so as in effect to steer the outcome which ought in any particular case to be arrived at. The evaluation of the impact on equality considerations of a particular decision clearly remains the responsibility of the primary decision-maker.[113]

It is clear that section 149 does not impose a requirement to actually achieve equality. This means that as long as the PSED has been considered, then a decision that may adversely affect those with a protected characteristic such as age or race can still be made. Laws LJ explained that the rationale for this restrained approach to the PSED is based on striking the appropriate balance between the judiciary and the other branches of government as required by the separation of powers:

> Much of our modern law, judge-made and statutory, makes increasing demands on public decision-makers in the name of liberal values: the protection of minorities, equality of treatment, non-discrimination, and the quietus of old prejudices. The law has been enriched accordingly. But it is not generally for the courts to resolve the controversies which this insistence involves. That is for elected government. The cause of constitutional rights is not best served by an ambitious expansion of judicial territory, for the courts are not

---

[111] Unreasonableness as a ground of judicial review is considered in Chapter 12. In outline the courts can intervene when a decision is 'so absurd that no sensible person could ever dream that it lay within the powers of the authority': Lord Greene MR, in *Associated Provincial Picture Houses Ltd v Wednesbury Corporation* [1948] 1 KB 223, 229.

[112] [2013] EWHC 2213 (QB).   [113] Ibid [73].

the proper arbiters of political controversy. In this sense judicial restraint is an ally of the [PSED], for it keeps it in its proper place, which is the process and not the outcome of public decisions.[114]

In the view of Laws LJ, issues of equality often raise matters of public spending which can be controversial, and politicians, rather than the courts, are better equipped to address these issues. The role of the courts should be limited to ensuring that when making decisions, public authorities comply with any requirements requested by Parliament when making the decision.

The remaining question is to consider what 'due regard' requires in practice. While there is no one clear test, it is clear from the case law that 'due regard' requires the 'regard that is appropriate in all the circumstances'.[115] As can be seen from the following case, if there is no evidence that the PSED has been engaged with, then the courts will find that the duty has not been fulfilled.

Case in depth: *Brackling v Secretary of State for Work and Pensions* **[2013] EWCA Civ 1345**

The Secretary of State had decided to close the Independent Living Fund, which was a benefit paid to severely disabled people, aimed at allowing recipients to live independently without requiring residential care. Although there had a been a consultation process that included consulting some groups that represented those affected, it was held that the PSED was not complied with. When the decision was made by the Minister for Disabled People (on behalf of the Secretary of State of Work and Pensions), it was accepted that she may have had a vague awareness that she owed legal duties to the disabled when making the decision, but there was no evidence that she had regard to the specific matters spelled out in section 149, in particular the need to advance equality of opportunity. As McCombe LJ stated:

> the 2010 Act imposes a heavy burden upon public authorities in discharging the PSED and in ensuring that there is evidence available, if necessary, to demonstrate that discharge. It seems to have been the intention of Parliament that these considerations of equality of opportunity (where they arise) are now to be placed at the centre of formulation of policy by all public authorities, side by side with all other pressing circumstances of whatever magnitude.[116]

Brackling makes clear that when a public authority makes a decision the specific obligations imposed by the PSED must be engaged with. Merely having an awareness of the need to take account of persons possessing protected characteristics is not sufficient. This is most easily satisfied by providing evidence that the PSED has been actively considered. This test is applied in the following case.

---

[114] Ibid [74].

[115] *R (Baker) v Secretary of State for Communities and Local Government (Equality and Human Rights Commission intervening)* [2009] PTSR 809 [31] Dyson LJ, considering the Race Relations Act 1976, s 71 which used almost identical language to that of the PSED.

[116] [2013] EWCA Civ 1345 [59]; referred to in *R (Carmichael) v Secretary of State for Work and Pensions* [2016] UKSC 58 [24], [67].

> ### Case in depth: *LDRA Ltd v Secretary of State for Communities and Local Government* [2016] EWHC 950 (Admin)
>
> In a planning appeal from the decision of a local authority, a planning inspector granted planning permission to build an office and warehouse which would replace a car park next to the River Mersey in Birkenhead. While the car park was open to the general public, there was evidence that this car park was specifically used by disabled people because of its easy access to the riverside. The decision by the inspector to grant planning permission was challenged by way of judicial review, on the basis that the PSED had not been complied with as the effect of the proposed development on disabled people had not been given 'due regard'. The planning inspector, in granting planning permission, accepted that the development would 'not preserve public access to the coast', but this was a matter that carried 'little weight' because only a short length of coastline would be affected and alternative access to the riverside was close by.
>
> However, Lang J held that the planning inspector had not complied with the PSED on the basis that this alternative access would have been extremely difficult or impossible for disabled people and there was no indication that this had been adequately considered by the planning inspector. Furthermore, there was no indication that the inspector had considered either expressly or impliedly the requirements imposed on him by the PSED. Emphasizing that the PSED requires an active consideration, Lang J further held that if the inspector felt that he had not received sufficient evidence to make a decision regarding the PSED 'he was under an obligation to seek the information requested'.[117]

On a first reading, section 149 of the Equality Act 2010 may appear to be straightforward. However, the case law has slowly teased out the subtleties of the law showing that the PSED is more nuanced than it may appear. As Laws LJ stated in *R (MA) v Work and Pension Secretary*, the PSED is now at the centre of the decision-making of public authorities. However, it does not require any particular outcome to be reached, merely that the effect of a decision on those with protected characteristics is taken into account. To satisfy the PSED it is important for the public authority to show that it has been taken into account when making the decision in question.

11.11 Summary

This chapter has explored the ground of judicial review known as illegality. As the discussion in this chapter has shown, this is a very broad heading of judicial review. The term illegality is essentially an umbrella term for the different ways to challenge a decision made by a public authority. This includes challenging a decision on the basis that it falls outside the scope of the power granted to the public authority. Often referred to as narrow or simple *ultra vires*, this requires considering the language used by Parliament in the statute when granting the power to the public authority.

---

[117] [2016] EWHC 950 [32].

Other ways to challenge a decision relate in particular to discretionary power. Discretionary power is necessary for modern government to operate and the courts have developed principles that can control the exercise of discretionary power. First, a discretionary power can only be used to further the purpose of the statute which granted the power to the public authority making the decision. Also, discretion cannot be 'fettered'. The fettering of discretion occurs when the public authority has not made a genuine exercise of their discretion. For example, this could be because they have stuck rigidly to an internal policy. Alternatively, it may appear that they have made the decision in question, but in substance the decision has been made elsewhere, as the public authority has allowed the decision to be made by someone else, or they have allowed themselves to be dictated and are required to reach a particular decision. Related to this is the requirement that unless expressly authorized, public authorities cannot delegate their powers to another person, although for pragmatic reasons, the *Carltona* principle means that government ministers can delegate their decision-making power to civil servants within their department without express authorization.

Finally, public authorities are required to take into account only relevant considerations and must ignore irrelevant considerations when making any decision. This also means that public authorities can only use their powers for their original and intended purpose and cannot manipulate the use of their powers to achieve other aims. Parliament may also require that certain factors are taken into account when a public authority is making any decision, such as the PSED.

Quick test questions

1. What do we mean by *ultra vires*?

2. What is an error of law and how is this different to an error of fact? When will the courts intervene?

3. What is a discretionary power? What are the advantages and disadvantages of giving discretionary powers to public authorities?

4. Is there any significant difference in the ways in which a discretionary power can be fettered?

5. In what circumstances can power be delegated? Are government ministers in a different position? If so, why?

6. What is the difference between the need for public authorities to consider only relevant considerations and pursue only those purposes intended by Parliament?

7. How significant is the Public Sector Equality Duty?

Further reading

Generally

Mark Elliott and Jason Varuhas, *Administrative Law: Text and Materials* (5th edn, OUP 2017) Chs 5 and 7

HWR Wade and Christopher Forsyth, *Administrative Law* (11th edn, OUP 2014) Chs 8, 10, and 11

Errors of law and errors of fact

*Christopher Forsyth, 'Error of Fact Revisited: Waiting for the '*Anisminic* Moment' (2018) 23(1) *Judicial Review* 1

Rebecca Williams, 'When Is an Error Not an Error? Reform of Jurisdictional Review of Error of Law and Fact' [2007] *Public Law* 793

Delegation

Mark Freedland, 'The Rule Against Delegation and the Carltona Doctrine in an Agency Context' [1996] *Public Law* 19

Rory Gregson, 'When Should there be an Implied Power to Delegate?' [2017] *Public Law* 408

Discretion

Chris Hilson, 'Judicial Review, Policies and the Fettering of Discretion' [2002] *Public Law* 111

*Christopher Knight, 'A Framework for Fettering' (2009) 14(1) *Judicial Review* 73

Public Sector Equality Duty

*Tom Hickman, 'Too Hot, Too Cold or Just Right? The Development of the Public Sector Equality Duties in Administrative Law' [2013] *Public Law* 325

Simonetta Manfredi, Lucy Vickers, and Kate Clayton-Hathway, 'The Public Sector Equality Duty: Enforcing Equality Rights through Second-generation Regulation' (2018) 47(3) *Industrial Law Journal* 365.

 Visit this book's **online resources** for additional materials relating to this chapter, including a full analysis of the start-of-chapter problem scenario.
www.oup.com/he/stanton-prescott2e

12

Judicial review: irrationality and proportionality

Pursuant to section 3(2) of the (fictitious) Criminal Evidence (Prison Life) Act 2024, Prison Boards are given significant power to punish misbehaving prisoners 'as they see fit'. At Her Majesty's Prison on the Isle of Grass (also fictitious), a disturbance is caused by three particularly troublesome prisoners. One breaks into the Warden's office and steals a prison officer's uniform. He wears it and proceeds to patrol the prison yard, shouting at his fellow prisoners. A second causes a fracas in the dining area, throwing chairs around and upturning tables. Finally, a third prisoner climbs the fence and tries to escape. Dealing with the three cases simultaneously, the Prison Board imposes the following punishment on the prisoners:

- they are forbidden from having visits from friends or family for two months;

- they are to be placed in solitary confinement for three weeks; and

- once out of solitary confinement, their cells are to be searched daily (for a period of six months), including diaries and private correspondence. During which time prisoners are to be excluded from their cells.

12.1 Introduction

The second ground for judicial review identified by Lord Diplock in *Council of Civil Service Unions and Others v Minister for the Civil Service*[1] is irrationality. This chapter explores the meaning of this principle, its foundation upon the test of unreasonableness, and the approach that the courts have adopted since that case.

Irrationality, and the notion of unreasonableness upon which it is based, is a particularly vague and ambiguous term, with a range of possible interpretations and meanings (something that is evident from the various cases and judgments that will be explored throughout this chapter). It has meant, however, that the courts have often considered judicial review claims, brought on the basis of irrationality, with varying degrees of caution, often employing the necessary tests with notable stringency. In part as a result of this and in part due to the increasing influence of European legal practices on the UK system, the test of proportionality has developed as a substantive ground for judicial review, often overlapping and sometimes conflicting with application of the irrationality doctrine. This chapter also explores the development of proportionality in UK law and as a further possible ground for judicial review, focusing in particular on the nature of its relationship with the test for irrationality.

The objectives for this chapter are:

- to explain irrationality and the manner in which it has developed as a substantive ground for judicial review;
- to consider the definition of unreasonableness, provided by Lord Greene in *Associated Provincial Picture Houses Ltd v Wednesbury Corporation* [1948] 1 KB 223 and to explore the manner in which the courts have come to interpret this test;
- to consider the development of proportionality as a ground for judicial review and the factors underpinning that development;
- to discuss, critically, the relationship between unreasonableness and proportionality and to explore arguments relating to the continuing relevance of unreasonableness and the use of proportionality as a ground for review in place of unreasonableness.

12.2 Defining irrationality and *Wednesbury* unreasonableness

In *GCHQ*, Lord Diplock explained the notion of irrationality in the following terms:

> By 'irrationality', I mean what can now be succinctly referred to as 'Wednesbury unreasonableness'. It applies to a decision which is so outrageous in its defiance of logic or of accepted moral standards that no sensible person who had applied his mind to the question to be decided could have arrived at it. Whether a decision falls within this category is a question that judges by their training and experience should be well equipped to answer

---

[1] [1985] AC 374. Hereinafter *GCHQ*, so called because of the case involved employees of Government Communications Headquarters (GCHQ).

. . . 'Irrationality' by now can stand upon its own feet as an accepted ground on which a decision may be attacked by judicial review.[2]

As Lord Diplock implies, the origins of 'irrationality' long pre-date the judgment in *GCHQ*, even though that case is notable for clarifying its role as an independent substantive ground for judicial review. In order that the doctrine might better be understood, then, it is necessary to look at the case of *Associated Provincial Picture Houses Ltd v Wednesbury Corporation*.[3]

Case in depth: *Associated Provincial Picture Houses Ltd v Wednesbury Corporation* [1948] 1 KB 223

Pursuant to section 1(1) of the Sunday Entertainments Act 1932, the Wednesbury Corporation had the power 'to grant licences under the Cinematograph Act 1909' and to 'allow places in that area licensed under the . . . Act to be opened and used on Sundays for the purpose of cinematograph entertainments, subject to such conditions as the authority think fit to impose'. Under this power, the Wednesbury Corporation granted the Associated Provincial Picture Houses Ltd permission to show films at the cinema on Sundays on the condition that no children under fifteen years of age should be permitted. The Picture House brought an action challenging this decision, arguing that to exclude those under the age of fifteen from Sunday performances was *ultra vires* and unreasonable. The court found that the Wednesbury Corporation had not acted unreasonably or *ultra vires* in setting out the policy, so the decision was held to be lawful.

In giving judgment in *Wednesbury*, Lord Greene MR discussed the nature of actions against councils and considered that there was a range of permissible grounds of attack in cases challenging exercises of local authority power.[4] Chief amongst these, however, Lord Greene singled out and discussed the notion of unreasonableness. He observed that:

It is true the discretion must be exercised reasonably . . . Lawyers familiar with the phraseology commonly used in relation to exercise of statutory discretions often use the word 'unreasonable' in a rather comprehensive sense. It has frequently been used and is frequently used as a general description of the things that must not be done. For instance, a person entrusted with a discretion must, so to speak, direct himself properly in law. He must call his own attention to the matters which he is bound to consider. He must exclude from his consideration matters which are irrelevant to what he has to consider. If he does not obey those rules, he may truly be said, and often is said, to be acting 'unreasonably'. Similarly, there may be something so absurd that no sensible person could ever dream that it lay within the powers of the authority.[5]

---

[2] Ibid 410–11, citing *Associated Provincial Picture Houses Ltd v Wednesbury Corporation* [1948] 1 KB 223. Throughout this chapter and, indeed, throughout wider literature in this area, the terms 'irrationality' and 'unreasonableness' are both used to reflect this head of judicial review. As Lord Diplock clarifies in *GCHQ*, 'irrationality' can be taken to mean 'unreasonableness' in the sense defined in *Wednesbury*.

[3] [1948] 1 KB 223.

[4] Ibid 229. Lord Greene there lists: 'Bad faith, dishonesty, unreasonableness, attention given to extraneous circumstances, [and] disregard of public policy' (at 229).

[5] Ibid 229.

This statement highlights the close link between what we now regard as the two separate grounds of illegality and irrationality. Noting that unreasonableness has 'frequently been used . . . as a general description of the things that must not be done',[6] Lord Greene goes on to identify two strands to this policing of discretionary power—the first, merely concerned with abuses of discretion and the second with absurd exercises of power. Challenges to alleged abuses of discretion are now covered by the ground of illegality as discussed in Chapter 11, when a decision can be challenged *inter alia*, on the basis of being used for an improper purpose, unauthorized delegation of power, or by taking into account irrelevant considerations. These grounds apply where a decision-maker can be said to have acted illegally, but not necessarily unreasonably. By contrast, the second strand of Lord Greene's approach accommodates challenges to exercises of discretionary authority that are so absurd as to be unreasonable. It is this second strand that is aligned with irrationality and is the focus of this chapter.

▶◀ Counterpoint: When irrationality overlaps with illegality

While Lord Greene differentiates between challenges to discretionary authority concerning abuses of discretion and challenges to discretionary authority concerning absurd exercises of power—a demarcation that lives on through the identification of the illegality ground for review separate from irrationality—there are in reality overlaps between these two areas. To put it another way, there are instances where abuses of discretionary power might feasibly be challenged under both illegality *and* irrationality.

A clear example of this is seen in the case of *Wheeler v Leicester City Council*.[7] Here, the local authority prevented the local rugby team from using a local recreation ground as a reaction to three players' involvement in an English rugby tour to South Africa during the apartheid regime. Leicester City Council's policy was to refuse to support sporting links with South Africa as a statement of protest at the apartheid. By contrast, while the club did not support the apartheid, they felt that sporting activities could be used as a force for good and that players could decide for themselves whether to join the tour or not. Consequently, the rugby club sought judicial review of the Council's decision to ban them from playing at the local recreation ground. Though the application was initially dismissed, it was later upheld in the House of Lords where Lord Roskill found 'that the actions of the council were unreasonable in the Wednesbury sense'.[8] Equally, though, the council's decision could be seen as falling under the illegality ground for review, and in particular, using powers for an improper purpose. Indeed, demonstrating this, Lord Templeman notes in his judgment that:

> the council could not use their statutory powers in the management of their property or any other statutory powers in order to punish the club. There is no doubt that the council intended to punish and have punished the club . . . In my opinion, this use by the council of its statutory powers was a misuse of power. The council could not properly seek to use its statutory powers of management or any other statutory powers for the purposes of punishing the club when the club had done no wrong.[9]

→

---

[6] Ibid.
[7] [1985] AC 1054, also discussed in 11.8.
[8] Ibid 1079.   [9] Ibid 1080–1.

→

As *Wheeler* demonstrates, while we might distinguish between abuses of discretion that merely fall under the illegality ground for review and those warranting the label of unreasonableness, there is sometimes an overlap between the two.

The notion of irrationality, drawn from Lord Greene's discussion of unreasonableness in *Wednesbury*, can be summarized as follows: that a decision is 'unlawful if it is one to which no reasonable authority could have come'.[10] At first glance, this is a particularly broad test covering, as Wade and Forsyth note, 'a multitude of sins'.[11] However, they limit the test by suggesting that cases that fall into this category 'commonly result from paying too much attention to the mere words of the Act and too little to its general scheme and purpose, and from the fallacy that unrestricted language naturally confers unfettered discretion'.[12]

We can see that unreasonableness, in the sense that it has come to be used as a substantive ground for judicial review, has its origins in the *Wednesbury* case and in Lord Greene's explanation of the principle. As explored in the next section, various cases have developed Lord Green's explanation into an independent ground of judicial review.

12.3 The development of unreasonableness

The idea that 'discretion must be exercised reasonably'[13] pre-dates the judgment in *Wednesbury*. In *Roberts v Hopwood*,[14] as discussed in 11.9, a local authority, using discretion granted under statute, set wages above local market rates through a desire to pay men and women the same, and that the level was what a model employer should pay. The District Auditor argued that the wages were too high. The House of Lords agreed with the Auditor. Lord Wrenbury explained that discretionary power must be exercised reasonably, stating that:

A person in whom is vested a discretion must exercise his discretion upon reasonable grounds. A discretion does not empower a man to do what he likes merely because he is minded to do so—he must in the exercise of his discretion do not what he likes but what he ought. In other words, he must, by use of his reason, ascertain and follow the course which reason directs. He must act reasonably.[15]

 Discussing the problem

With the facts of *Roberts v Hopwood* in mind, consider the power set out in the problem scenario at the start of this chapter, that means Prison Boards can 'punish misbehaving prisoners "as they see fit"'. Consider, in particular, the scope of this discretion and the extent to which it must be exercised reasonably.

→

[10] As summarized in HWR Wade and CF Forsyth, *Administrative Law* (10th edn, OUP 2009) 303.
[11] Ibid.   [12] Ibid.
[13] See the words of Lord Greene at [1948] 1 KB 223, 229.
[14] [1925] AC 578.   [15] Ibid 613.

> →
> The power set out in the 2024 Act is particularly broad. It ostensibly gives Prison Boards the authority to do whatever they think fit or appropriate in punishing misbehaving prisoners. With this in mind, and in setting the foundation for our discussion of this problem scenario, the need to ensure that this power is exercised reasonably, despite its apparently limitless scope, is helpfully provided by these words of Lord Wrenbury in *Roberts v Hopwood*.

Post-*Roberts v Hopwood*, however, and since *Wednesbury*, this notion of unreasonableness has continued to expand and develop. As already discussed, in *Wheeler v Leicester City Council*,[16] Lord Roskill, overturning judgments of the lower courts, held 'that the actions of the council [in banning the rugby club from the recreation ground] were unreasonable in the *Wednesbury* sense'.[17] Despite *Wheeler*, other cases demonstrate the reality that the test for unreasonableness has been set at a particularly high level. This stringency stems from the language used by Lord Greene in *Wednesbury* itself. To aid in explaining the concept, he cited the case of *Short v Poole Corporation*.[18] The issue there concerned the dismissal of an assistant mistress from a local school since she was a married woman and could be maintained by her husband. In the case, Warrington LJ discussed when a court could investigate the actions of a public body and considered the instances where an ostensibly lawful decision could be classified *ultra vires*. He said that:

> It may be . . . possible to prove that an act of the public body, though performed in good faith and without the taint of corruption, was so clearly founded on alien and irrelevant grounds as to be outside the authority conferred upon the body, and therefore inoperative.[19]

Coming a year after *Roberts v Hopwood*, such a statement was clearly not novel. The example that Warrington LJ provides, however, demonstrates the strict foundations of the unreasonableness test. He continues: 'To look for one example germane to the present case, I suppose that if the defendants were to dismiss a teacher because she had red hair, or for some equally frivolous and foolish reason, the Court would declare the attempted dismissal to be void.'[20] It is this last statement that is cited by Lord Greene in *Wednesbury* as an example of an unreasonable decision. It is an extreme example but one that arguably demonstrates how far a public body must go before it can be said to have acted unreasonably.

Statements further demonstrating the strict nature of the unreasonableness test can also be found elsewhere. In *Secretary of State for Education and Science v Tameside Metropolitan Borough Council*,[21] for instance, a case concerning a local authority's decision not to implement the government's education policy, Lord Denning stated that '[n]o one can properly be labelled as being unreasonable unless he is not only wrong but unreasonably wrong, so wrong that no reasonable person could sensibly take that view'.[22] Lord Diplock's categorization of irrationality in *GCHQ* also demonstrates this further. As noted, he says that irrationality exists where decisions are 'so outrageous in [their] defiance of logic

---

[16] [1985] AC 1054.

[17] Ibid 1079. As the discussion in 11.8 demonstrates, this case is also relevant to discussions of using power for an improper purpose.

[18] [1926] Ch 66.   [19] Ibid 91.   [20] Ibid.

[21] [1977] AC 1014.   [22] Ibid 1025–6.

or of accepted moral standards',[23] a statement that is drafted in particularly strict terms. The stringency of the unreasonableness test is clear to see. It is the purpose of this next section, however, to consider the underlying reason for this approach.

12.3.1 **Unreasonableness and the supervisory jurisdiction**

The strict nature of the unreasonableness test can, in part, be attributed to the jurisdiction that the courts exercise in entertaining applications for judicial review. It was discussed, in 10.2.1, that there is a distinction to be drawn between the courts' appellate jurisdiction and its supervisory jurisdiction. The former empowers courts to consider the merits of cases that it hears and allows them to pass judgment in respect of those merits. By contrast, the supervisory jurisdiction restricts the courts from looking at the merits of a particular issue, permitting them only to supervise the process. It is the latter which is exercised with regards to judicial review—courts review the process through which administrative decisions are made and actions taken, though they are not able to consider the merits of those decisions as to do so may usurp the role of the executive or other public bodies. It is this supervisory jurisdiction that arguably justifies the strict nature of the unreasonableness test, as illustrated by a number of cases.

The first case is *Nottinghamshire Country Council v Secretary of State for the Environment*.[24] The facts here involved a challenge by Nottingham County Council to the Secretary of State's Rate Support Grant Report, which set out guidance for local authority expenditure and which had been approved by the House of Commons. The challenge was brought, though, on the contention that the Secretary of State had allegedly failed to comply with the requirements set out in the Local Government Planning and Land Act 1980 and also on the basis that the guidance was unreasonable insofar as it disadvantaged certain local authorities. In the House of Lords, Lord Scarman explained the boundaries within which judges could decide on the unreasonableness of ministers' actions, putting great weight on the fact that the House of Commons' consent had been sought and granted. He stated that:

> If Parliament legislates, the courts have their interpretative role: they must, if called upon to do so, construe the statute. If a minister exercises a power conferred on him by the legislation, the courts can investigate whether he has abused his power. But . . . if a statute, as in this case, requires the House of Commons to approve a minister's decision before he can lawfully enforce it, and if the action proposed complies with the terms of the statute . . . it is not for the judges to say that the action has such unreasonable consequences that the guidance upon which the action is based and of which the House of Commons had notice was perverse and must be set aside. For that is a question of policy for the minister and the Commons, unless there has been bad faith or misconduct by the minister . . . Judicial review is a great weapon in the hands of the judges: but the judges must observe the constitutional limits set by our parliamentary system upon their exercise of this beneficent power.[25]

This extract from Lord Scarman's judgment is notable as it effectively seeks to exclude application of the unreasonableness test. His reasoning is based on the observation that the House of Commons authorized the decision, thereby making it a matter of policy and taking it outside the accepted jurisdiction of the court. In other words, if their Lordships

---

[23] [1985] AC 374, 410–11.   [24] [1986] AC 240.   [25] Ibid 250–1.

had sought to question whether or not the Secretary of State's decision was reasonable they would have been going beyond their supervisory jurisdiction. In a sense, this can be said to justify the strict nature of the *Wednesbury* test insofar as it suggests that only in the most extreme circumstances would the court seek to investigate executive action on the basis of unreasonableness. Indeed, this is supported by another extract from Lord Scarman's judgment in which he states that:

> I refuse in this case to examine the detail of the guidance or its consequences . . . Such an examination by a court would be justified only if a prima facie case were to be shown for holding that the Secretary of State has acted in bad faith, or for an improper motive, or that the consequences of his guidance were so absurd that he must have taken leave of his senses. The evidence comes nowhere near establishing any of these propositions.[26]

Five years after the *Nottinghamshire County Council* case, however, the House of Lords once again discussed the application of the unreasonableness test in the case of *R v Secretary of State for the Home Department, ex p Brind*,[27] this time expressly acknowledging and justifying its strict nature.

Case in depth: *R v Secretary of State for the Home Department, ex p Brind* [1991] 1 AC 696

Under the Broadcasting Act 1981, the Home Secretary prohibited the BBC, ITV, and Channel 4 from broadcasting the voices of individuals who represented terrorist organizations. This ban was challenged by way of an application for judicial review. The application argued that the decision was *ultra vires* and unlawful as it breached Article 10 of the European Convention on Human Rights[28] and conflicted with the duty, required by section 4 of the Broadcasting Act 1981, to ensure 'due impartiality . . . as respects matters of political or industrial controversy or relating to current public policy'. In addition, it was also argued that the actions were unreasonable and disproportionate to the objectives to be achieved ('namely to prevent intimidation by, or undeserved publicity and an appearance of political legitimacy for, such organisations'[29]).

The application for judicial review, however, was dismissed by the High Court, with the Court of Appeal dismissing a subsequent appeal. The House of Lords dismissed a further appeal on the grounds that, at that time, the ECHR was not incorporated into UK law and could therefore not be invoked in the case. In addition, the House of Lords held that applying a test of proportionality in considering the discretion exercised by the Secretary of State, would take the courts beyond their supervisory function. They instead applied the unreasonableness test and found that the Secretary of State had acted reasonably.

The issue relating to proportionality will be picked up again later on in this chapter. With regard to the House of Lords' assessment of the unreasonableness test, however, Lord Ackner stated in the House of Lords that:

> This standard of unreasonableness . . . has been criticised as being too high. But it has to be expressed in terms that confine the jurisdiction exercised by the judiciary to a supervisory, as opposed to an appellate, jurisdiction. Where Parliament has given to a minister

---

[26] Ibid 247.   [27] [1991] 1 AC 696.
[28] Hereinafter ECHR.   [29] [1991] 1 AC 696, 696–7.

or other person or body a discretion, the court's jurisdiction is limited, in the absence of a statutory right of appeal, to the supervision of the exercise of that discretionary power, so as to ensure that it has been exercised lawfully. It would be a wrongful usurpation of power by the judiciary to substitute its . . . judicial view, on the merits and on that basis to quash the decision. If no reasonable minister properly directing himself would have reached the impugned decision, the minister has exceeded his powers and thus acted unlawfully and the court in the exercise of its supervisory role will quash that decision. Such a decision is correctly, though unattractively, described as a 'perverse' decision.[30]

12.3.2 Difficulties with the strict approach

According to Lord Ackner, the strict nature of the unreasonableness test is not only rooted in, but also justified by, the need to maintain the supervisory jurisdiction of the court and to ensure that judges do not err into more appellate functions and adjudicate administrative matters on their merits. There are occasions, however, where this can sometimes give rise to difficult and sensitive decisions, as is shown by *R v Ministry of Defence, ex p Smith*;[31] a case which, through its appeal to the European Court of Human Rights[32] in Strasbourg, provided a platform on which the development of proportionality in judicial review could develop, as the chapter later goes on to discuss.

Case in depth: *R v Ministry of Defence, ex p Smith* [1996] QB 517

The Ministry of Defence, in 1994, set out a policy which stated that 'homosexuality was incompatible with service in the armed forces and that personnel known to be homosexual or engaging in homosexual activity would be administratively discharged'.[33] The policy had been debated at length in both Houses of Parliament and had been discussed by Select Committees on two separate occasions. In these instances, the policy had been approved and deemed to be 'consistent with advice received from senior members of the services'.[34]

In the case, four individuals, all serving members of the armed forces, were discharged from duty on the basis of their homosexuality. They brought actions for judicial review in respect of the decision to discharge, claiming that it was irrational and contrary to Article 8 ECHR. Though the application failed in the High Court, the individuals appealed.

Dismissing the appeal, it was held in the Court of Appeal that, as the policy involved human rights issues, greater justification would be needed before the court would be satisfied that the decision was unreasonable. It was found that because the policy had been so widely approved in Parliament and by Select Committees at various stages and, consequently, found to be consistent with advice received, the policy could not be deemed unreasonable.

In *Smith*, in both the Divisional Court and, later, the Court of Appeal, the judgment from *ex p Brind* featured prominently. Indeed, Simon Brown LJ, in the lower court, cited and endorsed wholeheartedly the words of Neill LJ, who had stated in *R v*

---

[30] Ibid 757–8.　　[31] [1996] QB 517.　　[32] Hereinafter ECtHR.
[33] [1996] QB 517, 517.　　[34] Ibid.

Secretary of State for the Environment, ex p National and Local Government Officers' Asso-ciation[35] that:

> In the light of the decision in *Brind* . . . I am quite satisfied that it is not open to a court below the House of Lords to depart from the traditional Wednesbury grounds when re-viewing the decision of a minister of the Crown who has exercised a discretion vested in him by Parliament . . . The constitutional balance in this country between the courts and the executive is a delicate one . . . . As the law stands at present, however, I have no hesitation in saying that on the facts of this case I can see no basis whatever for this court lowering the 'threshold of unreasonableness.[36]

Applying the strict unreasonableness test, Simon Brown LJ went on to find that 'the minister's stance cannot properly be held unlawful. His suggested justification for the ban may to many seem unconvincing; to say, however, that it is outrageous in its defiance of logic is another thing'.[37] On appeal to the Court of Appeal, rejection of the application was something with which Bingham MR, Henry LJ, and Thorpe LJ all agreed. Indeed, Bingham MR stated that:

> The Divisional Court rejected this argument and so do I. The greater the policy content of a decision, and the more remote the subject matter of a decision from ordinary judicial expe-rience, the more hesitant the court must necessarily be in holding a decision to be irrational. That is good law and, like most good law, common sense. Where decisions of a policy-laden, esoteric or security-based nature are in issue even greater caution than normal must be shown in applying the test, but the test itself is sufficiently flexible to cover all situations.[38]

This statement, then, confirms the view set out by Lord Ackner in *Brind*. The supervisory jurisdiction appears to justify the strict nature of the unreasonableness test to the effect that where matters are deemed to be far from the court's jurisdiction and expertise, the *Wednesbury* test can be applied as a safeguard to prevent the courts interfering.

 Pause for reflection

Do you agree with the Court of Appeal's judgment in *R v Ministry of Defence, ex p Smith*? In separating themselves from the merits of the decision at issue, was the court successful merely in examining the reasonableness of the governmental process behind the decision?

The judgment in *Smith* provides not only an example of the strict nature of the unrea-sonableness test, justified as that is by the need to preserve the court's supervisory juris-diction, but also an example of the difficult consequences to which this can give rise. Though appeal to the House of Lords in *Smith* was rejected, the applicants took their case to the ECtHR where judgment was handed down four years later in the case of *Smith and Grady v UK*.[39] There, the ECtHR criticized the strict application of the *Wednesbury* unrea-sonableness test, stating that:

> the threshold at which the High Court and the Court of Appeal could find the Ministry of Defence policy irrational was placed so high that it effectively excluded any consideration

---

[35] (1992) 5 Admin LR 785. [36] Ibid 797–8, cited at [1996] QB 517, 537.
[37] [1996] QB 517, 541. [38] Ibid 556. [39] (1999) 29 EHRR 493.

by the domestic courts of the question of whether the interference with the applicants' rights answered a pressing social need or was proportionate to the national security and public order aims pursued, principles which lie at the heart of the Court's analysis of complaints under Article 8 of the Convention.[40]

Though *Smith and Grady v UK* will be discussed further for its influence in developing proportionality as a ground for judicial review, it here demonstrates the issues presented by the domestic courts' application of unreasonableness. Indeed, and with the development of case law up to this point in mind, *Smith* can perhaps be regarded as the high water mark in terms of the *Wednesbury* test, with the Strasbourg Court's decision highlighting the extent to which the scope for finding a decision unreasonable had become increasingly limited.

The *Wednesbury* unreasonableness test has undergone significant development since Lord Greene first set it out in 1948. Over the years, the courts became increasingly stringent, in part out of a concern to preserve the supervisory jurisdiction within which judicial review operates. As described in the next section, *Smith* shows how the strict nature of the unreasonableness test caused difficulties, particularly when the ECHR was incorporated into UK law in 1998, and with it the requirement to take into account the jurisprudence of the Strasbourg Court,[41] which includes proportionality, rather than unreasonableness, as a substantive ground for review.

 Discussing the problem

Having now seen the strict nature of the *Wednesbury* test and the way in which it has been applied in numerous cases over the years, have another look at the problem scenario. Do you think the actions of the Prison Board would be deemed reasonable in light of Lord Greene's test?

Whether the punishment handed down by the Prison Board can be seen as reasonable is, of course, a question of judgement. Though there are potential arguments to make regarding human rights, we consider these in 12.4 and leave them aside for the moment. For now we need to consider whether the punishments could be seen as 'so absurd that no sensible person could ever dream that it lay within the powers of the authority'[42] or 'so outrageous in [their] defiance of logic or of accepted moral standards'.[43]

In dealing with misbehaving prisoners, under the power set out in the 2024 Act, it is perhaps understandable that the Prison Board would withhold certain privileges or impose stricter conditions of imprisonment. Furthermore, while some features of this punishment might seem somewhat harsh—three weeks in solitary confinement, for instance—this is not the same thing as 'unreasonable'. It could therefore be argued that the actions of the Prison Board fall short of the high standard of the *Wednesbury* test. Indeed, recalling the House of Lords' judgment in *Nottinghamshire Country Council v Secretary of State for the Environment*,[44] we can use Lord Scarman's reasoning to consider whether the Board 'has acted in bad faith, or for an improper motive, or . . . [in] so absurd [a way] that [they] must have taken leave of [their] senses'.[45] On the basis of these questions, the answer would most probably be no.

---

[40] Ibid [138].
[41] See s 2 of the Human Rights Act 1998, discussed in greater detail in 15.5.3.
[42] [1948] 1 KB 223, 229.   [43] [1985] AC 374, 410–11.   [44] [1986] AC 240.
[45] Ibid 247.

12.4 The development of proportionality

The judgments of the House of Lords in *ex p Brind* and the Court of Appeal in *ex p Smith* were notable in upholding the strict nature of the *Wednesbury* unreasonableness test and in respecting the supervisory jurisdiction of the courts. Both cases also rejected arguments suggesting that the ECHR gave rise to legally binding obligations in UK courts, avoiding the proportionality test that has become central to jurisprudence of the Strasbourg Court.

In *Brind*, Lord Ackner, noting the extent to which the proportionality doctrine has been a part of the ECtHR's approach, stated that 'until Parliament incorporates the Convention into domestic law . . . there appears to me to be at present no basis upon which the proportionality doctrine applied by the European Court can be followed by the courts of this country'.[46] Simon Brown LJ endorsed this view in in *Smith*[47] and, as Craig discusses, this rejection of proportionality is echoed in a number of other cases post-*Brind*.[48]

Yet, in *GCHQ*—which predates both *Brind* and *Smith*—Lord Diplock accepted that the three grounds for review which he identified as illegality, irrationality, and procedural impropriety were not exhaustive and that in time, proportionality could develop into a fourth ground of judicial review. Lord Diplock stated that 'I have in mind particularly the possible adoption in the future of the principle of "proportionality" which is recognised in the administrative law of several of our fellow members of the European Economic Community'.[49]

With Lord Diplock's words in mind, this section explores the development of proportionality in UK law. It identifies the origins of the principle, which, as Lord Diplock notes, are largely attributed to influences in Europe, and it considers the way in which it has grown to be a part of judicial review, particularly as a result of the Human Rights Act 1998 and incorporation of the ECHR. Following this, the next section discusses the place of proportionality within UK administrative law, and its relationship with *Wednesbury* unreasonableness.

Consideration of proportionality in UK law can be traced back to the mid-1970s. In 1976, Lord Denning considered the proportionality of permanently revoking a street trader's licence as punishment for urinating in public,[50] with Sir John Pennycuick stating in the case that 'the isolated and trivial incident . . . is manifestly not a good cause justifying the disproportionately drastic step of depriving Mr Hook of his licence, and indirectly of his livelihood'.[51] For this reason, and others not relevant to this discussion, the application to quash the revocation was successful.

For the most part, however, the development of proportionality in UK law stems from international legal jurisprudence.[52] As a result of the UK's membership of the European Union, for instance, and the use of proportionality in the Court of Justice, 'in cases that have a EU law dimension, an English court must . . . use proportionality to avoid reaching

---

[46] [1991] 1 AC 696, 763.   [47] [1996] QB 517, 538.

[48] See Paul Craig, *Administrative Law* (7th edn, Sweet and Maxwell 2012) 653–4. Craig there cites *R v International Stock Exchange, ex p Else* [1992] BCC 11; *R v Chief Constable of Kent, ex p Absalom*, 5 May 1993; and *R v Secretary of State for the Home Department, ex p Hargreaves* [1997] 1 All ER 397.

[49] [1985] AC 374, 410.

[50] See *R v Barnsley Metropolitan Council, ex p Hook* [1976] 1 WLR 1052 (see Lord Denning's judgment at 1057).

[51] Ibid 1064.   [52] [1985] AC 374, 410.

a decision out of kilter with the rulings of the ECJ'.[53] Similarly, though rather more indirectly,[54] as a result of section 2 of the Human Rights Act 1998, which has already been identified as expecting UK courts to 'take into account' judgments of the ECtHR, the use of proportionality at Strasbourg has also encouraged greater acceptance and use of the doctrine in the UK domestic courts.[55]

In particular, the ECtHR's application of the proportionality test in *Smith and Grady v UK* was particularly significant.[56] As noted above, the ECtHR considered that the unreasonableness test imposed an unnecessarily high threshold, unsuitable for considering 'whether the interference with the applicants' rights answered a pressing social need or was proportionate to the national security and public order aims pursued'.[57] Though by the time judgment was given in *Smith and Grady v UK* the Human Rights Act had been enacted, the Strasbourg judgment encouraged the UK courts 'to use the Act to extend the traditional parameters of judicial review to enable greater scrutiny of the proportionality of decisions being challenged'.[58]

It did not take long for this to begin, as shown by how the House of Lords considered proportionality in *R (Daly) v Secretary of State for the Home Department*.[59]

Case in depth: *R (Daly) v Secretary of State for the Home Department* [2001] UKHL 26

It was routine practice that prisoners' cells were searched by prison staff, with prisoners during that time being excluded from their cells. As part of those searches, correspondence between the prisoner and their legal team, including their solicitor could be checked but not read. Daly, a prisoner, sought judicial review of the decision to allow his legal correspondence to be checked in his absence, claiming that this breached Article 8 ECHR (which protects a right to respect for correspondence). The Court of Appeal dismissed Daly's claim. The House of Lords allowed Daly's appeal, holding that the right of the prisoner to be able to freely and confidentially correspond with a solicitor was disproportionately limited by the policy.

In the House of Lords, Lord Steyn discussed at length the use of proportionality in judicial review. He cited Lord Clyde's Privy Council judgment in *de Freitas v Permanent Secretary of Ministry of Agriculture, Fisheries, Lands and Housing*[60] as setting out the mechanics of the test, explaining that:

in determining whether a limitation (by an act, rule or decision) is arbitrary or excessive the court should ask itself: 'whether: (i) the legislative objective is sufficiently important to justify limiting a fundamental right; (ii) the measures designed to meet the legislative objective are rationally connected to it; and (iii) the means used to impair the right or freedom are no more than is necessary to accomplish the objective'.[61]

---

[53] Christopher Knight, 'The Test that Dare Not Speak its Name: Proportionality Comes Out of the Closet?' (2007) *Judicial Review* 117, 117.

[54] Ibid 117.

[55] See, on this and for discussion of the European foundation to the UK's use of proportionality, ibid 117.

[56] (1999) 29 EHRR 493.   [57] Ibid [138].

[58] Lord Irvine of Laing, 'The Impact of the Human Rights Act: Parliament, the Courts and the Executive' (2003) *Public Law* 308, 315.

[59] [2001] UKHL 26.   [60] [1999] 1 AC 69.   [61] [2001] UKHL 26 [27], citing [1999] 1 AC 69, 80.

This test of proportionality was, Lord Steyn noted, materially different from 'the *Wednesbury* and *Smith* grounds of review' and should be used wherever cases involving human rights come before the courts.[62] Indeed, on this last point he stated that the question to be asked in such cases is whether 'the limitation of the right was necessary in a democratic society, in the sense of meeting a pressing social need, and . . . whether the interference was really proportionate to the legitimate aim being pursued'.[63] This means that the effect of the judgment in *Daly* is notable. Though there were clear limitations to its application, as explained by Lord Steyn, the effect of the House of Lords' decision is that we now recognize a test of proportionality in UK Administrative Law, albeit only within the realms of ECHR and EU Law. This demonstrates a marked shift in the law compared with that which prevailed at the time of the judgment in *Brind*, a decade earlier, that shift being in no small part attributable both to the Strasbourg decisions already discussed and, more broadly, the influence of the ECHR and the need to establish uniformity in human rights cases domestically and across Europe. Summing up the process of this development and the impact that the ECHR has had on judicial review in the UK, Boughey notes that:

> The adoption of proportionality in English law is an example of how the Human Rights Act 1998 . . . has expanded administrative law . . . well beyond its traditional scope, causing Lord Cooke to remark that 'the common law of England is becoming gradually less English'. Prior to the adoption of the HRA, courts applied the deferential *Wednesbury* unreasonableness test to determining the legality of administrative decisions . . . [while] Proportionality was thought to be based on such foreign, civil law principles as to be incapable of transplantation into English law. However, following the ECtHR's criticism that the Wednesbury test was inadequate to protect human rights, a proportionality standard has been incorporated into English law. In essence the proportionality test allows for a 'somewhat greater' intensity of judicial review, requiring that limits placed on rights by administrators go no further than necessary to accomplish justifiable legislative objectives. In other words, English courts have accepted that the protection of human rights requires a more intrusive standard of review than Wednesbury provided, thereby expanding the scope of judicial review.[64]

Setting out the legal position of the law post-*Daly*, this statement emphasizes the acceptance into UK law of the proportionality test. Since 2001, however, the test that is used in the UK has itself evolved. In the case of *Bank Mellat v HM Treasury*,[65] for instance, the Supreme Court drew from a number of existing authorities, including *de Freitas*, *R v Oakes*,[66] and the later case of *Huang v Secretary of State for the Home Department*,[67] in setting out a modified version of the proportionality test. The case concerned an application to strike down an order from the Treasury to the effect that UK financial institutions should

---

[62] Ibid [26].   [63] Ibid [27].

[64] Janina Boughey, 'Administrative Law: The Next Frontier for Comparative Law' (2013) *International and Comparative Law Quarterly* 55, 89, citing Robin Cooke, 'The Road Ahead for the Common Law' (2004) 53(2) *The International and Comparative Law Quarterly* 274, Sophie Boyron, 'Proportionality in English Administrative Law: A Faulty Translation' (1992) 12 *Oxford Journal of Legal Studies* 237; *Smith and Grady v UK* (1999) 29 EHRR 493; Thomas Poole, 'Between the Devil and the Deep Blue Sea: Administrative Law in an Age of Rights' in Linda Pearson, Carol Harlow, and Michael Taggart (eds), *Administrative Law in a Changing State: Essays in Honour of Mark Aronson* (Hart Publishing 2008) 35; *R v Secretary of State for the Home Department, ex p Daly* [2001] UKHL 26; *Huang v Secretary of State for the Home Department* [2007] 2 AC 167 [19]; *R (Razgar) v Secretary of State for the Home Department* [2004] 2 AC 368 [20].

[65] [2013] UKSC 39.   [66] [1986] 1 SCR 103.   [67] [2007] UKHL 11.

be prevented from dealing with Iranian bank, Bank Mellat, to ensure separation from the funding of Iran's nuclear programme.[68] In finding the Treasury's order to be disproportionate, however, the Court considered that, in assessing proportionality:

> it is necessary to determine (1) whether the objective of the measure is sufficiently important to justify the limitation of a protected right, (2) whether the measure is rationally connected to the objective, (3) whether a less intrusive measure could have been used without unacceptably compromising the achievement of the objective, and (4) whether, balancing the severity of the measure's effects on the rights of the persons to whom it applies against the importance of the objective, to the extent that the measure will contribute to its achievement, the former outweighs the latter.[69]

This statement represents an up-to-date explanation of the questions a court must consider in applying the proportionality test in UK law. In order that we might further understand how this test applies in respect of judicial review, however, it is necessary now to consider the manner in which it relates to *Wednesbury* unreasonableness and to explore the way in which the courts have continued to apply and develop it, as the next section seeks to do.

Discussing the problem

In the last 'Discussing the problem' box, it was considered that the actions of the Prison Board, as set out in the problem scenario, could be argued as falling short of the *Wednesbury* unreasonableness test. With the development of proportionality in mind, however, particularly within the sphere of human rights, do you think a court would now take a different view in light of that test?

Probably, yes. For two connected reasons. First, the more structured proportionality test would be likely to permit a more intense level of review and scrutiny of the Board's actions. Secondly, the actions of the Prison Board engage certain Convention rights. We consider these reasons in reverse.

Though the ECHR is discussed in Chapters 15 and 16, we can here identify certain rights that are engaged by this problem scenario. Being forbidden from seeing friends or family for two months touches on the right protected in Article 8 ECHR, which sets out a right to a private and family life, while being placed in solitary confinement for three weeks amounts to a greater limitation of the Article 5 right to liberty (than that ordinarily imposed on prisoners), even arguably touching upon the Article 3 right to freedom from inhuman or degrading treatment. Finally, and as in the *Daly* case, the cell-searching and examination of private correspondence potentially amounts to a breach of confidentiality (depending on the nature of any such correspondence). With these rights identified and explained, we can now consider the proportionality test and determine whether the Prison Board's actions would be held lawful on that basis. For this, we can

→

---

[68] See for fuller discussion David Hart, 'An ABC on Proportionality—With Bank Mellat as our Primer' (*UK Human Rights Blog*, 22 June 2013), http://ukhumanrightsblog.com/2013/06/22/an-abc-on-proportionality-with-bank-mellat-as-our-primer/.

[69] [2013] UKSC 39 [74].

→

draw from the test set out in *Bank Mellat v HM Treasury*.[70] This is set out again here for ease of reference. The questions to consider are:

> (1) whether the objective of the measure is sufficiently important to justify the limitation of a protected right, (2) whether the measure is rationally connected to the objective, (3) whether a less intrusive measure could have been used without unacceptably compromising the achievement of the objective, and (4) whether, balancing the severity of the measure's effects on the rights of the persons to whom it applies against the importance of the objective, to the extent that the measure will contribute to its achievement, the former outweighs the latter.[71]

In answering these questions in light of the problem scenario, it could be argued that the punishment imposed by the Prison Board is disproportionate to the objective to be achieved (this being the punishment of prisoners for their misdemeanours). While the need to impose some form of punishment in the circumstances can be accepted as necessary, the argument is that these actions go too far and that there are 'less intrusive measures' that could have been used for the same purpose. The refusal of friend and family visits for a couple of weeks for instance, or the imposition of solitary confinement for a couple of days,[72] or, indeed, searching cells, excluding private and confidential correspondence, might all be deemed acceptable forms of punishment. Remission of sentence has even been used before.[73] The degrees of punishment here imposed are arguably a disproportionate infringement of the rights of prisoners.

12.5 Unreasonableness and proportionality

To consider the relationship between *Wednesbury* unreasonableness and proportionality, in *Daly* Lord Steyn noted that:

> there is an overlap between the traditional grounds of review and the approach of proportionality. Most cases would be decided in the same way whichever approach is adopted. But the intensity of review is somewhat greater under the proportionality approach. I would[, then,] mention three concrete differences without suggesting that my statement is exhaustive. First, the doctrine of proportionality may require the reviewing court to assess the balance which the decision maker has struck, not merely whether it is within the range of rational or reasonable decisions. Secondly, the proportionality test may go further than the traditional grounds of review inasmuch as it may require attention to be directed to the relative weight accorded to interests and considerations. Thirdly, even the heightened scrutiny test developed in *R v Ministry of Defence, Ex p Smith* . . . is not necessarily appropriate to the protection of human rights.[74]

---

[70] [2013] UKSC 39.   [71] [2013] UKSC 39 [74].

[72] The 'Council of Europe's Committee on the Prevention of Torture and Inhuman or Degrading Treatment or Punishment (CPT) has advised that for punitive purposes any stint [of solitary confinement] should be limited to 14 days' (Fraser Simpson, 'Unauthorised Solitary Confinement Incompatible with Prisoner's Rights' (UK Human Rights Blog, 15 October 2015), https://ukhumanrightsblog.com/2015/10/15/unauthorised-solitary-confinement-incompatible-with-prisoners-rights/, citing: CPT, '21st General Report' (Strasbourg, November 2011) 40, https://rm.coe.int/1680696a88).

[73] See *O'Reilly v Mackman* [1983] 2 AC 237, discussed in 10.5.

[74] [2001] UKHL 26 [27].

The relationship between unreasonableness and proportionality is a complex one. As Lord Steyn notes, there are certain overlaps between the two tests and in the manner in which they can assess similar situations. A consequence of this is that application of the two tests can sometimes give rise to the same result. Equally, though, the greater intensity of review afforded under the proportionality test can also mean that different results are achieved, as the House of Lords and Strasbourg judgments in *Smith and Grady* demonstrate. These two opposing realities give rise to differing arguments with regards to the potential for proportionality in judicial review cases. Some argue, on the one hand, that the increased intensity of review means that proportionality is ill-suited to application in general review and that it should be restricted to use under EU Law and the ECHR. Since unreasonableness and proportionality can often lead to the same or similar results, there is a strong case supporting the latter's limited use in domestic judicial review applications.[75] On the other hand, though, it is also argued that the more balanced proportionality test should be widely recognized as an independent ground for judicial review, perhaps even in place of the particularly stringent *Wednesbury* unreasonableness. These two competing views will now be explored in turn, starting with the latter.

12.5.1 Proportionality as a replacement for unreasonableness as a ground for judicial review

The case for proportionality as a ground for judicial review and as a replacement for *Wednesbury* unreasonableness rests on a number of points. The first that we shall consider relates to growing scepticism for *Wednesbury* unreasonableness and concern for its continued relevance in judicial review applications. In *Daly*, where the House of Lords applied the test of proportionality, rather than unreasonableness, Lord Cooke stated that:

> I think that the day will come when it will be more widely recognised that *Associated Provincial Picture Houses Ltd v Wednesbury Corpn* was an unfortunately retrogressive decision in English administrative law, in so far as it suggested that there are degrees of unreasonableness and that only a very extreme degree can bring an administrative decision within the legitimate scope of judicial invalidation. The depth of judicial review and the deference due to administrative discretion vary with the subject matter.[76]

The view that the decision in *Wednesbury* was 'unfortunate' must be seen in light of its use and application on countless occasions since 1948. Lord Cooke's real concern is that the test has become so strict as to become an inadequate tool for the courts, when scrutinizing exercise of administrative discretion in the range of contexts that applications for judicial review now involve. As Craig notes on this, the 'test, if taken seriously, constitutes an almost insurmountable hurdle for claimants'.[77]

The overlap between unreasonableness and proportionality and the realization that they can often be used to achieve the same result, noted by Lord Steyn, means that a strong case can be made for replacing the *Wednesbury* test with proportionality. In *R (Association of British Civilian Internees: Far East Region) v Secretary of State for Defence*,[78] for

[75] See, generally: James Goodwin, 'The Last Defence of Wednesbury' (2012) *Public Law* 445.
[76] [2001] UKHL 26 [32], citing [1948] 1 KB 223.
[77] Paul Craig, *Administrative Law* (7th edn, Sweet and Maxwell 2012) 665.
[78] [2003] EWCA Civ 473.

instance, a challenge was brought to the lawfulness of a scheme set up to compensate British nationals, either born in the UK or with parents or grandparents born in the UK, who had been held captive by the Japanese during the Second World War. In giving judgment, Dyson LJ not only noted the overlap between unreasonableness and proportionality, but also went further and suggested that there was a consequent case to be made for replacing the *Wednesbury* test with proportionality. He stated that '[t]he Wednesbury test is moving closer to proportionality and in some cases it is not possible to see any daylight between the two tests . . . we have difficulty in seeing what justification there now is for retaining the Wednesbury test'.[79]

Similarly, in the case of *R (Alconbury Developments Ltd and others) v Secretary of State for the Environment*,[80] Lord Slynn suggested that '[t]rying to keep the *Wednesbury* principle and proportionality in separate compartments seems to me to be unnecessary and confusing'.[81] The benefits of proportionality over unreasonableness have also been noted by Craig. He suggests that, with proportionality used under both EU law and ECHR jurisprudence, it offers greater simplicity and consistency for the test to be used in 'non-HRA domestic law challenges'.[82] Moreover, he notes that proportionality allows for a more structured and reasoned inquiry, which has 'often been lacking when the "monolithic" *Wednesbury* test has been applied'.[83] What Craig means by this is that the question the courts consider, in applying the proportionality test, permits a more measured and balanced analysis of the given issues, compared with the simple question as to whether or not something can be deemed reasonable. With Craig's call for more expansive use of proportionality in mind, it is hardly surprising that the House of Lords, in *Alconbury Developments Ltd*, saw fit to acknowledge the growing relevance of the test in UK Administrative law, even in cases that do not involve consideration of human rights. Lord Slynn noted that:

> I consider that even without reference to the Human Rights Act 1998 the time has come to recognise that this principle [proportionality] is part of English administrative law, not only when judges are dealing with Community acts but also when they are dealing with acts subject to domestic law.[84]

 Pause for reflection

Taking into account the cases of *Smith*, *Smith and Grady v UK*, and *Daly*, and the judgments handed down in those cases, do you think that the time has come for proportionality to replace *Wednesbury* unreasonableness as a ground for judicial review?

The position with regards to proportionality is quite clear. It has developed and expanded beyond the realm of human rights cases and is gradually being acknowledged by the courts as an independent ground for judicial review, perhaps at times even in preference to *Wednesbury* unreasonableness. Equally, though, there is also authority that supports retention of Lord Greene's 1948 test, as the next section now discusses.

---

[79] Ibid [34], citing Leonard Hoffman, 'A Sense of Proportionality' (Third John Maurice Kelly Memorial Lecture, University College Dublin, 14 November 1996) 13.
[80] [2001] UKHL 23.   [81] Ibid [51].
[82] Paul Craig, *Administrative Law* (7th edn, Sweet and Maxwell 2012) 668.
[83] Ibid.   [84] [2001] UKHL 23 [51].

12.5.2 The retention of *Wednesbury* unreasonableness

Though the case for proportionality to be recognized as a ground for review is a persuasive one and an approach that offers 'a degree of continuity and deference',[85] drawbacks remain.[86] There are concerns with regards to the use of the proportionality test in judicial review, with a consequent case often made for retention of *Wednesbury* unreasonableness, with both judicial and academic statements supporting that case. Indeed, regardless of the developments as regards proportionality, the unreasonableness test remains good law as can be seen in the following case.

Key case: *R (D and Others) v Parole Board* [2018] EWHC 694

John Warboys was convicted of nineteen serious sexual offences committed against twelve victims while working as a black cab driver in London between October 2006 and February 2009. He was sentenced to an indeterminate sentence with a minimum imprisonment of eight years. There was evidence of at least another eighty cases which had not gone to trial. Six years into his sentence, Warboys admitted his guilt for the nineteen offences for which he was convicted, but not in relation to the other cases. Once his minimum term expired, the Parole Board decided that his imprisonment was no longer necessary for the protection of the public and that Warboys (who had since changed his name to John Radford) should be released on licence. Psychologist reports indicated some inconsistencies about Warboys' own account of his offending and that he appeared to have minimalized the extent of his offending and the impact his actions had on his victims. In coming to its decision, the Parole Board placed much emphasis on the fact that Warboys had admitted his guilt to the offences for which he was imprisoned.

The High Court, in applying the Wednesbury test as explained by Lord Diplock in *GCHQ*, found that, although the decision to release Warboys was 'surprising and concerning', it was not irrational.[87] The Parole Board was fully aware of what it was doing, including that it was rejecting the assessments of psychological experts who had dealt with Warboys while in prison. However, the Court did find that it was irrational of the Board not to ask further questions about the case, including the extent of other offences he had committed, as a means of testing the honesty and veracity of Warboys' broader account of his offending. This was particularly important because Warboys' honesty was the key question as regards his continuing risk to the public, and this was not sufficiently investigated by the Board.[88]

The Court of Appeal has made clear that it is not for them to dispense with the *Wednesbury* test. In *R (Association of British Civilian Internees: Far East Region) v Secretary of State for Defence*, Dyson LJ noted, that regarding *Wednesbury* unreasonableness, 'it is not for this court to perform its burial rites. The continuing existence of the Wednesbury test has been acknowledged by the House of Lords on more than one occasion'.[89] Clearly, the Court of Appeal is unable to overrule a principle established by the House of Lords, or the Supreme Court. Dyson LJ's words indicate a general reluctance to depart from unreasonableness.

---

[85] Ian Leigh, 'Taking Rights Proportionately: Judicial Review, the Human Rights Act and Strasbourg' (2002) *Public Law* 265, 278.

[86] See Paul Craig, *Administrative Law* (7th edn, Sweet and Maxwell 2012) 670–3.

[87] [2018] EWHC 694 [130].   [88] Ibid [155]–[164].

[89] [2003] EWCA Civ 473 [35].

Yet, if the Court of Appeal cannot give *Wednesbury* unreasonableness its burial rites, apparently, neither can a five-justice panel of the Supreme Court.[90] In *Keyu v Secretary of State for Foreign and Commonwealth Affairs*,[91] the highest court in the UK once again discussed and considered the relationship between the two tests. The facts of the case concerned a refusal by the Foreign Secretary and Secretary of State for Defence to hold an inquiry into the death of unarmed civilians in the Federation of Malaya (now part of Malaysia) in the late 1948, which was then part of the British Empire.[92] Under the Inquiries Act 2005, the government has the power to hold an inquiry where it appears that certain events have caused 'public concern'[93] and the question turned on the refusal by the two ministers to exercise their discretion and hold an inquiry under the 2005 Act. While the majority of the Supreme Court held that the decision was lawful, in hearing the appeal, the Supreme Court was invited to consider the continued relevance of *Wednesbury* unreasonableness, including the question of whether it should 'be replaced by a more structured and principled challenge based on proportionality'.[94] On this issue, Lord Neuberger stated that:

> It would not be appropriate for a five-Justice panel of this court to accept, or indeed to reject, this argument, which potentially has implications which are profound in constitutional terms and very wide in applicable scope. Accordingly, if a proportionality challenge to the refusal to hold an inquiry would succeed, then it would be necessary to have this appeal (or at any rate this aspect of this appeal) re-argued before a panel of nine Justices. However, in my opinion, such a course is unnecessary because I consider that the appellants' third line of appeal would fail even if it was and could be based on proportionality.[95]

The Supreme Court, with just five justices on the bench, felt inadequately empowered to decide that *Wednesbury* unreasonableness, as a substantive ground for judicial review, should be replaced by proportionality. While interesting, in one sense, that nothing less than a nine-justice Supreme Court is desired to consider questions with potentially profound constitutional consequences, there is also an air of reluctance too easily to discard the well-established test of unreasonableness, suggesting that it still has a place in UK Administrative Law.[96] As Lord Kerr suggested, however, it is a question that the Supreme Court must soon consider, and when it does it must explore existing authorities to decide:

> whether irrationality and proportionality are forms of review which are bluntly opposed to each other and mutually exclusive; whether intensity of review operates on a sliding scale, dependent on the nature of the decision under challenge . . . whether there is any place in modern administrative law for a 'pure' irrationality ground of review . . . and whether proportionality provides a more structured and transparent means of review.[97]

---

[90] See Mark Elliott, 'Q: How Many Supreme Court Justices Does it Take to Perform the Wednesbury Doctrine Burial Rites? A: More than Five' (*Public Law for Everyone,* 27 November 2015), http://publiclaw-foreveryone.com/2015/11/27/q-how-many-supreme-court-justices-does-it-take-to-perform-the-wednes-bury-doctrines-burial-rites-a-more-than-five/#more-3313.

[91] [2015] UKSC 69.   [92] [2015] UKSC 69 [5].

[93] See s 1(1) of the Inquiries Act 2005.

[94] [2015] UKSC 69 [131].   [95] Ibid [132].

[96] It must be pointed out that eleven justices of the Supreme Court heard *R (Miller) v Secretary of State for Exiting the European Union* [2017] UKSC 5 and *R (Miller) v Prime Minister* [2019] UKSC 41.

[97] [2015] UKSC 69 [278].

Indeed, if proportionality is to replace *Wednesbury* unreasonableness, then there are secondary questions to explore surrounding the continued application of the *Bank Mellat* test. Lord Kerr in *Keyu*, for instance, questions the feasibility of applying the existing proportionality test 'in place of rationality in all domestic judicial review cases', envisaging instead 'a more loosely structured proportionality' test.[98] Until the Supreme Court is called upon to settle such issues more directly, however, *Wednesbury* unreasonableness sits alongside proportionality and remains good law.[99]

Arguments in favour of the continued relevance of *Wednesbury* unreasonableness are often founded on suggestions that proportionality is ill-suited to application in domestic judicial review cases and that it should be restricted to its application under EU Law and cases concerning the ECHR. Craig, for one, notes that '[p]roportionality should be the test in rights-based cases, with narrow rationality review remaining for what [Taggart] described as "public wrongs"'.[100] Similarly, Knight observes that '[t]he courts [have] maintained the strict separation of the proportionality spheres from ordinary domestic administrative law',[101] going on to highlight the case of *R v Chief Constable of Sussex, ex p International Trader's Ferry*.[102] Here, the House of Lords 'had to juggle the two spheres simultaneously . . . decid[ing] whether a policing manpower decision was irrational under domestic law (on *Wednesbury* grounds) but also whether the decision was proportionate under European . . . laws'.[103] The underlying rationale for arguments that proportionality is not best suited for domestic judicial review is that it offers 'too great an intrusion into the merits' of decisions.[104]

This brings us back to the distinction to be drawn between the courts' supervisory and appellate jurisdictions, discussed in previous sections and in 10.2.1. It is recalled that while courts in many cases exercise an appellate jurisdiction, deciding cases on their legal and factual merits, in judicial review applications use of the supervisory jurisdiction ensures that the courts merely supervise the legality of administrative acts and decisions and are not called upon to decide questions of merit to prevent them from engaging in potentially political matters. With this in mind, the argument in respect of proportionality is that if the courts are considering the application of the test then they are going beyond this supervisory jurisdiction and assessing the merits of political acts and decisions of a political nature.[105] Explaining this argument further, Goodwin notes a distinction between primary and secondary decision-making, which is drawn on similar lines to that between the appellate and supervisory jurisdiction:

> Primary decision-making is the essence of administrative decision-making; it is the making
> of a policy . . . Primary decisions are made by reference to their *merits*, and judged by their

---

[98] Ibid [281] and [282].

[99] See Mark Elliott, 'Q: How Many Supreme Court Justices Does it Take to Perform the Wednesbury Doctrine Burial Rites? A: More than Five' (*Public Law for Everyone*, 27 November 2015).

[100] Paul Craig, *Administrative Law* (7th edn, Sweet and Maxwell 2012) 664, citing Michael Taggart, 'Proportionality, Deference, Wednesbury' (2008) *New Zealand Law Review* 423, 471–2, and 477–9.

[101] Christopher Knight, 'The Test that Dare Not Speak its Name: Proportionality Comes Out of the Closet?' (2007) *Judicial Review* 117, 118.

[102] [1999] 2 AC 418.

[103] Christopher Knight, 'The Test that Dare Not Speak its Name: Proportionality Comes Out of the Closet?' (2007) *Judicial Review* 117, 118. Knight notes that the 'House of Lords held that the decision was neither irrational nor disproportionate' (see n 4).

[104] Paul Craig, *Administrative Law* (7th edn, Sweet and Maxwell 2012) 670.

[105] See, for contrasting arguments, Tom Hickman, *Public Law after the Human Rights Act* (Hart Publishing 2010) 261–4, and ch 9 generally.

accordance with the *public interest* . . . Conversely, secondary decision-making is deciding on the *lawfulness* of the primary decision. This is the essence of judicial review. The secondary decision is made by reference to legality, according to whichever standard of *legality* is applicable.[106]

Primary decision-making is carried out by ministers, secondary decision-making by judges.[107] The concern with regards to the application of the proportionality test is that it 'improperly blurs' the distinction between the two.[108] Goodwin further explains that:

> *Daly* exemplifies how the proportionality methodology requires the court to assess the balance of interests and accord weight to justifications. This is the very *essence* of primary decision-making, not secondary decision-making. The idea that *weight* would ever be considered in *Wednesbury* review is heretical, as made clear by Lord Steyn in distinguishing reasonableness review and proportionality.[109]

Arguments in favour of the retention of *Wednesbury* unreasonableness are based in part on the concern that proportionality invites courts to err from their supervisory jurisdiction and to consider the merits of potentially political decisions, thereby going outside their ordinary function in judicial review cases. Whether or not this is the case would need to be assessed in individual cases where the proportionality test has been employed. It is notable, though, that Lord Sumption in *Bank Mellat*, in setting out the proportionality test, stressed that '[n]one of this means that the court is to take over the function of the decision-maker'.[110]

 Pause for reflection

Do you think there are sufficient arguments in favour of retaining the *Wednesbury* test for unreasonableness? Aside from questions concerning the size of the panel hearing the case, can you think of circumstances in which the Supreme Court might finally perform its 'burial rites'?

The relationship between *Wednesbury* unreasonableness and proportionality is clearly a complex one. While an analysis of recent case law shows growing support for the development of proportionality in judicial review, arguments grounded in preserving the supervisory jurisdiction of the Administrative Court and ensuring judges are not granted too great a power to enquire as to the use of executive power support the retention of the unreasonableness test. Before long, the Supreme Court may be called upon to consider more directly the place of both proportionality and unreasonableness in judicial review. Until that day comes, we are left in the uncertain position of retaining *Wednesbury* unreasonableness and allowing for the application of the proportionality test, with the courts in any one case having the authority to decide the most suitable test.

---

[106] James Goodwin, 'The Last Defence of Wednesbury' (2012) *Public Law* 445, 451.

[107] Ibid, citing *R v Secretary of State for the Home Department, ex p Brind* [1991] 1 AC 696, 749.

[108] Ibid 453.

[109] Ibid 453, citing *R (on the application of Daly) v Secretary of State for the Home Department* [2001] UKHL 26 [27].

[110] [2013] UKSC 39 [21].

12.6 **Summary**

This chapter has explored and considered the second ground for judicial review identified by Lord Diplock, in *Council of Civil Service Unions and Others v Minister for the Civil Service*, as irrationality. This is a ground that builds on Lord Greene's principle of unreasonableness, espoused in the case of *Associated Provincial Picture Houses Ltd v Wednesbury Corporation*.[111] On this foundation, the chapter has explored the nature of the test, tracing its roots back to *Roberts v Hopwood* and it has examined the manner in which it has come to be interpreted by the courts since both *Wednesbury* and *GCHQ*. The general attitude with regard to the unreasonableness test has been one of strictness. In order that the supervisory jurisdiction of the court—itself arguably fundamental to the foundation of judicial review—might be preserved and protected, the courts have been reluctant to entertain questions relating to the merits of cases and, as a consequence, have been inclined to interpret Lord Greene's test with caution and stringency, most notably in the case of *Smith*.[112] While true to the notion that the courts should not look at the merits of a particular decision or engage with the matters that they raise, however, this judgment does raise broader concerns, as noted on appeal to the ECtHR. As a consequence of this, and motivated in part by the Strasbourg Court's judgment, the concept of proportionality has emerged as a growing ground for judicial review. Lord Steyn in *Daly* later noted that proportionality should always be used wherever human rights are at issue and, since that case, the test of proportionality has developed and expanded to an even greater degree, with questions now being considered with regard to whether or not it should replace *Wednesbury* unreasonableness or whether Lord Greene's test should be retained alongside proportionality.

Quick test questions

1. How did Lord Greene MR define unreasonableness in *Associated Provincial Picture Houses Ltd v Wednesbury Corporation*?

2. Why do you think the courts have applied the test for unreasonableness so strictly?

3. What are the circumstances underpinning the development of proportionality in judicial review?

4. What is the test for proportionality, as set out in *Bank Mellat v HM Treasury*?

5. Do you think that there is scope for both unreasonableness and proportionality to work alongside each other within the field of judicial review?

---

[111] [1948] 1 KB 223.
[112] [1996] QB 517.

Further reading

Generally

Paul Craig, *Administrative Law* (8th edn, Sweet and Maxwell 2016) Ch 20

HWR Wade and CF Forsyth, *Administrative Law* (11th edn, OUP 2014) Ch 11

Wednesbury

Mark Elliott, 'Q: How many Supreme Court Justices Does It Take to Perform the Wednesbury Doctrine Burial Rites? A: More than Five' (*Public Law for Everyone,* 27 November 2015) available at http://publiclawforeveryone.com/2015/11/27/q-how-many-supreme-court-justices-does-it-take-to-perform-the-wednesbury-doctrines-burial-rites-a-more-than-five/#more-3313

James Goodwin, 'The Last Defence of Wednesbury' (2012) *Public Law* 445

Michael Taggert, 'Proportionality, Deference and Wednesbury' [2008] *New Zealand Law Review* 423

*Rebecca Williams, 'Structuring Substantive Review' [2017] *Public Law* 99

Proportionality

*Tom Hickman, 'The Substance and Structure of Proportionality' (2008) *Public Law* 694

*Tom Hickman, *Public Law after the Human Rights Act* (Hart Publishing 2010) Chs 6 and 7

Christopher Knight, 'The Test that Dare Not Speak its Name: Proportionality Comes Out of the Closet?' (2007) 12(2) *Judicial Review* 117

Ian Leigh, 'Taking Rights Proportionately: Judicial Review, the Human Rights Act and Strasbourg' [2002] *Public Law* 265

 Visit this book's **online resources** for additional materials relating to this chapter, including a full analysis of the start-of-chapter problem scenario.
www.oup.com/he/stanton-prescott2e

13

Judicial review: procedural impropriety

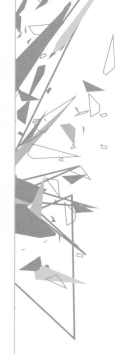

Problem scenario

Under section 3 of the (fictitious) Food Distribution Act 2024, should anyone wish to open a restaurant, they must apply to the local authority. Under section 3, the local authority must deal with the application according to a special procedure.

Under section 3(1), on receiving an application, the local authority must send a notice to all properties within 250 metres of the proposed restaurant and place a further notice outside the property where the restaurant is proposed. The notices must state that any comments about the application for the proposed restaurant must be made within twenty-eight days.

Under section 3(2) any decision made by the local authority, must be communicated to the applicant in writing. Finally, under section 3(3), the local authority must hear any appeal against the decision, which should be considered by a specially convened independent committee.

Louise owns a property which is currently empty in the town centre of Nanchester and has decided that she should open a seafood restaurant on the ground floor. She applies to the Council, but after six weeks, she receives a letter informing her that her application has been rejected.

It is also the case that Louise has since learned that Ryan, the chairman of the committee of the Council making the decision, owns two restaurants in Nanchester City Centre with one restaurant, called Fish Face, specializing in fish.

In order to prepare her appeal, Louise has requested from the Council the reasons for their decision. In their response, the Council has rejected Louise's request.

Finally, it also appears that the Council sent letters informing those within 250 metres of Louise's building about her application to open a restaurant; however, no public notice was placed on the outside of the building.

Louise is disappointed about the decision and feels that she has not been treated fairly. She has come to you for advice as she prepares her appeal.

13.1 **Introduction**

This chapter considers procedural impropriety, the final of the three grounds outlined by Lord Diplock in *Council of Civil Service Unions and Others v Minister for the Civil Service*.[1] Lord Diplock explained procedural impropriety in the following terms:

> I have described the third head as 'procedural impropriety' rather than failure to observe basic rules of natural justice or failure to act with procedural fairness towards the person who will be affected by the decision. This is because susceptibility to judicial review under this head covers also failure by an administrative tribunal to observe procedural rules that are expressly laid down in the legislative instrument by which its jurisdiction is conferred, even where such failure does not involve any denial of natural justice.[2]

We can see from Lord Diplock's statement that procedural impropriety has several elements. The first is a failure to comply with any procedural requirements set out in statute. Secondly, there is a broader heading of failing to act 'fairly', the core of which are the rules of natural justice. As will be seen in this chapter, these rules can be summarized as the right to be heard and the right to a fair hearing. Yet, even with Lord Diplock's statement in mind, a clear understanding of procedural impropriety and in particular the idea of fairness, still remains elusive. A more detailed explanation was made by Lord Mustill in *R v Secretary of State for the Home Department, ex p Doody*,[3] who distilled procedural impropriety into the following six principles:

1. Where an Act of Parliament confers an administrative power there is a presumption that it will be exercised in a manner which is fair in all the circumstances.

2. The standards of fairness are not immutable. They may change with the passage of time, both in the general and in their application to decisions of a particular type.

3. The principles of fairness are not to be applied by rote identically in every situation. What fairness demands is dependent on the context of the decision, and this is to be taken into account in all its aspects.

4. An essential feature of the context is the statute which creates the discretion, as regards both its language and the shape of the legal and administrative system within which the decision is taken.

5. Fairness will very often require that a person who may be adversely affected by the decision will have an opportunity to make representations on his own behalf either before the decision is taken with a view to producing a favourable result; or after it is taken, with a view to procuring its modification; or both.

6. Since the person affected usually cannot make worthwhile representations without knowing what factors may weigh against his interests fairness will very often require that he is informed of the gist of the case which he has to answer.[4]

From the outset, Lord Mustill explains that the concept of 'fairness' is an 'intuitive' concept, meaning that what 'fairness' or 'acting fairly' requires depends on the context. However, the principles that Lord Mustill describes are a key consideration in determining

---

[1] [1985] AC 374. Hereinafter called *GCHQ*, because the case involved employees of one of the intelligence services—Government Communications Headquarters.

[2] Ibid 411.   [3] [1994] AC 531.   [4] Ibid 560.

what is fair. First, the issue of fairness arises from the underlying assumption that when Parliament grants powers to a public authority, they will be exercised 'fairly'. However, the requirements of fairness may change over time and will differ depending on the decision being made. It is against this backdrop that cases are decided and more significant decisions are likely to have to meet a higher standard of fairness. The fourth principle makes clear that a key feature as to what is required by fairness is the statute that grants the public authority to make the decision in the first place. The final two principles show that before someone is adversely affected by the decision, fairness will often require that they have an opportunity to make representations to the decision-maker, allowing them to explain their point of view. This requirement will only have any substance, if in turn, that person is at least informed of the 'gist of the case' against them.

Together, Lord Diplock's and Lord Mustill's statements form a relatively more detailed picture as to what procedural impropriety (and consequently this chapter) covers. This picture includes complying with any statutory requirement to make decisions according to a specific procedure, the rules of natural justice, in particular the right to be heard and the rule against bias. We can also see that someone likely to be negatively affected by a decision should have an opportunity to put their views to the decision-maker. This could be through a hearing, but as we can see from Lord Mustill's approach, what constitutes a fair hearing is likely to depend on the nature of the decision in question. This has also been influenced by the European Convention on Human Rights, Article 6, and this chapter will consider the relationship between the common law and the requirements imposed by Article 6 on public authorities.

In addition, since both Lord Mustill and Lord Diplock laid down these principles there have been significant debates about other aspects of fairness—in particular, whether there is a duty on public authorities to give reasons for the decisions they have made. Finally, there is the requirement that the legitimate expectations of a claimant are fulfilled. This is when the public authority has acted in such a way, either through past practice, a policy, or a promise to generate an expectation that either a decision will be made following a specific procedure or in rare cases that the public authority will reach a particular conclusion.[5]

This is the third ground of judicial review and, in a similar manner to the other two grounds of illegality and unreasonableness or proportionality, discussed in Chapters 11 and 12, the overall objective of the courts is to ensure that the rule of law is maintained. This can be based on the interpretation of an Act of Parliament, when a public authority does not follow a procedural requirement laid down in legislation. However, the other sections of this chapter are based on a broader presumption based on the rule of law, that 'unless there is the clearest provision to the contrary, Parliament must be presumed not to legislate contrary to the rule of law. And the rule of law enforces minimum standards of fairness, both substantive and procedural'.[6] Consequently, the rules of natural justice and giving effect to legitimate expectations ensure that public authorities exercise their powers fairly according to the requirements of the rule of law.

The objectives of this chapter are as follows:

- to explore the consequences of when a public authority fails to comply with a procedure imposed by an Act of Parliament;

---

[5] This was expressly considered to be part of procedural impropriety by Lord Diplock in *GCHQ* [1994] AC 374, 411.

[6] *R v Home Secretary, ex p Pierson* [1998] AC 539, 591 (Lord Steyn).

- to consider the rules of natural justice: the rule against bias and the right to a fair hearing and how Article 6 of the European Convention on Human Rights has influenced the development of the common law in this area;

- to consider the requirement of an oral hearing and then, if required, what form an oral hearing takes;

- to consider when the action of a public authority gives rise to a legitimate expectation and when public authorities are required to give reasons for their decisions.

13.2 Failing to follow statutory procedure

Very often, when an Act of Parliament grants the power to a public authority to *make* a particular decision, it also imposes requirements as to *how* that decision should be made. This could be a requirement to serve a notice on any interested party or to require a consultation exercise before reaching a decision. The issue is what happens if those procedural requirements have not been met. This is an exercise of statutory interpretation, ensuring that the intention of Parliament is being respected.

13.2.1 Mandatory or directory procedural requirements?

From the outset, it must be emphasized that not every procedural error will invalidate a decision. To decide whether a procedural defect should invalidate the decision, the courts must consider carefully the relevant legislation, in order 'to ascertain the purpose of [the] statutory procedures'.[7] If, after this exercise, the view is that the procedural failure invalidates the decision, then the requirement is deemed to be 'mandatory' and it is the failure to comply with the requirement that makes the decision void. If the failure to comply is less serious, then the condition is described as 'directory'. This means that the condition is expected to be complied with, but the failure to comply with the requirement has not invalidated the decision. Yet, as Wade and Forsyth state, 'it should be made crystal clear that there is no suggestion here that affixing the label "mandatory" or "directory" to a condition enables the judge to determine the validity of an act mechanically without having regard to the relevant statute'.[8] Essentially, Wade and Forsyth confirm that the main task for the judge is to interpret the legislation to determine the importance of the procedural requirement that has not been complied with.

The distinction between mandatory and directory requirements can be seen in the following two cases. In *Bradbury v Enfield London Borough Council*,[9] secondary education was largely organized between grammar schools and secondary moderns, with students who passed the '11-plus' going to grammar schools. The policy of the government was to abolish this system and replace these schools with comprehensive schools which admitted all students regardless of ability. The local authority, in fulfilling its duties for secondary education within its area, sought to reorganize its schools and introduce comprehensive schools in accordance with government policy. However, the local authority had misinterpreted the statute and failed to give notice to the parents of pupils attending eight of the schools to be closed. The purpose of the notice was to allow these parents to raise any

---

[7] *Director of Public Prosecutions of the Virgin Islands v Penn* [2008] UKPC 29 [18] Lord Mance.
[8] HWR Wade and CF Forsyth, *Administrative Law* (11th edn, OUP 2014) 184.
[9] [1967] 1 WLR 1311.

objections they had to the proposals. This lack of consultation meant that the procedure required by statute was not complied with. This led to the Court of Appeal finding that the local authority had acted unlawfully. Danckwerts LJ stated:

> it is imperative that the procedure laid down in the relevant statutes should be properly observed. The provisions of the statutes in this respect are supposed to provide safeguards for Her Majesty's subjects. Public Bodies and Ministers must be compelled to observe the law; and it is essential that bureaucracy should be kept in its place.[10]

The requirement of the public notice was a mandatory requirement, meaning that the incorrect procedure had been followed by the public authority.

Bradbury can be contrasted to *Coney v Choyce*,[11] another case about the reorganization of secondary education into comprehensive schools. In this case, public notice of the proposals was given in the local newspapers and had been detailed in letters sent to the parents. In addition, public meetings to discuss the issue had been held. However, with two schools, a requirement that a notice was posted at or near the main entrance of the school had not been complied with. The scheme of reorganization was challenged on the basis that the statutory requirements had not been met. This argument was rejected, because the procedural requirements breached were minor and the breach did not prejudice the interests of the parties involved. The requirements not complied with were merely directory and did not invalidate the decision made.[12] Templeman J reached this decision after finding that the relevant legislation, the Education Act 1944 was 'concerned with the administration of education'[13] and that it would be 'lamentable if the carrying out of the purposes of the Education Act 1944 . . . were hampered by a strict insistence on the letter of the regulations being carried out subject to the dire penalty of the whole thing being invalid'.[14] Templeman J considered that as there had been 'substantial compliance with the regulations',[15] the failure to comply with the precise requirements did not cause 'substantial prejudice' as the purpose of the regulations, to inform parents about the proposed changes, had been achieved. In these 'circumstances it be quite wrong to hold that the technical defects in compliance with the regulations make the [decision] invalid'.[16]

13.2.2 Substantial compliance?

The breach of procedural requirements was of a minor nature in *Coney v Choyce*. This was clear because the intention of the requirements imposed was to ensure that parents were informed about the proposals. Because this objective was achieved through other methods, it was relatively easy to categorize the contested requirements as 'directory'. However, the distinction could be arbitrary and can be very much a matter of judgment. For this reason, Lord Hailsham suggested that these categories of 'mandatory' and 'directory' are 'not so much a stark choice of alternatives but a spectrum of possibilities in which one compartment or description fades gradually into another'.[17]

For this reason, later cases have questioned whether the terms 'mandatory' and 'directory' are still appropriate. This is because deciding whether a procedural requirement is mandatory or directory arises at the end of a process, which starts by determining whether the statute requires that the particular requirement is complied with in order for

---

[10] Ibid 1325.   [11] [1975] 1 WLR 422.   [12] Ibid 434.
[13] Ibid.   [14] Ibid.   [15] Ibid.   [16] Ibid.
[17] *London & Clydeside Estates Ltd v Aberdeen District Council* [1980] 1 WLR 182, 189.

it to be considered as mandatory. Consequently, the Australian High Court, when considering this issue in *Project Blue Sky Inc v Australian Broadcasting Authority*,[18] concluded that:

> The classification is the end of the inquiry, not the beginning. That being so, a court, determining the validity of an act done in breach of a statutory provision, may easily focus on the wrong factors if it asks itself whether compliance with the provision is mandatory or directory and, if directory, whether there has been substantial compliance with the provision. A better test for determining the issue of validity is to ask whether it was a purpose of the legislation that an act done in breach of the provision should be invalid. In determining the question of purpose, regard must be had to the 'language of the relevant provision and the scope and object of the whole statute'.[19]

In *R v Soneji*,[20] Lord Steyn approved the views of Lord Hailsham and of the Australian High Court in *Blue Sky*, considering that the 'rigid mandatory and directory distinction . . . have outlived their usefulness'.[21] Instead 'the emphasis ought to be on the consequences of non-compliance, and posing the question whether Parliament can fairly be taken to have intended total invalidity'.[22] This modern approach can be seen in the following case.

Case in depth: *R v Secretary of State for the Home Department, ex p Jeyeanthan* **[2000] 1 WLR 354**

An asylum seeker, whose claim had been rejected, appealed successfully before the adjudicator. The Secretary of State applied to appeal against the adjudicator's decision by letter rather than using the specified form as required by rule 13(3) of the Asylum Appeals (Procedure) Rules 1993. Other than the statement of trust as detailed on the form, the letter provided all the information required. Lord Woolf MR set out the approach that courts should take, following Lord Hailsham's guidance in *London & Clydeside Estates Ltd v Aberdeen District Council*.[23] Lord Woolf MR stated:

> I suggest that the right approach is to regard the question of whether a requirement is directory or mandatory as only at most a first step. In the majority of cases there are other questions which have to be asked which are more likely to be of greater assistance than the application of the mandatory/directory test. The questions which are likely to arise are as follows.
>
> 1. Is the statutory requirement fulfilled if there has been substantial compliance with the requirement and, if so, has there been substantial compliance in the case in issue even though there has not been strict compliance? (The substantial compliance question.)
> 2. Is the non-compliance capable of being waived, and if so, has it, or can it and should it be waived in this particular case? (The discretionary question.)
> 3. If it is not capable of being waived or is not waived then what is the consequence of the non-compliance? (The consequences question.)

Which questions arise will depend upon the facts of the case and the nature of the particular requirement. The advantage of focusing on these questions is that they should avoid the unjust and unintended consequences which can flow from an approach solely dependent on dividing requirements into mandatory ones, which oust jurisdiction, or directory, which do not.[24]

---

[18] (1998) 194 CLR 355.   [19] Ibid para 93.   [20] [2006] 1 AC 340.
[21] Ibid para 23.   [22] Ibid.   [23] [1980] 1 WLR 182, 188–90.   [24] [2000] 1 WLR 354, 362.

Lord Woolf considered that the breach in this case was a 'pure technicality' which had not affected the claimant in any way.[25] Lord Woolf also made clear that not objecting to a breach of procedure may mean that the procedural failure has been waived. The final issue regarding 'substantial compliance' is that fulfilling a procedural requirement must as a matter of substance, be genuine rather than merely tokenistic. For example, in *Lee v Department of Education*, giving notice only four days before the decision was made was deemed not to comply with the requirement to give public notice.[26]

Discussing the problem

Look again at the problem scenario set at the beginning of the chapter. Did the local authority comply with the statutory procedure set out in the Food Distribution Act 2024? Would a failure to comply invalidate the decision made about Louise's application?

It is clear the Council have complied with the requirement in section 3(1) of sending a notice to all properties within 250 metres of Louise's property, but the Council has failed to comply with the requirement that a public notice is placed outside the building. This raises the distinction between *Bradbury v Enfield Borough Council* and *Coney v Choyce*. On the facts, this appears to be closer to *Coney v Choyce*, as it appears that the purpose of section 3(1) is that those close to the property are informed about the proposal for a restaurant and that they are given the opportunity to do so. They will have been given this opportunity through the notices they each received. In this way, it appears that there has been substantial compliance with the section as required by the *Jeyeanthan* case.

13.2.3 A statutory duty to consult

A particularly common duty imposed by statute is the duty to consult with interested groups or the public. This allows for the public to engage with the decision-making process and have an input into decisions that are likely to affect them. The requirements of a statutory duty to consult were reviewed by the Supreme Court in the following case.

Case in depth: *R (Moseley) v Haringey LBC* [2014] UKSC 56

Some council taxpayers' bills were either reduced in part or entirely through the government's Council Tax Benefit Scheme. This was replaced by the 'Council Tax Reduction Scheme', provided for by section 13A of the Local Government Finance Act 1992. Haringey LBC was required to consult with taxpayers.[27] However, before starting the consultation process, Haringey LBC had already taken the view that a shortfall in government funding would have to be made up by reducing the amount of money available in its Council Tax Reduction Scheme and not change the level of council tax paid. This meant that the consultation exercise did not ask taxpayers for their views on increasing council tax to make up the funding gap and leave untouched the amount of money available for the Council Tax Reduction Scheme.

→

---

[25] Ibid 366.   [26] (1967) 66 LGR 211.
[27] Local Government Finance Act 1992, Sch 1A, para 3.

→

The Supreme Court held that the consultation exercise was unlawful, finding that the exercise fell below what was required by the Sedley criteria,[28] which were explicitly approved by the Supreme Court.[29] These are as follows:

1. The consultation must take place when the proposals are at a formative stage.
2. The body conducting the consultation must give reasons for any proposal to allow intelligent consideration and response.
3. The consultation must allow for adequate time for consideration and response.
4. The outcome of the consultation must be 'conscientiously taken into account' when finalizing any proposals.

Because the decision not to increase council tax had already been made, the consultation exercise did not comply with the criteria set out by the court.

It is important to note that in *Moseley* the duty to consult was imposed by statute. However, the requirements of procedural fairness may mean that at common law, a public body is under a duty to conduct a consultation exercise before making a decision. If such a duty is imposed by the common law, then the Sedley criteria apply with as much force to the consultation exercise as they do consultation exercises required by statute. This means that the remaining issue is when a duty to consult arises at common law.

13.2.4 A common law duty of consultation

This was considered in *R (BAPIO Action Ltd) v Secretary of State for the Home Department*.[30] The Home Secretary had decided to change the Immigration Rules, with the changes making it more difficult for foreign medical students who had completed their studies to take up a training post in the UK. The change to the rules had been made without any consultation with those likely to be affected. It was argued by BAPIO Action Ltd, a group called the British Association of Physicians of Indian Origin, that the government should have consulted with groups such as theirs before making this change, under a general common law duty to consult.

This argument was rejected by the Court of Appeal. Sedley LJ expressed concern that a general common law duty to consult would be too open-ended, stating that:

The appellants have not been able to propose any limit to the generality of the duty. Their case must hold good for all such measures, of which the state at national and local level introduces certainly hundreds, possibly thousands, every year. If made good, such a duty would bring a host of litigable issues in its train: is the measure one which is actually going to injure particular interests sufficiently for fairness to require consultation? If so, who is entitled to be consulted? Are there interests which ought *not* to be consulted? How is the exercise to be publicised and conducted? Are the questions fairly framed? Have the responses been conscientiously taken into account? The consequent industry of legal challenges would generate in its turn defensive forms of public administration. All of this, I accept, will have to be lived with if the obligation exists; but it is at least a reason for being cautious.[31]

---

[28] The Sedley criteria were first accepted by *R v Brent London Borough Council, ex p Gunning* (1985) 84 LGR 168.

[29] [2014] UKSC 56 [25].

[30] [2007] EWCA Civ 1139.   [31] Ibid [44].

Sedley LJ was clear that if such a duty should be imposed, it should be by Parliament and not the courts.[32] Parliament has the flexibility not available to the courts to tailor the consultation requirement for each decision made, as it can 'abandon or modify obligations to consult which experience shows to be unnecessary or unworkable and extend those which seem to work well. The courts, which act on larger principles, can do none of these things'.[33]

It should not be assumed that just because there is no statutory duty to consult or any such duty at common law no procedural safeguards at all exist. Instead, the matter as a whole needs to be looked at in the round: as Maurice Kay LJ considered, 'I doubt that, as a matter of principle, a duty to consult can generally be superimposed on a statutory rule making procedure which requires the intended rules to be laid before Parliament and subjected to the negative resolution procedure'.[34] Essentially, Parliament had considered and enacted a procedure by which the Immigration Rules could be changed and chose not to impose further procedural safeguards beyond requiring them to be presented to Parliament. The courts should not contravene the implied intention of Parliament by imposing further procedures, such as a consultation exercise.

This reluctance by the courts to act as a legislator can also be seen in the unusual case of *R (Plantagenet Alliance Ltd) v Secretary of State for Justice*.[35] Following the astonishing discovery of the remains of Richard III beneath a Leicester car park,[36] there was a public debate regarding where his remains should reinterred, with debate between whether Leicester Cathedral or York Minister would be most appropriate. The Plantagenet Alliance argued that given the considerable public interest, a process of public consultation should be undertaken before the government reached a decision. Unsurprisingly given *BAPIO Action*, this argument was rejected by the High Court. However, the court set out clearly the circumstances when consultation would be required:

1. There is no general duty to consult at Common Law. The government of the country would grind to a halt if every decision-maker were required in every case to consult everyone who might be affected by his decision …

2. There are four main circumstances where a duty to consult may arise. First, where there is a statutory duty to consult. Second, where there has been a promise to consult. Third, where there has been an established practice of consultation. Fourth, where, in exceptional cases, a failure to consult would lead to conspicuous unfairness. Absent these factors, there will be no obligation on a public body to consult . . . [37]

Both *BAPIO Action* and *Plantagenet Alliance* are examples of the courts recognizing their constitutional limitations and that a key role of judicial review is to interpret existing procedural requirements, rather than creating new ones unless, exceptionally, they are required by the overall need to act fairly. Compared with other aspects of procedural impropriety, the courts appear to be 'less inclined to push the institutional envelope so far as the judicial role is concerned because they are not (as) convinced as the normative

---

[32] Ibid [45].   [33] Ibid.   [34] Ibid [58].   [35] [2014] EWHC 1662 (QB).

[36] Richard III was King of England from 1483 to 1485.

[37] [2014] EWHC 1662 (QB) [98]. An example of when a failure to consult can be seen in *R (Holborn Studios Ltd) v Hackney LBC* [2017] EWHC 2823. A planning application had been made to which objections were made. The applicant then amended their planning application, and the Council approved the amended plans. It was held to be unfair that those who objected to the initial application had not been consulted on the amended application. Consequently, the court quashed the grant planning permission for the amended plans.

case for consultation'.[38] This is arguably because the duty to consult can raise a series of open-ended issues as Sedley LJ suggests in *BAPIO Action*. This reflects that, usually, questions regarding consultations do not involve individual rights as they are part of the policy-making processes within government. As can be seen with the right to be heard, discussed below, the courts are more eager to protect individual rights. Consequently, the courts are circumspect about introducing a general common law duty requiring consultation. This means that, in line with much of this ground of judicial review, the courts restrict themselves to considering whether a duty to consult arises on a case-by-case basis. Alternatively, if individual rights are at stake, there is the possibility that a legitimate expectation to consult with a particular person has arisen. Legitimate expectations are considered in 13.8.

13.3 Rules of natural justice: introduction

The focus on individual rights can be seen with the rules of natural justice, which can be summarized as the right to be heard[39] and the rule against bias.[40] They are considered essential to ensuring that fair decisions are made. They are so fundamental that, as Wade and Forsyth state, '[i]n courts of law and in statutory tribunals it can be taken for granted that these rules must be observed'.[41] In the context of public authorities, the courts have developed the principles of the right to be heard and the rule against bias so as to place a series of requirements on public authorities, which when taken together ensure that decisions are made fairly, so fulfilling the requirements of the rule of law as explained in 13.1.

For a decision-making process to be sustainable, it must be accepted by those who are negatively affected by those decisions. This can only be achieved if those subject to the decision in question have been involved with the decision-making process to an appropriate and proportionate degree. Being involved will usually mean being able to put your arguments to the decision-maker. The precise manner in which this takes place will depend on the nature of the decision in question. Given that natural justice applies to many different types of decision-making (and the requirements of natural justice can be implied into contracts),[42] what the right to be heard requires in any specific case will significantly depend on the context. The context can vary widely, from a local authority granting a taxi licence to a parole board deciding how long a prisoner should serve in jail; however, cases from one context are instructive as to the approach taken in other contexts. It is also the case that some decisions by public authorities engage Article 6 of the European Convention on Human Rights. In outline, this requires that civil rights and obligations should be determined by 'a fair and public hearing within a reasonable time by an independent and impartial tribunal established by law'. This is considered in 13.6.7.

---

[38] Mark Elliott and Jason Varuhas, *Administrative Law: Text and Materials* (5th edn, OUP 2017) 408.

[39] Sometimes referred to as '*audi alteram partem*' which is Latin for 'hear the other side'.

[40] Sometimes referred to as '*nemo iudex in causa sua*' which is Latin for 'no one should be a judge in his own cause'.

[41] HWR Wade and CF Forsyth, *Administrative Law* (11th edn, OUP 2014) 374.

[42] For example, into contracts between athletes or professional sportsmen and their governing body, *R v Disciplinary Committee of the Jockey Club, ex p Aga Khan* [1993] 1 WLR 909; *R (Mullins) v Appeal Board of the Jockey Club* [2005] EWHC 2197 (Admin).

Generally, as Lord Reed states in *R (Osborn) v Parole Board*,[43] as 'intuitively understood', justice requires

> a procedure which pays due respect to a person whose rights are significantly affected by decisions taken in the exercise of administrative or judicial functions. Respect entails that such persons ought to be able to participate in the procedure by which the decision is made.[44]

Similarly, a negative decision is only likely to be accepted by those disappointed with the outcome if the decision-maker was impartial or free from bias. Decisions tainted by bias are unlikely to be accepted as legitimate and harm confidence in decision-making more generally. This is reflected in the famous dictum of Lord Hewart CJ in *R v Sussex Justices, ex p McCarthy*, that 'justice should not only be seen to be done, but should manifestly and undoubtedly be seen to be done'.[45] To ensure that decisions are reached with the confidence of those affected by them, Lord Hewart CJ shows that it is not sufficient for the process to be fair, in that instance free from bias, but the process is undoubtedly fair and not a mere facade hiding an unfair process. The consequences of this fundamental maxim on the rule against bias are discussed in 13.6.

The combined effect of these rules is to increase the democratic nature of decision-making by encouraging those potentially affected by a decision to make representations in the confidence that not only do they have the opportunity to make such representations, but their views will be taken seriously by someone who is not pursuing their own personal interest.

These factors can be described as the *dignitarian reason* for the rules on natural justice. This is explained by Jeremy Waldron as follows:

> [applying] a norm to a human individual is not like deciding what to do about a rabid animal or a dilapidated house. It involves paying attention to a point of view and respecting the personality of the entity one is dealing with. As such it embodies a crucial dignitarian idea—respecting the dignity of those to whom the norms are applied as beings capable of explaining themselves.[46]

Further, some decisions, such as the decision whether to build a new airport runway in the South East of England, have the potential to affect hundreds of thousands of people. By encouraging participation in such decisions, not only does the process become more democratic, but such participation helps fulfil the rule of law. As Jowell states:

> If the Rule of Law is concerned to protect individuals from being deprived of their rights without an opportunity to defend themselves, the concern is only narrowly stretched to protect group interests from being overridden without the opportunity to express views on the matter to be decided.[47]

The final rationale for the rules of natural justice is that they lead to improved decision-making. This can be described as the *instrumental reason*. If the decision is a matter of policy, the increased inputs into the process, as encouraged through the right

---

[43] [2013] UKSC 61.   [44] Ibid [68].   [45] [1924] 1 KB 256, 259.

[46] Jeremy Waldron, 'How Law Protects Dignity' [2012] CLJ 200, 2010. Approved by Lord Reed in *R (Osborn and others) v Parole Board* [2013] UKSC 61 [69].

[47] Jeffrey Jowell, 'The Rule of Law' in Jeffrey Jowell and Dawn Oliver (eds), *The Changing Constitution* (7th edn, OUP 2011) 21–2.

to be heard, will allow the decision-maker to make that decision based on a wider range of evidence. If the decision involves a dispute between the individual and the state, then the rules of natural justice make it more likely that a correct decision has been reached. As Megarry J stated, in *Rees v John*:[48]

> As everybody who has anything to do with the law well knows, the path of the law is strewn with examples of open and shut cases which, somehow, were not; of unanswerable charges which, in the event, were completely answered; of inexplicable conduct which was fully explained …[49]

Clearly, the rules of natural justice can impose burdens on decision-makers and are likely to increase the costs of decision-making. For example, holding an oral hearing will inevitably be more expensive than simply deciding a case on documentary evidence. There is also the argument that the rules of natural justice benefit the officials who make decisions. Requiring that decisions are made free from bias and hearing the views of those who may be negatively affected by it will result in better decision-making.[50]

The following three sections discuss in detail the two main rules of natural justice: the right to be heard and the rule against bias.

 Pause for reflection

Do the rules of natural justice matter if the merits of the case are clear from the start? Why should decision-makers just not deal with straightforward cases as quickly as possible?

13.4 Rules of natural justice: the right to be heard

13.4.1 Pre-*Ridge v Baldwin*

At its core, the right to be heard is a centuries old principle. This can be seen from *Baggs Case*, decided in 1615.[51] James Bagg, a freeman of the Borough of Plymouth, was described as acting at times with 'an evil disposition', and repeatedly hurled public insults and threats at the Mayor and others.[52] When he was expelled from the Corporation (a precursor to the modern day local authority), the courts declared that the expulsion was void because no hearing had taken place beforehand. This shows the importance the court places on the right to be heard, as even though the decision appears certain, the lack of a hearing can make such a decision void. As was held in *Dr Bentley's Case*, quoting Seneca, 'a dismissal without hearing held intrinsically unfair, even though fully justified'.[53]

---

[48] [1970] Ch 345.   [49] Ibid 402.

[50] HWR Wade and CF Forsyth, *Administrative Law* (11th edn, OUP 2014) 372.

[51] *Baggs Case* (1615) 11 Co Rep 93b.

[52] Bagg was described in the report at 95b, as 'turning the hinder part of his body in an inhuman and uncivil manner towards the [Mayor of Plymouth], scoffingly, contemptuously, and uncivilly, with a loud voice, said to the [Mayor] "Come and kiss".' Cited in HWR Wade and CF Forsyth, *Administrative Law* (11th edn, OUP 2014) 403.

[53] *R v University of Cambridge* (1723) 1 Str 557, 561. Translated from the Latin '*quicunque aliquid statuerit parte inaudita altera, aequo licet statuenti, haud aequus guerita*'.

Cooper v Wandsworth Board of Works[54] provides a clear example of how the right to be heard can act as protection against the coercive power of the state. In an early example of planning regulation, the Metropolis Local Management Act 1855, section 76, gave the power to the local board (in this case Wandsworth) to demolish a building built within London, if the builders had not given the local board seven days' notice of their intention to build it. Cooper started constructing his building without giving notice. However, as the building reached the second storey, the local board without warning in the middle of the night demolished the building. On a reading of the legislation it appeared that the local board acted lawfully; however, Cooper sought damages on the basis that the local board should have given him notice of their intention to demolish the building.

The court agreed, implying into the statute, a requirement that the local board was required to give notice. Erle CJ considered that as the exercise of the power carried 'enormous consequences',[55] justice requires that those subject to its power should be heard before it is exercised. This is because there could have been several reasons why Cooper had not given the required notice. Cooper may even have intended to comply with the requirement, but notice may not have been received by the local board by accident.

> I cannot conceive any harm that could happen to the district board from hearing the party before they subjected him to a loss so serious as the demolition of his house; but I can conceive a great many advantages which might arise in the way of public order, in the way of doing substantial justice, and in the way of fulfilling the purposes of the statute, by the restriction which we put upon them, that they should hear the party before they inflict upon him such a heavy loss.[56]

Also significant is Willes J, who, agreeing with Erle CJ stated, 'that a tribunal which is by law invested with power to affect the property of one of Her Majesty's subjects, is bound to give such subject an opportunity of being heard before it proceeds: and that that rule is of universal application, and founded upon the plainest principles of justice'.[57] It is clear that this is a rule of wide application. The issue remained just how wide.

It appeared that the broad approach from *Cooper v Wandsworth Board of Works* lasted until the Second World War, during which it came under increasing pressure. During wartime, the pressures of secrecy and speed may prevail over the principles of natural justice.[58] This is most clearly seen in the notorious case of *Liversidge v Anderson*.[59] During the Second World War, the Home Secretary had the power to detain anyone if they had 'reasonable cause' to believe that they had associations with those hostile to the national interest. The House of Lords held that this should be given its natural meaning, so that the courts could not scrutinize the reasoning of the Home Secretary for detaining an individual. Importantly for present purposes, neither was a hearing of any sort required. This approach appeared to hang over into the post-war period. This period saw cases such as *Nakkuda Ali v Jayaratne*, a Privy Council case from Ceylon (now Sri Lanka) where a textile trader had their licence revoked without a hearing,[60] and *R v Metropolitan Police Commissioner, ex p Parker*, which stated that a London taxi driver's licence could be withdrawn by

---

[54] (1863) 14 CB (NS) 180.   [55] Ibid 188.   [56] Ibid.

[57] See also, Lord Loreburn LC in *Board of Education v Rice* [1911] AC 179, 182 'must in act in good faith and listen fairly to both sides, for that is a duty lying upon every one who decides anything'.

[58] In *Ridge v Baldwin* [1964] AC 40, 73 (Lord Reid).

[59] [1942] AC 206. This case is also discussed in 3.5.1.   [60] [1951] AC 66.

the Commissioner without any inquiry or hearing.[61] Lord Goddard CJ simply stated 'that a licence is nothing but a permission, and if one gives a man permission to do something it is natural that the person who gives the permission will be able to withdraw the permission'.[62] During this period, it appeared that the courts were seeking to rein in the scope of the right to be heard. Yet, any doubts as to the scope of the doctrine were comprehensively removed in the seminal case of *Ridge v Baldwin*.

13.4.2 *Ridge v Baldwin*

> ### Case in depth: *Ridge v Baldwin* [1964] AC 40
>
> Ridge, the Chief Constable of Brighton Police, had been acquitted of a charge of conspiracy to obstruct the course of justice. Two other officers were convicted. The judge of the criminal trial had raised serious doubts about Ridge's fitness for office as Chief Constable. The Watch Committee, responsible for overseeing the Brighton Police, decided to dismiss Ridge without granting him a hearing or giving him any notice. Ridge argued that his dismissal was void because he had not had the opportunity to present a defence.
>
> Lord Reid gave the leading judgment. After stating that 'the authorities on the applicability of the principles of natural justice are in some confusion',[63] Lord Reid systematically reasserted the traditional approach to natural justice. Lord Reid stated that the right to be heard:
>
>> goes back many centuries in our law and appears in a multitude of judgments of judges of the highest authority. In modern times opinions have sometimes been expressed to the effect that natural justice is so vague as to be practically meaningless. But I would regard these as tainted by the perennial fallacy that because something cannot be cut and dried or nicely weighed or measured therefore it does not exist . . . It appears to me that one reason why the authorities on natural justice have been found difficult to reconcile is that insufficient attention has been paid to the great difference between various kinds of cases in which it has been sought to apply the principle. What a minister ought to do in considering objections to a scheme may be very different from what a watch committee ought to do in considering whether to dismiss a chief constable.[64]
>
> The issues that Ridge's dismissal raised were not as simple as whether or not he should be dismissed. Instead there were three options available: he could be reinstated, dismissed, or required to resign. While there was no question of Ridge being reinstated, there was a real question over the last two options. If Ridge was dismissed he would lose his pension rights; if he resigned he would retain them. Rather than being reinstated, that was his primary concern.
>
> As Lord Reid stated:
>
>> even if as a general rule a watch committee must hear a constable in his own defence before dismissing him, this case was so clear that nothing that the appellant could have said could have made any difference. It is at least very doubtful whether that could be accepted as an excuse. But, even if it could, the respondents would, in
>
>   →

---

[61] [1953] 1 WLR 1150.   [62] Ibid 1154 (Lord Goddard CJ).
[63] *Ridge v Baldwin* [1964] AC 40, 64.   [64] Ibid 64–5.

> → my view, fail on the facts. It may well be that no reasonable body of men could have reinstated the appellant. But as between the other two courses open to the watch committee the case is not so clear. Certainly on the facts, as we know them, the watch committee could reasonably have decided to forfeit the appellant's pension rights, but I could not hold that they would have acted wrongly or wholly unreasonably if they had in the exercise of their discretion decided to take a more lenient course.[65]

Ridge v Baldwin made clear that the scope of the right to be heard can be extensive when the matters involved are serious. As Lord Reid highlighted, it was highly unlikely that the Watch Committee would seek to reinstate Ridge, but this did not remove the duty on the Watch Committee to grant Ridge an oral hearing. This was because there were still significant issues to resolve, in particular whether Ridge should be dismissed with or without his pension rights. This issue was far less clear, meaning that to resolve this an oral hearing was required so that Ridge could put his case to the Watch Committee.

13.4.3 The modern law—*Ridge v Baldwin* applied

Ridge v Baldwin made clear that when the actions of a public body affect an individual, they must exercise those powers 'fairly'. This principle has been applied in a wide range of circumstances; however, as stated by Lord Reid in *Ridge v Baldwin*, what 'fairness' requires in the context of a particular decision will vary widely.[66] In the classic example of *Re HK (An Infant)*,[67] an immigration officer refused to grant entry to an individual who claimed to be under sixteen years of age into the UK. If he was aged under sixteen, he would be entitled entry into the UK, as a dependent of his father, who was a Commonwealth citizen. However, he was refused entry because the immigration officer suspected that the individual was older. The individual sought a judicial review of the decision to refuse him entry. It was held that fairness in this context required putting the concerns of the immigration officer to the claimant and his father and giving them the opportunity to respond. As they had been given the opportunity to respond to the immigration officer's concerns, the requirements of fairness had been complied with.

An attempt to clarify what fairness requires in any given circumstances was made in *McInnes v Onslow-Fane*.[68] In this case, an application for a boxing manager's licence was refused by the British Boxing Board of Control. The applicant challenged this decision on the basis that the decision had been reached unfairly because there had been no oral hearing. Megarry VC suggested the following categories as a guide; the categories being based on the nature of the decision itself:

> I do not suggest that there is any clear or exhaustive classification; but I think that at least three categories may be discerned. First, there are what may be called the forfeiture cases. In these, there is a decision which takes away some existing right or position, as

---

[65] Ibid 68.   [66] Ibid 64.   [67] [1967] 2 QB 617.
[68] [1978] 1 WLR 1520.

where a member of an organisation is expelled or a licence is revoked. Second, at the other extreme there are what may be called the application cases. These are cases where the decision merely refuses to grant the applicant the right or position that he seeks, such as membership of the organisation, or a licence 'to do' certain acts. Third, there is an intermediate category, which may be called the expectation cases, which differ from the application cases only in that the applicant has some legitimate expectation from what has already happened that his application will be granted. This head includes cases where an existing licence-holder applies for a renewal of his licence, or a person already elected or appointed to some position seeks confirmation from some confirming authority.[69]

Megarry VC made clear that the 'forfeiture' cases and 'application' cases are clearly different. With a forfeiture case, a right is at risk of being taken away, whereas with an application case, this is an attempt to acquire that right in the first place. For this reason, with forfeiture cases, the right to be heard plays an important role in protecting rights and by ensuring that issues are heard before an unbiased tribunal, rights are only taken away when the person affected has had the opportunity to argue their case. An example of this is *Cooper v Wandsworth Board of Works*. By contrast, with an application case, 'nothing is being taken away'.[70] The difference between the two can be explained by comparing applications to a university to when universities decide to expel a student. When an application to a university is rejected, no reasons or an oral hearing are required. However, in the rare cases when a university feels compelled to expel a student, this is a forfeiture case, which requires an oral hearing with the student in question, with the student being notified of the charges against them in advance. This is because expelling a student involves taking away from that student the right to attend the university, sit exams, and graduate with a degree. With an application, none of these rights are acquired until the application has been accepted.

The intermediate category, described as an 'expectation' case, may arise in a renewal situation, where there is an expectation that an existing right will continue. For example, a renewal of a licence with no salient change in circumstances from the date of the original application, or where there has been some indication that an application will be accepted. This is an example of a legitimate expectation, which since *McInnes v Onslow Fane* has become an important area in its own right and is discussed in 13.8 of this chapter.

 Discussing the problem

Have a look at the problem scenario set at the beginning of the chapter. Using the categories from *McInnes v Onslow Fane*, how would you characterize Louise's issue? Is it an application, expectation, or forfeiture case?

On the face of it, this is clearly not a forfeiture or expectation case, as there is no question of any rights being taken away from Louise, nor does Louise have any expectation that her application will be granted. Consequently, this is an application case, as Louise has no pre-existing right to open a restaurant, but is applying for that right.

[69] Ibid 1528–9.   [70] Ibid.

13.4.4 **Relationship between Parliament and the right to be heard**

A constitutionally interesting question regarding the relationship between the role of Parliament and the right to be heard was raised in *Bank Mellat v HM Treasury*.[71] The case concerned the decision of the Treasury, acting under the Counter-Terrorism Act 2008 to ban Bank Mellat from having access to the banking and financial system in the UK. The Treasury suspected that Bank Mellat provided services to those engaged in providing nuclear weapons to Iran. The decision of the Treasury was implemented through secondary legislation, made under powers granted by the 2008 Act. However, the Bank had no advance notice of this decision, which was effective almost immediately for twenty-eight days until approved permanently by Parliament. The Bank challenged the decision on the basis of the right to be heard and to make representations on their behalf before such decision could be made.

Lord Sumption, giving the leading judgment for the majority, agreed, echoing the older case law including *Cooper v Wandsworth Board of Works*, finding that 'the duty to give advance notice and an opportunity to be heard to a person against whom a draconian statutory power is to be exercised is one of the oldest principles of what would now be called public law'.[72] Just like in *Cooper*, Lord Sumption was clear that the serious consequences of the power meant that a right to be heard was implied before the Treasury could make the decision. This was because the decision was targeted at Bank Mellat itself and deprived it 'of the effective use of the goodwill of their English business and of the free disposal of substantial deposits in London. It had, and was intended to have, a serious effect on their business, which might well be irreversible.'[73]

The argument of the Treasury was that notice was not required because the decision was implemented by making delegated legislation approved by Parliament. This argument raises issues that relate to the separation of powers and the ability of the courts to intervene on the grounds of natural justice when a decision has been approved by Parliament. Yet, Lord Sumption largely avoided these broader constitutional issues by basing his decision on ordinary judicial review principles. He concluded that delegated legislation is created by a minister acting under powers by the enabling Act to make it and 'the approval of Parliament does not alter that. The focus of the court is therefore on his decision to make it, and not on Parliament's decision to approve it.'[74] In essence, Lord Sumption focused on the process before the order was introduced into Parliament and its impact on the individual rights of the bank, concluding that that process was defective, which could not be cured by the later approval of both Houses of Parliament. Lord Sumption was also mindful of the nature of the decision. The decision of the Treasury was 'a measure targeted against identifiable individuals'[75] and had it 'not been required to be made by statutory instrument, there would have been every reason . . . to say that the Treasury had a duty to give prior notice to the Bank and to hear what they had to say'.[76] Yet, the limits of such an approach were also clear. Lord Sumption was very clear that approval by Parliament of a measure which was more general in application which affected a large section of the population would be sufficient, and the right to be heard or consulted before the decision was made would not apply.[77]

---

[71] [2013] UKSC 39. This case is also discussed in 12.4.   [72] Ibid [29].
[73] Ibid [32].   [74] Ibid [43].   [75] Ibid [46].
[76] Ibid.   [77] Ibid [44].

Counterpoint: Lord Reed's dissent in *Bank Mellat*

In *Bank Mellat*, Lord Reed gave a dissenting judgment disagreeing with Lord Sumption. He concluded that Parliament had excluded the right to be heard when enacting the Counter Terrorism Act 2008. Lord Reed stated that:

> Parliament has laid down . . . a detailed scheme for the making of orders such as the order with which this appeal is concerned. That scheme contains no provision entitling the person designated in the order to be given a hearing before the order is made by the Treasury or approved by Parliament. The absence of such provision does not in itself automatically entail that Parliament intended that there should be no such entitlement, but in the context of such detailed procedural provisions it is a pointer towards such an intention: if Parliament had intended that there should be consultation prior to the making of an order, one would expect that also to have been specified in the provisions.[78]

Lord Reed also stated that the context in which this power was exercised meant that 'prior consultation with the person who maybe affected by a direction, including . . . persons believed to be involved in terrorism, is liable to be inappropriate or impossible'.[79] Lord Reed took the view that in devising the procedure by which the statutory instrument is to be made, Parliament decided against allowing those subject to the order from being able to participate in the parliamentary process by not including in the procedure the ability for them to make representations to Parliament.[80] Consequently, if it was intended that the designated person should be entitled to participate in the procedure leading to the making of the order, it would make little sense to enact a provision specifically preventing him from participating in the procedure leading to its approval by Parliament.

Do you agree with Lord Reed, who concluded that Parliament had chosen to prioritize other considerations instead of the right to be heard and that the decision of the majority was tantamount to 're-writing the scheme intended by Parliament'?[81]

13.4.5 The limits of fairness

The debate between Lord Sumption and Lord Reed in *Bank Mellat* reflects two core elements of determining the extent of the right to be heard in any given case. These were best explained by Lord Bridge in *Lloyd v McMahon*.[82] The first element is as explained in the introduction to this chapter and it is clear from the cases discussed so far that what the rules of natural justice or 'fairness' impose is not fixed and does not apply in the same manner to every decision reached. As Lord Bridge stated:

> My Lords, the so-called rules of natural justice are not engraved on tablets of stone. To use the phrase which better expresses the underlying concept, what the requirements of fairness demand when any body, domestic, administrative or judicial, has to make a decision which will affect the rights of individuals depends on the character of the decision making body, the kind of decision it has to make and the statutory or other framework in which it operates.[83]

---

[78] Ibid [56].   [79] Ibid [57].   [80] Counter-Terrorism Act 2008, Part 4.
[81] [2013] UKSC 39 [61].   [82] [1987] AC 625.   [83] Ibid 702.

It is clear from this statement that the seriousness of the decision in question, the nature of the decision, and the statute creating the decision are all key elements in determining what fairness requires. Lord Bridge further explained:

> In particular, it is well-established that when a statute has conferred on any body the power to make decisions affecting individuals, the courts will not only require the procedure pre-scribed by the statute to be followed, but will readily imply so much and no more to be intro-duced by way of additional procedural safeguards as will ensure the attainment of fairness.[84]

In *Bank Mellat*, the difference between Lord Sumption and Lord Reed is the emphasis they chose to apply to each of those elements. Lord Sumption was mindful of the serious consequences that the decision had on the bank, whereas Lord Reed took account of the statute that gave the power to make the decision. This meant that Lord Reed was satisfied that the Counter-Terrorism Act 2008 gave sufficient protection to those subject to the orders, whereas Lord Sumption felt that fairness required that making the order was subject to the right to be heard.

13.5 The hearing

Having established the right to a hearing, the next issue is what form that hearing should take in order to comply with the requirements of fairness. What is required depends very much on the nature of the issues involved, but a range of features must be discussed. These include whether an oral hearing is required, the right to know the opposing case, and whether legal representation should be allowed for a fair decision to be made.

13.5.1 Right to an oral hearing

Usually, the notion of a 'hearing' indicates an oral hearing, with each side being able to present their 'side' of the issue. However, as shown in *Lloyd v McMahon*,[85] this is not always the case. Giving effect to the right to be heard can involve making written rep-resentations which the decision-maker then considers. Whether this is sufficient for the requirements of fairness and the right to be heard will depend on the overall facts of the case and the nature of the decision to be made. *Lloyd v McMahon* is discussed below.

Case in depth: *Lloyd v McMahon* [1987] AC 625

In 1985, the district auditor responsible for scrutinizing the accounts of Liverpool City Council was concerned that the councillors had not set a budget for the year 1985–86 and warned them that the councillors responsible would be disqualified and be required to make up any financial loss this caused the Council. After a further warning, the district auditor then started to take the necessary steps to recover the money lost. This involved sending his report and notices to the councillors involved, informing them that he had to determine whether the councillors should be required to pay back the money the Council had lost through their wilful misconduct, which

→

---

[84] Ibid 702–3.   [85] Ibid.

→

was a deliberate refusal to set a budget and a breach of their duties. The councillors made a response collectively on behalf of all those accused, in writing. They did not seek an oral hearing. The district auditor found the councillors responsible for the financial loss their actions had caused the Council. The councillors challenged this on the basis that an oral hearing is required. However, the court held that the procedure carried out by the district auditor was sufficiently fair and an oral hearing was not required, as the councillors had sufficient opportunity to express their concerns and meet the case that the district auditor had made against them.

Lord Keith considered the issue as to whether an oral hearing would be required.

> In the present case the district auditor had arrived at his provisional view upon the basis of the contents of documents, minutes of meetings and reports submitted to the council from the auditor's department and their own officers . . . If the appellants had attended an oral hearing they would no doubt have reiterated the sincerity of their motives from the point of view of advancing the interests of the inhabitants of Liverpool. It seems unlikely, having regard to the position adopted by their counsel on this matter before the Divisional Court, that they would have been willing to reveal or answer questions about the proceedings of their political caucus. The sincerity of the appellants' motives is not something capable of justifying or excusing failure to carry out a statutory duty, or of making reasonable what is otherwise an unreasonable delay in carrying out such a duty. In all the circumstances, I am of opinion that the district auditor did not act unfairly, and that the procedure which he followed did not involve any prejudice to the appellants.[86]

Counterpoint: The basis of the decision in *Lloyd v McMahon*: confusing the merits with the process?

As Fenwick, Phillipson, and Williams state:

> The real basis of the decision seemed to have been that, first, the councillors had not requested an oral hearing at the time, which cast some doubt on their subsequent contention that it was essential for a fair decision to be made. Secondly, as seen above, the House of Lords found that the application had lost nothing by not having an oral hearing; they had been given a full opportunity to make written representations with full knowledge of the case against them, and an oral hearing would have added nothing of relevance.[87]

Although perhaps understandable for the reasons that Fenwick, Philipson, and Williams state, the curious feature of *Lloyd v McMahon* is that the court appears to be focused on the result of the case as justifying the procedure used to make the decision. Elsewhere within this ground of judicial review, such an approach is generally avoided as the merits of the case should be a separate consideration to the procedure used to decide the case.

General guidance on when an oral hearing is required was provided in *R (Osborn) v Parole Board*.[88] Three separate cases (heard together by the Supreme Court) involved the question of

---

[86] Ibid 696.

[87] Helen Fenwick, Gavin Phillipson, and Alexander Williams, *Text, Cases and Materials on Public Law and Human Rights* (4th edn, Routledge 2017) 686.

[88] [2013] UKSC 61.

whether the parole board was required to grant three prisoners an oral hearing. In the first case, the prisoner had been released on licence, but breached its terms on the first day of release, meaning that he was recalled back to prison. The other two cases involved prisoners whose minimum sentence had expired, but the Parole Board had decided not to grant their release. In all three cases, a request for an oral hearing was declined by the Parole Board.

The Supreme Court allowed all three appeals, developing the following set of principles as to when the Parole Board should grant a hearing:

- When fairness to the prisoner requires that an oral hearing is held considering the facts of the case, and the importance of what is at stake.[89]

- Oral hearings are required when important facts are in dispute, or need to be explained or mitigated.[90]

- Oral hearings 'reflect the prisoner's legitimate interest in being able to participate in a decision of considerable importance to him, where he has something useful to contribute'.[91]

- Oral hearings allow the prisoner (or their representatives) to put their case to the board or to test the views presented to the board.[92]

- The board must not refuse oral hearings for the reason of saving time, trouble, and expense.[93]

These factors provide a good summary of the benefits of an oral hearing more generally. The more important the decision to be made, the more likely that fairness will require an oral hearing. This is because oral hearings, through airing any disputes over salient facts, can improve the quality of decision-making. In addition, such hearings can ensure that the person involved can take part in the decision. This in turn reflects the dignitarian purpose of the rules of natural justice as explained in 13.3. However, if an oral hearing is required, this in turn raises a series of other questions about the nature of how an oral hearing should be held. These include the right to call witnesses and cross-examine opposing witnesses, whether legal representation is required, and the right to know the opposing case. Each is looked at in turn below. However, the fundamental approach in each of these issues is the same. The concern of the court is to establish in all the circumstances what is required in the interests of fairness.

13.5.2 The right to cross-examine opposing witnesses and to call witnesses

Generally well known in the criminal context, but equally applicable to public law disputes, is that the main benefit of an oral hearing is the ability to determine questions of fact. Each side has the opportunity to call witnesses to further their respective cases and cross-examine the other side's witnesses by asking them questions. The purpose of this is to allow each party to present their case, but also to test the strength of the opposing case, through testing the credibility of the witnesses or prising out inconsistencies in the opposing case. This allows the decision-maker, after hearing the available evidence, to make the findings of fact necessary to make their decision. The level of formality by which this process takes place depends on the seriousness of the decision to be made; the more serious the decision, the more formal the process is likely to be.

---

[89] Ibid [81].   [90] Ibid [85].   [91] Ibid [82].   [92] Ibid.   [93] Ibid [91].

In *R v Board of Visitors of Hull Prison, ex p St Germain and Others (No 2)*,[94] a riot in a prison led to disciplinary charges being made against seven prisoners. If the charges were proven, the prisoners would serve a longer prison sentence. The Board of Visitors heard the hearings, but refused to allow the prisoners to call certain witnesses. In addition, witness statements of prison officers were referred to, but these officers did not attend the hearing which meant that their evidence could not be challenged through cross-examination. The court held that this was a breach of natural justice and that the requirements of fairness 'may oblige the board not only to inform the accused of the hearsay evidence but also to give the accused a sufficient opportunity to deal with that evidence'.[95]

The court invoked an example of a prisoner, in breach of prison rules, taking to the roof of the prison. The accused argues that he was not on the roof at the time and argues that he has been incorrectly identified. The prisoner may well 'wish to elicit by way of questions all manner of detail, e.g. the poorness of the light, the state of confusion, the brevity of the observation [or] the absence of any contemporaneous record'.[96] Such questions would be aimed at undermining the reliability of the witness. This can only take place through cross-examining that witness. 'To deprive [the accused] of the opportunity of cross-examination would be tantamount to depriving him of a fair hearing.'[97]

13.5.3 Legal representation

Linked to the question of cross-examining and calling witnesses is the issue of legal representation. Statute will often allow for legal representation; however, if the relevant statute is silent then question of legal representation is at the discretion of the decision-maker. In *R v Secretary of State for the Home Department, ex p Tarrant*,[98] the High Court suggested that the following factors should be considered:

(1) the seriousness of the charge and of the potential penalty;

(2) whether any points of law are likely to arise;

(3) the capacity of a particular prisoner to present his own case;

(4) procedural difficulties;

(5) the need for reasonable speed in making their adjudication, which is clearly an important consideration;

(6) the need for fairness as between prisoners and as between prisoners and prison officers.[99]

In *Tarrant* itself, the factors were applied with the conclusion that legal representation should be allowed in order for the prisoner in question to answer a charge of 'mutiny'. This was held to mean 'a concerted act of indiscipline involving more than person relating to the overthrow or supplanting of constituted authority'.[100] The legal issue arose as to whether the actions of the prisoner, together with others, satisfied the definition of mutiny. The need to answer this legal question meant that fairness required that the prisoner have access to legal representation. This case can be contrasted to *R v Board of Visitors of HM Prison, the Maze, ex p Hone*.[101] In this case, no right to legal representation

[94] [1979] 1 WLR 1401.   [95] Ibid 1419.   [96] Ibid 1409.   [97] Ibid 1419.
[98] [1985] QB 251.   [99] Ibid 285–6.
[100] Ibid 287, citing Lord Goddard CJ in *R v Grant* [1957] 1 WLR 906, 908.
[101] [1988] 1 AC 379.

was found on the basis that the prisoners charged with assault were able to defend themselves as no legal questions arose. The right to a fair hearing can also be subject to other considerations. For example, in this case, the House of Lords were mindful of the need to reach a timely decision.

> ### 🔰 Discussing the problem
>
> **Consider the facts of the scenario outlined at the beginning of the chapter. What sort of hearing should Louise be entitled to?**
>
> The Food Distribution Act 2024 gives no details as to the type of hearing that is required. Consequently, we have to consider what fairness would require at common law.
>
> This is an issue which relates to Louise's business interests and so is a relatively serious matter and it would seem that the principles from *R (Osborn) v Parole Board* would apply. There is a need for the Council to explain why her application for a licence has been rejected and Louise has a legitimate interest in participating in the decision. An oral hearing would also allow her to put her case before an independent panel and test the reasoning of the council most effectively.
>
> It may also be that she would be entitled to be legally represented at the hearing, should she so choose. It appears that the test in *R v Secretary of State for the Home Department, ex p Tarrant* applies, particularly given that the facts raise a legal question, as Ryan being the chair of the committee who decided her application may fall under one of the categories of bias. This is discussed in 13.6.

13.5.4 Know the opposing case

The right to be heard is of limited value unless the person seeking the hearing is aware of the nature of the case against them. If someone seeking to overturn a decision against them does not know the reasons for the decision in the first place, how can they address the concerns of the decision-maker? For this reason, natural justice can require that decision-maker discloses the factors that lie against the person challenging the decision. This was vividly explained in the *Fayed* case.[102]

> ### Case in depth: *R v Secretary of State for the Home Department, ex p Fayed* [1998] 1 All ER 763
>
> Mohammed al Fayed and his brother were both Egyptian nationals with high-profile business interests in the UK. They both applied for British citizenship under section 6(2) of the British Nationality Act 1981. The Home Secretary rejected both applications and, under section 44(2) of the 1981 Act, was expressly *not* required to give reasons for his decision.[103]
>
> →

---

[102] [1998] 1 All ER 763.

[103] Section 44(2) of the British Nationality Act 1981 stated that the Secretary of State 'shall not be required to assign any reason for the grant or refusal of any application under this Act the decision on which is at his discretion; and the decision of the Secretary of State or a Governor or Lieutenant-Governor on any such application shall not be subject to appeal to, or review in, any court'. Section 44(2) has since been repealed by the Nationality, Immigration and Asylum Act 2002, s 7(1).

The al Fayeds argued that despite section 44(2) the Home Secretary was still required to inform the applicants of the gist of the case against them. A majority agreed holding that although section 44(2) did remove any duty on the Home Secretary to give reasons, the section did not relieve them from the broader obligation to act fairly. In this instance, that required the applicants receiving notice of the matters that weighed against their applications being successful.

Lord Woolf MR stated:

> The suggestion that notice need not be given although this would be unfair involves attributing to Parliament an intention that it has not expressly stated that a minister should be able to act unfairly in deciding that a person lawfully in this country should be refused citizenship without the courts being able to do anything about it. This involves attributing to the protection which section 44(2) gives in relation to reasons far greater status than that to which it is entitled. English law has long attached the greatest importance to the need for fairness to be observed prior to the exercise of a statutory discretion.[104]

Aware of the potential consequences of this decision, Lord Woolf continued:

> I appreciate there is also anxiety as to the administrative burden involved in giving notice of areas of concern . . . I would emphasise that my remarks are limited to cases where an applicant would be in real difficulty in doing himself justice unless the area of concern is identified by notice. In many cases less complex than the Fayeds the issues may be obvious. If this is the position notice may well be superfluous.[105]

Counterpoint: Was section 44(2) undermined?

In *Fayed*, section 44(2) meant that the Home Secretary did not need to give reasons for his decision. As Kennedy LJ stated:

> in order to give effect to those words it seems to me that the Secretary of State when called upon to exercise his discretion must be relieved not only of any obligation to give reasons at the time of or immediately after he makes his decision, but also of any duty to indicate to an applicant at any earlier stage why he is minded to refuse.[106]

Kennedy LJ's argument is that, if the Home Secretary is not under a duty to give reasons, yet natural justice requires the disclosure of the factors against them, then those factors are surely going to be the reasons why application has been rejected. In substance, the approach of Lord Woolf that required notice of the factors against granting the applicants a British citizenship undermined the wording of the statute.

Whose view should be preferred? Lord Woolf's or Kennedy LJ's? Should fairness prevail over the wording of the statute?

A feature of the *Al Fayed* case was that the applicants need to be informed of the 'gist' or the essential features of the case against them. Considering the earlier case of *R v Gaming Board for Great Britain, ex p Benaim and Khaida*[107] further develops this point. The

[104] [1998] 1 All ER 763, 774.   [105] Ibid 777.   [106] Ibid 782–3.
[107] [1970] 2 QB 417.

applicants applied for a gaming licence from the Gaming Board which was rejected. They were informed of the Board's concerns about their application and had the opportunity to address them. However, these concerns were triggered by confidential information, and the Board did not disclose to the applicants the identity of their sources. The court found that this did not make the procedure unfair because the applicants were presented with all the information the Board had against them and had an opportunity to respond to the objections against them that the information raised. The Board were not required to disclose the source of the information.

13.5.5 Article 6 ECHR and its relationship with the common law

One question is the role of Article 6 ECHR, which is incorporated into UK law under the Human Rights Act 1998. Article 6 requires that in 'the determination of his civil rights and obligations . . . everyone is entitled to a fair and public hearing within a reasonable time by an independent and impartial tribunal'. Lord Reed in *Osborn v Parole Board* made clear that despite Article 6, the starting point should remain the common law. This is because Article 6 is 'expressed at a very high level of generality', which needs to be supplemented by a 'substantial body of much more specific domestic law'.[108] This should ensure that the rights protected by Article 6 are 'protected primarily by a detailed body of domestic law'.[109] This means that in substance, the focus in this area of law is still on the common law rather than on the Article 6 case law. However, to obtain a complete picture of this area of law, an understanding of Article 6 is needed. This section outlines the key issues with Article 6: first its scope and then what Article 6 requires if it is engaged.

Scope of Article 6

The core difficulty with Article 6 is that it only applies when determining a person's 'civil rights and obligations'. At first glance this could be taken to mean private law rights, such as those arising out of contract, meaning that relatively few decisions made by a public authority would engage Article 6. However, this is not how 'civil rights and obligations' have been interpreted by the European Court of Human Rights, which makes this a complex area of law.

In *Ali v Birmingham City Council*,[110] after reviewing the Strasbourg Court's jurisprudence, the Supreme Court explained when Article 6 would apply in the context of social security benefits and social housing. Article 6 is engaged when the eligibility for the benefit in question is defined with sufficient precision so as to become a 'civil right'. In contrast, benefits which are dependent on the judgment or discretion of the public authority in question do not engage Article 6. This meant that the Supreme Court considered that a claim to housing was not a 'civil right' under Article 6 because whether someone was entitled to housing depended on the 'evaluative judgement' of the public authority. By contrast, the ECHR has held that a claim for housing benefit payments and some non-contributory social benefits does engage Article 6.[111] In these instances, the rules were sufficiently clear to hold that those potentially entitled to such benefits had a right once they complied with the criteria as laid down in the law. This meant that their entitlement to the benefit is a 'civil right' for the purposes of Article 6.

---

[108] [2013] UKSC 61 [55].   [109] Ibid [56].
[110] [2010] UKSC 8.
[111] *Tsfayo v United Kingdom* (2009) 48 EHRR 18; *Salesi v Italy* (1998) 26 EHRR 187.

It is also the case that the seriousness of the matter can affect whether Article 6 is engaged. In *Kulkarni v Milton Keynes Hospital NHS Foundation Trust*,[112] a disciplinary panel was convened to hear an allegation that a junior doctor had inappropriately touched a patient. It was held that the hearing would engage Article 6, as the issue involved the doctor's 'civil rights'. This was because a guilty verdict would effectively cause the doctor to lose his livelihood, as he would be unable to complete his training and work in the NHS, which is the sole provider of public healthcare in the country. The court held that in general, that if the issue was whether a particular job was lost, this would not engage Article 6, but in a case such as this, where access to an entire profession was at stake, Article 6 would be engaged.[113] By contrast in *R (G) v Governors of X School*,[114] a disciplinary hearing of the board of governors to hear an allegation that a teaching assistant had an inappropriate relationship with a child did not engage Article 6 because the governors were not determining the civil rights and obligations of the accused. A finding of guilt by the board of governors would not deprive the accused of their livelihood, because they would pass the case on to another party that had the power to ban the accused from working with children. This also meant that the accused had no right to legal representation.

What protection does Article 6 grant?

Article 6 states that if it is engaged, then when determining someone's 'civil rights and obligations' there should be a 'fair and public hearing, within a reasonable time by an independent and impartial tribunal'. This could be taken to mean that decisions made involving civil rights and obligations should be made by a court or tribunal. This is plainly not the intention, for this 'would cause chaos in public administration',[115] as most decisions are not made by courts or tribunals, but by administrators or bureaucrats within government departments or local government. To understand the nature of Article 6, a broader perspective looking at the overall process is required. Consequently, as long as the initial decision can be appealed to an independent court or tribunal, Article 6 will be complied with.[116] For example, someone may apply to the Department of Work and Pensions for a social security benefit, such as Jobseeker's Allowance. The application is decided administratively by the Department of Work and Pensions, but the decision can be appealed to a tribunal.[117]

As regards how such hearings should be conducted, the requirements of the common law and the ECHR are broadly similar. However, one area of difference is that if Article 6 is engaged, then the courts have suggested that a right to legal representation exists under Article 6 rather than under the common law, where this can be at the discretion of the decision-maker. In *Kulkarni v Milton Keynes Hospital NHS Foundation Trusts*,[118] it was held as obiter that in circumstances where someone is in effect facing a criminal charge, although being dealt with by disciplinary proceedings, then a right to legal representation could be implied.[119]

Article 6 makes clear that a hearing must be held 'within a reasonable time'. This led the ECtHR to find that the five-and-a-half years it took for the Secretary of State to determine whether someone could be disqualified from acting as a company director breached Article 6.[120] The fact that the requirement of a reasonable time is explicit in Article 6

---

[112] [2009] EWCA Civ 789.   [113] Ibid [65].   [114] [2011] UKSC 30.

[115] Peter Cane, *Administrative Law* (5th edn, OUP 2011) 94.

[116] *R (on the application of Alconbury Developments Ltd) v Secretary of State for the Environment, Transport and the Regions* [2003] 2 AC 295.

[117] Tribunals are discussed in 14.2.   [118] [2009] EWCA Civ 789.   [119] Ibid [68].

[120] *Davies v UK* (2002) 35 EHRR 29.

means that this 'adds significantly to the common law', where 'timeliness is probably implicit'.[121]

Finally, Article 6 requires 'an independent and impartial tribunal'. The common law has traditionally taken seriously the need for decision-makers to be impartial to the extent that Lord Steyn in *Lawal v Northern Spirit Ltd* stated that 'there is now no difference between the common law test of bias and the requirements under article 6 of the Convention of an independent and impartial tribunal'.[122] The common law rules against bias are considered in detail in the next section of this chapter.

Summary

Overall, the relationship between the common law and Article 6 is a complex one. To some extent, the broad principles of Article 6 infuse the common law; however, the common law has always taken these issues seriously. If Article 6 is engaged, which is not an easy question to answer, Article 6 may grant further procedural safeguards in addition to those currently provided for by the common law.

13.6 **Rules of natural justice: rule against bias**

13.6.1 **What is 'bias'?**

The rule against bias is the second key element of the rules of natural justice. This is the requirement that a decision-maker should not have their own personal interest in the outcome or the decision they are making. If a decision-maker does have such an interest, then the decision will not be considered to be fair. Consequently, it is necessary to consider first what is meant by bias. In *Re Medicaments and Related Classes of Goods (No 2)*[123] Lord Phillips provided a useful summary:

> Bias is an attitude of mind which prevents the judge from making an objective determination of the issues that he has to resolve. A judge may be biased because he has reason to prefer one outcome of the case to another. He may be biased because he has reason to favour one party rather than another. He may be biased not in favour of one outcome of the dispute but because of a prejudice in favour of or against a particular witness which prevents an impartial assessment of the evidence of that witness. Bias can come in many forms. It may consist of irrational prejudice or it may arise from particular circumstances which, for logical reasons, predispose a judge towards a particular view of the evidence or issues before him.[124]

We can see from this that bias is linked to impartiality, in that if a decision-maker possesses bias, they are no longer impartial because, for some reason, they are 'willing to decide a matter for reasons which are unrelated to legitimate reasons'.[125] If the decision-maker is no longer impartial, this means the process can only be illegitimate because the 'absence of impartiality is a fundamental flaw'.[126] This is because by making a decision motivated by bias, the decision-maker is not applying legitimate reasons when deciding the question. This means that those to whom the decision applies are being treated unfairly.[127]

---

[121] Peter Cane, *Public Law* (5th edn, OUP 2011) 95.

[122] [2003] UKHL 35 [14].

[123] [2001] 1 WLR 700.   [124] Ibid [37].

[125] DJ Galligan, *Due Process and Fair Procedures* (OUP 1996) 441.   [126] Ibid.   [127] Ibid.

It is clear that decisions *actually* motivated by bias clearly do not comply with the requirement of fairness. However, as explained in the following case, the scope of the rule against bias is far greater than it may first appear.

In *R v Sussex Justices, ex p McCarthy*,[128] following a road traffic accident, McCarthy was subject to a claim for damages and a criminal charge of dangerous driving in the magistrates' court. The claim for damages was brought by the victim through his solicitor. McCarthy was found guilty and a fine was imposed. McCarthy challenged his conviction on the basis that the clerk to the magistrates was a partner of the same firm that was representing the victim. In evidence, the magistrates were clear that they did not discuss the case with the clerk, or consult him when reaching their decision. This meant that there was no suspicion that the decision against McCarthy was actually motivated by any bias.

Yet, as explained earlier, Lord Hewart CJ stated that justice 'should manifestly and undoubtedly be seen to be done'.[129] This meant that the concern was not whether the clerk to the court had actually acted improperly, but 'what might appear to be done'.[130] Essentially, perception matters as much as reality.[131] It did not matter that there was no question that the clerk had attempted to influence the decision, what mattered was how this appeared to those watching the proceedings. In this way, the rule against bias not only ensures that decisions are made impartially, but that this is unquestionably the case. The purpose behind this rule is to maintain confidence in decision-making, whether that is in a judicial or administrative context.

One concern is that the terminology of this area has been confused, with a range of different terms sometimes being used interchangeably. The following discussion revolves around the three main categories of bias: actual bias, the automatic disqualification rule, and apparent bias.

13.6.2 **Actual bias**

As stated by Lord Philips *In Re Medicaments and Related Classes of Goods (No 2)*, 'actual bias' has been applied when 'a judge has been influenced by partiality or prejudice in reaching his decision and . . . where it has been demonstrated that a judge is actually prejudiced in favour of or against a party'.[132] Any situation which falls within the definition of bias in 13.6.1 would be likely to fall within actual bias.

Examples of actual bias on the part of a judge are rare. As Lord Bingham states in *Locabail (UK) Ltd v Bayfield Properties Ltd*,[133] this is because:

> [hopefully] the existence of actual bias is very rare, but partly for other reasons also. The proof of actual bias is very difficult, because the law does not countenance the questioning of a judge about extraneous influences affecting his mind; and the policy of the common law is to protect litigants who can discharge the lesser burden of showing a real danger of bias without requiring them to show that such bias actually exists.[134]

It is essentially for this last reason that the real focus of this area of law is on the automatic disqualification rule and apparent bias. Both focus on circumstances which have the potential for bias to exist, such as a decision-maker having a financial interest. The law then takes a precautionary approach in finding that if these circumstances exist then

[128] [1924] 1 KB 256.   [129] Ibid 259.   [130] Ibid.

[131] Mark Elliott and Jason Varuhas, *Administrative Law: Text and Materials* (5th edn, OUP 2017) 318.

[132] [2001] 1 WLR 700 [38].   [133] [2000] QB 451.

[134] Ibid [3]. See also, Denis Galligan, *Due Process and Fair Procedures* (OUP 1996) 442: 'prejudice or personal preference which often constitutes bias can easily be concealed from outside scrutiny.'

that decision-maker must step aside, or their decision is void. When this applies, evidence of actual bias is irrelevant, as the focus is on the existence of the interest in the first place. It is the very potential of bias that taints the decision.

13.6.3 Automatic disqualification rule

This rule applies in two main circumstances, either when the decision-maker has a financial interest in the decision to be made or when a non-financial interest is so closely connected to the issues involved that they should be treated *as if* they had a financial interest. It is described as the automatic disqualification rule because a decision-maker that falls within its scope is automatically disqualified from making the decision in question.

Financial interests

Dimes v The Proprietors of the Grand Junction Canal is commonly seen as the foundation for the automatic disqualification rule.[135] Lord Cottenham, the Lord Chancellor, affirmed an order made by the Vice-Chancellor in favour of the Grand Junction Canal. However, the Lord Chancellor held shares in the company. The House of Lords held that his interest meant that he should not have heard the appeal. Lord Campbell stated that it was clear that the Lord Chancellor's decision was not 'in the remotest degree' influenced by his interest in the company, but 'it is of the last importance that the maxim that no man is to be a judge in his own cause should be held sacred. And that is not to be confined to a cause in which he is a party, but applies to a cause in which he has an interest.'[136]

Unlike with actual bias, there was no indication that the Lord Chancellor's decision in favour of the company was motivated by his interest in it. However, having such a financial interest places the decision-maker in a position that is taken to be as if they are acting as a judge in their own cause. Decision-makers in this situation are automatically disqualified from making the decision in question.

It had been generally felt that the rule applied to any financial or pecuniary interest, no matter how small.[137] However, this appears to be no longer the case. In *R v Bristol Betting and Gaming Licensing Committee, ex p O'Callaghan* (heard with *Locabail*), following a dispute over the validity of a bet with Coral Racing Ltd, the claimant sought a judicial review over the renewal of Coral's permit to operate as a bookmaker. The only issue was the payment of £5,000 of legal costs. The judge, Dyson J, refused the claim for judicial review. It then emerged that Dyson J was a director of a property company that included Coral amongst its commercial tenants. This was not declared at the hearing and O'Callaghan argued that had Dyson J declared this, he would have objected. It was held that the automatic disqualification rule did not apply because 'it cannot be said that the judge had anything more than a nominal and indirect interest because of his directorship and shares in the company. Such an interest does not establish a bar to the judge sitting.'[138] It is clear from this case and the others heard alongside *Locabail* that for the financial interest to trigger the automatic disqualification rule it must be more than *de minimis*.[139]

The effects of the automatic disqualification rule can be waived by the parties, meaning that a judge to whom the rule applies can nevertheless continue to hear the case.

---

[135] (1852) 3 HL Cas 759.   [136] Ibid 793.

[137] In *R v Rand* (1866) LR 1 QB 230, 232, Blackburn J stated that there 'is no doubt that any direct pecuniary interest, however small, in the subject of inquiry, does disqualify a person from acting as a judge in the matter'. See also *R v Camborne Justices, ex p Pearce* [1955] 1 QB 41, 47 (Slade J).

[138] *Locabail (UK) Ltd v Bayfield Properties Ltd* [2000] QB 451 [108].

[139] This means that it should be more than a merely minimal interest. Ibid [10].

The waiver must be 'clear and unequivocal, and made with full knowledge of all the facts relevant to the decision whether to waive or not'.[140] Should a judge declare a financial interest, and the parties decide against seeking the judge's recusal from the case, they may be prevented from invoking the automatic disqualification rule at a later stage. In *Locabail* itself, the trial judge declared to both parties a potential financial interest, neither party objected at the time. When the losing party later sought to raise the trial judge's financial interest before the Court of Appeal they were prevented from doing so. Similarly, a party can be deemed to have waived their right to object to a judge hearing a case, if after the judge declares a financial interest, the parties choose not to object or seek his recusal. Any such objection must be made when the financial interest is discovered and not wait until after judgment has been delivered. Doing so gives the impression of seeking to use the financial interest tactically, only raising it after losing before the trial judge. This can raise suspicions of wanting to 'have the best of both worlds . . . [which] the law will not allow'.[141]

Non-financial interests

It had been generally thought that the automatic disqualification rule applied to financial interests only. Perhaps surprisingly, the automatic disqualification rule was applied to non-financial interests in the unusual case of *Pinochet (No 2)*.

Case in depth: *R v Bow Street Metropolitan Stipendiary Magistrate, ex p Pinochet (No 2)* [2000] 1 AC 119

The former military ruler of Chile, General Pinochet, was facing extradition to Spain, against which Pinochet claimed immunity as a former Head of State. The leading human rights organization, Amnesty International, intervened in the case as a third party. The House of Lords decided he was not entitled to immunity. After making the decision, it emerged that one of the Law Lords who heard the appeal, Lord Hoffmann was a director of a charity connected to Amnesty International. The House of Lords held that Lord Hoffmann was effectively a 'judge in his own cause', meaning that the automatic disqualification rule should apply even though he had no financial interest. Lord Browne-Wilkinson explained that this was due to the 'striking and unusual' facts of this case.[142] Lord Hoffmann was not a member of Amnesty International itself, he was a director of Amnesty International Charitable Limited, a charitable company created for tax reasons, which had amongst its purposes, the aim of carrying out some of the functions of Amnesty International. In the view of the House of Lords, due to the close links between Amnesty International Charitable Limited and Amnesty International, which intervened in the case, Lord Hoffmann was automatically disqualified from hearing it.

Lord Browne-Wilkinson summed up the situation when stating:

> The substance of the matter is that [Amnesty International, Amnesty International Limited and Amnesty International Charitable Limited] are all various parts of an entity or movement working in different fields towards the same goals. If the absolute impartiality of the judiciary is to be maintained, there must be a rule which automatically disqualifies a judge who is involved, whether personally or as a director of a company, in promoting the same causes in the same organisation as is a party to the

→

---

[140] Ibid [15].   [141] Ibid [69].
[142] [2000] 1 AC 119, 134.

> → suit. There is no room for fine distinctions if Lord Hewart C.J.'s famous dictum is to be observed: it is 'of fundamental importance that justice should not only be done, but should manifestly and undoubtedly be seen to be done'.[143]

The controversial aspect of this decision is that there was no financial interest. However, Lord Browne-Wilkinson was clear that the automatic disqualification rule should not be limited to financial interests.

> The rationale of the whole rule is that a man cannot be a judge in his own cause. In civil litigation, the matters in issue will normally have an economic impact; therefore a judge is automatically disqualified if he stands to make a financial gain as a consequence of his own decision of the case. But if, as in the present case, the matter at issue does not relate to money or economic advantage but is concerned with the promotion of the cause, the rationale disqualifying a judge applies just as much if the judge's decision will lead to the promotion of a cause in which the judge is involved together with one of the parties.[144]

This passage of Lord Browne-Wilkinson's judgment makes clear that the non-financial interest has to be of such a direct nature that it is something extremely similar to having a financial interest. In *Helow v Secretary of State for the Home Department*,[145] a Palestinian refugee appealed against the refusal of her claim for asylum. This was rejected by the judge. It later emerged that the judge was a member of the International Association of Jewish Lawyers and Jurists, which through a magazine had carried pro-Israeli articles. It was held that *Pinochet* did not apply because the interest was 'a long way away from *ex p Pinochet*', because the Association was not a party to the proceedings and mere membership is insufficient to make *Pinochet (No 2)* relevant.[146]

Discussing the problem

Consider Louise's application to open a restaurant under the Food Distribution Act 2024 outlined at the start of the scenario. Is there any evidence that may give rise to actual bias or the possibility that the automatic disqualification rule applies?

The issue is Ryan, the man who chaired the committee that decided Louise's application and owns two restaurants, one of which is a seafood restaurant. This clearly raises questions as to why Louise's application has been rejected. The concern is that Ryan has his own interest in ensuring that Louise's restaurant does not open, as it could compete with his restaurants, especially his Fish Face restaurant, which serves the same type of food as Louise's proposed restaurant.

The question is whether there is actual bias or the automatic disqualification rule applies. It is very difficult to prove actual bias, as Louise has no evidence that the decision to reject her application has been motivated by bias against her. It is far easier to apply the automatic disqualification rule. Here, Ryan has a financial interest in the decision, this means that Ryan is automatically disqualified from being part of the committee that determined Louise's application. It is also likely that Ryan's interest is more than being merely *de minimis*.

---

[143] Ibid 135.   [144] Ibid.   [145] [2008] UKHL 62.
[146] *Helow v Secretary of State for the Home Department* [2008] UKHL 62 [40].

13.6.4 **Apparent bias**

There are circumstances when even if not automatically disqualified, a particular judge or other decision-maker may undermine public confidence in the process if they continue, or their decision is allowed to stand. This recalls Lord Hewart's notion that justice must 'manifestly and undoubtedly be seen to be done'.[147] Apparent bias arises when the facts are such that there is a perception that the decision-maker may no longer be impartial. Given the objective of ensuring that public confidence is maintained in the decision-making process, this perception is sufficient to mean that any decision is tainted by apparent bias. The controversy has been to establish the test for apparent bias, with the cases sometimes interchangeably using phrases such as whether there is a 'probability', 'danger', or 'possibility' of bias.

The law was placed into some confusion in this area in *R v Gough*,[148] when Lord Goff stated that the test was whether the court (personifying the reasonable man), on ascertaining the relevant circumstances from the evidence, concludes that there was a *real danger* of bias.[149] Lord Goff was clear that he preferred a test of 'real danger rather than real likelihood, to ensure that the court is thinking in terms of possibility rather than probability of bias'.[150] As Elliott and Varuhas state, this suggested that the law was moving away from Lord Hewart's principle that the overriding purpose of the rule against bias to maintain public confidence in decision-making and instead, by using language of 'possibility' and 'danger', the law was concerned with cases of actual bias.[151] This was particularly the case with the shift to the assessment being made by the court rather than the reasonable person. This can lead to some cases concluding that even though there was an allegation of bias, if on an investigation of the facts, no injustice was caused, then the decision will stand.[152] This uncertainty between real danger, likelihood, or possibility was resolved in the following case.

> ### Case in depth: *Porter v Magill* [2001] UKHL 67
>
> Westminster City Council had adopted a policy of selling council houses to tenants in marginal council wards, in the belief that property owners are more likely to vote Conservative. The auditor investigated and found the leader and deputy leader of the council, Dame Shirley Porter and David Weeks, guilty of wilful misconduct and liable for the £31 million that their actions had cost the council. Porter and Weeks argued that the auditor's decision could not stand because it was tainted by apparent bias. This was due to a press conference the auditor held during the investigation, when he used 'florid language' to describe Porter and Weeks and indicated that he believed the claimants were guilty of misconduct.
>
> The House of Lords, after considering developments since *R v Gough*, stated that the test was as follows. That, first, the court 'must first ascertain all the circumstances which have a bearing on the suggestion that the judge was biased. It must then ask whether those circumstances would lead a *fair-minded and informed observer to conclude that there was a real possibility* . . . that the tribunal was biased'.[153] Indeed, to put the issue beyond doubt, Lord Hope expressly rejected the use of any language such as real danger, even though this had been
>
> →

---

[147] [1924] 1 KB 256, 259.   [148] [1993] AC 646.   [149] Ibid 670.
[150] Mark Elliott and Jason Varuhas, *Administrative Law: Text and Materials* (5th edn, OUP 2017) 332.
[151] Ibid.   [152] *R v Inner West London Coroner, ex p Dallaglio* [1994] 4 All ER 139, 151.
[153] *Porter v Magill* [2001] UKHL 67, 103, emphasis added.

> interpreted in some cases to mean the same as real possibility.[154] Consequently, it is now clear that the test is whether there is a *real possibility* of bias.
>
> Applying this real possibility test to the facts, it was clear that however 'unwise' the auditor's language was at the press conference, this did not give rise to apparent bias. This was due to his overall conduct throughout the investigation and the fact that the auditor emphasized that his findings were preliminary.

The *Porter v Magill* test differs from *R v Gough* more significantly than it may first appear. It clearly places public confidence rather than the courts at the heart of the test and it is clear that a 'real possibility' of bias is sufficient for apparent bias to apply. The controversy now revolves around what attributes can be given to the 'fair-minded and informed observer'.

It was stated in *Gilles v Secretary of State for Work and Pensions*[155] that the 'fair-minded and informed observer' is assumed to be aware of 'all the facts that are capable of being known by members of the public generally' and be capable of exercising their judgment as to the weight to be given to relevant facts.[156] The allegation in this case was that a doctor sitting on the Disability Benefit Tribunal was biased because they also provided medical reports to the Benefits Agency, who would consider these reports when deciding whether applicants were eligible for a disability benefit. Appeals against the decisions of the Benefits Agency went to the Disability Benefit Tribunal. The allegation of apparent bias was that the doctor would favour the medical reports received by the Benefits Agency provided by other doctors. The House of Lords concluded that no apparent bias existed. The fair minded and informed observer would be aware that the doctor, when providing reports to the Benefits Agency, was doing so as an independent expert adviser. Further, the observer would appreciate that when a doctor provides a report to the Benefits Agency and later acts as a member of a disability benefit tribunal they would act with 'professional detachment and the ability to exercise her own independent judgment on medical issues'.[157]

The danger is that the greater reasoning power the 'fair-minded and informed observer' is said to have, the more likely that results from the test are likely to reflect the views of the judge, creating the risk that the test departs from its purpose, which is to reflect public perceptions and maintain confidence in the fairness of decision-making. This can perhaps be seen in *Taylor v Lawrence*.[158] The night before delivering his judgment, a judge changed his will free of charge using the same firm of solicitors that represented the claimant in the case. The judge found in favour of the claimant. This gave rise to an allegation of apparent bias on the part of the judge. Lord Woolf CJ stated that the 'fair-minded and informed observer' was expected to be aware of the traditions of the legal profession, including dining together in the Inns of Court and the links between the practitioners and the judiciary as promoting 'an atmosphere which is totally inimical to the existence of bias'.[159] Consequently, the Court of Appeal considered that it was 'unthinkable that an informed observer would regard it as conceivable that a judge would be influenced to favour a party in litigation with whom he has no relationship merely because that party happens to be represented by a firm of solicitors who are acting for the judge in . . . connection with a will'.[160]

---

[154] *In re Medicaments and Related Classes of Goods (No 2)* [2001] 1 WLR 700, 726–7.
[155] [2006] UKHL 2. [156] Ibid [17]. [157] Ibid [18].
[158] [2002] EWCA Civ 90. [159] Ibid [63]. [160] Ibid [73].

The difficulty with this approach is that the observer is imputed with knowledge regarding the legal profession far beyond that possessed by an ordinary person. Such was the level of knowledge imputed, that the informed observer's 'perceptions are likely to be substantially at odds with those of ordinary members of the public—whose perceptions are supposed to be paramount in this context'.[161]

Counterpoint: Is the fair-minded and informed observer wreally a judge in disguise?

The way in which attributes have been grafted onto the 'fair-minded and informed observer' has led to calls to return to the *R v Gough* test. Olowofoyeku argues that essentially, the 'fair-minded and informed observer' has become a fictional middle-man between the lay person and the judges,[162] with the judges placing unrealistic knowledge on the observer to give a pretence of basing their decisions on the observer when instead they are making decisions based on their own views. This is perhaps clear in *Virdi v Law Society of England and Wales*, where Stanley Burton LJ concluded that 'if on examination of all the relevant facts, there was no unfairness or any appearance of unfairness, there is no good reason for the imaginary observer to be used to reach a different conclusion'.[163]

If this is the view of courts and the imaginary observer is really disguising how judges are applying their own standards, then what purpose does the imaginary observer serve? Does this make Olowofoyeku correct to argue for a return to the test in *R v Gough*, which places the emphasis on the courts making the assessment of whether apparent bias exists?

The approach of *Taylor v Lawrence* and *Virdi v Law Society of England and Wales* can be contrasted with two Privy Council decisions which apply the *Porter v Magill* test in a more straightforward and objective manner. In *Yiacoub v The Queen*,[164] two defendants located in the Sovereign Base Area of Akrotiri and Dhekelia, on Cyprus,[165] were convicted of criminal offences. At first instance, the case was heard by three judges, including the Presiding Judge of the appeal court. On conviction the defendants appealed to the appeal court. However, the Presiding Judge of the appeal court, having heard the case at first instance, made arrangements for the appeal, in particular choosing the chair of the three-judge panel, who then selected two other judges to sit with him. The Privy Council found that the Presiding Judge's actions gave rise to apparent bias under the *Porter v Magill* test. Essentially, the problem is that the Presiding Judge was 'nominating a judge to hear an appeal from himself', and although there was no evidence of any wrongdoing in this case, the Privy Council concluded that 'under other regimes . . . such a process could be open to abuse', and that the objective observer would say 'that surely cannot be right' about such a process.[166]

Similarly, *Stubbs v The Queen*, a Privy Council case from The Bahamas, found apparent bias on the part of a judge who heard an appeal from a criminal trial, when they acted as the trial judge on an earlier but aborted trial for the same charges.[167] The presence of

---

[161] Mark Elliot and Robert Thomas, *Public Law* (2nd edn, OUP 2014) 469.

[162] Abimbola Olowofoyeku, 'Bias and the Informed Observer: A Call for Return to Gough' [2009] CLJ 388, 406–7.

[163] [2010] EWCA Civ 100 [38].   [164] [2014] UKPC 22,

[165] The Sovereign Base Areas of Akrotiri and Dhekelia is a British Overseas Territory on Cyprus, governed by the UK and primarily used as military bases for the armed forces.

[166] [2014] UKPC 22 [15].   [167] [2018] UKPC 30.

the judge on the appeal meant that a fair-minded and informed observer would conclude that there was a real possibility that the judge had pre-judged the issues on appeal from when he heard the aborted trial, meaning that the appeal 'did not have the appearance of a fresh tribunal of three judges' as required.[168]

The approach of *Yiacoub v The Queen* and *Stubbs v The Queen* should be preferred to cases such as *Taylor v Lawrence*. In neither case did the Privy Council seek to bestow the 'fair-minded and informed observer' with special attributes that would distinguish them from ordinary members of the public. This is important when the ultimate aim is to ensure public confidence in the judicial process, and if this approach is taken, then this would address the concerns of Olowofoyeku discussed above.

 Pause for reflection

In *Emerald Supplies Ltd v British Airways*,[169] a complex competition law dispute, the trial judge, Peter Smith J, repeatedly and robustly questioned counsel for British Airways for reasons as to why his luggage was lost when he flew with the airline on a flight to Florence. It also emerged that he had escalated his complaint by emailing the chairman of the airline, with the email referring to the fact that he was sitting on this case. This was described by one leading legal commentator as 'a profound misjudgement',[170] as this raised questions of potential bias or a lack of impartiality on behalf of the judge. These issues were not pursued further because, shortly afterwards, Peter Smith J decided to recuse himself from the case, leaving the case to be heard by an alternative judge.[171]

However, do potential issues of bias arise from these facts? Does it involve actual or apparent bias?

13.7 A duty to give reasons?

The issue of giving notice, as explained in *Al Fayed*, relates to giving an indication regarding any issues of concern before a decision is taken. A duty to give reasons, if it arises, means giving reasons for the decision after it has been made. *Al Fayed* highlights how in practice these issues can be intertwined, because the issues of concern are extremely likely to be the reasons why the decision has been taken. However, conceptually these issues are different, and the courts view the duty to give reasons following a decision that has been made differently to the duty to give notice before making the decision. This section focuses on the common law duty to give reasons, although reasons can be required by statute or if the decision has engaged Article 6.

13.7.1 Benefits of reason-giving

As Le Sueur explains, there are three main benefits to requiring public bodies to give reasons for their decision.

---

[168] Ibid [34].
[169] [2015] EWHC 2201 (Ch).
[170] Joshua Rozenberg, 'Scrutiny of Judicial Conduct', *The Law Society Gazette*, 6 June 2016.
[171] [2015] EWHC 2201 (Ch).

Reinforcing the rule of law

'A lack of knowledge about the reasons for a decision will often make it difficult to mount an effective challenge to an administrative decision even though there may be grounds on which that decision can be challenged.'[172] Giving reasons provides those subject to the decision the basis for the decision: if they believe that the decision has been reached incorrectly, then there is the possibility of an appeal (eg to a tribunal, if provision for one is made by statute) or a judicial review. However, it can be very difficult to determine the basis for an appeal or application for judicial review without the reasons for the decision in the first place. Giving reasons facilitates the legal accountability of decision-making, thereby reinforcing the rule of law.

Ensure consistency of decision-making

If reasons are given for a particular decision then, in principle, when the decision-maker later makes a decision for similar case, those reasons from the first case should apply. This leads Le Sueur to state that 'reason-giving . . . is a type of rule-making'.[173] These rules should then lead to the creation of 'settled rules, policies, or standards', which should ensure that like cases are treated alike.

Legitimizes government decision-making

Out of the three, this is perhaps the most abstract benefit, but giving reasons allows for the tacit acceptance of the decision. As Le Sueur states, when:

> a public body gives you a reason for its decision, it is trying to persuade you that it has done the correct thing. A tyrant does not seek to persuade; he simply asserts authority backed by force. To state a reason is also to issue an invitation to question: reasons declare 'this is what I say; do you agree?' A person who declines to question the reasons tacitly consents to the decision.[174]

In this way, the decision is made more legitimate because the reasons for the decision have acquired some form of 'acceptance' from the person subject to the decision. This 'acceptance' is not readily available if reasons for the decision are not communicated to that person.

13.7.2 **Duty to give reasons at common law?**

Given these benefits of reason-giving it may appear strange that, as explained in *Doody*, the common law 'does not at present recognise a *general* duty to give reasons for an administrative decision'.[175] However, it remains open to the courts to impose a duty to give reasons in individual cases on the grounds of fairness. The next two cases establish when this duty arises.

---

[172] Andrew Le Sueur, 'Legal Duties to Give Reasons' (1999) 52 CLP 150, 153.
[173] Ibid 155.   [174] Ibid 156.
[175] *R v Secretary of State for the Home Department, ex p Doody* [1994] AC 531, 564.

> **Case in depth: *R v Civil Service Appeal Board, ex p Cunningham* [1992] ICR 816**
>
> After serving twenty-three years, a civil servant was unfairly dismissed from his position in the prison service. The Civil Service Appeal Board decided that he should be awarded £6,500 in compensation. Considering his salary of £16,000 and length of service, this was considerably lower than the sum that the claimant could reasonably have expected. However, the board gave no reasons for their decision. The Court of Appeal held that reasons for their decision needed to be disclosed.
>
> McCowan LJ described the decision as one that 'cries out for some explanation from the board'.[176] Furthermore, the lack of reasons meant that 'not only is justice not seen to have been done but there is no way, in the absence of reasons from the board, in which it can be judged whether in fact it has been done'.[177] As this failed to comply with the requirements of fairness, the way the court remedied this was by requiring that the board gave reasons for its decision.

The decision in *Cunningham* was approved by the House of Lords in *Doody* itself, which also considered the situations in which the common law will impose a duty to give reasons.

> **Case in depth: *R v Secretary of State for the Home Department, ex p Doody* [1994] 1 AC 531**
>
> The four applicants had each received a mandatory life sentence for murder. Under the Criminal Justice Act 1967, section 61, the Home Secretary would consult with the Lord Chief Justice and the trial judge before setting a minimum period before they would be eligible for parole. This was known as the 'tariff'. The prisoners could not make their own representations to the Home Secretary and did not know the period recommended by the judges or whether the Home Secretary imposed a different tariff to that recommended by the judges or the reasons why the tariff was imposed in the first place.
>
> Lord Mustill stated that within the framework by which these decisions were made, the Secretary of State must act as fairly as possible. On conviction, the prisoners knew that they were going to serve a very long sentence, but even a reduction of one year would have a profound impact on the prisoners. As Lord Mustill explained, 'a difference of a year or years: [is] a long time for anybody, and longer still for a prisoner'.[178] Given the importance of the decision, not giving reasons for the minimum tariff could not be fair. 'The announcement of his first review date arrives out of thin air, wholly without explanation. The distant oracle has spoken, and that is that.'[179] Further, giving reasons provides 'an effective means of detecting the kind of error which would entitle the court to intervene, and in practice I regard it as necessary for this purpose that the reasoning of the Home Secretary should be disclosed'.[180] This would be particularly the case if the Home Secretary differed from the minimum period recommended by the judges and, consequently, any 'reasoning is bound to include, either explicitly or implicitly, a reason why the Home Secretary has taken a different view'.[181]

---

[176] *R v Civil Service Appeal Board, ex p Cunningham* [1992] ICR 816, 831.

[177] Ibid 831.

[178] *R v Secretary of State for the Home Department, ex p Doody* [1994] 1 AC 531.

[179] Ibid.   [180] Ibid 565.   [181] Ibid.

The effects of *Cunningham* and *Doody* were summarized in *R v Higher Education Funding Council, ex p Institute of Dental Surgery*[182] as establishing the following propositions:

'1. There is no general duty to give reasons for a decision, but there are classes of case where there is such a duty.

2. One such class is where the subject matter is an interest so highly regarded by the law (for example, personal liberty), that fairness requires that reasons, at least for particular decisions, be given as of right.

3. (a) Another such class is where the decision appears aberrant. Here fairness may require reasons so that the recipient may know whether the aberration is in the legal sense real (and so challengeable) or apparent; (b) it follows that this class does not include decisions which are themselves challengeable by reference only to the reasons for them. A pure exercise of academic judgment is such a decision; and (c) procedurally, the grant of leave in such cases will depend upon prima facie evidence that something has gone wrong.'[183]

In this case, the Institute of Dental Surgery sought a judicial review of the Universities Research Funding Council to cut the Institute's research grant, following the Funding Council's in-depth review process, which lowered the Institute's research rating. It was held that reasons were not required to be granted because of the interests at stake. Also, the decision relied on academic judgment, which is not readily reviewable by the court; neither was the subject of the decision as serious as it was in *Doody*, nor did the decision cry out for an explanation as in *Cunningham*.

Discussing the problem

Return again to the scenario at the beginning of the chapter. Can the Council's refusal to give reasons explaining their refusal of Louise's application for a licence be justified?

It remains the case that there is no duty at common law to give reasons and there is no statutory requirement to give reasons. However, under section 3(3) of the 2024 Act, Louise is given the right to appeal against the decision. This right can only be exercised fairly if Louise is aware of the factors that meant her application was rejected. This is a strong indication that in this case, reasons should be given to Louise. Both the *Cunningham* and *ex p Institute of Dental Surgery* cases support the conclusion that reasons should be given: there is no way to determine whether the decision has been reached fairly without any details of the reason given.

13.7.3 If reasons are given, they must be adequate

It follows that if a duty to give reasons is imposed at common law, the question is how to comply with that duty. It is suggested that a reasonable approach should be taken, in that the reasons should give the broad basis for the decision. In *Clarke Homes Limited v Secretary of State for the Environment and East Staffordshire District Council*,[184] Sir Thomas Bingham MR stated:

---

[182] [1994] 1 WLR 242.   [183] Ibid 263.
[184] (1993) 66 P & CR 263, 272–3.

I hope I am not over-simplifying unduly by suggesting that the central issue in this case is whether the [reasons provided] leaves room for genuine as opposed to forensic doubt as to what he has decided and why. This is an issue to be resolved as the parties agree on a straightforward down-to-earth reading of his decision letter without excessive legalism or exegetical sophistication.

Sir Thomas Bingham's statement was approved by the House of Lords in *South Bucking-hamshire District Council v Porter (No 2)*,[185] when Lord Nicholls stated that the reasons must be 'intelligible and they must be adequate', which allow the reader to understand why the matter was decided in that way, indicating the conclusions on the 'principal important controversial issues'.[186] When relevant, the reasons should explain how issues of law or fact were resolved. The level of detail required will depend on the nature of the decision, with more serious decisions, for example, those involving liberty of the person, requiring more detail than decisions that are relatively minor.

13.7.4 A general duty to give reasons?

The courts continue to impose a duty to give reasons in individual cases. However, in *Oakley v South Cambridgeshire District Council*,[187] the Court of Appeal considered whether this case-by-case approach should be replaced with a general duty to give reasons. The Court concluded that 'it may be more accurate to say that the common law is moving to the position whilst there is no universal obligation to give reasons in all circumstances, in general they should be given unless there is a proper justification for not doing so'.[188] Indeed, Elias LJ admitted that he was 'strongly attracted' to the argument that there is a general common law duty to give reasons. However, he declined the opportunity to reach this conclusion, preferring to continue with the existing case-by-case approach. He continued that the 'courts develop the common law on a case by case basis, and I do not discount the possibility that there may be particular circumstances, other than where the reasoning is transparent in any event, where there is a justification for not imposing a common law duty'.[189]

The Supreme Court reviewed the situation in *Dover District Council v CPRE Kent*.[190] Affirming the approach of the Court of Appeal in *Oakley*, the Court decided once again that a duty to give reasons was imposed at common law. In this instance, reasons were required because the Council had decided to grant planning permission despite being advised by the planning officer to reject it.

In some senses, this is surprising because the decision was in the planning context (as was *Oakley*), an area of law tightly regulated by statute, meaning that if Parliament wanted to impose a duty to give reasons, it had the opportunity to do so. However, the Supreme Court found that the correct approach is to interpret 'the statute [as] underpinned by general principles, properly referred to as derived from the common law'.[191] The Supreme Court then highlighted how this was not unusual, for the *Doody* case itself 'involved such an application of the common law principle of "fairness" in a statutory context, in which the giving of reasons was seen as essential to allow effective supervision by the courts'.[192]

---

[185] [2004] UKHL 33 [36].   [186] Ibid.
[187] [2017] EWCA Civ 71.   [188] Ibid [30].   [189] Ibid [55].   [190] [2017] UKSC 79.
[191] Ibid [54].   [192] Ibid [54].

Concerns about the lack of certainty as to when a duty to give reasons applies in any particular case were also brushed aside by the Supreme Court, stating that it should not be difficult for councils and their officers to identify cases which call for a formulated statement of reasons, beyond the statutory requirements. Typically, they will be cases where, as in *Oakley* and the present case, permission has been granted in the face of substantial public opposition or against the advice of officers. In other words, these are decisions which for one reason or another simply cry out for an explanation. Members of the planning committee remain 'entitled to depart from their officer's recommendation for good reasons, but their reasons for doing so need to be capable of articulation, and open to public scrutiny'.[193]

The Supreme Court has continued with the basic common law approach that there is no general common law duty to give reasons, but that in specific cases, requiring reasons ensures that decision-makers are accountable.

 Counterpoint: A general duty to give reasons at common law?

In *Oakley v South Cambridgeshire District Council*, Sales LJ, while agreeing that reasons were required in that particular case, disagreed with Elias LJ in the Court of Appeal about the desirability of a general duty to give reasons at common law. He stated:

> The need to prepare and agree reasons might also introduce an unwelcome element of delay into the planning system . . . These sorts of [factors] are difficult for a court to assess and I think this court should be wary of stepping in to impose a general duty where Parliament has chosen not to do so. In my view, the common law should only identify a duty to give reasons where there is a sufficient accumulation of reasons of particular force and weight in relation to the particular circumstances of an individual case.[194]

Given the benefits of reasons outlined in 13.7.1, has the time come for the courts to recognize a general duty to give reasons at common law as Elias LJ suggests or retain the case-by-case approach as argued by Sales LJ and the Supreme Court in *Dover*?

13.8 Legitimate expectations

13.8.1 What are legitimate expectations?

Lord Diplock in the *GCHQ* case stated that a legitimate expectation is when someone is deprived of:

> some benefit or advantage which either (i) he had in the past been permitted by the decision-maker to enjoy and which he can legitimately expect to be permitted to continue to do until there has been communicated to him some rational grounds for withdrawing it on which he has been given an opportunity to comment; or (ii) he has received assurance from the decision-maker will not be withdrawn without giving him first an opportunity of advancing reasons for contending that they should not be withdrawn.[195]

[193] Ibid [60].   [194] [2017] EWCA Civ 71 [76].
[195] [1985] AC 374, 408.

Usually, a legitimate expectation will arise when an individual is enjoying (or expecting to enjoy) a right, and they have been assured by a public body that the right will continue until they are informed that it is to be withdrawn. However, if it is proposed that the benefit may be withdrawn, then that person will be able to comment on the reasons as to why he should be allowed to retain the benefit. What is meant by 'assurance' can be relatively broad, and can include a policy, past practice, or a statement made by the public authority. The 'benefit' could be the granting or the renewal of a licence.

The basic rationale behind recognizing and enforcing legitimate expectations is that the courts are ensuring that public authorities comply with promises that they make. This reflects the broader requirement that public authorities exercise their powers fairly, in this context, by dealing with the public appropriately. As Laws LJ stated in *R (Nadarajah) v Secretary of State for the Home Department*:[196]

> Where a public authority has issued a promise or adopted a practice which represents how it proposes to act in a given area, the law will require the promise or practice to be honoured unless there is good reason not to do so. What is the principle behind this proposition? It is not far to seek. It is said to be grounded in fairness, and no doubt in general terms that is so. I would prefer to express it rather more broadly as a requirement of good administration, by which public bodies ought to deal straightforwardly and consistently with the public ...[197]

In *R v North and East Devon Health Authority, Ex p Coughlan*,[198] Lord Woolf MR identified three categories of case:

(1) When the public authority is '*only required to bear in mind its previous policy or other representation, giving it the weight, it thinks right, but no more, before deciding whether to change course*'.[199] Decisions in this category are subject to review on the ordinary *Wednesbury* unreasonableness test.

(2) When the promise or practice of a public authority '*induces a legitimate expectation of, for example, being consulted before a particular decision is taken*'. In these circumstances, the courts will require that the legitimate expectation is fulfilled (such as consultation) unless there is an overriding reason that permits the public authority to resile from their representation. The courts will judge for themselves what constitutes an overriding reason taking into account the requirements of fairness.

(3) When the promise or practice of a public authority induces '*a legitimate expectation of a benefit which is substantive, not simply procedural*'. The courts will decide whether frustrating the expectation would be 'so unfair' that it would 'amount to an abuse of power'.[200]

Category (2) can be described as covering procedural legitimate expectations, with Category (3) explaining substantive legitimate expectations. Cases that fall into Category (1) are not legitimate expectation cases and are decided under the ordinary reasonableness test.[201] The next section outlines procedural legitimate expectations before moving on to discuss the substantive version of the doctrine.

---

[196] [2005] EWCA Civ 1363.   [197] Ibid [78].   [198] [2001] QB 213.
[199] Ibid [57].   [200] Ibid.   [201] See Chapter 12.

13.8.2 Procedural legitimate expectations

A classic example of a procedural legitimate expectation is *R v Liverpool Corporation, ex p Liverpool Taxi Fleet Operators' Association*.[202] The local authority, the Liverpool Corporation, had the power to grant taxi licences. The Operators' Association, representing the drivers, told the Corporation that they wanted the number of licences to remain at 300. The town clerk of Liverpool wrote to the Operators' Association, informing them that no decision had been made and that they would be consulted. However, without any consultation, the Corporation then made a decision that there should be a limit of 350 licences, which later would be increased to 450, and ultimately the limit would be removed entirely. The Court of Appeal agreed with the Operators' Association, that the Corporation should have complied with their promise of consultation. The undertaking was compatible with their public duties and that:

> they ought not to depart from it except after the most serious consideration and hearing what the other party has to say: and then only if they are satisfied that the overriding public interest requires it . . . It is better to hold the corporation to their undertaking than to allow them to break it.[203]

Liverpool Taxi Fleet Operators' Association is an example of a procedural legitimate expectation. The Operators' Association had a legitimate expectation that the decision regarding the number of licences would be made only after the Operators' Association had been consulted. In this case, the expectation arose out of a specific representation by the Corporation.

Past practice

A legitimate expectation can arise out of previous practice. This is shown with the *GCHQ* case. The Minister for the Civil Service, an office held by the Prime Minister, had decided that on the grounds of national security, members of staff at one of the intelligence services, the General Communications Headquarters would no longer be allowed to be members of a trade union. This was a significant change to employment conditions. The Civil Service Unions argued that previous changes to employment conditions had only been implemented following consultation with the unions. This meant that the unions and their members had a legitimate expectation that further changes could only be implemented following consultation. The House of Lords agreed that a legitimate expectation of consultation had arisen, because 'the evidence shows that, ever since GCHQ began in 1947, prior consultation has been the invariable rule when conditions of service were to be significantly altered'.[204] However, the House of Lords agreed with the government that it was in the interests of national security that they did not consult with the Unions, because in light of industrial relations over the previous years when strike action had taken place, consultation was likely to have resulted in further strikes, which would have interrupted GCHQ's operations.

In finding that the government was not required to consult on the grounds of national security, despite a legitimate expectation arising through previous practice, *GCHQ* is an example of how the courts balance an overriding interest which outweighs the requirements of fairness to give effect to the legitimate expectation in question. Had the case involved a more typical employment context, then the government would have been required to give effect to the legitimate expectation of consultation before making a decision.

---

[202] [1972] 2 QB 299.   [203] Ibid 308.
[204] [1985] AC 374, 401.

Policy statement

R v Secretary of State for the Home Department, ex p Khan[205] is an example of a policy statement giving rise to a legitimate expectation. The claimants wanted to adopt their nephew from Pakistan. They received a circular published by the Home Office which explained its policy on adoption. This document indicated that the Home Secretary would consider four criteria when deciding whether to grant entry to the nephew. Entry was refused despite the couple complying with the criteria. Instead, the Home Secretary had changed the policy and relied on a fifth criterion which was not discussed in the circular. The Court of Appeal held that the claimants had a legitimate expectation that either the terms of the circular were complied with, or if the new, fifth criteria was to be applied, then the claimants must have the opportunity to argue that it should not apply to them.

The unfairness of the situation is quite plain. The claimants, on seeing the circular, had acted according to that policy in the belief that that policy would be applied to them. The change in the policy had not been communicated to them and so they were judged according to criteria of which they had no knowledge. This highlights how fairness is at the core of the doctrine of legitimate expectations. As explained by Parker LJ:

> if the new policy is to continue in operation, the sooner the Home Office letter is redrafted and false hopes cease to be raised in those who may have a deep emotional need to adopt, the better it will be. To leave it in its present form is not only bad and grossly unfair administration but, in some instances at any rate, positively cruel.[206]

An interesting issue was raised in *R (Rashid) v Secretary of State for the Home Department*[207] when it was decided that an asylum seeker should be returned to Iraq. This decision went against published Home Office policy. However, neither the claimant nor the officials dealing with the case were aware of the policy. Yet the claimant managed to establish that he had a legitimate expectation that he should not be treated in a manner that was in breach of the policy, despite his lack of knowledge of it.

The issue here is whether someone needs to be aware of the policy, as in *Khan* or *Coughlan* (discussed in 13.8.4), in order to give rise to the legitimate expectation. In *Mandalia v Secretary of State for the Home Department*, the Supreme Court has since described the application of legitimate expectations in these circumstances as 'strained'.[208] Arguably, *Rashid* is better explained as an example of requiring public authorities to comply with a policy they have published, unless there is a compelling reason to depart from it.[209] This would mean that there would be no need to 'strain' the concept of legitimate expectations to cover circumstances when the party invoking the doctrine has no knowledge of the rule or policy they are seeking to rely on.

13.8.3 **When a legitimate expectation arises**

Generally, in order for a legitimate expectation to arise, the statement relied on must be 'clear, unambiguous and devoid of relevant qualification'. However, particular issues have arisen regarding statements made by politicians. In *R v Secretary of State for Education*

---

[205] [1984] 1 WLR 1337.   [206] Ibid 1348.   [207] [2005] EWCA Civ 744.
[208] [2015] UKSC 59 [29].
[209] See *R (Lumba) v Secretary of State for the Home Department* [2011] UKSC 1 [35] (Lord Dyson); *R (SK Zimbabwe) v Secretary of State for the Home Department* [2011] UKSC 23 [36] (Lord Hope DPC).

and Employment, ex p Begbie,[210] the issue was whether promises made by Labour Party politicians generated a legitimate expectation once elected into government in 1997. One of Labour's promises was to abolish the 'assisted places scheme'. This gave public funding for some children to attend independent schools, instead of a state school. During the election campaign, Labour Party politicians, in newspaper interviews and letters, emphasized that no one would 'lose out' as a consequence of adopting this policy. The Labour Government implemented the Education (Schools) Act 1997 to abolish the scheme. As a transitional measure, the Act allowed those already in primary education to continue at their school under the scheme until they reached eleven and those in secondary education could continue at their school under in the scheme until they reached eighteen. The claimant was at an 'all through school', a school that educated children from the age of five until eighteen. The claimant, aged nine, argued that she should remain at her school under the scheme until she was eighteen, arguing that she had a legitimate expectation, triggered by statements made during the election campaign that no one would 'lose out'.

The claimant's argument was rejected on two grounds. First, that to give effect to her legitimate expectation would go against the terms of the 1997 Act, which only guaranteed that she could have the benefit of the scheme until she reached eleven years of age. Secondly, statements made by politicians when in opposition and not in government could not generate a legitimate expectation as they lacked the necessary authority to form the basis of a legitimate expectation. Any consequences for a politician failing to keep their election promises upon entering government should be 'political and not legal'.[211]

The second case is *R (on the application of Association of British Civilian Detainees: Far East Region) v Secretary of State for Defence*.[212] A junior Defence Minister announced to Parliament a compensation scheme for British subjects who were imprisoned by the Japanese during the Second World War.[213] However, the scheme was later clarified, restricting the scheme to those who were born, or had one parent or grandparent born, in the United Kingdom. This meant that some who, on hearing the minister's announcement believed that they would be entitled to compensation, would not be entitled as they did not satisfy the criteria. The Court of Appeal held that the statement by the minister was too vague to generate a legitimate expectation, as it did not contain a clear and unequivocal statement and it should have been understood by the claimants as needing clarification as provided by the detailed criteria was published.

13.8.4 Substantive legitimate expectations

Most cases, certainly the examples discussed in this section so far, have involved a legitimate expectation regarding the procedure by which a decision would be made—for example, that they would be consulted beforehand or that the decision would be made in accordance with the decision-maker's published policy. Far more controversial are

---

[210] [2000] 1 WLR 1115.   [211] Ibid 1125.   [212] [2003] QB 1397.

[213] The minister stated that those 'who will be entitled to receive the payment are former members of Her Majesty's armed forces who were made prisoners of war, former members of the merchant navy who were captured and imprisoned, and British civilians who were interned. Certain other former military personnel in the colonial forces, the Indian army and the Burmese armed forces who received compensation in the 1950s under United Kingdom auspices will also be eligible. As I said earlier, in cases in which a person who would have been entitled to the payment has died, the surviving spouse will be entitled to receive it instead': HC Deb, 7 November 2000, vol 356, cols 159–60.

legitimate expectations regarding the actual decision itself. For instance, that someone received an assurance that they will continue to receive a benefit or a particular decision after making an application. While giving effect to procedural expectations may delay a decision, the actual decision remains for the decision-maker, who can still exercise their discretion. Giving effect to a substantive expectation is more controversial because this involves the courts requiring the decision-maker to give effect to the legitimate expectation and so removes any discretion from the decision-maker. The courts are usually reluctant to do this, because the role of the courts is to ensure that public authorities act in the public interest and making a public authority bound by a previous promise can raise serious issues of allocation of resources, which are usually questions that require political rather than legal accountability. This is because if the courts give effect to someone's substantive legitimate expectation, this may mean that others will lose out. The most significant case regarding substantive legitimate expectations remains *Coughlan*.

Case in depth: *R v North and East Devon Health Authority, ex p Coughlan* [2001] QB 213

In 1971, the claimant was seriously injured in a road accident. She would require residential care for the rest of her life. In 1993, she moved from her previous home to Mardon House. The health authority assured her and other patients that they could stay there for 'as long as they wished' and that it would be their 'home for life'. In 1998, on the grounds of cost, the health authority decided to close Mardon House. The claimant argued that they had a legitimate expectation that they could remain there for life.

The House of Lords agreed, holding that the courts are willing to give effect to substantive legitimate expectations, but must weigh the 'requirements of fairness against any overriding interest relied upon for the change of policy'.[214] This means that once the court has found the legitimate expectation, the court must then consider whether there are compelling reasons to depart from the previously stated policy. In this case, the legitimate expectation should be protected and the promise of a 'home for life' honoured. Lord Woolf MR stated that this was because of:

> the importance of what was promised to Miss Coughlan; . . . second, the fact that promise was limited to a few individuals, and the fact that the consequences to the health authority of requiring it to honour its promise are likely to be financial only.[215]

Clearly, the House of Lords was keen to stress that this was an exceptional case. This was a promise made to a small number of individuals, so the broader policy implications of requiring the health authority to maintain its promise of a 'home for life' were likely to be relatively minor. The factor of the promise being made to a small number of people was discussed in *R (Patel) v General Medical Council*. The Court of Appeal stated:

> while in theory there may be no limit to the number of beneficiaries of a promise for the purpose of a substantive legitimate expectation, in reality it is likely to be small if the expectation is to be upheld because, first, it is difficult to imagine a case in which government will be held legally bound by a representation or undertaking made generally or to a diverse class and, secondly because the broader the class claiming the benefit of the expectation the more likely it is that the supervening public interest will be held to justify the change of position of which complaint is made.[216]

[214] [2001] QB 213 [57].   [215] Ibid [60].   [216] [2013] EWCA Civ 327 [50].

In terms of the standard of review, the court in *Patel* approved the following statement of Laws LJ in *Begbie*: the facts should 'steer the court to a more or less intrusive quality of review'.[217] Some changes of policy, despite a previous assurance generating a substantive legitimate interest, will raise 'questions of general policy affecting the public at large or a significant section of it (including interests not represented before the court)'.[218] In such a case, the court can only intervene on a *Wednesbury* basis, meaning that the decision would have to be so unreasonable as to be outside the scope of the power of the public authority, which would very rarely occur in practice.[219] By contrast, in cases such as *Coughlan* itself 'few individuals were affected by the promise in question. The case's facts may be discrete and limited, having no implications for an innominate class of persons. There may be no wide-ranging issues of general policy, or none with multi-layered effects, upon whose merits the court is asked to embark.'[220] In such a case, the courts would be able to determine the consequences of the order it makes. This means that if the court views a proposed action as amounting to an abuse of power, the court should only decline to intervene if there is an overriding public interest against such intervention.

To show this notion of a sliding scale the *Patel* case itself is helpful.[221] The claimant decided to train as a doctor through a distance learning course at the International University of Health Sciences, St Kitts and Nevis. Before he started the course, it was accepted by the General Medical Council (GMC) for a provisional registration as a doctor in the UK. This registration is required to practise as a doctor in the UK. In email correspondence, when specifically asked about whether they accepted the course, the GMC told the claimant that they did. The claimant enrolled onto the course and obtained the degree. He sought provisional registration, but was refused by the GMC because they had since changed their criteria which meant that the claimant's degree was no longer accepted. The claimant argued that following the email correspondence, they had a substantive legitimate expectation that their degree would be accepted by the GMC.

The Court of Appeal agreed with the claimant. The representation in the form of the emails from the GMC to the claimant were clear, unambiguous, and unqualified and amounted to a specific undertaking that his degree would be accepted, if he completed his degree within a reasonable time. While it was accepted that the GMC would from time to time adopt new criteria, the GMC should have made transitional provisions for those in the claimant's position. The lack of transitional provisions caused unfairness in that the substantive legitimate expectation of the claimant had not been fulfilled and there was no sufficient public interest which outweighed that unfairness.

From the *Patel* case, it might be thought that, in a parallel to estoppel from private law, the party invoking a substantive legitimate expectation must show that they have relied on the promise to their detriment. However, this is not the case. Instead, reliance is relevant as to the issue of fairness. This is explained by Lord Hoffmann in R *(Bancoult) v Secretary of State for Commonwealth Affairs (No 2)*, '[i]t is not essential that the applicant should have relied upon the promise to his detriment, although this is a relevant consideration in deciding whether the adoption of a policy in conflict with the promise would be an abuse of power'.[222] This approach has recently been approved in obiter by the Supreme Court in *Re Finucane's application for Judicial Review (Northern Ireland)*.[223]

---

[217] [2000] 1 WLR 1115, 1130.   [218] Ibid 1131.   [219] See Chapter 12.

[220] [2000] 1 WLR 1115, 1131.   [221] [2013] EWCA Civ 327.

[222] [2009] AC 453 [60], citing Laws LJ in *R v Secretary of State for Education and Employment, Ex p Begbie* [2000] 1 WLR 1115, 1131.

[223] [2019] UKSC 7 [63], [72] (Lord Kerr); [157] (Lord Carnwath).

13.9 **Summary**

This chapter has explained procedural impropriety as a ground of judicial review. The overriding requirement is that decisions are reached fairly. As this requirement applies broadly across most forms of decision-making by public authorities, the requirements of fairness need to be considered flexibly, taking account of the nature and context of the decision.

The starting point for determining what is required for any given decision is the statute that grants the decision-maker the power to make the decision, with any statutory requirement a key consideration. However, not every failure to comply with a statutory requirement will result in the decision being invalid. In addition to this, the common law has imposed further requirements based on the need for fairness when public authorities are reaching decisions. These can include the need for the public authority to consult with interested parties before a decision is made, or giving reasons once the decision has been taken. The fundamental debate regards how far the courts go in imposing these requirements above and beyond the statutory criteria (if any).

Two core rules historically derived from the rules of natural justice are the right to be heard and the rule against bias. Particularly with the right to be heard, what this requires will depend on the circumstances, but the more significant the issue is, the more likely an oral hearing will be required. Similarly, the rule against bias attempts to not only prevent decisions motivated by bias, but to maintain public confidence in the way decisions are made. These rules have been supplemented by Article 6 ECHR, although it is debatable as to how much the common law rules differ from what the article requires. Finally, procedural requirements can be imposed on a decision-maker through their own actions, giving rise to a legitimate expectation that a decision is going to be made in a particular manner. In some circumstances, the courts will give effect to this. In rarer circumstances, the expectation goes beyond mere procedure and to substance, where it is expected by someone that they will actually benefit in a particular way. If such an expectation is limited to a small number of individuals, the courts may require the public authority to maintain their promise.

Quick test questions

1. What are the benefits of the rules of natural justice?
2. When considering procedural requirements laid down by statute, do the mandatory/directory categories remain useful?
3. What is the significance of the judgment in *Ridge v Baldwin*?
4. To what extent does a duty to give reasons exist at common law?
5. What does Article 6 ECHR add to the common law requirements of fairness?
6. To what extent is there any difference in circumstances when the automatic disqualification rule and apparent bias apply?
7. How can the actions of a public authority give rise to a legitimate expectation?

Further reading

Generally

Mark Elliott and Jason Varuhas, *Administrative Law: Text and Materials* (5th edn, OUP 2017) Chs 6, 9, 10, and 11

William Wade and Christopher Forsyth, *Administrative Law* (11th edn, OUP 2014) Chs 12, 13, and 14

Duty to give reasons

Farrah Ahmed and Adam Perry, 'Expertise, Deference and Giving Reasons' [2012] *Public Law* 221

Joanna Bell, 'Kent and Oakley: a re-examination of the common law duty to give reasons for grants of planning permission and beyond' (2017) 22(2) *Judicial Review* 105

*Andrew Le Sueur, 'Legal Duties to Give Reasons' (1999) 52 *Current Legal Problems* 150

Jeremy Waldron, 'How the Law Protects Dignity' (2012) 71(1) *Cambridge Law Journal* 200

Bias

*Abimbola Olowofoyeku, 'Bias and the Informed Observer: A Call for a Return to Gough' (2009) 68(2) *Cambridge Law Journal* 388

Lord Roger of Earlsferry, 'Bias and Conflicts of Interests—Challenges for Today's Decision-Makers', 24th Sultan Azlan Shah Law Lecture 2010 (available at http://www.sultanazlanshah.com/pdf/2011%20Book/SAS_Lecture_24.pdf)

Legitimate expectations

Joe Tomlinson, 'The Narrow Approach to Substantive Legitimate Expectations and the Trend of Modern Authority' (2017) 17(1) *Oxford University Commonwealth Law Journal* 75

Rebecca Williams, 'The Multiple Doctrines of Legitimate Expectations' (2016) 132 *Law Quarterly Review* 639

 Visit this book's **online resources** for additional materials relating to this chapter, including a full analysis of the start-of-chapter problem scenario.
www.oup.com/he/stanton-prescott2e

14

Administrative justice: tribunals, ombudsmen, and public inquiries

Problem scenario

Consider the situations of Simon, Timothy, and Emeli.

Simon is fifty-five years old. Unfortunately, he has suffered a very serious stroke. While he is slowly recovering, he has very limited use of his right arm and his mobility is limited. Simon used to work as a builder, but inevitably he has been unable to work since his stroke. Simon has applied to the Department for Work and Pensions for Employment and Support Allowance, a social security benefit which provides support when someone is unable to work or has a limited capability to work. However, the Department of Work and Pensions has refused his claim on the basis that he is capable of doing some work.

Timothy owns a large farm. The government has announced that it intends to develop plans for a new railway line which will go through the middle of the farm. Timothy knew nothing about this announcement and is furious that he was not informed about this before the announcement was made. Timothy's anger increased when he discovered that his neighbour Frank has had meetings with the Department for Transport about their intention before the announcement was made. Timothy has written to his MP, James Baldock, who has also heard from several other constituents that they were not informed by the Department of Transport about the proposed railway line before the announcement.

Emeli is part of a group of families whose sons and daughters were killed during British military action in the Middle East. They are concerned that their relatives' deaths were at least partly due to using equipment unsuitable for warfare in the desert. They believe that the Secretary of State for Defence at the time, Alain Baird, had ordered his civil servants to purchase machine guns from Incerta Dynamics, who were not approved by the Ministry of Defence to supply machine guns. At the time of the deaths, military experts questioned why

→

→

these guns were being used, as they were unsuitable for desert conditions and at least five British military personnel were killed when using these guns. Two years after resigning from the government, it has now been announced that Alain Baird has taken up a position on the board of Incerta Dynamics. Following this announcement, rumours regarding Baird's period as Defence Secretary are now being reported in the newspapers. This includes photographs of Baird in a meeting with representatives of Incerta Dynamics at a hotel in Monaco.

14.1 Introduction: what is administrative justice?

The complexity and scale of modern government means that it is inevitable that sometimes things will go wrong. Public bodies make hundreds of thousands of decisions each year. The range of decisions stretch from matters which have national importance, such as whether to allow a new drug to be made available on the NHS, to decisions focused on the individual, for instance whether to accept an application for a social security benefit. Sometimes, the pressures of making thousands of decisions on finite resources means that public bodies may not treat members of the public appropriately and not fulfil the aims of good government. When things go wrong, some will wish to challenge decisions made by the public authorities. The instinctive response from a lawyer might be to suggest that such disputes should be resolved by the courts applying the principles of judicial review. While the principles of judicial review are clearly of importance, alternatives such as statutory tribunals and ombudsmen provide other ways to challenge decisions made by public bodies. In addition, when something has gone seriously wrong, or a major scandal has occurred, a public inquiry can be held.

Each of these three procedures deal with different issues. Tribunals provide a way in which an individual decision can be challenged without the need to go to court. They are meant to provide a cheap, accessible, and quick method for making such a challenge. The key advantage of tribunals over judicial review is that, unlike with an application for judicial review, they can overturn the decision in question. Ombudsmen investigate complaints made by individuals to establish whether injustice or 'maladministration'[1] has occurred. If the ombudsman agrees with the complainant, they can make recommendations aimed at remedying the injustice, by explaining what steps can be taken to prevent such injustice from reoccurring. This is in stark contrast to judicial review, where the primary concern of the courts is the dispute between the parties before the court. Exceptionally, the wrongdoing or a scandal within the government is of such seriousness that it gives rise to public concern causing the government to hold a public inquiry. An inquiry can establish the facts and make recommendations to the government that seek to remedy the consequences of the scandal and ensure that it does not happen again.

Together these three procedures form the basis of the system of administrative justice. One definition of administrative justice is that it covers:

the overall system by which decisions of an administrative or executive nature are made in relation between persons, including (a) the procedures for making such decisions, (b) the

---

[1] Which means poor decision-making and administrative practices. This is considered in detail in 14.3.5.

law under which such decisions are made, and (c) the systems for resolving disputes and airing grievances in relation to such decisions.[2]

Overall, this chapter will consider the following;

- the advantages of tribunals over the courts;
- the structure of tribunals;
- the contribution that tribunals make to administrative justice;
- the role and work of the ombudsman;
- the procedures of the ombudsman;
- potential reform to the ombudsman;
- the role of public inquiries;
- who should chair public inquiries;
- examples of public inquiries and their effectiveness.

Tribunals are discussed first in 14.2, followed by Ombudsmen in 14.3, with Public Inquiries being discussed last in 14.4.

14.2 Tribunals

14.2.1 Introduction

Tribunals are bodies created by statute that decide and hear appeals against decisions made by the government or determine certain disputes between private parties. The tribunal will hear the case by allowing the parties to submit written arguments and/or hold an oral hearing. The tribunal then reaches a decision which is binding on both parties. The importance of tribunals within the legal system cannot be overstated, as Hale LJ stated: 'In this day and age a right of access to a Tribunal . . . is just as important and fundamental as a right of access to the ordinary courts.'[3]

Arguably one could go further than Lady Hale and state that, rather than judicial review, tribunals provide the primary method by which decisions made by public bodies are challenged. This is supported by statistics for 2017–18 showing that the tribunal system received more than 480,000 cases.[4] This is 130 times greater than the 3,600 applications for judicial review lodged with the High Court during 2018.[5] This shows the practical importance of tribunals in providing a grass-roots form of justice where individual decisions can be challenged. Tribunals hear a very broad range of legal issues. Some can raise significant issues

---

[2] Tribunals, Courts and Enforcement Act 2007, Sch 17, para 13; repealed by Public Bodies (Abolition of Administrative Justice and Tribunals Council) Order 2013, SI 2013/2042, Sch 1, para 36.

[3] *R v Secretary of State for the Home Department, ex p Saleem* [2001] 1 WLR 443, 458.

[4] Ministry of Justice, 'Tribunals and gender recognition certificate statistics quarterly: October to December 2018' (14 March 2019), https://www.gov.uk/government/statistics/tribunals-and-gender-recognition-certificate-statistics-quarterly-october-to-december-2018.

[5] Ministry of Justice, 'Civil Justice Statistics Quarterly: April to June 2019' (5 September 2019), https://www.gov.uk/government/statistics/tribunals-and-gender-recognition-certificate-statistics-quarterly-october-to-december-2018.

of public law. For example, an appeal against a grant of asylum by the Home Office can raise issues of fundamental human rights. By contrast, other cases can involve millions of pounds, such as decisions regarding income tax made by Her Majesty's Revenue and Customs.[6] At the other end of the scale, tribunals deal with comparatively minor matters such as an appeal against a parking offence or a decision by the Department of Work and Pensions to refuse an application for a social security benefit. The common feature of all these issues is that they involve citizens challenging decisions made by the state.

However, tribunals also cover disputes between individuals that involve private law. These include employment law disputes between employees and employers, or some property law disputes, such as service charges attached to leases. The bewildering variety of cases means that the challenge for the tribunals system is to provide a coherent, overall structure, yet allowing sufficient flexibility to take account of the diversity of cases heard.

Why tribunals and not courts?

Before considering tribunals in detail, a prior question needs to be addressed. This is simply, why do we have tribunals in the first place, when there is the system of the ordinary courts available to deal with disputes? This question can be answered in several different ways. Appeals against a parking ticket or a refusal to grant a welfare benefit involve relatively small amounts of money, usually far less than the actual costs of going to court. If tribunals did not exist, the injustice caused by incorrect decisions would go uncorrected as for many, it would not be worth challenging the decision. Consequently, it is in the interests of administrative justice that alternative procedures are created. Tribunals are one of those processes which allow for these disputes to be resolved. The advantages of tribunals over the ordinary courts are as follows.

Cost—Appealing to some tribunals is free and in theory there is less need for legal representation, so avoiding legal fees.

Access—Tribunals sit in centres located around the country, rather than the High Court which is based in London.[7] Tribunals are also meant to follow procedures that avoid the complex procedural requirements that courts follow. Further, as explained in 14.2.4, tribunals can be more encouraging than the courts to those unused to legal process when they are making their case before them.

Expertise—Tribunals specialize in particular areas of law, which mean that they have a greater level of expertise in their areas when compared to the courts. For example, the Administrative Court deals with applications for judicial review from any area of public law. By contrast, individual tribunals focus on specific areas of public law, for example immigration, tax, or social security. By dealing solely with cases involving the same areas of law, tribunal judges can develop levels of expertise that the courts may not provide. This is important when it is considered that tribunals deal with some of the most complex areas of law such as tax or immigration. In addition, cases can be heard by both legally qualified specialists and experts in the relevant fields, for example doctors or accountants. Such expertise is not readily available to the courts.

---

[6] For example, *Bastionspark LLP v The Commissioners for Her Majesty's Revenue and Customs* [2016] UKUT 0425 (TCC).

[7] Although the Administrative Court, the specialist court that deals with applications for judicial review, also sits in Manchester, Birmingham, Cardiff, and Leeds.

Speed—The specialized nature of tribunals means tribunals can focus on the core issues of a case, whereas a court that comes across the issues less often may require a more detailed explanation of the law. Tribunals are also able to follow simpler and quicker procedures, meaning that they can deal with a large caseload more easily than the courts. This means that the courts are free to focus on judicial review cases.

The concept underpinning these considerations is *proportionate dispute resolution*, which is the idea that the level of resources used to determine a dispute should be related to the value of the dispute: 'serious and important disputes should call for more rigorous dispute resolution procedures than trivial and unimportant disputes.'[8] In addition to considering whether a case is best suited to be resolved by tribunals or the ordinary courts, this also has an impact within the tribunal system itself. As discussed in 14.2.4, a feature of the tribunals system is its ability to be flexible and adapt to the nature of the cases being considered. The more complex the case, the more formal and 'court-like' the procedure is likely to be.

Difference with judicial review

On the face of it, it appears that are similarities between judicial review and tribunals. They both involve a legal challenge before an independent body, be that a judge or a tribunal panel, who reaches a decision after hearing evidence from both parties. However, there are significant differences between appealing to a tribunal and seeking a judicial review in the High Court. Tribunals are created by statute which means that the scope of each tribunal is limited by the statute that creates them, whereas the courts have far greater control over their jurisdiction and will scrutinize very carefully attempts to limit their jurisdiction.[9] The biggest difference is that tribunals can overturn the initial decision of the public agency, imposing their own decision instead, which is binding on both parties.[10] By contrast, with judicial review, the court is exercising its inherent supervisory jurisdiction to consider the lawfulness of the decision by applying the principles of judicial review. If a decision is found to be unlawful, it is sent back to the decision-maker to be reconsidered. Finally, with judicial review the focus is on the legality of the decision and it is not designed to be a fact-finding process. By contrast, a tribunal can make findings of fact and then reach its decision by applying those facts to the law.

14.2.2 **The modern structure of tribunals**

History of tribunals

Tribunals are not a new feature of the legal landscape. The first modern form of tribunal, the General Commissioners of Income Tax, was established in 1798.[11] Tribunals gradually increased in number as the modern state grew and took on more activities and policy areas. This pattern accelerated during the twentieth century after the Second World War, as the scope of modern government increased dramatically with the creation of the

---

[8] Mark Elliott and Robert Thomas, 'Tribunal Justice and Proportionate Dispute Resolution' (2012) 71 *Cambridge Law Journal* 297, 299.

[9] See the discussion regarding ouster clauses in 10.2.2.

[10] Subject to appeal, as discussed in 14.2.2.

[11] The General Commissioner was only abolished in 2009 and cases involving income tax now heard by the Tax Chamber of the First-tier Tribunal (see Figure 14.1).

welfare state. Sir Carleton Allen summarized the position, stating that 'Nothing is more remarkable in our present social and administrative arrangements than the proliferation of tribunals of many different kinds. There is scarcely a new statute of social or economic complexion which does not add to the number.'[12] This statement highlights two aspects of the growth of tribunals. First, that tribunals a reset up on an individual and ad hoc basis by government departments when they decide that a particular area of policy requires a procedure to resolve disputes. This led to the second issue which was whether tribunals were part of their sponsoring government departments or whether they were part of the judicial process. In 1957, the Franks Report was commissioned to consider the role of tribunals given their increasing importance. Franks clearly took the view that tribunals should be independent from government departments, stating that:

> Tribunals are not ordinary courts, but neither are they appendages of Government Departments. Much of the official evidence . . . appeared to reflect the view that tribunals should properly be regarded as part of the machinery of administration, for which the Government must retain a close and continuing responsibility. Thus, for example, tribunals in the social services field would be regarded as adjuncts to the administration of the services themselves. We do not accept this view. We consider that tribunals should properly be regarded as machinery provided by Parliament for adjudication rather than as part of the machinery of administration.[13]

Holding that tribunals were not administrative meant the core principles of tribunals should be openness, fairness, and impartiality. Some of the recommendations of the Franks Report were implemented, such as the creation of the Council on Tribunals to monitor the operation of the tribunals system, that hearings should generally take place in public, and that there should be a right of appeal to the High Court on points of law. However, little systemic reform took place and this 'tribunals maze' continued to grow.[14] More tribunals were created in this ad hoc manner, each with varying jurisdictions, caseloads, procedures, and structures. Some tribunals operated in a two-tier system, with an initial hearing at a lower tribunal, whose findings could be appealed to a higher-level tribunal, while others only operated with one level.

By 2001, the Leggatt Report found that there were seventy different tribunals, dealing with nearly one million cases a year, but that 'only 20 hear more than 500 cases a year and many are defunct. Their quality varies from excellent to inadequate.'[15] Additionally, it remained the case that tribunals were created by the relevant department, meaning that their independence could be questioned. This was because a sponsoring department's fingerprints could be seen throughout some tribunals. The department created the tribunal in the first place, wrote the rules according to which hearings were held, and sometimes even chose the panel that heard individual cases. Overall, the Leggatt Report found that, although there was no suggestion of the government interfering in individual tribunal decisions, tribunals were not 'demonstrably independent':

> Indeed the evidence is to the contrary. For most tribunals, departments provide administrative support, pay the salaries of members, pay their expenses, provide accommodation,

---

[12] Sir Carleton Allen, 'Administrative Jurisdiction' [1956] *Public Law* 1, 13.
[13] *Report of the Committee on Administrative Tribunals and Enquiries* (Cmnd 218, 1957) para 40.
[14] Anthony Bradley, 'The Tribunals Maze' [2002] *Public Law* 200.
[15] Sir Andrew Leggatt, 'Tribunals for Users: One System, One Service' (2001) 5 (hereinafter 'Leggatt' or 'Leggatt Report') Overview, para 2.

provide IT support (which is often in the form of access to departmental systems), are responsible for some appointments, and promote the legislation which prescribes procedures to be followed. At best, such arrangements result in tribunals and their departments being, or appearing to be, common enterprises. At worst, they make the members of a tribunal feel that they have become identified with its sponsoring department, and they foster a culture in which the members feel that their prospects of more interesting work, of progression in the tribunal, and of appointments elsewhere depend on the departments against which the cases that they hear are brought.[16]

Given these difficulties, the Leggatt Report was radical. This proposed creating a unified structure for tribunals run independently from government via an executive agency under the control of a Senior President for Tribunals. The independence of tribunals would be enhanced with tribunal judges being appointed in a similar manner to judges. These proposals were accepted by the government in a White Paper[17] and were implemented in the Tribunals, Courts and Enforcement Act 2007, the key features of which we will now discuss.

Tribunals, Courts and Enforcement Act 2007

In the rest of this section, the key features of tribunals as established by the Tribunals, Courts and Enforcement Act 2007 are highlighted. The main feature is that the 'tribunals maze', with different tribunals operating in a variety of ways, is no more. Instead, tribunals have been streamlined into a single-coherent structure, with tribunals organized in two ways. First, the 2007 Act establishes two tiers of tribunal, with cases first being heard before the First-tier Tribunal with the possibility to appeal to the Upper Tribunal.[18] Secondly, both the First-tier Tribunal and Upper Tribunals are split into Chambers. The First-tier Tribunal is split into seven chambers, with each chamber having jurisdiction over a range of related matters. For example, there is the Health, Education and Social Care Tribunal, which deals with mental health, special educational needs, and disability appeals. Similarly, there is the Social Entitlement Chamber, which, amongst other cases, hears appeals regarding social security and child support. Appeals from either of these chambers are made to the Administrative Appeals Chamber of the Upper Tribunal. Significantly, the 2007 Act grants the Upper Tribunal the status of being a 'superior court of record'.[19] This means that it is of the same status as the High Court.

The two-tier structure created by the 2007 Act can be found in Figure 14.1.[20]

There is an inherent flexibility in the structure. Some first instance cases go straight to the Upper Tribunal avoiding the First-tier Tribunal completely.[21] Also, tribunals can be reallocated within the structure should the need arise.[22] However, it should be noted that not every tribunal has been incorporated into this structure—for example, parking appeals and employment tribunals still fall outside of this system.

---

[16] Leggatt Report, para 2.20.

[17] Department for Constitutional Affairs, *Transforming Public Services: Complaints, Redress and Tribunals* (Cm 6243, 2004).

[18] Tribunals, Courts and Enforcement Act 2007 (TCEA 2007), s 3.

[19] TCEA 2007, s 3(5).

[20] Courts and Tribunals Judiciary, 'Tribunals Organisation Chart', https://www.judiciary.uk/wp-content/uploads/2012/05/tribunals-chart-20180917-1.pdf.

[21] For example, appeals from the Financial Services and Markets regulator go straight to the Tax and Chancery Chamber.

[22] TCEA 2007, s 7(9).

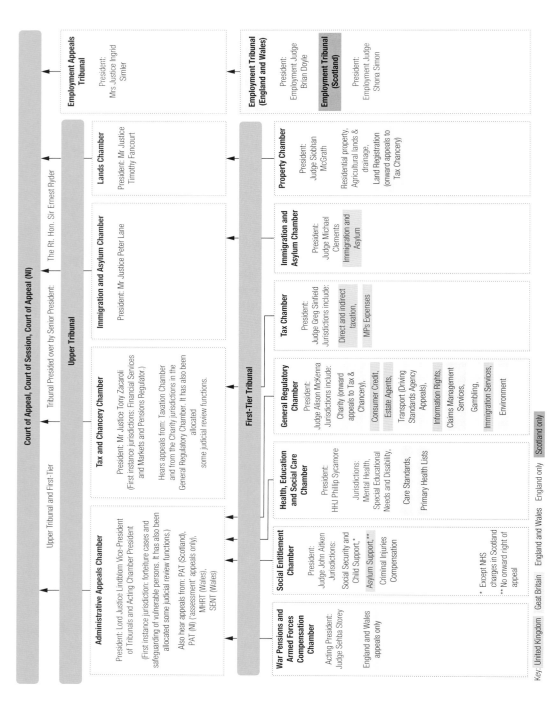

Figure 14.1 Tribunals organization chart as of September 2019

Source: Courts and Tribunals Judiciary (www.judiciary.uk). Content available under the Open Government Licence v3.0

> ⟩⟩ **Discussing the problem**
>
> Have a look at the scenario at the start of the chapter and consider the situations of Simon, Timothy, and Emeli. All three have a dispute with the government, but considering the discussion of tribunals in this section, who would you advise should go to a tribunal?
>
> The answer here is Simon. His concern is about a single decision, which does not appear to raise any broader issues. Simon has a right of appeal and the appeal would be heard by the Social Security and Child Benefit Tribunal within the Social Entitlement Chamber of the First-tier Tribunal. This is precisely the sort of decision that should be resolved through tribunals. Simon will want the matter to be resolved quickly, with the minimum of hassle. It will also be free to make the appeal.

Appeals from First-tier Tribunal to Upper Tribunal

The First-tier Tribunal makes findings of fact and law and reaches its decision.[23] An appeal to the Upper Tribunal from the First-tier Tribunal can only be made on a point of law.[24] Should the Upper Tribunal uphold the appeal, then it *may* set aside the original decision. The emphasis is on 'may'. It is open to the Upper Tribunal to uphold the original decision on the basis that it has not been invalidated by the error of law. However, should the Upper Tribunal decide that the original decision cannot stand, then it must then decide whether to send the case back to the First-tier Tribunal to be reconsidered or to remake the decision itself.[25]

Appeals from the Upper Tribunal to the Court of Appeal and Supreme Court

Appeals from the Upper Tribunal can be made to the Court of Appeal on any 'point of law arising from a decision made by the Upper Tribunal'.[26] However, an appeal can only be made with permission of either the Upper Tribunal itself or the Court of Appeal. Permission will only be granted by the Court of Appeal when the proposed appeal raises 'some important point of principle or practice', or there is 'some other compelling reason' for the appeal to be heard.[27] The Court of Appeal enjoys similar powers to that of the Upper Tribunal when hearing appeals from the First-tier Tribunal. If the Court of Appeal upholds the appeal from the Upper Tribunal, it may set that decision aside. If the Court of Appeal does so, then it can send the case back to the Upper Tribunal or remake the

---

[23] Exceptionally, under TCEA 2007, s 9, the First-tier Tribunal can review its own decision to correct any accidental errors in the decision itself, in the record of the decision, amend its reasoning or set its decision aside and then make a new decision. Under s 10, the Upper Tribunal has similar procedures available to it regarding its own decisions. These procedures are to be used sparingly, as tribunal decisions, subject to appeal, should be final.

[24] TCEA 2007, s 11(1). However, under s 11(5) the right to appeal against the First-tier Tribunal's decision is excluded.

[25] Ibid s 12.

[26] Ibid s 13(1), for appeals from England and Wales. Appeals in Northern Ireland are heard by the Northern Ireland Court of Appeal; Scottish Appeals are heard by the Court of Session.

[27] Ibid s 13(6), Appeals from the Upper Tribunal to the Court of Appeal Order 2008, SI 2008/2834.

decision itself.[28] Recent amendments to the 2007 Act have made it possible to make an appeal directly from the Upper Tribunal to the Supreme Court. Yet this will only be possible in very narrow circumstances.[29]

Appeals on a point of law and the relationship between the First-tier Tribunal, Upper Tribunal, and the courts

As discussed, appeals from the First-tier Tribunal to the Upper Tribunal and from the Upper Tribunal to the Court of Appeal are made on 'points of law'. This is contrasted to a finding of fact. An outline as to what is often considered to be a point of law was provided by Brooke LJ in *R (Iran) v Secretary of State for the Home Department*.[30] He stated that the most common examples of an error of law include:

(i) making perverse or irrational findings on a matter or matters that were material to the outcome (material matters);

(ii) failing to give reasons or any adequate reasons for findings on material matters;

(iii) failing to take into account and/or resolve conflicts of fact or opinion on material matters;

(iv) giving weight to immaterial matters;

(v) making a material misdirection of law on any material matter;

(vi) committing or permitting a procedural or other irregularity capable of making a material difference to the outcome or the fairness of the proceedings;

(vii) making a mistake as to a material fact which could be established by objective and uncontentious evidence, where the appellant and/or his advisers were not responsible for the mistake, and where unfairness resulted from the fact that a mistake was made.[31]

What should be apparent from this list is that a mistake of law is far broader than it may initially appear and goes beyond the interpretation of a legislation or case law. Overall, the dividing line between questions of fact and law remains (perhaps surprisingly) elusive. However, as Brooke LJ noted, one of the limiting factors is that each of these points include the word 'material', indicating that 'errors of law [that] would have made no difference to the outcome do not matter'.[32] Notwithstanding this, the question remains: when should the Upper Tribunal overturn a First-tier Tribunal decision and when should the Court of Appeal do likewise to an Upper Tribunal decision? This issue was discussed by the Supreme Court in the following case.

Case in depth: *R (Jones) v First-tier Tribunal (Social Entitlement Chamber)* [2013] UKSC 19

After suffering injuries in a road traffic accident, Jones applied for compensation from the Criminal Injuries Compensation Authority. The Authority rejected Jones's claim on the basis that Jones's

→

---

[28] Ibid s 14(2).   [29] Ibid s 14A–C.   [30] [2005] EWCA Civ 982 [9].
[31] Ibid.   [32] [2005] EWCA Civ 982 [10].

injuries had not resulted from a 'crime of violence' as defined by the scheme. Jones appealed against this decision to the Social Entitlement Chamber of the First-tier Tribunal, who dismissed the claim. Jones then appealed to the Upper Tribunal who upheld the decision of the First-tier Tribunal. Jones then appealed to the Court of Appeal, who overturned the decision of the First-tier Tribunal on the basis that they had made an error of law when interpreting a 'crime of violence'. The Supreme Court then reinstated the original decision made by the First-tier Tribunal on the basis that its interpretation was a rational and reasonable conclusion to reach. Given the specialist expertise available, when decisions made within the tribunal system are rational and reasonable, they should not be reopened by the appellate courts.

Lord Hope stated that:

> A pragmatic approach should be taken to the dividing line between law and fact, so that the expertise of tribunals at the first tier and that of the Upper Tribunal can be used to best effect. An appeal court should not venture too readily into this area by classifying issues as issues of law which are really best left for determination by the specialist appellate tribunals.[33]

Lord Hope is emphasizing how the courts should be reluctant to intervene in decisions made by the tribunals, given that they have expertise accumulated from their experience in hearing cases in this area. Essentially, the courts are exploiting the flexibility inherent in the 'error of law' test to take a step back and consider whether the interpretation that was placed on the law was a reasonable. On this occasion, The Supreme Court appeared content to defer to the specialist tribunal.

Jones is not the only case with such reasoning. It was held in *AH (Sudan) v Secretary of State for the Home Department* that the decision of tribunals 'should be respected unless it is clear that they have misdirected themselves in law. Appellate courts should not rush to find such misdirections simply because they might have reached a different conclusion on the facts.'[34]

This approach is clearly desirable for ensuring that the courts and tribunals system operate effectively. The entire rationale of the tribunals system would be undermined if the 'generalist' courts routinely overturned their decisions. This reflects the confidence that the highest courts have in the quality of decisions delivered by the system of tribunals. A key reason for this is as expressed by Lord Carnwath in *Jones*; as he explored the relationship between the First-tier Tribunal and the Upper Tribunal, focusing on the nature of the two-tier system:

> Where, as here, the interpretation and application of a specialised statutory scheme has been entrusted by Parliament to the . . . tribunal system, an important function of the Upper Tribunal is to develop structured guidance on the use of expressions which are central to the scheme, and so as to reduce the risk of inconsistent results by different panels at the First-tier level.[35]

Considering the structure created by the 2007 Act, the Upper Tribunal is the specialist body that hears appeals from the First-tier Tribunal and, rather than being for the

---

[33] [2013] UKSC 19 [16].   [34] [2007] UKHL 49 [30].   [35] Ibid [41].

appellate courts to intervene, it is for the Upper Tribunal to set precedents and guidance for the First-tier Tribunal. The underlying rationale is that while the courts should retain a supervisory jurisdiction, the very reason for creating tribunals would be undermined if recourse to the courts was required to obtain a final definitive decision.

Upper Tribunal's 'Judicial Review' jurisdiction

In addition to hearing appeals, the 2007 Act also grants the Upper Tribunal a 'Judicial Review' jurisdiction. This gives the Upper Tribunal similar powers to the High Court when hearing a judicial review claim.[36] This addition to the Upper Tribunal's powers means that the expertise of the Upper Tribunal available for ordinary appeals is also available for judicial review applications. An application for judicial review can start in the Upper Tribunal if the following conditions are met:

- *Condition One*—The remedy sought is one that the Upper Tribunal is able to grant;[37]

- *Condition Two*—The application must not call into question anything done by the Crown Court;[38]

- *Condition Three*—The application falls within a class of application specified by the Lord Chief Justice, under the Constitutional Reform Act 2005.[39] So far this has involved decisions regarding criminal injuries compensation and most types of immigration decisions;

- *Condition Four*—The judge presiding at the time of the hearing is either a judge of the High Court or Court of Appeal.[40]

If an application for judicial review has been made to the High Court, and the first three conditions have been met, it must be transferred to the Upper Tribunal.[41] If only the first two conditions are met, then the High Court *may* transfer the matter to the Upper Tribunal.

These reforms have the most significant effect with immigration cases. On the face of it, the benefit to applicants is that the specialist judges of the Upper Tribunal can deal with applications for judicial review that involve immigration law more quickly than the generalist judges of the High Court. As a significant majority of judicial review applications involved immigration issues, the transfer of judicial review from the High Court to the Upper Tribunal has dramatically reduced the number of cases reaching the High Court. The benefit for the High Court is that its resources can be devoted to cases which may have broader legal implications than those that involve the interpretation of ever more complex provisions of immigration law.

---

[36] TCEA 2007, s 15.

[37] TCEA 2007, s 18(4), refers to s 15(1), which lists mandatory, prohibiting, and quashing orders as well as declarations and injunctions. Of note is that this does not include the ability to make a declaration of incompatibility under Human Rights Act 1998, s 4.

[38] TCEA 2007, s 18(5).

[39] This includes decisions made by the First-tier Tribunal regarding the Criminal Injuries Compensation Scheme; and many forms of decisions made in the Immigration and Asylum Chamber, see *Practice Direction (Upper Tribunal: Judicial Review Jurisdiction)* [2009] 1 WLR 327 and *Practice Direction (Upper Tribunal: Judicial Review Jurisdiction) (No 2)* [2012] 1 WLR 16.

[40] TCEA 2007, s 18(6). If in Scotland, from the Court of Session; If in Northern Ireland, from the High Court or Court of Appeal of Northern Ireland.

[41] Senior Courts Act 1981, s 31A(2).

Counterpoint: The importance of the Upper Tribunal's 'Judicial Review' jurisdiction

Robert Thomas describes the creation of the Upper Tribunal's 'Judicial Review' jurisdiction as an important constitutional development. Thomas states:

> High Court has, for centuries, provided the forum for legal challenges against executive action affecting personal liberty. Its jurisdiction is based upon common law tradition, the court's own high status and the quality and independence of High Court judges . . . By contrast, [the Upper Tribunal] is a relatively new judicial institution and remains untested.[42]

Given that attempts to oust the High Court's jurisdiction to judicial review are generally controversial, as shown in Chapter 11, is it concerning that a significant part of the High Court's judicial review function has been transferred to the Upper Tribunal?[43]

Can the Upper Tribunal be judicially reviewed?

The final issue to consider the relationship between the tribunal system is whether the Upper Tribunal *itself* can be judicially reviewed. This is a different question to that just discussed, which was whether the Upper Tribunal can judicially review decisions made by a public body; rather, the question here is whether the Upper Tribunal as a body created by statute is itself subject to judicial review. In general, the availability of a further appeal precludes the need to seek a judicial review, which means that usually someone aggrieved at a decision made by the Upper Tribunal should seek to appeal to the Court of Appeal. However, as discussed above, in order to appeal to the Court of Appeal, the Upper Tribunal needs to grant permission. If permission is refused by the Upper Tribunal, then as discussed above, permission will only be granted by the Court of Appeal in very limited circumstances.[44] However, under the 2007 Act, a decision of the Upper Tribunal to refuse permission to appeal cannot itself be appealed. Does this mean that given that there is no other remedy, or is judicial review available in these circumstances? The issue arose in the following case.

Case in depth: *R (Cart) v Upper Tribunal* [2011] UKSC 28

The Child Support Agency refused Cart's claim. Cart then appealed to (what has now become) the First-tier Tribunal. They dismissed the appeal. Cart then sought permission from the Upper Tribunal to make a further appeal. The Upper Tribunal refused permission. The 2007 Act does not make any provision for appealing against that decision. This meant that the only option for Cart was to argue that this decision of the Upper Tribunal was subject to judicial review. The case reached the Supreme Court.

→

---

[42] Robert Thomas, 'Immigration judicial reviews', UK Constitutional Law Association Blog (12 September 2013), http://ukconstitutionallaw.org.

[43] Mark Elliott and Jason Varuhas, *Administrative Law: Text and Materials* (5th edn, OUP 2017) 747.

[44] See (n 36).

→

The Supreme Court held, overturning the decision of the Court of Appeal, that although the 2007 Act designates the Upper Tribunal as a 'superior court of record', this did not mean that the Upper Tribunal should be outside the scope of the High Court's ordinary supervisory jurisdiction. This was particularly the case when the 2007 Act did not contain any clear language, or an 'ouster clause' to indicate that Parliament's intention was that unappealable decisions of the Upper Tribunal should not be reviewed. This meant unappealable decisions of the Upper Tribunal could be subject to judicial review. However, to maintain the appropriate relationship between the Upper Tribunal and the courts, the Supreme Court limited the availability of judicial review by stating it would only be available if criteria known as the 'second appeal criteria' are fulfilled. The criteria are either that the application raises some important point of principle or practice, or that there is some other compelling reason for granting the application.[45]

The concern of the Supreme Court was that if the Upper Tribunal was not subject to judicial review, then there was the risk that it became the final arbiter of the law. Without the possibility of judicial review, there was a real risk that if the Upper Tribunal made an error of law it could not be corrected by the ordinary courts. The Supreme Court took the view that the courts can provide an external check to tribunals, guarding against errors of law from being perpetuated through the tribunals system. However, as discussed with ordinary appeals, there is a delicate balancing act to strike when considering the relationship between the ordinary courts and the Upper Tribunal. For the limited capacity of the High Court to be deployed appropriately, it should not become overburdened with applications for judicial review that lack any merit. Consequently, the Supreme Court took the view that applying the second appeals criteria as a filter would ensure that the courts retain some limited oversight of the Upper Tribunal, yet avoid any risk of duplicating the work of the Upper Tribunal. As Lady Hale stated:

> the adoption of the second-tier appeals criteria would be a rational and proportionate restriction upon the availability of judicial review of the refusal by the Upper Tribunal of permission to appeal to itself. It would recognise that the new and in many ways enhanced tribunal structure deserves a more restrained approach to judicial review than has previously been the case, while ensuring that important errors can still be corrected. It is a test which . . . is capable of encompassing both the important point of principle affecting large numbers of similar claims and the compelling reasons presented by the extremity of the consequences for the individual.[46]

 Pause for reflection

Underpinning the decision of the Supreme Court is the concept of proportionate dispute resolution. Lord Brown colourfully described this as follows: 'The rule of law is weakened, not strengthened, if a disproportionate part of the courts' resources is devoted to finding a very occasional

→

---

[45] These rules have now been incorporated into the Civil Procedure Rules, r 54.7A.
[46] [2011] UKSC 28 [57].

→

grain of wheat on a threshing floor full of chaff'.[47] As Elliott and Thomas highlight, the decision of the Supreme Court means that some errors of law made by the Upper Tribunal are 'acceptable' because of other demands placed on the justice system such as the need to decide quickly.

> [The approach of the Supreme Court] expressly recognises that there is an acceptable level of legal error because of the competing demands placed upon the limited re-sources of the judicial process. In other words, only some legal errors—namely, those which have broader significance—are worth correcting; by providing guidance on a general point of principle or practice, the judicial resources invested are justified be-cause of the implications for other cases.[48]

Yet if it remains the case that incorrect decisions may not be remedied, does this not harm the rule of law? Or is Lord Brown correct in saying that the decision in Cart furthers the rule of law?

14.2.3 The tribunal judiciary

Decisions by the senior judiciary in cases such as *Cart* and *Jones* also indicate how much faith they place in the tribunal judges operating within the reformed system. This is largely due to the reforms to the selection and training of the tribunal judiciary made under the 2007 Act.

The most significant figure within the tribunal judiciary is the Senior President of Tri-bunals. Since its creation, the office has always been held by a Lord Justice of Appeal. Primarily the Senior President presides over both the First-tier and Upper Tribunals. His responsibilities include ensuring that tribunals are accessible, follow fair procedures, han-dle cases quickly and efficiently, and that members of the tribunals have the necessary expertise in the subject matter and the law of the cases they decide.[49] The Senior President must report annually on the overall tribunals system.[50]

The links between the First-tier Tribunal, the Upper Tribunal, and the courts are high-lighted by the fact that judges of the Court of Appeal and High Court are automatically judges of the First-tier and Upper Tribunals. Occasionally, High Court judges sit within the tribunals system if the case is particularly complex.[51]

Far more commonly, cases are heard by specialist tribunal judges, who are recom-mended for appointment by the Judicial Appointments Commission in a similar man-ner to judges in the ordinary courts.[52] This means that government departments, which once were heavily involved in the selection of tribunal judges, now have no role in the appointments process. This further bolsters the independence of tribunals from the gov-ernment departments whose decisions are being challenged.

These reforms show how the aim of the 2007 Act was not only for tribunals to become unambiguously independent from the government, but also to become as much part of the judicial branch as the courts. This is shown by the extension of the duty of the

---

[47] Ibid [100].

[48] Mark Elliott and Robert Thomas, 'Tribunal Justice and Proportionate Dispute Resolution' [2012] CLJ 291, 315.

[49] TCEA 2007, s 2.   [50] Ibid s 43.

[51] Senior President of Tribunals, *Annual Report* 2016 (2016) 9. It is also the case that for the Upper Tribunal to exercise its judicial review jurisdiction the case must be heard by a High Court or Court of Appeal judge.

[52] Constitutional Reform Act 2005, ss 85–93 and Sch 14.

Lord Chancellor to uphold the independence of the judiciary to include the tribunals judiciary.[53]

The reliance that some tribunals had on their sponsoring department as highlighted by Leggatt was removed through the creation of the Tribunal Service as an executive agency of the Ministry of Justice. In 2011, this was merged with the Courts Service to create Her Majesty's Courts and Tribunals Service.[54] This was considered appropriate as the Ministry of Justice rarely makes decisions that are challenged through the tribunals system. In addition, the Lord Chancellor is under a duty to ensure that tribunals are supported by 'an efficient and effective system to support the carrying on of the business [of tribunals]'.[55] This means that tribunals should be given sufficient resources for its needs. Unlike before the TCEA 2007, it is no longer questioned that tribunal judges are part of the judiciary. Indeed, there are now proposals, discussed in 14.2.6, to combine the judiciary of the courts and tribunals into a single judiciary as part of broader reforms to civil justice.

14.2.4 **Tribunal procedure**

From the outset, when considering the procedure of tribunals, it is important to bear in mind the words of the first Senior President of Tribunals, Sir Robert Carnwath, when he stated:

> When talking about tribunals, generalisations are dangerous. Tribunals vary greatly in the complexity of the cases before them, their financial significance, and the degree of procedural formality appropriate to them. *Gillies*[56] was concerned with the role of the medical member of a social security tribunal in assessing disability benefit. In such cases, no doubt, cheapness, accessibility and freedom from technicality are desirable and achievable objectives. But there is no obvious parallel with, for example, a major case before the Special Commissioners of Tax or the Lands Tribunal. The sums there involved may be as great as in any case in the High Court, and the legal and factual issues equally complex. A degree of procedural formality is unavoidable if justice is to be done, and the specialist expertise of the tribunal is unlikely to be an adequate substitute for expert representation of the parties. There may be little in reality to distinguish such a 'tribunal' case from a case before a specialist 'court', such as the Technology and Construction Court [a specialist court within the High Court].[57]

This section will seek to give a flavour of the procedures that various tribunals follow.

Reconsidering the initial decision and relationship with tribunals

Usually, if someone disagrees with a decision, they should first ask the government department concerned to reconsider their decision before pursuing an appeal to the relevant tribunal. This has become mandatory for social security and benefits cases. The aim is that this should serve as a check against plainly incorrect decisions and mean that fewer cases reach tribunals. Yet despite going through this review process,

---

[53] Constitutional Reform Act 2005, s 3, as amended by Tribunals, Courts and Enforcement Act 2007, s 1.
[54] This has since been merged with the courts service to create Her Majesty's Courts and Tribunals Service.
[55] TCEA 2007, s 39.
[56] *Gilles v Secretary of State for Work and Pensions* [2006] UKHL 2.
[57] Sir Robert Carnwath, 'Tribunal Justice—A New Start' [2009] *Public Law* 48, 53.

for some benefits as many as 60 per cent of appeals heard by the Social Security and Child Benefit Tribunals are still successful.[58] This indicates that if the reconsideration is carried out internally, by the same government department that made the initial decision, then it may be treated as no more than a 'rubber stamping' exercise.[59] It is possible that a mandatory review merely 'filters out the clearly wrong decisions, while more borderline cases proceed to tribunals, and tribunals take a different view'.[60] Yet it appears a review of the initial decision still leads to many cases being overturned by a tribunal on appeal. It is possible that there are several reasons for this. Claimants may receive advice when preparing their appeal or submit new evidence to the tribunal, meaning that tribunals are making decisions on a different basis to the government department.

Despite these considerations, reconsidering original appeals should be encouraged, as they are cheaper, quicker, and can avoid the stress or hassle of an appeal. Yet it must be borne in mind that there is only so much a mandatory review can achieve and that complex borderline cases should progress to a tribunal. Indeed, if the mandatory review process became more elaborate, the benefits of speed and cost would be lost. A common theme throughout this discussion of tribunals is the 'inherent trade-off between quality and efficiency'.[61] Once again, the core issue is proportionate dispute resolution and the idea that the resources deployed to resolve the dispute should be proportionate to the issues at stake.

Written or oral hearings

When it comes to tribunal hearings themselves, a key issue is whether tribunals should deal with cases through a traditional hearing or decide the matter based on written evidence submitted by the parties. Some tribunals, such as the Traffic Penalty Tribunal which considers appeals against parking tickets, conduct cases remotely through the internet or phone.[62] Yet, this remains an exception and tribunals generally use oral hearings, although this may be on an opt-in basis, with the appellant having to request an oral hearing. Appellants are advised that they have a greater chance of success with an oral hearing. There are many reasons for this. Appellants are more likely to be able to present their case more effectively at a hearing, particularly if there is a dispute over the facts, as the questioning that forms the key part of an oral hearing makes it more likely that the evidence is tested. If only written evidence is considered then opportunities to see the evidence in a new light are less likely to arise.

The right to an oral hearing has long been held to be an important right. For example, in *FP (Iran) v Secretary of State for the Home Department*,[63] a procedural rule that meant the appellant lost their right to an oral hearing through the fault of their legal representative

---

[58] See 14.2.6.

[59] This was a concern in the House of Commons Constitutional Affairs Committee, *Asylum and Immigration Appeals* (HC 2003–04, 211) para 107.

[60] Robert Thomas, 'Mandatory reconsideration: what do the latest stats tell us?' UK Administrative Justice Institute Blog (16 June 2016), https://ukaji.org/2016/06/16/mandatory-reconsideration-what-do-the-latest-stats-tell-us/.

[61] Ibid.

[62] Traffic Penalty Tribunal—England and Wales, https://www.trafficpenaltytribunal.gov.uk/.

[63] [2007] EWCA Civ 13.

was struck down due to its inherent unfairness on the appellant. Again, the concern with oral hearings is the cost and speed. Paper hearings are quicker and cheaper than an oral hearing, which allows for many more decisions to be made. The essential issue is striking the right balance between these two competing objectives.

Conduct of tribunal hearings

The Leggatt Report discussed three main ways in which tribunal hearings could be held: these are described as the adversarial, enabling, or inquisitorial approaches. Each have their benefits or disadvantages, but given the diversity within the tribunals system, what is appropriate for one tribunal may not be appropriate for another. The difference in the approaches is the role of the judge or panel hearing the case.

Adversarial approach—This is the approach that common law courts tend to follow and so is the approach most familiar to lawyers. The judge allows each side to present its case and to challenge the other side's case. The judge or panel sparingly intervenes to maintain his independence from the parties. If one party, usually the appellant, is unrepresented by a lawyer, then there is an inequality of arms and they could be at a significant disadvantage if they are unfamiliar with the relevant law and the procedure to follow.

Inquisitorial approach—The hearing is solely conducted through the panel, with the panel or judge essentially asking each side questions, with the aim of establishing the necessary facts. While this may reduce any problems that arise if only one party is legally represented, it has the converse problem of risking the independence of the judge or panel if they appear to favour one side over another.

Enabling approach—This was the approach that was recommended in the Leggatt Report,[64] and this approach aims to provide a hybrid between the other two procedures. The judge supports the parties, particularly those that are unrepresented, to make their own representations and make allowances for the lack of legal knowledge of unrepresented parties. This may involve intervening to ensure that certain key facts are properly discussed.

 Discussing the problem

Consider the scenario of Simon. How will his appeal be conducted?

Simon will have a right to request an oral hearing. This is likely to be to his advantage as the tribunal panel will be able to see the extent of his condition, in addition to the medical evidence sent. The tribunal would be likely to follow the enabling approach and allow Simon to explain his case. Should Simon struggle, the tribunal panel could become more inquisitorial by asking him questions to ensure that the relevant issues have been discussed.

Legal representation

The Leggatt Report concluded that if the enabling approach was used, then the need for legal representation would be reduced. Leggatt argued that representation added delay and cost to proceedings which ran contrary to the accessibility of tribunal users. It was of fundamental

---

[64] Leggatt Report, para 7.5.

importance that tribunals should be as accessible as possible to users. If hearings are well-conducted, by a well-trained chair with appellants given good quality advice before the hearing, then the need for legal representation would be significantly reduced.[65] While this is a laudable aim, particularly in cases when the stakes are relatively low, it is important to bear in mind the statement of Sir Robert Carnwath that not all tribunals are alike. Certainly, the enabling approach has a key role to play in areas such as social security cases. However, in areas such as property law and tax, the stakes can be more than the equivalent of any case before the High Court meaning that the parties would benefit from legal representation leading to the tribunal being held according to the traditional adversarial approach.

The issue of representation arises more frequently in areas such as immigration and social security. In these contexts, for many, legal representation is not an option due to its cost. It used to be the case that Legal Aid would could provide funding for representation before some tribunals. However, since the Legal Aid, Sentencing and Punishment of Offenders Act 2012, Legal Aid is now extremely restricted and only available for tribunals that deal with cases of detention and asylum. In addition, section 10 of the 2012 Act makes it possible for Legal Aid to be available under the exceptional case category. This would apply if a failure to provide Legal Aid would breach an appellant's human rights, as determined by the Human Rights Act. The most relevant article of the ECHR is Article 6, which protects the right to a fair hearing when determining an individual's civil rights and obligations. However, the intention of the government is that Legal Aid would only be exceptionally granted on this basis.[66] This means that overall, the availability of Legal Aid has become extremely limited.

 Pause for reflection

In *AA (Nigeria) v Secretary of State for the Home Department*,[67] Longmore LJ expressed concern about the complexity of immigration law, which can be changed by the Home Secretary by amending the Immigration Rules. He stated that he was 'left perplexed and concerned how any individual whom the Rules affect . . . can discover what the policy of the Secretary of State actually is at any particular time if it necessitates a trawl through Hansard or formal Home Office correspondence as well as through the comparatively complex Rules themselves. It seems that it is only with expensive legal assistance, funded by the taxpayer, that justice can be done.'

As Legal Aid is no longer available for many immigration cases, does this fundamentally undermine the aim of the Leggatt Reforms, which was to be accessible to appellants, or is the system sufficiently accessible for appellants to represent themselves?

Inevitably, the restrictions on Legal Aid mean that many appellants represent themselves. This creates further pressures on Tribunal judges. For example, in the interests of fairness, judges should ensure that unrepresented appellants understand the legal issues and the arguments from the other side. This may give rise to questions about their independence.

---

[65] Leggatt Report, para 4.21.

[66] The government's original guidance regarding when legal aid was available under s 10 was declared unlawful in *Gudanaviciene v The Director of Legal Aid Casework* [2014] EWCA Civ 1622. The new guidance makes clear that the key consideration is whether funding is necessary, https://martinpartington.com/2015/06/16/legal-aid-exceptional-cases-funding-recent-developments/. The existing guidance is available at https://www.gov.uk/guidance/funding-and-costs-assessment-for-civil-and-crime-matters.

[67] [2010] EWCA Civ 773 [88].

Finally, it is also the case that the government department whose decision is being challenged should be present at the hearing. Usually, a presenting officer from the department will seek to defend the original decision and explain why the appeals should fail. If appellants are unrepresented then this raises an inequality between the parties. The presenting officer is likely to have expertise on the law and experience in presenting cases before tribunals. By contrast, it is likely that any hearing will be the appellant's sole experience of the tribunal system and will be far less knowledgeable about the process. Again, tribunal judges must strike a delicate balance between ensuring that the process is fair for the appellant, while maintaining their impartiality. It must also be noted that recent years have seen a slightly counterintuitive development, whereby in some areas, particularly in immigration and social security, the department's case is not made at the hearing by a presenting officer. This means that there is no one to argue the department's case beyond the written evidence submitted in advance of the hearing. This means that the emphasis will be on the tribunal judge to test the evidence of the appellant. However, there is a further balance to strike between asking questions which step into cross-examining the witnesses, as this could suggest that the tribunal judge is no longer independent.[68]

Overall, this discussion has shown that the enabling approach, with its flexibility to deal with such a range of different approaches should generally be followed. It allows a tribunal judge to intervene when necessary, while ensuring that the submission of each party's case remains a matter for them.

Tribunal procedure rules

Before the introduction of the reformed structure, each tribunal developed its own procedural rules. These were usually made by the Lord Chancellor or Secretary of State of the department that sponsored the tribunal. In common with many other features of tribunals in the unreformed system, this meant that there could be little commonality between the different tribunals and there was no overall coherent structure. The Leggatt Report considered that this approach could not continue.[69] Consequently, the 2007 Act created the Tribunal Procedure Committee, whose role it is to make the Tribunal Procedure Rules for the First-tier and Upper Tribunals.[70] The Rules must ensure that the tribunal system is accessible, by developing rules that are simple and simply expressed, which allow for cases to be handled quickly and efficiently. Each chamber has its own rules, however there is much similarity between them. For example, the rules for the Social Entitlement Chamber and General Regulatory Chamber within the First-tier Tribunal both have the same overriding objectives. These include the need to:

* deal with cases proportionately, based on the importance and complexity of the case;

* avoid any unnecessary informality and be flexible;

* ensure that the parties are able to participate fully in the proceedings.[71]

[68] Mark Elliott and Robert Thomas, *Public Law* (2nd edn, OUP 2014) 641.
[69] Leggatt Report, para 2.27.
[70] TCEA 2007, s 22.
[71] The Tribunal Procedure (First-Tier Tribunal) (General Regulatory Chamber) Rules 2009, SI 2009/1976, r 2 and the Tribunal Procedure (First-Tier Tribunal) (Social Entitlement Chamber) Rules 2008, SI 2008/2685, r 2.

Pause for reflection

Writing to *The Times* newspaper, the eminent public lawyer of his generation, William Wade, wrote in 1954: 'No one should belittle the work of tribunals; but they suffer from the system, or lack of system in which they have to operate . . . Tribunals have been created in a higgledy-piggledy fashion, united by no system and bound by no common procedural code.'[72]

To what extent is this still an accurate statement regarding tribunals today given the reforms introduced by the Tribunals, Courts and Enforcement Act 2007?

14.2.5 Reform of tribunal procedure: an electronic revolution for courts and tribunals?

This section discussing tribunal procedure concludes with a look to the future. In September 2016, the Lord Chancellor, the Lord Chief Justice, and the Senior President of Tribunals announced the reform programme Transforming Our Justice System. Aimed at both courts and tribunals, the ultimate aim is for courts and tribunals to form 'a single justice system with a single judiciary'.[73] Both courts and tribunals are to make a significantly greater use of digital procedures, with the ultimate aim of tribunals becoming 'digital by default'.[74]

Initially, this means that aspects of cases, such as serving evidence and giving notice of appeal to a tribunal, will increasingly take place through an IT system maintained by the HMCTS. The Joint Statement by the Lord Chancellor, Lord Chief Justice, and the Senior President of Tribunals argue that moving online 'will allow people to lodge a claim more easily'.[75] Sharing evidence online means that the 'tribunals and the parties will have all the right information to allow them to deal with claims promptly and effectively, saving time for both tribunal panels and claimants'. Achieving this change requires a simplified procedural code which guides the tribunal users through their case. The Joint Statement argues that:

> Those who use tribunals will have access to specialist judicial expertise using tools and technology that they use routinely in other parts of their lives. This will allow the nub of a case to be identified quickly, wrong decisions resolved, and hopeless causes weeded out – improving justice for everyone involved.[76]

These reforms apply to the civil courts as well. This raises the issue that if cases are being considered either partially or entirely online, in both tribunals and the civil courts, then the distinction between the tribunals and courts will arguably become less important.

[72] *The Times*, 23 December 1954, quoted in Anthony Bradley, 'The Tribunals Maze' [2002] *Public Law* 200, 200.

[73] Ministry of Justice, 'Transforming Our Justice System, By the Lord Chancellor, the Lord Chief Justice and the Senior President of Tribunals' (September 2016), https://www.gov.uk/government/uploads/system/uploads/attachment_data/file/553261/joint-vision-statement.pdf 15.

[74] Ministry of Justice, 'Transforming Our Justice System, By the Lord Chancellor, the Lord Chief Justice and the Senior President of Tribunals' (September 2016), https://www.gov.uk/government/uploads/system/uploads/attachment_data/file/553261/joint-vision-statement.pdf 15.

[75] Ibid.   [76] Ibid.

Indeed, this appears to be encouraged. The Lord Chief Justice and Senior President for Tribunals, said that these reforms 'will also change the way the judiciary works. The development of common processes will bring together the courts and tribunals into one system and one judiciary'.[77] It is already the case that High Court judges are hearing cases within the tribunals system and the High Court will seek to take advantage of the expertise of the Tribunals in complex areas of law. This sharing of 'skills and experience [provides] the opportunity for the litigant to resolve related problems before one specialist judge or panel'.[78]

There are some considerable concerns. Most obviously, the proposals assume a level of digital literacy which some users are not likely to have. Digital literacy is lowest amongst those from poorer backgrounds, the social group who are most likely to encounter the Social Security and Child Support Tribunal, which will be one of the first to move (at least partly) online. This concern has been noted by the proposals, but it is unclear how this will be addressed.[79] Additionally, it remains to be seen how the shift to online tribunals will deal with the fact that appellants at an oral hearing have a far greater chance of success than those who only pursue paper hearings. The question is whether the lower rate of successful appeals simply transfers from paper hearings to online hearings.

Clearly, as the internet and communications technology pervades ever more areas of life, tribunals (and the broader justice system) cannot be immune to this development. Indeed, online tribunals could achieve Leggatt's original aim of a single and accessible tribunal system, with members of the public challenging decisions without the need for legal advice. These reforms seek to achieve the goal of proportionate dispute resolution by introducing new procedures such as online decision-making and virtual hearings in addition to the traditional oral hearing. All these procedures would be available as and when cases require them. If the Leggatt Report was intended to provide a structure through which the cases that reach the tribunal system can be considered proportionately, these proposals have the potential to tailor the process to individual cases in an increasingly bespoke fashion.

The Prison and Courts Bill would have enabled the procedural reforms required for courts and tribunals to operate electronically according to a set of common rules. However, this legislation was lost when Parliament was dissolved for the surprise general election held in June 2017. Since then, some elements of the bill have been enacted separately as the reform project continues.[80] Yet the Courts and Tribunals (Online Procedure) Bill which focused on the procedural reforms of the original bill was also lost at the end of the 2017–19 session. As the bill was not mentioned in the Queen's Speech following the December 2019 General Election, it is unclear whether and when this will return to Parliament, although the government still intends for the project to conclude by 2023.

---

[77] House of Commons Public Bill Committee on the Prisons and Courts Bill 2016–17, Lord Chief Justice and Senior President of Tribunals, Memorandum: Prisons and Courts Bill 2017, para 8, https://www.publications.parliament.uk/pa/cm201617/cmpublic/PrisonsCourts/memo/PCB19.pdf.

[78] Ibid.

[79] Ministry of Justice, 'Transforming Our Justice System, By the Lord Chancellor, the Lord Chief Justice and the Senior President of Tribunals' (September 2016), https://www.gov.uk/government/uploads/system/uploads/attachment_data/file/553261/joint-vision-statement.pdf 7.

[80] Courts and Tribunals (Judiciary and Functions of Staff) Act 2018.

14.2.6 Tribunals and administrative justice—obtaining a correct decision

One significant area for concern is the high rate of successful appeals. This is a serious concern in the field of social security. Statistics show that as many as 70 per cent of appeals in the Social Security and Child Support Chamber of the First-tier Tribunal are successful.[81] The Public Accounts Committee from the House of Commons has expressed concern that the Department of Work and Pensions simply gets the decision wrong far too many times.[82] While some cases are explainable on the basis that complex medical evidence needs to be considered and in borderline cases the tribunal may simply have reached a different view, the number of successful appeals suggests more significant problems with how initial decisions are made. It also appears that departments have been unable to improve the accuracy of their decisions. The Public Accounts Committee has highlighted how the rate of successful appeals suggests that the Department of Work and Pensions has failed to make any significant progress in improving the accuracy of its decisions.[83] This also appears to be a problem across several areas of government, with 44 per cent of immigration appeals overturning the original result, 44 per cent of tax cases resolved in the taxpayer's favour without a hearing, and 22 per cent of cases that reach a hearing overturning the initial decision.[84]

These issues prompted the Administrative Justice and Tribunals Council (AJTC) to investigate this issue in its report, *Right First Time*. The AJTC took the view that aiming to get a decision right the first time should be a priority across government. As the Leggatt Report stated, the benefits from getting initial decisions correct are obvious. A correct decision means a 'a better result for the individual, less work for appeal mechanisms and lower cost for departments'.[85] The individual is aware of their rights and obtains a conclusive decision far more quickly, which in turn leads to fewer cases reaching tribunals and so delivers a saving to the public purse. It is also the case that if a department obtains a reputation for making decisions which are overturned by a tribunal, this decreases confidence in initial decisions made by the department.[86] Overall, a system that relies on tribunals to make correct decisions by overturning the initial wrong decisions is a very inefficient and expensive form of decision-making.

It seems obvious that decisions overturned by tribunals could form a key source of information about what has gone wrong about a department's decision-making process and many may contain lessons for the department about what could be done to improve initial decision-making. This could be through sending decision letters that are confusing or that those making the decisions miss key facts or have misconceptions

[81] Ministry of Justice, 'Tribunals and gender recognition certificate statistics quarterly: October to December 2018' (14 March 2019), https://www.gov.uk/government/statistics/tribunals-and-gender-recognition-certificate-statistics-quarterly-october-to-december-2018.

[82] Public Accounts Committee, *Department for Work and Pensions: Contract Management of Medical Services* (HC 744 2012–13) [3].

[83] Ibid [4].

[84] Robert Thomas, 'Administrative Justice, Better Decisions, and Organisational Learning' [2015] *Public Law* 111, 115.

[85] Leggatt Report, para 6.32.

[86] Administrative Justice and Tribunals Council, 'Right First Time' (London 2011), para 44.

about what the law requires.[87] The difficulty is that this feedback loop is difficult to achieve in practice. As the Leggatt Report itself stated, 'providing feedback for decision-makers is an undeveloped practice'.[88] Essentially, at its core, the main role of a tribunal is to determine the issue before it. This means that it is the responsibility of the government department involved to take it upon itself and learn from tribunal decisions. Leggatt was writing in 2001, and it appears that despite the reforms of the 2007 Act, little has changed. The AJTC's report in 2011 highlighted 'a lack of organisational commitment to learn from mistakes and the absence of processes and procedures to listen carefully and respond to feedback'.[89]

As Elliott and Thomas state, 'tribunals provide feedback to government agencies responsible for initial decision making on the standard of decisions many times every day by making their decisions and passing them back to the agency to put into effect'.[90] Indeed, the quality of this feedback should be all the greater given that the agency or government department could be represented before the tribunal responsible for defending the decision. Yet departments frequently do not send a presenting officer, meaning that this opportunity for feedback is lost. It is also the case that the presenting officer may not have been responsible for making the initial decision.[91] The difficulties in changing these practices are budgetary and the politics of 'austerity' and continuing restrictions on the budgets of government departments mean that this is unlikely to change soon.

An alternative is to look at the issue at a higher level, where tribunals and government departments have a formalized feedback process. This could take the form of a report where tribunals highlight situations in their decisions where cases indicate that a systemic problem may exist. These could be referred to in the Annual Report of the Senior President of Tribunals.[92] Some tribunals could be reluctant to engage in such a process as it may cause some to question the independence of the tribunal from the department. However, as the Leggatt Report concludes, drawing on experience in Australia, that 'clear structural independence from departments facilitates the development of relationships that are well managed, transparent, and able to dispel any appearance of improper collaboration'.[93]

Perhaps lurking behind the reasons for poor initial decisions is simply the challenge of making hundreds of thousands of decisions on a limited budget and under political pressure to reach decisions in a timely manner.[94] This led the AJTC to recommend (in line with the Leggatt Report) a 'polluter pays' model to make it in the interests of departments to make decisions that are right first time. This means that departments

---

[87] Leggatt Report, para 9.11.

[88] Ibid para 9.12.

[89] Administrative Justice and Tribunals Council, 'Right First Time' (London 2011), para 3.

[90] Mark Elliott and Robert Thomas, *Public Law* (3rd edn, OUP 2017) 714.

[91] Ibid 647. However, some evidence suggests that decision-making is improved if the original decision-maker is required to defend their decision before the tribunal, see Wikeley and Young, 'The Administration of Benefits in Britain: Adjudication Officers and the Influence of Social Security Appeal Tribunals' [1992] *Public Law* 238.

[92] Administrative Justice and Tribunals Council, 'Right First Time' (London 2011), para 87.

[93] Leggatt Report, para 9.14.

[94] At one point, it took the Department of Work and Pensions more than forty weeks to make decisions regarding applications for Personal Independence Payment.

should contribute to the cost of tribunals based on the number of successful appeals they cause. However, to date, there has been little indication of the government adopting this approach.

In some ways, getting decisions right the first time is the holy grail of an administrative justice system. It is very difficult to achieve, but more could be done to move closer to this ideal.

14.2.7 Conclusion

Overall, this section has shown why tribunals are created and has outlined their main differences with judicial review. Since the passing of the Tribunals, Courts and Enforcement Act 2007, the past ten years have seen extensive reform to tribunals. These reforms include the introduction of the two-tier system, aimed at increasing the effectiveness of tribunals and reforms to the appointment of tribunal judges. It is now unquestioned that tribunals are part of the judicial system. A key feature of tribunals is their procedural flexibility which allows tribunals to deal with a broad range of different legal issues. The senior courts are content to rely on the expertise within the tribunal system and maintain a supervisory role over tribunal decisions. There is still a concern that some government departments are making too many incorrect decisions in the first place, leading to more cases reaching tribunals. Yet, there has been little evidence of any significant improvement in initial decision-making. Finally, a move to provide more tribunal services online is likely to bring further significant change to the system, creating an even closer connection between the tribunals and the courts.

14.3 Ombudsmen

14.3.1 Introduction

As discussed in the introduction to this chapter, the term 'ombudsman' means 'complaints man', which indicates the main function of the role. The ombudsman is an independent person, responsible for investigating complaints made by members of the public against public bodies through a non-legal inquisitorial process. The benefit of such a service to the complainant is that it is free, devoid of the adversarial nature of court proceedings, and the ombudsman conducts the investigation on their behalf. If the ombudsman upholds the complaint, concluding that maladministration has occurred, then they recommend a remedy to correct the situation. Often the ombudsman will make further recommendations outlining how the public body involved could avoid such maladministration reoccurring in the future.

This highlights the dual role of ombudsmen. First, they seek to secure redress for individuals who have suffered injustice caused by maladministration. This can take the form of recommending that the public body concerned make an apology or otherwise 'put things right'. The ombudsman's second role is to consider the reasons behind the maladministration. This generally involves looking at the decision-making process within the public body concerned. This may involve the ombudsman embarking on a detailed investigation to discover how the public body acted and to make recommendations as to how the public body's procedures can be improved to avoid future occurrences of maladministration. Potentially, these two functions could conflict, as a greater focus on individual complaints may come at the expense of investigating the systemic reasons for the maladministration, or the reverse may be true. In practice, the two roles are complimentary. Systemic issues are discovered by pursuing individual complaints, and those investigations can reveal common failures that require further investigation. For example, the Parliamentary Ombudsman received numerous complaints regarding the system of tax credits, a form of social security benefit. It was through considering these individual complaints that an understanding of the systemic issues emerged. Consequently, the ombudsman released a report that, in addition to addressing individual cases, included recommendations about how the broader issues could be corrected.[95]

14.3.2 Ombudsmen in the UK

In 1967, the first ombudsman, the Parliamentary Commissioner for Administration, was created in Britain. The Commissioner is most commonly known as the Parliamentary Ombudsman and this term is used throughout the rest of this chapter. Since then a complex patchwork of ombudsmen has sprung up, with different ombudsmen having responsibility for specific areas of the public sector. A complicating factor has been devolution, which has resulted in different ombudsmen with different responsibilities in each nation of the UK. This is explained within Figure 14.2.

The Parliamentary Ombudsman is responsible for complaints regarding UK central government departments and agencies. In addition, for England only, the Parliamentary Ombudsman also acts as the Health Service Ombudsman,[96] responsible for complaints into NHS departments. Consequently, the ombudsman is known as the Parliamentary and Health Service Ombudsman. In addition, there is the Local Government Ombudsman, which is responsible for complaints about local authorities,[97] and the Independent Housing Ombudsman Service deals with complaints that involve public housing.[98] In

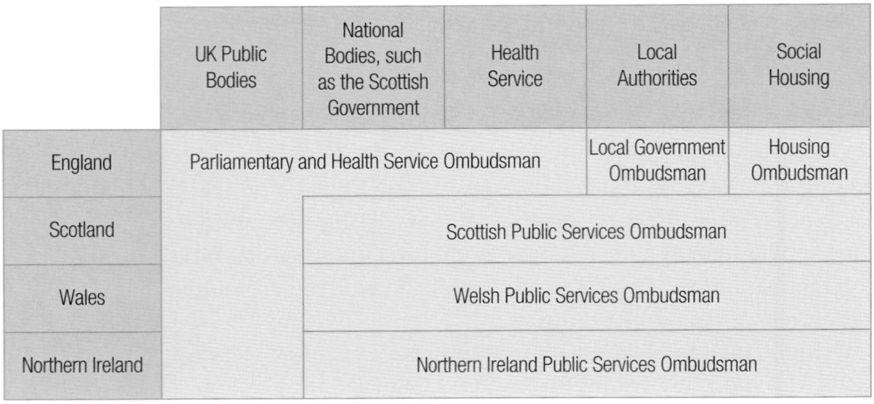

	UK Public Bodies	National Bodies, such as the Scottish Government	Health Service	Local Authorities	Social Housing
England	Parliamentary and Health Service Ombudsman			Local Government Ombudsman	Housing Ombudsman
Scotland		Scottish Public Services Ombudsman			
Wales		Welsh Public Services Ombudsman			
Northern Ireland		Northern Ireland Public Services Ombudsman			

Figure 14.2 Geographical responsibilities of different ombudsmen within the UK

---

[95] Parliamentary Ombudsman, *Tax Credits: Putting Things Right* (HC 2004–05, 124).
[96] Health Service Commissioner Act 1993.
[97] Local Government Act 1974, ss 23–34.
[98] Housing Act 1996, s 51 and Sch 2.

Scotland and Wales a single ombudsman fulfils the role of these three ombudsmen in England, with a public service ombudsman considering complaints into the NHS, local government, and housing. In addition, the Welsh or Scottish Public Service Ombudsmen have jurisdiction to deal with complaints into the departments and agencies of the Scottish or Welsh Governments. Northern Ireland has a Public Services Ombudsman, which is similar to the Scottish and Welsh counterparts, but does not consider complaints regarding social housing.

The more integrated and unified approach in Scotland, Wales, and Northern Ireland has the benefit of clarity and ease of use, as the single ombudsman provides a 'one stop shop' for complaints and avoids difficult questions of how who should handle a complaint that could be heard by more than one ombudsman. This has led to various reform proposals being made, and these are discussed in 14.3.10.

Finally, it should be noted that the ombudsman model has reached the private sector, with ombudsmen in fields as diverse as legal services (Legal Services Ombudsman), financial services (Financial Ombudsman), and even areas including professional football (Independent Football Ombudsman) and canals (Waterways Ombudsman). Individuals with a complaint against a business in a sector with an ombudsman can seek redress through the ombudsman instead of going to court.[99] However, the focus of this section is on the public sector ombudsman, particularly the Parliamentary Ombudsman.

14.3.3 The Parliamentary Ombudsman

The Parliamentary Ombudsman, officially known as the Parliamentary Commissioner for Administration, was created by the Parliamentary Commissioner Act 1967. The Parliamentary Ombudsman is appointed by the Crown and holds the office for seven years.[100] The independence of the ombudsman from the executive is reflected in that, in a similar manner to judges, the ombudsman can only be removed from by a vote of both Houses of Parliament.[101] Since 1993, the office has been combined with the role of Health Service Ombudsman (for England) and describes itself as the Parliamentary and Health Service Ombudsman. For ease, Parliamentary Ombudsman or ombudsman is used in the rest of this section to refer to the Parliamentary and Health Service Ombudsman.

The constitutional position of the Parliamentary Ombudsman is unusual. As Sir Cecil Clothier, the Parliamentary Ombudsman between 1978 and 1984, stated, the Ombudsman 'stands curiously poised between the legislative and the executive, while discharging an almost judicial function in the citizen's dispute with the government; and yet it forms no part of the judiciary'.[102] The ombudsman has a special relationship with Parliament which can only be explained by considering the reasons why the ombudsman was created in the first place.

The concern was that Parliament lacked the capacity to conduct 'a really impartial and really searching investigation into the workings of Whitehall' designed to address 'acts of injustice against the individual'.[103] It was, and still is, difficult for MPs to take on this role.

---

[99] For more details see the Ombudsman Association, http://www.ombudsmanassociation.org.
[100] Parliamentary Commissioner Act 1967 (PCA 1967), s 1(2), (2B).
[101] PCA 1967, s 1(3).
[102] Sir Cecil Clothier, 'The Value of an Ombudsman' [1986] *Public Law* 204, 205.
[103] HC Deb 18 October 1966, vol 734, col 44, Richard Crossman.

The electoral process does not guarantee that winning candidates have the capacity and capability to investigate complex administrative matters, and once in office, MPs have many other competing demands for their time, such as enacting legislation and holding the government to account.[104] These functions of Parliament reduce its capacity and capability to conduct the necessary investigations.[105]

To address this gap, the Parliamentary Ombudsman was created with the intention of being a 'servant of the House', fulfilling this function on behalf of Parliament.[106] This is reflected in the design of the Parliamentary Ombudsman.

The ombudsman is most clearly seen as part of the political process, in that complaints must go through the 'MP filter' (see 14.3.6) and that any recommendations made are not legally binding. However, the ombudsman can encourage Parliament to pressurize the government to comply with their recommendations. The Parliamentary Ombudsman achieves this by placing a special report before Parliament to draw its attention to the issue.[107] Finally, the Parliamentary Ombudsman has a strong working relationship with the Public Administration and Constitutional Affairs Select Committee, which itself can increase the political pressure on the government to accept the ombudsman's findings. These issues and other key elements of the Parliamentary Ombudsman's role and powers are discussed in the rest of this section.

14.3.4 Access to the Parliamentary Ombudsman

The scope of the Parliamentary Ombudsman is largely defined by section 5 of the 1967 Act, which states that the ombudsman may investigate action which has resulted 'in a written complaint . . . made to a member of the House of Commons by a member of the public who claims to have sustained injustice in consequence of maladministration'. From this, access to the Parliamentary Ombudsman is predicated on the fact that a member of the public claims to have suffered some form of injustice *as a result* of maladministration and has made a complaint to an MP regarding this. The importance of maladministration is shown here, as it is insufficient for the injustice to have occurred in isolation; it must have occurred as a consequence of the maladministration experienced by the complainant. The jurisdiction of the ombudsman is relatively broad when its understood that 'injustice' is interpreted flexibly and goes far beyond what might be considered as injustice in a legal context. Injustice can include a sense of 'outrage' caused by incompetent administration, even though no financial loss has been suffered.[108]

The following two sections discuss the concept of maladministration and the MP Filter.

14.3.5 Maladministration

For the Parliamentary Ombudsman to act, there needs to be a complaint of maladministration. Given the importance of the concept to the scheme of the Parliamentary Ombudsman, it is perhaps surprising that 'maladministration' is not defined in the 1967 Act.

---

[104] The functions of Parliament are described in detail in Chapter 8.
[105] Sir Cecil Clothier, 'The Value of an Ombudsman' [1986] *Public Law* 204, 205.
[106] HC Deb 18 October 1966, vol 734, col 43, Richard Crossman.
[107] PCA 1967, s 10(2).
[108] *R v Parliamentary Commissioner for Administration, ex p Balchin (No 1)* [1997] JPL 917, 926, per Sedley J.

Guidance can be gleaned by the so-called 'Crossman Catalogue'. Richard Crossman, the minister responsible for introducing the legislation into the House of Commons, stated that maladministration included 'neglect, inattention, delay, incompetence, ineptitude, perversity, arbitrariness and so on'.[109]

It can be seen from this that maladministration is not meant to be an exclusively legal concept and that the focus should be placed on the process by which decisions are made, rather than the merits of decisions themselves.[110] This is confirmed by section 12 which states that the Ombudsman is not authorized 'to question the merits of a decision taken without maladministration by a government department or other authority'.[111] Consequently, complaining to the ombudsman should not be viewed as an equivalent to an appeal. Although, it must be stated that in practice the distinction between the process used to make a decision and the merits of that decision can be subtle.

Leaving maladministration undefined allows its meaning to develop over time. In 1993, twenty-five years after Richard Crossman's statement, the ombudsman elaborated on the Crossman Catalogue, with maladministration taken to include the following:[112]

- rudeness (though that is a matter of degree);
- unwillingness to treat the complainant as a person with rights;
- refusal to answer reasonable questions;
- neglecting to inform a complainant on request of his or her rights or entitlement;
- knowingly giving advice, which is misleading or inadequate;
- ignoring valid advice or overruling consideration which would produce an uncomfortable result for the overruler;
- offering no redress or manifestly disproportionate redress;
- showing bias whether because of colour, sex, or any other grounds;
- omission to notify those who thereby lose a right of appeal;
- refusing to inform adequately of the right of appeal; and
- faulty procedures.

Clearly, this update to the Crossman Catalogue is undoubtedly useful. However, the problem with this approach to maladministration is its negative nature, as it merely informs public bodies what they should not do, rather than what they should seek to achieve. This does not necessarily reflect the dual role of an ombudsman system which is not only to seek redress for original complaints but to improve and promote good administration. As a former Parliamentary Ombudsman stated:

> The grievances that citizens bring to my Office put me on notice of where things are going wrong and of where improvement is most needed; they make it possible for me to prescribe values and behaviours that will reduce the likelihood of repetition; and they also enable me to tackle future breaches. In this way, a virtuous circle is established, the ultimate

---

[109] HC Deb, 18 October 1966, vol 734, col 51. Approved in *R v Local Commissioner for Administration for the North and East Area of England, ex p Bradford Council* [1979] 1 QB 287, 311.

[110] A point made in the House of Commons by Crossman himself; HC Deb, 18 October 1966, vol 734, col 51.

[111] PCA 1967, s 12(3).

[112] Parliamentary Commissioner for Administration, *Annual Report 1993* (1993–94, HC 290) para 7.

objective being not so much the retrospective eradication of maladministration but the prospective promotion of good administration, prevention rather than cure.[113]

For this reason, the ombudsman developed the Principles of Good Administration,[114] which, unlike the Crossman Catalogue, are positive in nature and inform public bodies as to the standards they should strive to achieve. If these principles are fulfilled, then they would avoid maladministration. It is also the case that any recommendations that the ombudsman makes will seek to uphold these principles. The principles can be described as follows:

1. Getting it right
   - Public bodies must comply with the law and act according to their statutory powers and duties.
   - Follow their own policies and procedural guidance.
   - In particular, public bodies should have regard to the relevant legislation and take account of all relevant considerations and ignoring any irrelevant considerations.

2. Being customer focused
   - Public bodies should provide services that are easily accessible to their customers. This means that policies should be accurate, complete, and understandable.
   - Public bodies should also ensure that customers are clear as to what they can and cannot expect from them and what the customer's own responsibilities are.
   - Public bodies maintain any commitment they enter into; should they be unable to do so, they must explain why they cannot keep it.

3. Being open and accurate
   - Public bodies should be as transparent as possible. This involves giving information to the public and when appropriate giving advice that is clear, accurate, relevant, and timely.
   - Public bodies should be open and truthful when accounting for decisions and actions, stating the criteria applied and the reasons for their decisions.
   - Public bodies should create and maintain records as evidence of their processes.

4. Acting fairly and proportionately
   - Public bodies should deal with people fairly and with respect. This means that they should listen to their customers and not be defensive when things go wrong.
   - Public bodies should act free from bias and prejudice; treat people equally, impartially, and without any unlawful discrimination.
   - If applying the law, regulations or procedures strictly would lead to unfairness, the public body should address this unfairness, bearing in mind that they do not exceed their legal powers.
   - When imposing a penalty, the penalty should be proportionate to the objectives pursued and appropriate in the circumstances.

---

[113] Ann Abraham, 'The Ombudsman as Part of the UK Constitution: A Contested Role?' (2008) 61 *Parliamentary Affairs* 206, 210.

[114] Parliamentary and Health Service Ombudsman, 'Principles of Good Administration' (Parliamentary and Health Service Ombudsman 2009), https://www.ombudsman.org.uk/sites/default/files/page/0188-Principles-of-Good-Administration-bookletweb.pdf.

5. Putting things right

- Public bodies should acknowledge when things go wrong and put things right quickly and effectively. This may require any decisions found to be incorrect put right.

- Decisions of a public body should be applied flexibly when they bear more heavily on an individual due to their particular circumstances even though the public body has met their statutory duties and policies.

- Public bodies should provide clear and timely information about how people can appeal or complain. This may involve providing information about how a customer can find assistance, if they are likely to find the complaints process daunting.

- Public bodies should operate an effective complaints procedure to investigate complaints thoroughly, quickly, and impartially.

- The remedy provided should include an apology and an explanation and, when necessary, seek to put the complainant back in the position they would have been in if nothing had gone wrong.

6. Seeking continuous improvement

- Public bodies should regularly review their policies and procedures and actively seek feedback to improve the performance and delivery of the public body. This also involves reviewing lessons from complaints.

As Ann Abraham, the Parliamentary Ombudsman who developed the principles of good government stated, 'it was a deliberate policy on my part to shift attention from the ill-defined concept of "maladministration" to the more positive notion of good administration, to a genuine sense of what "getting it right" and "acting fairly and proportionately" may mean'.[115] The further benefit of this is that the ombudsman is being open about what they expect from public authorities, so they are aware by what standards their actions will be judged.

 Discussing the problem

Take a moment to consider the problem scenario at the start of the chapter. Out of Simon, Timothy, or Emeli, who could make a complaint to the Parliamentary Ombudsman? Who has suffered maladministration?

The clearest answer is Timothy. Simon would not be able to make a complaint to the ombudsman because he has not exhausted the legal process as it would be reasonable for him to pursue his claim before the Tribunal. It appears that the Department for Transport may be guilty of maladministration here. They have treated Timothy less favourably than Frank for no apparent reason. The Department of Transport have been inconsistent in how they have approached consulting with landowners when developing the proposals for the new railway. It generally appears that they have not complied with the standards of good governance.

---

[115] Ann Abraham, 'The Parliamentary Ombudsman and Administrative Justice: Shaping the Next 50 Years', JUSTICE Tom Sargant Memorial Annual Lecture, 13 October 2001, 26.

Pause for reflection

In introducing the Parliamentary Commissioner Act 1967 into Parliament, Richard Crossman stated that '[a] positive definition of maladministration is far more difficult to achieve. We might have made an attempt in this Clause to define, by catalogue, all of the qualities which make up maladministration, which might count for maladministration by a civil servant . . . It would be a wonderful exercise . . . [and] a long and interesting list.'[116]

In publishing the Principles of Good Administration, to what extent has the Parliamentary Ombudsman established a positive definition of maladministration that Crossman thought would be difficult?

The concept of maladministration was central to the 'Debt of Honour' issue, which explained the relationship between maladministration and judicial review.

Case in depth: *R (Association of British Civilian Internees: Far East Region) v Secretary of State for Defence* [2003] EWCA Civ 473 ('Debt of Honour')

The government announced that it was going to establish a compensation scheme for 'British' civilians imprisoned by the Japanese during the Second World War. The initial announcement led many with British passports to believe that they would be entitled to compensation. However, this was later clarified and the scope of 'British' was clarified to mean those who were either born in the UK themselves or had a parent or grandparent born in the UK. Those who were now going to fall outside the scope of the scheme and not receive compensation sought a judicial review. The argument was that the initial announcement gave rise to a legitimate expectation that they would benefit and that this should be given effect. The Court of Appeal held that the claim should fail on the basis that the initial announcement was not sufficiently clear to generate a legitimate expectation.[117]

Following the Court of Appeal's decision, a complaint was made to the Parliamentary Ombudsman. The ombudsman found that maladministration had occurred because the initial announcement of the scheme was not sufficiently precise and criteria for inclusion into the scheme had been applied inconsistently. The ombudsman's recommendation was to reconsider the operation of the scheme in general, but also to reconsider the position of those who were now losing out.[118]

The 'Debt of Honour' case is significant because the Ombudsman found that maladministration had occurred even though the Court of Appeal had found the government's actions to be lawful. This shows that the concept of maladministration is broader than the principles applied by the courts when hearing an application for judicial review. This can clearly be seen by the principles of good administration.

---

[116] HC Deb, 18 October 1966, vol 734, col 51.

[117] The concept of legitimate expectation is discussed in 13.8.

[118] Parliamentary and Health Service Ombudsman, *'A Debt of Honour': The Ex Gratia Scheme for British Groups Interned by the Japanese during the Second World War* (HC 2005–06, 324) 212.

14.3.6 **MP filter**

As stated in 14.3.4, the ombudsmen can only investigate complaints of maladministration that have been made to a Member of Parliament. This is described as the 'MP filter' and reflects the close relationship between the ombudsman and Parliament. It maintains a traditional approach to ministerial accountability, with the government being accountable to the electorate through their MP. In this way, the MP filter was to ensure that the ombudsman complimented, rather than supplanted, the role of MPs. The filter was an attempt to protect the constituency—MP relationship, whereby constituents can continue to raise concerns about government with their MP, with MPs then exercising their 'independent judgment to the question of whether or not refer . . . no doubt largely for the purpose of preventing the ombudsman from being overwhelmed with the complaints direct from members of the public'.[119]

However, the MP filter has come under increasing criticism in recent years. The MP filter means that individuals have no direct access to the ombudsman and may discourage some from making a complaint in the first instance or some complaints may depend on finding a sympathetic MP in order to reach the ombudsman.[120] In any event, the filter may not be effective, as evidence suggests that over half of MPs automatically refer complaints to the ombudsman when asked to do so.[121]

It could be argued that removing the MP filter may in some way undermine the role of the MP, because they should have the primary responsibility for holding public bodies to account and they act on behalf of their constituents. Yet, it does not follow that removing the MP filter would sideline MPs. The problem is that routing the complaint via an MP remains the only way in which a complaint can be made to the ombudsman.

If direct access to the ombudsman was allowed, MPs could still be involved and be informed of complaints sent by their constituents. In addition, MPs, with the complainant's consent, could still forward complaints on to the ombudsman when necessary. The Public Administration Committee[122] and the Parliamentary Ombudsman have both called for the MP filter to be removed.[123] Indeed, the recent Gordon Review has also recommended that the MP filter should be removed and, going one step further, found that the ombudsman should be able to receive complaints submitted via electronic communication including social media.[124] The draft Bill introduced into Parliament before the 2017 General Election, which would have reformed the ombudsman, removed the requirement for complaints to be routed via an MP. The draft Bill is discussed in 14.3.10.

---

[119] *R (Murray) v Parliamentary Commissioner for Administration* [2002] EWCA Civ 1472 [17].

[120] *R (Murray)*, ibid, makes clear that the decision of an MP not to refer is not subject to judicial review.

[121] Philip Collcutt and Mary Hourihan, *Review of the Public Sector Ombudsmen in England: A Report by the Cabinet Office* (April 2000) para 3:45.

[122] Public Administration Select Committee, *Parliament and the Ombudsman* (HC 2009–10, 107) [2]–[6].

[123] Parliamentary and Health Service Ombudsman, *Report on Direct Access to the Parliamentary Ombudsman* (2011).

[124] Robert Gordon, *Better to Serve the Public: Proposals to restructure reform, renew and reinvigorate public services ombudsman* (October 2014) [129] and [132] ('the Gordon Review').

Counterpoint: Removing the MP filter?

The Public Administration Committee consider that the:

> continuing prohibition of direct access for all complaints is the denial of equal access to administrative justice and is an anachronism which is at odds with the expectations of today's citizens. This defies all logic. It disempowers citizens, obstructs access to their rights, and deters people from making complaints.[125]

Do you agree that the MP filter should be removed?

Discussing the problem

Would the MP filter pose a problem for Timothy?

Considering Timothy's scenario, as long as his MP is willing to pass his complaint on to the ombudsman, then he will be unlikely to have any problems. If the reforms of the Gordon Review are implemented, Timothy would be able to complain to the ombudsman directly. Even if Timothy made a direct complaint, he would be well advised to inform his MP, who could give publicity to this issue. This may cause others to complain, and multiple complaints will alert the ombudsman to the fact that there could be a systemic issue with how the Department of Transport has acted. This would make it more likely that the ombudsman would make a full investigation.

There is also the question as to whether a complaint should be necessary in the first place. The Public Administration Committee has recommended that the ombudsman should have the power to initiate their own inquiries without the need for a complaint in the first place.[126] In their evidence to the Committee, the Parliamentary Ombudsman gave the following reasons in favour:

- the ombudsman could investigate issues of immediate concern to Parliament and citizens;
- it would allow the ombudsman to respond to early warnings, maximizing the preventative (and not merely the reactive) role;
- it would extend access to justice to those least likely to complain, for example, the most vulnerable and marginalized in society;
- prevent first-tier complaints systems being over-burdened with complaints that are identical or similar in substance;
- enable trends across a particular sector to be addressed in a single investigation; and
- gain insight into service failures and use that insight to recommend systemic remedies.[127]

While there may be concern about the ombudsman usurping the role of MPs, these arguments remain compelling, particularly if the power to initiate investigations is used

---

[125] Public Administration Committee, *Time for a People's Ombudsman Service* (HC 2013–14, 655) [55].
[126] Ibid [71].   [127] Ibid [72].

sparingly. This would form a useful addition to the tools of the ombudsman in seeking to ensure good governance within public bodies.

14.3.7 Restrictions on the ombudsman

Under section 4 of the 1967 Act, the Parliamentary Ombudsman may investigate any of the public bodies listed in Schedule 2. While this approach does avoid the difficulties of attempting to develop a generic definition of public body, it does mean that this list needs to be constantly updated as public bodies merge or change names.[128] The list contains all government departments, for example, the Department for Health, Department for Work and Pensions, and the Cabinet Office, but also non-ministerial departments such as the Charity Commission and Food Standards Agency.

However, even if the body is listed in Schedule 2, the 1967 Act at Schedule 3 expressly excludes certain matters from the scope of an ombudsman investigation. These include:

- international relations;
- matters relating to civil or criminal legal proceedings;[129]
- matters relating to appointments to, or discipline within the armed forces or the civil service;
- the grant of honours by the Crown.

The most significant exclusion in practice, is matters 'relating to contractual or other commercial transactions, whether within the United Kingdom or elsewhere, being transactions of a government department or authority'.[130] This reference to 'contractual' means that the decision of a government department to 'contract out' the provision of public services to a commercial company is outside the remit of the ombudsman. Modern government involves a considerable amount of 'contracting out', so that instead of providing services directly, the department enters into a contract with a company such as ATOS or Capita who provide services on their behalf for a price as determined by the contract. This is significant because these contracts often involve large sums of public money.

This has become a far more significant restriction on the ombudsman than would have been envisaged when enacting the legislation in 1967. The effect of this is mitigated to some extent by section 5(1), which gives the ombudsman the power to investigate actions taken on behalf of a public body. This means that the activities of a company providing services for the government can be investigated. The concern is that the exclusion of contractual transactions means that underlying decision by a government department to contract out in the first place cannot be considered by the ombudsman. This means that should the government award a large contract to a company that then performs poorly, the ombudsman can investigate the actions of the company, but not the decision of the Department to award the contract to that company.[131] This is an unsatisfactory reduction in the scope of the ombudsman's power, given that a reason for poor performance or

---

[128] The list can be amended by secondary legislation under PCA 1967, s 4(2).

[129] Although the non-performance of duties owed to victims of violent or sexual offences is specifically included, PCA 1967, s 5(1A)–(1C).

[130] PCA 1967, Sch 3, para 9.

[131] Mark Elliott and Robert Thomas, *Public Law* (2nd edn, OUP 2014) 591.

decision-making could be the contract under which a company is acting on behalf of the government.

A more complex restriction is that under section 5(2). This states that the ombudsman shall not investigate a matter if the complainant has or had any right to appeal before a tribunal or to seek a remedy in the courts. However, the section then states that the ombudsman can investigate the matter 'if they are satisfied in the particular circumstances that it is not reasonable to expect him to resort or have resorted to it'. Consequently, the issue is whether the ombudsman should exercise their discretion to investigate a matter even though the complainant could have pursued an alternative remedy. The emphasis is that the complainant should have exhausted all *reasonable* avenues before making a complaint to the ombudsman. This could be through making a complaint according to the public body's own complaints procedure or appealing to the relevant tribunal. This means that the ombudsman exercises their discretion so that complainants are not expected to embark on speculative litigation or when the matter cannot be satisfactorily resolved by the courts.[132] In any event, as the Public Administration Committee has remarked, the whole idea of the ombudsman is to consider a matter in a broader context than that possible through the courts or at a tribunal, and the 'fact that legality has been established through judicial review may be irrelevant to maladministration'.[133]

Another restriction of note is that the complaint must be first made to an MP one year from the date that the complainant first had knowledge of the issue.[134] However, in special circumstances, this period can be extended at the ombudsman's discretion.

14.3.8 The procedure and powers of the ombudsman

The ombudsman adopts a three-stage process.

- The first stage is the initial enquiry. Inquiries are received by telephone, by post, or digitally. Most enquiries progress no further, as the enquirer has not made a complaint to the public body or organization involved. The ombudsman can advise the enquirer on who and how to make the complaint.

- The second stage is the formal complaint. These are the enquiries which may benefit from the assistance of the ombudsman and are considered in more detail. However, many complaints conclude at this stage because the ombudsman is unable to investigate. This could be because the time limit in which to make the complaint has been exceeded, legal action is a more viable option, or the complainant has not been personally affected by what happened.

- The third stage is the investigation and resolution of the complaint. There are usually four outcomes:

(1) *Resolution*—when the ombudsman can resolve the issue for the complainant without the need for a formal investigation.

---

[132] *R v Commissioner for Local Administration, ex p Croydon London Borough Council* [1989] 1 All ER 1033, 1044–5.
[133] Public Administration Select Committee, *Debt of Honour* (HC 2005–06, 735) para 20.
[134] PCA 1967, s 6(3).

(2) *No action*—the complaint has been assessed and the ombudsman cannot improve the situation by investigating. This could be because there has not been a failure or the organization involved has already taken appropriate steps to put things right.

(3) *Complaint not upheld*—when the ombudsman has conducted an investigation and found no wrongdoing or failure on the part of the organization involved.

(4) *Complaint upheld*—after an investigation, the ombudsman has found a failing on the part of the organization that has not been addressed. A complaint could either be fully or partially upheld.

The following diagram shows how the ombudsman addressed all enquiries and complaints in 2018–19.[135]

If a formal investigation is pursued, then the 1967 Act imposes a formal procedure that must be followed. The general principle of fairness is expressed in section 7 which requires that the public body must have the opportunity to comment on any allegation contained in the complaint. The investigation is conducted in private in a manner the

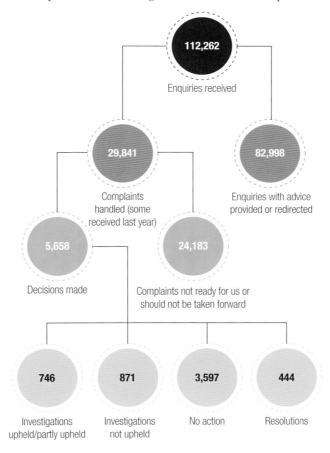

Figure 14.3 The outcome of enquiries and complaints to the ombudsman in 2018–19

[135] Diagram adapted from Parliamentary and Health Service Ombudsman, *The Ombudsman's Annual Report and Accounts 2018-2019* (HC 2017–19, 2918) 27.

ombudsman considers appropriate.[136] This will usually involve considering documents from the public body and interviewing members of staff involved.

The ombudsman has extensive powers to obtain evidence from the organization involved. By law, they must cooperate with the ombudsman, granting access to any documents requested.[137] If necessary, the ombudsman can compel witnesses to give evidence using similar powers to the courts.[138] This includes information that would ordinarily be protected by the Official Secrets Act 1989.[139] The main exception to disclosure is information relating to the Cabinet or a Cabinet Sub-Committee.[140] The rights of an ombudsman to access documents are further supported by section 9 which makes the obstruction of an investigation the equivalent to a contempt of court, an offence which could result in imprisonment.

14.3.9 The findings and remedies of the Parliamentary Ombudsman

Recommendations

When the ombudsman has concluded their investigation, they will determine whether maladministration has occurred and what recommendations they should make. These will be contained in a report, which the ombudsman is required to send to both the MP who referred the initial complaint and the public body who was subject to the complaint.[141] As the ombudsman has stated themselves, when determining the remedy, the 'underlying principle is to ensure that the public body restores the complainant to the position they would have been in if the maladministration or poor service had not occurred'.[142] As regards the initial complaint, recommended remedies can include an apology, reviewing the initial decision, or financial compensation. Should the ombudsman decide to make recommendations about any broader issues that have resulted from the investigation, these will also be included in their report.

It should be noted that in the same manner as decisions of other public bodies, the decision of the ombudsman as to whether maladministration has occurred is subject to judicial review. This was shown in the *Balchin* litigation which resulted in three successful judicial review claims against the decision of the ombudsman that no maladministration had occurred.

Case in depth: *Balchin* litigation

The local authority had decided to construct a new road near the complainant's house. This would reduce the value of the property. The Department of Transport refused to purchase the house at its original value. The ombudsman concluded that no maladministration had occurred. In *R v Parliamentary Commissioner for Administration, ex p Balchin (No 1)* [1997] JPL 917, this conclusion was quashed because the ombudsman had failed to consider a relevant consideration, which was that the Department of Transport should have informed the local authority that

➡

---

[136] Ibid s 7(2).   [137] Ibid s 8(1).   [138] Ibid s 8(2).

[139] PCA 1967, s 8(3). Although should the ombudsman refer to such information in their report, this may constitute a breach of the Official Secrets Act: see s 11(2).

[140] PCA 1967, s 8(4).   [141] PCA 1967, s 10(1)–(2).

[142] Parliamentary and Health Service Ombudsman, *Principles for Remedy* (2009) 3.

they had the statutory power to purchase the complainant's property. When the ombudsman reconsidered the issue, they again concluded that no maladministration had occurred. This again was successfully judicially reviewed on the basis that the ombudsman had failed to give adequate reasons for its reasoning on the essential issues of the matter.[143]

The trilogy of cases was completed in *R (Balchin) v Parliamentary Commissioner for Administration (No 3)* [2002] EWHC 1876 (Admin). This held that the ombudsman, who again had concluded no maladministration had taken place during a particular phase of the lengthy dispute, was not supported by adequate reasoning.

In *Balchin (No 2)*, the court was clear that because the ombudsman is considering matters of policy, they should enjoy a very wide area of discretion and judgment over whether maladministration has occurred. However, Dyson J was clear that this was subject to the need to provide adequate reasons. He stated:

> Where the court finds that there is a real shortcoming in the reasoning of the [ombudsman], it seems to me that it is not passing judgment on the substance of a policy decision. It is criticising the reasoning on grounds which do not depend in any way on the policy element of the decision.[144]

 Counterpoint: The risks of *Balchin* to the nature of the ombudsman process

As Giddings states, the danger of decisions such as *Balchin* is that if 'judges require the Ombudsman to meet the decision-making standards set for courts, then what was an informal, non-judicial mechanism for complaint-handling will become a formal, judicial one—with consequent costs in time and resources which are likely to deter some potential complainants from pursuing their case'.[145]

The concern is that meeting standards imposed by courts could require a more formalized process. Such a process which puts at risk the very purpose of the ombudsman which is to deal with complaints informally and in an accessible manner to potential complainants. Arguably such an intensive oversight by the courts, akin to the actions of government departments, is inappropriate. The rule of law requires that government governs according to the law, whereas the ombudsman does not govern, but merely investigates complaints of maladministration making recommendations when necessary.[146]

Enforcing the ombudsman's recommendations

The ombudsman's recommendations are not legally binding; however, this does not mean that recommendations are ignored. On the contrary, evidence suggests that as many as 99 per cent of recommendations are accepted by public bodies, including how

---

[143] *R v Parliamentary Commissioner for Administration, ex p Balchin (No 2)* (2000) 79 P & CR 157.

[144] Ibid 169.

[145] Philip Giddings, 'Ex P. Balchin: Findings of Maladministration and Injustice' [2000] *Public Law* 201, 203.

[146] Mark Elliott and Robert Thomas, *Public Law* (2nd edn, OUP 2014) 596.

the public body should resolve the complaint.[147] This reflects the relationship between the ombudsman and the public bodies they investigate, as the ombudsman's role is to support the public body, enabling them to improve rather than providing a disciplinary or penal function. The relationship is one of persuasion rather than compulsion.[148] As Kirkham, Thompson, and Buck state:

> Ombudsmen working in constructive partnerships with public bodies are in a stronger position to secure workable solutions than if the Ombudsmen were seen as a hostile force imposing solutions. Moreover, any short-term gains in securing redress would have to be offset against the long-term costs involved in discouraging public bodies from being amenable partners in the process of resolution and in working towards future improvements in the quality and fairness of administration.[149]

In 2018–19, the Ombudsman made the following recommendations:[150]

- 510 apologies;
- 345 compensation payments, £263,038 from NHS organizations and £16,435 from UK Government departments and other public organizations;
- 450 service improvements (this included changing procedures or training staff);
- 103 actions to put things right—for example, asking a GP practice to correct errors on medical records or asking public bodies such as government departments to review a decision.[151]

The issue is the 1 per cent of cases when the public bodies choose not to accept or comply with the ombudsman's recommendations. Given the policy nature of the issues, there is the inherent possibility that the public body just simply takes a different view to the ombudsman. This is especially the case when the ombudsman has recommended that compensation be paid, but the government is mindful of its limited resources and other demands on the public finances.

However, this should not be the sole reason for rejecting an ombudsman's recommendations. The special weapon in the ombudsman armoury is to lay a special report before Parliament. Under section 10(3), if the Ombudsman considers 'that injustice has been caused to the person aggrieved in consequence of maladministration and that the injustice has not been, or will not be, remedied, he may, if he thinks fit, lay before each House of Parliament a special report upon the case'. This process draws the attention of Parliament to the issue, particularly when the recommendations of the ombudsman have been rejected. This rarely happens, with only seven special reports being laid before Parliament since 1967. Yet, five of these have been published since 2005, which indicates that disagreements regarding the ombudsman's recommendations are increasing in frequency.

---

[147] Parliamentary and Health Service Ombudsman, *Annual Report and Accounts 2018–19* (HC 2017–19, 2198) 36.

[148] Welsh Affairs Committee, *Public Services Ombudsman (Wales) Bill* (HC 2004–05, 234) Ev 30, Q164 (Ann Abraham).

[149] Richard Kirkham, Brian Thompson, and Trevor Buck, 'When Putting Things Right Goes Wrong: Enforcing the Recommendations of the Ombudsman' [2008] *Public Law* 510, 522.

[150] As the Parliamentary Ombudsman is also the Health Service Ombudsman for England, the statistics are presented together.

[151] Parliamentary and Health Service Ombudsman, Annual Report and Accounts 2015–16 (2016–17, HC 779) 17.

The special report procedure reflects how the ombudsman is part of the political process. Once the special report is laid, it becomes the role of Parliament to pressurize the government to comply with the recommendations. The Public Administration Committee may hold an inquiry into the issue. As Kirkham states, this elevates the matter to one of ministerial responsibility to Parliament, as the responsible minister must account to Parliament for their non-compliance with the ombudsman's report. In this way, the Public Administration Committee 'bring to the process a degree of moral and political clout that would otherwise be absent'.[152] The government's acceptance of the ombudsman's recommendations was a significant issue following their investigation into Equitable Life.

Equitable Life

This was an investigation into Equitable Life Assurance Scheme, which promised policyholders a certain level of pension. It then emerged that Equitable Life was unable to meet the promised level of pension payments. The complaints to the ombudsman were based on the failure of the relevant public bodies to regulate Equitable Life properly to such an extent that maladministration occurred. The ombudsman agreed, finding that there had been a 'serial regulatory failure' as the public bodies responsible for regulating Equitable Life had been complacent in their approach and allowed Equitable Life to descend into the difficulties in which it found itself. The ombudsman recommended that a compensation scheme should be created, which would put all those who suffered loss back in the position they would have been had the maladministration not occurred. The potential bill for such a scheme was more than £1 billion.

The government's response was twofold. First, it did not accept all the Ombudsman's findings of maladministration and, secondly, the government did not fully implement the recommendation for a total compensation scheme as it was limited to those who were most affected. The ombudsman gave the following views on the government's response:

> I am disappointed to see the Government picking over and re-interpreting my findings of maladministration and injustice, re-arranging the evidence, re-doing the analysis and acting as judge on its own behalf . . . It seems to me the Government did not need to do that. It might have said, 'We do not see this in the same way as the Ombudsman sees it, but out of respect for the constitutional position of her office, we will accept her findings of maladministration and injustice.' The Government could then have gone on to consider the question of remedy. It could then have brought into play legitimate considerations of public policy and public purse.[153]

Here, the ombudsman highlights the essential features of the role of the ombudsman. The ombudsman believes their finding of maladministration should be binding, but their recommendations should not be. This is based on the idea that it is for the ombudsman, as required to do so by Parliament through legislation, to determine whether maladministration has taken place. This should not be a question for the government as that would be tantamount to government acting as its own judge. By contrast, when it comes to recommendations, these are not binding. Instead as part of the political process, the government must justify to Parliament its refusal to follow any recommendation.

---

[152] Richard Kirkham, 'Challenging the Authority of the Ombudsman: The Parliamentary Ombudsman's Special Report on Wartime Detainees' (2006) 69 (5) MLR 792, 815.

[153] Public Administration Committee, *Justice Denied? The Government's Response to the Ombudsman's Report on Equitable Life* (HC 2008–09, 219) Ev 1.

The non-binding nature of the ombudsman's recommendations is shown by how the government refused to yield on Equitable Life, despite criticism from the Public Administration Committee and a special report being laid before Parliament by the Ombudsman. Eventually, it took a change of government for a compensation scheme to be introduced. After taking office in 2010, the Coalition Government enacted the Equitable Life (Payments) Act 2010, which created a £1.5 billion compensation fund for affected policy holders.

Pause for reflection

Is it satisfactory that despite the political pressure placed on the government they can still refuse to implement the recommendations of the ombudsman?

'Pensions Promise'

This distinction between accepting a finding of maladministration and the ombudsman's recommendations was a critical issue in the 'Pensions Promise' case. Occupational pensions held by thousands of people were ultimately worth significantly less than they had been promised. This was due to a range of reasons, including several failures by the public bodies such as the Department of Work and Pensions. It was found that the Department of Work and Pensions had provided information which was 'sometimes inaccurate, often incomplete, largely inconsistent and therefore potentially misleading'.[154] The ombudsman recommended that the government should make good the losses caused by the maladministration by restoring the pension benefits that the holders were entitled to expect. This was to be achieved by 'whichever means is most appropriate, including if necessary, by payment from public funds, to replace the full amount lost by those individuals'.[155]

In response, the government rejected both the finding of maladministration and the recommendation as to how to remedy the injustice the maladministration had caused. Some of those affected sought a judicial review of the government's decision to reject both the finding of maladministration and the recommended remedy. The case reached the Court of Appeal.

Case in depth: *R (Bradley) v Secretary of State for Work and Pensions* [2008] EWCA Civ 36

The argument in the Court of Appeal revolved around the circumstances in which the government could reject the findings of the ombudsman. The Parliamentary Ombudsman argued that the government should always accept a finding by the ombudsman unless it has been quashed by the courts on an application for judicial review.[156] Sir John Chadwick, giving the leading judgment, rejected this argument entirely, on the basis that it was never the intention of the 1967 Act to require the government to pursue a judicial review against a finding of maladministration before they could reject it.

→

---

[154] Parliamentary and Health Service Ombudsman, *Trusting in the Pensions Promise* (HC 2005–06, 984) para 5.164.

[155] Ibid para 6.15.   [156] [2008] EWCA Civ 36 [135].

Instead, the purpose of the 1967 Act was for such matters to be resolved through ministerial accountability to Parliament rather than the law. This meant that the focus should not be on whether the ombudsman's findings were rational, but rather whether the government's decision to reject the ombudsman's report was rational. This is likely to be a high threshold to meet, as Sir John stated:

> it is not enough that the Secretary of State has reached his own view on rational grounds: it is necessary that his decision to reject the ombudsman's findings in favour of his own view is, itself, not irrational . . . he must have a reason (other than simply a preference for his own view) for rejecting a finding which the ombudsman has made after an investigation . . . [157]

Applying this stricter test, Sir John concluded that the government had acted irrationally in rejecting the ombudsman's finding of maladministration. However, this did not mean that the policyholders received any compensation. The focus of the Court of Appeal decision was on the ability of the government to reject a finding of maladministration. The Court of Appeal effectively required the government to accept this finding, but it remained open to the government to reject the ombudsman's recommendation regarding the remedy.

 Pause for reflection

The effect of the *Bradley* case is to make it difficult for the government to reject a finding of maladministration. However, it remains the case that governments can reject the ombudsman's recommendations. As Elliott suggests, this is the appropriate balance to strike, as this approach 'stops ministers from evading political responsibility' by dismissing the ombudsman's conclusions 'while recognising that whether such conclusions should be acted upon remains a policy question for government and Parliament'.[158] If Parliament wants the government to give effect to the ombudsman's recommendations, but is unable to place the government under sufficient pressure to do so, then that is an argument for 'strengthening the role of Parliament, not for legal enforcement of the Ombudsman's recommendations'.[159]

Essentially, the decision in *Bradley* is consistent with the notion that the ombudsman is part of the political rather than legal process.

14.3.10 Reform of the ombudsman

As mentioned in this section, there have been proposals for reform of the Parliamentary Ombudsman. Since 2000, there has been a groundswell of support for significant reform as shown by several reports and inquiries, the most notable being the Cabinet Office Review,[160] a Law Commission inquiry,[161] and the Public Administration Committee's

[157] Ibid [91].
[158] Mark Elliott, 'The Government Versus the Ombudsman: What Role for Judicial Review' [2010] *Cambridge Law Journal* 1, 3.
[159] Ibid 3.
[160] Philip Collcutt and Mary Hourihan, *Review of Public Sector Ombudsman in England* (2000).
[161] Law Commission, *Public Services Ombudsman* (Law Com No 329, 2011).

proposal for a People's Ombudsman Service.[162] However, no significant change had resulted. The government commissioned the Gordon Review, to examine the case for a single public service ombudsman in England.[163] The Gordon Report was published in 2014 and made the following recommendations.

First, the Parliamentary and Health Service Ombudsman (itself a combination of two roles) should be combined with the Local Government and Housing Ombudsman for England. This new unified ombudsman would still be able to hear complaints from government agencies that are ultimately accountable to the UK Parliament, but would also cover local government and the NHS within England. This means that complaints into matters devolved to Northern Ireland, Scotland, or Wales should still be sent to the relevant ombudsman in those nations. However, complaints would be able to be referred to each other when necessary.[164] This cooperation between the different ombudsmen should also be encouraged, including joint investigations with each other.

In addition, access to the new ombudsman should be as wide as possible. This means abolishing the MP Filter, so that complaints could be sent to the new ombudsman without the need for any input from an MP.[165] However, this should not mean that MPs no longer have a role, as they could continue to encourage complaints, through their contact with constituents.[166] Removal of the MP filter also means that the new ombudsman can be open to receiving complaints in different ways. At present, where the Parliamentary and Health Service Ombudsman can only receive complaints by letter, the new ombudsman would be able to receive complaints orally or electronically. The Gordon Review even mentions gathering complaints through social media.[167] The more positive approach pursued by the Parliamentary Ombudsman in adopting its principles of good government has been given recognition by the recommendation that the new ombudsman should issue guidance to government agencies on how to handle complaints.[168] Finally, and perhaps most controversially, the new ombudsman should, in limited circumstances, be able to initiate its investigations without the need for a complaint.[169]

The government published the Draft Public Service Ombudsman Bill in December 2016. Generally, the structure of the Act is an updated version of the original 1967 Act creating the Parliamentary Ombudsman and many features of the draft bill will be familiar to those with a knowledge of the 1967 Act. One proposal not fully implemented in the draft bill was the recommendation that the ombudsman can initiate its own investigations. Instead, the draft bill makes provision for the ombudsman to investigate an 'additional matter' that arises during an investigation made following a complaint.[170]

Potentially, the draft bill misses some opportunities for further reform. Given that the Parliamentary Ombudsman has felt it necessary to lay special reports more frequently in recent years because the government has been slow to implement the ombudsman's recommendations, it is disappointing to find that there are no changes to this process. Recommendations such as requiring a debate on the ombudsman's report have not been included in this bill.[171] The draft bill was introduced into Parliament in December 2016;

---

[162] Public Administration Committee, *Time for a People's Ombudsman Service* (HC 2013–14, 655).
[163] Gordon Review, Annex A, 54.   [164] Gordon Review, para 80.
[165] Gordon Review, para 129.   [166] Ibid para 128.   [167] Ibid para 132.
[168] Ibid para 26.   [169] Ibid para 139.
[170] Cabinet Office, *Draft Public Service Ombudsman Bill* (Cm 9374) Clause 13.
[171] Public Administration Committee, *Parliament and the Ombudsman* (HC 2009–10, 107) para 12.

but by the start of the new session of Parliament in October 2019, the bill had not progressed any further and it is unclear whether the government intends to continue with ombudsman reform.

14.3.11 Conclusion

The ombudsman has proven to be an effective method through which individual complaints against government departments are resolved without the need for legal proceedings. The core role of ombudsman remains investigating allegations of maladministration, which as shown by the 'Debt of Honour' case is a broader inquiry than considering the lawfulness of the decision-making process at a judicial review. Through their investigations, the ombudsman seeks to uphold the principles of good administration, which means that the ombudsman seeks to make recommendations which prevent maladministration from reoccurring. While most recommendations are accepted, sometimes the government disagrees. As shown by this section, resolving this disagreement is a matter of politics rather than law. Proposed reforms to the Parliamentary Ombudsman would further increase the effectiveness of the ombudsman process.

14.4 Public inquiries

14.4.1 Introduction

Inquiries are perhaps the most flexible of the three 'types' of administrative justice discussed in this chapter. While they take many forms, at their core, they investigate a matter and then compile a report which makes recommendations for the government to consider. There are two main types of inquiry. Some inquiries are held as part of the process of making a decision. A common example is planning inquiries, where if a planning application has been refused by the local authority, it can be appealed to the Secretary of State. However, before the Secretary of State determines the appeal, an inquiry is held by a planning inspector. The inspector makes a recommendation to the Secretary of State who is free to accept or ignore the inspector's recommendations.

The second type of inquiry is of a much higher profile and usually arises after some major political scandal or matter which has become an issue of public concern. They can be extremely high profile and have increasingly become a key method by which the government is held to account. In these circumstances, the aim of these inquiries is to discover what went wrong and what policies or changes to the law or policy are necessary to prevent the scandal from reoccurring. The inquiry will usually make recommendations which the government considers and choose whether or not to implement them. If the matter is politically controversial, then the government can come under considerable political pressure to hold an inquiry. This section discusses this second type of inquiry in more detail.

It will be useful for the discussion ahead to discuss some examples. It will be seen that each public inquiry is different, being held in response to specific circumstances and concerns. Elements of these inquiries will be discussed when relevant in the rest of this section.

- *The Leveson Inquiry*—It appeared that the voicemails of a murdered teenager had been hacked by journalists from a tabloid newspaper. This caused public disgust and it later emerged that journalists had hacked hundreds of people's phones. Those involved included celebrities, politicians, and members of the public who had become involved in major news stories. This raised fundamental questions about the conduct of the press and the legal framework under which they operated. This developed into broader questions about the ethics of the press and the relationship between the police, politicians, and the media. Leveson LJ led the inquiry, sessions of which were televised live. The inquiry recommended a new regulatory system for the newspapers, which has proven controversial.

- *Mid-Staffordshire Hospital*—An inquiry by Sir Robert Francis QC into very serious failures of care provided by the Mid-Staffordshire NHS Trust, including some patients suffering degrading and inhumane treatment. The inquiry held that this was due to a series of regulatory failures and mismanagement. Nearly 300 recommendations were made, with the main aim to change the culture of the NHS to ensure that patients are the primary priority of the system rather than meeting regulatory targets.

- *Iraq Inquiry*—An inquiry led by Sir John Chilcot, a former senior civil servant, into the overall conduct of the Iraq War, including the run-up to the conflict, the military action and its aftermath. After seven years of investigation, the report concluded that Britain entered the conflict without necessarily exploring all peaceful options before commencing military action, meaning that it had not become the last resort. In addition, the government's belief that Iraq had weapons of mass destruction was presented as more of a certainty than could be justified by the intelligence. Finally, the inquiry concluded that the planning for Iraq after the conflict was 'wholly inadequate'.

- *The Denning Inquiry into the Profumo Affair*—During the Cold War in 1961, the Secretary of State for War, John Profumo, had a sexual relationship with Christine Keeler. It later emerged that Keeler also had a relationship with a Soviet spy. This caused a huge scandal, with rumours of other impropriety circling the government. After denying the allegations in the House of Commons, Profumo later resigned when he admitted that he lied to Parliament. After pressure from MPs, the Prime Minister, Harold Macmillan, called on Lord Denning to conduct an inquiry into the affair. The inquiry, who concluded that no security risk arose out of Profumo's relationship with Keeler.

- *Bloody Sunday Inquiry*—This is notable for being the longest and most expensive inquiry in British history: it took twelve years and cost £192 million. The British Army killed thirteen people on the streets of Londonderry/Derry in Northern Ireland following a protest march. An initial inquiry was quickly held by the Lord Chief Justice. However, this failed to gain public acceptance, as it was viewed as too favourable to the government. After a campaign for a new inquiry, Lord Saville was appointed to chair a new inquiry, which concluded that the killings were unjustified. The Prime Minister, David Cameron, made an apology on behalf of the government before the House of Commons and criminal investigations into the killings began after the inquiry.

- *The Litvinenko Inquiry*—An inquiry into the circumstances surrounding the death of Alexander Litvinenko, a former officer for the Russian intelligence services, first the KGB and then the FSB. Litvinenko left Russia and moved to the UK after being dismissed for marking allegations of illegality within the FSB. Six years later, Litvinenko was poisoned at a London hotel, with his blood containing a high level of the radioactive substance polonium 210. The inquiry concluded that the poisoning was an FSB operation, which was 'probably approved by President Putin'.[172]

14.4.2 The role of inquiries

As can be seen from the examples we have discussed, public inquiries are held in a range of different circumstances, meaning that they do not fulfil any one key role, but are created for a range of reasons. A committee of the House of Lords, building upon earlier discussion,[173] considered that inquiries usually fulfil at least some of the following functions:[174]

- establishing the facts, especially where these are disputed, or the chain of causation is unclear;

- determining accountability;

- learning lessons and making recommendations to prevent recurrence, often by improving the constitution and powers of regulatory bodies;

- allaying public disquiet and restoring public confidence;

- catharsis: an opportunity for reconciliation between those affected by an event and those whose action caused it or whose inaction failed to prevent it;

- developing public policy.[175]

It must also be stated that inquiries can be created by the government for political purposes. Should a situation or scandal prove particularly controversial, the opposition and media may lead demands for a public inquiry to be held to consider the issue. This can be tempting for the government, as holding a public inquiry can, in the short term, suspend such scrutiny as all those concerned must wait for the inquiry to release their report. Ministers can cite the inquiry as evidence that they have taken the matter seriously, they have 'done something' in response, but cannot respond further until the inquiry has concluded. However, governments will only sparingly seek recourse to a public inquiry because they ultimately prolong the issue, as the release of the report may reopen the controversy. In addition, government has little control over the process, the independence of the inquiry means that the report could be embarrassing for the government.

Out of the inquiries discussed at the start of this section, inquiries such as the Francis Report into Mid-Staffordshire Hospital fit many of the reasons discussed earlier in this chapter. It established the facts and exposed the shocking scale of mistreatment at the hospital and made recommendations to ensure that such mistreatment does not reoccur within the NHS. When such recommendations are followed by the government, the

---

[172] The Litvinenko Inquiry, 'Report into the death of Alexander Litvinenko' (HC 2015–16, 695) para 10.16.

[173] Particularly, Lord Howe, 'The Management of Public Inquiries' (1999) 70 *Political Quarterly* 294.

[174] House of Lords Select Committee on the Inquiries Act 2005, *The Inquiries Act 2005: post legislative scrutiny* (HL 143, 2013–14), para 9.

[175] In addition, a public inquiry can be required for the UK to satisfy obligations under the European Convention on Human Rights, in particular Article 2, the right to life and Article 3, the prevention of torture or of inhuman or degrading treatment or punishment.

inquiry becomes part of the policy-making process. It is also the case that the mere existence of the inquiry has the aim of restoring public confidence in the NHS by showing the public that the issues were being taken seriously. Finally, inquiries such as this serve a cathartic purpose, as the inquiry provides closure for the families and friends of those involved, as they get to express their concerns to an independent person, who takes them seriously. In this case, finding that their concerns were vindicated.

14.4.3 The creation of public inquiries

There are three ways in which an inquiry can be created.

First, inquiries can be held under a specific statutory power. For example, the Stephen Lawrence inquiry, which investigated claims of racism against the Metropolitan Police, was established under the Police Act 1996.[176] Other inquiries include the investigation in the Southall Rail Accident, which was established under the Health and Safety at Work etc. Act 1974.[177] However, given the circumstances under which inquiries are held, statutory provisions such as these are unlikely to cover all the situations which give rise to inquiries.

This creates the need for stand-alone, generic legislation. Replacing earlier legislation, the Inquiries Act 2005 creates a set of common rules for ad hoc inquiries. This means that if necessary, an inquiry can be created relatively quickly.[178] The features of this Act are discussed in the rest of this section. The overall view is that, 'by and large', the Act has worked well.[179] The main concern with the Act is that, unlike the legislation it has replaced, the 2005 Act places the question as to whether to create an inquiry lies with the government, with the minister establishing the inquiry merely being under a duty to inform Parliament that an inquiry is to be held.[180]

Finally, inquiries can be held on a non-statutory basis under the royal prerogative. These are usually held when the inquiry is considering the actions of government or public bodies. The constitutional concern is that there is even less of an obligation on the government to involve Parliament with a non-statutory inquiry. The House of Lords have expressed concern that some inquiries have been created under the royal prerogative rather than the Inquiries Act 2005, for no good reason.[181] There are two main differences between statutory and non-statutory inquiries. First, a statutory inquiry can compel a witness to attend, and secondly there is a presumption that a statutory inquiry is held in public, whereas a non-statutory inquiry can be held in private. The House of Lords suggest that the presumption should be that the Inquiries Act 2005 (or other relevant statutory provision) should be used to create a public inquiry unless there is a good reason to use the royal prerogative. One example of a non-statutory inquiry is the Butler Inquiry which considered the use of intelligence information in the run up to the Iraq War. This

---

[176] Police Act 1996, s 49.

[177] Health and Safety at Work etc. Act 1974, s 14(2)(b).

[178] The Ministerial Code requires that the Prime Minister is consulted 'in good time' about any proposal to set up a public inquiry under the 2005 Act; Cabinet Office, *Ministerial Code* (August 2019) para 4.12.

[179] House of Lords Select Committee on the Inquiries Act 2005, *The Inquiries Act 2005: post-legislative scrutiny* (HL 2013–14, 143), 7.

[180] Inquiries Act 2005, s 6.

[181] House of Lords Select Committee on the Inquiries Act 2005, *The Inquiries Act 2005: post-legislative scrutiny* (HL 2013–14, 143) [81]–[82].

sat in private for reasons of national security as the inquiry involved hearing evidence from the intelligence agencies.

As explained by Lord Philips PSC in *Re McCaughey's application for judicial review* [2012] 1 AC 725, Article 2 ECHR, the right to life may also require a public inquiry:

> Article 2 by implication [gives] rise not merely to a substantive obligation on the state not to kill people but, where there was an issue as to whether the state had broken this obligation, a procedural obligation on the state to carry out an effective official investigation into the circumstances of the deaths (the procedural obligation).

This requirement for an 'official investigation' can take many forms, including a criminal trial. However, when that is not possible, or proves inconclusive, a public inquiry may be required. The issue of a public inquiry is required under Article 2 ECHR was addressed in the following case.

Case in Depth: *Re Finucane's Application for Judicial Review* [2019] UKSC 7

In 1989, Patrick Finucane, a human rights lawyer, was murdered by terrorists in Belfast. There was evidence that the UK security services had colluded in the murder. The initial police investigation, the inquest, and two reviews by John Stevens (then Deputy Chief Constable of the Cambridgeshire Constabulary) into collusion between the security services and terrorists did not specifically consider the allegation that the security services were involved in the murder. In 2002, the European Court of Human Rights found that the lack of a prompt and effective investigation into the allegations breached the right to life as protected by the ECHR.[182] Eventually, in 2004, the Secretary of State for Northern Ireland wrote to the widow, Geraldine Finucane, promising that a public inquiry would be held under the Inquiries Act 2005 once this legislation was enacted. Mrs Finucane objected to this, but years of discussions between the UK Government and Mrs Finucane failed to reach agreement. When the Coalition Government took office in 2010, in light of the Bloody Sunday inquiry, the government was concerned to avoid lengthy and costly public inquiries into the past in Northern Ireland. After a consultation exercise, the Prime Minister, David Cameron, decided not to hold a public inquiry. Instead a review would be conducted by Sir Desmond de Silva, a former UN war crimes prosecutor. Although invited, Mrs Finucane took no part in the review.

Mrs Finucane sought a judicial review of the government's refusal to hold a public inquiry, based on two grounds: (1) legitimate expectation and (2) Article 2 ECHR. The Supreme Court found that the promise of a public inquiry had given rise to a legitimate expectation, meaning that the question was whether the government could resile from its undertaking. The Court concluded that it could. In such a politically sensitive context, the courts will be reluctant to undermine the judgment of politicians that a 'bona fide decision is taken on genuine policy grounds',[183] and the Prime Minister had acted appropriately. As regards Article 2 ECHR, the Supreme Court concluded that an inquiry that complied with Article 2 ECHR had still not taken place and made a declaration to that effect. The de Silva review was not sufficient, as he lacked the power to compel the attendance of witnesses, or had any way of testing the evidence he was presented

→

---

[182] *Finucane v UK* (2003) 37 EHRR 29 [84].   [183] Ibid [76].

→

with. In short, it was not equivalent to a criminal trial or a public inquiry tasked with uncovering the truth.

However, the consequence of the Supreme Court's decision and whether a public inquiry will be held remains a matter for the government, who will have to consider the feasibility of an inquiry that could comply with Article 2, given the amount of time that has now passed since the murder in 1989. By November 2019, no decision had been taken by the UK Government, despite pressure from the Irish government.[184]

Terms of reference

When an inquiry is established, the government has a considerable discretion as to the terms of reference of the inquiry. This is arguably the most important consideration when establishing an inquiry as the terms of reference determine its scope. They are effectively an instruction to the inquiry panel as to what they should investigate. This raises the concern that if the government creates a public inquiry for political reasons, as an attempt to cool the political temperature, they can limit the terms of reference so that key issues cannot be considered.

This became a controversial issue with the Iraq War, which was (and remains) a hugely controversial decision. The war was justified on the basis that intelligence suggested that Iraq possessed weapons of mass destruction which posed a risk to national security. When this turned out not to be the case, many calls were made for a public inquiry to establish the facts and what lessons could be learned for the future from this failure in intelligence. The government responded by establishing two inquiries, the Hutton Inquiry and the Butler Inquiry, both of which considered specific aspects of the decision to go to war. Although the Butler Inquiry was critical of the government, the existence of these two reports was frequently used by the government to reject calls for a wider-ranging inquiry that considered the Iraq War in general. It was six years after the invasion of Iraq that the government established the Chilcot Inquiry, with a broad remit to consider the entire conduct of the Iraq War. When the inquiry concluded its report in 2016, thirteen years after the decision to go to war, nearly all the main protagonists had left office, limiting the impact of the report. The Public Administration and Constitutional Affairs Select Committee stated that the Chilcot Inquiry 'was set up in order to provide some closure to the controversy, but for many, it has failed to do so'.[185]

Another controversy is that the Chilcot Inquiry took seven years to conclude its report. Gordon Brown, the Prime Minister who established the inquiry, believed that it would take a year.[186] The inquiry took far longer than anyone expected. Sir John Chilcot, speaking after his report was published, believed that the broad terms of reference were the

---

[184] Marie O'Halloran, Dennis Staunton, and Vivienne Clarke, 'Government continues to press for Finucane murder inquiry despite UK court ruling', (*The Irish Times*, 27 February 2019), https://www .irishtimes.com/news/ireland/irish-news/government-continues-to-press-for-finucane-murder-inquiry-despite-uk-court-ruling-1.3808038.

[185] Public Administration and Constitutional Affairs Committee, *Lessons still to be learned from the Chilcot Inquiry* (HC 2016–17, 656) [2].

[186] HC Deb 15 June 2009, vol 494, col 23.

key reason for the delay.[187] The Public Administration Committee recommended that inquiries with such broad terms of reference should be split into stages, which would have allowed conclusions on some key issues to have been published far more quickly.[188]

 Discussing the problem

Take a moment to consider the scenario at start of this chapter. Whose situation would be most suitable to be investigated by the public inquiry? What could a public inquiry achieve?

Out of the three, the answer is Emeli and the other members of her group. This has become a high-profile issue and there is the potential for a major scandal to emerge out of these facts. Potentially Alain Baird, a former Secretary of State for Defence, when in office, forced the Ministry of Defence to purchase unsuitable equipment. The suspicion is that he may have done so for his own personal gain. This is particularly controversial as the equipment purchased may have contributed to the death of British soldiers. This is clearly a matter of public concern. The inquiry would seek to establish the facts and would be likely to investigate whether the guns used did, as a matter of fact, contribute to British soldiers losing their lives. The inquiry could also consider whether Alain Baird forced the Ministry of Defence to purchase the faulty equipment and his relationship with Incerta Dynamics. It may also fulfil a policy function by considering how contact between senior ministers and arms companies should be conducted in the future to avoid allegations of impropriety. However, what the inquiry would be able to investigate would very much depend on its terms of reference.

14.4.4 Membership and procedure of public inquiries

Alongside the setting of the terms of reference, the other key decision when establishing a public inquiry is to decide who should chair it. Here there are a variety of considerations. What sort of issues will the inquiry cover? Who has the necessary experience and expertise? Alongside this, there appears to be an increasing trend of judges chairing inquiries, with judges being used to chair the Harold Shipman inquiry, the Stephen Lawrence Inquiry, the Bloody Sunday Inquiry, the Leveson Inquiry, and the Hutton Inquiry.

Judges chairing inquiries has a beguiling attraction; judges have the skills and experience of deciding factual disputes based on the evidence presented. Given that inquiries are frequently fact-finding exercises, judges form an attractive pool from which to choose a potential chair. The independence of the judiciary also means that by choosing a judge to chair an inquiry, the government is making a clear indication to the public that the inquiry will be independent and impartial as between different witnesses and interest groups. It also ensures that any legal considerations will be more than amply dealt with. Leveson LJ himself considered that judges can bring benefits to the inquiry process, stating that they have:

> experience of fact finding about past events . . . [judges] are very used to listening to witnesses speak about past events and making up their mind about what happened . . . they have the ability to deal with legal and procedural complexity . . . they

---

[187] Foreign Affairs Committee, *Progress of the Iraq Inquiry* (HC 2014–15, 1027) Q1.
[188] Public Administration and Constitutional Affairs Committee, *Lessons still to be learned from the Chilcot Inquiry* (HL 656, 2016–17) [24].

are very used to running trials, running hearings, and avoiding unnecessary diversions and keeping focus . . . they are very used to analysing large amounts of data and making recommendations.[189]

The Leveson Inquiry, chaired by the Court of Appeal judge Leveson LJ, investigated the practices, conduct, and ethical standards of the press, and sat amidst ongoing police investigations into allegations of 'phone hacking', a criminal activity. Having a chair with a legal background ensured that the inquiry did not compromise these police investigations and ensured that the two issues remained separate.[190] In addition, one aim of the inquiry was to make recommendations for potential reforms to the criminal and civil law, in light of its findings.

By contrast, Lord Hutton, then a Law Lord, chaired the Hutton Inquiry. In the context of the Iraq War, this was an investigation into the circumstances surrounding the death of Dr David Kelly, a scientist working for the Ministry of Defence. Dr Kelly was revealed as the source of a BBC report that claimed the government exaggerated or (to use the key phrase of the time) 'sexed up' the arguments that Iraq had weapons of mass destruction and so were overstating the case for military action in Iraq. Lord Hutton found that the allegation made in the BBC report was unfounded. Lord Hutton's report was severely criticized by some for narrowly interpreting its terms of reference as one of fact-finding to the expense of investigating broader political issues. Lord Hutton exhibited a natural judicial tendency of not wanting to engage with the broader political issues that some felt was required. By finding so strongly in favour of the government, the Hutton Inquiry was criticized by some as a 'whitewash'. However, at the time, the findings justified the government's actions.

This raised a broader constitutional issue raised by Blom-Cooper and Munro, who doubted whether 'a Law Lord's "borrowed authority" should have been lent to such an inquiry . . . When its subject-matter is considered, the Hutton Inquiry may represent the classic instance of why we should question the public's ready acceptance of asking a senior judge to hold a public inquiry.'[191]

 Counterpoint: The separation of powers and judge-led inquiries

Iain Steele in his article 'Judging Public Inquiries'[192] argues that judges should not chair public inquiries because this contravenes the separation of powers. Steele argues that the 'three branches of government—executive, legislature and judiciary—ought to be entirely independent of each other. There should be no overlap between any two branches, in terms of either function or personnel. Furthermore, each branch of government should ensure that the other branches do not stray beyond the boundaries of their respective roles.'[193] By making policy recommendations

→

---

[189] House of Lords Select Committee on the Inquiries Act 2005, *The Inquiries Act 2005: post-legislative scrutiny* (HL 2013–14, 143) [117].

[190] Although to assist with this, the Inquiry was split into two 'modules', with the specific issue of phone hacking being reserved to the second module. This would start once all police investigations and legal proceedings had been completed. To date, this second module has yet to start.

[191] Louis Blom-Cooper and Colin Munro, 'The Hutton Inquiry' [2004] *Public Law* 472, 476.

[192] Iain Steele, 'Judging Public Inquiries' [2004] *Public Law* 738.   [193] Ibid 747.

to the government, judges are blurring the boundaries between the judicial and executive, as they are performing a policy function. When the policy area involved is the most controversial of all policy areas, namely the decision as to whether to go to war or the independence of the press from the government, expecting a judge to act as a 'firefighter' to 'douse the flames of scandal',[194] is expecting too much. If judges are frequently involved in such controversial political matters, this may have a cumulative effect of reducing public confidence in the senior judiciary.[195]

Do you agree with Steele or do the benefits of judges chairing public inquiries outweigh the potential constitutional costs?

There is also the question of judicial resources; a judge chairing a public inquiry is not available to hear cases. Almost the entirety of Lord Saville's period as a Law Lord and Supreme Court Judge was spent chairing the Bloody Sunday Inquiry. For this reason, the Inquiries Act 2005 requires that before a judge can be appointed, the Lord Chief Justice, as Head of the Judiciary must first be consulted.[196] This process allows for the Lord Chief Justice to intervene when a proposed appointment would be wrong and share his views as to whether it is appropriate to appoint a particular judge. However, as Beatson LJ stated, this section 'appears to be the only example in the statute book of a government minister being empowered to deploy a serving judge . . . it should not be for government alone to decide that a serving judge is to be used and to choose the judge who is to chair or conduct the inquiry'.[197] For this reason it has been recommended that it would be more constitutionally appropriate for section 10 to be amended so that the consent of the Lord Chief Justice is *required* rather than merely being *consulted*.

Non-judicial chairs and assessors

It is also the case that public inquiries may raise issues that involve the procedures within public sector bodies, of which judges, with their legal background, are unlikely to have any significant experience. If an inquiry is investigating failures within public bodies, a judicial chair may struggle to frame appropriate recommendations that the public body could implement because they lack experience in that field. In such cases, a non-judicial chair is perhaps most appropriate. An example of this is the Butler Report, which considered the use of intelligence material in the lead-up to the Iraq War. This inquiry raised sensitive questions of national security and the use of intelligence material within government. The inquiry had less of a legal focus, but required knowledge of the intelligence community. Consequently, the inquiry was chaired by Lord Butler, a former Cabinet alongside a former Chief of the Defence Staff,[198] a senior civil servant,[199] and two MPs who were members of the Intelligence and Security Committee.[200] All had experience of dealing with intelligence matters.

---

[194] Ibid 748.   [195] Ibid 749.

[196] Inquiries Act 2005, s 10.

[197] House of Lords Select Committee on the Inquiries Act 2005, *The Inquiries Act 2005: post-legislative scrutiny* (HL 2013–14, 143) [124].

[198] Field Marshal Lord Inge.

[199] Sir John Chilcot.

[200] Ann Taylor and Michael Mates.

This in turn is an example of the fact that inquiries are often conducted with a panel of assessors, in addition to a chairman.[201] The intention is that the inquiry can benefit from a range of expertise which is broader than that provided by the chair alone. For example, with the Leveson Inquiry, Leveson LJ was supported by a panel with expertise in the press, regulation, and the police. Using panel members gives rise to the concern that they add to the cost of an inquiry and it takes longer for the inquiry to conclude its report as it needs to be agreed between the chair and the assessors. This may mean that compromises are reached that water down the report.[202] An alternative is for expertise to be incorporated into the inquiry by inviting evidence to be submitted by experts who can openly take part in the inquiry. Consequently, it has been recommended that the default position should be for a single chair of an inquiry unless there are compelling reasons to suggest the contrary.[203]

However, it must be remembered that no matter who is appointed to chair a public inquiry, there is very little they can do to prevent controversy, for that is the very point of the inquiry. If the subject of a public inquiry was subject to broad agreement, there would be no controversy and no need for the inquiry in the first place.

 Discussing the problem

Consider the potential inquiry that Emeli's facts could give rise to. Should a judge chair this inquiry?

On the face of it, a judge could be a likely candidate. They would be able to consider the evidence reaching a conclusion as to facts. The scandal would have the potential to be seriously embarrassing for the government and the appointment of a judge would indicate that they would be taking it seriously. This potential inquiry would have to be careful to avoid determining any criminal or civil liability of Alain Baird. The judge could be assisted by experts, particularly when reaching conclusions as to the future relationships between senior ministers and the arms industry. A factor against a judicial involvement is the political controversy that the inquiry is likely to give rise to.

14.4.5 Procedure

In general, it is up to the inquiry chair to decide the procedure that the inquiry is to follow.[204] Such flexibility is necessary given the different circumstances behind each public inquiry. However, there are some common concerns that can be addressed.

Public or private?

The first issue is whether the inquiry should hear evidence in private or public. If the inquiry is created under the royal prerogative then it can sit entirely in private. With inquiries established under the Inquiries Act 2005, the situation is more complex. The

---

[201] Inquiries Act 2005, s 11.
[202] House of Lords Select Committee on the Inquiries Act 2005, *The Inquiries Act 2005: post-legislative scrutiny* (HL 2013–14, 143) [135].
[203] Ibid [136].   [204] Inquiries Act 2005, s 17.

presumption is that evidence should be heard in public, with the chair being required to 'take such steps as he considers reasonable' to ensure that members of the public and the media can attend the inquiry or 'to see and hear a simultaneous transmission' of proceedings.[205] A simultaneous transmission does not necessarily mean that the inquiry will be televised by broadcasters. While this was the case with the Leveson Inquiry, the Hutton Inquiry allowed some limited public access to the hearing room itself, but also a live link to another room with a greater capacity. This presumption of public access surely makes sense if the aim of an inquiry is to restore public confidence and avoid any suspicions of a cover-up, as all the evidence is available to the public.

An inquiry may restrict public access if it would enable the inquiry to fulfil its terms of reference or is necessary in the public interest. A restriction can be imposed after balancing several considerations. At all times the impact any restriction will have on the 'allaying of public concern'[206] must be considered against the factors in favour of restricting access. These factors include a risk of death or injury, damage to national security or the economic interests of the UK, or damage caused by the release of commercially sensitive information. In addition, the benefits that a restriction will have for the speed and cost of the inquiry are also relevant.[207]

Inquiries held in public are meant to ensure that the relevant information comes to light and it is more visible to the public that action is being taken. The process can also serve an educative function for the public and interested parties such as politicians and the media. With the evidence released in the public domain, they can make their own conclusions as to the evidence. These factors were significant in the following case.

Case in depth: *R v Secretary of Health, ex p Wagstaff* **[2001] 1 WLR 292**

The Harold Shipman Inquiry considered the circumstances surrounding Dr Harold Shipman, a GP who was found guilty of murdering at least fifteen of his patients. It was a matter of enormous public concern, not only for the families but also for the general public, as to how the actions of Dr Shipman went uncovered for so long. The Secretary of State for Health decided that the inquiry should be held in private. This was challenged through an application for judicial review on the grounds of irrationality by the families of the deceased who wished for the inquiry to be held in public. The judicial review was successful and the decision of the Health Secretary was found to be irrational. Holding the inquiry in public would have many positive benefits, including allowing for it to be reported in the media and the report would foster greater public confidence than if the inquiry was carried out in private. In the context of this inquiry, the need to restore the confidence of the public was particularly important, given the trust they place in the medical profession. Overall, there should be a presumption of holding an inquiry in public unless there were persuasive reasons for holding it in private. In this case, the arguments for holding an inquiry in public were compelling.

---

[205] Inquiries Act 2005, s 18(1).   [206] Ibid.   [207] Ibid.

Discussing the problem

Consider the nature of the inquiry that Emeli's facts could give rise to. Should this inquiry be held in public or private?

It is possible that the answer is both. If the inquiry was established under the Inquiries Act 2005, then there is a presumption that it would be held in public, but that some elements could be 'restricted' and held in private. It is likely that parts of the inquiry would raise questions of national security. Under section 19 of the 2005 Act these issues could be considered in private.

Holding an inquiry in public or private is likely to have an impact on witnesses. In public, witnesses who are more perhaps more distantly connected to the issues may be less likely to blame others, particularly if they feel that it may harm their careers and may find being in the spotlight distinctly uncomfortable. By contrast, the publicity may pressurize witnesses who were more deeply involved to reveal the facts as they understand them, knowing that other witnesses will be under a similar pressure.

Inquisitorial model and Maxwellization

Inquiries generally follow an inquisitorial model rather than the adversarial process usually followed in the courts. Fundamentally, most inquiries are fact-finding exercises and are not the forum by which any civil or criminal liability is determined. The general view is that the inquisitorial model:

> allows the inquiry to remain focused on its terms of reference . . . It allows the inquiry to focus on the issues that are of concern to it, to the chairman or the panel members, because an inquisitorial model has the inquisitor at its centre. Lastly, it allows often contentious and difficult issues to be examined and determined in a relatively dispassionate environment, without the extra heat that is brought to an affair when people are adversaries to each other.[208]

Questioning is often conducted not by the chair of the inquiry, but by a barrister who is appointed as Counsel to the Inquiry, asking questions on behalf of the inquiry. This means there is a separation between the chair and the questioning of witnesses. This allows for the questioning to take its natural course without giving the impression that the chair has made their mind up on certain issues. Answering questions may pose certain risks to some witnesses. If involved in a matter of great controversy, a witness's career or reputation could be at risk. In certain circumstances, it is also possible that the findings of the inquiry could later lead to a criminal or civil investigation depending on what a witness says. The concern is that, because it is not a full judicial process, there is no requirement for witnesses to be legally represented and there is no opportunity for witnesses to cross-examine the evidence. Despite this, it is expected that inquiries follow the general

---

[208] House of Lords Select Committee on the Inquiries Act 2005, *The Inquiries Act 2005: post-legislative scrutiny* (HL 2013–14, 143) [213] Jason Beer QC.

principles of fairness. For this reason, many inquiries have a process where the counsel to the inquiry meets witnesses before giving evidence. At this meeting they discuss the evidence and the sorts of questions that are likely to be asked, and gain any feedback from the witness. The extent of such a procedure would depend on the involvement of the witness in the issues of the inquiry.[209]

Finally, when it comes to writing the report, fairness indicates that those who are going to be criticized in the report should have an opportunity to address those criticisms. For inquiries created under the Inquiries Act 2005, a system of 'warning letters' applies. This is sometimes known as the 'Maxwellization Process'. The rules are detailed; however, they require that the inquiry must send anyone who is going to be explicitly criticized in the report a warning letter, which states what the criticism is, the facts that have led the inquiry to reach that conclusion, and refer to any evidence that supports those facts. This should be done in sufficient time to allow the witness to respond to the letter, which can be considered by the inquiry when finalizing their report.[210] This can take time and was seen to be a major reason why the Chilcot Inquiry took so long to report. Chilcot himself stated that this was not because any witness sought to obstruct or delay the inquiry, but the responses to the warning letters alerted the inquiry to documents and information they had not previously seen and needed to consider.[211]

14.4.6 Publication of inquiry and acceptance of recommendations

Publication of the report and its impact?

Once the report is concluded, it is sent to the minister who initiated the inquiry. Generally, reports should be published in full, but parts of some reports can be withheld if this is in the public interest.[212] The report will be laid before Parliament, the Scottish Parliament, Northern Ireland Assembly, or the Welsh Parliament as appropriate. Usually, the government will make a statement outlining its response to the inquiry. If the inquiry is particularly significant, the release of a report can be a significant political event attracting widespread media coverage. The release of the Chilcot Inquiry was particularly notable. The government made a statement to Parliament, outlining the key findings of the report. This was followed by a two-day debate in the House of Commons. Also, Tony Blair, who was Prime Minister during the period covered by the report, held a press conference giving his interpretation of Chilcot's findings. The sheer scale of some reports mean that reading them is not for the faint-hearted. For instance, the Chilcot Report contains more than 2.6 million words, split into thirteen volumes.

---

[209] Ibid [231].

[210] Inquiry Rules 2006, SI 2006/1838, rr 13–15.

[211] Public Administration and Constitutional Affairs Committee, *Lessons still to be learned from the Chilcot Inquiry* (HL 656, 2016–17) [29].

[212] Inquiries Act 2005, s 25(4) and (5). Public interest includes the following factors: the risk of death or injury to a person, potential damage to national security or the economic interests of the UK, or the damage caused by disclosing commercially sensitive information.

Impact of inquiries

After all of this, do inquiries have any impact? Inevitably, given the variety of circumstances in which inquiries are held, the precedents are mixed. By not being part of the judicial process, inquiries have no legal powers to enforce their recommendations. Generally, the implementation of an inquiry's recommendations is a matter for the government or the public agencies involved. This means that the real issue is how to scrutinize what actions the government has taken in light of the report. The scrutiny process should seek to establish which recommendations have been implemented and, if some have yet to be implemented, to discover why.

The obvious candidate to scrutinize the government is the inquiry itself. However, if a judge has been used to chair the inquiry, this risks involving them in the political process and potentially party political controversy. This would be highly inappropriate and would compromise the independence of the judiciary. Leveson LJ expressed this view, stating:

> I am a serving judge. It would be absolutely inappropriate for me to come back into the question of my report or regulation of the press. I was given a job to do. It was to examine the facts and to make recommendations. I examined the facts. I set them out in what might be described as extremely tedious detail. I reached a series of conclusions, which was my very best shot. I have said all I can say on the topic.[213]

There are problems even with non-judicial chairs. The Inquiries Act 2005 makes clear that once an inquiry has completed its report and has fulfilled its terms of reference then the inquiry comes to an end.[214] This makes it difficult for the inquiry to play any formal role once it has concluded its report. For this reason, the House of Lords has concluded that post inquiry scrutiny is not the responsibility of the inquiry chairman.[215]

Yet, the issue remains, and there are instances of recommendations not being implemented, when the recommendation has been vindicated by later events. For example, a report into the King's Cross fire in 1987 made recommendations to improve communications between the emergency services. This had still not been implemented by time of the 7/7 London bombings in 2005, when the lack of a common communication network between the emergency services compromised the effectiveness of their initial response to the attack.[216] Similarly, some have stated that if the recommendations of an earlier report into Bristol Royal Infirmary had been implemented, then the failings of care at Mid-Staffordshire Hospital may not have occurred.

Arguably, the most likely vehicle to scrutinize whether the government has implemented the recommendations of an inquiry are select committees in Parliament. This seems appropriate as ultimately whether to implement or reject a recommendation is a political decision for which ministers are accountable to Parliament. Select committees are one of the key ways in which Parliament holds the government to account and

---

[213] House of Lords Select Committee on the Inquiries Act 2005, *The Inquiries Act 2005: post-legislative scrutiny* (HL 2013–14, 143) [269].

[214] Inquiries Act 2005, s 14.

[215] House of Lords Select Committee on the Inquiries Act 2005, *The Inquiries Act 2005: post-legislative scrutiny* (HL 2013–14, 143) [278].

[216] Ibid [280].

following up on an inquiry is similar to the work select committees already undertake. Through its reports and its members asking parliamentary questions, select committees are also able to inform the rest of Parliament as to how the recommendations have been implemented. Some committees already undertake this work; for example, ten years after the Stephen Lawrence inquiry, the Home Affairs Committee investigated how well the Metropolitan Police had implemented the recommendations over those ten years.[217]

The final issue is to consider how successful inquiries have been. Some have led to legislation being passed: for example the inquiry into Alder Hay Hospital led to the Human Tissue Act 2004 being enacted. The Francis Report into Mid-Staffordshire Hospital has been strongly supported by the government, although, as many of its recommendations were made with the aim of changing the culture within the NHS, this is difficult to measure. The Francis Report suggested that the Health Committee should regularly review how its recommendations have been implemented. The Committee has indicated that it is willing to take on this role.[218]

14.4.7 Conclusions

Public inquiries have become an increasingly important way in which the government is held to account. No two inquiries are alike, as each considers a particular set of issues. While they are mostly fact-finding, they serve a range of different functions, from taking the political heat out of a situation, to investigating where the law or policy has failed in a particular situation. Although the Inquiries Act 2005 establishes a generic framework for inquiries, it is still the case that inquiries are being created under the royal prerogative. The concern is that Parliament plays little role in the creation of an inquiry or establishing its terms of reference. Judges have frequently been used to chair inquiries, although their use is constitutionally controversial. A significant issue is the implementation of an inquiry's recommendations; there is no legal requirement for the government to follow them and there is no systemic way to scrutinize the government's response. The most appropriate way is for select committees within Parliament to hold the government to account for their response through asking questions and holding its own investigations into the government's response.

14.5 Summary

Tribunals, ombudsmen, and public inquiries each perform complimentary functions and in different ways, straddle the boundary between the fields of law and administration. Tribunals consider appeals against individual decisions through a legal process. The tribunal's process is usually less formal than the courts and has a caseload which is far beyond the capacity of the ordinary courts. They clearly provide one form of administrative justice, in that they can overturn incorrect decisions made by government departments. The concern is that the high rates of successful appeals do not appear to feed into the decision-making process of the government department. While the ombudsman can provide redress in individual situations beyond when legal wrongdoing has occurred, the ombudsman has the capability to

---

[217] Home Affairs Committee, *The Macpherson Report: Ten Years On* (HC 2007–08, 427).
[218] Health Committee, *After Francis: making a difference* (HC 2013–14, 657).

consider the broader systemic concerns in a manner that tribunals simply cannot. Ombudsmen can delve deeply into the administrative processes of government departments and make recommendations as to how internal processes can be improved. Public inquiries can also provide investigations into government departments, but at a higher, policy level where failures of law or policy are pursued. While there is no unified system of administrative justice, tribunals, ombudsmen, and inquiries form its three key elements. They each allow scrutiny of the many millions of decisions made by government each year, ranging from a mere parking offence to the deployment of the armed forces in combat overseas.

Quick test questions

Tribunals

1. Why do we have tribunals? What advantages do they have over the ordinary courts?

2. What key reforms did the Tribunals, Courts and Enforcement Act 2007 introduce? Are these reforms an improvement on the previous structures?

3. 'The courts have taken the principle of proportionate dispute resolution very seriously when considering the relationship between the courts and tribunals.'

    To what extent do you agree?

Ombudsman

1. What is the role of the Parliamentary Ombudsman?

2. What is the meaning of maladministration?

3. Explain the relationship between the Parliamentary Ombudsman and Parliament. In what way can this relationship be improved?

4. 'As the recommendations of the ombudsman are not legally binding, government departments are free to ignore any recommendation they like without any consequences.' Do you agree?

Public inquiries

1. Why are public inquiries held?

2. Lord Morris, a former Attorney-General, stated that 'when a judge enters the marketplace of public affairs outside his court and thrown coconuts, he is likely to have the coconuts thrown back at him. If one values the standing of the judiciary, the less they are used [to chair public inquiries] the better it will be'. (HL Deb 21 May 2003, vol 648 col 883). Do you agree?

3. Should inquiries be held in public or private?

Further reading

Tribunals

Michael Alder, 'Tribunal Reform: Proportionate Dispute Resolution and the Pursuit of Administrative Justice' (2006) 69(6) *Modern Law Review* 984

*Robert Carnwath, 'Tribunal Justice: New Start?' [2009] *Public Law* 49

Mark Elliott and Thomas Robert, 'Tribunal Justice and Proportionate Dispute Resolution' (2012) 71(2) *Cambridge Law Journal* 297

Robert Thomas, 'Administrative Justice, Better Decisions and Organisational Learning' [2015] *Public Law* 111

Robert Thomas and Joe Tomlinson, 'A Different Tale of Judicial Power: Administrative Review as a Problematic Response to the Judicialisation of Tribunals' [2019] *Public Law* 537

Ombudsman

*Ann Abraham, 'The Ombudsman as Part of the UK Constitution: A Contested Role' (2008) 61(3) *Parliamentary Affairs* 206

Mark Elliott, 'The Government versus the Ombudsman: What Role for the Judicial Review?' (2010) 69(1) *Cambridge Law Journal* 1

Michael Everett and Sarah Piddy, 'Draft Public Service Ombudsman Bill' (House of Commons Library, CBP 07864, 5 December 2016), available at https://researchbriefings.parliament.uk/ResearchBriefing/Summary/CBP-7864

Robert Gordon, *Better to Serve the Public: Proposals to restructure reform, renew and reinvigorate public services ombudsman*, available at https://assets.publishing.service.gov.uk/government/uploads/system/uploads/attachment_data/file/416656/Robert_Gordon_Review.pdf

Richard Kirkham, 'Challenging the Authority of the Ombudsman: The Parliamentary Ombudsman's Special Report on Wartime Detainees' (2006) 69(5) *Modern Law Review* 792

*Richard Kirkham, Brian Thompson, and Trevor Buck, 'When Putting Things Right Goes Wrong: Enforcing the Recommendations of the Ombudsman' [2008] *Public Law* 510

Public inquiries

Jason Beer, *Public Inquiries* (OUP 2011)

*House of Lords Select Committee on the Inquiries Act 2005, *The Inquiries Act 2005: post legislative scrutiny* (HL 2013–14, 143), available at https://publications.parliament.uk/pa/ld201314/ldselect/ldinquiries/143/143.pdf

Lord Howe, 'The Management of Public Inquiries' (1999) 70(3) *Political Quarterly* 294

Emma Ireton, 'The Ministerial Power to Set up a Public Inquiry: Issues of Transparency and Accountability' (2016) 67(2) *Northern Ireland Legal Quarterly* 209

Emma Ireton, 'How Public is a Public Inquiry?' [2018] *Public Law* 277

Iain Steele, 'Judging Public Inquiries' [2004] *Public Law* 738

*Lord Thomas of Cwmgiedd, 'The Future of Public Inquiries' [2015] *Public Law* 225

Visit this book's **online resources** for additional materials relating to this chapter, including a full analysis of the start-of-chapter problem scenario.
www.oup.com/he/stanton-prescott2e

15

The European Convention on Human Rights and the Human Rights Act 1998

Problem scenario

Martha Pugwood, a (fictitious) Member of Parliament and Secretary of State for Justice, seeks to introduce into the House of Commons a Bill to enact more stringent restrictions on the lives enjoyed by prisoners in the UK—entitled the Prisoners Reform Bill 2023. It comes following criticism from the public, various interest groups, and MPs in Parliament, who all argue that the quality of life in prisons is so good that the experience is less and less about the punishment of offenders. To this end, the Bill includes the following features:

- Section 1: prison wardens have the power to open and inspect ALL incoming and outgoing prisoner correspondence.

- Section 2: where a prisoner is serving a sentence of five years or more, the Secretary of State for Justice has the power to restrict the right to vote in any election. In exercising this power, the Secretary of State must take into consideration the nature of the offence of which the prisoner has been convicted, and this restriction must be reviewed every two years.

- Section 3: the Home Secretary has the power to limit the amount of time prisoners are permitted to leave their cells each day.

- Section 4: Prison Boards have the power to refuse prisoners visits from family and friends 'as they see fit'.

→

→

The prisoners find themselves in the following situations:

* The Home Secretary decides that Prisoner W should be kept locked in his cell for twenty-three hours a day.

* The Prison Board at Prisoner X's jail decide that Prisoner X should not be allowed to have visits from her friends or family for six months.

* The Secretary of State for Justice decides to restrict Prisoner Y's right to vote. He is just starting a fifteen-year sentence.

* Prison Wardens open Prisoner Z's correspondence, reading through letters to her lawyer and to her partner.

15.1 Introduction

One of the most fundamental aspects of any constitution are the provisions and measures that protect the rights and freedoms of individuals. The emphasis placed on these rights and the importance of their protection is evident from the words of Thomas Jefferson, who, in 1776, when declaring the independence of the United States of America, stated:

> We hold these truths to be self-evident, that all men are created equal, that they are endowed by their Creator with certain unalienable Rights, that among these are Life, Liberty and the pursuit of Happiness—That to secure these rights, Governments are instituted among Men, deriving their just powers from the consent of the governed—That whenever any Form of Government becomes destructive of these ends, it is the Right of the People to alter or to abolish it, and to institute new Government, laying its foundation on such principles and organizing its powers in such form, as to them shall seem most likely to effect their Safety and Happiness.[1]

This declaration places the protection of individual rights at the foundation of modern government, emphasizing that where such systems fail to respect and uphold these rights, citizens have the power and ability to seek a new form of government. The unalienable rights of which Jefferson speaks—including 'Life, Liberty and the pursuit of Happiness'— are, by their very nature, a fundamental part of human life; they cannot be altered or eroded by governments and law-makers. The question of the inalienability of rights in the US Constitution is not a discussion for this book, though the entrenched nature of the US Bill of Rights—contained within the first ten amendments to the Constitution—exemplifies and underlines the importance of individual rights in a constitutional system.

Rights protection in the UK is markedly different to that in America, in chief because there is no entrenched Bill of Rights. Though we might fairly regard rights with importance in terms of their value to individuals, the uncodified nature of the constitution, coupled with the domestic sovereignty of Parliament, means that, at present, rights are not accorded any special or entrenched legal status. While, historically, the ordinary

[1] The Declaration of Independence, 1776.

courts protected individual rights through what is known as a civil liberties approach, nowadays, rights protection in the UK is dominated by the European Convention on Human Rights,[2] incorporated by the Human Rights Act 1998,[3] which sets out a number of positive rights that are actionable in the UK courts.

This chapter seeks to explain and explore the way in which these rights are protected in the UK Constitution. It discusses the courts' historic civil liberties approach and common law protection of rights, before then examining closely the development, incorporation, and application of the ECHR. The chapter also explores the way in which the various sections of the Human Rights Act 1998 work to ensure appropriate enforcement and protection of rights in UK law, also considering the consequent effect that the Act has on the constitution more widely. As with previous chapters, this discussion is framed around the issues drawn from the problem scenario.

The objectives of this chapter are:

- to define 'human rights' and identify the different classifications of rights;

- to explain the development underpinning the creation of the ECHR, including exploration of the institutions of the Council of Europe;

- to discuss the nature of the civil liberties approach to rights protection in the UK;

- to outline the contents of and discuss the impact of the Human Rights Act 1998, with a particular emphasis on the way in which it is invoked and treated in the courts;

- to consider, briefly, the future of Human Rights protection in the UK Constitution, including the potential introduction of a new Bill of Rights.

15.2 What are human rights?

Before this chapter can explore the nature of human rights protection in the UK Constitution, it is necessary first to address a particularly complex and theoretical question: 'what are human rights?'

This chapter opened with a quote from the US Declaration of Independence. In this, Thomas Jefferson emphasized the unalienable rights, 'life, liberty and the pursuit of happiness', and noted that man has been endowed with these rights by his Creator.[4] This means that these rights are an integral part of the natural human condition and cannot be taken away or eroded by legislative or governmental provision. Such inalienable rights might be contained within positive law, but they are by no means derived from express legal provision and are, in fact, often identified as a precondition of just government.[5] In the UK Constitution, though we might point to Magna Carta and the 1688 Bill of Rights as key constitutional documents representing limitation of sovereign power for the protection

---

[2] Hereinafter ECHR.

[3] The ECHR was not incorporated in the sense that the ECHR rights became directly enforceable or a part of UK law (ie as in the case of EU law) but rather—as this chapter will make clear—it sets up a scheme of interpretation whereby judges must always have regard for the Convention rights and public authorities are now under a legal duty to act compatibly with these rights.

[4] The Declaration of Independence, 1776.

[5] See, for example, Thomas Paine, *The Rights of Man,* 1791, and for further discussion: Martin Loughlin, *The Foundations of Public Law* (OUP 2010) ch 12.

of individual liberties and prevention of arbitrary power, both these sources reflect more 'concessions yielded by the sovereign',[6] rather than any notable claim to individual rights.

Loughlin suggests that the notion of rights is 'a recent phenomenon . . . [with] intellectual origins [that] go back quite a way. Most roads lead back to the Enlightenment . . . [and] a belief in some notion of natural rights'.[7] Specifically, it is Hobbes and Locke that are identified most prominently as developing the notion of individuals possessing rights, with both considering the idea of the social contract through which citizens place trust in a governing state, whose reciprocal duty it is to protect certain natural rights. Locke, for instance, identified some of these rights as follows:

> Man being born, as has been proved, with a title to perfect freedom and an uncontrolled enjoyment of all the rights and privilege of the law of Nature, equally with any other man, or number of men in the world, hath by nature a power not only to preserve his property—that is, his life, liberty, and estate, against the injuries and attempts of other men, but to judge of and punish the breaches of that law in others, as he is persuaded the offence deserves.[8]

In the years since the eighteenth century, others have offered their own accounts of rights theories with varying and inconclusive views concerning their derivation.[9] Some—including Locke—consider fundamental rights to have derived from God, an idea that is rooted in natural law theory. Others, notably Dworkin, see rights as rooted in a different fashion. He states:

> The institution of rights against the Government is not a gift of God, or an ancient ritual, or a national sport . . . Anyone who professes to take rights seriously . . . must accept, at the minimum, one or both of two important ideas. The first is the vague but powerful idea of human dignity. This idea, associated with Kant, but defended by philosophers of different schools, supposes that there are ways of treating a man that are inconsistent with recognizing him as a full member of the human community, and holds that such treatment is profoundly unjust.

> The second is the most familiar idea of political equality. This supposes that the weaker members of a political community are entitled to the same concern and respect of their government as the most powerful members have secured for themselves, so that if some men have freedom of decision whatever the effect on the general good, then all men must have the same freedom.[10]

Rights theories, as you can see, are diverse. They all, however, underline the importance of the protection of individual rights—regardless of where these might derive—and identify the role of government as being central to their protection. Returning to the US Declaration of Independence, for example, this provides a realization of the notion that individuals have certain rights and that it is the state's job to protect these.[11]

---

[6] Martin Loughlin, *The Idea of Public Law* (OUP 2003) 119.

[7] Ibid 114.

[8] John Locke, *Two Treatises of Government* Bk II, 1689.

[9] See Martin Loughlin, *The Idea of Public Law* (OUP 2003) ch 7 for discussion of varying theories.

[10] Ronald Dworkin, *Taking Rights Seriously* (first published 1977, Bloomsbury 1997) 239–40.

[11] See, for further discussion, Jerome J Shestack, 'The Philosophical Foundations of Human Rights' (1998) 20 *Human Rights Quarterly* 201, 204; and, generally, Scott Davidson, *Human Rights* (Open University Press 1993) ch 2; Jack Donnelly, *Universal Human Rights in Theory and Practice* (2nd edn, Cornell University Press 2002).

In terms of the human rights themselves, however, we tend to recognize different categories of rights depending on what it is we seek to protect. Some rights we might appropriately regard as being central to daily human life in a democratic society; others seek merely to enrich and improve the quality of life. With this in mind, a distinction is often drawn between political and civil rights on the one hand and social, economic, and cultural rights on the other, with varying degrees of protection offered in respect of each.[12]

✦✦ Counterpoint: Political, civil, economic, social, and cultural rights, and the UN Declaration

Political and civil rights are those that are essential for the operation of democratic society and individuals' place in that society. They include, for example, core rights such as those protecting life, due process, and fair trial, the right to vote and the protection of privacy; and certain freedoms, such as those allowing for free expression, association and assembly, and religion. By contrast, social, economic, and cultural rights cover aspects of life including the right to work and to leisure, as well as the rights to certain standards of living and well-being.

The main difference between political and civil rights, compared with economic, social, and cultural rights, is the level of protection they are regarded as requiring. Though, as we shall see, political and civil rights and freedoms invariably find themselves protected in relevant documents and declarations, they are widely regarded as being so essential to individuals' place in democratic society that they do not require positive provision but can instead be protected merely through laws preventing state institutions from violating the values they uphold. By contrast, economic, social, and cultural rights require some form of positive provision, through appropriate legal measures, before they can be said to offer protection to individuals. Despite the contrasting ways in which these different categories of rights are protected at law, there are overlaps that might be seen as exceptions to this typical trend. The right to a fair trial, for instance, while regarded as a political and civil right, also includes the right to funding for legal representation, thereby also serving as an economic right.

This distinction between political, civil, economic, social, and cultural rights is particularly evident from the example provided by the United Nations Universal Declaration on Human Rights. This came into force in 1948, shortly after and as a result of the experience of the Second World War and it represents worldwide consensus on the importance of rights and the manner in which they should be protected. The Declaration itself is an international statement of rights protection, setting out a range of rights and providing the foundation for more regionalized protections of rights—including the ECHR, discussed later in this chapter. The Articles of the Declaration, though, make provision for a wide range of rights, falling within these distinctions. Early articles, for instance, offer protection of the right to life, liberty, and security; freedoms from slavery and from torture, and the right to fair trials and hearings. Later articles, by contrast, cover economic, social, and cultural rights. Article 25 of the Declaration, for example, provides that:

1. Everyone has the right to a standard of living adequate for the health and well-being of himself and of his family, including food, clothing, housing and medical care and necessary

→

---

[12] See, for example, the preamble to the International Covenant on Civil and Political Rights, 16 December 1966 (entry into force 23 March 1976), http://www.ohchr.org/en/professionalinterest/pages/ccpr.aspx.

→

    social services, and the right to security in the event of unemployment, sickness, disability, widowhood, old age or other lack of livelihood in circumstances beyond his control.

2. Motherhood and childhood are entitled to special care and assistance. All children, whether born in or out of wedlock, shall enjoy the same social protection.

The often drawn distinction between political, civil, economic, social, and cultural rights not only provides insight into the nature of the rights against which we seek protection, but more importantly enables us to establish consensus on those rights that we hold most dear.[13] On this last point, it is noteworthy that the ECHR contains just political and civil rights, with no provision for the economic, social, and cultural freedoms contained in the UN Declaration.

Having explored both the origins and nature of the rights we seek to protect, it is necessary now to examine closely the development and provisions of the ECHR. This will enable the chapter later to discuss the manner in which rights are protected in the UK Constitution through the Human Rights Act's domestic incorporation of the ECHR.

15.3 The Council of Europe and the European Convention on Human Rights

By 1945, Europe had been at the centre of two world wars within the space of just thirty years and through both had witnessed mass devastation and widespread loss of life. As a consequence, it was felt that action needed to be taken to ensure that such abuses could never be repeated and, to this end, various international bodies were established—both in Europe and across the wider world—to guard and protect democratic values and to foster peaceful relations between different countries. One such organization was the Council of Europe, 'formed by the governments of 25 states with the broad aim of fostering democratic government within western Europe'.[14] The Council of Europe's stated aim was 'to achieve a greater unity between its members for the purpose of safeguarding and realising the ideals and principles which are their common heritage and facilitating their economic and social progress'.[15] To this end, it stated that signatory states 'must accept the principles of the rule of law and of the enjoyment by all persons within its jurisdiction of human rights and fundamental freedoms'.[16] On this foundation, the Council of Europe set out a document containing basic rights and fundamental freedoms. This was

---

[13] Identification of this distinction between political, civil, economic, social, and cultural rights, though, is contested. Both academics and policy-makers do not see such a clear and sharp divide. See, for more in-depth discussion, Matthew Craven, *The International Covenant on Economic, Social and Cultural Rights: A Perspective on its Development* (OUP Clarendon Press 1998) 7–16; and Virginia Mantouvalou, 'The Case for Social Rights' (2010) *Georgetown Public Law Research Paper No 10–18*, 2–3, http://scholarship.law.georgetown.edu/facpub/331/.

[14] Ann Lyon, *Constitutional History of the UK* (Cavendish Publishing 2003) 443.

[15] Statute of the Council of Europe, Arts 1 and 3, cited in Keith Syrett, *The Foundations of Public Law: Principles and Problems of Power in the British Constitution* (2nd edn, Palgrave Macmillan 2014) 219–20.

[16] Ibid.

the ECHR, introduced in 1951 and ratified by ten states in 1953.[17] Since the early 1950s, many more states have signed and ratified the Convention, with a total of forty-eight countries now committed to rights protection in its name.

The articles of the ECHR set out a number of rights and freedoms, for the most part inspired by the political and civil rights contained within the UN Declaration on Human Rights, and are as follows:

Article 2—Right to life

Article 3—Prohibition of torture

Article 4—Prohibition of slavery and forced labour

Article 5—Right to liberty and security

Article 6—Right to a fair trial

Article 7—No punishment without law

Article 8—Right to respect for private and family life

Article 9—Freedom of thought, conscience, and religion

Article 10—Freedom of expression

Article 11—Freedom of assembly and association

Article 12—Right to marry

Article 13—Right to an effective remedy

Article 14—Prohibition of discrimination[18]

Article 15—Derogation in time of emergency

Article 16—Restrictions on political activity of aliens

Article 17—Prohibition of abuse of rights

Article 18—Limitation on use of restrictions on rights

A number of these rights and their application in the UK Constitution are explored in greater detail in Chapter 16. One provision that is necessary to explain further here, however, is Article 15. This provides:

> In time of war or other public emergency threatening the life of the nation any High Contracting Party may take measures derogating from its obligations under this Convention to the extent strictly required by the exigencies of the situation, provided that such measures are not inconsistent with its other obligations under international law.

Whether a particular derogation is 'to the extent strictly required by the exigencies of the situation' is for a court to examine in any one case. Understanding this provision, though, is important here since in respect of the various rights and freedoms listed above,

---

[17] The European Convention on Human Rights is often confused with and thought to be a part of the network of institutions and laws that make up the European Union. It is important to note, though, that the European Union and the Council of Europe (responsible for the ECHR) are entirely separate entities, operating within different spheres and relating to entirely different institutions, Member States, and jurisdictions. Indeed, the ratification of the ECHR pre-dates the formation of what is now the European Union.

[18] Unlike the other ECHR rights, Art 14's prohibition of discrimination is not free-standing. If an action is to be brought on the basis of this right, it must be brought alongside another right.

we distinguish between three categories: absolute rights, limited rights, and qualified rights. The difference between each of these relates to the manner in which they are to be protected and valued by domestic constitutions and the extent to which states are permitted to derogate from their obligations under those articles.

Absolute rights are the most fundamental insofar as they can never be qualified. This means that there is never a situation in which they should not be protected or circumstances in which it would be permissible to derogate from them under Article 15. Absolute rights in the ECHR are limited to Article 3 (prohibition of torture), Article 4 (prohibition of slavery and forced labour), and Article 7 (no punishment without law). Qualified rights, by contrast, are those that, though protected by the ECHR, it is permissible and acceptable to interfere or derogate from the rights in order that competing rights or interests might be protected. Article 8 (right to private and family life), Article 9 (freedom of thought, conscience and religion), Article 10 (freedom of expression), and Article 11 (freedom of assembly and association) are examples of qualified rights in the ECHR. With regards to these qualified rights, it is important to distinguish between the notions of interference and derogation. Whereas derogation—as already explained—permits a High Contracting Party to take action that might ordinarily be regarded as contrary to ECHR rights, but which is necessary in time of emergency, interferences are lawful limitations or restrictions that are expressly set out in certain specific ECHR articles themselves. Article 8(2), for instance, states that '[t] here shall be no interference by a public authority with the exercise of this right [to private and family life] except such as in accordance with the law and is necessary in a democratic society in the interests of national security, public safety or the economic well-being of the country, for the prevention of disorder or crime, for the protection of health or morals, or for the protection of the rights and freedoms of others'. Similar provisions appear elsewhere, in respect of other qualified rights, set out in Articles 8 to 11 ECHR. A consequence of these stated limitations or restrictions, though, is that there are many instances in UK law where it is necessary to balance particular rights with competing concerns and interests. For example, the Article 11 right to assemble in protest and associate with union groups must be balanced alongside the need to maintain public order; while the protection of private and family life must be seen alongside the right of the press to publish under Article 10.

 Counterpoint: The importance of proportionality

One of the most important mechanisms that the European Court of Human Rights[19] employs in upholding and protecting the ECHR rights across the forty-eight Member States is ensured by the principle of proportionality. Permitting the court to assess whether or not a particular limitation or restriction imposed in respect of a right is proportionate, the test is often 'used to establish whether a limitation on Convention rights is justifiable' in a given situation.[20] This includes those interferences that are specifically noted in the ECHR itself in respect of the qualified rights contained in Articles 8 to 11. Indeed, and for example, it is recalled that Article 8(2) (similar to other

→

---

[19] Hereinafter ECtHR.
[20] Aileen Kavanagh, *Constitutional Review under the UK Human Rights Act* (Cambridge University Press 2009) 234.

→

qualified rights) states that '[t]here shall be no interference by a public authority with the exercise of this right except such as in accordance with the law and is necessary in a democratic society'. In determining whether a particular interference is 'necessary in a democratic society', the ECtHR must consider whether a given limitation is proportionate to the action being pursued. Explaining this, in the case of *Sunday Times v UK*,[21] the Strasbourg Court took the phrase 'necessary in a democratic society' as requiring enquiry as to 'whether [the limitation] was proportionate to the legitimate aim being pursued'.[22] In this way, proportionality permits the ECtHR to adopt a case-by-case approach to the assessment of whether particular limitations on ECHR rights can be seen as justifiable or legitimate.

In between these categories of absolute and qualified rights lies a third distinction: limited rights. Limited rights are those that can be restricted or qualified, but only in certain lawful circumstances set out in the ECHR provision itself. The Article 5(1) right to liberty and security, for instance, is an example of a limited right. This states that:

1. Everyone has the right to liberty and security of person. No one shall be deprived of his liberty save in the following cases and in accordance with a procedure prescribed by law:

   (a) the lawful detention of a person after conviction by a competent court;

   (b) the lawful arrest or detention of a person for noncompliance with the lawful order of a court or in order to secure the fulfilment of any obligation prescribed by law;

   (c) the lawful arrest or detention of a person effected for the purpose of bringing him before the competent legal authority on reasonable suspicion of having committed an offence or when it is reasonably considered necessary to prevent his committing an offence or fleeing after having done so;

   (d) the detention of a minor by lawful order for the purpose of educational supervision or his lawful detention for the purpose of bringing him before the competent legal authority;

   (e) the lawful detention of persons for the prevention of the spreading of infectious diseases, of persons of unsound mind, alcoholics or drug addicts or vagrants;

   (f) the lawful arrest or detention of a person to prevent his effecting an unauthorised entry into the country or of a person against whom action is being taken with a view to deportation or extradition.

In this example, the article clearly sets out that the only instances where the Article 5 right can be violated are where such a sentence or order has been imposed by a court of law, if an individual is being detained pending legal proceedings or is attempting to

---

[21] (1979–80) 2 EHRR 245.

[22] Ibid [59]–[62], also see Aileen Kavanagh, *Constitutional Review under the UK Human Rights Act* (Cambridge University Press 2009) 234. Also see *Handyside v UK* (1979–80) 1 EHRR 737, in which the Strasbourg Court noted that 'every "formality", "condition", "restriction", or "penalty" imposed in this sphere must be proportionate to the legitimate aim pursued' [49].

enter a country unlawfully, or for health or educational reasons. With regards to these limited rights, Article 5 exemplifies that applicable restrictions are more limited than in respect of qualified rights. Rather than setting out broader qualifications in which it is permissible to interfere with the application of a rights, these limited rights merely set out certain specific instances where the rights might lawfully be set aside. In addition to these specific instances, though, it is also possible to derogate from limited rights, as Article 15 itself explains. So, there are two ways to reduce the application of limited rights in any given individual case.

Since the original ECHR rights were set out and ratified, various additions have been introduced to the document in the form of Protocols, the most recent of these (Protocol 14) coming into force in 2010.[23] With each protocol, a number of further rights and freedoms have been added to the text of the ECHR, some taking the Convention beyond its initial scope of purely political and civil rights. There have been a number of protocols introduced over the course of the past sixty years. Some notable examples are listed below:

Protocol 1 (1954)

Article 1: Protection of Property

Article 2: Right to education

Article 3: Right to free elections

Protocol 4 (1968)

Article 2: Freedom of movement

Article 3: Prohibition of expulsion of nationals

Protocol 7 (1988)

Article 3: Compensation for wrongful conviction

Article 4: Right not to be tried or punished twice

Protocol 12 (2005)

Article 1: General prohibition of discrimination

Protocol 13 (2003)

Article 1: Abolition of the death penalty[24]

Some of these protocols do not contain substantive rights as such but merely introduce procedural amendments to the processes and machinery of the ECHR. Protocol 15, for example, makes an addition to the ECHR's preamble by including reference to the principle of subsidiarity[25] and the doctrine of the margin of appreciation,[26] while Protocol 16 introduces a procedure whereby the highest domestic courts in Member States can request advisory opinions from the European Court of Human Rights regarding interpretation of the ECHR rights.[27] In addition, and like the ECHR articles themselves, it is possible for states to ratify certain selected protocols for application in their domestic law. With regards to the UK, for instance, the only Protocols actually 'conferring additional rights

---

[23] Protocols 15 and 16 have not yet come into force.

[24] Though Protocol 6 also prohibits the death penalty, it states—in Art 2—that it can be lawfully permitted during time of war. Protocol 13 introduces a blanket prohibition for the death penalty.

[25] See 5.3.3 for discussion of the principle of subsidiarity.

[26] Explored later in this section.

[27] See Protocols 15 and 16 to the ECHR.

that the UK has ratified are Protocol 1 and Protocols 6 and 13.[28] Nonetheless, the protocols have a very important role to play alongside the Convention, adding further rights to the ECHR's provisions and amending the various procedures within which the Council of Europe's institutions operate. It is to these institutions that we now turn to explore.

„ Discussing the problem

Have a look at the Prisoners Reform Act 2023 in the problem scenario. Which ECHR articles and protocols, if any, are relevant to the sections of the 2023 Act?

The scenario potentially engages a number of ECHR rights with regards to the ways in which the prisoners will be affected by the new legislation. We look at each prisoner in turn.

Prisoner W

One of the primary objectives of imprisonment is to limit an individual's freedom and liberty, as a means of punishment and to provide opportunity for rehabilitation. Indeed, Article 5(1)(a) makes clear that, while '[e]veryone has the right to liberty', of which they 'shall [not] be deprived', a lawful exception to this is detention, following conviction for an offence. This said, it could be argued that a further limitation of an individual's liberty, such as to require Prisoner W to remain in his cell for twenty-three hours a day, engages the Article 5 right to liberty. Indeed, depending on the conditions and size of Prisoner W's cell, as well as the number of prisoners therein detained, it is likely that Article 3 would also be engaged, as a string of cases serves to exemplify.[29]

Prisoner X

Preventing Prisoner X from having visits from friends or family for a period of six months potentially engages Article 8. While prisoners should expect limitations of their rights while serving time in prison, keeping in mind that any infringements of ECHR rights must be proportionate, depriving Prisoner X from seeing her friends or family for such a long period of time would engage the right to a private and family life.

Prisoner Y

This aspect of the scenario concerns the right to vote. The right to vote is protected through Article 3 of the First Protocol to the ECHR. This states that '[t]he High Contracting Parties undertaking to hold free elections at reasonable intervals by secret ballot, under conditions which will ensure the free expression of the opinion of the people in the choice of the legislature'. This is the provision that is relevant to section 2 of the 2023 Act. We return to the issue of Prisoner Y's ban from voting in 15.5.3.

---

[28] Alice Donald, Jane Gordon, and Philip Leach, 'The UK and the European Court of Human Rights' (*Equality and Human Rights Commission Research Report 83*, 2012), https://www.equalityhumanrights.com/sites/default/files/83._european_court_of_human_rights.pdf. The Equality and Human Rights Commission here explains that the UK has not ratified Protocols 4, 7, or 12.

[29] European Court of Human Rights, 'Detention Conditions and Treatment of Prisoners' (2017), http://www.echr.coe.int/Documents/FS_Detention_conditions_ENG.pdf.

→

Prisoner Z

The Prison Warden's opening of Prisoner Z's correspondence is reminiscent of the case of *R (Daly) v Secretary of State for the Home Department*,[30] discussed in 12.4 and where judicial review proceedings were brought in respect of a prison's searching of prison cells, including confidential legal correspondence. The House of Lords held in that case that the Article 8 right to a private family life, which includes respect for correspondence, was unreasonably infringed. Similarly, in this instance the 2023 Act potentially engages the same right insofar as it potentially denies Prisoner Z any respect for her correspondence.

15.3.1 The European Court of Human Rights, the Plenary Court, and the Committee of Ministers

Having considered the various provisions and contents of the ECHR and the manner in which it came into being as part of the Council of Europe's commitment to ensuring 'the enjoyment by all persons within its jurisdiction of human rights and fundamental freedoms',[31] it is necessary now to look at some of the institutions tasked with enforcing and upholding the ECHR rights in practice.

There were, initially, three main institutions: the ECtHR, the Committee of Ministers, and the European Commission of Human Rights. While the first two of these survive, albeit in slightly changed form, the European Commission of Human Rights was abolished in the late 1990s pursuant to the amendments brought in by Protocol 11 to the ECHR. Its functions—chiefly concerned with assessing the admissibility of applications to the Court—were assumed by the court itself.

European Court of Human Rights

It is the ECtHR that we explore first. At a domestic level, Council of Europe Member States have their own individual institutions and facilities through which to enforce and uphold Convention rights. At Council level, however, the ECtHR serves as an international court, ruling on 'individual or State applications alleging violations of the civil and political rights'.[32] Set up in 1959 and located in Strasbourg, the ECtHR has operated as a full time, permanent court since 1998 and the amendments brought in by Protocol 11 to the ECHR.[33]

The provisions of the ECHR make comprehensive provision for the operation and composition of the ECtHR,[34] including the requirements for judicial office and the process

---

[30] [2001] UKHL 26.

[31] Statute of the Council of Europe, Arts 1 and 3, cited in Keith Syrett, *The Foundations of Public Law: Principles and Problems of Power in the British Constitution* (2nd edn, Palgrave Macmillan 2014) 219–20.

[32] Council of Europe and the European Court of Human Rights, 'The Court in brief', http://www.echr.coe.int/Documents/Court_in_brief_ENG.pdf.

[33] The introduction of a permanent court, by Protocol 11 to the ECHR, replaced the work of the Commission (now abolished) that served to determine the admissibility of applications to the ECtHR. A full-time court was deemed better placed to deal with the increased workload brought by a greater number of Council of Europe members.

[34] See Arts 19–52 ECHR.

through which applications can be deemed admissible in the court itself. Pursuant to Article 20, for instance, '[t]he Court shall consist of a number of judges equal to that of the High Contracting Parties', currently forty-eight. They are elected[35] and serve terms of nine years, without opportunity for re-election and with the requirement that they retire upon reaching the age of seventy.[36] The number of judges sitting depends on the level of the court. The court is divided into two main levels: individual Chambers, each consisting of seven judges, and the Grand Chamber, which sits as a court of seventeen judges. Applications to the ECtHR are brought under Article 33 (states) or 34 (individuals) of the ECHR, but are only done so where and once all appropriate domestic remedies have been exhausted, and—where relevant where—it is less than four months since the final decision of the domestic court.[37] Finally, and before the substance of an application is examined and heard, the court must first be satisfied that it is admissible. This is considered under Article 35, which provides in paragraphs (2)–(4):

2. The Court shall not deal with any application submitted under Article 34 that

   (a) is anonymous; or

   (b) is substantially the same as a matter that has already been examined by the Court or has already been submitted to another procedure of international investigation or settlement and contains no relevant new information.

3. The Court shall declare inadmissible any individual application submitted under Article 34 if it considers that:

   (a) the application is incompatible with the provisions of the Convention or the Protocols thereto, manifestly ill founded, or an abuse of the right of individual application; or

   (b) the applicant has not suffered a significant disadvantage, unless respect for human rights as defined in the Convention and the Protocols thereto requires an examination of the application on the merits and provided that no case may be rejected on this ground which has not been duly considered by a domestic tribunal.

4. The Court shall reject any application which it considers inadmissible under this Article. It may do so at any stage of the proceedings.

Once an issue has been deemed admissible, it is usually heard and decided by one of the seven-judge chambers. Where a question of Convention interpretation or understanding is raised in the proceedings, however, or one of the parties wishes to request an appeal of the decision (within the stipulated three-month period),[38] the case can then be referred to the full Grand Chamber. Hearings of both the Chambers and the Grand Chamber take place in public, 'unless the Court in exceptional circumstances decides otherwise'.[39] The finality of Grand Chamber judgments is set out in Article 44(1), with those of the individual Chambers becoming final either when a referral to the Grand Chamber is not made or is refused, or once three months have passed from the date of the judgment. European Court of Human Rights judgments are binding on the parties to a case—enforced by the Committee of Ministers—and judges must give reasons for their decisions.[40] It is worth pointing out, though, that ECtHR judgments do not generally prescribe what a Member

---

[35] Article 22 ECHR.   [36] Article 23 ECHR.
[37] Article 35(1) ECHR. Reduced to four months by Protocol 15 to the ECHR.
[38] Article 43 ECHR.   [39] Article 40(1) ECHR.   [40] Articles 45 and 46 ECHR.

State needs to do to meet the terms of its particular judgment by, for example, ordering a particular change in the law, but it is instead, consistent with the principle of subsidiarity, left to the Member State to decide how the outcomes of the judgment will be met and satisfied. Where these outcomes are not met, then an individual will be free to take a case back to Strasbourg on that basis.

Margin of appreciation

One of the inherent difficulties faced by the ECtHR, however, is caused by the fact that it is a court tasked with enforcing and implementing the ECHR rights across a wide number of countries, all with very different legal systems, political establishments, views and foundations, and very different societies. Enforcement or interpretation of a particular Convention right in one particular way might work well for certain countries and less well for others. To accommodate this, the principle of the margin of appreciation has been developed by the court to temper these differences and to afford each state a margin within which the rights can be interpreted and applied in a manner appropriate to the prevailing circumstances and broader constitutional context. In the Council of Europe's own words, the margin of appreciation:

> refers to the space for manoeuvre that the Strasbourg organs are willing to grant national authorities, in fulfilling their obligations under the [ECHR] . . . [and it] gives the flexibility needed to avoid damaging confrontations between the Court and the Member States and enables the Court to balance the sovereignty of Member States with their obligations under the Convention.[41]

In practice, this means that instead of interpreting and enforcing a given ECHR right in strict and literal terms, the ECtHR might adopt a broader, more flexible interpretation, mindful of the different constitutional, political, and governmental circumstances prevalent in the relevant Member State and impacting on their relationship with that particular right. Only where a state's activities are disproportionate to ECHR rights and values will the court step in. A commonly cited case exemplifying the court's use of this margin of appreciation is *Handyside v United Kingdom*.[42] Here, the defendant was convicted under the Obscene Publications Acts of 1959 and 1964 for publishing and distributing a book that was deemed to be obscene. He applied to the ECtHR, claiming, amongst other things, infringement of his Article 10 right to free expression. Though the court went to great lengths to explain the value and breadth of the freedom to expression in a democratic society—noting, in particular, that '[f]reedom of expression . . . is applicable not only to "information" or "ideas" that are favourably received or regarded as inoffensive . . . but also to those that offend, shock or disturb the State or any sector of the population'[43] —they ultimately found no violation of the Article 10 right. Demonstrating application of the margin of appreciation in this case, the ECtHR held that:

> it is not possible to find in the domestic law of the various Contracting States a uniform European conception of morals. The view taken by their respective laws of the requirements of morals varies from time to time and from place to place, especially in our era

---

[41] Council of Europe, *The Margin of Appreciation*, https://www.coe.int/t/dghl/cooperation/lisbonnetwork/themis/echr/paper2_en.asp.
[42] (1979–80) 1 EHRR 737.   [43] Ibid [49].

which is characterised by a rapid and far-reaching evolution of opinions on the subject. By reason of their direct and continuous contact with the vital forces of their countries, State authorities are in principle in a better position than the international judge to give an opinion on the exact content of these requirements as well as on the 'necessity' of a 're-striction' or 'penalty' intended to meet them . . . it is for the national authorities to make the initial assessment of the reality of the pressing social need implied by the notion of 'necessity' in this context.[44]

Handyside's conviction, based as that was on the 1959 and 1964 Acts, was found to be within the margin of appreciation. Understanding the particular circumstances under-pinning both the law and its enforcement, the ECtHR was satisfied that the UK had not infringed the Article 10 right. As this case demonstrates, the margin of appreciation serves a valuable purpose in regulating the application of ECHR rights in the various Member States, seeking to ensure a balance between enforcement of that right, on the one hand, and prevailing and unique domestic circumstances on the other. It is interesting to note, though, the differing trends as regards the ECtHR's adoption of a wide or narrow margin of appreciation. Generally speaking, the Strasbourg Court appears to adopt a strict or narrow margin of appreciation in a number of circumstances.[45] The court said in *Evans v UK*,[46] for instance, that '[w]here a 'particularly important facet of an individual's existence or identity is at stake, the margin allowed to the State will be restricted'.[47] This might be seen to include 'a most intimate aspect of private life', with respect to which the court said in *Dudgeon v UK*[48] that 'there must exist particularly serious reasons before interfer-ences on the part of the public authorities can be [regarded as] legitimate'.[49] For further example, where '[t]he domestic law and practice of the Contracting States reveal a fairly substantial measure of common ground . . . a more extensive European supervision cor-responds to a less discretionary power of appreciation'.[50]

By contrast, a wide margin of appreciation is often adopted where 'there [is] no con-sensus within the Member States of the Council of Europe, either as to the relative impor-tance of the interest at stake or as to the best means of protecting it'.[51] In this regard, and in the case of *Brannigan and McBride v UK*,[52] for instance, it was noted that '[i]n assessing the presence of a public emergency, each Contracting State maintains a wide . . . margin of appreciation'.[53] Equally, in *Klass v Germany*,[54] concern for national security enabled the Strasbourg Court to offer a liberal reading of Article 8. The extent to which the ECtHR's differing approach to the margin of appreciation differs across various areas highlights the flexibility that it must adopt in ensuring that the rights are appropriately protected across the various Member States.

---

[44] Ibid [48].

[45] For further discussion on all this, see: Open Society Justice Initiative, 'Margin of Appreciation' (*ECHR Reform*, April 2012), https://www.opensocietyfoundations.org/sites/default/files/echr-reform-margin-of-appreciation.pdf.

[46] (2008) 46 EHRR 34.   [47] Ibid [77].   [48] (1982) 4 EHRR 149.

[49] Ibid [52].

[50] *Sunday Times v UK* (1979–80) 2 EHRR 245 [59]. Also see Steven Greer, 'The Margin of Appreciation: Interpretation and Discretion under the European Convention on Human Rights' (*Human Rights Files No 17*, Council of Europe Publishing 2000) 29, http://www.echr.coe.int/LibraryDocs/DG2/HRFILES/DG2-EN-HRFILES-17(2000).pdf.

[51] (2008) 46 EHRR 34 [H12].   [52] (1994) 17 EHRR 539.

[53] Ibid [2] (and see [43]).   [54] (1979–80) 2 EHRR 214.

Plenary Court

Above and beyond hearing cases brought in the manner explained, there is one additional function that the ECtHR fulfils as a Plenary Court. While the Chambers and Grand Chamber together entertain and deal with applications concerning interpretation and enforcement of ECHR rights, the Plenary Court does not fulfil any formal judicial function. Composed of all the ECtHR judges, sitting as an assembly, it is tasked instead with administrative functions of the court's day-to-day business, these being listed in Article 25 of the ECHR. The functions include: the election of the President and Vice-Presidents of the court; establishment of the Chambers; adoption of the rules of the court; and election of the Registrar and Deputy Registrars.[55]

The Committee of Ministers

Alongside the ECtHR, there is just one other institution that works to enforce and implement the ECHR rights, namely the Committee of Ministers. This is the Council of Europe's political decision-making institution and is composed of the Foreign Ministers from each of the Council's Member States. Though it fulfils functions relevant to the full scope of the Council of Europe's activities, with particular regards to the ECHR, it plays an important role in enforcing the ECtHR's judgments and decisions, including by helping with questions of interpretation and dealing with Member States that refuse to abide by particular judgments.[56]

The ECtHR and the Committee of Ministers fulfil important functions, enforcing the ECHR rights in the various Member States of the Council of Europe. While the story of ECHR enforcement in each individual country is different and often dependent on the unique constitutional arrangements prevailing in that state, this chapter is concerned with human rights protection under the UK Constitution, which the rest of the chapter now explores, starting with the legal position before the ECHR was incorporated.

15.4 Human rights protection in the UK pre-1998: the common law and the road to incorporation

15.4.1 The common law protection of rights

Though British lawyers played a pivotal role in drafting the ECHR in the 1950s, it was not until the late 1990s that the rights it protects were eventually incorporated into UK domestic law with the enactment of the Human Rights Act 1998. Also, it was not until 1966 that the UK Government started permitting individuals access to the Strasbourg Court to challenge violations of their ECHR rights. Before the 1998 Act came into force, rights protection in the UK was founded on a very different culture, relying more on the role of the courts in a civil liberties tradition.

The basis of the civil liberties tradition in the UK was the courts protecting individuals from arbitrary and abusive exercises of power. We have already explored this theme, most notably in 3.3.3 and 3.5.3 through our examination of the rule of law. Indeed, two things

---

[55] Article 25 ECHR.   [56] Article 46 ECHR.

there discussed are worth highlighting again to exemplify the nature of the court's role in this tradition. First, the words of Dicey in defining the rule of law. While he identified three parts to this definition, it is the last of these that is useful here. He says:

> We may say that the constitution is pervaded by the rule of law on the ground that the general principles of the constitution . . . are . . . the result of judicial decisions determining the rights of private persons in particular cases brought before the Courts; whereas under many foreign constitutions the security . . . given to the rights of individuals results, or appears to result, from the general principles of the constitution.[57]

Dicey here effectively describes the civil liberties tradition that existed under the UK Constitution. While in some constitutions, such as the USA, the protection of rights is ensured through an entrenched constitutional document, such as the Bill of Rights, historically in the UK the protection of rights has stemmed not from the positive provisions of a legal instrument but from judges 'determining the rights of private persons in particular cases'.[58] A prime example of this at work is demonstrated by our second recollection to Chapter 3: the case of *Entick v Carrington*.[59] By way of a reminder, the facts are that King's messengers unlawfully entered Entick's property, under an illegal warrant, to search for and seize papers believed to contain seditious writings. In holding that there was no lawful authority for that warrant, the court sought to protect the rights of Entick from the arbitrary exercises of power by the executive. In this way, and in the absence of a law justifying the issuing of a warrant, the court found that Entick's rights had been violated. There are other more recent examples, too. Indeed, another case discussed in Chapter 3 is *R v Lord Chancellor, ex p Witham*,[60] which shows—even immediately before the enactment of the 1998 Act—the important role that the courts played in protected individual rights at common law. Concerning the Lord Chancellor's use of secondary legislative powers to repeal a statutory instrument relieving those on income support from payment of court fees, the court found in favour of Witham in order that his 'constitutional right of access to the court' be protected.[61] A third example of the UK courts protecting individual rights through the common law is provided by the case of *Derbyshire County Council v Times Newspapers Ltd*.[62] Here, Derbyshire County Council sought to bring an action against the Times Newspapers for defamation on the basis that two articles, published in the newspaper in September 1989, had 'question[ed] the propriety of certain investments made by the council of moneys in its superannuation fund'.[63] The case was dismissed in the House of Lords, with Lord Keith explaining that:

> It is of the highest public importance that a democratically elected governmental body, or indeed any governmental body, should be open to uninhibited public criticism. The threat of a civil action for defamation must inevitably have an inhibiting effect on freedom of speech.[64]

---

[57] AV Dicey, *Introduction to the Study of the Law of the Constitution* (JWF Allison ed, first published 1885, OUP 2013) 97–114.

[58] Ibid.   [59] (1765) 95 ER 807. See 3.2.   [60] [1998] QB 575. Also discussed in 3.4.2.

[61] Ibid 576.   [62] [1993] AC 534.

[63] Ibid 542, citing Balcombe LJ in the Court of Appeal [1992] QB 770, 802.

[64] Ibid 547.

In other words, to permit a local authority to sue a newspaper—or, indeed, anybody else—for defamation in respect of comments made about a local governmental scheme would serve to dissuade members of the press and the public from exercising a valuable right to free speech.

As these cases demonstrate, the underlying principle at the heart of the common law's protection of individual rights is, as Sir Robert Megarry explains, that 'everything is permitted except what is expressly forbidden'.[65] In other words, citizens and other entities of the state are free to do whatever they wish, so long as it is not expressly prohibited at law. In *Entick v Carrington*, there was no law prohibiting *Entick's* printing of the writings thought to be of a seditious nature; in *Witham*, there was no law expressly denying the applicant a right to free access to the court; and in *Derbyshire County Council*, there was no law forbidding *The Sunday Times* from expressing its views about the council's investments. Though challenges were in each case—and many more—brought, the courts acknowledged and upheld the importance of individual rights and liberties in the UK system through their decisions in those cases.

The notion that 'everything is permitted except what is expressly forbidden',[66] however, does work the other way as well. Indeed, the case from which Megarry's words are taken exemplifies an instance of government activity endorsed by the court on the basis that there was no express law prohibiting its taking place. The case is *Malone v Metropolitan Police Commissioner*.[67]

Case in depth: *Malone v Metropolitan Police Commissioner* [1979] Ch 344

Malone was on trial for handling stolen property. During the course of the proceedings, it transpired that Malone's phone had been tapped by the police. Though it was supported by a warrant, signed by the Secretary of State, Malone argued that the phone tapping was unlawful and he brought an action for breach of privacy and confidentiality. The court held, however, that not only could the tapping be justified under existing non-statutory powers, but also that the right to privacy and confidentiality was not recognized by the law of England. Consequently, the tapping in this case could not be deemed unlawful.

Though the Article 8 ECHR right to 'respect for private and family life' was highlighted in the case and considered by Sir Robert Megarry VC, the fact that the Convention was not at that time incorporated in UK domestic law meant that it created no legal obligations or rights that could be protected and enforced by the UK courts. Malone later appealed to the ECtHR in Strasbourg where his Article 8 right was deemed sufficient to render the tapping unlawful.[68] Insofar as the domestic court's decision is concerned, though, it highlights the uncertain nature of the common law's protection of human rights and the manner in which it is ultimately determined by the law as it stands and as enacted by Parliament. Though it was to be another nineteen years before Parliament would finally incorporate the ECHR and enact the Human Rights Act 1998, the need for positive legal rights, enforced by the Convention, was apparent as early as the late 1960s.[69]

---

[65] *Malone v Metropolitan Police Commissioner* [1979] Ch 344, 357.   [66] Ibid 357.
[67] Ibid.   [68] *Malone v UK* (1984) 7 EHRR 14.   [69] See 15.5.1.

15.4.2 The Convention rights in UK law pre-1998

Though, as the court in *Malone* rightly acknowledged, the ECHR did not create any legal obligations or rights applicable in the domestic legal system in the UK, the fact that the government had ratified the Convention in the early 1950s meant that the presence and relevance of the ECHR rights was keenly felt by both judges and politicians alike from a relatively early stage, with cases—particularly in the early 1990s—raising issues and questions relevant to Convention provisions. In the *Spycatcher* case,[70] for example, in which the government sought to stop the publication of a retired secret service employee's memoirs, the House of Lords noted that they could refer to the provisions of the ECHR in developing the common law, but that ultimately individuals were free to act in any way they choose, within the confines of the law of the land, as enacted by Parliament.

One of the most notable rejections of the ECHR in a domestic UK case pre-1998, however, was in *R v Secretary of State for the Home Department, ex p Brind*.[71] Discussed at length—for different reasons—in 12.3.1, this case concerned the Home Secretary's prohibition of the broadcasting of material associated with organizations identified under the Prevention of Terrorism (Temporary Provisions) Act 1984 and the Northern Ireland (Emergency Provisions) Act 1978. Though the House of Lords deemed such prohibition to be reasonable, in line with the principles established in the *Wednesbury* case, it is their consideration of the relevance of ECHR rights that is most pertinent to this discussion. It was made clear by their Lordships that the ECHR gave rise to no legal obligations or rights in domestic UK law and that to impose on the Secretary of State a duty to 'have proper regard to the Convention' would be to incorporate 'the Convention into English domestic law by the back door'.[72] This said, however, the House of Lords did at least acknowledge the relevance of Article 10 to the facts of the case and argued that the Home Secretary should have had regard to the right of free expression when implementing this policy.[73] Indeed, going further, the House of Lords also hinted at a presumption that Parliament would always seek to enact law in line with the ECHR rights and that, in interpreting statutes, judges should always seek to interpret legislation in line with this presumption.[74]

Later, in the case of *Derbyshire County Council v Times Newspapers Ltd*, Lady Justice Butler-Sloss, in the Court of Appeal, held the view that the ECHR should be used as an aid to interpretation. She stated that:

> where there is an ambiguity, or the law is otherwise unclear as so far undeclared by an appellate court, the English court is not only entitled but, in my judgment, obliged to consider the implications of article 10.[75]

Throughout the 1980s and 1990s the judiciary were acutely aware of the duties to which the UK Government had assented in the early 1950s and the obligations this ultimately placed on public bodies in the UK.[76] Concurrent with this judicial acceptance of the need to acknowledge or consider the ECHR, various parliamentarians were simultaneously exploring ways in which it could be incorporated into UK domestic law, as the next section explains.

---

[70] *AG v Guardian Newspapers (No 2)* [1990] 1 AC 109.   [71] [1991] 1 AC 696.
[72] Ibid 761–2.   [73] Ibid 747–8.   [74] Ibid 748.
[75] [1992] QB 770, 830.
[76] Indeed, and for example, 12.4 has already explained the extent to which human rights have impacted on the courts' use of *Wednesbury* unreasonableness.

15.5 **Human Rights Act 1998**

15.5.1 **The road to incorporation and bringing rights home**

Though it is not for this chapter to offer a thorough and detailed exploration of the various calls for and attempts at incorporation of the ECHR into UK domestic law that took place during the 1960s, 1970s, and 1980s, it is important at least to understand the frequency with which such calls were made, particularly by members of the judiciary. As Lester and Beattie explain:

> The first public call for . . . incorporation . . . was made in 1968. In 1974, Lord Scarman gave his great authority to the campaign to make the Convention directly enforceable, in his radical Hamlyn lectures. In 1976, the Home Secretary, Roy Jenkins, published a little-noticed discussion paper on the subject, and gave his personal support for incorporation. In 1977, the Northern Ireland Standing Advisory Committee on Human Rights published a report . . . recommending incorporation. In 1978, a Lords Select Committee also recommended incorporation.[77]

Despite these various calls for incorporation, it is the Conservatives' and Labour Party's own opposition to the idea of incorporation that ultimately delayed its taking place until the late 1990s, with the Labour Party under John Smith and then Tony Blair eventually placing it at the centre of their policy proposals and manifesto for the 1997 General Election.[78] Even before 1997, though, there had been attempts at introducing legislation to incorporate the ECHR rights. Lester and Beattie continue:

> In 1994, Lord Lester . . . introduced in the House of Lords the first of two Private Member's Bills to incorporate the Convention into UK law. The first Bill adopted a strong form of incorporation; it sought to give the Convention a similar status in UK law as is given to directly effective European Community law under the European Communities Act 1972, empowering the courts to disapply inconsistent existing and future Acts of Parliament, and creating effective remedies for breaches of Convention rights. The Bill had a turbulent passage through the Lords, and was mutilated by wrecking amendments supported by Conservative ministers
>
> …
>
> Lord Lester's second Bill, introduced in 1996 . . . was to be influential in shaping what became the Human Rights Act 1998.[79]

The nature of Lord Lester's first proposed Bill highlights one of the key issues that troubled those exploring incorporation of the ECHR—namely, the question of entrenchment and the manner in which any positive rights would sit with parliamentary sovereignty. On the

---

[77] Anthony Lester and Kate Beattie, 'Human Rights and the British Constitution' in Jeffrey Jowell and Dawn Oliver (eds), *The Changing Constitution* (6th edn, OUP 2007) 59, 66, citing Anthony Lester, 'Democracy and Individual Rights' (*Fabian Tract No 390*, November 1968); Lord Scarman, 'English Law—The New Dimension' in *Hamlyn Lectures, 26th Series* (Stevens and Sons 1974); Home Office, *Legislation on Human Rights with Particular Reference to the European Convention on Human Rights* (HMSO 1976); Northern Ireland Office, *The Protection of Human Rights in Northern Ireland* (Cmnd 7009, 1977); *Report of the Select Committee on a Bill of Rights* (HL 1978, 176).

[78] See Anthony Lester and Kate Beattie, 'Human Rights and the British Constitution' in Jeffrey Jowell and Dawn Oliver (eds), *The Changing Constitution* (6th edn, OUP 2007) 59, 66.

[79] Ibid 59, 66, citing Human Rights Bill debates: HL Deb, 25 January 1995, vol 560, col 144 and HL Deb, 5 February 1997, vol 568, cols 1725–30.

understanding that rights and freedoms are—as this chapter opened by highlighting—'a fundamental part of human life' and 'at the foundation of modern governments' and constitutions, the question of entrenchment was based on the concern that, if legislation purporting to protect such rights were to be introduced, is it right that it could be easily susceptible to ordinary repeal by Parliament? Equally, though, how might such legislation be protected from repeal by Parliament, all the while ensuring that its continuing sovereignty be maintained? It is a complex conundrum and one with no easy solution. As this chapter goes on later to discuss, though, the various provisions and mechanisms set out in the 1998 Act sought to strike a very careful balance, affording rights the necessary respect and protection they should enjoy, at the same time as protecting the sovereignty of Parliament. For now, however, we move to consider the White Paper that was introduced by Tony Blair's Labour Government in 1997.

One of the issues underpinning the government's eventual incorporation of the ECHR was the number of occasions on which the UK had been taken to the Strasbourg Court for alleged infringement of the Convention rights, such actions impacting both on the individuals seeking the application and the government itself. Indeed, the White Paper—entitled *Rights Brought Home: The Human Rights Bill*—itself stated that:

> the time has come to enable people to enforce their Convention rights against the State in the British courts, rather than having to incur delays and expense which are involved in taking a case to the European Human Rights Commission and Court in Strasbourg and which may altogether deter some people from pursuing their rights.[80]

15.5.2 The Act

On this basis, and on the back of the Government's White Paper, the Human Rights Bill was introduced into Parliament in November 1997. The Act then received Royal Assent on 9 November 1998 and came into force on 2 October 2000. As this section of the chapter will explore and explain in detail, since 2000 the mechanisms in the Act, designed to create legal means through which individual rights could be protected in courts of law, have inspired much debate and discussion and have generated a great deal of case law. Before the Act's important provisions are explored, however, it is necessary first to explain the broader features of the Act.

The Act itself neither creates nor contains any legal rights. It is merely an Act that facilitates the incorporation of the rights set out in the Convention to the extent that it imposes a duty on public authorities to act in accordance with the ECHR rights, also requiring the courts to interpret legislative provisions in a way that is consistent with the Convention. The rights themselves are set out in Schedule 1 to the Act, though are here merely a statement of the ECHR rights incorporated into UK law; they are here called 'Convention rights'. Looking at the list of rights set out in Schedule 1, however, it is notable that not all the ECHR rights are set out as applying in UK law. Specifically, there is no provision for Article 13 ECHR. As noted, Article 13 provides that '[e]veryone whose rights and freedoms as set forth in this Convention are violated shall have an effective remedy before a national authority notwithstanding that the violation has been committed by persons acting in an official capacity'.[81] In simple terms, this provides that individuals whose rights have been

---

[80] Home Office, *Rights Brought Home: The Human Rights Bill* (Cm 3782, 1997) para 1.18.
[81] Article 13 ECHR.

violated should have the opportunity to address an appropriate forum to seek redress for that violation. The main reason underpinning the UK's omission of this right is based on the fact that the Act essentially makes its own provision for people to seek redress for alleged violations of their rights. The other key rights are, however, protected through the Act, as are a couple of the protocols—noted in 15.3. In terms of understanding the manner in which these rights are protected at UK law, however, it is necessary to explore certain key provisions of the 1998 Act that regulate: the way in which courts interpret the rights and deal with potential incompatibilities; the powers and duties it affords government ministers; and the effect of ECtHR jurisprudence on UK law. The chapter now explores each of these issues in turn. Before it does, however, it is necessary to highlight one important feature of the Act. Noting the issue, concerning the preservation of parliamentary sovereignty, there is no legal requirement that legislation passed after the coming into force of the Human Rights Act be compatible with the ECHR rights. Parliament remains free to legislate in any way it chooses, even if this means going against the Convention rights. This being the case, though, section 19 of the Act does require a minister introducing any bill into the Houses of Parliament to make a statement either declaring that the provisions of his or her bill are compatible with the ECHR rights, or noting that they are incompatible but that the government wishes to proceed nonetheless.[82] This is a carefully and cleverly drafted provision that, while fully appreciative of Parliament's sovereign ability, sets out a political requirement that the ECHR rights be kept in mind throughout the debates and discussions on the bill. Other sections, too, help to ensure the continued sovereignty of Parliament, as the chapter now explains in exploring sections 2, 3, and 4. We start with the first of these.

 Discussing the problem

Have another look at the scenario set out at the beginning of the chapter. On the understanding that the various provisions of the Prisoners Reform Act 2023 are not entirely compatible with rights set out in the ECHR (as the last 'Discussing the problem' box has shown), what declaration, under section 19, might Martha Pugwood MP make to the House of Commons?

On the basis that provisions of the 2023 Act infringe various ECHR rights and protocols, Martha Pugwood MP would have to make a declaration in the House of Commons to the effect that the legislation is incompatible with the Convention. As the example of the Communications Act 2003 demonstrates, Parliament can decided to proceed nonetheless (as, indeed, it has done given that the 2023 Act has already been passed). This, though, highlights the purely political nature of the section 19 requirement. While it is intended to encourage MPs to consider their obligations under the ECHR and to demonstrate this through making a statement to the effect that legislation is compatible with the Convention rights, it by no means has the effect of legally binding Parliament to pass Convention-compliant laws. Parliament remains sovereign and can pass any law it so chooses, including a law that infringes upon individuals' human rights.

---

[82] Instances of Parliament proceeding on the basis of an admission that legislation goes against the ECHR are rare. The Communications Act 2003, for example, imposed certain bans on political advertising. Though it was the subject of two reports of the JCHR and was thought potentially to breach Article 10 ECHR, Parliament decided to proceed nonetheless (Richard Bellamy, 'Political Constitutionalism and the Human Rights Act' (2011) 9(1) *International Journal of Constitutional Law* 86, 100).

15.5.3 Strasbourg judgments in UK courts: section 2

Section 2 of the Human Rights Act is intended to make clear the relationship between the UK courts and the ECtHR, dealing as it does with the domestic courts' use of Strasbourg jurisprudence. It states, in section 2(1)(a), that '[a] court or tribunal determining a question which has arisen in connection with a Convention right must take into account any . . . judgment, decision, declaration or advisory opinion of the European Court of Human Rights'. This clarifies the way in which jurisprudence of the Strasbourg Court is said to impact upon the UK courts, by emphasizing that UK judges 'must take into account' judgments of the ECtHR. They are not, however—according to the Act—*bound* to follow their decisions and judgments.

While this provision might seem capable of relatively straightforward interpretation, it has generated a great deal of academic and judicial discussion, with much focusing on the precise meaning of 'take into account'. On this, for instance, Kavanagh suggests that the issue requires consideration of two questions: 'Would it suffice simply to consider the case law only then to disapply it? Or is the Strasbourg jurisprudence binding in the same way as domestic precedents of our higher courts?'[83] The issue is further complicated by the fact that, whilst the wording of section 2 would seem to lean more towards the first extreme in permitting 'a rather weak obligation . . . [and] minimal persuasive force', members of the judiciary have at times erred towards the other extreme, almost according 'the Strasbourg jurisprudence a binding status similar to that accorded by the House of Lords to its own precedents'.[84]

Section 2 of the 1998 Act poses a difficult question. It arises chiefly due to the status of the Convention in UK law, combined with the way in which the Human Rights Act 1998, in section 6, places upon the courts a duty to abide by the rights set out in the ECHR. To explain: the Convention is not of itself a binding legal force, but rather a political declaratory statement of rights, in respect of which the Member States are permitted a broad discretion in terms of application and incorporation. At the same time, however, section 6(1) of the 1998 Act provides that '[i]t is unlawful for a public authority to act in a way which is incompatible with a Convention right', adding in section 6(3)(a) that a 'public authority includes—a court or tribunal'. As a result, whilst the status of the Convention and the wording of section 2 of the 1998 Act might permit a broad margin in which Strasbourg jurisprudence can be applied or disapplied in the UK courts, the duty imposed on the courts themselves always to abide by the ECHR rights means that the permitted boundaries of interpretation are somewhat narrower. The consequent effect is a presumption in favour of following the decisions of the Strasbourg Court, evident from an examination of a string of case law that seems consistently to acknowledge that Strasbourg jurisprudence should ordinarily be applied by the domestic courts, save for those instances where certain and special circumstances justify a departure from what the ECtHR has held.[85]

The first case to consider is one previously discussed in 12.5.1—*R (Alconbury Developments Ltd) v Secretary of State for the Environment*.[86] Concerning the compatibility of the

---

[83] Aileen Kavanagh, *Constitutional Review under the UK Human Rights Act* (Cambridge University Press 2009) 144.

[84] Ibid.

[85] Where the UK Supreme Court (or, historically, the House of Lords) has departed from a Strasbourg decision, the lower domestic courts are bound by the Supreme Court/House of Lords and not by the ECtHR.

[86] [2001] UKHL 23.

Secretary of State for the Environment's planning procedures with Article 6, the House of Lords considered not only the test for proportionality but also the application of Strasbourg case law in the UK domestic courts. Of note, Lord Slynn acknowledged the possibility of a case proceeding from a domestic UK court to Strasbourg itself and the ECtHR there upholding its own previous decisions. He stated:

> In the absence of special circumstances it seems to me that the court should follow any clear and constant jurisprudence of the European Court of Human Rights. If it does not do so there is at least a possibility that the case will go to that court which is likely in the ordinary case to follow its own constant jurisprudence.[87]

This encouragement to 'follow any clear and constant' decisions has, on occasion, given the courts reason to depart from Strasbourg jurisprudence. In *R (Hicks and others) v Commissioner of Police of the Metropolis*,[88] for instance, the Court of Appeal felt 'wholly unconvinced' that there was 'clear and constant' authority for the proposition set out by the ECtHR in *Ostendorf v Germany*[89] and *Jecius v Lithuania*,[90] in relation to the scope of Article 5(1)(c), the Court of Appeal departing from the ECtHR decision on this basis.[91]

The view set out by Lord Slynn in *Alconbury Developments Ltd* was echoed shortly after by Lord Bingham in the case of *R (Anderson) v Secretary of State for the Home Department*.[92] Involving consideration of the Home Secretary's increase of a convicted murderer's prison sentence, Lord Bingham said that in the House of Lords that:

> While the duty of the House under section 2(1) of the Human Rights Act 1998 is to take into account any judgment of the European Court, whose judgments are not strictly binding, the House will not without good reason depart from the principles laid down in a carefully considered judgment of the court sitting as a Grand Chamber.[93]

This was ultimately a view which the House of Lords unanimously upheld and set out in the later case of *R (Ullah) v Special Adjudicator*,[94] one that has now become the leading authority on section 2 of the 1998 Act.

Case in depth: *R (Ullah) v Special Adjudicator* [2004] UKHL 26

This case concerned two individuals—Mr Ullah and Miss Do. Mr Ullah was a Pakistani citizen and also a member of the Ahmadhiya community, whilst Miss Do was Vietnamese and of the Roman Catholic faith. Arriving in the UK in 2001, they both sought asylum on the basis that they feared religious persecution in their native lands. The Secretary of State, however, refused both applications for asylum on the grounds that neither 'qualified for permission to remain in this country by

→

---

[87] Ibid [26]. Also see Aileen Kavanagh, *Constitutional Review under the UK Human Rights Act* (Cambridge University Press 2009) 146. For further consideration of the words 'clear and constant' in this context, see *R (Hicks and others) v Commissioner of Police of the Metropolis* [2014] EWCA Civ 3.

[88] [2014] EWCA Civ 3.   [89] (2013) 34 BHRC 738.   [90] (2000) 35 EHRR 400.

[91] The Supreme Court dismissed a further appeal ([2017] UKSC 9).

[92] [2002] 3 WLR 1800.

[93] Ibid [18]. Also see Aileen Kavanagh, *Constitutional Review under the UK Human Rights Act* (Cambridge University Press 2009) 146.

[94] [2004] UKHL 26.

⟶

reason of any article of the European Convention'.[95] Appeals, by both, to an adjudicator were also dismissed on the basis that it would not be in contravention of Mr Ullah's and Miss Do's Convention rights (specifically, Articles 3, 5, and 9) to return them to their native countries. Further appeals were made by both individuals, first to the Court of Appeal, where they were again dismissed, and eventually to the House of Lords where their Lordships held that, whilst human rights could be invoked to support arguments that the appellants should not be sent back to their native countries, on the facts, Mr Ullah and Miss Do did not have a strong enough case. Their appeals were also dismissed.

In the course of setting out their judgments, the Law Lords considered existing case law from Strasbourg, which generated discussion as to the meaning of section 2 of the Act and the extent to which such authorities should impact upon judgments in the domestic courts. On this, Lord Bingham's leading judgment set out what has since become known as 'the mirror principle'. He stated:

> [T]he House is required by section 2(1) of the Human Rights Act 1998 to take into account any relevant Strasbourg case law. While such case law is not strictly binding, it has been held that courts should, in the absence of some special circumstances, follow any clear and constant jurisprudence of the Strasbourg court . . . From this it follows that a national court subject to a duty such as that imposed by section 2 should not without strong reason dilute or weaken the effect of the Strasbourg case law. It is indeed unlawful under section 6 of the 1998 Act for a public authority, including a court, to act in a way which is incompatible with a Convention right. It is of course open to member states to provide for rights more generous than those guaranteed by the Convention, but such provision should not be the product of interpretation of the Convention by national courts, since the meaning of the Convention should be uniform throughout the states party to it. The duty of national courts is to keep pace with the Strasbourg jurisprudence as it evolves over time: no more, but certainly no less.[96]

 Pause for reflection

To what extent is the Ullah principle consistent with the wording of section 2 of the Human Rights Act? Do you think that the courts should be permitted to depart from Strasbourg jurisprudence more freely or be bound more tightly to its decisions?

Lord Bingham in *Ullah* sought to clarify the position under section 2, taking account of the precise wording, the court's duty under section 6 of the 1998 Act, and—more broadly—in view of the Convention's authority in the UK system, as an international instrument to which the UK Government has subscribed and the Parliament incorporated. Lord Bingham's mirror principle, so called because it notes the duty of the courts to adopt an approach that offers 'no more, but certainly no less' than the Strasbourg Court,[97]

---

[95] Ibid [2].

[96] Ibid [20], citing *R (Alconbury Developments Ltd) v Secretary of State for the Environment, Transport and the Regions* [2001] UKHL 23 [26].

[97] [2004] UKHL 26 [20]. Also see Lady Hale, 'What's the Point of Human Rights?' (Warwick Law Lecture, 2013), https://www.supremecourt.uk/docs/speech-131128.pdf.

remains good law today, though it has been further supplemented by more recent cases and statements. In *Smith v Ministry of Defence*,[98] for example, a case alleging negligence on the part of the Ministry of Defence, giving rise to the death of three soldiers, Lord Hope drew from Lord Bingham's judgment in *Ullah* and made clear that, whilst Strasbourg jurisprudence must be 'taken into account':

> Parliament never intended by enacting the Human Rights Act 1998 to give the courts of this country the power to give a more generous scope to the Convention rights than that which was to be found in the jurisprudence of the Strasbourg Court. To do so would have the effect of changing them from Convention rights, based on the Treaty obligation, into free-standing rights of the court's own creation.[99]

Of course, this could, on occasion, create the possibility for difficult decisions that might even go against the grain of prevailing political policy or opinion. In *R (Chester) v Secretary of State for Justice*,[100] for example, and despite the Prime Minister's clear line on the issue, the Supreme Court held that the UK's refusal to afford prisoners a right to vote was in contravention of the ECHR.[101] In reaching this decision, the Court was following the decision of the ECtHR in *Hirst v UK (No 2)*,[102] where a blanket ban on prisoners' voting rights was held to be contrary to Protocol 1, Article 3 of the ECHR.

 Discussing the problem

Mindful of the ECtHR's decision in *Hirst v UK (No 2)*, how successful do you think Prisoner Y might be in challenging the Secretary of State's decision to restrict his right to vote?

The case of *R (Chester) v Secretary of State for Justice*[103] has been considered in which the UK Supreme Court held that the UK's blanket ban on prisoner voting was found to be incompatible with Article 3 of the First Protocol to the ECHR, a decision that followed the ECtHR judgment in *Hirst v UK (No 2)*.[104] The circumstances in the problem scenario, however, are different. Under the 2023 Act, where a prisoner is serving a sentence of five years or more, the Secretary of State for Justice has the power to restrict the right to vote in any election. In exercising this power, the Secretary of State must take into consideration the nature of the offence of which the prisoner has been convicted, and this restriction must be reviewed every two years. It is on the basis of this power that Prisoner Y has had his right to vote restricted. The Secretary of State has acted within the power set out in the 2023 Act.

In *Hirst*, the ECtHR noted that Article 3 of Protocol 1 was not absolute and that there could be instances where the right to vote was limited, provided this 'did not impair the very essence of the right . . . [and provided it was] imposed in pursuit of a legitimate aim, and . . . proportionate'.[105]

→

---

[98] [2014] AC 52.   [99] Ibid [43].   [100] [2013] UKSC 63.

[101] The basis of this refusal to permit prisoners the vote is s 3(1) of the Representation of the People Act 1983 and s 8 of the European Parliamentary Elections Act 2002. Despite its finding, the court did not grant a declaration of incompatibility.

[102] (2006) 42 EHRR 41.   [103] [2013] UKSC 63.   [104] (2006) 42 EHRR 41.

[105] Ibid [H6], also see [62].

→

The Strasbourg Court also pointed out that '[w]hether or not an offender was . . . deprived of the right to vote depended entirely on whether the judge imposed a custodial sentence . . . there was no direct link between the facts of any individual case and the removal of the right to vote'.[106] By empowering the Secretary of State to restrict the right to vote, mindful of the offence of which the prisoner has been convicted, and ensuring that any restriction be reviewed every two years, however, the 2023 Act would ensure that there was a greater link between the facts of an individual case and the removal of the right to vote. The exercise of discretion would ensure that the proportionality of the restriction might be considered in each case. Section 2 of the 2023 Act could arguably be seen as compatible with ECHR rights and the Secretary of State's restriction of Prisoner Y's right to vote legitimate.

Despite this established approach under section 2 of the 1998 Act, there remains the question of those instances where the domestic courts feel moved to err from Strasbourg jurisprudence. Indeed, there are potentially any number of reasons why a UK domestic court might deem it necessary and appropriate to depart from an established decision and judgment of the ECtHR. It could, as Kavanagh observes, simply be a case of distinguishing the authority 'in light of factors specific to the UK political, legal and social context'.[107] She cites, by way of an example, the case of *R (Animal Defenders International) v Secretary of State for Culture, Media and Sport*,[108] in which the House of Lords distinguished the Strasbourg case of *Verein gegen Tierfabriken v Switzerland*,[109] thereby departing from the ECtHR's decision.[110] On other occasions, it might be because the Strasbourg authority is regarded as unsatisfactory.[111] In *Brown v Stott*,[112] for instance, a case concerning the implications under Article 6 ECHR of certain requirements under the Road Traffic Act 1988 with regards to self-incrimination, the driver in this case having driven a vehicle under the influence of alcohol. In finding against the defendant, the Privy Council considered existing Strasbourg jurisprudence, notably their decision in the case of *Saunders v UK*,[113] which the Council ultimately decided not to follow. In explaining this, Lord Steyn noted that '[w]ith due respect I have to say that the reasoning in *Saunders* is unsatisfactory and less than clear'.[114]

Another, more recent, circumstance in which the UK courts have shown an inclination to 'go . . . beyond existing Strasbourg authority' concerns instances where there has been a need for domestic law to offer a more expansive protection of rights than that ensured

---

[106] Ibid [H8], also see [77].

[107] Aileen Kavanagh, *Constitutional Review under the UK Human Rights Act* (Cambridge University Press 2009) 149.

[108] [2008] UKHL 15, cited at ibid 149.   [109] (2001) 34 EHRR 159, cited at ibid 149.

[110] Ibid 149.   [111] On this, again, see ibid 152.   [112] [2003] 1 AC 681.

[113] (1997) 23 EHRR 313. Also see Aileen Kavanagh, *Constitutional Review under the UK Human Rights Act* (Cambridge University Press 2009) 152.

[114] [2003] 1 AC 681, 711. Lord Steyn here cites John Andrews 'Hiding Behind the Veil: Financial Delinquency and the Law' (1997) 22(4) *European Law Review* 369; Morten Eriksen and Tarjei Thorkildsen, 'Self-Incrimination, the Ban on Self-incrimination after the Saunders Judgment' (1997) 5(2) *Journal of Financial Crime* 182; and Haydn Davies, 'Do Polluters have the Right not to Incriminate Themselves?' (1999) 143(38) *Solicitors Journal* 924.

under the ECHR. ~~...~~ for instance, explains in the case of *Commissioner of Police of the Metropolis* ~~...~~ *her*:[116]

> In more recent ~~...~~re from the mirror principle can be detected. . . . [I]n *Rabone v Pennine Care* ~~...~~ *Trust (INQUEST intervening)* [2012] UKSC 2 . . . it was held that there was a positive obligation to protect the life of a mentally ill young woman who had been admitted to hospital informally because of serious attempts to take her own life. This decision was reached notwithstanding the fact that there was no authority from ECtHR to that effect. In *Surrey County Council v P (Equality and Human Rights Commission intervening)* [2014] UKSC 19, . . . para 62 Lord Neuberger said that where there was no Strasbourg authority which dealt precisely with the issues before this court, this court could rely on principles expressed by ECtHR, even if only indirectly relevant, and apply them to the cases which it had to decide. And in *Moohan v Lord Advocate (Advocate General for Scotland intervening)* [2014] UKSC 67 . . . Lord Wilson suggested . . . [a]t para 105 . . . [that]:
>
> . . . where there is no directly relevant decision of the ECtHR with which it would be possible (even if appropriate) to keep pace, we can and must do more. We must determine for ourselves the existence or otherwise of an alleged Convention right . . .[117]

All this notwithstanding, though, it is still generally uncommon for the UK courts to depart from judgments of the Strasbourg Court, the judgment in *Ullah* reflecting—for now—the established approach. Having explored the manner in which the courts see themselves affected by decisions of the ECtHR, an issue that is yet more significant and that we now move to discuss is the provisions concerning judicial interpretation of primary and secondary legislation in light of the Convention, set out in sections 3 and 4 of the 1998 Act.

15.5.4 Interpreting the Convention under section 3

Section 3(1) of the Human Rights Act 1998 provides that '[s]o far as it is possible to do so, primary legislation and subordinate legislation must be read and given effect in a way which is compatible with the Convention rights'. The wording of this section is such as to impose upon the courts an interpretative duty to construe legislation compatibly with the ECHR rights. Section 4 then follows on from this and provides that, where such interpretation is not possible, the courts have the ability to make a 'declaration of incompatibility' to Parliament and the government.[118]

In imposing this duty on the courts, section 3 makes provision for the statutory interpretative measures and standards judges should employ when dealing with legislation that raises questions of compatibility with the ECHR rights. Though this is notable, in the first instance, in that the rules of statutory interpretation are usually left to the courts, not Parliament, to establish,[119] more significant is the *nature* of the interpretative duty imposed upon the courts. Ordinarily, the traditional rules of statutory interpretation—the

---

[115] *Commissioner of Police of the Metropolis v DSD and another* [2018] UKSC 11 [153]. For further discussion on this see Andrew Le Sueur, Maurice Sunkin, and Jo Eric Khushal Murkens, *Public Law* (OUP 4th edn, 2019), 686–8.

[116] [2018] UKSC 11.

[117] [2018] UKSC 11 [77]. See further: Andrew Le Sueur, Maurice Sunkin, and Jo Eric Khushal Murkens, *Public Law* (OUP 4th edn, 2019), 686–8.

[118] Section 4 of the Human Rights Act 1998.

[119] See Keith Syrett, *The Foundations of Public Law: Principles and Problems of Power in the British Constitution* (2nd edn, Palgrave Macmillan 2014) 222.

literal rule, golden rule, and mischief rule—are employed in those instances where there is an ambiguity in the law and the courts are tasked with determining an interpretation consistent with the intention of Parliament and the desire to achieve a sensible outcome. By contrast, the rules regarding statutory interpretation on the basis of section 3 are there not for those instances where Parliament's intention must be sought to clarify ambiguities in the law, but for where there is a potential incompatibility with the ECHR and a compatible interpretation is desired. Indeed, the government itself noted in the *Rights Brought Home* White Paper that this interpretative duty 'goes far beyond the present rule which enables the courts to take the Convention into account in resolving any ambiguity in a legislative provision'.[120] Explaining this further, Lord Nicholls stated in *Ghaidan v Godin-Mendoza*[121] that:

> It is now generally accepted that the application of section 3 does not depend upon the presence of ambiguity in the legislation being interpreted. Even if, construed according to the ordinary principles of interpretation, the meaning of the legislation admits of no doubt, section 3 may . . . require a court to read in words which change the meaning of the enacted legislation, so as to make it Convention-compliant.[122]

Pursuant to section 3 the courts must attempt to achieve a convention-compliant reading, even if that means altering the wording of an otherwise clear and unambiguous provision. The only boundary imposed on the power is that judges read legislative provisions 'so far as it is possible to do so . . . in a way which is compatible with the Convention rights'.[123] It is here, however, that the real issue lies. This is a particularly broad standard of interpretation, with little by way of guidance in suggesting the point at which judges should deem a convention-compliant reading impossible and a section 4 declaration of incompatibility to be suitable.[124] It is not surprising that the question of how far judges can and should go under the section 3 duty has inspired much discussion, both academic and judicial. Before this is explored, however, it is helpful to explain briefly the governmental and parliamentary rationale for this duty and, in particular, the form of words used in section 3.

Looking, again, to the *Rights Brought Home* White Paper, underpinning the drafting of section 3 was a discussion concerning whether or not the courts should be afforded the power to strike down legislation found to be incompatible with the ECHR, or whether a broad interpretative duty, coupled with the ability to make declarations of incompatibility, would suffice and be more appropriate. In exploring the possible options, the government looked to legal frameworks for human rights in Canada, Hong Kong, New Zealand, as well as the laws underpinning the domestic effect afforded to European Union law at that time. Eventually, and noting both the importance of maintaining parliamentary sovereignty and the reality that, unlike EU Law, the ECHR sets out no requirement that the rights be seen as legally binding, '[t]he Government . . . reached the conclusion that courts should not have the power to set aside primary legislation, past or future, on the ground of incompatibility with the Convention'.[125] Instead, it provided for 'a new basis for judicial

---

[120] Home Office, *Rights Brought Home: The Human Rights Bill* (Cm 3782, 1997) para 2.7.
[121] [2004] UKHL 30.   [122] Ibid [29] and [32].   [123] Section 3 of the Human Rights Act 1998.
[124] During the bill's passage through Parliament, opposition parties tabled an amendment suggesting that the test should include a question as to whether the interpretation was a reasonable one. This was rejected by the government and by Parliament, however.
[125] Home Office, *Rights Brought Home: The Human Rights Bill* (Cm 3782, 1997), para 2.13.

interpretation of all legislation',[126] which can now be seen from the wording of section 3 as enacted. Even once enacted, however, the section has also generated a great deal of further discussion, as we shall now explore. The first case to look at is *R v A (No 2)*.[127]

Case in depth: *R v A (No 2)* [2001] UKHL 25

This case concerned a prosecution for rape, the defence for which was that the defendant believed the complainant had consented to sexual intercourse. Relevant to the admissibility of evidence in rape trials is section 41 of the Youth Justice and Criminal Evidence Act 1999, which provides that the past sexual behaviour of the complainant may not be adduced or challenged during the course of the trial, without the leave of the court. The defendant in this case, however, sought to challenge this restriction, arguing that the admissibility of such evidence was crucial to the success of his defence. On this basis, he also argued that the restriction breached his Article 6 ECHR right to a fair trial. The Court of Appeal, and later, the House of Lords, accepted this argument and found in favour of the defendant. Their Lordships held that reading section 41 of the 1999 Act in light of the court's interpretative duty and, in particular, Article 6 ECHR, allowed a reading that permitted evidence of a complainant's past sexual behaviour to be adduced where to exclude such evidence would be in breach of the right to a fair trial.

Explaining the manner in which the section 3 interpretative duty assisted in establishing this reading of section 41 of the 1999 Act, Lord Steyn explained in the case that:

> The effect of [this] . . . decision . . . is that under section 41(3)(c) of the 1999 Act, construed where necessary by applying the interpretative obligation under section 3 of the Human Rights Act 1998, and due regard always being paid to the importance of seeking to protect the complainant from indignity and from humiliating questions, the test of admissibility is whether the evidence (and questioning in relation to it) is nevertheless so relevant to the issue of consent that to exclude it would endanger the fairness of the trial under article 6 of the convention. If this test is satisfied the evidence should not be excluded.[128]

The majority decision in *R v A (No 2)*, in particular Lord Steyn's judgment, has been said to represent a particularly broad approach to interpretation of the section 3 duty. In explaining this, Lord Steyn felt in the case that a wide reading was necessary to give effect to the will of Parliament and to ensure that declarations of incompatibility would be seen as a measure of last resort. On this he stated:

> In accordance with the will of Parliament as reflected in section 3 it will sometimes be necessary to adopt an interpretation which linguistically may appear strained. The techniques to be used will not only involve the reading down of express language in a statute but also the implication of provisions. A declaration of incompatibility is a measure of last resort. It must be avoided unless it is plainly impossible to do so.[129]

While Lord Steyn's judgment reflects the unanimous decision of the court, however, his approach to statutory interpretation under section 3 was open to criticism. Lord Hope,

---

[126] Ibid paras 2.13 and 2.14.   [127] [2001] UKHL 25.
[128] Ibid [46].   [129] Ibid [44].

for instance, favoured a more restrained approach, with the consequence being a potentially more liberal attitude towards the making of declarations of incompatibility. He stated that:

> I should like to add . . . that I would find it very difficult to accept that it was permissible under section 3 of the Human Rights Act 1998 to read in to section 41(3)(c) a provision to the effect that evidence or questioning which was required to ensure a fair trial under article 6 of the Convention should not be treated as inadmissible. The rule of construction which section 3 lays down is quite unlike any previous rule of statutory interpretation. There is no need to identify an ambiguity or absurdity. Compatibility with Convention rights is the sole guiding principle. That is the paramount object which the rule seeks to achieve. But the rule is only a rule of interpretation. It does not entitle the judges to act as legislators. As Lord Woolf CJ said in *Poplar Housing and Regeneration Community Association Ltd v Donogue* [2001] EWCA Civ 595, section 3 does not entitle the court to legislate; its task is still one of interpretation. The compatibility is to be achieved only so far as this is possible. Plainly this will not be possible if the legislation contains provisions which expressly contradict the meaning which the enactment would have to be given to make it compatible.[130]

The judgment in *R v A (No 2)* highlights the debate on this point, with Lord Steyn and Lord Hope adopting differing approaches regarding the scope of section 3. This case also highlights, however, the judicial division on the point at which the line should be drawn between sections 3 and 4, something that becomes further evident upon consideration of the next case, *Re S (Minors) (Care Order: Implementation of Care Plan)*.[131] Here, in the Court of Appeal, judges used section 3 of the Human Rights Act to interpret provisions of the Children Act 1989 relating to care orders particularly broadly. The effect of this was twofold. First, it sought 'to give trial judges a wider discretion to make an interim care order, rather than a final care order'.[132] Secondly, it introduced a whole new procedure, setting out the 'essential milestones of a care plan' and a starred system on the basis of which satisfaction of that plan would be based; a local authority having to step in '[i]f a starred milestone was not achieved within a reasonable time'.[133] As a result of the breadth of the Court of Appeal's interpretation under section 3, however, the decision was overturned in the House of Lords and a declaration of incompatibility was made. In setting out the leading judgment, Lord Nicholls offered the following explanation:

> In applying section 3 courts must be ever mindful of . . . [the fact that the i]nterpretation of statutes is a matter for the courts; the enactment of statutes, and the amendment of statutes, are matters for Parliament.
>
> . . .
>
> For present purposes [in the interpretation of statutes] it is sufficient to say that a meaning which departs substantially from a fundamental feature of an Act of Parliament is likely to have crossed the boundary between interpretation and amendment.
>
> . . .
>
> [In the Children Act,] Parliament entrusted to local authorities, not the courts, the responsibility for looking after children who are the subject of care orders. To my mind the new starring system would depart substantially from this principle.

---

[130] Ibid [108].   [131] [2002] UKHL 10.

[132] Ibid [17].   [133] Ibid [17].

. . .

I consider this judicial innovation passes well beyond the boundary of interpretation . . . [and] constitute[s] amendment of the Children Act, not its interpretation.

. . .

These are matters for . . . Parliament, not the courts . . . In my view, [therefore,] in the present case the Court of Appeal exceeded the bounds of its judicial jurisdiction under section
3 in introducing this new scheme.[134]

The House of Lords judgment in *Re S*, compared with that which came in *R v A (No 2)*,
demonstrates the point at which the courts deem interpretation to have become amendment; this ostensibly being the limits of the interpretative duty set out in the Human
Rights Act 1998. As broad as Lord Steyn's use of section 3 was in *R v A*, it was ultimately
a reading down of an existing statutory provision—in certain circumstances—to ensure
compatibility with ECHR rights. By contrast, the Court of Appeal's decision in *Re S* goes
further and constitutes amendment to existing legislation, their judgment effectively
adding in provisions to the Children Act 1989, hence the House of Lords rejection of
that approach. In addition, what the House of Lords' judgment in *Re S* provides is an
indication of this 'outer limit' of section 3. Lord Nicholls there makes clear that where an
interpretation results in a departure from the fundamental features of an Act, then the
section 3 duty has been exceeded and a section 4 declaration of incompatibility will be
the appropriate course of action.[135] Of course, what might constitute the fundamental
features of legislation will be down to judicial interpretation in each given case and it
may also require examination not just of the particular legislation at issue but also the
broader, systemic implications susceptible to being drawn from the consequent interpretation, a point that is evident in the case of *Bellinger v Bellinger*.[136]

Case in depth: *Bellinger v Bellinger* [2003] UKHL 21

This case concerned a transsexual individual who had been born male but who, following a period of time regarding herself as and living as a woman, had undertaken the necessary treatment
and sex-change operation involved to become female. Shortly thereafter, the individual—Mrs
Bellinger—was married to a man, Mr Bellinger. The case arose, however, because section 11(c)
of the Matrimonial Causes Act 1971 provides that a marriage is void unless the two parties are
male and female; Mrs Bellinger was seeking a declaration that the marriage described could
be regarded at law as valid. As Lord Nicholls explained, the question ultimately was whether
Mrs Bellinger could be regarded as female within the accepted meaning of the term. In giving
the leading judgment of a unanimous House of Lords, however, Lord Nicholls went on to find
that section 3 of the Human Rights Act 1998 did not permit a reading such as would allow Mrs
Bellinger to be regarded as female for the purposes of her marriage, issuing a declaration of
incompatibility in respect of section 11(c) of the 1971 Act.

The underlying reason for this decision, however, was not so much that the House felt
unable to stretch section 3 to accommodate such circumstances, but more that there

---

[134] Ibid [39]–[44].   [135] Ibid [40].   [136] [2003] UKHL 21.

would be broader precedential implications if a transsexual individual, such as Mrs Bellinger, were to be regarded as female. Explaining this point, Lord Nicholls observed that:

> the recognition of gender reassignment for the purposes of marriage is part of a wider problem which should be considered as a whole and not dealt with in a piecemeal fashion. There should be a clear, coherent policy. The decision regarding recognition of gender reassignment for the purpose of marriage cannot sensibly be made in isolation from a decision on the like problem in other areas where a distinction is drawn between people on the basis of gender. These areas include education, child care, occupational qualifications, criminal law (gender-specific offences), prison regulations, sport, the needs of decency, and birth certificates. Birth certificates, indeed, are one of the matters of most concern to transsexual people, because birth certificates are frequently required as proof of identity or age or place of birth.[137]

A comparison of the court's decision in both *Re S* and *Bellinger* demonstrates the case-by-case nature of this particular area and the different factors that can weigh on the courts' minds when considering interpretation of legislation under section 3 of the Human Rights Act 1998. Whereas in *Re S*, the House of Lords were concerned more with preserving the 'outer limits' of the interpretative duty, in *Bellinger*, the primary consideration was for the broader, fundamental features of the Matrimonial Causes Act 1971 and the systemic implications of their interpretation. The most recent case considering the interpretative duty under section 3, however, is *Ghaidan v Godin-Mendoza*.[138]

Case in depth: *Ghaidan v Godin-Mendoza* [2004] UKHL 30

A Mr Wallwyn-James lived in a London flat pursuant to a protected tenancy that he had with the landlord. Upon the death of Wallwyn-James, the defendant—Godin-Mendoza—who had been in a same-sex relationship with the tenant, living with him at the same address, was subjected to proceedings by the landlord, claiming possession of the property. Godin-Mendoza attempted to claim that he had become a statutory tenant by succession and was entitled to remain at the property, even upon the death of his partner. The Rent Act 1977 provides that where an original tenant dies, a person can claim succession of the lease, provided they were at least living with the original tenant 'as his or her wife or husband',[139] such wording presupposing the need for a heterosexual relationship. Indeed, in the case of *Fitzpatrick v Sterling Housing Association Ltd*,[140] the House of Lords confirmed that this wording could not apply to same-sex couples.

On the basis that the facts before the court, however, had taken place after the coming into force of the Human Rights Act 1998, Godin-Mendoza claimed breach of Articles 8 and 14 ECHR. The House of Lords, reading the relevant provisions of the Rent Act 1977 with section 3 of the Human Rights Act 1998 in mind, held that Godin-Mendoza must be entitled to claim succession of the tenancy, reading down the provision of the 1977 Act to include same-sex couples.

The facts and decision in *Mendoza* are, in one sense, fairly uncontentious. That a 1970s piece of legislation designed to benefit a heterosexual deceased's partner in connection

---

[137] Ibid [45].   [138] [2004] UKHL 30.
[139] Ibid [1].   [140] [1999] UKHL 42.

with the property they previously rented together should apply to homosexual couples is a reasonable development in the law and, for the most part, free from broader systemic implications that, by contrast, hindered the court's use of section 3 in *Bellinger*. The most notable aspect of the *Mendoza* judgment, however, is Lord Nicholls' consideration of the section 3 interpretative duty, which he describes as 'unusual and far-reaching'.[141] Adding flesh to this statement, he goes on to discuss the manner in which Parliament's intention 'in enacting section 3 was that, to an extent bounded only by what is "possible", a court can modify the meaning, and hence the effect, of primary and secondary legislation'.[142] Qualifying this, Lord Nicholls goes on to endorse the proviso highlighted in *Bellinger* in suggesting that 'Parliament . . . cannot have intended that in the discharge of this extended interpretative function the courts should adopt a meaning inconsistent with a fundamental feature of legislation'.[143] This would, he said, 'be to cross the constitutional boundary section 3 seeks to demarcate and preserve', emphasizing as a consequence that 'Parliament has retained the right to enact legislation in terms which are not Convention-compliant'.[144] Drawing from preceding authority, Lord Nicholls here stresses the breadth of section 3, noting that the ultimate limit to the courts' interpretative duty is that they remain within the 'fundamental features' of the Act in question.[145]

 Pause for reflection

To what extent do you think that the judgments in *R v A (No 2)*, *Re S*, *Bellinger v Bellinger*, and *Mendoza* reflect a changed relationship between the legislature, executive, and judiciary in light of section 3 of the Human Rights Act 1998? Is the court's power a potential usurpation of the legislative function or merely an opportunity to influence the governmental process underpinning the legislative process?

Section 3 of the Human Rights Act is a key provision, setting out as it does the manner in which the courts are required to interpret legislation in light of the ECHR rights. An exploration of the case law also highlights the particular approach that the courts have adopted with regards to putting section 3 into practice. Consistent with the government's intentions in introducing the broad wording of the provisions, the courts appear to have taken a relatively broad approach in their application of the interpretative duty. Lord Steyn's judgment in *R v A (No 2)*, for instance, seen alongside Lord Nicholls' judgment in *Mendoza*, demonstrates a willingness to interpret provisions broadly so as to achieve the necessary compatibility with the ECHR rights. All this notwithstanding, in view of the varying approaches taken by individual judges over the course of these recent cases—the difference between Lord Hope and Lord Steyn's judgments in *R v A*, for example—Lord Millet's dissenting observation in *Mendoza* that different judges often have different views on when the point of judicial law-making has been reached is a remark that ultimately rings true where this particular issue is concerned.

---

[141] [2004] UKHL 30 [30].   [142] Ibid [32].   [143] Ibid [33].
[144] Ibid.   [145] Ibid.

Counterpoint: Different perspectives on how the courts have used section 3

The interesting questions that the courts have had to consider with regards to section 3 of the 1998 Act have also inspired lively academic debate. Nicol, for instance, explores various cases in which the section 3 interpretative duty was discussed—including *R v A (No 2)*, *Re S*, and *Bellinger*—and suggests that whilst the first of these decisions is notable for being controversially broad, straying 'far from both the wording of the [legislative] provision and Parliament's clear intention',[146] the cases that follow exemplify a more settled approach, through which the House of Lords has restricted its use of section 3.[147]

Kavanagh, by contrast, and exploring a similar line of cases, suggests that the courts have adopted more of a case by case approach to their consideration of section 3, rather than establishing 'any fundamental change of mind' or settled approach.[148] She also argues that the approach adopted in *R v A (No 2)* is not as radical as some have argued, something she substantiates by recourse to judicial statements in *Mendoza* that seek to defend the court's line in *R v A (No 2)*.[149]

Having explored various cases throughout this section, how would you categorize the court's approach to the section 3 interpretative duty? Do you think Lord Steyn's judgment in *R v A (No 2)* was especially broad?

15.5.5 Declarations of incompatibility: sections 4 and 10

While section 3 of the Human Rights Act requires the courts—where possible—to seek an interpretation of legislation that is compatible with the Convention, section 4(2) makes provision for those instances where it is not possible, empowering the courts with the ability to make 'declarations of incompatibility'. The procedure through which incompatibilities are dealt with, following such a declaration, is set out in section 10 of the 1998 Act, which empowers a minister 'by order[to] make such amendments to the legislation as he considers necessary to remove the incompatibility'.

Section 4 is notable, though, for the manner in which it has been drafted so as to preserve the sovereignty of Parliament, something that is evident from two key features: first, the provision falls short of affording the courts the power to set aside primary legislation where they establish an incompatibility. Instead, it serves to make Parliament merely aware that a particular statute or sections of that statute are incompatible with the Convention. It is then up to Parliament to rectify the incompatibility, there being no legal obligation to do so. Secondly, section 4 also does not *require* courts to make declarations of incompatibility, but merely sets out the option to do so. In this way, the sovereign power of Parliament is protected—its enactments are not susceptible to being struck out by the courts, and the courts are not under a duty to notify them of incompatibilities in their legislation. In short, section 4 intentionally falls short of legal entrenchment on the basis that it would be against the orthodox principle of parliamentary sovereignty

---

[146] Danny Nicol, 'Statutory Interpretation and Human Rights after Anderson' (2004) *Public Law* 274, 276.
[147] Ibid 274.
[148] Aileen Kavanagh, 'Statutory Interpretation and Human Rights After Anderson: A More Contextual Approach' (2004) *Public Law* 537, 537.
[149] See Aileen Kavanagh, 'Unlocking the Human Rights Act: The "Radical" Approach to Section 3(1) Revisited' (2005) 3 *European Human Rights Law Review* 259, 260.

if Parliament had to amend legislation consistent with the ECHR rights or if the courts had the ability to strike down legislation found to be in breach of those rights. Offering a constitutional explanation of declarations of incompatibility in the case of *R (on the application of Nicklinson and another) v Ministry of Justice*,[150] Lord Kerr noted that:

> An essential element of the structure of the Human Rights Act 1998 is the call which Parliament has made on the courts to review the legislation which it passes in order to tell it whether the provisions contained in that legislation comply with ECHR. By responding to that call and sending the message to Parliament that a particular provision is incompatible with the Convention, the courts do not usurp the role of Parliament, much less offend the separation of powers. A declaration of incompatibility is merely an expression of the court's conclusion as to whether, as enacted, a particular item of legislation cannot be considered compatible with a Convention right. In other words, the courts say to Parliament, 'This particular piece of legislation is incompatible, now it is for you to decide what to do about it.' And under the scheme of the Human Rights Act it is open to Parliament to decide to do nothing.[151]

Notwithstanding the above, though, where incompatibilities are found, and are not able to be dealt with under section 3, then the courts *usually* do make a declaration under section 4. When this happens, it can be possible to appeal the decision and have it overturned, though where declarations have been upheld as final, they have invariably been addressed and rectified either through the primary legislative process or through the process set out in section 10 of the Act. As of July 2018 and since the Human Rights Act's entry into force in October 2000, thirty-nine declarations of incompatibility have been made by the UK courts.[152] Ten of these have been overturned on appeal, with the remaining twenty-nine either under consideration or subject to being remedied either by legislation or by the procedure set out in section 10 of the 1998 Act.[153] It is rare that the courts choose not to make a declaration and rare, too, that declarations are not addressed either by Parliament or by a minister acting under the section 10 power.

One of the most recent examples of a declaration of incompatibility being made is in the case of *R (Steinfeld and Keidan) v Secretary of State for International Development*.[154]

Case in depth: *R (Steinfeld and Keidan) v Secretary of State for International Development* **[2018] UKSC 32**

Since the passing of the Marriage (Same Sex couples) Act 2013, same-sex couples have had the option formally to marry or to enter into a civil partnership. Heterosexual couples can only get married; no provision being made in their regard in the Civil Partnership Act 2004. In light of this, this case concerned an action for judicial review, challenging the government's failure to widen the scope of the law relating to civil partnerships. It was argued that preventing different-sex couples from entering civil partnerships breached articles 8 and 14 of the ECHR. Though the case was dismissed in the High Court and the Court of Appeal, the Supreme Court upheld the challenge and issued a declaration of incompatibility in respect of sections 1 and 3 of the 2004 Act.

---

[150] [2014] UKSC 38.   [151] [2014] UKSC 38 [343].

[152] See Ministry of Justice, *Responding to Human Rights Judgments: Report to the Joint Committee on Human Rights on the Government's Response to Human Rights Judgments 2017–2018* (Cm 9728, 2018) 28. Also see, for a decision in which two appealed declarations were affirmed by the Supreme Court: *R (on the application of P) v Secretary of State for the Home Department and others* [2019] UKSC 3.

[153] Ibid 28.   [154] [2018] UKSC 32.

One of the arguments raised in the case concerned whether the nature of the subject matter at issue should have precluded the court from issuing a section 4 declaration. Lord Kerr explains:

> This court was encouraged to refrain from making a declaration of incompatibility because . . . the decision not to take action about extending or abolishing civil partnerships was one which fell squarely within the field of sensitive social policy which the democratically-elected legislature was pre-eminently suited to make.[155]

The court rejected this view, however, with Lord Kerr going on to give examples of the sort of matters the courts might consider relevant in deciding *not* to issue a declaration:

> [T]he court is not obliged to make a declaration of incompatibility when it finds that a particular provision is not compatible with a Convention right . . . [t]he provision clearly contemplates [therefore] that there will be circumstances in which the court considers that . . . it is not appropriate to have recourse to the section 4(2) power . . . An obvious example . . . was the case of [*Nicklinson*] . . . where what was at stake was the compatibility of section 2 of the Suicide Act 1961 (which makes encouraging or assisting a suicide a criminal offence) with article 8 of the Convention. At the time of this court's decision, Parliament was due to debate the issues arising in the appeal in the context of the Assisted Dying Bill . . . It was argued that the court should defer expressing any final view of its own regarding the compatibility of section 2 . . . until Parliament had first considered the Bill.[156]

In *Steinfeld*, though, Lord Kerr noted:

> In my view, there is no reason that this court should feel in any way reticent about the making of a declaration of incompatibility. To the contrary, I consider that we have been given the power under section 4 of HRA to do so and that, in the circumstances of this case, it would be wrong not to have recourse to that power.[157]

The *Steinfeld* case, therefore, not only provides a recent example of the courts issuing a declaration of incompatibility but, moreover, it demonstrates the courts' approach to the power and the scope of matters that the court can consider in its execution. The manner in which section 4 is interpreted and used in practice is also directly linked to the operation of section 3. Section 15.5.4 has highlighted the generally broad approach that judges take in interpreting legislation under section 3, and a consequence of this is that section 4 effectively becomes seen as 'a measure of last resort';[158] only used in those instances where the courts deem it *impossible* to find an interpretation under section 3. Indeed, this was the approach that the government expected when it first set out the planned provisions of the Act. During debates in the House of Commons, for instance, back in 1998, the Home Secretary noted that '[w]e expect that, in almost all cases, the courts will be able to interpret the legislation compatibly with the Convention' through use of section 3.[159] Similarly, during debates in the House of Lords, the Lord Chancellor suggested that 'in 99% of the cases that arise, there will be no need for judicial declaration

---

[155] [2018] UKSC 32 [54].   [156] [2018] UKSC 32 [56]–[57].   [157] [2018] UKSC 32 [61].

[158] See *R v A (No 2)* and the *Mendoza* case (see, further: Aileen Kavanagh, *Constitutional Review under the UK Human Rights Act* (Cambridge University Press 2009) 118).

[159] HC Deb, 16 February 1998, vol 306, col 778, as cited in Aileen Kavanagh, *Constitutional Review under the UK Human Rights Act* (Cambridge University Press 2009) 121.

of incompatibility'.[160] While it is notable, though, that a list annexed to the House of Lords' 2004 judgment in *Ghaidan v Godin-Mendoza* 'revealed that courts issued a declaration of incompatibility more often than they used their interpretative powers under section 3(1)',[161] members of the judiciary appear at least to agree with the government that the possibility of interpretation under section 3 should be sought and considered first, before a section 4 declaration is made. In *Wilson v First County Trust Ltd (No 2)*,[162] for example, a case in which the court was considering the compatibility of section 127(3) of the Consumer Credit Act 1974 with Article 6 ECHR and Article 1 of the First Protocol. Lord Nicholls emphasized the relationship between sections 3 and 4 in noting that:

> [I]t is only when a court is called upon to interpret legislation in accordance with section 3(1) that the court may proceed, where appropriate, to make a declaration of incompatibility. The court can make a declaration of incompatibility only where section 3 is available as an interpretative tool.[163]

With this in mind, it is notable that, since the observation in *Ghaidan v Godin-Mendoza* to the effect that declarations of incompatibility had—to that point—outnumbered interpretations under section 3, the number of declarations has significantly reduced. At the time of *Mendoza* in 2004, fifteen declarations had been made, with only another fourteen or so coming over the course of the next decade.[164] Indeed, '[d]uring the 2010–2015 Parliament . . . only three declarations of incompatibility [were] . . . made'.[165] More recent attitudes with regards to the issuing of declarations of incompatibility appear to support the broader view that they should be considered as a last resort, only where interpretation under section 3 is not possible.

 Discussing the problem

Having now explored sections 3 and 4 of the 1998 Act, have another look at the problem scenario. If Prisoner W were to bring a challenge against the Home Secretary, do you think the courts would be able to find a compatible reading of section 3 of the 2023 Act, using the interpretative duty, or should a declaration of incompatibility be issued?

The wording of section 3 (of the 2023 Act) is unquestionably broad. The result is that the Home Secretary has imposed particularly stringent restrictions on Prisoner W's freedom, contrary to Article

→

---

[160] HL Deb, 5 February 1998, vol 585, col 840, as cited in Aileen Kavanagh, *Constitutional Review under the UK Human Rights Act* (Cambridge University Press 2009) 121.

[161] Aileen Kavanagh, *Constitutional Review under the UK Human Rights Act* (Cambridge University Press 2009) 121. Kavanagh explains that: 'At that time, section 3(1) was only used in ten cases, a declaration of incompatibility was issued in fifteen cases, with five declarations reversed on appeal to the House of Lords' (121).

[162] [2003] UKHL 40.   [163] Ibid [23].

[164] Ministry of Justice, *Responding to Human Rights Judgments: Report to the Joint Committee on Human Rights on the Government's Response to Human Rights Judgments 2014–16* (Cm 9360, 2016) 48–62. Also see Merris Amos, 'Proposals for the Reform of Sections 3 and 4 of the Human Rights Act 1998' (2016) Queen Mary School of Law Legal Studies Research Paper No 238/2016, https://papers.ssrn.com/sol3/papers.cfm?abstract_id=2814973.

[165] Joint Committee on Human Rights, *Human Rights Judgments* (2014–15, HL 130, HC 1088), para 4.1.

→

5 and even potentially amounting to a breach of Article 3, as the first 'Discussing the problem' box explained. That the Home Secretary has infringed Prisoner W's ECHR rights, therefore, is fairly clear to see. But it might be argued that he was merely acting within the power set out in the 2023 Act. In protecting Prisoner W's (and others) rights, it would be incumbent upon the courts to determine whether or not section 3 could be read compatibly or whether a declaration of incompatibility should be issued under section 4. The case of *R v A (No 2)*[166] provides authority supporting use of the section 3 interpretative duty in this instance. In that case, a measure (section 41 of the Youth Justice and Criminal Evidence Act 1999) was read in such a way that permitted evidence of a complainant's past sexual behaviour to be adduced where to exclude such evidence would be in breach of the right to a fair trial. Similarly, here, section 3 of the 2023 Act could be read in such a way that permits the Home Secretary to limit the amount of time prisoners are permitted to leave their cells each day, up until the point when the infringement on Article 5—and possibly Article 3—would be so great as to render the limitation disproportionate. At that point, such action could be held unlawful.

On the basis of this reading, the Home Secretary's actions could be held to amount to an infringement of Prisoner W's ECHR rights, whilst the interpretative duty could ensure that section 3 of the 2023 Act be read compatibly with the Convention.

Sections 3 and 4 of the 1998 Act set out important provisions determining the courts' interpretation of legislation in view of the ECHR rights. Indeed, the relationship between these two sections is an important one with a great deal of case law discussing the approach that the courts take to their application and consideration. Drafted in such a way that serves to protect the sovereignty of Parliament, the sections give judges a great deal of discretion both in the task of interpreting legislation broadly and in deciding whether or not to make declarations of incompatibility, as the case law explored throughout this section demonstrates. The chapter moves on now, though, to consider sections 6 and 7.

 Counterpoint: A declaration of incompatibility may lead to no effective remedy

One final consideration in respect of section 4 relates to the concerns that it does not provide an effective remedy for those party to cases in which the declarations are made. During the course of court proceedings and when faced with an incompatibility that is not capable of being interpreted under section 3, the courts have the option to make a declaration of incompatibility under section 4. From that moment, however, the present case might continue and apply the given law with the incompatibility still in place; the courts have no power or ability to set aside the law themselves. The argument is often made that declarations of incompatibility fail to provide an effective remedy since they do not benefit those challenging violations of human rights in cases where the law is itself incompatible with the ECHR and in need of amendment. Indeed, this is sometimes a justification for 'strong judicial incentive to adopt a section 3(1) interpretation in situations where either a section 4 declaration of incompatibility would be unable to provide a remedy for the individual litigant'.[167]

---

[166] [2001] UKHL 25.

[167] Aileen Kavanagh, *Constitutional Review under the UK Human Rights Act* (Cambridge University Press 2009) 119.

15.5.6 **HRA and public bodies: sections 6 and 7**

Sections 2, 3, and 4 of the 1998 Act, which have dominated the discussion to this point, are chiefly concerned with the way in which the courts deal both with potential incompatibilities, arising under domestic law and the jurisprudence of the ECtHR as it applies in the UK. By contrast, sections 6 and 7 set out and clarify the procedure and basis on which applications can be brought before the courts, challenging alleged breaches of the ECHR rights. We deal with each of these sections in turn. Section 6(1) states that '[i]t is unlawful for a public authority to act in a way which is incompatible with a Convention right'. Section 6(3) then adds that a '"public authority" includes—(a) a court or tribunal, and (b) any person certain of whose functions are functions of a public nature, but [it] does not include either House of Parliament or a person exercising functions in connection with proceedings in Parliament'.

This is, in short, a duty on public authorities to act in a way that is compatible with the ECHR. Section 7 follows this and sets out the legal proceedings through which cases can be brought where a public authority has acted in breach of this duty. In setting out the duty on public authorities always to act in a way compatible with the ECHR, section 6 defines what is here meant by a 'public authority'. On this point there are two matters to consider. First, the vague wording and the consequent ability of the court to interpret this in broad terms and, secondly, the express inclusion of courts as public authorities for the purposes of section 6, which raises questions about the horizontal nature of the ECHR rights. We deal with each of these issues in turn.

Defining a public authority

Section 6(3) provides very little by way of a definition of a public authority. Aside from expressly including courts and excluding Parliament, the only other thing the section offers is consideration of people 'certain of whose functions are functions of a public nature', going on to give no indication of specifically what functions might be deemed public in nature. As a result of this, it has often fallen to the courts to assess and determine whether a particular body at issue can be regarded as a public authority for the purposes of the Act. In doing this and through a number of cases, the courts have come to recognize a distinction between core public authorities and hybrid public authorities, as we shall now explain.

One of the first opportunities the courts had to consider this issue arose in *Poplar Housing and Regeneration Community Association Ltd v Donoghue*.[168] Here, Donoghue—a homeless individual—had been housed by the local council. Later, however, ownership of the house was transferred to the Housing Association who, upon learning that Donoghue was intentionally homeless, sought to evict her from the property. Donoghue resisted this, claiming that the eviction contravened her Article 8 right to a private life. This brought into question the status of the Housing Association as regards section 6 of the 1998 Act and, considering this point, Lord Woolf CJ held:

> that while activities of housing associations need not involve the performance of public functions, in this case, in providing accommodation for the defendant and then seeking possession, the role of Poplar is so closely assimilated to that of Tower Hamlets that it was performing public and not private functions. Poplar therefore is a functional public authority, at least to that extent.[169]

---

[168] [2001] EWCA Civ 595.   [169] Ibid [66].

In finding that the Housing Association's functions were 'closely assimilated' with those of the local council, the court felt that it was capable of being regarded as a public authority for the purpose of section 6. This being so, the appellant's case was dismissed as the court felt that the legal process of repossessing the property did not interfere with the Article 8 right. Another case in which the courts were called upon to assess whether or not a body could be classified as public for the purposes of the 1998 Act is *R (Heather) v Leonard Cheshire Foundation*.[170] The Foundation was a private charity that provided accommodation for disabled persons, some of whom were funded by the local authority. On the question as to whether or not the Article 8 ECHR right to a private life could be invoked against the care home in respect of its decision to close, however, the Court of Appeal rejected the application. With regards to the issues raised by section 6, the court found that whilst ECHR rights could be invoked against a local authority, the Foundation was providing a private care home and was not exercising a public function or even, said the court, 'standing in the shoes of the local authority'.[171] The home, therefore, fell outside the scope of section 6. Both these cases concern typically private institutions exercising functions that are argued as being public in nature. While the Leonard Cheshire Foundation was found clearly to be fulfilling a private function, the Housing Association, in *Donoghue*, whilst typically fulfilling private functions, was on these particular facts, working closely with the local authority and thereby susceptible to review under the Human Rights Act.

These two cases, however, are by no means representative of the full scope of discussion and debate raised by section 6. On this very point, a number of important cases have been brought, the next is *Aston Cantlow PCC v Wallbank*.[172]

Case in depth: *Aston Cantlow PCC v Wallbank* [2003] UKHL 37

Mr and Mrs Wallbank were the owners of property that was once rectorial land (that is, land previously owned by the local church), their farmhouse being situated next to the church in Aston Cantlow, Warwickshire. On this basis, and pursuant to section 2(1) of the Chancel Repairs Act 1932, the local Parochial Church Council (PCC) sought to claim the costs of repairing the church chancel from Mr and Mrs Wallbank through the serving of notices authorized by the Act. Section 2(1) of the Chancel Repairs Act 1932 states that:

> Where a chancel is in need of repair, the responsible authority may serve upon any person, who appears to them to be liable to repair the chancel, a notice in the prescribed form . . . stating in general terms the grounds on which that person is alleged to be liable as aforesaid, and the extent of the disrepair, and calling on him to put the chancel in proper repair.

When the Wallbanks refused to pay for the costs of the repair, however, proceedings were brought against the couple. Though the judge at first instance held in favour of the PCC, finding the Wallbanks liable for the costs of the repair, the Court of Appeal overturned this judgment on the grounds that it breached the right contained in the First Protocol to the ECHR, protecting

➡

---

[170] [2002] EWCA Civ 366.   [171] Ibid [35].   [172] [2003] UKHL 37.

→

the Wallbanks' peaceful enjoyment of their property, that decision being predicated on the view that the PCC could be regarded as a public authority for the purposes of section 6 of the Human Rights Act 1998. The House of Lords, however, overturned the Court of Appeal's decision, finding again in favour of the PCC and with the consequence being that the Wallbanks would have to pay for the costs of the chancel repairs.

The crux of the issue in the House of Lords in *Wallbank* was the definition of a public authority under section 6 and whether a PCC could appropriately be regarded as falling within the scope of the 1998 Act on this point. The court held that, under section 6, two classes of public authority could be identified: a core public authority, that is, one whose activities are wholly of a public nature; and a hybrid public authority, which exercises functions of both a public and private nature, depending on the circumstances.[173] Their Lordships agreed that the PCC fell into the latter category and, more than this, that in respect of the issues arising in *Wallbank*, the PCC was acting not as a public authority, but as a private body dealing with private issues. As Lord Hope explained:

> [The PCC] plainly has nothing whatever to do with the process of either central or local government. It is not accountable to the general public for what it does. It receives no public funding, apart from occasional grants from English Heritage for the preservation of its historic buildings. In that respect it is in a position which is no different from that of any private individual. The statutory powers which it has been given by the Chancel Repairs Act 1932 are not exercisable against the public generally or any class or group of persons which forms part of it.[174]

There was, in effect, nothing that the PCC had done in this particular situation that could be said to amount to a broader public function. It was, to all intents and purposes, acting in a wholly private capacity. Lord Nicholls goes on further to explain:

> If a parochial church council enters into a contract with a builder for the repair of the chancel arch, that could be hardly be described as a public act. Likewise when a parochial church council enforces, in accordance with the provisions of the Chancel Repairs Act 1932, a burdensome incident attached to the ownership of certain pieces of land: there is nothing particularly 'public' about this.[175]

In deciding whether or not bodies can be classed as public authorities for the purposes of the Human Rights Act, the courts look beyond their basic functions and more broadly to the nature of their relationships with those affected by their actions in any one particular instance. While the Church of England has long had established links with central government, and other institutions of the state, the PCC in *Wallbank* was dealing specifically with a contractual arrangement with private, not public, parties.

One of the most recently important cases concerning the question of a public authority under section 6 of the Human Rights Act, however, is *YL v Birmingham City Council and others*.[176]

---

[173] Ibid [8] and [11].   [174] Ibid [59].   [175] Ibid [16].   [176] [2007] UKHL 27.

> ### Case in depth: *YL v Birmingham City Council and others* [2007] UKHL 27
>
> YL was an elderly woman who was suffering from Alzheimer's disease. Pursuant to a duty set out in section 21 of the National Assistance Act 1948, Birmingham City Council arranged for her to be placed in a private care home, run by Southern Cross. When YL's behaviour became disruptive, however, Southern Cross moved to terminate the contract on the basis of which she stayed in the care home. YL argued that such termination breached her right to a private and family life, protected under Article 8 ECHR. This argument was predicated on the view that Southern Cross, as provider of the care home, was providing a public function within the wording of section 6 of the Human Rights Act 1998, the issue that the court was asked to consider. A majority in the House of Lords, however, held that Southern Cross could not be classified as a public authority for the purposes of the Act since whilst it was carrying out a function that had formerly been undertaken by the local council, it was so doing pursuant to a private contract and not as a consequence of any statutory duties.

One thing that is highlighted by the decision in *YL*, especially when seen alongside *Wallbank*, is that there is not one single test for determining the classification of a public authority under section 6 of the 1998 Act. It is, instead, an issue that the courts must consider in each case on its own merits, having due regard not only for the functions of the body in question but also the relationship it has with those benefiting from its functions, and the legal basis on which it offers those functions. Indeed, as Lord Scott noted in *YL*:

> it cannot be enough simply to compare the nature of the activities being carried out at privately owned care homes with those carried out at local authority owned care homes. It is necessary to look also at the reason why the person in question, whether an individual or corporate, is carrying out those activities. A local authority is doing so pursuant to public law obligations. A private person, including local authority employees, is doing so pursuant to private law contractual obligations.[177]

The majority decision in *YL*, however, sat somewhat uneasily with those dissenting.[178] Of note, Lord Bingham felt that the circumstances that had arisen in *YL* were precisely of the sort that section 6(3)(b) had been 'intended to embrace'—that is, those affected by a local council's subcontracting of a particular public function to a private authority.[179] The concern was that public authorities, more widely, might be able to avoid their responsibilities and duties under the 1998 Act by subcontracting out certain of their functions to private institutions. Indeed, and in going further, in the aftermath of the case some noted that the majority judgment left over 300,000 elderly people across the UK living in private care homes without any ECHR protection.[180]

---

[177] Ibid [31].

[178] It has also been widely criticized in academic literature. See, for instance, Jonny Landau, 'Functional Public Authorities after YL' (2007) *Public Law* 630.

[179] [2007] UKHL 27 [20].

[180] Jon Robins, 'Law Lords leave elderly out in cold' *The Guardian* (London, 24 June 2007), https://www.theguardian.com/money/2007/jun/24/housinginretirement.longtermcare.

Pause for reflection

Do you agree with the House of Lords' decision in *YL v Birmingham City Council*? What might be the broader consequences of finding that private bodies, carrying out functions pursuant to subcontracts with public authorities, are susceptible to review in line with ECHR rights?

While *YL* highlights the flexible nature of section 6, and identifies certain matters that the courts might be called upon to consider when deciding the classification of public authorities for the purposes of the 1998 Act, it could well be that the judgment has served equally to limit the scope of the Act and the application of the ECHR rights.

Nonetheless, the more recent case of *R (Weaver) v London and Quadrant Housing*,[181] again highlights the different factors that the courts consider, which demonstrates the limited precedent that *YL* perhaps provides. Here, a Housing Association brought proceedings against Weaver for possession of her property on a number of grounds, including significant rent arrears. In response, Weaver sought to argue a breach of Article 8 ECHR, contesting that in bringing action for possession, the Housing Association was interfering with her right to a private and family life. The challenge on the basis of Article 8, however, raised the question as to whether the Housing Association could be regarded as a public authority under section 6 of the Human Rights Act. The Court of Appeal held that the Housing Association was a public authority, a decision that was reached in consideration of a number of factors. These included its 'significant reliance on public finance . . . [through] substantial public subsidy'; its operation 'in very close harmony with' the local council; and its 'provision of subsidised housing, as opposed to the provision of housing itself . . . [which] can properly be described as governmental'.[182] What is more, Elias LJ noted that 'the trust is acting in the public interest [rather than for profit] and has charitable objectives'.[183] The decision to class the Housing Association as a public authority, for the purposes of the 1998 Act, and on the basis of these specific grounds, has been noted as not sitting easily with the decision in *YL*, particularly in view of the decision that its charitable status contributed to its being a public authority.[184] Nonetheless, and particularly keeping in mind the criticisms levied at the majority decision in *YL*, *Weaver* has raised some interesting issues. While it may be for the Supreme Court, in time, to clarify the law, as Alderson notes in respect of *Weaver*, '[a]ssessing whether a particular act of a particular charity is a private act or not will always be fact-sensitive'.[185]

One final issue to consider in respect of those authorities that fall within the remit of section 6 of the 1998 Act relates to the government acting under the prerogative powers. In short, the effect of section 6 is such that the prerogative has to be exercised subject to

---

[181] [2009] EWCA Civ 587.

[182] Ibid [68]–[70]. Also see Ian Alderson, 'R (Weaver) v London and Quadrant Housing Trust' (2013–14) 16 *The Charity Law & Practice Review* 129, 136.

[183] [2009] EWCA Civ 587 [71]. Also see Ian Alderson, 'R (Weaver) v London and Quadrant Housing Trust' (2013–14) 16 *The Charity Law & Practice Review* 129, 143.

[184] Ian Alderson, 'R (Weaver) v London and Quadrant Housing Trust' (2013–14) 16 *The Charity Law & Practice Review* 129, 143.

[185] Ibid 146.

the requirements of the Human Rights Act. This said, given that many prerogative pow-ers deal with politically sensitive issues,[186] such as foreign policy and national security, the courts are likely to remain cautious when faced with a challenge to the exercise of prerogative powers that relates to such issues. This can be seen in the following case.

Case in depth: *R (Abbasi) v Foreign Secretary* **[2002] EWCA Civ 1598**

This case involved two British citizens who were detained by the US Government in Guantánamo Bay, without the ability to challenge their incarceration. It was argued that this detention contra-vened their human rights, including the right to liberty, under Article 5 ECHR. This meant that under the Human Rights Act, the government should make attempts to procure their release by providing diplomatic assistance, and that the government's failure to do so meant that as a public authority they were not fulfilling their duty to comply with Convention rights. The Court of Appeal was unmoved, stating that the government was under no such duty to take positive action beyond considering a request for the assistance provided.[187]

Despite the outcome of this case, it nonetheless highlights how exercise of the preroga-tive powers might engage the ECHR rights. This said, it is also clear from this decision that there remain some prerogative powers, such as negotiating treaties, granting hon-ours, and appointing ministers where the courts are unlikely to intervene. This has con-tinued to be the case under the Human Rights Act, as the courts are mindful that many areas of the royal prerogative can relate to politically sensitive matters.

Horizontality and the Human Rights Act

The second issue presented by section 6 refers to the courts' inclusion within the Act's definition of a public authority. While, in the first instance, this demonstrates that courts—like other public bodies—must honour and abide by the ECHR rights, it also raises questions regarding the horizontal effect of the ECHR rights.

The notion of horizontal effect, with regards to the Human Rights Act, refers to the question of whether the ECHR rights can be invoked horizontally, that is, against private individuals. It is contrasted with vertical effect, on the basis of which the rights can only be raised in challenges vertically, against emanations of the state. Historically, the ECHR was only ever intended to have vertical effect. Before the 1998 Act, the only way in which individuals could challenge alleged violations of their rights was through action against the state in the ECtHR, and even once the Act was passed, section 6 only makes provision for actions against public authorities. There is an argument, however, that the inclusion of the courts within the scope of section 6 means that the Act effectively gives ECHR rights horizontal effect. This argument is predicated on the view that courts hearing all manner of cases between private individuals must, under section 6, always keep in mind the ECHR rights and act consistently with them. As a result, and in resolving a dispute be-tween private individuals, a court must reach its decision in such a way that upholds the rights of the individuals before the court. Consequently, it can be argued that the Human Rights Act affords the ECHR a degree of horizontal effect.

---

[186] See 10.2.1.   [187] [2002] EWCA Civ 1598 [104].

This is an issue that has generated a great deal of academic discussion,[188] much of which it is not for this chapter to explore in fine detail. Worth a mention, however, is an often-quoted article by Wade, who was a notable proponent of the view that the Act permits horizontal effect. He states in simple terms that 'if a Convention right is relevant, a court deciding a case must decide in accordance with it, no less in a case between private parties than in a case against a public authority'.[189]

Wade's view is in stark contrast, however, to that of Buxton LJ, who states that:

> It . . . has never been seriously doubted that the rights created by the E.C.H.R. are rights only against national governments, or their public law emanations, and not rights against other citizens. There are a number of strands to this argument: quite apart from its being moderately clear that the creation of rights in private law was far from the minds of those who drafted and agreed the original treaty. First, the rights that the E.C.H.R. creates can only be asserted against a national government, by complaint to the Strasbourg organs. A complaint brought simply against an individual will fail *in limine* and be dismissed by the Commission on that ground. Secondly, the content of several articles of the E.C.H.R. is plainly directed at acts by state authorities, and is simply inept if directed at acts by private individuals or corporate bodies.[190]

Plainly, it is an issue that sparks a great deal of debate. While Buxton LJ's argument that horizontal effect is inconsistent with the ECHR carries weight, there is, in fact, domestic case law that supports the view that ECHR rights have horizontal effect. The cases of *Douglas v Hello! Ltd*[191] and *Venables v News Groups Newspapers Ltd*,[192] for instance, are both often cited as exemplifying the possible horizontality of ECHR rights. In the first of these, Michael Douglas and Catherine Zeta-Jones sought an injunction against *Hello!* magazine, preventing publication of their wedding photographs (*OK!* magazine had been allowed exclusive rights to the photos). The court considered both Article 8 and 10 and held that publication should be permitted since, because another national magazine was already permitted to take and publish pictures of the wedding, the argument that *Hello!* should be prevented on privacy grounds was weak. Damages were awarded and deemed to be sufficient. In *Venables*, the convicted murderers of Jamie Bulger sought injunctions preventing the publication of their new identities, following their releases from prison. In line with Article 2 ECHR, the court granted the injunction 'against the whole world'.[193] While *Douglas v Hello!* also involved consideration of relevant common law rights, both of these cases at least exemplify consideration of ECHR rights in cases involving private companies, not public authorities.

Whether the ECHR rights can be invoked against private persons is an issue inspiring much debate. That there is an increasing wealth of case law on the issue, however, shows not only the extent to which the rights have become embedded within the common law, but also the court's willingness and determination to uphold individual rights. Having considered section 6 of the Act in detail, it is important in the next section briefly to highlight the procedures through which cases can be brought under the 1998 Act.

---

[188] See, for example, Gavin Phillipson, 'The Human Rights Act, "Horizontal Effect" and the Common Law: A Bang or a Whimper?' (1999) 62(6) *Modern Law Review* 824 and Murray Hunt, 'The "Horizontal Effect" of the Human Rights Act' (1998) *Public Law* 423.

[189] HWR Wade, 'Horizons of Horizontality' (2000) 116 *Law Quarterly Review* 217, 217–18.

[190] Richard Buxton, 'The Human Rights Act and Private Law' (2000) 116 *Law Quarterly Review* 48, 50–51.

[191] [2005] EWCA Civ 595.   [192] [2001] Fam 430.   [193] Ibid 431.

15.5.7 Proceedings under the Human Rights Act

Section 7 of the 1998 Act sets out the basis on which applications can be brought, contending contravention of the ECHR rights. It provides, in paragraph (1), that:

> A person who claims that a public authority has acted (or proposes to act) in a way which is made unlawful by section 6(1) may –
>
> (a) bring proceedings against the authority under this Act in the appropriate court or tribunal, or
>
> (b) rely on the Convention right or rights concerned in any legal proceedings.

The consequences of this section are notably broad. It means, in the first sense and under paragraph (a), that individuals are able to bring actions against a public authority for breaching the duty set out in section 6.[194] In this way, section 7 effectively sets out a new form of judicial review. Under paragraph (b), though, ECHR rights can also be relied upon or addressed in any other public or private legal proceedings against a public authority. An example of this at work is seen in the case of *Campbell v MGN Ltd*,[195] where Articles 8 and 10 were discussed and explored as part of an action brought by Naomi Campbell for an alleged breach of confidence by the Mirror News Group. Another effect of section 7(1)(b), though, is that ECHR rights can be used by individuals collaterally in existing proceedings brought against them by public or private bodies. In the case of *Mendoza*, for instance, in the proceedings brought by the landlord, claiming possession of the property in question, Godin-Mendoza claimed breach of Articles 8 and 14, as already discussed; whereas in *Turner v East Midland Trains*,[196] proceedings in which a train conductor was dismissed for issuing hundreds of faulty tickets to train passengers and keeping the proceeds included a defence on the basis that Article 8 had been infringed through damage to the conductor's reputation. Section 7 provides the tools through which the incorporation of the ECHR can become a practical reality.

Coming back to the observation that section 7 effectively sets out a new form of judicial review, with the courts empowered to examine acts and decisions of public bodies in view of claims that they have breached ECHR rights, there are a number of points to be made as regards the effect the 1998 Act has had on judicial review as a form of action. Different from judicial review under common law (explored in Chapters 10–13), there are rather different procedural requirements under the Human Rights Act. Of note, the test for standing is much stricter. Under the common law rules, applications can be brought to review acts and decisions of the executive where there is 'sufficient interest' in the matter at issue.[197] Pursuant to section 7(3), by contrast, where an application is brought under the 1998 Act, 'the applicant is to be taken to have a sufficient interest in relation to the unlawful act only if he is, or would be, a victim of that act'. The time limit within which applications must be brought before the court is also different. Whereas under the common law, applications for judicial review must typically be brought promptly within

---

[194] See, for instance, *R (Pretty) v DPP* [2001] UKHL 61 and *R (Prolife Alliance) v BBC* [2003] UKHL 23.

[195] [2004] UKHL 22.

[196] [2012] EWCA Civ 1470. For more on this, see Rosalind English, 'Facebook faux pas and disciplinary proceedings—when do human rights come in?' (*UK Human Rights Blog*, 21 November 2012), https://ukhumanrightsblog.com/2012/11/21/facebook-faux-pas-and-disciplinary-proceedings-when-do-human-rights-come-in/#more-16115.

[197] See s 31(3) of the Senior Courts Act 1981 and, for fuller discussion, 10.4.

three months, under the 1998 Act, section 7(5) provides that 'proceedings . . . must be brought' within 'one year beginning with the date on which the act complained of took place'.

Where an application under section 7 is successful then the court has the power under section 8(1) to 'grant such relief or remedy, or make such order, within its powers as it considers just and appropriate'. A court can also award damages, where it has that power.[198]

One of the most notable changes to judicial review that has been effected by the Human Rights Act and the applicability of the ECHR in UK law, though, is the incoming tide of proportionality as a ground for judicial review. Though historically, and on the basis of the decisions in *Wednesbury* and *GCHQ*, decisions of public authorities were susceptible to review on the grounds of illegality, irrationality, and procedural impropriety, the increasing prominence of human rights jurisprudence has meant that the courts have been permitted to review decisions of public authorities on the ground of proportionality, as a line of cases serves to demonstrate.[199] This incoming tide of proportionality and the extent to which it has become established as a ground for judicial review is discussed in detail in 12.4.

One issue that can arise when a court hears applications under section 7 relates to the political nature of government and the unavoidable reality that judges are often being called upon to explore and scrutinize political acts and decisions of the executive to assess their compatibility with the ECHR rights. Under common law judicial review, the notion of justiciability permits a court to gauge whether or not it has the jurisdiction to review matters that might touch upon political or administrative matters of state.[200] Under the 1998 Act, by contrast, the level of judicial review is widely acknowledged as being much more stringent than at the common law, chiefly due to the constitutional importance attached to individual rights. As such, the courts often have to ask more probing questions in assessing the lawfulness of executive action. To ensure that they do not go too far, however, and acknowledge the expertise of government or the peculiar powers they are able to exercise, the courts have developed a principle of judicial deference. This permits judges to defer to the government, for example, 'where the subject-matter in hand is peculiarly within their constitutional responsibility' or if 'the subject-matter lies more readily within the actual or potential expertise of the democratic powers',[201] in so doing, leaving it to the government's own discretion how far they wish to exercise their powers mindful of the ECHR rights.

This section has explored the practical implications of the Human Rights Act—the duty it imposes on public authorities and the procedures through which applications can be brought in respect of infringements of ECHR rights. Though the Human Rights Act has become a fundamental feature of the UK's constitutional arrangements, however, possibilities for reform in the coming years could see the legal framework setting out rights protection changing, as the next, final section explores.

---

[198] Section 8(2) of the Human Rights Act 1998.

[199] See, for example, *R (Daly) v Secretary of State for the Home Department* [2001] UKHL 26 and *R (Alconbury Developments Ltd and others) v Secretary of State for the Environment* [2001] UKHL 23.

[200] See, for more discussion, 6.5.3.

[201] *International Transport Roth GmbH v Home Secretary* [2002] EWCA Civ 158 [85] and [87]. For more on this, see Keith Syrett, *The Foundations of Public Law: Principles and Problems of Power in the British Constitution* (2nd edn, Palgrave Macmillan 2014) 236–7.

15.6 The future of human rights in the UK: a British Bill of Rights?

Ever since its enactment, the Human Rights Act has divided opinion and attracted a great deal of criticism. The Conservative Party, for instance, list a number of complaints, including concern that the ECHR and ECtHR undermine both 'the role of the UK courts' and 'the sovereignty of Parliament, and democratic accountability to the public'; whilst '[t]here is mounting concern at Strasbourg's attempts to overrule decisions of . . . Parliament and overturn UK courts' careful applications of Convention rights', of which prisoner voting and the right of foreign nationals, convicted of terrorist offences, to remain in the UK are just two examples.[202] As a result of this, there has been much discussion in recent years regarding the possible repeal of the Human Rights Act—and perhaps even departure from the Council of Europe—and the subsequent introduction of a British Bill of Rights. Such discussion began under the 2010–15 Coalition Government and has continued under subsequent governments (though it was reported in 2016 that plans to proceed with the reform were delayed due to the priority and importance of Brexit).[203] Indeed, in response to a request for an update on the government's plans in this area, the then Parliamentary Under-Secretary of State for Justice, Edward Agar, explained that '[i]t is right that we wait until the process of leaving the EU concludes before considering the matter [of human rights reform] further'.[204]

As a consequence, as of October 2019, we have yet to see formal plans for this British Bill of Rights and, indeed, uncertainty within the government as to the future role and impact of the ECHR needs to be clarified. For now, however, the Conservative Party has provided some indication of the reforms that it may seek to promote in the coming years.[205] These include:

● a limitation of the UK courts' ability effectively to re-write legislation through their interpretative duty, with plans to ensure that '[i]n future, the UK courts will interpret legislation based upon its normal meaning and the clear intention of Parliament';[206]

● a break in 'the formal link between British courts and the' ECtHR.[207] The rationale here is to permit the UK courts 'the final say in interpreting Convention Rights, as clarified by Parliament';[208]

● a clarification of the sovereignty of Parliament, ensured through putting 'the text of the original Human Rights Convention into primary legislation' and through leaving it with Parliament to decide whether laws incompatible with the ECHR should be amended to correct the incompatibility.[209]

---

[202] Conservative Party, 'Protecting Human Rights in the UK: The Conservatives' Proposals for Changing Britain's Human Rights Laws' (Conservative Party, 2014) 2–3.

[203] Owen Bowcott, 'UK Bill of Rights delayed further by Brexit and supreme court case' *The Guardian* (London, 9 December 2016), https://www.theguardian.com/law/2016/dec/09/uk-bill-of-rights-delayed-further-brexit-supreme-court-case-jeremy-wright.

[204] Adam Bloodworth, 'What is the Human Rights Act and why is Theresa May "considering scrapping" it?' *Rights Info* (London, 22 January 2019), https://rightsinfo.org/what-is-the-human-rights-act-scrapping-human-rights-act-theresa-may-british-bill-of-rights/.

[205] Conservative Party, 'Protecting Human Rights in the UK: The Conservatives' Proposals for Changing Britain's Human Rights Laws' (Conservative Party, 2014).

[206] Ibid 6.   [207] Ibid.   [208] Ibid.   [209] Ibid 5–6.

Through these and other suggested proposals, the Conservative Party plans to take forward the case for reform of human rights law in the UK. While the legal and political questions encircling the UK's departure from the European Union will inevitably take much time and energy in the immediate future, it is likely that repeal and replacement of the Human Rights Act 1998 will not be too far behind.

Pause for reflection

Having explored the various discussions throughout this chapter, what are the supposed problems with the Human Rights Act and how, if at all, do you think a British Bill of Rights will fix them? In considering these questions, think in particular about the problems that stem from the 1998 Act itself and problems that perhaps stem more from the ECHR and the Strasbourg Court.

15.7 Summary

The protection of individual human rights is a fundamental role of a constitution. The Bill of Rights in the US Constitution, for instance, exists as the first ten amendments to the codified Constitution and is thereby entrenched. The peculiar nature of our own constitutional arrangements, however, means that rights protection takes on a rather different form. Historically, and as Dicey explained, rights were protected through the courts. The enactment of the Human Rights Act 1998, however, incorporating as that did some of the rights set out in the ECHR, effected a significant change in the UK Constitution's own respect for individual rights. As this chapter has explored, the Act sets out various provisions that enable rights to be protected. Sections 2, 3, and 4, on the one hand, empower the courts to uphold individual rights, both mindful of Strasbourg jurisprudence and the intentions of the sovereign Parliament, whilst sections 6 and 7 impose on public authorities a duty to honour and abide by the ECHR rights in all that they do, also providing a procedure through which infringements of these rights can be challenged. There are numerous criticisms of the 1998 Act, however, and as a consequence the UK Constitution could see yet further development of its protection of individual rights in the coming years. For now, though, the next chapter explores in greater detail the manner in which certain ECHR rights are protected and balanced under UK law.

Quick test questions

1. Explain the rationale underpinning the introduction of the ECHR.

2. What do sections 3 and 4 of the Human Rights Act 1998 provide? Do you think that section 4 provides an effective remedy?

3. Describe the civil liberties tradition in the UK that existed before the 1998 Act. How does the protection of civil liberties differ from the protection of human rights?

4. Explain the 'mirror' principle from the case of *Ullah*.

5. What is the difference between political, civil, social, economic, and cultural rights?

6. How have the courts interpreted the notion of a 'public authority' for the purposes of section 6 of the Human Rights Act?

7. What is the rationale behind proposals for a British Bill of Rights?

Further Reading

Human rights in the UK

*Merris Amos, 'Problems with the Human Rights Act and How to Remedy Them: Is a Bill of Rights the Answer?' (2009) 72 *Modern Law Review* 883

*Conor Gearty, *On Fantasy Island: Britain, Europe and Human Rights* (OUP 2016)

Tom Hickman, *Public Law after the Human Rights Act* (Hart Publishing 2010)

*Aileen Kavanagh, *Constitutional Review under the UK Human Rights Act* (Cambridge University Press 2013)

Anthony Lester and Kate Beattie, 'Human Rights and the British Constitution' in Jeffrey Jowell and Dawn Oliver (eds), *The Changing Constitution* (6th edn, OUP 2007) 59

Alison L Young, *Parliamentary Sovereignty and the Human Rights Act* (Hart Publishing 2009)

The interpretative duty and declarations of incompatibility

*Aileen Kavanagh, 'Statutory Interpretation and Human Rights After Anderson: A More Contextual Approach' (2004) *Public Law* 537

*Aileen Kavanagh, 'Unlocking the Human Rights Act: The "Radical" Approach to Section 3(1) Revisited' (2005) 3 *European Human Rights Law Review* 259

*Danny Nicol, 'Statutory Interpretation and Human Rights after Anderson' (2004) *Public Law* 274

Public authorities and horizontal effect under the Human Rights Act

*Richard Buxton, 'The Human Rights Act and Private Law' (2000) 116 *Law Quarterly Review* 48

Murray Hunt, 'The "Horizontal Effect" of the Human Rights Act' (1998) *Public Law* 423

*Jonny Landau, 'Functional Public Authorities after YL' (2007) *Public Law* 630

Dawn Oliver, 'The Frontiers of the State: Public Authorities and Public Functions under the Human Rights Act' (2000) *Public Law* 476

Gavin Phillipson, 'The Human Rights Act, "Horizontal Effect" and the Common Law: A Bang or a Whimper?' (1999) 62(6) *Modern Law Review* 824

*HWR Wade, 'Horizons of Horizontality' (2000) 116 *Law Quarterly Review* 217

 Visit this book's **online resources** for additional materials relating to this chapter, including a full analysis of the start-of-chapter problem scenario.
www.oup.com/he/stanton-prescott2e

Human rights in the UK: public order and police powers

16.1 Introduction

Chapter 15 explored the development of human rights in the UK Constitution. From its common law foundation and civil liberties approach, to the development and incorporation of the ECHR and enactment of the Human Rights Act 1998, human rights have come to form a central feature of the constitution. Building on this exploration of the legal basis for human rights and the manner in which they empower and impose duties and expectations on the institutions of the state, it is necessary now to explore how certain specific rights are protected within UK law. In doing this, this chapter focuses particularly, though not exclusively, on rights contained within Article 10 ECHR (freedom of expression), Article 11 (freedom of association and assembly), Article 5 (the right to liberty), and Article 8 (the right to a private and family life). It considers the domestic application of these rights as well as some of the cases in which they have been raised, thereby permitting examination of the manner in which the 1998 Act enables rights to be upheld and protected by the courts. The prevailing theme in this chapter is to explore the balance that must be struck between certain rights on the one hand and competing interests and needs on the other. With this in mind, the chapter focuses on two areas: first, the freedoms of association and assembly, balanced against the need to ensure public order; and secondly, the freedom of liberty and right to a fair trial, against the need to ensure that the police can carry out their functions and responsibilities appropriately. The chapter deals with each of these areas in turn, focusing on a specific problem scenario separate for each area as a basis for discussion. Though there are other areas of law and policy that might be included in a chapter such as this, public order and police powers have been chosen as they connect with a number of ECHR rights, thereby ensuring that—following Chapter 15—it is possible to see how the Human Rights Act functions in practice. The objectives of this chapter are:

- to discuss the freedoms of expression, association, and assembly as set out in the ECHR and applicable in UK law;
- to explore the case law and legislation pertaining to the protection of public order;
- to explain the freedom of liberty and the right to a private and family life, as set out in the ECHR and applicable in UK law;
- to consider legislation and case law setting out the rights and responsibilities of the police, including the Police and Criminal Evidence Act 1984.

16.2 Public order and the freedoms of association and assembly

Problem scenario: public order

Following a vote in the House of Commons, the UK Government decides to increase the tuition fees of students attending English and Welsh universities to £15,000 a year. This decision is met with much unhappiness and marches are planned across Central London in protest at the decision. During the marches, the following events occur.

- A group of thirteen individuals plan and launch an attack on two police vans that are parked on the street in Whitehall. They throw bottles, stones, and other objects at the vehicle and use sledgehammers to smash the windows. Later, at trial, two of the individuals make an agreement with prosecuting authorities whereby their charges are dropped in return for evidence against the remaining eleven protestors.

- One particularly disgruntled student—Don—breaks away from the procession and starts hurling abuse at passers-by, threatening to 'break their legs' and 'smash their faces in'.

- Finally, a group of ten students are sitting on the pavement opposite Downing Street, chanting and waving placards. Amy, one of the group, is holding a sign that says 'Rob us of a free education and we'll rob you'. Jane, an elderly tourist, sees this and is distressed. As she hurries past the group, Peter, another protestor, shouts 'Oi, Granny, give us your money or we'll mug you'.

16.2.1 Freedoms of expression, association, and assembly and the right to protest

The freedoms of expression, association, and assembly together protect two of the most important civil rights in democratic society; namely, the right to express yourself freely and without limitation, either by speech or in writing, and the right to be a member of a political group and engage in peaceful protest with that group. At the heart of these rights is the fundamental value that individuals should be free and able to form their own political views, and associate with other citizens in support or opposition of particular political causes. These values are central to the workings of our democratic system since, because we live in a society that relies heavily on the views, decisions, and judgment of those in elected office, it is crucial that citizens have the means through which to impress their political views, criticisms, and concerns peacefully upon those in power. Articles 10 and 11 ECHR seek to protect these particular rights.

The first of these articles sets out a freedom of expression, which ensures that individuals are free to hold and express their own opinions, without any restriction or influence by public authorities. It is a right that is subject to very few limitations. Alongside this, Article 11 protects a freedom to assemble and associate, entitling citizens to join groups, unions, and other such organizations, so that they can assemble in support or opposition of a particular cause, thereby ensuring a right to peaceful protest. The ECHR, through the Human Rights Act 1998, makes provision for these freedoms in UK law, most notably through both the section 6 duty on public authorities to act in a way that is consistent with the Convention and the section 3 interpretative duty, which ensures that the courts interpret legislation consistently with ECHR provisions. Before we come to explore the workings of these Convention rights, however, it is important to note that the courts' efforts to protect a right to peaceful protest long predates incorporation of the ECHR. As Tugendhat J said in *Austin v Metropolitan Police Commissioner*:

> Political demonstrations have long been a central feature of English life. Before the extension of the franchise in the nineteenth century they were the only means by which the public could make known their views. But they were generally treated as rebellions, whether they were violent or not. Out of the upheavals in the 16th and 17th centuries there came to be recognised a right of free speech and a free assembly. There are repeated re-affirmations by the Courts of the importance of these rights in a democracy. Large modern democracies operate through representation and elections. Political demonstrations are one of the few ways that members of the public can impress upon their representatives and upon candidates the importance of issues in which they might otherwise not take an interest.[1]

There are many pre-Human Rights Act cases that demonstrate the courts' willingness to uphold and protect this right and while it is not the focus of this chapter to explore all of these in detail, it is helpful to draw from a couple to demonstrate the historic importance of these rights in UK law. In the case of *Beatty v Gillbanks*,[2] the Divisional Court held that a Salvation Army march, which took place at the same time as an opposing demonstration, against the order of the Magistrates' Court and the police (who feared disturbance to public order), was lawful. The Court found that just because the two marches were taking place simultaneously, it did not automatically mean that a disturbance would occur. There were no grounds on which the Salvation Army should have been prevented from marching. More recently, in *Redmond-Bate v DPP*,[3] three preachers were protesting outside Wakefield Cathedral in Yorkshire. Though the police warned them not to stop any passers-by in the course of their demonstrations, a large crowd soon gathered, with some people behaving violently. The protestors were arrested after they refused to stop their preaching, and they were later convicted for the disturbance that they caused and for obstructing a police officer. The Divisional Court, however, overturned their convictions finding that there was no lawful basis for the arrest. Noting that the crowd had

---

[1] [2005] EWHC 480 [80].   [2] (1882) 9 QBD 308.   [3] [1999] Crim LR 998

gathered voluntarily, rather than by invitation, the court also stressed that the preachers had a right to protest and a freedom of speech, both of which should be protected by law. Equally, though, there are other historic cases that demonstrate a tendency by the courts to permit interference with the right to protest in certain instances. In the Irish case of *Humphries v Connor*,[4] for example, the court held that a police officer had acted lawfully by removing an orange lily from Humphries' clothing as it was an emblem that was 'tended to provoke animosity between different classes of Her Majesty's subjects'.[5] Action in trespass against the officer therefore failed. Similarly, in another Irish case, *O'Kelly v Harvey*,[6] the court upheld the actions of a Member of Parliament who had laid a hand on the defendant in an attempt to disperse a protest in which he was participating because he feared a breach of the peace. Even before the incorporation of the ECHR rights, therefore, the courts were concerned with individuals' right to protest and freedom of expression. They developed a wealth of case law, making provision for certain common law offences and powers, as the next section explores. With this in mind, it is in the context of Articles 10 and 11 ECHR that this first half of the chapter proceeds to consider the way in which the courts have sought to protect the freedoms of expression, association, and assembly and to balance these rights against the need to preserve and ensure public order.

16.3 Common law public order offences and powers

16.3.1 Breach of the peace

One of the most important features of the Article 11 freedom of association and assembly is that it represents a right to *peaceful* protest and assembly. This requirement that peace be maintained during the exercise of this right has given rise to various offences over the years, these serving to police the boundaries between lawful exercises of the rights and what might be regarded as disturbances or breaches of public order. In this half of the chapter we look at some of these offences, focusing first on those established at common law.

One of the most historically notable public order offences has been the common law notion of a 'breach of the peace'. This refers to the causing of a disturbance to the Queen's peace, at a time when the country is not at war. The offence can be traced back to the sixteenth century and a case in 1593, during which Popham CJ held that '[a] constable is one of the most ancient officers of the realm for the conservation of the peace, and by his office he is a conservator of the peace; and if he see any breaking of the peace, he may take and imprison him'.[7] A breach of the peace was found to have occurred here by a man abandoning a baby, though since that case, and over the centuries, there have been various other examples of conduct that has been found to amount to a breach of the peace. Despite the historic foundation underpinning the concept, however, and the wealth of case law exemplifying its nature, the courts have often been reluctant to offer any clear and concrete understanding of what a breach of the peace broadly means and what type

---

[4] (1864) 17 ICLR 1.

[5] Ibid and also cited at *R (Laporte) v Chief Constable of Gloucestershire Constabulary* [2006] UKHL 55 [97].

[6] (1882) 10 LR lr 287.

[7] Anon. (1593) Poph 12, 79 ER 1135. Discussed in: David Clark, 'Filling in the Doughnut? Police Operational Discretion and the Law in Australia' (2014) 14(2) *Oxford University Commonwealth Law Journal* 195, 199.

of behaviour it is designed to prevent. The leading case on this and one in which the Court of Appeal offered a clearer idea of the concept is *R v Howell*.[8]

Case in depth: *R v Howell* [1982] QB 416

This case involved a conviction for assault occasioning actual bodily harm. This occurred when a party that had spilled out onto the street was deemed by the police to be causing a disturbance. The officers asked the partygoers to go home, accusing them of breaching the peace. The defendant, however, taking issue at the police's actions, refused and continued to cause disruption. When the police attempted to arrest the defendant, he assaulted them. Though the prosecution alleged that the defendant committed the assault in the course of resisting lawful arrest, the defendant alleged that no breach of the peace had occurred and that he was acting reasonably in resisting an unlawful arrest. Despite this argument, the defendant was convicted, this being upheld on appeal. The court found that the police had a power of arrest for both threatened and actual breaches of the peace.

In the course of the Court of Appeal's judgment, Watkins LJ explained the offence of breach of the peace, stating that:

> [W]e cannot accept that there can be a breach of the peace unless there has been an act done or threatened to be done which either actually harms a person, or in his presence his property, or is likely to cause such harm, or which puts someone in fear of such harm being done. There is nothing more likely to arouse resentment and anger in him, and a desire to take instant revenge, than attacks or threatened attacks upon a person's body or property.[9]

A breach of the peace, then, is committed where an act or a threatened act causes harm to an individual or their property, or is likely to cause harm to that person or their property. It need not always take place in public, but can also be committed on private premises too.[10] The definition of breach of the peace, set out in *R v Howell*, has since been more widely accepted and it is in these terms that the common law offence still exists today. Indeed, and as subsequent case law shows, it can be committed by a range of activities. In *Steel and Others v United Kingdom*,[11] for instance, a number of incidents in which a breach of the peace was alleged to have occurred, were considered by the court. These included: where a woman protested against a grouse shoot by walking in front of the shooters, preventing them from firing; and where another woman protested against the building of a motorway by placing herself under the bucket of a digger, preventing the vehicle from being used for the motorway's construction.[12] The case went to the European Court of Human Rights[13] which, finding that arrests in both these instances were lawful and reasonable, went to great lengths to explain how a breach of the peace could be committed. Endorsing Watkins LJ's definition from *Howell*, the Strasbourg Court cited the case of *Percy v DPP*,[14] in which Collins J had stated that '[t]he conduct in question does not itself have to be disorderly or a breach of the criminal law. It is sufficient if its natural consequence would, if persisted in, be to provoke others to violence, and so some actual danger to the peace is

---

[8] [1982] QB 416.   [9] Ibid 426.
[10] See, for example, *McLeod v UK* [1998] 27 EHRR 493 and *R v Lamb* [1990] Crim LR 58.
[11] (1999) 28 EHRR 603.   [12] Ibid.   [13] Hereinafter ECtHR.   [14] [1995] 1 WLR 1382.

established'.[15] In the instances noted, impeding a grouse shoot or delaying the construction of a motorway could be seen as action provoking violence in others. Despite the historic foundation to the common law offence of breach of the peace, the courts have been increasingly willing—over the course of the past thirty years—to explain more clearly the particulars of the offence and to provide examples of where and how it can be committed.

 Discussing the problem

Have a look at the problem scenario set out at the start of this chapter. Do you think any of the protestors have committed a breach of the peace?

Using Watkins LJ's words from *R v Howell*,[16] we can take a breach of the peace to occur when an act or a threatened act causes harm to an individual or their property, or is likely to cause harm to that person or their property. On this basis, it could be argued that each of the three scenarios in the problem involve a breach of the peace: the group of thirteen individuals attacking the police vans; Don's abuse to passers-by threatening to 'break their legs' and 'smash their faces in'; and Peter's threatened attack on Jane to the effect that he would mug her if she did not give him some money. Each of these scenarios involves either action or threatened action that causes harm or that would be likely to cause harm. As later 'Discussing the problem' boxes will show, however, legislative reform in the area of public order has meant that each of these specific offences is more suitably dealt with under statutory provisions.

16.3.2 Powers to deal with and prevent breaches of the peace

The common law not only provides the basis for the notion of breach of the peace, however, but also sets out the powers that the police have to control breaches of the peace. Returning to the case of *Howell*, Watkins LJ also stated in the case that 'there is a power of arrest for breach of the peace' in three situations.[17] These are where:

(1) a breach of the peace is committed in the presence of a person making the arrest or (2) the arrestor reasonably believes that such a breach will be committed in the immediate future by the person arrested although he has not yet committed any breach or (3) where a breach has been committed and it is reasonably believed that a renewal of it is threatened.[18]

This broad power is, in Watkins LJ's words, to ensure that a police officer has the ability to keep the peace, something he must be able to do in the public interest.[19] The second aspect of this power, however, is particularly interesting, namely the power to arrest an individual for a breach of the peace that has not yet occurred and 'where the person arrested has not acted unlawfully'.[20] On this, Watkins LJ notes 'that a constable has a power of arrest where there is reasonable apprehension of imminent danger of a breach of the peace'.[21] Stated in these terms, this aspect of the common law power of arrest raises two points of

---

[15] Ibid 1392, as cited in *Steel and Others v UK* (1999) 28 EHRR 603 [27].
[16] [1982] QB 416.   [17] Ibid 426.
[18] Ibid. Also see *R v Podger* [1979] Crim LR 524.   [19] [1982] QB 416, 426.
[20] Richard Stone, *Civil Liberties and Human Rights* (10th edn, OUP 2014) 111.
[21] [1982] QB 416, 426. Also see ibid 110.

interest. First, at what point and in what circumstances might a police officer be said reasonably to apprehend a breach of the peace? Sedley LJ noted, in the case of *Redmond-Bate v DPP*,[22] that the question the courts should consider here is 'whether in the light of what [the police officer] knew and perceived at the time the court is satisfied that it was reasonable for him to fear an imminent breach of the peace'.[23] It is, then, a question of fact that the courts must decide in each case, taking into account a range of factors while seeking to maintain a balance between the need to keep the peace against the right of individuals to exercise their right to protest. In *Walker v Commissioner of Police of the Metropolis*,[24] for instance, a claimant's 'agitated and irate' state upon a visitation from the police to investigate complaints of domestic violence might, in the view of Tomlinson LJ, have led the police reasonably to apprehend an imminent breach of the peace.[25] Elsewhere, in the case of *Duncan v Jones*,[26] the fact that previous meetings held by Mrs Duncan at a particular location had caused a disturbance in the past was sufficient basis for a reasonable apprehension of breach of the peace when another meeting was planned.

The second point of interest, stemming from the terms of this common law power of arrest as stated in *Howell*, is this notion of imminence and the condition that a police officer arrest an individual where he has reasonable apprehension that a breach of the peace is *imminent*. The question that the courts have had to consider in this regard is at what point can a breach of the peace be said to be imminent? Keeping in mind that, in seeking to arrest an individual for a breach of the peace that has not yet occurred, the police must strike a careful balance between keeping the peace and protecting the public interest, this is a matter that the courts have often been called upon to consider. One notable case is *Moss v McLachlan*.[27]

Case in depth: *Moss v McLachlan* [1985] IRLR 76

The facts for this case are set in the context of the miners' strikes that took place during the 1980s. A car containing four striking miners was en route to a planned demonstration at one of the mines. The police, who knew of the demonstration and had set up a road block, stopped the car a short distance from the mine and ordered the protestors to turn back. The police feared that, if the miners were allowed to proceed to the mine and the demonstration, a breach of the peace would occur. The miners, however, tried to push their way through the police cordon and proceed to the pit. They were arrested for obstructing a police office in the execution of his duty, a charge for which they were later convicted. The case was appealed, unsuccessfully.

In determining the basis on which a police officer might take action to prevent a breach of the peace occurring, the court held that that officer must 'honestly and reasonably form the opinion that there is a real risk of a breach of the peace in the sense that it is in close proximity both in place and time'.[28] In this case, the cars were stopped less than two miles from the nearest mine, a distance that would take just a matter of minutes to cover by car, and, as such, the court was satisfied that a potential breach of the peace was imminent. This decision was approved, though qualified, in the more recent case of *R (Laporte) v Chief Constable of Gloucestershire Constabulary*.[29]

---

[22] [1999] Crim LR 998.   [23] (1999) 163 JP 789, 791.   [24] [2014] EWCA Civ 897.
[25] Ibid [49].   [26] [1936] 1 KB 218.   [27] [1985] IRLR 76.   [28] Ibid 78.
[29] [2006] UKHL 55.

> **Case in Depth:** *R (Laporte) v Chief Constable of Gloucestershire Constabulary* [2006] UKHL 55
>
> A number of coaches were making the journey from London to a US Air Force base in Gloucestershire so that protestors could participate in a demonstration that was taking place in opposition to the Iraq war. In light of information received by the police that a number of the protestors were likely to cause a breach of the peace, officers were ordered to stop the coaches and search the protestors under a power set out in section 60 of the Criminal Justice and Public Order Act 1994. The order was not, however, to arrest protestors as it was not felt that a breach of the peace was at that time imminent. Following the search, the police were satisfied that some of the protestors were prepared and intent upon causing a breach of the peace at the demonstration, so the coaches were ordered to return to London under police escort. The case was brought by Ms Laporte, one of the protestors, through an application for judicial review. She contested that her freedoms of expression, association, and assembly had been violated by the police's actions. The Divisional Court, and subsequently the Court of Appeal, dismissed the claim, however, finding that the actions short of arrest were appropriate to preventing participation in the planned demonstration, also holding—against the police—that the detention on the coach was unlawful since any breach of the peace was not imminent. The House of Lords, however, upheld Mrs Laporte's appeal, overruling the Court of Appeal on the first point and dismissing a cross-appeal from the police on the second. Since no breach of the peace had occurred or was deemed to be imminent, there was no basis on which any preventive action could lawfully be taken.

In reaching this decision and in commenting on the question of imminence, Lord Brown stated in the House of Lords that:

> I regard the decision in *Moss v McLachlan* as going to the furthermost limits of any acceptable view of imminence, and then only on the basis that those prevented from attending the demonstration were indeed manifestly intent on violence and were not . . . quite possibly intent only on peaceful demonstration . . . the course taken by the police here in preventing Ms Laporte from proceeding further [is] . . . plainly unsustainable . . . because [the police officer] Mr Lambert did not in fact regard a breach of the peace as then imminent.[30]

Beyond approving—and qualifying—the decision in *Moss v McLachlan*, the House of Lords also took time to consider a test to determine the requirement of imminence. Lord Bingham stated that 'I would observe . . . that *Albert v Lavin* laid down a simple and workable test . . . It recognises the power and duty to act in an emergency to prevent something which is *about to happen*.'[31] *Laporte*, then, is the leading authority on the procedural requirements that must be satisfied in dealing with or preventing a breach of the peace, with the courts in subsequent cases continuing to uphold the principles there set out by the House of Lords.[32] More broadly, though, the judgment in *Laporte*, combined with Lord Brown's qualification of the decision in *Moss*, also highlights the extent to which the courts strike a balance between the need to prevent breaches of the peace that police

---

[30] Ibid [118].

[31] Ibid [49], citing [1982] AC 546. Emphasis added.

[32] See, for example, *R (on the application of Moos and McClure) v Commissioner of the Metropolis* [2011] HRLR 24 and *Walker v Commissioner of Police of the Metropolis* [2014] EWCA Civ 897.

officers reasonably believe are about to occur and the freedom of individuals to participate peacefully in demonstrations. As Lord Bingham went on to note in *Laporte*, because
there was no lawful basis on which Ms Laporte's attendance at the protest could be prevented, '[i]t was wholly disproportionate to restrict her exercise of her rights under articles 10 and 11 [ECHR]'.[33]

Balancing ECHR rights with actions taken to prevent a breach of the peace was also a
central issue in the final case that we shall here consider: *Austin v Commissioner of Police
for the Metropolis*.[34]

Case in depth: *Austin v Commissioner of Police for the Metropolis* [2009] UKHL 5

On 1 May 2001, there was a large demonstration in Central London. By mid-afternoon, about
3,000 protestors had marched into and around Oxford Circus. Aware that previous May Day
demonstrations had resulted in disturbances, the police, fearing that a breach of the peace
would occur on this occasion, decided to impose a cordon around the protestors that had gathered in the Circus. The cordon remained in place for seven hours, during which time nobody
was permitted to leave. Once the cordon was dismantled, the protestors were allowed to return
home. The actions of the police, however, were later challenged in proceedings brought by Ms
Austin, a protestor who had made repeated requests to leave the cordon so that she could
collect her child; requests that were refused. Her challenge was brought under section 7 of the
Human Rights Act 1998—which, to recall from 15.5.7, permits a challenge by a victim arguing
that a public authority has acted in violation of someone's Convention rights—on the basis that
she had been falsely imprisoned and that her right to liberty, protected under Article 5 ECHR, had
been violated. Her claim failed, however, with the Divisional Court holding that the deprivation of
liberty was within the exceptions listed in Article 5(1)(c) (which permits lawful detention to prevent
the commission of an offence). The police, they said, had acted reasonably and in good faith.
The Court of Appeal and, later, the House of Lords dismissed Ms Austin's further appeal, holding
that the 'sole purpose of the cordon was to maintain public order, [and] that it was proportionate
to that need',[35] and even went further in finding that Article 5 ECHR had not been engaged by the
police's actions. That view was subsequently endorsed by the ECtHR.[36]

In reaching these various decisions, the courts gave great consideration to the fact that
the police had been constantly monitoring the situation in Oxford Circus throughout the
afternoon to see if the threat of serious injury or damage had lessened, thereby assessing whether the cordon was still needed and their preventive actions reasonable. As the
ECtHR noted:

> where the police kept the situation constantly under close review, but where substantially
> the same dangerous conditions which necessitated the imposition of the cordon . . . con-
> tinued to exist throughout the afternoon and early evening, the Court does not consider
> that those within the cordon can be said to have been deprived of their liberty.[37]

---

[33] [2006] UKHL 55 [55].   [34] [2009] UKHL 5.
[35] Ibid [2].   [36] *Austin v United Kingdom* (2012) 55 EHRR 14.
[37] Ibid [67]. See, for further discussion, Richard Stone, *Civil Liberties and Human Rights* (10th edn, OUP
2014) 433.

The cordon imposed by the police in *Austin*, designed to prevent a violent disturbance, is an example of a crowd control measure known as 'kettling'. The Strasbourg Court in *Austin*, though holding that the police were correct in taking such action in the circumstances, went on to limit the situations in which kettling should be used. They said that '[i]t must be underlined that measures of crowd control should not be used by the national authorities directly or indirectly to stifle or discourage protest, given the fundamental importance of freedom of expression and assembly in all democratic societies'.[38] They can only be used, they said, to 'prevent serious injury or damage'.[39] The case of *Austin* shows, therefore, that the common law powers to control **protests** and prevent breaches of the peace must always and constantly be balanced against the ECHR freedoms of expression, association, and assembly, as well as the right to liberty protected under Article 5. In *Austin*, the threat to public safety throughout the afternoon of 1 May 2001 was constantly assessed and ultimately deemed by the police to be sufficient to justify the cordon that was put in place, with the courts not only endorsing their actions but going so far as to find that the Article 5 freedom of liberty was not even engaged in the circumstances. Though notable, this judgment has been subjected to academic criticism. Stone, for instance, states that:

> It may well be that this is an understandable outcome in terms of the practical demands of policing large demonstrations, but it nevertheless seems bizarre to hold that a group of people, including bystanders who had no part in the demonstration, held in one place for six to seven hours should be regarded as not having their liberty infringed.[40]

Mead, focusing inter alia on the court's examination of the police's motives for the cordon as well as the broader implications of the judgment, goes further in suggesting that:

> One conclusion to be drawn from *Austin* is that much of art.5(1) will become increasingly redundant. A concentration on the purpose of the deprivation is likely to mean that states need not justify detentions and arrests by reference to art.5(1)(a)–(f) since they would be defined out by earlier considerations of state of mind.[41]

The *Austin* case is a particularly important one. While the decision by the courts that Article 5 ECHR was not engaged on the facts has attracted debate and discussion, the case is itself important for further considering the scope of the police's powers in dealing with and preventing breaches of the peace and the manner in which these should be balanced against individuals' freedoms of expression and protest.

 Pause for reflection

Do you agree with the decision in *Austin v Commissioner of Police for the Metropolis*? At what point do you think the police's actions in keeping protestors in a cordon would have become disproportionate or unreasonable?

[38] (2012) 55 EHRR 14 [68].   [39] Ibid [68].

[40] Richard Stone, 'Deprivation of Liberty: The Scope of Article 5 of the European Convention of Human Rights' (2012) 1 *European Human Rights Law Review* 46, 56.

[41] David Mead, 'Of Kettles, Cordons and Crowd Control—Austin v Commissioner of Police for the Metropolis and the Meaning of "Deprivation of Liberty"' (2009) 3 *European Human Rights Law Review* 376, 392–3.

Alongside the common law protection of the freedom of speech and the right to peaceful protest, therefore, the courts have developed the rules concerning breach of the peace, as this section has explained. The cases discussed demonstrate that it is for the courts in each case to determine the point at which exercise of these rights and freedoms becomes unlawful, at that point justifying proportionate and reasonable actions by the police in maintaining public order and protecting public safety. Furthermore, and even since the development of statutory safeguards for public order and the legislative incorporation of the ECHR through the Human Rights Act 1998, the common law basis for these rights and the notion of the breach of the peace has continued to play an important role in UK law. Having explored these common law rules, however, it is necessary now to discuss the statutory provisions in this area.

16.4 The Public Order Acts

The most prominent, though certainly not the only, pieces of legislation seeking to balance the freedoms of expression, association, and assembly with the need to 'keep the peace' are the Public Order Acts. These contain certain offences which together, and to varying degrees, police the boundaries between peaceful activity and public order, as this section will explore. In addition, and as this chapter will later go on to address, the Acts also contain an administrative framework that governs the manner in which marches and demonstrations should lawfully be executed.

The first Act to consider is the Public Order Act 1936, which was enacted amidst concern for the growing fascist movements that were emerging in the UK and across Europe in the years before the Second World War. In particular, the British Union of Fascists was a political party of the time that espoused increasingly far right-wing and anti-Semitic views, these sometimes causing violent clashes in London. The 1936 Act was in part a reaction both to the views of the British Union of Fascists and other such movements, and to the violence that their beliefs were motivating.

Section 1 of the 1936 Act states that 'any person who in any public place or at any public meeting wears uniform signifying his association with any political organisation or with the promotion of any political object shall be guilty of an offence'. This was a feature of the Act that was inspired by the British Union of Fascists themselves, who all wore black shirts as a uniform. Despite the apparently broad scope of this offence, where a uniform is worn on a ceremonial occasion or an anniversary and is, as a result, not thought likely to cause a risk of public disorder, the police can, with the consent of the Secretary of State, permit the wearing of that uniform.[42] Despite the offence it contains, section 1 fails to offer any definition of the term 'uniform', though this is something that has, on occasion, been considered by the courts. In *O'Moran v DPP*,[43] for instance, a group of eight men all wearing black or dark blue berets, dark glasses, dark jumpers, and other items of dark clothing, was deemed sufficient to amount to a uniform for the purposes of the Act.

---

[42] Section 1 of the Public Order Act 1936.   [43] [1975] QB 864.

Counterpoint: The Public Order Act 1936 and its relationship with the Human Rights Act 1998

In respect of the offence set out in section 1 of the 1936 Act, we see the potential for the Human Rights Act 1998 to operate in support of those charged with such an offence, thereby serving to permit a balance to be struck between public order and individual rights. Imagine a hypothetical scenario, for instance, in which a group of fifteen students walk peacefully through a city centre wearing t-shirts that show the face of a divisive politician and display a slogan supporting that politician's policies. Under the wording of section 1 of the 1936 Act, an offence has been committed. Equally, though, and in view of the ECHR, it could be argued that to press charges in such circumstances would infringe upon the students' freedom of expression and association. On that basis, and in entertaining any subsequent criminal proceedings, the courts could use the interpretative duty, set out in section 3 of the 1998 Act, to read in a defence to section 1 to the effect that an offence under that section has only been committed provided the Article 10 and 11 ECHR rights have not—in the view of the court—been infringed. Indeed, and notwithstanding the power of the judges to read in such a defence, the students, as defendants in any subsequent criminal trial, could use section 7(1)(b) of the 1998 Act to raise the defence using Articles 10 and 11 themselves.[44] This scenario shows the manner in which the Human Rights Act 1998 works in UK law, protecting individuals from actions or charges that might be seen as infringing upon their human rights.

Despite the motivation behind the offence contained within section 1 of the 1936 Act being a particular threat, prominent in the late 1930s, the provision still remains in force today (though it is worth noting that the offence overlaps with section 13(1) of the Terrorism Act 2000, which makes it an offence to wear an item of clothing or carry or display an article 'in such a way or in such circumstances as to arouse reasonable suspicion that he is a member or supporter of a proscribed organisation'). This is not, however, the only offence still provided in the 1936 Act. Section 2(1) prohibits the establishment of quasi-military organizations, and states that:

If the members or adherents of any association of persons, whether incorporated or not, are—

(a) organised or trained or equipped for the purpose of enabling them to be employed in usurping the functions of the police or of the armed forces of the Crown; or

(b) organised and trained or organised and equipped either for the purpose of enabling them to be employed for the use or display of physical force in promoting any political object, or in such manner as to arouse reasonable apprehension that they are organised and either trained or equipped for that purpose;

then any person who takes part in the control or management of the association, or in so organising or training as aforesaid any members or adherents thereof, shall be guilty of an offence under this section.

---

[44] See, for more in-depth discussion on this, David Mead, *The New Law of Peaceful Protest* (Hart Publishing 2010) 214–15.

As with the section 1 offence, many of these 'quasi-military organisations' will also be covered and prohibited under more recent terrorism legislation.[45] The offence, though, is still in force and, indeed, its broad scope is notable and evident from the case of *R v Jordan and Tyndall*.[46] Here, members of a fascist anti-Semitic group that practised Nazi salutes and had access to bomb-making resources were found to fall within this section.[47]

Sections 1 and 2 of the 1936 Act are the only offences still in force from the 1936 Act. Sections 3 to 5,[48] when enacted, set out certain powers and offences that have since been replaced by and expanded upon by the Public Order Act 1986. For the purposes of our discussion, it is the newer Act that is particularly interesting. It was passed at the height of Thatcher's Government, amidst growing concern regarding demonstrations, riots, and disputes. To this end, it contains provisions that not only create offences for the protection of public order, but it also sets out various powers enabling the police to control and regulate the holding of protests and demonstrations. We start by looking at the offences, of which there are six. We deal with these three at a time. The first group, contained within sections 1–3, relate to the threatened or use of unlawful violence, while the second trio, contained in sections 4, 4A, and 5, deal with the various consequences of using threatening, abusive words or behaviour.

16.4.1 Threatened or use of unlawful violence

There is a common theme running through the offences contained in sections 1, 2, and 3 of the Public Order Act 1986. That is, they all prohibit the use or threatening of unlawful violence, such as 'would cause a person of reasonable firmness present at the scene to fear for his or her personal safety'. The differences between the sections relate to the number of people required for the commission of the offence. Section 1, for instance, sets out the offence of riot, which requires '12 or more persons . . . present together [to] use or threaten unlawful violence'. By contrast, section 2, which sets out the offence of violent disorder, requires '3 or more persons . . . present together [to] use or threaten unlawful violence'. Section 3, by further contrast and making provision for the offence of affray, requires just one person to use or threaten unlawful violence. The maximum sentences that these offences attract are commensurate to their severity, riot attracting the potentially most serious punishment as up to ten years in prison or a fine.[49] Those convicted of violent disorder could receive a maximum prison sentence of five years (on indictment) or six months (on summary),[50] or have to pay a fine,[51] while individuals convicted of affray could be imprisoned (on indictment) for a maximum of three years or (on summary) six months, or receive a fine.[52]

---

[45] See Steve Foster, *Human Rights and Civil Liberties* (3rd edn, Pearson Education Ltd 2011) 506.

[46] [1963] Crim LR 124.

[47] See, for further discussion, Steve Foster, *Human Rights and Civil Liberties* (3rd edn, Pearson Education Ltd 2011) 506–7.

[48] Section 3 set out police powers for the preservation of public order during processions; section 4 set out an offence to be found with offensive weapons at a public meeting or procession; section 5 prohibited offensive conduct conducive to breaches of the peace.

[49] Section 1(6) of the Public Order Act 1986.

[50] Indictable offences are those that are tried before a judge and a jury; summary offences are those that are tried before a single judge in the Magistrates' Court.

[51] Section 2(5) of the Public Order Act 1986.

[52] Section 3(7) of the Public Order Act 1986.

These public order offences seek to deal with demonstrations, protests, and mere gatherings that come to involve violent disturbance in some way.[53] Indeed, this is evident from the added requirement—in sections 1 and 2—that it is the conduct of all the people taken together (ie not individually) that is considered as part of the offence. (Section 3(2) similarly states that '[w]here 2 or more persons' commit an affray, 'it is the conduct of them taken together that must be considered'.) Added to this, section 1 also requires that a riot be committed by twelve persons who are acting towards a common purpose. This need not necessarily be pre-planned or specific but can, instead, arise as a result of a spontaneous disruption. In *R v Sherlock (Kyle)*,[54] for instance, a planned 'and co-ordinated attack by a great number of prisoners taking control of the entire prison block for six hours and with a common purpose of seeking to destroy it'[55] was sufficient to satisfy this aspect of the offence of riot. It is also a key part of these offences that the violence used or threatened actually be directed towards another person. In the case of *I v DPP*,[56] for example, while the House of Lords held that the mere act of carrying petrol bombs in public, without actual threats to use them, could amount to affray, it was necessary to prove that people present in the vicinity felt threatened. The test with which such threats are assessed is an objective one, the court asking: if a person of reasonable firmness were present at the scene, would they fear for his or her personal safety?[57] It is not a requirement that a person of reasonable firmness actually be present at the scene of the incident; the court merely asks the question hypothetically, considering: *if* he or she were there, *would* they have feared for their personal safety?[58] This test is, as Stone notes, 'the standard of "disorderliness" that appears at a number of points in the [Public Order Act] 1986 as the test of criminality'.[59]

One issue relevant to these three offences, and on which the courts have particularly focused, relates to the number of people required to be involved for each offence. Though the legislative provisions are themselves relatively clear in requiring twelve (or more), three (or more), or one person, there are a number of cases in which not all the individuals alleged to have been involved in the threatening or use of unlawful violence were convicted, causing complications for the satisfaction of the particulars of the relevant offence. In *R v Mahroof*,[60] for instance, four men turned up at a house armed with a can of petrol and threatened to set fire to the house if the occupant did not repay them money that was owed. Violence ensued, in respect of which three of the men were charged with violent disorder, pursuant to section 2 of the 1986 Act. Though one of the men (the appellant) was convicted, the other two were acquitted. Just one man, therefore, was convicted of an offence that stipulates the requirement that '3 or more persons . . . present together [to] use or threaten unlawful violence'.[61] On this very point, the case was appealed to the Court of Appeal, which allowed the appeal and quashed the conviction, holding that while 'there [was] evidence before the jury that there were three people involved in the criminal behaviour' it was not necessarily those listed on the indictment.[62] One person could not be convicted of the offence under section 2. Noting, at the same

---

[53] Note, though, that these offences can be committed on private premises as well as in public (see section 3(5) of the Public Order Act 1986).

[54] [2014] EWCA Crim 310.   [55] Ibid [17].   [56] [2001] UKHL 10.

[57] See ss 1–3 of the Public Order Act 1986.

[58] See ss 1(4), 2(3), and 3(4) of the Public Order Act 1986.

[59] Richard Stone, *Civil Liberties and Human Rights* (10th edn, OUP 2014) 406–7.

[60] (1989) 88 Cr App R 317.   [61] Section 2 of the Public Order Act 1986.

[62] (1989) 88 Cr App R 317, 321.

time, however, that 'there was no miscarriage of justice in the circumstances' and that the jury had unanimously found the appellant guilty of wrongdoing, the Court of Appeal in the circumstances turned to section 7(3) of the 1986 Act.[63] This states that '[i]f on the trial on indictment of a person charged with violent disorder or affray the jury find him not guilty of the offence charged, they may . . . find him guilty of an offence under section 4'. The Court found that the appellant could be convicted of this lesser offence, which prohibits 'threatening, abusive or insulting word or behaviour . . . with intent to cause that person to believe that immediate unlawful violence will be used against him'.[64] This decision was followed in another case shortly after, the established rule there being stated as follows: if a jury cannot be sure that three or more defendants named on the indictment were using or threatening unlawful violence, it should be directed to acquit all of the defendants.[65] It is then open to the court, as we have seen in the case of *Mahroof*, to substitute any possible conviction for a more suitable one. In *R v Fleming and R v Robinson*, the court substituted a possible conviction for violent disorder for one with affray under the authority of section 3 of the Criminal Appeal Act 1968.[66]

Discussing the problem

In the scenario set at the beginning of this section, a group of thirteen individuals attack two police vans, throwing bottles, stones, and other objects at the vehicle and smashing its windows. Do you think these individuals could be convicted of an offence under the Public Order Act 1986? If so, which offence? What is the significance of two of the protestors having their charges dropped?

The thirteen individuals who attacked two police vans by throwing stones and other objects at the vehicle, and using sledgehammers to smash the windows, could potentially be convicted of committing a riot. As per section 1 of the 1986 Act, there are at least twelve individuals, acting violently towards a common purpose (ie destruction of the police van), and it would be a reasonable view to hold that a person of reasonable firmness, present in the vicinity of the police vans, would fear for their safety. On this basis, the individuals could serve as much as ten years in prison or receive a fine.

It is significant, though, that—at trial—two of the protestors have their charges dropped in exchange for evidence against the other eleven individuals. This significance is linked to the number of people allegedly committing the offence; there are now fewer than twelve—the number required for the offence of riot. Relevant to this issue is the case of *R v Mahroof*,[67] in which only

→

---

[63] Ibid 321.   [64] Section 4(1) of the Public Order Act 1986.

[65] See *R v Fleming and R v Robinson* [1989] Crim LR 658, 658–9.

[66] Ibid. Section 3 of the 1968 Act states that: '(1) This section applies on an appeal against conviction, where the appellant has been convicted of an offence to which he did not plead guilty and the jury could on the indictment have found him guilty of some other offence, and on the finding of the jury it appears to the Court of Appeal that the jury must have been satisfied of facts which proved him guilty of the other offence. (2) The Court may, instead of allowing or dismissing the appeal, substitute for the verdict found by the jury a verdict of guilty of the other offence, and pass such sentence in substitution for the sentence passed at the trial as may be authorised by law for the other offence, not being a sentence of greater severity.'

[67] (1989) 88 Cr App R 317.

→

one man was convicted (and two acquitted) of the offence of violent disorder. While, as the Court of Appeal noted, 'there [was] evidence before the jury that there were three people involved in the criminal behaviour', it was not necessarily those listed on the indictment.[68] The individual was convicted under section 4. Our situation here, however, is slightly different insofar as there would be evidence before the jury that thirteen individuals took part in the attack on the police vans, this evidence also potentially showing that the two individuals whose charges have been dropped were a part of that group. Keeping in mind the words of the Court of Appeal in *Mahroof*, the jury could still potentially find the eleven individuals guilty of taking part in a riot.

The offences of riot, violent disorder, and affray are important in ensuring the protection of public order, insofar as they prohibit the use or threatening of violence that stems from protests, demonstrations, and gatherings. In assessing whether the particulars of each of these offences has been committed in each case, however, the courts must carefully ensure and maintain a balance between the right to protest against the need for public safety and order. While, as this chapter has already explained, freedoms contained in Articles 10 and 11 are important in permitting individuals a right to express themselves through protest, the severity of the offences in sections 1, 2, and 3 of the 1986 Act are such that to satisfy the particulars of the offences, citizens will have departed someway from acceptable and peaceful protests. Indeed, the extent to which the courts go in ensuring and maintaining public safety against the right to protest is emphasized by the Northern Irish case of *Re E (A Child)*,[69] in which school children were terrorized by loyalist protestors in Belfast. The police here were found to have acted insufficiently to protect the children from protestors, to the extent that the House of Lords found a breach of Article 3 ECHR, namely a duty to protect citizens from inhuman and degrading treatment. This shows that even where the ECHR rights are framed negatively—that is, where they are committed by a failure sufficiently to respect that given right—they are still capable of being interpreted in such a way that creates positive duties to facilitate or to effect.

16.4.2 Use of threatening, abusive words or behaviour

Having now looked at the offences contained within sections 1, 2, and 3 of the Public Order Act 1986, it is time to consider those set out in sections 4, 4A, and 5, which deal with less serious disturbances of public order. As with sections 1, 2, and 3, there is a common theme that runs through these offences, namely, the prohibition of 'threatening, abusive or insulting words or behaviour'[70] or the distribution or displaying of 'any writing, sign or other visible representation which is threatening, abusive or insulting' (though section 57 of the Crime and Courts Act 2013 removed the word 'insulting' from the section 5 offence).[71] The difference in each of the offences comes when we consider the motivation behind the actions that fall within these provisions. Section 4, for instance, requires that such words, behaviour, or visible representation be done either with

---

[68] Ibid 321.   [69] [2008] UKHL 66.

[70] Sections 4A and 5 also state the inclusion of 'disorderly behaviour' at this point.

[71] See ss 4, 4A, and 5 of the Public Order Act 1986 and s 57 of the Crime and Courts Act 2013.

the intent 'to cause [a] person to believe that immediate unlawful violence will be used against him or another by any person, or to provoke the immediate use of unlawful violence by that person or another, or whereby that person is likely to believe that such violence will be used or it is likely that such violence will be provoked'. By contrast, section 4A—which was inserted into the 1986 Act by the Criminal Justice and Public Order Act 1994—requires that the individual committing such an offence have 'intent to cause a person harassment, alarm or distress'. Finally, section 5 of the 1986 Act merely requires that the words, behaviour, or visible representations necessary to satisfy the offence, take place 'within the hearing or sight of a person likely to be caused harassment, alarm or distress thereby'. These offences are designed to ensure that those engaging in demonstrations and protests do not use words, behaviour, or signs that would cause varying degrees of upset to passers-by in the vicinity. A further dimension is added to all three of these offences, though, by section 31(1) of the Crime and Disorder Act 1998. This states that a 'person is guilty of an offence . . . if he commits' an offence under section 4, 4A, or 5 of the Public Order Act 1986, 'which is racially or religiously aggravated'. This added element brings with it potentially more severe sentences. While the 1986 Act provides that conviction for these offences in the form there provided carries a maximum of six months in prison, commission of the offence along with the racially or religiously aggravated element, as provided by the 1998 Act, takes the possible sentence to maximum of two years' imprisonment.

The offences in sections 4, 4A, and 5 of the 1986 Act raise a number of issues that are necessary to explore here in greater detail. The first, specific to section 4, is the requirement of intent, that is, intention 'to cause [a] person to believe that immediate unlawful violence will be used against him or another by any person, or to provoke the immediate use of unlawful violence by that person or another, or whereby that person is likely to believe that such violence will be used or it is likely that such violence will be provoked'.[72] The wording of this section shows that any words, behaviour, or visible representations engaged by this section must be directed at a particular person and, furthermore, that person must fear immediate, unlawful violence. Such words or actions that are not directed at any particular person would more likely fall within section 5,[73] while a person feeling merely harassed, alarmed, or distressed, rather than in fear of immediate unlawful violence, could fall within sections 4A or 5. Indeed, the appropriateness of section 5 in instances where words, behaviour, or visible representation are not directed at a particular person is evident from the case of *R (on the application of Owusu-Yianoma) v Chief Constable of Leicestershire*.[74] Here, an individual under the influence of alcohol was being disruptive and shouting loudly at the door to a particular bar. The Divisional Court explained that section 5 contained the most appropriate offence in these circumstances, with Treacy LJ stating that '[i]t is to be noted that under this section there is no requirement to prove that any person was harassed, alarmed or distressed. It is sufficient if the abusive words were uttered within the hearing or sight of a person likely to be caused harassment, alarm or distress.'[75]

The particulars of the section 4 offence are quite specific. There is case law, though, that adds further clarification to these particulars. In *Atkin v DPP*,[76] for instance, a bailiff and two Customs and Excise officers attended a property to seek payment of debts that were

---

[72] Section 4(1) of the Public Order Act 1986.

[73] Section 4A also requires words or actions to be directed at a particular individual.

[74] [2017] EWHC 576 (Admin).   [75] Ibid [15].   [76] (1989) 89 Cr App R 199.

owed. While the bailiff waited outside in the car, the Customs and Excise officers entered the house whereupon Atkin said: '[i]f the bailiff gets out of the car he's a dead "un".'[77] Though Atkin was initially convicted in the Magistrates' Court under section 4, this was later overturned by the Divisional Court on the basis that the words, though pertinent to the bailiff, were neither directed towards the bailiff nor said while within his earshot. They were said to the Customs and Excise officers. This outcome emphasizes not only that words or behaviour should actually be directed at a particular individual, but, more-over, the immediacy of the offence. A potential victim must be there, hearing the words or seeing the behaviour first hand, and fearing immediate unlawful violence as a result. The requirement of immediacy was relevant in the case of *R v Horseferry Road Magistrates, ex p Siadatan*.[78] This involved a challenge to the publication and distribution of Salman Rushdie's book *The Satanic Verses* on the grounds that the book would, in time, be likely to provoke unlawful violence. The Magistrates' Court had refused to issue summons in respect of this offence, giving rise to an application for judicial review. The Divisional Court, however, refused this application on the basis that section 4 of the 1986 Act required such unlawful violence to be *immediate*. While they said this did not necessarily mean it should be instantaneous, it did at least mean that there had to be sufficient proximity in time and place.[79] Consequently section 4 did not apply.

More broadly, and focusing on aspects of all three of these public order offences, despite the fact that the words *threatening, abusive and insulting* words or behaviour run as a common theme through the provisions, they are not defined in the 1986 Act. The courts, however, have provided historic indication for the ways in which such words should be interpreted. Though it pre-dates the 1986 Act, the case of *Brutus v Cozens*[80] discusses these terms, as they appeared in similar offences under the Public Order Act 1936.

Case in depth: *Brutus v Cozens* [1973] AC 854

In this case, during a tennis match at the Wimbledon Championships, a protestor—Brutus—walked onto the court, blowing a whistle and attempting to distribute leaflets, including to one of the players. Other protestors then joined Brutus, bringing placards and banners onto the court, eventually causing play to be stopped. Brutus was charged under (the now repealed) section 5 of the Public Order Act 1936, which made it an offence to use 'threatening, abusive or insulting words or behaviour with intent to provoke a breach of the peace or where a breach of the peace is likely to be occasioned'. Though the Magistrates' Court initially found that Brutus' behaviour was not insulting, this was overturned on appeal by the Divisional Court. Upon further appeal, the House of Lords agreed with the Magistrates' Court, stating that '[t]he spectators may have been very angry and justly so. The appellant's conduct was deplorable. Probably it ought to be punishable. But I cannot see how it insulted the spectators'.[81]

Much of the case, both in the lower courts and in the House of Lords, turned on the definition of 'insulting'. The matter was clarified by Lord Reid, who stated that the word was 'intended to have its ordinary meaning'.[82] It was, he emphasized, a question of fact

---

[77] Ibid 199.   [78] [1991] 1 QB 260.   [79] Ibid 269.   [80] [1973] AC 854.
[82] Ibid 861.
[81] Ibid 863. In view of the change introduced by the Crime and Courts Act 2013 such a charge could not now be brought.

whether or not the alleged victims in any particular case could be said to be *insulted* by the words or actions in question. Even after the enactment of the 1986 Act, *Brutus v Cozens* still provides the authority on this point, though the courts have also shown a willingness to interpret the requirements of section 5 quite broadly. In *Percy v DPP*,[83] for instance, a woman had defaced the American flag and trampled on it at a US Air Force base, in front of American citizens. Though she was convicted under section 5, the Divisional Court later held that the conviction was not compatible with the right to freedom of expression. That the conviction was quashed on the basis of incompatibility with the Article 10 right provides further example of the Human Rights Act in action. Even when faced with the clear words of section 5 of the 1986 Act, the court—keeping in mind its role under the Human Rights Act—felt that to uphold a conviction in the circumstances would have been contrary to Percy's ECHR rights. Above and beyond this, though, and in discussing the question of insulting words or behaviour, the court said:

> What one person finds insulting and distressing may be water off a duck's back to another. A civilised society must strike an appropriate balance between the competing rights of those who may be insulted by a particular course of conduct and those who wish to register their protest on an important matter of public interest. The problem comes in striking that balance, giving due weight to the presumption in the accused's favour of the right to freedom of expression.[84]

More recently, in *Gough v DPP*,[85] a walker was convicted under this offence having walked through a busy town centre in the middle of the day with no clothes on. The conviction was upheld by the Divisional Court who felt that '[i]t was not necessary to decide whether the district judge was right to conclude that [Gough] was threatening, abusive or insulting. The district judge was clearly entitled to conclude that, by walking through the town centre entirely naked, [Gough] was violating public order and was thus disorderly.'[86] These two cases show the manner in which the courts have considered the word 'insulting' in the context of these public order offences.

Discussing the problem

Return to the scenario set at the beginning of the Public Order section. Which, if any, of these offences set out in sections 4, 4A, and 5 of the Public Order Act 1986 could apply in respect of Amy or Peter's actions? Has Don committed any of these offences?

We deal with each of these individuals in turn.

Amy

Amy is holding a sign that says 'Rob us of a free education and we'll rob you'. The sign is not necessarily aimed at any specific individual but is instead designed to convey the message of their demonstration to passers-by generally. On this basis, section 5 of the Public Order Act 1986

→

---

[83] [2001] EWHC 1125 (Admin).   [84] Ibid [28].   [85] [2014] ACD 49.   [86] Ibid [H19].

→

contains the most relevant offence. This states that '[a] person is guilty of an offence if he—(a) uses threatening or abusive words or behaviour, or disorderly behaviour, or (b) displays any writing, sign or other visible representation which is threatening or abusive, within the hearing or sight of a person likely to be caused harassment, alarm or distress thereby'. Since Amy's sign includes a threat to rob, it could arguably fall within paragraph (b) of this offence. It is not necessary to show that any individual walking along Whitehall was actually harassed, alarmed, or distressed by Amy's placard, but—pursuant to Treacy LJ's judgment in *R (on the application of Owusu-Yianoma) v Chief Constable of Leicestershire*[87]—it suffices to show that the sign was displayed within the sight of a person likely to be harassed, alarmed, or distressed. Given that this demonstration was taking place on a busy street, in Central London, it is not inconceivable to think that such an individual would be in the vicinity.

Peter

Peter's actions are more serious than Amy's. He singles out a passer-by (Jane, who is an elderly tourist) and shouts at her: 'Oi, Granny, give us your money or we'll mug you'. On the basis that his words are aimed at a particular individual, these words could bring Peter within the offence contained in section 4 of the Public Order Act 1986. His threatening words are directed at a specific individual and could be taken as intending to cause Jane to believe that immediate unlawful violence will be used against her.

Don

Don breaks away from the main march and begins hurling abuse at passers-by, threatening to 'break their legs' and 'smash their faces in'. We are perhaps given insufficient information here. If Don makes these threats towards specific individuals or groups of people, then his words might suffice to bring him within section 4 or 4A of the 1986 Act; that directness being sufficient—with the other particulars—to satisfy those offences. If we interpret his behaviour, however, as general disruption, with these threats being offered to the public generally, then it is more likely to be section 5. Indeed, in *R (on the application of Owusu-Yianoma) v Chief Constable of Leicestershire*, an individual's alcohol-fuelled shouts and disruption came within section 5.

Sections 4, 4A, and 5 of the Public Order Act 1986 provide a further category of offences, less serious than those in sections 1, 2, and 3, but designed and graded nonetheless to regulate public order and ensure—in particular—that individuals seeking to exercise their ECHR freedoms of expression, association, and assembly do so peacefully and lawfully.

16.4.3 The Public Order Act, processions, and assemblies

The Public Order Act 1986 is not merely about offences, however. It also seeks to set out—in Part II of the Act—provisions permitting police control and supervision over the holding of public processions and assemblies. This section of the chapter now looks at these provisions, drawing from appropriate case law in exploring and considering the manner in which these powers have been used.

---

[87] [2017] EWHC 576 (Admin).

Under section 11 of the 1986 Act, a person organizing a public procession is required to provide written notice to the police of processions that are intended to demonstrate support for or opposition to the views or actions of any person or body; to publicize a cause or campaign; or to mark or commemorate an event.[88] Such notice is not required where it is 'not reasonably practicable to give any advance notice of the procession',[89] or—under section 11(2)—where 'the procession is one commonly or customarily held in the . . . area'. The rationale behind this section is not so much to restrict or hinder individuals' right to protest, but rather to ensure that the police are not only aware of any possible processions but that they also have sufficient time to prepare and assemble any necessary police presence for the protection of public order. This is evidenced by the wording of the provision itself, which does not require that protestors seek permission for their proposed processions but that they merely notify the police of their intentions,[90] including the date of the planned procession, its start time, its route, and the details of the individual responsible for its organization.[91]

With regards to the exception contained within section 11(2) of the Act, the courts have often been called upon to consider whether or not a procession can be classified as 'one commonly or customarily held'. On this, the judgment in *Kay v Commissioner of the Police of the Metropolis* is of particular interest.[92]

Case in depth: *Kay v Commissioner of the Police of the Metropolis* [2008] UKHL 69

This case concerned the holding of a cycle ride through the streets of Central London, which had taken place on a monthly basis for many years. Though the event always started from the same South Bank location, its route or destination was never planned and there was never a fixed finishing time. At the heart of the case, however, is a letter that was handed to participants in this cycle ride by the police. This letter stated that the cycle ride was unlawful because, pursuant to section 11(3) and (5) of the Public Order Act 1986, such events were classified as processions and must be brought to the attention of the police at least six days in advance, there outlining the proposed date, timings, and route, as well as the contact details of the organizer. Proceedings for judicial review were sought by the cyclists, who argued that section 11 of the 1986 Act could not apply to their ride since there was no organizer and no pre-ordained route about which the police could be notified. They also argued that, under the terms of section 11(2), the cycle ride was a procession commonly or customarily held and, as such, notice was not required to be given. It was on the strength of this last point that the Administrative Court found in favour of the cyclists, a decision that was ultimately upheld by the House of Lords.

---

[88] It is interesting to note that, in Northern Ireland, a different framework operates. Under s 6(7) of the Public Processions (Northern Ireland) Act 1998, it is not just the organizers of processions who commit offences when the police are not notified, but all those who participate in such processions (see further *DB v Chief Constable of Police Service of Northern Ireland* [2017] UKSC 7).

[89] Section 11(1) of the Public Order Act 1986.

[90] See, for further discussion on this, Helen Fenwick and Gavin Phillipson, *Text, Cases and Materials on Public Law and Human Rights* (3rd edn, Routledge 2011) 1094.

[91] Section 11(3) of the Public Order Act 1986.   [92] [2008] UKHL 69.

In the House of Lords, the case turned on the meaning of section 11(2)'s exception for processions 'commonly or customarily held'. In considering both this section and the specific features of the monthly cycle ride in question, Lord Phillips stated that:

> I am in no doubt that the . . . cycle rides that take place month after month have so many common features that any person would consider that each month the same procession takes place and, giving the English language its natural meaning, that it is a procession that is 'commonly or customarily held' in the Metropolitan Police area.[93]

It is a question of fact for the courts to consider in each case, taking the words of section 11(2) in their ordinary and natural meaning, whether a procession can be classed as being 'commonly or customarily held'.

The requirement, in section 11 of the 1986 Act, to give written notice of processions is complemented by the police's power, under section 12, to impose conditions on public processions. In view of the importance of the ECHR freedom to associate and assemble, this provision sets out the specific circumstances in which conditions might be imposed on public processions so as not to give the police too broad a power that might be used to restrict or limit unnecessarily the right to protest. Section 12(1) states, on this basis, that the police must have 'regard to the time or place at which and the circumstances in which any public processions is being held or is intended to be held and to its route or proposed route'. The provision also states that conditions can only be imposed if a police officer 'reasonably believes that' the procession 'may result in serious public disorder, serious damage to property or serious disruption to the life of the community' or that 'the purpose of the persons organising it is the intimidation of others with a view to compelling them not to do an act they have a right to do, or to do an act they have a right not to do'.[94] This ensures that conditions are only imposed where they 'appear . . . necessary to prevent such disorder, damage, disruption or intimidation'.[95] Section 12 empowers the police with valuable authority to preserve and uphold public order. Where, though, this power is insufficient 'to prevent . . . [a] public procession . . . from resulting in serious public disorder', then the police also have the power, under section 13(1) of the 1986 Act, to apply to the local council for an order prohibiting the holding of processions in the area for a maximum three-month period.

The monthly London cycle ride, which was at issue in the case of *Kay v Commissioner of the Police of the Metropolis*, once again came before the courts in *Powlesland v DPP*,[96] this time on a point raised under section 12 of the 1986 Act. The circumstances of the ride were unchanged from *Kay*, there being a monthly cycle ride across the capital, starting from a set time and place but thereafter with no fixed end-time or route. In July 2012, the established date of the ride was due to coincide with the day of the 2012 Olympic Games Opening Ceremony, to be held at a stadium in Stratford, East London. So as to ensure that the cycle ride did not create any more disruption or congestion than was already predicted to occur, the police imposed a condition, under section 12 of the Public Order Act, which forbade the cycle ride from crossing the River Thames to the north. This condition was ignored by the cyclists, actions that resulted in a charge under section 12(5) of the Act, which states that '[a] person who takes part in a public procession and knowingly fails to comply with a condition imposed under this section is guilty of

[93] Ibid [16].   [94] Section 12(1) of the Public Order Act 1986.
[95] Ibid.   [96] [2014] 1 WLR 2984.

an offence'. Powlesland was convicted of this offence, a conviction that was appealed to the Divisional Court. In their judgment, the court clarified two key issues concerning the scope and workings of the section 12 power. First, they said, section 12 does not merely apply to those processions about which the police have been notified under section 11, but can apply to any appropriate procession that falls within the wording of the section.[97] Secondly, the court held that conditions can be imposed by the police, under section 12, even where the procession in question has no specifically planned route.[98] The Divisional Court upheld the original conviction and agreed that the section 12 conditions were appropriate and lawful in this case. Section 12, with section 13, serves as a potential limit on individuals' right to participate in processions, ensuring as it does that the police have adequate provision to maintain and uphold public order.

Sections 11, 12, and 13 of the 1986 Act, however, deal specifically with public processions. This is a term that is defined in the Act in particularly vague terms, with section 16 stating that a public procession is constituted by 'processions in a public place'. This is a term, though, that the courts have also been called upon to consider, offering further guidance and definition. In the case of *Flockhart v Robinson*,[99] for instance, Lord Goddard CJ asked: 'When a person organizes a procession, what does he do? A procession is not a mere body of persons: it is a body, of persons moving along a route.'[100] Indeed, we have already seen in the cases of *Kay v Commissioner of the Police of the Metropolis* and *Powlesland v DPP* that a procession might not merely be constituted by a procession of people, perhaps marching in support or opposition of a particular cause, but also by a mass cycle ride. The term is broadly understood and widely interpreted on a case-by-case basis. With sections 11, 12, and 13 of the 1986 Act dealing specifically with processions, though, the Act makes separate provision for assemblies. Section 16 states that '"public assembly" means an assembly of 2 or more persons in a public place which is wholly or partly open to the air'.[101]

Pause for reflection

Do you agree with the broad manner in which the courts have interpreted the notion of 'processions'? Can you think of any other instances of 'a body of persons moving along a route' that could fall within these provisions?

Police powers to control public assemblies are dealt with in sections 14 and 14A of the Act. Section 14 mirrors section 12 insofar as it empowers the police to impose conditions on assemblies where there is a reasonable belief that the assembly 'may result in serious public disorder, serious damage to property or serious disruption to the life of the community', or if 'the purpose of the . . . [assembly] is the intimidation of others with a view to compelling them not to do an act they have a right to do, or to do an act they have a right not to do'.[102] The extent to which this power sits alongside the ECHR freedoms of expression, association, and assembly was considered by the Administrative Court in the

---

[97] Ibid [15].   [98] Ibid [22].   [99] [1950] 2 KB 498.   [100] Ibid 502.
[101] Section 16 of the Public Order Act 1986, as amended by s 57 of the Anti-Social Behaviour Act 2003.
[102] Section 14(1) of the Public Order Act 1986.

case of *R (Brehony) v Chief Constable of Greater Manchester Police*.[103] Here, opposing political assemblies that often took place close to each other in the centre of Manchester raised concern for public disorder. As a result, police in Manchester sought to impose conditions on both demonstrations, pursuant to section 14 of the 1986 Act, instructing them to protest in another location during the Christmas period, when the city centre would be particularly busy. Brehony, one of the protestors, brought a judicial review application under section 7(1)(a) of the Human Rights Act 1998, challenging the lawfulness of the police's restriction under Articles 10 and 11 ECHR. The application was rejected, however, the court finding that since Articles 10 and 11 were not absolute rights, but necessary to be balanced with competing interests, the police's conditions were a proportionate interference in order that public order might be maintained.[104] Similarly, in the case of *James v DPP*,[105] protestors had failed to comply with directions issued by a police officer under section 14 of the Public Order Act 1986. The Court discussed at length the basis on which prosecution for public order offences should be considered and the extent to which ECHR rights should be relevant to that. While it was argued in the case that the court must always consider, in public order cases, 'whether the action taken by the police was proportionate to the disturbance caused by the demonstration, as their action engaged articles 10 and 11 of the Convention',[106] Ouseley J rejected this argument. The court held that, provided a particular statutory offence is compatible with the ECHR and the particulars of that offence have been satisfied by the actions in question, then there is no need to go further and 'to consider whether the prosecution breaches articles 10 or 11'.[107]

One of the more recent instances of the police imposing conditions on assemblies is in respect of the Extinction Rebellion protests prominent in London in October 2019. Extinction Rebellion is a movement committed to encouraging government action in respect of climate change. To this end, mass protests—dubbed the 'Autumn Uprising'—were planned in London from 7 October 2019. A day after the protests began, the Metropolitan Police Service imposed a condition under section 14 of the Public Order Act 1986, requiring that '[a]ny assembly linked to the Extinction Rebellion "Autumn Uprising" . . . MUST go to Trafalgar Square and only assemble in the pedestrianised area around Trafalgar Column'.[108] In the days that followed, the police made a large number of arrests of protestors refusing to abide by these conditions and, in fact, on 14 October 2019, a further condition was imposed under section 14. This provided that '[a]ny assembly linked to the Extinction Rebellion "Autumn Uprising" . . . must now cease . . . within London by 21.00hrs [on Monday] 14th October 2019'.[109] Though protestors were given time to comply with the updated conditions, further arrests were made in its regard in subsequent days. This provides a recent example of the way in which the police can

---

[103] [2005] EWHC 640 (Admin).

[104] See, for further discussion, 'R (Brehony) v Chief Constable of Greater Manchester Police (2005)' (*Solicitors Journal*, 1 April 2005), https://www.solicitorsjournal.com/node/206170.

[105] [2015] EWHC 3296 (Admin).

[106] Ibid [15].

[107] Ibid [19], citing *Bauer v DPP (Liberty intervening)* [2013] 1 WLR 3617 and dismissing *Dehal v CPS* (2005) 169 JP 581.

[108] Metropolitan Police, 'Conditions imposed on Extinction Rebellion protests', 15 October 2019, http://news.met.police.uk/news/conditions-imposed-on-extinction-rebellion-protests-384627.

[109] Metropolitan Police, 'Conditions imposed on Extinction Rebellion protests', 15 October 2019, http://news.met.police.uk/news/conditions-imposed-on-extinction-rebellion-protests-384627.

impose conditions under section 14 of the Public Order Act 1986 to 'prevent . . . demonstrations from causing serious disruption to the community'.[110]

The power to prohibit the holding of assemblies, however, compared with that relating to processions, is more narrow in scope. Section 14A of the Act states that a police officer may apply to a local council for an order prohibiting the holding of assemblies of '20 or more persons',[111] only where the assembly is:

> to be held . . . at a place on land to which the public has no right of access or only a limited right of access and . . . (a) is likely to be held without the permission of the occupier . . . or to conduct itself in such a way as to exceed the limits of any permission . . . and (b) may result–(i) in serious disruption to the life of the community, or (ii) where the land, or a building or monument on it, is of historical, architectural, archaeological or scientific importance, in significant damage to the land, building or monument.[112]

Sections 14B and 14C then cover offences connected to trespassory assemblies and the power of the police to stop people participating in such assemblies. Protestors in the case of *DPP v Jones and Lloyd*,[113] for instance, were charged with having committed a trespassory assembly under section 14B of the 1986 Act by protesting on the roadside, close to Stonehenge. Though they were initially convicted, this was overturned on appeal, the House of Lords finding that a peaceful assembly which did not unreasonably interfere with or obstruct the highway was not a trespassory assembly, adding that a public right of way—such as that which existed in respect of the highway—did not merely entitle the public to pass and repass, but also included a right to assemble, so long as any assembly did not obstruct the highway.

The first half of this chapter has sought to explore in detail the extent to which rights protected in Articles 10 and 11 ECHR operate and are protected under UK law. The Public Order Acts, along with other legislative provisions, provide the courts with the means through which a balance can be struck between these rights and the need to ensure and maintain public order. The chapter now moves on, though, to explore another area in which ECHR rights have to be balanced with competing interests, namely the powers of the police effectively to fulfil their duties and responsibilities in investigating and dealing with the commission of crimes. In order that this section can be explored, though, we start now with another problem scenario.

16.5 Powers of the police and the law

Problem scenario: police powers

Donald is on his way home from work. Wearing a baggy grey hoodie, black jeans, and blue trainers, he carries a plastic bag from the shop where he works containing some items he bought on his lunch break. To get home, Donald has to walk through a part of town that is

→

---

[110] Metropolitan Police, 'Conditions imposed on Extinction Rebellion protests', 15 October 2019, http://news.met.police.uk/news/conditions-imposed-on-extinction-rebellion-protests-384627.

[111] See s 14A(9) of the Public Order Act 1986.

[112] Section 14A(1) of the Public Order Act 1986.

[113] [1999] UKHL 5.

➜

notorious for its crime rate and for the presence of drug dealing gangs. Carrying out a routine patrol of the area, PC Smith and WPC Jones catch sight of Donald. Knowing the area and not liking his scruffy appearance, they approach Donald and ask him to stop 'for a chat'. Donald does so, reluctantly. The police officers say to Donald 'We're carrying out a routine patrol of the area and we'd like to search your bag, we have good reason to suspect that you are carrying stolen items'. At this point, Donald becomes aggressive. He pushes the officers out the way and attempts to walk off, refusing the requests to search his bag. Straight away WPC Jones grabs Donald and says, 'You'd better come with us, hadn't you?' When Donald asks why, PC Smith responds 'I think you know why; you're nicked, mate'.

Once at the police station, Donald is thrown straight away into a cell without any further information. While Donald is in detention, PC Smith and WPC Jones drive to his house. Approaching the door, they hear muffled gunshots and a number of screams. They kick the door in and enter hurriedly, to find a teenage boy (Donald's son) watching an action film on the television. Realizing that their suspicions of a violent crime are misplaced, PC Smith and WPC Jones turn to leave. As they do they spot an unmarked bag of DVDs and CDs in the hall, still in the wrappers and with the prices on. Suspecting these to have been stolen, the officers seize the bag and return to the station. It later transpires that the bag of DVDs and CDs was the result of Donald's son's recent trip to the shops.

The prevailing theme throughout the first half of this chapter was the need to ensure a balance of certain ECHR rights—in this case, the freedoms of expression, association, and assembly—with competing interests, in this instance, public order and safety. This focus on maintaining a balance between rights and competing interests is unchanged for this second half of the chapter, which moves now to consider how the rights of liberty and to a private and family life are impacted upon by laws setting out the powers and duties of the police to fulfil their role and ensure public safety. For the most part this involves consideration and exploration of the Police and Criminal Evidence Act 1984, though further legislation is cited where relevant. Before we come to examine the provisions of that Act, however, it is important to consider the ECHR rights that are relevant to this discussion.

16.6 The right to liberty and the right to a private and family life

Articles 5 and 8 of the ECHR set out and protect two fundamental rights, namely, the right to liberty and security and the right to respect for private and family life. We consider each of these in turn before exploring the way in which they are balanced alongside police powers.

Article 5 ECHR, which protects the right to liberty and security, states that '[e]veryone has the right to liberty and security of person' and that '[n]o one shall be deprived of his liberty' save in the event of certain stated exceptions 'and in accordance with a procedure prescribed by law'. The exceptions to this right, stated in Article 5(1) and already discussed in 15.3, mean that the right to liberty can be legitimately compromised in the following, limited circumstances:

(a) the lawful detention of a person after conviction by a competent court;

(b) the lawful arrest or detention of a person for noncompliance with the lawful order of a court or in order to secure the fulfilment of any obligation prescribed by law;

(c) the lawful arrest or detention of a person effected for the purpose of bringing him before the competent legal authority on reasonable suspicion of having committed an offence or when it is reasonably considered necessary to prevent his committing an offence or fleeing after having done so;

(d) the detention of a minor by lawful order for the purpose of educational supervision or his lawful detention for the purpose of bringing him before the competent legal authority;

(e) the lawful detention of persons for the prevention of the spreading of infectious diseases, of persons of unsound mind, alcoholics or drug addicts or vagrants;

(f) the lawful arrest or detention of a person to prevent his effecting an unauthorised entry into the country or of a person against whom action is being taken with a view to deportation or extradition.

In the case of *Austin v Commissioner of Police for the Metropolis*, for example, while the appeal courts found that Article 5 had not been engaged by the police cordon placed around the protestors in Oxford Circus, it is recalled that the Divisional Court found the cordon—or kettling—to be lawful under Article 5(1)(c) of the ECHR, the exception that permits detention to prevent an offence from being committed.

In addition, Article 5 also sets out various procedural requirements that must be fulfilled in the event of legitimate infringement of the right to liberty. When arrested, for example, an individual must be 'informed promptly . . . of the reasons for his arrest and of any charge against him'[114] and they should 'be brought promptly before a judge' or other judicial officer and 'entitled to trial within a reasonable time or to release pending trial'.[115] Finally, the article provides that an individual is entitled to bring proceedings testing the legality of his detention, which, if deemed to be unlawful, will lead to immediate release and a right to compensation.[116] Article 5, through its various exceptions and procedural requirements, seeks to ensure that, depending on the facts of a given case, the courts are able to strike a balance between protection of the right to liberty and justification of legitimate detentions and restrictions on individual liberty. As Lord Toulson stated in the case of *R (Hicks and others) v Commissioner of Police of the Metropolis*,[117] '[t]he fundamental principle underlying article 5 is the need to protect the individual from arbitrary detention, and an essential part of that protection is timely judicial control, but at the same time article 5 must not be interpreted in such a way as would make it impracticable for the police to perform their duty to maintain public order and protect the lives and property of others. These twin requirements are not contradictory but complementary.'[118]

---

[114] Article 5(2) ECHR.   [115] Article 5(3) ECHR.   [116] Article 5(4) and (5) ECHR.

[117] [2017] UKSC 9. This is a protest case, so could have been at home in the earlier part of this chapter.

[118] Ibid [29].

The second ECHR right relevant to our discussions in this section of the chapter is the right to respect for private and family life, protected under Article 8 of the Convention. This provision states that:

1. Everyone has the right to respect for his private and family life, his home and his correspondence.

2. There shall be no interference by a public authority with the exercise of this right except such as is in accordance with the law and is necessary in a democratic society in the interests of national security, public safety or the economic well-being of the country, for the prevention of disorder or crime, for the protection of health or morals, or for the protection of the rights and freedoms of others.

Though the exceptions to the right, listed in the second paragraph, cover a range of potential instances in which a right to a private and family life can be legitimately compromised, we are chiefly concerned with the manner in which actions of the police, in dealing with and investigating crimes, coincides with this right and the instances in which it is necessary to balance the values it protects with police action.

 Counterpoint: The importance of Article 6 ECHR

In considering the powers of the police to deal with and investigate crimes, it is also important to keep in mind Article 6 of the ECHR, which states, in paragraph (1), that '[i]n the determination of his civil rights and obligations or of any criminal charge against him, everyone is entitled to a fair and public hearing within a reasonable time by an independent and impartial tribunal established by law'. One of the most fundamental features of this right is the presumption of innocence. Article 6(2) provides that '[e]veryone charged with a criminal offence shall be presumed innocent until proved guilty according to law'. Despite the importance that the ECHR places on this presumption, it long pre-dates the Human Rights Act 1998 and, indeed, the ECHR's 1950s ratification. The presumption is, in most cases, taken to mean that the prosecution bears the burden of proof, meaning that it is required to satisfy a jury of the defendant's guilt, rather than the defendant of his innocence.[119] Above and beyond the common law foundation to the presumption of innocence, though, Article 6 also sets out various requirements which ensure that '[e]veryone charged with a criminal offence has' certain 'minimum rights' protected.[120] These include the right 'to be informed promptly' of the case against them; the right to defend oneself, or legal assistance to that end, with that assistance free of charge 'when the interests of justice so require'; 'adequate time and facilities for the preparation' of a defence; the right to examine witnesses giving evidence for the prosecution and the right to call upon witnesses in defence; and, finally, should the need arise, 'the free assistance of an interpreter'.[121] We see a manifestation of some of these requirements within the laws regulating police powers.

These rights are fundamental in protecting the liberty, privacy, and innocence of free individuals and, more than this, the rights of those suspected of committing criminal offences. Notwithstanding the importance of Articles 5, 8, and 6 of the ECHR, however,

---

[119] See Viscount Sankey in *DPP v Woolmington* [1935] AC 462, 481.
[120] Article 6(3) ECHR.   [121] Ibid.

in the interests of justice and of public safety, it is also important that the police be able to carry out their duties and responsibilities appropriately, with sufficient power and authority to investigate and deal with the commission of crimes. The powers of the police in this regard and the manner in which these sit alongside the rights contained in the ECHR, is our focus for the remainder of this chapter. We look now at the Police and Criminal Evidence Act 1984.

16.7 The Police and Criminal Evidence Act 1984

The Police and Criminal Evidence Act 1984[122] makes 'provision in relation to the powers and duties of the police, persons in police detention, criminal evidence, police discipline and complaints against the police'.[123] In doing this, it ensures that there are limits to these powers for the protection of fundamental human rights. Indeed, as Leon Brittan, the Home Secretary at the time of the Act, stated in the House of Commons:

> First, the present state of the law is unclear and contains many indefensible anomalies. Secondly, the police need to have adequate and clear powers to conduct the fight against crime on our behalf and the public need to have proper safeguards against any abuse of such powers if they are to have confidence in the police. Thirdly, these measures play an essential part in an overall strategy designed to create more effective policing. They do not solve, or pretend to solve, all the problems of policing in Britain today, but they have an important part to play alongside administrative and other measures . . . [that] ensure that the police can operate efficiently, fairly and with the active support of the public.[124]

The motivation behind PACE's enactment was the need to clarify previously unclear laws relating to the duties and responsibilities of the police and to set out the discretionary powers of the police in dealing with, preventing, and investigating crimes. The Act was preceded by the Royal Commission on Criminal Procedure, which was itself established in response to the 1977 Fisher Report. This report explored, in detail, the police procedures used during the investigation and preparation of the case brought following the murder of a man named Maxwell Confait in the early 1970s. In the case—*R v Lattimore*[125]—two boys were wrongly convicted of the murder, with allegations of suspicious police behaviour underpinning questionable confessions. On this foundation, the 1984 Act was just as much about clarifying police powers as it was about framing these powers in such a way that would serve to protect individuals' rights and prevent such miscarriages of justice in the future.

The provisions of the Act are accompanied by extensive Codes of Practice, which, while not legally binding, provide further guidance on the way in which the powers of the police contained not only in PACE, but in other relevant statutes as well, should be exercised. There are eight codes of practice, which cover:

Code A: Powers of stop and search

Code B: Searching premises and the seizure of property

Code C: Detention, treatment, and questioning of suspects

---

[122] Hereinafter PACE.   [123] Long Title to the 1984 Act.
[124] HC Deb, 7 November 1983, vol 48, cols 25–6.   [125] (1976) 62 Cr App R 53.

Code D: Identification matters

Code E: Tape-recorded interviews

Code F: Video-recorded interviews

Code G: Statutory powers of arrest

Code H: Detention of terrorist suspects

These Codes of Practice can be revised and added to at any time by the Secretary of State, pursuant to requirements and procedures set out in sections 60, 60A, and 66 of the 1984 Act. They are revised or introduced by statutory instrument and following consultation of various relevant bodies.[126]

PACE is an important piece of legislation, providing comprehensive regulation of police powers and serving as a step towards their full codification.[127] Vast as it is, though, in this chapter we focus only on certain specific sections of the Act, looking at three key areas: stop and search; arrest; and entry, search, and seizure. We start, now, with the first of these.

16.7.1 Stop and search powers

Pursuant to section 1(2)(a) of PACE, a police constable may search a person or a vehicle for stolen or prohibited articles. Such a search can only be carried out where the constable has reasonable grounds for suspecting that stolen or prohibited articles will be found[128] and the search must take place in public and must not require the removal of any clothing other than an outer coat, jacket, or gloves.[129] If the police officer is not in uniform then they must produce some form of documentation that substantiates their power to carry out the search.[130] In exercising the power, the police are able to detain the individual or the vehicle for the purposes of the search[131] and, pursuant to section 117 of the Act, they can use reasonable force in carrying out the search. Details of the search must be appropriately documented[132] and if any stolen or prohibited articles are found in the course of the search, these can be seized.[133] Notable as this power is, it is not the only stop and search power at the police's disposal. Under section 23(2) of the Misuse of Drugs Act 1971, for instance, there is a power to search anyone who a police officer has reasonable grounds of suspecting to be in possession of a controlled drug; while section 163 of the Road Traffic Act 1988 permits the police to stop vehicles. Section 60 of the Criminal Justice and Public Order Act 1994 gives police the authority to stop and search individuals or vehicles for 'offensive or dangerous instruments' where there is a reasonable belief that serious violence will occur in the locality. Finally, section 47A of the Terrorism Act 2000 empowers the police to stop and search individuals or vehicles for the purposes 'of discovering whether there is anything which may constitute evidence' of terrorist activities.[134] While this 2000 Act 'power . . . may be exercised whether or not the constable reasonably suspects that there is such evidence',[135] it can only be used where a senior officer has given authorisation, which itself must be founded on a

---

[126] These include the Bar Council, the Law Society, the Association of Police Authorities, and the Association of Chief Police Officers of England, Wales, and Northern Ireland.

[127] See, for further discussion, Richard Stone, *Civil Liberties and Human Rights* (10th edn, OUP 2014) 90.

[128] Section 1(3) of PACE.   [129] Sections 1(1) and 2(9) of PACE.   [130] Section 2 of PACE.

[131] Section 1(2)(b) of PACE.   [132] Section 3 of PACE.   [133] Section 1(6) of PACE.

[134] Inserted by the Protection of Freedoms Act 2012.

[135] Section 47A(5) of the Terrorism Act 2000.

reasonable suspicion 'that an act of terrorism will take place'.[136] Though repealed by the Protection of Freedoms Act, sections 44 and 45 of the Terrorism Act 2000 are also worth identifying here, these sections formerly empowering the police to stop individuals for the purposes of 'searching for articles of a kind which could be used in connection with terrorism'.[137] The police, therefore, have extensive powers at their disposal to carry out stop and searches.

Exercise of a stop and search power falls short of an arrest. This is reflected in the reality that a stop and search takes place in public, with various requirements designed to ensure the relevant officer can do no more than is necessary to carry out the required search. Despite this, however, stops and searches can still involve an infringement of a person's liberty. Explaining this, the Strasbourg Court in *Gillan v UK*[138] stated that the individuals in question, who were being stopped and searched under the provisions of the Terrorism Act 2000, 'were entirely deprived of any freedom of movement. They were obliged to remain where they were and submit to the search and if they had refused they would have been liable to arrest, detention at a police station and criminal charges. This element of coercion is indicative of a deprivation of liberty within the meaning of art. 5(1).'[139] Though stop and searches often take place in a public place and involve only momentary investigation by a police officer, therefore, they can still be regarded as an interference with the Article 5 right.

There are, then, extensive requirements accompanying stop and search powers, which ensure that they are exercised appropriately and proportionate to the right to liberty. The importance of these requirements is evident in the case of *Osman v DPP*.[140] Here, a search was being carried out pursuant to section 60 of the Criminal Justice and Public Order Act 1994. In the course of the search, the police officer failed to notify the individual being searched of their name and the police station at which they were based, as required by section 2 of PACE, which was sufficient to make the search unlawful. The defendant's initial conviction for assaulting a police officer was therefore quashed. It is important, then, that these powers are exercised in such a way that is balanced and proportionate to ECHR rights. One of the fundamental ways in which this is assessed, though, is through the requirement of reasonable suspicion.

Reasonable suspicion

It is a fundamental requirement of *some* of these stop and search powers that the police show reasonable suspicion. That is, reasonable grounds for suspecting, for example, that stolen or prohibited articles will be found by searching the individual or the vehicle in question (section 1 of PACE), or for suspecting that a person is in possession of a controlled drug (section 23(2) of the Misuse of Drugs Act). The importance of this reasonable suspicion requirement is significant in human rights terms as, keeping the balance in mind, it permits a point of examination to assess whether a search is compatible with ECHR rights. Reasonable suspicion must exist before a search begins and cannot be satisfied by items or evidence that might be obtained during the course of the search itself. Code A of the PACE Codes of Practice provides further guidance on this particular requirement. It states that reasonable suspicion:

> means that there must be an objective basis for that suspicion based on facts, information and/or intelligence which are relevant to the likelihood that the object in question will be

---

[136] Section 47A(1) of the Terrorism Act 2000.   [137] Section 45(1) of the Terrorism Act 2000.
[138] (2010) 50 EHRR 45.   [139] Ibid [57].   [140] [1999] EWHC 622 (Admin).

found, so that a reasonable person would be entitled to reach the same conclusion based on the same facts and information and/or intelligence. . . Reasonable suspicion can never be supported on the basis of personal factors. This means that unless the police have information or intelligence which provides a description of a person suspected of carrying an article for which there is a power to stop and search, the following cannot be used, alone or in combination with each other, or in combination with any other factor, as the reason for stopping and searching any individual, including any vehicle which they are driving or are being carried in: (a) A person's physical appearance . . . or the fact that the person is known to have a previous conviction; and (b) Generalisations or stereotypical images that certain groups or categories of people are more likely to be involved in criminal activity.[141]

Despite Code A's coverage of this particular requirement, it is also an issue to which the courts have paid a great deal of attention. In the case of *Lodwick v Sanders*,[142] for instance, two policemen stopped a lorry under a power contained in section 159 of the Road Traffic Act 1972, on the grounds that it had no rear registration plate and because its rear brake lights were not working. Upon questioning the driver about ownership of the vehicle, a vague answer was given and an attempt made at that point to drive off and leave the search. This was, in the opinion of the Divisional Court, sufficient to give rise to a reasonable suspicion that the lorry had been stolen. Later, in the unreported case of *Black v DPP*,[143] during a search of premises pursuant to the Misuse of Drugs Act 1971, the defendant arrived carrying a bag. Given the nature of the search (ie drug related) the police suspected that the defendant had arrived either to sell or buy drugs and asked to search him on that basis. When he became aggressive, however, and attempted to leave, he was charged and later convicted under section 23(4)(a) of the 1971 Act for obstructing exercise of the search power. This was quashed by the Divisional Court, however, who held that merely arriving at the property of a known drug dealer could not give rise to a reasonable suspicion that the defendant himself was in possession of drugs.

The notion of reasonable suspicion, therefore, has been interpreted broadly by the courts in assessing whether or not police searches are legitimate. This discussion of reasonable suspicion notwithstanding, however, it is also notable from a human rights perspective that the powers contained in sections 44 and 45 (now repealed) and 47A of the Terrorism Act 2000 and section 60 of the Criminal Justice and Public Order Act 1994 permit the police to stop and search individuals *without* this need for reasonable suspicion.[144] It is the powers in sections 44 and 45 of the 2000 Act that is our focus in the case of *R (on the application of Gillan) v Commissioner of Police of the Metropolis*.[145]

Case in depth: *R (on the application of Gillan) v Commissioner of Police of the Metropolis* [2006] UKHL 12

In the summer of 2003, officers of the Metropolitan Police in London were authorized and instructed to use the stop and search powers contained in sections 44 and 45 of the 2000 Act to stop members of the public randomly in search of items that could be connected with terrorist

➡

---

[141] PACE Codes of Practice, Code A, paras 2.2 and 2.2B.   [142] [1985] 1 WLR 382.

[143] (1995), unreported.

[144] As already noted, s 47A must be based on an authorization that is given on the basis of reasonable suspicion that an act of terrorism will take place (s 47A(1)).

[145] [2006] UKHL 12.

> → offences. The power was used to stop two individuals in East London who were on their way to a demonstration. No items were found. The individuals, though, brought claims for judicial review of both the search and the authorization that it should be carried out, arguing that they were excessive and disproportionate responses to the threat of terrorist activities at that time. Their applications were dismissed by the Divisional Court, with subsequent appeals to the Court of Appeal and the House of Lords also dismissing their case.

In giving their judgment, the House of Lords noted the significance of the stop and search power and its lack of any requirement of reasonable suspicion, going on to identify that there were other constraints within the 2000 Act that would serve to ensure that the power was used appropriately. Lord Bingham stated that:

> It is true . . . that section 45(1)(b), in dispensing with the condition of reasonable suspicion, departs from the normal rule applicable where a constable exercises a power to stop and search . . . [But t]here is . . . every indication that Parliament appreciated the significance of the power it was conferring but thought it an appropriate measure to protect the public against the grave risks posed by terrorism, provided the power was subject to effective constraints. The legislation embodies a series of such constraints.[146]

Such constraints included, said Lord Bingham, the fact that 'an authorisation under section 44(1) or (2) may be given only if the person giving it [reasonably] considers . . . it expedient "for the prevention of acts of terrorism". [Adding that t]he authorisation must be directed to that overriding objective'.[147] In addition, the power could only be authorized by a very senior police officer, for a limited period of twenty-eight days, and it had to be reported to the Secretary of State, who had the power to shorten or cancel its application.[148]

On further appeal to the ECtHR, the House of Lords' decision in *Gillan* was reversed. The Strasbourg Court, commenting on the power's lack of any requirement of reasonable suspicion, stated that:

> In the Court's view, there is a clear risk of arbitrariness in the grant of such a broad discretion to the police officer . . . such a widely framed power could be misused against demonstrators and protestors in breach of Article 10 and/or 11 of the Convention . . . [I]n the absence of any obligation on the part of the officer to show a reasonable suspicion, it is likely to be difficult if not impossible to prove that the power was improperly exercised . . . [T]he Court considers[, therefore,] that the powers of authorisation and confirmation as well as those of stop and search under sections 44 and 45 of the 2000 Act are neither sufficiently circumscribed nor subject to adequate legal safeguards against abuse. They are not, therefore, 'in accordance with the law' and it follows that there has been a violation of Article 8 of the Convention.[149]

Gillan v UK was later considered by the UK Supreme Court in *R (Roberts) v Commissioner of Police of the Metropolis and another (Liberty intervening)*,[150] a case concerning use of the power set out in section 60 of the 1994 Act and also permitting searches without the need for reasonable suspicion.

---

[146] Ibid [14].   [147] Ibid.   [148] Ibid [14].
[149] (2010) 50 EHRR 1105 [85]–[87].   [150] [2015] UKSC 79.

> **Case in depth:** *R (Roberts) v Commissioner of Police of the Metropolis and another (Liberty intervening)* **[2015] UKSC 79**
>
> In response to an increase in gang violence across certain London Boroughs, police officers were authorized and instructed to exercise the stop and search powers contained in section 60 of the Criminal Justice and Public Order Act 1994. Roberts was travelling on the bus without a fare and, when confronted by a ticket inspector, she gave a false name and address. When the police were called, suspicious of her nervous behaviour and her insistence in clinging on to her bag, they effected a search under the section 60 power, suspecting Roberts to be in possession of offensive weapons. The officer, however, found no offensive weapons. Roberts sought judicial review of the stop and search under the Human Rights Act, claiming that the power under section 60 was arbitrary and incompatible with her Article 8 right to a private life.[151] She sought a section 4 declaration of incompatibility on this basis. Her claim was dismissed by the Divisional Court, however, a decision that was upheld on appeal to both the Court of Appeal and the Supreme Court. No declaration of incompatibility was made.

In considering whether or not the lack of a requirement of reasonable suspicion could be deemed compatible with the ECHR, Baroness Hale considered in the Supreme Court the ECtHR's finding in *Gillan*, noting that 'it cannot be concluded from the Gillan case that the Strasbourg court would regard every "suspicionless" power to stop and search as failing the Convention requirement of lawfulness'.[152] She then went on to cite the post-*Gillan* case of *Colon v The Netherlands*,[153] in which a broadly drafted search power—also not requiring any reasonable suspicion to be established—was found to be compatible with the ECHR.[154] With this authority in mind, Baroness Hale went on to comment on the compatibility of section 60 of the 1994 Act, stating that:

> Any random 'suspicionless' power of stop and search carries with it the risk that it will be used in an arbitrary or discriminatory manner in individual cases . . . whatever the scope of the power in question, [though,] it must be operated in a lawful manner. It is not enough simply to look at the content of the power. It has to be read in conjunction with section 6(1) of the Human Rights Act 1998, which makes it unlawful for a police officer to act in a manner which is incompatible with the Convention rights of any individual. It has also to be read in conjunction with the Equality Act 2010 . . . [There are] other features, contained in a mixture of the Act itself, PACE and the force Standard Operating Procedures, which [also] guard against the risk that the officer will not, in fact, have good reasons for the decision. The result of breaching these will in many cases be to render the stop and search itself unlawful and to expose the officers concerned to disciplinary action . . . All of these requirements . . . should make it possible to judge whether the action was 'necessary in a democratic society . . . for the prevention of disorder or crime'.[155]

It was found, therefore, on the strength of Strasbourg jurisprudence and broader statutory safeguards, that a stop and search power that included no requirement for reasonable suspicion to be shown could be compatible with ECHR rights.

---

[151] She had also alleged violation of Arts 5 and 14, though these were dealt with in the earlier appeals.
[152] [2015] UKSC 79 [21].   [153] (2012) 55 EHRR SE45.
[154] [2015] UKSC 79 [21].   [155] Ibid [41]–[47].

Pause for reflection

Do you agree with the decision in *Roberts*? What are the dangers—from a human rights perspective—in empowering the police to carry out stops and searches without a need for reasonable suspicion?

The requirement—or lack thereof—of reasonable suspicion is one of the main ways in which stop and search powers engage with and impact upon the ECHR rights. Where the requirement exists, it provides a mechanism through which the proportionality of the use of the stop and search powers can be assessed by the courts.[156] Conversely, and where there is no requirement for reasonable suspicion, then the broader requirements of the particular power in question need to be sufficient to ensure that an individual's rights are not infringed by exercise of the power, as the respective House of Lords and Supreme Court judgments in *Gillan* and *Robert* demonstrate.

Discussing the problem

Look back to the problem scenario at the start of the police powers section of this chapter. Did PC Smith and WPC Jones have reasonable suspicion for the stop and search that they attempted to carry out on Donald?

What difference would it make if a fellow police officer had given them a tip-off that an individual fitting Donald's description was walking through the area with a bag of stolen goods?

On the facts of the problem scenario as they stand, any reasonable suspicion that PC Smith and WPC Jones have is somewhat questionable. Code A of the Codes of Practice makes clear that 'there must be an objective basis for that suspicion based on facts, information and/or intelligence which are relevant to the likelihood that the object in question will be found . . . [it] can never be supported on the basis of personal factors'.[157] Donald is stopped largely on the basis of his appearance, factors which are subjective, rather than objective. Indeed, '[a] person's physical appearance' is noted in Code A as being a basis on which reasonable suspicion cannot be legitimately founded. There could arguably be grounds to question the lawfulness of his stop and search.

Considering whether it would make a difference if a fellow police officer had given PC Smith and WPC Jones a tip-off that an individual fitting Donald's description was walking through the area, the answer is yes. Code A also makes clear that if 'the police have information or intelligence which provides a description of a person suspected of carrying an article for which there is a power to stop and search',[158] then this can legitimately form the basis of a reasonable suspicion.

[156] Ibid [43].   [157] PACE Codes of Practice, Code A, paras 2.2 and 2.2B.
[158] Ibid.

16.7.2 **Arrest**

Unlike the powers of stop and search set out in the opening sections of PACE and other statutes, powers and provisions relating to the arrest of suspected criminals are more significant from a human rights perspective since they involve a more substantial deprivation of an individual's liberty. It is important that where such powers are exercised, they are done so legitimately and lawfully so as not to fall outside the scope of Article 5 ECHR. Arrest is not itself a single act, but in the words of Lord Diplock it is:

> a continuing act: it starts with the arrester taking a person into custody (so by action or words restraining him from moving anywhere beyond the arrester's control), and it continues until the person so restrained is either released from custody or, having been brought before a magistrate, is remanded in custody by the magistrate's judicial act.[159]

It is also important that this process of arrest and the ongoing deprivation of liberty that it can bring is legitimate and supported by appropriate legal authority. In terms of the powers of arrest, this chapter has already explained and explored the common law basis for arresting individuals and does not seek to do so again here. We are concerned here with the statutory basis for arrest and, in particular, the power contained in PACE.

The 1984 Act used to distinguish between arrestable and non-arrestable offences, offering powers of arrest on this basis.[160] Following a Home Office consultation, however, changes were introduced by the Serious Organised Crime and Policing Act 2005 to effect 'a straightforward, universal framework which focuses on the nature of an offence in relation to the circumstances of the victim, the offender and the needs of the investigation'.[161] Following these reforms, PACE now distinguishes between arrests that are carried out by the police and those carried out by 'other persons'.[162] Both of these powers are to effect an arrest without a warrant (the power to arrest with a warrant is covered by section 1(1) of the Magistrates' Court Act 1980). On the basis that this chapter's focus is specifically on the powers of the police, we look now at the police's power to arrest, set out in section 24 of PACE.

Section 24(1) of the 1984 Act provides that '[a] constable may arrest without a warrant— (a) anyone who is about to commit an offence; (b) anyone who is in the act of committing an offence; (c) anyone whom he has reasonable grounds for suspecting to be about to commit an offence; (d) anyone whom he has reasonable grounds for suspecting to be committing an offence'. Section 24(2) and (3) add that where an offence has been committed, or a police officer, having reasonable grounds for suspecting that an offence has been committed, may arrest anybody that he has reasonable grounds for suspecting to have committed that offence.

Such is the severity of any potential deprivation of liberty under this power, pursuant to sections 24(4) and (5), an arrest without a warrant can only be made if the police officer in question has reasonable grounds for believing that the arrest is necessary for one

---

[159] *Holgate-Mohammed v Duke* [1984] AC 437, 441. The notion of arrest as a process is contested, though. It does not necessarily sit easily with s 28 of PACE, which appears to be premised on arrest being an event, not a process. Also see *R v Fiak* [2005] EWCA Crim 2381.

[160] This distinction no longer exists—all offences are now potentially arrestable.

[161] Home Office, *Policing: Modernising Police Powers to Meet Community Needs* (2004), http://www.statewatch.org/news/2004/aug/police-powers-consult.pdf.

[162] See ss 24 and 24A of PACE.

of a number of reasons. These reasons are: to obtain the suspect's name and address; to prevent them causing or suffering injury, loss, or damage to property, or to prevent them from committing an offence against public decency or an unlawful obstruction of the highway; to protect a child or vulnerable person; to ensure prompt and effective investigation; or to keep the suspect from disappearing and thereby avoiding prosecution.[163]

There are a number of requirements, then, that must be satisfied if a lawful arrest is to be effected under the power set out in PACE, and an individual deprived of their liberty for one of the reasons stated under subsection (5). Above and beyond these provisions, however, the courts have, on occasion, been called upon to assess the lawfulness of arrests and, in so doing, have elucidated tests for determining whether an arrest can be regarded as lawful. In the case of *Hayes v Chief Constable of Merseyside Constabulary*,[164] a claimant brought proceedings against the police for wrongful arrest following his detention and subsequent release in light of harassment allegations that were later withdrawn. Though Hayes lost his case at first instance, he appealed to the Court of Appeal, arguing that arrest should have been a last resort and that the police should have considered appropriate alternatives before arresting him. Though the Court of Appeal rejected this argument, Hughes LJ explained the test that should be applied in examining the lawfulness of an arrest under section 24 of PACE. The first requirement is that, if a police officer has reasonable grounds for suspecting that an individual has committed an offence, they must reasonably believe that the individual's arrest is necessary within section 24(5) of PACE.[165] Added to this, the second requirement is that the belief that an arrest is necessary must be objectively reasonable.[166] In the case of *Commissioner of Police of the Metropolis v MR*,[167] the arrested individual had voluntarily turned himself into a police station in connection with an allegation of harassment. He was arrested and remanded in custody. The arrest was found to be unlawful, however, since—as Mrs Justice Thornton explained—'there was no objective need to arrest MR, given his voluntary attendance at the police station'.[168] Adding context and explanation to this finding, the court said that an 'officer who has given no thought to alternatives to arrest is exposed to the risk of being found by a Court to have had objectively no reasonable grounds for his belief that arrest was necessary'.[169]

Above and beyond the requirements contained in section 24 of PACE, section 28(1) of the Act also sets out another important requirement. It states that 'the arrest is not lawful unless the person arrested is informed that he is under arrest as soon as is practicable after his arrest'. This is supplemented by section 24(3), which adds that 'no arrest is lawful unless the person arrested is informed of the ground for the arrest at the time of, or, as soon as is practicable after, the arrest'. Both of these requirements must be honoured, even if the offence or the circumstances of the arrest make the reason obvious,[170] though the information does not necessarily have to be provided by the police officer actually carrying out the arrest.[171] Where this information is not provided, the arrest is unlawful from the point at which the court thinks that it would have been practicable to provide the information.[172]

---

[163] Section 24(5) of PACE.   [164] [2011] EWCA Civ 911.   [165] Ibid [16].   [166] Ibid.
[167] [2019] EWHC 888 (QB).   [168] [2019] EWHC 888 (QB) [50].
[169] [2019] EWHC 888 (QB) [49], citing *Hayes* [34] and [40].   [170] Sections 28(2) and (4) of PACE.
[171] *Dhesi v Chief Constable of West Midlands* (9 May 2000) The Times.
[172] See *DPP v Hawkins* [1988] 1 WLR 1166.

The importance of this requirement is underlined by the fact that it actually pre-dates PACE, its pre-1984 authority lying at common law. In the case of *Christie v Leachinsky*,[173] an individual was arrested, pursuant to the Liverpool Corporation Act 1921, for theft. The suspect, however, was not given any reason for the arrest, an omission which was sufficient to render the arrest unlawful. In the House of Lords, Viscount Simon explained the fundamental principle in the following terms:

> If a policeman arrests without warrant upon reasonable suspicion of felony . . . he must in ordinary circumstances inform the person arrested of the true ground of arrest . . . a citizen is entitled to know on what charge or on suspicion of what crime he is seized. If the citizen is not so informed but is nevertheless seized, the policeman . . . is liable for false imprisonment . . . [I]n this country a person is, prima facie, entitled to his freedom and is only required to submit to restraints on his freedom if he knows in substance the reason why it is claimed that this restraint should be imposed.[174]

Another one of the requirements for arrest under PACE is the need for reasonable suspicion. Indeed, it was noted above that section 24(2) and (3) of the Act make clear that where an offence has been committed, or where a police officer has reasonable grounds for suspecting that an offence has been committed, the officer may arrest anybody that they have reasonable grounds for suspecting to have committed that offence. As we have discussed, this need for reasonable suspicion is rooted in the balance that must be struck between the need for the police to be able to carry out and effect a lawful arrest, and against this, the individual's right to liberty and freedom, protected under the ECHR. In the case of *Castorina v Chief Constable of Surrey*,[175] an individual was arrested on suspicion of burglary following a break-in at the company from which she had recently been sacked. She was later released without charge. In proceedings later brought by Castorina for wrongful arrest, the Court of Appeal explained the requirement of reasonable suspicion in respect of the power of arrest. The Court emphasized that '[s]uspicion by itself . . . will not justify an arrest. There must be a factual basis for it of a kind which a court would adjudge to be reasonable.'[176] In *Kandamwala v Cambridgeshire Constabulary HQs*,[177] for instance, a woman calling the police to allege that a man had touched her daughter's bottom was a sufficient basis for reasonable suspicion. In explaining more fully the test to be applied, though, the court in *Castorina* elucidated a three-stage test, which should be used in assessing the reasonableness of an arrest. The first question to ask, said Woolf LJ, is '(a) [d]id the arresting officer suspect that the person arrested was guilty of the offence?'[178] This, he stated, 'depends entirely on the findings of fact as to the officer's state of mind' and is consequently a subjective test.[179] The second question is '(b) [a]ssuming the officer had the necessary suspicion, was there reasonable cause for [that] suspicion?'.[180] This, said Woolf LJ, is 'a purely objective requirement'.[181] The final element of the test is as follows: '(c) [i]f the answer to the two previous questions is in the affirmative, then the officer has a discretion which entitles him to make an arrest and in relation to that discretion has been exercised in accordance with the principles laid down by Lord Greene MR in *Associated Provincial Picture Houses Ltd v Wednesbury Corporation*'.[182] The combined subjective and objective elements of this test were confirmed by the House of Lords in *O'Hara v Chief*

[173] [1947] AC 573.   [174] Ibid 587–8.   [175] (1988) LG Rev R 241.   [176] Ibid.
[177] (2017), unreported.   [178] (1988) LG Rev R 241.   [179] Ibid.   [180] Ibid.
[181] Ibid.   [182] Ibid, citing [1948] 1 KB 223.

Constable for the Royal Ulster Constabulary.[183] Lord Hope, there discussing the power of arrest set out within section 12(1) of the Prevention of Terrorism (Temporary Provisions) Act 1984, noted that it is '[i]n part . . . a subjective test, because he [the police officer] must have formed a genuine suspicion in his own mind that the person has been concerned in acts of terrorism. In part also, it is an objective one, because there must also be reasonable grounds for the suspicion which he has formed.'[184] More recently, in the case of *McCann v DPP*, the Divisional Court explained:

> The arresting officer must have formed a genuine suspicion that the person being arrested had been concerned in offending and there had to be reasonable grounds for forming such a suspicion. Such grounds did not have to be based on the officer's own observations but could arise from information he had received even if it was subsequently shown to be false, provided that a reasonable man, having regard to all the surrounding circumstances, would regard them as reasonable grounds for suspicion.[185]

This last point is demonstrated both by the case of *O'Hara*, in which an anonymous tip-off was sufficient to amount to a lawful reasonable suspicion and by the case of *Alford v Chief Constable of Cambridgeshire*,[186] in which a briefing provided by a fellow police officer was found to be sufficient basis for a reasonable suspicion. In other cases, though, the courts have been more restrictive in their interpretation of the reasonable suspicion requirement. In *Raissi v Commissioner of Police of the Metropolis*,[187] for example, a woman and her brother were arrested under section 41 of the Terrorism Act 2000, questioned and later released without charge. The basis for reasonable suspicion was that the man's brother was himself a suspected terrorist and that he lived close by. The Court of Appeal held that this was insufficient.[188] The requirement, made clear in *O'Hara*, that the police officer 'must have formed a genuine suspicion in his own mind that the person' has committed an offence[189] was not satisfied in the case of *Parker v Chief Constable of Essex*.[190] Here, the arrest was unlawful since, though the investigating officer had reasonable grounds of suspicion that Parker had committed an offence and that his arrest was necessary, she was delayed and therefore unable to carry out the arrest. A surveillance officer was instead asked to arrest Parker in her place. As a result, 'it was admitted on . . . behalf [of the Chief Constable] that the arrest was unlawful . . . [since] the arresting officer did not personally have reasonable grounds for the necessary suspicion to justify arrest as required by s. 24(2) of the Police and Criminal Evidence Act 1984'.[191]

As the tests discussed in *Castorina* and *O'Hara* emphasize, along with the various cases explored throughout this section, whether there are reasonable grounds for an arrest is a question to be considered by the courts in each case. The requirement, though, is a vital part of the power of arrest and in ensuring that, where an individual is deprived of their liberty to the extent that they are arrested, that power is exercised on a reasonable suspicion that arrest is necessary.

---

[183] [1997] AC 286.   [184] Ibid 298.   [185] [2015] EWHC 2461 (Admin) at para 20.
[186] [2009] EWCA Civ 100.   [187] [2008] EWCA Civ 1237.
[188] Similar to *O'Hara*, this is another case in which the arresting officer had undertaken no inquiries of his own but was simply going on what he had been told by superiors, who in turn had learned the facts of the allegations from the FBI.
[189] Ibid 298.   [190] [2018] EWCA Civ 2788.
[191] [2018] EWCA Civ 2788 [6]. In view of this admission, it is important to note that this case concerned the level of damages due to Parker following the unlawful arrest.

Discussing the problem

Have another look at the police powers problem scenario. Is there anything wrong with the arrest carried out on Donald?

Under section 24 of PACE, the police have the power to arrest without a warrant anyone they have reasonable grounds for suspecting to have committed an offence. The requirement of reasonable suspicion is, again, notable in this regard. As the judgment in *O'Hara* explains, this is an issue involving both subjective and objective questions. PC Smith and WPC Jones 'must have formed a genuine suspicion' in their minds that Donald was carrying a bag of stolen goods, but there must also be objectively reasonable grounds for the suspicion.[192] It could be argued that PC Smith and WPC Jones have the requisite reasonable suspicion on the basis that Donald starts acting aggressively when a bag-search is mentioned. He also pushes the officers and attempts to walk off, refusing the requests to search his bag. Subjectively, his specific behaviour can be regarded as suspicious, while his refusal to show the officers his bag and attempts to walk off might objectively be seen as actions to hide something.

The main problem with Donald's arrest, however, relates to the requirement in section 28(1) of PACE, which states that 'arrest is not lawful unless the person arrested is informed that he is under arrest as soon as is practicable after his arrest'. This is supplemented by section 24(3), which adds that 'no arrest is lawful unless the person arrested is informed of the ground for the arrest at the time of, or, as soon as is practicable after, the arrest'. When PC Smith simply tells Donald 'you're nicked, mate', this fails to satisfy the statutory requirement. Donald must be told of the offence of which they suspect him having committed. On this basis, the arrest could be argued as unlawful.

Having now considered the extent to which the powers of arrest under PACE impact upon and are balanced against individual's rights, it is necessary now to consider the powers of the police to enter and search premises belonging to another individual and the power to seize items found in the course of that search.

16.7.3 Entry, search, and seizure

At law, there is a presumption in favour of the sanctity of a person's private property. Another individual can only enter your property with your consent or with appropriate legal authority. There is much to support this, including the famous words of Sir Edward Coke in *Semayne's Case*:[193] '[t]he house of every one is his castle.'[194] This is a principle that later found expression in the case of *Entick v Carrington*,[195] in which a King's messenger entered Entick's property under the authority of a general warrant that had been unlawfully issued by the Secretary of State. Emphasizing, even in 1765, the principle that you can only enter the property of another with lawful authority, Lord Camden CJ stated that '[b]y the laws of England, every invasion of private property, be it ever so minute, is a trespass. No man can set his foot upon my ground without my licence',[196] a principle that remains unchanged in UK law to this day. In this final section, and in the context both of

---

[192] [1997] AC 286 at 298.   [193] (1604) 5 Coke Rep 91.   [194] Ibid 91a.
[195] (1765) 95 ER 807.   [196] Ibid 817.

this historic principle and of this chapter's focus on police powers, we are here concerned with the provisions of PACE that provide the necessary legal authority for police to enter the property of another for the purposes of carrying out their duties and responsibilities and the provisions that permit police to seize items upon such entry. This legal authority can be found in four different sections, which we consider in turn. Before this, however, it is important to identify the importance of section 78 of PACE, which concerns the exclusion of evidence at trial. This section states:

> In any proceedings the court may refuse to allow evidence on which the prosecution proposes to rely to be given if it appears to the court that, having regard to all the circumstances, including the circumstances in which the evidence was obtained, the admission of the evidence would have such an adverse effect on the fairness of the proceedings that the court ought not to admit it.

The effect of this provision is essentially to permit the courts a discretion to exclude evidence in a criminal trial where it is felt that it would have a detrimental effect on the fairness of the trial, a discretion that is consistent with duties under the Human Rights Act, which make it incumbent upon the judiciary to ensure that human rights—including those of an accused individual—are upheld in the course of any such proceedings.[197] There are a number of ways in which evidence could be deemed unlawfully obtained—including through a breach of the Codes of Conduct. Relevant to the discussion in this section, though, concerning the legal bases on which the police can enter property belonging to another and seize certain items there found, section 78 ensures that where evidence is obtained in the course of a search that falls outside the sections now explored, the courts can exclude its admission in the course of the trial, thereby protecting the human rights of the accused. With section 78 in mind, this chapter now proceeds to examine the powers concerning entry, search, and seizure set out in PACE.

Section 8 of the 1984 Act empowers a magistrate to issue a warrant, authorizing a police officer to enter and search premises specified in that warrant. Unlike sections 18 and 32, discussed below, exercise of this power is premised on prior judicial involvement and sanction, rather than the police simply authorizing themselves to enter and search particular premises. Such a warrant can be issued, following an application by the police, where the magistrate has reasonable grounds for believing that an indictable offence has been committed and that there is material on the premises likely to be of value to the investigation and relevant evidence in any subsequent trial.[198] Entry with the warrant must be deemed necessary by the magistrate, on the grounds that 'it is not practicable to communicate with any person entitled to grant entry to the premises . . . [or] access to the evidence'; if the occupier's permission to enter is contingent upon a warrant being produced; or if 'the purpose of a search [would] be frustrated or seriously prejudiced unless' the police 'can secure immediate entry'.[199] The materials likely to be found at the premises cannot be subject to legal privilege,[200] but under section 8(2) can be seized and retained by the police. The Serious Organised Crime and Police Act 2005 introduced certain changes to this power, including permitting 'entry to and search of premises on more than one occasion', provided the magistrate deems it necessary to authorize multiple entries.[201] The 2005 Act

---

[197] See s 3 of the Human Rights Act 1998.   [198] Section 8(1) of PACE.
[199] Section 8(3) of PACE.   [200] Section 8(1)(d) of PACE.   [201] Section 8(1C) of PACE.

also provided that the warrant need not merely apply to one specific premises, but potentially to any premises controlled by a person named in the warrant.[202]

There are, then, a number of requirements that must be satisfied if entry and search of a premises, pursuant to one of these warrants, is to be lawful. If all of the various conditions are not met, then the warrant could potentially be deemed unlawful. In *Redknapp v Commissioner of Police of the Metropolis*,[203] for instance, football manager Harry Redknapp was suspected of committing various fraud offences relating to false accounting in the buying and selling of football players during his time at Portsmouth Football Club. In the investigation of the alleged offence, the police sought to enter his house by virtue of a warrant issued under section 8 of PACE, Redknapp's wife admitting the officers for the search. The legality of the warrant was challenged, however, on the grounds that some of the pre-conditions had not been satisfied, potentially rendering the warrant defective. The court accepted the challenge and quashed the warrant, stressing that the issuing of a warrant should not be a formality as it involves invasion of a person's home and private life; it should be drafted carefully, satisfying all the necessary requirements and conditions. Provided all such requirements and conditions are met, however, then the courts have generally been happy to regard warrants as lawful under this section. They have dismissed claims of varying types that argue that execution of a warrant carries with it certain other rights and expectations. In *R (Haralambous) v Crown Court at St Albans and another*,[204] for instance, the Divisional Court rejected a claim suggesting that the subjects of warrants should be entitled to see the material and information used in applying for the warrant; while in *R (Cabot Global Ltd and others) v Barkingside Magistrates' Court and Another*,[205] the same court interpreted the term 'materials', under section 8, broadly.[206] Fulford LJ noted that section 8 of the Act referred to 'material which is likely to be relevant evidence', and so found that this did not always require items sought in a particular search to be specifically identified in the warrant.[207] These cases highlight the balance that must be struck between the issuing of warrants to carry out police work on the one hand, such as the gathering of evidence, and an individual's right to a private and family life, protected under Article 8 ECHR on the other.

The second provision of PACE, authorizing a police officer's entry to premises belonging to another, is section 17. This is of much more limited scope than the power set out in section 8 insofar as it permits entry *without* a warrant, but only in certain specific instances. These are: for the purposes of carrying out an arrest; for the purposes of recapturing an escaped individual; or to save life or limb of an individual in the property or prevent serious damage from being caused.[208] An indication of the courts' interpretation of the last of these justifications is explained by the case of *AA v Chief Constable of Thames Valley*.[209] Here, an individual, who had heard loud music and children screaming from a neighbouring property, called the police. The officers attended the property but were unable to gain entry. Hearing the loud music, they proceeded to the back of the house and entered through the unlocked back door. The police officers entered pursuant to section 17(1)(e), that is, to save 'life and limb' or to prevent 'serious damage to property'. Upon entry, the police encountered AA, who was intoxicated, but they could hear no children.

---

[202] Section 1A(b) of PACE.   [203] [2008] EWHC 1177 (Admin).
[204] [2016] EWHC 916 (Admin).   [205] [2015] EWHC 1458 (Admin).   [206] Ibid [34].
[207] Ibid [34], citing Keene LJ in *R (Faisaltex Ltd) v Preston Crown Court and Others* [2008] EWHC 2832 (Admin).
[208] Section 17(1) of PACE.   [209] [2019] EWHC 1499 (QB).

AA was arrested and the children located. Police felt 'that the children were at risk, there being only heavily intoxicated people in the premises'.[210] It was argued in court that entry on the basis of section 17 was improper since that section 'was confined to situations where there was a serious threat to life or limb'.[211] The court rejected this argument, however, explaining that:

> The police concern did . . . meet the necessary threshold in section 17(1)(e). These were very young children. They had been heard shouting 'Mummy, mummy' for some period by the neighbour. There was silence when the police arrived. And there was good reason for the police to be concerned, both by the apparent large quantities of alcohol that had been consumed, the presence of such young children and the open door, which would both have allowed access into the premises but also, potentially at least, allowed the children to exit from the premises unless properly supervised.[212]

A police officer carrying out a search under section 17 must do so in uniform and that officer must have reasonable grounds for believing that the person they are seeking is on the premises (except for the purposes of 'saving life and limb', which does not require entry to seek a specific individual).[213] In addition, and as the court explained in the case of *O'Loughlin v Chief Constable of Essex*,[214] entry under this power is only lawful if the police have sought to explain or justify to the owner of the property their need to enter.

Entry to another person's premises without a warrant potentially engages Article 8 ECHR much more prominently than the power set out in section 8 of PACE. It is important that when an officer arrives to enter the property, they must first request entry and explain the grounds on which entry is requested. Only where entry is refused can reasonable force be used to gain access to the property.[215] Even where such force is deemed necessary, though, it must still fall in line with the requirements of the 1984 Act. In the case of *Syed v DPP*,[216] for instance, the police forced their way into a property because they 'feared for the welfare of a person or persons within the house'.[217] The Divisional Court, however, held that this was not lawful under section 17. Collins J stated that '[i]t is plain that Parliament intended that the right of entry by force without a warrant should be limited to cases where there was an apprehension that something serious was otherwise likely to occur, or perhaps had occurred, within the house . . . [t]he test applied by the officers . . . in this case, was a concern for the welfare of someone within the premises. Concern for welfare is not sufficient to justify an entry within the terms of' section 17.[218] With regards to the other justifications noted in section 17, where this power is being used to recapture an escaped individual, it is not permitted simply to arrive at the premises suspecting an escaped individual to be on the premises, entry for these circumstances under this power must be immediately required as part of a pursuit. In the case of *D'Souza v DPP*,[219] for instance, the House of Lords held that turning up at a property three-and-a-half hours after the individual sought had absconded from a hospital could not be held to fall within the remit of section 17 of PACE.

---

[210] [2019] EWHC 1499 (QB) [5].   [211] [2019] EWHC 1499 (QB) [7].
[212] [2019] EWHC 1499 (QB) [8]–[9].   [213] Section 17(2)(a) of PACE.
[214] [1998] 1 WLR 374.
[215] In view of discussions in Chapters 12 and 15, and since the coming into force of the Human Rights Act 1998, bringing with it the increased influence of Strasbourg, the notion of reasonable force might now be interpreted as proportionate force.
[216] [2010] EWHC 81 (Admin).   [217] Ibid.
[218] Ibid [11] and [12].   [219] [1992] 1 WLR 1073.

The third provision through which PACE authorizes entry onto the premises belonging to another is section 18. Under this section, and following an arrest, a police officer can 'enter and search any premises occupied or controlled by' the arrested person, provided 'he has reasonable grounds for suspecting that there is on the premises evidence, other than items subject to legal privilege, that relates' either to that particular offence, or to some other similar or connected offence.[220] A clear condition of entry effected under this particular provision is an arrest of the person who 'occupied or controlled' the premises in question. This chapter has already explained that section 24(5)(e) of PACE permits arrest 'to allow the prompt and effective investigation of the offence or of the conduct of the person in question', and this could be used in conjunction with section 18—or indeed, section 32—to effect an arrest before police enter and search a property. In the case of *R (on the application of TL) v Surrey Police*,[221] for instance, following allegations of rape and sexual assault, the police arrested the suspect under the section 24(5)(e) power in order that a search could be effected under section 18 of PACE. While the Divisional Court did not decide on whether the need to carry out such a search could be the sole justification for an arrest,[222] they did find that the lack of urgency meant that a section 8 search, with a warrant, would have been preferable.[223] These circumstances demonstrate that the courts have been minded to interpret section 18 as providing an immediate search power, not one that could be exercised later on—a point at which a warrant might reasonably have been obtained—an issue that was made clear by the courts in the case of *R v Badham*.[224] The section 18 power also permits the police to seize any items found at the premises.[225] This power is subject to limitation, though, insofar as a police officer can only enter and search such premises where he or she has written authorization from 'an officer of the rank of inspector or above' explaining the basis for the entry.[226] The importance of this limitation is highlighted in the case of *R v Badham*, where verbal authorization for a search was deemed insufficient. Crucially, though, in *R v Emu*,[227] the Court of Appeal held that failure to provide such authorization did not automatically render any evidence obtained inadmissible in court. It is inadmissible only, they said, 'if its admission would have such an effect on the fairness of the proceedings that it ought to be excluded'.[228]

Finally, section 32(2)(b) is the fourth way in which PACE provides legal authority for entry and search of another's premises. Upon the arrest of a suspect, section 32 empowers the police not only to search the individual,[229] but also (provided the offence in question is indictable) 'to enter and search any premises in which [the suspect] was when arrested or immediately before he was arrested for evidence relating to the offence'.[230] It is, in a sense, similar to the section 18 power. However, whereas that permits the police to enter premises belonging to or controlled by a suspect at some point after an arrest, section 32(2)(b) enables the police to search any premises where the suspect was actually found and arrested. This does not only apply to houses or offices, but also, as in *R v Kelleher*,[231] to a car. In this case, police attended an address following an alleged assault. The individual in question was spoken to by the police, thereafter driving off in his car. A later search of the car, under section 32 of the 1984 Act, revealed possession of firearms. Under subsection (6),

---

[220] Section 18(1) of PACE.   [221] [2017] EWHC 129 (Admin).   [222] Ibid [71].
[223] Ibid [73].   [224] [1987] Crim LR 202.   [225] Section 18(2) of PACE.
[226] Section 18(4) of PACE.   [227] [2004] EWCA 2296.   [228] Ibid [28].
[229] Section 32(1) of PACE.   [230] Section 32(2)(b) of PACE.   [231] [2015] EWCA Crim 691.

it is only permissible to search such premises where an officer 'has reasonable grounds for believing that there is evidence' relating to the offence in question.[232]

Pause for reflection

On the basis of section 32(6), if the police have a reasonable suspicion that a suspect—for example—has stolen a large object, such as a bike, what issues would arise if the police, in the course of a subsequent search, had tipped out a chest of drawers containing clothes in apparent search for that bike? What view would the law take if the police found other prohibited items in searching the chest of drawers?

It has already been noted that some of the entry and search powers permit the police to seize items found on premises relevant to an offence in question. These are supplemented, however, by section 19 of PACE. This provision permits a police officer to seize items he reasonably believes to have been obtained through the commission of an offence or if it is evidence relating to an offence. It is a power that has been used on a number of occasions. In the case of *R (on the application of Pearce) v Commissioner of Police of the Metropolis,*[233] for instance, in the execution of a search warrant under section 16 of PACE, police entered premises in search of stolen goods. In the course of this search, which took place on the day before the wedding between the Duke and Duchess of Cambridge, anti-monarchy flyers were found on the premises and seized under section 19, actions that were endorsed by the Divisional Court and, later, the Court of Appeal.

Discussing the problem

Have another look at the police powers problem scenario. On the basis of which provision of PACE did the police officers enter Donald's house? Did their actions and suspicions satisfy the requirements set out in that provision? Finally, did the officers have the power to seize the DVDs under the 1984 Act?

Following Donald's arrest, PC Smith and WPC Jones' arrival at and entry to Donald's house would initially be argued as founded on the power set out in section 18 of PACE. This permits entry on to an arrested person's property, provided the police officers have 'reasonable grounds for suspecting that there is on the premises evidence, other than items subject to legal privilege, that relates' either to that particular offence, or to some other similar or connected offence.[234] Similar to the case of *R (on the application of TL) v Surrey Police*, a court could find that the lack of urgency in this instance might mean that a section 8 search, with a warrant, would be preferable.[235] Indeed, in *Badham*, the court made clear that section 18 is an immediate search power, not one to be exercised later.

Upon their arrival, however, PC Smith and WPC Jones hear muffled gunshots and screams, kicking the door in and barging in quickly. On this basis, their actual entry could be justified under

→

---

[232] Section 32(6) of PACE.   [233] [2013] EWCA Civ 866.
[234] Section 18(1) of PACE.   [235] [2017] EWHC 129 (Admin) [73].

→

section 17 of PACE, which permits entry 'to save life or limb of an individual in the property', this being reasonably justified by what the officers heard while outside the property. Upon realizing, however, that the gunshots and screams were from an action film on the television, PC Smith and WPC Jones did the right thing in moving to leave the property, their entry under section 17 no longer being justified.

Finally, with regards to the DVDs and CDs that PC Smith and WPC Jones removed from the property, if entry were to be justified under section 18 then the items could be seized pursuant to that provision. Since the officers are seemingly in the property under section 17, however, seizure of the DVDs and CDs would need to be justified on the basis of section 19.

There are a number of ways in which the police can enter the property belonging to another to effect a search and, where relevant, to seize items. On the basis, though, that the power involves interference with the property belonging to another, the extent to which the police are permitted to enter such property is strictly regulated by both the provisions of the 1984 Act and the courts in applying them.

16.8 Summary

This final chapter of the book has sought to explore in detail the way in which certain ECHR rights are protected and dealt with under UK law. While it is by no means a comprehensive exploration of the area, its consideration of the freedoms of expression, association, and assembly (protected in Articles 10 and 11 ECHR) and the right to liberty and security and to respect for private and family life (protected under Articles 5 and 8 ECHR) has shown the extent to which the courts have to strike a balance between the values ensured by the specific ECHR right in question and competing interests, such as the need to maintain public order or the need to ensure that the police can deal with and investigate crimes.

Quick test questions

1. How did Watkins LJ define a breach of the peace in *R v Howell*?

2. On what basis can a police officer arrest an individual for an anticipated breach of the peace?

3. What are the facts of *Austin v Commissioner of Police for the Metropolis*?

4. Explain the offences set out in sections 4, 4A, and 5 of the Public Order Act 1986.

5. What does section 1 of the Police and Criminal Evidence Act 1984 provide? How do similar powers, set out in other legislation, differ from this provision?

6. What are the crucial differences between riot, violent disorder, and affray, all set out in the Public Order Act 1986?

7. Explain the different powers with which the police can enter the property belonging to another.

Further reading

Public order

Steve Foster, 'Breach of the Peace, the Right to Demonstrate and the European Convention on Human Rights' (2004) 9(1) *Coventry Law Journal* 63

Richard Glover, 'Keeping the Peace and Preventive Justice – A New Test for Breach of the Peace?' (2018) *Public Law* 444

Richard Glover, '"When we smash windows . . ." Black Blocs and Breaches of the Peace' (2017) 11 *Criminal Law Review* 830

*David Mead, 'Of Kettles, Cordons and Crowd Control—Austin v Commissioner of Police for the Metropolis and the Meaning of "Deprivation of Liberty"' (2009) 3 *European Human Rights Law Review* 376

*David Mead, *The New Law of Peaceful Protest: Rights and Regulation in the Human Rights Act Era* (Hart Publishing 2010)

Police powers

*Ed Cape, 'R. (on the application of Roberts) v Commissioner of Police of the Metropolis' (2016) 4 *Criminal Law Review* 278

Geoff Monaghan, 'Searching for Stolen or Prohibited Articles under PACE: An Open-and-Shut Case?, (2016) 180(24) *Criminal Law & Justice Weekly* 427

Home Office, *Policing: Modernising Police Powers to Meet Community Needs* (2004), http://www.statewatch.org/news/2004/aug/police-powers-consult.pdf

*Richard Stone, 'Deprivation of Liberty: The Scope of Article 5 of the European Convention of Human Rights' (2012) 1 *European Human Rights Law Review* 46

Michael Zander, *Police and Criminal Evidence Act 1984* (7th edn, Sweet & Maxwell 2015)

 Visit this book's **online resources** for additional materials relating to this chapter, including a full analysis of the two problem scenarios.
www.oup.com/he/stanton-prescott2e

Glossary

Absolute rights This refers to the most serious classification of rights. Absolute rights are absolute insofar as they can never be qualified or compromised under any circumstances.

Accountability In the context of government, this refers to the notion of a government having to explain its decisions and policies, answering questions, and submitting itself to scrutiny.

Acts of Parliament The laws that are passed by Parliament. They are the highest form of law in the UK Constitution and will typically be passed by the House of Commons and the House of Lords with the monarch's Royal Assent enacting them as law.

Administrative Court This Court is a part of the Queen's Bench Division of the High Court and it specializes in administrative law. One of its main functions is to entertain judicial review applications.

Administrative Justice This concerns the way in which administrative decisions and policies are made, ensuring that proper and just procedures are followed, that the decisions and policies are made with lawful foundation, and that there are appropriate means of redress where it is needed.

Administrative Law The body of law that concerns the administration of the state. It includes areas such as judicial review, tribunals, public inquiries, and ombudsmen.

Appellate Committee of the House of Lords This no longer exists. It used to be a Committee of the House of Lords, serving as the highest appellate court in the country. It was replaced by the UK Supreme Court in October 2009.

Arrest This is the process through which an individual suspected of having committed a criminal offence is brought into detention and thereby deprived of their liberty. This may be so that they can be prepared for trial or so that evidence can be gathered.

Assembly This refers to a body of people who gather together in support for or opposition against a particular idea or value as an act of protest.

Association Refers to the right that individuals have to be able join and associate themselves with bodies or people that represent and support similar views, such as unions or political parties.

Attorney-General A legal adviser to the government.

Backbenchers This refers to MPs in the House of Commons who do not hold positions within the government or (on the opposite side of the house) positions within the shadow government.

Bicameral This term refers to the fact that the UK Parliament (like other legislatures around the world) has 'two chambers'.

Bill Before an Act of Parliament receives Royal Assent and during its passage through Parliament, it is referred to as a bill. Once Royal Assent is granted, it becomes an Act.

Breach of the peace A common law offence pertaining to public order, which is committed by an act or threatened act that causes harm, or is likely to cause harm (*R v Howell* [1982] QB 416, 426).

Brexit The term coined to reflect Britain's exit from the European Union.

By-elections These take place where an MP resigns (or is no longer able to act as MP, for whatever reason) and another election in that one constituency is needed to replace them.

Cabinet The Cabinet is made up of the senior ministers in government, with the

Prime Minister at its head, and it makes key policy decisions that shape and determine the way in which the government functions and operates. It meets every week.

Cabinet Manual This sets out various rules and principles relevant to the day-to-day operation of government, with particular focus on how a government should conduct itself around elections.

Cardinal Convention This rule states that the monarch will always act on the advice of their government.

Case law Law and legal principles that have been established and developed through case judgments.

Checks and balances This refers to the UK's approach to the separation of powers principle. There is a good degree of overlap between the various institutions, which enables the different bodies of the state to check and scrutinize one another.

Civil Procedure Rules Rules governing civil procedure, brought in in 1999.

Civil servant They work in the civil service. They are 'servants of the Crown', rather than employed by any one minister, therefore highlighting their permanent nature as working for the government.

Civil service The permanent and professional body of people who work in the various and numerous government departments.

Coalition Government Where a government is made up of more than one political party. When no one party wins a General Election, two parties may join forces to achieve the necessary majority in the House of Commons to form a government. This happened in 2010–15 when, following a Hung Parliament, the Conservatives and Liberal Democrats formed a Coalition Government.

Codification Codification refers to the process through which different sources or instruments are brought together to form one, codified document.

Codified constitutions This refers to a constitution that is predominantly set out in one, single document. The US Constitution, though it has been amended over the centuries, is still found in one place since it is codified.

Collective responsibility A convention that provides that the members of the Cabinet collectively take responsibility for decisions that are made by the Cabinet.

Combined authorities A model of local government in England that is created by existing councils joining together to form one, region-wide authority.

Commencement Orders A form of delegated legislation through which a Secretary of State brings an Act, or certain sections of an Act, into force.

Common law See **Case law**.

Competence This refers to 'legal ability'.

Confidentiality A common law principle relating to keeping things private.

Congress The legislature in the US Constitution. It is a bicameral institution, composed of the House of Representatives and the Senate. The President also has a power of veto over the passing of laws of the Congress.

Constituency A geographical area that corresponds to one seat in the House of Commons. Each MP therefore represents one constituency.

Constitutional conventions These refer to the various conventional rules and practices that have evolved and become established over the centuries. They play a key role in shaping the way in which the Constitution operates on a day-to-day basis.

Constitutional law This refers to the broad area of law that relates to the allocation and use of power in the system. It is concerned with the various constitutional institutions that wield that power and the manner in which they operate and relate to one another and to citizens.

Constitutional monarchy This refers to a state that has an unelected monarch as Head of State, with a separate, elected individual, as Head of Government.

Constitutionalism The notion of acting and behaving in line with established constitutional principles.

Contempt of court An offence that is committed by disobeying court orders or rules.

Continuing sovereignty This is a school of thought, based on orthodox views of parliamentary sovereignty, which supposes that Parliament's sovereignty is continuing and ongoing. Parliament can never be bound or affected by previous enactments.

Council of Europe The body that set out, *inter alia*, the European Convention on Human Rights (ECHR).

County Councils The upper tier of local government in non-metropolitan two-tier areas, providing administration and services at county level.

Court of Appeal The second-highest court of appeal in the country. It operates in two divisions: the civil division and the criminal division.

Crossbenchers Members of the House of Lords who do not belong to any political party.

Crown This refers to the monarch. Historically, the Crown has been seen as the seat of executive power. Royal prerogative powers still exist that are exercised by the government in the name of the Crown.

Decentralization The process of dispersing power away from the centre, typically to local government.

Declaration of incompatibility This refers to the declarations that courts can make, under the authority of section 4 of the Human Rights Act 1998, which informs the government and Parliament that a legislative provision is incompatible with the European Convention on Human Rights.

Democracy This refers to the value that reflects popular views and free choice, ensuring that these contribute in some way to the process of government (either through the selection of representatives or the more active participation of government itself).

Demonstrations Gatherings or assemblies that protest in support of or in opposition to certain views and policies.

Derogation This refers to an exemption that Member States can, in exceptional circumstances, seek in respect of certain ECHR rights.

Devolved matters/powers Refers to the powers that have been devolved to the institutions in Edinburgh, Cardiff, and Belfast.

Devolution The process of dispersing power from central government and the UK Parliament and transferring it to regional institutions in Scotland, Wales, and Northern Ireland.

Directives A form of secondary EU legislation. These are not directly applicable, but are binding as to the objective to be achieved.

Direct applicability This refers to the notion of EU laws applying in Member States' domestic legal systems immediately and automatically, without any need for further enactment.

Direct effect This refers to the possibility of individuals enforcing measures of EU law against emanations of the state (or sometimes other individuals or institutions).

Discretionary authority/power This refers to power that is bestowed with a degree of choice as to how it is to be exercised.

Dissolution of Parliament Parliament is dissolved ahead of a General Election. This means that it is dismissed and will no longer sit until after the election has provided a fresh cohort of MPs.

District Councils The lower tier of local government in non-metropolitan two-tier areas, providing administration and services at district level. A number of District Councils function within the geographical area overseen by one County Council.

Divine right of Kings A historic notion, popular with some of the Stuart Kings, who argued that they derived their monarchical authority from God and could therefore pass laws, without Parliament's involvement.

Dualism This refers to a state—such as the UK—where international laws and national laws exist, as it were, on two different levels. Only national laws have domestic legal force. If international laws are also to have force, then they will have to be incorporated into national law by an Act of Parliament.

Elections The democratic process through which MPs (or, at the local level, councillors and mayors, etc) are chosen by the people. Votes are cast on a given day and in a given area, typically on a political party basis.

English Question See **West Lothian Question**.

Entrenchment This refers to the notion of laws being protected from ordinary repeal. With procedural entrenchment, an Act might contain provisions requiring an extraordinary process to be satisfied for repeal. With substantive entrenchment, there might be a particular topic or subject/policy area that is 'off limits' and, therefore, protected from ordinary parliamentary activity. Entrenchment does not sit easily with parliamentary sovereignty in the UK Constitution.

Errors of law A sub-category of the illegality ground for judicial review. In this context, the term refers to instances where a public authority has made an error in interpreting the scope of their legal powers.

European Union A supra-national organization that exists in Europe, with its own legal system and institutions that are superior to domestic laws and bodies. The European Union currently has twenty-seven Member States.

Excepted matters/powers This refers to the powers, set out under the Northern Ireland Act 1998, which are reserved for the exclusive competence of the UK Parliament and government. The Northern Ireland Assembly cannot pass laws or make decisions in matters that are excepted.

Exclusivity This refers to the principle espoused by Lord Diplock in the case of *O'Reilly v Mackman* ([1983] 2 AC 237) which stated that public decisions, made by public authorities, must be challenged at public law (ie through a claim for judicial review). It was, in that sense, an exclusive form of action.

Executive The body within a constitution that executes decisions and policies. Government is a branch of the executive.

Express repeal The process through which legislation is revoked by measures that explicitly acknowledge the Act (or sections of an Act) being repealed.

Federal This refers to a constitutional system in which power is not concentrated at one, central level. Instead, power is shared between the central level and a regional, or state level. Powers at both the centre and at the regional/state level are the exclusive domain of the relevant institutions, typically protected by a constitution. All the regions/states have the same powers.

Fettered (referring to discretion) Used as a sub-category of the illegality ground for judicial review. In this context, it refers to the notion of restricted or limited use of discretion.

Formal conceptions of the rule of law A school of thought that espouses the notion that the rule of law refers to adherence to procedural characteristics, which determine the way in which a system of government should operate. It is distinct from a substantive conception of the rule of law.

General power of competence This is a general power, set out in section 1 of the Localism Act 2011 that permits councils 'to do anything that individuals generally may do'.

Government The branch of the constitution that is tasked with making decisions and executing policies to govern a country or area. This includes, though is not restricted to, public service provision and the levying of taxes.

Government departments Central government is divided into a number of departments that each deal with different policy areas. The Ministry of Defence, the Ministry of Justice, and the Ministry for Housing, Communities and Local Government are some examples.

Greater London Authority The upper tier of local government in London. The Greater London Authority consists of the Mayor of London and a twenty-five-strong London Assembly.

Henry VIII Clauses These refer to powers given to government ministers to amend primary legislation.

Hereditary peer In the House of Lords there are ninety-two hereditary peers (substantially reduced in number by the House of Lords Act 1999). These are peers whose peerages were inherited from a previous generation.

High Court One of the senior courts in the country. It is divided into three divisions: Chancery Division, Queen's Bench Division, and Family Division.

Home Rule This term has often been used with regard to questions of Northern Ireland's place in the UK. It refers to the idea of self-government.

House of Commons The lower chamber in the Houses of Parliament. It consists of 650 Members of Parliament (MPs) who belong to different political parties and who are voted into the Commons after a General Election, representing their constituencies in the House.

House of Lords The upper chamber in Parliament. The House of Lords is made up of about 800 unelected peers. The majority of these hold life peerages.

Hung Parliament This refers to Parliament following the result of a General Election at which no party has succeeded in winning a majority of the seats in the House of Commons.

Illegality A ground for judicial review identified by Lord Diplock in *Council for Civil Service Unions v Minister for the Civil Service* ([1985] AC 374). It concerns instances where public authorities have misused or abused their given powers, thereby using them illegally.

Implied repeal A doctrine employed by the courts to acknowledge that, where two pieces of legislation conflict with or contradict one another, the most recent Act is said to impliedly repeal the earlier Act.

Incorporation This refers to the notion of giving domestic effect to provisions of international law.

Individual ministerial responsibility The convention that states that ministers are individually responsible for everything that happens in their government departments.

Irrationality A ground for judicial review identified by Lord Diplock in *Council for Civil Service Unions v Minister for the Civil Service* ([1985] AC 374). It is based on *Wednesbury* unreasonableness and concerns instances where public authorities are using their powers irrationally or unreasonably.

Judicial Appointments Commission The body created by the Constitutional Reform Act 2005 to make selections and appointments for judicial office.

Judicial Committee of the Privy Council The highest court of appeal for former Commonwealth countries, Crown dependencies, and the overseas territories.

Judicial independence A principle, connected with the rule of law, which reflects the idea that the judiciary and the courts should function and operate independently, separate from other institutions and organisations of the state (such as the government).

Judicial review This refers to the action through which decisions and policies of public authorities can be challenged in the courts. There are various procedural requirements, which must be satisfied for an action to be brought, and applications must be based on one of the grounds for review (illegality, irrationality, proportionality, and procedural impropriety).

Judiciary This refers to the courts and represents the institution of the state, which, *inter alia*, adjudicates disputes, interprets legislation, and generates case law.

Junior Ministers Ministers who are not Secretaries of State/senior ministers. They have a role within the government and often a specific portfolio within a government department. There are typically a number of junior ministers within a given department.

Legal constitution The legal rules, provisions, and principles that make up a constitution. It is contrasted with a political constitution.

Legislature The body within a constitution that makes the law.

Legitimate expectation Under the procedural impropriety ground for judicial review, it is possible to bring an application against a public authority, claiming that you had a legitimate expectation of certain behaviour or benefits. Such claims must be based on past practice or a given policy.

Life peer These are awarded peerages in honour of their service or expertise in a particular field. They are not hereditary; the peerage ceases upon the recipient's death.

Limited rights Limited rights come between absolute and qualified rights. They are rights that can be qualified or limited, but only in specific circumstances set out in the ECHR provisions themselves.

Local authority This refers to a specific local governmental body. It is made up of councillors who are elected by local people.

Local council See **Local authority**.

Local government This refers to a level of government beneath the centre and beneath regional (devolved) bodies. It is made up of councils that provide governance, leadership, and administration to local areas.

London Borough Councils This is a level of local government in London. The thirty-two London Boroughs (if we include the City of London Corporation) function in specific localities across Greater London, under the level of the Greater London Authority.

Lord Chancellor Now also known as the Secretary of State for Justice, the Lord Chancellor is responsible for the work of the Ministry of Justice. Historically, the Lord Chancellor was also the head of the judiciary and the speaker of the House of Lords. The Constitutional Reform Act 2005 effected changes to the role to ensure a clearer separation of powers.

Lords Spiritual These are the twenty-six most senior bishops of the Church of England who sit in the House of Lords.

Majority Government A government formed by the political party that commands a majority in the House of Commons.

Maladministration This refers to poor or bad administrative practices.

Manifesto A document published by political parties in the run up to an election, outlining their proposed policies, reforms, and actions that they would pursue if elected to government.

Manner and form Theories supportive of self-embracing theories of sovereignty, these espouse the notion that Parliament is capable of enacting legislation that binds future Parliaments as to the manner and form in which they may thereafter legislate.

Margin of appreciation A doctrine employed within the jurisdiction of the European Convention on Human Rights. It permits the Strasbourg Court to recognize that different rights might be protected to different degrees across the various Member States.

Mayor of London The directly elected leader of the Greater London Authority.

Member States Typically used in respect of the European Union, this refers to the countries who are members of the European Union.

Members of Parliament (MPs) The name given to the 650 individuals/politicians who are elected to represent their constituencies in the House of Commons.

Metropolitan District Councils Created as the lower tier of local government in metropolitan two-tier areas, though following the abolition of Metropolitan County Councils in the 1980s, they now exist as a single tier of government.

Ministerial Code This is a code that sets out the way in which government ministers are expected to behave in a full range of circumstances relevant to the day-to-day operation of government.

Ministerial prerogatives Royal prerogative powers that are exercised by government ministers.

Minority Government A government formed by a political party that does not command a majority in the House of Commons.

Monism The opposite of dualism. In a monist state, international laws exist at the same level as domestic laws and apply automatically. They do not require incorporation.

Natural justice A subcategory of the procedural impropriety ground for judicial review. Natural justice refers to the common law rules of procedure. It includes a right to be heard, rules against bias, a duty to act fairly, and many others.

Ombudsman An independent position that receives and investigates complaints made against specific public bodies.

Opposition Parties The political parties in the House of Commons, other than the party that forms the government.

Orders in Council A form of secondary/delegated legislation that is enacted by the Queen and the Privy Council.

Parish councils The lowest level of local government. Not everywhere has parish councils, but where they do exist, they fulfil very local functions in small geographical areas.

Parliament The legislative body of the UK Constitution. Parliament is made up of the House of Commons and the House of Lords, with the monarch as its formal head.

Parliamentary Private Secretary An unpaid assistant to a Government Minister who communicates between ministers and backbench MPs.

Personal prerogatives Royal prerogative powers that still reside personally with the monarch.

Political constitution This reflects the way in which the political machinery and the political goings on form a part of the UK's uncodified constitution.

Pre-Action Protocol In the context of the judicial review procedure, this refers to the protocol that must be followed before the formal proceedings can be initiated. It includes consideration of alternative forms of dispute resolution.

Prerogative remedies The public law remedies that can be awarded in respect of successful judicial review applications. They are quashing orders, mandatory orders, and prohibition orders.

President In a republic, the President is the Head of State (and, in some cases—eg USA—the Head of Government, too).

Prime Minister The Head of the Government. The Prime Minister is the leader of the political party that commands the confidence of (ie has a majority of seats in) the House of Commons following a General Election. On this basis, he or she will be asked to form a government and will become Prime Minister.

Principle of conferral This refers to the powers of the European Union only to act within the authority conferred on it by the Member States through the Treaties.

Private law Contrasted with public law, this refers to areas of law where laws apply to private individuals or parties, rather than to public authorities or governments.

Procedural impropriety A ground for judicial review identified by Lord Diplock in *Council for Civil Service Unions v Minister for the Civil Service* ([1985] AC 374). It concerns those instances where public authorities have neglected to follow the correct procedures in exercising their powers. These include the rules of natural justice.

Proclamation This refers to an announcement by the monarch, as required by law. For example, under the Fixed-term Parliaments Act, when the date that the new Parliament sits is set out, it is done so by royal proclamation. Historically, and before the Bill of Rights 1688, the monarch had the power to legislate by proclamation.

Proportionality This refers to a test that is employed by the courts to determine whether particular actions or measures are appropriate with regard to their stated objective. It is arguably a fourth ground for judicial review.

Prorogation This refers to the legal power to end a parliamentary session.

Protests See **Demonstrations**.

Public Bill Committee A committee within the House of Commons that is responsible for the Committee Stage of a bill's legislative process. The provisions of the bill are here studied and examined in fine detail.

Public inquiry These are held in the event of particularly serious scandals or allegations in the process of government.

Public order The notion of order and peace being maintained in public. It is often identified as an objective in dealing with breaches of the peace or disturbances in the course of demonstrations.

Qualified rights Unlike absolute rights, qualified rights can be limited if it is necessary to seek a balance against some competing interests or rights. Article 8 (right to private and family life) might be limited to give way to Article 10 (freedom of expression).

Question Time This takes place in both the House of Commons and the House of Lords and provides an opportunity for members of both Houses to put questions to the government about their decisions and policies.

Referendums These are democratic exercises where a specific policy question is put to a public vote in order that wider public opinion can be canvassed.

Regulations A form of secondary EU legislation. They are directly effective and directly applicable.

Republic A state in which the Head of State is an elected President, rather than an unelected monarch.

Reserved matters/powers This refers to the powers, set out under the Scotland Act 1998 and Wales Act 2017, which are reserved for the exclusive competence of the UK Parliament and government. The Scottish Parliament and government, and the Welsh Parliament cannot pass laws or make decisions in matters that are reserved.

Royal Assent This is the final stage of the legislative process. It represents the monarch's assent to a bill, thereby enacting it into law as an Act of Parliament.

Royal prerogative Powers that formally lie in the hands of the monarch. Nowadays, many such powers are exercised by the government (ministerial prerogatives).

Rule of judicial obedience The notion, particularly prominent in Wade's explanation of parliamentary sovereignty (HWR Wade, 'The Basis of Legal Sovereignty' (1955) 13(2) *Cambridge Law Journal* 172), which explains that judges obey the laws set out in parliamentary enactments and thereby provide the legal basis for sovereignty.

Rule of law This refers to the principle that the law should rule. It is fundamental to the operation of constitutional and governmental systems, though there are a number of theories that seek to explain what it means and how it operates.

Salisbury Convention Where a proposed bill was included in the government's manifesto, and therefore, part of the basis on which the public elected the government, that bill will always be given a second reading in the House of Lords.

Secondary/delegated legislation Distinct from primary legislation (ie Acts of Parliament). These are laws passed under the authority of Acts of Parliament.

Secretary of State A Secretary of State, or a Senior Minister, is the head of a government department. They sit in the Cabinet.

Select Committees These are permanent committees, in both the House of Commons and the House of Lords, which exist to scrutinize government activity in particular areas.

Self-embracing sovereignty A school of thought that rests on the argument that the sovereign Parliament is capable of passing laws that bind itself and future Parliaments.

Senior Ministers See **Secretary of State**.

Separation of powers A principle that espouses the notion that the three core constitutional functions (legislative, executive, and judicial) should be independent and separate from one another to prevent any potential abuses of power.

Sewel Convention This was established in the aftermath of the devolution settlements in the late 1990s and is designed to deal with the fact that there are now legislatures in Edinburgh, Belfast, and Wales, but also a sovereign legislature in Westminster. The Sewel Convention states that the UK Parliament would not normally legislate on matters devolved to the various regions.

Shadow Cabinet On the front row of the Opposition benches in the House of Commons is the Shadow Cabinet. This contains various Shadow Ministers, whose portfolios mirror those of the ministers in the government and whose role it is to scrutinize their opposite number. The Shadow Cabinet is headed by the Leader of the Opposition.

Sinecure titles Ministerial positions within government that give the holder a seat in Cabinet, but unlike other Secretaries of State do not come with the responsibility of heading a government department. Examples include the Lord Privy Seal, Chancellor of the Duchy of Lancaster, and Lord President of the Council.

Social contract A theory that is founded on the notion that citizens place their trust in a government, which in turn governs and protects citizens' rights. It was a theory espoused by, *inter alia*, Locke, Hobbes, and Rousseau.

Sovereign power This is the fundamental authority within a given constitution. In the UK, the sovereign power is exercised by Parliament.

Special advisers These work for government ministers, advising and representing them. They work alongside civil servants.

Standing (or *locus standi*) This refers to the question of whether an individual bringing an application for judicial review can be said to have a 'sufficient interest' in the matter at issue, thereby legitimizing the bringing of the application.

Statutory instruments See **Secondary/ delegated legislation**.

Subsidiarity The notion that power should be exercised at the most appropriate level. Prominent within European Union law.

Substantive conceptions of the rule of law A school of thought that espouses the notion that the rule of law requires the law to include certain moral content. For example, adherence to fundamental rights.

Supervisory jurisdiction This refers to the jurisdiction of the court in judicial review cases. In exercising their supervisory jurisdiction, the courts are merely supervising decision- and policy-making processes of public authorities.

Supremacy This refers to a force of law that is superior over other laws. European Union law, for instance, is supreme over the domestic laws of the EU Member States.

Treaties In the context of European Union law, these are primary legislation, setting out and laying down the way in which the EU works, operates, and relates to its Member States. In this regard—as well as in broader application—treaties set out internationally agreed and ratified provisions of international law.

Tribunals These are statutory bodies that resolve disputes or hear appeals against government decisions, operating in particular and specific areas of focus.

UK Supreme Court Since October 2009, this has served as the highest court in the UK. It replaced the Appellate Committee of the House of Lords and is the final court of appeal.

Ultra vires A Latin term meaning 'outside the powers'. It can refer to public authorities who have gone beyond their given powers and who, as a result, are susceptible to judicial review.

Uncodified constitution This refers to the constitution that prevails in the UK. Unlike those systems with a codified constitutional document, the UK's constitution is found in numerous sources (such as Acts of Parliament, case law, and constitutional conventions), which have been developed over the centuries.

Unicameral This term is contrasted with bicameral. It refers to legislative institutions that have just one chamber. The Scottish Parliament is unicameral.

Unitary This refers to the way in which the UK Constitution is structured. It is unitary in the sense that authority ultimately derives from the centre—from Central Government and the UK Parliament. While we have devolved and local systems of government, these are subordinate to Westminster.

Unitary authorities A single level of local government. It is contrasted with two-tier areas, in which both District Councils and County Councils operate.

United Kingdom (or UK) The union of four separate countries: England, Wales, Scotland, and Northern Ireland, which are united under one sovereign, one Parliament, and one centralized government.

US Supreme Court The highest court in the USA. Unlike the UK Supreme Court, it has the power to review primary legislation against the constitution, also having the power to set it aside on that basis.

Warrant These are issued by magistrates to permit certain activities, such as arrest or entry onto another's property.

Wednesbury unreasonableness This refers to a test espoused by Lord Greene in the case of *Associated Provincial Picture Houses Ltd v Wednesbury Corporation* ([1948] 1 KB 223) which has come to serve as the test for unreasonableness. It is used under the irrationality ground for judicial review.

West Lothian Question The question presented by the reality that, post-devolution, MPs in Scottish, Welsh, and Northern Irish constituencies have the ability to debate and vote on laws affecting only England. Due to the work of the devolved institutions, however, English MPs have no input into laws debated and passed in Scotland, Wales, or Northern Ireland.

Index

Tables and figures are indicated by an italic *t* and *f* following the page number. Cases are cited where they are discussed in detail. For a complete list of cases, and the full names of those cited in the index, see the Table of Cases.

A

A and others v Secretary of State for the Home Department (HL) 81–2, 112
A (No. 2) case (HL) 649–50, 651, 653, 654, 658
Abbasi case (CA) 664
abdication of powers 465–6; *see also* delegation of powers
abortion law in Northern Ireland 385
Abraham, Ann 589
absolute rights 627–8
abuse, threats, and insults prohibitions 686–90
access to courts, *see* right of access to courts
accountability:
   civil servants 298
   constitutionalism principle 10, 152
   executive, *see* executive's accountability to Parliament
   local government officials 475–6, 478
   media scrutiny of government 290, 296, 333
   ministers, *see* collective ministerial responsibility; individual ministerial responsibility
   MPs, recall of 313–14
   PM's weekly audience with monarch 39, 220, 262
   Prime Minister's Questions 10, 49, 349–50
   see also administrative justice; judicial review
Act of Settlement 1700 42, 121, 207, 254
Act of Union with Ireland 1800 19, 362
Act of Union with Scotland 1707 18, 361–2, 363, 365
Acts of Parliament, *see* primary legislation
Acts of the Scottish Parliament, judicial review of 366–71
actual bias 538–9
additional members electoral system 320
Administrative Court, *see* judicial review

administrative justice 559–61, 617–19; *see also* ombudsmen; public inquiries; tribunals
administrative law:
   definition 2
   glossary of terms 719–28
adversarial approach:
   to politics 307–8, 322
   of tribunals 576, 577
Advisory Council on the Misuse of Drugs 301–2
affirmative resolution procedure 347
affray offence 683–6
Aga Khan case (CA) 439–40
Agar, Edward 668
Al Fayed case (CA) 533–4, 545
Allan, T.R.S. 66, 83, 88, 96, 179
Allen, Sir Carleton 564
alternative vote electoral system 283, 320
American Revolution 6
Anisminic case (HL) 53, 109, 134–5, 415–16, 452–3
Anne, Queen 237, 339
Anufrijeva case (HL) 93
apparent bias 542–5
appeals:
   immigration decisions 570, 577–8
   right to appeal, effect on Parliamentary Ombudsman's jurisdiction 594
   Supreme Court, *see* Supreme Court
   from tribunals 567–70, 581
   to tribunals, *see* tribunal procedures
appointments:
   judges 23, 55, 58–9, 64, 573
   ministers 46, 47
      Cabinet ministers 264–7, 268–70
   PM, *see* Prime Minister (PM), appointment of
Aristotle 41, 69, 74–5, 79, 113, 414
armed forces:
   deployment overseas 49, 221–3, 224*t*, 236, 263
   sexual orientation discrimination 495–6
   see also military action
arrest, police powers and duties 706–10
Arts Council 301
assemblies and processions 690–5; *see also* public order policing

Assembly legislation (National Assembly for Wales) 378–80, 381
assessors at public inquiries 612
association and assembly, freedom of, *see* freedom of association and assembly (ECHR Article 11)
Aston Cantlow PCC v Wallbank (HL) 660–1
asylum seekers, *see* immigration, asylum seekers
Attlee, Clement 457
Attorney-General 382
   power to stop prosecutions 214, 216
   Upper Tribunal decisions, power to overturn 43–4, 52–3, 109
Attorney-General of New South Wales v Trethowan (PC) 143–4
Attorney-General v De Keyser's Royal Hotel Ltd (HL) 210–11, 230, 231
Attorney-General v Fulham Corporation (Ch D) 450, 451
Austin v Commissioner of Police for the Metropolis (HL) 679–80, 697
Australia:
   Attorney-General of New South Wales v Trethowan (PC) 143–4
   Australia Act 1986 130, 131
automatic disqualification rule 539–41
AXA Insurance v Lord Advocate (Sup Ct) 367–8, 386

B

backbench MPs, *see* Members of Parliament (MPs), backbenchers
Bagehot, Walter 46
Bailey, Stephen 395–6, 399, 403
Balchin litigation (Admin) 596–7
Bancoult (Chagos Islands) litigation (HL) 228, 413, 556
Bank Mellat v HM Treasury (SC) 500–2, 508, 527–9
Bank of England 273, 300
BAPIO Action Ltd case (CA) 518–20
Barber, Nicholas W. 44–5, 46–7, 56–7
Barendt, Eric 8, 42, 58, 66
Barnard v National Dock Labour Board (CA) 470, 471
Barnett, Hilaire 3

BBC 217, 494, 610
Beattie, Kate 639
Belfast Agreement 1998 (Good Friday Agreement) 382–3, 387
Bellinger v Bellinger (HL) 651–2, 653
benefits, *see* social security benefits
Bentham, Jeremy 29
Benton, Meghan 353
Bercow, John 321, 324, 352
bias, rule against 520–2, 557
    bias definition and types 537–8
        actual bias 538–9
        apparent bias 542–5
        automatic disqualification rule 539–41
    civil servants' political neutrality 279, 280, 296, 297
    monarch's political neutrality 220, 239, 254
    right to independent and impartial tribunal 57, 520, 535, 536, 537, 698
    Speaker's political neutrality 322
    see also judicial independence; procedural impropriety; right to fair trial (ECHR Article 6)
Bill of Rights 1688:
    executive authority under 38, 205, 207
    individual liberties under 24, 622–3
    parliamentary sovereignty principle 16, 42, 76, 117, 120–1, 123, 149–50
Bill of Rights proposal (Human Rights Act 1998 replacement) 668–9
bills, *see* legislative proceedings; primary legislation
Bingham, Lord Tom 74, 78, 87, 92, 458–9, 462
bishops (Lords Spiritual) 326
Black case (Sup Ct) 213
Blackburn, Robert 318
Blackstone, William 207
Blair, Tony 19, 26, 48, 91, 239, 299, 328, 615
    Cabinet government under 272, 273–4, 277
    devolution initiatives, *see* devolution
    Gordon Brown, relationship with 266, 268, 269
    Human Rights Act 1998, *see* Human Rights Act 1998
Blom-Cooper, Louis 610
Bloody Sunday Inquiry (2000–10) 604, 609, 611
Bogdanor, Vernon 65, 269
Bonham's Case (Ct Common Pleas) 119
borough authorities, *see* local government
Boughey, Janina 500
Bourgass case (Sup Ct) 99–100

Brackling v Secretary of State for Work and Pensions (CA) 483
Bracton, Henry de 75
Bradley, A.W. 218
Bradley case (CA) 600–1
Brady, Baroness Karren 327
Brazier, Rodney 212, 290, 330
    on Cabinet government 267, 272, 283
    on constitutional conventions 218, 219, 221
breach of the peace:
    offence 674–6
    police powers to prevent 676–81
    see also public order policing
Brent LBC case (CA) 397–8
Brexit 9–10, 200–2
    Brexit referendum (2016) 155, 182–4, 200
    Department for Exiting the European Union 279
    and devolution, *see* Brexit and devolution
    EU law 'retained' after, *see* EU law 'retained' after Brexit
    EU withdrawal process (TEU Article 50) 184–5
    House of Commons proceedings 187–8, 194–5, 233, 237, 242, 321, 324–5
    Miller litigation, *see* Miller, Gina
    UK–EU future relationship 199–200, 263
    Withdrawal Agreement, *see* European Union (Withdrawal) Act 2018
Brexit and devolution:
    devolved institutions, role in Brexit process denied 186, 371–2
    Northern Ireland Backstop 194–5, 197–8, 199
    Scottish Government's opposition 186, 369–70, 371–2, 374, 375
Brind case (HL) 494–5, 496, 498, 500, 638
British Bill of Rights proposal 668–9
British Oxygen Company Ltd v Minister of Technology (HL) 464–5, 469
British Railways Board v Pickin (HL) 137, 147
British Union of Fascists 681
Brittan, Leon 699
Brown, Gordon 240–1, 266, 268, 269, 273, 608
Brutus v Cozens (HL) 688–9
Burmah Oil Co Ltd v Lord Advocate (HL) 53–4, 108, 132, 208–9
Burns Report on size of House of Lords (2017) 331
Butler Review on use of intelligence before Iraq war (2004) 274, 606–7, 608, 611

Buxton, Richard 665
by-elections 313, 314
Byers, Stephen 290

C

Cabinet 25, 38–9
    Cabinet ministers, *see* Cabinet ministers
    Cabinet Office 264; see also *Cabinet Manual; Ministerial Code*
    committees 276–7
    historical development 204
    leaks from 283–4
    ministers bound by Cabinet decisions 272, 282
    PM's relationship with, *see* Prime Minister's relationship with Cabinet
    role 270–2
    Shadow Cabinet 322
    see also executive; government departments; ministers
Cabinet Manual 30, 38, 219, 261
    on Cabinet's role 270–2
    on hung Parliaments 239–40, 244
    see also constitutional conventions
Cabinet ministers:
    appointment 264–7, 268–70
    Chancellor of the Exchequer 218, 264, 298
    collective responsibility, *see* collective ministerial responsibility
    Foreign Secretary 265, 298
    Home Secretary 265, 298
    individual responsibility, *see* individual ministerial responsibility
    Lord Chancellor 22–3, 57–8
    Members of the House of Lords 46, 265
    as Privy Councillors 217
    see also ministers
Cable, Vince 285
Callaghan, James 245
Cameron, David 328
    and Brexit referendum (2006) 182–4, 200, 239
    Coalition Government (2010–15), *see* Coalition Government (2010–15)
Canada Act 1982 130, 131
Cane, Peter 411, 420, 472
cardinal convention 26, 219–20, 237
care homes 660, 661–3
Carltona principle 471–3, 485
Carnwath, Sir Robert 574, 577
Carrington, Lord Peter 289, 290
Cart case (Sup Ct) 571–3
central government, *see* executive
Chagos Islands *(Bancoult)* litigation (HL) 228, 413, 556

Chancellor of the Exchequer 218, 264, 298

Chandler, J.A. 389

Charles, HRH Prince of Wales 253, 254
Evans case (Sup Ct) 43–4, 52–3, 109–10, 254
see also Prince of Wales

Charles I 76, 119–20, 123

Charles II 120

checks and balances principle 35, 65–9, 412; *see also* separation of powers

Chilcot Inquiry on Iraq war (2009–16) 604, 608–9, 616

Childcare Act 2016 345–6

Chowdhury, Tanzil 236

Churchill, Sir Winston 220

Civil Service 12, 39, 296–8
Civil Service Code 296–7
GCHQ case (HL) 227, 413, 488–9, 492–3, 498, 512, 550, 552
government departments, civil servants in 280
mistakes, ministerial responsibility for 289–92
PM's role respecting 262
political neutrality of civil servants 279, 280, 296, 297
special advisers to ministers 261, 280–1, 292, 298–300
see also government departments

Clarke, Charles 291

Clarke, Kenneth 60, 218, 267

Clegg, Nick 22, 268, 277

Clothier, Sir Cecil 585

Coalition Government (2010–15):
airstrikes on Syria, Commons vote against 49, 222
Cabinet government 268–9, 276–7, 278, 282–3, 285, 303
electoral reform referendum (2011) 283, 320
establishment of 240–1
EU, policy towards 183
Fixed-term Parliaments Act 2011, *see* Fixed-term Parliaments Act 2011
House of Lords reform initiative 22, 329
Scottish independence referendum (2014) 18, 183, 220, 312, 373–4, 375

codified constitutions 5–9, 116
UK codification proposals 30–1

Coke, Sir Edward 75–6

collective ministerial responsibility 281–2
as constitutional convention 10, 26
formal setting aside 282–3
informal setting aside (leaks) 283–4
ministers bound by Cabinet decisions 272, 282
public inquiries, *see* public inquiries

public support for government policy 268, 273–4, 282
ministerial dissent, consequences 285–7
see also individual ministerial responsibility

combat, *see* military action

combined authorities 394–5; *see also* local government

commencement orders 344, 345

***Commissioner of Police of the Metropolis v DSD and another* (Sup Ct)** 647

Committee of Ministers (Council of Europe) 635

committees:
Cabinet committees 276–7
Parliamentary Liaison Committee 353
Select Committees 12, 49–50, 251, 352–3
to 'sift' post-Brexit amendment legislation 193

common law constitutionalism 152
common law rights 24, 85–6, 111–12, 535–7, 635–7, 673–4

Commonwealth 181, 216, 253, 263, 267, 311

community and parish councils 401–3; *see also* local government

conferral principle of EU law 165–6

confidence in government votes 246–7, 250, 281, 308–9, 323

constituency representation by MPs 318–19

Constitution, UK, *see* UK Constitution

Constitution, US, *see* US Constitution

constitutional conventions 25–7, 215, 217
armed forces, deployment overseas 49, 221–3, 224t, 236, 263
cardinal convention 26, 219–20, 237
collective ministerial responsibility, *see* collective ministerial responsibility
identification of 217–18
individual ministerial responsibility, *see* individual ministerial responsibility
Sewel Convention 371–2, 374, 380–1, 388
sources
Cabinet Manual, see *Cabinet Manual*
Civil Service Code 296–7
Erskine May: Parliamentary Practice (25th ed. 2019) 307, 350
Ministerial Code, see *Ministerial Code*
see also personal prerogatives of monarch; royal prerogative powers

constitutional law 2
codified and uncodified constitutions distinction 5–9, 116
UK Constitution, *see* UK Constitution, uncodified nature
'constitution' definition and purpose 3–5, 6, 27–8
constitutional conventions, *see* constitutional conventions
constitutional monarchies 13, 14, 16
constitutional statutes, *see* constitutional statutes
constitutionalism principle 10, 152
federalism 11–12, 359–60, 388
'flexible' and 'rigid' constitutions distinction 7–8
legal and political constitutions distinction 9–10
republics 13–14
separation of powers, *see* separation of powers
unitary constitutions 11, 19, 359–60

Constitutional Reform Act 2005:
Judicial Appointments Commission establishment 23, 55, 58–9
Lord Chancellor's role revision 22–3, 56–8, 59–60, 74
rule of law principle 74
Supreme Court establishment 22, 55

Constitutional Reform and Governance Act 2010 203, 214, 215, 225–6, 230, 296–7, 345

constitutional statutes 179–81
Act of Union 1707 as 361–2
European Communities Act 1972 as 179–81
Northern Ireland Act 1998 as 383

consult, duty to, *see* duty to consult

contempt of court by ministers (*M* case (HL)) 62–3, 84–5, 105–6

continuing sovereignty theory 141

Conventions (international law), *see* treaties

conventions, constitutional, *see* constitutional conventions

Cook, Robin 274, 285, 294

***Cooper v Wandsworth Board of Works* (Ct CP)** 523, 526, 527

***Corner House Research* case (HL)** 467–8

***Costa v ENEL* (6/64) (ECJ)** 167–8

***Coughlan* case (CA)** 551, 555, 556

Council of Europe 625, 631
Committee of Ministers 635
ECHR, *see* European Convention on Human Rights 1950 (ECHR)
ECtHR, *see* European Court of Human Rights (ECtHR)

county councils 391; *see also* local government

courts 39
  access to, *see* right of access to courts
  Administrative Court, *see* judicial review
  court structure, England and Wales 40*f*
  ECtHR, *see* European Court of Human Rights (ECtHR)
  Judicial Committee of the Privy Council 216
  jurisdiction of 451–2
  online procedures 579–80
  Supreme Court, *see* Supreme Court
  see also judiciary; tribunals
Crabb, Stephen 286, 294
Craig, Paul P. 88, 89, 95, 441, 498, 503, 504, 507
Cranborne, Viscount Robert 340
Crewe, Ivor 292, 297
Crichel Down affair (1949) 289
Cromwell, Oliver 6, 120, 123
crossbenchers in House of Lords 50, 326, 327, 331
Crossman, Richard 587, 590
'Crown' concept 204–5, 255;
  see also monarch; royal prerogative powers
Cunningham case (CA) 547, 548

D

D and Others case (Div Ct) 505
Daly case (HL) 499–500, 501, 502, 503, 508
Dalyell, Tam 376
damages as judicial review remedy 442
Datafin Plc case (CA) 437–9
Davies, Christopher 314
de Bracton, Henry 75
De Montfort, Simon 307
de Smith, Stanley 65, 212
'Debt of Honour' case (CA) 590, 603
decentralization 19; *see also* devolution; local government
Declaration of Independence (US) 4–5, 6, 621, 622, 623
declarations as judicial review remedy 442
declarations of incompatibility 53, 647, 654–8
delegated legislation, *see* secondary legislation
delegation of powers 469–71
  by ministers (*Carltona* principle) 471–3, 485
  outsourcing by local authorities 659–60, 661–3
democracy:
  constitutional law, *see* constitutional law
  democratic values 4
  elections, *see* elections
  EU's perceived democratic deficit 165

local democracy, *see* devolution; local government
  rule of law, *see* rule of law
  separation of powers, *see* separation of powers
Democratic Unionist Party 242, 243, 244, 281, 319, 323, 386
demonstrate, right to 672–4, 694;
  see also public order policing
Denning Inquiry into the Profumo Affair (1963) 604
departments, government, *see* government departments
deployment of armed forces overseas 49, 221–3, 224*t*, 236, 263
Derbyshire County Council v Times Newspapers Ltd (HL) 636–7, 638
derogations from human rights law 81–2, 626–7
  wartime emergency powers, *see* wartime emergency powers
detention:
  arrest, police powers and duties 706–10
  imprisonment, *see* imprisonment
  mental health patients 474
  terrorist suspects, detention without trial 81–2, 112
  under wartime emergency powers 104–5
devolution 11, 19–20, 356, 357–60, 363, 387, 407–8
  and Brexit, *see* Brexit and devolution
  to English regions 19, 394–5
  English Votes for English Laws 322, 341, 342–3, 342*f*, 375–6
  federalism and devolution distinction 11–12, 359–60, 388
  in Northern Ireland, *see* Northern Irish executive and Assembly
  PM's relationship with devolved administrations 263
  reserved powers model, *see* reserved powers model
  in Scotland, *see* Scottish executive and Parliament
  Sewel Convention 371–2, 374, 380–1, 388
  subsidiarity principle 11, 166, 358
  in Wales, *see* Welsh executive and Assembly
  see also local government
Dicey, A.V. 24
  on constitutional conventions 25
  parliamentary sovereignty theory, *see* parliamentary sovereignty, Dicey's theory on
  on royal prerogative powers 208
  rule of law theory, *see* rule of law, Dicey's theory on
dictation, discretionary powers exercised under 467–8

Dilhorne, Viscount (Reginald Manningham-Buller) 54
direct effect of EU law 170–2, 190*t*, 196
Directives, EU 163, 171–2
'directory' and 'mandatory' rules distinction 514–15
  'substantial compliance' test alternative 515–17
  see also procedural impropriety
discretionary powers 457–8, 469
  advantages and disadvantages 459–62
  definition 458–9
  delegation of 469–71
    by ministers (*Carltona* principle) 471–3, 485
  Dicey on 80, 89, 106–7, 462
  exercise of 462, 485
    fettering discretion 464–9
    purpose of Act conferring power 462–3
    reasonable use 491–2
  and human rights 98
  of local authorities 395, 397–9
  see also rule of law
discrimination:
  public sector equality duty 481–4
  sexual orientation discrimination, *see* sexual orientation discrimination
dissolution of Parliament:
  Fixed-term Parliaments Act 2011, *see* Fixed-term Parliaments Act 2011
  prerogative power 244–5
  see also prorogation of Parliament
district councils 391; *see also* local government
divine right of Kings 75, 118
Donoghue case (CA) 659–60
Doody case (HL) 512, 546, 547–8, 549
Dover District Council v CPRE Kent (Sup Ct) 549–50
Dr Bonham's Case (Ct Common Pleas) 119
drone strikes 263, 264
dualist and monist states distinction 128–9, 170
due process, *see* procedural impropriety; right to fair trial (ECHR Article 6)
Dugdale, Sir Thomas 289, 290
Duncan Smith, Iain 285–6
DUP (Democratic Unionist Party) 242, 243, 244, 281, 319, 323, 386
duty to consult:
  at common law 518–20
  as procedural legitimate expectation 552
  statutory duties 517–18
  see also procedural impropriety
duty to give reasons:
  adequacy of reasons 548–9
  benefits of duty 545–6

common law duty 546–8
before decisions are taken 533–5, 545
general duty 549–50
see also procedural impropriety
DVLA (Driver and Vehicle Licensing Agency) 302
Dworkin, Ronald 95, 96–7, 623

E

Early Parliamentary General Election Act 2019 248, 309
ECHR, *see* European Convention on Human Rights 1950 (ECHR)
ECtHR, *see* European Court of Human Rights (ECtHR)
Edinburgh and Dalkeith Railway Company v Wauchope (HL) 135–6
effective remedy, right to (ECHR Article 13) 640–1
Ekins, Richard 110
elections:
  by-elections 313, 314
  candidates, eligibility criteria 46, 312–13
  electoral systems, *see* electoral systems
  electorate 311–12
    prisoners' voting rights 312, 630, 645–6
  general elections, *see* general elections
  local government elections 399–401, 475–6
  manifesto commitments, *see* manifesto commitments
  referendums, *see* referendums
electoral systems:
  additional members 320
  alternative vote 283, 320
  first-past-the-post, *see* first-past-the-post electoral system
  party list 321
  single transferable vote 321, 384
  supplementary vote 320
electronic communications:
  ombudsman complaints via 591, 602
  online court and tribunal procedures 579–80
Elizabeth I 118
Elizabeth II 206, 220, 253, 254; *see also* monarch
Ellen Street Estates Ltd v Minister of Health (CA) 140
Elliott, Mark:
  on judicial review 228, 417, 418, 472, 542, 573
  on local government 399, 403
  on Parliamentary Ombudsman 601
  on parliamentary sovereignty 110, 151, 237
  on tribunal system 573, 582
employment tribunal fees 95

enabling approach of tribunals 576–7, 578
English regions, devolution to 19, 394–5
English Votes for English Laws 322, 341, 342–3, 342f, 375–6
Enrolled Bill Rule 135–8, 145
Entick v Carrington (KB) 62, 76–7, 79, 80, 84, 87, 104, 636–7, 710
entrenchment:
  codified constitutions, entrenchment of rights 23, 28–9
  constitutional statutes, *see* constitutional statutes
  ECHR rights entrenched in UK 639–40; *see also* Human Rights Act 1998
  legislation entrenched by Parliament 141–5
entry, search, and seizure:
  police powers and duties 710–16
  as rule of law issue
    Entick v Carrington (KB) 62, 76–7, 79, 80, 84, 87, 104, 636–7, 710
    Inland Revenue Commissioners v Rossminster Ltd (HL) 80–1, 105
Equality Act 2010 138, 189
  public sector equality duty 481–4
Equitable Life investigation (Parliamentary Ombudsman, 2004–8) 599–600
errors:
  civil servant mistakes, ministerial responsibility 289–92
  of law and fact 451–6, 568–9; *see also* illegality
Erskine May: Parliamentary Practice (25th ed. 2019) 307, 350
ethics, *see* morality
EU law 162–3
  conferral principle 165–6
  direct effect doctrine 170–2, 190t, 196
  free movement rights 158, 160, 168–9
  legislative competencies 165–6
  Member State withdrawal process (TEU Article 50) 184–5
  ordinary legislative procedure 163, 164–5, 164f
  proportionality principle 167, 498–9
  Regulations and Directives 163, 169–70, 171–2
  'retained' after Brexit, *see* EU law 'retained' after Brexit
  subsidiarity principle 166, 358
  supremacy doctrine, *see* supremacy of EU law
  UK, given effect in 172, 173–4, 173f, 229–30
  see also European Union
EU law 'retained' after Brexit 189–91
  amending 'retained EU law' 192–4, 348–9

case study (protected designations of origin) 154, 166, 172, 175, 188, 193–4, 198, 199–200
  see also Brexit
European Communities Act 1972 16, 150
  case law under, *see* supremacy of EU law, case law
  as a constitutional statute 179–81
  EU law given effect in UK 172, 173–4, 173f, 229–30
  repeal 189, 195–6; *see also* European Union (Withdrawal) Act 2018
European Convention on Human Rights 1950 (ECHR) 626
  Article 2: right to life 607–8
  Article 3: freedom from inhuman or degrading treatment or punishment 627, 630, 658, 686
  Article 5, *see* right to liberty and security (ECHR Article 5)
  Article 6, *see* right to fair trial (ECHR Article 6)
  Article 8, *see* right to respect for private and family life/ correspondence (ECHR Article 8)
  Article 10, *see* freedom of expression (ECHR Article 10)
  Article 11, *see* freedom of association and assembly (ECHR Article 11)
  Article 13: right to effective remedy 640–1
  Article 15: derogation in times of emergency 81–2, 626–7
  Protocol 1 Article 1: right to peaceful enjoyment of possessions 367–8, 660–1
  Protocol 1 Article 3: right to vote 645–6
  Protocols 629–30
  horizontal effect 664–5
  rights application, *see* European Court of Human Rights (ECtHR); Human Rights Act 1998
  see also human rights law
European Court of Human Rights (ECtHR) 631–3
  admissibility criteria 632
  jurisprudence use by UK courts 642–7
  margin of appreciation doctrine 629, 633–4
  Plenary Court function 635
  proportionality principle 499, 627–8
European Union:
  EU law, *see* EU law
  institutions 161–2
  origins and development 156–9
  treaties establishing 159–61, 162
  UK's accession 16, 155, 158, 172, 181–2, 200; *see also* European Communities Act 1972
  UK's withdrawal, *see* Brexit

European Union (Withdrawal) Act
    2018 17, 48, 155–6
  amendments of 2020 Act, *see*
      European Union (Withdrawal
      Agreement) Act 2020
  repeal of European Communities Act
      1972 189, 195–6
  'retained EU law', *see* EU law
      'retained' after Brexit
European Union (Withdrawal
    Agreement) Act 2020 188,
    194–5, 336
  citizens' rights 196–7
  direct effect and supremacy of the
      Withdrawal Agreement 196
  Northern Ireland Backstop 197–8
  transition period 195–6, 198, 199
Evans case (Sup Ct) 43–4, 52–3,
    109–10, 254
evidence:
  in public inquiries 614–15
  rape cases, complainant's sexual
      history 649–50, 651
  right to call and cross-examine
      witnesses 531–2
  unfairly obtained 711
Ewing, Keith 187
excepted matters (Northern Ireland
    Assembly) 384–6
exclusive competences of UK
    executive, *see* reserved powers
    model
exclusivity principle 434–6
executive 37–9, 260–1, 302–4
  accountability, *see* executive's
      accountability to Parliament
  authority derived from statute 39
  bills proposed by 37
  Cabinet, *see* Cabinet
  Civil Service, *see* Civil Service
  delegated legislative powers, *see*
      secondary legislation
  devolution, *see* devolution
  discretionary powers, *see*
      discretionary powers
  government departments, *see*
      government departments
  judiciary's independence from, *see*
      judicial independence
  local government, relations with
      403–6
  monarch, *see* monarch
  in Northern Ireland, *see* Northern
      Irish executive and Assembly
  Parliament, accountability to, *see*
      executive's accountability to
      Parliament
  PM, *see* Prime Minister (PM)
  public bodies, *see* public bodies
  royal prerogative powers exercised
      by 26, 204–5, 208, 215
  rule of law, executive power checked
      by 101–6, 414–18;

  see also judicial review
  in Scotland 372–3
  special advisers 261, 280–1, 292,
      298–300
  in Wales 381–2
  see also rule of law; separation of
      powers
executive agencies 302
executive's accountability to
    Parliament 37, 45–51, 63, 68,
    234–6, 306, 354
  ministerial questions 350–1
  opposition business debates 351
  parliamentary executive system
      12–13, 37, 107
  Prime Minister's Questions 10, 49,
      349–50
  Select Committees 12, 49–50,
      251, 352–3
  urgent questions 352
  see also executive; Parliament
expertise:
  Civil Service, *see* Civil Service
  crossbenchers in House of Lords 50,
      326, 327, 331
  groups, standing for judicial
      review 429–33
  legislative proceedings, expert
      contributions 333, 334, 336
  Lord Chancellor, non-lawyers in
      role 60
  non-departmental public
      bodies 301–2
  of public inquiry members 609–12
  special advisers to ministers 261,
      280–1, 292, 298–300
  of tribunals 562, 569, 573, 574, 580
expression, freedom of, *see* freedom of
    expression (ECHR Article 10)
Extinction Rebellion protests
    694–5
extra-territorial effect of
    legislation 129–31

F

Factortame litigation 17, 175–9, 181
fair procedures, *see* procedural
    impropriety; right to fair trial
    (ECHR Article 6)
Falconer, Lord Charles 56
Falkner, Robert 437–8
Fallon, Sir Michael 294
false imprisonment of
    protestors 679–80
Fayed case (CA) 533–4, 545
federalism 11–12, 359–60, 388
Feldman, David 27
Fenwick, Helen 530
fettering discretion 464–9;
    see also discretionary powers
feudal system 15–16
Finer, S.E. 289, 290

*Finucane's Application for Judicial
    Review* (Sup Ct) 607–8
Fire Brigades Union case (HL) 211–12
First Lord of the Treasury, *see* Prime
    Minister (PM)
First Ministers:
  Northern Ireland 384
  Scotland 372
  Wales 381–2
  see also Prime Minister (PM)
first-past-the-post electoral system:
  arguments in favour
    avoiding extremism 318
    constituency representation 318–19
    majority governments more
        likely 319–20
    simplicity 318
  disproportionality of 314–18, 330
  see also electoral systems
First-tier Tribunals 565, 566f,
    573, 578
  appeals from 567, 568–9, 581
  see also tribunals
Fisher, Mark 252
Fisher Report (1977) 699
Fixed-term Parliaments Act 2011 30,
    215, 233, 245–6, 263
  early elections under
    Early Parliamentary General
        Election Act 2019 248, 309
    66% MPs vote in favour 247,
        248–9, 250, 309
    votes of no confidence 246–7,
        250, 281, 308–9, 323
  prerogative power to dissolve
      Parliament 244–5
  principled defence of 249
'flexible' constitutions 7–8
Foreign Secretary 265, 298
formal conceptions of the rule of
    law 87–95, 111
Forsyth, Christopher 110, 416, 448,
    456, 457, 491, 514, 520
Foster, Arlene 386
Foster, Christopher 276
Fox, Liam 292, 293
France 13
franchise 311–12
  prisoners' voting rights 312, 630,
      645–6
Francis Report (Mid-Staffordshire
    Hospital Inquiry, 2010–3) 604,
    605–6, 617
Franks Report (1957) 564
free movement rights of EU law 158,
    160, 168–9
Freedland, Mark 473
freedom from inhuman or degrading
    treatment or punishment (ECHR
    Article 3) 627, 630, 658, 686
freedom of association and assembly
    (ECHR Article 11) 671–2
  processions and assemblies 690–5

right to protest 672–4, 694
see also public order policing
**freedom of expression (ECHR Article
10)** 633–4, 638, 671–2
media reporting restrictions 494–5
political uniforms 681–2
right to protest 672–4, 694
see also public order policing

G

Galligan, D.J. 458
GCHQ case (HL) 227, 413, 488–9,
492–3, 498, 512, 550, 552
Geddes, Marc 350
gender reassignment 651–2
general elections 12, 311
appointment of PM after, *see*
Prime Minister (PM),
appointment of
candidates, eligibility criteria 46,
312–13
dissolution of Parliament for
Fixed-term Parliaments Act 2011,
see Fixed-term Parliaments
Act 2011
prerogative power 244–5
electorate 311–12
prisoners' voting rights 312, 630,
645–6
first-past-the-post system,
see first-past-the-post electoral
system
hung Parliaments, *see* hung
Parliaments
manifesto commitments, *see*
manifesto commitments
results (2005–19) 314*t*
Speaker seeking re-election 322
see also elections; Members of
Parliament (MPs)
George II 260
George III 204
George V 340
George VI 220
German Constitution 8
Ghaidan v Godin-Mendoza (HL) 52,
648, 652–3, 654, 657, 666
Giddings, Philip 597
Gillan litigation (HL and
ECtHR) 701, 702–3
gist of opposition case, right to
know 512, 513, 534
Glorious Revolution (1688) 16, 38,
75, 76, 117, 120–1
glossary of public law terms
719–28
Goldsmith, Lord Peter 222
Goldsworthy, Jeffrey 124–5
Good Friday Agreement 1998 382–3,
387
Goodwin, James 507–8
Gordon, Michael 183, 372

Gordon Review on Public Service
Ombudsman proposal
(2014) 591, 592, 602
government, *see* executive; local
government
government departments 278–9
Cabinet Office 264; see also *Cabinet
Manual; Ministerial Code*
civil servants in 280
Department for Exiting the European
Union 279
Department of Work and
Pensions 279
departmental Select
Committees 352–3
maladministration complaints, *see*
Parliamentary Ombudsman
Ministry of Justice 23, 58, 574
mistakes, ministerial responsibility
for 289–92
non-ministerial departments 261, 301
reorganizations of 279–80
Scottish Government
Directorates 372–3
Secretaries of State, *see* Cabinet
ministers
special advisers to 261, 280–1, 292,
298–300
Treasury 264
see also Civil Service; executive;
ministers
Government of Wales Act 1998 377–8
Government of Wales Act 2006 378–80
Grayling, Chris 60
**Great Reform Acts (1832, 1867, and
1884)** 307, 390
Greater London Authority 392–3,
394, 400; *see also* local
government
Green, Damien 294–5
Green, David Allen 60
Green Papers 333
Greenpeace case (QBD) 430–2
Griffith, J.A.G. 9, 30, 65, 455
**groups, standing for judicial
review** 429–33
Guernsey 57

H

Hadfield, Brigid 365
Hailsham, Lord Quintin 48, 317, 319
Haldane Committee 270, 271, 272
Hammond, Philip 269–70
Hansard Society 350
harassment:
sexual harassment complaints
against MPs 294–5
threats, abuse, and insults
prohibitions 686–90
Harlow, Carol 106
Harold Shipman Inquiry (2000)
609, 613

Harrison, Brian 181
Harry, HRH Duke of Sussex 255
Hayek, Friedrich 89
Hazell, Robert 218
**head of state and nation roles of
monarch** 253
**health functions of local
authorities** 396
Health Service Ombudsman 584,
585, 602;
see also Parliamentary Ombudsman
hearings:
fair procedures, *see* procedural
impropriety; right to fair trial
(ECHR Article 6)
oral hearings 529–31, 575–6
public inquiry hearings 612–14
right to be heard, *see* right to be
heard
tribunal hearings 575–6
Henderson, Edith 43
Hennessy, Peter 218
Henry VIII 118
Henry VIII clauses 39, 47–8, 193,
345, 349
hereditary peers 325–6
Heseltine, Michael 275
**historical development of UK
Constitution** 24–5
allocation of sovereign power 15–18,
75–6, 118–21, 123, 204–5, 207
institutional arrangements 20–3,
38–9, 42–3
judicial review 411, 418–19
local government 390–1
Parliament 20–1, 307
rights protection 15–16, 23–4, 75,
621–3, 635–8
rule of law 75–7
tribunals 563–5
UK formation 18–19, 361–2, 382
Hitler, Adolf 318
HM Loyal Opposition 322
opposition business debates 351
opposition party members 48–9,
307–8, 337, 354
pairing system 323
Shadow Cabinet 322
HM Revenue and Customs 301
Hobbes, Thomas 623
Hogg, Quintin (Lord Hailsham) 48,
317, 319
Home Secretary 265, 298
House of Commons 44, 306, 310–11,
332
Brexit, Commons proceedings 187–
8, 194–5, 233, 237, 242, 321,
324–5
enactment of laws alone, *see*
Parliament Acts 1911 and 1949
executive's accountability to, *see*
executive's accountability to
Parliament

House of Commons (*Cont.*)
  historical development 307
  Leader of 265
  legislative proceedings, *see* legislative
    proceedings
  MPs, *see* Members of Parliament
    (MPs)
  Speaker 309, 321–2
  votes, whip system and pairing 322–3
  see also Parliament
House of Lords 306, 325, 332
  Appellate Committee 55, 327
    abolition 22, 55; *see also* Supreme
      Court
  historical development 20, 307
  Leader 265
  legislative powers, *see* House of
    Lords, legislative powers
  Members, *see* Members of the House
    of Lords
  political parties in 327
  Question Time 50
  reform initiatives 21–2, 127,
    329–31
  unelected nature 44, 50, 330
  see also legislative proceedings;
    Parliament
House of Lords, legislative
  powers 339
  bills introduced in House 334
  committee stage in House 337
  consideration of amendments 'ping
    pong' 338
  Parliament Acts limiting, *see*
    Parliament Acts 1911 and 1949
  Salisbury Convention limiting
    339–40, 347
  scrutiny of secondary
    legislation 347–8
  see also legislative proceedings
Housing Associations 659–60, 663
Howard, Michael 302
Howe, Geoffrey 218, 275
***Howell* case (CA)** 675–6
HS2 case (Sup Ct) 149–51, 181
Huhne, Chris 293
Human Rights Act 1998 7, 24, 30, 86,
  128, 640–1
  background to 24, 639–40
    ECHR application prior to
      Act 637–8
  Rights Brought Home White Paper
    (Cm 3782, 1997) 640, 648–9
  repeal proposals 668–9
  section 2: use of ECtHR
    jurisprudence 642–7
  section 3: statutory
    interpretation 52, 647–54
  section 4: declarations of
    incompatibility 53, 647, 654–8
  section 6: public authorities'
    duties 642, 659–65
  section 7: public authorities,
    proceedings against 659, 666–7

  section 10: legislative
    amendments 48, 654, 655
human rights law 2, 620–2, 669–70
  absolute, limited, and qualified
    rights distinction 627–9
  British Bill of Rights proposal 668–9
  common law rights 24, 85–6,
    111–12, 535–7, 635–7, 673–4
  derogation in times of
    emergency 81–2, 626–7
    wartime emergency powers, *see*
      wartime emergency powers
  ECHR, *see* European Convention on
    Human Rights 1950 (ECHR)
  ECtHR, *see* European Court of
    Human Rights (ECtHR)
  historical development 15–16, 23–4,
    75, 621–3, 635–8
  Human Rights Act 1998, *see* Human
    Rights Act 1998
  'human rights' definition 622–5
  judicial review, effect on 666–7
  prisoners' rights, *see* prisoners' rights
  proportionality principle, *see*
    proportionality
  'public authorities' and public
    functions 437–40, 659–64
  public order policing, *see* public
    order policing
  public sector equality duty 481–4
  and rule of law 111–12, 635–7
  sexual orientation discrimination,
    see sexual orientation
    discrimination
hung Parliaments 48, 239–44, 245,
  319–20, 323
  Cabinet Manual on 239–40, 244
  Coalition Government (2010–15),
    see Coalition Government
    (2010–15)
  Johnson minority government
    (September–November
    2019) 243, 324–5
  May premiership (2017–19) 48,
    241–2, 243, 281, 319, 323
Hurd, Lord Douglas 252
Hutton Inquiry on death of Dr David
  Kelly (2003) 610, 613

I

illegality 101–2, 445–9, 449*f*, 484–6
  delegation of powers 469–71
    by ministers (*Carltona*
      principle) 471–3, 485
  discretionary powers exercise,
    see discretionary powers,
      exercise of
  errors of fact 453–6
  errors of law 451–3, 568–9
  improper purposes 473–7, 480
  irrationality, overlaps with 490–1
  irrelevant considerations 477–81
  public sector equality duty 481–4

ultra vires doctrine 395, 396, 414, 447–9
  'simple' or 'narrow' *ultra vires* 450–1
  see also judicial review; rule of law
immigration:
  appeals against decisions 570, 577–8
  asylum seekers
    benefits entitlement 93
  deportation 454, 643–4
  right to be heard 525
  discretionary powers *vs.* objective
    decision-making criteria
    459–61, 465, 466
  Immigration Rules 459, 460, 461,
    518–19, 577
  M case (HL) 62–3, 84–5, 105–6
  passports, grant or revocation 214,
    215, 227, 229, 250
  policy statements 553
  Windrush scandal (2018) 288
immunities and privileges 83, 105,
  306, 412, 540–1
impartiality, *see* bias, rule against
Imperial Tobacco v Lord Advocate
  (Sup Ct) 368–9
implied repeal doctrine 138–40,
  179–81
imprisonment:
  overseas 664
  Parole Board decisions 505, 530–1
  prison discipline
    Board of Visitors' inquiries 532–3
    solitary confinement 99–100, 497
  prisoners' rights, *see* prisoners' rights
  sentencing, *see* sentencing
  smoking ban in prisons 213
  under wartime emergency
    powers 104–5
  see also detention
improper purposes 473–7, 480;
  see also illegality
independence, grants of 130–1
individual ministerial
  responsibility 287, 303
  constitutional conventions 10
  for departmental mistakes 289–92
  Ministerial Code, see *Ministerial Code*
  misleading Parliament 288
  private conduct 292–3
    sexual misconduct 288, 293–6
  public inquiries, *see* public inquiries
  public sector equality duty 481–4
  see also collective ministerial
    responsibility
inhuman or degrading treatment or
  punishment, freedom from
  (ECHR Article 3) 627, 630,
  658, 686
injunctions as judicial review
  remedy 441
Inland Revenue Commissioners v
  National Federation of Self-
  Employed and Small Businesses
  ***Ltd* (HL)** 420, 422–4, 427,
  428, 429

Inland Revenue Commissioners v Rossminster Ltd (HL) 80–1, 105
inquiries, *see* public inquiries
inquisitorial approach:
  of ombudsmen 583
  of public inquiries 614–15
  of tribunals 576
insults, abuse, and threats prohibitions 686–90
intelligence services 252
  GCHQ case (HL) 227, 413, 488–9, 492–3, 498, 512, 550, 552
  Iraq war (2003), intelligence use, *see* Iraq war (2003)
  PM's role respecting 263, 264
intention of Parliament, *see* parliamentary intention
international law:
  independence, grants of 130–1
  international relations, PM's role and powers 263
  treaties, *see* treaties
  Universal Declaration on Human Rights 1948 624–5
interpretation of legislation, *see* statutory interpretation
Iraq war (2003):
  Butler Review on use of intelligence (2004) 274, 606–7, 608, 611
  Chilcot Inquiry (2009–16) 604, 608–9, 615
  Hutton Inquiry on death of Dr David Kelly (2003) 610, 613
  justiciability 67
  ministerial dissent 274, 285
  Parliament's role in deployment decision 221–2
  see also intelligence services; military action
Ireland:
  Brexit, Northern Ireland Backstop 194–5, 197–8, 199
  Good Friday Agreement 1998 382–3, 387
  Irish citizens, voting and candidacy rights in UK 311, 312
  union with/independence from UK 19, 362
  see also Northern Ireland
irrationality 102, 455, 487–8, 509–10
  illegality, overlaps with 490–1
  proportionality, relationship with 502–8
  unreasonableness test
    historical development 491–3
    and supervisory jurisdiction of courts 493–7
    Wednesbury unreasonableness 488–91, 496–7, 502–8
  see also judicial review
irrelevant considerations 477–81; *see also* illegality

Irvine, Lord Derry 57
Israeli Constitution 5

J

Jackson case (HL) 21, 122, 127, 134, 146–9, 151
James I 76, 118
James II 16, 120, 123
Jefferson, Thomas 621, 622
Jennings, Sir Ivor 28, 80
  on constitutional conventions 25, 218, 222
  on parliamentary sovereignty 123–5, 126, 129, 132, 133, 142, 144, 145–6
Jeyeanthan case (CA) 516–17
John, King 15, 24, 75
Johnson, Boris:
  appointment as PM 155, 187–8, 194, 238, 239, 266
  Brexit strategy 155, 188, 194–5, 197, 199, 247–8, 287, 336
  minority government (September–November 2019) 243, 324–5
  prorogation of Parliament 63, 234, 310
    R. (Miller) v Prime Minister (Sup Ct) 63, 77, 151–2, 232–6, 238, 310, 413
Johnson, Jo 287
Jones case (Sup Ct) 568–9
Jones, George 403
Jowell, Jeffrey 74, 83, 85–6, 87, 101–2, 521
Judge, David 121
Judge, Lord Igor 345, 348, 349
judges, *see* judiciary
Judicial Appointments Commission 23, 55, 58–9, 64, 573
judicial independence 44–5, 56, 61–4
  in appointments process 23, 58–60, 64
  Entick v Carrington (KB) 62, 76–7, 79, 80, 84, 87, 104, 636–7, 710
  judicial review, *see* judicial review
  Lord Chancellor, revision of role 22–3, 56–8, 59–60, 74
  M case (HL) 62–3, 84–5, 105–6
  R (Miller) v Prime Minister (Sup Ct) 63, 77, 151–2, 232–6, 238, 310, 413
  statutory interpretation, *see* statutory interpretation
  see also bias, rule against; separation of powers
judicial review 66–8, 409–10, 442–4
  of Acts of the Scottish Parliament 366–71
  courts' supervisory jurisdiction 67, 412–13, 493–7, 563
  definition 410–11

  grounds for, *see* illegality; irrationality; legitimate expectations; procedural impropriety; proportionality, as judicial review ground
  historical development 411, 418–19
  human rights law, effect on judicial review 666–7
  justiciability, *see* justiciability
  of Northern Irish legislation 385, 386
  procedure 419–20, 421*f*, 666–7
  public/private law divide 434
    exclusivity principle 434–6
    'public authorities' and public functions 437–40, 659–64
  remedies 418, 434, 441–2
    'makes no difference' principle 418
  rule of law upheld by 101–6, 414–18, 448–9
  of secondary legislation 348
  standing rules
    group standing 429–33
    liberal approach 424–8, 433
    sufficient interest test 421–4
  statutory interpretation, *see* statutory interpretation
  Upper Tribunal
    'judicial review' jurisdiction of 570–1
    review of Tribunal's decisions 571–3
  US Supreme Court 8–9, 40, 51
  of Welsh National Assembly legislation 379–80
judiciary 39
  appointments 23, 55, 58–9, 64, 573
  bias, *see* bias, rule against
  at ECtHR 632
  independence, *see* judicial independence
  Law Lords 327
  law-making function 54–5
  obedience of;
  see also parliamentary sovereignty
    Enrolled Bill Rule 135–8, 145
    H.W.R. Wade on 122–3
  public inquiries, judicial members 609–11, 616
  statutory interpretation, *see* statutory interpretation
  Supreme Court Justices 22, 55, 327
  tribunal judiciary 59, 573–4
  see also courts; tribunals
junior ministers 39, 267
justiciability 9, 67–8, 226–9, 234–5
  case law, *see* justiciability, case law
  judicial review, courts' supervisory jurisdiction 67, 412–13, 493–7
  sovereignty of primary legislation 132–8, 174, 177–9, 361–2
  see also judicial review

justiciability, case law:
 Anisminic case (HL) 53, 109, 134–5, 415–16, 452–3
 Bancoult (Chagos Islands) litigation (HL) 228, 413, 556
 GCHQ case (HL) 227, 413, 488–9, 492–3, 498, 512, 550, 552
 parliamentary sovereignty cases, *see* parliamentary sovereignty, case law

K

Kavanagh, Aileen 642, 646, 654, 658
Kay v Commissioner of the Police of the Metropolis (HL) 691–2, 693
Keeler, Christine 288, 604
Kelly, Dr David 610
'kettling' protestors 679–80; *see also* public order policing
Keyu v Secretary of State for Foreign and Commonwealth Affairs (SC) 506, 507
Khawaja case (HL) 454
King, Anthony 274, 292, 297
Kirkham, Richard 598, 599
Knight, Christopher 507

L

Laidlaw Review (HC 2012–13, 809) 291
Laporte case (HL) 678–9
Lavender & Son Ltd v Minister of Housing and Local Government (QBD) 466, 468
Law Lords 327
law reform:
 constitutional amendments 6–8
 Constitutional Reform Act 2005, *see* Constitutional Reform Act 2005
 House of Lords reform initiatives 21–2, 127
 UK Constitution codification proposals 30–1
Lawrence, Stephen 606, 609, 617
Lawson, Nigel 273, 275
LDRA Ltd case (Admin) 484
Le Sueur, Andrew 545–6
Leadsom, Andrea 239, 294
leaks from Cabinet 283–4
Lee v Showmen's Guild of Great Britain (CA) 454
legal aid restrictions 577
legal constitutionalism 9, 152
legal privileges and immunities 83, 105, 306, 412, 540–1
legal representation, right to 532–3, 536, 576–8
Leggatt, Sir Andrew 564–5, 574, 576–7, 580, 582
legislation:
 immoral or unconstitutional 87–8, 126, 133–5

 interpretation of, *see* statutory interpretation
 primary, *see* primary legislation
 secondary, *see* secondary legislation
legislative proceedings 36, 332
 backbench legislation 324–5
 bills proposed by Government 37, 333–4
  flowchart 335*f*
  first reading 334
  second reading 334, 336
  committee stage 336–8
  report stage 338
  third reading 338
  consideration of amendments 'ping pong' 338
  Royal Assent 25–6, 36, 216, 236–8, 339, 345
  English Votes for English Laws 322, 341, 342–3, 342*f*, 375–6
 consultations on government proposals 333
 Enrolled Bill Rule 135–8, 145
 EU law given effect in UK 172, 173–4, 173*f*, 229–30
 EU ordinary legislative procedure 163–5
 expert contributions 333, 334, 336
 House of Lords powers, *see* House of Lords, legislative powers
 human rights compatibility, declarations of 641
 policy-making process 332–3
 Private Member's bills 332
 Queen's Speech 233, 235, 240, 245, 309–10, 334
 secondary legislation, *see* secondary legislation
 see also Parliament; primary legislation
legislature, *see* Parliament
legitimate expectations 102, 526, 550–1
 procedural legitimate expectations 552–4
 substantive legitimate expectations 554–6
 see also judicial review
Lester, Lord Anthony 639
Leveson Inquiry on press culture and practices (2011–12) 604, 609–10, 612, 616
Lewis, Derek 302
liberty and security, right to, *see* right to liberty and security (ECHR Article 5)
'life' of a Parliament 308
 dissolution
  Fixed-term Parliaments Act 2011, *see* Fixed-term Parliaments Act 2011
  prerogative power 244–5
 meeting of new Parliament 309
 parliamentary sessions 310

 prorogation 119–20, 310
  R (Miller) v Prime Minister (Sup Ct) 63, 77, 151–2, 232–6, 238, 310, 413
 recall for extraordinary sittings 321–2
 State Opening 309–10
 see also Parliament
life peers 22, 127, 326–7, 328, 331
life, right to (ECHR Article 2) 607–8
limited rights 628–9
Lincoln, Abraham 5
Litvinenko Inquiry (2015–16) 604–5
Liversidge v Anderson (HL) 104–5, 523
Lloyd v McMahon (HL) 528–9, 529–30
local government 11, 356–7, 389–90, 407–8
 accountability of local government officials 475–6, 478
 judicial review, *see* judicial review
 central–local relations and local government finance 403–6
 elections 399–401, 475–6
 English regions, devolution to 19, 394–5
 historical development 390–1
 local authority types 391–2, 392–5, 392*f*, 401–3
 in London 392–3, 394, 400
 in Northern Ireland 391, 393, 396, 399, 400, 401, 405
 powers and functions of local authorities 395–7
  delegation, *see* delegation of powers
  discretionary powers 395, 397–9
 public sector equality duty 481–4
 in Scotland, *see* Scotland, local government
 in Wales 391, 393, 398, 400, 401, 402, 405
 see also devolution
Locke, John 41, 623
locus standi of judicial review, *see* judicial review, standing rules
London, local government in 392–3, 394, 400
Lord Chancellor 22–3, 56–8, 59–60, 74
Lords Spiritual 326
Loughlin, Martin 75, 390–1, 395, 623

M

M case (HL) 62–3, 84–5
Macarthy's Ltd v Smith (CA) 174–5
McGuinness, Martin 386
MacMillan, Harold 181
Madison, James 12
Magna Carta 15–16, 24, 75, 76, 79, 101, 622–3
Maitland, F.W.R. 205
Major, Sir John 235, 238, 267, 268
maladministration complaints, *see* ombudsmen

Malone v Metropolitan Police Commissioner (Ch D) 111–12, 637
'mandatory' and 'directory' rules distinction 514–15
  'substantial compliance' test alternative 515–17
  see also procedural impropriety
mandatory orders 441
manifesto commitments 279, 319, 332, 333
  Salisbury Convention 339–40, 347
  whether binding 400
'manner and form' theory 124, 144–5, 148, 152; *see also* parliamentary sovereignty
Manningham-Buller, Reginald (Viscount Dilhorne) 54
margin of appreciation doctrine 629, 633–4
marriage validity, transgender persons 651–2
Marshall, Geoffrey 26, 218
Mary II and William III 16, 120–1, 123, 254
material errors of fact 455
Maxwell Fyfe, Sir David 289–90
May, Theresa:
  appointment as PM 194, 239
  authorization of air strikes on Syria without Commons vote 222–3
  Brexit strategy and resignation as PM 155, 187, 194, 231, 233, 239, 247, 277–8, 324, 336
  Cabinet government under 266, 269–70, 277–8, 283–4, 286, 287, 303
  confidence and supply agreement with DUP 48, 241–2, 243, 281, 319, 323
  dissolution of Parliament (2017) 247, 309
  government departments reorganization 279–80
Mayor of London 392, 393, 394, 400
Mead, David 680
media:
  BBC 217, 494, 610
  government briefing of 299
  Leveson Inquiry on press culture and practices (2011-12) 604, 609–10, 612, 616
  reporting restrictions 494–5
  scrutiny of government 290, 296, 333
Mellor, David 293–4
Members of Parliament (MPs) 311
  backbenchers 322–3
    backbench legislation 324–5
    Private Member's bills 332
  constituency representation 318–19
  disqualification criteria 46, 312–13
  election of
    by-elections 313, 314
    general elections, *see* general elections

government party members 281–2, 307
Members of Northern Ireland Assembly 384
Members of Scottish Parliament 365, 373
Members of Welsh National Assembly 378
opposition party members 48–9, 307–8, 337, 354
Parliamentary Ombudsman, MP filter 591–3, 602
privileges and immunities 83, 306
recall of 313–14
retirement 313
Select Committee service 353
voting, whip system and pairing 322–3
see also Parliament; political parties
Members of the House of Lords:
  as Cabinet members 46, 265
  composition and proposals to reduce numbers 328–9, 331
  crossbenchers 50, 326, 327, 331
  hereditary peers 325–6
  ineligibility to serve as MP 46, 312
  Law Lords 327
  life peers 22, 127, 326–7, 328, 331
  Lords Spiritual 326
Mendoza case (HL) 52, 648, 652–3, 654, 657, 666
mental health patients' detention 474
mercy, royal prerogative of 205, 214, 215, 216, 226
metropolitan district councils 391; *see also* local government
Mid-Staffordshire Hospital Inquiry (2010-13) 604, 605–6, 617
military action:
  armed forces, *see* armed forces
  declaration of war 26
  drone strikes 263, 264
  Iraq war (2003), *see* Iraq war (2003)
  PM's powers of 263, 264
  quasi-military organizations, bans of 682–3
  Syria, airstrikes on 49, 222–3
  wartime emergency powers, *see* wartime emergency powers
Mill, John Stuart 318
Miller, Gina:
  R (Miller) v Prime Minister (Sup Ct) 63, 77, 151–2, 232–6, 238, 310, 413
  R (Miller) v Secretary of State for Exiting the European Union (Sup Ct) 6, 29, 58, 181, 185–7, 229–32, 372
  see also Brexit
Ministerial Code 30, 38, 261, 288
  on duty not to mislead Parliament 292
  on private conduct of ministers 292, 293, 295

on public support for government policy 282, 285
ministerial prerogatives, *see* royal prerogative powers
ministers:
  appointment of 46, 47
    Cabinet ministers 264–7, 268–70
    Cabinet ministers, *see* Cabinet ministers
  collective responsibility, *see* collective ministerial responsibility
  in contempt of court (*M* case (HL)) 62–3, 84–5, 105–6
  delegation of powers (*Carltona* principle) 471–3, 485
  individual responsibility, *see* individual ministerial responsibility
  junior ministers 39, 267
  Ministerial Code, see *Ministerial Code*
  parliamentary private secretaries 267
  parliamentary questions to 350–1
  special advisers to 261, 280–1, 292, 298–300
  see also Cabinet; government departments
Ministry of Justice 23, 58, 574
minority governments, *see* hung Parliaments
mistakes:
  civil servant mistakes, ministerial responsibility 289–92
  of law and fact 451–6, 568–9;
  see also illegality
Mitchell, Andrew 293
monarch:
  allocation of sovereign power, historical development 15–18, 75–6, 118–21, 123, 204–5, 207
  cardinal convention 26, 219–20, 237
  constitutional monarchies 13, 14, 16
  'Crown' concept 204–5, 255
  as head of state and head of nation 253
  immunity from prosecution 83, 105, 412
  personal prerogative powers, *see* personal prerogatives of monarch
  PM's weekly audience with 39, 220, 262
  political neutrality 220, 239, 254
  primary legislation, binding effect on Crown 212–13
  Queen's Speech 233, 235, 240, 245, 309–10, 334
  regents, appointment of 253–4
  royal prerogative powers, *see* royal prerogative powers
  royal proclamations 76, 118, 309
  State Opening of Parliament 309–10
  succession, line of 254–5
  as Supreme Governor of the Church of England 253, 255
  taxation, exemption from 212–13
  see also Prince of Wales

money bills 341

monist and dualist states
distinction 128–9, 170

Montesquieu, Charles de Secondat:
separation of powers doctrine 41–2,
43, 45, 65
separation of powers in UK
compared 48, 51, 54, 56, 64,
68, 69

Montfort, Simon De 307

Moore, Jo 290, 299

morality:
and constitutional conventions 26–7
immoral legislation 87–8, 126,
133–5
and rule of law 73, 74, 90–1, 95–100

Morris, Estelle 290

Mortensen v Peters (HCJ) 128–9

Moseley case (Sup Ct) 517–18

Moss v McLachlan (Div Ct) 677,
678–9

MPs, *see* Members of Parliament (MPs)

municipal authorities, *see* local
government

Munro, Colin 3, 610

N

National Assembly for Wales 378–9,
381, 382

National Health Service (NHS) 297–8,
339, 560
Health Service Ombudsman 584,
585, 602; *see also* Parliamentary
Ombudsman
Mid-Staffordshire Hospital Inquiry
(2010-13) 604, 605–6, 617

national security services, *see*
intelligence services

natural justice rules 520–2, 557; *see
also* bias, rule against; right to
be heard

natural law theory 623

negative resolution procedure 347

Neuberger, Lord David 52

New Magna Carta? (HC 2014–15,
463) 31

New Zealand Constitution 5, 8

NHS, *see* National Health Service (NHS)

Nicol, Danny 654

no confidence in government votes
246–7, 250, 281, 308–9, 323

no man is above the law
principle 82–5

no punishment without breach of
law 79–82, 102–4

non-departmental public
bodies 301–2

non-discrimination:
public sector equality duty 481–4
sexual orientation discrimination,
see sexual orientation
discrimination

non-ministerial departments 261, 301

non-retroactivity principle, *see*
retrospective effect

Northern Ireland:
abortion law 385
Bloody Sunday Inquiry (2000–10)
604, 609, 611
Brexit, Northern Ireland
Backstop 194–5, 197–8, 199
Democratic Unionist Party 242, 243,
244, 281, 319, 323, 386
devolved executive and Assembly,
see Northern Irish executive and
Assembly
establishment of 19, 362, 382
Good Friday Agreement 1998 382–3,
387
local government 391, 393, 396,
399, 400, 401, 405
Northern Irish Public Services
Ombudsman 584–5
Sinn Fein 386

Northern Irish executive and
Assembly 19
background to devolution 382–3
judicial review of Northern Irish
legislation 385, 386
Northern Ireland Act 1998 383,
384–6
Northern Ireland Assembly 321,
384–6
re-centralization of executive powers
(2017-20) 360, 386
reserved and excepted powers 384–6
see also devolution

Northumbria Police Authority case
(CA) 209–10

notice requirements 514–17, 523,
527, 534, 545
for public processions and
assemblies 691–2
see also procedural impropriety

O

*Oakley v South Cambridgeshire
District Council* (CA) 549–50

obedience, judicial:
Enrolled Bill Rule 135–8, 145
H.W.R. Wade on 122–3
see also parliamentary sovereignty

Ofqual (Office of Qualification
and Examinations
Regulations) 300

Oliver, Dawn 307, 414

Olowofoyeku, Abimbola 544

ombudsmen 583–4, 584f, 585
'maladministration' definition 586–90
Parliamentary Ombudsman, *see*
Parliamentary Ombudsman
Public Service Ombudsman proposal
(2014) 591, 592, 602

Onasanya, Fiona 314

online procedures of courts and
tribunals 579–80

opposition, *see* HM Loyal Opposition

oral hearings, right to 529–31, 575–6

oral questions in Parliament 351

Orders in Council 47, 216–17, 228,
233, 384

Orders of Council 217, 344

O'Reilly v Mackman (HL) 434–6,
440, 452

Osborne, George 37, 266, 269

outsourcing by local authorities
659–60, 661–3

P

*Padfield v Minister of Agriculture,
Fisheries and Food* (HL) 462–3,
473–4

Paine, Thomas 4, 6, 29

pairing of MPs 323

Paisley Jr, Ian 314

pardons 205, 214, 215, 216, 226

parish and community
councils 401–3

Parkinson, Cecil 293

Parliament 36–7, 305–8, 354–5
dissolution of
Fixed-term Parliaments Act 2011,
see Fixed-term Parliaments
Act 2011
prerogative power 244–5
Erskine May: Parliamentary Practice
(25th ed. 2019) 307, 350
executive's accountability to, *see*
executive's accountability to
Parliament
historical development 20–1, 307
House of Commons, *see* House of
Commons
House of Lords, *see* House of Lords
hung Parliaments, *see* hung
Parliaments
legislative proceedings, *see* legislative
proceedings
meeting of new Parliament 309
ministerial accountability to,
see collective ministerial
responsibility; individual
ministerial responsibility
MPs, *see* Members of Parliament (MPs)
Northern Ireland Assembly 321,
384–6
parliamentary sessions 310
prorogation of 119–20, 310
R (Miller) v Prime Minister (Sup Ct) 63,
77, 151–2, 232–6, 238, 310, 413
questions in, *see* questions in
Parliament
recall for extraordinary sittings 321–2
Scottish Parliament, *see* Scottish
executive and Parliament
Select Committees 12, 49–50, 251,
352–3
sovereignty of, *see* parliamentary
sovereignty

State Opening 309–10
Welsh National Assembly 378–9, 381, 382
see also separation of powers
Parliament Acts 1911 and 1949 20–1, 126–7, 306, 329, 340–1
Jackson case (HL) 21, 122, 127, 134, 146–9, 151
secondary legislation, non-application to 347
parliamentary intention:
discretionary powers 462–3
improper purpose assessments 473–7, 480
see also statutory interpretation
Parliamentary Liaison Committee 353
Parliamentary Ombudsman 319, 584, 585–6
access to 586
'maladministration' definition 586–90
MP filter 591–3, 602
Equitable Life investigation (2004-8) 599–600
investigations initiated by 592–3
jurisdiction, restrictions on 593–4
outcomes of investigations 594–5, 595f, 596
procedures 594
recommendations and their enforcement 596–601
reform proposals 601–3
parliamentary private secretaries 267
parliamentary sovereignty 51–2, 61, 76, 115–16, 152–3
Bill of Rights 1688 on 16, 42, 76, 117, 120–1, 123, 149–50
case law, *see* parliamentary sovereignty, case law
common law constitutionalism, *see* common law constitutionalism
Constitutional Reform Act 2005, effect on 55–6
continuing sovereignty theory 141
court judgments, power to overturn 53–4, 93–4, 108
and devolution
reserved powers model, *see* reserved powers model
Sewel Convention 371–2, 374, 380–1, 388
Dicey's theory on 106–7, 117, 125
no Parliament can bind its successors 138–46, 174
Parliament can make and unmake any law on any subject matter 126–32
sovereignty of primary legislation 132–8, 174, 177–9, 361–2
historical development 15–18, 75–6, 118–21, 123;
see also Bill of Rights 1688

and human rights 641
declarations of incompatibility 53, 647, 654–8
international law, relationship with 127–9
legal justifications (Wade, Jennings and Goldsworthy's theories) 121–5
'manner and form' theory 124, 144–5, 148, 152
parliamentary intention, *see* parliamentary intention
and royal prerogative powers
constitutional conventions limiting powers, *see* constitutional conventions
Parliament's power to abolish or restrict powers 210–12, 225–6
and rule of law 106–11, 448–9
self-embracing sovereignty theory 142–6
supremacy of EU law doctrine limiting, *see* supremacy of EU law, and parliamentary sovereignty
see also separation of powers
parliamentary sovereignty, case law:
Attorney-General of New South Wales v Trethowan (PC) 143–4
Bank Mellat v HM Treasury (SC) 500–2, 508, 527–9
Dr Bonham's Case (Ct Common Pleas) 119
Edinburgh and Dalkeith Railway Company v Wauchope (HL) 135–6
Evans case (Sup Ct) 43–4, 52–3, 109–10, 254
HS2 case (Sup Ct) 149–51, 181
Jackson case (HL) 21, 122, 127, 134, 146–9, 151
Miller litigation, *see* Miller, Gina
Mortensen v Peters (HCJ) 128–9
Pickin case (HL) 137, 147
Privacy International case (Sup Ct) 416–17, 452, 453
Vauxhall Estates v Liverpool Corporation (KBD) 139–40
Parole Board decisions 505, 530–1
party list electoral system 321
passports, grant or revocation 214, 215, 227, 229, 250
Patel case (CA) 555–6
Patel, Priti 293
peaceful enjoyment of possessions, right to (ECHR Protocol 1 Article 1) 367–8, 660–1
personal prerogatives of monarch 205, 256–8
constitutional conventions limiting, *see* constitutional conventions
dissolution of Parliament 244–5
Fixed-term Parliaments Act 2011, *see* Fixed-term Parliaments Act 2011
list of 214

PM appointment, *see* Prime Minister (PM), appointment of
prorogation of Parliament 119–20
R (Miller) v Prime Minister (Sup Ct) 63, 77, 151–2, 232–6, 238, 310, 413
reform or abolition proposals 250–2
Royal Assent 25–6, 36, 216, 236–8, 339, 345
see also royal prerogative powers
Petition of Right 1628 75–6
Phillips, Lord Nicholas 61
Pickin case (HL) 137, 147
Pierson case (QBD) 103–4, 108
Pimlott, Ben 220
Pinochet (No 2) case (HL) 540–1
planning inquiries 603
Plantagenet Alliance Ltd case (QBD) 519–20
PM, *see* Prime Minister (PM)
police:
phone tapping by 111–12, 637
Police Commissioners, delegation of powers 473
powers and duties, *see* police powers and duties
public order policing, *see* public order policing
Stephen Lawrence Inquiry (1997–9) 606, 609, 617
police powers and duties 716–17
arrest 706–10
entry, search, and seizure, *see* entry, search, and seizure
Police and Criminal Evidence Act 1984 (PACE) 699–700
public order policing, *see* public order policing
stop and search 695–6, 700–5
use of force 209–10
policy-making 464–5, 469
policy statements 553
see also discretionary powers
political constitutionalism 9–10, 152
political parties 307–8, 311
Democratic Unionist Party 242, 243, 244, 281, 319, 323, 386
in House of Lords 327
largest opposition party, *see* HM Loyal Opposition
in local government elections 399–400, 475–6
minor parties, disadvantaged by first-past-the-post system 316–17
policy-making processes 332–3
Scottish Nationalist Party 244, 317, 375
Sinn Fein 386
UKIP (United Kingdom Independence Party) 316
whip system 322–3
see also Members of Parliament (MPs)
political uniforms 681–2
Pollard, David 251

Porter v Magill (HL) 475–6, 542–3
Powlesland v DPP (Div Ct) 692–3
precedent facts 454
prerogative powers 255–8
    human rights law application 663–4
    justiciability, *see* justiciability
    personal prerogative powers,
        see personal prerogatives of
        monarch
    reform or abolition proposals 250–2
    royal prerogative, *see* royal
        prerogative powers
prerogative remedies at judicial
    review 441–2
Prescott, John 274, 294
presidential systems 12–13, 271
presumption of innocence 698
primacy of EU law, *see* supremacy of
    EU law
primary legislation:
    Acts of the Scottish Parliament
        366–71
    Assembly Acts (National Assembly
        for Wales) 378–80, 381
    constitutional statutes, *see*
        constitutional statutes
    Crown, binding effect on 212–13
    EU Regulations and Directives 163,
        169–70, 171–2
    with extra-territorial effect 129–31
    Henry VIII clauses to amend 39,
        47–8, 193, 345, 349
    immoral or unconstitutional
        legislation 87–8, 126, 133–5
    interpretation of, *see* statutory
        interpretation
    legislative proceedings, *see* legislative
        proceedings
    Parliament's power to enact and
        repeal 126–32
        implied repeal doctrine 138–40,
            179–81
    sovereignty of 132–8, 174, 177–9,
        361–2
    see also parliamentary sovereignty;
        secondary legislation
Prime Minister (PM) 37–8
    appointment of 13, 14, 25, 27, 214,
        238, 262
        hung Parliaments 239–42, 243–4
        single party majority
            governments 238–9
    Cabinet, relationship with, *see* Prime
        Minister's relationship with
        Cabinet
    dismissal of 245
    First and Deputy First Ministers of
        Northern Ireland 384
    First Minister of Scotland 372
    First Minister of Wales 381–2
    monarch, weekly audience with 39,
        220, 262
    origins of position 38, 260
    parliamentary questions to 10, 49,
        349–50

resignation of
    after losing support of
        Cabinet 267, 275, 302–3
    after losing vote of no
        confidence 246–7, 250, 281
    between general elections 239
    office held until resignation 240,
        241, 243
    role and powers 13, 25–6, 260, 262–4
        government departments,
            reorganization 279–80
        ministerial appointments, *see*
            ministers, appointment of
    see also executive
Prime Minister's relationship with
    Cabinet 262, 271, 275–6, 278
    Blair premiership (1997–2007) 272,
        273–4, 277
    Cabinet reshuffles 268–70
    Coalition Government (2010–
        15) 268–9, 276–7, 278, 282–3,
        285, 303
    May premiership (2016–19) 266,
        269–70, 277–8, 283–4, 286, 287,
        303
    modern practice 272–3
    Thatcher's resignation (1990) 267,
        275, 302–3
    traditional approach 271–2
Prince of Wales:
    Evans case (Sup Ct) 43–4, 52–3,
        109–10, 254
    as first in line of succession 254
    regents, appointment of 253–4
    see also monarch
prisoners' rights 501–2, 620–1
    under ECHR Article 5 81–2, 112,
        630, 657–8, 664
    to leave cells 630, 657–8
    to receive friend and family
        visits 630
    respect for correspondence 499–500,
        501, 631
    voting rights 312, 630, 645–6
    see also imprisonment; right to liberty
        and security (ECHR Article 5)
privacy, *see* right to respect for private
    and family life/correspondence
    (ECHR Article 8)
Privacy International case (Sup
    Ct) 416–17, 452, 453
private conduct of ministers 292–3
    sexual misconduct 288, 293–6
Private Member's bills 332
private/public law divide, *see* public/
    private law divide
privileges and immunities 83, 105,
    306, 412, 540–1
Privy Council:
    historical role 118, 204, 207
    Judicial Committee 216
    Orders in Council 47, 216–17, 228,
        233, 384
procedural impropriety 101–2, 448,
    511–14, 557–8

consultation duty, *see* duty to
    consult
legitimate expectations, *see*
    legitimate expectations
'mandatory' and 'directory' rules
    distinction 514–15
    'substantial compliance' test
        alternative 515–17
natural justice rules 520–2, 557;
see also bias, rule against; right to be
    heard
reasoned decision-making, *see* duty
    to give reasons
see also judicial review
processions and assemblies 690–5;
see also public order policing
proclamations, royal 76, 118, 309
Profumo, John 288, 604
prohibition orders 441
proportionality:
    ECtHR proportionality
        principle 499, 627–8
    EU law proportionality
        principle 167, 498–9
    as judicial review ground 498–502,
        509
    irrationality, relationship
        with 502–8
    proportionate dispute
        resolution 563, 575;
    see also tribunals
    see also human rights law; judicial
        review
prorogation of Parliament 119–20,
    310
    R (Miller) v Prime Minister (Sup
        Ct) 63, 77, 151–2, 232–6, 238,
        310, 413
protected designations of origin
    (post-Brexit case study) 154,
    166, 172, 175, 188, 193–4, 198,
    199–200
protest, right to 672–4, 694; *see also*
    public order policing
'public authorities' and public
    functions 437–40, 659–64
public bodies 300
    executive agencies 302
    non-departmental public
        bodies 301–2
    non-ministerial departments 261, 301
public health functions of local
    authorities 396
public inquiries 603, 617
    examples 604–5
    impact 616–17
    inquisitorial model and
        Maxwellization process 614–15
    judicial and lay members 609–12, 616
    public or private hearings 612–14
    report publication 615
    role 605–6
    statutory and non-statutory
        inquiries 606–8
    terms of reference 608–9

public interest litigation 425, 428, 429–33; *see also* judicial review
public law:
 definition 2
 glossary of terms 719–28
Public Order Act offences 681–3
 racially or religiously aggravated offending 687
 riot, violent disorder, and affray 683–6
 threats, abuse, and insults 686–90
public order policing 671–2
 breach of the peace
  offence 674–6
  police powers to prevent 676–81
 processions and assemblies control 690–5
 Public Order Act offences, *see* Public Order Act offences
 right to protest 672–4, 694
 use of force 209–10
 see also police
public/private law divide 434
 exclusivity principle 434–6
 'public authorities' and public functions 437–40, 659–64
 see also human rights law; judicial review
public processions and assemblies 690–5;
 see also public order policing
public sector equality duty 481–4
Public Service Ombudsman proposal (2014) 591, 592, 602
Pym, John 120

Q

qualified rights 627–8
quashing orders 441–2
'quasi-federalism' 388
quasi-military organizations, bans of 682–3
Queen, HM (Elizabeth II) 206, 220, 253, 254; *see also* monarch
Queen's Speech 233, 235, 240, 245, 309–10, 334
questions in Parliament 50
 in House of Lords 50
 ministerial questions 350–1
 Prime Minister's Questions 10, 49, 349–50
 urgent questions 352
 written or oral 351
 see also executive's accountability to Parliament

R

Raab, Dominic 287
racially or religiously aggravated offending 687
Raz, Joseph 79–80, 83, 89–91, 95, 96, 97, 100, 414–15

reasonableness, *see* irrationality
reasons, duty to give, *see* duty to give reasons
recall of MPs 313–14
recall of Parliament 321–2
Redcliffe-Maud Commission 391
Rees-Mogg case (Div Ct) 426–7, 428
referendums:
 on Brexit (2016) 155, 182–4, 200
 on continued EEC membership (1975) 182, 282
 on electoral reform (2011) 283, 320
 local referendums 401
 on Scottish independence (2014) 18, 183, 220, 312, 373–4, 375
 see also elections
reform of law, *see* law reform
regents, appointment of 253–4
regions, devolution to 19;
 see also local government
regulations, *see* secondary legislation
Regulations, EU 163, 169–70, 171, 172
Reilly (No. 2) case (Admin) 93–4, 107, 108
religiously or racially aggravated offending 687
repeal of legislation 131
 after Brexit, *see* European Union (Withdrawal) Act 2018
 implied repeal doctrine 138–40, 179–81
republics 13–14
reserved powers model:
 Northern Ireland 384–6
 Scotland 365–6, 370
 Wales 380–1
 see also devolution
reshuffles of Cabinet 268–70
residence rights after Brexit 196–7
resignation of ministers, *see* individual ministerial responsibility
resignation of PM, *see* Prime Minister (PM), resignation of
retrospective effect:
 no punishment without breach of law 79–82, 102–4
 Parliament's power to overturn judgments 53–4, 93–4, 108
Ridge v Baldwin (HL) 524–5
Ridley, F.F. 28–9, 30
Right First Time (Administrative Justice and Tribunals Council, 2011) 581–3
right of access to courts:
 employment tribunal fees 95
 legal aid restrictions 577
 standing for judicial review, *see* judicial review, standing rules
 Witham case (QBD) 98, 636–7
 see also right to fair trial (ECHR Article 6)
right to be heard 520–4, 557

application, forfeiture, and expectation cases distinction 525–6
 legal representation 532–3, 536, 576–8
 oral hearings 529–31, 575–6
 and parliamentary sovereignty 527–9
 Ridge v Baldwin (HL) 524–5
 right to fair trial (ECHR Article 6), relationship with 535–7
 right to know opposition case 533–5, 545; *see also* duty to give reasons
 witnesses, right to call and cross-examine 531–2
 see also procedural impropriety
right to effective remedy (ECHR Article 13) 640–1
right to fair trial (ECHR Article 6) 520, 698
 common law, relationship with 535–7
 immigration cases, legal aid restrictions 577
 non-retroactivity principle, *see* retrospective effect
 presumption of innocence 698
 rape cases, complainant's sexual history evidence 649–50, 651
 right of access to courts, *see* right of access to courts
 right to independent and impartial tribunal 57, 520, 535, 536, 537, 698
 scope of right 535–6
 unfairly obtained evidence 711
 see also bias, rule against; procedural impropriety
right to liberty and security (ECHR Article 5) 628–9, 696–7
 false imprisonment of protestors 679–80
 police powers to restrict, *see* police, powers and duties
 of prisoners 81–2, 112, 630, 657–8, 664
 see also detention; imprisonment
right to life (ECHR Article 2) 607–8
right to peaceful enjoyment of possessions (ECHR Protocol 1 Article 1) 367–8, 660–1
right to protest 672–4, 694;
 see also public order policing
right to respect for private and family life/correspondence (ECHR Article 8) 698
 abortion law in Northern Ireland 385
 accommodation duties outsourced by local authorities 659–60, 661–3
 phone tapping by police 111–12, 637
 police searches, *see* entry, search, and seizure; stop and search

right to respect for private and family life (*Cont.*)
of prisoners 499–500, 501, 631
proportionality principle application 627–8
weekend leisure 371
Rights Brought Home White Paper (Cm 3782, 1997) 640, 648–9
'rigid' constitutions 7–8
riot offence 683–6
RM v Scottish Ministers (Sup Ct) 474
Roberts case (Sup Ct) 703–5
Roberts v Hopwood (HL) 478, 491–2
Rogers, Robert 323
Rose Theatre Trust case (QBD) 429–30, 431–2
Royal Assent 25–6, 36, 216, 236–8, 339, 345
Royal Marriages Act 1772 255
royal prerogative powers 206–7, 255–8
armed forces, deployment overseas 49, 221–3, 224*t*, 236, 263
constitutional conventions limiting, *see* constitutional conventions
exercise of, justiciability 226–9
exercised by executive 26, 204–5, 208, 215
identifying existence of 208–10
list of 213–14
ministerial appointments, *see* ministers, appointment of
nature of 207–8
pardons 205, 214, 215, 216, 226
Parliament's power to abolish or restrict 210–12, 225–6
passports, grant or revocation 214, 215, 227, 229, 250
public inquiries 606–7
reform or abolition proposals 250–2
statutes, binding effect on Crown 212–13
treaties, entry and ratification 214, 215, 224–6
war declaration 26
wartime emergency powers, *see* wartime emergency powers
withdrawal from EU (power contested) 6, 29, 58, 181, 185–7, 229–32
see also executive; personal prerogatives of monarch
royal proclamations 76, 118, 309
Rozenberg, Joshua 59–60
Rudd, Amber 287, 288
rule of law 43, 72–3, 112–14
case law, *see* rule of law, case law
constitutionalism principle 10, 152
definitions 73–5
formal conceptions 87–95, 111
substantive conceptions 95–100, 111
Dicey's theory on 78, 87

constitutional rights protection by courts 85–6, 111–12, 636
discretionary powers 80, 89, 106–7, 462
no man is above the law 82–5
no punishment without breach of law 79–82, 102–4
discretionary powers, *see* discretionary powers
executive power checked by 101–6, 414–18; *see also* judicial review
historical development 75–7
and human rights protection 111–12, 635–7
illegality, *see* illegality
and morality 73, 74, 90–1, 95–100
immoral or unconstitutional legislation 87–8, 126, 133–5
and parliamentary sovereignty 106–11, 448–9
reasoned decision-making, *see* duty to give reasons
separation of powers, *see* separation of powers
rule of law, case law:
A and others v Secretary of State for the Home Department (HL) 81–2, 112
Anufrijeva case (HL) 93
Bourgass case (Sup Ct) 99–100
Entick v Carrington (KB) 62, 76–7, 79, 80, 84, 87, 104, 636–7, 710
Inland Revenue Commissioners v Rossminster Ltd (HL) 80–1, 105
Liversidge v Anderson (HL) 104–5, 523
M case (HL) 62–3, 84–5, 105–6
Pierson case (QBD) 103–4, 108
Reilly (No. 2) case (Admin) 93–4, 107, 108
Unison case (Sup Ct) 95, 107
Wheeler v Leicester City Council (HL) 102–3, 474–5, 477, 490–1, 492
Witham case (QBD) 98, 636–7
Rushdie, Salman 688
Russell, Meg 337, 353

S

S case (CA) 465, 466
S (Minors) (Care Order: Implementation of Care Plan), Re (HL) 650–1
Salisbury Convention 339–40, 347
Salmond, Alex 373–4
Salmond, John W. 122–3
Sandford, Mark 396, 401
Saville Inquiry into Bloody Sunday (2000–10) 604, 609, 611
Schiemann, Konrad 422, 427
Schuman, Robert 157
Scotland:
Act of Union 1707 18, 361–2, 363, 365
devolved executive and Parliament, *see* Scottish executive and Parliament

independence referendum (2014) 18, 183, 220, 312, 373–4, 375
local government 321, 391, 393, 405
elections 321, 400, 401
powers and functions of local authorities 396, 398–9, 402
Scottish Nationalist Party 244, 317, 375
Scottish Public Services Ombudsman 584–5
Scottish executive and Parliament 19, 377
background to Scottish devolution 363–4
Brexit opposition 186, 369–70, 371–2, 374, 375
judicial review of Acts of the Scottish Parliament 366–71
Members of Scottish Parliament 365, 373
reserved powers model 365–6, 370
Scotland Act 1998 181, 364–5
Scotland Act 2016 374–5
Scottish Government 372–3
Sewel Convention 371–2, 374, 380–1, 388
see also devolution
Scottish Nationalist Party 244, 317, 375
Scrap Metal Dealers Act 2013 343, 344
scrutiny:
for accountability purposes, *see* accountability
of secondary legislation 346–8
searches by police, *see* entry, search and seizure; stop and search
secondary legislation 39, 47, 343–4
affirmative resolution procedure 347
to amend 'retained EU law' after Brexit 192–4, 348–9
Assembly Measures (National Assembly for Wales) 378, 379–80, 381
commencement orders 344, 345
concerns about 345–6
data on 344*t*
EU Directives implementation by 189
Henry VIII clauses 39, 47–8, 193, 345, 349
negative resolution procedure 347
Orders in Council 47, 216–17, 228, 233, 384
Orders of Council 217, 344
purposes 344
scrutiny of 346–8
'skeleton bills' 348, 349
see also legislative proceedings; primary legislation
Secretaries of State, *see* Cabinet ministers
Sedley, Sir Stephen 2, 41, 42
Select Committees 12, 49–50, 251, 352–3

self-embracing sovereignty theory 142–6
sentencing:
  for public order offences 683, 687
  reasons, duty to give 547–8
  sentences extended retrospectively 102–4, 479, 643
  see also imprisonment
separation of powers 10–11, 34–6, 69–71
  checks and balances principle 35, 65–9, 412
  definition 41–3
  Evans case (Sup Ct) 43–4, 52–3, 109–10, 254
  executive and judiciary relationship, see judicial independence
  justifications for 43–5
  Parliament and executive relationship 37, 45–51, 68
    executive accountability, see executive's accountability to Parliament
    parliamentary executive system 12–13, 37, 107
  Parliament and judiciary relationship, see parliamentary sovereignty
  'pure' and 'partial' separation of powers distinction 35, 65–9
  in US 11
  see also executive; judiciary; Parliament
service personnel:
  deployment overseas 49, 221–3, 224t, 236, 263
  sexual orientation discrimination 495–6
  see also military action
Sewel Convention 371–2, 374, 380–1, 388
sex scandals involving ministers 288, 293–6
sexual orientation discrimination:
  armed forces 495–6
  opposite-sex couples, civil partnerships 655–6
  tenants' succession rights 652–3
Shadow Cabinet 322
Sharp, Dan 362
Shipman, Dr Harold 609, 613
Short, Claire 274, 285
sinecure titles of ministers 265
single transferrable vote electoral system 321, 384
Sinn Fein 386
'skeleton bills' 348, 349
Smith and Grady v UK (ECtHR) 496–7, 499, 503
Smith case (CA) 495–6, 498, 509
Smith Commission 374
Smith, John 639
Smith, Stanley de 65, 212
Smith, Thomas B. 362

SNP (Scottish Nationalist Party) 244, 317, 375
social contract theory 623
social security benefits:
  appeals against decisions
    high rate of successful tribunal appeals 581–3
    initial reviews of decisions 574–5
  asylum seekers' entitlement 93
  as a 'civil right' 535
  Independent Living Fund closure 483
  Universal Credit system 285–6
sources of the UK Constitution 5, 6
sovereignty of Parliament, see parliamentary sovereignty
Speaker of House of Commons 309, 321–2
special advisers to ministers 261, 280–1, 292, 298–300
standing for judicial review, see judicial review, standing rules
Statute of Westminster 1931 130, 131
statutes, see primary legislation
statutory instruments, see secondary legislation
statutory interpretation:
  delegation provisions 348
  in human rights compliant manner 52, 647–54
    declarations of incompatibility 53, 647, 654–8
  judicial activism by 52–3, 109–10
  parliamentary intention, see parliamentary intention
  rules of 51
  statutes, binding effect on Crown 212–13
  words, meaning of 450–1
statutory procedure, failure to follow, see procedural impropriety
Steele, Iain 610–11
Steinfeld and Keidan case (Sup Ct) 655–6
Stephen Lawrence Inquiry (1997–9) 606, 609, 617
Stephen, Sir Leslie 87, 126, 133
Stewart, John 403
Stone, Richard 680
stop and search 695–6, 700–5
Straw, Jack 251
Street, Harry 65
Sturgeon, Nicola 375
subordinate legislation, see secondary legislation
subsidiarity principle 11, 166, 358
substantive conceptions of the rule of law 95–100, 111
Succession to the Crown Act 2013 255
sufficient interest test 421–4;
  see also judicial review, standing rules
Sugar, Lord Alan 327

supplementary vote electoral system 320
supremacy of EU law:
  case law, see supremacy of EU law, case law
  direct applicability of Regulations 163, 169–70, 171, 172
  direct effect doctrine 170–2, 190t, 196
  and parliamentary sovereignty 16–17, 155, 173–4, 177–9, 200–2
    after Brexit 191
    in Brexit transition period 196
    European Communities Act 1972 as constitutional statute 179–81
    political controversy over 182–3, 200
    rationale 167–9
    UK, EU law given effect in 172, 173–4, 173f, 229–30
  see also Brexit; European Union; parliamentary sovereignty
supremacy of EU law, case law:
  Costa v ENEL (6/64) (ECJ) 167–8
  Factortame litigation (HL) 17, 175–9, 181
  HS2 case (Sup Ct) 149–51, 181
  Macarthy's Ltd v Smith (CA) 174–5
  Thoburn v Sunderland City Council (Admin) 180–1, 372
  Van Gend en Loos (26/62) (ECJ) 170–1
Supreme Court 9
  appeals from Upper Tribunal 568
  establishment 22, 55
  Justices 22, 55, 327
  US Supreme Court compared 40, 51
Supreme Court (US) 8–9, 40, 51
suspension of Parliament 119–20, 310
  R (Miller) v Prime Minister (Sup Ct) 63, 77, 151–2, 232–6, 238, 310, 413
Syrett, Keith 69, 79, 412
Syria, airstrikes on 49, 222–3

T

Tameside MBC case (HL) 455, 492
Taming the Prerogative: Strengthening Ministerial Accountability (HC 2003–4, 422) 250–1, 252
taxation:
  HM Revenue and Customs 301
  monarch's exemption 212–13
Taylor, A.J.P. 457
terrorism:
  counter-terrorist financing 500–2, 508, 527–9
  detention of suspects without trial 81–2, 112
  media reporting restrictions 494–5
  quasi-military organizations, bans of 682–3
  stop and search of suspects 700–1, 702–3

Thatcher, Margaret 267, 272, 273, 275, 302–3
Thoburn v Sunderland City Council (Admin) 180–1, 372
Thomas, Robert 571, 573, 582
threats, abuse, and insults prohibitions 686–90
Tomkins, Adam 42–3, 74, 121–2, 210, 282, 411
transgender persons 651–2
treaties:
  EU treaties 159–61, 162
  monist and dualist states distinction 128–9, 170
  and parliamentary sovereignty 127–9
  royal prerogative power to enter and ratify 214, 215, 224–6
tribunal procedures 574
  adversarial, enabling, or inquisitorial approaches 576
  initial reviews of decisions 574–5
  legal representation 576–8
  online procedures 579–80
  rules of procedure 578–9
  written or oral hearings 575–6
tribunals 561–2, 583
  and administrative justice 581–3
  advantages over courts 562–3
  appeals from 567–70, 581
  expertise of 562, 569, 573, 574, 580
  First-tier Tribunals 565, 566f, 573, 578
    appeals from 567, 568–9, 581
  historical development 563–5
  judiciary of 59, 573–4
  jurisdiction 563
  procedures, *see* tribunal procedures
  structure of tribunal system 565, 566f
  Upper Tribunal, *see* Upper Tribunal
  see also courts
Truss, Liz 58, 60
Turpin, Colin 282

U

UK Constitution 1–2, 32–3
  amendment process 7
  'constitution' definition and purpose 3–5, 6, 27–8
  constitutional conventions, *see* constitutional conventions
  constitutional monarchy 13, 14, 16; *see also* monarch
  Constitutional Reform Act 2005, *see* Constitutional Reform Act 2005
  constitutional statutes, *see* constitutional statutes
  devolution, *see* devolution
  existence debated 27–30
  historical development, *see* historical development of UK Constitution

legal and political nature 9–10
parliamentary sovereignty, *see* parliamentary sovereignty
rule of law, *see* rule of law
separation of powers, *see* separation of powers
sources 5, 6
structure 10–14
Supreme Court, *see* Supreme Court
uncodified nature 5–9, 27–30, 35, 116
  codification proposals 30–1
unitary nature 11, 19, 359–60; *see also* devolution
UK Withdrawal from the European Union (Legal Continuity) (Scotland) Bill, Re (Sup Ct) 369–70
UKIP (United Kingdom Independence Party) 316
UK's accession to EU 16, 155, 158, 172, 181–2, 200; *see also* European Communities Act 1972
UK's exit from EU, *see* Brexit
Ullah case (HL) 643–5, 647
ultra vires doctrine 395, 396, 414, 447–9
  'simple' or 'narrow' *ultra vires* 450–1
  see also illegality
uncodified constitutions 5–9, 116
  UK Constitution, *see* UK Constitution, uncodified nature
unconstitutional acts 10
  legislation 87–8, 126, 133–5
uniforms, political 681–2
Unison case (Sup Ct) 95, 107
unitary authorities 391; *see also* local government
unitary constitutions 11, 19, 359–60
United States:
  Constitution, *see* US Constitution
  Declaration of Independence 4–5, 6, 621, 622, 623
  Supreme Court 8–9, 40, 51
  treaty ratification 225
  War Powers Act 223
Universal Declaration on Human Rights 1948 624–5
unlawful violence offences 683–6
unlawfulness, *see* illegality
unreasonableness, *see* irrationality
unwritten (uncodified) constitutions 5–9, 116
  UK Constitution, *see* UK Constitution, uncodified nature
Upper Tribunal 565, 566f
  appeals from 567–9
  appeals to 567, 568–9, 581
  decisions of
    Attorney-General's power to overturn 43–4, 52–3, 109
    judicial review of 571–3
  'judicial review' jurisdiction 570–1
  see also tribunals

urgent questions in Parliament 352
US Constitution 4, 6
  amendment process 6–7
  codified nature 5–9, 116
  federal structure 11–12, 359, 360, 388
  presidential executive system 12–13, 13–14
  rights protection 23, 621, 622, 623, 636, 669
  separation of powers 11
  see also United States

V

Van Gend en Loos (26/62) (ECJ) 170–1
Varuhas, Jason 228, 542
Vauxhall Estates v Liverpool Corporation (KBD) 139–40
Venables case (HL) 479
Victoria, Queen 237
Vile, M.J.C. 388
violent disorder offence 683–6
votes in Parliament 322–3
voting rights 311–12
  of prisoners 312, 630, 645–6

W

Wade, H.W.R. (aka William Wade):
  on human rights law 665
  on judicial review 416, 457, 491, 514, 520
  on parliamentary sovereignty 122–3, 124–5, 141, 178–9
  on tribunal system 579
Wagstaff case (Div Ct) 613
Waldron, Jeremy 521
Wales:
  devolved executive and Assembly, *see* Welsh executive and Assembly
  English conquest of (1282) 18, 361
  local government 391, 393, 398, 400, 401, 402, 405
  Welsh Public Services Ombudsman 584–5
Wales Act 2017 380–1
Walpole, Robert 260
Walters, Rhodri 323
war, *see* military action
wartime emergency powers:
  Attorney-General v De Keyser's Royal Hotel Ltd (HL) 210–11, 230, 231
  Burmah Oil Co Ltd v Lord Advocate (HL) 53–4, 108, 132, 208–9
  Liversidge v Anderson (HL) 104–5, 523
  see also royal prerogative powers
Weaver case (CA) 663
Wednesbury unreasonableness 488–91, 496–7, 502–8; *see also* irrationality
welfare benefits, *see* social security benefits

Welsh executive and
  Assembly 19
  background to Welsh
    devolution 377
  judicial review of Assembly
    legislation 379–80
  National Assembly for Wales 378–9,
    381, 382
  reserved powers model 380–1
  Welsh Government 381–2
  see also devolution
Werritty, Adam 292
West Lothian Question (English
  Votes for English Laws) 322,
  341, 342–3, 342*f*, 375–6
Westland Plc 275
Westminster, *see* Parliament
*Westminster Corporation v London
  & North Western Railway Co*
  (HL) 476–7
Wheare, K.C. 3, 28

Wheeler v Leicester City Council
  (HL) 102–3, 474–5, 477,
  490–1, 492
whip system 322–3; *see also* political
  parties
White Papers 333
Whitehall, *see* executive
Wicks, Elizabeth 7, 15–16, 21, 75
William, HRH Duke of
  Cambridge 254, 255
William III and Mary II 16, 120–1,
  123, 254
Williams, D.G.T. 364
Williamson, Gavin 284
Wilson, Harold 363–4
Windrush scandal (2018) 288
Witham case (QBD) 98, 636–7
Withdrawal Agreement, *see* European
  Union (Withdrawal) Act 2018
witnesses:
  in public inquiries 614–15

rape cases, complainant's sexual
  history evidence 649–50, 651
right to call and cross-examine 531–2
Woodhouse, Diana 290
Woolf, Lord Harry 108–9, 133–4, 149
World Development Movement case
  (Div Ct) 432–3
written (codified) constitutions 5–9,
  116
  UK codification proposals 30–1
written questions in Parliament 351
written tribunal hearings 575–6

Y

*YL v Birmingham City Council and
  others* (HL) 661–3
Yong, Ben 218
Young, Alison L. 92, 148
young persons, voting rights 312
Young, Sir George 222, 223